# One-Stop Internet Resources

## Log on to wh.mt.glencoe.com

### ONLINE STUDY TOOLS

- Study Central
- Chapter Overviews
- ePuzzles and Games
- Self-Check Quizzes
- Vocabulary E-Flashcards
- Multi-Language Glossaries

### ONLINE RESEARCH

- Student Web Activities
- Web Resources
- Current Events
- State Resources
- Beyond the Textbook Features

### ONLINE STUDENT EDITION

- Complete Interactive Student Edition

### FOR TEACHERS

- Teacher Forum
- Web Activity Lesson Plans
- Literature Connections

# Honoring America

For Americans, the flag has always had a special meaning. It is a symbol of our nation's freedom and democracy.

## Flag Etiquette

Over the years, Americans have developed rules and customs concerning the use and display of the flag. One of the most important things every American should remember is to treat the flag with respect.

- The flag should be raised and lowered by hand and displayed only from sunrise to sunset. On special occasions, the flag may be displayed at night, but it should be illuminated.

- The flag may be displayed on all days, weather permitting, particularly on national and state holidays and on historic and special occasions.

- No flag may be flown above the American flag or to the right of it at the same height.

- The flag should never touch the ground or floor beneath it.

- The flag may be flown at half-staff by order of the president, usually to mourn the death of a public official.

- The flag may be flown upside down only to signal distress.

- The flag should never be carried flat or horizontally, but always carried aloft and free

- When the flag becomes old and tattered, it should be destroyed by burning. According to an approved custom, the Union (stars on blue field) is first cut from the flag; then the two pieces, which no longer form a flag, are burned.

★   ★   ★   ★   ★   ★   ★   ★

## The Star-Spangled Banner

O! say can you see, by the dawn's early light,
What so proudly we hail'd at the twilight's last gleaming?
Whose broad stripes and bright stars through the perilous fight,
O'er the ramparts we watched, were so gallantly streaming?
And the rockets' red glare, the bombs bursting in air,
Gave proof through the night that our flag was still there;
O! say, does that star-spangled banner yet wave
O'er the land of the free and the home of the brave?

## The Pledge of Allegiance

I pledge allegiance to the Flag of the United States of America and to the Republic for which it stands, one Nation under God, indivisible, with liberty and justice for all.

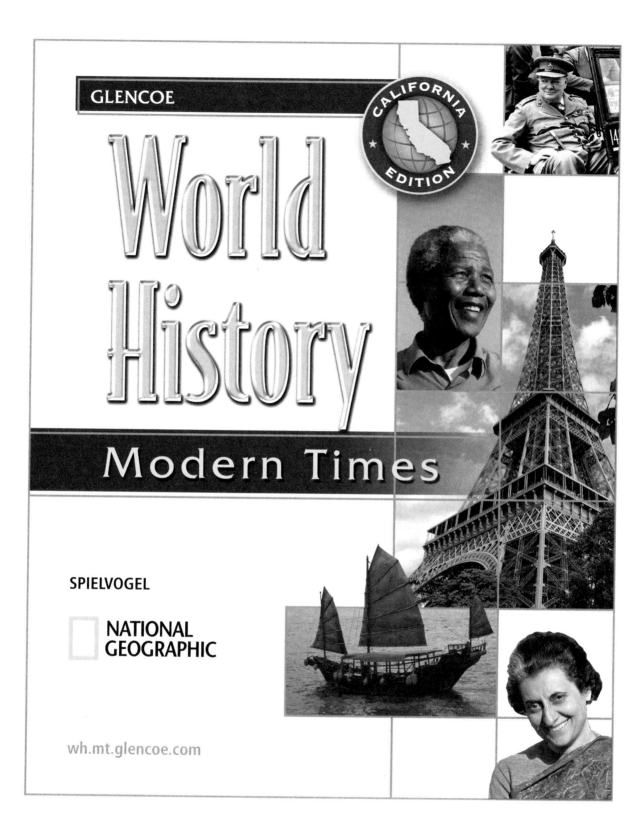

GLENCOE

# World History

## Modern Times

CALIFORNIA EDITION

SPIELVOGEL

NATIONAL GEOGRAPHIC

wh.mt.glencoe.com

McGraw Hill Glencoe

New York, New York   Columbus, Ohio   Chicago, Illinois   Peoria, Illinois   Woodland Hills, California

# Authors

## Jackson J. Spielvogel

Jackson J. Spielvogel is associate professor emeritus of history at The Pennsylvania State University. He received his Ph.D. from The Ohio State University, where he specialized in Reformation history under Harold J. Grimm. His articles and reviews have appeared in such journals as *Moreana, Journal of General Education, Archiv für Reformationsgeschichte,* and *American Historical Review.* He has also contributed chapters or articles to *The Social History of the Reformation, The Holy Roman Empire: A Dictionary Handbook, Simon Wiesenthal Center Annual of Holocaust Studies,* and *Utopian Studies.* His book *Hitler and Nazi Germany* was published in 1987 (fourth edition, 2001). His book *Western Civilization* was published in 1991 (fourth edition, 2000). He is the co-author (with William Duiker) of *World History,* published in 1994 (third edition, 2001). Professor Spielvogel has won five major university-wide teaching awards, and in 1997, he became the first winner of the Schreyer Institute's Student Choice Award for innovative and inspiring teaching.

The National Geographic Society, founded in 1888 for the increase and diffusion of geographic knowledge, is the world's largest nonprofit scientific and educational organization. Since its earliest days, the Society has used sophisticated communication technologies, from color photography to holography, to convey geographic knowledge to a worldwide membership. The School Publishing Division supports the Society's mission by developing innovative educational programs—ranging from traditional print materials to multimedia programs including CD-ROMs, videos, and software.

## One-Stop Internet Resources

This textbook contains one-stop Internet resources for teachers, students, and families. Log on to wh.mt.glencoe.com for more information. Online study tools include Study Central, ePuzzles and Games, Self-Check Quizzes, Vocabulary E-Flashcards, and multi-language glossaries. Online research tools include Student Web Activities, Current Events, Beyond the Textbook Features, Web Resources, and State Resources. The interactive online student edition includes the complete Interactive Student Edition. Especially for teachers, Glencoe offers an online Teacher Forum, Web Activity Lesson Plans, and Literature Connections.

Copyright © 2006 by The McGraw-Hill Companies, Inc. All rights reserved. Except as permitted under the United States Copyright Act, no part of this publication may be reproduced or distributed in any form or by any means, or stored in a database or retrieval system, without prior permission of the publisher.

National Geographic contributions, identified by the trademark, were designed and developed by National Geographic School Publishing. Copyright © 2006 National Geographic Society. All rights reserved. The name "National Geographic Society" and the Yellow Border Rectangle are trademarks of the Society, and their use, without prior written permission, is strictly prohibited.

Send all inquiries to:
Glencoe/McGraw-Hill
8787 Orion Place
Columbus, Ohio 43240-4027

X 20407

ISBN 0-07-867855-2 (Student Edition)

Printed in the United States of America.

4 5 6 7 8 9 10   079/055        08 07 06

# Contributing Authors, Consultants, and Reviewers

## Contributing Authors

**Stephen F. Cunha**
Humboldt State University
Arcata, CA

**Douglas Fisher**
San Diego State University
San Diego, CA

**Nancy Frey**
San Diego State University
San Diego, CA

**Robin C. Scarcella**
University of California, Irvine
Irvine, CA

**Emily M. Schell**
San Diego State University
San Diego, CA

**David Vigilante**
National Center for History in the Schools
San Diego, CA

**Ruben Zepeda II**
Los Angeles Unified School District
Los Angeles, CA

## Academic Consultants

**W. Lindsay Adams**
University of Utah
Salt Lake City, UT

**Stephen F. Dale**
The Ohio State University
Columbus, OH

**Jonathan Grant**
Florida State University
Tallahassee, FL

**Marilynn J. Hitchens**
University of Colorado
Denver, CO

**Farid Mahdavi**
San Diego State University
San Diego, CA

**Frances Malino**
Wellesley College
Wellesley, MA

**Rev. Marvin O'Dell**
Faith Baptist Church
Thousand Oaks, CA

**Joseph R. Rosenbloom**
Washington University
St. Louis, MO

**Guy Welbon**
University of Pennsylvania
Philadelphia, PA

## Reading Consultants

**Maureen D. Danner**
Project CRISS
Kalispell, MT

**ReLeah Cossett Lent**
University of Central Florida
Orlando, FL

**Steve Qunell**
Montana Academy
Kalispell, MT

**Carol M. Santa**
Montana Academy
Kalispell, MT

**Bonnie Valdes**
Project CRISS
Largo, FL

## Teacher Reviewers

**Larayne Anderson**
Hudson's Bay High School
Vancouver, WA

**Joan Arno**
George Washington High School
Philadelphia, PA

**Michele Austin**
La Reina High School
Thousand Oaks, CA

**Wendell Brooks**
Berkeley High School
Berkeley, CA

**Linda Clark**
Padua Franciscan High School
Parma, OH

**Timothy Connell**
Laurel School
Shaker Heights, OH

**W. Dean Eastman**
Beverly High School
Beverly, MA

**William Everdell**
St. Ann's School
Brooklyn, NY

**Sam Gellens**
Horace Mann School
Riverdale, NY

**Helen Grady**
Springfield High School
Philadelphia, PA

**Roy Sunada**
Marshall Fundamental Secondary
Pasadena, CA

**Bonnie Sussman**
Bishop O'Dowd High School
Oakland, CA

**Andrew Turay**
Evander Childs High School
Bronx, NY

**Jeff Wright**
John Marshall High School
Rochester, MN

# California Advisory Board

**Helen Ligh**
Social Studies and
Language Arts Teacher
Macy Intermediate
Montebello Unified School District
Monterey Park, CA

**Barbara S. Lindemann, Ph.D.**
Professsor of History and
Ethnic Studies
History Department Chair
Santa Barbara City College
Santa Barbara, CA

**Reynaldo Antonio Macías**
World History Teacher
Mark Twain Middle School
Los Angeles Unified School District
Los Angeles, CA

**Jennifer Metherd**
Program Coordinator
Tehama County Department
of Education
Red Bluff, CA

**Derrick K. Neal**
Social Studies Department Chair
Patrick Henry Middle School
Los Angeles Unified School District
Los Angeles, CA

**Robin C. Scarcella, Ph.D.**
Professor and Director
Academic English/ESL
University of California, Irvine
Irvine, CA

**Emily M. Schell, Ed.D.**
Visiting Professor, San Diego
State University
Social Studies Education Director
SDSU City Heights Educational
Collaborative
San Diego, CA

**Dale Steiner, Ph.D.**
Professor of History
California State University, Chico
Chico, CA

**Roy Sunada**
Social Studies Teacher/AP Coordinator
Marshall Fundamental Secondary School
Pasadena Unified School District
Pasadena, CA

**David Vigilante**
Associate Director
National Center for History in the Schools
San Diego, CA

**Ruben Zepeda II, Ed.D.**
Adviser, Instructional Support Services
Los Angeles Unified School District
Los Angeles, CA

# Contents

**NATIONAL GEOGRAPHIC**

## Reference Atlas

**NATIONAL GEOGRAPHIC**

## Geography Handbook

**UNIT 1**

## The World Before Modern Times, *3000 B.C.–1800*

# UNIT 2

## An Era of European Imperialism, *1800-1914*

# UNIT 3

## The Twentieth Century

# Contents

## Toward a Global Civilization

## Appendix

## Primary Sources Library

## SKILLBUILDER Handbook

# Features

# Features

# Primary Source Quotes

# Primary Source Quotes

# Primary Source Quotes

# Charts, Graphs, & Tables

## Three Dictators: Mussolini, Stalin, and Hitler

| | Benito Mussolini (1883–1945) | Joseph Stalin (1879–1953) | Adolf Hitler (1889–1945) |
| --- | --- | --- | --- |
| Country | Italy | USSR | Germany |
| Political Title | Prime Minister | General Secretary | Chancellor |
| Date in Power | 1922 | 1929 | 1933 |
| Political Party | Fascist Party | Communist Party | National Socialist German Workers' Party (NSDAP, or Nazi) |
| Type of Government | Fascist | Communist | Fascist |
| Source(s) of Support | Middle-class industrialists and large land owners | Party officials | Industrial leaders, landed aristocrats, military, and bureaucracy |
| Methods of Controlling Opposition | Secret police (OVRA), imprisonment, outlawing other parties, propaganda, censorship of the press | Purges, prison camps, secret police, state-run press, forced labor camps, executions | *Schutzstaffeln* (SS) police force, propaganda, state-run press, terror, repression, racial laws, concentration and death camps |
| Policies | Support for Catholic Church, nationalism, antisocialism, anticommunism | Five-Year Plans for rapid industrialization, collectivization of farms | Rearmament, public projects to put people to work, anti-Semitism, racism, Social Darwinism, extreme nationalism |

xv

# NATIONAL GEOGRAPHIC Maps

## NATIONAL GEOGRAPHIC Reference Atlas

## Unit 1

## NATIONAL GEOGRAPHIC Middle East, 1919–1935

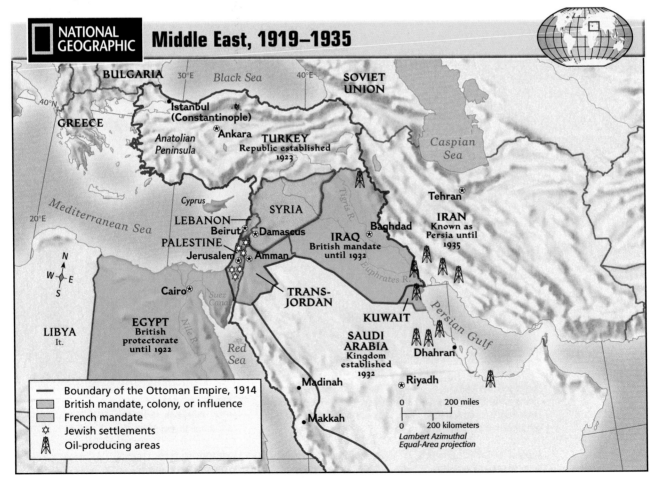

## Unit 2

## Unit 3

## Unit 4

NATIONAL GEOGRAPHIC

**Expansion of the European Union**

Original members, 1957
Additional members:
by 1973
by 1986
by 1995
by 2004
Candidate countries

# A Guide to Students and Families

## How do I succeed in World History?

**W**elcome to World History, Culture, and Geography: The Modern World and to *Glencoe World History: Modern Times.* The content of this course focuses on the major turning points in the shaping of the modern world, from the late eighteenth century to the present. You will be viewing and interpreting periods in world history from various perspectives, including historical, geographic, political, economic, and cultural. Together, these perspectives can help you to understand how the past has led to the present and to appreciate your role in shaping the future.

Your textbook includes a variety of tools designed to help you be successful in the study of modern world history. One of the most valuable of these is a list of the standards and objectives that you will be expected to master by the end of the school year.

These are the California Grade 10 Content Standards for World History, Culture, and Geography: The Modern World, and are listed on pages 4–10 of this book. This book also lists the California Historical and Social Sciences Analysis Skills you will be expected to master. They are listed on pages 11–12.

Knowing what you are expected to learn from the very beginning of the year is an advantage. It will help you and your family see when you might need extra help. This should ensure that your world history course will be both enjoyable and successful.

▼ **Redwood National Forest**

## What are the California History–Social Science Standards?

The California State Board of Education approved the History–Social Science Framework, with Content Standards, on October 11, 2004. The purpose of the History–Social Science Framework and the Content Standards is to provide you, the student, with expectations for achievement in California. These standards spell out what you should learn in social sciences from kindergarten through grade twelve. These Content Standards represent the knowledge and skills you need to achieve in order to succeed in the world of work or college.

## Why do the California History–Social Science Standards matter to me?

The California History–Social Science Standards are the things you should learn and be able to do as you take the course. The standards are specific for each grade and subject. Your teachers base their lessons and tests on the California History–Social Science Standards. Teachers also pay special attention to the Historical and Social Sciences Analysis Skills. Unlike the Content Standards, the Analysis Skills are the same for grades nine through twelve.

So, to be successful in this course, you may want to read over the Content Standards and Analysis Skills with your family. (These Content Standards and Analysis Skills are listed on pages 4–12.) Although some of the names and terms may not be familiar to you at first, you and your family can outline some steps to take to achieve proficiency. As you take this course, review the standards from time to time to help the things you are learning fall into place.

## What is included on the following pages?

California History–Social Science Standards for Grade 10: World History, Culture, and Geography: The Modern World and Grades Nine Through Twelve Historical and Social Sciences Analysis Skills

- Pages 4–10 include a listing of all of the California Content Standards for this course.

- Pages 11–12 include a listing of the Historical and Social Sciences Analysis Skills for grades nine through twelve.

- Turn to page 13 to see how Glencoe's *World History: Modern Times* will help you learn the Content Standards, the Analysis Skills, and how to be successful in this course.

*The California Grade 10 Content Standards tell you what you need to learn and be able to do as you complete your course in World History, Culture, and Geography: The Modern World. The course is designed to cover important events that have shaped the modern world, from the late 1700s to the present. Reading through these standards with your parents or family will help you understand the goals for your course—and help you to achieve them.*

# Grade Ten

## World History, Culture, and Geography: The Modern World

**10.1** Students relate the moral and ethical principles in ancient Greek and Roman philosophy, in Judaism, and in Christianity to the development of Western political thought.

**10.1.1** Analyze the similarities and differences in Judeo-Christian and Greco-Roman views of law, reason and faith, and duties of the individual.

**10.1.2** Trace the development of the Western political ideas of the rule of law and the illegitimacy of tyranny, using selections from Plato's Republic and Aristotle's Politics.

**10.1.3** Consider the influence of the U.S. Constitution on political systems in the contemporary world.

**10.2** Students compare and contrast the Glorious Revolution of England, the American Revolution, and the French Revolution and their enduring effects worldwide on the political expectations for self-government and individual liberty.

**10.2.1** Compare the major ideas of philosophers and their effects on the democratic revolutions in England, the United States, France, and Latin America (e.g., biographies of John Locke, Charles-Louis Montesquieu, Jean-Jacques Rousseau, Simon Bolivar, Thomas Jefferson, James Madison).

**10.2.2** List the principles of the Magna Carta, the English Bill of Rights (1689), the American Declaration of Independence (1776), the French Declaration of the Rights of Man and the Citizen (1789), and the U.S. Bill of Rights (1791).

**10.2.3** Understand the unique character of the American Revolution, its spread to other parts of the world, and its continuing significance to other nations.

**10.2.4** Explain how the ideology of the French Revolution led France to develop from constitutional monarchy to democratic despotism to the Napoleonic empire.

**10.2.5** Discuss how nationalism spread across Europe with Napoleon but was repressed for a generation under the Congress of Vienna and the Concert of Europe until the Revolutions of 1848.

**10.3** Students analyze the effects of the Industrial Revolution in England, France, Germany, Japan, and the United States.

**10.3.1** Analyze why England was the first country to industrialize.

**10.3.2** Examine how scientific and technological changes and new forms of energy brought about massive social, economic, and cultural change (e.g., the inventions and discoveries of James Watt, Eli Whitney, Henry Bessemer, Louis Pasteur, Thomas Edison).

**10.3.3** Describe the growth of population, rural to urban migration, and growth of cities associated with the Industrial Revolution.

**10.3.4** Trace the evolution of work and labor, including the demise of the slave trade and effects of immigration, mining and manufacturing, division of labor, and the union movement.

**10.3.5** Understand the connections among natural resources, entrepreneurship, labor, and capital in an industrial economy.

**10.3.6** Analyze the emergence of capitalism as a dominant economic pattern and the responses to it, including Utopianism, Social Democracy, Socialism, and Communism.

▼ **Golden Gate Bridge, San Francisco**

# History–Social Science Standards

**10.3.7** Describe the emergence of Romanticism in art and literature (e.g., the poetry of William Blake and William Wordsworth), social criticism (e.g., the novels of Charles Dickens), and the move away from Classicism in Europe.

**10.4** **Students analyze patterns of global change in the era of New Imperialism in at least two of the following regions or countries: Africa, Southeast Asia, China, India, Latin America and the Philippines.**

**10.4.1** Describe the rise of industrial economies and their link to imperialism and colonialism (e.g., the role played by national security and strategic advantage; moral issues raised by the search for national hegemony, Social Darwinism, and the missionary impulse; material issues such as land, resources, and technology).

**10.4.2** Discuss the locations of the colonial rule of such nations as England, France, Germany, Italy, Japan, the Netherlands, Russia, Spain, Portugal, and the United States.

**10.4.3** Explain imperialism from the perspective of the colonizers and the colonized and the varied immediate and long-term responses by the people under colonial rule.

**10.4.4** Describe the independence struggles of the colonized regions of the world, including the role of leaders, such as Sun Yat-sen in China, and the role of ideology and religion.

**10.5** **Students analyze the causes and course of the First World War.**

**10.5.1.** Analyze the arguments for entering into war presented by leaders from all sides of the Great War and the role of political and economic rivalries, ethnic and ideological conflicts, domestic discontent and disorder, and propaganda and nationalism in mobilizing citizen population in support of "total war."

▼ **Vineyard, Napa**

**10.5.2** Examine the principal theaters of battle, major turning points, and the importance of geographic factors in military decisions and outcomes (e.g., topography, waterways, distance, climate).

**10.5.3** Explain how the Russian Revolution and the entry of the United States affected the course and outcome of the war.

**10.5.4** Understand the nature of the war and its human costs (military and civilian) on all sides of the conflict, including how colonial peoples contributed to the war effort.

**10.5.5** Discuss human rights violations and genocide, including the Ottoman government's actions against Armenian citizens.

**10.6** Students analyze the effects of the First World War.

**10.6.1** Analyze the aims and negotiating roles of world leaders, the terms and influence of the Treaty of Versailles and Woodrow Wilson's Fourteen Points, and the causes and the effects of United States' rejection of the League of Nations on world politics.

**10.6.2** Describe the effects of the war and resulting peace treaties on population movement, the international economy, and the shifts in the geographic and political borders of Europe and the Middle East.

**10.6.3** Understand the widespread disillusionment with prewar institutions, authorities, and values that resulted in a void that was later filled by totalitarians.

# History–Social Science Standards

**10.6.4** Discuss the influence of World War I on literature, art, and intellectual life in the West (e.g., Pablo Picasso, the "lost generation" of Gertrude Stein, Ernest Hemingway).

**10.7** **Students analyze the rise of totalitarian governments after the First World War.**

**10.7.1** Understand the causes and consequences of the Russian Revolution, including Lenin's use of totalitarian means to seize and maintain control (e.g., the Gulag).

**10.7.2** Trace Stalin's rise to power in the Soviet Union and the connection between economic policies, political policies, the absence of a free press, and systematic violations of human rights (e.g., the Terror Famine in Ukraine).

**10.7.3** Analyze the rise, aggression, and human costs of totalitarian regimes (Fascist and Communist) in Germany, Italy, and the Soviet Union, noting their common and dissimilar traits.

**10.8** **Students analyze the causes and consequences of World War II.**

**10.8.1** Compare the German, Italian, and Japanese drives for empire in the 1930s, including the 1937 Rape of Nanking and other atrocities in China and the Stalin-Hitler Pact of 1939.

**10.8.2** Understand the role of appeasement, non-intervention (isolationism), and the domestic distractions in Europe and the United States prior to the outbreak of World War II.

**10.8.3** Identify and locate the Allied and Axis powers on a map and discuss the major turning points of the war, the principal theaters of conflict, key strategic decisions, and the resulting war conferences and political resolutions, with emphasis on the importance of geographic factors.

**10.8.4** Describe the political, diplomatic, and military leaders during the war (e.g., Winston Churchill, Franklin Delano Roosevelt, Emperor Hirohito, Adolf Hitler, Benito Mussolini, Joseph Stalin, Douglas MacArthur, Dwight Eisenhower).

**10.8.5** Analyze the Nazi policy of pursuing racial purity, especially against the European Jews; its transformation into the Final Solution; and the Holocaust that resulted in the murder of six million Jewish civilians.

**10.8.6** Discuss the human costs of the war, with particular attention to the civilian and military losses in Russia, Germany, Britain, the United States, China, and Japan.

**10.9** **Students analyze the international developments in the post-World War II world.**

**10.9.1** Compare the economic and military power shifts caused by the war, including the Yalta Pact, the development of nuclear weapons, Soviet control of Eastern European nations, and the economic recoveries of Germany and Japan.

**10.9.2** Analyze the causes of the Cold War, with the free world on one side and Soviet client states on the other, including competition for influence in such places as Egypt, the Congo, Vietnam, and Chile.

**10.9.3** Understand the importance of the Truman Doctrine and Marshall Plan, which established the pattern for America's postwar policy of supplying economic and military aid to prevent the spread of Communism and the resulting economic and political competition in arenas such as Southeast Asia (i.e., the Korean War, Vietnam War), Cuba, and Africa.

**10.9.4** Analyze the Chinese Civil War, the rise of Mao Tse-tung, and the subsequent political and economic upheavals in China (e.g., the Great Leap Forward, the Cultural Revolution, and the Tiananmen Square uprising).

**10.9.5** Describe the uprisings in Poland (1952), Hungary (1956), and Czechoslovakia (1968) and those countries' resurgence in the 1970s and 1980s as people in Soviet satellites sought freedom from Soviet control.

▼ **Stovepipe Wells, Death Valley National Park**

**10.9.6** Understand how the forces of nationalism developed in the Middle East, how the Holocaust affected world opinion regarding the need for a Jewish state, and the significance and effects of the location and establishment of Israel on world affairs.

**10.9.7** Analyze the reasons for the collapse of the Soviet Union, including the weakness of the command economy, burdens of military commitments, and growing resistance to Soviet rule by dissidents in satellite states and the non-Russian Soviet republics.

**10.9.8** Discuss the establishment and work of the United Nations and the purposes and influences of the Warsaw Pact, SEATO, and NATO, and the Organization of American States.

**10.10** Students analyze instances of nation-building in the contemporary world in two of the following regions or countries: the Middle East, Africa, Mexico, and other parts of Latin America, and China.

**10.10.1** Understand the challenges in the regions, including their geopolitical, cultural, military, and economic significance and the international relationships in which they are involved.

**10.10.2** Describe the recent history of the regions, including political divisions and systems, key leaders, religious issues, natural features, resources, and population patterns.

**10.10.3** Discuss the important trends in the region today and whether they appear to serve the cause of individual freedom and democracy.

**10.11** Students analyze the integration of countries into the world economy and the information, technological, and communications revolutions (e.g., television, satellites, computers).

▼ **Marina Del Rey**

*The California Content Standards also address the skills you need to master the study of world history. Read over these skills standards so you can be familiar with them. This will give you a good idea of the skills you will acquire as you complete your course in modern world history.*

# Historical and Social Sciences Analysis Skills

The intellectual skills noted below are to be learned through, and applied to, the content standards for grades nine through twelve. They are to be assessed only in conjunction with the content standards in grades nine through twelve.

*In addition to the standards for grades nine through twelve, students demonstrate the following intellectual, reasoning, reflection, and research skills.*

## *Chronological and Spatial Thinking*

**CS 1** Students compare the present with the past, evaluating the consequences of past events and decisions and determining the lessons that were learned.

**CS 2** Students analyze how change happens at different rates at different times; that some aspects can change while other remain the same; and understand that change is complicated and affects not only technology and politics but also values and beliefs.

**CS 3** Students use a variety of maps and documents to interpret human movement, including major patterns of domestic and international migration, changing environmental preferences and settlements patterns, the frictions that develop between population groups, and the diffusion of ideas, technological innovations, and goods.

**CS 4** Students relate current events to the physical and human characteristics of places and regions.

## *Historical Research, Evidence, and Point of View*

**HR 1** Students distinguish valid arguments from fallacious arguments in historical interpretations.

**HR 2** Students identify bias and prejudice in historical interpretations.

# History–Social Science Standards

**HR 3** Students evaluate major debates among historians concerning alternative interpretations of the past, including an analysis of authors' use of evidence and the distinctions between sound generalizations and misleading oversimplifications.

**HR 4** Students construct and test hypotheses; collect, evaluate, and employ information from multiple primary and secondary sources; and apply it in oral and written presentations.

## Historical Interpretation

**HI 1** Students show the connections, causal and otherwise, between particular historical events and larger social, economic, and political trends and developments.

**HI 2** Students recognize the complexity of historical causes and effects, including the limitations of determining cause and effect.

**HI 3** Students interpret past events and issues within the context in which an event unfolded rather than solely in terms of present-day norms and values.

**HI 4** Students understand the meaning, implication, and impact of historical events while recognizing that events could have taken other directions.

**HI 5** Students analyze human modifications of a landscape, and examine the resulting environmental policy issues.

**HI 6** Students conduct cost/benefit analyses and apply basic economic indicators to analyze the aggregate economic behavior of the U.S. economy.

▼ **Mushroom Rock, Lake Tahoe**

# How Does *Glencoe World History: Modern Times* Help Me Practice the Standards?

**G**lencoe World History: Modern Times has been designed to ensure that it provides comprehensive coverage of all History–Social Science standards for Grade Ten. To further help you, Glencoe has reproduced the History–Social Science Standards in the previous pages for your reference.

Each History–Social Science Standard begins with a general statement identifying the broad time period and subject you are to master. For example, if you turn back to page 6, you will find the following:

**10.5  Students analyze the causes and course of the First World War**

Underneath the standard, you will find a number of supporting standards. The supporting standards for 10.5 divide the main standard into specific topics related to the causes of the First World War. If you look again at pages 6–7, you will see the supporting standards for 10.5:

**10.5.1**  Analyze the arguments for entering into war presented by leaders from all sides of the Great War and the role of political and economic rivalries, ethnic and ideological conflicts, domestic discontent and disorder, and propaganda and nationalism in mobilizing the civilian population in support of "total war."

**10.5.2**  Examine the principal theaters of battle, major turning points, and the importance of geographic factors in military decisions and outcomes (e.g., topography, waterways, distance, climate).

## How should I use the standards?

You will see that each chapter is divided into several sections. Each section is then introduced by a Guide to Reading that lists the California standards that apply to what you are about to read. Try these strategies:

• Read through the standards before you begin a chapter. Make it your goal to understand them by the end of the chapter.

• Take notes on the chapter with the standards in mind.

• Review the standards after you complete the chapter to see if you understand the chapter content.

# A Guide to Students and Families

## *How Does* Glencoe World History: Modern Times *Strengthen My Reading and Writing Skills?*

**A**s you study world history, you build your understanding of today's world, a world where countries and regions with different traditions and cultures are coming into closer contact.

At the same time, your study of history can strengthen your reading and writing skills. These skills are important to your Language and Arts courses, but they are valuable tools for success in other courses, too. As you hone your reading and writing skills, you will be able to perform better on a math test, write a solid report on Napoleon's military strategies, or summarize a lab report for your biology teacher.

## *Why are the English–Language Arts Standards Important?*

The English-Language Arts Standards for California focus on the essential skills for succeeding in school, but also in life. Almost all jobs require a good mastery of these skills, and they are, of course, essential for college and other advanced training.

*Glencoe World History: Modern Times* provides many opportunities for you to practice reading, writing, and speaking. For example, each chapter focuses on a different reading strategy that you can practice with the history content in that chapter. In addition, every section and chapter assessment includes activities that allow you to practice your reading, writing, and presentation skills.

**Glencoe World History: Modern Times** *will help you practice many of the California English–Language Arts Standards for tenth grade. The standards which are addressed in your textbook are listed below. Activities and questions that reflect the standards are identified in the textbook with a small lozenge-shaped symbol that includes the number of the standard.*

## Reading

### 1.0 Word Analysis, Fluency, and Systematic Vocabulary Development

**10RW1.1** Identify and use literal and figurative meanings of words and understand word derivations.

### 2.0 Reading Comprehension

**10RC2.3** Generate relevant questions about readings on issues that can be researched.

**10RC2.4** Synthesize the content from several sources or works by a single author dealing with a single issue; paraphrase ideas and connect them to other sources and related topics to demonstrate comprehension.

**10RC2.8** Evaluate the credibility of an author's argument or defense of a claim by critiquing the relationship between the generalizations and evidence, the comprehensiveness of evidence, and the way in which the author's intent affects the structure and tone of the text (e.g., in professional journals, editorials, political speeches, primary source material).

### 3.0 Literary Response and Analysis

**10RL3.5** Compare works that express a universal theme and provide evidence to support the ideas expressed in each work.

**10RL3.9** Explain how voice, persona, and the choice of a narrator affect characterization and the tone, plot, and credibility of a text.

**10RL3.12** Analyze the way in which a work of literature is related to the themes and issues of its historical period. (Historical approach)

## Writing

### 1.0 Writing Strategies

**10WS1.3** Use clear research questions, and suitable research methods (e.g., library, electronic media, personal interview) to elicit and present evidence from primary and secondary resources.

### 2.0 Writing Applications (Genres and Their Characteristics)

**10WA2.1** Write biographical or autobiographical narratives or short stories.
**a.** Relate a sequence of events and communicate the significance of the events to the audience.

**10WA2.2** Write responses to literature.

**10WA2.3** Write expository compositions, including analytical essays and research reports:
**a.** Marshal evidence in support of a thesis and related claims, including information on all relevant perspectives.
**b.** Convey information and ideas from primary and secondary sources accurately and coherently.

**10WA2.4** Write persuasive compositions in a sustained and logical fashion.
**a.** Structure ideas and arguments in a sustained and logical fashion.
**c.** Clarify and defend positions with precise and relevant evidence, including facts, expert opinions, quotations, and expressions of commonly accepted beliefs and logical reasoning.

**10WA2.5** Write business letters:
**c.** Highlight central ideas or images.

## Listening and Speaking

### 1.0 Listening and Speaking Strategies

**1.10** Analyze historically significant speeches (e.g., Abraham Lincoln's "Gettysburg Address," Martin Luther King, Jr.'s "I Have a Dream") to find the rhetorical devices and features that make them memorable.

### 2.0 Speaking Applications (Genres and Their Characteristics)

**2.3** Apply appropriate interviewing techniques.

# How Does *Glencoe World History: Modern Times* Help Me Practice the Standards?

**W**hen you study world history with *Glencoe World History: Modern Times*, you are also practicing many of the English–Language Arts Standards for tenth grade. Your textbook includes many opportunities to practice reading, writing, and speaking skills.

- Each Section Assessment includes a writing prompt in the Writing About History box. The writing prompts can be short journal entries, letters, or brief reports.

- Each Chapter Assessment contains a Writing About History component with several activities. Many of these activities require you to do research either on the Internet or in the library and ask you to give a presentation about your research to your class.

- The World Literature feature in each unit, along with other features in your textbook, gives you the opportunity to develop critical reading skills, as well as writing exercises.

- The SkillBuilder Handbook on pages 779–796 provides additional practice in critical thinking and in technology and writing skills. Each Skillbuilder explains a specific skill and gives you an exercise so you can practice what you have learned.

### WORLD LITERATURE

#### from Shooting an Elephant
**George Orwell**

**George Orwell** was the pen name of English author Eric Arthur Blair, who was born in Motihari, India, on June 25, 1903. He lived for 46 years, and during that time, he wrote many influential essays, novels, and newspaper articles. His two most famous works are *1984* and *Animal Farm*, both of which are commentaries against totalitarianism. He served for several years as an assistant superintendent in the Indian Imperial Police but resigned due to his distaste of imperialism. In *Shooting an Elephant*, Orwell describes an incident that happened to him, and he satirizes the problems of colonial rule.

**Read to Discover**
Examine the ways in which George Orwell describes the relationship between the British colonial officer and the "natives." Can you think of a modern parallel to this situation?

**Reader's Dictionary**
**mahout:** a keeper and driver of an elephant

**dominion:** rule, control

**sahib:** title meaning "sir" or "master"

*I*n Moulmein, in lower Burma, I was hated by large numbers of people—the only time in my life that I have been important enough for this to happen to me. I was subdivisional police officer of the town, and in an aimless, petty kind of way anti-European feeling was very bitter. No one had the guts to raise a riot, but if a European woman went through the bazaars alone somebody would probably spit betel juice over her dress. As a police officer I was an obvious target and was baited whenever it seemed safe to do so. . . .

All this was perplexing and upsetting. For at that time I had already made up my mind that imperialism was an evil thing and the sooner I chucked up my job and got out of it the better. Theoretically—and secretly, of course—I was all for the Burmese and all against their oppressors, the British. . . . But I could get nothing into perspective. . . .

One day something happened which in a roundabout way was enlightening. . . . Early one morning the subinspector at a police station the other end of the town rang me up on the phone and said that an elephant was ravaging the bazaar. Would I please come and do something about it? . . .

The Burmese subinspector and some Indian constables were waiting for me in the quarter where the elephant had been seen. . . . We began questioning the people as to where the elephant had gone and,

◄ **Colonial hunter**

# A Guide to Glencoe's Standards Practice for Your World History Course

The History-Science Standards adopted by the California State Board of Education highlight important developments in modern world history. That is why you are expected to master these standards by the time you have finished your world history course.

Glencoe's *At-Home Standards Practice* is designed to help you become familiar with the California standards. If you use this Standards Practice as you are taking the course, you will know whether you are learning the material of your World History course.

How does the Standards Practice work?

- For each two-week period, you will focus on a single standard. Each day of the school week, you can try to answer a question on one standard. By the end of the course, you will have completed a practice session on every standard!

- You will notice that each question tells you which standard you are practicing. This also helps familiarize you with the content of the standards.

- After most questions, the Standards Practice refers you to the Chapter and Section of your textbook where you can find the answer. This will help you review material quickly.

- Each practice session includes questions based on primary sources, maps, charts, and illustrations. These questions will help you acquire the history and analysis skills you need to master world history.

- Finally, you can check your understanding by consulting the Answer Key at the back of the Standards Practice pages.

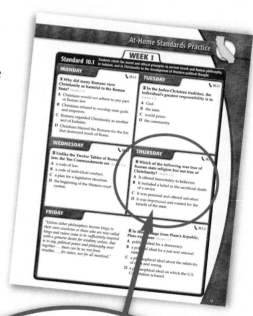

## THURSDAY 📞 10.1.1

**4** **Which of the following was true of Roman state religion but not true of Christianity?** *(Section 1.3)*

A It offered immortality to believers.

B It included a belief in the sacrificial death of a savior.

C It was personal and offered salvation.

D It was impersonal and existed for the benefit of the state.

## WEEK 1

**Standard 10.1** Students relate the moral and ethical principles in ancient Greek and Roman philosophy, in Judaism, and in Christianity to the development of Western political thought.

### MONDAY
📞 10.1.1

**1** **Why did many Romans view Christianity as harmful to the Roman State?** *(Section 1.3)*

A Christians would not adhere to any part of Roman law.

B Christians refused to worship state gods and emperors.

C Romans regarded Christianity as another sect of Judaism.

D Christians blamed the Romans for the fire that destroyed much of Rome.

### TUESDAY
📞 10.1.1

**2** **In the Judeo-Christian tradition, the individual's greatest responsibility is to** *(Section 1.3)*

A God.

B the state.

C world peace.

D the community.

### WEDNESDAY
📞 10.1.1

**3** **Unlike the Twelve Tables of Roman law, the Ten Commandments are** *(Section 1.1)*

A a code of law.

B a code of individual conduct.

C a plan for a legislative structure.

D the beginning of the Western court system.

### THURSDAY
📞 10.1.1

**4** **Which of the following was true of Roman state religion but not true of Christianity?** *(Section 1.3)*

A It offered immortality to believers.

B It included a belief in the sacrificial death of a savior.

C It was personal and offered salvation.

D It was impersonal and existed for the benefit of the state.

### FRIDAY
📞 10.1.2

*"Unless either philosophers become kings in their own countries or those who are now called kings and rulers come to be sufficiently inspired with a genuine desire for wisdom; unless, that is to say, political power and philosophy meet together . . . there can be no rest from troubles . . . for states, nor for all mankind."*

**5** **In this passage from Plato's *Republic*, Plato expresses** *(Section 1.2)*

A political ideal for a democracy.

B a political ideal for a just and rational state.

C a philosophical ideal about the relativity of right and wrong.

D a philosophical ideal on which the U.S. Constitution is based.

# At-Home Standards Practice

## Standard 10.1
Students relate the moral and ethical principles in ancient Greek and Roman philosophy, in Judaism, and in Christianity to the development of Western political thought.

### MONDAY
🔊 10.1.2

*The best man, then, must legislate, and laws must be passed, but these laws will have no authority when they miss the mark, though in all other cases retaining their authority. But when the law cannot determine a point at all, or not well, should the one best man or should all decide? . . . the state is made up of many individuals. . . . a feast to which all the guests contribute is better than a banquet furnished by a single man . . .*

—*Aristotle,* Politics

**1** This passage would best support the idea of *(Section 1.2)*

A  a supreme ruler

B  an anarchist state

C  a constitutional government

D  an absolute monarchy

### TUESDAY
🔊 10.1.2

**2** Who first suggested that citizens had not only rights but also responsibilities to the state? *(Section 1.2)*

A  Moses

B  Jesus

C  Plato

D  Aristotle

### WEDNESDAY
🔊 10.1.3

**3** One similarity between the Mexican Constitution enacted in 1917 and U.S. Constitution is *(Section 6.4)*

A  it established limits on foreign investors.

B  an agenda to help workers.

C  the inclusion of land reforms.

D  a government led by a president.

### THURSDAY
🔊 10.1.3

**4** In its principles, the Declaration of the Rights of Man and the Citizen most resembled *(Section 3.1)*

A  the Magna Carta.

B  the U.S. Constitution.

C  the philosophy of Aristotle.

D  Plato's *Republic*.

### FRIDAY
🔊 10.1.3

**5** Many countries in Latin America began to build democratic governments in the 1980s EXCEPT *(Section 14.2)*

A  Mexico.

B  Cuba.

C  Brazil.

D  Chile.

## WEEK 3

**Standard 10.2**
Students compare and contrast the Glorious Revolution of England, the American Revolution, and the French Revolution and their enduring effects worldwide on the political expectations for self-government and individual liberty.

### MONDAY
10.2.1

**1** What was Montesquieu's most lasting contribution to political thought? *(Section 2.2)*

A analysis of the system of checks and balances through separation of powers

B the concept of a social contract

C introduction of laissez-faire economics

D reform of the social justice system

### TUESDAY
10.2.1

**2** Which Latin American leader developed revolutionary ideas based on the principles of the equality of all people? *(Section 6.4)*

A Antonio López de Santa Anna

B Porfirio Díaz

C Simón Bolívar

D Mohandas Gandhi

### WEDNESDAY
10.2.1

*"We hold these truths to be self-evident: that all men are created equal, that they are endowed by their Creator with certain unalienable rights, that among these are life, liberty, and the pursuit of happiness."*

**3** The ideas expressed in the quotation are based primarily on the writings of
*(Section 2.1)*

A Niccolò Machiavelli.

B Charles Darwin.

C Charlemagne.

D John Locke.

### THURSDAY
10.2.2

**4** The Magna Carta was significant because it *(Section 1.4)*

A limited the power of the king.

B established the Parliament.

C extended the right to vote to nobles and bishops.

D led to the limited power of the king's vassals.

### FRIDAY
10.2.4

**5** The French Revolution, which tried to create both a new social order and a new political order, *(Sections 3.1 and 3.2)*

A failed to create a new constitution.

B aimed to create democratic despotism.

C was compromised by a movement to radicalism.

D created only a new political order.

## WEEK 4

**Standard 10.2** — Students compare and contrast the Glorious Revolution of England, the American Revolution, and the French Revolution and their enduring effects worldwide on the political expectations for self-government and individual liberty.

### MONDAY — 10.2.3

**1** Revolutions against colonial rule in Latin America were inspired, in part, by the ideals of *(Section 6.4)*

A  a majority of *peninsulares.*

B  the African nationalist movement.

C  the ideas of Augustín de Iturbide.

D  the French and American revolutions.

### TUESDAY — 10.2.3

**2** The American Revolution was NOT a conflict about *(Section 2.3)*

A  rights of man.

B  religion.

C  taxes.

D  representation.

### WEDNESDAY — 10.2.4

**3** Napoleon rose to power in France primarily because *(Section 3.3)*

A  he preached Enlightenment principles.

B  he had great leadership abilities during a period of instability.

C  he used military skills to undermine the monarchy.

D  he had no opposition when he ran for consulate.

### THURSDAY — 10.2.5

**4** A main goal of the Congress of Vienna was to *(Section 4.2)*

A  keep France powerless.

B  keep any one country from dominating Europe.

C  diminish the power of the monarchies.

D  create a defensive alliance against Germany.

### FRIDAY — 10.2.5

French are hated as oppressors

France shows the power of the nation-in-arms

**5** Which of the following best completes this organizer? *(Section 3.3)*

A  Napoleon enlarges his empire.

B  Nationalism spreads across Europe.

C  Nations embrace their common destiny.

D  Napoleon changes France for the better.

## WEEK 5

## Standard 10.3
Students analyze the effects of the Industrial Revolution in England, France, Germany, Japan, and the United States.

### MONDAY
10.3.1

**1** All these were reasons why the Industrial Revolution began in Britain **EXCEPT** *(Section 4.1)*

A natural resources were plentiful.

B there was a ready supply of capital.

C a growing population was available to work in industry.

D agricultural production had dropped.

### TUESDAY
10.3.2

**2** Which of these revolutionized the spinning and weaving of cotton? *(Section 4.1)*

A the steam engine.

B the spinning jenny.

C the water-powered loom.

D the process called puddling.

### WEDNESDAY
10.3.3

**3** The rapid growth of cities during the first half of the nineteenth century led **most immediately** to *(Section 4.1)*

A the rise of industrial capitalism.

B poor living conditions in the cities.

C widespread famine.

D child labor laws.

### THURSDAY
10.3.4

**4** Which of the following best describes the new industrial working class? *(Section 4.1)*

A It consisted mainly of children between the ages of nine and fourteen.

B It included very few women.

C Many of its members worked in cotton mills or mines.

D Hours were long, and conditions were dangerous, but minimum wages were guaranteed.

### FRIDAY
10.3.5

- natural resources
- labor
- capital

**5** Study the list at left. What item should be added to this list of critical factors in industrialization? *(Section 4.1)*

A cottage industries

B secularization

C natural selection

D entrepreneurship

## WEEK 6

**Standard 10.3** Students analyze the effects of the Industrial Revolution in England, France, Germany, Japan, and the United States.

### MONDAY    📞 10.3.4

**1 Early trade unions are best characterized as** *(Section 5.1)*

A capitalist.

B communist.

C socialist.

D industrialist.

### TUESDAY    📞 10.3.6

**2 When early socialists responded to the conditions created by the Industrial Revolution, what did they propose?** *(Section 4.1)*

A cooperation instead of competition

B communes instead of cities

C farms instead of factories

D manual labor instead of machines

### WEDNESDAY    📞 10.3.6

**3 In response to conditions created by the Industrial Revolution, Karl Marx proposed** *(Section 4.1)*

A a global economy.

B the oppression of the bourgeoisie.

C the end of technology.

D a new social order.

### THURSDAY    📞 10.3.7

**4 The romantic poetry of William Wordsworth celebrated** *(Section 4.4)*

A the Industrial Revolution.

B Enlightenment principles.

C nature.

D civilization.

### FRIDAY    📞 10.3.7

*It was a town of red brick, or of brick that would have been red if the smoke and ashes had allowed it; but, as matters stood, it was a town of unnatural red and black like the painted face of a savage. It was a town of machinery and tall chimneys, out of which interminable serpents of smoke trailed themselves for ever and ever, and never got uncoiled.*

**5 This excerpt from a novel by Charles Dickens could best be described as** *(Section 4.4)*

A modernism.

B classicism.

C realism.

D stream of consciousness.

## WEEK 7

**Standard 10.4** Students analyze patterns of global change in the era of New Imperialism in at least two of the following regions or countries: Africa, Southeast Asia, China, India, Latin American, and the Philippines.

### MONDAY 📞 10.4.1

**1** In the philosophy called Social Darwinism, Charles Darwin's theories were used to justify *(Section 5.4)*

A nationalist agendas and racism.

B psychoanalysis.

C secularization and modernism.

D theories set forth in the *Communist Manifesto.*

### TUESDAY 📞 10.4.1

**2** The primary economic motivation for the new imperialism was *(Section 6.1)*

A spreading democracy around the world.

B finding waterways and trade routes.

C converting conquered people to Christianity.

D finding raw materials and establishing new markets.

### WEDNESDAY 📞 10.4.2

*During the era of "New Imperialism," the German Chancellor said: "For Germany to acquire colonies would be like a poverty-stricken Polish nobleman providing himself with silks and sables when he needed shirts." A German writer countered by saying, "What was and is valid for England is also valid for us."*

**3** Which statement best represents the assumptions of both men about Germany? *(Section 6.2)*

A Germany was not rich enough for colonies.

B Germany should cut other budget costs in order to afford colonies.

C Germany is or is not different from England.

D Since England was getting all the colonies, Germany needed to compete.

### THURSDAY 📞 10.4.1

**4** Colonial economies depended on *(Section 6.1)*

A developing industry.

B direct rule.

C indirect rule.

D exporting raw materials.

### FRIDAY 📞 10.4.2

**5** At the beginning of the nineteenth century, the two major colonial powers in Latin America were *(Section 6.4)*

A the United States and Spain.

B Spain and Portugal.

C Spain and Germany.

D Spain and the Netherlands.

# At-Home Standards Practice

## WEEK 8

**Standard 10.4**  Students analyze patterns of global changes in the era of New Imperialism in at least two of the following regions or countries: Africa, Southeast Asia, China, India, Latin America, and the Philippines.

### MONDAY

📞 10.4.2

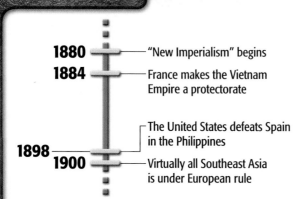

1880 — "New Imperialism" begins
1884 — France makes the Vietnam Empire a protectorate

1898 — The United States defeats Spain in the Philippines
1900 — Virtually all Southeast Asia is under European rule

**1** The number of years that passed between the beginning of the new imperialism and the virtually complete colonization of Southeast Asia is approximately *(Section 6.1)*

A  ten years.

B  sixteen years.

C  twenty years.

D  thirty years.

### TUESDAY

📞 10.4.3

**2** The phrase "white man's burden" refers to *(Section 6.1)*

A  the costs of extracting raw materials.

B  the "moral" responsibility to "civilize" others.

C  the economic responsibility to spread capitalism.

D  the costs of creating new markets.

### WEDNESDAY

📞 10.4.3

**3** By the beginning of the twentieth century, reaction against colonial rule in Africa had shown itself in *(Section 6.2)*

A  the rise of nationalism, especially among educated Africans.

B  widespread rebellion.

C  a growing socialist movement, especially among plantation workers.

D  economic gains for most members of the middle class.

### THURSDAY

📞 10.4.4

**4** What is another name for the revolt that Indians call their First War of Independence against Britain? *(Section 6.3)*

A  the Kanpur Uprising

B  the Sepoy Mutiny

C  the Mumbai Rebellion

D  the Indian National Revolt

### FRIDAY

📞 10.4.4

**5** Which of the following accurately describes Sun Yat-sen? *(Section 7.2)*

A  He agreed with most ruling principles of the Qing dynasty.

B  He believed in democracy but did not think it could be accomplished immediately.

C  He hoped to make himself a permanent dictator.

D  He primarily followed the teachings of Empress Ci Xi.

## WEEK 9

**Standard 10.5** Students analyze the causes and the course of the First World War.

### MONDAY
 10.5.1

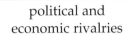

```
political and
economic rivalries
```

```
ethnic and
ideological conflicts
```    →    World
                War I

```
alliances
```

```
[                    ]
```

**1** **Which of the following best completes the graphic organizer?** *(Section 8.1)*

**A** economic discontent and disorder

**B** instability resulting from the Russian Revolution

**C** genocide in Armenia

**D** the rising threat of communism in China, Russia, and Southeast Asia

### TUESDAY
 10.5.1

**2** **During the period from 1900 to 1914, European political leaders believed that peace throughout the world could best be maintained by** *(Section 8.1)*

**A** policies of isolationism.

**B** international organizations.

**C** systems of alliances.

**D** policies of appeasement.

### WEDNESDAY
 10.5.2

**3** **The geographic factor that contributed most significantly to the "great slaughter" of World War I was** *(Section 8.2)*

**A** mountains.

**B** open fields.

**C** rushing rivers.

**D** polluted streams.

### THURSDAY
 10.5.2

**4** **Which of these major battles occurred on the Eastern Front?** *(Section 8.2)*

**A** Marne

**B** Somme

**C** Verdun

**D** Tannenberg

### FRIDAY
 10.5.3

**5** **What effect did the Russian Revolution have on World War I?** *(Section 8.4)*

**A** Russia withdrew from the war.

**B** Russia became more vulnerable to German invasion.

**C** Russia switched loyalties, aligning itself with Germany.

**D** The Russian army was destroyed by fighting two wars.

## WEEK 10

**Standard 10.5** Students analyze the causes and the course of the First World War.

### MONDAY
10.5.1

ENLIST

**1** All of the following are true of this poster EXCEPT *(Section 8.1)*

A it refers to the sinking of the *Lusitania*.

B it is an example of propaganda.

C it was used to motivate Americans to go to war.

D it is meant to suggest the importance of motherhood.

### TUESDAY
10.5.3

**2** Which of the following best describes the effect of the United States entry into World War I in April 1917? *(Sections 8.2 and 8.4)*

A The tide of war turned immediately.

B The tide of war turned by the end of 1917.

C The tide of war turned in 1918.

D The United States helped the Allies to win the war they had already just begun to win.

### WEDNESDAY
10.5.4

**3** The impact of World War I on most European nations included all of the following EXCEPT *(Section 8.4)*

A the development of planned economies.

B increased government powers.

C new roles for women.

D destruction of the middle class.

### THURSDAY
10.5.4

**4** From which nation or nations did Britain mobilize the efforts of colonial peoples during World War I? *(Section 8.2)*

A India

B Australia

C New Zealand

D all of the above

### FRIDAY
10.5.5

**5** How did the Ottoman Turks deal with their Armenian minority in 1915? *(Section 10.1)*

A by resettling Armenians in Georgia

B by massacring one million Armenians

C by granting them autonomy

D by forcing them to learn Turkish

## WEEK 11

## Standard 10.6 Students analyze the effects of the First World War.

### MONDAY 📞 10.6.1

**1** **Which of the following best describes the Fourteen Points?** *(Section 8.4)*

**A** an installment plan of fourteen payments for German reparations

**B** the fourteen terms of the Treaty of Versailles

**C** Wilson's fourteen main ideas for a just and lasting peace

**D** fourteen disputed territories to be discussed at the Paris Peace Conference in 1919

### TUESDAY 📞 10.6.1

**2** **The main reason for the U.S. failure to join the League of Nations was** *(Section 9.1)*

**A** French demands for more German territory.

**B** Americans' desire to stay out of European affairs.

**C** dissatisfaction with Woodrow Wilson.

**D** suspicion of other member nations.

### WEDNESDAY 📞 10.6.1

**3** **The new map of Europe after World War I created all of the following new nation-states EXCEPT** *(Section 8.4)*

**A** Serbia, Croatia, and Slovenia.

**B** Latvia, Lithuania, and Estonia.

**C** Austria and Hungary.

**D** Poland, Czechoslovakia, and Finland.

### THURSDAY 📞 10.6.2

**4** **The Treaty of Versailles with Germany included all of the following EXCEPT**
*(Section 8.4)*

**A** a war guilt clause.

**B** a reduced army and navy.

**C** the return of Alsace and Lorraine to France.

**D** the return of the Rhineland to France.

### FRIDAY 📞 10.6.1

**5** **This painting was created in response to** *(Section 9.2)*

**A** the horrors of the Spanish Civil War.

**B** a request by Francisco Franco.

**C** the Russian Revolution.

**D** the rise of surrealism.

## WEEK 12

### Standard 10.6 Students analyze the effects of the First World War.

#### MONDAY
✎ 10.6.2

*Certain communities formerly belonging to the Turkish Empire have reached a stage of development where their existence as independent nations can be provisionally recognised subject to the rendering of administrative advice and assistance by a Mandatory until such time as they are able to stand alone. The wishes of these communities must be a principal consideration in the selection of the Mandatory.*

—*Treaty of Versailles, Article 22, 1919*

**1** **This article expresses all of these ideas EXCEPT** *(Section 8.4)*

A that the Ottoman Empire will be broken up.

B that nation-states should develop on their own.

C that Western powers will annex new territory.

D that tyranny is still a principal concern.

#### TUESDAY
✎ 10.6.3

**2** **The Turkish leader who overturned prewar institutions and values was** *(Section 10.1)*

A Mustafa Kemal.

B T. E. Lawrence.

C Abdulhamid II.

D Ibn Saud.

#### WEDNESDAY
✎ 10.6.3

**3** **Which of these best states the main goal of Reza Shah Pahlavi?** *(Section 10.1)*

A to unify the northern part of the Arabian Peninsula

B to create a modern Iran

C to create a Zionist movement

D to issue the Balfour Declaration

#### THURSDAY
✎ 10.6.3

**4** **Fascism arose in Italy primarily as a result of** *(Section 9.2)*

A severe economic problems.

B fear of a communist takeover.

C division created by agricultural and industrial strikes.

D all of the above.

#### FRIDAY
✎ 10.6.4

**5** **After World War I, a widespread sense of purposelessness was best reflected in the art form called** *(Section 9.4)*

A the uncertainty principle.

B stream of consciousness.

C surrealism.

D dadaism.

## WEEK 13

## Standard 10.7 — Students analyze the rise of totalitarian governments after World War I.

### MONDAY
10.7.2

*"We must gradually, but systematically and persistently, place our agriculture on a new technical basis, the basis of large-scale production, and bring it up to the level of socialist industry. Either we accomplish this task-in which case the final victory of socialism in our country will be assured, or we turn away from it and do not accomplish it—in which case a return to capitalism may become inevitable."*

**1 In this statement on his Five-Year Plan, Stalin expresses his belief that**

A the Soviet agricultural system is advanced.

B the modernization of agricultural production is necessary.

C industry and capitalism can't be separated.

D tradition is in danger from technology.

### TUESDAY
10.7.1

**2 By which means did Lenin gain control of Russia?** *(Section 8.3)*

A parliamentary or legislative procedure

B popular vote

C military overthrow of the government

D czarist abdication

### WEDNESDAY
10.7.1

**3 Why did German military leaders ship V.I. Lenin to Russia in 1917?** *(Section 8.3)*

A Lenin tried to overthrow the German government.

B German leaders believed Lenin would defeat the Bolsheviks.

C Russia demanded the return of Lenin from a German prison.

D German military leaders hoped to create disorder in Russia.

### THURSDAY
10.7.2

**4 In general, Stalin's economic policies led to** *(Section 8.3)*

A suffering for the masses.

B a slight increase in real wages.

C suffering for some peasants who lost their farms.

D the end of famine in Russia.

### FRIDAY
10.7.2

**5 Stalin dealt with political opposition primarily by means of** *(Section 9.2)*

A industrialization.

B collectivization.

C purges.

D the Politburo.

## WEEK 14

**Standard 10.7** Students analyze the rise of totalitarian governments after World War I.

### MONDAY ☎ 10.7.3

**1 The dictator who developed Five-Year Plans and collectivized agriculture was** *(Section 9.2)*

A Stalin.

B Hitler.

C Franco.

D Mussolini.

### TUESDAY ☎ 10.7.2

**2 How did Stalin's program of collectivization lead to widespread famine?** *(Section 9.2)*

A It caused peasants to protest by hoarding crops and killing livestock.

B It prohibited the use of machinery in peasant farming.

C It limited crop production to only those crops that could be used in industry.

D It attempted to eliminate agricultural efforts in favor of industrialization.

### WEDNESDAY ☎ 10.7.3

**3 Mussolini created the OVRA, which was** *(Section 9.2)*

A a secret police force.

B a new cabinet.

C a national bank.

D an arts council.

### THURSDAY ☎ 10.7.3

**4 Totalitarian regimes tried to gain the loyalty of their people through** *(Section 9.2)*

A isolation and misinformation.

B conventions and elections.

C propaganda and modern communication.

D promoting individual achievements and innovations.

### FRIDAY ☎ 10.7.3

| Leader | Party | Core Supporters |
|---|---|---|
| Mussolini | Fascist | business, landowners, military |
| Stalin | Communist | workers, party bureaucrats |
| Hitler | Nazi | small business-people, anti-Semites |

**5 According to the chart, which of the following was a key difference between the communist regime of Stalin and the fascist regimes of Hitler and Mussolini?** *(Sections 9.2 and 9.3)*

A Stalin's regime was authoritarian, not totalitarian.

B Stalin's regime was supported by party officials.

C Stalin's regime used secret police.

D Stalin's regime was supported by large landowners.

## WEEK 15

### Standard 10.8 Students analyze the causes and consequences of World War II.

---

### MONDAY 🔌 10.8.1

**1** When Hitler sent troops into the Rhineland, it was a first step toward war because *(Section 11.1)*

A Hitler invaded France.

B Hitler broke the terms of the Treaty of Versailles.

C Great Britain controlled the Rhineland as a mandate.

D Mussolini supported Hitler's action.

### TUESDAY 🔌 10.8.1

**2** What did the agreement that Hitler made with Stalin in 1939 allow Hitler to do? *(Section 11.1)*

A invade Stalingrad

B conquer the Balkans

C invade Poland

D declare war on Britain

---

### WEDNESDAY 🔌 10.8.1

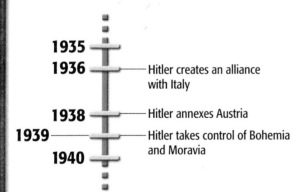

1935
1936 — Hitler creates an alliance with Italy
1938 — Hitler annexes Austria
1939 — Hitler takes control of Bohemia and Moravia
1940

**3** What is the best title for this time line? *(Section 11.1)*

A Germany Moves Toward War

B Europe Prepares for War

C Europe Abandons Appeasement

D New Alliances Change Europe

---

### THURSDAY 🔌 10.8.2

**4** Great Britain responded to German aggression in the 1930s with *(Section 11.1)*

A demilitarization.

B annexation.

C ethnic cleansing.

D appeasement.

### FRIDAY 🔌 10.8.3

**5** In addition to fierce resistance, what halted the German advance on the Soviet Union? *(Section 11.2)*

A the Black Sea

B harsh winter weather

C the Volga River

D the distance across the Caucasus

# At-Home Standards Practice

## Standard 10.8 Students analyze the causes and consequences of World War II.

### MONDAY 🎧 10.8.3

**1** Put these events in order.
1 Attack on Pearl Harbor
2 Battle of Britain
3 Fall of France
4 Attack on Poland *(Section 11.2)*

A 4, 1, 3, 2

B 2, 4, 3, 1

C 4, 1, 2, 3

D 4, 3, 2, 1

### TUESDAY 🎧 10.8.3

**2** The turning point of the war in the Asian Theater occurred at *(Section 11.2)*

A Midway Island.

B Iwo Jima.

C Okinawa.

D Wake Island.

### WEDNESDAY 🎧 10.8.6

| Battle Deaths in World War II | |
|---|---|
| **Country** | **Battle Deaths** |
| USSR | 7,500,000 |
| Germany | 3,500,000 |
| Yugoslavia | 410,000 |
| Poland | 320,000 |
| Romania | 300,000 |
| United States | 292,000 |
| United Kingdom | 245,000 |
| France | 210,000 |
| Hungary | 140,000 |

**3** Which of the following conclusions is accurately drawn from this data? *(Section 11.2)*

A Germany lost the most soldiers in World War II.

B The United Kingdom had greater losses than the United States.

C The losses of the USSR were greater than the combined losses of all other nations.

D France lost more soldiers than Hungary and Finland combined.

### THURSDAY 🎧 10.8.4

**4** Generals Douglas MacArthur and Dwight Eisenhower were *(Section 11.2)*

A the American commanders of the D-Day invasion.

B the British and American commanders of the D-Day invasion.

C American commanders in the Pacific and Europe.

D American commanders who argued against dropping the atomic bomb.

### FRIDAY 🎧 10.8.5

**5** The extermination of six million Jews during the Holocaust was carried out *(Section 11.3)*

A at death camps.

B by the *Einsatzgruppen.*

C by a method of gassing called the Final Solution.

D by a variety of means, including mass murder at death camps.

## WEEK 17

## Standard 10.9 Students analyze the international developments in the post-World War II world.

### MONDAY 10.9.1

**1** **Like Germany after World War II, Japan also experienced** *(Section 16.3)*

A an "economic miracle."

B an inability to rebuild its industrial base.

C a period of occupation.

D political division by means of an "iron curtain."

### TUESDAY 10.9.1

**2** **What issue remained unresolved after the Yalta Conference?** *(Section 11.4)*

A Stalin's control of the Sakhalin and Kuril Islands

B the creation of the United Nations

C the division of Germany into four zones

D free elections in Eastern Europe

### WEDNESDAY 10.9.2

**3** **What political theory influenced United States involvement in the conflict in Vietnam?** *(Section 12.1)*

A the Arms Theory

B the Roosevelt Corollary

C the Domino Theory

D the Marshall Plan

### THURSDAY 10.9.3

**4** **Both the Truman Doctrine and the Marshall Plan** *(Section 12.1)*

A provided economic aid in the hopes of fighting communist aggression.

B provided military rather than economic aid to anti-communist nations.

C offered aid to Western European nations only.

D refused aid to Germany.

### FRIDAY 10.9.6

Egypt, Israel, and Surrounding Nations

SYRIA
LEBANON
ISRAEL
IRAQ
JORDAN
EGYPT
SAUDI ARABIA

**5** **Based on this map, which issue would NOT lead to territorial disputes?** *(Section 15.2)*

A access to waterways

B Saudi Arabia's size

C a Jewish homeland

D Pan-Arabism

# At-Home Standards Practice

## WEEK 18

**Standard 10.9** Students analyze the international developments in the post-World War II world.

### MONDAY
10.9.7

| 1 Ukraine votes for independence |
| 2 Brezhnev Doctrine enacted |
| 3 Revolutionary movement in Eastern Europe |
| 4 Soviet Union invades Afghanistan |

**1** Put the events at left in chronological order. *(Section 13.1)*

A 2, 4, 3, 1
B 1, 3, 2, 4
C 1, 2, 3, 4
D 3, 1, 4, 2

### TUESDAY
10.9.8

**2** Which two major hostile alliances had arisen in Europe by 1955? *(Section 12.1)*

A NATO and SEATO
B SEATO and CENTO
C CENTO and the Warsaw Pact
D The Warsaw Pact and NATO

### WEDNESDAY
10.9.4

**3** Who led the People's Liberation Army, which fought the Nationalists in the Chinese Civil War? *(Section 10.3)*

A Chiang Kai-shek
B Mao Zedong
C Sun Yat-sen
D Ho Chi Minh

### THURSDAY
10.9.4

**4** In 1958, China's Great Leap Forward *(Section 16.1)*

A increased agricultural productivity.
B abandoned the principles of industrial expansion.
C restored a capitalist economic system.
D resulted in widespread famine.

### FRIDAY
10.9.5

**5** The events that took place in Hungary in the 1950s and in Czechoslovakia in the 1960s demonstrated the Soviet Union's *(Section 12.2)*

A support of nationalism among satellite states.
B influence on the economies of developing nations.
C determination to maintain political control over Eastern Europe at that time.
D attempts to promote its artistic and literary achievements in Western Europe.

## WEEK 19

**Standard 10.10** Students analyze instances of nation-building in the contemporary world in at least two of the following regions or countries: the Middle East, Africa, Mexico and other parts of Latin America, and China.

### MONDAY ⬛ 10.10.1

**1** Which major economic problem have Latin American countries faced throughout their histories that continues to be an issue now? *(Sections 14.1, 14.2, and 14.3)*

**A** lack of capital for industrial development

**B** declining birthrate

**C** widespread acceptance of Marxist economic principles

**D** lack of labor for factories in urban centers

### TUESDAY ⬛ 10.10.1

**2** What group has most frequently opposed social and economic change in Latin American and continues to be a force against change today?

*(Sections 14.1, 14.2, 14.3)*

**A** landowners

**B** students

**C** mestizos

**D** peasants

### WEDNESDAY ⬛ 10.10.2

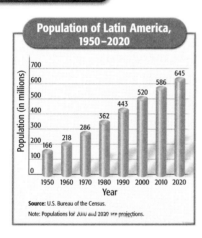

Population of Latin America, 1950–2020

Source: U.S. Bureau of the Census.
Note: Populations for 2010 and 2020 are projections.

**3** According to this graph, the rate of growth of the Latin American population

*(Section 14.4)*

**A** spiked in some decades and held steady in others.

**B** is projected to grow at a fairly steady rate until at least 2020.

**C** is projected to decrease slightly after 2010.

**D** doubled between 1950 and 2020.

### THURSDAY ⬛ 10.10.1

**4** The war between Israel and Egypt ended in 1979 with the signing of the

*(Section 15.2)*

**A** Camp David Accords.

**B** Treaty of Locarno.

**C** INF Treaty.

**D** Truman Doctrine.

### FRIDAY ⬛ 10.10.1

**5** Which of the following is most characteristic of today's Africa? *(Section 15.1)*

**A** fundamentalist Islamic governments

**B** isolation from the influence of the West

**C** widespread existence of democratic governments based on the principles of the French and American Revolutions

**D** tension between rural and urban and between traditional and modern ways of life

# At-Home Standards Practice

## WEEK 20

**Standard 10.10** Students analyze instances of nation-building in the contemporary world in at least two of the following regions or countries: the Middle East, Africa, Mexico and other parts of Latin America, and China.

### MONDAY
📞 10.10.2

**1** **A legacy of colonialism that continues to be a problem for today's African nations is** *(Section 15.1)*

A the system of apartheid.

B political borders that unite conflicting ethnic groups.

C the Pan-African movement.

D schools that teach traditional African values.

### TUESDAY
📞 10.10.2

**2** **Which leader became the head of the Palestinian Authority in 1993?** *(Section 15.2)*

A Ayatollah Ruhollah Khomeini

B Menachem Begin

C Gamal Abdel Nasser

D Yasir Arafat

### WEDNESDAY
📞 10.10.3

*"We shall build a society in which . . . both black and white, will be able to walk tall, without any fear in their hearts, assured of their inalienable right to human dignity—a rainbow nation at peace with itself and the world."*

**3** **Who spoke these words at his presidential inaugural?** *(Section 15.1)*

A Jomo Kenyatta

B Julius Nyerere

C Kwame Nkrumah

D Nelson Mandela

### THURSDAY
📞 10.10.3

**4** **Which statement best describes the Middle East at the beginning of the twenty-first century?** *(Section 15.2)*

A Palestinians in the occupied territories want greater integration into Israeli society.

B The nations of the Middle East have adopted a common foreign policy.

C Arab unity has not been achieved.

D International cooperation has brought about an era of peace in the region.

### FRIDAY
📞 10.10.3

**5** **During the 1980s, one of China's major goals was to** *(Section 16.1)*

A accelerate economic growth.

B encourage the growth of religions.

C establish a federal system.

D protect individual liberties.

## WEEK 21

**Standard 10.11** Students analyze the integration of countries into the world economy and the information, technological, and communications revolutions (e.g., television, satellites, computers).

### MONDAY 📞 10.11

**1** Which is the MOST accurate statement about the global economy? *(Section 17.1)*

A It has narrowed the gap between rich and poor nations.

B It has intensified environmental and health problems for all developing nations.

C It is an economy in which the production, distribution, and sale of goods occur on a worldwide scale.

D It is likely to increase the spread of democracy around the world.

### TUESDAY 📞 10.11

**2** What is true about the World Trade Organization? *(Section 17.1)*

A It is a trade agreement between the nations of Western Europe.

B It developed the North American Free Trade Agreement.

C It is more concerned with the environment than with commercial interests.

D It is the only global international organization that deals with the rules of trade between nations.

### WEDNESDAY 📞 10.11

**3** What event in the 1980s reduced the chances of a major nuclear war? *(Section 17.1)*

A the end of the Cold War

B the proliferation of bomb shelters

C the elimination of nuclear research throughout the world

D the election of President Ronald Reagan

### THURSDAY 📞 10.11

**4** Some scientists believe that experimentation in which field may accidentally create new, uncontrollable strains of bacteria? *(Section 17.1)*

A mechanical heart valves

B organ transplants

C computer imaging

D genetic engineering

### FRIDAY 📞 10.11

*"We'll continue our quest in space. There will be more shuttle flights and more shuttle crews and, yes, more volunteers, more civilians, more teachers in space. Nothing ends here; our hopes and our journeys continue."*

—President Ronald Reagan's Address to the Nation on the Space Shuttle "Challenger"

**5** In this excerpt, Reagan expresses all beliefs EXCEPT

A America dominates space exploration.

B technological setbacks won't stop exploration.

C a trust in progress.

D space exploration is attainable for all people.

# At-Home Standards Practice

**Standard 10.11** Students analyze the integration of countries into the world economy and the information, technological, and communications revolutions (e.g., television, satellites, computers).

## MONDAY

10.11

### Highest Adult Literacy Rates

| Country | Rate of Literacy (percent) |
|---------|----------------------------|
| Andorra | 100 |
| Niger | 14 |
| Estonia | 100 |
| Czech Republic | 99.9 |
| Somalia | 24 |
| Nepal | 28 |

**1** Using the table at left, which of the nations would be considered developed, based on their literacy rate?

A Niger and Czech Republic

B Andorra and Nepal

C Nepal and Somalia

D Czech Republic and Estonia

## TUESDAY

10.11

**2 What caused drastic food shortages in the Sudan in the 1980s and 1990s?** *(Section 17.1)*

A trade restrictions

B civil war

C drought

D wildfires

## WEDNESDAY

10.11

**3 What development in the 1990s made the Internet accessible to people everywhere?** *(Section 17.1)*

A Internet Explorer

B the personal computer

C the World Wide Web

D direct satellite links

## THURSDAY

10.11

**4 Which is the MOST accurate statement about the technological revolution?** *(Section 17.1)*

A It has generally brought great benefits to humankind, including cures for diseases.

B It has had little effect on the world, although rich nations have grown richer.

C It has brought alarming consequences, such as bioterrorism and environmental threats.

D It has brought great advances in medicine, agriculture, and other fields, while also creating new threats and problems.

## FRIDAY

10.11

**5 What is true about the effort of developing nations to establish industrial economies?** *(Section 17.1)*

A Rapid population growth has placed burdens on the economies of developing nations, making industrialization difficult.

B Citizens of developing nations are resistant to changing from agriculture to industry.

C Developing nations do not have sufficient population numbers to industrialize.

D The climates of most developing nations do not support large industry.

# Answer Key

**Week 1**
1. B
2. A
3. B
4. D
5. B

**Week 2**
1. C
2. D
3. D
4. B
5. B

**Week 3**
1. A
2. C
3. D
4. A
5. C

**Week 4**
1. D
2. B
3. B
4. B
5. B

**Week 5**
1. D
2. A
3. B
4. C
5. D

**Week 6**
1. C
2. A
3. D
4. C
5. C

**Week 7**
1. A
2. D
3. C
4. D
5. B

**Week 8**
1. C
2. B
3. A
4. B
5. B

**Week 9**
1. A
2. C
3. B
4. D
5. A

**Week 10**
1. D
2. C
3. D
4. D
5. B

**Week 11**
1. C
2. B
3. A
4. D
5. A

**Week 12**
1. B
2. A
3. B
4. D
5. D

**Week 13**
1. B
2. C
3. D
4. A
5. C

**Week 14**
1. A
2. A
3. A
4. C
5. B

**Week 15**
1. B
2. C
3. A
4. D
5. B

**Week 16**
1. D
2. A
3. C
4. C
5. D

**Week 17**
1. C
2. A
3. C
4. A
5. B

**Week 18**
1. A
2. D
3. B
4. D
5. C

**Week 19**
1. A
2. A
3. B
4. A
5. D

**Week 20**
1. B
2. D
3. D
4. C
5. A

**Week 21**
1. C
2. D
3. A
4. D
5. A

**Week 22**
1. D
2. B
3. C
4. D
5. A

# Previewing Your Textbook

*Your textbook has been organized to help you learn about the significant events and people that make up world history. Before you start reading, though, here's a road map to help you understand what you will encounter in the pages of this textbook. Follow this road map before you read so that you can understand how this textbook works.*

## Units

Your textbook is divided into 4 units. Each unit begins with two pages of information to help you start your study of the topics.

**WHY IT MATTERS**

Each unit begins with *Why It Matters.* This is a short summary about the important topics and what you will study in the unit.

**QUOTATION**

A short quotation gives a glimpse of the ideas of a key figure from the era.

**PRIMARY SOURCES LIBRARY**

This tells you where to find the *Primary Sources Library* readings that accompany the unit.

**VISUALS**

A photograph or painting suggests what life was like during the time period.

# Chapters

Each unit in *Glencoe World History: Modern Times* is made up of chapters. Each chapter starts by providing you with background information to help you get the most out of the chapter.

## CHAPTER TITLE

The chapter title tells you the main topic you will be reading about.

## BIG IDEAS

The *Big Ideas* identify major themes in history for each section of the chapter.

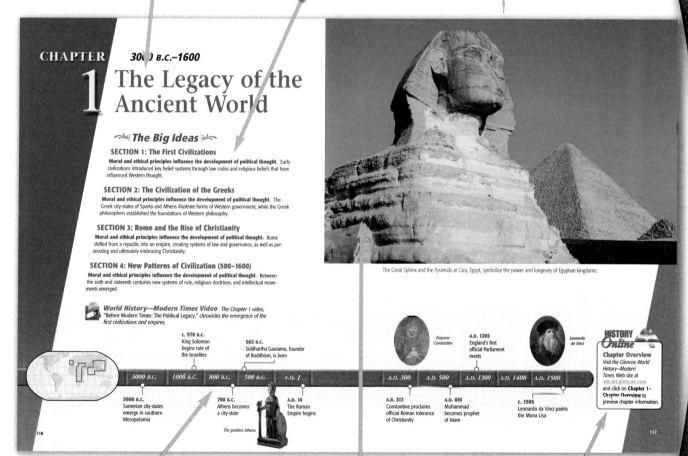

CHAPTER

3000 B.C.–1600

## 1 The Legacy of the Ancient World

### ✺ The Big Ideas ✺

**SECTION 1: The First Civilizations**
**Moral and ethical principles influence the development of political thought.** Early civilizations introduced key belief systems through law codes and religious beliefs that have influenced Western thought.

**SECTION 2: The Civilization of the Greeks**
**Moral and ethical principles influence the development of political thought.** The Greek city-states of Sparta and Athens illustrate forms of Western government, while the Greek philosophers established the foundations of Western philosophy.

**SECTION 3: Rome and the Rise of Christianity**
**Moral and ethical principles influence the development of political thought.** Rome shifted from a republic into an empire, creating systems of law and governance, as well as persecuting and ultimately embracing Christianity.

**SECTION 4: New Patterns of Civilization (500–1600)**
**Moral and ethical principles influence the development of political thought.** Between the sixth and sixteenth centuries new systems of rule, religious doctrines, and intellectual movements emerged.

**World History—Modern Times Video** The Chapter 1 video, *"Before Modern Times: The Political Legacy,"* chronicles the emergence of the first civilizations and empires.

The Great Sphinx and the Pyramids at Giza, Egypt, symbolize the power and longevity of Egyptian kingdoms.

c. 970 B.C.
King Solomon begins rule of the Israelites

563 B.C.
Siddhartha Gautama, founder of Buddhism, is born

*Emperor Constantine*

A.D. 1295
England's first official Parliament meets

*Leonardo da Vinci*

3000 B.C.   1000 B.C.   800 B.C.   500 B.C.   A.D. 1   A.D. 300   A.D. 500   A.D. 1300   A.D. 1400   A.D. 1500

3000 B.C.
Sumerian city-states emerge in southern Mesopotamia

700 B.C.
Athens becomes a city-state

A.D. 14
The Roman Empire begins

A.D. 313
Constantine proclaims official Roman tolerance of Christianity

A.D. 610
Muhammad becomes prophet of Islam

c. 1505
Leonardo da Vinci paints the Mona Lisa

*The goddess Athena*

**HISTORY Online**
**Chapter Overview**
Visit the *Glencoe World History—Modern Times* Web site at **wh.mt.glencoe.com** and click on **Chapter 1– Chapter Overview** to preview chapter information.

116     117

## TIME LINE

The time line shows you when and where events happened during the period of time covered in the chapter.

## VISUALS

A photograph or painting depicts a scene from the chapter's era.

## WEB SITE

*History Online* directs you to the Internet, where you can find activities and quizzes, along with more information about the chapter's topic.

# Previewing Your Textbook

# Sections

A section is a division, or part, of the chapter. The first page of the section, the section opener, helps you set a purpose for reading.

## SECTION PREVIEW AND MAIN IDEA

The *Section Preview* and *Main Idea* summarize the ideas in the section and in each subhead.

## VOCABULARY

The *Content Vocabulary* words are the section's key terms and will be defined in the text. *Academic Vocabulary* consists of words you should know to be successful in school and life.

## READING STRATEGY

Completing the *Reading Strategy* activity will help you organize information as you read the section.

## TIME LINE

The time line identifies important events you will study in the section.

## CALIFORNIA STANDARDS

The California Standards covered in each section can be found here.

---

SECTION 1 **The First Civilizations**

### Guide to Reading

**Section Preview**
Early civilizations introduced key belief systems through law codes and religious beliefs that have influenced Western thought.

**Main Idea**
• In ancient Mesopotamia, city-states elaborated the concept of the law code and divine kingship. (p. 122)
• The divinity of the pharaoh and religious belief contributed to the long life of Egyptian civilization. (p. 124)
• Key beliefs of Judaism that became important to the West developed during ancient times. (p. 125)
• Hinduism became a conservative force in Indian society that has lasted to this day. (p. 127)

• The lessons of Confucius influenced basic Chinese attitudes of deference and loyalty to family. (p. 128)

**Content Vocabulary**
civilization, patriarchal, pharaoh, Judaism, monotheistic, covenant, prophet, caste system, Hinduism, Buddhism, Confucianism

**Academic Vocabulary**
code, focus, network, core

**People to Identify**
Hammurabi, King Solomon, Aryans, Siddhartha Gautama, Confucius

**Places to Locate**
Israel, Judah, Indus River, China

**Reading Objectives**
1. Trace how the law codes and religious beliefs developed in ancient civilizations.
2. Describe how the caste system influenced the lives of people in ancient India.

**Reading Strategy**
**Compare and Contrast** As you read this section, prepare a Venn diagram like the one below to show the similarities and differences between Hinduism and Buddhism.

Hinduism / Buddhism

**Preview of Events**

| ♦ 3000 B.C. | ♦ 2500 B.C. | ♦ 2000 B.C. | ♦ 1500 B.C. | ♦ 1000 B.C. | ♦ 500 B.C. | ♦ A.D. 1 |
|---|---|---|---|---|---|---|
| c. 3000 B.C. Sumerians establish independent city-states | 1792 B.C. Hammurabi comes to power | | 1200 B.C. Israelites emerge as a distinct group of people | c. 500 B.C. Buddhism develops | | 202 B.C. Han dynasty begins |

### California Standards in This Section

*Reading this section will help you master these California History–Social Science standards.*

**10.1:** Students relate the moral and ethical principles in ancient Greek and Roman philosophy, in Judaism, and in Christianity to the development of Western political thought.

**10.1.1:** Analyze the similarities and differences in Judeo-Christian and Greco-Roman views of law, reason and faith, and duties of the individual.

# Previewing Your Textbook

## Reading Roadmap

You will get more out of your textbook if you recognize the different elements that help you understand what you read.

### VOICES FROM THE PAST

*Voices from the Past* is usually a quote from an eyewitness to the event or development you will read about.

### OUTLINE

Think of the headings as forming an outline. The red titles are the main headings. The blue titles that follow are the subheadings.

### MAIN IDEA

The *Main Idea* ties the text under the heading to the big idea for the section.

### READING CONNECTION

The *Reading Connections* help you connect to what you are about to read.

### VISUAL AIDS

Photographs, maps, and charts provide visual information about the section. Questions help you interpret them and relate them to content.

### SECTION ASSESSMENT

The *Section Assessment* is the last item in every section. Completing the assessment can help you evaluate your comprehension.

---

**Ancient Mesopotamia**

**Main Idea** In ancient Mesopotamia, city-states elaborated the concept of the law code and divine kingship.

**Reading Connection** What are the motives behind the system of American laws? Read to learn how the goals of Hammurabi shaped his law code.

The first civilizations were born near rivers in four areas—Mesopotamia, Egypt, India, and China. None is part of the Western world. The people in these areas were building cities, writing, and creating laws while people in the area now called Europe were still living in huts and caves. What do we mean when we say *European civilization* or *Mesopotamian civilization*? A **civilization** is a complex culture in which large numbers of people share basic elements, such as a social structure, religion, and art.

*Voices from the Past*

A civilization is defined partly by its geography. A land lies open to invasion, as Mesopotamia did, may experience many invasions, and that will affect the social and religious attitudes. The following poem reflects the despair of the people of Ur after their city was sacked and burned:

❝Ur is destroyed, bitter is its lament. The country's blood now fills its holes like hot bronze in a mould. Bodies dissolve like fat in the sun. Our temple is destroyed, the gods have abandoned us, like migrating birds. Smoke lies on our city like a shroud.❞

Geography is not the only basic influence on civilization. Its sheer age can affect its traditions and customs. A civilization that dates from 3000 B.C. is rooted in a time when people knew and understood only certain things. Their customs developed in a certain way because of what they knew.

Perhaps they treated their elders with respect, or perhaps they expected children to grow up faster. Perhaps parents and families had the role in deciding on the man their daughter married. Although all civilizations advance over time, old social and cultural attitudes can survive to a degree even in the modern world.

The modern world came about in Europe with the Industrial and French Revolutions, but to un...

122　CHAPTER 1　The Legacy of the Ancient World

---

**New Centers of Civilization: The Israelites**

**Main Idea** Key ideas of Judaism that became important to the West developed during ancient times.

**Reading Connection** Have you read that explorers have "conquered" space? Read to discover one source for the belief that Westerners should conquer nature.

By 1200 B.C., neither Mesopotamia nor Egypt dominated western Asia. Because there was no single dominant power, it was possible for a number of peoples to emerge and build small states. One of these groups was the Israelites. The Israelites were a group of Semitic-speaking people. They left an important legacy in the religion of Judaism. Judaism flourished as a world religion and later influenced Christianity and Islam. The spiritual heritage of the Israelites is a basic pillar of Western civilization.

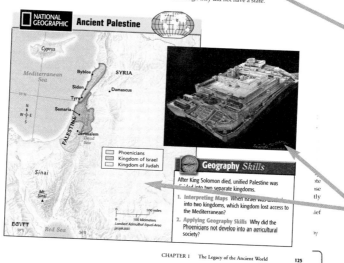

**NATIONAL GEOGRAPHIC** — **Ancient Palestine**

Cyprus
Mediterranean Sea
Byblos
SYRIA
Sidon
Damascus
Tyre
Samaria
PALESTINE
Jerusalem
Dead Sea
Sinai
Mt. Sinai
EGYPT
Red Sea

Phoenicians
Kingdom of Israel
Kingdom of Judah

0　100 miles
0　100 kilometers
Lambert Azimuthal Equal-Area projection

**Geography Skills**

After King Solomon died, unified Palestine was divided into two separate kingdoms.

1. **Interpreting Maps** When Israel was divided into two kingdoms, which kingdom lost access to the Mediterranean?

2. **Applying Geography Skills** Why did the Phoenicians not develop into an agricultural society?

---

**History of the Israelites** Under King Solomon, who ruled from about 970 B.C. to 930 B.C., the Israelites established control over all of Palestine. Jerusalem became the capital of a united kingdom, known as Israel. This great king expanded the government and army and encouraged trade. Solomon is best known for building the temple in Jerusalem, which Israelites viewed as the symbol for their religion and for the kingdom itself.

The tribes that made up Solomon's kingdom did not stay united after his death. Israel split into two kingdoms, **Israel** and **Judah**. Stronger powers, the Assyrians and the Persians, eventually destroyed both kingdoms, but the people of Judah survived. They became known as Jews, and their religion was thus called Judaism. Judaism became a stateless religion. Jews did not believe that God was fixed to any one place: Yahweh was lord of the whole world. Over the centuries, the Jews took strength from their faith. It helped them maintain their identity as a people even though they did not have a state.

CHAPTER 1　The Legacy of the Ancient World　125

---

...*idiotes,* meaning "idiot," by which they meant a fool who lives in his own private world.

For help with the concepts in this section of *Glencoe World History–Modern Times,* go to wh.mt.glencoe.com and click on Study Central.

### SECTION 2 ASSESSMENT

**Checking for Understanding**

1. **Vocabulary** Define: polis, goal, adult, tyrant, democracy, oligarchy, direct democracy, philosophy, Socratic method, foundation.

2. **People** Identify: Pericles, Socrates, Plato, Aristotle.

3. **Places** Locate: Sparta, Athens.

**Reviewing Big Ideas**

4. **Explain** how the systems of government in Sparta and Athens influenced Western political thought. Be sure to discuss how the two systems differed.

**Critical Thinking**

5. **Historical Analysis** **Interpreting** How did the governments favored by Plato and Aristotle differ? Which view makes more sense to you? **CA HR 2**

6. **Organizing Information** Using a table like the one below, identify the reforms that led to democracy in Athens and the leaders who initiated them.

| Leader | Reforms |
|---|---|
| Solon | |
| Cleisthenes | |
| Pericles | |

7. **Examine** the photo of the Parthenon shown on page 135. Where is the Parthenon located? Why was this famous temple situated on high ground?

**Writing About History**

8. **Descriptive Writing** Imagine that you are a 25-year-old male living in Sparta in 700 B.C. Create a diary in which you record your activities for one week. Write one diary page for each day. **CA 10WA2.1**

CHAPTER 1　The Legacy of the Ancient World　141

45

# Previewing Your Textbook

## Special Features

A variety of special features will help you as you study *Glencoe World History: Modern Times.*

**READING SKILL**

Use the *Reading Skills* to learn strategies for reading and comprehension.

### Preparing to Read Chapter 6

**Reading Skill** Comparing and Contrasting

Good readers look for similarities and differences in new information they read. This helps them figure out what it means. You do this subconsciously in everyday life. If you meet someone new, you probably compare that person to people you know. Is the person the same or different? If different, what makes that person different?

When you read, comparing and contrasting helps you get a handle on new information. Luckily, certain signal words tell you when the author is comparing and contrasting information to what you already know. Some signal words for showing similarity are *still* and *alike.* Some signal words differences are *however, but,* and *on the other hand.*

**HISTORICAL ANALYSIS SKILL**

*Historical Analysis Skills* teach you valuable skills to help you understand and interpret historical events.

**Historical Analysis Skill** Evaluating Evidence

Historical Research, Evidence, and Point of View: CA Sta Students evaluate major debates among historians concerni pretations of the past, including an analysis of authors' use distinctions between sound generalizations and misleading

When historians try to understand historical events, they w kinds of evidence. Then, like judges who have sifted thro they come to a verdict. Unlike the judge, a historian's "verdict" simple "Guilty" or "Innocent." Read these statements from pag British rule affected India and the Indian people.

**PRIMARY SOURCES**

For each chapter, this feature presents excerpts from three sources on an important topic in history.

## PRIMARY SOURCE
### EYEWITNESS TO HISTORY

*An American president, a Chinese politician, and a Japanese scholar each had their o importance of East-West contacts. Read them to understand this period in Asian histo*

**SOURCE 1: U.S. Trade with Japan**

*When U.S. Commodore Matthew C. Perry arrived in Tokyo Bay on his first visit to Japan in July 1853, he carried a letter from Millard Fillmore, the president of the United States. This excerpt is from that letter to the emperor of Japan.*

I have directed Commodore Perry to assure your Imperial Majesty that I entertain the kindest feelings towards your Majesty's person and government; and that I have no other object in sending him to Japan, but to propose to your Imperial Majesty that the United States and Japan should live in friendship, and have [trade] with each other. . . . I have particularly charged Commodore Perry to **abstain**[1] from any act, which could possibly disturb the peace of your Imperial Majesty's lands.

[1]**abstain:** refrain; keep from

The United States of A ocean, and our territory o nia lie directly opposite t Imperial Majesty. Our stea nia to Japan in eighteen fornia produces about six every year, besides silver, and many other valuable

Japan is also a rich an many very valuable artic two countries should tra benefit both of Japan an

We know that the anc Majesty's government d except with the Dutch. changes, and new gove to be wise from time t

**SOURCE 2: Weste**

*The Chinese politician (1873–1929) petitione exam system, to resist f embrace Western techn and promoted progres including in the excerp*

What is our duty? It with that of the West lization with ours to them to make a new . . . In the past, the ern civilization have f and materialism have gionists have one-sid life. . . . The reaction swept over the world and threw overboa ideals. . . . Now **pragmatism**[3] and evolutionism are being promoted, the aim being to embrace the ideal

[2]**dominions:** royal lands
[3]**pragmatism:** philosophical method of inquiry

*Pu Yi, China's last emperor, standing in a courtyard*

404  CHAPTER 7  East Asia Under Challenge

**WORLD LITERATURE**

*World Literature* analyzes poems and excerpts from biographies, world literature, and other writings and describes their historical lessons.

## WORLD LITERATURE

### *from* Shooting an Elephant

**George Orwell**

**George Orwell** was the pen name of English author Eric Arthur Blair, who was born in Motihari, India, on June 25, 1903. He lived for 46 years, and during that time, he wrote many influential essays, novels, and newspaper articles. His two most famous works are *1984* and *Animal Farm,* both of which are commentaries against totalitarianism. He served for several years as an assistant superintendent in the Indian Imperial Police but resigned due to his distaste of imperialism. In *Shooting an Elephant,* Orwell describes an incident that happened to him, and he satirizes the problems of colonial rule.

**Read to Discover**
Examine the ways in which George Orwell describes the relationship between the British colonial officer and the "natives." Can you think of a modern parallel to this situation?

**Reader's Dictionary**
**mahout:** a keeper and driver of an elephant

**dominion:** rule, control

**sahib:** title meaning "sir" or "master"

In Moulmein, in lower Burma, I was hated by large numbers of people—the only time in m that I have been important enough for this to hap to me. I was subdivisional police officer of the tow and in an aimless, petty kind of way anti-European feeling was very bitter. No one had the guts to raise riot, but if a European woman went through the bazaars alone somebody would probably spit betel juice over her dress. As a police officer I was an obvi ous target and was baited whenever it seemed safe to do so. . . .

All this was perplexing and upsetting. For at that time I had already made up my mind that imperialism was an evil thing and the sooner I chucked up my job and got out of it the better. Theoretically—and secretly of course—I was all for the Burmese and all against their oppressors, the British. . . . But I could get nothing into perspective. . . .

One day something happened which in a roundabout way was enlightening. . . . Early one morning the subinspector at a police station the other end of the town rang me up on the phone and said that an elephant was ravaging the bazaar. Would I please come and do something about it? . . .

The Burmese subinspector and some Indian constables were waiting for me in the quarter where the elephant had been seen. . . . We began questioning the people as to where the elephant had gone and,

◄ *Colonial hunter*

408

46

# Scavenger Hunt

*Glencoe World History: Modern Times* contains a wealth of information. The trick is to know where to look to access all the information in the book. If you run through this scavenger hunt exercise with your teachers or parents, you will see how the textbook is organized, and how to get the most out of your reading and study time. Let's get started!

1. How many chapters and how many units are in the book?

2. What time period does Unit 2 cover?

3. Name the places you can find time lines for Chapter 6.

4. In what two places can you find the Content Vocabulary for Section 2 of Chapter 6?

5. Where can you find the graphic organizer summarizing the Age of Imperialism discussed in Chapter 6?

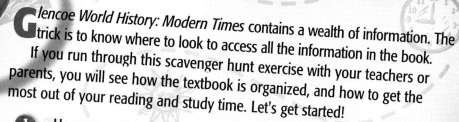

6. How are the Academic Vocabulary words for Section 4 of Chapter 6 highlighted in the narrative?

7. There are six Web sites in Chapter 6. The first previews the chapter. The second quizzes you on the entire chapter. What do the others do?

8. Where do you look if you want to quickly find all the maps in the book?

9. Most sections of a chapter open with an excerpt from a primary source—a document or other testimony dating from the period. Where else can you find extended primary sources in the textbook?

10. Where can you learn the definition of a physical map, a political map, and a special purpose map?

# What Is History?

*World history is more than just a series of dramatic events. It is the story of the human community—how people lived on a daily basis, how they shared ideas, how they ruled and were ruled, and how they fought. World history includes big subjects like economics, politics, and social change, but it is also the story of dreams fulfilled or unfulfilled, personal creativity, and philosophical and religious inspiration.*

Y*ou may think of history as a boring list of names and dates, an irrelevant record of revolutions and battles, or the meaningless stories of kings, queens, and other rulers. History is not, however, just what happens to famous and infamous people. History includes everything that happens to everyone, including you.*

## A Record of the Past

The most common definition of history is "a record of the past." To create this record, historians use documents (what has been recorded or written); artifacts, such as pottery, tools, and weapons; and even artworks. History in this sense really began five thousand to six thousand years ago, when people first began to write and keep records. The period before written records we call *prehistory*.

Herodotus, a Greek who lived in the fifth century B.C., was one of the first historians. In his history of the Greek and Persian wars, he used evidence, tried to tell a good story, and showed concern for the causes and effects of events. Today's historians still try to discover what happened (the factual evidence).

Early movie camera ▶

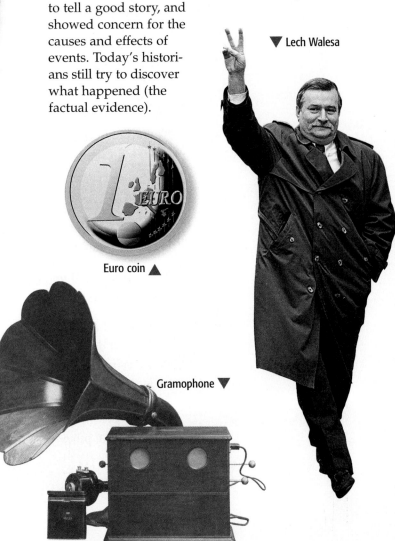

▼ Lech Walesa

Euro coin ▲

Gramophone ▼

They also want to know it happened. They use critical thinking and detailed investigation to explain the cause-and-effect relationships that exist among facts, and they look for new discoveries that might change our view of the past.

All of us are involved in the making of history. Alex Haley, the editor of *The Autobiography of Malcolm X*, grew up in Tennessee listening to his grandmother tell stories of Kunta Kinte, a family ancestor kidnapped in Africa during the 1700s and taken to America as a slave. Haley's search for his family's history led to his famous book, *Roots: The Saga of an American Family*. The book was turned into one of the most-watched television miniseries of all time. Although Haley's family was a small part of larger historical events, the personal family history had universal appeal.

You will find, with some investigation, that history has been made by your own family and by the families of your friends. You are who you are because of the choices and experiences of your ancestors. Their experiences guide your choices and actions, just as

yours will guide your children's and grandchildren's. You are an important link in a chain that stretches back into your ancestors' history and forward into your descendants' future.

In this book, you will read one account of the history of the world, as well as documents that historians use to create their own pictures of the past. Reading the documents will enable you to develop your critical skills and to evaluate the material in this book—in a sense, to be a historian yourself. The study of history will give you the tools to examine not only the lives of others, but also your own life. As Socrates, an ancient Greek philosopher, said, "The unexamined life is not worth living."

Alex Haley, ▲
*Roots: The Saga of an American Family*

# Big Ideas in World History

As you read, you will see a number of "big ideas" —broad themes that can be glimpsed behind the events and developments of the modern period. These big ideas are described briefly below.

1. **Moral and Ethical Principles**
2. **Struggle for Rights**
3. **New Technologies**
4. **Competition Among Nations**

5. **Devastations of War**
6. **Human Rights**
7. **Cold War Conflicts**
8. **Nationalism**

 **Moral and ethical principles influence the development of political thought.** Throughout history, people have sought to find a deeper meaning to human life. Religion, cultural values and codes of ethics have always influenced social customs, laws, and forms of government. Conflicts among people of opposing religions and moral principles have often been at the heart of many controversies and conflicts. The principles found in religions like Hinduism, Buddhism, Judaism, Christianity, and Islam have influenced thousands of people for generations.

**Throughout history people have struggled for rights.** The struggle for rights has been reflected in many ways: in the actions of individual men and women, as well as in organizations and informal groups. Examples of this struggle for rights include the campaign for the vote, for economic freedom, for personal liberties, and for national independence. It has been said that without struggle, nothing is possible and that struggle is endless. There are few nations in the world whose history has not been marked by a struggle for rights among its people.

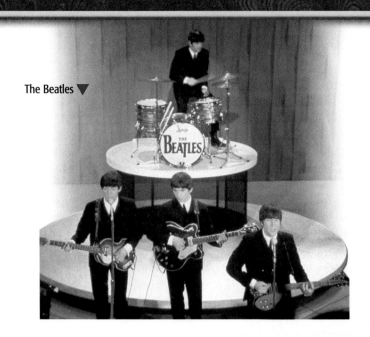

The Beatles ▼

**3** **New technologies can revolutionize the way people live, work, interact and govern.**
For thousands of years, people around the world have made scientific discoveries and technological innovations that have changed the world. Usually, economies have become prosperous after a new invention or discovery, but some people may lose out, too, in the transition to a new economy. In the modern era, machines and computers have forever altered how humans relate to the world, and to one another.

**4** **Nations compete for natural resources and strategic advantages over other nations.** Competition among nations has led to the development of stable economies in some cases, but also to the depletion of economies that have become sources of raw materials. Strong economies tend to mean stronger governments, and this provides a sense of safety for citizens. During the 1800s, especially, the competition for resources and power led many Western powers to colonize other parts of the world. Through these colonies, they were able to gain access to critical natural resources, as well as to find markets for their own products.

**5** **War causes immeasurable devastation.**
In the modern period, wars have usually brought greater devastation than in earlier epochs. It is estimated that more than ten million soldiers and civilians were killed during World War I, and World War II was the most devastating war in history, claiming more than 50 million lives. Genocide and ethnic cleansing have also characterized the wars of the twentieth century. Physical devastation—to factories, homes, roads, and bridges—also has been extreme. Recovering from such losses is costly, and the desire for revenge or triumph can color the attitudes of an entire generation.

United States

**6** **A totalitarian system violates human rights in pursuit of political power.** By definition, the totalitarian state smothers the individuality of its citizens. This system seeks to control the political, economic, social, intellectual, and cultural areas of life and does so through propaganda and through force. Totalitarian governments have a single leader who does not tolerate dissent. They place the state's need for power above the concerns of their people.

**7** **International rivalry between superpowers and growing nationalism in the Third World led to major conflicts in the Cold War.** In the period of the Cold War, the United States and the Soviet Union opposed each other around the world. Both powers worked to find allies who supported their beliefs and positions: the United States supported a capitalist democracy, while the Soviet Union supported state-controlled communism. Conflicts resulting from this Cold War rivalry were found in China, in Korea, and Vietnam, as well as in civil conflicts in many Latin American nations.

**8** **The quest for national self-determination is universal.** Free will is the cornerstone of humanity, so it is no wonder that peoples around the world want to have an independent nation to express their free will. People unite as a nation because they feel that independence is essential to freedom and that freedom is essential to leading a full life. The past century has been a landmark in the quest for independence for many nations, and the struggle continues in many parts of the world.

# Historians and the Dating of Time

In recording the past, historians try to determine the exact time when events occurred. World War II in Europe, for example, began on September 1, 1939, when Adolf Hitler sent German troops into Poland. The war in Europe ended on May 7, 1945, when Germany surrendered. By using dates, historians can place events in the order they occurred and try to determine the development of patterns over periods of time.

The dating system most commonly used in the Western world (Europe and the Western Hemisphere) is based on the assumed date of the birth of Jesus Christ (the year 1). An event that took place 400 years before the birth of Jesus would be dated 400 B.C. ("before Christ"). Dates after the birth of Jesus are labeled A.D. These letters stand for the Latin words *anno Domini*, which mean "in the year of the Lord." An event that took place 250 years after the birth of Jesus is written A.D. 250. It can also be written as 250.

Because B.C. and A.D. are so Western and Christian-oriented, some historians now prefer to use the abbreviations B.C.E. ("before the common era") and C.E. ("common era"). Thus, 1850 B.C. could be written as 1850 B.C.E.

Historians use other terms to refer to time. A decade is 10 years, a century is 100 years, and a millennium is 1,000 years. The fourth century B.C. is the fourth period of 100 counting backward from 1, the assumed date of the birth of Jesus. The first century B.C. encompasses the years 100 to 1 B.C. Therefore, the fourth century B.C. refers to the years 400 to 301 B.C. We say, then, that an event in 650 B.C. took place in the seventh century B.C.

The fourth century A.D. is the fourth period of 100 years after the birth of Jesus. The first period of 100 years includes the years 1 to 100, so the fourth hundred-year period, or the fourth century, encompasses the years 301 to 400. For example, we say that an event in 750 took place in the eighth century. Just as the first millennium B.C. spans the years 1000 to 1 B.C., the first millennium A.D. spans the years 1 to 1000.

General Dwight D. Eisenhower ▶ speaks to his troops just before the invasion of France in June 1944.

# Reading for Information

When you read this textbook, you are reading for information, but you are also gaining insights into the world around you, the how and why of events that have happened. History is nonfiction writing—it describes real-life events, people, ideas, and places. Here is a menu of reading strategies that will help you become a better textbook reader. As you come to passages in your textbook that you do not understand, refer to these reading strategies for help.

## ✓ Before You Read

### Set a Purpose
- Why are you reading the textbook?
- How does the subject relate to your life?
- How might you be able to use what you learn in your own life?

### Preview
- Read the chapter title to find what the topic will be; then look over the section titles to see how the topic will be organized.
- Skim the photos, charts, graphs, or maps. How do they support the topic?
- Look for words and terms that are highlighted in yellow and bolded in your textbook. These include Content Vocabulary and important people and places discussed in each section.
- Look for words that are bolded only. Understanding these Academic Vocabulary words will strengthen your ability to read and write in all your subjects.

### Draw from Your Own Background
- What have you read or heard about on the topic?
- How is the new information different from what you already know?
- How will the information you know help you understand the new information?

## Question

- What is the main idea?
- How do the photos, charts, graphs, and maps support the main idea?

## Connect

- Think about people, places, and events in your own life. Are there any similarities with those in your textbook?
- Can you relate the textbook information to other areas of your life?

## Predict

- Predict events or outcomes by using clues and information that you already know.
- Change your predictions as you read and gather new information.

## Visualize

- Pay careful attention to details.
- Create graphic organizers to show relationships in the reading. Use the graphic organizer in the Guide to Reading to help organize the information in each section.

## Look for Clues

### Compare and Contrast Sentences

- Look for clue words and phrases that signal comparison, such as *similarity, just as, both, in common, also,* and *too.*
- Look for clue words and phrases that signal contrast, such as *on the other hand, in contrast to, however, different, instead of, rather than, but,* and *unlike.*

### Cause-and-Effect Sentences

- Look for clue words and phrases such as *because, as a result, therefore, that is why, since, so, for this reason,* and *consequently.*

### Chronological Sentences

- Look for clue words and phrases such as *after, before, first, next, last, during, finally, earlier, later, since,* and *then.*

## Summarize

- Describe the main idea and how the details support it.
- Use your own words to explain what you have read.

## Assess

- What was the main idea?
- Did you learn anything new from the material?
- Can you use this new information in other school subjects or at home?
- What other sources could you use to find more information about the topic?

# READING TO LEARN

**T**his handbook focuses on skills and strategies that can help you understand the words you read. The strategies you use to understand whole texts depend on the kind of text you are reading. In other words, you do not read a textbook the way you read a novel. You read a textbook mainly for information; you read a novel for the story and the characters. To get the most out of your reading, you need to choose the right strategy to fit the reason you are reading. This handbook can help you learn about the following reading strategies:

- how to identify new words and build your vocabulary;
- how to adjust the way you read to fit your reason for reading;
- how to use specific reading strategies to better understand what you read;
- how to use critical thinking strategies to think more deeply about what you read; and
- how to understand text structures to identify an author's ideas.

## TABLE OF CONTENTS

# Identifying Words and Building Vocabulary

**W**hat do you do when you come across a word you do not know as you read? Do you skip over the word? If you are reading a novel, you use the context to understand the meaning of the word. But if you are reading for information, an unfamiliar word may get in the way of your understanding. When that happens, follow the strategies below to learn how to say the word and what it means.

## Reading Unfamiliar Words

**Sounding Out the Word** One way to figure out how to say a new word is to sound it out, syllable by syllable. Look carefully at the word's beginning, middle, and ending. For example, in the word *coagulate,* what letters make up the beginning sound or beginning syllable of the word? *Co* rhymes with *so.* Inside *coagulate,* do you see a word you already know how to pronounce? The syllable *ag* has the same sound as the *ag* in *bag,* and the syllable *u* is pronounced like the letter *u.* What letters make up the ending sound or syllable? *Late* is a familiar word you already know how to pronounce. Now try pronouncing the whole word: ***co ag u late.***

## Determining a Word's Meaning

**Using Syntax** Like all languages, the English language has rules and patterns for the way words are arranged in sentences. The way a sentence is organized is called the syntax. If English is your first language, you have known this pattern since you started using sentences. If you are learning English now, you may find that the syntax is different from the patterns you know in your first language.

In a simple sentence in English, someone or something (the subject) does something (the predicate or verb) to or with another person or thing (the object): *The soldiers attacked the enemy.* Sometimes adjectives, adverbs, and phrases are added to add details to the sentence: *The courageous young soldiers fearlessly attacked the well-entrenched enemy shortly after dawn.*

Knowing about syntax can help you figure out the meaning of an unfamiliar word. Just look at how syntax can help you figure out the following nonsense sentence: *The blizzy kwarkles sminched the flerky fleans.* Your experience with English syntax tells you that the action word, or verb, in this sentence is *sminched.* Who did the *sminching?* The *kwarkles.* What kind of *kwarkles* were they? *Blizzy.* Whom did they *sminch?* The *fleans.* What kind of *fleans* were they? *Flerky.* Even though you don't know the meaning of the words in the nonsense sentence, you can make some sense of the entire sentence by studying its syntax.

**Using Context Clues** You can often figure out the meaning of an unfamiliar word by looking at its context, the words and sentences that surround it. To learn new words as you read, follow these steps for using context clues.

- Look before and after the unfamiliar word for a definition or a synonym, a general topic associated with the word, a clue to what the word is similar to or different from, or an action or a description that has something to do with the word.
- Connect what you already know with what the author has written.
- Predict a possible meaning.
- Use the meaning in the sentence.
- Try again if your guess does not make sense.

**Using Types of Reference Materials**
Dictionaries and other reference sources can help you learn new words and how to use them. Check out these reference sources. You can find these in your local public or school library as well as on the Internet.

- A **dictionary** gives the pronunciation, the meaning or multiple meanings, and often examples of how to use the words. Some dictionaries also provide illustrations or diagrams to help define words, other forms of words, their parts of speech, and synonyms. You might also find the historical background of a word, such as its Greek, Latin, or Anglo-Saxon origins.
- A **glossary** is a word list that appears at the end—or Appendix—of a book or other written work and includes only words that are in that work. Like dictionaries, glossaries include the pronunciation and definitions of words.
- A **thesaurus** lists groups of words that have the same, or almost the same, meaning. Words with similar meanings are called synonyms. Seeing the synonyms of words can help you build your vocabulary.

## Recognizing Word Meanings Across Subjects

Have you ever learned a new word in one class and then noticed it in your reading for other subjects? The word probably will not mean exactly the same thing in each class. But you can use what you know about the word's meaning to help you understand what it means in a different subject area. Look at the following example from three different subjects:

- **Social studies:** One *product* manufactured in the southern part of the United States is cotton cloth.
- **Math:** After multiplying the numbers five and five, explain how you arrived at the *product*.
- **Science:** One *product* of photosynthesis is oxygen.

### CHECKING YOUR UNDERSTANDING

The following sentence does not include real English words, but you can use what you have learned about English syntax to decode the sentence. First read the sentence. Then answer the questions that follow.

*The shabs smatously graled the mul-bulowed rotfabs.*

1. What is the verb in the sentence?
2. What is the subject?
3. What is the object?

## Reading for a Reason

**W**hy are you reading that paperback mystery? What do you hope to get from your world history textbook? And are you going to read either of these books in the same way that you read a restaurant menu? The point is, you read for different reasons. The reason you are reading something helps you decide on the reading strategies you use with a text. In other words, how you read will depend on why you are reading.

## Knowing Your Reason for Reading

In school and in life, you will have many reasons for reading, and those reasons will lead you to a wide range of materials:

- **To learn and understand new information,** you might read news magazines, textbooks, news on the Internet, books about your favorite pastime, encyclopedia articles, primary and secondary sources for a school report, instructions on how to use a calling card, or directions for a standardized test.
- **To find specific information,** you might look at the sports section for the score of last night's game, a notice on where to register for a field trip, weather reports, bank statements, or television listings.
- **To be entertained,** you might read your favorite magazine, e-mails or letters from friends, the Sunday comics, or even novels, short stories, plays, or poems!

## Adjusting How Fast You Read

How quickly or how carefully you should read a text depends on your purpose for reading it. Because there are many reasons and ways to read, think about your purpose and choose the strategy that works best. Try out these strategies:

- **Scanning** means quickly running your eyes over the material, looking for key words or phrases that point to the information you are looking for. Scan when you need to find a particular piece or type of information. For example, you might scan a newspaper for movie show times.
- **Skimming** means quickly reading a piece of writing to find its main idea or to get a general overview of it. For example, you might skim the sports section of the daily newspaper to find out how your favorite teams are doing. Or you might skim a chapter in your textbook to prepare for a test.
- **Careful reading** involves reading very slowly and paying close attention with a purpose in mind. Read carefully when you are learning new concepts, following complicated directions, or preparing to explain information to someone else.

 **CHECKING YOUR UNDERSTANDING**

If you were working on a research paper on the American Revolution, how would you adjust the speed at which you were reading for each of the following cases?

1.  You have just found a 1,200-page work that covers the entire colonial and revolutionary era of the British colonies in North America.

2.  You have discovered an article in a leading history magazine that supports every point that you are trying to make.

## Understanding What You Read

**R**eading without understanding is like trying to drive a car on an empty gas tank. Fortunately, there are techniques you can use to help you concentrate on and understand what you read. Skilled readers adopt a number of strategies before, during, and after reading to make sure they understand what they read.

# Preparing to Read

*It is important to set the stage before you read. Following these steps will make the reading process more rewarding.*

**Previewing** If you were making a preview for a movie, you would want to let your audience know what the movie is like. When you preview a piece of writing, you are trying to get an idea about the piece. Follow these steps to preview your reading assignments.

- Look at the title and any illustrations that are included.
- Read the headings, subheadings, and anything in bold letters.
- Skim the passage to see how it is organized.
- Set a purpose for your reading.

**Using What You Know** You already know quite a bit about what you are going to read. You bring knowledge and personal experience to a selection. Drawing on what you learned in a previous class is called *activating prior knowledge,* and it can help you create meaning in what you read. Ask yourself, *What do I already know about this topic?*

**Predicting** *Predicting* requires using background and prior knowledge, as well as the ability to make educated guesses. Make educated guesses before you read and while you read to figure out what might happen in the story or article you are reading.

# Reading the Text

*Following these suggestions while you read will help ensure that you get the most out of your reading.*

**Visualizing** Creating pictures in your mind as you read—called *visualizing*—is a powerful aid to understanding. As you read, set up a movie theater in your imagination. Picture the setting—city streets, the desert, or the moon. If you can visualize, selections will be more vivid, and you will recall them better later on.

**Identifying Sequence** When you discover the logical order of events or ideas, you are identifying *sequence.* Do you need to understand step-by-step directions? Are you reading a persuasive speech with the reasons listed in order of importance? Look for clues and signal words that will help you find the way information is organized.

**Determining the Main Idea** When you look for the *main idea* of a selection, you look for the most important idea. The examples, reasons, and details that further explain the main idea are called *supporting details.* Some main ideas are clearly stated within a passage—often in the first sentence of a paragraph, or sometimes in the last sentence of a passage. Other times, however, an author does not directly state the main idea. Instead, he or she provides details that help readers figure out what the main idea is.

**Questioning** By learning how to analyze questions, you will quickly learn where to look for information as you read. Questions vary in many ways. One of the ways that questions vary is by how explicit or implied the question is compared with the text. These types of questions fall into four categories:

- **Right there** questions can be answered based on a line from the text.
- **Think and search** questions can be answered by looking in a few different places in the text.
- **Author and you** questions can be answered by thinking about the text but that also require your prior knowledge.
- **On your own** questions cannot be answered by the text and rely on the reader.

**Clarifying** Clear up, or clarify, confusing or difficult passages as you read. When you realize you do not understand something, try these techniques to help you clarify the ideas. *Reread* the confusing parts slowly and carefully. *Look up* unfamiliar words. Simply *talk out* the part to yourself.

**Monitoring Your Comprehension** As you read, check your understanding by using the following strategies.

- **Summarize** what you read by pausing from time to time and telling yourself the main ideas of what you have just read. Answer the questions *Who? What? Where? When? Why?* and *How?* Summarizing tests your comprehension by encouraging you to clarify key points in your own words.
- **Paraphrase** what you have just read to see whether you really got the point. Paraphrasing is retelling something in your own words. If you cannot explain it clearly, you should probably reread the text.

 **CHECKING YOUR UNDERSTANDING**

1. How does visualizing help you understand what you read in your textbook or when you read for pleasure?

2. How can you determine the main idea of a selection if the author never explicitly explains what it is?

3. Why is clarifying an important skill for you to develop?

# Thinking About Your Reading

**S**ometimes it is important to think more deeply about what you have read so you can get the most out of what the author says. These critical thinking skills will help you go beyond what the words say and get at the important messages of your reading.

## Interpreting

When you listen to your best friend talk, you do not just hear the words he or she says. You also watch your friend, listen to the tone of voice, and use what you already know about that person to put meaning to the words. In doing so, you are interpreting what your friend says. Readers do the same thing when they interpret as they read. *Interpreting* is asking yourself *What is the writer really saying here?* and then using what you know about the world to help answer that question.

## Inferring

You may not realize it, but you make inferences every day. Here is an example: You run to the bus stop a little later than usual. No one is there. "I have missed the bus," you say to yourself. You might be wrong, but that is the way our minds work. You look at the evidence (you are late; no one is there) and come to a conclusion (you have missed the bus).

When you read, you go through exactly the same process because writers do not always directly state what they want you to understand. They suggest certain information by providing clues and interesting details. Whenever you combine those clues with your own background and knowledge, you are making an inference.

## Drawing Conclusions

Skillful readers are always *drawing conclusions,* or figuring out much more than an author says directly. The process is like a detective solving a mystery. You combine information and evidence that the author provides to come up with a statement about the topic. Drawing conclusions helps you find connections between ideas and events and gives you a better understanding of what you are reading.

## Making Connections

One way that you can remember what you have read is by making connections with the text. Your teacher often expresses these connections aloud so that you and your classmates have a model. Your teacher may also ask you to make connections with the text and share them with the class. The most common connections include:

- **Text-to-self** connections, in which you remember something from your own life that serves as a connection with what is being read. *(While reading about the Civil War, you think about a fight you had with a relative.)*
- **Text-to-world** connections, in which you remember something that is happening or has happened in the world that serves as a connection with what is being read. *(While reading about the Civil War, you remember reading a newspaper article about the civil war in Somalia.)*
- **Text-to-text** connections, in which you remember something you have read elsewhere that serves as a connection with what is being read. *(While reading about the Civil War, you recall the novel* The Red Badge of Courage.*)*

# Analyzing

*Analyzing,* or looking at separate parts of something to understand the entire piece, is a way to think critically about written work. In analyzing persuasive *nonfiction,* you might look at the writer's reasons to see if they actually support the main point of the argument. In analyzing *informational text,* you might look at how the ideas are organized to see what is most important.

# Distinguishing Fact From Opinion

Distinguishing between fact and opinion is an important reading skill. A *fact* is a statement that can be proved. An *opinion,* on the other hand, is what a writer believes on the basis of his or her personal viewpoint. Writers can support their opinions with facts, but an opinion is something that cannot be proved.

# Evaluating

When you form an opinion or make a judgment about something you are reading, you are *evaluating.* If you are reading informational texts or something on the Internet, it is important to evaluate how qualified the author is to be writing about the topic and how reliable the information is that is presented. Ask yourself whether the author seems biased, whether the information is one-sided, and whether the argument presented is logical.

# Synthesizing

When you *synthesize,* you combine ideas (maybe even from different sources) to come up with something new. It may be a new understanding of an important idea or a new way of combining and presenting information. For example, you might read a manual on coaching soccer, combine that information with your own experiences playing soccer, and come up with a winning plan for coaching your sister's team this spring.

 **CHECKING YOUR UNDERSTANDING**

1. How does making connections with what you have read help you remember more?

2. How do analyzing and synthesizing differ?

3. How do facts and opinions differ? Why is it important to differentiate between the two as you study history?

# Understanding Text Structure

**G**ood writers do not just put together sentences and paragraphs in any order. They structure each piece of their writing in a specific way for a specific purpose. That pattern of organization is called text structure. When you know the text structure of a selection, you will find it easier to locate and recall an author's ideas. Here are four ways that writers organize text.

## Comparison and Contrast

Comparison-and-contrast structure shows the *similarities* and *differences* among people, things, and ideas. Maybe you have overheard someone at school say something like "He is better at throwing the football, but I can run faster than he can." This student is using comparison-and-contrast structure. When writers use comparison-and-contrast structure, they often want to show you how things that seem alike are different or how things that seem different are alike.

**Signal words and phrases:** *similarly, on the one hand, on the other hand, in contrast to, but, however*

## Cause and Effect

Just about everything that happens in life is the cause or the effect of some other event or action. Sometimes what happens is pretty minor: You do not look when you are pouring milk *(cause);* you spill milk on the table *(effect).* Sometimes it is a little more serious: You do not look at your math book before the big test *(cause);* you mess up on the test *(effect).*

Writers use cause-and-effect structure to explore the reasons for something happening and to examine the results of previous events. This structure helps answer the question that everybody is always asking: *Why?* A historian might tell us why an empire rose and fell. Cause-and-effect structure is all about explaining why things are as they are.

**Signal words and phrases:** *so, because, as a result, therefore, for the following reasons*

# Problem and Solution

How did scientists overcome the difficulty of getting a person to the moon? How will I brush my teeth when I have forgotten my toothpaste? These questions may be very different in importance, but they have one thing in common: Each identifies a problem and asks how to solve it. *Problems and solutions* are part of what makes life interesting. Problems and solutions also occur in fiction and nonfiction writing.

**Signal words and phrases:** *how, help, problem, obstruction, difficulty, need, attempt, have to, must*

# Sequence

Take a look at three common forms of sequencing, the order in which thoughts are arranged.

- **Chronological order** refers to the order in which events take place. First, you wake up; next, you have breakfast; then, you go to school. Those events do not make much sense in any other order.
  **Signal words:** *first, next, then, later, finally*

- **Spatial order** tells you the order in which to look at objects. For example, consider this description of an ice-cream sundae: *At the bottom of the dish are two scoops of vanilla. The scoops are covered with fudge and topped with whipped cream and a cherry.* Your eyes follow the sundae from the bottom to the top. Spatial order is important in descriptive writing because it helps you as a reader to see an image the way the author does.
  **Signal words:** *above, below, behind, next to*

- **Order of importance** is going from most important to least important or the other way around. For example, a typical news article has a most important to least important structure.
  **Signal words:** *principal, central, important, fundamental*

## CHECKING YOUR UNDERSTANDING

**Read the following paragraph and answer the questions about the selection's text structure below.**

*The Huntington City Council recently approved an increase in the city sales tax. Recognizing the need to balance the city's budget, the council president Matt Smith noted that the council had no choice. The vote ended more than a year of preparing voters for the bad news. First, the council notified citizens that there would be a public discussion last April. Then, the council issued public statements that the vote would take place in November. Finally, the council approved the increase last week even though many residents opposed it. On one hand, the increase will increase revenues. On the other hand, more taxes could lead to fewer shoppers in the city's struggling retail stores.*

1. **How does the writer use comparison and contrast text structure?**

2. **How does the writer use problem and solution text structure?**

3. **What signal words show that the writer is setting the chronological order of events?**

# Geography's Impact On History

*Throughout this text, you will discover how geography has shaped the course of events in world history. Landforms, waterways, climate, and natural resources all have helped or hindered human activities. Usually people have learned either to adapt to their environment or to transform it to meet their needs. Here are some examples of the role that geographic factors have played in the story of humanity.*

Roman aqueduct, an example of humans' adapting their environment

## Unit 1: The World Before Modern Times

Rivers contributed to the rise of many of the world's early civilizations. By 3000 B.C., the Sumerians of Southwest Asia had set up 12 prosperous city-states in the Tigris-Euphrates River valley. The area is often called the Fertile Crescent because of its relatively rich topsoil and its curved shape.

Fertile land produced abundant food supplies and led to population growth. The river valleys of Mesopotamia, Egypt, India, and China became some of the great food-producing areas of the ancient world.

Landforms and waterways also affected the political relationship of the world's developing civilizations. For example, the rugged landscape of Greece divided the ancient Greeks into separate city-states instead of uniting them into a single nation.

Climatic changes had an important impact as well. In Europe during the Middle Ages, for example, improving climates resulted in better agricultural conditions and increased food production, resulting in a growth in population.

Singapore skyline ▶

Civilizations also developed at trade crossroads. From about A.D. 400 to A.D. 1500, the city of Makkah (Mecca) in the Arabian Peninsula was a crossroads for caravans from North Africa, Palestine, and the Persian Gulf.

At the dawn of the modern era, Asians and Europeans came into contact with one another partly because Europeans wanted Asia's spices and silks. When the Asiatic people known as the Mongols could no longer guarantee safe passage for traders on overland routes, Europeans were forced to consider new water routes to Asia. This began a new global age.

Climate often affects the way a country interacts with its neighbors. For example, many of Russia's harbors stay frozen during the long winter months. In the past, Russia has gone to war to capture land for warmer ports.

Climate was one reason the Russians were able to stop the invasions of the French ruler Napoleon Bonaparte in 1812 and the German dictator Adolf Hitler in 1941. The Russians were used to the cold and snow of their country's winter, while the invaders were not.

## Unit 2:
## An Era of
## European Imperialism

Utilizing natural resources, such as coal and iron, was an important factor in the growth of the Industrial Revolution. Modern industry started in Great Britain, which had large amounts of coal and iron ore for making steel. Throughout Europe and North America, the rise of factories that turned raw materials into finished goods prompted people eager for employment to move from rural areas to urban centers.

Also, the availability of land and the discovery of minerals in the Americas, Australia, and South Africa caused hundreds of thousands of Europeans to move to these areas in hopes of improving their lives. These mass migrations were possible because of improvements in industrial technology and transportation that enabled people to overcome geographic barriers.

## Unit 3:
## The Twentieth-Century
## Crisis

Environmental disasters during the first part of the 1900s affected national economies in various parts of the world. For example, during the 1930s, winds blew away so much of the soil in the Great Plains of central North America that the area became known as the Dust Bowl. It took many years of normal rainfall and improved farming techniques to transform the Great Plains from a Dust Bowl into productive land once again.

## Unit 4:
## Toward a
## Global Civilization

The world's peoples have become more aware of the growing scarcity of nonrenewable resources. Oil takes millions of years to form and the earth's supply is limited. Industrialized countries like the United States consume far more oil than they produce and must import large amounts. Many experts agree that consumption must be limited and alternative energy sources found.

Environmental problems are no longer limited to a single nation or region. For example, deforestation in one area and pollution in another area may be responsible for climate changes that cause floods and droughts all over the world. Global problems require global solutions, and nations are beginning to work together to ensure solutions that will work for all.

# REFERENCE ATLAS

## ATLAS KEY

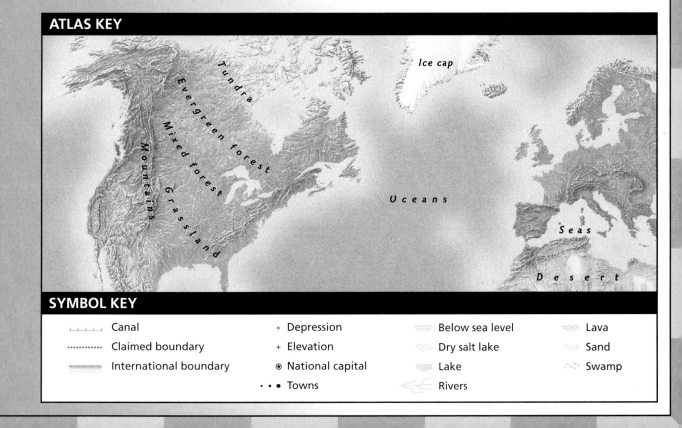

### SYMBOL KEY

| | | |
|---|---|---|
| ⌐⌐⌐ Canal | ○ Depression | ～ Below sea level | ～ Lava |
| ·········· Claimed boundary | + Elevation | ～ Dry salt lake | ～ Sand |
| ～～～ International boundary | ⊛ National capital | ▱ Lake | ⤍ Swamp |
| | • • ● Towns | ≼ Rivers | |

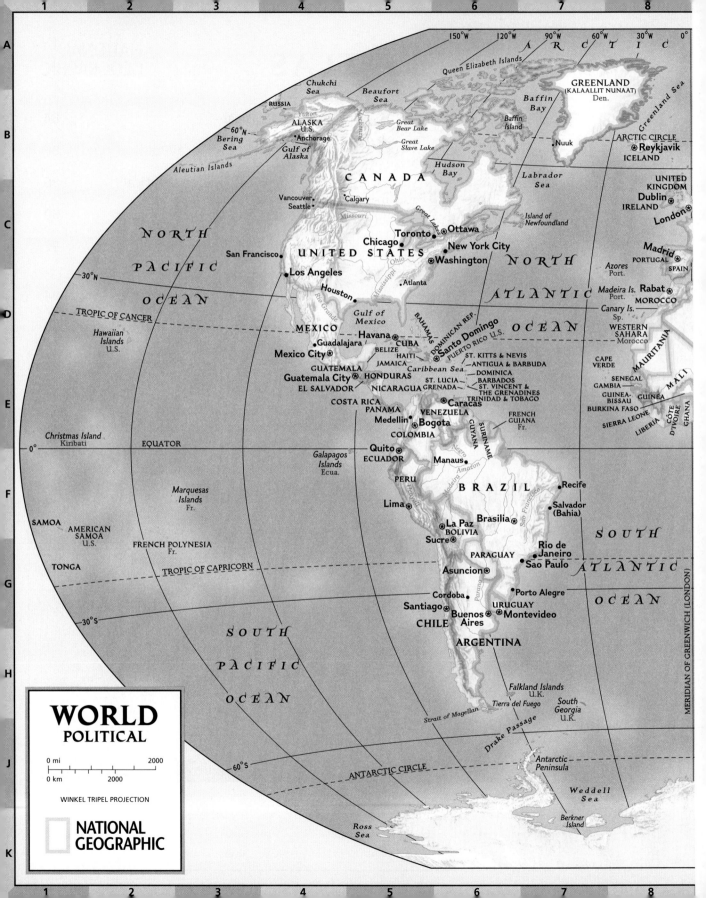

# WORLD
## POLITICAL

0 mi — 2000
0 km — 2000

WINKEL TRIPEL PROJECTION

## NATIONAL GEOGRAPHIC

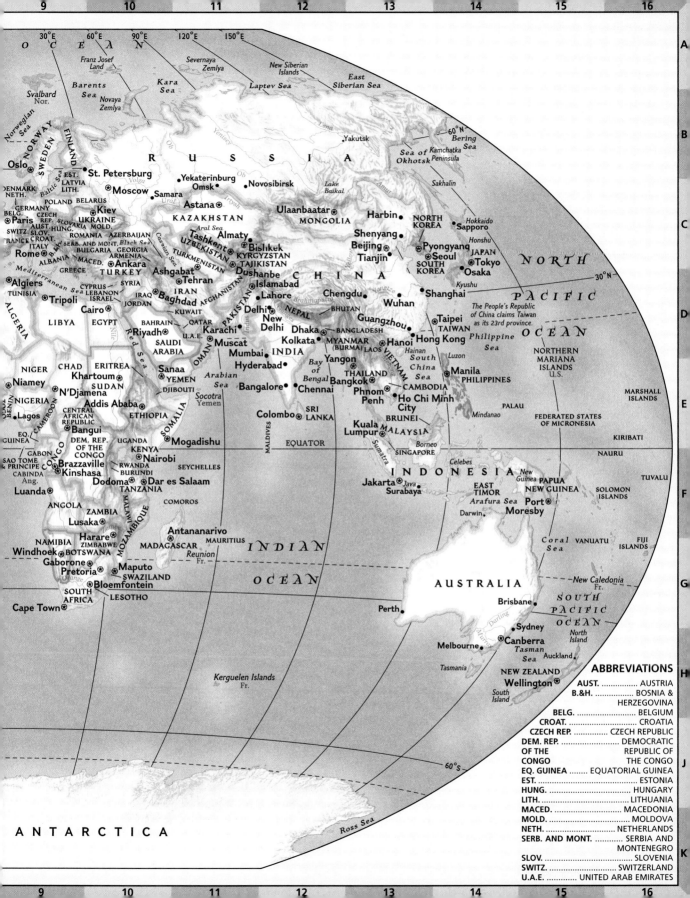

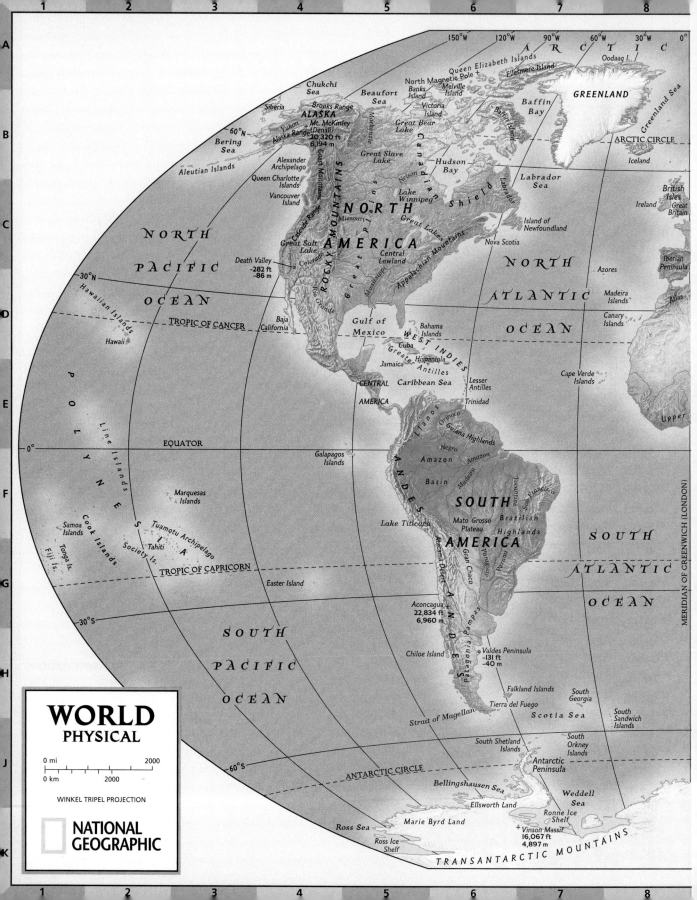

# WORLD
## PHYSICAL

0 mi        2000

0 km       2000

WINKEL TRIPEL PROJECTION

## NATIONAL GEOGRAPHIC

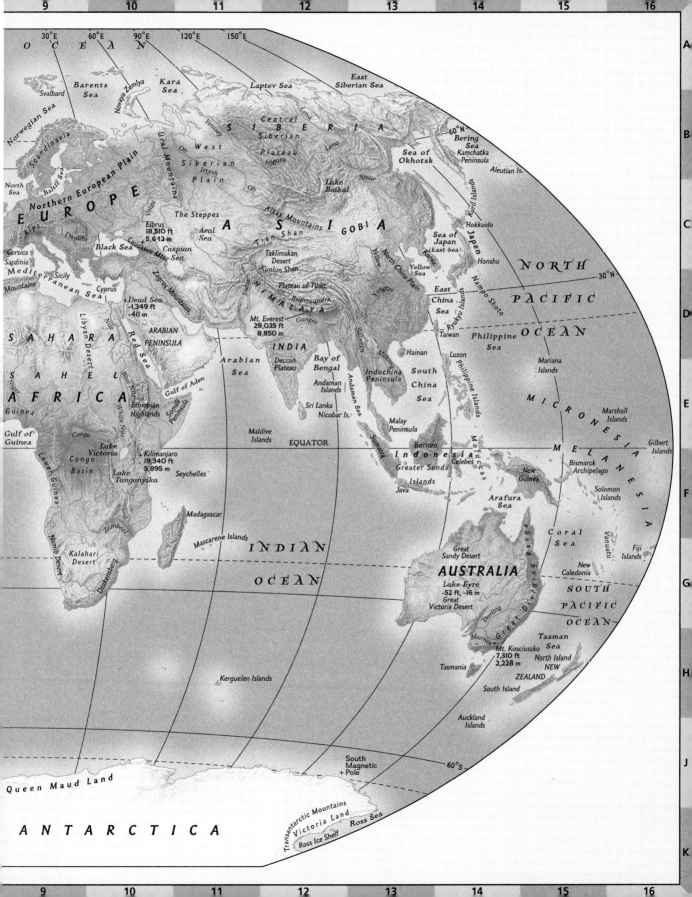

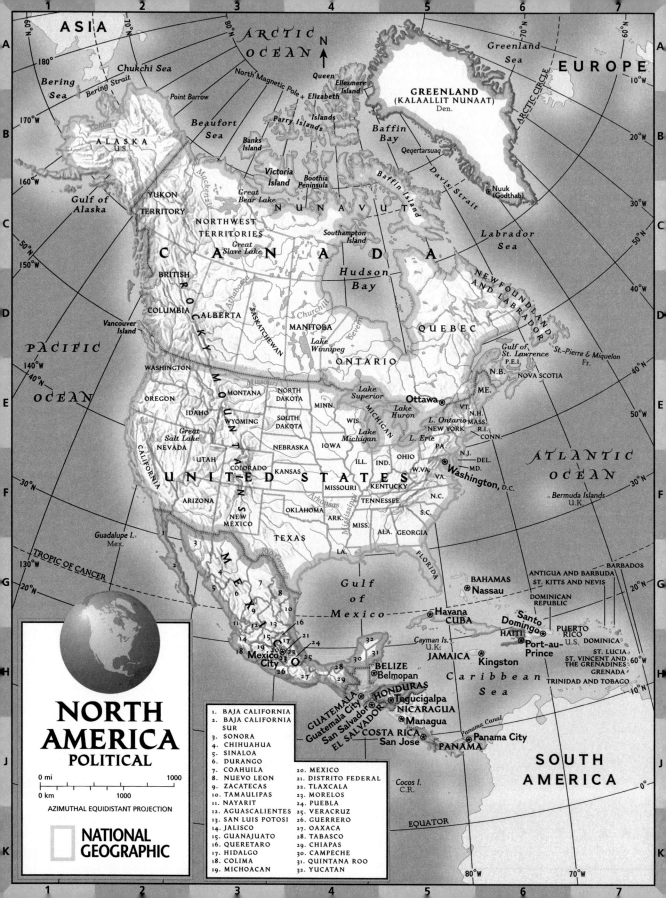

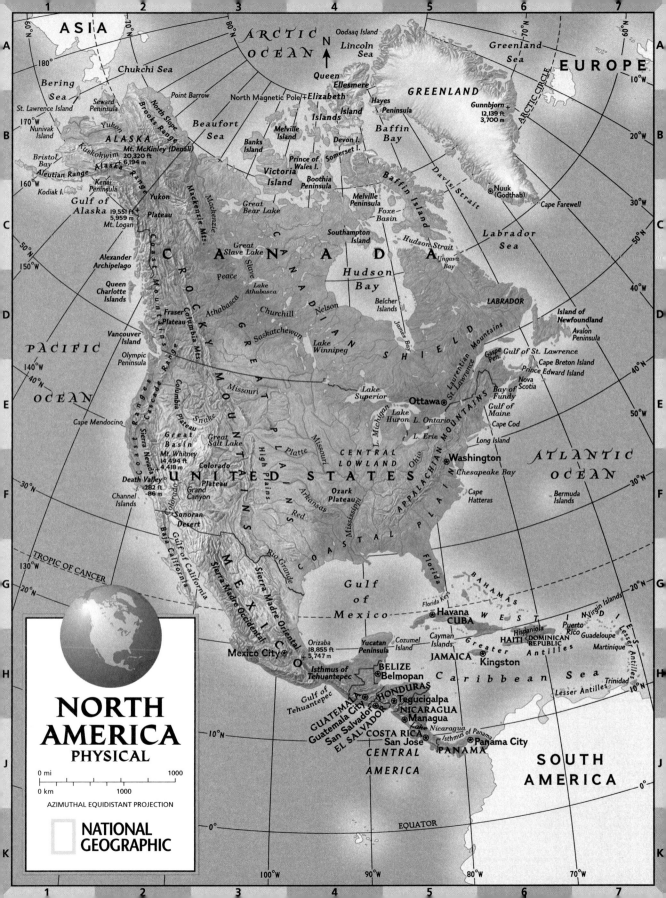

# NORTH AMERICA

## PHYSICAL

0 mi            1000

0 km        1000

AZIMUTHAL EQUIDISTANT PROJECTION

## NATIONAL GEOGRAPHIC

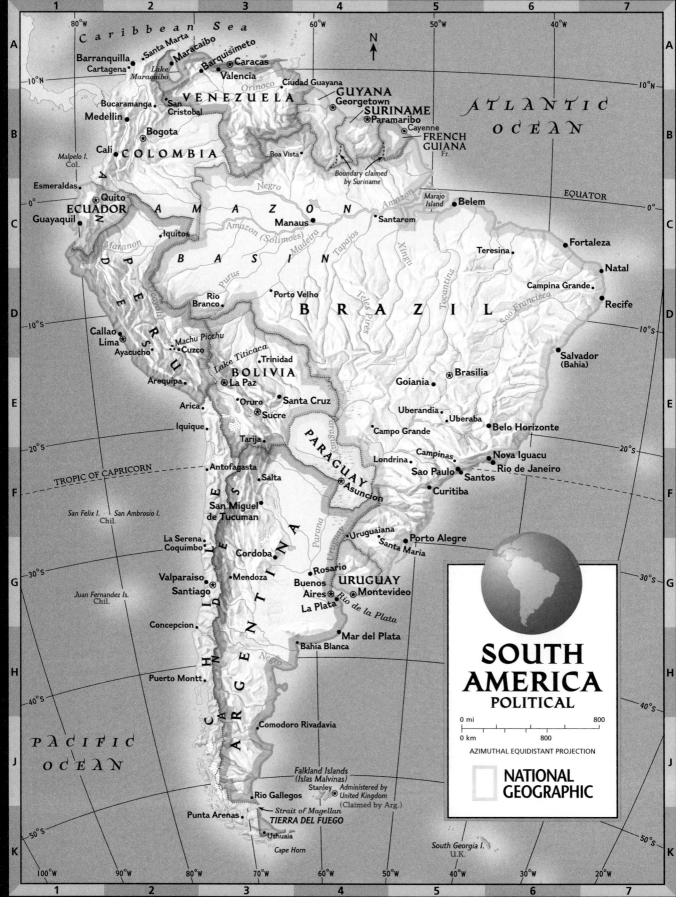

## SOUTH AMERICA
### POLITICAL

0 mi · · · · · · · · 800
0 km · · · · · · · · 800

AZIMUTHAL EQUIDISTANT PROJECTION

## NATIONAL GEOGRAPHIC

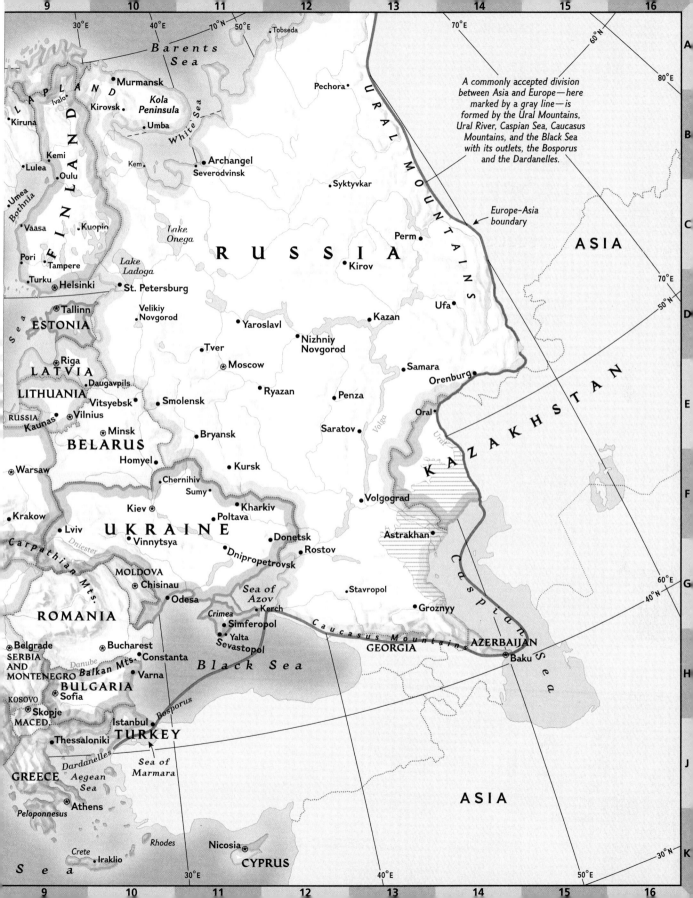

A commonly accepted division between Asia and Europe—here marked by a gray line—is formed by the Ural Mountains, Ural River, Caspian Sea, Caucasus Mountains, and the Black Sea with its outlets, the Bosporus and the Dardanelles.

Europe-Asia boundary

**Barents Sea**

Tobseda

Pechora

*U R A L  M O U N T A I N S*

**ASIA**

Murmansk

Kirovsk

*Kola Peninsula*

Umba

*White Sea*

Kiruna

Ivalo

*L A P L A N D*

Kemi

Kem

Archangel

Severodvinsk

Syktyvkar

Lulea

Oulu

*Lake Onega*

**R U S S I A**

Perm

Umea

*Gulf of Bothnia*

Vaasa

Kuopio

*F I N L A N D*

Kirov

Ufa

Pori

Tampere

*Lake Ladoga*

Turku

Helsinki

St. Petersburg

Kazan

Tallinn

**ESTONIA**

Velikiy Novgorod

Yaroslavl

Samara

Orenburg

Riga

**LATVIA**

Tver

Nizhniy Novgorod

**LITHUANIA**

Daugavpils

Moscow

Oral

**RUSSIA**

Vitsyebsk

Vilnius

Smolensk

Ryazan

Penza

*Ural*

**K A Z A K H S T A N**

Kaunas

Minsk

Saratov

*Volga*

**BELARUS**

Bryansk

Warsaw

Homyel

Kursk

Volgograd

Chernihiv

Sumy

Krakow

Kiev

Kharkiv

Astrakhan

Lviv

Poltava

**U K R A I N E**

Donetsk

*Caspian Sea*

Vinnytsya

Dnipropetrovsk

Rostov

*Carpathian Mts.*

*Dniester*

**MOLDOVA**

Chisinau

*Sea of Azov*

Stavropol

Odesa

Kerch

*Crimea*

Groznyy

**ROMANIA**

Simferopol

Yalta

Sevastopol

*Caucasus Mountains*

**GEORGIA**

**AZERBAIJAN**

Belgrade

Bucharest

**SERBIA AND MONTENEGRO**

*Danube*

*Balkan Mts.*

Constanta

Baku

**BULGARIA**

Varna

*Black Sea*

**KOSOVO**

Sofia

Skopje

**MACED.**

Istanbul

*Bosporus*

Thessaloniki

**TURKEY**

*Dardanelles*

*Sea of Marmara*

**GREECE**

*Aegean Sea*

Athens

**ASIA**

*Peloponnesus*

*Crete*

Iraklio

*Rhodes*

Nicosia

**CYPRUS**

EUROPE
PHYSICAL

0 mi          400
0 km          400

AZIMUTHAL EQUIDISTANT PROJECTION

NATIONAL
GEOGRAPHIC

**ICELAND** ⊙ Reykjavik

Faroe
Islands

Shetland
Islands

Orkney
Islands

*Norwegian Sea*

N

ARCTIC CIRCLE

MERIDIAN OF GREENWICH (LONDON)

S C A N D I N A V I A

S W E D E N

N O R W A Y

⊗ Oslo

⊗ Stockholm

Gulf of

*Outer Hebrides*

*British
Isles*

*Highlands*

⊙ Edinburgh

⊗ Belfast
**UNITED**
**IRELAND**
Dublin ⊗   *Irish
Sea*

*Great
Britain*

**KINGDOM**

Cardiff ⊗

London ⊗

⊗ Amsterdam
**NETH.**

*North
Sea*

*Jutland*
**DENMARK**
Copenhagen ⊗   *Zealand*

Berlin ⊗

*Baltic*

**ATLANTIC
OCEAN**

*English Channel*

*Brittany*

*Seine*
⊙ Paris

*Loire*

**FRANCE**

**BELGIUM**
⊙ Brussels
**LUX.**

*Rhine*

**GERMANY**

N O R
**POLAND**

*Oder*

*Elbe*
⊙ Prague
**CZECH REP.**

Bratislava ⊗ **SLOVAKIA**

*Danube*

**LIECH.**
Vienna ⊗

Bay of
Biscay

Mont Blanc
15,771 ft
4,807 m

⊗ Bern
**SWITZ.**

A   L   P   S

**AUSTRIA**

Budapest ⊗

**HUNGARY**

*Massif
Central*

*Rhône*

**SLOVENIA**
Ljubljana ⊗
*Po*

Zagreb ⊗
**CROATIA**

*Drava*

*Sava*

*Danube*

**MONACO.**

*Riviera*

**SAN MARINO**

*Adriatic
Sea*

**BOSNIA &
HERZEGOVINA**
Sarajevo ⊗

*Cantabrian Mountains*

*Pyrenees*

**ANDORRA**

**PORTUGAL**

*Douro*

Madrid ⊗

**IBERIAN**

*Ebro*

**SPAIN**

**PENINSULA**

*Corsica*

**VATICAN
CITY**
Rome ⊙

**ITALY**

*Apennines*

Tirana ⊗
**ALBANIA**

Lisbon ⊗

*Tagus*

*Sardinia*

*Tyrrhenian
Sea*

*Ionian
Sea*

**GIBRALTAR**   *Baetic Mountains*
*Strait of Gibraltar*

*Balearic Islands*

M  e  d  i  t  e  r  r  a  n  e  a  n

*Sicily* + *Etna*
10,902 ft
3,323 m

Valletta ⊗
**MALTA**

**AFRICA**

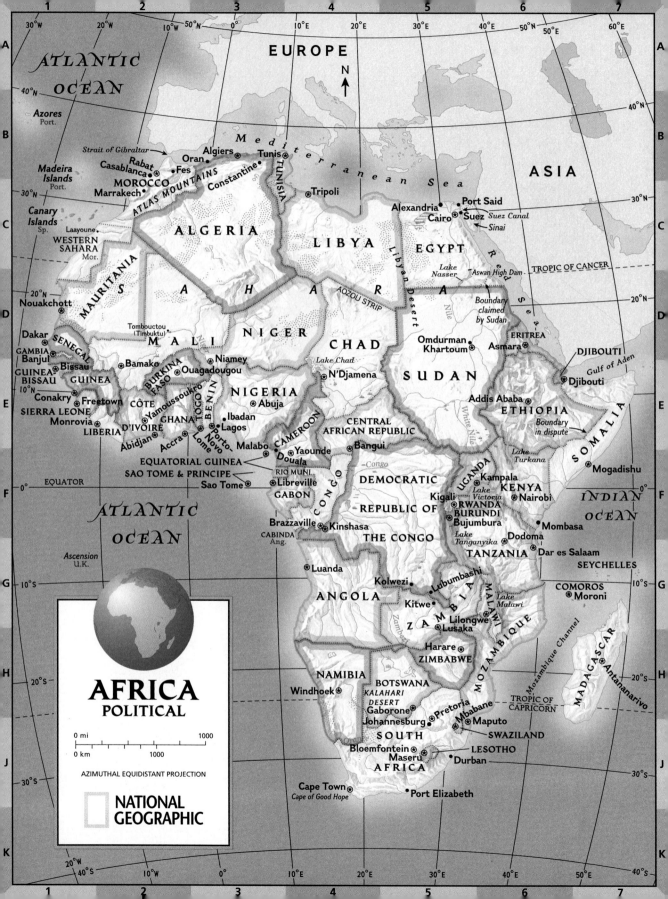

# AFRICA
## POLITICAL

0 mi        1000
0 km       1000

AZIMUTHAL EQUIDISTANT PROJECTION

# NATIONAL
# GEOGRAPHIC

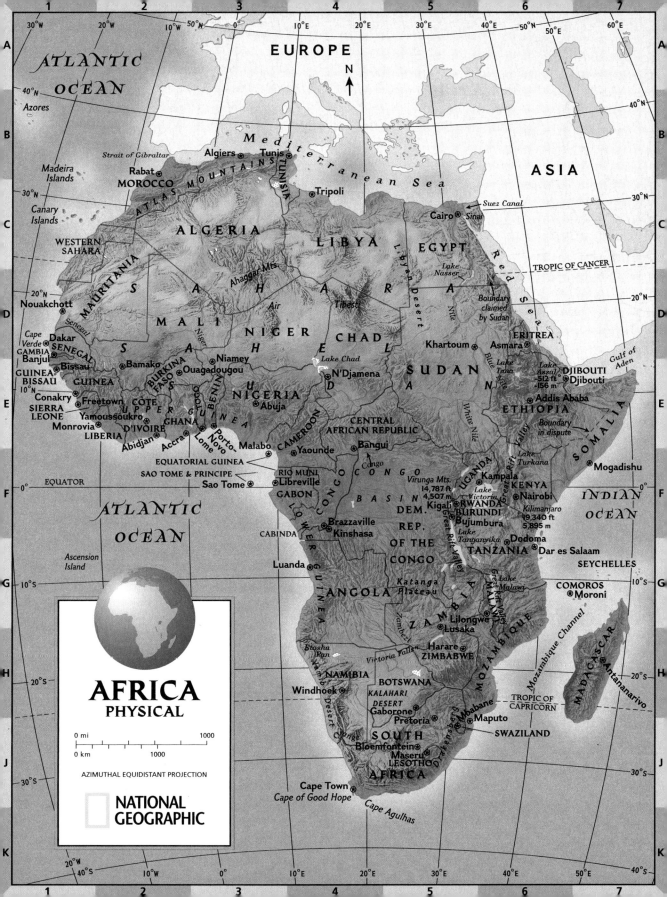

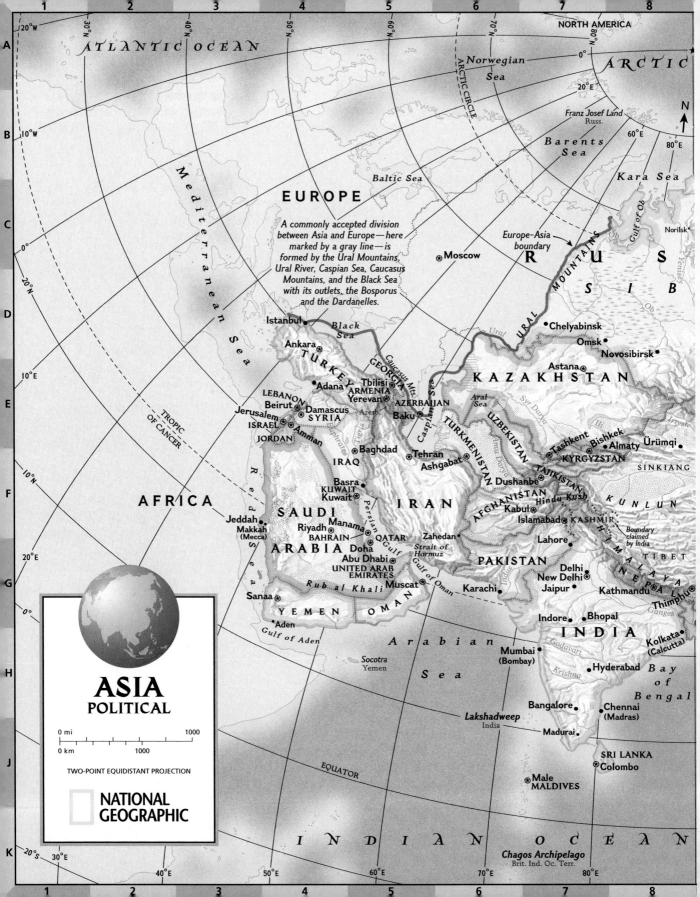

**9** **10** **11** **12** **13** **14** **15** **16**

North Pole

NORTH AMERICA
Bering Strait

Chukchi
Sea

O C E A N
180°
Wrangel I.

East
Siberian
Sea

160°E

Gulf of
Anadyr
Anadyr

B E R I N G

S e a

North
Land
120°E
100°E

Laptev
Sea

New Siberian
Islands

Cherskiy Range

Kolyma Range

Commander Is.

Kamchatka
Peninsula

Verkhoyansk Range

Magadan

Sea of
Okhotsk

S I A
E R I A

Lena

Yakutsk

Aldan

Sakhalin

Kuril Islands

Irkutsk

Lake
Baikal

MANCHURIA

Hokkaido
Sapporo

P A C I F I C   O C E A N

Yenisey

Herlen

Changchun

Sea of
Japan

Vladivostok

JAPAN
Tokyo

Marcus I.
Jap.

TROPIC OF CANCER

MONGOLIA

Ulaanbaatar

GOBI

Shenyang
Pyongyang

NORTH
KOREA

Seoul
SOUTH
KOREA

Honshu
Kyoto
Osaka
Hiroshima

ALTAY MTS.

Beijing

Bonin Is.
Jap.

Kyushu

SHAN

Lanzhou

Shijiazhuang

Xi'an

Qingdao

Yellow
Sea

East
China

Volcano Is.
Jap.

Xuzhou

Yellow

Chengdu

Nanjing

Shanghai

Ryukyu Islands

Okinawa

C H I N A

Yangtze

Nanchang

Fuzhou

Sea

Parece Vela
Jap.

Guiyang

Changsha

Taipei

TAIWAN

Boundary
claimed
by China

BHUTAN

BANGLADESH
Dhaka

Kunming

Guangzhou

Hong Kong
Macau

The People's Republic of China claims
Taiwan as its 23rd province.

Brahmaputra

Hanoi

Haiphong

South

P h i l i p p i n e

MYANMAR
(BURMA)

LAOS

Vientiane

Hainan

Da Nang

China

Luzon

Quezon City
Manila

S e a

Yangon
(Rangoon)

THAILAND

Sea

Mindoro

Samar

PHILIPPINES

Leyte

Bangkok

CAMBODIA

VIETNAM

Phnom Penh

Palawan

Panay
Negros

Andaman
Islands
India

Gulf of Thailand

Ho Chi Minh City

Mindanao

Andaman Sea

Bandar Seri
Begawan
BRUNEI

SABAH

Morotai

Biak

Jayapura

Halmahera

New Guinea

Nicobar
Islands
India

Kuala Lumpur

MALAYSIA

SARAWAK

MALAYSIA

Buru

Ceram

Aru
Is.

Kepi
Merauke
Dolak

Medan

SINGAPORE

Borneo

Celebes

M o l u c c a s

Sumatra

I N D O N E S I A

G R E A T E R

Tanimbar
Is.

Jambi

S U N D A   I S L A N D S

Dili
EAST
TIMOR

Mentawai
Islands

Jakarta

Java Sea

Java

Timor Sea

AUSTRALIA

100°E

110°E

120°E

Kupang

130°E

140°E

150°E

N.80

N.70

N.60

50 N

N.40

30 N

160°W

170°W

180°

20 N

170°E

10 N

160°E

0°

10°S

20°S

A
B
C
D
E
F
G
H
J
K

**9** **10** **11** **12** **13** **14** **15** **16**

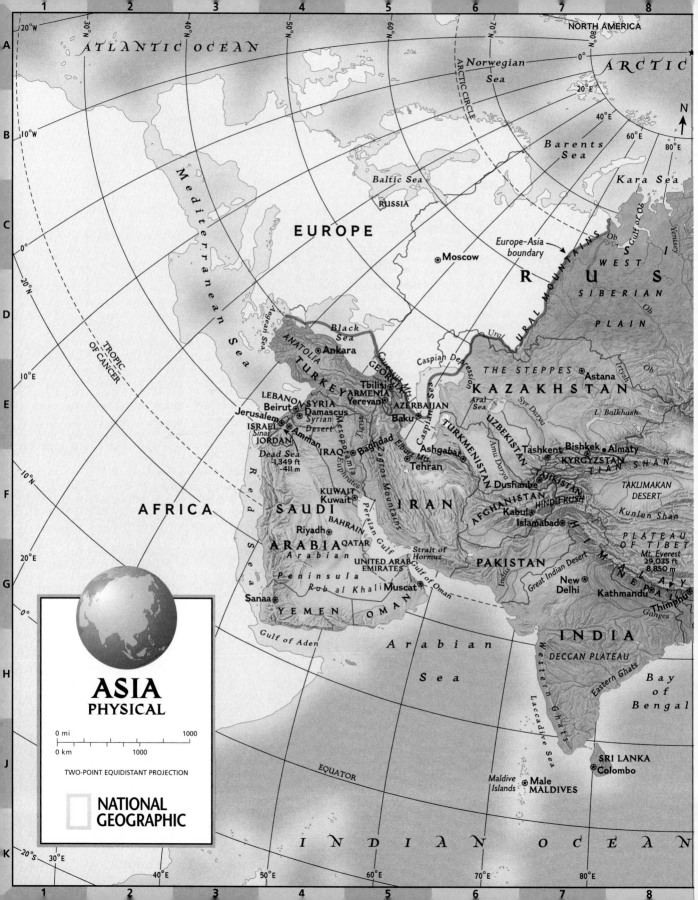

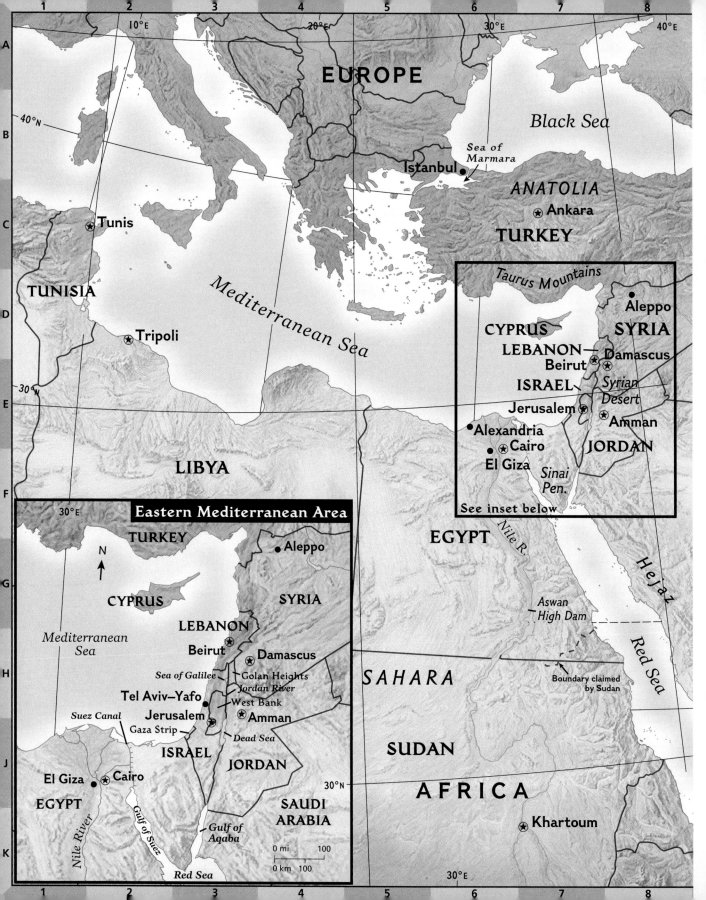

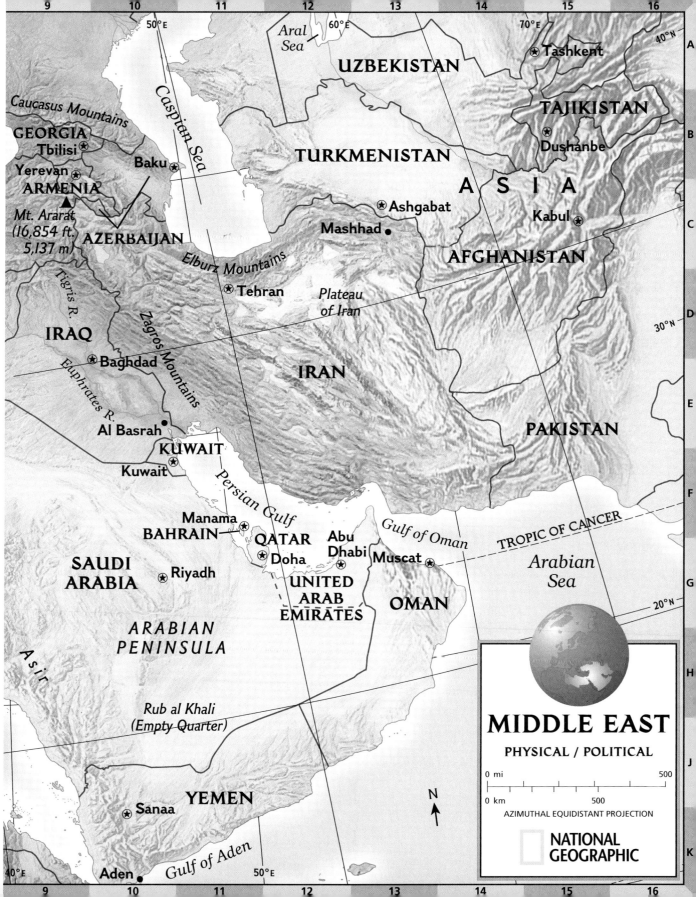

## MIDDLE EAST
### PHYSICAL / POLITICAL

0 mi                    500

0 km            500

AZIMUTHAL EQUIDISTANT PROJECTION

**NATIONAL GEOGRAPHIC**

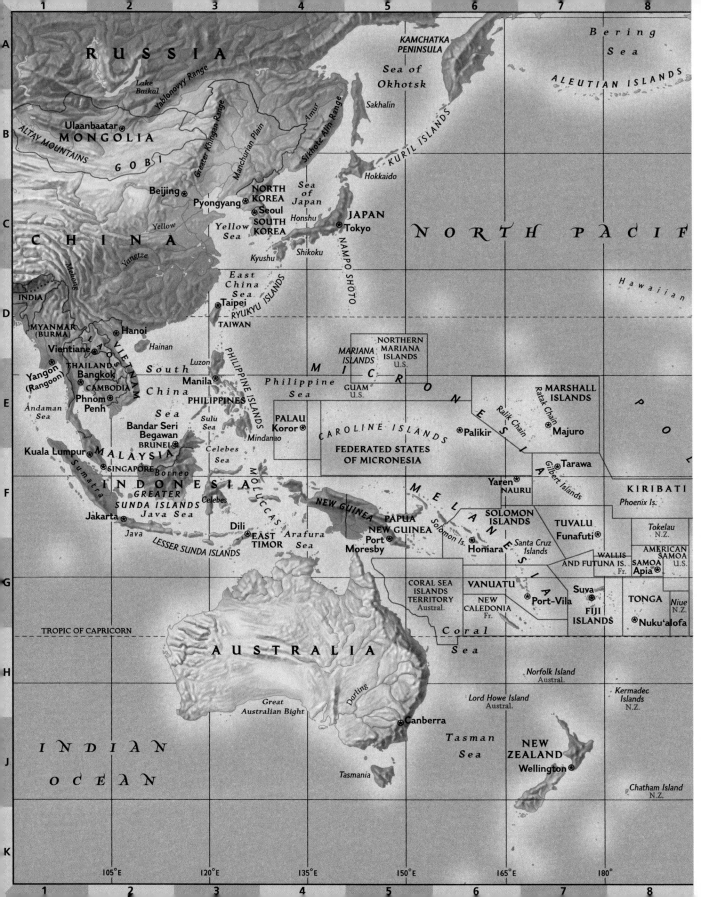

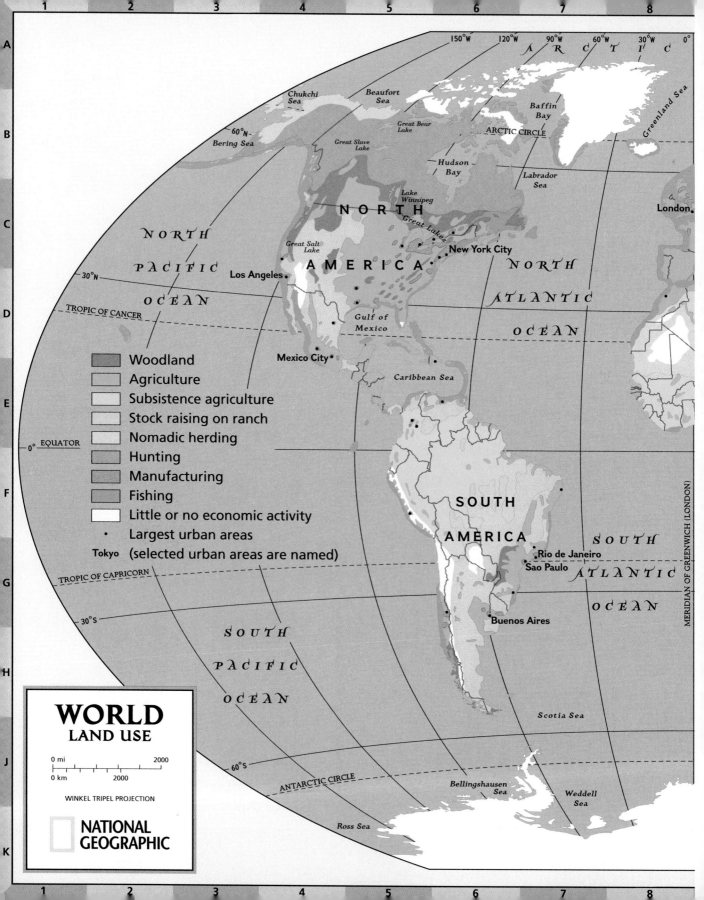

# WORLD
## LAND USE

Woodland
Agriculture
Subsistence agriculture
Stock raising on ranch
Nomadic herding
Hunting
Manufacturing
Fishing
Little or no economic activity
• Largest urban areas
Tokyo (selected urban areas are named)

0 mi       2000
0 km      2000

WINKEL TRIPEL PROJECTION

**NATIONAL GEOGRAPHIC**

ARCTIC
150°W 120°W 90°W 60°W 30°W 0°

Chukchi Sea
Beaufort Sea
Baffin Bay
Greenland Sea
60°N
Bering Sea
Great Bear Lake
Great Slave Lake
ARCTIC CIRCLE
Hudson Bay
Labrador Sea

N O R T H
Lake Winnipeg
Great Lakes
London

N O R T H
London

N O R T H   P A C I F I C
A M E R I C A
New York City
N O R T H
30°N
Great Salt Lake
Los Angeles
A T L A N T I C

O C E A N
Gulf of Mexico
O C E A N
TROPIC OF CANCER

Mexico City
Caribbean Sea

0° EQUATOR

S O U T H
A M E R I C A
S O U T H
Rio de Janeiro
Sao Paulo
A T L A N T I C

TROPIC OF CAPRICORN
30°S
Buenos Aires
O C E A N

S O U T H
P A C I F I C
O C E A N

Scotia Sea

60°S
ANTARCTIC CIRCLE
Bellingshausen Sea
Weddell Sea

Ross Sea

MERIDIAN OF GREENWICH (LONDON)

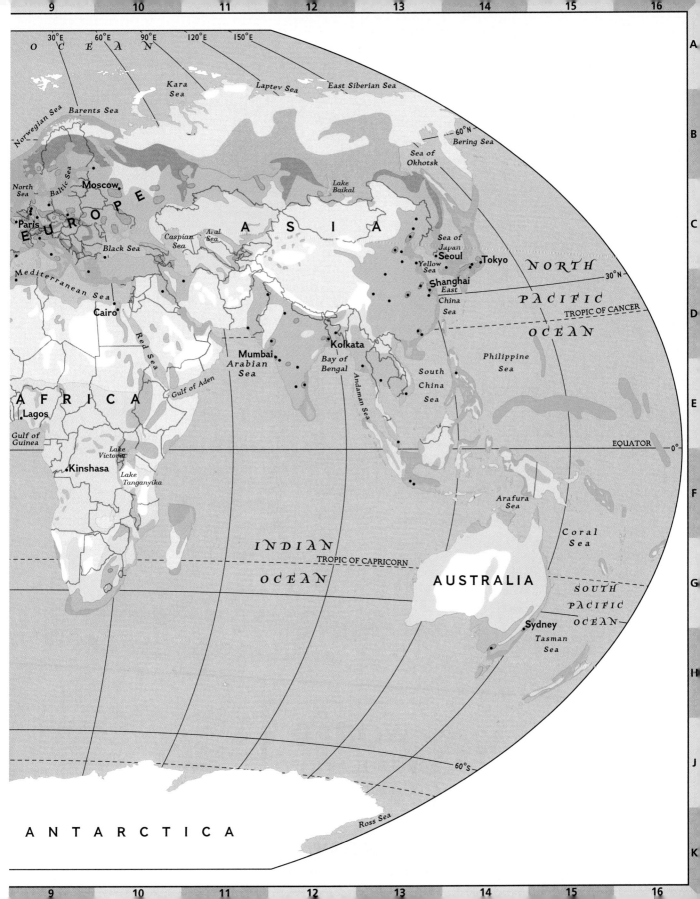

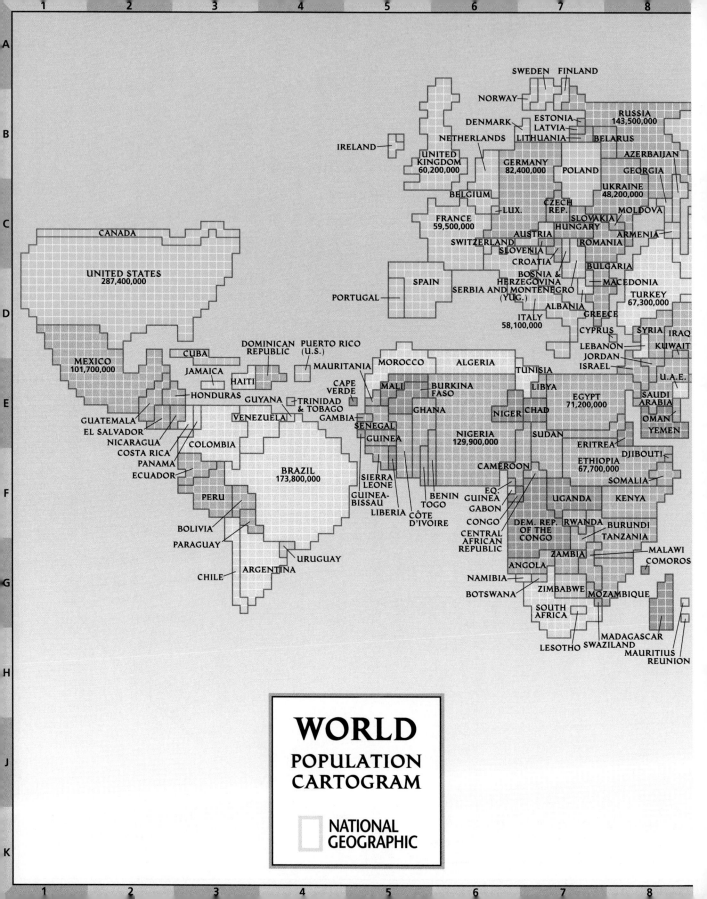

# WORLD
## POPULATION
## CARTOGRAM

NATIONAL
GEOGRAPHIC

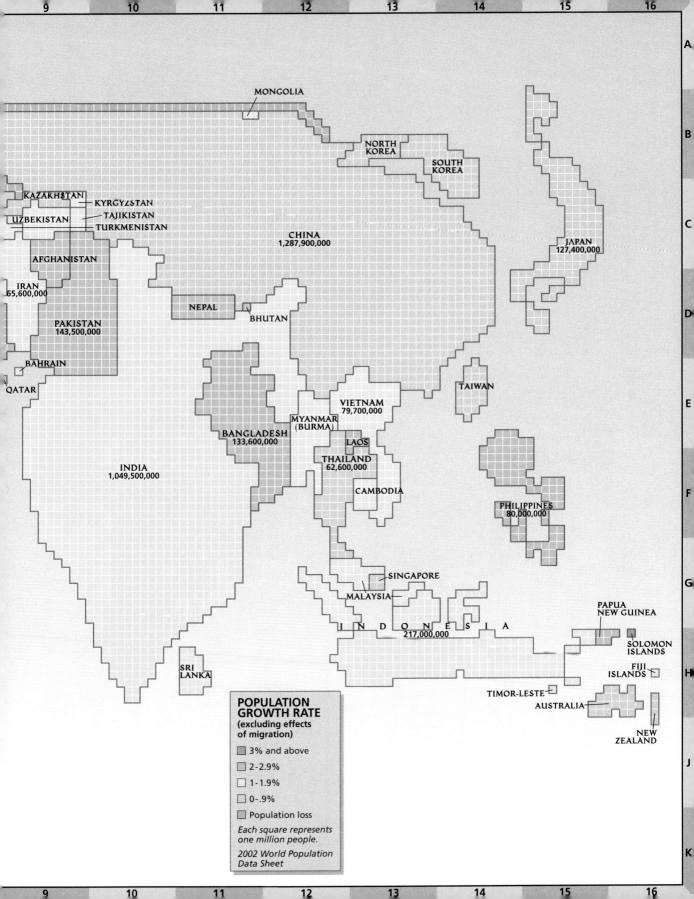

MONGOLIA

NORTH
KOREA

SOUTH
KOREA

JAPAN
127,400,000

KAZAKHSTAN

KYRGYZSTAN

UZBEKISTAN

TAJIKISTAN

TURKMENISTAN

AFGHANISTAN

CHINA
1,287,900,000

IRAN
65,600,000

NEPAL

BHUTAN

PAKISTAN
143,500,000

BAHRAIN

QATAR

TAIWAN

VIETNAM
79,700,000

MYANMAR
(BURMA)

BANGLADESH
133,600,000

LAOS

THAILAND
62,600,000

INDIA
1,049,500,000

CAMBODIA

PHILIPPINES
80,000,000

SINGAPORE

MALAYSIA

PAPUA
NEW GUINEA

I N D O N E S I A
217,000,000

SOLOMON
ISLANDS

FIJI
ISLANDS

SRI
LANKA

TIMOR-LESTE

AUSTRALIA

NEW
ZEALAND

**POPULATION
GROWTH RATE**
(excluding effects
of migration)

3% and above

2-2.9%

1-1.9%

0-.9%

Population loss

*Each square represents
one million people.*

*2002 World Population
Data Sheet*

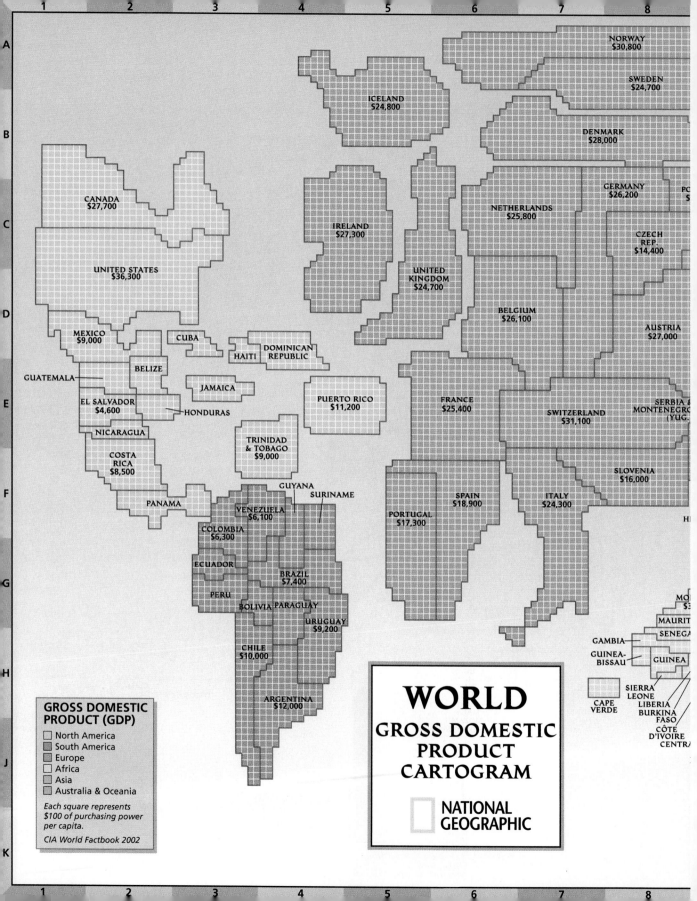

# WORLD

## GROSS DOMESTIC PRODUCT CARTOGRAM

NATIONAL GEOGRAPHIC

**GROSS DOMESTIC PRODUCT (GDP)**

- North America
- South America
- Europe
- Africa
- Asia
- Australia & Oceania

*Each square represents $100 of purchasing power per capita.*

*CIA World Factbook 2002*

NORWAY $30,800

SWEDEN $24,700

ICELAND $24,800

DENMARK $28,000

GERMANY $26,200

NETHERLANDS $25,800

PO...

CZECH REP. $14,400

CANADA $27,700

IRELAND $27,300

UNITED STATES $36,300

UNITED KINGDOM $24,700

BELGIUM $26,100

AUSTRIA $27,000

MEXICO $9,000

CUBA

DOMINICAN REPUBLIC

HAITI

GUATEMALA

BELIZE

JAMAICA

EL SALVADOR $4,600

HONDURAS

PUERTO RICO $11,200

FRANCE $25,400

SWITZERLAND $31,100

SERBIA & MONTENEGRO (YUG.)

NICARAGUA

SLOVENIA $16,000

COSTA RICA $8,500

TRINIDAD & TOBAGO $9,000

PANAMA

GUYANA

SURINAME

VENEZUELA $6,100

PORTUGAL $17,300

SPAIN $18,900

ITALY $24,300

COLOMBIA $6,300

ECUADOR

BRAZIL $7,400

PERU

BOLIVIA PARAGUAY

URUGUAY $9,200

MO... $3...

MAURIT...

SENEGA...

GAMBIA

GUINEA-BISSAU

GUINEA

CHILE $10,000

ARGENTINA $12,000

CAPE VERDE

SIERRA LEONE

LIBERIA

BURKINA FASO

CÔTE D'IVOIRE

CENTRA...

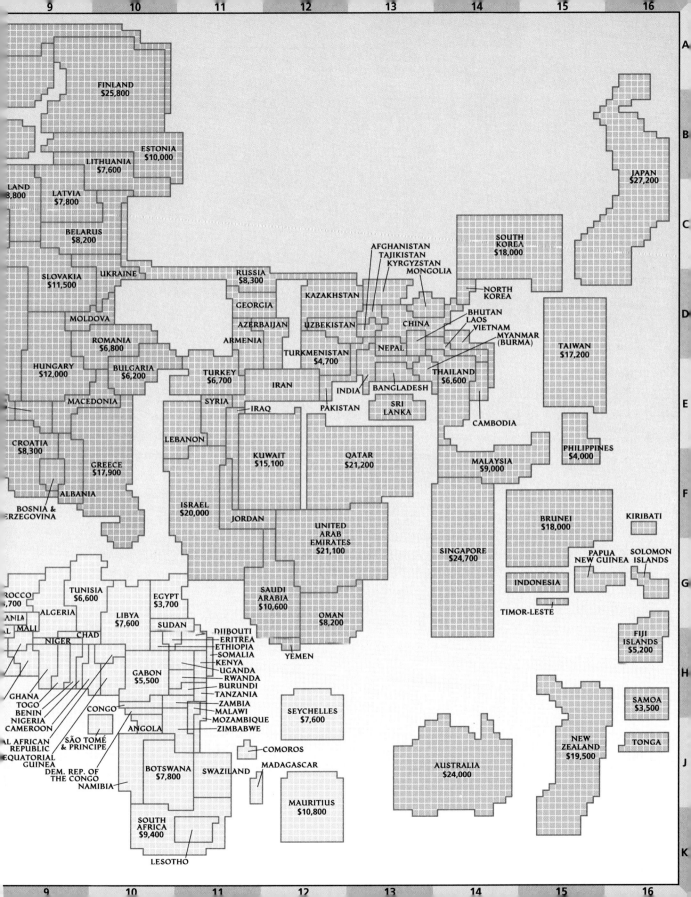

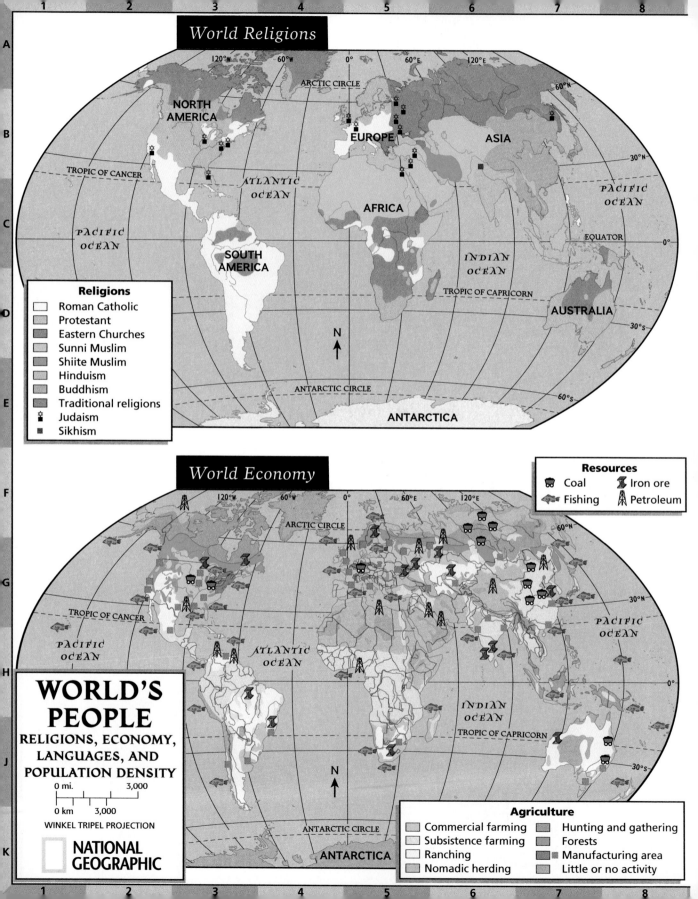

# World Religions

NORTH AMERICA

EUROPE

ASIA

AFRICA

SOUTH AMERICA

PACIFIC OCEAN

ATLANTIC OCEAN

PACIFIC OCEAN

INDIAN OCEAN

AUSTRALIA

ANTARCTICA

ARCTIC CIRCLE
TROPIC OF CANCER
EQUATOR
TROPIC OF CAPRICORN
ANTARCTIC CIRCLE

N

120°W 60°W 0° 60°E 120°E
60°N 30°N 0° 30°S 60°S

**Religions**
- Roman Catholic
- Protestant
- Eastern Churches
- Sunni Muslim
- Shiite Muslim
- Hinduism
- Buddhism
- Traditional religions
- ✡ Judaism
- ■ Sikhism

# World Economy

**Resources**
- Coal
- Iron ore
- Fishing
- Petroleum

ARCTIC CIRCLE
TROPIC OF CANCER
TROPIC OF CAPRICORN
ANTARCTIC CIRCLE

PACIFIC OCEAN

ATLANTIC OCEAN

PACIFIC OCEAN

INDIAN OCEAN

ANTARCTICA

N

120°W 60°W 0° 60°E 120°E
60°N 30°N 0° 30°S

# WORLD'S PEOPLE
## RELIGIONS, ECONOMY, LANGUAGES, AND POPULATION DENSITY

0 mi. 3,000
0 km 3,000

WINKEL TRIPEL PROJECTION

**NATIONAL GEOGRAPHIC**

**Agriculture**
- Commercial farming
- Subsistence farming
- Ranching
- Nomadic herding
- Hunting and gathering
- Forests
- ■ Manufacturing area
- Little or no activity

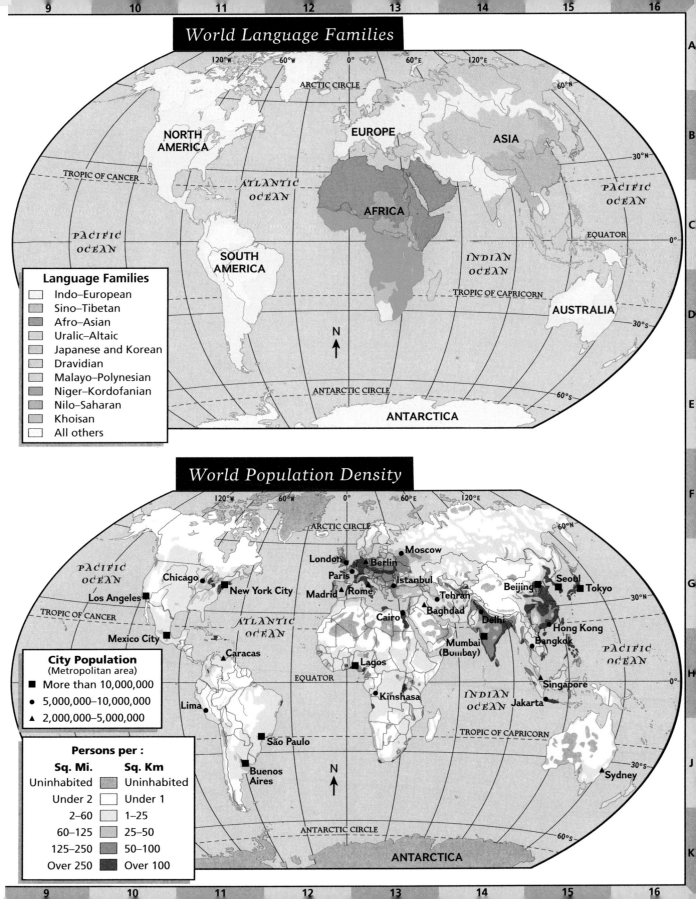

# World Language Families

**Language Families**
- Indo–European
- Sino–Tibetan
- Afro–Asian
- Uralic–Altaic
- Japanese and Korean
- Dravidian
- Malayo–Polynesian
- Niger–Kordofanian
- Nilo–Saharan
- Khoisan
- All others

NORTH AMERICA

EUROPE

ASIA

AFRICA

SOUTH AMERICA

AUSTRALIA

ANTARCTICA

ATLANTIC OCEAN

PACIFIC OCEAN

PACIFIC OCEAN

INDIAN OCEAN

ARCTIC CIRCLE

TROPIC OF CANCER

EQUATOR

TROPIC OF CAPRICORN

ANTARCTIC CIRCLE

N

# World Population Density

**City Population**
(Metropolitan area)
- ■ More than 10,000,000
- ● 5,000,000–10,000,000
- ▲ 2,000,000–5,000,000

**Persons per :**

| Sq. Mi. | Sq. Km |
|---|---|
| Uninhabited | Uninhabited |
| Under 2 | Under 1 |
| 2–60 | 1–25 |
| 60–125 | 25–50 |
| 125–250 | 50–100 |
| Over 250 | Over 100 |

Chicago · London · Moscow · Berlin · Paris · Istanbul · Madrid · Rome · Tehran · Baghdad · Cairo · Beijing · Seoul · Tokyo · Delhi · Hong Kong · Bangkok · Mumbai (Bombay) · Los Angeles · New York City · Mexico City · Caracas · Lagos · Kinshasa · Singapore · Jakarta · Lima · São Paulo · Buenos Aires · Sydney

PACIFIC OCEAN · ATLANTIC OCEAN · INDIAN OCEAN

ARCTIC CIRCLE · TROPIC OF CANCER · EQUATOR · TROPIC OF CAPRICORN · ANTARCTIC CIRCLE

ANTARCTICA

N

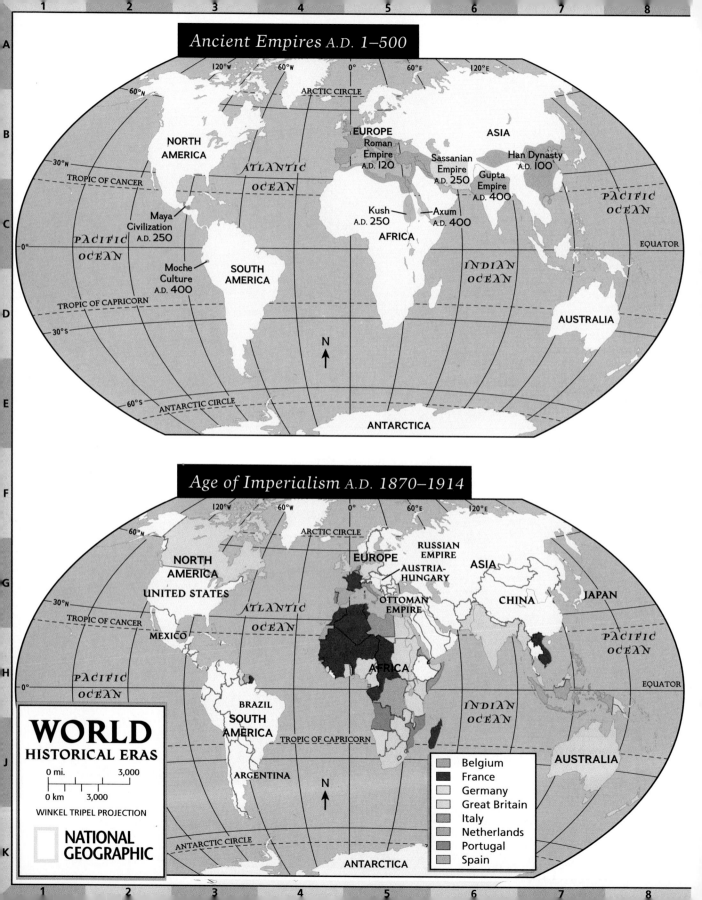

## Ancient Empires A.D. 1–500

**NORTH AMERICA**

*ATLANTIC OCEAN*

**EUROPE**
Roman Empire A.D. 120

**ASIA**

Sassanian Empire A.D. 250

Han Dynasty A.D. 100

Gupta Empire A.D. 400

Maya Civilization A.D. 250

Kush A.D. 250

Axum A.D. 400

*PACIFIC OCEAN*

**AFRICA**

Moche Culture A.D. 400

**SOUTH AMERICA**

*INDIAN OCEAN*

*PACIFIC OCEAN*

**AUSTRALIA**

N

**ANTARCTICA**

ARCTIC CIRCLE
TROPIC OF CANCER
EQUATOR
TROPIC OF CAPRICORN
ANTARCTIC CIRCLE
60°N 30°N 0° 30°S 60°S
120°W 60°W 0° 60°E 120°E

## Age of Imperialism A.D. 1870–1914

**NORTH AMERICA**
**UNITED STATES**

*ATLANTIC OCEAN*

**EUROPE**

**RUSSIAN EMPIRE**

AUSTRIA-HUNGARY

**ASIA**

OTTOMAN EMPIRE

**CHINA**

**JAPAN**

MEXICO

**AFRICA**

*PACIFIC OCEAN*

*PACIFIC OCEAN*

**BRAZIL**
**SOUTH AMERICA**

ARGENTINA

*INDIAN OCEAN*

**AUSTRALIA**

N

**ANTARCTICA**

ARCTIC CIRCLE
TROPIC OF CANCER
EQUATOR
TROPIC OF CAPRICORN
ANTARCTIC CIRCLE
60°N 30°N 0°
120°W 60°W 0° 60°E 120°E

### WORLD HISTORICAL ERAS

0 mi. 3,000
0 km 3,000

WINKEL TRIPEL PROJECTION

**NATIONAL GEOGRAPHIC**

- ◻ Belgium
- ◻ France
- ◻ Germany
- ◻ Great Britain
- ◻ Italy
- ◻ Netherlands
- ◻ Portugal
- ◻ Spain

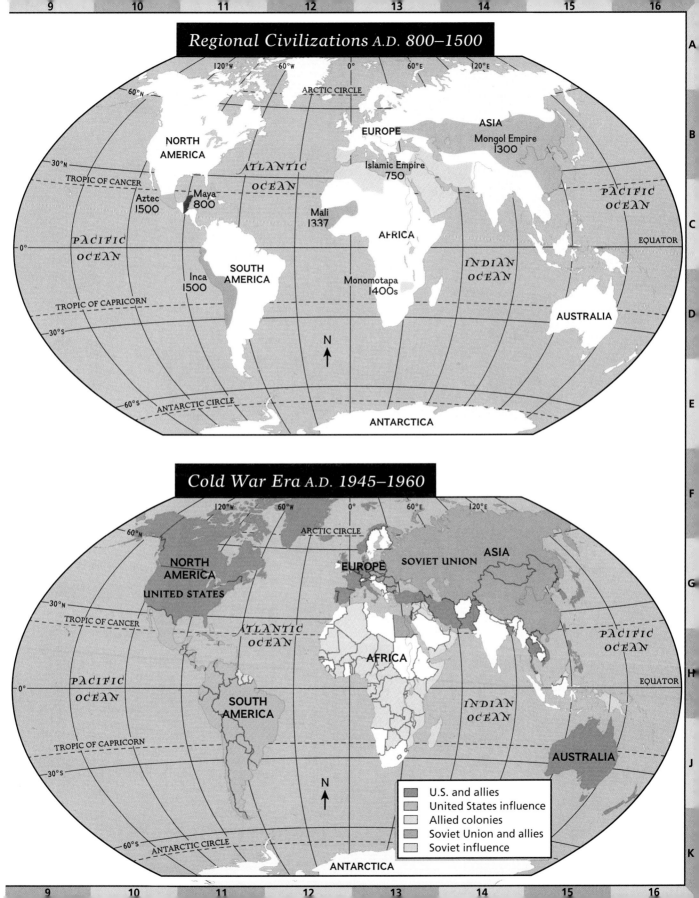

## Regional Civilizations A.D. 800–1500

ARCTIC CIRCLE

NORTH AMERICA

EUROPE

ASIA
Mongol Empire
1300

ATLANTIC OCEAN

Islamic Empire
750

PACIFIC OCEAN

Aztec
1500

Maya
800

Mali
1337

AFRICA

PACIFIC OCEAN

EQUATOR

Inca
1500

SOUTH AMERICA

INDIAN OCEAN

Monomotapa
1400s

TROPIC OF CANCER

TROPIC OF CAPRICORN

30°S

AUSTRALIA

N

ANTARCTIC CIRCLE

ANTARCTICA

60°N
30°N
0°
120°W
60°W
0°
60°E
120°E

## Cold War Era A.D. 1945–1960

ARCTIC CIRCLE

NORTH AMERICA
UNITED STATES

EUROPE

SOVIET UNION

ASIA

ATLANTIC OCEAN

TROPIC OF CANCER

PACIFIC OCEAN

AFRICA

PACIFIC OCEAN

EQUATOR

SOUTH AMERICA

INDIAN OCEAN

TROPIC OF CAPRICORN

AUSTRALIA

30°S

N

60°N
30°N
0°
120°W
60°W
0°
60°E
120°E

ANTARCTIC CIRCLE

ANTARCTICA

Legend:
- U.S. and allies
- United States influence
- Allied colonies
- Soviet Union and allies
- Soviet influence

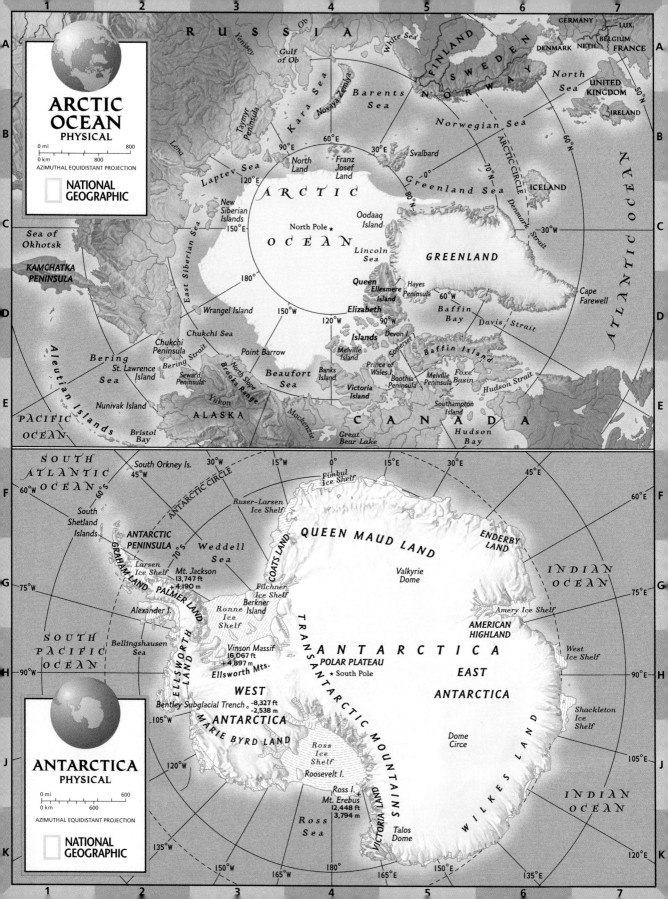

# NATIONAL GEOGRAPHIC

# Geography Handbook

*The story of the world begins with geography—the study of the earth in all of its variety. Geography describes the earth's land, water, and plant and animal life. It is the study of places and the complex relationships between people and their environment.*

*The resources in this handbook will help you get the most out of your textbook—and provide you with skills you will use for the rest of your life.*

The Gui River, Guilin, China ▼

▲ Saharan sand dunes, Morocco

The Amazon, Brazil ▶

# How Do I Study Geography?

To understand how our world is connected, some geographers have divided the study of geography into five themes. **The Five Themes of Geography are** (1) location, (2) place, (3) human/environmental interaction, (4) movement, and (5) regions.

## Six Essential Elements

Recently geographers have broken down the study of geography into **Six Essential Elements.** Being aware of these elements will help you better understand and organize what you are learning about geography.

### Element 2

**Places and Regions**
**Place** has a special meaning in geography. It means more than where a place is. It also describes what a place is like. Physical characteristics such as landforms, climate, and plant or animal life help geographers distinguish different kinds of places. Human characteristics, including language and way of life, also describe places.

Geographers often group places or areas into regions. **Regions** are united by one or more common characteristics.

### Element 1

**The World in Spatial Terms**
Geographers first take a look at where a place is located. **Location** serves as a starting point by defining where a place is. Knowing the location of places helps you develop an awareness of the world around you.

### Element 3

**Physical Systems**
When studying places and regions, geographers analyze how **physical systems**—such as hurricanes, volcanoes, and glaciers—shape the earth's surface. As part of their study of physical systems, geographers look at communities of plants and animals that depend upon one another and their surroundings for survival.

## Element 4

### Human Systems

Geographers also examine **human systems,** or how people have shaped our world. Geographers look at how boundary lines are determined and analyze why people settle in certain places and not in others. A key theme in geography is the continual **movement** of people, ideas, and goods.

## Element 5

### Environment and Society

How does the relationship between people and their natural surroundings influence the way people live? Geographers study how people use the **environment** and how their actions affect the environment.

## Element 6

### The Uses of Geography

How does a war in the Middle East affect the economy of the United States? Knowing **how to use geography** helps people understand the relationships between people, places, and environments over time. Learning how to study geography also prepares you for life in our modern society.

# Globes and Maps

**P**hotographs from space show Earth in its true form—a great ball spinning around the Sun. The most accurate way to depict the earth is as a **globe,** a spherical scale model of the earth. A globe gives a true picture of the continents' relative sizes and the shapes of landmasses and bodies of water. Globes are proportionately correct, accurately representing distance and direction.

A **map** is a flat drawing of all or part of the earth's surface. Unlike globes, maps can show small areas in great detail. People use maps to locate places, plot routes, and judge distances. Maps can also display useful information, such as political boundaries, population densities, or even voting returns.

## From Globes to Maps

Maps, however, do have their limitations. As you can imagine, drawing a round object on a flat surface is very difficult. Think about the surface of the earth as the peel of an orange. To flatten the peel, you might have to cut it like the globe shown here. **Cartographers,** or mapmakers, use mathematical formulas to transfer information from the three-dimensional globe to a two-dimensional map. However, when the curves of a globe become straight lines on a map, distortion of size, shape, distance, or area occurs.

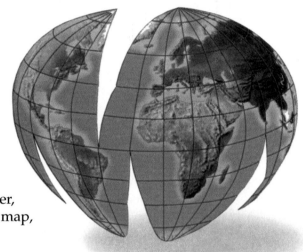

## How Map Projections Work

To create maps, cartographers *project* the round earth onto a flat surface—making a **map projection.** There are more than a hundred kinds of map projections, each with some advantages and some degrees of accuracy. The purpose of the map usually dictates which projection is used. Three of the basic categories of projections used are shown here: **planar, cylindrical,** and **conic.**

### Planar Projection

Planar projections show the earth centered in such a way that a straight line going from the center to any other point on the map represents the shortest distance. Since they are most accurate at the center, they are often used for maps of the Poles.

# Great Circle Routes

A *great circle* is an imaginary line that follows the curve of the earth. A line drawn along the Equator is an example of a great circle. Traveling along a great circle is called following a **great circle route.** Airplane pilots use great circle routes because they represent the shortest distances from one city to the next.

The idea of a great circle shows one important difference between a globe and a map. Because a globe is round, it accurately shows great circles. On a flat map, however, the great circle route between two points may not appear to be the shortest distance. For example, on map A the great circle distance (dotted line) between Tokyo and Los Angeles appears to be far longer than the true direction distance (solid line). In fact, the great circle distance is 345 miles (555 km) shorter, which is evident on map B.

# Geographic Information Systems

Technology has changed the way maps are made. Most cartographers use software programs called **geographic information systems (GIS).** A GIS uses data from maps, satellite images, printed text, and statistics. Cartographers can program the GIS to produce the maps they need, and it allows them to make changes quickly and easily.

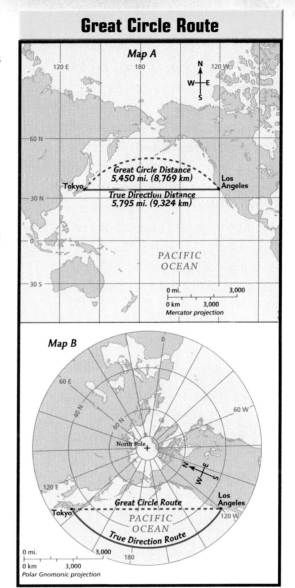

**Great Circle Route**

Map A

Great Circle Distance
5,450 mi. (8,769 km)

Tokyo

Los Angeles

True Direction Distance
5,795 mi. (9,324 km)

PACIFIC OCEAN

0 mi. 3,000
0 km 3,000
Mercator projection

Map B

North Pole

Great Circle Route

Tokyo

Los Angeles

PACIFIC OCEAN

True Direction Route

0 mi. 3,000
0 km 3,000
Polar Gnomonic projection

## Cylindrical Projection

Cylindrical projections are based on the projection of the globe onto a cylinder. They are most accurate near the Equator, but shapes and distances are distorted near the Poles.

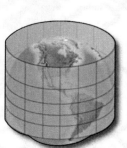

EQUATOR

## Conic Projection

Conic projections are made by placing a cone over part of the globe. They are best suited for showing east-west areas that are not too far from the Equator. For these uses, a conic projection can indicate distances and directions fairly accurately.

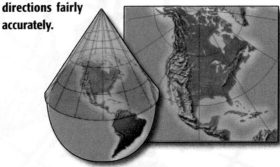

# Common Map Projections

F our of the most popular map projections are named for the cartographers who developed them. These are the **Winkel Tripel** projection, the **Robinson** projection, **Goode's Interrupted Equal-Area** projection, and the **Mercator** projection. Remember, all map projections have some degree of inaccuracy in distance, shape, or size because the curved surface of the earth cannot be shown accurately on a flat map. Every map projection stretches or breaks the curved surface of the earth in some way.

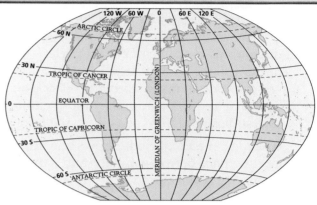

▲ Most reference world maps use the Winkel Tripel projection. Adopted by the National Geographic Society in 1998 for use in most maps, this projection provides a better balance between the size and shape of land areas as they are shown on the map. Even the polar areas are depicted with little distortion of size and shape.

# Reading a Map

Maps include several important tools to help you interpret the information contained on a particular map. Learning to use these map tools will help you read the symbolic language of maps more easily.

**Compass Rose**   A compass rose is a marker that indicates directions. The four cardinal directions—north, south, east, and west—are usually indicated with arrows or points of a star. Sometimes a compass rose may point in only one direction because the other directions can be determined in relation to the given direction. The compass rose on this map indicates all four cardinal directions.

**Key** Cartographers use a variety of symbols to represent map information. Because these symbols are graphic and commonly used, most maps can be read and understood by people around the world. To be sure that the symbols are clear, however, every map contains a key—a list that explains what the symbols stand for. This key shows symbols used for a battle map. It indicates troop movements, supply lines, and U.S. bases.

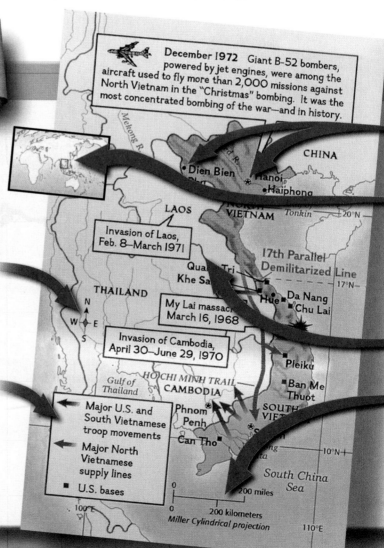

December 1972   Giant B-52 bombers, powered by jet engines, were among the aircraft used to fly more than 2,000 missions against North Vietnam in the "Christmas" bombing. It was the most concentrated bombing of the war—and in history.

## Robinson Projection

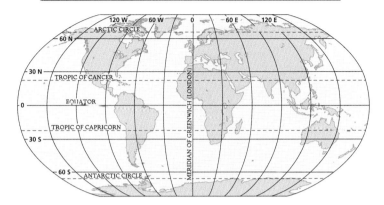

▲ The Robinson projection has minor distortions. The sizes and shapes near the eastern and western edges of the map are accurate, and the outlines of the continents appear much as they do on the globe. However, the shapes of the polar areas appear somewhat flat.

## Goode's Interrupted Equal-Area Projection

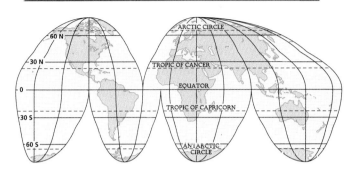

▲ An interrupted projection looks something like a globe that has been cut apart and laid flat. Goode's Interrupted Equal-Area projection shows the true size and shape of the earth's landmasses, but distances are distorted.

**Cities and Capitals** Cities are symbolized by a solid circle. Sometimes the relative sizes of cities are shown with circles of different sizes. Capitals are represented by a star within a circle.

**Relative Location** People use relative direction to indicate location. You may be told, for example, to look for a street that is "two blocks north" of another street. Relative location is the location of one place in relation to another place, while absolute location indicates the exact position of a place on the earth's surface. On this map, the relative position of where the Vietnam War took place is given in relation to the rest of the world.

**Boundary Lines** On political maps of large areas, boundary lines highlight the borders between different countries, states, provinces, or counties.

**Scale Bar** Every map is a representation of a part of the earth. The scale bar shows the relationship between map measurements and actual distance. Scale can be measured with a ruler to calculate actual distances in standard or metric measurements. On this map, three-fourths inch represents 200 miles (322 km).

## Mercator Projection

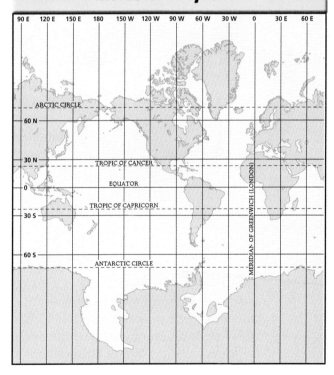

▲ The Mercator projection, once the most commonly used projection, increasingly distorts size and distance as it moves away from the Equator. This makes areas such as Greenland and Antarctica look much larger than they would appear on a globe. However, Mercator projections do accurately show true directions and the shapes of landmasses, making these maps useful for sea travel.

# Understanding Latitude and Longitude

**L**ines on globes and maps provide information that can help you easily locate places on the earth. These lines—called **latitude** and **longitude**—cross one another, forming a pattern called a grid system.

## Latitude

Lines of latitude, or **parallels,** circle the earth parallel to the **Equator** and measure the distance north or south of the Equator in degrees. The Equator is at 0° latitude, while the Poles lie at latitudes 90°N (north) and 90°S (south).

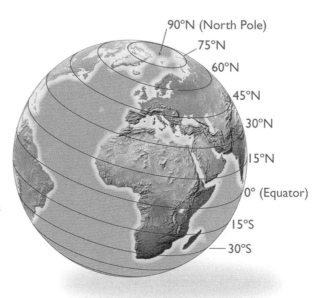

90°N (North Pole)
75°N
60°N
45°N
30°N
15°N
0° (Equator)
15°S
30°S

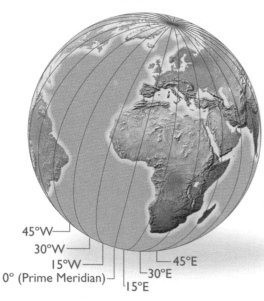

45°W
30°W
15°W
0° (Prime Meridian)
15°E
30°E
45°E

## Longitude

Lines of longitude, or **meridians,** circle the earth from Pole to Pole. These lines measure distances east or west of the starting line, which is at 0° longitude and is called the **Prime Meridian.** The Prime Meridian runs through the Royal Observatory in Greenwich, England.

## Absolute Location

The grid system formed by lines of latitude and longitude makes it possible to find the absolute location of a place. Many places can be found along a line of latitude, but only one place can be found at the point where a certain line of latitude crosses a certain line of longitude. By using degrees and minutes (points between degrees), people can pinpoint the precise spot where one line of latitude crosses one line of longitude—an absolute location.

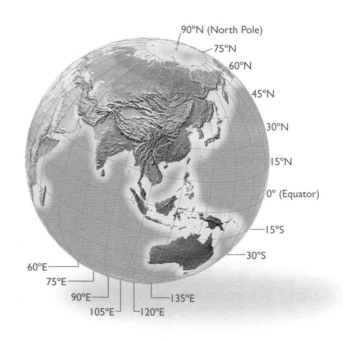

90°N (North Pole)
75°N
60°N
45°N
30°N
15°N
0° (Equator)
15°S
30°S
60°E
75°E
90°E
105°E
120°E
135°E

# Types of Maps

**M**aps are prepared for many uses. The information depicted in the map depends on how the map will be used. Learning to recognize a map's purpose will help you make the best use of its content.

## General-Purpose Maps

Maps that show a wide range of general information about an area are called **general-purpose** maps. Two of the most common general-purpose maps are physical maps and political maps.

**Physical maps** show the location and the topography, or shape, of the earth's physical features. They use colors or patterns to indicate relief—the differences in elevation, or height, of landforms.

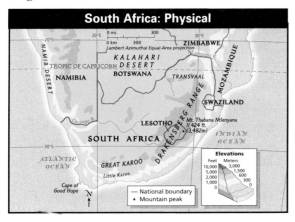

**Political maps** show the boundaries between countries. Smaller internal divisions, such as states or counties, may also be indicated by different symbols. Political maps usually feature capitals and other cities.

## Special-Purpose Maps

**Special-purpose** maps show information on specific topics, such as climate, land use, or vegetation. Human activities, such as exploration routes, territorial expansion, or battle sites, also appear on special-purpose maps. Colors and map key symbols are especially important on this type of map.

## LANDSAT Maps

LANDSAT maps are made from photographs by camera-carrying LANDSAT satellites in space. The cameras record millions of energy waves invisible to the human eye. Computers then change this information into pictures of the earth's surface. With LANDSAT images, scientists can study whole mountain ranges, oceans, and geographic regions. Changes to the earth's environment can also be tracked using the satellite information.

LANDSAT image, Mt. St. Helens, Washington ▼

# NATIONAL GEOGRAPHIC
# Geographic Dictionary

As you read about world history, you will encounter the terms listed below. Many of the terms are pictured in the diagram.

**Labels in diagram:** Volcano, Mountain peak, Strait, Sound, Valley, Cape, Island, Ocean, Cliff, Isthmus, Bay, Harbor, Gulf, Delta, Peninsula, Seacoast

**absolute location** exact location of a place on the earth described by global coordinates

**basin** area of land drained by a given river and its branches; area of land surrounded by lands of higher elevation

**bay** part of a large body of water that extends into a shoreline, generally smaller than a gulf

**canyon** deep and narrow valley with steep walls

**cape** point of land that extends into a river, lake, or ocean

**channel** wide strait or waterway between two landmasses that lie close to each other; deep part of a river or other waterway

**cliff** steep, high wall of rock, earth, or ice

**continent** one of the seven large landmasses on the earth

**cultural feature** characteristic that humans have created in a place, such as language, religion, housing, and settlement pattern

**delta** flat, low-lying land built up from soil carried downstream by a river and deposited at its mouth

**divide** stretch of high land that separates river systems

**downstream** direction in which a river or stream flows from its source to its mouth

**elevation** height of land above sea level

**Equator** imaginary line that runs around the earth halfway between the North and South Poles; used as the starting point to measure degrees of north and south latitude

**glacier** large, thick body of slowly moving ice

**gulf** part of a large body of water that extends into a shoreline, generally larger and more deeply indented than a bay

**harbor** a sheltered place along a shoreline where ships can anchor safely

**highland** elevated land area such as a hill, mountain, or plateau

**hill** elevated land with sloping sides and rounded summit; generally smaller than a mountain

**island** land area, smaller than a continent, completely surrounded by water

**isthmus** narrow stretch of land connecting two larger land areas

**lake** a sizable inland body of water

**latitude** distance north or south of the Equator, measured in degrees

**longitude** distance east or west of the Prime Meridian, measured in degrees

**lowland** land, usually level, at a low elevation

**map** drawing of the earth shown on a flat surface

**meridian** one of many lines on the global grid running from the North Pole to the South Pole; used to measure degrees of longitude

**mesa** broad, flat-topped landform with steep sides; smaller than a plateau

**mountain** land with steep sides that rises sharply (1,000 feet

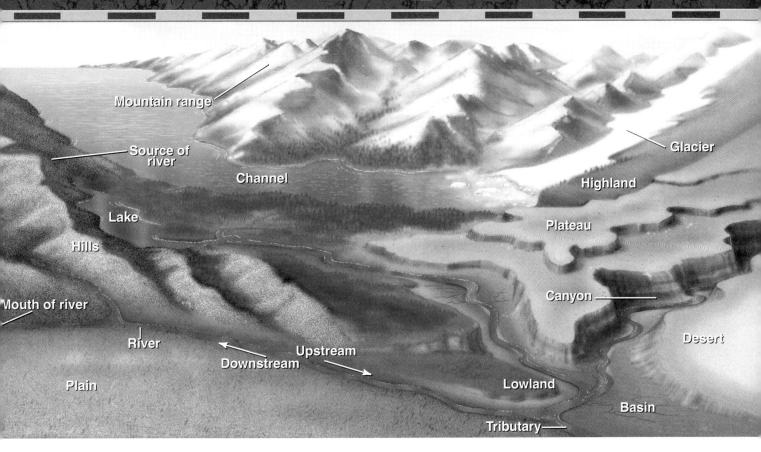

Mountain range

Source of river

Channel

Glacier

Highland

Lake

Plateau

Hills

Mouth of river

Canyon

Desert

River

Upstream

Downstream

Plain

Lowland

Basin

Tributary

[305 m] or more) from surrounding land; generally larger and more rugged than a hill

**mountain peak**  pointed top of a mountain

**mountain range**  a series of connected mountains

**mouth**  (of a river) place where a stream or river flows into a larger body of water

**ocean**  one of the four major bodies of salt water that surround the continents

**ocean current**  stream of either cold or warm water that moves in a definite direction through an ocean

**parallel**  one of many lines on the global grid that circle the earth north or south of the Equator; used to measure degrees of latitude

**peninsula**  body of land jutting into a lake or ocean, surrounded on three sides by water

**physical feature**  characteristic of a place occurring naturally, such as a landform, body of water, climate pattern, or resource

**plain**  area of level land, usually at a low elevation and often covered with grasses

**plateau**  area of flat or rolling land at a high elevation, about 300–3,000 feet  (91–914 m) high

**Prime Meridian**  line of the global grid running from the North Pole to the South Pole at Greenwich, England; starting point for measuring degrees of east and west longitude

**relief**  changes in elevation over a given area of land

**river**  large natural stream of water that runs through the land

**sea**  large body of water completely or partly surrounded by land

**seacoast**  land lying next to a sea or ocean

**sea level**  position on land level with surface of nearby ocean or sea

**sound**  body of water between a coastline and one or more islands off the coast

**source**  (of a river) place where a river or stream begins, often in highlands

**strait**  narrow stretch of water joining two larger bodies of water

**tributary**  small river or stream that flows into a larger river or stream; a branch of a river

**upstream**  direction opposite the flow of a river; toward the source of a river or stream

**valley**  area of low land between hills or mountains

**volcano**  mountain created as liquid rock or ash erupts from inside the earth

# The World Before Modern Times

## 3000 B.C.–1800

# **W**hy It Matters

Around 3000 B.C., civilizations began to emerge in four different areas of the world—western Asia, Egypt, India, and China—and give rise to the great empires of the ancient world. By the beginning of the first millennium A.D., however, the great states of the ancient world were mostly in decline or at the point of collapse. On the ruins of the ancient empires, new patterns of civilization began to take shape.

In Western Europe, the legacy of the ancient Roman world was preserved in a new medieval society firmly based on Christianity. During the Renaissance, Europeans rediscovered the ideas of the Greeks, and the rebirth of civilization created a dynamic society. The Western outlook laid the foundation for Western political ideas and Western global dominance in the modern era.

### Primary Sources Library

See pages 770–771 for primary source readings to accompany Unit 1.

Use The World History **Primary Source Document Library CD-Rom** to find additional primary sources about The World Before Modern Times.

▲ Grecian urns and pottery were often used to portray mythological scenes.

▶ The temple at Delphi was built to honor the Greek god Apollo.

"...*let no day pass without discussing goodness*..."

—*Socrates*, The Apology

# Looking Back...

## Systems of Law

Law is a code of conduct and rights recognized by a society. It provides social control, order, and justice, and it enables people to know their rights and responsibilities. Law is also the cornerstone of a constitutional government, helping to ensure justice and fair treatment of all citizens. "Where law ends, tyranny begins," said William Pitt, an English leader in 1770.

**451–450 B.C.**
Twelve Tables posted
in Rome

**A.D. 120**
Roman law governs
the Mediterranean world

**A.D. 533–534**
Justinian Code
established

### ❶ *Roman Republic*

## Laying the Foundation

Around 451–450 B.C., a group of judges posted 12 tablets in Rome's main forum, or marketplace. According to legend, the common people of Rome had demanded that the laws be written down for all to see, so that they would then know their rights.

The Twelve Tables, as they were called, remained in effect for almost 1,000 years. When Roman armies conquered other nations, they brought their laws with them. By A.D. 120, the entire Mediterranean world was governed by Roman law.

The Romans developed important legal principles: the law applied to all people regardless of wealth or power, and people should be ruled by law rather than the whims of their leaders. In A.D. 533–534, the Byzantine emperor Justinian consolidated all Roman law into a single written code. The Justinian Code, *The Body of Civil Law* as it is properly named, became the foundation of today's civil law system.

*Justinian Code*

# to See Ahead

Preamble to the
United States Constitution

## ❷ *The United States*

## A Model for Constitutional Government

The founders of the United States knew about and admired the Romans and their belief in limiting the power of government. When it came time to draw up a plan of government, the Framers wrote a constitution that balanced the powers of government among three branches.

To ensure that elected leaders did not place themselves above the law, the Framers included a provision that made the Constitution "the supreme law of the land." The Constitution was adopted on June 21, 1788.

**A.D. 1788**
United States
Constitution adopted

**A.D. 1804**
Napoleonic Code
established in France

## ❸ *France*

## Unifying the Law

In 1799, a French general named Napoleon Bonaparte set out to build an empire even larger than Rome's. To rule this empire, Napoleon followed the Roman example. He appointed a commission to write a uniform code of laws. This code, known as the Napoleonic Code, was completed in 1804.

Although Napoleon ruled as emperor, he drew upon many of the legal precedents first introduced by the Romans. This included the principle that the same laws should be used to govern all people. Under Napoleon, this code was adopted in areas across the globe, such as present-day Belgium, Spain, and Latin America.

*Napoleon Bonaparte*

## Why It Matters

The Romans developed the principle that people should be ruled by law rather than by the whims of leaders. How did the United States ensure that leaders would not place themselves above the law?

# *3000 B.C.–1600*

# The Legacy of the Ancient World

## ❧ *The Big Ideas* ❧

### SECTION 1: The First Civilizations

**Moral and ethical principles influence the development of political thought.** Early civilizations introduced key belief systems through law codes and religious beliefs that have influenced Western thought.

### SECTION 2: The Civilization of the Greeks

**Moral and ethical principles influence the development of political thought.** The Greek city-states of Sparta and Athens illustrate forms of Western government, while the Greek philosophers established the foundations of Western philosophy.

### SECTION 3: Rome and the Rise of Christianity

**Moral and ethical principles influence the development of political thought.** Rome shifted from a republic into an empire, creating systems of law and governance, as well as persecuting and ultimately embracing Christianity.

### SECTION 4: New Patterns of Civilization (500–1600)

**Moral and ethical principles influence the development of political thought.** Between the sixth and sixteenth centuries new systems of rule, religious doctrines, and intellectual movements emerged.

***World History—Modern Times Video*** *The Chapter 1 video, "Before Modern Times: The Political Legacy," chronicles the emergence of the first civilizations and empires.*

**c. 970 B.C.**
King Solomon
begins rule of
the Israelites

**563 B.C.**
Siddhartha Gautama, founder
of Buddhism, is born

| 3000 B.C. | 1000 B.C. | 800 B.C. | 500 B.C. | A.D. 1 |
|---|---|---|---|---|

**3000 B.C.**
Sumerian city-states
emerge in southern
Mesopotamia

**700 B.C.**
Athens becomes
a city-state

**A.D. 14**
The Roman
Empire begins

*The goddess Athena*

The Great Sphinx and the Pyramids at Giza, Egypt, symbolize the power and longevity of Egyptian kingdoms.

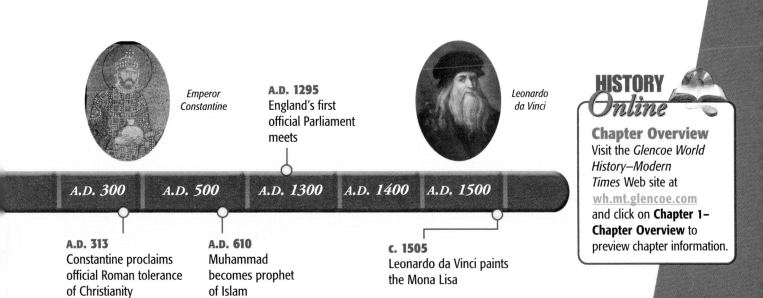

*Emperor Constantine*

**A.D. 1295**
England's first official Parliament meets

*Leonardo da Vinci*

| A.D. 300 | A.D. 500 | A.D. 1300 | A.D. 1400 | A.D. 1500 |

**A.D. 313**
Constantine proclaims official Roman tolerance of Christianity

**A.D. 610**
Muhammad becomes prophet of Islam

**c. 1505**
Leonardo da Vinci paints the Mona Lisa

**HISTORY Online**

**Chapter Overview**
Visit the *Glencoe World History–Modern Times* Web site at wh.mt.glencoe.com and click on **Chapter 1– Chapter Overview** to preview chapter information.

**Reading Skill** — **Predicting**

Good readers make predictions as they read. Predictions are educated guesses, based on what you know or the author has already told you. Even though your predictions may not always be correct, they are valuable because they cause you to think further about the topic.

You can make predictions at many points in a text. For example, if an author is stating a position, you might be predicting the kinds of arguments that will be given to support that position. One common place to make a prediction is just after you read a topic sentence in a paragraph. A topic sentence suggests what will be discussed in the paragraph.

*Read the paragraphs below from this chapter and write down your prediction on what information the author will discuss next. Discuss your prediction with your partner.*

## PREDICTING

four: Number words are very useful in predictions. Make sure you can account for the stated number of ideas, categories, or people in the description that follows.

Then, beginning around 1500 B.C., a new people, the Aryans, began to dominate. They fought with metal-tipped spears and were able to gain control of most of the subcontinent. The Aryans created an Indian civilization whose social structure has very distinct divisions.

. . . When the Aryans arrived, they brought their own social system. It divided society into four varnas, or broad social classes ranking people from high to low.

### Apply the Skill

Did you predict that the author would tell you more about the four social classes? Turn to page 127 in your text to find out if your prediction was right. As you read the chapter, stop from time to time and make a prediction about what you think the author will tell you next.

**Historical Interpretation: Standard HI 1** *Students show the connections, causal and otherwise, between particular historical events and larger social, economic, and political trends and developments.*

Historians search for connections between civilizations to explain how ideas and technologies evolve over time. Because the interactions of people during war and peace create ways for new ideas to spread, historians can sometimes trace the path of an idea through many generations and societies. This is especially true of thoughts about ethics and values. Ideas about right and wrong, the creation of the world, and the importance of family varied from society to society. When people interacted with one another, they shared these thoughts, sometimes resulting in important changes to a civilization.

This chapter focuses on the influence of ancient civilizations on the modern world. Ideas about ethics and values can be traced back to these times.

*Read the following excerpt from Chapter 1 and consider how this idea is still seen in the justice systems of the modern world.*

- **The Code of Hammurabi, a collection of 282 laws, was based on strict justice.**

- **Hammurabi wanted to keep order and prevent conflict.**

- **Penalties for criminal offenses were severe and took no account of motive or accidental circumstances.**

- **Retaliation—"an eye for an eye, tooth for a tooth"—was fundamental to the code.**

### Apply the Skill

Although Hammurabi came to power nearly 4,000 years ago, this idea of retaliation still exists in law today. What are some examples? What are important differences? As you read this chapter, look for other examples of thoughts that influenced other civilizations.

# A Story That Matters

*Pericles giving his famous Funeral Oration*

# Pericles Addresses Athens

*I*n 431 B.C., war erupted in Greece as two very different Greek states—Athens and Sparta—fought for domination of the Greek world. Strengthened by its democratic ideals, Athens felt secure behind its walls.

In the first winter of the war, the Athenians held a public funeral to honor those who had died in combat. On the day of the ceremony, the citizens of Athens joined in a procession. The relatives of the dead mourned their loved ones.

As was the custom in Athens, one leading citizen was asked to address the crowd. On this day it was Pericles who spoke to the people. He talked about the greatness of Athens and reminded the Athenians of the strength of their political system.

"Our constitution," Pericles said, "is called a democracy because power is in the hands not of a minority but of the whole people. When it is a question of settling private disputes, everyone is equal before the law; when it is a question of putting one person before another in positions of public responsibility, what counts is not membership in a particular class, but the actual ability which the man possesses. No one . . . is kept in political obscurity because of poverty. And, just as our political life is free and open, so is our day-to-day life in our relations with each other. . . . Here each individual is interested not only in his own affairs but in the affairs of the state as well."

## Why It Matters

In his famous speech, called the Funeral Oration, Pericles describes the Greek ideal of democracy and the importance of the individual. This is but one example of how the Greeks laid the intellectual foundations of Western civilization. They asked basic questions about the purpose of life, divine forces, and truth. The Greeks not only strove to answer these questions, they also created a system of logical thought for answering such questions. This system of thought remains worthwhile today.

**History and You** Reread the quote by Pericles. What portions of Athenian democracy described in this passage are found in the Constitution of the United States? Prepare a written report explaining and supporting your position with examples from the United States Constitution.

# The First Civilizations

## Guide to Reading

### Section Preview
Early civilizations introduced key belief systems through law codes and religious beliefs that have influenced Western thought.

**Main Idea**

- In ancient Mesopotamia, city-states elaborated the concept of the law code and divine kingship. (p. 122)

- The divinity of the pharaoh and religious belief contributed to the long life of Egyptian civilization. (p. 124)

- Key beliefs of Judaism that became important to the West developed during ancient times. (p. 125)

- Hinduism became a conservative force in Indian society that has lasted to this day. (p. 127)

- The lessons of Confucius influenced basic Chinese attitudes of deference and loyalty to family. (p. 128)

### Content Vocabulary
civilization, patriarchal, pharaoh, Judaism, monotheistic, covenant, prophet, caste system, Hinduism, Buddhism, Confucianism

### Academic Vocabulary
code, focus, network, core

### People to Identify
Hammurabi, King Solomon, Aryans, Siddhartha Gautama, Confucius

### Places to Locate
Israel, Judah, Indus River, China

### Reading Objectives
1. Trace how the law codes and religious beliefs developed in ancient civilizations.
2. Describe how the caste system influenced the lives of people in ancient India.

### Reading Strategy
**Compare and Contrast** As you read this section, prepare a Venn diagram like the one below to show the similarities and differences between Hinduism and Buddhism.

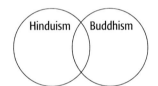

Hinduism   Buddhism

### Preview of Events

| ♦3000 B.C. | ♦2500 B.C. | ♦2000 B.C. | ♦1500 B.C. | ♦1000 B.C. | ♦500 B.C. | ♦A.D. 1 |
|---|---|---|---|---|---|---|

**c. 3000 B.C.**
Sumerians establish independent city-states

**1792 B.C.**
Hammurabi comes to power

**1200 B.C.**
Israelites emerge as a distinct group of people

**c. 500 B.C.**
Buddhism develops

**202 B.C.**
Han dynasty begins

## California Standards in This Section

*Reading this section will help you master these California History–Social Science standards.*

**10.1:** Students relate the moral and ethical principles in ancient Greek and Roman philosophy, in Judaism, and in Christianity to the development of Western political thought.

**10.1.1:** Analyze the similarities and differences in Judeo-Christian and Greco-Roman views of law, reason and faith, and duties of the individual.

# Ancient Mesopotamia

**Main Idea** In ancient Mesopotamia, city-states elaborated the concept of the law code and divine kingship.

**Reading Connection** What are the motives behind the system of American laws? Read to learn how the goals of Hammurabi shaped his law code.

The first civilizations were born near rivers in four areas—Mesopotamia, Egypt, India, and China. None is part of the Western world. The people in these areas were building cities, writing, and creating laws while people in the area now called Europe were still living in huts and caves. What do we mean when we say *European civilization* or *Mesopotamian civilization?* A **civilization** is a complex culture in which large numbers of people share basic elements, such as a social structure, religion, and art.

## Voices from the Past

A civilization is defined partly by its geography. If a land lies open to invasion, as Mesopotamia did, it may experience many invasions, and that will affect the social and religious attitudes. The following poem reflects the despair of the people of Ur after their city was sacked and burned:

> 66 Ur is destroyed, bitter is its lament. The country's blood now fills its holes like hot bronze in a mould. Bodies dissolve like fat in the sun. Our temple is destroyed, the gods have abandoned us, like migrating birds. Smoke lies on our city like a shroud. 99

Geography is not the only basic influence on a civilization. Its sheer age can affect its traditions and customs. A civilization that dates from 3000 B.C. is rooted in a time when people knew and understood only certain things. Their customs developed in a certain way because of what they knew.

Perhaps they treated their elders with great respect, or perhaps they expected children to grow up faster. Perhaps parents and families had the main role in deciding on the man their daughter married. Although all civilizations advance over time, these social and cultural attitudes can survive to some degree even in the modern world.

The modern world came about in Europe with the Industrial and French Revolutions, but to understand what is meant by *modern*, it is helpful to remember what is not modern. It is also helpful to remember the contributions of early civilizations. Ancient civilizations created law **codes** and the idea of divine kingship. They also created major religions that have endured in the modern world.

**The City-States of Mesopotamia** One of the world's earliest civilizations developed in the city-states of southern Iraq, known in ancient times as Mesopotamia. City-states were cities which had control of the surrounding countryside.

By 3000 B.C., the Sumerians had created a number of city-states. These city-states began to fight over land and water, resources that were in short supply in this ancient region.

The flatness of Mesopotamia's land made Sumerian city-states vulnerable to invaders. Some city-states took over others and created empires—governments powerful enough to rule over many peoples.

**The Empire of Hammurabi** In 1792 B.C., a new empire controlled much of Mesopotamia. It was based in Babylon, a city-state north of Akkad, where a man named **Hammurabi** had come to power. Hammurabi had a well-disciplined army of foot soldiers. He was able to divide and conquer his opponents and created a new Mesopotamian kingdom. After his conquests, he called himself "the sun of Babylon, the king who has made the four quarters of the world subservient."

Hammurabi was not just a great warrior. He built temples, defensive walls, and irrigation canals. He encouraged trade and brought an economic revival.

▼ *A detail of a stele, or stone monument, representing Hammurabi standing in front of the seated sun god*

Hammurabi's empire collapsed after his death in 1750 B.C., but he is still remembered because he created the earliest law code that has been preserved.

The Code of Hammurabi, a collection of 282 laws, was based on strict justice. Hammurabi wanted to keep order and prevent conflict. Penalties for criminal offenses were severe and took no account of motive or accidental circumstances. Retaliation—"an eye for an eye, tooth for a tooth"—was fundamental to the code.

Another feature of Hammurabi's code had to do with penalties. Since there was no concept of equality of individuals, penalties for the same crime differed among social classes. For example, a man who stole from a noble was punished more harshly than if he stole from a commoner. A direct comparison of two laws in the code makes it clear that punishments depended not only on the crime, but on the social class of the victim. Law 196 of the code says: "If a free man has destroyed the eye of a member of the aristocracy, they shall destroy his eye." Yet law 198 describes a lesser punishment for the same crime against a commoner: "If [a free man] has destroyed the eye of a commoner or broken the bone of a commoner, he shall pay one mina of silver."

The importance of family to Mesopotamian civilization can be judged from the fact that many laws in the code **focused** on it. Parents arranged marriages for their children, and parties signed a marriage contract. Without this contract, a couple was not legally married.

Society in Mesopotamia was **patriarchal**, that is, it was dominated by men. Women had far fewer privileges and rights in marriage than men. A woman's duties were in the home, and if she failed to fulfill them, her husband could legally divorce her. He could also divorce her if she did not bear children or tried to engage in business. Even more harsh, a wife who was a "gadabout, . . . neglecting her house [and] humiliating her husband," could be drowned.

In a patriarchal society, the man ruled his children as strictly as he ruled his wife. Obedience was expected: "If a son has struck his father, he shall cut off his hand." If a son committed a serious enough offense, his father could disinherit him. Obviously, Hammurabi's law code covered almost every aspect of people's lives.

✓ **Reading Check** **Describing** What are three examples of patriarchal behavior in Mesopotamian society?

▼ *In Sumerian cities, the temple sat at the top of a massive stepped tower called a ziggurat. A restored ziggurat at Ur is seen here.*

**Hatshepsut**

Ruled 1503–1482 B.C.

**Egyptian pharaoh**

Hatshepsut was the daughter of the pharaoh Thutmose I. She married her half-brother, who became the pharaoh Thutmose II. When he died, Hatshepsut assumed the full power of pharaoh. Statues show Hatshepsut clothed and bearded as a king would be. She was addressed as "His Majesty."

Hatshepsut's reign was a prosperous one. She is best known for the temple dedicated to herself at Deir el Bahri on the west bank of the Nile at Thebes. One of the inscriptions she had placed there reads: "Now my heart turns to and fro, in thinking what will the people say, they who shall see my monument in later years, and shall speak of what I have done."

## Egypt and Divine Kingship

**Main Idea** The divinity of the pharaoh and religious belief contributed to the long life of Egyptian civilization.

**Reading Connection** Do you ever attribute superhuman traits to a famous person? Read to learn about how early Egyptians revered their pharaohs.

Egypt is one of the oldest civilizations in the world and, like that of Mesopotamia, developed near a river, the Nile. This civilization was very stable and lasted a very long time. In part this came from the fact that the Nile flooded at regular intervals. Farmers could plan, and people felt secure. Early on, the Egyptians developed a sophisticated irrigation system. To irrigate, Egyptians had to keep flood records and plan together. This alone proves that the Egyptians had an advanced civilization.

Egyptian history is often divided into three major periods called the Old Kingdom, Middle Kingdom, and New Kingdom. These were periods of long-term stability marked by strong leadership, freedom from invasion, the building of pyramids, and great cultural activity. Between these stable periods, Egyptians suffered from chaotic government and foreign invasion.

During the Old Kingdom, which lasted from around 2700 B.C. to 2200 B.C., powerful monarchs presided over a unified, prosperous, and splendid kingdom. Egyptian monarchs had many titles, but the most common became **pharaoh**, originally meaning "great house" or "palace."

Kingship was thought to be divine and the pharaoh was considered equal to other deities—Egyptians were not monotheistic but worshipped many gods. The pharaoh was seen as part of the universal order: "What is the king of Upper and Lower Egypt? He is a god by whose dealings one lives, the father and mother of all men, alone by himself, without an equal." By obeying their divine pharaoh, Egyptians believed they were helping to maintain a prosperous society.

The Middle Kingdom came to an end about 1652 B.C., when the Hyksos people from western Asia invaded. The Hyksos drove horse-drawn chariots and overwhelmed Egyptian soldiers, who fought from donkey carts. The Egyptians showed another trait that can contribute to a civilization's survival—they learned from their conquerors. From the Hyksos, the Egyptians learned how to make bronze weapons and the war chariot. Eventually, they drove the Hyksos out.

During the New Kingdom that followed, Egypt built an empire. For a while, Egypt was the most powerful state in Southwest Asia, but it grew too large and could not maintain its frontiers. In modern times, too, there are examples of an empire's growing so big that it eventually collapses. A number of surrounding peoples invaded from time to time, but in the thirteenth century B.C., one last group of invaders—the "Sea Peoples," who may have been from the area around the Aegean Sea—dealt the final blow. The New Kingdom collapsed in 1085 B.C.

**✓ Reading Check** **Analyzing** How might geography influence how a civilization develops?

# New Centers of Civilization: The Israelites

**Main Idea** Key beliefs of Judaism that became important to the West developed during ancient times.

**Reading Connection** Have you read that explorers have "conquered" space? Read to discover one source for the belief that Westerners should conquer nature.

By 1200 B.C., neither Mesopotamia nor Egypt dominated western Asia. Because there was no single dominant power, it was possible for a number of peoples to emerge and build small states. One of these groups was the Israelites. The Israelites were a group of Semitic-speaking people. They left an important legacy in the religion of Judaism. Judaism flourished as a world religion and later influenced Christianity and Islam. The spiritual heritage of the Israelites is a basic pillar of Western civilization.

**History of the Israelites** Under **King Solomon**, who ruled from about 970 B.C. to 930 B.C., the Israelites established control over all of Palestine. Jerusalem became the capital of a united kingdom, known as Israel. This great king expanded the government and army and encouraged trade. Solomon is best known for building the temple in Jerusalem, which Israelites viewed as the symbol for their religion and for the kingdom itself.

The tribes that made up Solomon's kingdom did not stay united after his death. Israel split into two kingdoms, **Israel** and **Judah**. Stronger powers, the Assyrians and the Persians, eventually destroyed both kingdoms, but the people of Judah survived. They became known as Jews, and their religion was thus called **Judaism**. Judaism became a stateless religion. Jews did not believe that God was fixed to any one place: Yahweh was lord of the whole world. Over the centuries, the Jews took strength from their faith. It helped them maintain their identity as a people even though they did not have a state.

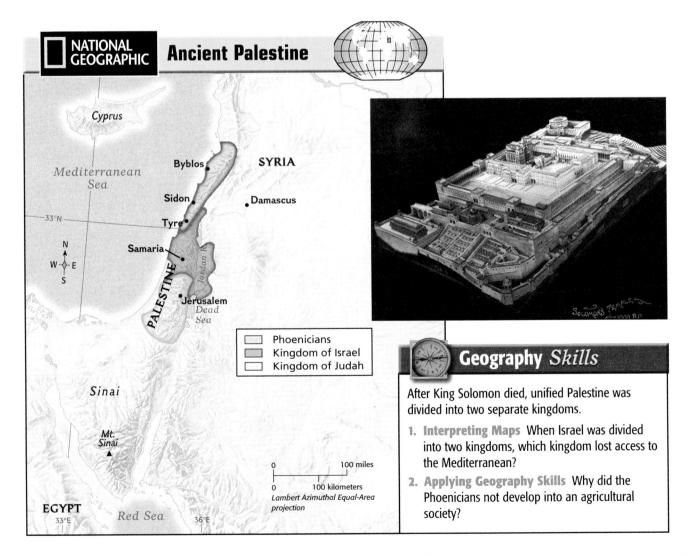

## NATIONAL GEOGRAPHIC — Ancient Palestine

Phoenicians
Kingdom of Israel
Kingdom of Judah

0 — 100 miles
0 — 100 kilometers
Lambert Azimuthal Equal-Area projection

### Geography Skills

After King Solomon died, unified Palestine was divided into two separate kingdoms.

1. **Interpreting Maps** When Israel was divided into two kingdoms, which kingdom lost access to the Mediterranean?

2. **Applying Geography Skills** Why did the Phoenicians not develop into an agricultural society?

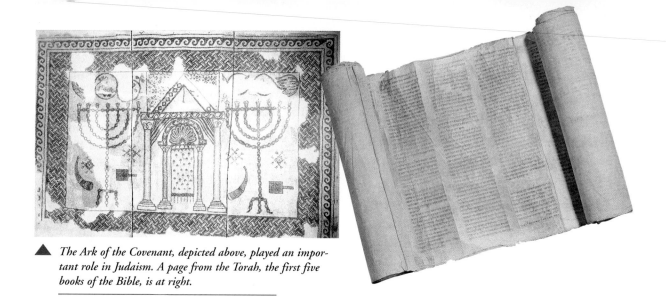

▲ *The Ark of the Covenant, depicted above, played an important role in Judaism. A page from the Torah, the first five books of the Bible, is at right.*

**The Spiritual Dimensions of Israel** Jews were **monotheistic**: they believed in one God, not many. They called their God Yahweh. According to Jewish belief, Yahweh was Creator and ruler of the world. All peoples were his servants, whether they knew it or not.

Unlike many religions in Eastern civilizations, this powerful creator was not in the sun or stars, but above everything in nature. Even so, he watched over his creatures. He punished them for wrongdoing, but he was merciful, too. Since human beings were God's special creatures, they were expected to rise above nature. In Judaism, if humans fail to do so, they have done wrong, or sinned.

These Jewish beliefs are markers of the Western tradition: human beings are separate from nature and must struggle against it; human beings have a particular relationship to a Supreme Being, who watches over them. These beliefs are not prominent in civilizations of the East.

Jewish ideas can be traced in three aspects of their religion—the covenant, law, and the prophets. In Jewish tradition, God made a **covenant**, or contract, with his people when Moses led them out of bondage into the promised land. The covenant said that Yahweh would guide them if they obeyed the Ten Commandments Moses received on Mount Sinai. The Jews could choose whether to follow these moral laws, but if they did not, suffering and evil would follow.

The prophets were the second important element in Jewish tradition. Jews believed that God used the **prophets**, or religious teachers, as a voice to speak to his people. The prophets flourished from roughly 900 B.C. to 500 B.C., a time that coincided with threats to the Israelites or even their conquest. The message of the prophets was that the Jews had not been faithful, but if they turned from evil, God would be merciful.

Unjust actions brought punishment, as the Book of Isaiah in the Bible made clear:

> ❝The Lord enters into judgment against the elders and leaders of his people: 'It is you who have ruined my vineyard; the plunder from the poor is in your houses. What do you mean by crushing my people and grinding the faces of the poor?' declares the Lord, the Lord Almighty. The Lord says, 'The women of Zion are haughty . . . with ornaments jingling on their ankles. Therefore the Lord will bring sores on the heads of the women of Zion; the Lord will make their scalps bald. . . . Instead of fragrance there will be a stench; . . . instead of fine clothing, sackcloth. . . .'❞

The prophet Isaiah had another message, the concern for all humanity and a vision of a peaceful world. In the words of Isaiah: "He will judge between the nations and will settle disputes for many people. They will beat their swords into plowshares and their spears into pruning hooks. Nation will not take up sword against nation, nor will they train for war anymore."

Finally, the prophets cried out against social injustice. They condemned the rich for making the poor suffer. The rich should share with their neighbors and care for the unfortunate. The prophets thus became a source for ideals of social justice.

Judaism was unique among the religions of ancient western Asia and Egypt in being monotheistic. It was also unique because it gave all people, not just a ruler and priests, access to God's wishes. God's wishes were communicated to the people through the prophets and were written down in the Bible. No leader could claim that he alone knew God's will.

✓**Reading Check** **Examining** Did Jews believe that other peoples belonged to their spiritual community?

# Ancient India

**Main Idea** Hinduism became a conservative force in Indian society that has lasted to this day.

**Reading Connection** What kind of thinking makes us feel that some people are worth more? Read to learn about the social distinctions in ancient India.

In the fertile **Indus River** valley, another of the world's earliest civilizations arose. It was known as the Harappan or Indus civilization and emerged sometime after 3000 B.C. The cities of Harappa and Mohenjo-Daro were its center. The Harappans were advanced. Their cities were well planned, and they had a piped water supply and bathrooms. Bathing and washing seem to have been important to rituals of their religion.

Internal problems, perhaps a flooding of the agricultural plain, brought an end to the Harappan civilization. Then, beginning around 1500 B.C., a new people, the **Aryans,** began to dominate. They fought with metal-tipped spears and were able to gain control of most of the subcontinent. The Aryans created an Indian civilization whose social structure has very distinct divisions.

Most scholars believe the Aryans originally came from central Asia, but one theory suggests they could have been from the Indus Valley. If this second theory is true, the Aryans would then have had to spread north and west over time. Only such a movement could explain why many words in languages spoken from Greece to India have common roots. Today we refer to these as Indo-European languages.

**The Caste System** When the Aryans arrived, they brought their own social system. It divided society into four varnas, or broad social classes ranking people from high to low. At the top were the Brahmins, the priestly class. Kshatriyas (ku•SHA•tree•yuhs), the warriors, were next in importance. The Vaisyas (VYSH•yuhz) were commoners who were usually merchants. The fourth large class were the Sudras (SHOO•druhz), or peasants. The word *varna* itself means "color." Thus discrimination based on skin color likely played a role in Aryan social divisions.

Over centuries, a caste system of social and religious discrimination evolved in India within the four varnas. A **caste system** is based on occupation and extended family **networks**. There are thousands of castes. With rare exceptions, a person is born into a caste and remains in it for life.

In many traditional societies, as in medieval Europe, people were born into their social station. India's caste system was more difficult to escape because it was based on beliefs about religious purity—higher castes had greater religious purity, while castes at the bottom were "polluted." The Untouchables were seen as the most polluted group and not part of the caste system at all. Untouchables were given menial, degrading tasks that other Indians would not accept, such as collecting trash and handling dead bodies. The life of the Untouchables was extremely difficult. When they traveled outside their quarters, they were required to tap two sticks together so that others could move away from their path.

Some people have suggested that a benefit of the caste system was that it gave a sense of order during chaotic periods. In modern times, India's government has worked to end the caste system. It is a very old tradition, however, with religious roots, and has survived in varying degrees, especially in rural villages.

*Picturing* **History**

Siva is the god of destruction, transformation, and change. Siva creates with the right hand and destroys with the left hand. Compassion and healing are offered with the lower hands. How does this bronze statue illustrate Siva's role in Hinduism?

**Hinduism and Buddhism** India was home to two world religions, Hinduism and Buddhism. Hinduism developed from several sources. One of these was the religion of the Aryans, but Hinduism included a number of other beliefs, too. Some early Hindus stressed that there was a single force, or ultimate reality in the universe, the Brahman. If the individual self, the Atman, sought to know the Brahman in this life, the self would merge with the Brahman after death.

By the sixth century B.C., other important ideas appeared in Hinduism. One is reincarnation, the belief that after death, each person's soul is reborn in another form. After a number of earthly lives, union with the Brahman is achieved. Karma refers to the belief that what a person does in this life affects this future life. If people are dutiful, they will have good karma and move closer to the Brahman in each succeeding life.

These beliefs have tended to support the caste system, justifying the privileges of higher castes—people in them must have lived a dutiful life in past lives. What did people in the lower castes find attractive in this belief? It gave them hope that if they were dutiful in their current status, they might improve their condition in their future life.

Another world religion also developed in India, **Buddhism**. It was the product of one man, **Siddhartha Gautama**. Born around 563 B.C., he is better known as the Buddha. In his lifetime he gained thousands of devoted followers. People would come to him seeking to know more about him. They asked, "Are you a god?" "No," he answered. "Are you an

*The Buddha*

angel?" "No." "Are you a saint?" "No." "Then what are you?" The Buddha replied, "I am awake."

Thus Buddhism began with a man who claimed that he had awakened and seen the world in a new way. His simple message of achieving wisdom created a new spiritual philosophy. Both Buddhism and Hinduism were crucial to the civilization that flourished in India, and they remain influential today.

✓ **Reading Check** **Analyzing** Why would it be more difficult to escape your caste in rural India today?

## Ancient China

**Main Idea** The lessons of Confucius influenced basic Chinese attitudes of deference and loyalty to family.

**Reading Connection** What do Americans mean by "family values"? Read about how family values were shaped in Chinese civilization.

The first flourishing Chinese civilization came about during the Shang dynasty, which ruled from about 1750 B.C. to 1045 B.C. It was the next dynasty, the Zhou, however, that saw the development of recognizable ideas in Chinese culture. During their long reign from 1045 B.C. to 256 B.C., for example, the belief in the "Mandate from Heaven" came about. This political belief said that a ruler *was* the ruler because Heaven had given him a mandate. If the country was invaded, or the economy was in crisis, the people had reason to doubt his mandate and withdraw their support.

Under the long Zhou dynasty, Chinese society took shape. In **China**, the family is the **core** of society, and within the family the father's place was very high. Devotion to family and to one's ancestors made China a stable society, but also a conservative one.

China's powerful position in the world today stems from its great size and cultural influence. These factors trace back as far as the Han dynasty. The Han, the dynasty that reigned from 202 B.C. to A.D. 221, extended the boundaries of its empire far into the sands of central Asia and southward along the coast of the South China Sea into what is modern-day Vietnam. Chinese culture appeared to be unrivaled, and its scientific achievements were unsurpassed.

Chinese civilization is closely tied to **Confucius**, a philosopher who lived in the sixth century B.C. Confucius traveled the length of China, observing society and seeking employment as a political counselor. He never received a political appointment, but became a teacher to hundreds of students.

▲ *This early nineteenth-century painting illustrates scenes from the life of Confucius, who is shown here with his followers.*

Confucius lived at a time of great confusion in China. Rival armies were constantly fighting one another, and Confucius wanted to answer a moral question: How do we restore order to our society?

The most important thing to Confucius was not the supernatural world, but how to act morally in the real world. He believed people were naturally good. Every person could acquire knowledge and virtue, but this was not likely to happen unless they had virtuous leaders. Obedience to superiors became very important in **Confucianism.**

Student disciples recorded the sayings of Confucius, which guided the Chinese and other peoples in the Chinese Empire for centuries. Confucianism remains an important cultural influence to this day.

✓**Reading Check** **Explaining** When did the Chinese feel it was justifiable to turn against a ruler?

**HISTORY** *Online* **Study Central**

For help with the concepts in this section of *Glencoe World History–Modern Times,* go to wh.mt.glencoe.com and click on **Study Central.**

# SECTION 1 ASSESSMENT

### Checking for Understanding

1. **Vocabulary** Define: civilization, code, focus, patriarchal, pharaoh, Judaism, monotheistic, covenant, prophet, caste system, network, Hinduism, Buddhism, core, Confucianism.

2. **People** Identify: Hammurabi, King Solomon, Aryans, Siddhartha Gautama, Confucius.

3. **Places** Locate: Israel, Judah, Indus River, China.

### Reviewing Big Ideas

4. **Explain** how the Code of Hammurabi influenced political thought.

### Critical Thinking

5. **Historical Analysis** **Connecting Ideas** Analyze how the Hindu system of reincarnation supported the Indian caste system. **CA HI 1**

6. **Compare and Contrast** Create a chart like the one below to compare the contributions of Isaiah, the Buddha, and Confucius to religious beliefs.

| Religious Leader | Contributions | Effects on Beliefs |
|------------------|---------------|--------------------|
| Isaiah | | |
| the Buddha | | |
| Confucius | | |

### Analyzing Visuals

7. **Examine** the photo on page 123. What does this image teach us about Sumerian religious attitudes?

### Writing About History

8. **Expository Writing** Explain why Hammurabi's code was significant. Develop a set of laws based on the Code of Hammurabi that would apply to your community. Explain why your code differs from that of Hammurabi, or why it is similar. **CA 10WA2.3**

# MORE THAN
# MYTH TO THE *ILIAD*

1

In Homer's epic poem the *Iliad*, the rich and powerful city-state of Mycenae headed a united Greek attack against "windy Ilion"—the wealthy city of Troy—to avenge the kidnapping of "lovely-haired Helen," wife of Sparta's king Menelaus. For centuries, the fabled treasures of these legendary cities were thought to exist—like the Trojan War itself—in imagination only. But modern archaeology suggests there may be more than myth to Homer's classic tale.

Greeks in antiquity considered the *Iliad* to be a historical account of their past. Alexander the Great, for example, traced his mother's family back to the hero Achilles. We know today that the poem is not a true story of a war in Greece's late Bronze Age (about 1600 to 1100 B.C.). For one thing, the *Iliad* was not written during this period. It is the result of more than 500 years of oral tradition, handed down by generations of professional poets. Credit for the final masterpiece went to someone the Greeks called "divine Homer," but they knew nothing more about this person than his supposed name—and neither do we.

Still, myths often spring from a kernel of historical truth, and in the late nineteenth century, the Trojan War's mythic rival cities entered the real world of history. Between 1870 and 1890 German businessman and amateur archaeologist Heinrich Schliemann carried out archaeological digs that put Troy and Mycenae on the map. Since then, archaeologists and scholars have uncovered numerous details suggesting that Homer's *Iliad* records many aspects of the Greek Bronze Age (known to historians as the Mycenaean Age, for the city that dominated the period). The giant walls of Mycenae and its fabulous treasure, for example, and the geography around Troy itself in northwestern Turkey, all support descriptions you can find in the poem's stirring rhythms.

Descendants of Greek-speaking peoples who appeared on the Greek mainland around 1900 B.C., the Mycenaeans eventually developed societies that revolved around a central palace. In addition to Mycenae itself, Schliemann and later archaeologists have discovered major Mycenaean centers whose names appear in the *Iliad*: "sacred" Pylos, Tiryns "of the huge walls," and "thirsty" Argos, to list only a few of them. Researchers have also discovered hundreds of settlements and tombs—all with a shared culture.

The historical Mycenae dominated the plain of Argos, a wealthy region that controlled much of the trade

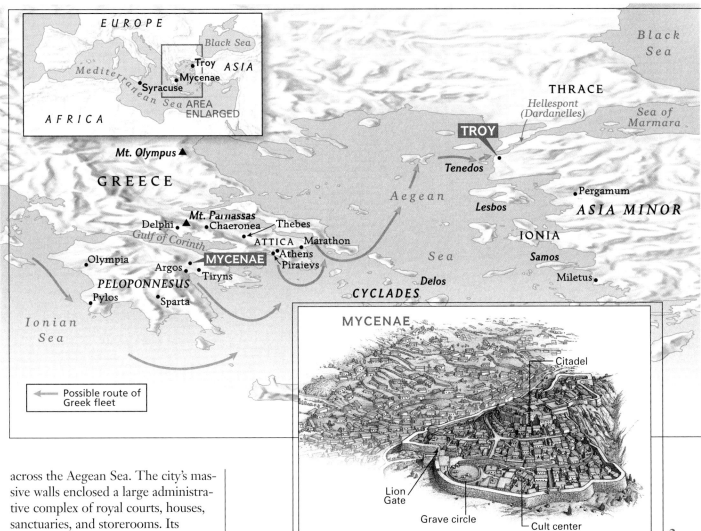

across the Aegean Sea. The city's massive walls enclosed a large administrative complex of royal courts, houses, sanctuaries, and storerooms. Its famous grave circle, unearthed by Schliemann in 1876, revealed rich treasures suggesting that as early as the sixteenth century B.C. the Mycenaean ruling class possessed a treasure trove of silver, gold, and ivory.

From archaeological digs at both Mycenae and Troy came signs that Homer's *Iliad* told of real things in the ancient world. Among the items found at Mycenae, for example, was a small gold ring. Carved on its face is a miniature battle scene showing a man protecting his entire body behind a huge shield, the kind that Homer describes the Greek hero Ajax holding in front of him "like a wall." The *Iliad's* heroes were known across the sea in Asia as well. Tomb art found in Turkey and dating from the fourth century

B.C. depicts a scene from the Trojan siege (opposite page).

◼

Troy's location at the mouth of the Dardanelles, the strait that Homer called the Hellespont, gave it command of the water route into central Asia. From this vantage point, the historical Trojans traded skillfully throughout central Asia. What remains of Troy's walls still overlooks a plain crossed by willow-lined rivers mentioned in the *Iliad*.

Heinrich Schliemann's excavation of Troy was crude and impatient. He sank trenches straight to bedrock, believing Homer's "windy Ilion" would lie at the bottom, thus destroy-

**1  A scene etched in stone on a fourth century B.C. tomb found in Turkey suggests the *Iliad's* tragic final battle, between Hector of Troy and Achilles, hero of the Greeks.**

**2  Prosperous Mycenae traded throughout the Aegean. The reconstruction above shows the city's fortress in the late thirteenth century B.C., at the peak of its power. Some 250 miles (402 km) away, its rival Troy commanded the strait called the Dardanelles (Homer's Hellespont), a key link to the Black Sea. Today Troy's ruins lie 3 miles (4.8 km) inland, but in the late Bronze Age, the city sat on the edge of a bay that opened directly onto the Hellespont.**

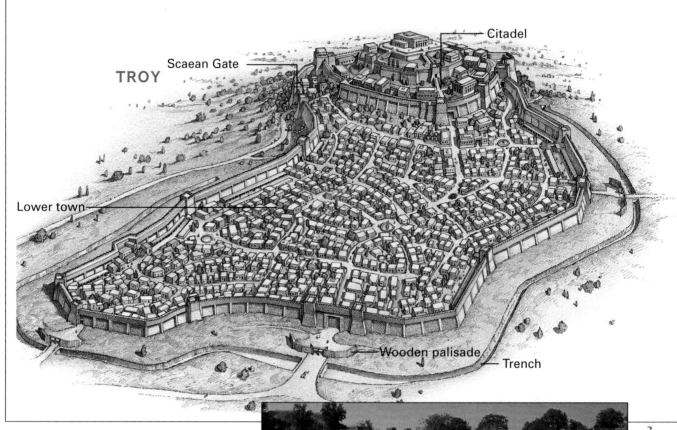

TROY

Scaean Gate

Citadel

Lower town

Wooden palisade

Trench

3

ing several layers of history. Today an international team of archaeologists directed by Manfred Korfmann of Germany's Tubingen University is reexcavating the entire site—nine levels ranging from 3000 B.C. to the Roman city of New Ilium in the early sixth century A.D. The sixth and seventh levels straddle the years 1250 to 1150 B.C., the era of Homer's war.

Whether or not the Greeks actually launched an invasion or entered Troy by means of the famous Trojan horse ruse (opposite page), evidence shows that the two peoples were in trading contact. Mycenaean pottery found at Troy dates back to 1500 B.C.

Some 1,300 feet (396 m) beyond the citadel first uncovered by Schliemann, Korfmann's team of archaeologists has made a most exciting find. They uncovered an extensive trench 8 feet (2.4 m) deep and 10 feet (3 m) wide encircling an entire lower town

of wooden houses. The reconfigured city (reconstruction above)—which increases the known area of the sixth level of Troy by as much as 50 acres (20.25 ha)— is almost ten times as large as the citadel and held a population of at least 6,000. This finding makes Troy an opponent more equal to the mighty Mycenae than Schliemann's hilltop fortress.

Farther afield, in a nearby sand cove, lies evidence to support speculation that the Trojans took advantage of their commanding position at this crossroads of trade between Europe and Asia. Because of prevailing northeasterly winds, shallow-keeled Bronze Age merchant ships would have been forced to wait at Troy for a favorable breeze before proceeding north of the Dardanelles to the Black Sea.

Korfmann's team has located burials in the cove that reflect different cultural influences, suggesting that

4

the crews of stranded vessels may have died while waiting for the wind to change. Korfmann says later texts confirm that "occupants of the region exacted tolls from incoming vessels." If Troy grew rich with this practice, it would have made bitter enemies of merchants like the Mycenaeans.

Indeed, some historians speculate that conflict over trade routes, rather than Helen's legendary beauty, may have sparked the Trojan War. As Korfmann sees it, "It is possible that Troy experienced several commercial skirmishes, if not one Trojan War."

**3** Stone walls believed to be the citadel of Troy were first unearthed in the 1870s. Troy holds the remains of at least nine settlements spanning 3,500 years. In the early 1990s, archaeologists discovered several wooden palisades and a 10-foot (3 m) trench encircling a lower town (reconstruction). Earlier only the hilltop citadel was known.

**4** The Tumulus of Ajax is one of more than 40 mounds on the plain of Troy said to honor fallen heroes of the Trojan War.

**5** A seventh-century B.C. amphora from Mykonos shows the earliest known depiction of the wooden horse that bore "death and doom for the Trojans."

5

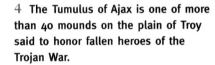

## INTERPRETING THE PAST

1. Was there a Trojan War? If so, what was its likely cause?

2. What is significant about the strait called the Dardanelles?

# The Civilization of the Greeks

## Guide to Reading

### Section Preview
The Greek city-states of Sparta and Athens illustrate forms of Western government, while the Greek philosophers established the foundations of Western philosophy.

**Main Idea**

• The polis created a model for active citizenship, while the Athenian polis laid the foundations for democracy. (p. 135)

• Greek thinkers left an important legacy to the West in their commitment to rational inquiry. (p. 139)

### Content Vocabulary
polis, tyrant, democracy, oligarchy, direct democracy, philosophy, Socratic method

### Academic Vocabulary
goal, adult, foundation

### People to Identify
Pericles, Socrates, Plato, Aristotle

### Places to Locate
Sparta, Athens

### Reading Objectives
1. Describe the groups who lived in the polis.
2. Identify how Athens and Sparta differed.

### Reading Strategy
**Organizing Information** Use a concept map like the one below to show ideas on government that the Greeks contributed.

> Greek ideas on government

### Preview of Events

| ◆800 B.C. | ◆750 B.C. | ◆700 B.C. | ◆650 B.C. | ◆600 B.C. | ◆550 B.C. | ◆500 B.C. | ◆450 B.C. |
|---|---|---|---|---|---|---|---|

**c. 800 B.C.**
Sparta is a powerful city-state

**c. 700 B.C.**
Athens becomes a unified polis

**508 B.C.**
Cleisthenes comes to power

**461 B.C.**
The Age of Pericles begins

## California Standards in This Section

*Reading this section will help you master these California History–Social Science standards.*

**10.1:** Students relate the moral and ethical principles in ancient Greek and Roman philosophy, in Judaism, and in Christianity to the development of Western political thought.

**10.1.1:** Analyze the similarities and differences in Judeo-Christian and Greco-Roman views of law, reason and faith, and duties of the individual.

**10.1.2:** Trace the development of the Western political ideas of the rule of law and illegitimacy of tyranny, using selections from Plato's Republic and Aristotle's Politics.

# The Polis: Center of Greek Life

**Main Idea** The polis created a model for active citizenship, while the Athenian polis laid the foundations for democracy.

**Reading Connection** Has a parent or friend taken part in a city council meeting? Read to understand the workings of a direct democracy.

By the eighth century B.C., the Greek city-state, or **polis**, became central to Greek life. Our word *politics* is derived from *polis*. In a physical sense, the polis was a town, city, or even a village, along with its surrounding countryside. The town, city, or village was the center of the polis where people met for political, social, and religious activities. In some of them, this central meeting point was a hill, like the Acropolis at Athens, which served as a place of refuge during an attack. Sometimes this high ground also became a religious center where temples and public monuments were erected.

At a lower level, below the acropolis, there was the agora. The agora was an open place that served as a place for citizens to assemble and a market area.

City-states could cover a few square miles or a few hundred square miles. They also varied in population. Athens had a population of more than 250,000 by the fifth century B.C., but most city-states consisted of only a few hundred to several thousand people. Above all, the polis was a community with a common identity and common **goals.**

## Voices from the Past

The sense of common goals in the polis was especially evident in Athens. In a speech to the people of the city at the beginning of the Peloponnesian War, the Athenian leader Pericles proclaimed:

> ❝I could tell you a long story about what is to be gained by beating the enemy back. What I would prefer is that you should fix your eyes every day on the greatness of Athens as she really is, and should fall in love with her. When you realize her greatness, then reflect that what made her great was men . . . who knew their duty. . . . If they ever failed in an enterprise, they made up their minds that at any rate the city should not find their courage lacking to her, and they gave to her the best contribution that they could.❞

A polis was made up of three groups: citizens with political rights (**adult** males), citizens with no political rights (women and children), and noncitizens (slaves and resident aliens).

Citizens had rights, but rights were coupled with responsibilities, such as passing laws and making government decisions. The Greek philosopher Aristotle argued that a citizen did not just belong to himself or herself: "We must rather regard every citizen as belonging to the state." In all Greek states, citizens had the duty to fight and die, if necessary, for the polis. The fierce loyalty of citizens to their polis had a negative side, however. Greece's independent city-states did not trust one another, and their conflicts ultimately brought about their ruin.

In the seventh and sixth centuries B.C., many Greek city-states fell under the control of tyrants. They were not necessarily oppressive or wicked, as our word *tyrant* implies. Greek **tyrants** were rulers who seized power by force and were not subject to the law.

Tyrants stayed in power because they had the support of the rich traders and of poor peasants in debt to landholding aristocrats. Both groups were tired of aristocratic rule.

▼ *The temple of the Parthenon on top of the Acropolis in Athens*

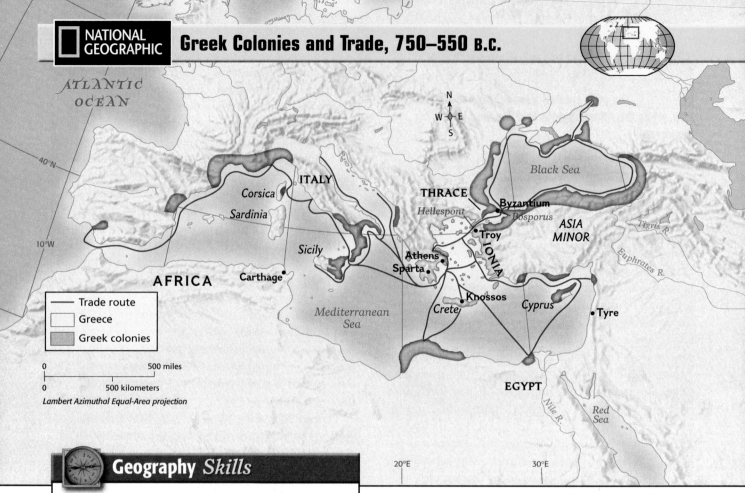

# Greek Colonies and Trade, 750–550 B.C.

ATLANTIC
OCEAN

40°N

10°W

ITALY

Corsica

Sardinia

Sicily

AFRICA    Carthage

Mediterranean
Sea

THRACE

Byzantium

Hellespont    Bosporus

Troy

ASIA
MINOR

Tigris R.

Euphrates R.

Athens

Sparta    IONIA

Knossos    Cyprus    Tyre

Crete

EGYPT

Nile R.    Red
Sea

Black Sea

— Trade route
☐ Greece
■ Greek colonies

0        500 miles
0    500 kilometers
*Lambert Azimuthal Equal-Area projection*

20°E        30°E

## Geography *Skills*

Over a period of 200 years, the Greeks spread across Europe and northern Africa, bringing Greek civilization to areas more than 1,500 miles (2,400 km) from Greece.

1. **Interpreting Maps** Analyze the relationship between Greek trading routes and Greek colonies.
2. **Applying Geography Skills** Find a map of the contemporary world. Name all the modern countries where Greece had colonies.

The tyrants used hired soldiers to stay in power, and often built new marketplaces, temples, and walls. These projects made them popular, but by the end of the sixth century B.C., Greeks turned against them because they felt tyranny was an insult to the ideal of law.

Tyranny's role in ending the rule of Greek aristocrats was important because democracy could begin to flourish in some city-states. **Democracy** is government by the people or rule of the many. Other city-states remained committed to rule by an **oligarchy**, rule by the few. The differences in these forms of government can be understood by examining the most famous city-states, Sparta and Athens.

✓ **Reading Check** **Evaluating** In the polis, are citizens' rights the same as in the United States?

**Sparta** The powerful city-state of **Sparta** conquered neighboring peoples, the Laconians and Messenians. To prevent these peoples from rebelling, the Spartans made a conscious decision to create a military state.

Between 800 B.C. and 600 B.C., the lives of Spartans were rigidly organized and controlled—our word *spartan* means highly self-disciplined. Boys spent their childhood learning military discipline and enrolled in military service at age 20. They might marry, but lived in the military barracks until age 30. At 30, Spartan males could vote in the assembly and live at home, but they stayed in the army until age 60.

All meals were eaten in public dining halls with fellow soldiers. Meals were simple: the famous Spartan black broth consisted of a piece of pork boiled in

**HISTORY Online**

**Web Activity** Visit the *Glencoe World History—Modern Times* Web site at <u>wh.mt.glencoe.com</u> and click on **Chapter 1–Student Web Activity** to learn more about the Greek city-states.

animal blood, salt, and vinegar. A visitor who ate some of the black broth once remarked that he now understood why Spartans were not afraid to die.

While their husbands lived in the barracks, Spartan women lived at home. This separation gave them greater freedom of movement and power in the household than was usual in other parts of Greece. Spartan women were expected to exercise so they could bear and raise healthy children.

Most women upheld the Spartan values as strongly as their husbands. The women expected bravery from their husbands and sons. One famous story shows this very well. It describes a Spartan woman who was ready to see her son off to war. As she handed him his shield, she is supposed to have told him he should return carrying it—or being carried on it.

Spartan government was an oligarchy headed by two kings, who led the Spartan army on its campaigns. Five citizens were elected each year as ephors to supervise education and conduct in the polis.

Another body in the government was a council of elders. This council was made up of two kings and 28 citizens who were over the age of 60. It had the power to decide on what issues would be presented to an assembly of male citizens. The assembly's only role was to vote on those issues, not to debate them.

It is clear then that this government structure was conservative. A relatively small group of older men had great authority over the policies of Sparta.

Sparta remains a historic symbol of the impact of a closed society. Intent on military might and security against the Messenians and Laconians, the Spartans turned their backs on the outside world. Foreigners, who might have brought in new ideas, were discouraged from visiting.

For the same reason, most Spartans were not allowed to travel abroad. They were also discouraged from studying philosophy, literature, or the arts—subjects that might encourage critical thinking. The art of war was the Spartan ideal. All other arts were frowned upon.

**Athens** Athens was the other major city-state in ancient Greece. By 700 B.C., it was a unified polis on the peninsula of Attica, a location that would make Athens a strong sea power with an empire.

Early Athens was ruled by a king. By the seventh century B.C., it was an oligarchy with aristocrats in control. They owned the best land and dominated political decisions. Economic problems at the end of the seventh century B.C., however, brought a crisis to Athens. Athenian farmers could not pay their debts to aristocrats and were being sold into slavery. Over and over, there were cries to cancel the debts and give land to the poor. Athens was on the verge of civil war.

▼ *The importance of military skill to the Greeks is reflected on this* kylix, *or two-handled drinking cup.*

This crisis is significant for the modern world. The events the crisis set in motion eventually led to democratic government. First, in 594 B.C., the Athenian aristocrats gave full power to Solon, a trusted aristocrat who knew reforms must be made. Solon canceled land debts and released farmers from slavery. However, Solon would not go further—he would not take land from the rich and give it to those with no land. Since only landowners could vote in the assembly, many still had no voice in government. Unrest continued.

Then, in 508 B.C., another reform-minded aristocrat, Cleisthenes (KLYS•thuh•neez), came to power. Cleisthenes restructured the assembly and laid the foundation for Athenian democracy.

Cleisthenes created a Council of 500 whose members came from local districts. All male citizens voted to elect the Council, which controlled foreign policy and the treasury. The Council also prepared legislation. Our ideal of Greek democracy is best symbolized by how the polis decided on its laws. Legislation was debated openly in the assembly, and all male citizens voted on it. Since citizens participated directly in decision making, Athens had a **direct democracy**.

Athenian democracy was more limited than in modern times, however, because whole groups did not qualify as active or voting citizens—women, for-

▲ *Democracy crowning a figure that symbolizes Athens*

eign residents, and slaves. In 450 B.C., the population might have been about 250,000, but probably only about 43,000 were male citizens over 18 who voted.

In another sense, democracy was less limited than in modern nations because so many citizens actively participated. Every ten days, the assembly met on a hillside east of the Acropolis, the city's fortified public area. On average, about 6,000 men attended. They passed all laws, elected all officials, and made final decisions on war and peace.

The most glorious period of Athenian democracy is associated with **Pericles**, who dominated politics from 461 B.C. to 429 B.C. Pericles also advanced democracy. By paying salaries, he made it possible for many more citizens to serve in public office. In the Age of Pericles, the Athenians became deeply attached to their political system. The officials who ran the city's daily business were also a fairly large group, but ten men known as generals had overall direction of policy.

Under Pericles, Athens became the leading center of Greek culture. New temples and statues soon made the greatness of Athens visible to everyone. Art and architecture flourished, and Pericles boasted that Athens had become the "school of Greece." The achievements of three Athenian philosophers have been especially important to Western culture.

✓ **Reading Check** **Analyzing** What was the chief economic problem Cleisthenes wanted to solve?

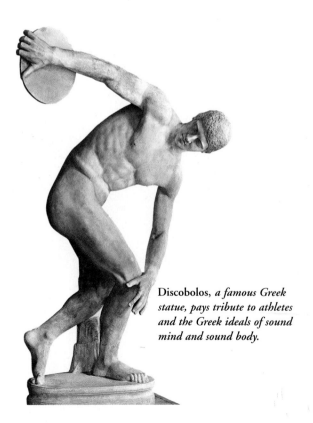

*Discobolos, a famous Greek statue, pays tribute to athletes and the Greek ideals of sound mind and sound body.*

# The Greek Love of Wisdom

**Main Idea** Greek thinkers left an important legacy to the West in their commitment to rational inquiry.

**Reading Connection** Has a teacher ever asked you questions to draw out an idea? Read to learn why Socrates believed in this teaching method.

**Philosophy** refers to an organized system of thought. The term comes from the Greek word meaning "love of wisdom." Early Greek philosophers were devoted to thinking critically and rationally about the nature of the universe. To this day, three Greek philosophers—Socrates, Plato, and Aristotle—are usually named as the greatest thinkers of the Western world.

**Socrates** Because he left no writings, we know about **Socrates** only from his pupils. Socrates was an Athenian stonemason whose true love was philosophy. Socrates believed that education had no other goal than improving human understanding. In Socrates' words, "the unexamined life is not worth living." He also urged his students to "let no day pass without discussing goodness."

Socrates used a teaching method still known by his name, the **Socratic method**. Socrates presumed that all knowledge was already present in each person,

and that careful questioning could draw it out. Thus the Socratic method used a question-and-answer format to lead pupils to see things for themselves.

Socrates placed great emphasis on the ability to reason, and this Greek tradition has been key to Western civilization. Socrates questioned all things, including authority, and this led him into trouble.

Athenians had had a tradition of free thought, but when they were defeated in war, they began to fear free debate. Socrates was accused and convicted of corrupting the youth by encouraging critical thinking. An Athenian jury sentenced him to die by drinking hemlock, a poison.

**Plato** One of Socrates' students was **Plato**, considered by many the greatest philosopher of Western civilization. Unlike Socrates, who did not write down his thoughts, Plato wrote a great deal. Plato explained his ideas about government in a work entitled *The Republic*. Plato thought political life in Athens was too rowdy. No one would be able to lead the good life—a virtuous life—in such a democracy. Plato therefore described what an ideal state would look like. There would be three groups in society. At the top was an upper class of philosopher-kings. These men would have political power because they were wise. In Plato's words, the good society could be achieved only when "political power and philosophy meet together."

The second group were the warriors who protected society. The third group included everyone else—the masses who were driven not by wisdom or courage but only by their desires. Contrary to the prevailing Greek view, Plato believed that men and women should have the same education and access to all positions in society.

**History** *through Art*

In early times, the Greeks watched the rituals of their religion while seated on theater-style benches. Greek plays grew out of these rituals. Plays were staged in outdoor amphitheaters, such as this one. How does this amphitheater differ from modern theaters?

**Aristotle** The third great Greek philosopher was **Aristotle**. Just as Plato was a student of Socrates, Aristotle was a student of Plato. Aristotle studied at Plato's famous Academy in Athens for 20 years. Aristotle focused on analyzing and classifying things based on observation and investigation. He wrote about many subjects, including ethics, logic, politics, poetry, astronomy, geology, biology, and physics. His careful methods contributed greatly to Western science, which was based largely on Aristotle until the Scientific Revolution.

Like Plato, Aristotle thought critically about a rational form of government. Unlike Plato, he did not seek an ideal state but analyzed existing ones to find what was best. In his *Politics*, Aristotle looked at the constitutions of 158 states and concluded that there were three good forms of government: monarchy, aristocracy, and constitutional government. He felt that constitutional government was best for most people.

### The Greeks and Western Civilization

With their brilliant civilization, the ancient Greeks were the principal source of Western culture. Socrates, Plato, and Aristotle established the **foundations** of Western philosophy. The rational method of inquiry, so

*" . . . a life guided by intelligence is the best and most pleasant for man, inasmuch as intelligence, above all else, is man."*

—**Aristotle's** *Ethics*

*Aristotle*

important to modern science, was first conceived in ancient Greece. Western literature, too, is largely derived from the poetry and drama of the ancient Greeks. In art and architecture, the Greek principles of harmony and proportion have remained the touchstones in Western culture.

# CONNECTIONS Around The World

## Rulers and Gods

All of the world's earliest civilizations believed that there was a close connection between rulers and gods. In Egypt, pharaohs were considered gods whose role was to maintain the order and harmony of the universe in their own kingdoms. In Mesopotamia, India, and China, rulers were thought to rule with divine assistance. Kings were often seen as rulers who derived their power from the gods and who were the agents or representatives of the gods. Many Romans certainly believed that their success in creating an empire was a visible sign of divine favor. As one Roman stated, "We have overcome all the nations of the world, because we have realized that the world is directed and governed by the gods."

The rulers' supposed connection to the divine also caused them to seek divine aid in the affairs of the world. This led to the art of *divination*—an organized method to figure out the intentions of the gods. In Mesopotamian and Roman society, divination took the

form of examining the livers of sacrificed animals or the flights of birds to determine the will of the gods. The Chinese used oracle bones to receive advice from the gods. The Greeks consulted oracles.

Underlying all of these practices was a belief in a supernatural universe—a world in which divine forces were in charge and human well-being depended on those divine forces. It was not until the Scientific Revolution of the 1600s that many people began to believe in a natural world that was not governed by spiritual forces.

▲ *An Athenian king consults the oracle at Delphi.*

## Comparing Cultures

Why were rulers of early civilizations considered to have divine powers? How did this affect their systems of government?

Essential Western political ideas also owe a great deal to the ancient Greeks. These ideas were passed down in different ways from the Greeks to the Romans, from the Romans to Western Europeans, and from Western Europe to the United States. Many modern political terms—*politics, monarchy, oligarchy, aristocracy, tyranny,* and *democracy*—come from the Greek.

For the Greeks, being a citizen in a democracy brought with it a strict sense of duty. As Pericles said, "We do not say that a man who takes no interest in politics minds his own business; we say he has no business here at all." The Greeks called such a man *idiotes,* meaning "idiot," by which they meant a fool who lives in his own private world.

In the United States, there is no direct democracy. Citizens elect representatives who propose and vote on laws. American citizens have the right to choose their representatives, but they are not directly involved in making policy. In fact, many U.S. citizens even choose not to vote, thus removing their chief source of power.

✓**Reading Check** **Evaluating** Why might a person say Aristotle is the most modern of philosophers?

**HISTORY** *Online* **Study Central**

For help with the concepts in this section of *Glencoe World History–Modern Times,* go to wh.mt.glencoe.com and click on **Study Central.**

# SECTION 2 ASSESSMENT

### Checking for Understanding

1. **Vocabulary** Define: polis, goal, adult, tyrant, democracy, oligarchy, direct democracy, philosophy, Socratic method, foundation.

2. **People** Identify: Pericles, Socrates, Plato, Aristotle.

3. **Places** Locate: Sparta, Athens.

### Reviewing Big Ideas

4. **Explain** how the systems of government in Sparta and Athens influenced Western political thought. Be sure to discuss how the two systems differed.

### Critical Thinking

5. **Historical Analysis** **Interpreting** How did the governments favored by Plato and Aristotle differ? Which view makes more sense to you? **CA HR 2**

6. **Organizing Information** Using a table like the one below, identify the reforms that led to democracy in Athens and the leaders who initiated them.

| Leader | Reforms |
|---|---|
| Solon | |
| Cleisthenes | |
| Pericles | |

7. **Examine** the photo of the Parthenon shown on page 135. Where is the Parthenon located? Why was this famous temple situated on high ground?

### Writing About History

8. **Descriptive Writing** Imagine that you are a 25-year-old male living in Sparta in 700 B.C. Create a diary in which you record your activities for one week. Write one diary page for each day. **CA 10WA2.1**

# YOUNG PEOPLE IN . . .

## Ancient Greece

In Sparta, boys were trained to be soldiers. At birth, each child was examined by state officials, who decided whether the child was fit to live. Those who were judged unfit were left on a mountainside to die. Boys judged fit were taken from their mothers at the age of seven and put under control of the state. These boys lived in military-style barracks, where they were subjected to harsh discipline to make them tough. Their education stressed military training and obedience to authority. The Greek historian Plutarch described the handling of young Spartans:

"After they were twelve years old, they were no longer allowed to wear any undergarments, they had one coat to serve them a year; their bodies were hard and dry, with but little acquaintance of baths; these human indulgences they were allowed only on some few particular days in the year. They lodged together in little bands upon beds made of the rushes which grew by the banks of the river Eurotas, which they were to break off with their hands with a knife."

Spartan girls received an education similar to that of the boys. Girls, too, underwent physical training, including running, wrestling, and throwing the javelin. The purpose was clear: to strengthen the girls for their roles as healthy mothers.

Well-to-do Athenians raised their children very differently. Athenian children were nurtured by their mothers until age 7, when a male servant called a *pedagogue* took charge.

The purpose of an education for upper-class Athenian boys was to create a well-rounded person. To that end, a boy had three teachers. One taught him reading, writing, and arithmetic. Another taught physical education, a necessity to achieve the ideal of a sound mind in a sound body. A third taught him music, which consisted of playing the lyre (a stringed instrument) and singing. Education ended at 18, when an Athenian male formally became a citizen.

Girls of all classes remained at home. Their mothers taught them how to run a home. Only in some wealthy families did girls learn to read, write, and perhaps play the lyre.

◄ This relief—a sculpture that stands out from a flat surface—shows young Greeks enjoying their pets. It decorated the base of a statue. By the 500s B.C., Greek artists were already demonstrating their skill at showing human anatomy.

◄ Greek ideals and art remained a powerful influence on Western culture for centuries. This illustration appears on a French vase of the early 1800s. The artist, who depicted a footrace, idealized the physical training of Greek youths during the classical age.

In Sparta girls and boys were ► trained to be athletes, as is shown by this bronze statue, which was part of a vase lid.

▼ The Greeks were famous for celebrating physical as well as mental excellence. This young man is grasping weights as he vaults. The depiction appears on a cup that dates from about 480 B.C.

### CONNECTING TO THE PAST

1. **Summarizing Information** Describe a Spartan upbringing. How does this differ from the childhood of an American child?

2. **Compare and Contrast** Compare a well-educated Spartan boy with a well-educated Athenian and a well-educated American. What are the differences?

3. **Writing about History** Does your education today incorporate any Spartan or Athenian ideas? If so, give specific examples.

# Rome and the Rise of Christianity

## Guide to Reading

### Section Preview
Rome shifted from a republic into an empire, creating systems of law and government, as well as persecuting and ultimately embracing Christianity.

**Main Idea**

- The Romans made an important contribution to the West with their universal standards of justice. (p. 145)

- The vast extent of the Roman Empire explains why Roman culture has had such great influence in the West. (p. 146)

- Christianity was able to spread rapidly through the Roman imperial network, while both Roman and Christian values influenced the West. (p. 148)

### Content Vocabulary
patricians, plebeians, republic, Senate, Christianity, Catholic Church

### Academic Vocabulary
estate, potential, minority

### People to Identify
Augustus, Jesus, Nero, Constantine

### Places to Locate
Rome, Mediterranean Sea

### Reading Objectives
1. Examine why Rome became an empire.
2. Describe why Christianity grew so quickly.

### Reading Strategy
**Categorizing Information** As you read this section, complete a chart like the one shown below listing the government officials and the legislative bodies of the Roman Republic.

| Officials | Legislative Bodies |
|-----------|--------------------|
|           |                    |
|           |                    |

### Preview of Events

| ♦500 B.C. | ♦250 B.C. | ♦A.D. 1 | ♦A.D. 250 | ♦A.D. 500 |
|-----------|-----------|---------|-----------|-----------|

**509 B.C.**
Roman Republic created

**133 B.C**
Rome controls entire Mediterranean

**27 B.C**
Augustus becomes first Roman emperor

**A.D. 180**
*Pax Romana* ends

**A.D. 313**
Constantine proclaims official tolerance of Christianity

**A.D. 476**
Collapse of the Roman Empire in the West

## California Standards in This Section

*Reading this section will help you master these California History–Social Science standards.*

**10.1:** Students relate the moral and ethical principles in ancient Greek and Roman philosophy, in Judaism, and in Christianity to the development of Western political thought.

**10.1.1:** Analyze the similarities and differences in Judeo-Christian and Greco-Roman views of law, reason and faith, and duties of the individual.

# The Roman State

**Main Idea** The Romans made an important contribution to the West with their universal standards of justice.

**Reading Connection** Do you know anyone who has been involved in a civil suit? Read to learn about the Roman origins for Western legal traditions.

Roman history is the story of the Romans' conquest of the area around Rome, then of Italy, and finally of the entire Mediterranean world. Through the centuries, while the Roman form of government changed, it is the fame of the Roman Senate that has lasted.

## *Voices from the Past*

In the second century B.C., a Jewish military leader, Judas Maccabaeus, explained why he was impressed by the Romans:

> 66 He had been told of their wars and of the brave deeds that they were doing. . . . They had defeated Antiochus the Great, king of Asia, who went to fight against them with one hundred twenty elephants and with cavalry and chariots and a very large army. He was crushed by them. . . . Yet for all this not one of the Romans has put on a crown, but they have built for themselves a senate chamber, and every day three hundred senators constantly deliberate concerning the people, to govern them well. 99

Early **Rome** was divided into two groups or orders —the patricians and the plebeians. The **patricians** were great landowners, who became Rome's ruling class. Less wealthy landholders, craftspeople, merchants, and small farmers were part of a larger group called **plebeians**. In 509 B.C., Rome overthrew its last king and created a republic. A **republic** is a form of government in which the leader is not a monarch and certain citizens have the right to vote. Both patricians and plebeians could vote, but only patricians could be elected to office.

The chief officers of the Roman Republic were the consuls and praetors. Two consuls, chosen every year, ran the government and led the Roman army. The praetor was in charge of civil law, the law as it applied to Roman citizens. As Roman territory expanded, another praetor was added to judge cases in which one or both people were noncitizens.

The Roman **Senate** came to hold an especially important position in the Roman Republic. It was a select group of about 300 landowners who served for life. At first, its only role was to advise officials. Still, its advice was taken very seriously, and by the third century B.C. it had the force of law.

Besides the Senate, the Roman Republic had several people's assemblies. By far the most important was the centuriate assembly. The centuriate assembly elected the chief officials, such as consuls and praetors, and passed laws. Because it was organized by classes based on wealth, the wealthiest citizens always had a majority. The council of the plebs was for plebeians only, and it came into being as a result of the struggle between patricians and plebeians.

**The Struggle of the Orders** In the early Roman Republic, the two orders often had conflicts because the plebeians were looked down upon. Children of plebeians could not even marry patricians. Plebeians resented this situation, especially since they were the ones who served in the army that protected the republic. Plebeians felt they deserved both political and social equality with the patricians.

The struggle between the groups dragged on for hundreds of years, but the plebeians won a significant victory when the council of the plebs was created in 471 B.C. New officials, known as tribunes of the plebs, had the power to protect plebeians. In the

▼ *Judas Maccabaeus*

fourth century B.C., plebeians were permitted to become consuls, and in 287 B.C., the council of the plebs had the right to pass laws for all Romans.

By 287 B.C., all male Roman citizens were supposedly equal under the law. In reality, a few wealthy patrician and plebeian families in the Senate were the ruling class. Unlike the Athens assembly, the Roman Republic had not become democratic. Instead Roman citizens chose representatives to their assemblies where wealthy citizens had a majority. Furthermore, the representatives were always from Rome's wealthiest families.

**Roman Law** One of Rome's chief gifts to the Mediterranean world of its day and to later generations was its system of law. Rome's first code of laws was the Twelve Tables, which was adopted in 450 B.C. This code was a product of a simple farming society and proved inadequate for later Roman needs.

From the Twelve Tables, the Romans developed a more sophisticated system of civil law, but it applied only to Roman citizens. As Rome expanded, legal issues arose that involved Romans and non-Romans. Roman civil law could be used for some of these issues, but not for all. Special rules were created, and these became a body of law, the Law of Nations. The Romans came to identify the Law of Nations with natural law, a universal law based on reason. These laws applied to all peoples. This was a major step forward in the development of Western law.

Roman standards of justice included many that are familiar to us. For example, a person was regarded as innocent until proved otherwise. People accused of wrongdoing were allowed to defend themselves before a judge. A judge, in turn, was expected to weigh evidence carefully in making his decision. These principles lived on long after the fall of the Roman Empire. They are, in fact, part of the legal system of many European countries and of the United States.

**Reading Check** **Identifying** Through what institution did the Roman elite preserve its power?

## The Influence of the Roman Empire

**Main Idea** The vast extent of the Roman Empire explains why Roman culture has had such great influence in the West.

**Reading Connection** Do you know Spanish, French, or Italian? Read about why these are called Romance languages.

The Roman Republic lasted for about five centuries, but in the first century A.D. Rome became an empire. Between 509 B.C. and 264 B.C., Rome had expanded to control almost all of what is now Italy. Even more dramatically, between 264 B.C. and 133 B.C., Rome expanded to the west and east and became master of the **Mediterranean Sea**. Rome's republican institutions were not adequate to rule an empire.

After a series of bloody civil wars, **Augustus** created a new order that began the Roman Empire. Between A.D. 14 and A.D. 180, the Roman Empire experienced a lengthy period of peace and prosperity. The latter part of this period was known as the *Pax Romana*, or "Roman Peace." Trade flourished, and the provinces were ruled in an orderly fashion. There was, however, an enormous gulf between rich and poor. The upper classes lived lives of great luxury in their villas and on their vast **estates.**

The Roman Empire was one of the largest empires in antiquity. The Roman talent for practical administration was developed to a high level because of their need to rule such a vast empire. Roman influence on Western civilization was strong, too, because Romans extended citizenship to the peoples they ruled. Many peoples were therefore integrated into Roman ways. Towns in Spain or Britain would have public circuses just like the Romans if they could afford it. They might also have the grid layout for their streets, and the aqueducts and bridges that Roman engineers had pioneered.

▼ *The great orator Cicero addressing the Roman Senate*

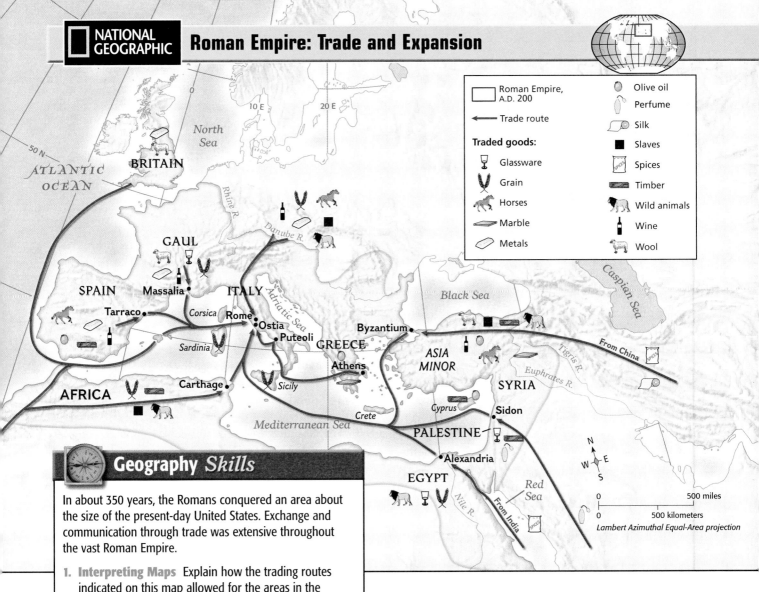

## NATIONAL GEOGRAPHIC — Roman Empire: Trade and Expansion

**Legend:**
- ☐ Roman Empire, A.D. 200
- ← Trade route

**Traded goods:**
- Glassware
- Grain
- Horses
- Marble
- Metals
- Olive oil
- Perfume
- Silk
- Slaves
- Spices
- Timber
- Wild animals
- Wine
- Wool

500 miles
500 kilometers
*Lambert Azimuthal Equal-Area projection*

### Geography *Skills*

In about 350 years, the Romans conquered an area about the size of the present-day United States. Exchange and communication through trade was extensive throughout the vast Roman Empire.

1. **Interpreting Maps** Explain how the trading routes indicated on this map allowed for the areas in the furthest reaches of the Roman Empire to trade with one another.
2. **Applying Geography Skills** Why would control of the Mediterranean region benefit Rome's economy? What are the names of the two chief Italian port cities of the Roman Empire?

Educated citizens everywhere in the empire spoke Latin. Over centuries, the languages of the peoples of Gaul, Spain, and other areas were Latinized. Today, French and Spanish are among the Romance languages—Romance referring to Roman.

Roman achievements in language, law, architecture, and engineering were adopted and adapted by the peoples who came after them. People looked to Roman law for basic principles of justice. Finally, the Romans preserved and grafted onto their own ideas the intellectual heritage of the Greeks, whom they admired so much. This is why we refer today to a Greco-Roman tradition.

The Roman Empire was also a means of spreading another set of beliefs and values, as well as the faith that inspired them. The birth and expansion of **Christianity** occurred within the Roman Empire. In the late empire, Christianity, in fact, became the official religion of the empire. Because it did so, the Christian Church and later the Catholic Church was organized in a way that reflected Roman institutions. Church law, especially, reflected some Roman ideas.

After A.D. 200, Roman influence and power declined because of internal and external factors. Goths, Visigoths, Vandals, and other Germanic tribes beyond the Rhine and Danube frontiers continued to threaten the empire. The tribes pressed south, looking for better land, and they succeeded finally in A.D. 476, the usual date given for the collapse of the Roman Empire in the West. Yet the tremendous influence of Roman institutions and Roman ways survived.

✓ **Reading Check** **Summarizing** List elements of Western culture the Romans helped to shape.

# The Development of Christianity

**Main Idea** Christianity was able to spread rapidly through the Roman imperial network, while both Roman and Christian values influenced the West.

**Reading Connection** Do you even feel lost in a big group? Read about how Christianity helped to form a sense of community in the vast Roman Empire.

During the early Roman Empire, a Jewish prophet named **Jesus** traveled and preached throughout Judaea and neighboring Galilee. His message was simple. He told his fellow Jews that he did not plan to harm their traditional religion: "Do not think that I have come to abolish the Law or the Prophets; I have not come to abolish them but to fulfill them." According to Jesus, what was important was not strict adherence to the letter of the law but the transformation of the inner person: "So in everything, do to others what you would have them do to you, for this sums up the Law and the Prophets."

God's command was to love God and one another. Jesus said: "Love the Lord your God with all your heart and with all your soul and with all your mind and with all your strength. This is the first commandment. The second is this: Love your neighbor as yourself." Jesus voiced the ethical concepts—humility, charity, and love toward others—that shaped the value system of the entire civilization of medieval Europe.

Jesus' preaching eventually stirred controversy. Some people saw Jesus as a **potential** revolutionary who might lead a revolt against Rome. Jesus' opponents finally turned him over to Roman authorities. The procurator Pontius Pilate ordered Jesus' crucifixion.

After the death of Jesus, his followers proclaimed that he had risen from death and had appeared to them. They believed Jesus to be the Messiah, or anointed one, the long expected deliverer who would save Israel from its foes.

**Christian Persecution and Final Triumph** At first, the Romans did not pay much attention to the Christians. They saw Christianity as just another sect within Judaism. As time passed, however, the Roman attitude toward Christians changed.

The Romans tolerated other religions so long as they did not threaten public order or public morals. All Romans were supposed to participate in public rituals honoring Roman gods and the emperor.

▼ The Last Supper *by Philippe de Champaigne, 1648*

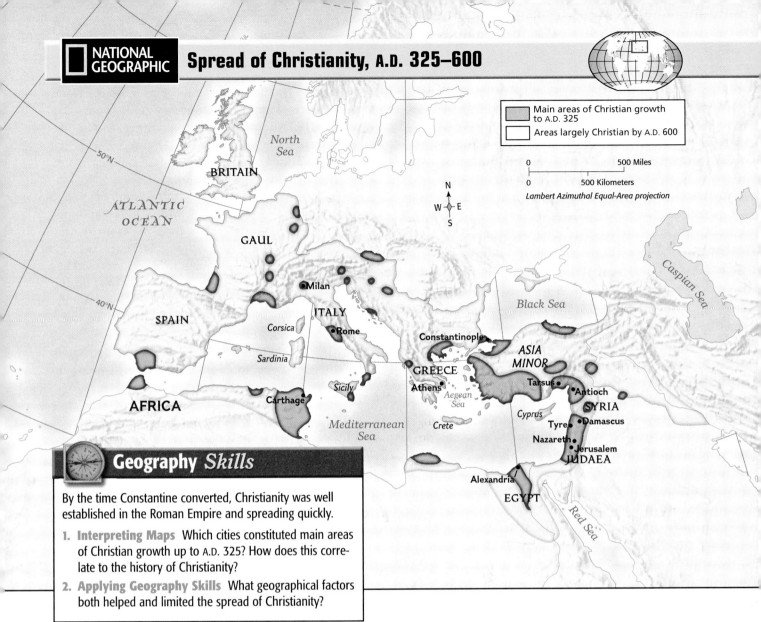

## Spread of Christianity, A.D. 325–600

NATIONAL GEOGRAPHIC

Main areas of Christian growth to A.D. 325

Areas largely Christian by A.D. 600

0        500 Miles

0        500 Kilometers

*Lambert Azimuthal Equal-Area projection*

### Geography *Skills*

By the time Constantine converted, Christianity was well established in the Roman Empire and spreading quickly.

1. **Interpreting Maps** Which cities constituted main areas of Christian growth up to A.D. 325? How does this correlate to the history of Christianity?

2. **Applying Geography Skills** What geographical factors both helped and limited the spread of Christianity?

---

Christians, however, believed in only one God and refused to take part in these ceremonies.

The Roman government saw this refusal as an act of treason, punishable by death. Christians could not comply with state religious rituals because they believed in only one God. If they worshipped the state's gods, they believed they would endanger their own salvation.

The government began persecuting Christians under Emperor **Nero,** who reigned from A.D. 54 to 68. Nero blamed the Christians for the fire that destroyed much of Rome and subjected them to cruel deaths. In contrast, in the second century A.D., persecution of Christians diminished. By the end of the second century A.D., Christians still represented a small **minority,** but one of considerable strength.

Christianity grew slowly in the first century, took root in the second, and by the third had spread widely. Why was Christianity able to attract so many followers?

First, the Christian message had much to offer the Roman world. The Roman religion was impersonal and existed for the good of the state. Christianity was personal and offered everyone an eternal life of happiness and bliss. In Greek religion, by contrast, an afterlife in the Elysian Fields was reserved for just a few, perhaps for a hero, who was already half-divine.

Second, Christianity was appealing because it contained elements familiar from other popular religions. This made it easy for people to understand. Some even identified it at first as one of the so-called mystery religions that offered immortality through the sacrificial death of a savior-god. Even the communal sharing of wine was familiar to followers of Dionysus, who believed that through this medium, the god's vital powers were transferred to mere mortals.

Finally, Christianity fulfilled a very human need to belong. Christians formed communities bound to one another. In these communities, people could express their love by helping each other and offering assistance to the poor and the sick. Christianity satisfied the need to belong in a way that the huge Roman Empire could never provide.

Christianity proved attractive to all classes, but especially to the poor and powerless. Eternal life was promised to everyone—rich, poor, aristocrats, slaves, men, and women. As Paul stated in his letters to the Colossians: "And [you] have put on the new self. … Here there is no Greek nor Jew … barbarian, Scythian, slave or free, but Christ is all, and is in all." Although Christianity did not call for revolution, it stressed a sense of spiritual equality for all people, which was a revolutionary idea.

Some emperors began new persecutions in the third century, but they could not suppress the new faith. In the fourth century A.D., Christianity prospered as never before because the emperor **Constantine** became a Christian. Although he was not baptized until the end of his life, in A.D. 313 Constantine issued the Edict of Milan, which proclaimed official tolerance of Christianity.

Under Theodosius the Great, who ruled from A.D. 378 to A.D. 395, Christianity became the state religion. Theodosius declared all other religions illegal.

*Minerva*

**Roman and Christian Values** There were many similarities in the ethical precepts of Romans and Christians. Both encouraged virtue. Both also encouraged duty to one's community and to the state. Jesus himself said, "Render unto Caesar the things that are Caesar's," but these famous words also show a distinction that Romans never made.

Jesus implies that only certain things belong to Caesar, or the state, and that therefore certain things do not. For the Christians, there was an internal world that did not belong to the state. That is because the individual relationship to a personal God lies at the heart of Christianity. This relationship must come above everything else—even the laws of the state. Roman persecution came about because of this difference. Romans did honor to Roman gods, but these gods were connected to the state—one honored and served them together.

The Roman sense of duty to the state and to the community was heightened by what they had learned from the Greeks. For the Greeks, the polis was an all-important community of ideas and fellowship. There were some exceptions in the Greek tradition, but most Greeks of the classical period would never understand that a person could be isolated in any sense from the polis—that would not be true life. Nor could a Greek have understood the Christian sense of being alone with one's God.

## Greek and Roman Gods

| Greek God | Roman God | Role |
| --- | --- | --- |
| Ares | Mars | god of war |
| Zeus | Jupiter | chief god |
| Hera | Juno | wife of chief god |
| Aphrodite | Venus | goddess of love |
| Artemis | Diana | goddess of the hunt |
| Athena | Minerva | goddess of wisdom |
| Hermes | Mercury | messenger god |
| Hades | Pluto | god of the underworld |
| Poseidon | Neptune | god of the sea |
| Hephaestus | Vulcan | god of fire |

## Chart *Skills*

The Romans adopted many of the gods of the peoples they conquered. Eventually the most important gods took on the characteristics of the Greek gods.

1. **Applying Chart Skills** Nike—the Greek goddess of victory—is the name of a sports shoe. What names in the chart do you recognize and what do you associate them with? In your examples, what is the connection to a particular god?

▲ *Catacombs for the Christian dead*

Christianity changed in some ways during the Middle Ages. Catholicism was the religion of most of Europe. The internal feeling for God was still an essential element of Catholicism, but as an institution the Church was also Roman. The **Catholic Church** became an institution that was an avenue between the individual and God. The Church would show the individual how to reach salvation.

Thus Christianity contained two traditions that could come into conflict—the emphasis on the individual conscience, and the emphasis on the public community or state. Christians might make good subjects of a state, but if the political community violated conscience, the Christian must stand up to the state. Many early martyrs had done so. Joan of Arc did so in 1431, Martin Luther did so in 1519, and Catholics did so in Communist Poland in the 1970s.

Christianity was not, of course, the only tradition that encouraged the virtue of standing up for one's ideas. Socrates had stood up to his polis because he believed he must abide by what his reason told him. It was because Greeks, Romans, and Christians shared a devotion to duty and virtue that their different traditions were able to blend in the modern West.

One element that cannot be found in Roman religion is probably the most powerful in Christianity: the emphasis on loving one's God. Romans honored and served their gods. They did not think in terms of loving a personal savior.

Jesus taught that Christians should treat others as they would like to be treated. This promoted tolerance to some degree, but ultimately Christians hoped to convert all people to their faith, forcibly if necessary. This belief inspired the Crusades. During the Middle Ages, Christians achieved their goal. Those who were not Christians, or whose beliefs did not match the Church doctrine, were seen as a threat.

✓**Reading Check** **Explaining** Why did the Romans believe that early Christians were traitors to the state?

**HISTORY** *Online* **Study Central**

For help with the concepts in this section of *Glencoe World History–Modern Times,* go to wh.mt.glencoe.com and click on **Study Central.**

---

# SECTION 3 ASSESSMENT

1. **Vocabulary** Define: patricians, plebeians, republic, Senate, estate, Christianity, potential, minority, Catholic Church.

2. **People** Identify: Augustus, Jesus, Nero, Constantine.

3. **Places** Locate: Rome, Mediterranean Sea.

### Reviewing Big Ideas

4. **Explain** the significance of the Twelve Tables and the Law of Nations to the development of political thought.

### Critical Thinking

5. **Historical Analysis** **Sequence and Change** How was the Roman Empire Latinized? How did Roman culture and politics spread? **CA CS 2**

6. **Summarizing Information** Create a table like the one below describing the contributions of the Greeks and Romans to Western civilization.

| Greek contributions | Roman contributions |
|---|---|
|  |  |
|  |  |
|  |  |

### Analyzing Visuals

7. **Examine** the photograph of the catacombs on this page. What does this space tell you about early Christian practices and what influenced them?

---

### Writing About History

8. **Expository Writing** Use the Internet or library sources to research the theories about why the Roman Empire fell. Summarize the theories in a brief essay and explain why some theories seem more convincing than others. **CA 10WA2.3**

# New Patterns of Civilization

## Guide to Reading

### Section Preview
Between the sixth and sixteenth centuries new systems of rule, religious doctrines, and intellectual movements emerged.

**Main Idea**

- In the seventh century, Muhammad spread a new faith that claimed to complete the promise of Judaism and Christianity. (p. 153)

- Charlemagne united the areas in Western Europe where European civilization took shape. (p. 154)

- The Magna Carta won rights mainly for nobles, but it established those rights in writing, and later they were extended to commoners. (p. 155)

- The High and Late Middle Ages traced a series of highs and lows for European agriculture, commerce, religion, and political stability. (p. 157)

- The Renaissance encouraged excellence in worldly pursuits, while its new ways of thinking encouraged trends that led to the Reformation. (p. 158)

### Content Vocabulary
Islam, feudalism, common law, Magna Carta, parliament

### Academic Vocabulary
grant, confer

### People and Events to Identify
Muhammad, Charlemagne, Middle Ages, Edward I, Renaissance, Leonardo da Vinci, Protestant Reformation, Martin Luther

### Places to Locate
Arabian Peninsula, Makkah, England, Worms

### Reading Objectives
1. Define the major beliefs and principles of Islam.
2. Identify the elements that formed European civilization.

### Reading Strategy
**Cause and Effect** Use a chart like the one below to show the effects of King John's weak leadership on medieval society.

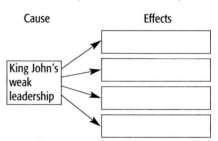

### Preview of Events

| ◆500 | ◆700 | ◆900 | ◆1100 | ◆1300 | ◆1500 |

**c. 500**
The Middle Ages begin

**610**
Muhammad receives first message

**800**
Charlemagne crowned Emperor of the Romans

**1215**
Magna Carta is signed

**1520**
Martin Luther stands trial

---

## California Standards in This Section

*Reading this section will help you master these California History–Social Science standards.*

**10.1:** Students relate the moral and ethical principles in ancient Greek and Roman philosophy, in Judaism, and in Christianity to the development of Western political thought.

# The World of Islam

**Main Idea** In the seventh century, Muhammad spread a new faith that claimed to complete the promise of Judaism and Christianity.

**Reading Connection** Do religious leaders today have a message inspired by social and economic problems? Read to learn what led Muhammad to pray and meditate.

From ancient times, Southwest Asia has been the site of great empires. In the seventh century, a new empire was being built by the Arabs—a people who believed that their efforts were aided by Allah, the supreme being of their religion, Islam.

In the **Arabian Peninsula**, the religion called **Islam**, which means "submission to Allah," spread rapidly. Its spread came about through a man named **Muhammad**, who is often called the Prophet. Muhammad was born in 570 in **Makkah**, a town of about three thousand located in the desert lands of the Arabian Peninsula. Orphaned as a small boy, he was raised by an uncle in the traditional Arabic religion. Muhammad was intelligent and hardworking and became a capable merchant. He married a widow, had children, and seemed to have a happy and comfortable life.

Muhammad, however, was not content. Deeply disturbed by social problems in Makkah, he spent days on end in a nearby cave on Mount Hira, praying and meditating. According to tradition, one night in 610, while Muhammad was deep in meditation, an angelic voice called out: "Recite!" A frightened Muhammad replied, "What shall I recite?" The voice responded, "In the name of thy Lord the Creator, who created mankind from a clot of blood, recite!" The voice then began to speak about the nature of God.

## 𝒱oices from the 𝒫ast

Allah speaks to Muslims through the Quran:

❝God had helped you at Badr, when you were a contemptible little band. So fear God and thus show your gratitude. Remember when you said to the Believers: 'Is it not enough for you that your Lord helped you with 3,000 angels sent down? Yes, and if you remain firm and aright, even if the enemy should come against you here in hot haste, your Lord would help you with 5,000 angels on the attack.'❞

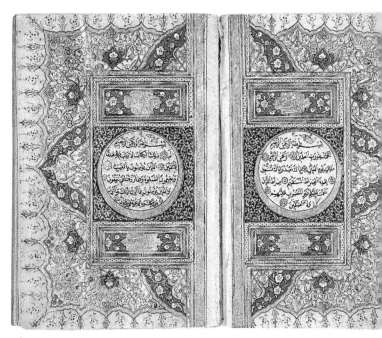

▲ *Fourteenth-century Quran pages*

Over a period of time, Muhammad memorized everything the voice revealed and began to preach these words to others: "Allah will bring to nothing the deeds of those who disbelieve.... As for the faithful who do good works and believe in what is revealed to Muhammad—which is the truth from their Lord—He will forgive them their sins and ennoble their state." These words were gathered together as the Quran, the sacred book of Islam. The message of Islam attracted many followers, who considered Muhammad a prophet of God. Believers were certain that they would be rewarded when the Day of Judgment came if they submitted to Allah by practicing the acts of worship known as the Five Pillars of Islam: belief, prayer, charity, fasting, and pilgrimage. Like Christianity, Islam was open to every person, and this encouraged a greater sense of equality in society.

Muhammad's life changed the course of world history. At the time of his birth, the empires that had once ruled the entire Middle East were only a memory. The region was now divided into many separate states, and the people worshipped many different gods.

Within a few decades of Muhammad's death, Islam united the Middle East once again. Arab armies marched westward across North Africa and eastward into Mesopotamia and Persia, creating a new empire that stretched from Spain to the Indus Valley. Arab rule also brought with it the new religion and the culture of Islam.

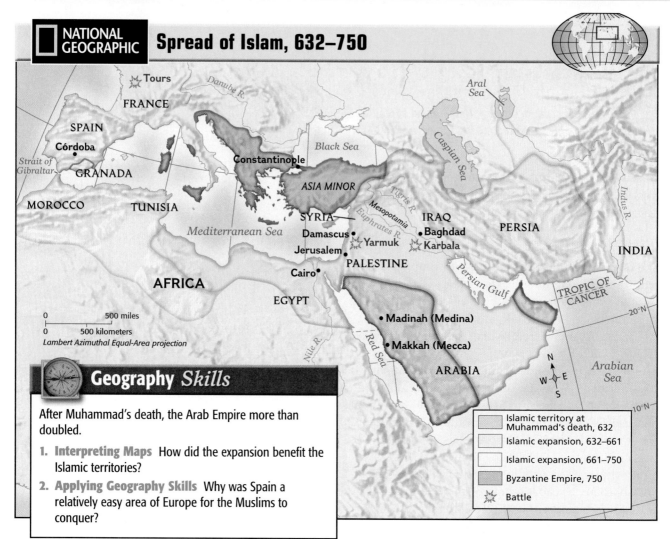

Tours
FRANCE
Danube R.
Aral Sea
SPAIN
Córdoba
Strait of Gibraltar
GRANADA
Constantinople
Black Sea
Caspian Sea
ASIA MINOR
MOROCCO
TUNISIA
Mediterranean Sea
Tigris R.
Mesopotamia
SYRIA
Euphrates R.
IRAQ
Damascus
Baghdad
PERSIA
Yarmuk
Karbala
Jerusalem
PALESTINE
INDIA
Indus R.
Cairo
AFRICA
EGYPT
Persian Gulf
TROPIC OF CANCER
20°N
Nile R.
Red Sea
• Madinah (Medina)
• Makkah (Mecca)
ARABIA
Arabian Sea
10°N

0    500 miles
0    500 kilometers
Lambert Azimuthal Equal-Area projection

N W E S

Islamic territory at Muhammad's death, 632
Islamic expansion, 632–661
Islamic expansion, 661–750
Byzantine Empire, 750
Battle

## Geography *Skills*

After Muhammad's death, the Arab Empire more than doubled.

1. **Interpreting Maps** How did the expansion benefit the Islamic territories?

2. **Applying Geography Skills** Why was Spain a relatively easy area of Europe for the Muslims to conquer?

Islamic beliefs made a powerful impact in all areas occupied by Arab armies, but the Arab Empire did not last. Internal struggles led first to its decline and then to its destruction at the hands of the Mongols in 1258. Still, the Arab conquest left a powerful legacy. The appeal of Islam remained strong throughout the Middle East and extended into areas not occupied by Arab armies, such as Africa, India, and Southeast Asia.

Islam and Christianity shared many values. In fact, Muslims stressed their connection to Jews and Christians—all three groups were "people of the book," or Torah. Judaism came first, Christianity perfected Judaism, and Islam was the final stage in God's plan.

These religious traditions **granted** the highest priority on God's will and on the individual's relationship to God. Because of their history in the Roman Empire, Christians had some room for the idea of separate recognition for state power. In the world of Muhammad, Islam and the state were virtually identical.

**✓ Reading Check** **Explaining** Why is Islam often said to be an egalitarian faith?

# European Civilization in the Middle Ages

**Main Idea** **Charlemagne united the areas in Western Europe where European civilization took shape.**

**Reading Connection** Are there rituals from earlier times that Americans use for a dignified occasion? Read about the ritual for Charlemagne's coronation.

In 800, **Charlemagne**, the king of a Germanic people known as the Franks, went to Rome to support the Catholic pope, Leo III. The pope was barely clinging to power in the face of rebellious Romans. On Christmas Day, Charlemagne, his family, and a host of visitors crowded into Saint Peter's Basilica to attend mass.

According to a Frankish writer, the assembled crowd was surprised when, "as the king rose from praying before the tomb of the blessed apostle Peter, Pope Leo placed a golden crown on his head." In keeping with ancient tradition, the people in the church shouted, "Long life and victory to Charles Augustus, crowned by God the great and peace-loving Emperor of the Romans."

It appeared that the Roman Empire in the West had been reborn, and Charles had become the first Roman emperor since 476. This "Roman emperor" was actually a German king, and he was crowned by a pope. Thus, his coronation did not signal that the Roman Empire had been reborn, but that a new civilization had emerged.

This new civilization, European civilization, was formed by the coming together of three major elements: the Roman legacy itself; the traditions of Germanic peoples who had settled the Western Roman Empire; and the Christian Church.

After 800, this new Europe became the center of the Western world. Its civilization developed during the **Middle Ages**, roughly from 500 to 1500. Later historians referred to this time as the "Middle Ages" because they saw the period as a transition between the ancient and modern worlds.

After his death, centralized control in Charlemagne's empire weakened. Medieval political institutions developed as **feudalism**. The feudal system put power into the hands of many different lords, who came to constitute a powerful group of nobles dominating the political, economic, and social life of Europe.

Medieval Europeans considered the Catholic Church to be the all-embracing institution for humanity. Lords and princes themselves bowed to churchmen, and to the pope, God's ruler on earth.

Quietly and surely within this world of castles, however, kings gradually began to extend their powers. As they did so, they fought the pope in order to have total control in their own kingdoms. Although they could not know it then, their actions laid the foundations for the European kingdoms that we know as European nations today. One of these kingdoms, England, created the first parliament that claimed rights against the king.

**✓Reading Check** **Explaining** Why was Charlemagne not truly the "Emperor of the Romans"?

## England in the High Middle Ages

**Main Idea** The Magna Carta won rights mainly for nobles, but it established those rights in writing, and later they were extended to commoners.

**Reading Connection** In what kind of situations do you want an agreement put into writing? Read to find out what English nobles wanted King John to sign.

On October 14, 1066, an army of heavily armed knights under William of Normandy landed on the coast of **England** and soundly defeated King Harold and the Anglo-Saxon foot soldiers. William was crowned king of England at Christmastime in London and then began a rule that combined Anglo-Saxon and Norman institutions in a new England. William made all nobles swear an oath of loyalty to him as sole ruler, and insisted that all subjects owed loyalty to the king.

▼ *A medieval depiction of the crowning of Charlemagne on Christmas Day, 800*

In the twelfth century, the power of the English monarchy was greatly enlarged during the reign of Henry II, who ruled from 1154 to 1189. Henry II was one of England's most able monarchs. The king was especially successful in strengthening royal courts. Many more criminal cases and property cases were now tried in royal courts, not the local courts of feudal lords. Henry appointed officials who toured the land, delivering royal justice. Henry's goal was clear: by expanding the power of royal courts, he expanded the king's power.

Another important result followed. Since royal courts were now found throughout England, a body of **common law**—law common to the whole kingdom—replaced local law codes that often varied from place to place.

## The Magna Carta

Henry was only the first of a number of English kings to build up their power. Because of this, many English nobles in the 1100s felt they were losing power, and they resented it.

When King John proved a weak leader in war, these discontented nobles rebelled. At Runnymede in 1215, they forced him to put his seal on the **Magna Carta,** or Great Charter. The Magna Carta was, above all, a feudal document. Its purpose was to **confer** more rights on nobles. Feudal custom had always recognized that the relationship between a king and his knights—vassals—was based on mutual rights and obligations. The Magna Carta, however, recognized this fact in writing.

In later centuries, the Magna Carta was used to strengthen the idea that a monarch's power was limited, not absolute. Through later interpretation, certain provisions of the Magna Carta acquired significance for commoners, as well as nobles.

One provision of the Magna Carta stands out. Chapter 39 reads: "No free man shall be taken or imprisoned or dispossessed, or outlawed, or banished, or in any way destroyed, nor will we go upon him, nor send upon him, except by the legal judgment of his peers or by the law of the land." In the fourteenth century, this provision gave rise to trial by jury.

When the Magna Carta was first signed, this provision did not apply to everyone. In 1215, the label of "free man" applied to fewer than half of the English population. Later, however, this statement was applied to all.

The principles of English common law and the Magna Carta were adopted by the American colonies. When the colonies became a new nation, these same principles of law would become part of the legal system of the United States.

## The Beginnings of Parliament

One of the most important institutions in the Western political tradition is a parliament. A **parliament** is a representative body of advisers to a king or other chief executive.

During the reign of **Edward I,** the English Parliament emerged. At first the word *parliament* referred to the king's Great Council, which was made up of the king's officials, nobles, and bishops. Since the Magna Carta, however, a pattern had been established that the king would turn to the local lords when he needed revenues.

Because he needed money, Edward I did turn to the lords in the counties and towns. These lords invited two knights from every county and two residents from each town to meet with the Great Council to consent to new taxes. This group was the first official Parliament and it met in 1295.

In time, Parliament had two houses, upper and lower. Nobles and church lords sat in the House of Lords; knights and townspeople formed the House of Commons. During the reign of Edward I, Parliament approved taxes, discussed politics, and passed laws. Parliament had emerged as an institution. The law of the English kingdom would be determined not by the king alone but by king and Parliament together. Much conflict and even open war ensued before Parliament gained the dominant political power it has today in England.

**Reading Check** **Connecting** How did Henry's goal to become more powerful affect the development of law?

**Feudal System**

**Kings**

Land (fief) ↓ ↑ Fees, loyalty, military support

**Lords**

*Medieval knight* Land ↓ ↑ Fees, loyalty, military support

**Knights**

Protection ↓ ↑ Fees, loyalty, labor

**Serfs**

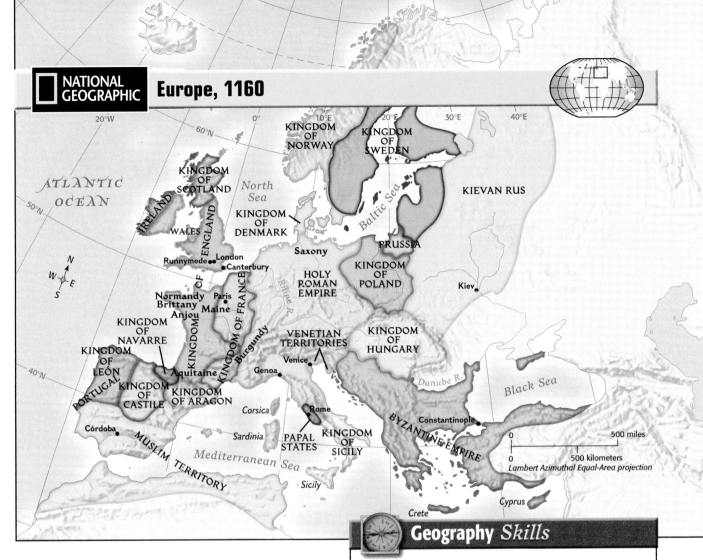

**Geography Skills**

Strong monarchies developed in France and England, while Germany and Italy consisted of independent states.

1. **Interpreting Maps** Locate Runnymede. What event occurred there and why was it significant?

2. **Applying Geography Skills** Create a bar graph of the sizes of kingdoms on this map.

## Europe in the High and Late Middle Ages

**Main Idea** The High and Late Middle Ages traced a series of highs and lows for European agriculture, commerce, religion, and political stability.

**Reading Connection** Do you plan on attending college after graduation? Learn about when universities first flourished.

The High Middle Ages lasted from about 1000 to 1300, and this era represents the peak of medieval culture and politics. European kingdoms experienced an incredible burst of energy and growth. New farming practices, the growth of cities and trade, and a growing population created a vigorous society.

Another reason for the vigor of the High Middle Ages was strong leadership by the popes. A new spiritual energy was found in the monasteries spreading across Europe. Intellectual and artistic activity was equally vigorous in this period. The spires of Gothic churches towered over growing cities as a beacon to

faith. Universities first flourished in this period. There, men like Thomas Aquinas developed a new system of Catholic thought on eternal questions about man's relationship to God.

All this changed in the Late Middle Ages, which lasted from 1300 to the early 1400s. Europe faced an overwhelming number of disasters—the devastating plague of the Black Death, a decline in commerce, seemingly constant warfare, political instability, and the decline of the Church. No doubt, to some people it appeared that the last days of the world were at hand. In the course of the fifteenth century, however, Europe experienced a revival or rebirth of civilization.

✓**Reading Check** **Analyzing** What elements of society might the growth in trade influence?

***School of Athens* by Raphael** Raphael created this painting for the pope to show the unity of Christian and classical works. Research the painting to discover the identities of the historical figures that Raphael depicted.

## The Renaissance and Reformation

**Main Idea** The Renaissance encouraged excellence in worldly pursuits, while its new ways of thinking encouraged trends that led to the Reformation.

**Reading Connection** Have you encountered Leonardo da Vinci in other classes besides history? Read to learn why he can be discussed in classes on several different subjects.

Between 1350 and 1550, Italian intellectuals believed that they were living in a new age. This new age, the **Renaissance**, was based on a rebirth of the culture of the Greeks and Romans. It began in Italy and continued some of the trends of the High Middle Ages. The Renaissance was also a new age, however, when intellectuals and artists proclaimed a new vision of the world and held up the value of the individual.

The Renaissance thinkers found glory in the idea that the individual had gifts that were almost divine. When they looked to Greek and Roman thinkers and artists, they saw a love of excellence and accomplishment. One Renaissance Italian, Leon Battista Alberti, summed up the faith in the individual by saying, "Men can do all things if they will."

This high regard for human worth and a realization of what individuals could achieve created a new optimism and a new social ideal, the "Renaissance man." There is probably no better example of this new ideal than **Leonardo da Vinci** (VIHN•chee). A painter, sculptor, architect, inventor, and mathematician, Leonardo developed his abilities to the highest level.

Many Renaissance artists remain models of accomplishment, and contemporary Western art is indebted to them. Their methods, their works, and their commitment to the vision of each individual artist are at the core of Western art.

The Renaissance affected not just art, but the whole intellectual world. By advocating a return to the early sources of Christianity and criticizing religious practices, the Renaissance humanists aroused fundamental questions about Catholicism and the Catholic Church, still a very important institution. In the sixteenth century, this intellectual revolution gave way to what we might call a religious renaissance, the **Protestant Reformation**. It touched the lives of many Europeans in profound ways.

On April 18, 1520, a lowly monk stood before the emperor and princes of Germany in the city of **Worms**. He had been called before this gathering to answer charges of heresy, charges that could threaten his very life. The monk was shown a pile of his books and asked if he wished to defend them all or reject a part. Courageously, **Martin Luther** defended them all and declared: "Since then Your Majesty and your lordships desire a simple reply, I will answer without horns and without teeth. Unless I am convicted by Scripture and plain reason . . . my conscience is captive to the Word of God. I cannot and I will not recant anything, for to go against conscience is neither right nor safe. Here I stand, I cannot do otherwise. God help me. Amen."

Luther's refusal to renounce his ideas on the basis of his conscience began the Protestant Reformation. 📖 *(See page 770 to read an excerpt on the religious debate in the Primary Sources Library.)* The movement begun by Martin Luther when he made his dramatic stand quickly spread across Europe. Within a short time, new Protestant churches were attracting supporters all over Europe. Although seemingly helpless to stop the new churches, the Catholic Church also underwent a religious rebirth and managed to revive its fortunes. By the mid-sixteenth century, the religious division had produced two militant faiths—Protestantism and Catholicism—that were prepared to do combat for the

*Martin Luther addressing the emperor in Worms*

souls of the faithful. An age of religious passion was soon followed by an age of religious warfare.

Religious wars were political wars, too. Kings and queens were motivated by their faith, but they were also motivated by the worldly goal of ruling over a strong state. The strongest nation-states vied with one another for wealth and power. The way these struggles played out, especially in England, affected the further development of constitutional government.

 **Identifying** What sources inspired the Renaissance thinkers?

---

**HISTORY Online** **Study Central**

For help with the concepts in this section of *Glencoe World History–Modern Times,* go to <u>wh.mt.glencoe.com</u> and click on **Study Central.**

---

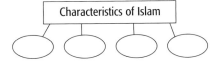

## Checking for Understanding

1. **Vocabulary** Define: Islam, grant, feudalism, common law, Magna Carta, confer, parliament.

2. **People and Events** Identify: Muhammad, Charlemagne, Middle Ages, Edward I, Renaissance, Leonardo da Vinci, Protestant Reformation, Martin Luther.

3. **Places** Locate: Arabian Peninsula, Makkah, England, Worms.

### Reviewing Big Ideas

4. Explain how the Quran influenced the government in Islamic civilization.

## Critical Thinking

5. **Historical Analysis** **Connecting Ideas** Explain how the qualities of a "Renaissance man" reflected the political and social values of the Renaissance. **CA HI 1**

6. **Summarizing Information** Create a diagram of the main characteristics of Islam.

```
┌──────────────────────────┐
│ Characteristics of Islam │
└──────────────────────────┘
     │     │      │      │
   ◯    ◯     ◯      ◯
```

## Analyzing Visuals

7. **Identify** the event illustrated in the painting on this page. Why was this event significant? How has the painter portrayed Martin Luther?

### Writing About History

8. **Informative Writing** Imagine that you are a journalist attending a meeting of the first English Parliament. What questions would you ask? Write a newsletter for people of your town explaining what happened. **CA 10WA2.2**

# PRIMARY SOURCES
## EYEWITNESS TO HISTORY

*In these excerpts, Plato and Aristotle discuss philosophers holding political office, a governing middle class, and the roles of citizens.*

## SOURCE 1: *The Republic* of Plato

*Plato, a pupil of Socrates, was one of the great philosophers of ancient Athens. Plato's* Republic *is written in the form of a dialogue about a perfect society governed by a philosopher-king.*

You will see then, Glaucon, that there will be no real injustice in compelling our philosophers to watch over and care for the other citizens. We can fairly tell them that . . . we have brought you into existence for your country's sake as well as your own, to be like leaders and king-bees in a hive; you have been better and more thoroughly educated than those others and hence you are more capable of playing your part both as men of thought and as men of action. . . . in truth, government can be at its best and free from dissension only where the destined rulers are least desirous of holding office.

*A mural by Puvis de Chavannes of Plato and a student*

Yes, my friend; for the truth is that you can have a well-governed society only if you can discover for your future rulers a better way of life than being in office; then only will power be in the hands of men who are rich, not in gold, but in the wealth that brings happiness, a good and wise life. All goes wrong when, starved for lack of anything good in their own lives, men turn to public affairs hoping to snatch from thence the happiness they hunger for. They set about fighting for power, and this conflict ruins them and their country. The life of true philosophy is the only one that looks down upon offices of state; and access to power must be confined to men who are not in love with it; otherwise rivals will start fighting. So whom else can you compel to undertake the guardianship of the **commonwealth**[1], if not those who, besides understanding best the principles of government, enjoy a nobler life than the politician's and look for rewards of a different kind?

There is no other choice.

## SOURCE 2: Aristotle: Government and the Middle Class

*In this excerpt from* Politics, *Aristotle analyzed what constitution was best. He concluded that power should rest in the hands of the middle class.*

In all states there are three sections of the community—the very well-off, the very badly-off, and those in between. Seeing therefore that it is agreed that moderation and a middle position are best, it is clear that in the matter of possessions to own a middling amount is best of all. This condition is most obedient to reason, and following reason is just what is difficult both for the exceedingly rich, handsome, strong, and well-born, and for the downtrodden. The former commit deeds of violence on a large scale, the latter are delinquent and wicked in petty ways. The misdeeds of the one class are due to [pride], the misdeeds of the other to **rascality**[2]. . . .

---

[1]**commonwealth:** the state

[2]**rascality:** low birth, social status

It is clear then that the political partnership which operates through the middle class is best, and also that those cities have every chance of being well-governed in which the middle class is large, stronger if possible than the other two together, or at any rate stronger than one of them.... For this reason it is a happy state of affairs when those who take part in the life of the state have a moderate but adequate amount of property; for where one set of people possesses a great deal and the other nothing, the result is either extreme democracy or a tyranny due to the excesses of the other two....

The superiority of the middle type of constitution is clear also from the fact that it alone is free from fighting among **factions**[3]. Where the middle element is large, there least of all arise faction and counter-faction among citizens. And for the same reason the larger states are free from danger of splitting; they are strong in the middle.... Democracies too are safer than **oligarchies**[4] in this respect and longer lasting thanks to their middle class, which is always more numerous and more politically important in democracies than in oligarchies.

## SOURCE 3: The *Politics* of Aristotle

*In this selection from his* Politics, *Aristotle examined the nature of a political community and the polis.*

From these considerations it is evident that the **polis**[5] belongs to the class of things that exist by nature, and that man is by nature an animal intended to live in a polis. He who is without a polis, by reason of his own nature and not of some accident, is either a poor sort of being, or a being higher than man: he is the man of whom Homer wrote in **denunciation**[6]: "Clanless and lawless and heartless is he." The man who is such by nature [i.e., unable to join in the society of a polis] at once plunges into a passion for war; he is in the position of a solitary advanced piece in a game of [chess].

---

[3]**factions:** parties or groups focused on their own interests
[4]**oligarchies:** governments run by a small group
[5]**polis:** Greek city-state
[6]**denunciation:** public condemnation

The reason why man is a being meant for political association, in a higher degree than bees or other **gregarious**[7] animals can ever associate, is evident. Nature, according to our theory, makes nothing in vain; and man alone of the animals is furnished with the faculty of language. The mere making of sounds serves to indicate pleasure and pain, is thus a faculty that belongs to animals in general: their nature enables them to attain the point at which they have perceptions of pleasure and pain, and can signify those perceptions to one another. But language serves to declare what is advantageous and what is the reverse, and it therefore serves to declare what is just and what is unjust. It is the peculiarity of man, in comparison with the rest of the animal world, that he alone possesses a perception of good and evil, of the just and the unjust, and of other similar qualities; and it is association in [a common perception of] these things which makes a family and a polis.

We now proceed to add that [though the individual and the family are prior in the order of time] the polis is prior in the order of nature to the family and the individual.

---

[7]**gregarious:** associating with others of one's kind or species

## DBQ Document-Based Questions

### Historical Analysis  CA HR 3

**Source 1:** Why does Plato believe that philosophers would make the best rulers? What men would make poor rulers?

**Source 2:** According to Aristotle, what makes the rich and downtrodden poor rulers?

**Source 3:** Why does Aristotle believe that man is meant for political association?

### Comparing and Contrasting Sources

1. What group do both authors agree would make poor rulers? Why?
2. Which author seems to possess a more positive view of human nature? Explain.

# CHAPTER 1

# ASSESSMENT and ACTIVITIES

## Chapter Summary

A series of causes and effects shaped the history of ancient and medieval civilizations.

| Cause | | Effect |
|---|---|---|
| Hammurabi creates a code of 282 laws. | → | Laws are established for almost every aspect of a person's life. |
| Cleisthenes gives the Athenian assembly the final authority to pass laws. | → | Male citizens play a central role in politics, creating the foundation for Athenian democracy. |
| The expansion of Rome weakens its republican rule and leads to civil wars. | → | Augustus gains control of the state and becomes the first emperor of the Roman Empire. |
| Christianity attracts many followers and quickly spreads throughout the Roman Empire. | → | Theodosius the Great makes Christianity the official religion of the Roman Empire. |
| Muhammad meditates and prays in a desert cave, contemplating social problems. | → | Islam unites the Middle East and remains a powerful religion after the Arab Empire's decline. |
| King John is unable to provide strong leadership or stand up to English nobles. | → | The Magna Carta limits a monarch's power and leads to the concept of a trial by jury. |

## Reviewing Content Vocabulary

*On a sheet of paper, use each of these terms in a sentence.*

1. civilization
2. patriarchal
3. pharaoh
4. Judaism
5. monotheistic
6. covenant
7. prophet
8. caste system
9. Hinduism
10. Buddhism
11. Confucianism
12. polis
13. tyrant
14. democracy
15. oligarchy
16. direct democracy
17. philosophy
18. Socratic method
19. patrician
20. plebeian
21. republic
22. Senate
23. Christianity
24. Catholic Church
25. Islam
26. feudalism
27. common law
28. Magna Carta
29. parliament

## Reviewing Academic Vocabulary

*On a sheet of paper, use each of these terms in a sentence that reflects the term's meaning in the chapter.*

30. code
31. focus
32. network
33. core
34. goal
35. adult
36. foundation
37. estate
38. potential
39. minority
40. grant
41. confer

## Reviewing the Main Ideas

### Section 1

42. How did Mesopotamian and Egyptian city-states develop concepts of law codes and divine kingship?

43. What were the major beliefs of Judaism and how did they influence Western culture?

### Section 2

44. How was citizenship connected to the Greek polis?

45. What is the Socratic method and what is its legacy?

### Section 3

46. What were the Roman standards of justice?

47. Why was Christianity able to spread so quickly throughout the Roman Empire, and how did Roman and Christian values combine?

### Section 4

48. How was Islam meant to complete what Judaism and Christianity had begun?

49. What was Charlemagne's influence on European civilization?

## Critical Thinking

**50. Comparing and Contrasting** How did Renaissance thinkers think the individual was defined? Explain how this idea can be compared with the value of an individual in ancient Roman and medieval European societies.

**51. Reading Skill** **Predicting** Based on what you have learned about the role of the English Parliament, how do you predict it will react to a controlling ruler?

## Writing About History

**52. Historical Analysis** **Connecting Ideas** Research the judicial system that Henry II introduced into England during the twelfth century. Compare the new law codes created to the local law codes they replaced. Present your findings in a carefully prepared essay. Be sure to link how this process strengthened royal courts over local courts, and what this meant for an individual's rights. **CA HI 1**

**53.** *Big Idea* You are a Roman patrician who wants to become a senator. Write a campaign speech explaining how you are qualified and what duties you know you must perform. **CA 10WA2.1**

**DBQ Document-Based Questions**

**Analyzing Sources** Read the following description of the feudal vow of loyalty between lords and vassals:

The man should put his hands together as a sign of humility, and place them between the two hands of his lord as a token that he vows everything to him and promises faith to him; and the lord should receive him and promise to keep faith with him. Then the man should say: 'Sir, I enter your homage and faith and become your man by mouth and hands (that is, by taking the oath and placing his hands between those of the lord), and I swear and promise to keep faith and loyalty to you against all others.'

**54.** Why is it significant that the vow was given to a particular person rather than a nation, written constitution, or religion?

**55.** What is meant by the phrase "and the lord should receive him and promise to keep faith with him"?

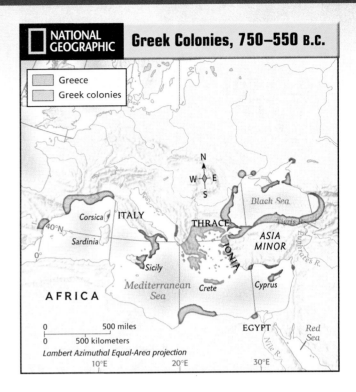

**NATIONAL GEOGRAPHIC** **Greek Colonies, 750–550 B.C.**

Greece
Greek colonies

## Analyzing Maps and Charts

Study the map above to answer the following questions.

**56.** Based on this map, how important was having a navy to the Athenian Empire?

**57.** What is the approximate maximum distance that a Greek citizen would have to travel to reach the Mediterranean Sea?

**Standards Practice**

**Directions: Choose the best answer to the following question.**

**58.** According to Plato, which was the best type of ruler for an ideal society?

**A** an absolute monarch

**B** a commoner

**C** a philosopher-king

**D** an emperor

**CA Standard 10.1.2** Trace the development of the Western political ideas of the rule of law and illegitimacy of tyranny, using selections from Plato's Republic and Aristotle's Politics.

# WORLD RELIGIONS

**H**ow was the universe created? What happens when we die? How do we become good people? These are some of the questions that religions attempt to answer. By creating an organized system of worship, religions help us make sense of our lives and our world.

Religion can be an individual belief. In some nations, religion is also state policy. Throughout history, religions have had both the power to unite people and to create terrible conflict. Today, there are thousands of religions practiced by about 6 billion people around the world.

| Major World Religions | |
|---|---|
| **Religion** | **Number of Followers** |
| Christianity | 2,000,000,000 |
| Islam | 1,226,403,000 |
| Hinduism | 828,130,000 |
| Chinese religions* | 398,555,000 |
| Buddhism | 364,014,000 |
| Judaism | 14,535,000 |

**Source:** *World Almanac and Book of Facts,* 2004.
*Includes Chinese folk religions, Confucianism, and Taoism

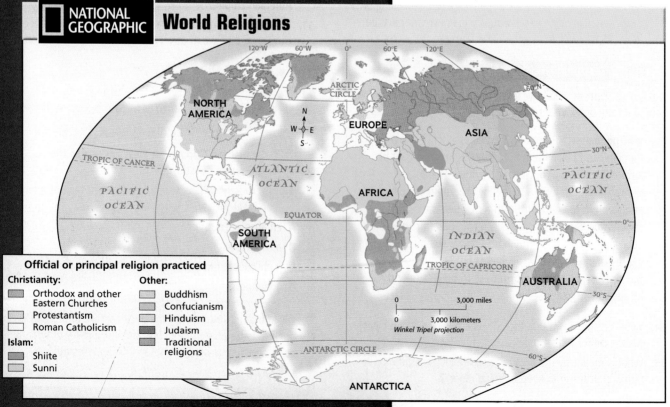

**NATIONAL GEOGRAPHIC** **World Religions**

**Official or principal religion practiced**

**Christianity:**
- Orthodox and other Eastern Churches
- Protestantism
- Roman Catholicism

**Islam:**
- Shiite
- Sunni

**Other:**
- Buddhism
- Confucianism
- Hinduism
- Judaism
- Traditional religions

*Winkel Tripel projection*

# Local Religions—⟶

Although some religions have spread worldwide, many people still practice religions that originated and developed in their own area.

## Australia

There are no deities in the traditional beliefs of the Aborigines of Australia. Their lives revolve around a belief known as the Dreamtime. According to Aboriginal mythology, ancestor heroes created the world and all it contains during the Dreamtime. The Aborigines also believe in spirits that inhabit the natural world and can be reborn or return to the earth many times.

## Africa

Many Africans south of the Sahara continue traditional religious practices. Because Africa has many ethnic groups, languages, customs, and beliefs, it is not surprising that local religions are just as diverse. Despite the differences, however, most Africans recognize one god whom they consider to be a supreme creator.

## Japan

In Japan there are over 80,000 Shinto shrines, such as the one shown to the left. Shintoism, which goes back to prehistoric times, has no formal doctrine. Believers worship *kami,* which are sacred spirits that take on natural forms such as trees or mountains. Followers also worship ancestors or protectors of families.

## North America

The Navajo religion is distinct in that it must be practiced in a particular geographical area. Navajo people believe that the Creator instructed them never to leave the land between four sacred mountains located in Colorado, New Mexico, and Arizona. Navajo dwellings, called hogans (at right), are sacred and constructed to symbolize their land: the four posts represent the sacred mountains, the floor is Mother Earth, and the dome-like roof is Father Sky.

# Major Religions—→ History and Beliefs

## Buddhism

Buddhism began in India around the sixth century B.C. and today is practiced by over 360 million people throughout Asia. It is based on the teachings of Siddhartha Gautama, known as the Buddha, or Enlightened One. The Buddha taught that to escape the suffering caused by worldly desires, people must follow the Eightfold Path, which prescribes a life of morality, wisdom, and contemplation. The Wheel of Law (at left) is an important Buddhist symbol, representing the endless cycle of life.

## Christianity

Christians believe in one God and that Jesus Christ is the Savior, the Son of God, who was sent to Earth and died on the cross to save humanity. Christians believe that faith in Jesus saves believers from God's penalty for sin and bestows eternal life. The cross remains a very potent symbol of the religion. For Christians, the Bible is the inspired word of God. Christianity began approximately 2,000 years ago. It is practiced by 2 billion people in nearly all parts of the world.

## Confucianism

Although many people consider Confucianism a religion, it is actually a philosophy based on the teachings of Confucius, a Chinese scholar who lived about 500 B.C. He believed that moral character and social responsibility were the way to lead a fulfilling life. Confucianism has been an important influence on Chinese life since its founding, and Confucius is often honored as a spiritual teacher.

# Major Religions——History and Beliefs

### Hinduism

Hinduism is the world's oldest organized religion, starting in India about 1500 B.C. It has influenced and absorbed many other religions. This has led to a wide variety of beliefs and practices among its followers, who number over 825 million and still live principally in India. Although Hindus worship a number of gods, today they primarily worship Siva and Vishnu (shown at left). Siva represents both the destructive and creative forces of the universe. Vishnu is considered the preserver of the universe.

### Islam

The followers of Islam, known as Muslims, believe in one God, *Allah.* They also accept all the prophets of Judaism and Christianity. Muslims follow the practices and teachings of the Quran, which the prophet Muhammad said was revealed to him by Allah beginning in A.D. 610. In 2003, there were about 1.2 billion Muslims, living mainly in Asia and Africa. Islam is often symbolized by a crescent moon, an important element of Muslim rituals, which depend on the lunar calendar.

### Judaism

Jews believe in only one God; in fact, their faith, Judaism, was the first monotheistic religion. Today, about 14.5 million people throughout the world practice Judaism, with most Jews living in Israel and the United States. The main laws and practices of Judaism are contained in the Torah, the first five books of the Hebrew Bible (the *Pentateuch*). The six-pointed star, known as the Star of David (see the Torah mantle at left), has often been a controversial symbol of Judaism, but today it is widely accepted and appears on the Israeli flag.

# *Major Religions* ⟶ *Worship and Celebrations*

### Buddhism

The ultimate goal of Buddhism is to reach nirvana, an enlightened state that frees an individual from the suffering that is found in life. Anyone might reach nirvana, but it is considered most attainable by Buddhist monks. These devout believers usually live in monasteries, leading a disciplined life of poverty, meditation, and study. Those who are not monks pursue enlightenment by making offerings and performing rituals such as walking clockwise around sacred domes, called *stupas*.

### Christianity

Christians gather weekly to worship God and pray. Christians also observe important and joyful holidays such as Easter, which celebrates the resurrection of Jesus Christ. Christians believe that his resurrection was the evidence of God's power over sin and death. Holy Week, the week before Easter, begins with Palm Sunday, which celebrates Jesus' arrival into Jerusalem. Maundy Thursday, or Holy Thursday, commemorates Jesus' last meal with his disciples. Good Friday is a somber day in remembrance of Jesus' death.

### Confucianism

Confucianism does not have a god or clergy and does not concern itself with what could be considered religious issues. It is more of a guide to ethical behavior and good government. Despite this, Confucius is venerated as a spiritual leader, and there are many temples dedicated to him. His teachings were recorded by his students in a book called the *Analects*, which have influenced Chinese people for generations.

# *Major Religions* ⟶ *Worship and Celebrations*

## Hinduism

Hindus believe that after death the soul leaves the body and is reborn in another person, animal, vegetable, or mineral. Where a soul is reborn depends upon its karma, or the accumulated merits or faults of its past lives. One of the ways Hindus increase "good" karma is through rituals such as washing away their sins. The Ganges is considered a sacred river to Hindus, and each year thousands come to bathe in the water to purify themselves.

## Islam

Ramadan is the ninth month of the Muslim calendar, commemorating the time during which Muhammad received the Quran from Allah. During Ramadan, Muslims read from the Quran and fast from dawn until sunset. Fasting helps believers focus on spiritual rather than bodily matters. The daily fast is broken with prayers and a meal called the *iftar*. People celebrate the end of Ramadan with the Feast of the Fast, *Eid-ul-Fitr.*

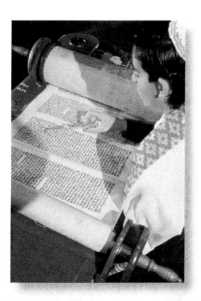

## Judaism

Observant Jews follow many strict laws that guide their daily lives and the ways in which they worship. They recite their prayers standing up and often wear a prayer shawl. Their heads are covered as a sign of respect for God. Every synagogue (place of worship) has a Torah, handwritten on a parchment scroll. During services, the Torah is read to the congregation, and the entire text is read in the course of a year.

**1600–1800**

# 2 Revolution and Enlightenment

## ~ *The Big Ideas* ~

### SECTION 1: The Glorious Revolution

**Throughout history people have struggled for rights.** During the English civil wars and the Glorious Revolution, nobles and wealthy commoners established the principle of representative government.

### SECTION 2: The Enlightenment

**Moral and ethical principles influence the development of political thought.** Enlightenment thinkers believed that human nature was rational and good, and wanted government and society to be based on reason.

### SECTION 3: The American Revolution

**Throughout history people have struggled for rights.** Inspired by a belief in natural rights theory, American colonists rebelled against Britain to found a new nation.

*World History—Modern Times Video* The Chapter 2 video, "Women of the Revolution," *chronicles the impact that women had on the course of the American Revolution.*

**1534**
English Parliament passes Act of Supremacy

**1603**
James I, first Stuart king, ascends English throne

**1687**
Isaac Newton publishes the *Principia*

**1689**
Toleratio Act and English B of Rights

1550    1575    1600    1625    1650    1675

*Henry VIII*

**1643**
Louis XIV becomes king of France

**1690**
Locke publishes *Two Treatises o Government*

*John Locke*

Louis XIV at the French Royal Academy of Sciences

*Denis Diderot*

**1751**
Diderot becomes editor of the *Encyclopedia*

**1788**
The Constitution of the United States is ratified by nine states

| 1700 | 1725 | 1750 | 1775 | 1800 | 1825 |
|------|------|------|------|------|------|

**1748**
Montesquieu publishes *The Spirit of the Laws*

**1776**
American colonies declare independence from Britain

**1792**
Mary Wollstonecraft publishes *A Vindication of the Rights of Woman*

*Mary Wollstonecraft*

**HISTORY Online**

**Chapter Overview**
Visit the *Glencoe World History–Modern Times* Web site at wh.mt.glencoe.com and click on **Chapter 2– Chapter Overview** to preview chapter information.

# Preparing to Read Chapter 2

## Reading Skill  Synthesizing

Careful readers piece together information as they read, remembering information from different places in the text. They spot ideas as they go—sometimes these are found in different sentences, pages, or even sections. When the reader makes sense of these related ideas, he or she is synthesizing.

By the end of a section, the reader can usually understand how the different ideas are related to one another. Sometimes authors include a paragraph at the end of a section that will trigger the connections that you, the reader, have already made. The ending paragraph might also forecast topics covered in upcoming sections to help you prepare for additional connections.

*Look at this concluding paragraph for Section 1 of Chapter 2. See which two historical groups are referred to in connection with the Glorious Revolution.*

### SYNTHESIZING

You synthesize when you connect events and ideas to reveal themes. Synthesizing the influences of the Glorious Revolution, Enlightenment, and the American Revolution demonstrates that rights and liberties are a major theme in this period.

. . . the Glorious Revolution of 1688 had a huge impact. It inspired French thinkers to speak out against absolutism. British colonists . . . applauded Parliament's fight, and saw their own parliaments in the colonies as having the same rights. Fully aware of events in England, the colonists expanded their concept of rights and liberties.

### Apply the Skill

As you read this chapter, keep track of the factors that led to the Glorious Revolution as well as the results. Do the same thing when you read about the Enlightenment and the American Revolution. When you are finished, look at your notes for all three developments. Consider the kind of factors that operated in each and think about how they are related to one another. Can you draw any overall conclusions? If so, you are synthesizing.

# Historical Analysis Skill Understanding Chronology

**Chronological and Spatial Thinking: Standard CS 1** *Students compare the present with the past, evaluating the consequences of past events and decisions and determining the lessons that were learned.*

One skill historians develop is the ability to examine a current idea or event and trace it back to its origins. They are then able to analyze all the consequences that came about. Tracking the influence of an idea through time allows historians to see what ideas and events have been crucial to determining our world today.

Read this selection from John Locke's *Two Treatises of Government,* an Enlightenment document published soon after the Glorious Revolution in England.

> **"Man being born . . . with a title to perfect freedom, and an uncontrolled enjoyment of all the rights and privileges of the law of nature, equally with any other man, or number of men in the world, hath by nature a power, not only to preserve his property, that is, his life, liberty and estate, against the injuries and attempts of other men; but to judge of, and punish the breaches of that law in others, as he is persuaded the offence deserves, even with death itself, in crimes where the heinousness of the fact, in his opinion, requires it."**

Locke wrote that all people were born with certain natural rights of life, liberty, and property. He was reacting to the rule of the Stuart kings in England, who seemed to be acting like absolutist rulers. Locke rejected that kind of rule. His ideas about the natural rights of all individuals influenced political thought in other parts of the world, especially in the American colonies.

## Apply the Skill

How do you think that Locke's ideas have influenced people's perceptions of themselves and society over time? Make a list of the natural rights that you have just by being human. How would you modify the list that Locke originally proposed?

# A Story That Matters

*British Parliament members offering the crown to William and Mary in 1689*

## The Birth of a Son

*I*n early June of 1688, as the late-spring sun warmed the English countryside, the royal family prepared for a birth. Queen Mary, the mother-to-be, was the second wife of King James II. The king, who had come to the throne in 1685, already had two grown daughters, Mary and Anne, by his first wife. Both were Protestant. Mary would succeed her father, but a male heir would take precedence. The problem was that any male heir would be Catholic, for the new queen was Catholic. So too was James II.

As king, James II was head of the Protestant, or Anglican, Church of England. Most of the English people were Protestant, but James wanted to return England to the Catholic fold. His attitude was, as he said, "Know I am your King, I will be obeyed." He even appointed Catholics as generals of the army. Would James then ignore the wishes of his Protestant Parliament? Would he take England back into the Catholic camp?

On June 10, the queen gave birth to a son. Some of the king's enemies argued—wrongly—that the child was not really the king's son but someone else's infant who had been smuggled into the queen's bedroom. Outraged at the thought of a Catholic king, seven leaders of Parliament signed a letter inviting William of Orange, the Dutch leader and husband of James's older daughter, Mary, to come and rule as a Protestant king. William came with an army, James II fled, and England experienced its Glorious Revolution.

### Why It Matters

The Glorious Revolution was an important turning point in English history. When William and Mary accepted the throne from Parliament, they agreed to a declaration of rights. This declaration, soon enacted into law as a Bill of Rights, affirmed Parliament's right to make laws and raise taxes. Parliament was now recognized as a vital part of government, thus laying the foundations for a constitutional monarchy. Years later, with the expansion of the right to vote to all males, England would become a democracy.

**History and You** In the United States, the legislature, or Congress, had power from the very beginning, but not everyone was represented in Congress. Make a chart showing when each of these groups attained representation: all adult males, women, African Americans, and 18-year-olds.

# The Glorious Revolution

## Guide to Reading

### Section Preview
During the English civil war and the Glorious Revolution, nobles and wealthy commoners established the principle of representative government.

### Main Idea
- In the 1600s, absolutist rulers in Europe were asserting that their power came directly from God, but in England Parliament was expanding its political power. (p. 176)
- Civil war broke out in England in 1642 between supporters of the king and the Parliament, and in 1649 Parliament proved victorious. (p. 179)
- England's Glorious Revolution created a constitutional, or limited, monarchy in which the monarch shared power with Parliament. (p. 181)

### Content Vocabulary
divine right of kings, commonwealth, natural rights

### Academic Vocabulary
attribute, restraint, consensus, hypothetical, mutual

### People to Identify
Elizabeth I, Puritans, Charles I, Oliver Cromwell, Charles II, James II, William of Orange, John Locke

### Reading Objectives
1. Identify problems that troubled Europe between 1560 and 1650.
2. Explain how the Glorious Revolution undermined the divine right of kings.

### Reading Strategy
**Summarizing Information** As you read this section, use a chart like the one below to summarize the rulers' positions on religion and power.

| Ruler | Position on issues of religion and power |
|---|---|
| Henry VIII | |
| Elizabeth I | |
| The Stuarts | |
| Oliver Cromwell | |
| William & Mary | |

### Preview of Events

| ♦1600 | ♦1620 | ♦1640 | ♦1660 | ♦1680 | ♦1700 |
|---|---|---|---|---|---|

**1603**
Elizabeth I dies

**1642**
Civil war in England begins

**1649**
Charles I is executed

**1688**
Glorious Revolution

## California Standards in This Section

*Reading this section will help you master these California History–Social Science standards.*

**10.2:** Students compare and contrast the Glorious Revolution of England, the American Revolution, and the French Revolution and their enduring effects worldwide on the political expectations for self-government and individual liberty.

**10.2.1:** Compare the major ideas of philosophers and their effects on the democratic revolutions in England, the United States, France, and Latin America (e.g., John Locke, Charles-Louis Montesquieu, Jean-Jacques Rousseau, Simón Bolívar, Thomas Jefferson, James Madison).

**10.2.2:** List the principles of the Magna Carta, the English Bill of Rights (1689), the American Declaration of Independence (1776), the French Declaration of the Rights of Man and the Citizen (1789), and the U.S. Bill of Rights (1791).

# Background to Revolution

**Main Idea** In the 1600s, absolutist rulers in Europe were asserting that their power came directly from God, but in England Parliament was expanding its political power.

**Reading Connection** Have you ever heard it said that someone acted as if he or she were "above the law"? Read to learn how the English Parliament challenged kings who claimed to be accountable only to God.

At the end of the seventeenth century, English nobles and landowners carried out an important political revolution called the Glorious Revolution. It forced the king to recognize that he must rule in accordance with the laws they approved.

This revolution was one of three great political events in the Western world in this period—the other two were the American Revolution and the French Revolution. Each made a different contribution to the ideas that have shaped the modern world.

## Voices from the Past

Jacques Bossuet, a seventeenth-century French bishop, explained a popular viewpoint:

> 66It is God who establishes kings. They thus act as ministers of God and His lieutenants on earth. It is through them that he rules. This is why we have seen that the royal throne is not the throne of a man, but the throne of God himself. It appears from this that the person of kings is sacred, and to move against them is a crime. Since their power comes from on high, kings . . . should exercise it with fear and restraint as a thing which has come to them from God, and for which God will demand an account.99

Bossuet's ideas about kings became reality during the reign of King Louis XIV.

The Glorious Revolution introduced the principle that the king must bow to the representative body in a nation. The American Revolution clearly spelled out the roles of government institutions and the rights of citizens in a republic. The French Revolution experimented with several forms of government, and went furthest in asserting the principles of liberty

and equality for all people, regardless of their economic status.

The Glorious Revolution was the first of these three great revolutions. During the sixteenth and seventeenth centuries, most European countries were governed by absolute rulers who asserted that their power came directly from God. Monarchs who believed in the **divine right of kings** did not consider themselves accountable to their citizens, but only to God. Individuals who dared to question a monarch's actions could be put to death. They might be considered sinners against an established religion because they had flaunted a king who was so close to God.

The most famous absolutist ruler was Louis XIV, who ruled France from 1643 to 1715. Louis had an unshakeable belief in divine right and saw no need to consult his subjects, not even his great nobles. Louis's reign can best be summed up by a famous saying **attributed** to him: "I am the state."

In England, the political system had developed in the opposite direction. During the Tudor dynasty of Henry VIII and Elizabeth I, the English monarchs discovered that having the support of Parliament—the body of nobles and wealthy commoners who claimed to represent the nation—was an advantage.

By 1700, however, English monarchs not only ruled with Parliament, but had to recognize that Parliament was the ultimate authority if there were disagreements. The idea that a parliament could limit the monarch's power is simple, but it took centuries and violent conflict before it was accepted. In England, the conflict began in the 1640s and was not settled until 1688.

*King Louis XIV of France*

**How the Tudors Ruled** From 1485 until 1603, England was governed by the Tudors, including King Henry VIII, who reigned from 1509 to 1547, and his daughter **Elizabeth I**, who reigned from 1558 to 1603. Both were strong and shrewd rulers who regularly consulted Parliament to get support for their policies. Their practices helped create an expectation that Parliament would be listened to.

Henry and Elizabeth needed Parliament's help in one area especially: religious policies. Conflicts over religion were dividing powerful interests in the kingdom. Henry really created the problem when he demanded that the pope approve a divorce from his first wife, Catherine. Catherine gave birth to several daughters, but Henry wanted a son to succeed him. He wanted the pope to declare his marriage invalid so he could remarry.

The pope refused, not only because declaring a marriage invalid was a rare event, but because Catherine's royal family in Spain were strong papal supporters. Henry finally decided to declare himself the head of the church in England. English archbishops and bishops were appalled, but Henry ignored them all—the pope, English church courts, and the advice of great nobles. He had Parliament pass the Act of Supremacy in 1534. The king was declared "the only supreme head on earth of the Church of England."

Why did Parliament agree? First, the king was still the most powerful authority in the kingdom. Second, the king gave many members in Parliament a good reason to support him. Church lands that were seized were sold to them. No family that had been enriched with land would ever want the Catholic Church reestablished in England.

Henry's church, the Anglican Church, was the product of a political struggle. By Elizabeth's reign, conflict over religious doctrine was more intense because the Reformation had spread to England. The established Anglican religion made England a Protestant power. England's rivals for world power, Spain and France, were Catholic. Thus England became firmly committed to Protestantism.

At home, Elizabeth moved to solve religious conflicts made worse by her half sister, Mary, a devout woman. Mary had passed laws to favor Catholicism during her five-year reign. Mary wanted to make England Catholic again and persecuted many people.

Elizabeth repealed these laws when she took the throne. Elizabeth wanted a national Anglican church because it gave the monarch more power. She did not want to upset Catholics too much, however—that might bring on bloody religious wars like those in France and the German states.

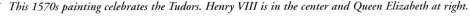

▼ *This 1570s painting celebrates the Tudors. Henry VIII is in the center and Queen Elizabeth at right.*

Her solution was to support a moderate Protestantism. In many ways, the Anglican Church still *was* very Catholic: The prayers were not much different, the services looked almost the same, and priests wore similar vestments.

As the Reformation intensified, Elizabeth's moderation was unacceptable to fervent Protestants. Puritans, especially, were horrified by Anglican services that looked so Catholic. **Puritans** were Calvinists who wanted to purify the Anglican Church. They thought that individual worshippers should focus on spiritual things at church, not indulge their senses with organ music, stained glass, and incense.

Equally important, the Puritans wanted a congregation to be independent of the government and of bishops who might be corrupted by their lust for power. If congregations elected their own ministers, they would be more godly. These ideas challenged the queen's power since the queen as head of the church appointed the bishops.

As the conflict heated up, Puritans in Parliament drafted legislation to change religious policies. In 1576, when one Puritan proposed to change the Anglican prayer book, Elizabeth imprisoned him. Government persecution increased, and many Puritans emigrated to found colonies in New England. There Puritanism made a significant contribution to how future generations of Americans felt about the relation between state and church.

**The Stuarts and Divine Right** The Tudor dynasty ended in 1603 because Elizabeth had no heir. Eliza-beth's cousin, the Stuart king of Scotland, then became James I of England.

The problems between Parliament and the monarch began when the Stuarts came to the English throne. The Stuarts did not understand how the Tudors had ruled. The Stuarts believed in the divine right of kings and wanted to be absolutist rulers like the glorious kings of France. The English Parliament knew a very different tradition.

Conflicts began under James I and intensified during the reign of his son, **Charles I.** Both kings looked to Louis XIV as their example. They believed they should be able to operate without any **restraint** from Parliament—to spend money as they wanted, to build fine buildings, or make alliances abroad if they felt like it.

Parliament was outraged. In 1628, Parliament passed a petition that said the king could not impose taxes without its consent. At first, Charles I accepted this petition, but later he realized that it restricted his freedom far too much. He retaliated the next year by not allowing Parliament to meet at all. Some members of Parliament were imprisoned. Others arrived at Parliament only to find that the doors had been bolted shut. They remained locked from 1629 until 1640. During this period—known as the Eleven Years' Tyranny—Charles ruled without Parliament.

**Reading Check** **Contrasting** How did the Stuarts' view of Parliament differ from that of the Tudors?

**History** *through Art*

In this 1861 work by Ferdinand Piloty, Queen Elizabeth I is shown rallying troops against Spain, England's traditional enemy. Why does the painting support national feeling?

*Cromwell Opening the Coffin of Charles I,* 1831
French artist Paul Delaroche was famous for this painting on an English history theme. If this event actually occurred, do you think the painting would realistically capture Cromwell's attitude toward the executed king? Why or why not?

# Civil War and Aftermath

**Main Idea** Civil war broke out in England in 1642 between supporters of the king and the Parliament, and in 1649 Parliament proved victorious.

**Reading Connection** If you felt a political leader was acting against the law, what would you do to show your opposition? Read to learn how English leaders expressed their opposition to Charles I.

The English Parliament was very important to governing the nation. From every county, the lords and wealthy landowners and townspeople traveled to London to sit in the House of Lords and the House of Commons. These men were not simply wealthy, but actively involved in serving as a network of officials, sheriffs, and judges in their counties. If a king wanted to govern without Parliament's support, he would have had to do it by military force.

In 1642 a civil war, known as the English Revolution, broke out between supporters of the king and supporters of Parliament. The king's supporters were called Cavaliers or Royalists. Parliament's supporters were called Roundheads because they disapproved of long fashionable curls and cut their hair short.

Parliament won largely because of the New Model Army of **Oliver Cromwell**, a military genius who knew how to use new tactics and discipline. Like their leader, the soldiers were zealous Puritans who were fighting for their religion. In Cromwell's words, "This is none other but the hand of God, and to Him alone belongs the glory."

The victorious forces lost no time in taking control. Cromwell concluded that Charles I could not be trusted and must be put to death. When Parliament hesitated, Cromwell purged Parliament of anyone who disagreed with him.

What was left—the 50 to 60 members of the "Rump Parliament"—had Charles I executed on January 30, 1649. The beheading of the king divided families and horrified much of Europe, especially members of the ruling classes. One writer recounted that "a man in a [mask] . . . held up to the spectators the head, streaming with blood, and cried aloud, 'This is the head of a traitor.'" Others saw Charles as a martyr. To this day, the British commemorate the anniversary of his death by carrying wreaths to his statue in London.

▲ *Cromwell is depicted dismissing Parliament in 1653, when he began his military dictatorship.*

**Cromwell's Puritan Commonwealth** Following Charles's execution, Parliament abolished the monarchy and the House of Lords and declared England a republic, or **commonwealth**.

Cromwell found it difficult to work with the Rump Parliament and finally dispersed it by force in 1653. As the members of Parliament departed, he shouted, "It is you that have forced me to do this, for I have sought the Lord night and day that He would slay me rather than put upon me the doing of this work." After eliminating both Parliament and the king, Cromwell set up a military dictatorship.

Under Cromwell's puritanical rule, the English had to give up going to the theater and most Sunday entertainment. The Puritans wanted a godly society. Used to a freer society, the English people became dissatisfied. When Cromwell died, his son was unable to maintain Cromwell's system.

**The Restoration** Soon after Cromwell's death, Parliament restored the Stuart heir to the English throne—**Charles II.** Most people were relieved to be done with Puritanism and dictatorship. Parliament had not forgotten, however, that the Stuarts had a tendency toward absolutism and got certain agreements that Charles II would respect its power.

England's time of troubles seemed at an end for a while, but Charles II was sympathetic to Catholicism.

Fears of Catholicism surfaced again. If Catholicism were restored, prominent Protestants would lose land and influence. The heir to the throne, Charles's brother James, did not hide the fact that he was Catholic.

To counter any danger, Parliament introduced the Exclusion Bill to bar James from the throne if he professed his Catholicism. This bill is famous because it created two political groups, later called parties: the Whigs, who did not want a Catholic on the throne; and the Tories, who wanted to follow the lawful succession to the throne.

To foil the Exclusion Bill, Charles dismissed Parliament in 1681. He died in 1685 and **James II,** a devout Catholic, succeeded him. Once again, religion was a cause of conflict with Parliament. James began favoring Catholics for high positions in the government, army, navy, and universities.

Parliament was unhappy, but they did not yet rebel. James was old, and they hoped that things would improve when one of his daughters, Mary or Anne, succeeded. Both girls had been born to his first wife and had been raised Protestant. In 1688, however, James had a son by his second wife, a Catholic. The possibility of a Catholic monarchy and a restored Catholic Church loomed large.

✔**Reading Check** **Explaining** What was the basis for the English civil war that broke out in 1642?

# Glorious Revolution and Limited Monarchy

**Main Idea** England's Glorious Revolution created a constitutional, or limited, monarchy in which the monarch shared power with Parliament.

**Reading Connection** Think of a recent conflict dividing your country and how it was settled. Read how English lords brought about a "bloodless revolution" in 1688.

By 1688, England had seen decades of struggle over what institution should have the final authority in the kingdom. It had also seen decades of struggle over religion. England's lords and landowners reached a quiet **consensus**. They did not want a king to dictate to them, and they did not want a Catholic king.

A coup was under way. A group of English noblemen invited the Dutch leader, **William of Orange**, who was married to James's Protestant daughter Mary, to come to England. William and Mary raised an army and in 1688 arrived without much opposition in England. James and his wife and infant son fled to France. With almost no bloodshed, England had undergone a "Glorious Revolution."

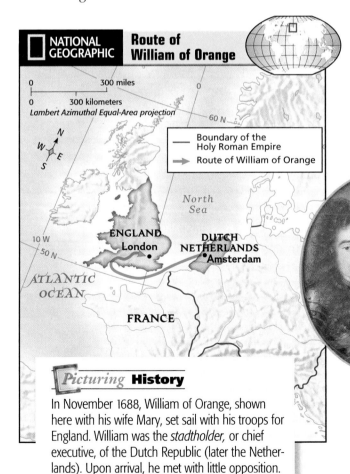

## Route of William of Orange

NATIONAL GEOGRAPHIC

0    300 miles
0    300 kilometers
Lambert Azimuthal Equal-Area projection

60 N

— Boundary of the Holy Roman Empire
→ Route of William of Orange

North Sea

ENGLAND
London

DUTCH NETHERLANDS
Amsterdam

10 W

50 N

ATLANTIC OCEAN

FRANCE

### Picturing History

In November 1688, William of Orange, shown here with his wife Mary, set sail with his troops for England. William was the *stadtholder*, or chief executive, of the Dutch Republic (later the Netherlands). Upon arrival, he met with little opposition.

Now the issue was who would be monarch. In January 1689, Parliament offered the throne to William and Mary if they would accept the Bill of Rights. It set forth Parliament's right to make laws and levy taxes. It also stated that standing armies could be raised only with Parliament's consent. The Bill of Rights also confirmed citizens' right to keep arms and have a jury trial.

The Bill of Rights helped create a system of government based on law and a freely elected Parliament. Many of its provisions were used a century later as a foundation for the American Bill of Rights.

The same year, Parliament also passed the Toleration Act of 1689. It granted Puritans, but not Catholics, the right to free public worship. Very few English citizens were ever again persecuted because of religion. England was one of the most tolerant nations in Europe, and many people persecuted elsewhere sought refuge there.

By deposing one king and establishing another, Parliament had destroyed the divine-right theory of kingship. William, after all, was king by the grace of Parliament, not the grace of God. Parliament also asserted its right to be part of the government.

**John Locke** The English struggles of the 1600s inspired **John Locke** to write *Two Treatises of Government*, published in 1690. This work criticized absolutism and defended the Glorious Revolution. Locke described how governments are formed, and what justifies them. He believed that before society was organized, human beings lived in a state of equality and freedom. In this state of nature, humans had certain **natural rights**—rights they were born with.

In the real world, Locke felt there were problems in this **hypothetical** idea of nature. People could not protect their rights very well. That is why they agreed to contract with a government to protect their rights.

Under this contract, the people and the government had **mutual** obligations. Government would protect the rights of the people, and the people would act reasonably toward government. If a government broke the contract by not protecting an individual's natural rights, then people were justified in rebelling and forming a new government.

To Locke, "people" meant the landholding elites, not common people who did not own land. Even though Locke did not advocate democracy, his ideas promoted democracy. In the American and French Revolutions, Locke's arguments were used to demand the rule of law and individual rights. 📖 (*See page 771 to read an excerpt from Locke's* Two Treatises of Government *in the Primary Sources Library.*)

The Glorious Revolution, the American Revolution, and the French Revolution all utilized natural rights theory. The Glorious Revolution was different in two ways from the two later revolutions, however. First, it was not violent—later historians have termed it the "bloodless revolution," although there had been much violence in the 1640s. Second, the Glorious Revolution was different because it was not the middle class and lower class who were demanding rights, but nobles and wealthy members of Parliament.

Still, the Glorious Revolution of 1688 had a huge impact. It inspired French thinkers to speak out against absolutism. British colonists also took an important lesson from the Glorious Revolution. They applauded Parliament's fight and saw their own parliaments in the colonies as having the same rights. Fully aware of events in England, the colonists expanded their concept of rights and liberties.

✔**Reading Check** **Describing** Trace the events of the late 1680s that led to the English Bill of Rights.

▲ *Enlightenment thinker John Locke (shown in oval) was a major influence on America's founders Benjamin Franklin, John Adams, and Thomas Jefferson.*

**HISTORY** *Online* **Study Central**

For help with the concepts in this section of *Glencoe World History–Modern Times,* go to wh.mt.glencoe.com and click on **Study Central**.

# SECTION 1 ASSESSMENT

### Checking for Understanding

1. **Vocabulary** Define: divine right of kings, attribute, restraint, commonwealth, consensus, natural rights, hypothetical, mutual.

2. **People** Identify: Elizabeth I, Puritans, Charles I, Oliver Cromwell, Charles II, James II, William of Orange, John Locke.

### Reviewing Big Ideas

3. **Explain** why Oliver Cromwell first purged Parliament and then declared a military dictatorship.

### Critical Thinking

4. **Historical Analysis** **Connecting Events** Summarize the reasons behind the formation of the Church of England. **CA HI 1**

5. **Compare and Contrast** the Catholic and Anglican Churches and explain why the Puritans rejected both of them.

### Analyzing Visuals

6. **Examine** the cameo of William and Mary shown on page 181. How does this painting compare to portraits of other rulers, such as the one of Louis XIV on page 176? How is the purpose of this painting different from the purpose of other royal portraits?

### Writing About History

7. **Persuasive Writing** Compose a letter to Oliver Cromwell. Using examples from history, attempt to convince him that winning the support of the English people is important and give him specific suggestions of how to do it. **CA 10WA2.4c**

# The Enlightenment

## Section Preview

Enlightenment thinkers, or philosophes, believed that human nature was rational and good, and wanted government and society to be based on reason.

### Main Idea

• The philosophes believed that they could copy the rational methods of scientists to eliminate unjust laws and create a better society. (p. 184)

• The philosophes' belief in logic and reason promoted the beginnings of the social sciences, such as economics and political science. (p. 187)

• Enlightenment ideas spread in France through salons and in the Western world through an expansion of the reading public. (p. 188)

### Content Vocabulary

philosophe, deism, separation of powers, social contract, laissez-faire, salon

### Academic Vocabulary

evidence, affect, concept

### People to Identify

Isaac Newton, Voltaire, Montesquieu, Rousseau, Adam Smith, Cesare Beccaria, Denis Diderot, Mary Wollstonecraft

### Places to Locate

Paris, London

### Reading Objectives

1. Define the central ideas of the Enlightenment.
2. Explain the role that religion played during the Enlightenment.

### Reading Strategy

**Summarizing Information** Use a diagram like the one below to list main ideas of the Enlightenment.

Major Ideas of the Enlightenment

## Preview of Events

♦1700　　♦1715　　♦1730　　♦1745　　♦1760　　♦1775　　♦1790

**1702**
The first daily newspaper is published in London

**1748**
Baron de Montesquieu publishes *The Spirit of the Laws*

**1762**
Rousseau publishes *The Social Contract*

**1763**
Voltaire writes his *Treatise on Toleration*

**1776**
Adam Smith publishes *The Wealth of Nations*

## California Standards in This Section

*Reading this section will help you master these California History–Social Science standards.*

**10.2:** Students compare and contrast the Glorious Revolution of England, the American Revolution, and the French Revolution and their enduring effects worldwide on the political expectations for self-government and individual liberty.

**10.2.1:** Compare the major ideas of philosophers and their effects on the democratic revolutions in England, the United States, France, and Latin America (e.g., John Locke, Charles-Louis Montesquieu, Jean-Jacques Rousseau, Simón Bolívar, Thomas Jefferson, James Madison).

**10.2.2:** List the principles of the Magna Carta, the English Bill of Rights (1689), the American Declaration of Independence (1776), the French Declaration of the Rights of Man and the Citizen (1789), and the U.S. Bill of Rights (1791).

**10.2.3:** Understand the unique character of the American Revolution, its spread to other parts of the world, and its continuing significance to other nations.

# The Enlightenment and the Philosophes

**Main Idea** The philosophes believed that they could copy the rational methods of scientists to eliminate unjust laws and create a better society.

**Reading Connection** Think of a time when you experienced an injustice. Read to learn how imprisonment and forced exile affected the ideas of Voltaire.

The Enlightenment was an intellectual movement that began in France. Its leaders were called **philosophes** (FEE•luh•ZAWFS). They were not philosophers in the strict sense of the term, but writers, professors, journalists, economists, and social reformers. They came chiefly from the nobility and the middle class.

## Voices from the Past

The French intellectual Voltaire attacked religious intolerance in *The Ignorant Philosopher*:

❝I say, there is scarce any city or borough in Europe, where blood has not been spilled for religious quarrels; I say, that the human species has been perceptibly diminished, because women and girls were massacred as well as men. I say that Europe would have a third larger population if there had been no theological disputes. In fine, I say, that so far from forgetting these abominable times, we should frequently take a view of them, to inspire an eternal horror for them. . . . It is for our age to make amends by toleration, for this long collection of crimes, which has taken place through the lack of toleration during sixteen barbarous centuries.❞

Religious toleration was one of the major themes of the Enlightenment.

These philosophes were amazed by the Scientific Revolution and saw that reason had enabled scientists to discover the secrets of the universe. Reason became their guide and motto. If reason was applied to politics and government, it would be a better, more just society for all.

Although the Enlightenment began in France, two of its heroes were Englishmen, **Isaac Newton** and John Locke. Newton's discoveries in math and astronomy showed **evidence** that the physical universe followed regular natural laws. The philosophes wanted to be like Newton and find the natural laws for human society.

John Locke was another powerful influence in the Enlightenment. He had analyzed how a government should rule in *Two Treatises of Government*, but in other essays he wrote about how people think and learn. Locke said that when infants were born, their minds were blank—they were a tabula rasa, or blank slate, on which anything could be written. Locke argued that people learned everything from their senses and experiences.

From Locke, Enlightenment thinkers concluded that if a more rational environment was created in society, then people would be rational and good. One writer said that the philosophe is one who "applies himself to the study of society with the purpose of making his kind better and happier."

The Enlightenment spanned almost a century. Centered in **Paris,** it was an international movement which evolved over time. For this reason, one can find disagreements on certain issues, but all of the philosophes focused on the themes of reason, natural law, hope, and progress.

▼ *Isaac Newton analyzing light rays*

**Voltaire** Of all the great names in the Enlightenment, the greatest was François-Marie Arouet, known simply as **Voltaire**. A Parisian, Voltaire came from a prosperous middle-class family. He wrote an almost endless stream of pamphlets, novels, plays, letters, essays, and histories, which brought him both fame and wealth.

In 1726, when he was 32, Voltaire clashed with a nobleman in France, who resented an insult Voltaire had directed at him. The nobleman had powerful connections and succeeded in having Voltaire imprisoned. Voltaire was released only when he agreed to leave France and go into exile in England.

This experience **affected** Voltaire deeply. After his release from prison, he often spoke out against censorship and unjust laws. In the three years he spent in England, he saw a society that he felt was superior. As a man of ideas, he liked the freer air in England—for the most part, men and women could express their opinions openly. On his return to France, he published a work that criticized French institutions as compared to the English. The French king banned the book immediately.

Voltaire was a strong opponent of the Catholic Church. His opposition had a lot to do with the fact that the Church in France supported absolutism. Voltaire opposed traditional Christianity, too, however, because he believed it did not encourage people to think rationally. He mocked what he termed superstition wherever he saw it and campaigned for religious toleration. His *Treatise on Toleration* of 1763 reminded governments that "all men are brothers under God."

Voltaire himself was a deist. **Deism** is based on reason and natural law. The Supreme Being is not a personal God, but an impersonal being. Deists imagined that God had created a world-machine that was perfect. Once set in motion, the universe ran according to natural laws, without the need for constant supervision or occasional miracles.

**Montesquieu** Charles-Louis de Secondat, the Baron de **Montesquieu**, came from the French nobility. His most famous work, *The Spirit of the Laws*, was published in 1748. Montesquieu used the scientific method to make a close study of governments. In a way, Montesquieu was the first political scientist.

Montesquieu identified three basic kinds of governments: (1) republics, suitable for small states; (2) despotism, appropriate for large states; and (3) monarchies, ideal for moderate-size states. He used England as an example of a monarchy.

▲ *A London coffeehouse, a typical setting for the discussion of politics and new ideas*

Montesquieu believed that England's government had three branches: the executive (the monarch), the legislative (Parliament), and the judicial (the courts of law). He thought that the English government functioned through a **separation of powers** in which the executive, legislative, and judiciary placed limits and controls on each other. By preventing one group from having too much power, and by creating a system of checks and balances, the English had created the most freedom and security for the nation.

Montesquieu was actually inaccurate in his analysis of English government. Power was not strictly separated as he claimed, but distributed in a much more complex way. As just one example, the king had many connections to Parliament through noble families. Yet essentially Montesquieu was right to say that power was balanced in the English system.

It was in America that Montesquieu's **concept** of separation of powers made a contribution. Montesquieu's work was translated into English, and Americans read it. They followed his ideas about separation of powers, and checks and balances, very closely in the United States Constitution.

**Rousseau** By the late 1760s, a new generation of philosophes had come to maturity. Most famous of these talented writers and thinkers was Jean-Jacques **Rousseau** (ru•SOH). Rousseau was very different from Voltaire, the sophisticated man of Paris, or from Montesquieu, an aristocrat.

*Jean-Jacques Rousseau*

**Geography** *Skills*

The intellectuals of the Enlightenment created a movement that influenced the entire Western world.

1. **Interpreting Maps** Examine the key for the map. What kind of information does it contain?

2. **Applying Geography Skills** Pose and answer two questions about the geographic distributions shown on the map. Create a thematic chart that represents the same information.

---

Rousseau was born into a poor middle-class family in Switzerland. As a young man, he wandered through France and Italy, making a living by holding odd jobs for low pay. Eventually he made his way to Paris, where he wrote several essays. His writings attracted the attention of Voltaire and other philosophes, but Rousseau was always the outsider. He did not like city life and often withdrew to be alone for long periods.

In *Discourse on the Origins of the Inequality of Mankind*, Rousseau argued that people had adopted laws and government to preserve their property. In doing so, they had become enslaved by government. What should people do to regain their freedom?

In his famous work *The Social Contract*, published in 1762, Rousseau presented a strikingly new idea about society. John Locke had written about a contract between people and the government. Rousseau's **social contract** was something different, an agreement among a whole society that it would be governed by the general will. Individuals who wanted to follow their own self-interests must be forced to abide by the general will. "This means nothing less than that [they] will be forced to be free," said Rousseau. In Rousseau's theory, the general will represents what is best for the entire community.

Another important work by Rousseau is *Emile*. Written in the form of a novel, Emile discusses the education of "the natural man." Rousseau argued that education should foster, and not restrict, children's natural instincts.

Most Enlightenment thinkers talked and wrote constantly about reason. Rousseau believed that emotion held another kind of truth and was also important to human development. His goal was a balance between heart and mind, between emotion and reason.

Rousseau's ideas about women were not very advanced. Women were "naturally" different from men: "To fulfill her functions, . . . [a woman] needs a soft life. . . . How much care and tenderness does she need to hold her family together." He thought women should learn obedience and nurturing skills so that they could care for their husbands and children. He once wrote that he preferred the traditional woman. "I would a thousand times have a homely girl, simply brought up than a learned lady and a wit who would make a literary circle of my house." Not everyone, however, agreed with Rousseau.

✓ **Reading Check** **Comparing** What were the major contributions of the Enlightenment thinkers?

# Toward a New Social Science

**Main Idea** The philosophes' belief in logic and reason promoted the beginnings of the social sciences, such as economics and political science.

**Reading Connection** Have you heard of studies that influence how politicians draft new laws? Read to learn about the time when studies in the social sciences first began to influence government.

The philosophes believed that scientific methods could be used to study society. In time, this conviction led to new fields of study, the social sciences. Economics and political science were two of the first social sciences to develop.

The founders of the modern social science of economics were the Physiocrats in France and the philosopher Adam Smith in Scotland.

The Physiocrats argued that if individuals were free to pursue their economic self-interest, everyone would be better off in the end. Believing in this principle, the Physiocrats argued that the state should not interrupt the free play of natural economic forces by imposing government regulations. The state should leave the economy alone.

This doctrine became known by its French name, **laissez-faire** (LEH•SAY FEHR), meaning "to let (people) do (what they want)." The best statement of laissez-faire was made in 1776 by **Adam Smith** in his famous work *The Wealth of Nations.* Like the Physiocrats, Smith believed that the state should not interfere in the economy. Instead, Smith argued that the law of supply and demand would naturally regulate the economy for everyone's best interest.

In fact, Smith argued that the government had only three very basic roles: protecting society from invasion (the army); keeping up certain public works, such as roads and canals, that private individuals could not afford; and defending citizens from injustice (the police).

The power of the Enlightenment ideas can be seen in writings on another aspect of society: crime and punishment. By the eighteenth century, most European states had developed a system of courts to formally sentence criminals. Punishments were often cruel. Governments felt extreme punishments were necessary to deter crime because their police forces were weak and thus unable to capture criminals.

Following the thinking of the philosophes, one man came up with different conclusions. **Cesare Beccaria** proposed a new approach to justice in *On Crimes and Punishments,* written in 1764. Beccaria argued that brutal punishments did not stop others from turning to crime. Moreover, it set an example of barbarism: "Is it not absurd, that the laws, which punish murder, should, in order to prevent murder, publicly commit murder themselves?"

✓**Reading Check** **Explaining** What is the concept of laissez-faire?

## People In History

### Mary Wollstonecraft
**1759–1797—English writer**

**M**ary Wollstonecraft is considered by many to be the founder of the European and American movements for women's rights. Wollstonecraft was largely self-educated. For a while, she earned a living as a governess but soon moved to a writing career and worked for a magazine publisher.

All along, Wollstonecraft continued to develop her ideas on education and women's rights. She wrote in 1792: "Make women rational creatures, and free citizens, and they will quickly become good wives; that is—if men do not neglect the duties of husbands and fathers!"

Mary Wollstonecraft married the philosopher William Godwin in 1797. She died shortly after the birth of their daughter, Mary Wollstonecraft Godwin Shelley, who wrote the famous novel *Frankenstein.*

# Spread of the Enlightenment

**Main Idea** Enlightenment ideas spread in France through salons and in the Western world through an expansion of the reading public.

**Reading Connection** Think about the careers open to American women today. Read to learn how the Enlightenment first promoted ideas about women's rights.

It was wealthy elites who experienced the Enlightenment to the fullest. However, the movement also spread to literate people in urban areas of Europe.

**Salons and the Growth of Reading** In the eighteenth century, many more books began to be published. In 1750, French publishers came out with about 300 titles, and by 1780, that number had climbed to about 1,600. Publishers were aiming at a new market, too, new readers among the middle class, which included women and artisans and even a few workers in the cities.

Between 1751 and 1772, a French philosophe named **Denis Diderot** published a 28-volume *Encyclopedia, or Classified Dictionary of the Sciences, Arts,*

**HISTORY Online**

**Web Activity** Visit the *Glencoe World History—Modern Times* Web site at **wh.mt.glencoe.com** and click on **Chapter 2–Student Web Activity** to learn more about the arts in the 1700s.

*and Trades.* The *Encyclopedia* became a major weapon in the philosophes' crusade against the old French society, attacking superstition and calling for political changes. Many copies were sold, spreading Enlightenment ideas. Magazines also changed ideas. In Great Britain, an important center for the new magazines, 25 periodicals were published in 1700, 103 in 1760, and 158 in 1780. Along with magazines came daily newspapers. The first was printed in **London** in 1702. Newspapers were relatively cheap and were even provided free in many coffeehouses.

Enlightenment ideas also spread through **salons.** Salons were the elegant drawing rooms of the wealthy upper class's great urban houses. Guests gathered in them to discuss ideas. Salons brought writers and artists together with aristocrats and wealthy middle-class people. This mixing of the classes was itself a sign of progress.

# CONNECTIONS Past To Present

## Magazines, Then and Now

Bookstores and newsstands carry thousands of magazines that appeal to an enormous variety of interests. We can find magazines on fishing, car racing, fashion, politics, television, furniture making, tourism, wrestling, and a host of other subjects.

The first magazines in Europe were a product of a growing reading public in the seventeenth and eighteenth centuries, especially among the middle classes. The first magazine was published in Germany in 1633. It contained poems and articles on religion, the chief interest of its editor, Johann Rist.

Many early magazines had serious goals. Joseph Addison and Richard Steele's *Spectator,* begun in 1711, aimed to "bring Philosophy out of the closets and libraries, schools and colleges, to dwell in clubs and assemblies, at tea-tables and coffeehouses."

Some publishers began to broaden the appeal of their magazines. Some attracted women readers. *Ladies' Mercury,* published in Britain, provided advice on marriage, sewing patterns, and gossip. Its success inspired a host of similar magazines.

▲ *Argentine magazine stand*

## Comparing Past and Present

Pretend you are an eighteenth-century magazine editor assigned to write an article for the next edition. Choose a person or an event discussed in Chapter 2 to be the subject of your article (use outside resources if necessary). You could also select one Enlightenment idea and present it to your readers.

**Women and the Enlightenment** Salons were always hosted by women. In this role, women found themselves in a position to sway political opinion and influence literary and artistic taste. At her fashionable home in Paris, for example, Marie-Thérèse de Geoffrin, the wife of a wealthy merchant, held gatherings that became the talk of France and of all Europe. Distinguished foreigners, including a future king of Sweden and a future king of Poland, competed to receive invitations.

For centuries, male intellectuals had argued that women were naturally inferior to men and so it was necessary for men to dominate women. By the time of the Enlightenment, however, female thinkers did not find that these ideas met the test of reason. The English writer **Mary Wollstonecraft** made the strongest statement for the rights of women. Many see her as the original founder of the movement for women's rights.

In *A Vindication of the Rights of Woman,* Wollstonecraft identified two problems with how some Enlightenment thinkers viewed women. She asked why the same people who argued that women must obey men without question also said that an absolutist government was wrong.

Wollstonecraft also argued that the Enlightenment was based on an ideal of reason in all human beings. Because women have reason, they too are entitled to natural rights. Women, Wollstonecraft declared, should have equal rights in education, as well as in economic and political life.

**The Enlightenment in America** The Enlightenment had a powerful effect on colonists in America. The British colonies were still part of European society in many ways, and educated men and women read the same books and journals as the elites of Europe—at least as soon as they could get them for their libraries or borrow them.

Thomas Jefferson, who drafted the Declaration of Independence, first encountered the writings of Enlightenment thinkers when he was a college student in the early 1760s. He and James Madison, another influential American leader, were both attracted to the ideas of John Locke.

One of the most obvious examples of Locke's influence can be seen in the Declaration of Independence. Numerous phrases in the Declaration bear a resemblance to statements in Locke's *Two Treatises of Government.* Perhaps Locke had the most impact through his argument that citizens were justified in rebelling against a government that causes harm to those it governs. Americans were certain that the British government of King George III had caused them harm, and that they were justified in rebelling.

✓**Reading Check** **Evaluating** How did Mary Wollstonecraft use the Enlightenment ideal of reason?

**HISTORY Online** **Study Central**

For help with the concepts in this section of *Glencoe World History–Modern Times,* go to **wh.mt.glencoe.com** and click on **Study Central.**

# SECTION 2 ASSESSMENT

### Checking for Understanding

1. **Vocabulary** Define: philosophe, evidence, affect, deism, separation of powers, concept, social contract, laissez-faire, salon.

2. **People** Identify: Isaac Newton, Voltaire, Montesquieu, Rousseau, Adam Smith, Cesare Beccaria, Denis Diderot, Mary Wollstonecraft.

3. **Places** Locate: Paris, London.

### Reviewing Big Ideas

4. **Explain** the influence of Isaac Newton and John Locke on Enlightenment thinkers.

### Critical Thinking

5. **Historical Analysis** **Connecting Ideas** What did Rousseau mean when he stated that if any individual wants to pursue his own self-interest at the expense of the common good, "He will be forced to be free"? **CA HI 1**

6. **Summarizing Information** Use a diagram like the one below to identify factors that helped spread Enlightenment ideas throughout Europe.

> Factors that Spread Enlightenment

### Analyzing Visuals

7. **Describe** the scene in the painting on page 182, which portrays Thomas Jefferson, Benjamin Franklin, and John Adams drafting the Declaration of Independence. Does the scene suggest the seriousness of what they were doing?

## Writing About History

8. **Persuasive Writing** Mary Wollstonecraft argued that women are entitled to the same rights as men. In an essay, present an argument for today's audience on the same issue, using evidence and logic. **CA 10WA2.4a,c**

# The American Revolution

## Section Preview

Inspired by a belief in natural rights theory, American colonists rebelled against Britain to found a new nation.

**Main Idea**

- In theory, the colonies were governed by the British, but in practice colonial legislatures often acted independently. (p. 191)
- After the French and Indian War, the British angered colonists by imposing new taxes to help pay for the war. (p. 191)
- Drawing on natural rights theory and the ideas of John Locke, the Declaration of Independence declared the colonies to be independent of the British Crown. (p. 192)

- Americans won their independence from Britain in 1783 and later ratified a constitution that clearly spelled out the rights of individuals and the limits of government. (p. 194)
- Americans struggled to find a balance between individual freedom and a unified central government. (p. 196)

## Content Vocabulary

colony, Stamp Act, Declaration of Independence, Articles of Confederation, federal system, Bill of Rights

## Academic Vocabulary

tension, correspondence, amendments, assembly

## People to Identify

William Pitt the Elder, King George III, George Washington, Thomas Jefferson

## Places to Locate

Yorktown

## Reading Objectives

1. Identify the causes of the American Revolution.
2. Describe the short-term and long-term impact of the American Revolution.

## Reading Strategy

**Summarizing Information** Use a chart like the one below to identify key aspects of the government created by the American colonists.

New American Government

### Preview of Events

| ◆1715 | ◆1730 | ◆1745 | ◆1760 | ◆1775 | ◆1790 |
|---|---|---|---|---|---|

**1721**
Robert Walpole becomes cabinet head in Britain

**1757**
William Pitt the Elder becomes cabinet head

**1776**
American Revolution begins

**1783**
Treaty of Paris recognizes American independence

## California Standards in This Section

*Reading this section will help you master these California History–Social Science standards.*

**10.1.3:** Consider the influence of the U.S. Constitution on political systems in the contemporary world.

**10.2:** Students compare and contrast the Glorious Revolution of England, the American Revolution, and the French Revolution and their enduring effects worldwide on the political expectations for self-government and individual liberty.

**10.2.2:** List the principles of the Magna Carta, the English Bill of Rights (1689), the American Declaration of Independence (1776), the French Declaration of the Rights of Man and the Citizen (1789), and the U.S. Bill of Rights (1791).

**10.2.3:** Understand the unique character of the American Revolution, its spread to other parts of the world, and its continuing significance to other nations.

# How the Colonies Learned Self-Government

**Main Idea** In theory, the colonies were governed by the British, but in practice colonial legislatures often acted independently.

**Reading Connection** What issues might make you want to declare independence from your parents, teachers, and friends? Read to discover why colonists took their first steps to political independence.

By 1750, more than one million people lived in the thirteen British **colonies** in North America. Located on the eastern coast of the present United States, they attracted many settlers and became prosperous.

## Voices from the Past

On July 2, 1776, the Second Continental Congress adopted a resolution declaring the independence of the American colonies. It read:

❝We hold these truths to be self-evident, that all men are created equal, that they are endowed by their Creator with certain unalienable Rights, that among these are Life, Liberty, and the pursuit of Happiness. That to secure these rights, Governments are instituted among Men, deriving their just powers from the consent of the governed. That whenever any Form of Government becomes destructive of these ends, it is the Right of the People to alter or to abolish it and to institute new Government.❞

The ideas of the Enlightenment had clearly made an impact on the colonies in North America. Despite their close ties to their European mother countries, the colonies of Latin America and British North America were developing in ways that sometimes differed significantly from those of Europe.

The colonies were established to supply raw materials to Britain and to be a market for British goods. In theory, the British Board of Trade, and ultimately the Parliament, were in charge of them, but the colonies had set up their own legislatures. For decades, these legislatures operated with little interference from Britain.

Each of the 13 legislatures functioned like a miniature Parliament and made its own laws. White male citizens who owned land elected the representatives. There were also county and local government institutions which passed laws for towns and villages.

✓**Reading Check** **Comparing** How did American and British views of their legislatures differ?

# British and French Rivalry in North America

**Main Idea** After the French and Indian War, the British angered colonists by imposing new taxes to help pay for the war.

**Reading Connection** Think about the various kinds of taxes that may affect your life. Read this section to see how colonists reacted to taxes they felt were unjust.

The French and British colonies in North America were set up differently. French North America, consisting of Canada and Louisiana, was run by the French government as a vast trading area. The French state was unable to get people to move to North America, so its colonies were thinly populated, in contrast to those of Britain.

Between 1756 and 1763, Britain and France fought one another in the Seven Years' War. The American phase of the war is known as the French and Indian War. The British and the French were fighting for control of North America, especially for control of the Ohio River valley. British settlers wanted to expand into this vast area, and French forts stood in their way.

▼ *Thomas Jefferson*

At first, the French, with the help of their Indian allies, scored some victories. British fortunes were revived by **William Pitt the Elder,** Britain's prime minister. Pitt was convinced that the French colonial empire would have to be destroyed for Britain to have its own empire. He used the British navy to defeat the weaker French fleet. The British had the advantage—the French now had a hard time reinforcing their troops in America.

In 1759, British forces defeated the French on the Plains of Abraham, outside Quebec. The French were forced to make peace. By the Treaty of Paris, they transferred Canada and the lands east of the Mississippi to Great Britain. Their ally Spain transferred Spanish Florida to British control. In return, the French gave their Louisiana territory to the Spanish. By 1763, Great Britain had become the world's greatest colonial power.

After achieving victory in the Seven Years' War, British leaders wanted to get new revenues from the colonies. These revenues would be used to cover war costs, as well as to pay for the expenses of maintaining an army to defend the colonies.

In 1765, Parliament imposed the **Stamp Act** on the colonies. This act required that certain printed materials, such as legal documents and newspapers, carry a stamp showing that a tax had been paid to Britain.

Opposition was widespread and often violent, and the act was repealed in 1766. The crisis was over, but the cause of the dispute was not resolved.

✓ **Reading Check** Why did British leaders impose the Stamp Act on colonists, and what response did it elicit?

## The American Revolution

**Main Idea** Drawing on natural rights theory and the ideas of John Locke, the Declaration of Independence declared the colonies to be independent of the British Crown.

**Reading Connection** What comes to mind when you celebrate the Fourth of July? Read to learn how and why the colonists took the bold and risky step of declaring independence.

The **tension** between Great Britain and the colonies had started before the Stamp Act was passed. The British expected the colonies to import mostly British goods. Parliament passed taxes on non-British goods to make them more expensive. To avoid these tariffs, the colonists had been smuggling them. The British then clamped down on smugglers,

▼ *The Battle of Quebec in 1759 was a great British victory over the French in the French and Indian War.*

even searching private homes for illegal goods. The colonists were angry because they thought of themselves as English citizens protected by English laws.

On the same day that Parliament repealed the Stamp Act, it passed the Declaratory Act. The Declaratory Act said that Parliament had the right to tax and make decisions for the colonies "in all cases." New taxes on basic goods were passed. The new taxes—and the undermining of the colonial legislatures—enraged the colonists. "No taxation without representation!" became the rallying cry behind anti-British demonstrations, boycotts, and even destruction of property.

As a result of the colonists' actions, the British sent more troops to the colonies. Clashes between the British soldiers and the colonists grew more volatile. One clash, the Boston Massacre, left five colonists dead and led to the spread of anti-British propaganda. In order to restore the peace and reestablish trade relations, the British repealed all taxes except for the tea tax, and the colonists put an end to boycotts on British goods. However, the push for economic independence was growing stronger.

After two years of relative calm, tension mounted when Parliament passed the Tea Act of 1773. This act allowed the struggling British East India Company to bypass American merchants and sell their tea directly to colonial shopkeepers. This made British tea cheaper than all other tea, gave the British a monopoly, and decreased profits for American merchants.

## The Colonists Unite in Protest

The colonists had had enough. Previously, at Thomas Jefferson's urging, the colonies had formed committees of **correspondence** to allow them to communicate with each other about the British. They used these committees to keep East India Company tea out of America. At Boston Harbor, two ships carrying the tea were forced to turn around and another had its cargo seized. In December 1773, colonists boarded one ship and dumped 342 chests of tea into the harbor, an event that became known as the Boston Tea Party. Despite this radical act, most colonists were still not ready to throw off British rule.

When **King George III** heard about the Boston Tea Party, he ordered Parliament to pass the Coercive Acts to punish Massachusetts and put an end to colonial rebellion. The acts—renamed the Intolerable Acts by the colonists—violated several traditional English rights, including the right to a trial by jury and the right to not be forced to quarter, or house, troops in one's own home.

## The Continental Congresses

To counteract British actions, the colonies organized the First Continental Congress, which met in Philadelphia in September 1774. The mood of many colonists could be summed up by the words of Patrick Henry, who said, "The distinctions between Virginians, Pennsylvanians, New Yorkers, and New Englanders are no more. . . . I am not a Virginian, but an American."

This Continental Congress called for the repeal of the 13 Parliament acts passed since 1763, the boycott of British goods, and the formation of colonial militias. It sent the king a Declaration of Rights and Grievances that stated their loyalty but condemned the Coercive Acts. The delegates agreed to meet again in 1775 if the crisis had not been resolved.

The reaction of King George III and Parliament did not calm the colonists. When colonial militias were formed, the king sent more British troops to the colonies. In the spring of 1775, British troops in Boston were sent to seize the arms and supplies of militias stored in Concord, Massachusetts. On their way, the British ran into colonial militias in Lexington. By the time the British got to Concord, they faced more militias and found that the supplies had been removed. The British were harassed all the way back to Boston, with 99 killed and 174 wounded. News of the fighting spread to other colonies. In Boston, the

▼ *A British cartoonist's image of the Boston Tea Party*

THE BOSTONIANS PAYING THE EXCISE-MAN OR TARRING & FEATHERING
Copied on stone by D.C. Johnston from a print published in London 1774 — Lith of Pendleton Boston 1830

▲ *At the Second Continental Congress in Philadelphia, Patriot leaders called for a Continental army.*

colonial militia began to stream in and soon the British were surrounded.

**The Second Continental Congress** These tensions led to the Second Continental Congress. It met in May 1775 and voted to form an army under the command of **George Washington**. Before this Continental Army could be organized, the British sent more soldiers to suppress the revolt in Boston. The colonial militia discovered the plan and met the British at the Battle of Bunker Hill. Although the colonists' supplies were low, they managed to kill or wound 1,000 British soldiers. The result was a military stalemate, but American confidence was rising.

Still, the colonists did not rush into war. After the Lexington and Concord fighting, more than a year passed before the colonists declared independence.

In July 1775, the Second Continental Congress sent the Olive Branch petition to King George III to assure him of their desire for peace. The colonists asked him to protect their rights as English citizens, which they felt Parliament had violated. The king refused to look at the petition. Instead, he sent 30,000 hired German troops to fight the rebellious colonists.

Although some colonists, called Loyalists, wanted to remain loyal English citizens, others, called Patriots, began calling for independence. Beginning in January 1776, Patriot Thomas Paine's pamphlets, called *Common Sense,* began circulating throughout the colonies. Paine's writings began to convince people that both Parliament and King George III were acting like tyrants, and complete independence from Great Britain was necessary if Americans were to secure their rights.

☑ **Reading Check** **Explaining** Why did the Declaratory Act upset the American colonists so much?

## The Birth of a New Nation

**Main Idea** Americans won their independence from Britain in 1783 and later ratified a constitution that clearly spelled out the rights of individuals and the limits of government.

**Reading Connection** Can you think of a time when a goal you had finally became a reality? Read to learn about the steps colonists took when they finally won independence.

On July 4, 1776, the Second Continental Congress approved a declaration of independence written by **Thomas Jefferson.** Based in large part on the ideas of John Locke, the **Declaration of Independence** declared the colonies to be "free and independent states absolved from all allegiance to the British Crown." Like Locke, Jefferson stated that life, liberty, and property are natural rights and it is the government's duty to protect those rights. When governments do not, they can be rightfully overthrown. The people of the American colonies reacted with celebration to the Declaration of Independence. The American Revolution had formally begun.

The Declaration of Independence amounted to a declaration of war against Great Britain. Such a declaration was an enormous gamble. The Continental Army was a brand-new creation. The soldiers were a motley group of ordinary citizens—small farmers, artisans, and merchants. They had no regular military training and usually agreed to serve for only a short time. These so-called Patriots faced the world's best military force, one supported by a rich nation with a healthy economy.

The Patriots had some important advantages, though. The British had to ship soldiers and supplies across the Atlantic, while the Patriots were fighting on home ground.

One of the most important advantages that the Patriots had was their motivation to fight. Most of the British and German soldiers were fighting as part of a job or for money. For the Patriots, it was a battle for their freedom.

A critical factor for the American victory was the financial support from other countries, especially France. The French, eager to inflict damage on the British in any way possible, gave arms and money to the Americans from early in the war. French officers and soldiers served under General Washington. One famous Frenchman, the Marquis de Lafayette, wrote this about the American Revolution: "The future of America is closely bound up with the future of all mankind." Spain and the Dutch Republic, other British rivals, were also eager to fight against Great Britain. The British had their hands full.

Both sides expected the war to be short, but it dragged on for about seven years, from 1776 to 1783. When the army of General Cornwallis was finally forced to surrender to combined American and French forces under Washington at **Yorktown** in 1781, the British decided to end the war.

The Treaty of Paris, signed in 1783, recognized the independence of the American colonies and granted the Americans control of the western territory from the Appalachians to the Mississippi River.

✓**Reading Check** **Explaining** Why did foreign countries support the American cause?

🎨 **History** *through Art*

***The March to Valley Forge, 1883*** was painted by William B.T. Trego. It conveyed the suffering General Washington and his Continental Army endured during the brutal winter of 1777 at their headquarters in Pennsylvania. How do you think the public felt about this event in the year it was painted?

▲ This 1867 painting depicts the signing in Philadelphia of a new plan of government for the former British colonies—the United States Constitution.

## Ruling a New Nation

**Main Idea** Americans struggled to find a balance between individual freedom and a unified central government.

**Reading Connection** Have you heard the phrase cost-benefit analysis? Read to learn how Americans balanced the costs and benefits of government.

The thirteen American colonies had gained their independence. The former colonies were now states which had to come together to form a country. Because they had just fought a war to free themselves from a king, the states feared the potential for concentrated power. Also, each state was primarily concerned for its own interests. For these reasons, the states had little enthusiasm for creating a united nation with a strong central government.

The **Articles of Confederation**, the nation's first constitution, thus did little to provide for a strong central government. It soon became clear that the government under the Articles lacked the power to deal with many problems. A movement for a different form of national government arose.

The Articles of Confederation had been approved in 1781. In the summer of 1787, 55 delegates met in Philadelphia to revise the Articles. The convention's delegates decided to throw out the Articles of Confederation and write a plan for an entirely new national government. That meeting became known as the Constitutional Convention.

**The Constitution** The proposed Constitution created a **federal system** in which power would be shared between the national government and the state governments. The national, or federal, government was given the power to levy taxes, raise an army, regulate trade, and create a national currency.

The Framers, or writers, of the Constitution used Montesquieu's ideas and divided the federal government into three branches, each with some power to check the workings of the others. The first branch was the executive branch, with a president serving as the chief executive. The president had the power to execute laws, veto the legislature's acts, supervise foreign affairs, and direct military forces.

Like the British Parliament, the second, or legislative, branch of government had two houses, a Senate and a House. State legislatures elected the Senate, while the people voted directly for the House of Representatives. Here, too, the Framers built in a system of checks and balances.

The Supreme Court and other courts deemed necessary by Congress made up the judiciary, or third branch of government. The courts would enforce the Constitution as the "supreme law of the land."

**The Bill of Rights** To take effect, the Constitution had to be ratified by nine states. The Constitution was finally approved, but in several states, the voting margin was slim. It was the promise that a bill of rights would be added to the Constitution that won sufficient supporters.

Why did many colonists insist on a bill of rights? Americans had just gone through a terrible war fighting the tyranny of the British king and Parliament. They wanted to be sure that there were written guarantees defining the limits of the government and the rights of the individual.

In 1789 the new Congress proposed 12 **amendments.** The 10 amendments the states approved became the **Bill of Rights.** They guaranteed freedom of religion, speech, press, petition, and **assembly.** The Bill of Rights clearly laid out a number of other rights that Americans considered absolute: the right against unreasonable searches and arrests, the right to bear arms, and the right to trial by jury. One of the most well-known of these rights is the right to due process.

A long history lies behind the Bill of Rights, including the Magna Carta set before King John in 1215. The natural rights theory of the Enlightenment was, however, the most direct influence on this document. Even at the time, American and European intellectuals felt that the U.S. Constitution embodied the ideas of the Enlightenment. The price of achieving equality and freedom had been high, but now the way was open to build a better society.

**A Model for Democracy** The American Revolution took place when Enlightenment ideas were gaining ground everywhere in the West. In France, the home of the Enlightenment, educated people wanted a society based on reason, not simply on outdated traditions from medieval times. There were other causes for the French Revolution, too—famine, a financial crisis, and nobles' discontent with the king. Yet the new American republic was a great inspiration to the French. In 1789, the same year the American Bill of Rights was proposed, the French Revolution broke out. It, too, created a new government, one based on representative institutions and individual rights.

The American experience inspired Latin America, too. Between 1807 and 1825, while Europe was in turmoil, landowners and middle-class merchants carried out revolts against Spain in Mexico, Argentina, Peru, Chile, Venezuela, and Bolivia.

In the twentieth century, the American legacy continued to inspire independence movements. Nationalist leaders in Africa and Southeast Asia looked to the United States for political principles and a model for constitutional government. The same was true for Eastern Europeans and Russians. Even in China, where there is still no representative government, the American Revolution has provided a stirring example for citizens who want a free and open society.

✓**Reading Check** **Contrasting** What was the main difference between the Articles of Confederation and the Constitution?

**HISTORY Online** **Study Central**

For help with the concepts in this section of *Glencoe World History–Modern Times,* go to wh.mt.glencoe.com and click on **Study Central.**

# SECTION 3 ASSESSMENT

### Checking for Understanding

1. **Vocabulary** Define: colony, Stamp Act, tension, correspondence, Declaration of Independence, Articles of Confederation, federal system, amendments, Bill of Rights, assembly.

2. **People** Identify: William Pitt the Elder, King George III, George Washington, Thomas Jefferson.

3. **Places** Locate: Yorktown.

### Reviewing Big Ideas

4. **List** the freedoms guaranteed under the American Bill of Rights.

### Critical Thinking

5. **Historical Analysis** **Analyzing Cause and Effect** Why did the American colonies declare their independence from the British Empire? **CA HI 2**

6. **Summarizing Information** Use a chart like the one below to identify the significant events and conflicts that led to the American Revolution.

| Conflicts Between British and Colonists |
|---|
| |
| |
| |

### Analyzing Visuals

7. **Examine** the painting *The March to Valley Forge* on page 195. Use details from the painting to explain whether this artist sympathizes with the Patriots or Loyalists.

### Writing About History

8. **Expository Writing** Do further research on how the French supported the colonies during the American Revolution. Then write an essay analyzing the importance of French assistance. **CA 10WS1.3**
**CA 10WA2.3a,b**

*Three influential Enlightenment authors wrote about how they thought progress should be recorded and maintained. Read about their eighteenth-century views on the triumphs of civilization.*

## SOURCE 1: The Progress of Man

*Edward Gibbon (1737–1794) published the first volume of* The History of the Decline and Fall of the Roman Empire *in 1776. Here, he celebrates how far mankind has progressed and his belief in future progress.*

. . . [A] philosopher may be permitted . . . to consider Europe as one great republic, whose various inhabitants have attained almost the same level of politeness and cultivation. . . . The savage nations of the globe are the common enemies of civilized society; and we may inquire with anxious curiosity, whether Europe is still threatened with a repetition of those **calamities**[1] which formerly oppressed the arms and institutions of Rome. . . .

. . . [From an] abject condition, perhaps the primitive and universal state of man, he has gradually arisen to command the animals, to fertilise the earth, to traverse the ocean, and to measure the heavens. His

▶ _____

[1]**calamities:** disasters; misfortunes

_____

*The Enlightenment love of knowledge as seen in a 1766 painting by Joseph Wright of Derby*

progress in the improvement and exercise of his mental and **corporeal**[2] faculties has been irregular and various, infinitely slow in the beginning, and increasing by degrees with redoubled velocity. . . . Yet the experience of four thousand years should enlarge our hopes, and diminish our apprehensions; we cannot determine to what height the human species may aspire in their advances towards perfection; but it may safely be presumed that no people, unless the face of nature is changed, will relapse into their original barbarism. . . .

Since the first discovery of the arts, war, commerce, and religious zeal have diffused, among the savages of the Old and New World, those inestimable gifts: they have been successfully **propagated**[3]; they can never be lost. We may therefore **acquiesce**[4] in the pleasing conclusion that every age of the world has increased, and still increases, the real wealth, the happiness, the knowledge, and perhaps the virtue, of the human race.

## SOURCE 2: *Encyclopédie*

*The* Encyclopédie *was published under the direction of Denis Diderot (1713–1784) in 28 volumes. More than 140 writers contributed articles. In defining* encyclopédie, *Diderot focuses on why sharing knowledge is important to progress.*

ENCYCLOPÉDIE, f. n. (Philosophy). This word means the *interrelation of all knowledge*. . . . [T]he aim of an *encyclopédie* is to collect all the knowledge scattered over the face of the earth, to present its general outlines and structure to the men with whom we live, and to transmit this to those who will come after us, so that the work of past centuries may be useful to the following centuries, that our children, by becoming more educated, may at the same time become

_____

[2]**corporeal:** physical; material
[3]**propagated:** reproduced; spread
[4]**acquiesce:** accept; be satisfied

more virtuous and happier, and that we may not die without having deserved well of the human race. . . .

It would be desirable for the government to authorize people to go into the factories and shops, to see the craftsmen at their work, to question them, to draw the tools, the machines, and even the premises. . . .

. . . What is the good of divulging the knowledge a nation possesses, its private transactions, its inventions, its industrial processes, its resources, its trade secrets, its enlightenment, its arts, and all its wisdom? This is what they [narrow minds] say; and this is what they might add: would it not be desirable if, instead of enlightening the foreigner, we could spread darkness over him or even plunge all the rest of the world into barbarism so that we could dominate more securely over everyone? These people do not realize that they occupy only a single point on our globe and that they will endure only a moment in its existence. To this point and to this moment they would sacrifice the happiness of future ages and that of the entire human race.

## SOURCE 3: *The Social Contract*

*The Social Contract, published in 1762, is one of the most famous works of Jean-Jacques Rousseau (1712–1778). It argues that each person must enter into a contract with everyone in the community to secure freedom. In this excerpt, Rousseau explains the difference between the general will and the individual will.*

. . . [T]he act of association consists of a reciprocal commitment between society and the individual, so that each person, in making a contract, as it were with himself, finds himself doubly committed, first as a member of the **sovereign**[5] body in relation to individuals, and secondly as a member of the state in relation to the sovereign. . . .

As soon as the multitude is united thus in a single body, no one can injure any one of the members without attacking the whole, still less injure the whole without each member feeling it. Duty and self-interest thus equally oblige the two contracting parties to give each other mutual aid; and the same men should

seek to bring together in this dual relationship, all the advantages that flow from it. . . .

For every individual as a man may have a private will contrary to, or different from, the general will that he has as a citizen. His private interest may speak with a very different voice from that of a public interest. . . .

There is often a great difference between the will of all [what all individuals want] and the general will; the general will studies only the common interest while the will of all studies private interest, and is indeed no more than the sum of individual desires. But if we take away from these same wills, the pluses and minuses which cancel each other out, the sum of the difference is the general will.

From the deliberations of a people properly informed, and provided its members do not have any communication among themselves, the great number of small differences will always produce a general will and the decision will always be good.

---

**DBQ** **Document-Based Questions**

**Historical Analysis** CA HR 2

**Source 1:** According to Gibbon, in what ways has "primitive man" progressed over time? What assures the author that this progress will continue?

**Source 2:** Why does Diderot believe that knowledge should be collected and shared among all people? Which group does he think will especially benefit from this shared knowledge?

**Source 3:** What is the difference between "general will" and "individual will"? Why does Rousseau claim the general will is always good?

### Comparing and Contrasting Sources

1. What do both Gibbon and Diderot agree is a necessary duty of man to contribute to the happiness of the human race? **CA 10RL3.5**
2. Would Gibbon view Diderot as a philosopher? How would he view Rousseau? Explain.

---

➤ _____

[5]**sovereign:** supreme; principal

Standards 10.1.3, 10.2, 10.2.1, 10.2.2, 10.2.3

## Reviewing Content Vocabulary

1. In the _____, power is shared between the national government and the state government.
2. The intellects, or thinkers, of the Enlightenment were generally called _____.
3. The doctrine that maintains that the state should not intervene in economics is called _____.
4. The belief that the monarch receives power directly from God is called _____.
5. John Locke believed people had certain _____ to life, liberty, and property.
6. Montesquieu believed that the government functioned through a _____, which allowed the branches of government to limit and control each other.
7. The first ten amendments to the U.S. Constitution, added to secure its ratification, are called the _____.
8. At the Constitutional Convention, the ineffective _____ were scrapped in order to create a new government.
9. According to Rousseau, through a _____ an entire society agrees to be governed by the general will.
10. Parliament abolished the monarchy and declared England a republic or _____.

## Reviewing Academic Vocabulary

*On a sheet of paper, use each of these terms in a sentence that reflects the term's meaning in the chapter.*

11. attribute
12. restraint
13. consensus
14. hypothetical
15. mutual
16. evidence
17. affect
18. concept
19. tension
20. correspondence
21. amendments
22. assembly

## Reviewing the Main Ideas

**Section 1**

23. What was the basic reason behind the Glorious Revolution?
24. Explain why Elizabeth demonstrated moderation in her religious policy.

**Section 2**

25. What was the Enlightenment?
26. List the primary occupations of the philosophes.

**Section 3**

27. What was the major accomplishment of the Second Continental Congress?
28. Explain the difference between French and British colonies.

## Chapter Summary

| Movement | Conflict | Political Outcome | Long-Term Outcomes | Related Documents |
|---|---|---|---|---|
| Glorious Revolution | Divine rights of kings v. nobles' representation | constitutional monarchy (also known as limited monarchy) | expansion of natural rights and social contract theories of government | English Bill of Rights |
| Enlightenment | tradition v. reason | end of absolutism; sovereignty lies with the people | growth of new social sciences, education, literacy | John Locke's *Second Treatise;* Adam Smith's *Wealth of Nations* |
| American Revolution | constitutional monarchy v. rights of colonial assemblies | American Revolution and new American Republic | spread of democratic ideals | Declaration of Independence; United States Constitution |

## Critical Thinking

29. **Reading Skill** **Synthesizing** Describe the connection between the principles of a limited monarchy, the U.S. Constitution, and the Enlightenment.

30. **Summarizing** Explain how separation of powers works in the American government today and give specific examples.

## Writing About History

31. **Historical Analysis** **Understanding Chronology** Writing a separate paragraph for each example, trace how the relationships between the English Parliament and rulers changed, covering Henry VIII, Elizabeth I, Charles I, Oliver Cromwell, and James II. **CA CS 1**

32. Although Enlightenment thinkers disagreed over certain issues, they all focused on the themes of *reason, natural law,* and *progress.* Explain the influence of any of these themes on the Enlightenment.

33. **Expository Writing** Analyze how John Locke, Montesquieu, Rousseau, and Voltaire influenced the United States Constitution. Which thinker(s) had the most impact on the writers of the Constitution? **CA 10WA2.3a,b**

**DBQ** **Document-Based Questions**

**Analyzing Sources** Read the following quote from John Locke's *Essay Concerning Human Understanding:*

> ❝Let us then suppose the mind to be, as we say, white paper, void of all character, without any ideas. How comes it to be furnished? Whence has it all the materials of reason and knowledge? To this I answer, in one word, from experience. . . . Our observation, employed either about external sensible objects or about the internal operations of our minds perceived and reflected on by ourselves, is that which supplies our understanding with all the materials of thinking.❞

34. According to Locke, how did the blank mind become knowledgeable? **CA 10WA2.3b**

35. How did one gain the experience necessary to nurture the mind? **CA 10WA2.3b**

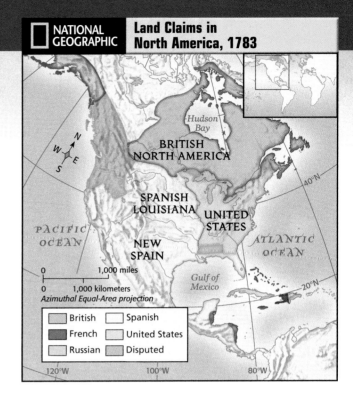

**NATIONAL GEOGRAPHIC** **Land Claims in North America, 1783**

Hudson Bay

BRITISH NORTH AMERICA

SPANISH LOUISIANA

UNITED STATES

PACIFIC OCEAN

NEW SPAIN

ATLANTIC OCEAN

Gulf of Mexico

0 1,000 miles
0 1,000 kilometers
Azimuthal Equal-Area projection

- British
- French
- Russian
- Spanish
- United States
- Disputed

## Analyzing Maps and Charts

Study the map above to answer the following questions.

36. After the Revolutionary War, what were the borders for the United States on the north? On the south? On the west?

37. What natural borders helped define the United States during this period?

38. How does the extent of the United States in 1783 compare to the extent of the United States today?

---

**Standards Practice**

**Directions: Choose the best answer to the following question.**

39. In England, the Glorious Revolution of 1688 led to

A the end of the Tudor reign.

B the end of Anglican influence in English political life.

C the dominance of Parliament in lawmaking.

D the restoration of the divine right of kings.

**CA Standard 10.2.2** List the principles of the Magna Carta, the English Bill of Rights (1689), the American Declaration of Independence (1776), the French Declaration of the Rights of Man and the Citizen (1789), and the U.S. Bill of Rights (1791).

# WORLD LANGUAGES

L anguage not only allows us to communicate, it affects the way we think and even how we may view ourselves. It creates an identity for a community of people and shapes their experiences.

Today about 6,500 languages are spoken around the world. Hundreds of these will disappear in this century because younger generations no longer speak them. Others will be overpowered by the influence of English, a language that has spread through technology, global commerce, telecommunications, and tourism.

## World Languages

| Language(s) | Native Speakers |
|---|---|
| Chinese languages | 1,198,000,000 |
| Spanish | 322,000,000 |
| English | 341,000,000 |
| Hindi/Urdu | 426,000,000 |
| Bengali | 207,000,000 |
| Arabic languages | 204,000,000 |
| Portuguese | 176,000,000 |
| Russian | 167,000,000 |
| Japanese | 125,000,000 |
| German | 100,000,000 |
| French | 77,000,000 |

Source: *World Almanac and Book of Facts,* 2004.

## NATIONAL GEOGRAPHIC  Major World Languages

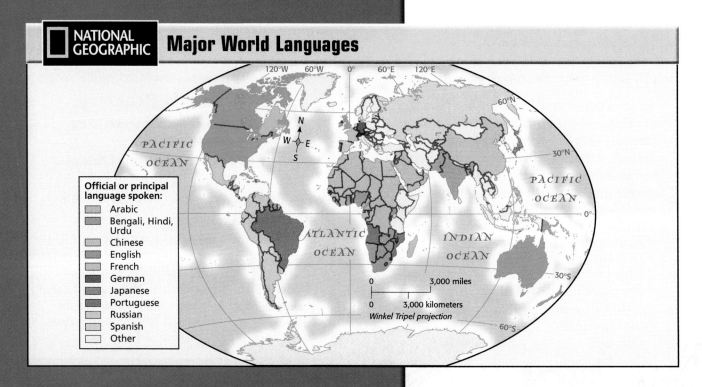

Official or principal language spoken:
- Arabic
- Bengali, Hindi, Urdu
- Chinese
- English
- French
- German
- Japanese
- Portuguese
- Russian
- Spanish
- Other

0  3,000 miles
0  3,000 kilometers
*Winkel Tripel projection*

# *English Spoken Here*

## Old English (5th–11th Centuries)

If you were to travel back in time to visit Robin Hood, you would not be able to understand him. Even though you would both be speaking English, the language you speak has changed a great deal since the days of Robin and his merry men. Can you recognize any words from this old English conversation?

**"Hast thu hafoc?"**
*Do you have a hawk?*
**"Ic habbe."**
*I have.*
**"Canst thu temian hig?"**
*Do you know how to tame them?*
**"Gea, ic cann. Hwat sceoldon hig me buton ic cuthe temian hig?"**
*Yes, I do. What use would they be to me if I could not tame them?*
—From a tenth-century lesson

## Middle English (11th–15th Centuries)

Middle English evolved when the Normans conquered England, bringing their language, French, with them. Many different dialects of English were spoken, but the dialect spoken in London became dominant. Geoffrey Chaucer's *Canterbury Tales* (1390) is an example.

**In this viage shal telle tales tweye
To Caunterbury-ward I mene it so,
And homward he shal tellen othere two,
Of aventures that whilom han bifalle.**

*On this trip [you each] shall tell two tales
On the way to Canterbury,
And homeward [you] shall tell another two,
Of adventures that once had happened.*
—From the Prologue of *Canterbury Tales*

## Modern English (15th Century–Present)

Although you might find Shakespeare difficult to understand, his English is essentially the language that evolved into the way we speak and read today.

JULIET: How camest thou
  hither, tell me, and wherefore?
  The orchard walls are high and hard
    to climb,
  And the place death, considering who
    thou art,
  If any of my kinsmen find thee here.

ROMEO: With love's light wings did I
  o'er perch these walls,
  For stony limits cannot hold love out,
  And what love can do, that dares
    love attempt,
  Therefore thy kinsmen are no stop to me.
—From *Romeo and Juliet*

# The ABCs of Language

**H**ow did writing begin? Early writing systems were derived from pictures. Every word would correspond to one or more symbols. For example, the word *house* might be written as a symbol that looked like a simplified house. Ancient Egyptian and Mayan hieroglyphics are examples.

The Phoenicians were among the first to develop an alphabet with characters that could be combined to make different sounds. The Greeks adapted it and passed it on to the Romans. The Roman alphabet is the alphabet most Western languages, such as English, use today.

**How would you write "How are you?" to the people you meet around the world through the Internet?**

## "How Are You?"

| Languages written from left to right → | |
| --- | --- |
| Danish | Hvordan gaar det? |
| Greek | Πῶς ɛιστε: |
| Hindi | आप कैसे है ? |
| Russian | Как поживаете? |
| Spanish | ¿Cómo está usted? |
| Swahili | Hujambo? |
| Tagalog (Philippines) | Kumusta po kayo? |
| Thai | สบายดีหรือ |
| Vietnamese | Anh (Chi) có khoe không? |

| Languages written from right to left ← | |
| --- | --- |
| Arabic | كيف حالكم؟ |
| Hebrew | מה שלומך? |
| Persian | چطورید؟ |

Languages written from top to bottom ↓

Chinese 你好吗？

Japanese お元気ですか

Korean 어떻게지내십니까?

## Reading Chinese Characters

Chinese characters are combined in thousands of ways to make new words. In this example, when the character for tree is inserted into the character for box, you have a tree growing in a box, which is the character for "be in trouble."

Here are some other Chinese words divided into their elements. See if you can figure out what these characters mean.

**EXAMPLE**

木 口 困

tree + box = be in trouble

1. 火 山 火山

fire + mountain = _____

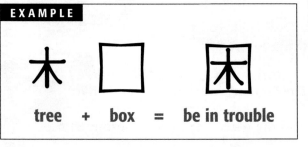

2. 木 木 木 森

tree + tree + tree = _____

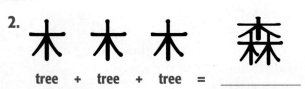

# Disappearing Languages

Before World War II, it is estimated that over 11 million Jews spoke Yiddish, a language based on German, Hebrew, and other languages. Many Yiddish speakers were killed in the Holocaust. Children of Holocaust survivors often forgot the language or chose not to use it in their new homelands. Today, the number of Yiddish speakers is approximately 2 million, most of whom are elderly. When these people die, there will be few people left who speak the language, even though it's preserved in literature and oral records.

Many minority cultures around the world face the same problem. Often, these people live in areas that were once subjugated or conquered by other countries. The new rulers forced native peoples to adopt a new culture, often by prohibiting the use of the local language. In the United States, Native American children were frequently sent to boarding schools where they were forced to speak English and were punished if they spoke their own language. Not surprisingly,

where there had once been hundreds of Native American languages, today there are only 175, and many of those will soon be extinct.

Fortunately, many struggling languages are making a comeback. In places like Ireland, northern Spain, and even Hawaii, schools are teaching traditional languages, and their usage is becoming widely accepted. Native Americans are also taking steps to revive their languages, as demonstrated by the Navajo newspaper at right. With language comes renewed interest in culture, and many ethnic groups who revive their language also find that they revive hope and self-worth within their people.

# English As an International Language

Mahesh is an Indian who lives in Trinidad. His wife is from Venezuela. To communicate they speak English. He works for an international oil company where he conducts business worldwide in English. On TV he watches CNN news, and he enjoys going to American movies.

English was first spread through colonization. Though usually unwelcome, English eventually became a way of communicating between ethnic groups who shared a country but not a common language. In the late twentieth century, English became even more dominant as American language and culture spread through global business (think Coca-Cola and McDonald's), media, and technology. The Israeli sign with English translations at left is an example of how English is being used worldwide.

Today, English is spoken in 115 countries as either the official language or as an important minority language. Although many people do not like it, the globalization of English has made communication and interaction between peoples easier. On the other hand, many smaller languages and cultures are being lost as the world becomes more homogeneous.

# CHAPTER 3

## 1789–1815

# The French Revolution and Napoleon

## ❦ The Big Ideas ❧

### SECTION 1: The French Revolution Begins

**Throughout history people have struggled for rights.** Social inequality and economic problems contributed to the French Revolution, a struggle for rights that has shaped the modern world.

### SECTION 2: Radical Revolution and Reaction

**Throughout history people have struggled for rights.** Radical groups controlled the revolution, which many people in France and abroad opposed.

### SECTION 3: The Age of Napoleon

**The quest for national self-determination is universal.** After the French Revolution, Napoleon built and lost an empire, and also spread ideas about nationalism.

*World History—Modern Times Video* The Chapter 3 video, *"Napoleon," chronicles the rise and fall of Napoleon Bonaparte.*

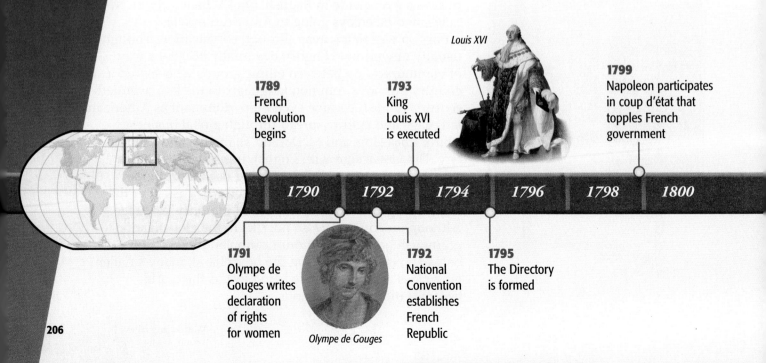

Louis XVI

**1789**
French Revolution begins

**1793**
King Louis XVI is executed

**1799**
Napoleon participates in coup d'état that topples French government

*1790*  *1792*  *1794*  *1796*  *1798*  *1800*

**1791**
Olympe de Gouges writes declaration of rights for women

*Olympe de Gouges*

**1792**
National Convention establishes French Republic

**1795**
The Directory is formed

*Napoleon Crossing the Great St. Bernard* by Jacques-Louis David  David was the leading artist of the French Revolution.

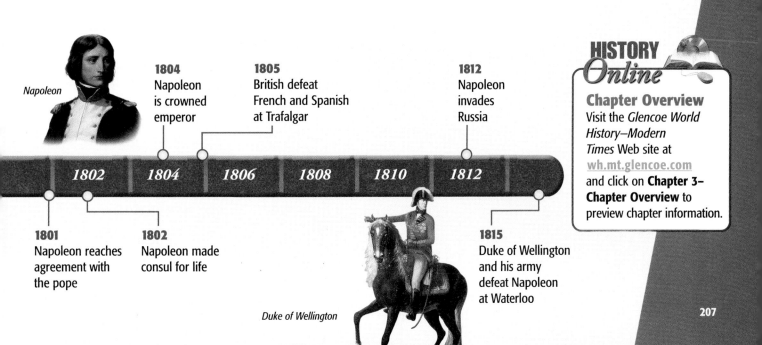

*Napoleon*

**1804**
Napoleon is crowned emperor

**1805**
British defeat French and Spanish at Trafalgar

**1812**
Napoleon invades Russia

1802    1804    1806    1808    1810    1812

**1801**
Napoleon reaches agreement with the pope

**1802**
Napoleon made consul for life

**1815**
Duke of Wellington and his army defeat Napoleon at Waterloo

*Duke of Wellington*

**HISTORY**
*Online*

**Chapter Overview**
Visit the *Glencoe World History–Modern Times* Web site at wh.mt.glencoe.com and click on **Chapter 3– Chapter Overview** to preview chapter information.

# Preparing to Read Chapter 3

**Reading Skill** **Identifying Complex Causation**

Authors structure texts in order to present information logically. They often do this by providing a number of causes, called complex causation, leading to a particular effect. This shows that a number of events or developments are interrelated. Together these things have a cumulative effect—they add up to a result that is highly significant.

You can understand complex causation through two steps: First, notice that the author presents multiple reasons for a specific outcome. Second, when you are finished reading the passage with this structure, ask yourself a focus question that will help identify the various events that led to the final result.

*Read the following excerpt from this chapter and use the focus question to find the causes that contributed to Napoleon's downfall.*

## IDENTIFYING COMPLEX CAUSATION

Notice the signaling phrase, One of the most important factors. If you didn't notice this at first, it gives you a cue to reread to see if the author is describing a chain of causes and effects.

So long as Britain ruled the waves, it was almost invulnerable. Napoleon gathered together ships, hoping to invade, but the British navy defeated the combined French-Spanish fleet at Trafalgar in 1805. . . . His next move was to make his allies cut off trade with Britain. . . . The Continental System failed. . . . One of the most important factors in Napoleon's defeat was nationalism. . . . The beginning of Napoleon's downfall can be dated to 1812 when he made the fateful decision to invade Russia. . . . Now that the French army was crippled, other European states joined in for the attack.

### Apply the Skill

A useful focus question for the excerpt could include: What events weakened Napoleon's power? List four causes based on the excerpt. Once you've read the chapter, go back to this question and think about how the causes are interconnected.

## Historical Analysis Skill | Interpreting History

**Historical Research, Evidence, and Point of View: Standard HR 2**
*Students identify bias and prejudice in historical interpretations.*

Do you believe everything you read and hear? Can you recall reading an e-mail or hearing someone interviewed about an event and thinking to yourself, "I don't think that could have happened like that"?

Historians are trained to recognize bias in firsthand accounts and to think about why an account might be biased. Learning to identify bias is vital for the study of history. Read this account of the execution of King Louis XVI of France. The writer, Henry de Firmont, was present at the events he describes:

> **"The path leading to the scaffold was extremely rough and difficult to pass; the King was obliged to lean on my arm, and from the slowness with which he proceeded, I feared for a moment that his courage might fail; but what was my astonishment, when arrived at the last step, he suddenly let go of my arm, and I saw him cross with a firm foot the breadth of the whole scaffold; and in a loud voice, I heard him pronounce distinctly these words: 'I die innocent of all the crimes laid to my charge; I pardon those who had occasioned my death; and I pray to God that the blood you are going to shed may never be visited on France."**

Is the writer for or against the king? Discuss your position with a classmate, explaining how you came to your conclusion. Identify words and phrases in the quote that led to your decision.

### Apply the Skill

As you read firsthand accounts in your textbook, remember that all of them have some bias or point of view. Practice looking for words and phrases that signal the author's bias.

# A Story That Matters

*The storming of the Bastille*

## Fall of the Bastille

On the morning of July 14, 1789, a Parisian mob of some eight thousand men and women in search of weapons streamed toward the Bastille, a royal armory filled with arms and ammunition. The Bastille was also a state prison. Although it contained only seven prisoners at the time, in the eyes of those angry Parisians it was a glaring symbol of the government's harsh policies. The armory was defended by the marquis de Launay and a small garrison of 114 men.

The assault began at one o'clock in the afternoon when a group of attackers managed to lower two drawbridges over the moat surrounding the fortress. The mob was joined by members of the French Guard, who began to bombard the fortress with cannonballs. After four hours of fighting, 98 attackers lay dead or dying. Only one defender had been killed.

As more attackers arrived, de Launay realized that he and his troops could not hold out much longer and surrendered. Angered by the loss of its members, the victorious mob beat de Launay to death, cut off his head, and carried it aloft in triumph through the streets of Paris.

When King Louis XVI returned to his palace at Versailles after a day of hunting, he was told about the fall of the Bastille by the duc de La Rochefoucauld-Liancourt. Louis exclaimed, "Why, this is a revolt." "No, Sire," replied the duke, "It is a revolution."

### Why It Matters

The French Revolution began a new age in European political life. The old political order in France was destroyed. The new order was based on individual rights, representative institutions, and loyalty to the nation rather than the monarch. The revolutionary upheaval of the era, especially in France, created new political ideals, summarized in the French slogan, "Liberty, Equality, and Fraternity." These ideals transformed France, then spread to other European countries and the rest of the world.

**History and You** Using print or Internet sources, familiarize yourself with the lyrics to *The Marseillaise*, *God Save the Queen*, and *The Star-Spangled Banner*. How do they vary in subject matter, tone, theme, and style, and how are they similar? Create a chart listing your findings.

# The French Revolution Begins

## Guide to Reading

### Section Preview
Social inequality and economic problems contributed to the French Revolution, a struggle for rights that has shaped the modern world.

**Main Idea**

- The Third Estate, which made up the vast majority of the French people, were heavily taxed and discontented. (p. 212)

- By meeting as a separate assembly, the Third Estate claimed the right to have their votes count as much as those of the clergy and nobles. (p. 214)

- The National Assembly affirmed the "rights of man" and set up a limited monarchy in the Constitution of 1791. (p. 215)

### Content Vocabulary
estate, *taille*, bourgeoisie, sans-culottes

### Academic Vocabulary
consumer, exclusion

### People and Events to Identify
Louis XVI, Tennis Court Oath, Declaration of the Rights of Man and the Citizen, Olympe de Gouges

### Places to Locate
Versailles, Paris, Austria, Prussia

### Reading Objectives
1. Describe how the population of France was divided into three estates.
2. Explain how the fall of the Bastille saved the National Assembly.

### Reading Strategy
**Cause and Effect** As you read this section, use a web diagram like the one below to list factors that contributed to the French Revolution.

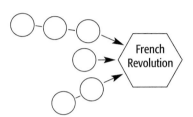

### Preview of Events

♦1785                          ♦1790                                    ♦1795

**1787**
Bad harvest leads to food shortages

**1788**
Bad harvest intensifies economic problems in France

**1789**
National Assembly adopts Declaration of the Rights of Man

**1791**
National Assembly completes new constitution

## California Standards in This Section

*Reading this section will help you master these California History–Social Science standards.*

**10.2.4:** Explain how the ideology of the French Revolution led France to develop from constitutional monarchy to democratic despotism to the Napoleonic empire.

# Background to the Revolution

**Main Idea** The Third Estate, which made up the vast majority of the French people, were heavily taxed and discontented.

**Reading Connection** What if you performed all the chores at your house, but had only bread to eat and no say-so in family concerns? Read to learn about the oppression of France's Third Estate.

The year 1789 witnessed two far-reaching events: the beginning of a new United States of America and the beginning of the French Revolution. Compared with the American Revolution, the French Revolution was more complex, more violent, and far more radical. From the start, it was clear that something extraordinary was occurring in world history.

## Voices from the Past

A London *Times* correspondent sent a report to his editor on July 20, 1789. He may not have realized the full significance of the events he reported, but the French Revolution had begun:

> 66 The number of armed men in Paris is supposed to amount to 300,000 men, and they called themselves the Militia. The way by which so many people have procured arms is, that all the public storehouses where weapons were lodged, have been broken open, as well as several private houses plundered, which they thought contained them. The Archbishop of Paris is among the number of those who have been sacrificed to the people's rage. He was assassinated at Versailles on Tuesday night. The city of Paris is entirely surrounded with a guard, and not a soul suffered to go out who has an appearance of wealth. 99

The French Revolution tried to create not only a new political order, but a new social order, too. This was different from the American Revolution, which created a new political system but did not change the existing social system. There was no huge resentment against a certain class. The American colonies had wealthy people and clergy, but neither group was given special status as they were in France.

The French Revolution was also more violent because the French had to decide what to do about the king. His ancestors had ruled France for centuries, and his royal cousins and neighbors threatened them with powerful armies. In the American colonies, there was no king whose dynasty had ruled for centuries. And the only king that had to be gotten rid of lived far across the Atlantic Ocean.

The French Revolution was a major turning point in world history. During the decade it occurred, many different forms of government were tried and many new social ideas were put forth. One of the most powerful ideas of the French Revolution was that the people were the nation. This idea continues to influence world politics in the twenty-first century.

Some causes of the French Revolution lay deep in the past, while others were attributed to more immediate problems. The long-range causes were found in the great inequality of French society. Since medieval times, each person belonged by law to one of three status groups, or **estates**.

**The Three Estates** The First Estate were the clergy, the Second Estate the nobles, and the Third Estate everyone else. Thus the Third Estate included anyone from the lowliest peasant to the wealthiest merchant.

The First Estate, or clergy, numbered about 130,000 out of a total population of 27 million and owned about 10 percent of the land. These owners were not poor parish priests, but cardinals, bishops, and the heads of monasteries. Usually, well-to-do clergy were from the noble families and shared their outlook and interests.

The Second Estate, or nobility, numbered about 350,000 and owned about 25 to 30 percent of the land. They played a crucial role in society in the 1700s. They held leading positions in the government, in the military, in the law courts, and in the Roman Catholic Church. Despite the fact that they controlled most of the wealth of the kingdom, neither the clergy nor the nobles had to pay the *taille* (TAH•yuh), the chief tax.

▼ *Conquerors of the Bastille*

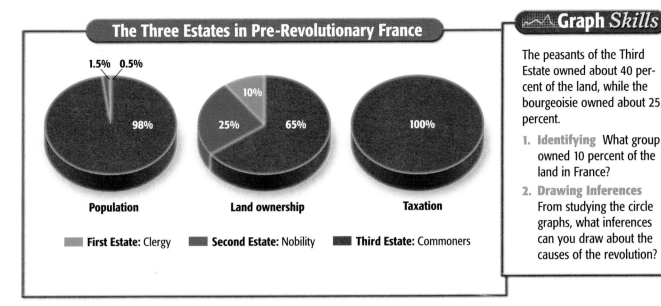

1.5%  0.5%

98%

**Population**

10%
25%  65%

**Land ownership**

100%

**Taxation**

■ **First Estate:** Clergy    ■ **Second Estate:** Nobility    ■ **Third Estate:** Commoners

**Graph** *Skills*

The peasants of the Third Estate owned about 40 percent of the land, while the bourgeoisie owned about 25 percent.

1. **Identifying** What group owned 10 percent of the land in France?

2. **Drawing Inferences** From studying the circle graphs, what inferences can you draw about the causes of the revolution?

Ever since French kings had gained absolute power, the nobles had been trying to regain some of their rights. Another goal of the nobles was to continue to be appointed to most important posts in the military, government, or Church. These positions were a source of the wealth every noble needed for his heirs.

Unlike the First and Second Estates, the Third Estate were divided by vast differences in occupation, level of education, and wealth. Peasants made up from 75 to 80 percent of the Third Estate and owned about 35 to 40 percent of the land; middle-class members of the Third Estate owned the rest. At least half of the peasants had little or no land to live on.

All peasants owed certain duties to the nobles. These duties were a holdover from medieval times when serfdom was widespread. For example, a peasant had to pay a fee to grind his flour or press his grapes because the local lord controlled the flour mill and wine press. When the busy harvest time came, the peasant had to work a certain number of days harvesting the noble's crop. French peasants fiercely resented these duties.

Another part of the Third Estate consisted of urban craftspeople, shopkeepers, and workers. These people too were struggling to survive. In the 1700s, the price of **consumer** goods rose much faster than wages. During the revolution, this group played an important role.

The **bourgeoisie** (BURZH•WAH•ZEE), or middle class, was another group in the Third Estate. They were merchants, bankers, manufacturers, and professional people—lawyers, public officials, doctors, and journalists. They made up about 8 percent of the population and owned about 20 percent of the land.

The middle class was unhappy with the privileges held by nobles. They did not want to abolish the nobility, however, but to better their own position. Some bourgeoisie had managed to become nobles by being appointed to public offices which conferred

noble status. About 6,500 new nobles had been created by appointment during the 1700s.

The bourgeoisie also shared certain ideas with the nobles. Both were drawn to the Enlightenment and disliked the rigid social system. Ultimately, the dissatisfaction of these elite groups led them to oppose the absolute monarchy of **Louis XVI.**

**Financial Crisis** The immediate cause of the revolution was the near collapse of the French budget. Although the economy had been expanding for fifty years, there were periodic crises. Bad harvests in 1787 and 1788 and a slowdown in manufacturing led to food shortages, rising prices for food, and unemployment. On the eve of the revolution, the number of poor—estimated at almost one-third of the population—reached crisis proportions.

One English traveler commented on the misery of French peasants: "All the country girls and women are without shoes or stockings; and the plowmen at their work have neither shoes nor stockings to their feet. This is a poverty that strikes at the root of national prosperity."

Despite these problems, the French king and his ministers continued to spend enormous sums on wars and court luxuries. When the government decided to spend huge sums to help American colonists against Britain, the budget went into total crisis.

With France on the verge of financial collapse, Louis XVI was forced to call a meeting of representatives of the Estates-General, or all three Estates meeting together, to raise new taxes. Before French kings had become so powerful, the Estates-General had been consulted more often. In 1789, however, this body had not met since 1614.

✓ **Reading Check** **Identifying** What groups were part of the Third Estate?

# From Estates-General to National Assembly

**Main Idea** By meeting as a separate assembly, the Third Estate claimed the right to have their votes count as much as those of the clergy and nobles.

**Reading Connection** Have you heard about a riot and thought about what made people take to the streets? Read to learn why Parisian workers rioted in the summer of 1789.

In the Estates-General, the First and Second Estates each had about 300 representatives. The Third Estate had almost 600 representatives, many of them lawyers from French towns and cities. To solve the financial crisis, most of the Third Estate wanted to set up a constitutional government that would make the clergy and nobility pay taxes.

The meeting of the Estates-General opened at **Versailles** on May 5, 1789. From the start, there were arguments about voting. Traditionally, each estate had one vote. That meant that the First and Second Estates could outvote the Third Estate two to one.

The Third Estate demanded that instead each deputy have one vote. With the help of a few nobles and clerics, that would give the Third Estate a majority. The king, however, stated that he favored the current system.

The Third Estate reacted quickly. On June 17, 1789, it boldly declared that it was the National Assembly and would draft a constitution. Three days later, on June 20, its deputies arrived at their meeting place, only to find the doors had been locked. They then moved to a nearby indoor tennis court and swore that they would continue meeting until they had a new constitution. The oath they swore is known as the **Tennis Court Oath**.

Louis XVI prepared to use force against the Third Estate. The actions of Parisians, however, saved the situation. On July 14, Parisian workers stormed the Bastille (ba•STEEL), an armory and prison in **Paris**, and dismantled it, brick by brick. Paris was abandoned to the rebels.

Louis XVI was soon informed that he could no longer trust royal troops to shoot at the mob. The king's authority had collapsed in Paris. Meanwhile, all over France, there were revolts in the towns and the countryside. Popular hatred of the entire land-holding system, with its fees and obligations, had finally spilled over into action.

In the countryside, peasant rebellions became part of the vast panic known as the Great Fear. The peasants feared that the work of the National Assembly would be stopped by foreign armies. Rumors spread from village to village that foreign troops were on the way to put down the revolution. The peasants reacted by breaking into the great houses of the lords to destroy the records of their obligations.

**Reading Check** **Examining** Why did the Third Estate believe voting in the Estates-General was unfair?

## Picturing **History**

Les Halles, the market area of Paris, is pictured with the Grand Chatelet in the background. Would this market have been quieter or busier twenty years before the revolution? Why?

**History** *through Art*

**The Tennis Court Oath by Jacques-Louis David** Members of the National Assembly swore that they would produce a French constitution. What caused members to fear that the National Assembly would be dissolved by force?

# The Destruction of the Old Regime

**Main Idea** The National Assembly affirmed the "rights of man" and set up a limited monarchy in the Constitution of 1791.

**Reading Connection** Remember how the English king reacted to the American Declaration of Independence. Read to see how Louis XVI reacted to the Declaration of the Rights of Man and the Citizen.

The National Assembly reacted to news of peasant rebellions and rumors of a possible foreign invasion. On August 4, 1789, the National Assembly decided to abolish all legal privileges of the nobles and clergy.

**Declaration of the Rights of Man** On August 26, the National Assembly adopted the **Declaration of the Rights of Man and the Citizen**. Inspired by the English Bill of Rights of 1689 and by the American Declaration of Independence and Constitution, this charter of basic liberties began with a ringing affirmation of "the natural and imprescriptible rights of man" to "liberty, property, security, and resistance to oppression."

The declaration proclaimed that all men were free and equal before the law, that appointment to public office should be based on talent, and that no group should be exempt from taxation. All citizens had the right to make laws. Freedom of speech and the press were affirmed.

The declaration raised an important issue. Should its ideal of equal rights include women? Many deputies insisted that it did, provided that, as one man said, "women do not hope to exercise political rights and functions."

One woman writer, **Olympe de Gouges**, refused to accept this **exclusion** of women from political rights. Echoing the words of the official declaration, she wrote a Declaration of the Rights of Woman and the Female Citizen.

> ❝Believing that ignorance, omission, or scorn for the rights of woman are the only causes of public misfortunes and of the corruption of governments, the women have resolved to set forth in a solemn declaration the natural, inalienable, and sacred rights of woman in order that this declaration, constantly exposed before all the members of the society, will ceaselessly remind them of their rights and duties.❞

The National Assembly ignored her completely. 📖
*(See page 771 to read an excerpt from de Gouge's Declaration of the Rights of Woman and the Female Citizen in the Primary Sources Library.)*

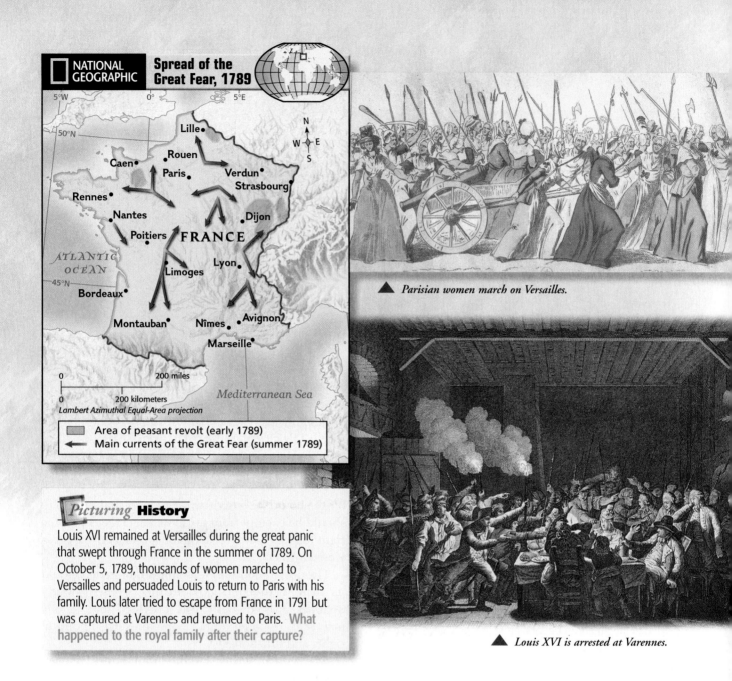

**Spread of the Great Fear, 1789**

Lille
Rouen
Caen
Paris
Verdun
Strasbourg
Rennes
Nantes
Dijon
Poitiers
FRANCE
ATLANTIC OCEAN
Limoges
Lyon
Bordeaux
Montauban
Nîmes
Avignon
Marseille
Mediterranean Sea

0       200 miles
0       200 kilometers
Lambert Azimuthal Equal-Area projection

Area of peasant revolt (early 1789)
Main currents of the Great Fear (summer 1789)

*Parisian women march on Versailles.*

*Picturing* **History**

Louis XVI remained at Versailles during the great panic that swept through France in the summer of 1789. On October 5, 1789, thousands of women marched to Versailles and persuaded Louis to return to Paris with his family. Louis later tried to escape from France in 1791 but was captured at Varennes and returned to Paris. What happened to the royal family after their capture?

*Louis XVI is arrested at Varennes.*

**The King Concedes** In the meantime, Louis XVI had remained at Versailles. Used to the absolutist system, he stubbornly refused to accept the National Assembly's decrees. On October 5, however, thousands of Parisian women—described by an eyewitness as "detachments of women coming up from every direction, armed with broomsticks, lances, pitchforks, swords, pistols and muskets"—marched to Versailles. Some of the women then met with the king. They told him that their children were starving because there was no bread. These hostile women forced Louis to accept the new decrees.

Now the crowd insisted that the king and his family return to Paris to show support for the National Assembly. If the king was not under their close watch, they feared he would rouse the kings and princes from other countries to oppose reform.

On October 6, the king and his family did return to Paris. As a goodwill gesture, they brought wagonloads of flour from the palace stores. Along their route, they were escorted by women armed with long, sharp pikes who chanted: "We are bringing back the baker and the baker's wife." The king and his family became virtual prisoners in Paris.

**Church Reforms** Under the old regime, the Catholic Church had been an important pillar of the social and political system. The revolutionaries felt they had to reform it too. The new revolutionary government was also motivated by the need for money. By seizing and selling off Church lands, the National Assembly was able to increase the state's revenues.

Finally, the Church was brought under the control of the state formally. A law was passed called the Civil Constitution of the Clergy. It said that bishops and priests were to be elected by the people, not appointed by the pope and the church hierarchy. The state would also pay the salaries of the bishops and priests.

This legislation affecting the Church upset many Catholics in France. They felt that state control was wrong. Many of them became permanent enemies of the revolution, and of all radical ideas in politics.

**A New Constitution and New Fears** The new Constitution of 1791 set up a limited monarchy. There was still a king, but the Legislative Assembly would make the laws. The new body was designed to be conservative. First, only men over 25 who paid a certain amount of taxes could vote. Second, the method of choosing its 745 representatives meant that only relatively wealthy people would serve.

By 1791, the old order had been destroyed, but the new government did not have enough support. On one hand were political radicals and economically disadvantaged people who wanted greater reform. On the other hand were the king and his court who resisted the new government. In June 1791, the king attempted to flee France. He almost succeeded but was captured and brought back to Paris. In this unsettled situation, the new Legislative Assembly met for the first time in October 1791. Soon, France's rocky relations with the rest of Europe led to the downfall of the king.

**War with Austria** A number of European leaders worried that revolution would spread to their lands. **Austria** and **Prussia** even threatened to use force to restore Louis XVI to full power. The Legislative Assembly decided it would act first and declared war on Austria in early 1792.

# CONNECTIONS Around The World

## A National Holiday

The French Revolution gave rise to the concept of the modern nation-state. With the development of the modern state came the celebration of one day a year as a national holiday—usually called Independence Day. The national holiday is a day that has special significance in the history of the nation-state.

In France, the fall of the Bastille on July 14, 1789, has been celebrated ever since as the beginning of the French nation-state. Independence Day in the United States is celebrated on July 4. On July 4, 1776, the Second Continental Congress approved the Declaration of Independence.

In Norway, people celebrate Constitution Day as a national holiday on May 17. On that day in 1814, Norway received a constitution, although it did not gain its independence from Sweden until 1905.

Most Latin American countries became independent of Spain or Portugal in the early nineteenth century. Mexico, for example, celebrates its Independence Day on September 16 with a colorful festival. On September 16, 1810, a crowd of local people attacked Spanish authorities in a small village near Mexico City. They were crushed, but their action eventually led to Mexico's independence from Spanish control in 1821.

Most nations in Africa and Asia gained their independence from Western colonial powers after World War II. India celebrates Independence Day on August 15. On that day in 1947, India won its independence from the British Empire.

*Bastille Day parade* ▶

## Comparing Cultures

Every nation celebrates its Independence Day with different kinds of festivities. For example, in the United States, many people have barbecues and watch fireworks displays. Choose two other nations and research how each nation and its people celebrate their Independence Day. Create an illustrated poster or chart showing your results.

At first, the French fared badly in the war. A frantic search for scapegoats began. One observer noted, "Everywhere you hear the cry that the king is betraying us, the generals are betraying us, that nobody is to be trusted; . . . that Paris will be taken in six weeks by the Austrians . . . we are on a volcano ready to spout flames."

**Rise of the Paris Commune** In the spring of 1792, angry citizens demonstrated to protest food shortages and defeats in the war. In August, Paris radicals again decided the fate of the revolution. They declared themselves a commune—a popularly run city council—and organized a mob attack on the royal palace and Legislative Assembly.

Members of the new Paris Commune took the king captive. They forced the Legislative Assembly to suspend the monarchy and to call for a National Convention. This time they wanted a more radical change: All male citizens would vote for the representatives who would decide the nation's future.

The French Revolution was entering a more radical and violent stage. Many members of the Paris Commune proudly called themselves the **sans-culottes**, ordinary patriots without fine clothes. They wore long trousers, not the knee-length breeches of the nobles. (In French, *sans-culottes* means "without breeches.") Often, sans-culottes are depicted as poor workers, but many were merchants or artisans—the elite of their neighborhoods.

▲ *A woman of the Third Estate painted by Jacques-Louis David*

✓ **Reading Check** **Evaluating** What was the significance of the Constitution of 1791?

**HISTORY** *Online* **Study Central**

For help with the concepts in this section of *Glencoe World History–Modern Times*, go to wh.mt.glencoe.com and click on **Study Central.**

# SECTION 1 ASSESSMENT

## Checking for Understanding

1. **Vocabulary** Define: estate, *taille*, consumer, bourgeoisie, exclusion, sans-culottes.

2. **People and Events** Identify: Louis XVI, Tennis Court Oath, Declaration of the Rights of Man and the Citizen, Olympe de Gouges.

3. **Places** Locate: Versailles, Paris, Austria, Prussia.

### Reviewing Big Ideas

4. **Explain** why the Catholic Church was targeted for reform.

## Critical Thinking

5. **Summarize** What were the main affirmations of the Declaration of the Rights of Man and the Citizen?

6. **Organizing Information** Equality was one of the slogans of the French Revolution. In a web diagram, identify five occasions when different groups expressed concern for equality during the revolution.

Expressions of Equality

## Analyzing Visuals

7. **Examine** the painting of the Tennis Court Oath shown on page 215. How does David's painting reflect the ideals of the French Revolution?

### Writing About History

8. **Persuasive Writing** Olympe de Gouges wrote that "ignorance, omission, or scorn for the rights of woman are the only causes of public misfortunes and of the corruption of governments." Do you agree or disagree? Write a paragraph supporting your point of view. **CA** 10WA2.4a,c

# Radical Revolution and Reaction

## Section Preview

Radical groups controlled the revolution, which many people in France and abroad opposed.

### Main Idea

- Some European countries opposed the revolution and threatened to invade France to keep the king in power. (p. 220)
- While the Committee of Public Safety was in power, thousands who opposed the government were executed. (p. 221)
- The revolutionary government raised a huge army that successfully defended France against invasion. (p. 223)
- The Constitution of 1795 set up a new government, but it was not able to inspire trust or solve the government's economic problems. (p. 224)

## Content Vocabulary

faction, elector, coup d'état

## Academic Vocabulary

domestic, external

## People and Events to Identify

Georges Danton, Jean-Paul Marat, Jacobins, Committee of Public Safety, Maximilien Robespierre, Reign of Terror, the Directory

## Places to Locate

Lyon, Nantes, Austrian Netherlands

## Reading Objectives

1. Identify the reasons why a European coalition fought together against France.
2. Explain why the Reign of Terror occurred.

## Reading Strategy

**Summarizing Information** As you read the section, use a table like the one below to list the actions of the National Convention.

| Actions taken by the National Convention |
|---|
| 1. |
| 2. |
| 3. |
| 4. |

## Preview of Events

| ♦1792 | ♦1793 | ♦1794 | ♦1795 |
|---|---|---|---|
| **1792**<br>National Convention splits into factions | **1793**<br>King Louis XVI is executed | **1794**<br>Reign of Terror ends | **1795**<br>New constitution is created |

## California Standards in This Section

*Reading this section will help you master these California History–Social Science standards.*

**10.2.4:** Explain how the ideology of the French Revolution led France to develop from constitutional monarchy to democratic despotism to the Napoleonic empire.

# The Move to Radicalism

**Main Idea** Some European nations opposed the revolution and threatened to invade France to keep the king in power.

**Reading Connection** What issues today might be used to justify sending American troops into another country? Read to find out what drove some European nations to consider invading France in 1793.

---

The Paris Commune had forced the Legislative Assembly to call a National Convention. Before the Convention met, the Paris Commune dominated the political scene. Led by the newly appointed minister of justice, **Georges Danton**, the sans-culottes sought revenge on those who had aided the king and resisted the popular will. Soon the life of the king himself was at risk.

## Voices from the Past

The execution of King Louis XVI in 1793 pushed the French Revolution into a new radical stage. Henry de Firmont reported on this dramatic event of January 21, 1793:

> ❝The path leading to the scaffold was extremely rough and difficult to pass; the King was obliged to lean on my arm, and from the slowness with which he proceeded, I feared for a moment that his courage might fail; but what was my astonishment, when arrived at the last step, he suddenly let go of my arm, and I saw him cross with a firm foot the breadth of the whole scaffold; and in a loud voice, I heard him pronounce distinctly these words: 'I die innocent of all the crimes laid to my charge; I pardon those who had occasioned my death; and I pray to God that the blood you are going to shed may never be visited on France.❞

The buildup to the king's execution began about the time elections were called for a new National Convention. Thousands were arrested and then massacred. New leaders of the people emerged, including **Jean-Paul Marat**, who published a radical journal called *Friend of the People.*

In September 1792, the newly elected National Convention began meeting. It had been called to draft a new constitution, but it also served as the ruling body of France. The Convention was dominated by lawyers, professionals, and property owners.

Two-thirds of its deputies were under the age of 45, but most had gotten some political experience as a result of the revolution. Almost all distrusted the king. It was therefore no surprise that the National Convention's first major step on September 21 was to abolish the monarchy and establish a republic, the French Republic.

*King Louis XVI*

The convention soon split into **factions**, or dissenting groups, however, over the fate of the king. The two main factions were the Girondins (juh•RAHN•duhns) and the Mountain. Both belonged to the **Jacobins** (JA•kuh•buhns), a network of national political clubs. The Girondins tended to represent areas outside Paris and favored keeping the king alive. The Mountain represented the interests of radicals in Paris. They felt the king needed to be executed to ensure he was not a rallying point for opponents of the republic.

In early 1793, the Mountain convinced the Convention to condemn Louis XVI to death. On January 21, he was beheaded on the guillotine. This machine was favored because it killed quickly and, the revolutionaries felt, humanely. The king's execution created new enemies for the revolution, both at home and abroad. A new crisis was at hand.

Disputes between the Girondins and the Mountain were only one reason France went through a **domestic** crisis in 1792 and 1793. In Paris, the Commune was constantly pressuring the National Convention to adopt more radical measures. In the country at large, there was serious resistance to the Convention in western France and in several important cities.

A crisis in foreign affairs was looming, too. When Louis XVI was executed, the crowned heads of Europe were outraged. Austria and Prussia were already threatening to invade in the summer of 1792. Now, with the king's execution, an informal coalition of Austria, Prussia, Spain, Portugal, Britain, and the Dutch Republic took up arms against France. The French armies began to fall back.

By late spring of 1793, the coalition was poised to invade. It seemed possible that the revolutionaries would be destroyed, and the old regime reestablished. The moment was decisive.

In order to meet the domestic and foreign crises, the National Convention gave broad powers to a special committee of 12, the **Committee of Public Safety.** It was dominated at first by Georges Danton, then by **Maximilien Robespierre.**

✓**Reading Check** **Examining** What were the differences between the Girondins and the Mountain?

# The Reign of Terror

**Main Idea** While the Committee of Public Safety was in power, thousands who opposed the government were executed.

**Reading Connection** Can you think of a modern-day government that has executed its critics? Read to learn how the threat of execution affected French people in the 1790s.

For roughly a year during 1793 and 1794, the Committee of Public Safety was in control of the government. It acted to defend France from **external** and domestic threats. To meet these threats, it adopted policies that created what came to be known as the **Reign of Terror.**

Revolutionary courts were set up and almost 40,000 people were killed. Of those, 16,000 people, including Marie Antoinette and Olympe de Gouges, died by the guillotine. Most executions occurred in towns and cities that had openly rebelled against the National Convention.

**Crushing Rebellion** Revolutionary armies were set up to bring rebellious cities back under the control of the National Convention. The Committee of Public Safety decided to make an example of **Lyon.** Some 1,880 citizens of that city were executed. When guillotining proved too slow, grapeshot (a cluster of small iron balls) was used to shoot the condemned into open graves. A German observer wrote:

❝Whole ranges of houses, always the most handsome, burnt. The churches, convents, and all the dwellings of the former patricians were in ruins. When I came to the guillotine, the blood of those who had been executed a few hours beforehand was still running in the street. . . . I said to a group of sans-culottes that it would be decent to clear away all this human blood. Why should it be cleared? one of them said to me. It's the blood of aristocrats and rebels. The dogs should lick it up.❞

## People In History

### Jean-Paul Marat
**1743–1793**
**French revolutionary**

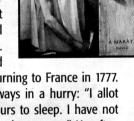

Jean-Paul Marat was a popular revolutionary leader in Paris at the beginning of the radical stage of the French Revolution. Born in Switzerland, he practiced medicine in London before returning to France in 1777. Marat was an intense man, always in a hurry: "I allot only two of the twenty-four hours to sleep. I have not had fifteen minutes play in over three years." He often worked in the bathtub because the water soothed the pain of a severe skin disorder.

In his journal, *Friend of the People,* Marat expressed his ideas, which were radical for his time. He called for mob violence and the right of the poor to take by force whatever they needed from the rich. He helped make the Jacobins more radical, especially by condemning the Girondins. This also led to his death: Charlotte Corday, a Girondin, stabbed him to death in his bathtub.

### Maximilien Robespierre
**1758–1794**
**French revolutionary**

Robespierre was one of the most important French revolutionary leaders. He received a law degree and later became a member of the National Convention, where he preached democracy and advocated suffrage (the right to vote) for all adult males. He lived simply and was known to be extremely honest. In fact, he was often known as "The Incorruptible." A believer in Rousseau's social contract idea, Robespierre thought that anyone opposed to being governed by the general will, as he interpreted it, should be executed.

One observer said of Robespierre, "That man will go far; he believes all that he says." Robespierre himself said, "How can one reproach a man who has truth on his side?" His eagerness and passion in pursuing the Reign of Terror, however, frightened many people. Eventually, he was arrested and guillotined.

In the west of France, too, revolutionary armies were brutal in defeating rebels. The commander of the revolutionary army ordered that no mercy be given: "The road is strewn with corpses. Women, priests, monks, children, all have been put to death. I have spared nobody." Perhaps the most notorious violence occurred in **Nantes**, where victims were executed by being sunk in barges in the Loire River.

People from all classes were killed during the Terror. Clergy and nobles made up about 15 percent of the victims, while the rest were from the bourgeoisie and peasant classes. The Committee of Public Safety held that all this bloodletting was only temporary. Once the war and domestic crisis were over, the true "Republic of Virtue" would follow, and the Declaration of the Rights of Man and the Citizen would be fully realized.

**The Republic of Virtue** The Committee of Public Safety took other steps to shape a new kind of French society. Robespierre called this the Republic of Virtue—a democratic republic composed of good citizens. As outward signs of support for the republic, the titles "citizen" and "citizeness" were to replace "mister" and "madame." Women wore long dresses inspired by the clothing of the ancient Roman Republic.

Good citizens would be formed by good education. A law aimed at primary education for all was passed but not widely implemented. Another law abolished slavery in French colonies.

Because people were alarmed about high inflation, the committee tried to control the prices of essential goods like food, fuel, and clothing. The controls did not work well, however, because the government had no way to enforce them.

During this radical stage of the revolution, women remained very active. They observed sessions of the National Convention and were not shy about making their demands known. In 1793, two women founded the Society for Revolutionary Republican Women in Paris. Most members were working-class women who asserted that they were ready to defend the republic. Men usually felt, however, that women should not be participating in politics or volunteering to fight.

# Opposing Viewpoints

## When Can Society Rightfully Break the Social Contract?

In a famous debate, two Englishmen, Edmund Burke and Thomas Paine, answered this question very differently. Burke, horrified by revolutionary violence, emphasized that people should be very cautious before breaking with tradition. Paine, a fervent supporter of the American Revolution, argued for great freedom in establishing a new government.

"Society is indeed a contract. Subordinate contracts for objects of mere occasional interest may be dissolved at pleasure—but the state ought not to be considered as nothing better than a partnership agreement in a trade of pepper and coffee . . . taken up for a little temporary interest, and to be dissolved by the fancy of the parties. . . . . As the ends of such a partnership cannot be obtained in many generations, it becomes a partnership not only between those who are living, but between those who are to be born. Each contract of each particular state is but a clause in the great primaeval contract of eternal society, linking the lower with the higher natures, connecting the visible and the invisible world, according to a fixed compact. . . . . "

—Edmund Burke,
*Reflections on the French Revolution* (1789)

The Convention also pushed a policy of de-Christianization. Its members believed that the Catholic Church encouraged superstition, rather than the use of reason. The word *saint* was removed from street names, churches were pillaged and closed by revolutionary armies, and priests were encouraged to marry. In Paris, the cathedral of Notre Dame was designated a "temple of reason." In November 1793, a public ceremony dedicated to the worship of reason was held in the former cathedral. Patriotic maidens in white dresses paraded before a temple of reason where the high altar had once stood.

Another example of de-Christianization was the adoption of a new calendar. Years would no longer be numbered from the birth of Christ but from September 22, 1792—the first day of the French Republic. The calendar contained 12 months. Each month consisted of three 10-day weeks, with the tenth day of each week a day of rest. This eliminated Sundays and Sunday worship services, as well as church holidays. Even the months were given new names. The new names often referred to agriculture or the climate. *Vendémiaire,* which was roughly the month of October, meant "vintage time."

> **"** Every age and generation must be as free to act for itself in all cases as the age and generations which preceded it. The vanity and presumption of governing beyond the grave is the most ridiculous and insolent of all tyrannies. Man has no property in man; neither has any generation a property in the generations which are to follow. Every generation is, and must be, competent to all the purposes which its occasions require. It is the living, and not the dead, that are to be accommodated. **"**
>
> —**Thomas Paine,**
> *The Rights of Man* (1792)

## You Decide

1. Based on these excerpts, how would Burke identify the people who make a social contract for a government? How would Paine do so?

2. With which of these arguments do you think most Americans would agree? Why do you think so?

Robespierre came to realize, however, that most French people would not accept these efforts at de-Christianization. France was still overwhelmingly Catholic.

**√ Reading Check** **Analyzing** How did the Committee of Public Safety identify enemies of the state?

## A Nation in Arms

**Main Idea** The revolutionary government raised a huge army that successfully defended France against invasion.

**Reading Connection** How would you feel if every young man in your town or city had to join the army? Read to find out French reaction to a national draft in 1793.

As foreign troops gathered on its borders, the revolution seemed to be in danger. To save the republic, the Committee of Public Safety issued a decree for universal mobilization on August 23, 1793:

> **"** Young men will fight, young men are called to conquer. Married men will forge arms, transport military baggage and guns and will prepare food supplies. Women, who at long last are to take their rightful place in the revolution and follow their true destiny, will forget their futile tasks: their delicate hands will work at making clothes for soldiers; they will make tents and they will extend their tender care to shelters where the defenders of the Patrie [homeland] will receive the help that their wounds require. Children will make lint of old cloth. It is for them that we are fighting: children, those beings destined to gather all the fruits of the revolution, will raise their pure hands toward the skies. And old men, performing their missions again, as of yore, will be guided to the public squares of the cities where they will kindle the courage of young warriors and preach the doctrines of hate for kings and the unity of the Republic. **"**

In less than a year, the French revolutionary government had raised a huge army—by September 1794, it was over a million. It was the largest army that had ever been seen in Europe, and it pushed the allied invaders back across the Rhine. It even conquered the **Austrian Netherlands.**

The French revolutionary army was very important in creating modern nationalism. In earlier times, wars were more the business of ruling dynasties who fought rivals with relatively small armies of paid professionals. This army was created by a people's government. Its wars were people's wars.

▼ Reign of Terror
execution list

▼ Model of a guillotine

LISTE
DES
GUILLOTINÉS

SUR la place de la Révolution, et au ci-devant
Carouzel

1. Louis-David Collenot, dit d'Angremont,
ci-devant secrétaire de l'administration de la garde
nationale à la maison-commune, commandant en
chef la bande assassine, convaincu de conspiration.

2. La Porte, ci-devant intendant de la liste-civile,
convaincu de conspiration.

3. Turnsoi, homme-de-lettres, et ci-devant rédac-
teur de la Gazette de Paris, et d'une autre feuille in-
titulée Le Royalisme, convaincu de conspiration.

4. Jean Julien, ci-devant charretier à Vaugirard,
convaincu de conspiration.

5. Jacques-Joseph-Antoine-Léger Backman, natif du
canton de Glaris, âgé de 59 ans, militaire depuis son
jeune âge, demeurant à Paris, rue Verte, fauxbourg
St-Honoré, ci-devant major-général des ci-devant
gardes-suisses, convaincu de conspiration.

6. Nicolas Roussel, natif de Ville-Rosoi, départe-
ment de la Moselle, âgé de 49 ans, ci-devant em-
ployé dans la régie générale, convaincu de conspiration.

7. Jeanne-Catherine Leclerc, âgée de 50 ans, cui-
sinière, convaincue de conspiration.

8. Anne-Hyacinthe Beaujour, ci-devant colonel du
3e. régiment d'infanterie commandé par Dumouriez,
A a

Fac-similé de la liste des guillotinés vendue dans les rues
sous la Terreur.

### 🖼 Picturing **History**

During the Reign of Terror, thousands of people, including aristocrats and the queen of France, were killed by the guillotine. Why did the revolutionaries decide to use the guillotine to execute people?

▲ Marie Antoinette
goes to her execution.

**End of the Terror** By mid-1794, most of France's enemies had been defeated. There was less need for the tight control of the Reign of Terror, but still it continued. The powerful Robespierre was obsessed with ridding France of every enemy and all corruption. Only then could the Republic of Virtue follow.

Now many deputies in the Convention decided to act against Robespierre: if they did not, he might execute them next. The deputies won enough votes to condemn Robespierre, and he himself went to the guillotine on July 28, 1794.

After the death of Robespierre, revolutionary fervor cooled. Gradually the Jacobins lost power and moderate leaders took control. The Reign of Terror came to a halt.

☑ **Reading Check** **Evaluating** How did the French revolutionary army help to create modern nationalism?

## The Directory

**Main Idea** The Constitution of 1795 set up a new government, but it was not able to inspire trust or solve the government's economic problems.

**Reading Connection** What kind of government did Americans set up after the Revolutionary War? Read to learn about the French government set up after the Reign of Terror.

With the terror over, the National Convention moved in a more conservative direction. First, it restricted the power of the Committee of Public Safety. Next, churches were allowed to reopen. Finally, a brand-new constitution was created.

To keep any one political group from gaining control, the Constitution of 1795 set up a legislative branch of two houses. A lower house, known as the Council of

500, drafted laws. An upper house of 250, the Council of Elders, accepted or rejected proposed laws.

The method for election shows that the new government was much more conservative than the government of Robespierre. Members of both houses were chosen by **electors**, or qualified voters. Only those who owned or rented property worth a certain amount could be electors—only 30,000 people in the whole nation qualified.

Under the new constitution, the executive was a committee of five termed **the Directory.** The upper house chose the Directors from a list presented by the lower house.

The Directory, which lasted from 1795 to 1799, became known mainly for corruption. Government officials and legislators often made fortunes through government contracts or by loaning the government money at very high interest rates.

The Directory faced massive challenges. First, like earlier governments, it had political enemies. Some people wanted to bring back the monarchy, while others plotted to create a more radical regime like Robespierre's. Second, economic problems continued with no solution in sight. Finally, France was still conducting an expensive war against foreign enemies.

To stay in power, the Directory began to rely on the military, but one military leader turned on the government. In 1799, General Napoleon Bonaparte toppled the Directory in a **coup d'état** (KOO DAY• TAH), a sudden overthrow of the government.

✓ **Reading Check** **Describing** Describe the government that replaced the National Convention.

**History** *through Art*

***The Eighteenth of Brumaire* by François Bouchot**
This painting depicts Napoleon's coup d'état, November 10, 1799. What factors helped Napoleon (shown center) overthrow the Directory?

**Study Central**

For help with the concepts in this section of *Glencoe World History–Modern Times*, go to wh.mt.glencoe.com and click on **Study Central.**

# SECTION 2 ASSESSMENT

### Checking for Understanding

1. **Vocabulary** Define: faction, domestic, external, elector, coup d'état.

2. **People and Events** Identify: Georges Danton, Jean-Paul Marat, Jacobins, Committee of Public Safety, Maximilien Robespierre, Reign of Terror, the Directory.

3. **Places** Locate: Lyon, Nantes, Austrian Netherlands.

### Reviewing Big Ideas

4. **Explain** both the similarities and the differences between the Girondins and the Mountain.

### Critical Thinking

5. **Historical Analysis** **Understanding Chronology** Did the French Republic live up to the revolution's ideals of Liberty, Equality, and Fraternity? Write a paragraph to support your opinion. **CA CS 1**

6. **Contrasting Information** Use a table like the one below to contrast government policy during and after Robespierre.

| During | After |
|--------|-------|
|  |  |
|  |  |
|  |  |

### Analyzing Visuals

7. **Examine** the painting shown on page 224. Explain whether or not you think this is a realistic depiction of Marie Antoinette before her execution, or whether the artist is promoting a particular version of events.

### Writing About History

8. **Expository Writing** Propaganda is the spreading of information to help or hurt a cause. How does the decree of universal mobilization quoted on page 223 fit the definition of propaganda? Support your argument in an essay. **CA 10WA2.3**

# YOUNG PEOPLE IN . . .

## Revolutionary France

In 1794, deputies in the National Convention proposed a new military school to train young boys aged 16 and 17 in the arts of war and the love of country. A few months later, the *École de Mars,* or School of Mars (the Roman god of war), opened on the outskirts of Paris.

The 3,400 recruits were expected to maintain high moral standards and become enthusiastic patriots, but many ignored the rules and expressed a wish to go home. After the death of Robespierre, the school shut down. The plan to train young people in a few weeks to be dedicated patriots had failed.

At the same time, many of these youths now became part of the reaction against the Reign of Terror. They formed what were called "golden youth," gangs of young men who attacked Jacobins and destroyed public statues of revolutionary figures, such as Jean-Paul Marat.

For many young people who had shared in the revolutionary enthusiasm, however, the reaction against the Reign of Terror was a disaster. One good example is Marc-Antoine Jullien. At 18, he had been an assistant to Robespierre. After the execution of Robespierre, he was hunted down and put in prison for two years.

In prison, Jullien wrote a diary on the hardships of a young revolutionary who had grown old before his time: "I was born in a volcano, I lived in the midst of its eruption. I will be buried in its lava." He expressed his pain: "My life is a dark and terrible story, but one that is touching and educational for inexperienced youth."

When Jullien was released from prison, he wrote, "I am leaving, I never wish to see Paris again, I want cows and milk. I am twenty-one years old, may the dawn of my life no longer be clouded by dark images."

Disillusioned by his troubles, Jullien came to long for a savior who would restore the freedom of the republic. When Napoleon came along, he believed that he had found his savior.

◄ In this image, young men are going off to practice using the cannon. During the eighteenth century, and even later, the cannon was the main artillery weapon in warfare. Cannon shot balls that could be blasted at targets as far away as a mile.

In the last years before the revolution broke out, French families could participate in entertainments like this fair in August that celebrated the feast of St. Lawrence. If you look closely, you can spot young people acting up during a theatrical performance.

▲ This image depicts a fierce sans-culotte, the name for the Parisian lower classes who took part in the revolution. Notice his red cap of liberty and the pike he carries. It was natural for sans-culottes to influence young boys to follow their lead.

◄ Closing of the Salle des Jacobins in Paris, symbolizing the end of the Reign of Terror

## CONNECTING TO THE PAST

1. **Examine** Why did the National Convention choose to open a school dedicated to training patriots? Are there comparable schools in the United States today?

2. **Writing about History** Marc-Antoine Jullien lived during troubled times. In the world today, many young people are undergoing similar experiences. Research an area of political unrest. Write a one-page paper describing the effect of that unrest on a person your age.

# The Age of Napoleon

## Guide to Reading

### Section Preview
After the French Revolution, Napoleon built and lost an empire, and also spread ideas about nationalism.

**Main Idea**
- Napoleon, a popular general, overthrew the Directory, helped set up a new government, and eventually held complete power. (p. 229)
- Napoleon brought stability to France and established a single law code that recognized the equality of all citizens before the law. (p. 230)
- By conquering much of Europe, Napoleon established an empire. (p. 231)

- A feeling of nationalism spread by France to other countries led to the opposition to French rule in these countries. (p. 233)
- After major losses in Russia and Austria, Napoleon met his final defeat at Waterloo and was exiled. (p. 234)

### Content Vocabulary
consulate, nationalism

### Academic Vocabulary
capable, liberal

### People and Events to Identify
Napoleon Bonaparte, Civil Code, Anne-Louise-Germaine de Staël, Duke of Wellington

### Places to Locate
Corsica, Moscow, Elba, Waterloo

### Reading Objectives
1. Explain why Napoleon wanted to stop British goods from reaching Europe.
2. Identify two reasons for the collapse of Napoleon's empire.

### Reading Strategy
**Summarizing Information** In a table like the one below, list Napoleon's achievements.

| Achievements of Napoleon's Rule |
|---|

### Preview of Events

| ♦1790 | ♦1800 | ♦1810 | ♦1820 |
|---|---|---|---|

**1799**
Napoleon takes part in coup d'état

**1804**
Napoleon is crowned emperor

**1805**
French are defeated at Trafalgar

**1815**
Napoleon is defeated at Waterloo

## California Standards in This Section

*Reading this section will help you master these California History–Social Science standards.*

**10.2.4:** Explain how the ideology of the French Revolution led France to develop from constitutional monarchy to democratic despotism to the Napoleonic empire.

**10.2.5:** Discuss how nationalism spread across Europe with Napoleon but was repressed for a generation under the Congress of Vienna and Concert of Europe until the Revolutions of 1848.

# The Rise of Napoleon

**Main Idea** Napoleon, a popular general, overthrew the Directory, helped set up a new government, and eventually held complete power.

**Reading Connection** What qualities do you look for in a government leader? Read to find out what qualities made people accept Napoleon as a powerful leader in the early 1800s.

**Napoleon Bonaparte** dominated French and European history from 1799 to 1815. His great military exploits, rapid rise to fame, and tragic end have made him a legend. Not the least of his qualities was his supreme self-confidence.

## Voices from the Past

Napoleon possessed an overwhelming sense of his own importance. He was convinced that he was the man of destiny who would save the French people. Napoleon once wrote:

> ❝But let that impatiently awaited savior give a sudden sign of his existence, and the people's instinct will divine him and call upon him. The obstacles are smoothed before his steps, and a whole great nation, flying to see him pass, will seem to be saying: 'Here is the man.'. . . A consecutive series of great actions never is the result of chance and luck; it always is the product of planning and genius. Great men are rarely known to fail in their most perilous enterprises. . . . Is it because they are lucky that they become great? No, but being great, they have been able to master luck.❞

Napoleon's role in the French Revolution is complex. In one sense, he brought it to an end when he came to power in 1799. Yet he was a child of the revolution, too. Without it, he would never have risen to power, and he himself never failed to remind the French that he had preserved the best parts of the revolution during his reign as emperor.

**Early Life** Napoleon was born in 1769 in **Corsica**, an island in the Mediterranean, only a few months after France annexed the island. His father came from minor nobility in Italy, but the family was far from rich. Napoleon was talented, however, and won a scholarship to a famous military school.

When he completed his studies, Napoleon was commissioned as a lieutenant in the French army. Although he turned out to be one of the world's greatest generals and a man beloved by his soldiers, there were few signs of his future success at this stage. He was short, spoke with an Italian accent, and was not popular with his fellow officers.

Napoleon devoted himself to his goals. He read what French philosophes had to say about reason, and he studied famous military campaigns. When revolution and war with Europe came about, there were many opportunities for Napoleon to use his knowledge and skills.

**Military Successes** Napoleon rose quickly through the ranks. In 1792, he became a captain. Two years later, at the age of 24, he was made a brigadier general by the Committee of Public Safety. In 1796, he was made commander of the French armies in Italy. There Napoleon won a series of battles with qualities he became famous for—speed, surprise, and decisive action.

During the Italian campaigns, Napoleon's energy and initiative earned him the devotion of his troops. His keen intelligence, ease with words, and supreme self-confidence allowed him to win the support of everyone around him.

In 1797, he returned to France as a hero. He was given command of an army in training to invade Britain, but he knew the French could not carry out that invasion. Instead, he suggested striking indirectly at Britain by taking Egypt. Egypt lay on the route to India, one of Britain's most important colonies.

Napoleon's goal of taking Egypt was never met, however. The British were a great sea power and controlled the Mediterranean. By 1799, the British cut off Napoleon's army in Egypt. With defeat certain, Napoleon abandoned his army and returned to Paris.

▼ *Napoleon Bonaparte*

**Consul and Emperor** In Paris, Napoleon took part in the coup d'état of 1799 that overthrew the Directory and set up a new government, the **consulate.** In theory, it was a republic, but in fact Napoleon held absolute power. Napoleon was called first consul, a title borrowed from ancient Rome. He appointed officials, controlled the army, conducted foreign affairs, and influenced the legislature. In 1802, Napoleon was made consul for life. Two years later, he crowned himself Emperor Napoleon I.

✓**Reading Check** **Describing** What personal qualities did Napoleon possess that gained him popular support?

# Napoleon's Domestic Policies

**Main Idea** Napoleon brought stability to France and established a single law code that recognized the equality of all citizens before the law.

**Reading Connection** How would you feel if a government official checked all your mail before you read it? Read to learn how many of Napoleon's policies reduced freedom.

Napoleon once claimed that he had preserved the gains of the revolution. Since he destroyed the republican form of government when he took power, how could Napoleon make this boast? This is an important question. As we look at Napoleon's domestic policies, it will be possible to judge whether the emperor's claims had any merit.

**Peace with the Church** One of Napoleon's most important domestic policies was his policy toward the Catholic Church. Very soon after the consulate was established, Napoleon set out to establish peace with the Church, the oldest enemy of the revolution. In matters of religion, Napoleon himself was a man of the Enlightenment. He believed in reason and felt that religion was at most a social convenience. Since most of France was Catholic, Napoleon felt it was good policy to mend relations with the Church.

In 1801, Napoleon came to an agreement with the pope. Catholicism would be recognized as the religion of the majority of the people. In return, the pope would not ask for the return of the church lands seized in the revolution.

With this agreement, the Catholic Church was no longer a formal enemy of the French government. It also meant that people who had acquired church land in the revolution became avid supporters of Napoleon.

*Picturing* **History**

In this painting, Napoleon is shown crowning his wife Josephine empress. During his own coronation, Napoleon seized the crown from Pope Pius VII and placed it on his own head. **How had Napoleon earlier made peace with the Catholic Church?**

**Codification of the Laws** Napoleon's most famous domestic achievement was to codify the law. Before the revolution, France had almost 300 different legal systems. During the revolution, efforts were made to organize them and make them consistent, but the work was not completed until Napoleon's reign.

Seven law codes were created, but the most important was the **Civil Code**, or Napoleonic Code. It reflected many of the principles that the revolutionaries had fought for: equality of all citizens before the law; the right of the individual to choose a profession; religious toleration; and the abolition of serfdom and all feudal obligations.

For women and children, the Civil Code was a step back. During the radical stage of the revolution, new laws had made divorce easier and allowed children, even daughters, to inherit property on an equal basis. The Civil Code undid these laws. It became more difficult for a woman to get a divorce. Women were "less equal than men" in other ways, too. When they married, they lost control over any property they had. They could not testify in court. In general, the code treated women something like children, beings who needed protection and who did not have a public role.

**A New Bureaucracy** Napoleon is also well known because he created a strong, centralized administration. He focused on developing a bureaucracy of **capable** officials. Early on, the regime showed that it did not care about rank or birth. Public officials and military officers alike were promoted based on their ability. Opening careers to men of talent was a reform that the middle class had clamored for before the revolution.

Napoleon also created a new kind of aristocracy, one based on meritorious service to the nation. Between 1808 and 1814, Napoleon created about 3,200 nobles. Nearly 60 percent were military officers, while the rest were civil service or state and local officials. Only 22 percent of this new aristocracy were from noble families of the old regime; about 60 percent were middle class.

**Preserver of the Revolution?** In his domestic policies, then, Napoleon did keep some major reforms of the French Revolution. Under the Civil Code, all citizens were

▲ *French marriage ceremony, nineteenth century*

equal before the law. The concept of opening government careers to more people was another gain of the revolution that he retained.

On the other hand, Napoleon destroyed some ideals of the revolution. He restricted liberty, for example, when he censored the free press. Despite protests from prominent writers like **Anne-Louise-Germaine de Staël**, he shut down 60 of France's 73 newspapers. Even government-approved newspapers had to have all their manuscripts examined before they were published. The government police kept busy censoring private mail as well.

✓ **Reading Check** **Evaluating** What was the overall effect of Napoleon's Civil Code?

## Napoleon's Empire

**Main Idea** By conquering much of Europe, Napoleon established an empire.

**Reading Connection** Can you remember how the empire of Charlemagne was built in Europe? Read to discover how Napoleon was able to build an empire.

Napoleon is known best not as a domestic reformer, but as a talented general who conquered much of Europe. His conquests began soon after he rose to power.

**Building the Empire** When Napoleon became consul in 1799, France was at war with a European coalition of Russia, Great Britain, and Austria. Napoleon realized the need for a pause in the war. "The French Revolution is not finished, " he said, "so long as the scourge of war lasts. . . . I want peace, as much to settle the present French government, as to save the world from chaos."

In 1802, a treaty was signed, but the peace did not last long. War with Britain broke out again in 1803. Gradually, Britain was joined by Austria, Russia, Sweden, and Prussia. In a series of battles at Ulm, Austerlitz, Jena, and Eylau from 1805 to 1807, Napoleon's Grand Army defeated the Austrian, Prussian, and Russian armies.

With all these victories behind him, Napoleon was able to create a new European order. From 1807 to 1812, Napoleon was the master of a Grand Empire of three main parts: the French Empire, the dependent states, and allied states. The French Empire was the core. It included an enlarged France extending to the Rhine River on its eastern boundary and the western half of Italy north of Rome.

The dependent states were kingdoms ruled by relatives of Napoleon. Eventually these included Spain, Holland, the kingdom of Italy, the Swiss Republic, the Grand Duchy of Warsaw, and the Confederation of the Rhine—an alliance of all the German states except Austria and Prussia.

The allied states were states Napoleon had defeated and then forced to join his struggle against Britain. These states included Prussia, Austria, Russia, and Sweden.

**Spreading the Principles of the Revolution**
Within his empire, Napoleon sought to spread some of the principles of the French Revolution, including legal equality, religious toleration, and economic freedom. He explained to his brother Jerome after he had made Jerome king of Westphalia:

66What the peoples of Germany desire most impatiently is that talented commoners should have the same right to your esteem and to public employments as the nobles, that any trace of serfdom and of an intermediate hierarchy between the sovereign and the lowest class of the people should be completely abolished. The benefits of the Code Napoleon, the publicity of judicial procedure, the creation of juries must be so many distinguishing marks of your monarchy. . . . The peoples of Germany, the peoples of France, of Italy, of Spain all desire equality and liberal ideas. . . . [T]he buzzing of the privileged classes is contrary to the general opinion. Be a constitutional king.99

Napoleon brought many revolutionary principles and practices to Europe. In the inner core and dependent states of his Grand Empire, Napoleon tried to destroy the old order. The nobility and the clergy everywhere in these states lost their privileges. All people were declared equal before the law, offices were to be open equally to talent, and a policy of religious toleration was announced. These revolutionary principles were important in developing **liberal** traditions in these countries.

✓ **Reading Check** **Identifying** What were the three parts of Napoleon's Grand Empire?

## People In History

### Anne-Louise-Germaine de Staël
**1766–1817—French writer**

Anne-Louise-Germaine de Staël was a prominent writer of the revolutionary and Napoleonic eras in France. She established a salon for the powerful that lasted from 1790 until 1804. It was said of her that she was "so spoiled by admiration for her wit that it [would] be hard to make her realize her shortcomings." During the Reign of Terror, she helped friends escape France. She also left France but returned in 1795.

Although she at first supported Napoleon, she clashed repeatedly with him. She once asked him, "Who was the greatest woman of history?" Napoleon responded, "The one who had the most children." Eventually, she denounced Napoleon's rule as tyrannical. Napoleon banned her books in France and exiled her to the German states, where she continued to write.

## Napoleonic Europe, 1799–1815

NATIONAL GEOGRAPHIC

**Map labels:**
KINGDOM OF DENMARK AND NORWAY, SWEDEN, North Sea, Baltic Sea, UNITED KINGDOM, Moscow R., Borodino 1812, Moscow, Smolensk, Kovno, Neman, Minsk, Friedland 1807, PRUSSIA, RUSSIAN EMPIRE, Berlin, GRAND DUCHY OF WARSAW, Kiev, Dnieper R., London, Rhine R., Leipzig 1813, Jena 1806, Brussels, Waterloo 1815, CONFEDERATION OF THE RHINE, Dniester R., ATLANTIC OCEAN, Paris, Versailles, Seine R., Ulm 1805, Vienna, Wagram 1809, Austerlitz 1805, AUSTRIAN EMPIRE, Black Sea, FRENCH EMPIRE, SWITZ., Danube R., ILLYRIAN PROVINCES, OTTOMAN EMPIRE, Marengo 1800, KINGDOM OF ITALY, Elba, Rome, Corsica, KINGDOM OF NAPLES, Madrid, PORTUGAL, Sardinia, SPAIN, Sicily, Mediterranean Sea, Trafalgar 1805, Strait of Gibraltar

**Legend:**
— France, 1799
French Empire, 1812
Dependent states, 1812
States allied with Napoleon, 1812
States allied against Napoleon, 1812
✹ French victory
✹ French defeat
← Napoleon's invasion of Russia, June–December 1812

300 miles
300 kilometers
Lambert Azimuthal Equal-Area projection

## The European Response

**Main Idea** A feeling of nationalism spread by France to other countries led to the opposition to French rule in these countries.

**Reading Connection** How would Americans today react to a foreign country's dictating trade policy to their government? Read to learn about the reaction Napoleon called forth when he tried to bar trade with Britain.

Like Hitler 130 years later, Napoleon hoped that his Grand Empire would last for centuries. Yet like Hitler's empire, the empire of Napoleon collapsed almost as rapidly as it was formed. Two major reasons explain this collapse: Britain's ability to resist Napoleon, and the rise of nationalism.

### Geography Skills

From 1807 to 1812, Napoleon controlled a vast empire in Europe.

1. **Interpreting Maps** Which of the dependent states in Napoleon's empire lies farthest east?

2. **Applying Geography Skills** Examine the locations of the states that were allied against Napoleon in 1812. What geographic factors would have helped these states to remain independent from Napoleon's control?

**British Resistance** Napoleon was never able to conquer Great Britain. To a great extent, this was because Britain was a sea power. So long as Britain ruled the waves, it was almost invulnerable. Napoleon gathered together ships, hoping to invade, but the British navy defeated the combined French-Spanish fleet at Trafalgar in 1805. Napoleon gave up on the idea of actually landing forces on British shores.

His next move was to make his allies cut off trade with Britain. He believed that if no British goods were sold to any of the European nations in the Grand Alliance, the British would be too poor to wage war. Napoleon called this the Continental System. The Continental System failed because the allied states resented it. Some began to cheat and traded secretly. The British also found new markets in the Middle East and in Latin America—so much so that by 1810, British overseas exports were at near-record highs.

**Nationalism** One of the most important factors in Napoleon's defeat was nationalism. **Nationalism** is the sense of unique identity of a people. That feeling has its foundations in a common language, common religion, and national symbols.

Nationalism would prove to be one of the most important forces of the nineteenth century, and it began with the French Revolution. A new era in history was born when the French people decided that *they* were the nation, not the king.

As Napoleon marched his armies through the Germanies, Spain, Italy, and Poland, the peoples in these countries learned about the revolutionary ideas of equality and liberty. Napoleon also roused new ideas of nationalism. This happened in two ways. First, the conquered peoples became united in their hatred of the invaders. Second, the conquered peoples were able to see the power and strength of national feeling. It was a lesson not lost on them or their rulers.

✔️ **Reading Check** **Explaining** Why did being a sea power help Britain to survive an attack by the French?

---

▼ The Crossing of the Beresina *by January Suchodolsky shows Napoleon's Grand Army in full retreat from Russia.*

# The Fall of Napoleon

**Main Idea** After major losses in Russia and Austria, Napoleon met his final defeat at Waterloo and was exiled.

**Reading Connection** Today there are some rulers who go into exile to avoid prosecution in their homelands. Read to see why in 1815 the French government felt safe only with Napoleon in exile.

---

The beginning of Napoleon's downfall can be dated to 1812 when he made the fateful decision to invade Russia. Within a few years, his fall was complete.

**Disaster in Russia** The Russians had refused to remain in the Continental System, leaving Napoleon with little choice but to invade. He knew the risks in invading vast Russia, but he also knew that if he did not punish the Russians for ignoring the Continental System, other nations would follow suit.

In June 1812, a Grand Army of more than 600,000 men crossed into Russia. Napoleon's hopes depended on a quick victory over the Russians. The Russian forces, however, refused to give battle. Instead they retreated for hundreds of miles. As they retreated, they burnt their own villages and countryside to keep Napoleon's army from finding food. When the Russians did stop to fight at Borodino, Napoleon's forces won an indecisive and costly victory.

When the Grand Army finally reached **Moscow**, they found that the city had been set on fire. Lacking food or supplies, Napoleon was forced to abandon the Russian capital in October. As the winter snows and storms began, Napoleon led the "Great Retreat" west

## What If...

### Napoleon had won at Waterloo?

Napoleon dominated much of the world stage until Waterloo, a close battle against the Duke of Wellington and the allied forces. Military strategists speculate that had Napoleon's commanders been better, Napoleon might have won.

**Consider the Consequences** Consider Napoleon's impact on history had he defeated Wellington. Explain why this victory might have marshaled enough support for Napoleon to have resumed his rule as emperor.

across Russia. Thousands of soldiers starved and froze along the way. Only 40,000 of the original 600,000 managed to make it to Poland in January 1813.

Now that the French army was crippled, other European states joined in for the attack. In March 1814, Paris itself was captured. Napoleon was sent into exile on the island of **Elba**, off the northwest coast of Italy. The victorious powers restored monarchy to France. The brother of the executed king was installed as Louis XVIII.

**The Final Defeat** The new king had little support—the French people were not ready to surrender the glory of empire. Nor was Napoleon ready to give up.

Restless in exile, he left the island of Elba and slipped back into France.

The new king sent troops to capture Napoleon, but he boldly addressed them: "Soldiers of the 5th regiment, I am your Emperor. . . . If there is a man among you [who] would kill his Emperor, here I am!"

No one fired a shot. Instead, they shouted "Vive l'Empereur! Vive l'Empereur!"—"Long live the Emperor! Long live the Emperor!"—and went over to his side. On March 20, 1815, Napoleon entered Paris in triumph.

Russia, Great Britain, Austria, and Prussia were worried. They pledged to defeat again the man they called the "Enemy and Disturber of the Tranquility of the World." Meanwhile, Napoleon raised another French army as devoted veterans rallied from all over France. He then readied an attack on the allies across the border in Belgium.

At **Waterloo** in Belgium, Napoleon met a combined British and Prussian army under the **Duke of Wellington** on June 18, 1815. Napoleon suffered a bloody defeat, and this time the consensus of the victorious allies was to exile him to St. Helena, a small island in the south Atlantic. Napoleon remained in exile until his death in 1821, but his memory haunted French political life for many decades.

✓**Reading Check** **Examining** Why did Napoleon invade Russia?

For help with the concepts in this section of *Glencoe World History–Modern Times*, go to wh.mt.glencoe.com and click on **Study Central.**

## SECTION 3 ASSESSMENT

### Checking for Understanding

1. **Vocabulary** Define: consulate, capable, liberal, nationalism.

2. **People and Events** Identify: Napoleon Bonaparte, Civil Code, Anne-Louise-Germaine de Staël, Duke of Wellington.

3. **Places** Locate: Corsica, Moscow, Elba, Waterloo.

### Reviewing Big Ideas

4. **List** the powers Napoleon exercised as first consul.

### Critical Thinking

5. **Historical Analysis** **Connecting Events** How did the principles of the French Revolution spread throughout Europe? **CA HI 1**

6. **Sequencing Information** Using a diagram like this one, identify the reasons for the rise and fall of Napoleon.

Napoleon's Rise and Fall

Rise ↗ / Fall ↘

### Analyzing Visuals

7. **Examine** the portrait on page 207. Napoleon commissioned it in 1800. How does David portray Napoleon, and why do you think Napoleon wanted artists to produce portraits like this one?

### Writing About History

8. **Persuasive Writing** Was Napoleon an enlightened ruler or a tyrant? Write a paper supporting your view. Be sure to include pertinent information about Napoleon's Civil Code. **CA 10WA2.4a,c**

*During a revolution, who makes the laws, and are they the same for everyone? Read how different people addressed these issues during the French Revolution.*

## SOURCE 1: *Preliminary to the French Constitution* August 1789

*Abbé Sieyès (1748–1836), an influential writer, described the difference between active and passive citizens in the* Preliminary to the French Constitution.

After having set forth the *natural and civil rights* of the citizen, the plan that we are following leads us to recognize their *political* rights.

The difference between these two kinds of rights consists in the natural and civil rights being those *for* which the maintenance and development of society is constituted and the political rights being those *by* which society is constitutes and maintains itself. It would be better for the clarity of language to call the first *passive* rights and the second *active* rights.

All the inhabitants of a country should enjoy the rights of a passive citizen: all have the right to protection of their person, their property, their liberty, etc.; but all do not have the right to take an active part in the formation of the public authorities: all are not active citizens. Women, at least in the present state, children, foreigners, those who contribute nothing to maintaining the public establishment, should have no active influence on public affairs. All can enjoy the advantages of society; but those alone who contribute to the public establishment are like the true shareholders in the great social enterprise. They alone are the true active citizens, the true members of the association.

## SOURCE 2: Robespierre Denouncing Restrictions on Citizenship

*In this speech, Maximilien Robespierre (1758–1794) opposed the National Assembly's categories of active and passive citizens.*

All citizens, whoever they are, have the right to aspire to all levels of officeholding. Nothing is more in line with your declaration of rights, according to which all privileges, all distinctions, all exception must disappear. The Constitution establishes that **sovereignty**[1] resides in the people, in all the individuals of the people. Each individual therefore has the right to participate in making the law which governs him and the administration of the public good which is his own. If not, it is not true that all men are equal in rights, that every man is a citizen. If he who only pays a tax equivalent to a day of work has fewer rights than he who pays the equivalent to three days of work, and he who pays at the level of ten days has more rights than he whose tax only equals that value of three, then he who enjoys 100,000 livres [French pounds] of revenue has 100

*Cartoon of 1789 showing king, noble, and priest riding comfortably on a road which is the Third Estate*

THE ESTATES. (Paris, 1789.)

---
[1]**sovereignty:** power; authority

times as many rights as he who only has 1,000 livres of revenue. It follows from all your **decrees**[2] that every citizen has the right to participate in making the law and consequently that of being an elector or eligible for office without the distinction of wealth.

## SOURCE 3: Women's Rights

*Etta Palm d'Aelders was a woman actively involved with the reformers known as the Cercle Social (Social Circle). She expressed frustration over women's position in her* Discourse on the Injustice of the Laws in Favor of Men, *written in 1790.*

Do not be just by halves, Gentlemen; . . . justice must be the first virtue of free men, and justice demands that the laws be the same for all beings, like the air and the sun. And yet everywhere, the laws favor men at the expense of women, because everywhere power is in your hands. What! Will free men, an enlightened people living in a century of enlightenment and philosophy, will they **consecrate**[3] what has been the abuse of power in a century of ignorance? . . .

The prejudices with which our sex has been surrounded—supported by unjust laws which only accord us a secondary existence in society and which often forces us into the humiliating necessity of winning over the **cantankerous**[4] and ferocious character of a man, who, by the greed of those close to us has become our master—those prejudices have changed what was for us the sweetest and most saintly of duties, those of wife and mother, into a painful and terrible slavery. . . .

Well! What could be more unjust! Our life, our liberty, our fortune are no longer ours; leaving childhood, turned over to a despot whom often the heart finds repulsive, the most beautiful days of our life slip away in moans and tears, while our fortune becomes prey to fraud and debauchery. . . .

Oh! Gentlemen, if you wish us to be enthusiastic about the happy constitution that gives back men their rights, then begin by being just toward us. From now on we should be your voluntary companions and not

your slaves. Let us merit your attachment! Do you believe that the desire for success is less becoming to us, that a good name is less dear to us than to you? And if devotion to study, if patriotic zeal, if virtue itself . . . is as natural to us as to you, why do we not receive the same education and the same means to acquire them?

I will not speak, Gentlemen, of those **iniquitous**[5] men who pretend that nothing can exempt us from an eternal subordination. Is this not an absurdity just like those told to the French on 15 July 1789: "Leave there your just demands; you are born for slavery; nothing can exempt you from eternally obeying an arbitrary will."

> ─────────────
> [5]**iniquitous:** wicked

## DBQ — Document-Based Questions

### Historical Analysis     CA HR 1, HR 3

**Source 1:** According to Sieyès, what is the difference between the rights of a *passive citizen* and an *active citizen*? Why does he explain that women, children, and foreigners should be excluded from possessing active rights?

**Source 2:** How does Robespierre use the Declaration of the Rights of Man and the Citizen and the French constitution to denounce the practice of giving more rights to citizens in France who pay more taxes?

**Source 3:** What does Etta Palm D'Aelders mean when she says "Will free men . . . consecrate what has been the abuse of power in a century of ignorance"?

### Comparing and Contrasting Sources

1. Even though Robespierre was not a defender of women's equality in France, how are his and Etta Palm d'Aelders's arguments similar?

2. When might Sieyès claim that women would be eligible for the equal rights that Etta Palm d'Aelders states that they rightfully deserve?

> ─────────────
> [2]**decrees:** authoritative decisions; declarations
> [3]**consecrate:** make sacred
> [4]**cantankerous:** bad disposition; quarrelsome

## Chapter Summary

The French Revolution was one of the great turning points in history. The years from 1789 to 1815 in France were chaotic, and change came in unexpected ways. The chart below will help you understand and remember some of the major events of this time and the changes they caused.

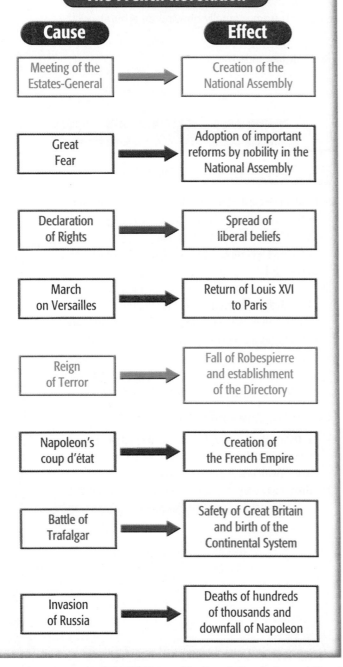

**The French Revolution**

**Cause** → **Effect**

| Cause | Effect |
|-------|--------|
| Meeting of the Estates-General | Creation of the National Assembly |
| Great Fear | Adoption of important reforms by nobility in the National Assembly |
| Declaration of Rights | Spread of liberal beliefs |
| March on Versailles | Return of Louis XVI to Paris |
| Reign of Terror | Fall of Robespierre and establishment of the Directory |
| Napoleon's coup d'état | Creation of the French Empire |
| Battle of Trafalgar | Safety of Great Britain and birth of the Continental System |
| Invasion of Russia | Deaths of hundreds of thousands and downfall of Napoleon |

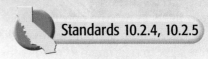

Standards 10.2.4, 10.2.5

## Reviewing Content Vocabulary

*On a sheet of paper, use each of these terms in a sentence.*

1. estate
2. *taille*
3. bourgeoisie
4. sans-culottes
5. faction
6. elector
7. coup d'etat
8. consulate
9. nationalism

## Reviewing Academic Vocabulary

*On a sheet of paper, use each of these terms in a sentence that reflects the term's meaning in the chapter.*

10. consumer
11. exclusion
12. domestic
13. external
14. capable
15. liberal

## Reviewing the Main Ideas

**Section 1**

16. What event started the French Revolution?

17. What reforms did the National Assembly make between 1789 and 1791?

**Section 2**

18. How did Robespierre and the Committee of Public Safety deal with opponents of the government? What was the effect of their policies?

19. List the members of the informal coalition that took up arms against France. What was the result of this conflict?

**Section 3**

20. How did Napoleon assume power in France and become emperor?

21. Why was the French invasion of Russia a failure?

## Critical Thinking

22. **Making Comparisons** Examine the different systems of government in France from 1789 to 1812. Which was the most democratic? Which form of government was the most effective and why?

23. **Evaluating** Evaluate which Enlightenment ideals affected the French Revolution.

24. **Analyzing** Explain why the National Convention decided to execute Robespierre. Can you think of another solution that would have addressed their concerns?

25. **Summarizing** During the radical phase of the French Revolution, there were a number of social customs that signaled the political change. Name some of these new customs.

**Self-Check Quiz**
Visit the *Glencoe World History–Modern Times* Web site at <u>wh.mt.glencoe.com</u> and click on **Chapter 3– Self-Check Quiz** to prepare for the Chapter Test.

**26.** **Reading Skill** **Identifying Complex Causation** How did the French Revolution first lead to war with other European nations?

**27.** **Drawing Conclusions** Was Napoleon's Continental System effective or not?

## Writing About History

**28.** **Historical Analysis** **Interpreting History** Write out this sentence, excerpted from a London *Times* correspondent's report at the beginning of the French Revolution. Highlight all the words that indicate a bias and explain why: "The Archbishop of Paris is among the number of those who have been sacrificed to the people's rage." **CA HR 2**

**29.** *Big Idea* Look ahead to Section 3 in Chapter 8. Compare and contrast the American, French, and Russian Revolutions. Consider their causes and effects, and summarize the principles of each revolution regarding ideas such as democracy, liberty, separation of powers, equality, popular sovereignty, human rights, constitutionalism, and nationalism. **CA 10WA2.3**

**DBQ** **Document-Based Questions**

**Analyzing Sources** Read the following quotation by Napoleon. Then answer the questions below.

What the peoples of Germany desire most impatiently is that talented commoners should have the same right to your esteem and to public employments as the nobles, that any trace of serfdom and of an intermediate hierarchy between the sovereign and the lowest class of the people should be completely abolished. The benefits of the Code Napoleon, the publicity of judicial procedure, the creation of juries must be so many distinguishing marks of your monarchy.99

**30.** What does Napoleon say that the people of Germany want and do not want?

**31.** What were Napoleon's views about how civil and military workers should be hired and promoted? Where in this quote does Napoleon refer to these views?

**32.** In the quotation, Napoleon addresses "the peoples of Germany." How would the nobles of various German states be likely to respond to what he is telling German peoples and why?

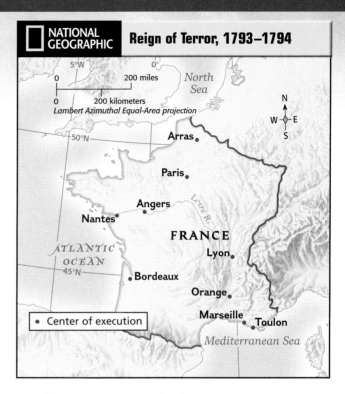

**NATIONAL GEOGRAPHIC** **Reign of Terror, 1793–1794**

• Center of execution

## Analyzing Maps and Charts

Study the map above to answer the following questions.

**33.** What cities served as centers of execution?

**34.** Approximately how far from Paris were centers of execution established?

**35.** Research one of the towns on the map and write a brief essay that describes the impact of the Reign of Terror on the people who lived there.

---

**Standards Practice**

**Directions: Choose the best answer to the following question.**

**36.** The rule of Robespierre was a time when the French Revolution

**A** was controlled by royalists who supported King Louis XIV.

**B** established a long-lasting constitutional monarchy.

**C** became a centralized force under Napoleon.

**D** grew more violent as extremists took control.

**CA Standard 10.2.4** Explain how the ideology of the French Revolution led France to develop from constitutional monarchy to democratic despotism to the Napoleonic empire.

# WORLD LITERATURE

## from Candide

### by Voltaire

**Voltaire** was born François-Marie Arouet on November 21, 1694. He assumed the pen name "Voltaire" in 1718. Voltaire was a critical and satiric writer who used his wit to attack both church and state. *Candide* is one of Voltaire's most brilliant and most well-known works.

### Read to Discover

Candide has been taught that "everything is for the best." However, his adventures usually prove the opposite. Here, he has just been cast out of a castle. The "men in blue" he meets are army recruiters for Frederick the Great, king of Prussia, who was at war with the French when Voltaire wrote *Candide*. How can you tell that Voltaire is making fun of the Prussian king and his army?

### Reader's Dictionary

**bulwark:** strong support or protection
**summarily:** done without delay or formality
**concatenated:** linked together in a series or chain

$C$andide . . . dragged himself into the neighboring village, which was called Waldberghofftrarbkdik-dorff; he was penniless, famished, and exhausted. At the door of a tavern he paused forlornly. Two men dressed in blue [Prussian soldiers] took note of him:

—Look, chum, said one of them, there's a likely young fellow of just about the right size.

They approached Candide and invited him very politely to dine with them.

—Gentlemen, Candide replied with charming modesty, I'm honored by your invitation, but I really don't have enough money to pay my share.

—My dear sir, said one of the blues, people of your appearance and your merit don't have to pay; aren't you five feet five inches tall?

—Yes, gentlemen, that is indeed my stature, said he, making a bow.

—Then, sire, you must be seated at once; not only will we pay your bill this time, we will never allow a man like you to be short of money; for men were made only to render one another mutual aid.

—You are quite right, said Candide; it is just as Dr. Pangloss always told me, and I see clearly that everything is for the best.

They beg him to accept a couple of crowns, he takes them, and offers an I.O.U.; they won't hear of it, and all sit down at table together.

—Don't you love dearly . . . ?

—I do indeed, says he, I dearly love Miss Cunégonde.

▲ *Prussian soldiers*

—No, no, says one of the gentlemen, we are asking if you don't love dearly the King of the Bulgars [Frederick the Great].

—Not in the least, says he, I never laid eyes on him.

—What's that you say? He's the most charming of kings, and we must drink his health.

—Oh, gladly, gentlemen; and he drinks.

—That will do, they tell him; you are now the bulwark, the support, the defender, the hero of the Bulgars; your fortune is made and your future assured.

Promptly they slip irons on his legs and lead him to the regiment. There they cause him to right face, left face, present arms, order arms, aim, fire, doubletime, and they give him thirty strokes of the rod. Next day he does the drill a little less awkwardly and gets only twenty strokes; the third day, they give him only ten, and he is regarded by his comrades as a prodigy.

Candide, quite thunderstruck, did not yet understand very clearly how he was a hero. One fine spring morning he took it into his head to go for a walk, stepping straight out as if it were a privilege of the human race, as of animals in general, to use his legs as he chose. He had scarcely covered two leagues when four other heroes [Prussian soldiers], each six feet tall, overtook him, bound him, and threw him into a dungeon. At the courtmartial they asked which he preferred, to be flogged thirty-six times by the entire regiment or to receive summarily a dozen bullets in the brain. In vain did he argue that the human will is free and insist that he preferred neither alternative; he had to choose; by virtue of the divine gift called "liberty" he decided to run the gauntlet thirty-six times, and actually endured two floggings. The regiment was composed of two thousand men. That made four thousand strokes. As they were preparing for the third beating, Candide, who could endure no more, begged as a special favor that they would have the

▲ **Frederick the Great, king of Prussia**

goodness to smash his head. His plea was granted; they bandaged his eyes and made him kneel down. The King of the Bulgars [Frederick the Great], passing by at this moment, was told of the culprit's crime; and as this king had a rare genius, he understood, from everything they told him of Candide, that this was a young metaphysician, extremely ignorant of the ways of the world, so he granted his royal pardon, with a generosity which will be praised in every newspaper in every age. A worthy surgeon cured Candide in three weeks with the ointments described by Dioscorides. He already had a bit of skin back and was able to walk when the King of the Bulgars went to war with the King of the Abares.

Nothing could have been so fine, so brisk, so brilliant, so well-drilled as the two armies. The trumpets, the fifes, the oboes, the drums, and the cannon produced such a harmony as was never heard in hell. First the cannons battered down about six thousand men on each side; then volleys of musket fire removed from the best of worlds about nine or ten thousand rascals who were cluttering up its surface. . . .

Candide made all the haste he could to [a] village, which belonged to the Bulgarians, and there he found the heroic Abares had enacted the same tragedy. Thence continuing to walk over palpitating limbs, or through ruined buildings, at length he arrived beyond the theater of war, with a little provision in his budget, and Miss Cunégonde's image in his heart. When he arrived in Holland his provision failed him; but having heard that the inhabitants of that country were all rich and Christians, he made himself sure of being treated by them in the same manner as the Baron's castle, before he had been driven thence through the power of Miss Cunégonde's bright eyes.

He asked charity of several grave-looking people, who one and all answered him, that if he continued

▲ *A scene from Leonard Bernstein's musical* Candide, *based on Voltaire's satire of French life before the revolution*

to follow this trade they would have him sent to the house of correction, where he should be taught to get his bread.

He next addressed himself to a person who had just come from haranguing a numerous assembly for a whole hour on the subject of charity. The orator, squinting at him under his broadbrimmed hat, asked him sternly, what brought him thither and whether he was for the good old cause?

"Sir," said Candide, in a submissive manner, "I conceive there can be no effect without a cause; everything is necessarily concatenated and arranged for the best. It was necessary that I should be banished from the presence of Miss Cunégonde; that I should afterwards run the gauntlet; and it is necessary I should beg my bread, till I am able to get it. All this could not have been otherwise."

"Hark ye, friend," said the orator, "do you hold the Pope to be Antichrist?"

"Truly, I never heard anything about it," said Candide, "but whether he is or not, I am in want of something to eat."

"Thou deservest not to eat or to drink," replied the orator, "wretch, monster, that thou art! hence! avoid my sight, nor ever come near me again while thou livest."

The orator's wife happened to put her head out of the window at that instant, when, seeing a man who doubted whether the Pope was Antichrist, she discharged upon his head a utensil full of water. Good heavens, to what excess does religious zeal transport womankind!

A man who had never been christened, an honest Anabaptist named James, was witness to the cruel and ignominious treatment showed to one of his brethren, to a rational, two-footed, unfledged being. Moved with pity he carried him to his own house, caused him to be cleaned, gave him meat and drink, and made him a present of two florins, at the same time proposing to instruct him in his own trade of weaving Persian silks, which are fabricated in Holland.

Candide, penetrated with so much goodness, threw himself at his feet, crying, "Now I am convinced that my Master Pangloss told me truth when he said that everything was for the best in this world; for I am infinitely more affected with your extraordinary generosity than with the inhumanity of that gentleman in the black cloak and his wife."

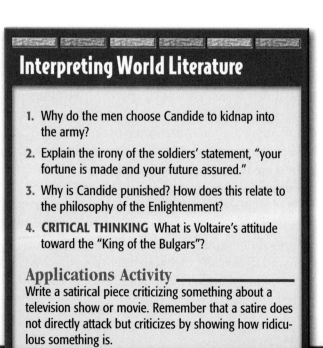

## Interpreting World Literature

1. Why do the men choose Candide to kidnap into the army?

2. Explain the irony of the soldiers' statement, "your fortune is made and your future assured."

3. Why is Candide punished? How does this relate to the philosophy of the Enlightenment?

4. **CRITICAL THINKING** What is Voltaire's attitude toward the "King of the Bulgars"?

### Applications Activity _____

Write a satirical piece criticizing something about a television show or movie. Remember that a satire does not directly attack but criticizes by showing how ridiculous something is.

# Reading on Your Own

*Here are several books you may want to read on your own.*
*These authors have explored some of the topics covered in this unit.*

### *Utopia* (Fiction)

**More, Thomas** (1477?–1535) More was a great lawyer and admired for his humanity. A contemporary described him as "a man of an angel's wit and singular learning . . . of marvelous mirth and pastimes, and sometimes of as sad gravity. . . . A man for all seasons." In 1529, he was appointed Lord Chancellor. His firm opposition to King Henry VIII's divorce and claim to be "Supreme Head" of the Church led to his execution. More's *Utopia*, published in 1516, rivals other famous works about an ideal society and government. It held up a picture of a society of equals where everyone shares in the work, but also in prayer and contemplation.

### *The Return of Martin Guerre* (Fiction)

**Davis, Natalie Zemon** (1928–) This noted historian has told the compelling story of the French peasant named Arnaud who successfully poses as another peasant, Martin Guerre. When the real Martin Guerre turns up to claim his wife and property, the local court and community all become involved. Based on a true event, Davis raises interesting questions about how people deceive themselves and others. She also faithfully reconstructs how ordinary French people lived in the sixteenth century.

### *Robinson Crusoe* (Fiction)

**Defoe, Daniel** (1660–1731) The son of a London tradesman and staunch Puritan, Defoe was active in politics. Dissatisfied with King James II, he ultimately supported William of Orange during the Glorious Revolution of 1688. Although Defoe wrote political journalism, he earned permanent fame with this 1719 novel about a shipwrecked sailor. The novel recounts the years the hero spends on an uninhabited island in the Pacific. A theme worthy of the philosopher Rousseau can be traced in its pages—how people are torn between civilization and nature, or the need for society and the need for solitude.

### *A Tale of Two Cities* (Fiction)

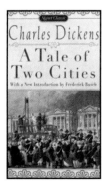

**Dickens, Charles** (1812–1870) One of the century's most beloved authors, Dickens produced this stirring novel of the French Revolution late in his career. First published in 1859, the story is set in both London and Paris. In many of his novels, Dickens was sympathetic to the oppressed, but his image of the Parisian revolutionaries is that they are a mob gone wild. Yet he has accurately captured the spirit and drama of one of history's most famous events.

# European Imperialism

## 1800–1914

# **W**hy It Matters

The period of world history from 1800 to 1914 was characterized by two major developments: the growth of industrialization and Western domination of the world. The Industrial Revolution became one of the major forces for change, leading Western civilization into the industrial era that has characterized the modern world. At the same time, the Industrial Revolution created the technological means, including new weapons, by which the West achieved domination over much of the rest of the world.

## Primary Sources Library

See pages 772–773 for primary source readings to accompany Unit 2.

Use The World History **Primary Source Document Library CD-ROM** to find additional primary sources about An Era of European Imperialism.

▲ Zulu lodging

► Zulu king Cetewayo meeting with British ambassadors

*"The world's surface is limited, therefore the great object should be to take as much of it as possible."*

—Cecil John Rhodes

# *Looking Back...*

# Industrialization

The rise of industry changed the world forever. So dramatic were the changes that historians have labeled the period the Industrial Revolution. Although the revolution began in Britain, it eventually touched every nation on Earth.

**1705**
Thomas Newcomen perfects the steam engine

**1769**
James Watt patents a more efficient steam engine

**1787**
Edmund Cartwright patents a power loom

## ① *Great Britain*

# Workshop of the World

The birth of industry needed certain preconditions: the technology, incentive, and money to build machines; a labor force to run them; raw materials and markets to make the system profitable; and efficient farms to feed a new group of workers. By the early 1700s, Great Britain possessed all these conditions.

Industry grew from the innovations of individuals who developed machines to do work formerly done by humans and animals. Inventors built upon each other's ideas. For example, in 1769 James Watt improved upon Thomas Newcomen's primitive steam engine. Other inventors then adapted Watt's engine to run cloth-making machines. Business owners soon brought machines and workers together in factories.

By the 1800s, industry had catapulted Great Britain into a position of world leadership. "[Britain has] triumphantly established herself as the workshop of the world," boasted one leader. Soon, however, America would be humming with its own workshops.

*James Watt's steam engine*

# to See Ahead

*Samuel Slater's mill*

## ❷ *The United States*

## The Revolution Spreads

Great Britain prohibited the export of machines and machine operators. In 1789, however, a factory supervisor named Samuel Slater escaped by disguising himself as a farmhand and boarding a ship to New York. Working from memory, Slater built a cotton mill in Rhode Island in 1793.

Soon after, the United States began churning out its own industrial inventors. Standardized parts and the assembly line led to mass production—a concept that would revolutionize people's lives around the globe.

**1793**
Samuel Slater opens the first machine-run cotton mill in the U.S.

**1855**
Henry Bessemer patents an inexpensive method of producing steel

**1913**
Henry Ford uses assembly lines to mass produce cars

**1914**
Japan expands foreign trade

## ❸ *Japan*

## The Search for Markets

In 1853, the Industrial Revolution traveled to Japan in the form of a fleet of United States steamships sent to open the islands to trade. "What we had taken as a fire at sea," recalled one Japanese observer, "was really smoke coming out of the smokestacks."

The military power produced by United States industry shook the Japanese. They temporarily gave in to American trade demands, but they also vowed that they too would possess industry. By 1914, Japan's merchant fleet was the sixth largest in the world, and its trade had increased one hundredfold in value in 50 years.

*Matthew Perry's steamship in Tokyo Bay*

## Why It Matters

The increase in industry made it necessary to find new sources of raw materials and new markets for manufactured goods. How could competition for resources and markets lead to the wars of the twentieth century?

# Industrialization and Nationalism

## ⤚ *The Big Ideas* ⤙

### SECTION 1: The Industrial Revolution

**New technologies can revolutionize the way people live, work, interact, and govern.** When coal and steam engines powered new industry, people migrated to expanding cities to find jobs.

### SECTION 2: Reaction and Revolution

**Throughout history people have struggled for rights.** In 1848, liberals and nationalists rebelled against many of the conservative governments of Europe.

### SECTION 3: National Unification and the National State

**The quest for national self-determination is universal.** In the mid-1800s, the German and Italian peoples succeeded in creating their own nations, but not all national groups were able to reach that goal.

### SECTION 4: Culture: Romanticism and Realism

**New technologies can revolutionize the way people live, work, interact, and govern.** Artistic movements were influenced by the society around them. Romanticism was a reaction to the Industrial Revolution, while progress in science contributed to realism.

 ***World History—Modern Times Video*** *The Chapter 4 video, "The Romantic Era," chronicles cultural and social changes in nineteenth-century Europe.*

**1814**
Congress of
Vienna meets

**1830**
First public railway
line opens in Britain

| 1800 | 1810 | 1820 | 1830 |

**1807**
Robert Fulton
builds the first
paddle-wheel
steamboat

*The* Clermont, *built
by Robert Fulton*

*Coalbrookedale by Night* by Philippe Jacques de Loutherbourg  Artists painted the dramatic changes brought on by the Industrial Revolution.

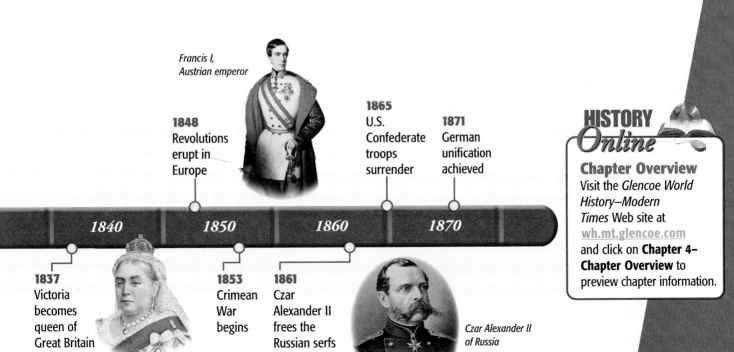

*Francis I, Austrian emperor*

**1848**
Revolutions erupt in Europe

**1865**
U.S. Confederate troops surrender

**1871**
German unification achieved

1840          1850          1860          1870

**1837**
Victoria becomes queen of Great Britain

**1853**
Crimean War begins

**1861**
Czar Alexander II frees the Russian serfs

*Czar Alexander II of Russia*

*Queen Victoria*

**HISTORY**
*Online*
**Chapter Overview**
Visit the *Glencoe World History–Modern Times* Web site at <u>wh.mt.glencoe.com</u> and click on **Chapter 4– Chapter Overview** to preview chapter information.

# Preparing to Read Chapter 4

Authors often use details and vivid description to create a picture of a person or event. They want to make the text come alive for the reader by appealing to the senses. When you form a picture in your mind, or hear a sound, or remember a smell while reading, you are visualizing. Good readers take the time to use their imagination and visualize.

You can visualize by noticing when an author is using specific details and language that appeals to the senses. You can also look for photos and other images in the text that further help you visualize what you are reading about.

*Read the following paragraph from this chapter describing industrial working conditions. Notice the number of details the author uses:*

## VISUALIZING

Use photographs, diagrams, and charts to support your ability to visualize. Look at the photograph on page 263 of the child miners. Does this help you imagine their situation better?

Coal miners also faced harsh and dangerous conditions. Steam-powered engines could lift the coal from the pits to the surface, but deep below ground, miners had to dig out this "black gold" with sledges, pick axes, and chisels. Horses, mules, women, and children worked underground, too, hauling carts full of coal on rails to the lift. Cave-ins, explosions, and gas fumes . . . were a way of life. The cramped conditions in mines—tunnels were often only three or four feet high—and their constant dampness led to deformed bodies and ruined lungs.

### Apply the Skill

After you visualize what life was like for a coal miner, discuss the image with a partner. How closely did your partner's image match your mental picture? Now read the passage again. Did your ideas change?

# Historical Analysis Skill  Interpreting Migration

 **Chronological and Spatial Thinking: Standard CS 3** *Students use a variety of maps and documents to interpret human movement, including major patterns of domestic and international migration, changing environmental preferences and settlement patterns, the frictions that develop between population groups, and the diffusion of ideas, technological innovations, and goods.*

One important way historians and geographers analyze change is by tracking large-scale migration—why it happens and the impact it has on societies. Sometimes people are moving from a rural area to an urban area. Sometimes they move across national, and even international, boundaries.

Read this excerpt from Chapter 4 about rural-to-urban migration and its effects in the early years of the Industrial Revolution in Great Britain:

- **In 1800, Great Britain had one major city, London, with a population of 1 million, and six more cities had populations of 50,000 to 100,000. Fifty years later, London's population had swelled to nearly 2,500,000. . . . nine cities had more than 100,000 residents. . . . By 1850, half of the people were urban residents.**

- **Cities grew faster than the basic facilities like a clean water supply and sewers. . . . industrial cities bred dirt and disease as workers crowded into ramshackle housing. . . . reformers called for government action. . . .**

Consider what kind of lifestyle changes had to occur to move from an agricultural to an industrial society. What do you think happened in the countryside when a large part of its population moved to urban areas?

## Apply the Skill

As you read this chapter, keep a running list of the causes and effects of the Industrial Revolution. Don't forget to notice primary sources, graphs, and maps. Once you've completed your list, focus on how migration was connected to the successes and problems of the Industrial Revolution.

# A Story That Matters

*Austrian emperor Francis I (left) hosted the Congress of Vienna.*

## The Congress of Vienna

*I*n the fall of 1814, hundreds of foreigners began to converge on Vienna, the capital city of the Austrian Empire. Many of these foreigners were members of European royalty—kings, archdukes, princes, and their wives—accompanied by their political advisers and scores of servants.

Their congenial host was the Austrian emperor Francis I, who was quite willing to spend a fortune to entertain the visitors. A Festivals Committee arranged entertainment on a daily basis for nine months. Francis I never tired of providing Vienna's guests with glittering balls, hunting parties, picnics, hot-air balloon displays, and sumptuous feasts.

A banquet for 40 tables of guests was held every night in the Hofburg Palace. Then, too, there were the concerts. Actors, actresses, singers, and composers were engaged to entertain, and Beethoven even composed a new piece of music for the event. One participant remembered, "Eating, fireworks, public illuminations. For eight or ten days, I haven't been able to work at all. What a life!"

Of course, not every waking hour was spent in pleasure during this gathering of notables, known to history as the Congress of Vienna. These people were representatives of all the states that had fought Napoleon. Their real business was to arrange a final peace settlement after almost 10 years of war.

### Why It Matters

The Congress of Vienna tried to find a way to undo the changes brought about by the French Revolution and Napoleon. However, the new forces of change had become too powerful to be contained. They called forth political revolutions that would shake Europe for years to come. At the beginning of the nineteenth century, another kind of revolution began to transform the economic and social structure of Europe. The Industrial Revolution led to the industrialization that shaped the modern world.

**History and You** List several inventions developed during your lifetime. What are their purposes? Do they save time or make manual work easier? Have they affected society as a whole? Have there been negative consequences to any of these inventions? Write a paper summarizing your thoughts.

# SECTION 1 The Industrial Revolution

## Guide to Reading

### Section Preview
When coal and steam engines powered new industry, people migrated to expanding cities to find jobs.

**Main Idea**

- Plentiful natural resources, workers, wealth, and markets explain why Great Britain was the country where the Industrial Revolution began. (p. 254)
- The pace of industrialization in Europe, the United States, and Japan depended on many factors, including government policy. (p. 257)

- Industrialization urbanized Europe and created new social classes, as well as the conditions for the rise of socialism. (p. 259)

### Content Vocabulary
enclosure movement, capital, entrepreneur, cottage industry, puddling, industrial capitalism, socialism

### Academic Vocabulary
dynamic, migrate

### People to Identify
James Watt, Robert Fulton

### Reading Objectives
1. Trace the advances that made the Industrial Revolution possible.
2. Describe how the Industrial Revolution affected women and children.

### Reading Strategy
**Categorizing Information** Use a table like the one below to name important inventors and their inventions.

| Inventors | Inventions |
|-----------|-----------|
|           |           |
|           |           |
|           |           |

### Preview of Events

| ♦1750 | ♦1770 | ♦1790 | ♦1810 | ♦1830 | ♦1850 |
|-------|-------|-------|-------|-------|-------|

**1764**
Hargreaves invents spinning jenny

**1782**
Watt builds steam engine to drive machinery

**1807**
Steamboats make transport easier

**1833**
Factory Act passed in Britain

**1840**
Steamships cross the Atlantic

## California Standards in This Section

*Reading this section will help you master these California History–Social Science standards.*

**10.3:** Students analyze the effects of the Industrial Revolution in England, France, Germany, Japan, and the United States.

**10.3.1:** Analyze why England was the first country to industrialize.

**10.3.2:** Examine how scientific and technological changes and new forms of energy brought about massive social, economic, and cultural change (e.g., the inventions and discoveries of James Watt, Eli Whitney, Henry Bessemer, Louis Pasteur, Thomas Edison).

**10.3.3:** Describe the growth of population, rural to urban migration, and growth of cities associated with the Industrial Revolution.

**10.3.4:** Trace the evolution of work and labor, including the demise of the slave trade and the effects of immigration, mining and manufacturing, division of labor, and the union movement.

**10.3.5:** Understand the connections among natural resources, entrepreneurship, labor, and capital in an industrial economy.

**10.3.6:** Analyze the emergence of capitalism as a dominant economic pattern and the responses to it, including Utopianism, Social Democracy, Socialism, and Communism.

# The Industrial Revolution in Great Britain

**Main Idea** Plentiful natural resources, workers, wealth, and markets explain why Great Britain was the country where the Industrial Revolution began.

**Reading Connection** Think about how computers are rapidly changing today's world. Read to understand how the Industrial Revolution changed life in the nineteenth century.

The Industrial Revolution began in Great Britain sometime around 1780. Within about fifty years, industrialization took hold in the rest of Western Europe, but why did it occur in Britain first?

When a nation industrializes, a major transformation occurs. A society is transformed from a stable agricultural world to an industrial society of constant growth. For the workers of the day, this transformation could be traumatic.

## *Voices from the Past*

The new factories forced employees to comply with a new kind of discipline. In 1844, a factory in Berlin posted the following rules:

66 The normal working day begins at all seasons at 6 A.M. precisely and ends, after the usual break of half an hour for breakfast, an hour for dinner and half an hour for tea, at 7 P.M. . . . Workers arriving 2 minutes late shall lose half an hour's wages; whoever is more than 2 minutes late may not start work until after the next break, or at least shall lose his wages until then. . . . No worker may leave his place of work otherwise than for reasons connected with his work. . . . All conversation with fellow-workers is prohibited. . . . 99

A number of factors are necessary in order for this **dynamic** process of industrialization to occur.

## Contributing Factors

First, Britain was producing much more food in the eighteenth century because its agriculture had improved. More farmland, better transportation, and new crops like the potato dramatically increased the food supply. More people could be fed at lower prices with less labor.

Second, with more abundant food supplies, the population increased dramatically. At the same time, Parliament passed laws in the 1700s that allowed landowners to fence off common lands. As a result of this **enclosure movement,** many peasants were forced to move to towns to find work. Britain thus had a plentiful supply of labor.

Third, Britain had a ready supply of money, or **capital,** to invest in the new industrial machines and the factories needed to house them. Some wealthy people, called **entrepreneurs,** sought new business opportunities and new ways to make profits.

Fourth, natural resources were plentiful in Britain. The country's many rivers provided the water power for the steam engine, as well as transportation for raw materials and finished products. The British landscape was also rich in the coal and iron ore that was necessary for manufacturing.

Fifth, Britain had a relatively free society. Its government did not heavily regulate the economy, and ideas also circulated freely. Inventors and capitalists felt they had the freedom to act on their ideas.

Finally, the British had a ready market in their vast empire, and British ships could transport manufactured goods anywhere in the world. At home, too, the market was growing because the population was growing. Since food was cheaper, the mass of the population were able to buy more than just their daily bread. With demand expanding, capitalists—those with money to invest—had a huge incentive to find methods to expand production.

▼ *Supervisors ensuring constant work*

▲ *Factory workers*

## Changes in Cotton Production
In the eighteenth century, Great Britain had already surged ahead of other countries in making inexpensive cotton goods. Making cotton cloth was a two-step process. First, spinners made thread from raw cotton. Then, weavers wove the thread into cloth on looms. In the eighteenth century, people performed this work in their rural cottages, so the production method was called a **cottage industry.**

A series of technological advances in the eighteenth century made the cottage industry inefficient and outdated. First, the invention of the "flying shuttle" made weaving faster. Now, the weavers needed spinners to produce thread more quickly since they could make cotton faster.

In 1764 James Hargreaves invented a machine called the spinning jenny, which met this need. Other inventors made similar contributions. The spinning process became so quick that thread was being produced faster than weavers could use it.

Yet another invention allowed the weavers to catch up. This was a water-powered loom, invented by Edmund Cartwright by 1787. It now became more efficient to bring workers to the new machines and have them work in factories near streams and rivers, whose water powered the early machines.

The cotton industry became even more productive when Scottish engineer **James Watt** improved the steam engine in the 1760s. Then, in 1782, Watt made changes that allowed the steam engine to drive machinery.

▲ *Women beating and lapping cotton by hand (above); (below) a machine performing the same function*

A series of complex developments brought about the Industrial Revolution—two of these developments included increased demand and the fact that some businesspeople had capital to invest. Another major step forward came when steam power could be used to spin and weave cotton.

Because steam engines were fired by coal, they did not need to be located near rivers. Before long, cotton mills powered by steam engines were found all over Britain.

British cotton cloth production increased dramatically. In 1760, Britain had imported 2.5 million pounds of raw cotton—or 1.14 million kilograms—for use in cottage industries. In 1787, imports rose to 22 million pounds (10 million kg), and by this time, most cotton was spun on machines. By 1840, 366 million pounds (166 million kg) were imported each year. Factory-made cotton cloth was Britain's most valuable product and was sold everywhere in the world.

**The Coal and Iron Industries** Since the steam engine was crucial to the Industrial Revolution, Britain had to have the coal for its engine. In Britain, coal seemed to lie everywhere under the ground. As more factories were built, more coal was needed. Inventors found ways to use coal more efficiently. These new methods aided another important industry—the iron industry.

Britain had plenty of iron ore as well as coal. In the early 1700s, the process of making iron had changed very little since the Middle Ages. In the 1780s, however, Henry Cort developed a way to produce better iron with a process called **puddling.**

In puddling, coke, a coal derivative, was used to purify crude iron. The result was higher-quality iron, and the iron industry boomed. In 1740, 17,000 tons (15,419 t) had been sold, but once the puddling process came into use, production jumped to about 70,000 tons (63,490 t). In 1852, Britain produced more iron than the rest of the world combined—almost 3 million tons (2.7 million t). The new iron was used to make machines and to build railroads.

**Railroads** In the eighteenth century, roads and canals had already made moving goods more efficient. It was railroads, however, that dramatically improved Britain's transportation.

In 1804, the first steam-powered locomotive ran on an industrial rail line. It pulled 10 tons (9 t) of ore and 70 people at 5 miles per hour (8.05 km per hour). Better locomotives followed. The *Rocket* moved on the first public railway line, which opened in 1830 between **Liverpool** and **Manchester.** Today the trip would take an automobile a half hour, but in 1830, it took the *Rocket* two hours as it sped along at 16 miles per hour (25.7 km per hour). Within 20 years, the speed of locomotives almost tripled. By 1850, railroads crisscrossed much of the country—about 6,000 miles (9,654 km).

Railroad expansion caused a ripple effect in the economy. Building railroads created more jobs and less expensive transport made goods cheaper to buy. Cheaper goods created more sales and more sales led to more factories. When business owners profited, they invested profits in new and better equipment, which increased economic growth. In the old agricultural society, growth was rare and intermittent. In an industrial society, economic growth is permanent.

### History *through Art*

**Biermeister and Wain Steel Forge by P.S. Kroyer**
Industry's raw power captured the imagination of many artists. Kroyer, a Norwegian-born Dane, painted this scene in 1875. **How do the conditions for workers compare to industry today?**

**The New Factories** The factory was very important to industrialization. Early on, factories were situated near water and powered by mills. When new energy sources were developed, however, factories could be located in cities near workers.

This new industrial economy created an entirely new labor system. Because factory owners wanted their machines producing goods constantly, workers were forced to work in shifts to keep the machines going.

Early factory workers **migrated** from rural areas. In the country, they were used to periods of hectic work, followed by periods of rest. Factory owners wanted workers to work without stopping. They disciplined workers to a system of regular hours and repetitive tasks. Anyone who came to work late was fined, or quickly dismissed for misconduct, especially for drunkenness. Child workers were often beaten.

☑ **Reading Check** **Describing** Why did employers feel they needed to discipline factory workers?

# The Spread of Industrialization

**Main Idea** The pace of industrialization in Europe, the United States, and Japan depended on many factors, including government policy.

**Reading Connection** Are some groups more willing to change than others? Read about the factors that help explain why nations adapt to change at different speeds.

By the mid-nineteenth century, Great Britain, the world's first industrial nation, was also the richest. It produced half the world's output of coal and manufactured goods. Its cotton industry alone was equal in size to the combined industries of all other European countries. Most of them were just beginning to industrialize.

The Industrial Revolution spread to continental Europe at different times and speeds. Countries with more urban areas and a tradition of trade industrialized earlier. Belgium and France did not have all of Britain's advantages, but both countries showed significant industrial growth after 1830. In the German states, it was another story. There was no single nation, but more than 30 states, many very small. Instead of selling goods in a national market, manufacturers had to face multiple governmental units and regulations.

In the early 1830s, Prussia, one of the largest German states, took an important

## Comparing Britain and the United States*

### Britain

Population (in millions): 1830: 24.0; 1870: 31.0; 1900: 41.0

### United States

Population (in millions): 1830: 12.9; 1870: 38.6; 1900: 76.0

### Britain

Railroad Track (in thousands of miles): 1830: .032; 1870: 11.0; 1900: 18.6

### United States

Railroad Track (in thousands of miles): 1830: .023; 1870: 53.0; 1900: 195.0

*As you compare, keep in mind the vast difference in area between Britain and the United States. Britain (England, Scotland, Wales, and Ireland) totals 94,548 square miles (244,879 sq km); the continental United States, 3,717,796 square miles (9,629,091 sq km).

## 📈 Graph Skills

Britain was the leading industrial nation in the early and mid-nineteenth century, but countries such as the United States eventually surpassed Britain in industrial production.

1. **Comparing** How did Britain's population growth, from 1830 to 1870 and 1870 to 1900, compare to the United States's growth? How did Britain's expansion in railroad tracks compare to that of the United States during the same period?

2. **Problem Solving** Which country had the highest percentage of railroad track miles in comparison to total square miles in 1870? In 1900?

**Geography Skills**

The Industrial Revolution spread throughout nineteenth-century Europe.

1. **Interpreting Maps** What was the predominant industry in the United Kingdom?
2. **Applying Geography Skills** What patterns do you see in the distribution of the major industries? What geographical factors could account for these patterns?

Legend:
- Manufacturing and industrial area
- Major industrial center
- Major railways by 1870

**Industry:**
- Coal mining
- Iron working
- Textile production

step by creating a free trading zone. Industrialization began, but it did not transform the economy until 1870 when Germany was united.

In Britain, a freer society, private entrepreneurs took the lead. In France, Belgium, and the German states, governments tended to be active in promoting industrialization. Often governments funded roads, canals, and railroads.

One of the most important facts in modern history is that Western Europe and the United States industrialized first. They therefore had an immense advantage in becoming wealthy, powerful nations, nations that soon dominated other parts of the world.

One Asian country, Japan, followed the Western example. Japan had seen the importance of industrial power in 1853. In that year, American admiral Matthew Perry steered his steam-powered ship into the Japanese harbor and demanded that Japan trade with the United States. Many Asian countries hesitated to change their culture and adopt some Western ways, but the new Japanese government of 1868 decided that it must copy Western technology to become a strong nation.

In the United States, the pace of industrializing was fairly quick, especially considering that Americans were also busy expanding across the continent. In 1800, six of seven American workers were farmers, and no city had more than 100,000 people. Between 1800 and 1860, the population of the United States grew from about 5 million to 30 million. In the same period, cities grew, too. Nine cities had populations over 100,000, and now only half of Americans worked as farmers.

Once the United States extended to the Pacific, a national transportation system was vital. Thousands of miles of roads and canals were built to link east and west. **Robert Fulton** built the first paddle-wheel steamboat, the *Clermont,* in 1807. By 1860, a thousand steamboats plied the Mississippi River and made transportation easier on the Great Lakes and along the Atlantic coast. It was the railroad that really brought the nation together. In 1830, there were fewer than 100 miles of track (160.9 km). By 1860, about 30,000 miles of track (48,270 km) had been built.

In the early years, factory workers came from the farms of the Northeast. Women and girls made up a

substantial majority of textile workers. Early capitalists even advertised for whole families. In Utica, New York, one newspaper ran this ad: "Wanted: A few sober and industrious families of at least five children each, over the age of eight years, are wanted at the cotton factory in Whitestown. Widows with large families would do well to attend this notice."

**Reading Check** **Evaluating** Why was the railroad important to the industrialization of the United States?

## Social Impact in Europe

**Main Idea** Industrialization urbanized Europe and created new social classes, as well as the conditions for the rise of socialism.

**Reading Connection** Do you know any entrepreneurs who run their own businesses? Read about how early entrepreneurs contributed to the Industrial Revolution.

The Industrial Revolution drastically changed the societies of Europe and, eventually, the world. The major signs of this change were the growth of cities and the emergence of two new social classes, the industrial middle class and the industrial working class.

**Growth of Population and Cities** In 1750, European population stood at an estimated 140 million. By 1850, the population had almost doubled to 266 million. The key to this growth was a decline in death

### Picturing History

This English train of the mid-1840s shows early passenger travel. The first line to handle both passengers and goods opened between Liverpool and Manchester in 1830. What does the style of the rail coaches remind you of?

rates, wars, and diseases such as smallpox and plague. Because of an increase in the food supply, more people were better fed and resistant to disease. Famine largely disappeared from Western Europe.

Cities and towns in Europe grew dramatically in the first half of the 1800s. The growth was directly related to industrialization. By 1850, especially in Great Britain and Belgium, many factories were located in cities, which now grew rapidly—factories were a magnet for anyone looking for work.

In 1800, Great Britain had one major city, London, with a population of 1 million, and six more cities had populations of 50,000 to 100,000. Fifty years later, London's population had swelled to nearly 2,500,000. Growth was seen all over Britain now—nine cities had more than 100,000 residents, and 18 had populations between 50,000 and 100,000. By 1850, half of the people were urban residents. This process of urbanization was going on in other European countries, but it happened more quickly and more completely in Britain than in many other countries.

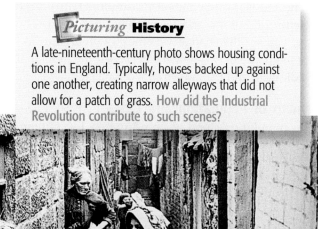

*Picturing* **History**

A late-nineteenth-century photo shows housing conditions in England. Typically, houses backed up against one another, creating narrow alleyways that did not allow for a patch of grass. How did the Industrial Revolution contribute to such scenes?

Cities grew faster than the basic facilities like a clean water supply and sewers. Thus industrial cities bred dirt and disease as workers crowded into ramshackle housing. Upset by disease and human suffering, reformers called for government action, but their pleas were not met until later in the century.

**The Industrial Middle Class** Capitalism had existed since the Middle Ages, when men with capital could invest in long-distance trade for profit. In this period, **industrial capitalism,** an economic system based on manufacturing, took hold. With a new kind of economy, a new social group emerged—the industrial middle class.

In earlier times the term *bourgeoisie,* or middle class, referred to burghers, or town dwellers. They were merchants, artisans, professionals such as lawyers or doctors, and government officials. The bourgeoisie were not noble, but they were not poor. Some were quite wealthy.

During the Industrial Revolution, a new group was added to the middle class. The industrial middle class were the men who built the factories, bought the machines, and figured out where the markets were. They had initiative, vision, ambition, and quite often, greed. As one manufacturer put it, "Getting of money . . . is the main business of the life of men."

**The Industrial Working Class** The Industrial Revolution also created a new kind of worker, the industrial worker. Industrial workers worked from 12 to 16 hours a day, six days a week, with only a half hour for lunch and dinner. They had no minimum wage and could be fired at a moment's notice.

In the cotton mills, the heat was stifling. "In the cotton-spinning work," it was reported, "these creatures are kept, 14 hours in each day, locked up, summer and winter, in a heat of from 80 to 84 degrees." Dirt and dust filled the air, and machines operated without safety codes for the workers.

Coal miners also faced harsh and dangerous conditions. Steam-powered engines could lift the coal from the pits to the surface, but deep below ground, miners had to dig out this "black gold" with sledges, pick axes, and chisels. Horses, mules, women, and children worked underground, too, hauling carts full of coal on rails to the lift. Cave-ins, explosions, and gas fumes (called "bad air") were a way of life. The cramped conditions in mines—tunnels were often only three or four feet high—and their constant dampness led to deformed bodies and ruined lungs.

As in the United States, women and children made up a high percentage of workers in the cotton industry

—about two-thirds by 1830. Reformers condemned the factories for enslaving children. The situation improved after the Factory Act of 1833. It set 9 years of age as the minimum for child labor, but children between 9 and 13 could still work 9 hours a day, and those between 13 and 18 years of age could work 12 hours.

As the number of working children declined, more women were employed, and before 1870 they made up half of the labor force in British textiles. Women were mostly unskilled and were paid half or less than half of what men received. Excessive working hours for women were outlawed in 1844.

One reason women and children began by working such long hours in factories was that families were accustomed to working together in cottage industry. When laws limited working hours for women and children, a new pattern began to be established. Men would be expected to work outside the home, while women took over running the home. Women continued to add to family income by taking low-paying jobs that could be done at home, such as washing laundry or sewing.

**Early Socialism** The transition to factory work was not easy. Although workers' lives eventually improved, they suffered terribly during the early decade of industrialization. Their family life was disrupted, they were separated from the countryside, hours were long, and pay was low.

Some reformers opposed a capitalist system which they saw as responsible for destroying people's lives. They advocated **socialism.** Socialism is an economic system in which society, usually in the form of the government, owns and controls important parts of the economy, such as factories and utilities. In socialist theory, this public ownership of the means of production would allow wealth to be distributed more equally to everyone.

Early socialists wanted to replace competition with cooperation. They wrote books about the ideal society that might be created, a hypothetical society where workers could use their abilities and where everyone would be cared for. Later socialists said that these ideas were impractical dreams. Karl Marx contemptuously called earlier reformers of this group utopian socialists. (He borrowed the term from *Utopia,* a medieval work describing an ideal society by Sir Thomas More.) To this day, we refer to the early socialists in this way.

One utopian socialist was Robert Owen, a British cotton manufacturer. Owen believed that if only people lived in a cooperative environment, they would show their natural goodness. At New Lanark in Scotland, Owen transformed a squalid factory town into a flourishing community. He created a similar community at New Harmony, Indiana, in the 1820s, which failed. Not everyone was as committed to sharing and caring as Owen himself, and New Harmony split up in the late 1820s.

✓**Reading Check** **Describing** How did socialists respond to new and harsh working conditions?

**HISTORY** *Online* **Study Central**

For help with the concepts in this section of *Glencoe World History—Modern Times,* go to wh.mt.glencoe.com and click on **Study Central.**

## SECTION 1 ASSESSMENT

### Checking for Understanding

1. **Vocabulary** Define: dynamic, enclosure movement, capital, entrepreneur, cottage industry, puddling, migrate, industrial capitalism, socialism.

2. **People** Identify: James Watt, Robert Fulton.

### Reviewing Big Ideas

3. **Describe** the importance of the railroads in the growth of cities in Europe and the United States.

### Critical Thinking

4. **Historical Analysis** **Connecting Ideas** Analyze how the Industrial Revolution changed the way families lived and worked. **CA HI 1**

5. **Cause and Effect** Use a diagram like the one below to list the causes and effects of the Industrial Revolution.

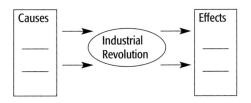

### Analyzing Visuals

6. **Examine** the picture of female textile workers shown on page 255 of your text. How does this picture reflect the role that women played in the Industrial Revolution?

### Writing About History

7. **Informative Writing** You are a nineteenth-century journalist. Write a brief article depicting the working conditions in cotton mills and an explanation of how mill owners defend such conditions. **CA WA2.3b**

# YOUNG PEOPLE IN . . .

## The Industrial Revolution

Children had been an important part of the family economy in preindustrial times. They worked in the fields or at home in cottage industries. In the Industrial Revolution, however, child labor was exploited.

Children represented a cheap supply of labor. In 1821, 49 percent of the British people were under 20 years of age. Hence, children made up a large pool of workers. Children were paid only about one-sixth to one-third of what a man was paid.

The owners of cotton factories in England found child labor especially useful. Children had a delicate touch as spinners. Their smaller size made it easier for them to move under machines to gather loose cotton. They were also more easily trained to factory work than adults.

In the cotton factories in 1838, children under the age of 18 made up 29 percent of the total workforce. In cotton mills, children as young as age seven worked 12 to 15 hours per day, six days a week.

Discipline was often harsh. A report from a British parliamentary inquiry into the condition of child factory workers in 1838 stated:

"It is a very frequent thing at Mr. Marshall's . . . for Mr. Horseman to start the mill earlier in the morning than he formerly did; and provided a child should be drowsy, the overlooker walks round the room with a stick in his hand, and he touches that child on the shoulder, and says, 'Come here.' In a corner of the room there is an iron cistern; it is filled with water; he takes this boy, and takes him up by the legs, and dips him over head in the cistern, and sends him to work for the remainder of the day. . . . What means were taken to keep the children to their work?—Sometimes they would tap them over the head, or nip them over the nose, or give them a pinch of snuff, or throw water in their faces, or pull them off where they were, and job them about to keep them awake."

The same inquiry also reported that, in some factories, children were often beaten with a rod or whip to keep them at work.

◄ The textile industry was the earliest to be industrialized. This young American textile worker stands next to the spinning machine that she worked at for long hours. In the 21st century, child labor can still be found in the textile industry, especially in Asia.

Boys who worked in coal mines were typically between the ages of 8 and 15. They often worked underground where they might lead horses dragging wagons, or help miners fill them. Above ground, they might pick out slate and other impurities from chutes of coal.

▲ In this engraving, a young boy of the upper class comforts a factory boy. The father in the background might be a reformer, asking the factory manager questions. The image was for an 1840 novel, *The Life and Adventures of Michael Armstrong, the Factory Boy.*

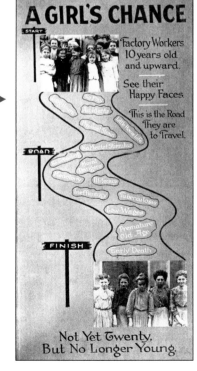

This American poster used sarcasm to convey its reform message: Fresh-faced girls of 10 are shown at the top, but their life of factory work will present them with the "delights" of tuberculosis, low wages, and early death.

### CONNECTING TO THE PAST

1. **Identifying** What kind of working conditions did children face in the factories during the early Industrial Revolution?

2. **Analyzing** Why did factory owners permit such conditions and child labor?

3. **Writing about History** Write an essay contrasting current factory conditions with those of 100 years ago.

# Reaction and Revolution

Guide to Reading

## Section Preview

In 1848, liberals and nationalists rebelled against many of the conservative governments of Europe.

### Main Idea

- After Napoleon's defeat, the victors met and redrew the map of Europe to create a balance of power and to strengthen conservatism. (p. 265)
- Liberals and nationalists opposed the existing political system and threatened conservative regimes. (p. 266)
- Beginning in France in 1848, the spirit of revolution spread quickly over Europe, but the uprisings were largely suppressed. (p. 268)

## Content Vocabulary

conservatism, principle of intervention, liberalism, universal male suffrage, multinational state

## Academic Vocabulary

stability, beneficial

## People and Events to Identify

Congress of Vienna, Klemens von Metternich, Bill of Rights, Louis-Napoleon, German Confederation

## Places to Locate

Vienna, Prague

## Reading Objectives

1. Evaluate the work of the Congress of Vienna.
2. Explain why revolutions broke out in Europe in 1848.

## Reading Strategy

**Cause and Effect** Use a chart like the one below to identify the causes of the revolutions in France in 1830 and 1848.

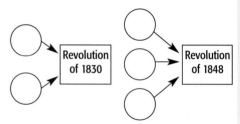

### Preview of Events

| ♦1810 | ♦1820 | ♦1830 | ♦1840 | ♦1850 | ♦1860 |
|---|---|---|---|---|---|

**1814**
Congress of Vienna meets to create balance of power

**1830**
Liberals overthrow Charles X and establish a constitutional monarchy in France

**1848**
Revolutions sweep through Europe

**1849**
Austria reestablishes control over Lombardy

## California Standards in This Section

*Reading this section will help you master these California History–Social Science standards.*

**10.2:** Students compare and contrast the Glorious Revolution of England, the American Revolution, and the French Revolution and their enduring effects worldwide on the political expectations for self-government and individual liberty.

**10.2.5:** Discuss how nationalism spread across Europe with Napoleon but was repressed for a generation under the Congress of Vienna and Concert of Europe until the Revolutions of 1848.

# The Congress of Vienna

**Main Idea** After Napoleon's defeat, the victors met and redrew the map of Europe to create a balance of power and to strengthen conservatism.

**Reading Connection** Does the United Nations intervene in international disputes? Read about Great Power decisions affecting European countries at the Congress of Vienna.

With Napoleon gone, representatives of the Great Powers—Great Britain, Austria, Prussia, and Russia—gathered in **Vienna** in September 1814. In that city's glittering palaces, they agreed at the **Congress of Vienna** to work to restore the old order. The most influential leader there was the haughty foreign minister of Austria, Prince **Klemens von Metternich** (MEH•tuhr•NIHK).

## *Voices from the Past*

For 30 years, Metternich worked tirelessly to repress the "revolutionary seed," as he called it, spread by Napoleon Bonaparte. In his memoirs, he wrote:

> ❝The first principle to be followed by the monarchs, united as they are by the coincidence of their desires and opinions, should be that of maintaining the stability of political institutions against the disorganized excitement which has taken possession of men's minds. . . . The first and greatest concern for the immense majority of every nation is the stability of the laws, and their uninterrupted action—never their change. Therefore, let the governments govern, let them maintain the groundwork of their institutions, both ancient and modern; for it is at all times dangerous to touch them.❞

Metternich claimed that he was guided by the principle of legitimacy. He meant that the lawful monarchs who had ruled before Napoleon swept through Europe should be restored to their thrones. This had already been done in France, where the Bourbon king had been put back on the throne.

The principle of legitimacy was used, however, only if it helped balance power in Europe. None of the victors—Great Britain, Russia, Austria, and Prussia—wanted France or any other nation, for that matter, to become too powerful.

To achieve a balance of power, some territories were divided up, and some boundaries were changed. As one example, land on the west bank of the Rhine River was taken away from France and given to Prussia. In this way, the strong Prussian army would be able to restrain France if it threatened to overrun Europe again.

The policies of the Congress were a victory for rulers who wanted to contain the new forces unleashed during the French Revolution. Like Metternich, these rulers believed in the political philosophy known as **conservatism.**

Conservatism is based on tradition and social **stability.** Conservatives of this period favored obedience to political authority. They also believed that established religions were **beneficial** to social order. They hated revolutions and were unwilling to accept demands for representative governments or more individual rights.

To maintain the new balance of power, Great Britain, Russia, Prussia, and Austria, and later France, agreed to meet occasionally if it was necessary to take action to maintain order. Their meetings came to be called the Concert of Europe.

Eventually, the Great Powers adopted a **principle of intervention.** It said that the Great Powers had the right to send armies into countries where there were revolutions in order to keep monarchs in power. Britain argued against this principle because it did not want to interfere in the internal affairs of other states, but Austria, Prussia, Russia, and France used military force to crush revolutions in Spain and Italy.

✓**Reading Check** **Analyzing** Explain the goals of European leaders at the Congress of Vienna.

▼ *Klemens von Metternich conferring with Napoleon*

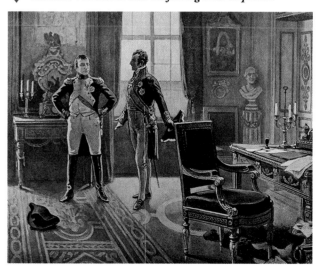

KINGDOM OF
NORWAY AND SWEDEN

North
Sea

UNITED
KINGDOM

DENMARK

Baltic Sea

RUSSIAN EMPIRE

NETH.

PRUSSIA

ATLANTIC
OCEAN

GERMAN
STATES

FRANCE

SWITZ.

Vienna

AUSTRIAN
EMPIRE

Black Sea

PORTUGAL

SPAIN

ITALIAN
STATES

Constantinople

OTTOMAN EMPIRE

— German Confederation

Mediterranean Sea

0        400 miles
0        400 kilometers
Lambert Azimuthal Equal-Area projection

## Geography Skills

The Congress of Vienna tried to create a new balance of power in Europe.

1. **Interpreting Maps** Within what political boundaries is Vienna located? Of what nation is Vienna the capital today?
2. **Applying Geography Skills** Compare this map to the map of Napoleonic Europe shown on page 233 of your text. What territories that belonged to the French Empire in 1812 were *not* part of France after the Congress of Vienna? What land did Russia gain?

## Forces of Change

**Main Idea** Liberals and nationalists opposed the existing political system and threatened conservative regimes.

**Reading Connection** Have you heard news reports about national conflicts in Bosnia? Read about the first stirrings of nationalism among ethnic groups in the Austrian Empire.

Between 1815 and 1830, conservative governments throughout Europe worked to maintain the old order. Powerful forces for change were also at work, however: liberalism and nationalism.

**Liberalism** Liberalism is a political philosophy that grew out of the Enlightenment. **Liberalism** held that people should be as free as possible from government restraint.

Liberals believed that all people had the right to basic civil liberties—equality before the law, and freedom of assembly, speech, and the press. Liberals wanted the rights of the individual to be protected in

a written document, as they were in the American **Bill of Rights.** Liberals were also committed to religious toleration and to separation of church and state.

A typical liberal favored a limited monarchy in which a king must follow the law. It was very important to liberals to have the basic laws for government embodied in a written constitution.

Finally, liberals were great supporters of a representative assembly, or legislature. This legislature was to be elected, but liberals did not think everyone should vote for representatives. Liberals were not democrats who believed in universal suffrage. They believed that only people with property should vote because property owners were the ones who had a long-term, serious interest in the community.

These attitudes were middle-class attitudes. It was the new industrial middle class that was acquiring wealth. They felt important and wanted representation, as well as protection from the mobs who might threaten their property. They said that workers should not have the vote until they became as educated and hardworking as the middle class.

**Nationalism** In the nineteenth century, nationalism was an even more powerful force than liberalism. Nationalism arose when people began to identify themselves as part of a community defined by a distinctive language, religion, and customs. In earlier centuries, people's loyalty went to a king, or their town or region. In this period, people began to feel that their chief loyalty was to the nation.

It was the French Revolution that made nationalism a potent force. Everywhere, people with a common language and traditions began to feel that they were the nation, not a royal ruler. Germans living in tiny states ruled by princes yearned for unity. Writers and poets writing about German folk legends and heroes urged national unity. Ethnic and religious groups in the Austrian and Ottoman Empires wanted to break away from the empire and be a nation. Nationalism was a particular threat to empires that contained many ethnic and language groups, but conservatives everywhere fought the forces of nationalism.

Nationalism was so strong that it eventually overcame some of the principles of liberalism. Liberals had argued that freedom could flourish only if each people had its own sovereign state. Nationalists became more and more passionate about their own nation. Often, they forgot about the rights of other national groups. They were willing to expand their

**Picturing History**

In 1830, Charles X of France dissolved the French legislature and suspended freedom of the press. Revolution followed. The rebels demanded a republic. How was Louis-Philippe involved in these events?

own nation at the expense of others. In this way, nationalism weakened some liberal principles.

**Revolutionary Outbursts** Beginning in 1830, the forces of change—liberalism and nationalism—began to break through conservative domination of Europe. In France, upper middle-class liberals overthrew the Bourbon monarch Charles X in 1830 because he ignored the law. The new government was a constitutional monarchy under Louis-Philippe, a cousin of Charles X.

## People In History

### Klemens von Metternich
**1773–1859—Austrian statesman**

There was no greater symbol of conservatism in the first half of the nineteenth century than Prince Klemens von Metternich. Born in the Rhineland of Germany, he fled to Austria in 1794 and joined the Austrian diplomatic service. He was made Austrian foreign minister in 1809.

An experienced diplomat, Metternich was conceited and self-assured. He described himself in his memoirs in 1819: "There is a wide sweep about my mind. I am always above and beyond the preoccupation of most public men; I cover a ground much vaster than they can see. I cannot keep myself from saying about twenty times a day: 'How right I am, and how wrong they are.'" When revolution erupted in 1848, Metternich fled to England.

In the same year, 1830, there were three more revolutions. Nationalism was the chief force in all of them. Belgium, which had been annexed to the former Dutch Republic in 1815, rebelled and created an independent state. Nationalists in Poland and Italy also tried to create their own nations, but they were not successful. Russian forces crushed the Poles' revolt, and the Austrian army put down revolts in a number of Italian states.

✓ **Reading Check** **Evaluating** How did liberalism and nationalism begin to break through the conservative domination of Europe?

## The Revolutions of 1848

**Main Idea** Beginning in France in 1848, the spirit of revolution spread quickly over Europe, but the uprisings were largely suppressed.

**Reading Connection** Did you know that popular revolutions in 1989 and 1990 destroyed communist governments in Eastern Europe? In 1848, popular revolutions also ignited, but they failed to achieve most of their goals.

In the first half of the nineteenth century, conservatism still dominated Europe. In 1848, however, liberalism and nationalism triggered another outburst against the status quo—the established groups in society that had long held power and expected to keep it.

**Another French Revolution** France again provided the spark for revolution. Severe problems in the French economy in 1846 brought untold hardship in France to the lower middle class, workers, and peasants. At the same time, members of the middle class clamored for the right to vote, but the government refused to make changes.

The monarchy was finally overthrown in 1848. A group of moderate and radical republicans set up a provisional, or temporary, government. The republicans were people who wished France to be a republic—a government in which leaders are elected and there is no monarch.

The provisional government called for the election of representatives to a Constituent Assembly that would draw up a new constitution. Election was to be by **universal male suffrage,** meaning all adult men could vote.

The provisional government also set up national workshops to provide work for the unemployed. From March to June, the number of unemployed enrolled in the national workshops rose from about 66,000 to almost 120,000. This emptied the treasury and frightened the moderates, who reacted by closing the workshops on June 21.

The workers refused to accept this decision and poured into the streets. In four days of bitter and bloody fighting, government forces crushed the working-class revolt. Thousands were killed, and thousands more were sent to the French prison colony of Algeria in northern Africa.

The new constitution, ratified on November 4, 1848, set up a republic, called the Second Republic. The new government had a single legislature elected by universal male suffrage. An elected president served for four years.

In December 1848, Charles Louis Napoleon Bonaparte, known as **Louis-Napoleon,** was elected president by a huge margin. His victory was attributed to the fact that everyone knew his famous uncle.

## Trouble in the German States

News from France led to upheaval in other parts of Europe. The Congress of Vienna in 1815 had recognized the existence of 38 independent German states called the **German Confederation.** Of these, Austria and Prussia were the two great powers. The other states varied in size.

In 1848, cries for change led many German rulers to promise constitutions, a free press, and jury trials. Revolutionists even formed an all-German parliament, the Frankfurt Assembly, to fulfill a liberal and nationalist dream—the preparation of a constitution for a united German nation. Deputies to the parliament were elected by universal male suffrage.

Ultimately, however, the Frankfurt Assembly failed to achieve its goal. The members drafted a constitution but had no real means of forcing the German rulers to accept it. German unification was not achieved.

## Revolutions in Central Europe

The Austrian Empire also had its problems. The empire was a **multinational state**—a collection of different peoples, including Germans, Czechs, the Magyars in Hungary, Slovaks, Romanians, Slovenes, Poles, Croats, Serbians, and Italians. Only the German-speaking Hapsburg dynasty held the empire together. German speakers played a lead role in the empire, although they represented only a quarter of the population.

In March 1848, popular demonstrations led to the dismissal of Metternich. In Vienna, revolutionaries took control of the capital and demanded a liberal constitution. To appease them, the government gave Hungary its own legislature. In Bohemia, the Czechs clamored for their own government.

Austrian officials made concessions, but they were determined to reestablish control. In June 1848, Austrian forces crushed the Czech rebels in **Prague.** By the end of October, the rebels in Vienna had been defeated as well. With the help of a Russian army of

# CONNECTIONS Past To Present

## Russian Troops in Hungary

On November 1, 1956, Imre Nagy, leader of Hungary, declared Hungary a free nation and promised new elections. Hungary was at that time under the control of the Soviet Union. Fearing that these elections would mean the end of Communist rule in Hungary, Nikita Khrushchev, leader of the Soviet Union, reacted dramatically.

On November 4, two hundred thousand Soviet (mostly Russian) troops and four thousand Soviet tanks invaded Budapest, Hungary's capital city. An estimated fifty thousand Hungarians died on that day. Nagy fled but was later arrested and executed. The Hungarian Revolution of 1956 had failed.

To Hungarians who knew their country's history, the use of Russian troops to crush their independence had an all-too-familiar ring. In 1848, Louis Kossuth had led a revolt that forced Hungary's Austrian rulers to grant Hungary its own legislature and a separate national army. In April 1849, the Hungarian legislature declared Hungary a republic. Kossuth was made the new president.

Meanwhile, the Austrians were unwilling to give up their control of Hungary. Unable to subdue the Hungarians, the Austrian government asked the Russians for help. Czar Nicholas I of Russia, who feared revolution anywhere, gladly agreed. A Russian army of 140,000 men crushed the Hungarian forces, and Kossuth fled abroad. The Hungarian Revolution of 1848–1849 had failed.

▲ *Soviet tanks in Hungary*

## Comparing Past and Present

There have been more recent revolts against repressive governments that have been violent. Review recent newsmagazines to locate one such event. Write a historical account of the event, using both primary and secondary sources.

## NATIONAL GEOGRAPHIC
### Revolutions in Europe, 1848–1849

※ Center of revolution

0 ———— 300 miles
0 ———— 300 kilometers
*Chamberlin Trimetric projection*

N W E S

PRUSSIA
Berlin ※
RUSSIA
BELGIUM Frankfurt ※ Dresden ※ ※ Warsaw
Paris ※ GERMANY ※ Prague ※ Kraków
FRANCE Munich ※
Vienna ※ ※ Buda
Lyon ※ AUSTRIAN EMPIRE
Milan ※ ※ Venice
Florence ※
Livorno ※ ※
PAPAL STATES
Corsica Rome ※
Sardinia ※ Naples
KINGDOM OF THE TWO SICILIES
Mediterranean Sea Palermo ※
※ Sicily
OTTOMAN EMPIRE
GREECE
50°N 45°N 40°N
5°E 10°E 20°E

### Geography *Skills*

In 1848 and 1849, revolution spread through Europe.

1. **Interpreting Maps** How far south did the revolutions of 1848 to 1849 extend?
2. **Applying Geography Skills** Pose and answer one question about the pattern in world history shown on this map.

---

140,000 men, the Hungarian revolutionaries were finally subdued in 1849. The revolutions in the Austrian Empire had failed.

**Revolts in the Italian States** The Congress of Vienna had set up nine states in Italy. They were the Kingdom of Piedmont in the north; the Kingdom of the Two Sicilies (Naples and Sicily); the Papal States; a handful of small states; and the northern provinces of Lombardy and Venetia as part of the Austrian Empire.

In 1848, Italians rebelled against the Austrian government in Lombardy and Venetia. Revolutionaries in other Italian states also took up arms and sought to create liberal constitutions and a unified Italy. By 1849, however, the Austrians had reestablished control over Lombardy and Venetia. The old order also won out in the rest of Italy.

In 1848, popular revolts at first succeeded. Middle-class liberals and radicals cooperated to achieve liberal governments and constitution. When these two groups began to fight over goals, however, the conservatives were able to regain control. Still the forces of nationalism and liberalism had been unleashed, and for the rest of the century, they remained a powerful political force.

✓ **Reading Check** **Identifying** What countries experienced revolutions in 1848?

### HISTORY *Online* — Study Central

For help with the concepts in this section of *Glencoe World History–Modern Times*, go to wh.mt.glencoe.com and click on **Study Central.**

---

## SECTION 2 ASSESSMENT

### Checking for Understanding

1. **Vocabulary** Define: conservatism, stability, beneficial, principle of intervention, liberalism, universal male suffrage, multinational state.

2. **People and Events** Identify: Congress of Vienna, Klemens von Metternich, Bill of Rights, Louis-Napoleon, German Confederation.

3. **Locate** Vienna, Prague.

### Reviewing Big Ideas

4. **Explain** the effect of conservatism in 1848.

### Critical Thinking

5. **Historical Analysis** **Sequence and Change** How did industrialization contribute to the spread of liberalism?
   **CA CS2**

6. **Compare and Contrast** Use a table like the one below to compare and contrast the ideologies of conservatism, liberalism, and nationalism.

| Conservatism | Liberalism | Nationalism |
|---|---|---|
|  |  |  |
|  |  |  |
|  |  |  |

### Analyzing Visuals

7. **Examine** the painting on page 268. Can you identify a worker and a middle-class person among the rebels? How is it possible to distinguish them?

### Writing About History

8. **Expository Writing** Select one ideology: conservatism, liberalism, or nationalism. Write an essay identifying contemporary ideas it has influenced. **CA 10WA2.3**

# National Unification and the National State

## Guide to Reading

### Section Preview
In the mid-1800s, the German and Italian peoples succeeded in creating their own nations, but not all national groups were able to reach that goal.

### Main Idea
- By taking opposite sides in the Crimean War, the Great Powers of Europe ended decades of cooperation. (p. 272)

- Italians wanted their own nation and drove their Austrian rulers out of Italy. (p. 273)

- Germany was united under Prussian leadership through three wars planned by the Prussian prime minister, Otto von Bismarck. (p. 274)

- After 1848, Great Britain liberalized, while the governments of France, Austria, and Russia grew more authoritarian. (p. 276)

- Unified by the War of 1812, the United States later split over slavery, but the Union survived a bloody civil war that lasted from 1861 to 1865. (p. 278)

### Content Vocabulary
militarism, kaiser, plebiscite, emancipation, abolitionism, secede

### Academic Vocabulary
reliance, levy, successor

### People to Identify
Giuseppe Garibaldi, Otto von Bismarck, Queen Victoria, Czar Alexander II

### Places to Locate
Piedmont, Alsace, Lorraine, Budapest

### Reading Objectives
1. Explain how Camillo di Cavour and Otto von Bismarck worked to unify their countries.
2. Outline the causes of the American Civil War.

### Reading Stategy
**Summarizing Information** Use a table like the one below to list changes in these countries during the nineteenth century.

| Great Britain | France | Austrian Empire | Russia |
|---|---|---|---|
| | | | |
| | | | |

## Preview of Events

| ◆1850 | ◆1855 | ◆1860 | ◆1865 | ◆1870 | ◆1875 |
|---|---|---|---|---|---|

**1852**
Second Empire begins in France

**1861**
Kingdom of Italy proclaimed

**1867**
The British North America Act is passed

**1870**
Franco-Prussian War begins

**1871**
William I becomes kaiser of a united Germany

## California Standards in This Section

*Reading this section will help you master these California History–Social Science standards.*

**10.2.5:** Discuss how nationalism spread across Europe with Napoleon but was repressed for a generation under the Congress of Vienna and Concert of Europe until the Revolutions of 1848.

# Breakdown of the Concert of Europe

**Main Idea** By taking opposite sides in the Crimean War, the Great Powers of Europe ended decades of cooperation.

**Reading Connection** Can you think of an example in recent times when access to water caused conflict? Read to learn what happened when nations fought for access to the Mediterranean Sea.

*Giuseppe Garibaldi*

The revolutions of 1848 had failed. By 1871, however, both Germany and Italy would be unified. Both countries had waited many decades to be united, and in each, nationalist feeling was passionate.

## Voices from the Past

One sign of the times was the response people gave to their leaders. On June 13, 1860, the *Times* of London described a public tour by Garibaldi, one of the most colorful leaders in the struggle to unify Italy:

> ❝In the afternoon, Garibaldi made a tour of inspection round [Palermo]. The popular idol [Garibaldi], in his red flannel shirt, with a loose colored handkerchief around his neck, was walking on foot among those cheering, laughing, crying, mad thousands; and all his few followers could do was to prevent him from being bodily carried off the ground. The people threw themselves forward to kiss his hands, or at least, to touch the hem of his garment. Children were brought up, and mothers asked on their knees for his blessing.❞

Why did these nations each finally unify after the 1850s? The answer lies partly with the Crimean War. This war shifted the balance of power in Europe, and allowed Germany and Italy to unify.

The Crimean War was the result of a very old struggle between Russia and the Ottoman Empire. The Ottoman Empire, centered in what is now Turkey, had long controlled most of the Balkan Peninsula in southeastern Europe. By the beginning of the nineteenth century, however, the Ottoman Empire was in decline, and its authority over the Balkans was weakening.

Russia was a nation with little access to warm-water ports. It had always coveted territory in the Balkans because having this would allow Russian ships to sail through the Dardanelles, the straits between the Black Sea and the Mediterranean. If Russians could achieve this goal, they would be a major power in eastern Europe and would even be able to challenge British control of the eastern Mediterranean. European powers feared Russian ambitions, and they, too, hoped to gain some territory if the Ottoman Empire collapsed.

In 1853, the Russians made a move. They invaded Moldavia and Walachia, Balkan provinces controlled by the Ottoman Turks. The Turks declared war on Russia. Britain and France were afraid that Russia would grow too powerful and so, in 1854, they too declared war on Russia.

This was the Crimean War, named for the Russian peninsula in the Black Sea where important battles took place. The war was poorly planned and poorly fought, but Russia lost so many troops that it finally asked for peace. In the Treaty of Paris, signed in March 1856, Moldavia and Walachia were placed under the protection of the Great Powers. The Ottoman Empire was weaker, and the Russians had been held back, but no single nation had gained a significant advantage.

The Crimean War ended the old Concert of Europe in which Russia and Austria had operated as the chief powers working for the conservative status quo. Now it was clear that Austria and Russia were rivals in eastern Europe. Austria too wanted territory in the Balkans and had refused to support Russia during the Crimean War.

A defeated and humiliated Russia withdrew from European affairs for the next 20 years. Austria was now without friends among the Great Powers. This new situation was very important for the forces of nationalism: It opened the door for the unification of Italy and of Germany.

**✔ Reading Check** **Explaining** How did the Crimean War destroy the Concert of Europe?

# Italian Unification

**Main Idea** Italians wanted their own nation and drove their Austrian rulers out of Italy.

**Reading Connection** If you had the power to start a war, could you justify doing so? Read to learn how and why the Italian state of Piedmont started a war with Austria.

In 1850, the Austrian Empire dominated the Italian Peninsula, as it had for decades. Often, Austrian control was exercised through the ties of the Austrian emperor with the kings and royalty of the many small Italian states.

After the failure of the 1848 revolts, Italian nationalists focused their hopes for independence on **Piedmont.** The royal house of Savoy was not connected to the Austrian emperor. In 1849, King Victor Emmanuel II took the throne of Piedmont, which included Nice, Savoy, and the island of Sardinia. In 1852, the king appointed Camillo di Cavour his prime minister.

Cavour was a skilled statesman. He wanted a strong state and a strong army so that Piedmont could lead the independence movement. Cavour knew, however, that no matter how much he could increase state revenues and build a stronger army, his king would need additional help to defeat the Austrians.

Cavour therefore made an alliance with the French emperor, Louis-Napoleon. If the emperor would help them against the Austrians, the Kingdom of Piedmont would give the areas of Nice and Savoy to the French. Once the agreement was signed, Cavour provoked the Austrians so that they invaded Piedmont in 1859. War soon broke out.

When the short war ended, the peace treaty gave Nice and Savoy to France. The Austrians kept control of Venetia, another small northern province, while Piedmont received the province of Lombardy. Cavour's success caused Italian nationalists living in other northern states—Parma, Modena, and Tuscany—to revolt and join their states with Piedmont.

While northern Italians were clamoring for greater unity, a new nationalist leader arose in southern Italy. **Giuseppe Garibaldi,** a dedicated Italian patriot, raised an army of a thousand volunteers to fight for independence. They were called Red Shirts because of the color of their uniforms.

One of the strongest states in the southern part of Italy was the Kingdom of the Two Sicilies, Sicily and Naples. This kingdom was ruled by a branch of the Bourbon dynasty. When a revolt broke out in Sicily against the king, Garibaldi's Red Shirts landed on the island of Sicily and by late July 1860, they were in control. In August, the revolutionary forces crossed over to the mainland and began a victorious march up the Italian peninsula. In early September, Naples and the entire Kingdom of the Two Sicilies fell.

Garibaldi was a man of the people. He had led revolts in South America and could inspire the common people. He might have fought for a popular republic to be created in a new Italian nation. Instead he chose to turn over his conquests to Piedmont. On March 17, 1861, a new kingdom of Italy was proclaimed under King Victor Emmanuel II. Unification was not yet complete. Venetia lay outside the new Italy. So too did the Papal States where the pope ruled from Rome. The Papal States had the strong backing of Catholic France.

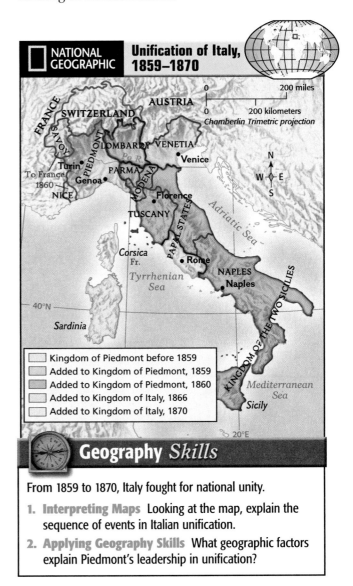

**NATIONAL GEOGRAPHIC**

**Unification of Italy, 1859–1870**

0      200 miles
0      200 kilometers
*Chamberlin Trimetric projection*

- ☐ Kingdom of Piedmont before 1859
- ☐ Added to Kingdom of Piedmont, 1859
- ☐ Added to Kingdom of Piedmont, 1860
- ☐ Added to Kingdom of Italy, 1866
- ☐ Added to Kingdom of Italy, 1870

## Geography *Skills*

From 1859 to 1870, Italy fought for national unity.

1. **Interpreting Maps** Looking at the map, explain the sequence of events in Italian unification.
2. **Applying Geography Skills** What geographic factors explain Piedmont's leadership in unification?

Once again, the Italians were successful in their cause because they took advantage of a rivalry between other powers. When Austria became involved in a war with Prussia, the Italians helped the Prussians. When the Prussians won, they rewarded the Italians with Venetia.

During this same war, French troops had to withdraw from Rome. This allowed the Italian army to move on Rome. It was annexed on September 20, 1870, and became the capital of the new Italian state.

✓ **Reading Check** **Explaining** How did Giuseppe Garibaldi contribute to Italian unification?

# German Unification

**Main Idea** Germany was united under Prussian leadership through three wars planned by the Prussian prime minister, Otto von Bismarck.

**Reading Connection** Have you heard arguments about the role of ethics in politics? Read to understand the policy of *realpolitik* Bismarck followed to unite Germany.

Germans had been longing for a unified national state for many decades. Like the Italians, Germans too had been disappointed by the events of 1848. Now they looked to Prussia for leadership in the cause of unification. In the course of the nineteenth century, Prussia had become a strong and prosperous state. Its government was authoritarian. The Prussian king had firm control over both the government and the army. Prussia was also known for its **militarism,** or **reliance** on armed force.

In the 1860s, King William I tried to enlarge the Prussian army. When the Prussian legislature refused to **levy** new taxes for the proposed military changes, William I appointed a new prime minister, Count **Otto von Bismarck.**

Bismarck has often been seen as the foremost nineteenth-century practitioner of *realpolitik*—the "politics of reality," or politics based on practical matters rather than on theory or ethics. Bismarck was open about his strong dislike of anyone who opposed him.

Bismarck ignored the legislative opposition to the military expansion. He declared that "Germany does not look to Prussia's liberalism but to her power."

Bismarck proceeded to collect taxes and strengthen the army. From 1862 to 1866, he governed Prussia without approval of the parliament. In the meantime, he followed an activist foreign policy, which soon led to war.

After defeating Denmark with Austrian help in 1864 and gaining control of the duchies of Schleswig and Holstein, Bismarck created tension with the Austrians and forced them into a war on June 14, 1866. The Austrians, no match for the well-disciplined Prussian army, were decisively defeated on July 3.

Prussia now organized the German states north of the Main River into a North German Confederation.

▼ *Bismarck stands at the center as William I is proclaimed emperor of the Second German Empire.*

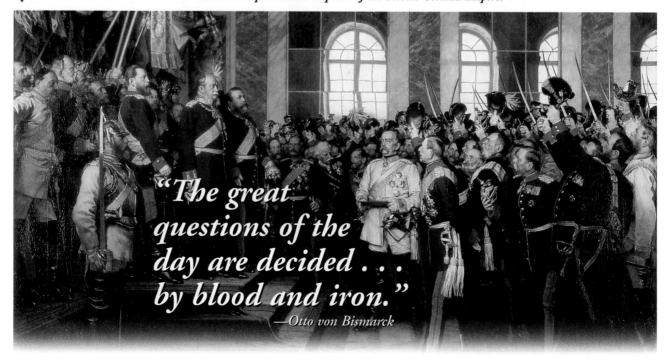

"*The great questions of the day are decided . . . by blood and iron.*"
—*Otto von Bismarck*

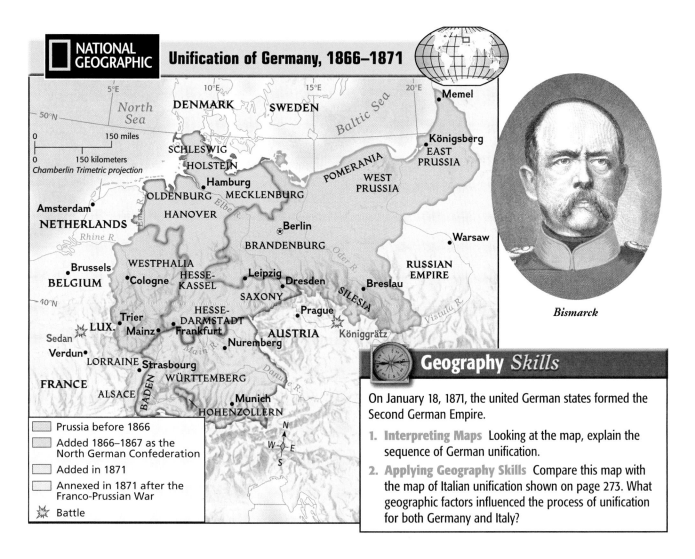

*Bismarck*

### Geography Skills

On January 18, 1871, the united German states formed the Second German Empire.

1. **Interpreting Maps** Looking at the map, explain the sequence of German unification.

2. **Applying Geography Skills** Compare this map with the map of Italian unification shown on page 273. What geographic factors influenced the process of unification for both Germany and Italy?

**Legend:**
- Prussia before 1866
- Added 1866–1867 as the North German Confederation
- Added in 1871
- Annexed in 1871 after the Franco-Prussian War
- ✹ Battle

---

The southern German states, which were largely Catholic, feared Protestant Prussia, but they also feared France, their western neighbor. As a result, they signed military alliances with Prussia for protection against France.

Prussia now dominated all of northern Germany, but problems with France soon arose. Bismarck realized that France would never be content with a strong Germany because it could threaten France. In 1870, Prussia and France became embroiled in a dispute over the candidacy of a relative of the Prussian king for the throne of Spain. Bismarck took advantage of the misunderstandings between the French and Prussians to goad the French into declaring war on Prussia on July 19, 1870. This conflict was called the Franco-Prussian War.

The French proved to be no match for the better-led and better-organized Prussian forces. The southern German states honored their military alliances with Prussia and joined the war effort against the French. Prussian armies advanced into France. At Sedan, on September 2, 1870, an entire French army and the French ruler, Napoleon III, were captured.

Paris finally surrendered on January 28, 1871, and an official peace treaty was signed in May. France had to pay 5 billion francs (about $1 billion) and give up the provinces of **Alsace** and **Lorraine.** This loss left the French burning for revenge.

Even before the war had ended, the southern German states had agreed to enter the North German Confederation. On January 18, 1871, Bismarck and six hundred German princes, nobles, and generals filled the Hall of Mirrors in the palace of Versailles, 12 miles outside Paris. William I of Prussia was proclaimed **kaiser,** or emperor, of the Second German Reich, or Empire. (The First German Reich was the medieval Holy Roman Empire.)

German unity had been achieved by the Prussian monarchy and the Prussian army. The authoritarian and militaristic values of Prussia were triumphant in the new German state. With its industrial resources and military might, the new state had become the strongest power on the European continent.

✓ **Reading Check** **Summarizing** What events led to German unification?

# Nationalism and Reform in Europe

**Main Idea** After 1848, Great Britain liberalized, while the governments of France, Austria, and Russia grew more authoritarian.

**Reading Connection** Have you ever been to Paris or seen it depicted in the movies? Read about why the wide boulevards and public squares were originally built.

While Italy and Germany were unifying, other states in Europe were also experiencing changes.

**Great Britain** Great Britain managed to avoid the revolutionary upheavals of the first half of the nineteenth century. At the time of the Congress of Vienna, the nation was governed by aristocratic landowning classes, which dominated both houses of Parliament. In 1832, Parliament passed a bill that increased the number of male voters, chiefly from the industrial middle class. By giving them a vote, Britain avoided revolution. In the 1850s and 1860s, Parliament continued to make reforms that helped the country to remain stable.

Another reason for Britain's stability was continuing economic growth. In 1851, the nation held the Crystal Palace Exhibition in London to show off its industrial production and prosperity. The middle class was already prosperous, but after 1850, working class income increased. From 1850 to 1870, the real wages of laborers increased more than 25 percent.

British national pride was reflected in **Queen Victoria,** whose reign from 1837 to 1901 was the longest in English history. Her sense of duty and moral respectability reflected her era, which ever since has been known as the Victorian Age.

**France** In France, events after the Revolution of 1848 moved toward the restoration of the monarchy. Four years after his election as president in 1848, Louis-Napoleon asked the people to approve a return to the empire. He held a **plebiscite,** an election in which people can vote only yes or no to a proposition, and 97 percent responded with a yes vote. On December 2, 1852, Louis-Napoleon assumed the title of Napoleon III, Emperor of France. (Although the first Napoleon's son had never ruled in France, the child's title had been Napoleon II.) The Second Empire had begun.

▼ *This image commemorating Victoria's golden jubilee in 1887 shows off Windsor and Balmoral castles and is decorated with the national flowers of the British Isles.*

**History** *through Art*

**La Place Clichy by Eugene Galien-Laloue**
Napoleon III had Baron Haussmann beautify
Paris with broad boulevards and public parks.
How does this reflect the economy of the era?

*Napoleon III*

As chief of state, Napoleon III controlled the armed forces, police, and civil service. Only he could introduce legislation and declare war. The Legislative Corps gave an appearance of representative government, because members were elected by universal male suffrage for six-year terms, but they could not initiate legislation or affect the budget.

Napoleon III completely controlled the government and limited civil liberties, but the first five years of his reign were a spectacular success. He focused on expanding the economy and subsidized the construction of railroads, harbors, roads, and canals. Napoleon III also carried out a vast rebuilding of Paris. Narrow streets and walls were replaced by broad boulevards, spacious buildings, public squares, an underground sewage system, a new public water-supply system, and gaslights. The new Paris served a military purpose as well. Broad streets made it difficult for rebels to throw up barricades and easier for troops to move through the city.

In the 1860s, opposition to some of Napoleon's policies arose. In response, he began to liberalize his regime. For example, he gave the legislature more power. In a plebiscite on his reign in 1870, the French voted their approval of Napoleon. This triumph was short-lived. Soon the French would be defeated in a war with the Prussians, and the Second Empire fell.

**The Austrian Empire** As we have seen, nationalism was a major force in nineteenth-century Europe.

However, one of Europe's most powerful states—the Austrian Empire—was a multinational empire that had been able to frustrate the desire of its ethnic groups for independence.

After the Hapsburg rulers crushed the revolutions of 1848 and 1849, they restored centralized, autocratic government to the empire. Austria's defeat at the hands of the Prussians in 1866, however, forced the Austrians to make concessions to the fiercely nationalistic Hungarians.

The result was the Compromise of 1867. This compromise created the dual monarchy of Austria-Hungary. Each of these two components of the empire now had its own constitution, its own legislature, its own government bureaucracy, and its own capital (Vienna for Austria and **Budapest** for Hungary). Holding the two states together were a single monarch (Francis Joseph was both emperor of Austria and king of Hungary) and a common army, foreign policy, and system of finances.

In domestic affairs, then, the Hungarians had become an independent nation. However, the compromise did not satisfy the other minorities that made up the multinational Austro-Hungarian Empire.

**HISTORY** *Online*

**Web Activity** Visit the *Glencoe World History–Modern Times* Web site at wh.mt.glencoe.com and click on **Chapter 4–Student Web Activity** to learn more about Queen Victoria.

▲ *Russian peasants had to pay for the poor-quality land they received from the government.*

**Russia** At the beginning of the nineteenth century, Russia was overwhelmingly rural, agricultural, and autocratic. The Russian czar was still regarded as a divine-right monarch with unlimited power. The Russian government—based on soldiers, secret police, repression, and censorship—withstood the revolutionary fervor of the first half of the nineteenth century.

Then, in 1856, the Russians suffered a humiliating defeat in the Crimean War described earlier. Even staunch conservatives now realized that Russia was falling hopelessly behind the western European powers. **Czar Alexander II** decided to make serious reforms.

Serfdom was the largest problem in czarist Russia. On March 3, 1861, Alexander issued an **emancipation** edict, which freed the serfs. Peasants could now own property and marry as they chose. The government provided land for the peasants by buying it from the landlords. 📖 *(See page 772 to read excerpts from Czar Alexander II's* Emancipation Manifesto *in the Primary Sources Library.)*

The new land system, however, did not help the peasants much. Landowners often kept the best lands. The peasants soon found that they did not have enough good land to support themselves. Emancipation of the serfs, then, led not to a free, landowning peasantry, but to an unhappy, land-starved peasantry that largely followed old ways of farming.

Alexander II attempted other reforms as well, but he soon found that he could please no one. Reform-

ers wanted more and faster change. Conservatives thought that the czar was trying to destroy the basic institutions of Russian society. When a group of radicals assassinated Alexander II in 1881, his son and **successor,** Alexander III, turned against reform and returned to the old methods of repression.

✓ **Reading Check**

**Examining** How was Great Britain able to avoid a revolution in 1848?

# Nationalism in the United States

**Main Idea** Unified by the War of 1812, the United States later split over slavery, but the Union survived a bloody civil war that lasted from 1861 to 1865.

**Reading Connection** Do you remember reading about the upheaval of the American and French Revolutions? Read to learn how the United States responded to national upheaval in the 1800s.

The government under the U.S. Constitution had committed the United States to two of the major forces of the first half of the nineteenth century: liberalism and nationalism. National unity had not come easily, however.

Two factions had fought bitterly about the division of power in the new government. The Federalists had favored a strong central government. The Republicans, fearing central power, had wanted the federal government to be subordinate to the state governments. These early divisions had come to an end when the War of 1812 against the British began. A surge of national feeling had served to cover over the nation's divisions.

The election of Andrew Jackson as president in 1828 had opened a new era in American politics. Property qualifications for voting had been reduced. The right to vote was eventually extended to almost all adult white males.

By the mid-nineteenth century, however, slavery had become a threat to American national unity. There were four million African American slaves in the South by 1860, compared with one million in 1800.

The South's economy was based on growing cotton on plantations, chiefly by slave labor. The invention of the cotton gin by Eli Whitney in 1793 had made it easier to clean cotton of its seeds, thus increasing cotton production. The South was determined to maintain both its cotton economy and plantation-based slavery. At the same time, **abolitionism,** a movement to end slavery, arose in the North and challenged the Southern way of life.

As opinions over slavery grew more divided, compromise became less possible. Abraham Lincoln said in a speech in Illinois in 1858 that "this government cannot endure permanently half slave and half free." When Lincoln was elected president in November 1860, war became certain.

On December 20, 1860, a South Carolina convention voted to **secede,** or withdraw, from the United States. In February 1861, six more Southern states did the same, and a rival nation—the Confederate States of America—was formed. In April, fighting erupted between North and South—the Union and the Confederacy.

The American Civil War was an extraordinarily bloody struggle which lasted from 1861 to 1865. More than 600,000 men died in battle or from deadly diseases spawned by filthy camp conditions. The Union's superior resources and population gradually wore down the Confederacy.

On January 1, 1863, Lincoln's Emancipation Proclamation declared most of the nation's slaves "forever free." The surrender of Confederate forces

▲ *Slavery challenged national unity in the United States.*

on April 9, 1865, meant that the United States would be "one nation, indivisible." National unity had prevailed in the United States.

 **Reading Check** **Explaining** How did the election of Andrew Jackson influence American politics?

**HISTORY Online** **Study Central**

For help with the concepts in this section of *Glencoe World History—Modern Times,* go to <u>wh.mt.glencoe.com</u> and click on **Study Central.**

# SECTION 3 ASSESSMENT

### Checking for Understanding

1. **Vocabulary** Define: militarism, reliance, levy, kaiser, plebiscite, emancipation, successor, abolitionism, secede.

2. **People** Identify: Giuseppe Garibaldi, Otto von Bismarck, Queen Victoria, Czar Alexander II.

3. **Locate** Piedmont, Alsace, Lorraine, Budapest.

### Reviewing Big Ideas

4. **List** the Prussian values and assets that caused the Second German Empire to become the strongest European state.

### Critical Thinking

5. **Historical Analysis** **Contextualizing** Explain how the forces of liberalism and nationalism affected events in the United States during the 1800s.
   **CA HI 3**

6. **Compare and Contrast** Use a Venn diagram like the one below to compare and contrast Bismarck's and Cavour's methods for achieving unification in Germany and Italy.

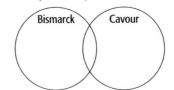

### Analyzing Visuals

7. **Examine** the photographs of a peasant and a slave family shown on pages 278 and 279. Based on the visual evidence of the two photographs, how do you think the living conditions of Russian peasants compared to living conditions of slaves in the United States?

## Writing About History

8. **Expository Writing** Write an essay comparing the events and outcomes of the reigns of Bismarck and Napoleon III. What personal characteristics did each man have that contributed to his accomplishments?
   **CA 10WA2.3**

# Culture: Romanticism and Realism

## Guide to Reading

### Section Preview
Artistic movements were influenced by the society around them. Romanticism was a reaction to the Industrial Revolution, while progress in science contributed to realism.

**Main Idea**

- In the arts, romanticism stressed individualism and emotion instead of the reason and universalism of the Enlightenment period. (p. 281)

- Rapid advances in science and technology fueled industrial growth, made medical care more effective, and challenged religious faith. (p. 283)

- The rise of science encouraged writers and artists to create realistic works that portrayed even the poor and degraded in society. (p. 284)

### Content Vocabulary
romanticism, secularization, organic evolution, natural selection, realism

### Academic Vocabulary
abandon, adapt, variation, controversy

### People to Identify
Ludwig van Beethoven, Louis Pasteur, Charles Darwin, Charles Dickens

### Reading Objectives
1. List the main features of romanticism and realism.
2. Trace a cause-and-effect path from the Scientific Revolution to secularization.

### Reading Strategy
**Summarizing Information** Use a table like the one below to list popular literature from the romantic and realist movements.

| Romanticism | Realism |
|---|---|
|  |  |
|  |  |
|  |  |

### Preview of Events

| ♦1820 | ♦1830 | ♦1840 | ♦1850 | ♦1860 | ♦1870 | ♦1880 |
|---|---|---|---|---|---|---|

**1820**
Walter Scott writes *Ivanhoe*

**1849**
Courbet paints *The Stonebreakers*

**1859**
Charles Darwin publishes *On the Origin of Species by Means of Natural Selection*

**1869**
Mendeleyev presents his classification of material elements

## California Standards in This Section

*Reading this section will help you master these California History–Social Science standards.*

**10.3:** Students analyze the effects of the Industrial Revolution in England, France, Germany, Japan, and the United States.

**10.3.2:** Examine how scientific and technological changes and new forms of energy brought about massive social, economic, and cultural change (e.g., the inventions and discoveries of James Watt, Eli Whitney, Henry Bessemer, Louis Pasteur, Thomas Edison).

**10.3.7:** Describe the emergence of Romanticism in art and literature (e.g., the poetry of William Blake and William Wordsworth), social criticism (e.g., the novels of Charles Dickens), and the move away from Classicism in Europe.

# Romanticism

**Main Idea** In the arts, romanticism stressed individualism and emotion instead of the reason and universalism of the Enlightenment period.

**Reading Connection** Do you know of any group that strives to show by their dress that they disagree with mainstream values? Read to learn about the values that romantics were expressing.

At the end of the eighteenth century, a new movement called **romanticism** emerged as a reaction against the Enlightenment. During that period, art and literature followed classicism. The ideals of classicism were reason, balance, and restraint in all things. Romantics went to the other extreme. They wanted the arts to express the feeling, emotion, and imagination of the individual artist or writer.

Many romantic writers in England lived during the early Industrial Revolution, and they often expressed a horror of the conditions they saw.

## Voices from the Past

In his novel *The Old Curiosity Shop*, Charles Dickens wrote about the English mill town of Birmingham. An element of romanticism pervaded his description:

> 66A long suburb of red brick houses—some with patches of garden ground, where coal-dust and factory smoke darkened the shrinking leaves, and coarse rank flowers; and where the struggling vegetation sickened and sank under the hot breath of kiln and furnace . . . —a long, flat, straggling suburb passed, they came by slow degrees upon a cheerless region, where not a blade of grass was seen to grow; where not a bud put forth its promise in the spring; where nothing green could live but on the surface of the stagnant pools, which here and there lay idly sweltering by the black roadside.99

To the romantics, the inner feelings of each person were unique, even mysterious. Romantic novelists tended to create characters who were misunderstood or rejected by the society around them. Isolated, their individual feelings and ideas were their only barometer for right and wrong. They did not bow to middle-class conventions. They wore their hair long and grew beards. A woman might dress in a man's pants and frock coat to show she was a poet.

Romantics loved to think about past ages, especially medieval times. They felt it had a mystery and interest in the soul that their own industrial age did not. Romantic architects revived medieval styles and designed castles, cathedrals, railway stations, and city halls in a style called neo-Gothic. The Houses of Parliament in London reflect this style.

Romantic literature was also inspired by the Middle Ages. Sir Walter Scott's *Ivanhoe*, for example, a best-seller in the early 1800s, told of clashes between knights in medieval England. By focusing on their nations' past, many romantic writers were also reflecting the nationalism that was so strong in the nineteenth century.

The exotic and unfamiliar also attracted many romantics. This attraction gave rise to Gothic literature. Chilling examples are Mary Shelley's *Frankenstein* and Edgar Allan Poe's short stories of horror. Some romantics even sought the unusual in their own lives by exploring their dreams and nightmares and seeking altered states of consciousness.

▼ *Built between 1869 and 1892, this Bavarian castle reflects the romantic love of medieval style.*

**Wanderer Above a Sea of Fog by Caspar David Friedrich** A sense of isolation and a tragic fate characterize this 1819 painting by this German romantic. How would you compare the feeling of this art to the image on page 225?

The romantics viewed poetry as the direct expression of the soul. Romantic poetry gave expression to one of the most important characteristics of the movement—its love of nature. Romantics believed that nature served as a mirror into which humans could look to learn about themselves.

This feeling is especially evident in the poetry of William Wordsworth, the foremost English romantic poet of nature. His experience of nature was almost mystical:

> ❝One impulse from a vernal wood
> May teach you more of man,
> Of moral evil and of good,
> Than all the sages can.❞

The worship of nature also caused Wordsworth and other romantic poets to be critical of eighteenth-century science, which they believed had reduced nature to a cold object of study. To Wordsworth, the scientists' dry, mathematical approach left no room for the imagination or for the human soul.

The human soul was a source of expression for William Blake, a poet and artist connected with romanticism, though he combined imagination with reality in a way other romantics did not. In two of his collections of lyric poems and their accompanying designs, *Songs of Innocence* and *Songs of Experience*, Blake uses a child's point of view to capture basic human emotions. He also used that point of view to write "The Chimney Sweeper," "London," and "The Tyger." In these poems, he criticized the church and the state because he felt these institutions did not bring out the best in people.

Like Blake, many romantics were convinced that industrialization would cause people to become alienated from their inner selves and from the natural world. This idea shows up in Mary Shelley's novel *Frankenstein:* When science dares to try and conquer nature, a monster is created.

Like the literary arts, the visual arts were deeply affected by romanticism. Romantic artists shared at least two features. First, to them, all art was a reflection of the artist's inner feelings. A painting should mirror the artist's vision of the world and be the instrument of the artist's own imagination. Second, romantic artists **abandoned** classical reason for warmth and emotion.

Eugène Delacroix (DEH•luh•KWAH) was one of the most famous romantic painters from France. His paintings showed two chief characteristics: a fascination with the exotic and a passion for color. His works reflect his belief that "a painting should be a feast to the eye."

In music, too, romantic trends dominated the first half of the nineteenth century. One of the most famous composers of this era was **Ludwig van Beethoven.** Some have called him a bridge between classical and romantic music. Others argue that he was such a rare genius, he cannot be easily classified. His early work fell within the classical framework. In his Third Symphony, first performed in 1805, however, the romantic elements were in place: powerful melodies and dramatic intensity.

In one way, Beethoven was definitely a romantic. He thought of himself as an artist, not a craftsman. He had an intense and difficult personality, but was committed to writing music that reflected his deepest feelings: "I must write, for what weighs on my heart, I must express."

**Reading Check** **Examining** How did the popularity of *Ivanhoe* reflect the interests of the nineteenth century?

# New Age of Science

**Main Idea** Rapid advances in science and technology fueled industrial growth, made medical care more effective, and challenged religious faith.

**Reading Connection** Have you heard of discoveries about our genetic makeup and its possible applications? Read to learn how discoveries changed society in the 1800s.

The Scientific Revolution had created a modern, rational approach to the study of the natural world. For a long time, only the educated elite understood its importance. By the 1830s, however, new discoveries in science had led to many practical benefits that affected all Europeans. In 1796, for example, the English doctor Edward Jenner had discovered a vaccine for smallpox, a widespread disease that killed mostly infants and young children.

In biology, the Frenchman **Louis Pasteur** proposed the germ theory of disease, which was crucial to the development of modern scientific medical practices. In chemistry, the Russian Dmitry Mendeleyev in the 1860s classified all the material elements then known on the basis of their atomic weights. In Great Britain, Michael Faraday put together a primitive generator that laid the foundation for the use of electric current.

Dramatic material benefits such as these led Europeans to have a growing faith in science. This faith, in turn, undermined the religious faith of many people. It is no accident that the nineteenth century was an age of increasing **secularization,** indifference to or rejection of religion in the affairs of the world. For many people, truth was now to be found in science and in the material existence of human beings.

More than anyone else, it was probably **Charles Darwin** who created the concept of humans as beings who were part of the natural world. In 1859, Darwin published *On the Origin of Species by Means of Natural Selection.* His basic theory was that each species, or kind, of plant or animal had evolved over millions of years from earlier, simpler forms of life. Darwin called this principle **organic evolution.**

How did this natural process work? According to Darwin, in every species, "many more individuals of each species are born than can possibly survive."

**History** *through Art*

***The Lion Hunt* by Eugene Delacroix (1861)**
This French romantic artist was known for lush color and exotic scenes. If you were alive in the 1800s, what elements would strike you as exotic?

This results in a "struggle for existence." Darwin believed that some organisms are better able to **adapt** to changes in the environment than others.

Those that are able to survive ("survival of the fittest") reproduce and thrive, while the unfit do not. Darwin called this process **natural selection.** Survivors pass on the **variations** that allowed them to survive until a new, separate species emerges. In *The Descent of Man,* published in 1871, Darwin argued that human beings had animal origins and were not an exception to the rule governing other species.

Darwin's ideas raised a storm of **controversy.** Some people objected that his theory made human beings ordinary products of nature, not unique creations of God. Other people were bothered because they felt he was saying that life was a mere struggle for survival. "Is there a place in the Darwinian world for moral values?" they asked. Some believers felt Darwin had not granted God a role in creation. Gradually, however, many scientists and other intellectuals came to accept Darwinism.

✓ **Reading Check** **Describing** How did the theory of natural selection influence the way people saw the world?

## Realism

**Main Idea** The rise of science encouraged writers and artists to create realistic works that portrayed even the poor and degraded in society.

**Reading Connection** Have you been to museums and noticed how technology is used in some modern art? Read how artists reflected intellectual trends at this time.

The belief that the world should be viewed realistically was closely related to the scientific outlook. In politics, Bismarck had practiced the "politics of reality." In the literary and visual arts, **realism** became a movement as well.

The literary realists of the mid-nineteenth century rejected romanticism. They wanted to write about ordinary characters from actual life rather than romantic heroes in exotic settings. They also tried to avoid emotional language by using precise description. They preferred novels to poems.

Many literary realists combined their interest in everyday life with an examination of social issues. These artists expressed their social views through their characters. Although this type of realistic writing occurred worldwide, the French led the way.

The realist novel was perfected by the French author Gustave Flaubert, who was a leading novelist of the 1850s and 1860s. His work *Madame Bovary* presents a critical description of small-town life in France.

In Great Britain, **Charles Dickens** became a huge success with novels that showed the realities of life for the poor in the early Industrial Age. Novels like *Oliver Twist* and *David Copperfield* created a vivid picture of the brutal life of London's poor, as well as of their humor and humanity. In fact, his characters were so sympathetic that they helped inspire social reform.

In art, too, realism became dominant after 1850. Realist artists sought to show the everyday life of ordinary people and the world of nature with photo-

*Picturing* **History**

This friendly cartoon drawing of Charles Darwin was published in the magazine *Vanity Fair* in 1871. It shows the scientist in the wheeled chair he used to propel himself round his work room.

**History** *through Art*

*The Stonebreakers* **by Gustave Courbet, 1849** As an artist of the realist school, Courbet broke with the mystical and imaginative romantic period. Which style do you prefer?

graphic realism. The French became leaders in realist painting, just as they had become the leaders in realist writing.

Gustave Courbet was the most famous painter of the realist school. He loved to portray scenes from everyday life. His subjects were factory workers, peasants, and the wives of saloon keepers. "I have never seen either angels or goddesses, so I am not interested in painting them," Courbet once commented.

One of Courbet's famous works, *The Stonebreakers*, shows two roadworkers engaged in the deadening work of breaking stones to build a road. There were those who objected to Courbet's "cult of ugliness" and who found such scenes of human misery scandalous. To Courbet, however, no subject was too ordinary, too harsh, or too ugly.

✓**Reading Check** **Evaluating** What factors helped to produce the movement known as realism?

**HISTORY Online** **Study Central**

For help with the concepts in this section of *Glencoe World History–Modern Times,* go to <u>wh.mt.glencoe.com</u> and click on **Study Central.**

# SECTION 4 ASSESSMENT

## Checking for Understanding

1. **Vocabulary** Define: romanticism, abandon, secularization, organic evolution, adapt, natural selection, variation, controversy, realism.

2. **People** Identify: Ludwig van Beethoven, Louis Pasteur, Charles Darwin, Charles Dickens.

### Reviewing Big Ideas

3. **Explain** how scientific developments affected the cultural movements of the nineteenth century.

## Critical Thinking

4. **Compare and Contrast** How did romanticism compare to the ideas of the Enlightenment?

5. **Organizing Information** Use a table like below to list scientists and their discoveries in the mid-nineteenth century.

| Scientist | Discovery |
|-----------|-----------|
| Pasteur | |
| Mendeleyev | |
| Faraday | |
| Darwin | |

## Analyzing Visuals

6. **Examine** the painting by Eugène Delacroix shown on page 283 of your text. How does this painting reflect the characteristics of the romantic movement?

### Writing About History

7. **Expository Writing** Read poetry by two different poets of romanticism. Write a paper describing the elements of romanticism found in the poems. Be sure to include quotations. **CA** 10WA2.2 **CA** 10RL3.12

# PRIMARY SOURCES
## EYEWITNESS TO HISTORY

*The Industrial Revolution did not appear overnight in England. A well-known author, a government report, and an economist trace the use of machinery and new styles of labor.*

## SOURCE 1: An Industrial Village

*Daniel Defoe (1660–1731), best known for his novel* **Robinson Crusoe,** *describes an early industrial village in* **A Tour Through England and Wales.**

. . . people all full of business; not a beggar, not an idle person to be seen, except here and there an alms-house, where people **antient**[1], decrepid, and past labour, might be found; for it is observable, that the people here, however **laborious**[2], generally live to a great age, a certain testimony to the goodness and wholesomness of the country, which is, without doubt, as healthy as any part of England; nor is the health of the people lessen'd, but help'd and establish'd by their being constantly employ'd, and as we call it, their working hard; so that they find a double advantage by their being in business . . .

> ───────────────
> [1]**antient:** ancient
> [2]**laborious:** industrious; hardworking

───────────────
*Gustave Doré's engraving of rooftops in 1870s London*

Having thus fire and water at every dwelling, there is no need to enquire why they dwell thus dispers'd upon the highest hills, the convenience of the manufactures requiring it. Among the manufacturers houses are likewise scattered an infinite number of cottages or small dwellings, in which dwell the workmen which are employed, the women and children of whom, are always busy carding, spinning, &c. so that no hands being unemployed, all can gain their bread, even from the youngest to the antient . . .

This is the reason also why we saw so few people without doors [outside]; but if we knock'd at the door of any of the master manufacturers, we presently saw a house full of lusty fellows, some at the dye-fat, some dressing the cloths, some in the loom, some one thing, some another, all hard at work, and full employed upon the manufacture, and all seeming to have sufficient business.

## SOURCE 2: Child Labor

*In the 1830s, the British Parliament formed the Sadler Committee to investigate factory conditions. William Cooper testified about his work in factories as a boy.*

William Cooper, called in; and Examined
What is your business?—I follow the cloth-dressing at present.
What is your age?—I was eight-and-twenty last February.
When did you first begin to work in mills or factories?—When I was about 10 years of age.
With whom did you first work?—At Mr. Benyon's flax mills, in Meadowland, Leeds.
What were your usual hours of working?—We began at five, and gave over at nine; at five o'clock in the morning.
And you gave over at nine o'clock?—At nine at night. . . .
At what time had you to get up in the morning to attend to your labour?—I had to be up soon after four o'clock.
Every morning?—Every morning.

What intermissions had you for meals?—When we began at five in the morning, we went on until noon, and then we had 40 minutes for dinner. . . .

To keep you at your work for such a length of time, and especially towards the termination of such a day's labour as that, what means were taken to keep you awake and attentive?—They strapped [beat] us at times, when we were not quite ready to be **doffing**[3] the frame when it was full. . . .

When your hours were so long, you had not any time to attend to a day-school?—We had no time to go to day-school, only to a Sunday-school, and then with working such long hours we wanted to have a bit of rest, so that I slept till the afternoon, sometimes till dinner, and sometimes after . . .

After working at the mill to this excess, how did you find your health at last?—I found it very bad indeed; I found illness coming on me a long-time before I fell down.

Did you at length become so ill as to be unable to pursue your work?—I was obliged to give it up entirely. . . .

When you were somewhat recovered, did you apply for labour?—I applied for my work again, but the overlooker said I was not fit to work; he was sure of that, and he would not let me have it. I was then obliged to throw myself on the parish. [The parish church administered poor relief, or welfare, at that time].

## SOURCE 3: The Division of Labor

*Adam Smith (1723–1790), is often called the father of economics. In this excerpt from* The Wealth of Nations, *Smith discusses the advantages of the division of labor.*

First, . . . the division of labor, by reducing every man's business to some one simple operation, and by making this operation the sole employment of his life, necessarily increases very much the dexterity of the workman. A common smith, who though accustomed to handling the hammer, has never been used to make nails, if upon some particular occasion he is obliged to attempt it, will scarcely, I am assured, be able to make above two or three hundred nails in a day, and those too, very bad ones. . . .

_____
[3]**doffing:** taking off; removing

Secondly, the advantage which is gained by saving the time commonly lost in passing from one sort of work to another is much greater than we should at first view be apt to imagine it. . . .

Thirdly and lastly, everybody must be sensible how much labor is facilitated and **abridged**[4] by the application of proper machinery. It is unnecessary to give any example. I shall only observe, therefore, that the invention of all those machines by which labor is so much facilitated and abridged seems to have been originally owing to the division of labor. Men are much more likely to discover easier and readier methods of attaining any object, when the whole attention of their minds is directed toward that single object, than when it is dissipated among a great variety of things. . . . A great part of machines made use of in those manufacturers in which labor is most subdivided were originally inventions of common workmen, who being each of them employed in some very simple operation, naturally turned their thoughts toward finding out easier and readier methods of performing it.

_____
[4]**abridged:** shortened

## DBQ Document-Based Questions

### Historical Analysis    CA HR 1, HR 2

**Source 1:** What is the general tone of Defoe's piece describing labor in the textile-manufacturing village?

**Source 2:** According to William Cooper, what hardships did child laborers face working in factories and mills?

**Source 3:** What three advantages does Adam Smith see in dividing labor among individuals?

### Comparing and Contrasting Sources

1. How does Defoe's description of workers' health differ from the testimony of William Cooper to the Sadler Committee?

2. How might Adam Smith criticize the system of labor described by Daniel Defoe?

Standards 10.2, 10.2.5, 10.3, 10.3.1, 10.3.2, 10.3.3, 10.3.4, 10.3.5, 10.3.6, 10.3.7

## Reviewing Content Vocabulary

*On a sheet of paper, use each of these terms in a sentence.*

1. capital
2. entrepreneur
3. cottage industry
4. puddling
5. industrial capitalism
6. socialism
7. conservatism
8. principle of intervention
9. liberalism
10. universal male suffrage
11. militarism
12. kaiser
13. plebiscite
14. emancipation
15. abolitionism
16. secede
17. romanticism
18. secularization
19. organic evolution
20. natural selection
21. realism

## Reviewing Academic Vocabulary

*On a sheet of paper, use each of these terms in a sentence that reflects the term's meaning in the chapter.*

22. dynamic
23. migrate
24. stability
25. beneficial
26. reliance
27. levy
28. successor
29. abandon
30. adapt
31. variation
32. controversy

## Reviewing the Main Ideas

### Section 1

33. List the members of the new industrial middle class.
34. What were the goals of early socialists?

### Section 2

35. What four nations were prepared to use military forces to crush revolts in other nations?
36. Name the social classes that tended to support liberalism.

### Section 3

37. What countries were involved in the Crimean War? What were the causes of the war?
38. Describe how Otto von Bismarck contributed to German unification.

### Section 4

39. What features can be found in paintings of the romantic style?
40. How did new discoveries in science in the 1800s provide practical benefits to Europeans?

## Critical Thinking

41. **Making Comparisons** Compare the motives for Czar Alexander II's emancipation of the serfs with Abraham Lincoln's motives for the Emancipation Proclamation in 1863.
42. **Cause and Effect** Describe how the Crimean War indirectly contributed to Italian and German unification.
43. **Reading Skill** Visualizing Imagine you are an Italian during Italy's struggle for a unified nation. What would life be like? Use the paintings, literature, and quotations in your chapter to write a brief essay on Italian nationalism.

## Chapter Summary

In this chapter, you have studied developments from industry to art, faith to science, and liberalism to conservatism. The chart below summarizes some of these developments.

| Advances | Conflict | Change | Reaction | Diversity |
|---|---|---|---|---|
| • Steam and coal are new sources of power.<br>• Higher-quality iron leads to better railroads. | • Nationalism and liberalism become forces for change.<br>• Conservatives attempt to suppress nationalism. | • People move to cities for factory work.<br>• Italy unifies.<br>• Germany emerges as a strong European power. | • Russian czars oppose the forces of liberalism and nationalism.<br>• Science has a greater impact on people, undermining religious faith. | • Austria-Hungary contains many different ethnic groups seeking self-rule.<br>• Romanticism and realism are opposite artistic styles. |

## Writing About History

44. **Historical Analysis** Interpreting Migration Write an essay exploring the pros and cons of leaving a farm to work in a factory. Be sure to consider social and economic factors and come to a conclusion on whether it is a positive or negative move. **CA CS 3**

45. *Big Idea* How did the political, economic, and social injustices that existed during the nineteenth century contribute to romanticism and realism?

**DBQ** **Document-Based Questions**

**Analyzing Sources** Read the following excerpt from the poetry of William Wordsworth:

> 66One impulse from a vernal wood
> May teach you more of man,
> Of moral evil and of good,
> Than all the sages can.99

46. What characteristic of romantic poetry is evident in Wordsworth's poem? **CA 10RL3.12**

47. What message is Wordsworth trying to convey? Do you agree?

**Analyzing Sources** Read the following lines from William Blake's "The Chimney-Sweeper":

> 66When my mother died I was very young,
> And my father sold me while yet my tongue
> Could scarcely cry 'Weep! weep! weep! Weep!
> So your chimneys I sweep, and in soot I sleep.
>
> There's little Tom Dacre, who cried when his head,
> That curled like a lamb's back, was shaved' so I said,
> 'Hush, Tom! never mind it, for, when your head's bare,
> You know that the soot cannot spoil your white hair.99

48. To whom is the chimney sweep speaking and why do you think Blake has him address that person?

49. According to Blake's poem, what is the effect of the Industrial Revolution on families?

50. Why do you think Tom's head is shaved?

## Analyzing Maps and Charts

Study the map, Industrialization of Europe by 1870, that appears on page 258. Then answer the following questions.

51. In which part of the United Kingdom is industrialization concentrated?

52. What relationship exists between railways and industrial centers?

# CHAPTER 5

## 1870–1914
# Mass Society and Democracy

### ❧ The Big Ideas ❧

### SECTION 1: The Growth of Industrial Prosperity

**New technologies can revolutionize the way people live, work, interact and govern.** Industrialization led to dramatic increases in productivity as well as to new political theories and social movements.

### SECTION 2: The Emergence of Mass Society

**New technologies can revolutionize the way people live, work, interact and govern.** The Second Industrial Revolution led to more leisure for all classes, and women began to expand their education and career opportunities.

### SECTION 3: The National State and Democracy

**Moral and ethical principles influence the development of political thought.** Democracy triumphed in Western Europe, authoritarianism prevailed in the East, the United States became an industrial powerhouse, and the European powers prepared for war.

### SECTION 4: Toward the Modern Consciousness

**New technologies can revolutionize the way people live, work, interact and govern.** Radical change in the economic and social structure of the West created equally dramatic intellectual and artistic change.

***World History—Modern Times Video*** *The Chapter 5 video,* "The Industrial Movement," *chronicles the impact of the development and advancements of the Second Industrial Revolution.*

*Transmitter and receiver used for first telephone call*

**1876**
Alexander Graham Bell invents the telephone

| 1835 | 1845 | 1855 | 1865 | 1875 |
|------|------|------|------|------|

*Karl Marx*

**1848**
*The Communist Manifesto* is published

**1861**
First Civil War battle fought in United States

**1871**
British unions gain legal recognition

*The Gare Saint-Lazare: Arrival of a Train* by Claude Monet, 1877  This painting illustrates Monet's fascination with light as it is reflected and absorbed by the sky, clouds, windows, and trains.

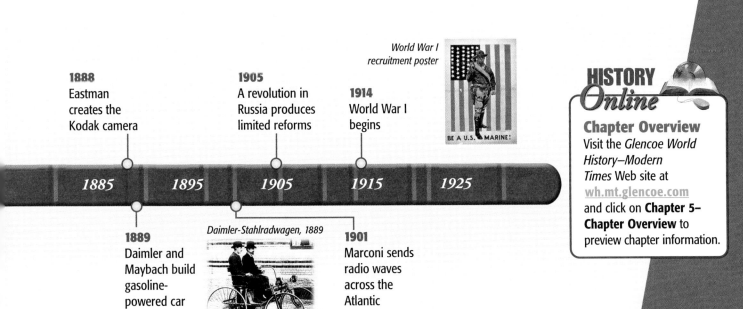

**1888**
Eastman creates the Kodak camera

**1905**
A revolution in Russia produces limited reforms

**1914**
World War I begins

*World War I recruitment poster*

BE A U.S. MARINE!

1885    1895    1905    1915    1925

**1889**
Daimler and Maybach build gasoline-powered car

*Daimler-Stahlradwagen, 1889*

**1901**
Marconi sends radio waves across the Atlantic

**HISTORY Online**

**Chapter Overview**
Visit the *Glencoe World History–Modern Times* Web site at wh.mt.glencoe.com and click on **Chapter 5– Chapter Overview** to preview chapter information.

## Reading Skill ⟩ Summarizing

Have you ever asked a friend to tell you what happened in an episode of a TV show? You were asking for a summary of the most important parts, not a description of every detail. Good readers summarize as they read. To do this, they use a few words of their own to capture the main ideas. Summarizing is useful for taking notes. It also helps you predict what will come next in the story.

When should you pause to summarize what you've been reading? Often, the end of a long paragraph or the end of a section is a good place to stop and summarize.

*Read the following excerpt from the chapter.*

## SUMMARIZING TIP

Try summarizing the most important points on paper and in your mind. Then talk to other students to find out how they summarized a specific section.

At the top of European society stood a wealthy elite. This group made up only 5 percent of the population but controlled between 30 and 40 percent of the wealth.... The middle classes consisted of a variety of groups. Below the upper middle class ... was a group that included lawyers [and] doctors.... The Second Industrial Revolution produced a new group. These were the white-collar workers who were seen as fitting in between the lower middle class and lower classes ... includ[ing] ... bookkeepers ... and secretaries.... Below the middle classes were the working classes, who made up almost 80 percent of Europe's population. In eastern Europe, the working classes were often landholding peasants, farm laborers, and sharecroppers....

## Apply the Skill

As you read the chapter, pause to summarize, especially when you feel there is a lot of information. If a paragraph or section is challenging, make a chart to show the most important facts or conclusions. This technique will help your mental ability to summarize.

## Historical Analysis Skill  Examining Trends

**Historical Interpretation: Standard HI 1** *Students show the connections, causal and otherwise, between particular historical events and larger social, economic, and political trends and developments.*

Historians examine trends in politics, economics, and social life so that they can draw larger conclusions about a certain time period. If they can see that the same kinds of things are happening in the political world—for example, political rallies for a certain cause—they would be alerted to a trend.

In the late 1800s, political institutions in some Western European countries were moving toward greater democracy. More and more people were pressing for the vote. In Great Britain, even women were campaigning for the vote. (In other European nations, France and Italy, for example, women did not achieve the vote until the 1940s.)

*Examine this excerpt from a speech by the British suffragist Emmeline Pankhurst in 1908 to see the connections being made between voting rights and representative governments:*

> **"[The vote] is a symbol of freedom, a symbol of citizenship, a symbol of liberty. It is a safeguard of all those liberties which it symbolizes. And in these later days it has come to be regarded more than anything else as an instrument, something with which you can get a great many more things than our forefathers who fought for the vote ever realised as possible to get with it. . . ."**

At this point in history, women did not have the right to vote. Based on her speech, why did Pankhurst think suffrage was so important? How representative is a government in which not everyone is able to vote?

### Apply the Skill

Discuss with another student what Pankhurst meant when she said that the vote was "an instrument." Do you think that voters have always thought of the vote in this way? Why or why not?

# A Story That Matters

*Steeplechase swimming pool at Coney Island, New York, c. 1919*

## The New Leisure

**B**y the second half of the nineteenth century, new work patterns had established the concept of the weekend as a distinct time of recreation and fun. New forms of transportation—railroads and streetcars—enabled workers to make brief trips to amusement parks. Coney Island was only eight miles from central New York City; Blackpool, in England, was a short train ride from nearby industrial towns.

With their Ferris wheels and other daring rides that threw young men and women together, amusement parks offered a whole new world of entertainment. Before leaving, people purchased picture postcards to remember the day's fun.

Thanks to the railroad, seaside resorts—once visited only by the wealthy—became accessible to more people for weekend visits. One upper-class seaside resort regular expressed his disgust with the new "day-trippers":

"They swarm upon the beach, wandering about with apparently no other aim than to get a mouthful of fresh air. You may see them in groups of three or four—the husband, a pale man, dressed in black coat, carries the baby; the wife, equally pale and thin, decked out in her best, labors after with a basket of food. And then there is generally another child . . . wandering behind."

Businessmen in resorts like Blackpool, however, welcomed the crowds of new visitors and built for them boardwalks laden with food, drink, and entertainment.

### Why It Matters

A new leisure was one part of the mass society that emerged in the late nineteenth century. The development of this new mass society helped improve the lives of the lower classes, who benefited from extended voting rights, a better standard of living, and public education. In addition, the European nation-states now fostered national loyalty and created mass armies. Political democracy grew as the right to vote was extended to all adult males.

**History and You** In 1850, a person born in the West could expect to live about 40 years. By 1910, life expectancy had increased to 54 years. Using a recent almanac, compare the life expectancy rates of people in the United States, United Kingdom, and Russia today with the rates in 1910. Create a bar graph with the data you find.

# The Growth of Industrial Prosperity

## Section Preview

Industrialization led to dramatic increases in productivity as well as to new political theories and social movements.

### Main Idea

• In Western Europe, the introduction of electricity, chemicals, and petroleum triggered the Second Industrial Revolution, and a world economy began to develop. (p. 296)

• Industrialization gave some a higher standard of living, but struggling workers turned to trade unions or socialism to improve their lives. (p. 298)

## Content Vocabulary

assembly line, mass production, proletariat, dictatorship, revisionist

## Academic Vocabulary

generator, transform, emerge

## People to Identify

Thomas Edison, Alexander Graham Bell, Guglielmo Marconi, Karl Marx

## Places to Locate

the Netherlands, Spain, Portugal, Russia, Austria-Hungary

## Reading Objectives

1. Define the Second Industrial Revolution.
2. List Karl Marx's main ideas.

## Reading Strategy

**Cause and Effect** As you read, complete a diagram like the one below showing the relationship between certain resources and the products that resulted from their use.

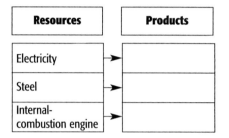

| Resources | Products |
|-----------|----------|
| Electricity | → |
| Steel | → |
| Internal-combustion engine | → |

## Preview of Events

| ◆1845 | ◆1855 | ◆1865 | ◆1875 | ◆1885 | ◆1895 | ◆1905 |
|-------|-------|-------|-------|-------|-------|-------|

**1848**
Marx and Engels publish *The Communist Manifesto*

**1875**
Creation of German Social Democratic Party

**1879**
Thomas Edison invents the lightbulb

**1889**
The Second International socialist association forms

**1903**
Wright brothers make first flight

## California Standards in This Section

*Reading this section will help you master these California History–Social Science standards.*

**10.3:** Students analyze the effects of the Industrial Revolution in England, France, Germany, Japan, and the United States.

**10.3.2:** Examine how scientific and technological changes and new forms of energy brought about massive social, economic, and cultural change (e.g., the inventions and discoveries of James Watt, Eli Whitney, Henry Bessemer, Louis Pasteur, Thomas Edison).

**10.3.3:** Describe the growth of population, rural to urban migration, and growth of cities associated with the Industrial Revolution.

**10.3.4:** Trace the evolution of work and labor, including the demise of the slave trade and the effects of immigration, mining and manufacturing, division of labor, and the union movement.

**10.3.5:** Understand the connections among natural resources, entrepreneurship, labor, and capital in an industrial economy.

**10.3.6:** Analyze the emergence of capitalism as a dominant economic pattern and the responses to it, including Utopianism, Social Democracy, Socialism, and Communism.

# The Second Industrial Revolution

**Main Idea** In Western Europe, the introduction of electricity, chemicals, and petroleum triggered the Second Industrial Revolution, and a world economy began to develop.

**Reading Connection** Does your life come to a halt when the power goes out? Read to learn what happened when electricity first became a part of everyday life.

In the late nineteenth century, the belief in progress was so strong in the West that it was almost a religion. Europeans and Americans had been converted by the stunning bounty of products of the Second Industrial Revolution. In the first Industrial Revolution, textiles, coal, iron, and railroads were major elements. In the Second Industrial Revolution, steel, chemicals, electricity, and petroleum were the keys to making economies even more productive.

## *Voices from the Past*

Guglielmo Marconi made one of the era's most striking discoveries, wireless telegraphy, on December 12, 1901. The scientist and inventor described it in these words:

> ❝Shortly before mid-day I placed the single earphone to my ear and started listening. . . . I was at last on the point of putting . . . my beliefs to test. The answer came at 12:30 when I heard, faintly but distinctly, pip-pip-pip. I handed the phone to Kemp: 'Can you hear anything?' I asked. 'Yes,' he said, 'the letter S'—he could hear it. . . . The electric waves sent out into space from Britain had traversed the Atlantic—the distance, enormous as it seemed then, of 1,700 miles—It was an epoch in history. I now felt for the first time absolutely certain the day would come when mankind would be able to send messages without wires . . . between the farthermost ends of the earth.❞

**New Products** One major industrial change between 1870 and 1914 was the substitution of steel for iron. New methods for shaping steel made it useful in building lighter and faster machines and engines, as well as railways, ships, and weapons. In 1860, Great Britain, France, Germany, and Belgium produced 125,000 tons (112,500 t) of steel. By 1913, the total was an astounding 32 million tons (29 million t).

Electricity was a major new form of energy. It could be easily converted into other forms of energy, such as heat, light, and motion, and could be sent over long distances by means of wires. In the 1870s, the first practical **generators** of electrical current were developed. By 1910, hydroelectric power stations and coal-fired, steam-driven generating plants enabled homes and factories alike to draw upon a reliable, versatile, clean, and convenient source of power.

Electricity gave birth to a series of inventions. The creation of the lightbulb by **Thomas Edison** in the United States and Joseph Swan in Great Britain opened homes and cities to electric lights. A revolution in communications began when **Alexander Graham Bell** invented the telephone in 1876 and **Guglielmo Marconi** sent the first radio waves across the Atlantic in 1901.

By 1900, streetcars and subways powered by electricity had appeared in major European cities. Electricity **transformed** the factory as well. Conveyor belts, cranes, and manufacturing machines could all be powered by electricity. With electric lights, factories could operate 24 hours a day.

The development of the internal-combustion engine, fired by oil or gasoline, provided a new source of power in transportation. This engine gave rise to ocean liners and warships with oil-fired engines, as well as to the airplane and the automobile. In 1903, Orville and Wilbur Wright made the first powered flight in a fixed-wing plane at Kitty Hawk, North Carolina. In 1908, Henry Ford produced his first Model T.

▼ *Edison in 1915 with his portable searchlight*

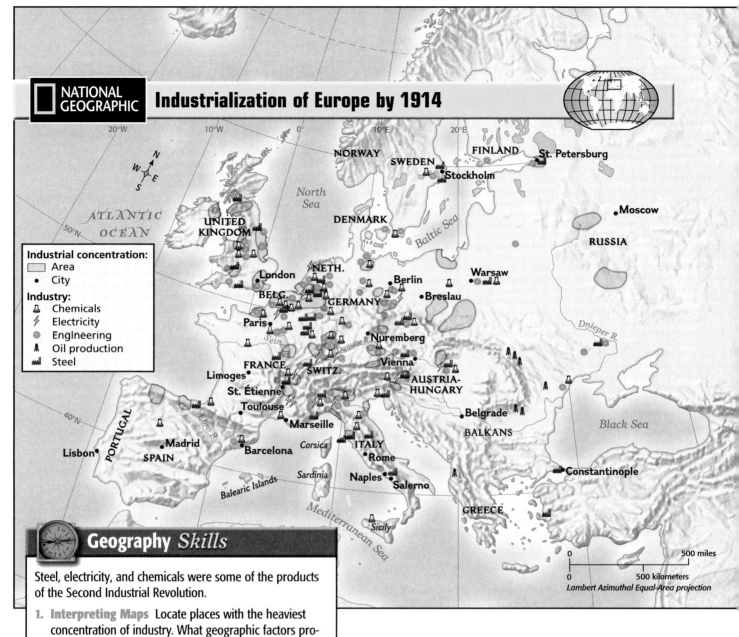

## NATIONAL GEOGRAPHIC
## Industrialization of Europe by 1914

**Industrial concentration:**
- ☐ Area
- • City

**Industry:**
- 🜀 Chemicals
- ⚡ Electricity
- ⊙ Engineering
- 🜛 Oil production
- ⛏ Steel

ATLANTIC OCEAN

North Sea

Baltic Sea

Black Sea

Mediterranean Sea

NORWAY
SWEDEN • Stockholm
FINLAND • St. Petersburg
DENMARK
• Moscow
RUSSIA
UNITED KINGDOM
• London
NETH.
BELG.
• Berlin
• Breslau
• Warsaw
GERMANY
• Paris
FRANCE
• Nuremberg
SWITZ.
• Vienna
AUSTRIA-HUNGARY
• Belgrade
BALKANS
• Limoges
• St. Étienne
• Toulouse
• Marseille
PORTUGAL
SPAIN
• Madrid
Lisbon•
• Barcelona
Corsica
ITALY
• Rome
Sardinia
Balearic Islands
Naples •
• Salerno
Sicily
GREECE
Constantinople
Dnieper R.
Danube R.
Seine
Ebro R.

0        500 miles
0        500 kilometers
Lambert Azimuthal Equal-Area projection

## Geography Skills

Steel, electricity, and chemicals were some of the products of the Second Industrial Revolution.

1. **Interpreting Maps** Locate places with the heaviest concentration of industry. What geographic factors promoted industry in these areas?

2. **Applying Geography Skills** Use the information provided in this map to create a chart that shows the types of industry in each country.

The Model T was very affordable and kicked off the era when many people owned cars.

**New Patterns** Industrial production grew at a rapid pace because the demand, or market, for goods was a mass market. Many more Europeans could afford to buy products. Their wages increased after about 1870. At the same time, manufactured goods were becoming cheaper: both production and transportation were more efficient. One of the biggest reasons for more efficient production was the **assembly line,** a new manufacturing method pioneered by Henry Ford in 1913. The assembly line allowed a much more efficient **mass production** of goods.

In the cities, the first department stores began to sell a new range of products made possible by the steel and electrical industries—clocks, bicycles, electric lights, and typewriters, for example. Glass technology also inspired stores to create eye-catching window displays of the latest fashions.

Not everyone benefited from the Second Industrial Revolution. By 1900, Europe was divided into two economic zones. Great Britain, Belgium, France, **the Netherlands,** Germany, the western part of the Austro-Hungarian Empire, and northern Italy made up an advanced industrialized core. These nations had a high standard of living and advanced transportation.

In the rest of Europe—southern Italy, **Spain, Portugal,** the Balkans, **Russia,** and most of **Austria-Hungary**—the economy was still largely agricultural. These countries provided food and raw materials for the industrial countries, and their peoples often had a much lower standard of living.

**Toward a World Economy** The period of the Second Industrial Revolution marked a major step toward a true world economy. Transportation by steamship and railroad contributed to this advance. A European living in 1900 had the benefit of products from faraway places—beef and wool from Argentina and Australia, coffee from Brazil, iron ore from Algeria, and sugar from Java in Indonesia.

Another part of the world economy was financial. European money was invested in other foreign enterprises that would produce a profit—railroads, mines, electric power plants, and banks. Of course, foreign countries also provided markets for the manufactured goods of Europe. With its capital, industries, and military might, Europe dominated the world economy by the beginning of the twentieth century.

✓ **Reading Check** **Explaining** What parts of Europe still had an agricultural economy in the early twentieth century?

## Organizing the Working Class

**Main Idea** Industrialization gave some a higher standard of living, but struggling workers turned to trade unions or socialism to improve their lives.

**Reading Connection** Do you hear news stories about life in a communist country such as China or Cuba? Read to learn about the first socialist movements in Europe.

The transition to an industrialized society was very hard on workers. It disrupted their lives and forced them to move to crowded slums. They had to give up occupations they knew and liked, and work long hours at mind-numbing tasks. Eventually this transformation gave workers a higher standard of living. This was not true at first, however, and for many workers, improved conditions took many decades.

# SCIENCE, TECHNOLOGY & SOCIETY

## The Automobile

**M**any new forms of transportation were created in the Industrial Revolution, but none affected more people on a daily basis than the automobile. It was the invention of the internal-combustion engine that made the automobile possible.

A German engineer, Gottlieb Daimler, invented a light, portable internal-combustion engine in 1885. In 1889, Daimler and Wilhelm Maybach produced an automobile powered by a gasoline engine that reached a speed of 10 miles [16 km] per hour. In 1926, Daimler and Karl Benz, another German, merged to form Daimler-Benz, an automotive company that would later manufacture the Mercedes-Benz.

Early cars were handmade and expensive. Only several hundred were sold between 1893 and 1901. Their slow speed, 14 miles [22.5 km] per hour, was a problem, too. Early models were not able to climb steep hills.

An American, Henry Ford, revolutionized the car industry in 1908 by using an assembly line to mass-produce his Model T. Before, it had taken a group of workers 12 hours to build a single car. Now, the same number of workers could build a car in an hour and a half. By cutting production costs, Ford lowered the price of the automobile. A Model T cost $850 in 1908 but only $360 by 1916. By 1916, Ford's factories were producing 735,000 cars a year. By 1925, Ford's Model T cars would make up half of the automobiles in the world.

**Analyzing** *Why were early cars expensive?*

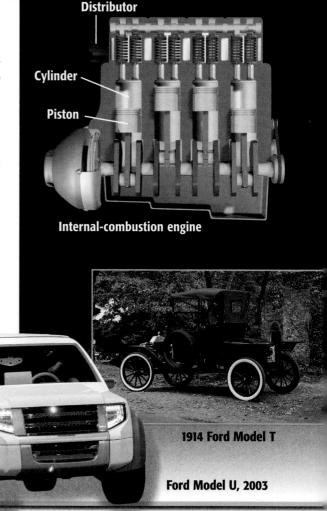

Distributor

Cylinder

Piston

**Internal-combustion engine**

**1914 Ford Model T**

**Ford Model U, 2003**

Reformers of this era believed that industrial capitalism was heartless and brutal. They wanted a new kind of society. Some reformers were moderates. They were willing to work within the system for gradual changes like fewer hours, better benefits, and safe working conditions. Often they used trade unions to achieve these practical goals.

Other reformers were more radical or even revolutionary. They wanted to abolish the capitalist system entirely and to create a socialist system. To achieve this goal, they supported socialist parties. Socialist parties **emerged** after 1870, but their theory for a new society came largely from Karl Marx. Marx was a socialist, and one form of Marxist socialism was eventually called communism (see Chapter 8).

**Marx's Theory** Karl Marx was one of the most influential theorists of the century. His socialist theory first came to light when *The Communist Manifesto* was published during the Revolution of 1848, just when workers were demonstrating in the streets.

In *The Communist Manifesto,* Marx and his friend and coauthor Friedrich Engels denounced the new industrial economy and predicted that it would be defeated. A workers' revolution was bound to occur. When the revolution came, it would destroy capitalism. Material wealth could then be distributed equally among all workers.

Marx believed that the oppressor and oppressed have "stood in constant opposition to one another" through all history. After the Industrial Revolution occurred, the oppressors were the capitalists with the capital, or money, to invest. They owned the land and the raw material; thus, they had total power over production. In Marx's view, the oppressed were the workers who owned nothing and who depended for their very survival on the capitalists.

Around him, Marx believed he saw a society that was "more and more splitting up into two great hostile camps, into two great classes directly facing each other: Bourgeoisie and Proletariat." The term *bourgeoisie* was well known as a way of referring to the middle class, but Marx popularized the term **proletariat** (PROH•luh•TEH•ree•uht) as a way of referring to the working class.

Marx predicted that the struggle between the two groups would finally lead to revolution. The proletariat would violently overthrow the bourgeoisie.

# CONNECTIONS Past To Present

## May Day

On May 1, 1997, parades and demonstrations took place around the world. Mexican workers poured into the streets of Mexico City to denounce the North American Free Trade Agreement (NAFTA). Workers believed it had caused a decline in their wages. In Seoul, Korean workers hurled rocks at police to protest government corruption in South Korea. In Berlin and Leipzig, union workers marched to protest high unemployment in Germany. In Beijing, people filled Tiananmen Square to praise workers at the beginning of a three-day vacation. In Japan, two million workers attended rallies across the country. Fifteen thousand workers marched in the streets of San Salvador to demand that the government pass laws to benefit the workers of El Salvador.

Why did these marches and demonstrations occur around the world on May 1? In the nineteenth century, the rise of socialist parties in Europe led to a movement to form an international organization. The purpose of this organization was to strengthen the position of socialist parties against international capitalism.

In 1889, leaders of various socialist parties formed the Second International, a loose association of national groups. Its first action was to declare May 1 as May Day, an international labor day to be marked by strikes and mass labor demonstrations. Although the Second International no longer exists, workers around the world still observe May Day.

◀ *May Day rally near St. Basil's cathedral in Moscow, May 1, 1997*

## Comparing Past and Present

Using outside sources, research what occurred last May 1. Were May Day celebrations held, and if so, where? Is May 1 still an international labor day?

Then a **dictatorship** of the proletariat would be formed to abolish capitalism and create a socialist economy. (A dictatorship is a government in which a person or small group has absolute power.) After this dictatorship abolished economic differences among classes, a classless society would come about. The state itself, which had been a tool of the bourgeoisie, would wither away.

**Socialist Parties** People inspired by Marx and by the goals of socialism began to form political parties to change society. The most important was the German Social Democratic Party (SPD), founded in 1875. The SPD advocated a Marxist revolution. Bismarck, the German prime minister, outlawed the SPD in 1878, but the party grew and in 1890 it was legalized.

In the German parliament, SPD representatives lobbied for laws to improve working conditions. In 1912, four million Germans voted for SPD candidates. It had become the largest party in Germany. Because the German constitution gave greater power to the upper house and the German emperor, the SPD was not able to bring about the kind of changes it wanted.

Socialist parties emerged in other European states, too. As early as 1862, the First International was founded to promote socialist goals. It died out quickly because its members could not agree on tactics.

In 1889, the Second International was founded, but socialist parties continued to disagree over precise goals and tactics. So-called pure Marxists thought that only a violent revolution could defeat capitalism. Other Marxists, **revisionists,** rejected the idea of violent revolution. They argued that workers could achieve socialism through the parliamentary system. If more and more workers won the right to vote, they said, the laws could be changed and workers would have better lives. In other words, socialism would be achieved gradually and by working through the system, not through violent revolution.

**Trade Unions** Another movement for workers focused on the trade union, or labor union. To improve their conditions, workers organized in a union. Then the union had to get the employer to recognize its right to represent workers in collective bargaining, negotiations with employers over wages and hours.

The right to strike was another important part of the trade union movement. In a strike, a union calls on its members to stop work in order to pressure employers to meet their demands for higher wages or improved factory safety. At first, laws were passed that made strikes illegal under any circumstances. In Great Britain, in 1870, unions won the right to strike. By 1914, there were almost four million workers in British trade unions. In the rest of Europe, trade unions had varying degrees of success in helping workers achieve a better life.

✓ **Reading Check** **Summarizing** How would you summarize Marx's theory as stated in *The Communist Manifesto?*

**HISTORY** *Online* **Study Central**

For help with the concepts in this section of *Glencoe World History—Modern Times,* go to wh.mt.glencoe.com and click on **Study Central.**

---

# SECTION 1 ASSESSMENT

### Checking for Understanding

1. **Vocabulary** Define: generator, transform, assembly line, mass production, emerge, proletariat, dictatorship, revisionist.

2. **People** Identify: Thomas Edison, Alexander Graham Bell, Guglielmo Marconi, Karl Marx.

3. **Places** Locate: the Netherlands, Spain, Portugal, Russia, Austria-Hungary.

### Reviewing Big Ideas

4. **Explain** how Marx's ideas came to directly affect society.

### Critical Thinking

5. **Historical Analysis** **Contextualizing** What is the relationship between the large number of technical innovations made during this period and the growing need for labor reforms and unions? **CA HI 3**

6. **Compare and Contrast** Use a Venn diagram like the one below to compare and contrast the first and second Industrial Revolutions.

First Industrial Revolution   Second Industrial Revolution

### Analyzing Visuals

7. **Compare** the photos of the two Ford vehicles on page 298. Do you think that style and practicality weighed equally with car buyers in the 1920s as it does today? Why or why not?

---

**Writing About History**

8. **Expository Writing** After Marconi's first transmission across radio waves, he said, "I now felt for the first time absolutely certain the day would come when mankind would be able to send messages without wires. . . ." Write a paragraph about this prophecy. **CA 10WA2.3b**

---

# The Emergence of Mass Society

## Section Preview

The Second Industrial Revolution led to more leisure for all classes, and women began to expand their education and career opportunities.

### Main Idea

- As workers migrated to cities, local governments had to solve urgent public health problems, and their solutions allowed cities to grow even more. (p. 302)
- European society settled into three broad social classes—upper, middle, and lower—but many subgroups existed within the three classes. (p. 304)

- Attitudes toward women changed as they moved into white-collar jobs, received more education, and began agitating for the vote. (p. 306)
- As a result of industrialization, the levels of education rose, and people's lives were more clearly divided into periods of work and leisure. (p. 308)

## Content Vocabulary

feminism, literacy

## Academic Vocabulary

innovation, objective

## People to Identify

Florence Nightingale, Emmeline Pankhurst

## Reading Objectives

1. Identify the main characteristics of the European middle class in the nineteenth century.
2. List the major changes in women's social status between 1870 and 1914.

## Reading Strategy

**Summarizing Information** As you read, complete a graphic organizer summarizing social class divisions.

| Social Classes | | |
|---------|--------|---------|
| Working | Middle | Wealthy |
|  |  |  |
|  |  |  |
|  |  |  |

## Preview of Events

♦1870    ♦1875    ♦1880    ♦1885    ♦1890    ♦1895    ♦1900

**1870**
British wives gain greater property rights

**1881**
First publication of London's *Evening News*

**1885**
10,000 people watch British Soccer Cup finals

**1903**
Women's Social and Political Union established

# California Standards in This Section

*Reading this section will help you master these California History–Social Science standards.*

**10.3:** Students analyze the effects of the Industrial Revolution in England, France, Germany, Japan, and the United States.

**10.3.2:** Examine how scientific and technological changes and new forms of energy brought about massive social, economic, and cultural change (e.g., the inventions and discoveries of James Watt, Eli Whitney, Henry Bessemer, Louis Pasteur, Thomas Edison).

**10.3.3:** Describe the growth of population, rural to urban migration, and growth of cities associated with the Industrial Revolution.

**10.3.4:** Trace the evolution of work and labor, including the demise of the slave trade and the effects of immigration, mining and manufacturing, division of labor, and the union movement.

**10.3.5:** Understand the connections among natural resources, entrepreneurship, labor, and capital in an industrial economy.

**10.3.6:** Analyze the emergence of capitalism as a dominant economic pattern and the responses to it, including Utopianism, Social Democracy, Socialism, and Communism.

# The New Urban Environment

**Main Idea** As workers migrated to cities, local governments had to solve urgent public health problems, and their solutions allowed cities to grow even more.

**Reading Connection** Have you heard adults in your community talk about landfill problems? Read to learn about government solutions to similar problems in the late 1800s.

By the end of the nineteenth century, the new industrial world had led to the emergence of a mass society in which the condition of the majority—the lower classes—was demanding some sort of governmental attention. The lower classes were concentrated in cities where, as voters, they became a political force.

Governments that used to be concerned only with the interests of the wealthier members of society now had to consider how to appeal to the masses. Housing was one area of great concern—crowded quarters could easily spread disease. An even bigger threat to health was public sanitation. From the 1850s on, this was an urgent mutual concern in many big cities.

## Voices from the Past

The government's failure to provide clean water was satirized in *Punch*, the famous humor magazine, in 1849. It was enough to make any Londoner think twice before drinking the next glass of water.

**"**This is the water that JOHN drinks.

This is the Thames with its cento* of stink,
That supplies the water that JOHN drinks.

These are the fish that float in the inky
stream of the Thames with its cento of stink,
That supplies the water that JOHN drinks.

This is the sewer from cesspool and sink,
That feeds the fish that float in the inky
stream of the Thames with its cento of stink,
That supplies the water that JOHN drinks.**"**

*Usually refers to a poetic blend of parts of literary works; here used sarcastically to refer to the mucky waters of the Thames River.

## NATIONAL GEOGRAPHIC  European Population Growth and Relocation, 1820–1900

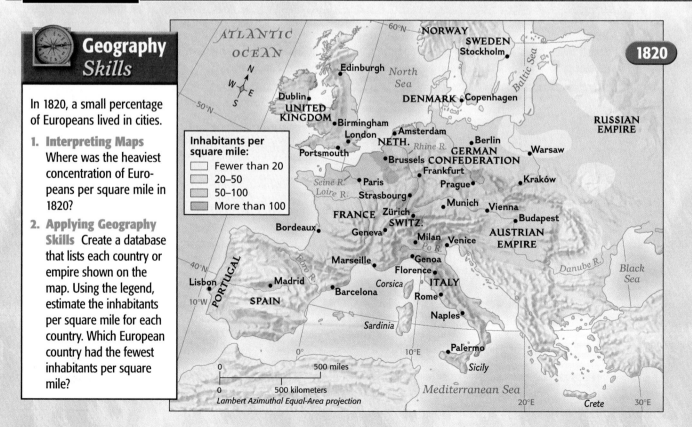

 **Geography Skills**

In 1820, a small percentage of Europeans lived in cities.

1. **Interpreting Maps** Where was the heaviest concentration of Europeans per square mile in 1820?

2. **Applying Geography Skills** Create a database that lists each country or empire shown on the map. Using the legend, estimate the inhabitants per square mile for each country. Which European country had the fewest inhabitants per square mile?

**1820**

Inhabitants per square mile:
- Fewer than 20
- 20–50
- 50–100
- More than 100

*Lambert Azimuthal Equal-Area projection*

The population figures tell the story. In the early 1850s, urban dwellers made up about 40 percent of the English population, 15 percent of the French, 10 percent of the population in Prussia (the largest of the German states), and 5 percent in Russia. By 1890, urban dwellers had increased to about 60 percent in England, 25 percent in France, 30 percent in Prussia, and 10 percent in Russia. In heavily industrialized nations, cities grew tremendously. Between 1800 and 1900, for example, the population of London grew from 960,000 to 6,500,000.

Cities grew quickly because vast numbers of people from rural areas migrated to them. In the countryside, they no longer had jobs, and in many countries, the land had never been theirs. In cities, they found work in factories and, later, in new white-collar jobs.

Cities also grew quickly after the 1850s because municipal governments had made **innovations** in public health and sanitation. Thus many more people could survive living close together.

Improvements had come only after reformers in the 1840s began urging local governments to do something about the filthy conditions that caused disease. Cholera, which is caused by a contaminated water supply, was the most deadly disease—a person might die in a matter of a few days. Cholera epidemics ravaged many European cities in the 1830s and 1840s.

Reformers blamed some problems on the lack of restraints on builders. City governments responded by creating boards of health to improve housing. Medical officers and building inspectors inspected dwellings for health hazards. Cities began requiring running water and internal drainage systems for new buildings.

Clean water and an effective sewage system were critical to public health. The need for fresh water was met by dams and reservoirs to store water and by the aqueducts and tunnels to carry it from the countryside to urban homes. By the 1860s, many more people could take regular hot baths, too, because gas heaters, and later electric heaters, were invented.

The treatment of sewage was improved by building mammoth underground pipes that carried raw sewage far from the city for disposal. The city of Frankfurt, Germany, began its program for sewers with a lengthy public campaign featuring the slogan "from the toilet to the river in half an hour."

**✓ Reading Check** **Explaining** Why did cities grow so quickly in the nineteenth century?

## Geography Skills

Two population changes occurred in Europe from 1820 to 1900: the overall population increased, and it shifted from rural to urban areas.

1. **Interpreting Maps** Which country has the greater population density: Spain or Italy?

2. **Applying Geography Skills** Analyze the relationship between the increased urban populations shown here and the areas of industrial concentration shown on the map on page 297.

▲ *The sumptuous lifestyle of the upper middle class featured formal dress for meals of multiple courses prepared by a kitchen staff.*

# Social Structure of Mass Society

**Main Idea** European society settled into three broad social classes—upper, middle, and lower—but many subgroups existed within the three classes.

**Reading Connection** Do you think of yourself as belonging to the large American middle class? Read to learn about how your great-grandparents might have viewed themselves in an earlier time.

After 1871, most people enjoyed an improved standard of living. Their meals more often included meat, their clothes were more often "store-bought," and they might even have a little money left over from their pay. Even so, poverty remained a serious problem.

Several classes can be identified in European society at this time. A very small number were very rich, many more were very poor, and substantial numbers belonged to different middle-class groups.

**The New Elite** At the top of European society stood a wealthy elite. This group made up only 5 percent of the population but controlled between 30 and 40 percent of the wealth. During the nineteenth century, the most successful industrialists, bankers, and merchants—the wealthy upper middle class—had joined with the landed aristocracy to form this new elite. Members of the elite, whether aristocratic or upper middle class in background, became leaders in the government and military.

Marriage also served to unite the two groups. Daughters of business tycoons gained aristocratic titles, and aristocratic heirs in financial difficulties gained new sources of cash. For example, when wealthy American Consuelo Vanderbilt married the British Duke of Marlborough, the new duchess brought approximately $10 million to the match.

**The Middle Classes** The middle classes consisted of a variety of groups. Below the upper middle class, which formed part of the new elite, was a group that included lawyers, doctors, members of the civil service, business managers, engineers, architects, accountants, and chemists. They made up a solid and comfortable middle-class group. Beneath them was a lower middle class. The lower middle class primarily consisted of small shopkeepers, traders, and prosperous farmers.

▲ *This family scene is typical of the middle class. It is much less formal than the scene on page 304. The aproned woman is probably a servant; if she served in an upper-class family, she would not seem to be participating, as she is here.*

The Second Industrial Revolution produced a new group. These were the white-collar workers who were seen as fitting in between the lower middle class and the lower classes. White-collar workers included traveling salespeople, bookkeepers, telephone operators, department-store salespeople, and secretaries. Their pay was relatively low, but they hoped to join the middle class and were committed to middle-class values.

The middle classes shared a certain lifestyle with values that dominated nineteenth-century society. The members of the middle class liked to preach their values not only to their children, but to the upper and lower classes. This was especially evident in Victorian Britain, often considered the model of middle-class society. In part, this was because British prosperity had created a very large middle class.

One of the chief **objectives** was the middle-class belief in hard work. Hard work was open to everyone and, in the minds of the middle classes, it was guaranteed to have positive results. They were also regular churchgoers who believed in Christian morality. Outward appearances were also very important to the middle classes. The etiquette book *The Habits of Good Society* was a best-seller.

**The Working Classes** Below the middle classes were the working classes, who made up almost 80 percent of Europe's population. In eastern Europe, the working classes were often landholding peasants, farm laborers, or sharecroppers.

In western Europe, the working classes were urbanized. They might be skilled artisans or semiskilled laborers, but most of them were unskilled. People with no skills were often day laborers or else domestic servants. In Great Britain in 1900, one of every seven employed persons was a domestic servant, and most servants were women.

After 1870, urban workers began to live more comfortably. Reforms had created better housing and cleaner streets. Their wages were rising—although wages were not rising as fast as production. And since the cost of consumer goods was less, workers were able to buy more than just food and housing. Now workers even had money to buy extra clothes or pay to entertain themselves in their few leisure hours. Because workers had organized and conducted strikes, they had won the 10-hour workday, with a Saturday afternoon off.

✓ **Reading Check** **Identifying** Name the major groups in the social structure of the late nineteenth century.

▲ *Women worked as operators and secretaries at the Paris telephone exchange in 1904.*

Governments had also expanded their services, and this, too, created new job opportunities. Women might be secretaries and telephone operators in government offices or work in public education or health. A few men worked in these jobs, but most of them were filled by working-class and lower middle-class women. For these women, the jobs offered a chance at a better life.

## Marriage and the Family

When women began working outside the home, it challenged older ideals about women. For many people, that ideal was best expressed in the lines of Lord Tennyson's *The Princess,* published in 1847:

## The Experiences of Women

**Main Idea** Attitudes toward women changed as they moved into white-collar jobs, received more education, and began agitating for the vote.

**Reading Connection** To what extent are jobs today stereotyped by gender? Read to learn about how women started to expand their options in the late 1800s.

In 1800, women were mainly defined by their family and household roles. Growing up, a girl received an education suited to becoming a mother and wife. As a married woman, she was legally inferior to her husband, as well as economically dependent on his income. In the course of the nineteenth century, women's roles and experiences changed dramatically.

**New Job Opportunities** During much of the nineteenth century, European men maintained the belief that women should remain at home to bear and nurture children and should not be allowed in the industrial workforce.

The Second Industrial Revolution, however, opened the door to new jobs for women. There were not enough men to fill the relatively low-paid white-collar jobs being created, so employers began to hire women. Many businesses, whether they were industrial plants or retail shops, needed clerks, typists, secretaries, file clerks, and salesclerks.

❝Man for the field and woman for the hearth:
Man for the sword and for the needle she:
Man with the head and woman with the heart:
Man to command and woman to obey. . . .❞

This view of the sexes was strengthened during the Industrial Revolution. As the main family wage earners, men worked outside the home. Women were left with the care of the family, and marriage was their only honorable or available career.

There was an important change, however. The number of children born to the average woman began to decline—the most significant development in the modern family. The decline in the birthrate was tied to improved economic conditions and to the increased use of birth control. In 1882, Europe's first birth control clinic was founded in Amsterdam.

The family was the central institution of middle-class life. With fewer children, mothers were able to devote more time to child care and domestic leisure.

The middle-class family fostered an ideal of togetherness. The Victorians created the family Christmas with its Yule log, tree, songs, and exchange of gifts. By the 1850s, Fourth of July celebrations in the United States had changed from wild celebrations to family picnics.

The lives of working-class women were very different from this middle-class ideal. Most working-class women had to earn money to help support their families. Daughters in working-class families were expected to work until they married. After marriage, they had to work at small jobs at home to help in the raising of younger children. The childhood of a working-class girl or boy was essentially over by the age of nine or ten when many became apprentices or worked at odd jobs. 📖 *(See page 773 to read an excerpt from an article on working women in the Primary Sources Library.)*

Between 1890 and 1914, however, family patterns among the working class began to change. Higher-paying jobs in heavy industry and improvements in the standard of living made it possible for these families to depend on the income of the husbands alone.

By the early twentieth century, some working-class mothers could afford to stay at home just like middle-class women. Working-class families, too, began to save up to buy new consumer products like a sewing machine or a cast-iron stove.

**Women's Rights** Modern **feminism,** or the movement for women's rights, had its beginnings during the Enlightenment, when some women advocated equality for women based on the doctrine of natural rights. In the 1830s, some women in the United States and Europe began arguing that women had the right to divorce their husbands and to own property—at that time, the law gave the husband almost complete control over his wife's property. These early efforts were not very successful, and married women in Britain did not win the right to own property until 1870.

The fight for property rights was only the beginning of the women's movement. Some middle- and upper middle-class women fought for and gained access to universities, while others fought to enter professions and occupations dominated by men.

Women could not become doctors, so women with an interest in medicine became nurses. In Germany, Amalie Sieveking was a nursing pioneer who founded the Female Association for the Care of the Poor and Sick in Hamburg. More famous is the British nurse **Florence Nightingale.** Her efforts during the Crimean War (1853–1856), combined with those of Clara Barton in the U.S. Civil War (1861–1865), transformed nursing into a profession of trained, middle-class "women in white."

By the 1840s and 1850s, the movement for women's rights expanded: Women now called for equal political rights. They believed that suffrage, the right to vote, was the key to improving their overall position.

In Europe, the British movement for women's suffrage led the way. The Women's Social and Political Union, founded in 1903 by **Emmeline Pankhurst** and her daughters, quickly learned how to call attention to its demands by using publicity stunts. Its members, called "suffragettes" by the press, pelted government officials with eggs, chained themselves to lampposts, burned railroad cars, and smashed the windows of fashionable department stores. British police answered with arrests and brutal treatment of leading activists. These suffragists, as they were more generally known, had one basic aim: the right of women to full citizenship in the nation.

Before World War I, demands for women's rights were being heard throughout Europe and the United States. At the time, women had the right to vote in only a few places—nations like Norway and Finland, and a few American states of the Far West. It took the dramatic upheaval of World War I to make male-dominated governments give in on this basic issue.

**Reading Check** **Identifying** What was the basic aim of the suffragists?

*Picturing* **History**

Shown below are Emmeline Pankhurst, her daughters, and a fellow suffragist. Why do you think women such as these had to fight so hard and long to obtain the right to vote?

# Changes in Education and Leisure

**Main Idea** As a result of industrialization, the levels of education rose, and people's lives were more clearly divided into periods of work and leisure.

**Reading Connection** How would our society change if a college education was required? Read to learn about the era when the government required an elementary education.

Universal education was the result of the mass societies of the late nineteenth and early twentieth centuries. Before that time, education was reserved mostly for the elite and the wealthier middle class. Between 1870 and 1914, most Western governments financed a system of primary education. Boys and girls between 6 and 12 years of age were required to attend these elementary schools.

Why did Western nations make a commitment to education at this time? One reason was that the Second Industrial Revolution helped create jobs that required a higher level of education than in the past. Boys and girls with an elementary education were able to work in white-collar jobs, any job that did not require work clothes. They might be clerks in a bank or a railway, or a teacher or nurse.

A second reason that governments backed public education was political. Since more people were going to vote, they needed to be able to read, and they needed to know about citizenship. Primary schools helped to instill patriotism. In fact, during this period, many people felt less attached to their town or region and more attached to their nation. This was a big change in people's loyalties and in how they identified themselves.

Compulsory elementary education created a demand for teachers, and most of them were women. Many men saw teaching as a part of women's "natural role" to be the nurturers of children. Women were also paid lower salaries than men, which in itself was a strong incentive for states to set up teacher-training schools for women. The first women's colleges were really teacher-training schools.

Better education led immediately to a corresponding increase in **literacy**, or the ability to read. By 1900, most adults in western and central Europe could read, but the story was very different where governments did not promote education. Only about 20 percent of adults in Serbia and Russia could read.

Once literacy expanded, a mass media developed. Newspapers sprang up to appeal to this new reading public. In London, papers like the *Evening News* (1881) and the *Daily Mail* (1896) sold millions of copies each day. They simplified their reporting and picked stories to appeal to people who read newspapers to entertain themselves after a long day of work. Newspapers for the general public were often sensationalistic—they peppered their columns with gossip, colorful anecdotes, and the gruesome details of violent crimes.

People read this new kind of newspaper in their leisure time. There were other new forms of leisure, too—amusement parks, dance halls, and organized team sports, for example.

▼ *In the late nineteenth century, holiday travel was widespread. As the presence of dogs suggests, these travelers were returning to London from a grouse-hunting holiday in Scotland.*

▲ *A poster advertising the newest sports craze*

These forms of leisure were new in several ways. First, leisure was now seen as what people did for fun after work. In an older era, work and leisure time were not so clearly defined. During the era of cottage industry, family members might chat or laugh while they worked on cloth in their homes. Now free time was more closely scheduled and more often confined to evening hours, weekends, and perhaps a week in the summer.

Second, the new forms of leisure tended to be passive, not participatory. Instead of doing a folk dance on the town square, a young woman sat in a Ferris wheel and was twirled around by a huge mechanized contrivance. Instead of playing a game of tug-of-war at the town fair, a young man sat on the sidelines at a cricket match and cheered his favorite team to victory.

A third change in leisure during this era was that people more often paid for many of their leisure activities. It cost money to ride a merry-go-round or Ferris wheel at Coney Island. This change was perhaps the most dramatic of all. Business entrepreneurs created amusement parks and professional sports teams in order to make a profit. Whatever would sell, they would promote.

✔**Reading Check** **Explaining** What motivated governments to provide public education?

**HISTORY** **Study Central**
*Online*

For help with the concepts in this section of *Glencoe World History–Modern Times,* go to wh.mt.glencoe.com and click on **Study Central.**

# SECTION 2 ASSESSMENT

### Checking for Understanding

1. **Vocabulary** Define: innovation, objective, feminism, literacy.

2. **People** Identify: Florence Nightingale, Emmeline Pankhurst.

### Reviewing Big Ideas

3. **Explain** what is meant by the term *universal education.* Why did the Industrial Revolution help to promote it?

### Critical Thinking

4. **Historical Analysis** **Contextualizing** Why have certain jobs, such as elementary teaching and nursing, historically been filled by women? **CA HI 3**

5. **Summarizing Information** Use a graphic organizer like the one below to summarize the results of urban reforms.

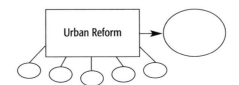

### Analyzing Visuals

6. **Examine** the clothing worn by the women in the photos on pages 304, 305, and 307. Do you think there is a connection between changes in women's dress and changes in their political rights?

## Writing About History

7. **Persuasive Writing** The feminist movement changed the role of women. In an essay, argue whether these changes had a positive or negative impact on society. **CA 10WA2.3**

# SPORTS AND CONTESTS

## The New Team Sports

Sports were by no means a new activity in the late nineteenth century. Soccer games had been played by peasants and workers, and these games had often been bloody and even deadly. However, in the late nineteenth century, sports became strictly organized. The English Football Association (founded in 1863) and the American Bowling Congress (founded in 1895), for example, provided strict rules and officials to enforce them.

The new sports were not just for leisure or fun. Like other forms of middle-class recreation, they were intended to provide excellent training, especially for youth. The participants could not only develop individual skills but also acquire a sense of teamwork useful for military service.

These characteristics were already evident in British schools in the 1850s and 1860s. Such schools as Harrow and Loretto placed organized sports at the center of education. At Loretto, for example, education was supposed to instill "First—Character. Second—Physique. Third—Intelligence. Fourth—Manners. Fifth—Information."

The new team sports rapidly became professionalized as well. The English Football Association, mentioned above, regulated professional soccer. In the United States, the first national association to recognize professional baseball players was formed in 1863. By 1900, the National League and the American League had complete control over professional baseball.

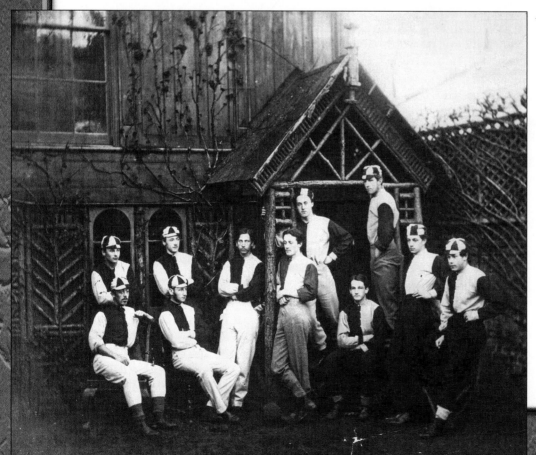

◄ This photo of the Eton rugby team dates from the early 1900s. The sport is said to have originated in the 1820s at Rugby, one of England's famed public schools—schools which are, in fact, private. Eton, another famous public school, is the oldest public school, founded in the 1400s. Rugby remains popular in England, but in the United States, football is the popular game.

▲ Croquet was popular in the nineteenth century. In the United States, there was something of a croquet craze in the 1860s. As the image suggests, it could be a sedate game for women to play, although some versions were more aggressive.

▲ In the late 1800s, women were thought too delicate to play vigorous sports. Eventually sports began to appear at some women's colleges and girls' public schools in England. This image is from a 1914 football (soccer) match.

◄ Ballparks were built once fans had to pay admission to watch a game. In the United States, baseball was so popular that more than 1.5 million fans watched American League games during the 1901 season.

## CONNECTING TO THE PAST

1. **Describing** What did sports offer middle-class men of the late nineteenth century?

2. **Evaluating** Why do you think spectator sports became such a big business?

3. **Writing about History** Write a brief essay comparing the educational goals at your school with those at Loretto. What are the differences and similarities?

# The National State and Democracy

## Section Preview

Democracy triumphed in Western Europe, authoritarianism prevailed in the East, the United States became an industrial powerhouse, and the European powers prepared for war.

### Main Idea

• Growing prosperity after 1850 contributed to the expansion of democracy in Western Europe. (p. 313)
• Although Germany, Austria-Hungary, and later Russia instituted elections and parliaments, real power remained in the hands of the emperors and elites. (p. 315)

• In the United States, the Second Industrial Revolution produced a wealthy society, and wealth was far more concentrated than in Europe (p. 316)
• After firing Bismarck, the German emperor pursued aggressive foreign policies that divided Europe into two hostile alliance systems. (p. 317)
• When Ottoman control over the Balkans weakened, Russia and Austria competed for power there, while Balkan peoples worked for independence. (p. 317)

## Content Vocabulary

ministerial responsibility, Duma

## Academic Vocabulary

crucial, compensation

## People to Identify

Otto von Bismarck, William II, Francis Joseph, Nicholas II, Queen Liliuokalani

## Reading Objectives

1. List the most serious problems in the American society of the time.
2. Trace the issues that lay behind the Balkan crises.

## Reading Strategy

**Summarizing Information** As you read this section, complete a diagram listing the countries in each alliance.

## Preview of Events

| ♦1860 | ♦1870 | ♦1880 | ♦1890 | ♦1900 | ♦1910 |
|---|---|---|---|---|---|
| **1867** Dual monarchy of Austria-Hungary created | **1870** France establishes the Third Republic | **1882** Triple Alliance created | | **1900** Labour Party emerges in Great Britain | **1907** Triple Entente formed |

## California Standards in This Section

*Reading this section will help you master these California History–Social Science standards.*

**10.3:** Students analyze the effects of the Industrial Revolution in England, France, Germany, Japan, and the United States.

**10.3.2:** Examine how scientific and technological changes and new forms of energy brought about massive social, economic, and cultural change (e.g., the inventions and discoveries of James Watt, Eli Whitney, Henry Bessemer, Louis Pasteur, Thomas Edison).

**10.4.1:** Describe the rise of industrial economies and their link to imperialism and colonialism (e.g., the role played by national security and strategic advantage; moral issues raised by the search for

national hegemony, Social Darwinism, and the missionary impulse; material issues such as land, resources, and technology).

**10.5:** Students analyze the causes and course of the First World War.

**10.5.1:** Analyze the arguments for entering into war presented by leaders from all sides of the Great War and the role of political and economic rivalries, ethnic and ideological conflicts, domestic discontent and disorder, and propaganda and nationalism in mobilizing the civilian population in support of "total war."

# Western Europe and Political Democracy

**Main Idea** Growing prosperity after 1850 contributed to the expansion of democracy in Western Europe.

**Reading Connection** Does a change in economic status help minorities in the United States increase their political power? Read to learn about the political advances of European workers in the later 1800s.

By the late nineteenth century in European nations, especially in Western Europe, democracy was becoming well established. These nations had already had representative government, but now the groups who were represented included the lower classes. The advance in democracy was underscored by comparing it to the situation in Eastern Europe and Russia. In Russia there was still no parliament at the beginning of the twentieth century.

## Voices from the Past

On January 22, 1905, a group of peaceful demonstrators in the Russian capital tried to present a petition of grievances to Czar Nicholas II. One witness described the result:

> ❝We were not more than thirty yards from the soldiers, being separated from them only by the bridge over the Tarakanovskii Canal, when suddenly, without any warning and without a moment's delay, was heard the dry crack of many rifle-shots. . . . A little boy of ten years, who was carrying a church lantern, fell pierced by a bullet. Both the [black]smiths who guarded me were killed, as well as all those who were carrying the icons and banners; and all these emblems now lay scattered on the snow. The soldiers were actually shooting into the courtyards of the adjoining houses, where the crowd tried to find refuge.❞

Russia never did achieve true representative government at this time. Instead the Bolshevik Revolution occurred in 1917, and a communist state was declared in 1918.

In the West, however, there were many signs that democracy was expanding. First, laws that granted universal male suffrage were passed. Second, the chief executive officer, usually called the prime minister, was responsible to the popularly elected legislative body, not to the king or president. This principle is called **ministerial responsibility** and it is **crucial** for democracy.

Mass political parties were another sign of expanding democracy. As more and more men, and later women, could vote, parties had to create larger organizations and find ways to appeal to many who were now part of the political process.

**Great Britain** By 1871, Great Britain had long had a working two-party parliamentary system. For roughly the next 50 years, the Liberal Party and the Conservative Party alternated in power. Both parties were led by a ruling class composed of aristocratic landowners and a wealthy upper middle class.

Universal male suffrage came about because Liberals and Conservatives competed with one another to win popular support. Laws of 1867 and 1884 increased the number of adult males who could vote. In 1918, as World War I was ending, another reform law passed which gave the vote to all men over the age of 21 as well as to most women who were over the age of 30.

With political democracy established, social reforms for the working class soon followed. In Britain, the working class supported the Liberals, but the Liberals were worried they would lose this support. Trade unions were growing, and they favored changes in the economic system that the middle classes did not like. In 1900, a new party—the Labour Party, which dedicated itself to the interests of workers—emerged.

The Liberals held the government from 1906 to 1914. To retain the support of the workers, they cooperated with the small Labour Party and also enacted many basic social reforms. The National Insurance Act of 1911, for example, provided benefits for workers when they were sick or lost their job.

*Czar Nicholas II*

313

Austria-Hungary
French Empire
German Empire
Kingdom of Italy
Ottoman Empire
Russian Empire

0          500 miles
0      500 kilometers
Lambert Equal-Area projection

NORWAY
SWEDEN
St. Petersburg
Stockholm
North Sea
Baltic Sea
DENMARK
Moscow
Copenhagen
RUSSIA
UNITED KINGDOM
Berlin
London
NETH.
Elbe R.
Rhine
Warsaw
Dresden
Kiev
Volga R.
BELG.
LUX.
POLAND
Dnieper R.
Paris
Prague
Seine R.
Munich
Vienna
ATLANTIC OCEAN
N W E S
FRANCE
SWITZ.
AUSTRIA
Budapest
Odessa
CRIMEA
Marseille
Venice
HUNGARY
ITALY
ROMANIA
Danube R.
Black Sea
Corsica
MONTENEGRO
Sinope
Madrid
Rome
BULGARIA
Lisbon
PORTUGAL
SPAIN
Sardinia
Naples
Constantinople
Sicily
GREECE
Athens
MOROCCO
ALGERIA
TUNISIA
Mediterranean Sea

## Geography Skills

Various empires dominated the European political scene in the late nineteenth century.

1. **Interpreting Maps** Which three empires extend beyond the boundaries shown on this map?
2. **Applying Geography Skills** Pose and answer your own question about how the geographic relationships shown on this map might result in major conflicts, such as the impending world war.

Other reforms provided a small pension for workers over age 70 and **compensation** for workers if they were injured on the job.

**France** During this general period, politics in France was not stable. The Second Empire government of Louis-Napoleon collapsed when the Prussians defeated France in 1871. In an atmosphere of bitter defeat, the French set up the Third French Republic, but it took five years for the republican constitution to be proclaimed.

The new government had a president and a legislature of two houses. The upper house, or Senate, was conservative. High-ranking officials elected its members, who served for nine-year periods. All adult males, however, voted for the members of the lower house, the Chamber of Deputies.

The powers of the president were not well defined in the constitution. A premier, or prime minister, actually led the government and there was ministerial responsibility. France failed to develop a strong parliamentary system, however. Since there were as many as a dozen political parties, the premier had to depend on coalitions to stay in power. Shifting political alliances led to frequent changes of gov-

ernment. Nevertheless, by 1914, the Third Republic commanded the loyalty of most voters.

**Italy** Italy had emerged by 1870 as a united national state. The nation had little sense of unity, however. In a sense there were two nations because a great gulf separated the poverty-stricken south from the industrialized north. Constant turmoil between labor and industry further weakened national unity. Widespread corruption among government officials prevented the government from dealing with these problems. Universal male suffrage was not granted until 1912, but this reform did little to stop corruption and weakness in the government.

✓ **Reading Check** **Summarizing** What is the principle of ministerial responsibility?

# Central and Eastern Europe: The Old Order

**Main Idea** Although Germany, Austria-Hungary, and later Russia instituted elections and parliaments, real power remained in the hands of emperors and elites.

**Reading Connection** Can a country have a constitution but not be a true democracy? Read to learn about the political structures in Central and Eastern Europe in the late 1800s.

In Central and Eastern Europe, governments were more conservative than in Western Europe. Germany, the Austro-Hungarian Empire, and Russia were less industrialized, and education was not widely available. It was easier, therefore, for the old ruling groups to continue to dominate politics.

**Germany** Germany became a united state in 1871 under the leadership of **Otto von Bismarck** and Emperor William I. The constitution of imperial Germany provided for a two-house legislature. In the upper house, or *Reichsrat,* there were representatives appointed by the 26 princely states. The lower house, or *Reichstag,* was elected by universal male suffrage.

There were two constitutional features that made the German Empire less democratic than nations like France and Great Britain. First, the upper house was a conservative body, and it could veto actions by the *Reichstag.* Second, government ministers were responsible not to the legislature, but to the emperor.

The emperor also controlled the armed forces, foreign policy, and the bureaucracy. Bismarck, the German prime minister, or chancellor, was determined to preserve the power of his king. He directed his policies toward preventing real democracy in the nation.

By the reign of **William II,** emperor from 1888 to 1918, Germany had become the strongest power in Europe. With the expansion of industry and cities came demands for greater democracy.

Conservative forces, the landowning nobility and big industrialists, tried to blunt the movement for democracy by supporting a strong foreign policy. They believed that expansion abroad would divert people from pursuing political reform. At the same time, it would increase their profits.

**Austro-Hungarian Empire** In 1867, the Austrian Empire became the Austro-Hungarian Empire. The constitution of this "dual monarchy" gave greater recognition to Hungary. In theory, it also set up a parliamentary system with ministerial responsibility. In reality, the emperor, **Francis Joseph,** largely ignored this system. He appointed and dismissed his own ministers and issued decrees, or laws, when the parliament was not in session.

The empire remained troubled by conflicts among its many ethnic groups. A German minority governed the empire but felt increasingly threatened by Czechs, Poles, and other Slavic groups. There were Czech, Polish, and Slavic representatives in the imperial parliament, and they continually made speeches demanding their own states.

Unlike Austria, Hungary had a parliament that worked, even though it was controlled by Magyar landowners who dominated the peasants and ethnic minority groups. Because Emperor Francis Joseph no longer had any say in internal Hungarian affairs, the acts of the parliament became effective law.

**Russia** Czar **Nicholas II** came to the throne in Russia in 1894. His grandfather, Alexander II, had been assassinated in 1882 by Russian radicals, and radical movements still flourished in the Russian Empire. Nicholas was totally devoted to upholding the absolute power of the czars: "I shall maintain the principle of autocracy just as firmly and unflinchingly as did my unforgettable father."

Industrialization, which progressed rapidly after 1890, was changing Russia, however. By 1900, Russia had become the fourth-largest producer of steel. With industrialization came an industrial working class and socialist parties. The two most popular, the Marxist Social Democratic Party and the Social Revolutionaries, were declared illegal and became underground movements. After Russia was defeated in the Russo-Japanese War, opposition to the czarist regime exploded into the Revolution of 1905.

On January 22, 1905, a massive procession of workers went to the Winter Palace in St. Petersburg to present a petition of grievances to the czar. Troops foolishly opened fire on the peaceful demonstration, killing hundreds. This "Bloody Sunday" caused workers throughout Russia to call strikes. Nicholas II was eventually forced to confer civil liberties and create a legislative assembly, called the **Duma.** By 1907, however, the czar had already curtailed the power of the Duma, and again used the army and bureaucracy to rule Russia.

**✓ Reading Check** **Identifying** What was the role of the Duma in the Russian government?

# The United States

**Main Idea** In the United States, the Second Industrial Revolution produced a wealthy society, and wealth was far more concentrated than in Europe.

**Reading Connection** Today American power is often exercised through a dominance of world markets. Read to learn about the era when Americans first exercised world power.

Between 1870 and 1914, the United States became an industrial power able to compete with the leading industrialized nations of Western Europe. Like them, it now wanted to expand the market for the wealth of goods it was producing. Thus the United States, too, became an imperialist nation.

**Aftermath of the Civil War** Four years of bloody civil war had preserved the American nation, but the social structure of the old South was destroyed. One-fifth of the adult white male population in the South had been killed, and four million African American slaves had been freed.

In 1865, the Thirteenth Amendment to the Constitution was passed, abolishing slavery. Later, the Fourteenth and Fifteenth Amendments gave citizenship to African Americans and the right to vote to African American males. New state laws in the South, however, soon stripped African Americans of the right to vote. By 1880, supporters of white supremacy were back in power everywhere, and a culture of racial oppression, called "Jim Crow," made daily life a nightmare for African Americans in the South for the next eight decades.

**Economy** Between 1860 and 1914, the United States made the shift from an agrarian to an industrial nation. American heavy industry, or steel and iron production, was the greatest in the world in 1900. In that year, the Carnegie Steel Company alone produced more steel than did Britain's entire steel industry. As in Europe, industrialization in the United States led to urbanization. In 1860, 20 percent of Americans lived in cities; in 1900, over 40 percent.

By 1900, the United States had become the world's richest nation, but wealth was very unevenly distributed. In 1890, the richest 9 percent of Americans owned an incredible 71 percent of the wealth.

Labor unrest over unsafe working conditions and regular cycles of devastating unemployment led workers to organize unions. By 1900, the American Federation of Labor had emerged as the voice of skilled labor.

The union lacked real power, however, because only 8.4 percent of the entire workforce were members. Most workers were unskilled and had no union.

**Expansion Abroad** In the late 1800s, the United States began to expand abroad. The Samoan Islands in the Pacific were the first important United States colony. By 1887, American settlers gained control of the sugar industry on the Hawaiian Islands.

As more Americans settled in Hawaii, they sought to gain political power. In 1893, American residents, aided by U.S. Marines from the ship U.S.S. *Boston,* then docked in a harbor on the Hawaiian island of Oahu, overthrew the monarchy of **Queen Liliuokalani** (lee•lee•oo•oh•kah•LAH•nee). Five years later, the United States formally annexed Hawaii.

In 1898, the United States also defeated Spain in the Spanish-American War. As a result, the United States acquired the former Spanish possessions of Puerto Rico, Guam, and the Philippines.

The Filipino people hoped for independence, but the United States refused to grant it. A fierce revolt broke out, and it took the United States three years to pacify the Philippines and establish control. By the beginning of the twentieth century, the United States, the world's richest nation, had an empire.

**Reading Check** **Identifying** Name the territories acquired by the United States in 1898.

▼ *Hawaiian royalty: Queen Liliuokalani*

# International Rivalries

**Main Idea** After firing Bismarck, the German emperor pursued aggressive foreign policies that divided Europe into two hostile alliance systems.

**Reading Connection** Remember how the Great Powers acted together in the early 1800s? Read to learn how the Great Powers divided into two hostile camps after the 1890s.

Otto von Bismarck realized that Germany's emergence in 1871 as the most powerful state in continental Europe had upset the balance of power established at Vienna in 1815. Fearing that France wanted to create an anti-German alliance, Bismarck made a defensive alliance with Austria-Hungary in 1879. In 1882, Italy joined this alliance. This Triple Alliance thus united Germany, Austria-Hungary, and Italy against France.

At the same time, Bismarck maintained a separate treaty with Russia. He calculated that such a treaty would prevent France from allying with Russia. Bismarck also tried to remain on good terms with Great Britain.

In 1890, the headstrong Emperor William II fired Bismarck and took control of foreign policy. The emperor embarked on an activist policy dedicated to enhancing German power. He wanted, as he put it, to find Germany's rightful "place in the sun."

One change he made in foreign policy was to drop the treaty with Russia. Almost immediately, in 1894, France concluded a military alliance with Russia. Germany thus had a hostile power on her western border and on her eastern border—exactly the situation Bismarck had feared!

Over the next 10 years, the German emperor acted in ways that caused the British to draw closer to France. By 1907, Europe was divided into two opposing alliances: the Triple Entente of Great Britain, France, and Russia, and the Triple Alliance of Germany, Austria-Hungary, and Italy.

Europe's two camps became more and more unwilling to compromise. A series of crises in the Balkans between 1908 and 1913 set the stage for World War I.

**✔ Reading Check** **Summarizing** What countries formed the Triple Alliance and the Triple Entente?

**Analyzing** *Political Cartoons*

In 1890, Emperor William II fired Otto von Bismarck and took control of Germany's relations with other countries. In this scene, the emperor is shown relaxing on a throne made of cannonballs and artillery, while Bismarck bids him good-bye. What do you think the cartoonist is trying to say?

# Crises in the Balkans

**Main Idea** When Ottoman control over the Balkans weakened, Russia and Austria competed for power there, while Balkan peoples worked for independence.

**Reading Connection** Can you locate the Balkans on a map? Learn why this region is called "the powder keg" of World War I.

During the nineteenth century, the Ottoman Empire that had once been strong enough to threaten Europe began to fall apart. Most of its Balkan provinces were able to gain their freedom.

As this was happening, however, two Great Powers saw their chance to gain influence in the Balkans: Austria and Russia. Their rivalry over the Balkans was one of the causes of World War I.

By 1878, Greece, Serbia, Romania, and Montenegro had become independent. Bulgaria did not become totally independent, but was allowed to operate

▲ *Francis Ferdinand, archduke of the Austro-Hungarian Empire, and his wife*

autonomously under Russian protection. The Balkan territories of Bosnia and Herzegovina were placed under the protection of Austria-Hungary.

In 1908, Austria-Hungary took a drastic step. It annexed Bosnia and Herzegovina outright. Serbia was outraged because Serbia hoped to take over these two Slavic-speaking territories itself. The Serbs wanted a large kingdom that would include most of the southern Slavs.

The Russians, self-appointed protectors of their fellow Slavs, supported the Serbs in opposing the Austrian annexation. Backed by the Russians, the Serbs prepared for war against Austria-Hungary. At this point, Emperor William II of Germany demanded that the Russians accept the annexation of Bosnia and Herzegovina or face war with Germany. Russia was forced to back down because it had just been defeated in the Russo-Japanese War in 1905. Humiliated, the Russians vowed revenge. More tension was created when two wars broke out—first in 1912, and then in 1913—among the Balkan states themselves.

The Serbs blamed Austria-Hungary for their inability to create an expanded Serbia. Austria-Hungary was convinced that Serbia was a mortal threat to its empire and must be crushed at some point. The Russians were determined not to back down again if there was another confrontation with Austria-Hungary. Finally, the allies of Austria-Hungary and of Russia were determined to stand fast in any crisis. By 1914, it would not take much to light the Balkan "powderkeg."

✓ **Reading Check** **Explaining** Why were the Serbs outraged when Austria-Hungary annexed Bosnia and Herzegovina?

**HISTORY** *Online* **Study Central**

For help with the concepts in this section of *Glencoe World History—Modern Times,* go to wh.mt.glencoe.com and click on **Study Central.**

# SECTION 3 ASSESSMENT

## Checking for Understanding

1. **Vocabulary** Define: ministerial responsibility, crucial, compensation, Duma.

2. **People** Identify: Otto von Bismarck, William II, Francis Joseph, Nicholas II, Queen Liliuokalani.

### Reviewing Big Ideas

3. **List** the series of events leading to unrest in Russia at the turn of the century. Then focus on the event known as "Bloody Sunday." Before this event, the Russian people thought of the czar as their "Little Father." Why did this event change their attitude?

## Critical Thinking

4. **Historical Analysis** **Evaluating** Which country do you think had a stronger democracy at the end of the nineteenth century, France or England? Why? **CA HR 3**

5. **Compare and Contrast** Use this chapter and Chapter 2 to create a Venn diagram like the one below comparing and contrasting the systems of government in France and the United States.

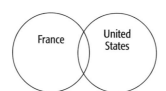

France | United States

## Analyzing Visuals

6. **Examine** the cartoon on page 317 of Bismarck leaving the presence of William II of Germany. What adjectives would you use to describe the attitude of William? Who is the woman in the background, and what is her attitude?

### Writing About History

7. **Expository Writing** Do some research about recent conflicts in the Balkans. Then write one or two paragraphs comparing the causes of the recent conflicts with the causes of the conflicts between Balkan countries in the early twentieth century. **CA 10WA2.3b**

# Toward the Modern Consciousness

## Section Preview

Radical change in the economic and social structure of the West created equally dramatic intellectual and artistic change.

**Main Idea**

- Scientific discoveries in this period had a profound impact on how people saw the world and themselves. (p. 320)
- In the late 1800s, extreme nationalism was reflected in the two movements of Social Darwinism and anti-Semitism. (p. 321)
- In the changing Europe of the late 1800s, dramatic innovation occurred in literature, the visual arts, and music. (p. 323)

## Content Vocabulary

psychoanalysis, Social Darwinism, pogrom, modernism

## Academic Vocabulary

discrimination, annually, reinforce

## People to Identify

Marie Curie, Albert Einstein, Sigmund Freud, Claude Monet, Pablo Picasso, Frank Lloyd Wright

## Places to Locate

Vienna, France

## Reading Objectives

1. Describe ways in which Einstein and Freud challenged the existing views of the world.
2. Explain the key effects of modernism on architecture.

## Reading Strategy

**Identifying Information** As you read this section, complete a chart like the one below. For each art movement, name an artist.

| | |
|---|---|
| Impressionism | |
| Post-Impressionism | |
| Cubism | |
| Abstract Expressionism | |

## Preview of Events

♦1890　　♦1895　　♦1900　　♦1905　　♦1910　　♦1915　　♦1920

**1896**
Herzl publishes *The Jewish State*

**1900**
Freud publishes *The Interpretation of Dreams*

**1905**
Einstein publishes his special theory of relativity

**1913**
Stravinsky's *The Rite of Spring* is performed in Paris

## California Standards in This Section

*Reading this section will help you master these California History–Social Science standards.*

**10.3.2:** Examine how scientific and technological changes and new forms of energy brought about massive social, economic, and cultural change (e.g., the inventions and discoveries of James Watt, Eli Whitney, Henry Bessemer, Louis Pasteur, Thomas Edison).

**10.4.1:** Describe the rise of industrial economies and their link to imperialism and colonialism (e.g., the role played by national security and strategic advantage; moral issues raised by the search for national hegemony, Social Darwinism, and the missionary impulse; material issues such as land, resources, and technology).

# From Certainty to Uncertainty

**Main Idea** Scientific discoveries in this period had a profound impact on how people saw the world and themselves.

**Reading Connection** Have you read about Einstein's theory of relativity in a science class? Read to put this theory into historical perspective.

Before 1914, many people in the Western world continued to believe in the values and ideals that had been put forth by the Scientific Revolution and the Enlightenment. *Reason, science,* and *progress* were still important words in Western societies. After 1870, however, radical ideas in the sciences and the arts opened the way to a modern consciousness.

## Voices from the Past

In the visual arts, the modern consciousness was summed up by Camille Pissarro, a French artist who worked during this period. Pissarro expressed his philosophy of painting in this way:

> ❝Do not define too closely the outlines of things; it is the brush stroke of the right value and color which should produce the drawing. . . . The eye should not be fixed on one point, but should take in everything, while observing the reflections which the colors produce on their surroundings. Work at the same time upon sky, water, branches, ground, keeping everything going on an equal basis. . . . Don't proceed according to rules and principles, but paint what you observe and feel. Paint generously unhesitatingly, for it is best not to lose the first impression.❞

The sciences made a dramatic assault on older ideas. Ever since the Enlightenment, science had been one of the chief pillars supporting an optimistic view of the world. Since science was seen as being based on hard facts and cold reason, it seemed to offer a clear basis for believing in the orderliness of nature. Science offered hope, too. By applying its laws, people believed they would eventually arrive at a complete understanding of the physical world and reality itself.

This Western attitude about science rested on the mechanical conception of the universe of Isaac Newton, the genius of the Scientific Revolution of the 1600s. In this perspective, the universe was regular and orderly. Time, space, and matter were objective realities. Matter was composed of solid, though infinitesimally small, material bodies called atoms.

In the late 1800s, leading scientists challenged this idea of the universe. Although educated people who were not scientists might not understand the new research, they recognized that their old certainty about the universe was gone.

**A New Physics** One of the first scientists to challenge older views was the French scientist **Marie Curie.** She discovered that an element called radium gave off energy, or radiation, that apparently came from within the atom itself. Atoms turned out to be not solid bodies of matter but small, active worlds.

The true revolutionary, however, was **Albert Einstein,** a man whose genius ranks with that of the great Newton. Einstein was German-born, but finished high school in Switzerland where he eventually became a citizen. As a young student, he was thought to be slow. Some suggest he may have been dyslexic. He worked in a patent office at first, but made his reputation when he published scientific articles that put forth radical new views of the universe.

In 1905, Einstein published his special theory of relativity, which stated that space and time are not absolute but are relative to the observer. According to this theory, neither space nor time has an existence independent of human experience. As Einstein later explained to a journalist, "It was formerly believed that if all material things disappeared out of the universe, time and space would be left. According to the relativity theory, however, time and space disappear together with the things." Furthermore, matter and energy reflect the relativity of time and space.

▼ *Marie Curie, c. 1910*

Einstein concluded that matter is nothing but another form of energy. This led to an understanding of the vast energies contained within the atom and to the Atomic Age. For many, however, a relative universe was a universe without certainty.

**Freud and Psychoanalysis** Einstein raised very basic questions about the nature of the universe. **Sigmund Freud** (FROYD), a doctor from **Vienna,** raised questions about another world, the world of the human mind. Like Einstein, Freud added to the uncertainties of the age.

Freud's major theories were published in 1900 in *The Interpretation of Dreams.* According to Freud, human behavior is strongly determined by past experiences and mental forces of which people are largely unaware. Freud argued that when painful or unsettling things happen, they are often repressed, hidden from our conscious awareness. Freud believed that these feelings continue to influence behavior, however.

Freud also claimed that repression of such experiences begins in childhood, so he devised a method—known as **psychoanalysis**—by which a therapist and a patient could probe deeply into the patient's memory. In this way, they could retrace the chain of repressed thoughts all the way back to their childhood origins. If the patient's conscious mind could be made aware of the unconscious and its repressed contents, the patient could be healed.

The full importance of Sigmund Freud's thought was not felt until after World War I. In the 1920s, his ideas gained worldwide acceptance. Freudian terms, such as *unconscious* and *repression,* became standard vocabulary words. Psychoanalysis, pioneered by Freud, developed into a major profession.

✔️**Reading Check** **Summarizing** What is Freud's theory of the human unconscious?

▼ *Sigmund Freud, c. 1938*

# Social Darwinism and Anti-Semitism

**Main Idea** In the late 1800s, extreme nationalism was reflected in the two movements of Social Darwinism and anti-Semitism.

**Reading Connection** What do you think qualifies someone to be an American? Read to learn how some thinkers in the late 1800s felt national identity should be determined.

Nationalism became more intense in many countries in the late 1800s. For some Europeans, loyalty to their nation became an anchor, almost a religious faith, in uncertain times. They began to feel that their nation should dominate other parts of the world, and that it should be highly competitive with other European nations. Preserving their nation's status and their national traditions counted above everything else.

Social Darwinism is a major example of extreme nationalism. **Social Darwinism** was a theory used to justify the dominance of Western nations in the late nineteenth century. Certain thinkers claimed that it was valid to apply Darwin's theory of evolution to modern human societies. In fact, this was not good science, but what today might be called "junk science."

The most popular exponent of Social Darwinism was the British philosopher Herbert Spencer. He argued that human progress was the result of "the struggle for survival," as the "fit"—the strong—advanced while the weak declined. Some prominent businessmen used Social Darwinism to explain their success. To them, the strong and fit—the able and energetic—had risen to the top; the stupid and lazy had fallen by the wayside. This kind of thinking allowed them to reject the idea that they should take care of the less fortunate.

Social Darwinists went even further in using faulty science. They said that nations were in a "struggle for existence" in which only the fittest nations or races would survive. Extreme nationalists tended to equate the nation with race. They spoke, for example, of "the Anglo-Saxon" race, a formula which has no basis in science. Social Darwinists even suggested that war was useful. In 1907, the German general Friedrich von Bernhardi argued, for example, as follows: "War is a biological necessity of the first importance . . . since without it an unhealthy development will follow, which excludes every advancement of the race, and therefore all real civilization. War is the father of all things."

▲ *The Dreyfus affair in France was notorious for showing that old prejudices were still strong in the 1890s. Dreyfus, shown here having his sword broken, was a Jewish officer falsely accused of treason.*

Nowhere was the combination of extreme nationalism and racism more obvious than in Germany. One of the main champions of German racism was Houston Stewart Chamberlain, a Briton who had become a German citizen.

Chamberlain believed that modern-day Germans were the only pure successors of the Aryans. Historically, *Aryan* is the term used to refer to many tribal peoples from central Asia who are thought to have migrated to northern India, Iran, and parts of Europe about 2000 B.C. Chamberlain falsely portrayed the Aryans as a race. He said that they were the original creators of Western culture, and that Jews were the racial enemy out to destroy the superior Aryans.

Anti-Semitism, or hostility toward and **discrimination** against Jews, was not new to Europe. Since the Middle Ages, Jews had been portrayed as the murderers of Christ and subjected to mob violence. In many places, they could not own land or practice certain professions. They were even physically separated from Christians and required to live in ghettos, or certain areas of the city.

By the 1830s, the lives of many Jews had improved. They had legal equality in many European countries. Many had left the ghettos. They became bankers, lawyers, scientists, and scholars, and assimilated into the national culture. Wherever they lived in Western Europe, they felt as patriotic as anyone else.

Old prejudices were still very much alive, though, and anti-Semitism grew stronger at the end of the century. One of the most famous examples of anti-Semitism was the Dreyfus affair in France. Alfred Dreyfus, a Jew, was a French army captain assigned to the general staff. In 1894, a military court, meeting behind closed doors, found him guilty of selling army secrets to Germany and condemned him to life imprisonment on Devil's Island, a brutal French penal colony off the coast of South America. During his trial, angry right-wing mobs roamed the streets of Paris, yelling anti-Semitic sayings, such as "Death to the Jews."

Soon after the trial, however, evidence emerged suggesting Dreyfus had been framed by anti-Semitic officers who did not accept that Jews should be part of the army. Another officer, a Catholic aristocrat, was more obviously the traitor. The army, claiming its honor was at stake, refused a new trial. For more than a decade, there were violent debates over the guilt or innocence of Captain Dreyfus. Finally, as evidence clearing him mounted, a wave of public protest forced the government to pardon him in 1899. The affair revealed the bitter divisions that still plagued French society many decades after the French Revolution.

Anti-Semitism was also seen in Germany and Austria-Hungary during the 1880s and 1890s. New parties appealed to voters who felt threatened by the economic problems and blamed those problems on Jews. The worst treatment of Jews, however, came at the turn of the century in eastern Europe, where most Jews lived. Russian Jews were forced to live in certain regions of the country. Persecutions and bloody **pogroms,** or organized massacres, were widespread.

Hundreds of thousands of Jews decided to emigrate to escape the persecution. Many went to the United States. Perhaps 25,000 Jews immigrated to

Palestine, which became the center of a Jewish nationalist movement called Zionism. Zionists wanted to establish a Jewish state in Palestine. The site of ancient Israel had long been the land of their dreams. A key figure in the growth of political Zionism was Theodor Herzl, who stated in his book *The Jewish State* (1896), "The Jews who wish it will have their state."

Settlement in Palestine was difficult, however, because it was then part of the Ottoman Empire, which was opposed to Jewish immigration. Although about 3,000 Jews went **annually** to Palestine between 1904 and 1914, the Zionist desire for a homeland in Palestine remained only a dream on the eve of World War I.

✓ **Reading Check** **Analyzing** Why did some Jews feel they needed their own nation?

# The Culture of Modernity

**Main Idea** In the changing Europe of the late 1800s, dramatic innovation occurred in literature, the visual arts, and music.

**Reading Connection** How can you recognize that student artwork is from your era? Read to learn how writers and other artists expressed the society they knew in the late 1800s.

Between 1870 and 1914, many writers and artists rebelled against the traditional literary and artistic styles that had dominated European cultural life since the Renaissance. The changes that they produced have since been called **modernism.**

**Literature** Western novelists and poets who followed the naturalist style felt that literature should be realistic and address social problems. Writers like Henrik Ibsen and Émile Zola explored issues such as the role of women in society. They might set their stories in a slum or show how many poor people drank their sorrows away in a dirty cafe.

The symbolist writers had a very different idea about what was real. This group liked the ideas of Freud and believed that it was not possible to know the objective world. The external world was really only a collection of symbols of the true reality—the human mind. Since the human mind was what was most important, symbolists believed that art did not need to examine society. Art should function for its own sake.

**Painting** The period from 1870 to 1914 was one of the most productive in the history of the visual arts. Since the Renaissance, artists had worked to represent reality as accurately as possible. By the late nineteenth century, artists were seeking new ways to express their changing ideas about the world.

**HISTORY Online**

**Web Activity** Visit the *Glencoe World History— Modern Times* Web site at wh.mt.glencoe.com and click on **Chapter 5– Student Web Activity** to learn more about Impressionism.

Impressionism was a movement that began in **France** in the 1870s, when a group of artists rejected the studios where artists had traditionally worked and went out into the countryside to paint nature directly. One important Impressionist was **Claude Monet** (moh•NAY), who painted pictures in which he sought to capture the interplay of light, water, and sky. Other well-known Impressionists were Pierre-Auguste Renoir (REHN•WAHR) and Berthe Morisot.

In the 1880s, a new movement, known as Post-Impressionism, arose in France and soon spread. Painters Paul Cezanne and Vincent van Gogh used

## People In History

### Berthe Morisot
**1841–1895—French painter**

**B**erthe Morisot was the first woman painter to join the Impressionists. She came from a wealthy French family that had settled in Paris when she was seven. Her dedication to the new style of painting won her the disfavor of more traditional French artists.

Morisot believed that women had a special vision, which was, as she said, "more delicate than that of men." She developed her own unique style, using lighter colors and flowing brushstrokes. Near the end of her life, she lamented the refusal of men to take her work seriously: "I don't think there has ever been a man who treated a woman as an equal, and that's all I would have asked, for I know I'm worth as much as they."

color and structure to express a mood. For van Gogh, art was a spiritual experience. He sacrificed everything to his painting. In his hands, color became almost a language—the intensity of his *Sunflowers* is a famous example of color matched to feeling.

By the beginning of the 1900s, artists were not convinced that their main goal was to represent reality. This was especially true in the visual arts. One factor in the decline of realism in painting was the spread of photography. Invented in the 1830s, photography became widely popular after George Eastman created the first Kodak camera in 1888.

Artists tended to focus less on mirroring reality, which the camera could do, and more on creating reality. Painters and sculptors, like the symbolist writers of the time, looked for meaning in individual consciousness. Between 1905 and 1914, this search for individual expression created modern art. One of the most outstanding features of modern art is the attempt of the artist to avoid "visual reality."

By 1905, one of the most important figures in modern art was beginning his career. **Pablo Picasso,** a Spaniard who settled in Paris, painted in a remarkable variety of styles and created a new style, cubism. Cubism used geometric designs to re-create reality in the viewer's mind. In his paintings, Picasso attempted to view the human form from many sides. In this respect, he was probably influenced by the theory of relativity.

Another major art trend, abstract painting, emerged around 1910. Abstract painting does not attempt to represent reality, but instead emphasizes form, color, line, and surface. Wassily Kandinsky, a Russian who worked in Germany, was the first painter to adopt this style. His vivid shapes conveyed strong emotion. He believed that art should speak directly to the soul and that to do so, it should use only line and color.

**Architecture** Modernism revolutionized architecture and gave rise to a new principle known as functionalism. Functionalism said that buildings, like machines, should be useful. They should fulfill the specific function or purpose for which they were built. No unnecessary ornamentation was allowed.

The United States, especially the city of Chicago, welcomed the new trends. Louis H. Sullivan led the Chicago school of the 1890s, which designed

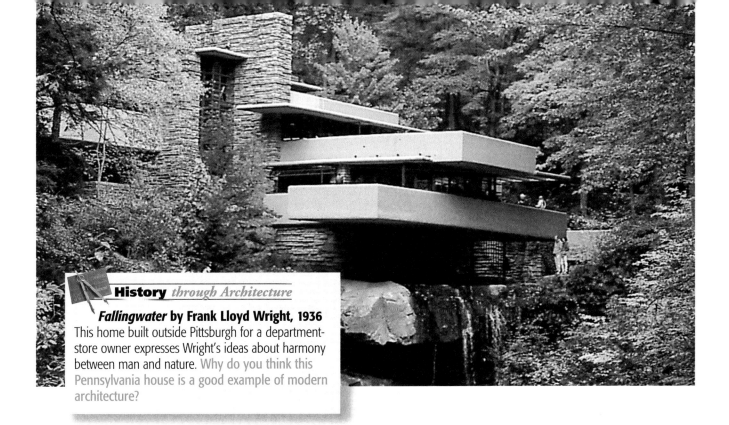

skyscrapers of **reinforced** concrete and steel free of external decoration. One of Sullivan's pupils, **Frank Lloyd Wright,** specialized in building homes with long geometric lines and overhanging roofs. He pioneered the modern American home.

**Music** In the early 1900s, musical trends followed the times. The Russian composer Igor Stravinsky exploited expressive sounds and bold rhythms. His *Rite of Spring* ballet was so revolutionary, the audience nearly rioted when it debuted in 1913. Mean-while, French composers Maurice Ravel and Claude Debussy created impressionist compositions with subtle and shifting harmonies.

 **Explaining** How did the Impressionists radically change the art of painting in the 1870s?

**HISTORY Online** **Study Central**

For help with the concepts in this section of *Glencoe World History–Modern Times,* go to wh.mt.glencoe.com and click on **Study Central.**

# SECTION 4 ASSESSMENT

### Checking for Understanding

1. **Vocabulary** Define: psychoanalysis, Social Darwinism, discrimination, pogrom, annually, modernism, reinforce.

2. **People** Identify: Marie Curie, Albert Einstein, Sigmund Freud, Claude Monet, Pablo Picasso, Frank Lloyd Wright.

3. **Places** Locate: Vienna, France.

### Reviewing Big Ideas

4. **Explain** why photography caused some artists to reject realism.

### Critical Thinking

5. **Historical Analysis** **Connecting Ideas** Why are times of political and economic change often associated with times of artistic change? **CA HI 1**

6. **Organizing Information** Use a web diagram to summarize the problems the Jews faced during this time.

Problems Faced by Jews

### Analyzing Visuals

7. **Compare** the painting by van Gogh on page 324 to other paintings of night scenes in art history books. Pick one such painting and tell why you enjoy that painting either more or less than the van Gogh painting.

## Writing About History

8. **Expository Writing** Research the symbolist writers. Who were they and what did they write about? Write a short biography of the symbolist who most interests you. **CA 10WA2.1**

# PRIMARY SOURCES
## EYEWITNESS TO HISTORY

*In the late 19th and early 20th century, the vote for women was a major political issue in Western societies. Women took various positions on the issue–and some even opposed it.*

## SOURCE 1: Women Against Women's Suffrage

*As the movement for women's suffrage gained momentum in Britain, an anti-suffrage movement also formed. In 1889, this document appeared in a leading journal,* The Nineteenth Century. *Signed by 104 notable women, it outlined arguments against suffrage.*

1. While desiring the fullest possible development of the powers, energies, and the education of women, we believe that their work for the State, and their responsibilities towards it, must always differ essentially from those of men, and that therefore their share in the working of the State machinery should be different from that assigned to men. To men belong the struggle of debate and legislation in Parliament; the hard and exhausting labour implied in the administration of the national resources and powers; the conduct of England's relations towards the external world; the working of the army and navy; all the heavy, laborious, fundamental industries of the State. . . . In all these spheres women's direct participation is made impossible either by the disabilities of sex, or by strong formations of custom and habit resting ultimately upon physical difference, against which it is useless to contend. . . .

2. . . . For whatever may be the duty and privilege of the parliamentary vote for men, we hold that citizenship is not dependent upon or identical with the possession of the suffrage. Citizenship lies in the participation of each individual in effort for the good of the community. And we believe that women will be more valuable citizens, will contribute more precious elements to the national life without the vote than with it.

5. We are convinced that the pursuit of a mere outward equality with men is for women not only vain but **demoralizing**[1]. It leads to a total misconception of woman's true dignity and special mission. It tends to personal struggle and rivalry, where the only effort of both the great divisions of the human family should be to contribute the characteristic labour and the best gifts of each to the common stock.

## SOURCE 2: A Suffragette Questions British Democracy

*In a 1908 speech in London, Emmeline Pankhurst argued that Britain needed to give women the vote to have truly representative government. She was leader of the militant* Women's Social and Political Union. (Suffragette *was the nickname British newspapers used to refer to women in the movement.*)

What, then, is the vote that we are hearing so much about just now, so much more than people have heard in discussion at least, for a great many years? I think we may give the vote a threefold description. We may describe the vote as, first of all, a symbol, secondly, a safeguard, and thirdly, an instrument. It is a symbol of freedom, a symbol of citizenship, a symbol of liberty. It is a safeguard of all those liberties which it symbolizes. And in these later days it has come to be regarded more than anything else as an instrument, something with which you can get a great many more things than our forefathers who fought for the vote ever realised as possible to get with it. . . .

Wherever masses of people are gathered together there must be government. Government without the vote is more or less a form of tyranny. Government with the vote is more or less representative according to the extent to which the vote is given. In this country they tell us we have representative government. So far as women are concerned, while you have representa-

> [1]**demoralizing:** weakening the spirit of

*Police taking suffragette to jail*

are now in touch with the most advanced development of the women's movement in Egypt, Palestine, India, Burma, China, Japan, Java, and the Philippine and Hawaiian Islands. . . .

Behind the **purdah**[3] in India, in the harems of Mohammedanism, behind veils and barred doors and closed **sedan chairs**[4], there has been rebellion in the hearts of women all down the centuries. . . . We spoke with many women all over the East who had never heard of a 'women's movement,' yet isolated and alone, they had thought out the entire program of woman's emancipation. . . .

We must give aid to these sisters. . . . When I review the slow, tragic struggle upward of the women in the West, I am overwhelmed with the awfulness of the task these Eastern women have assumed. . . . I would that we could put a protecting arm around these heroic women and save them from the cruel blows that they are certain to receive. . . . For every woman of every tribe and nation, every race and continent . . . we must demand deliverance.

➤ ────────────────────────────
[3]**purdah:** curtain screening women
[4]**sedan chairs:** portable chairs placed on poles

tive government for men, you have **despotic**[2] government for women. So it is in order that the government of the country may be made really representative, may represent not only all classes of the community, but both sexes of the community, that this struggle for the vote is going on on the part of women.

## SOURCE 3: A Voice for All Women

*American Carrie Chapman Catt, president of the* International Woman Suffrage Alliance, *an organization she helped found, reported in 1913 on women's suffrage issues around the globe.*

We held public meetings in many of the towns and cities of four continents, of four large islands, and on ships of three oceans, and had representatives of all the great races and nationalities in our audiences. We

➤ ────────────────────────────
[2]**despotic:** tyrannical; arbitrary

**DBQ** **Document-Based Questions**

**Historical Analysis** ◀ CA HI 1, HR 3, CS 2

**Source 1:** According to the document, why are men involved in politics, but women kept out of it?

**Source 2:** What does Pankhurst mean when she says a *representative government* exists for men in Great Britain, while women live under a *despotic government?*

**Source 3:** In the last sentence of Catt's report, what is she implying women need *deliverance* from?

### Comparing and Contrasting Sources

1. In document 1, the claim is made that women can be citizens without the vote. How would Pankhurst answer this claim?

2. Describe how the women in each source see the act of voting. **CA 10RL3.5**

# ASSESSMENT and ACTIVITIES

 Standards 10.3, 10.3.2, 10.3.3, 10.3.4, 10.3.5, 10.3.6, 10.4.1, 10.5, 10.5.1

## Reviewing Content Vocabulary

*On a sheet of paper, use each of these terms in a sentence.*

1. assembly line
2. mass production
3. proletariat
4. dictatorship
5. revisionist
6. feminism
7. literacy
8. ministerial responsibility
9. Duma
10. psychoanalysis
11. Social Darwinism
12. pogrom
13. modernism

## Reviewing Academic Vocabulary

*On a sheet of paper, use each of these terms in a sentence that reflects the term's meaning in the chapter.*

14. generator
15. transform
16. emerge
17. innovation
18. objective
19. crucial
20. compensation
21. discrimination
22. annually
23. reinforce

## Reviewing the Main Ideas

### Section 1

24. List one invention each of Guglielmo Marconi, Thomas Edison, and Alexander Graham Bell.
25. What is *The Communist Manifesto?* Who wrote it?

### Section 2

26. How did Florence Nightingale and Clara Barton transform nursing?
27. What purposes were served by compulsory education?

### Section 3

28. What was the name given to France's government after the adoption of a new constitution in 1875?
29. Explain how the United States became an industrial power.

### Section 4

30. List some of the modernist movements in art, music, and architecture and an individual associated with each of the movements.
31. Explain the theories of Social Darwinism.

## Critical Thinking

32. **Evaluating** Revisionist socialists believed they could achieve a socialist state gradually through legal means. Why was revisionist socialism more powerful in Western Europe than in Eastern Europe?

33. **Drawing Conclusions** Was the Revolution of 1905 in Russia a success or a failure? Why?

34. **Reading Skill** **Summarizing** Identify changes that resulted from the Second Industrial Revolution, and then briefly summarize them in a chart, list, or paragraph.

35. **Compare and Contrast** Reread the information in your text and examine the similarities and differences among the British Conservative, Liberal, and Labour parties of 1914. Decide which of these three parties you would belong to if you lived in England at that time. Explain your choice of parties, based on a comparison of their goals.

## Chapter Summary

Innovations in technology and production methods created great economic, political, social, and cultural changes between 1870 and 1914, as shown in the chart below. The development of a mass society led to labor reforms and the extension of voting rights. New scientific theories radically changed people's vision of the world. Change also brought conflict as tensions increased in Europe and new alliances were formed.

| Economics | Politics | Society | Culture | Conflict |
|---|---|---|---|---|
| • Industrial growth and the development of new energy resources lead to increased production of consumer goods. | • Growth of mass politics leads to the development of new political parties.<br>• Labor leaders use ideas of socialism and Marxism to form unions. | • Women fight for equal rights.<br>• Society adopts middle-class values.<br>• Unions fight for labor reforms.<br>• Mass leisure develops. | • Many artists reject traditional styles and develop new art movements.<br>• New scientific ideas radically change people's perception of the world. | • Nationalism and imperialism create conflict in the Balkans and eventually lead to World War I.<br>• Growth of nationalism leads to increased anti-Semitism. |

## Forms of Government, 1900

**Autocracy**
Rule by one
*auto* (self) + *kratos* (might)

*No public involvement in political decision making*

**Democracy**
Rule by the people
*demos* (people) + *kratos* (might)

*Direct public involvement in political decision making*

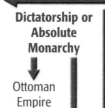

**Dictatorship or Absolute Monarchy**

Ottoman Empire

Russia

**Authoritarian State***

Austria-Hungary

Germany

*Austria-Hungary and Germany had parliaments chosen by the people.

**Constitutional Monarchy**

Italy

Great Britain

**Republic**

United States

France

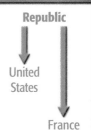

**Direct Democracy**

Switzerland

## Writing About History

**36. Analyzing** Leisure activities became more widespread and accessible during the Second Industrial Revolution. Give details of why leisure life became so popular and explain who profited most from the expanded culture.

**37. Explaining** What is the method or process that Sigmund Freud became famous for? Explain how the terms *unconscious* and *repression* are used in Freud's theory.

**38. Historical Analysis Examining Trends** In Great Britain, unions won the right to strike in the 1870s. Review what you have read and know about trade unions. Then write a short paper explaining how unions helped to expand workers' rights. **CA HI 1**

**39.** *Big Idea* Compare and contrast Einstein's and Newton's understandings of the universe.

### DBQ Document-Based Questions

**Analyzing Sources** Read the following quote from a regular visitor to a seaside resort.

❝They swarm upon the beach, wandering about with apparently no other aim than to get a mouthful of fresh air. You may see them in groups of three or four–the husband, a pale man, dressed in black coat, carries the baby; the wife, equally pale and thin, decked out in her best, labors after with a basket of food. And then there is generally another child . . . wandering behind.❞

**40.** What can you infer about the husband and the wife from the way in which they are described?

**41.** In what way do the ideas expressed in this quote reflect the class-consciousness of this time period? **CA 10RL3.12**

## Analyzing Maps and Charts

Use the chart above to answer the following questions.

**42.** According to the chart, what is the major difference between an autocratic government and a democratic form of government?

**43.** How are a constitutional monarchy and a republic similar? How do they differ?

**44.** Based on the chart, where was direct democracy practiced in 1900? Which earlier civilizations also practiced direct democracy?

### Standards Practice

**Directions: Choose the best answer to the following question.**

**45.** The emergence of different factions in the Balkan Peninsula at the end of the nineteenth century was a result of

**A** shifting power as the Ottoman Empire waned.

**B** Serbia's dominance of the region.

**C** America's victory in the Spanish-American War.

**D** Nicholas II of Russia's repressive regime.

**CA Standard 10.4.1** Describe the rise of industrial economies and their link to imperialism and colonialism (e.g., the role played by national security and strategic advantage; moral issues raised by the search for national hegemony, Social Darwinism, and the missionary impulse; material issues such as land, resources, and technology).

# 6

## *1800–1914*

# The Height of Imperialism

### ⊰ *The Big Ideas* ⊱

### SECTION 1: Colonial Rule in Southeast Asia

**Nations compete for natural resources and strategic advantages over other nations.** Through "New Imperialism," Westerners controlled vast territories, exploited native populations, and opened markets for European products.

### SECTION 2: Empire Building in Africa

**Nations compete for natural resources and strategic advantages over other nations.** Great Britain, France, Germany, Belgium, and Portugal placed virtually all of Africa under European rule.

### SECTION 3: British Rule in India

**Throughout history people have struggled for rights.** The British brought stability to India, but destroyed native industries and degraded Indians, while leaders like Mohandas Gandhi worked for independence through nonviolent action.

### SECTION 4: Nation Building in Latin America

**Throughout history people have struggled for rights.** Latin American countries served as a source of raw materials for Europe and the United States.

 ***World History—Modern Times Video*** *The Chapter 6 video, "Imperialism," chronicles imperialism on three continents.*

*Sir Thomas Raffles, founder of Singapore*

**1848**
Mexico loses almost half of its territory to the United States

**1855**
David Livingstone is first European to see Victoria Falls

| 1810 | 1820 | 1830 | 1840 | 1850 | 1860 |

**1819**
British colony of Singapore is founded

*Victoria Falls, in Zimbabwe*

British family celebrating Christmas in India, c. 1900

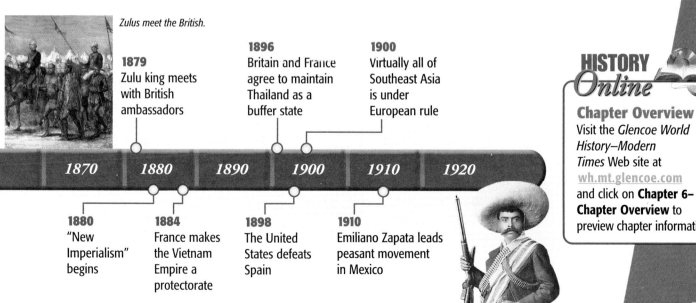

*Zulus meet the British.*

**1879**
Zulu king meets with British ambassadors

**1896**
Britain and France agree to maintain Thailand as a buffer state

**1900**
Virtually all of Southeast Asia is under European rule

| 1870 | 1880 | 1890 | 1900 | 1910 | 1920 |

**1880**
"New Imperialism" begins

**1884**
France makes the Vietnam Empire a protectorate

**1898**
The United States defeats Spain

**1910**
Emiliano Zapata leads peasant movement in Mexico

*Emiliano Zapata*

**HISTORY Online**

**Chapter Overview**
Visit the *Glencoe World History–Modern Times* Web site at wh.mt.glencoe.com and click on **Chapter 6–Chapter Overview** to preview chapter information.

## Reading Skill    Comparing and Contrasting

Good readers look for similarities and differences in new information they read. This helps them figure out what it means. You do this subconsciously in everyday life. If you meet someone new, you probably compare that person to people you know. Is the person the same or different? If different, what makes that person different?

When you read, comparing and contrasting helps you get a handle on new information. Luckily, certain signal words tell you when the author is comparing and contrasting information to what you already know. Some signal words for showing similarity are *still* and *alike*. Some signal words for showing differences are *however, but,* and *on the other hand.*

*Look at the paragraphs below from this chapter. Notice the signal words that focus your mind on the two attitudes Africans had toward Europeans and European ideas.*

### COMPARING

On the one hand: This phrase is one of the easiest to spot. It usually begins a listing of several factors that are similar. The whole paragraph is talking about why Africans had reason to be positive about Western culture.

As in Southeast Asia, a new class of leaders emerged in Africa by the beginning of the twentieth century. Educated in colonial schools or in Western nations, they were the first generation of Africans to know a great deal about the West.

On the one hand, the members of this new class admired Western culture and sometimes disliked the ways of their own countries. They were eager to introduce Western ideas and institutions into their own societies.

On the other hand, many came to resent the foreigners and their arrogant contempt for African peoples. . . . Westerners had exalted democracy, equality, and political freedom but did not apply these values in the colonies.

### CONTRASTING

On the other hand: This phrase is always used after an author says "on the one hand." It usually begins a listing of several factors that are on the opposing side of an argument. Here, the author uses it to introduce reasons Africans resented Westerners.

### Apply the Skill

Turn to page 339, and read the fourth paragraph under the heading Indirect and Direct Rule. What are the signal words that tell you a comparison is being made?

**Historical Research, Evidence, and Point of View: CA Standard HR 3:**
*Students evaluate major debates among historians concerning alternative inter-pretations of the past, including an analysis of authors' use of evidence and the distinctions between sound generalizations and misleading oversimplifications.*

When historians try to understand historical events, they weigh different kinds of evidence. Then, like judges who have sifted through testimony, they come to a verdict. Unlike the judge, a historian's "verdict" is not always a simple "Guilty" or "Innocent." Read these statements from pages 356–357 on how British rule affected India and the Indian people.

- British rule in India had several benefits for subjects. It brought order and stability to a society that had been divided into many states with different political systems. It also led to a fairly honest and efficient government.

- . . . a new school system was set up. . . . The new system served only elite, upper-class Indians, however. Ninety percent of the population remained illiterate.

- Railroads, the telegraph, and a postal service were introduced to India shortly after they appeared in Great Britain.

- British entrepreneurs and a small number of Indians reaped financial benefits from British rule. . . .

- British manufactured goods destroyed local industries.

- The introduction of British textiles put thousands of women out of work and severely damaged the Indian textile industry.

- The best jobs and the best housing were reserved for Britons.

- Despite their education, the Indians were never considered equals of the British.

## Apply the Skill

How did the evidence add up? What "verdict" is the author making on the British Raj? When you finish reading the section, look again at pages 356–357. Can you list the type of evidence the author used for his statements? Did he persuade you that he was a reasonable judge?

# A Story That Matters

*David Livingstone*

*Livingstone expedition in Africa, c. 1855*

## Livingstone in Africa

In 1841, the Scottish doctor and missionary David Livingstone began a series of journeys that took him through much of central and southern Africa. Livingstone was a gentle man whose goal was to find locations for Christian missions on behalf of the London Missionary Society. He took great delight in working with the African people.

Livingstone's travels were not easy. Much of his journey was done by foot, canoe, or mule. He suffered at times from rheumatic fever, dysentery, and malaria. He survived an attack by armed warriors and a mutiny by his own servants.

Back in Great Britain, his exploits made Livingstone a national hero. His book *Missionary Travels and Researches in South Africa* was a best-seller. People jammed into lecture halls to hear him speak of the beauty of Africa. As the *London Journal* reported, "Europe had always heard that the central regions of southern Africa were bleak and barren, heated by poisonous winds, infested by snakes . . . [but Livingstone spoke of] a high country, full of fruit trees, abounding in shade, watered by a perfect network of rivers."

Livingstone tried to persuade his listeners that Britain needed to send both missionaries and merchants to Africa. Combining Christianity and commerce, he said, would achieve civilization for Africa.

### Why It Matters

During the nineteenth and early twentieth centuries, Western colonialism spread throughout the non-Western world. Great Britain, Spain, Holland, France, Germany, Russia, and the United States competed for markets and raw materials for their expanding economies. By the end of the nineteenth century, virtually all of the peoples of Asia and Africa were under colonial rule. Although Latin America successfully resisted European control, it remained economically dependent on Europe and the United States.

**History and You** Territorial and trade dominance are among the primary goals of imperialist nations. Create a map of either Asia or Africa to help you understand how the various imperialists viewed those regions. Code the territories according to exports or European dominance.

# Colonial Rule in Southeast Asia

## Guide to Reading

### Section Preview
Through "New Imperialism," Westerners controlled vast territories, exploited native populations, and opened markets for European products.

**Main Idea**
- Under New Imperialism, European countries began to seek additional territory. (p. 336)
- Rivalries for overseas territories led to Western dominance of Southeast Asia. (p. 337)
- European countries controlled the governments and economies of their colonies in Southeast Asia. (p. 339)

- Native peoples had varying levels of success resisting colonial rule in Southeast Asia. (p. 340)

### Content Vocabulary
New Imperialism, protectorate, indirect rule, direct rule

### Academic Vocabulary
exploit, impose, regime

### People to Identify
King Mongkut, King Chulalongkorn, Commodore George Dewey, Emilio Aguinaldo

### Places to Locate
Singapore, Burma, Thailand, Philippines

### Reading Objectives
1. Describe why Westerners were so determined to colonize Southeast Asia.
2. Explain the chief goal of the Western nations.

### Reading Strategy
**Identifying Information** Make a chart like this one showing which countries controlled what parts of Southeast Asia.

| | |
|---|---|
| Spain (until 1898) | |
| Holland | |
| United States (after 1898) | |
| France | |
| Great Britain | |

### Preview of Events

| ♦1850 | ♦1870 | ♦1890 | ♦1910 | ♦1930 | ♦1950 |
|---|---|---|---|---|---|

**1887**
France completes its control of Indochina

**1896**
France and Great Britain agree to maintain Thailand as a buffer state

**1930**
Saya San leads Burma uprising

## California Standards in This Section

*Reading this section will help you master these California History–Social Science standards.*

**10.4:** Students analyze patterns of global change in the era of New Imperialism in at least two of the following regions or countries: Africa, Southeast Asia, China, India, Latin America, and the Philippines.

**10.4.1:** Describe the rise of industrial economies and their link to imperialism and colonialism (e.g., the role played by national security and strategic advantage; moral issues raised by the search for national hegemony, Social Darwinism, and the missionary impulse; material issues, such as land, resources, and technology).

**10.4.2:** Discuss the locations of the colonial rule of such nations as England, France, Germany, Italy, Japan, the Netherlands, Russia, Spain, Portugal, and the United States.

**10.4.3:** Explain imperialism from the perspective of the colonizers and the colonized and the varied immediate and long-term responses by the people under colonial rule.

**10.4.4:** Describe the independence struggles of the colonized regions of the world, including the roles of leaders, such as Sun Yat-sen in China, and the roles of ideology and religion.

# The New Imperialism

**Main Idea** Under New Imperialism, European countries began to seek additional territory.

**Reading Connection** Do you remember how the Industrial Revolution created demand for raw materials and new markets? Read to learn how European countries used "New Imperialism" to meet these needs.

In the nineteenth century, a new phase of Western expansion into Asia and Africa began. European nations began to view Asian and African societies as a source of industrial raw materials and a market for Western manufactured goods. No longer were Western gold and silver traded for cloves, pepper, tea, and silk. Now the products of European factories were sent to Africa and Asia in return for oil, tin, rubber, and the other resources needed to fuel European industries.

## Voices from the Past

In 1860, E. Douwes Dekker wrote a book that described the effects of this newest phase of imperialism. Although he was a colonial official himself, Dekker concluded that the Dutch rulers had wreaked havoc on the native people of Java:

> 66The [Dutch government] compels [the Javanese farmer] to cultivate certain products on his land; it punishes him if he sells what he has produced to any purchaser but itself; and it fixes the price actually paid. The expenses of transport to Europe through a privileged trading company are high; the money paid to the chiefs for encouragement increases the prime cost; and because the entire trade must produce profit, that profit cannot be got in any other way than by paying the Javanese just enough to keep him from starving, which would lessen the producing power of the nation.99

Beginning in the 1880s, European states began an intense scramble for overseas territory. Imperialism, the extension of a nation's power over other lands, was not new. Europeans had set up colonies in North and South America and trading posts around Africa and the Indian Ocean by the sixteenth century.

The imperialism of the late nineteenth century was different, however. Earlier, European states had been content to set up a few trading posts where they could carry on trade and perhaps some missionary activity. Under **New Imperialism,** as it is often called, Europeans sought nothing less than direct control over vast territories, mainly in Africa.

Why did Westerners intensify their search for colonies after 1880? One motive was economic. Capitalist states in the West were looking for markets and raw materials, such as rubber and oil, for their industries. They also wanted more direct control of areas with raw materials and markets.

The motives were not simply economic. European nations competed with one another for power and influence. As the rivalries intensified, each nation tried to acquire colonies to gain an advantage over its rivals. Colonies were a source of national prestige. To some people, a nation could not be great without colonies. One German historian wrote that "all great nations in the fullness of their strength have the desire to set their mark upon barbarian lands and those who fail to participate in this great rivalry will play a pitiable role in time to come."

Imperialism was also tied to Social Darwinism and racism. Social Darwinists believed that in the struggle between nations, the fit are victorious. Racism holds that certain races are superior and that this justifies their use of force against other races or nations. As one British professor put it in 1900: "The path of progress is strewn with the wrecks of nations; traces are everywhere to be seen of the [slaughtered remains] of inferior races. Yet these dead people are, in very truth, the stepping stones on which mankind has arisen to the higher intellectual and deeper emotional life of today."

Some Europeans took a more religious and humanitarian approach to imperialism. They felt that Europeans had a moral responsibility to civilize

▼ *Dutch plantation in Java, mid-1800s*

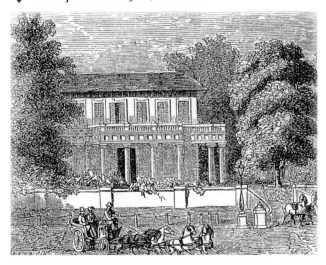

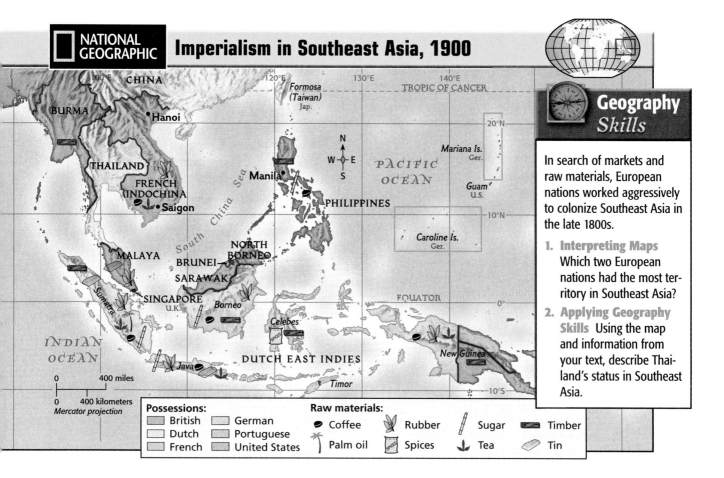

**Geography Skills**

In search of markets and raw materials, European nations worked aggressively to colonize Southeast Asia in the late 1800s.

1. **Interpreting Maps** Which two European nations had the most territory in Southeast Asia?

2. **Applying Geography Skills** Using the map and information from your text, describe Thailand's status in Southeast Asia.

**Possessions:**
- British
- Dutch
- French
- German
- Portuguese
- United States

**Raw materials:**
- Coffee
- Palm oil
- Rubber
- Spices
- Sugar
- Tea
- Timber
- Tin

---

primitive people. Some people called this duty "the white man's burden." The phrase was borrowed from a famous poem (see page 346). They believed that the West should bring progress to Asian and African countries. To some, this meant bringing the Christian message to the "heathen masses." To others, it meant introducing Western democracy and capitalism to Asian and African societies.

**Reading Check** **Describing** What motivated European countries to engage in New Imperialism?

## Colonial Takeover in Southeast Asia

**Main Idea** Rivalries for overseas territories led to Western dominance of Southeast Asia.

**Reading Connection** Does your school have a sports rivalry with another school? Read to learn how the rivalry between Great Britain and France led to conquests in Southeast Asia.

The New Imperialism of the late nineteenth century was evident in Southeast Asia. In 1800, only two societies in this area were ruled by Europeans: the

Spanish Philippines and the Dutch East Indies. By 1900, virtually the entire area was under Western rule.

**Great Britain** The process began with Great Britain. In 1819, Great Britain, under Sir Thomas Stamford Raffles, founded a new colony on a small island at the tip of the Malay Peninsula called **Singapore** ("city of the lion"). In the new age of steamships, Singapore soon became a major stopping point for traffic going to or from China. Raffles was proud of his dynamic city and wrote to a friend in England, "Here all is life and activity; and it would be difficult to name a place on the face of the globe with brighter prospects."

During the next few decades, the British advanced into Southeast Asia. Next to fall was the kingdom of **Burma** (modern Myanmar). Britain wanted control of Burma to protect its possessions in India and to gain a land route to China. The British did not find this land route because the terrain was too rugged, but British activity in Burma led to the fall of the Burmese monarchy. Soon, Britain controlled the entire country.

**France** The British advance into Burma was watched nervously by France, which had some missionaries operating in Vietnam. The French missionaries were persecuted by the local authorities, who viewed Christianity as a threat to Confucian doctrine. Vietnam could not stop the Christian missionaries, however. Vietnamese internal rivalries divided the country into two separate governments, in the north and the south.

France was especially alarmed by British attempts to monopolize trade. To stop any British move into Vietnam, the French government decided in 1857 to force the Vietnamese to accept French protection.

The French eventually succeeded in making the Vietnamese ruler give up territories in the Mekong River delta. The French occupied the city of Saigon and, during the next 30 years, extended their control over the rest of the country. In 1884, France seized the city of Hanoi and made the Vietnamese Empire a French **protectorate**—a political unit that depends on another government for its protection.

In the 1880s, France extended its control over neighboring Cambodia, Annam, Tonkin, and Laos. By 1887, France included all of its new possessions in a new Union of French Indochina.

### Thailand—The Exception

After the French conquest of Indochina, **Thailand** (then called Siam) was the only remaining free state in Southeast Asia. During the last quarter of the nineteenth century, British and French rivalry threatened to place Thailand, too, under colonial rule.

Two remarkable rulers were able to prevent that from happening. One was **King Mongkut** (known to theatergoers as the king in *The King and I*), and the other was his son **King Chulalongkorn.** Both promoted Western learning and maintained friendly relations with the major European powers. In 1896, Britain and France agreed to maintain Thailand as an independent buffer state between their possessions in Southeast Asia.

### The United States

One final conquest in Southeast Asia occurred at the end of the nineteenth century. In 1898, during the Spanish-American War, United States naval forces under **Commodore George Dewey** defeated the Spanish fleet in Manila Bay.

Believing it was his moral obligation to "civilize" other parts of the world, President William McKinley decided to turn the **Philippines,** which had been under Spanish control, into an American colony. This action would also prevent the area from falling into the hands of the Japanese. In fact, the islands gave the United States a convenient jumping-off point for trade with China.

This mixture of moral idealism and desire for profit was reflected in a speech given in the Senate in January 1900 by Senator Albert Beveridge of Indiana:

> ❝Mr. President, the times call for candor. The Philippines are ours forever. And just beyond the Philippines are China's unlimited markets. We will not retreat from either. We will not abandon an opportunity in [Asia]. We will not renounce our part in the mission of our race, trustee, under God, of the civilization of the world.❞

The Filipinos did not agree with the American senator. **Emilio Aguinaldo** (ah•gee•NAHL•doh) was the leader of a movement for independence in the

## Major Regions of European Control

| | Southeast Asia | Africa | India |
|---|---|---|---|
| **Britain** | 🇬🇧 | 🇬🇧 | 🇬🇧 |
| **Belgium** | | ▮▮ | |
| **France** | 🇫🇷 | 🇫🇷 | |
| **Germany** | | ≈ | |
| **Italy** | | 🇮🇹 | |
| **Netherlands** | ≈ | ≈ | |
| **Portugal** | 🇵🇹 | 🇵🇹 | |
| **Spain** | ≈ | ≈ | |

### Chart Skills

In the late 1800s a "New Imperialism" flourished, with most of the major European countries attempting to take control of territories in Asia and Africa.

1. **Identifying** Look at a political map of Europe in Chapter 5. Which European countries did *not* try to colonize parts of Asia or Africa?

2. **Analyzing** It has been said about one of the countries identified in the chart that "the sun never sets" on this particular empire. To which country does this phrase refer? Why?

*Emilio Aguinaldo*

▲ *Scene from decisive Manila Bay battle*

Philippines. He began his revolt against the Spanish. When the United States acquired the Philippines, Aguinaldo continued the revolt and set himself up as the president of the Republic of the Philippines. Led by Aguinaldo, the guerrilla forces fought bitterly against the United States troops to establish their independence. The United States defeated the guerrilla forces, however, and President McKinley had his stepping-stone to the rich markets of China.

✓ **Reading Check** **Comparing** How was the rule of the British in Burma similar to or different from the rule of the French in Vietnam?

## Colonial Regimes in Southeast Asia

**Main Idea** European countries controlled the governments and economies of their colonies in Southeast Asia.

**Reading Connection** Does your school's student council have the power to run the school? Read to learn how European countries ruled their colonies in Southeast Asia.

Western powers governed their new colonial empires through either indirect or direct rule. Their goals were to **exploit** natural resources and open up markets for their manufactured goods. As they pursued their goals, they often spoke of bringing the blessings of civilization to colonial peoples.

**Indirect and Direct Rule** Sometimes, a colonial power could reach its goals most easily by getting the cooperation of local political leaders. In these cases,

**indirect rule** was used. Local rulers were allowed to maintain their authority and status.

In Southeast Asia, colonial powers, wherever possible, tried to work with other local elites—the religious, merchant, and social leaders in an area. This made it easier to gain access to the region's natural resources. Indirect rule also lowered the cost of government because fewer officials had to be trained. Finally, indirect rule was an advantage because it maintained the local culture and therefore did not interfere with the customs of the people.

One example of indirect rule can be seen in the Dutch East Indies. The Dutch East India Company allowed landed aristocrats in the East Indies to control local government. The company paid these aristocrats to maintain order and collect taxes.

Indirect rule, then, was convenient and cost less. Indirect rule was not always possible, especially when local elites resisted conquest. If that happened, the local elites were removed from power and replaced with officials from Britain, France, or other colonial power. This system is called **direct rule.**

In Burma, for example, the monarchy staunchly opposed colonial rule. As a result, Great Britain abolished the monarchy and administered the country directly through its colonial government in India.

In Indochina, France used both direct and indirect rule. It **imposed** direct rule on the southern provinces in the Mekong delta, which had been ceded to France as a colony after the first war from 1858 to 1862. The northern parts of Vietnam, seized in the 1880s, were governed as a protectorate. The emperor still ruled from his palace in Hue, but he had little power.

▲ *Local peasants, shown here in Ceylon in the late 1800s, worked at poverty-level wages for foreign plantation owners during the colonial period.*

To justify their conquests, Western powers had spoken of bringing the blessings of advanced Western civilization to their colonial subjects. Many colonial powers, for example, spoke of introducing representative institutions and educating the native peoples in the democratic process. However, many Westerners came to fear the idea of native peoples (especially educated ones) being allowed political rights.

**Colonial Economies** The colonial powers did not want their colonists to develop their own industries. Thus, colonial policy stressed the export of raw materials—teakwood from Burma; rubber and tin from Malaya; spices, tea, coffee, and palm oil from the East Indies; and sugar from the Philippines. In many cases, this policy led to some form of plantation agriculture, in which peasants worked as wage laborers on plantations owned by foreign investors.

Plantation owners kept the wages of their workers at poverty levels in order to increase the owners' profits. Conditions on plantations were often so unhealthy that thousands died. In addition, the peasants suffered from a heavy tax burden. Colonial governments taxed peasants in order to pay the salaries of their officials and other administrative costs. In effect, the subjects paid the costs of being ruled.

Nevertheless, colonial rule did bring some benefits to Southeast Asia. It led to the beginnings of a modern economic system. Colonial governments built railroads, highways, and other structures that could benefit native peoples as well as colonials. The development of an export market helped to create an entrepreneurial class in rural areas. In the Dutch East Indies, for example, small growers of rubber, palm oil, coffee, tea, and spices began to share in the profits of the colonial enterprise. Most of the profits, however, were taken back to the colonial mother country.

✓ **Reading Check** **Explaining** Why did colonial powers prefer that colonists not develop their own industries?

## Resistance to Colonial Rule

**Main Idea** Native peoples had varying levels of success resisting colonial rule in Southeast Asia.

**Reading Connection** Do you know of any occupied countries currently objecting to being governed by another power? Read to learn how those in Southeast Asia resisted the colonial rule of European powers.

Many subject peoples in Southeast Asia were quite unhappy with being governed by Western powers. At first, resistance came from the existing ruling class. In Burma, for example, the monarch himself fought Western domination. By contrast, in Vietnam, after the emperor had agreed to French control of his country, a number of government officials set up an organization called Can Vuoug ("Save the King"). They fought against the French without the emperor's help.

Sometimes, resistance to Western control took the form of peasant revolts. Under colonial rule, peasants were often driven off the land to make way for plantation agriculture. Angry peasants then vented their anger at the foreign invaders. For example, in Burma, in 1930, the Buddhist monk Saya San led a peasant uprising against the British colonial **regime** many years after the regime had completed its takeover.

Early resistance movements failed, overcome by Western powers. At the beginning of the twentieth century, a new kind of resistance began to emerge that was based on the force of nationalism. The leaders were often a new class that had been created by colonial rule: westernized intellectuals in the cities.

In many cases, this new urban middle class—composed of merchants, clerks, students, and professionals—had been educated in Western-style schools. They were the first generation of Asians to understand the institutions and values of the West. Many spoke Western languages and worked in jobs connected with the colonial regimes.

At first, many of the leaders of these movements did not focus clearly on the idea of nationhood but simply tried to defend the economic interests or religious beliefs of the native peoples. In Burma, for example, the first expression of modern nationalism came from students at the University of Rangoon. They formed an organization to protest against official persecution of the Buddhist religion and British lack of respect for local religious traditions. They protested against British arrogance and failure to

▲ *In 1907, Vietnamese prisoners await trial for plotting against the French.*

observe local customs in Buddhist temples. Not until the 1930s, however, did these resistance movements begin to demand national independence.

 **Reading Check** **Summarizing** Explain three forms of resistance to Western domination.

---

**HISTORY** **Online** **Study Central**

For help with the concepts in this section of *Glencoe World History–Modern Times,* go to wh.mt.glencoe.com and click on **Study Central.**

---

**SECTION 1 ASSESSMENT**

**Checking for Understanding**

1. **Vocabulary** Define: New Imperialism, protectorate, exploit, indirect rule, direct rule, impose, regime.

2. **People** Identify: King Mongkut, King Chulalongkorn, Commodore George Dewey, Emilio Aguinaldo.

3. **Places** Locate: Singapore, Burma, Thailand, Philippines.

**Reviewing Big Ideas**

4. **Explain** how the New Imperialism differed from old imperialism. How did imperialism come to be associated with Social Darwinism?

**Critical Thinking**

5. **Historical Analysis** **Evaluating Evidence** Why were resistance movements often led by Southeast Asians who had been educated in the West? Initially, what were the goals of these resistance leaders? How did their goals change over time? **CA HR 3**

6. **Cause and Effect** In a diagram like the one below, identify the effects of colonial rule on the colonies.

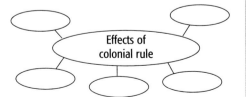

Effects of colonial rule

**Analyzing Visuals**

7. **Describe** the situation being endured by the Vietnamese prisoners in the photo above. Be specific in your description. Based on what you have read about the poverty of native peoples at this time, would you have risked this type of punishment if you had been in their position?

---

**Writing About History**

8. **Expository Writing** Use varied media to determine what the United States's relationship is today with the Philippines and how Filipino political groups view this relationship. Write an essay based on your findings. **CA 10WA2.3**

---

# Empire Building in Africa

## Guide to Reading

### Section Preview

Great Britain, France, Germany, Belgium, and Portugal placed virtually all of Africa under European rule.

**Main Idea**

- European countries exercised increasing control over West Africa. (p. 343)
- The completion of the Suez Canal played a major role in the growth and colonization of Egypt. (p. 343)
- The explorations of Livingstone and Stanley led Belgium to colonize Central Africa. (p. 345)
- Germany and Great Britain dominated the colonization of East Africa. (p. 346)

- European powers quickly came to dominate South Africa. (p. 347)
- European powers ruled their colonies in Africa through both direct and indirect rule. (p. 348)
- European exploitation of Africa stimulated the growth of African nationalism. (p. 349)

### Content Vocabulary

annex, indigenous

### Academic Vocabulary

conflicting, consequence

### People to Identify

Muhammad Ali, David Livingstone, Henry Stanley, Zulu

### Reading Objectives

1. Describe the new class of Africans which colonialism inspired.
2. Explain the relationship between the Boers and the Zulu.

### Reading Strategy

**Categorizing Information** Make a chart like the one below showing which countries controlled what parts of Africa.

| Western Power | Area of Africa |
|---|---|
| Belgium | |
| Britain | |
| France | |
| Germany | |

### Preview of Events

| ♦1860 | ♦1870 | ♦1880 | ♦1890 | ♦1900 | ♦1910 | ♦1920 |
|---|---|---|---|---|---|---|

**1869**
Suez Canal completed

**1884–1885**
Berlin Conference divides Africa among Europeans

**1896**
Ethiopia defeats Italian forces

**1914**
Egypt becomes British protectorate

## California Standards in This Section

*Reading this section will help you master these California History–Social Science standards.*

**10.3.4:** Trace the evolution of work and labor, including the demise of the slave trade and the effects of immigration, mining and manufacturing, division of labor, and the union movement.

**10.4:** Students analyze patterns of global change in the era of New Imperialism in at least two of the following regions or countries: Africa, Southeast Asia, China, India, Latin America, and the Philippines.

**10.4.1:** Describe the rise of industrial economies and their link to imperialism and colonialism (e.g., the role played by national security and strategic advantage; moral issues raised by the search for national hegemony, Social Darwinism, and the missionary impulse; material issues such as land, resources, and technology.)

**10.4.2:** Discuss the locations of the colonial rule of such nations as England, France, Germany, Italy, Japan, the Netherlands, Russia, Spain, Portugal, and the United States.

**10.4.3:** Explain imperialism from the perspective of the colonizers and the colonized and the varied immediate and long-term responses by the people under colonial rule.

**10.4.4:** Describe the independence struggles of the colonized regions of the world, including the roles of leaders, such as Sun Yat-sen in China, and the roles of ideology and religion.

# West Africa

**Main Idea** European countries exercised increasing control over West Africa.

**Reading Connection** Have you ever wanted something just because someone else did? Read to learn about competitive motives behind European imperialism in Africa.

Before 1880, Europeans controlled little of the African continent directly. They were content to let African rulers and merchants represent them on the continent. Between 1880 and 1900, however, fed by intense rivalries among themselves, Great Britain, France, Germany, Belgium, Italy, Spain, and Portugal placed virtually all of Africa under European rule. In their race to control the continent, Europeans did not hesitate to deceive native Africans.

## *Voices from the Past*

A southern African king, Lobengula, wrote a letter to Queen Victoria about how he had been cheated:

> 66Some time ago a party of men came to my country, the principal one appearing to be a man called Rudd. They asked me for a place to dig for gold, and said they would give me certain things for the right to do so. I told them to bring what they could give and I would show them what I would give. A document was written and presented to me for signature. I asked what it contained, and was told that in it were my words and the words of those men. I put my hand to it. About three months afterwards I heard from other sources that I had given by the document the right to all the minerals of my country.99

The Europeans had a keen interest in the raw materials of Africa, and in West Africa that included peanuts, timber, hides, and palm oil. Earlier in the nineteenth century, Europeans had made money in this part of Africa through the slave trade. By the late 1800s, however, trade in slaves had virtually ended, and as slavery declined, Europe's interest in other forms of trade increased.

Early in the nineteenth century, the British had set up settlements in West Africa along the Gold Coast and in Sierra Leone. A more permanent presence allowed the British and other European nations to protect their trade interests.

The growing European presence in West Africa led to increasing tensions with African governments in the area. For a long time, most African states were able to maintain their independence. In 1874, however, Great Britain stepped in and **annexed** (incorporated a country within a state) the west coastal states as the first British colony of Gold Coast. At about the same time, Britain established a protectorate over warring groups in Nigeria. By 1900, France had added the huge area of French West Africa to its colonial empire. This left France in control of the largest part of West Africa. In addition, Germany controlled Togo, Cameroon, German Southwest Africa, and German East Africa.

✓ **Reading Check** **Describing** What was the importance of the decline in the slave trade?

# North Africa

**Main Idea** The completion of the Suez Canal played a major role in the growth and colonization of Egypt.

**Reading Connection** Do you take the long way to get to a destination, or do you look for shortcuts? Read about how quicker transportation affected Europe's interest in Egypt.

Egypt had been part of the Ottoman Empire, but as Ottoman rule declined, the Egyptians sought their independence. In 1805, an officer of the Ottoman army named **Muhammad Ali** seized power and established a separate Egyptian state.

During the next 30 years, Muhammad Ali introduced a series of reforms to bring Egypt into the modern world. He modernized the army, set up a public school system, and helped create small industries in refined sugar, textiles, munitions, and ships.

▼ *King Lobengula, seated, c. 1880*

# Imperialism in Africa, 1914

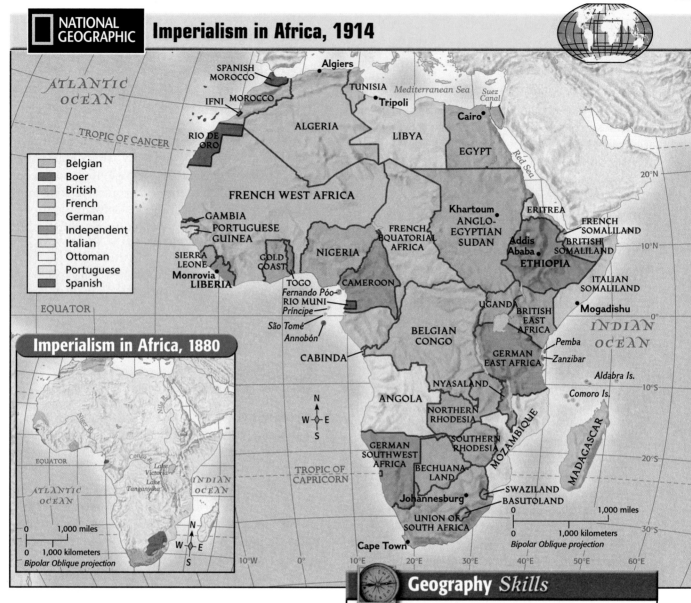

Belgian
Boer
British
French
German
Independent
Italian
Ottoman
Portuguese
Spanish

**Imperialism in Africa, 1880**

## Geography *Skills*

More so in Africa than in Asia, European countries strongly competed in their attempts to colonize new territories.

1. **Interpreting Maps** Identify the two independent countries in Africa in 1914.
2. **Applying Geography Skills** Describe the changes that occurred in Africa from 1880 to 1914 for the Ottoman Empire, France, Britain, and the Boers.

The growing economic importance of the Nile Valley in Egypt, along with the development of steamships, gave Europeans the desire to build a canal east of Cairo to connect the Mediterranean and Red Seas. In 1854, a French entrepreneur, Ferdinand de Lesseps, signed a contract to begin building the Suez Canal. The canal was completed in 1869.

The British took an active interest in Egypt after the Suez Canal was opened. Believing that the canal was its "lifeline to India," Great Britain sought as much control as possible over the canal area. In 1875, Britain bought Egypt's share in the Suez Canal. When an Egyptian army revolt against foreign influence broke out in 1881, Britain suppressed the revolt. Egypt became a British protectorate in 1914.

The British believed that they should also control the Sudan, south of Egypt, to protect their interests in Egypt and the Suez Canal. In 1881, Muslim cleric

Muhammad Ahmad, known as the Mahdi ("the rightly guided one," in Arabic), launched a revolt that brought much of the Sudan under his control.

Britain sent a military force under General Charles Gordon to restore Egyptian authority over the Sudan. However, Gordon's army was wiped out at Khartoum in 1885 by Muhammad Ahmad's troops. Gordon himself died in the battle. Not until 1898 were British troops able to seize the Sudan.

The French also had colonies in North Africa. In 1879, after about 150,000 French people had settled in the region of Algeria, the French government established control there. Two years later, France imposed a protectorate on neighboring Tunisia. In 1912, France established a protectorate over much of Morocco to the west of Algeria.

Italy joined in the competition for colonies in North Africa by attempting to take over Ethiopia, but Italian forces were defeated by Ethiopia in 1896. Italy now was the only European state defeated by an African state. This humiliating loss led Italy to try again in 1911. Italy invaded and seized Turkish Tripoli, which it renamed Libya.

✓ **Reading Check** **Explaining** Great Britain was determined to have complete control of the Suez Canal. Why?

**History** *through Art*

**Gordon's Last Stand by George William Joy**
British general Gordon is portrayed fighting off nationalists in the Sudan. What does the perspective of the image suggest about Gordon and the Sudanese Muslims?

# Central Africa

**Main Idea** The explorations of Livingstone and Stanley led Belgium to colonize Central Africa.

**Reading Connection** What motivates countries today to attempt to control other nations? Read to learn how European nations justified occupying Central Africa in the 1880s.

Central African territories were soon added to Europe's list of colonies, too. It was explorers who first roused popular interest in the dense tropical jungles of Central Africa. **David Livingstone,** as we have seen, was one such explorer. He arrived in Africa in 1841. For 30 years he trekked through uncharted regions. He spent much of his time exploring the interior of the continent.

When Livingstone disappeared for a while, the *New York Herald* hired a young journalist, **Henry Stanley,** to find him. Stanley did, on the eastern shore of Lake Tanganyika, and greeted the explorer with the now famous words, "Dr. Livingstone, I presume."

Stanley remained in Africa as the great explorer's successor after Livingstone's death in 1873. Unlike Livingstone, however, Stanley had a strong dislike of Africa. He once said, "I detest the land most heartily."

In the 1870s, Stanley explored the Congo River in Central Africa and sailed down it to the Atlantic Ocean. Soon, he was encouraging the British to send settlers to the Congo River basin. When Britain refused, he turned to King Leopold II of Belgium.

King Leopold II was the real driving force behind the colonization of Central Africa. He rushed enthusiastically into the pursuit of an empire in Africa. "To open to civilization," he said, "the only part of our globe where it has not yet penetrated, to pierce the darkness which envelops whole populations, is a crusade, if I may say so, a crusade worthy of this century of progress." Profit, however, was equally important to Leopold. In 1876, he hired Henry Stanley to set up Belgian settlements in the Congo.

Leopold's claim to the vast territories of the Congo aroused widespread concern among other European states. France, in particular, rushed to plant its flag in the heart of Africa. Leopold ended up with the territories around the Congo River. France occupied the areas farther north.

✓ **Reading Check** **Examining** What effect did King Leopold II of Belgium have on colonization of the Congo River basin?

## East Africa

**Main Idea** Germany and Great Britain dominated the colonization of East Africa.

**Reading Connection** Would a nation today have no say-so in its political future at an international conference? Read to learn how European nations divided East Africa at the Berlin Conference.

By 1885, Britain and Germany had become the chief rivals in East Africa. Because Germany became united only in 1870, that nation joined the imperial competition late.

At first, the German chancellor Otto von Bismarck had downplayed the importance of colonies. As more and more Germans called for a German empire, however, Bismarck became a convert to colonialism. As he expressed it, "All this colonial business is a sham, but we need it for the elections."

Besides its holdings in West Africa, Germany wanted colonies in East Africa. Most of East Africa had not yet been claimed by any other power. For strategic reasons, the British were also interested in the area, however—East Africa lay between the two British-controlled areas of South Africa and Egypt. To add to the problem of competing powers, Portugal and Belgium were also claiming parts of East Africa.

To settle the **conflicting** claims, the Berlin Conference was called in 1884–1885. The agreement reached recognized British and German claims to specific territory in East Africa, while Portugal received a clear claim on Mozambique. At the Berlin Conference, the European nations adopted an agreement that described how a European nation could lay claim to an area of Africa. No African delegates were present at the conference.

**Reading Check** **Evaluating** What role did African representatives play at the Berlin Conference?

# Opposing Viewpoints

## Who Benefited from the New Imperialism?

Europeans justified colonization of Africa and Asia in many ways. Native peoples viewed the takeover of their lands differently. Rudyard Kipling and Edward Morel were British journalists who held opposing viewpoints about imperialism.

"Take up the White Man's burden—
Send forth the best ye breed—
Go bind your sons to exile
To serve your captives' needs;
To wait in heavy harness,
On fluttered folk and wild—
Your new-caught sullen peoples,
Half-devil and half-child. . . .
Take up the White Man's burden—
And reap his old reward:
The blame of those ye better,
The hate of those ye guard—
The cry of hosts ye humour
(Ah, slowly;) toward the light: —
'Why brought he us from bondage,
Our loved Egyptian night?'"

—**Rudyard Kipling, 1899**
*The White Man's Burden*

"It is [the Africans] who carry the 'Black man's burden. . . .' In hewing out for himself a fixed abode in Africa, the white man has massacred the African in heaps. . . .

## South Africa

**Main Idea** European powers quickly came to dominate the region of South Africa.

**Reading Connection** Do you remember studying about early explorers who sailed round the Cape of Good Hope? Read to learn about why Europeans wanted to control South Africa in the 1800s.

Nowhere in Africa did the European presence grow more rapidly than in the south. By 1865, the white population of the area had risen to about 200,000.

Since the 1600s, descendants of early Dutch settlers, known as Boers or Afrikaners, had lived in Cape Town and surrounding areas. During the Napoleonic Wars, the British seized these lands from the Dutch. Later the British government encouraged British settlers to move to this area, which they named Cape Colony.

What the partial occupation of his soil by the white man has failed do; . . . what the [machine gun] and the rifle, the slave gang, labour in the bowels of the earth and the lash, have failed to do; what imported measles, smallpox and syphilis have failed to do; whatever the overseas slave trade failed to do; the power of modern capitalistic exploitation, assisted by modern engines of destruction, may yet succeed in accomplishing. . . .

Thus the African is really helpless against the material gods of the white man, as embodied in the trinity of imperialism, capitalistic exploitation, and militarism.**"**

—**Edward Morel, 1903**
*The Black Man's Burden*

## You Decide

1. What was the impact of imperialism on the colonized territories in Africa, according to Morel?

2. Quote lines in Rudyard Kipling's poem that reflect his view of colonized peoples. What values did Kipling assume his readers shared with him?

**The Boer Republics** Disgusted with British rule, the Boers moved north in the 1830s. This "Great Trek" took them to the region between the Orange and Vaal (VAHL) Rivers and north of the Vaal as well. Here they formed two republics—the Orange Free State and the Transvaal, later called the South African Republic. The Boers, who believed white superiority was ordained by God, put many of the **indigenous** (native to a region) peoples living in the republics on reservations.

The Boers had frequently battled one of the indigenous groups, the **Zulu** people. In the early nineteenth century, under the talented ruler Shaka, the Zulu carved out their own empire. The Zulu were not completely subdued until the late 1800s, when the British finally defeated them.

In the 1880s, British policy in South Africa was influenced by Cecil Rhodes. Rhodes had started diamond and gold companies operating in South Africa that made him a fortune. He gained control of a territory north of the Transvaal, which he named Rhodesia after himself.

Rhodes was a great champion of British expansion. He said once, "I think what [God] would like me to do is to paint as much of Africa British red as possible." Rhodes wanted a series of British colonies "from the Cape to Cairo," all linked by a railroad.

Rhodes had such influence that he was appointed prime minister of Cape Colony. In 1896, however, he was forced to resign when the British government discovered that Rhodes had planned to overthrow the South African Republic of the Boers without British approval. The British removal of Rhodes from office came too late to avoid a war between the British and the Boers.

**The Boer War** The Boer War lasted from 1899 to 1902. Fierce Boer resistance angered the British. They burnt crops and forced about 120,000 Boer women and children into detention camps where as many as 20,000 died. Eventually the much larger British army won.

In 1910, the British created an independent Union of South Africa, which combined the old Cape Colony and the Boer republics. The new state was a self-governing nation within the British Empire. To appease the Boers, the British agreed that only whites would vote, excluding all but a few propertied Africans.

**✓ Reading Check** **Explaining** How did European influence lead to the Boer War?

# Colonial Rule in Africa

**Main Idea** European powers ruled their colonies in Africa through both direct and indirect rule.

**Reading Connection** How is the American government organized and run? Read to learn about the methods European nations used to govern African colonies.

By 1914, Great Britain, France, Germany, Belgium, Italy, Spain, and Portugal had divided up Africa. Only Liberia and Ethiopia remained free states. Native peoples who dared to resist were simply devastated by the superior military force of the Europeans.

As was true in Southeast Asia, most European governments ruled their new territories in Africa with the least effort and expense possible. Indirect rule meant relying on existing political elites and institutions. The British especially followed this approach. At first, in some areas, the British simply asked a local ruler to accept British authority and to fly the British flag over official buildings.

The concept of indirect rule was introduced in the Islamic state of Sokoto, in northern Nigeria, beginning in 1903. This system of indirect rule in Sokoto had one good feature: it did not disrupt local customs and institutions. However, it did have some unfortunate **consequences.**

The system was basically a fraud because British administrators made all major decisions. The native authorities served chiefly to enforce those decisions. Another problem was that indirect rule kept the old African elite in power. Such a policy provided few opportunities for ambitious and talented young Africans from outside the old elite. In this way British indirect rule sowed the seeds for class and tribal tensions, which erupted after independence came in the twentieth century.

Most other European nations governed their African possessions through a form of direct rule. This was true in the French colonies. At the top was a French official, usually known as a governor-general. He was appointed from Paris and governed with the aid of a bureaucracy in the capital city of the colony.

The French ideal was to assimilate Africans into French culture rather than preserve local traditions. Africans could run for office and even serve in the French National Assembly in Paris. A few were appointed to high positions in the colonial administration.

✓**Reading Check** **Comparing** How did the French system of colonial rule differ from that of Great Britain?

# CONNECTIONS Around The World

## The Role of Quinine

Before 1850, the fear of disease was a major factor in keeping Europeans from moving into Africa. Especially frightening was malaria, an often fatal disease spread by parasites. Malaria is especially devastating in tropical and subtropical regions, which offer good conditions for breeding the mosquitoes that carry and spread the malaria parasites.

By 1850, European doctors had learned how to treat malaria with quinine, a drug that greatly reduced the death rate from the disease. Quinine is a bitter drug obtained from the bark of the cinchona tree, which is native to the slopes of the Andes in South America. The Indians of Peru were the first people to use the bark of the cinchona tree to treat malaria.

The Dutch took the cinchona tree and began to grow it in the East Indies. The East Indies eventually became the chief source of quinine. With the use of quinine and other medicines, Europeans felt more secure about moving into Africa.

By the beginning of the twentieth century, more than 90 percent of African lands were under the control of the European powers. A drug found in the bark of Latin American trees, which were then grown in Asia, had been used by Europeans to make possible their conquest of Africa.

*The bark from cinchona ▶ trees dries in the sun.*

## Comparing Cultures

Fear of disease kept Europeans from moving into Africa. Once quinine was discovered, Europeans felt safer about Africa.

1. What fears do we have today that prevent or inhibit exploration or research?
2. What technological advances would be required to overcome those fears?

# Rise of African Nationalism

**Main Idea** European exploitation of Africa stimulated the growth of African nationalism.

**Reading Connection** Did American colonial governments want the kind of power that the British Parliament had? Read to learn how Africans wanted to set up their own governments on the Western model.

As in Southeast Asia, a new class of leaders emerged in Africa by the beginning of the twentieth century. Educated in colonial schools or in Western nations, they were the first generation of Africans to know a great deal about the West.

On the one hand, the members of this new class admired Western culture and sometimes disliked the ways of their own countries. They were eager to introduce Western ideas and institutions into their own societies.

On the other hand, many came to resent the foreigners and their arrogant contempt for African peoples. These intellectuals recognized the gap between theory and practice in colonial policy. Westerners had exalted democracy, equality, and political freedom but did not apply these values in the colonies.

Native Africans were able to obtain only low-paying jobs in the colonial bureaucracy. Colonialism for most meant that they had lost their farms and were now employed on foreign-run plantations or factories.

Middle-class Africans suffered somewhat less, but they, too, had grievances. At best, they filled clerical jobs in government or business offices. Even then, they were paid less than Europeans in similar jobs.

Europeans expressed their superiority in other ways. Clubs, schools, and churches were segregated. Europeans, even the children in a European family, often addressed Africans by their first names or by calling an adult male "boy."

Such conditions led many of the new urban educated class of Africans to have mixed feelings toward colonialists and Western culture. Educated Africans were willing to admit the superiority of many aspects of Western culture, but they had a fierce hatred of colonial rule. They were determined to assert their own nationality. Out of this mixture of hopes and resentments emerged the first stirrings of modern nationalism in Africa.

During the early part of the twentieth century, resentment turned to action. Across Africa, native peoples began to organize political parties and movements to bring an end to foreign rule. In 1908, for example, Nigerians formed the People's Union to work for more rights. The Young Senegalese Club was founded in 1910. In South Africa, African leaders founded what would become the African National Congress (ANC) in 1912. This organization was designed to protect African rights in the Rhodesias (modern Zambia and Zimbabwe), Basutoland (modern Lesotho), Bechuanaland (modern Botswana), and Swaziland.

**Reading Check** **Evaluating** Why were many African intellectuals frustrated by colonial policy?

## HISTORY Online Study Central

For help with the concepts in this section of *Glencoe World History–Modern Times,* go to wh.mt.glencoe.com and click on **Study Central.**

---

# SECTION 2 ASSESSMENT

## Checking for Understanding

1. **Vocabulary** Define: annex, conflicting, indigenous, consequence.

2. **People** Identify: Muhammad Ali, David Livingstone, Henry Stanley, Zulu.

### Reviewing Big Ideas

3. **Explain** why the British were interested in East Africa. What other countries claimed parts of East Africa?

## Critical Thinking

4. **Historical Analysis** **Interpreting History** What can you conclude from the fact that African delegates were not at the 1884 Berlin Conference? **CA HR 2**

5. **Organizing Information** Using a chart like the one below, identify key figures of African resistance to colonial rule.

| Leader | Country opposed | Dates of resistance |
|--------|-----------------|---------------------|
|        |                 |                     |
|        |                 |                     |

## Analyzing Visuals

6. Consider the painting on page 345 again. Does modern-day war coverage present the same opportunity to present an interpretation of events that this artist's illustration did of conflict in Sudan? Why or why not?

### Writing About History

7. **Expository Writing** Research the importance of the Suez Canal today. Write a paper comparing the present-day significance of the canal to its historical significance. **CA 10WA2.3**

# STANLEY AND LIVINGSTONE
# IN AFRICA

AFRICA.—THE MEETING BETWEEN STANLEY AND LIVINGSTONE, AT UJIJI.

1

More than three years had passed with no word from Dr. David Livingstone. The renowned Scottish missionary and explorer had left Britain in August 1865, bound for East Africa, where the Royal Geographical Society had asked him, among other things, to try to determine the source of the Nile River. The explorer Richard Burton favored Lake Tanganyika while the late John Hanning Speke had been certain the Nile arose in Lake Victoria. The 52-year-old Livingstone had arrived at the island of Zanzibar in January 1866. He and his party of about 60 men were taken to the mainland some six weeks later and were known to have headed into the interior. Months later, the first rumors of his death reached the coast.

In October 1869, James Gordon Bennett, son of the publisher of the *New York Herald*, met with reporter Henry M. Stanley in the Grand Hotel in Paris. "Go and find him wherever you may hear that he is and get what news you can of him," Bennett told Stanley. "And perhaps the old man may be in want; take enough with you to help him should he require it. Of course, you will act according to your own plans, and do what you think best—but find Livingstone!"

The man Stanley was supposed to find was known and admired both for his achievements as an explorer and for his dedicated efforts to end the slave trade. Since going out to Africa in 1841 as a 27-year-old medical missionary, David Livingstone had covered thousands of miles of territory previously unexplored by Europeans. Sometimes he traveled by canoe or on the back of an ox, but mostly he went on foot. In the early years he traveled with his wife, Mary, and their young children.

Though he suffered from malaria and had lost the use of his left arm after being attacked by a wounded lion, Livingstone remained determined. He made detailed notes and reports, which he sent to London whenever he could. The information he sent was used to revise the maps of Africa.

All the exploration that Livingstone did in the mid-1850s had one goal: to find a navigable river that would open the center of Africa to legitimate European commerce and to Christianity. In so doing, Livingstone hoped to drive out the slave trade, an evil that he called "this open sore of the world."

In the spring of 1852, Livingstone sent his family back to England. Then, starting from Cape Town, South Africa, he trekked north to the Upper Zambezi and then west to Luanda on the Atlantic coast (in present-day Angola). After a brief rest, he headed to Quelimane on the east coast (now in Mozambique). The trip of some 4,300 miles (6,919 km) finally ended in May 1856. Livingstone traveled with a small party of 25 or so

3

Africans. In contrast to other European expedition leaders, the missionary regarded the men not as his servants but as his friends. His loyalty to them was returned manyfold.

The expedition traveled light, although Livingstone always carried his navigational instruments, a Bible, a nautical almanac, and his journal. He also carried a magic lantern (an early slide projector) and slides, so he could tell Bible stories to any who would listen. On the second half of the journey, from the interior to the mouth of the Zambezi River, Livingstone became the first European to see the spectacular waterfall the Africans called "Mosi-oa-tunya" (the smoke that thunders).

2

Livingstone named it Victoria Falls, after the British queen.

■

When the missionary got back to Britain in late 1856, he found that word of his explorations and discoveries had preceded him. He was now famous. The following year Livingstone turned his journals into a book—*Missionary Travels and Researches in South Africa*—which quickly became a best-seller. In his book and at every public opportunity he could find, he raised the issue of the slave trade. He condemned those who tolerated it and profited by it.

When he sailed back to Africa in the spring of 1858, Dr. Livingstone was the newly appointed British Con-

**1** Tipping his pith helmet, Henry Morton Stanley greets the explorer with his restrained inquiry: "Dr. Livingstone, I presume?"

**2** The scarcity of paper did not prevent Livingstone from recording his observations in meticulous detail, as seen in this fragment from his journals. He would also record topographical measurements taken with the sextant.

**3** "It had never been seen before by European eyes," Livingstone wrote of his first view of Victoria Falls, "but scenes so lovely must have been gazed upon by angels in their flight." His drawing of the falls and the meandering Zambezi River below it (inset) hardly does the scene justice.

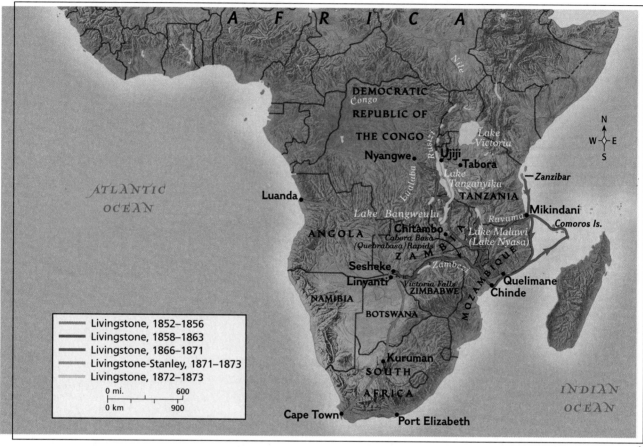

Livingstone, 1852–1856
Livingstone, 1858–1863
Livingstone, 1866–1871
Livingstone-Stanley, 1871–1873
Livingstone, 1872–1873

0 mi.          600
0 km          900

4

sul for the East Coast of Africa. With substantial government backing and far more equipment and personnel than he had previously enjoyed, he continued to explore the Zambezi and its tributaries. His wife sailed with him but then fell ill and went to rest in Cape Town.

Despite its advantages, this expedition was plagued with problems. There was quarreling among Livingstone's six European assistants, and the fuel-eating boat he had been given was more trouble than it was worth.

Worst of all was the discovery that on his previous trip down the Zambezi he had bypassed a bend in the river that held big problems. When the party headed upriver from the east coast of Africa, they came around that bend only to be stopped by the Quebrabasa Rapids. Try as he might—and Livingstone insisted on trying, until

everyone in his expedition was exhausted— this was an obstacle no boat could get past.

Even though his efforts were adding daily to European knowledge of the African interior and would be of benefit to all who came after him, Livingstone was frustrated at not finding the navigable river that would surely bring an end to the slave trade.

Then, tragedy struck. In early 1862, Mary Livingstone was well enough to join her husband, but a few months later she fell ill again. In April, she died. Grief stricken, Livingstone threw himself into his work, but his increased efforts did not pay off. In July 1863, the expedition was ordered to return home.

Livingstone stayed in Britain only long enough to write a second book, *The Zambezi and Its Tributaries*, and to drum up support for his next expedi-

tion. On his third and final trip to Africa, the great explorer disappeared.

Henry Stanley left to carry out his employer's orders soon after the Paris meeting. He took a roundabout route to Africa to cover other stories for the *Herald*, including the opening of the Suez Canal in Egypt. James Bennett hoped that by delaying Stanley's arrival in Africa, the reporter would come back with definite news of Livingstone—that he was dead or alive and not just missing. ("If he is dead," Bennett had said, "bring back every possible proof of his death.")

By the time Stanley finally reached Africa in late January 1871, Livingstone had been struggling with near-starvation, chronic dysentery, sore-covered feet, and hostile groups. Of the 60 men he had started with, only a small handful remained, including Chuma, a freed slave, and

Susi, a Yao servant. Both of them had been with him for years. Desperately sick and without medicine, Livingstone had been repeatedly nursed back to relatively good health by Arab slave traders. The passionate anti-slavery activist owed his life to the very people he wished to banish from Africa.

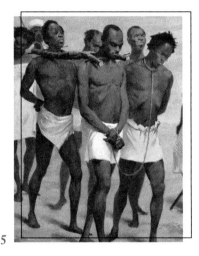

5

In July 1871, ill and discouraged, Livingstone headed to Ujiji, on the east bank of Lake Tanganyika. He expected to find several months' worth of supplies, medicine, and mail waiting for him there. In late October, "reduced to a skeleton," as he put it, he hobbled into the village—only to learn that all his supplies and precious medicines had been plundered by the headman of the place. Extremely depressed, he felt he couldn't do anything but wait for a miracle.

Several weeks later, the miracle arrived under a waving Stars and Stripes. Henry Stanley could hardly contain his emotion as he approached the pale white man."I would have run to him, only I was a coward in the presence of such a mob," Stanley later wrote, "[I] would have embraced him, only he being an Englishman, I did not know how he would receive me; so I did what cowardice and false pride suggested was the best thing— walked deliberately to him, took off my hat, and said: 'Dr. Livingstone, I

presume?' 'Yes,' said he, with a kind smile, lifting his cap slightly."

Stanley remained with Livingstone for five months and explored Lake Tanganyika with him. That trip proved that Burton was wrong about the Ruzizi, the river he thought led from the lake to become the Nile. Livingstone was now determined to prove his own theory, which was that the Nile originated with the headwaters of a river called the Lualaba. (As it turns out, the Lualaba is actually part of the Congo River system. Speke was right all along: The Nile's source is Lake Victoria.)

Unable to persuade the older man to return to Britain, Stanley left in March 1872. Reaching the coast in May, his news of finding Livingstone reached Europe and America in August. At about that time, Livingstone received the fresh supplies and men that Stanley had promised to send back to him. He promptly set off toward Lakes Tanganyika and Bangweulu.

The old explorer's will was great, but his long-suffering body was no longer up to the demands of the trip. By April 22, 1873, he was being carried in a litter. On the night of April

6

30, in the village of Chitambo, Susi helped him to bed, last speaking with him at midnight. The next morning, his companions found Livingstone kneeling by the bed, his head in his hands in prayer—dead.

Resolving that Livingstone should be returned to Britain, they buried his heart under a large tree near the hut where he died. Then they filled the body with salt, smeared it with brandy, and left it to dry for two weeks before beginning the long journey to the coast. Eight months and a thousand miles (1,609 km) later, they delivered Livingstone's body to the British Consul in Zanzibar. April 18, 1874, was declared a national day of mourning and all of London came to a halt as Dr. Livingstone was buried in Westminster Abbey.

4 **Livingstone made two significant crossings of the African continent—from the interior west to Luanda in 1853–1854, and then east to Quelimane in 1855–1856. On his expedition in 1866 to find the source of the Nile, illness and other difficulties hampered his progress. Henry Stanley found him at Ujiji on November 10, 1871.**

5 **The all-too-familiar sight of captives in chains drove Livingstone to denounce the collaboration of European authorities in the widespread traffic in slaves.**

6 **Henry Morton Stanley developed a great interest in exploring Africa after he found Livingstone.**

## INTERPRETING THE PAST

1. What were two of Dr. Livingstone's reasons for exploring Africa?

2. What waterfall did Livingstone encounter on his trip from the interior to the mouth of the Zambezi River ?

3. What were the main obstacles that Livingstone faced?

# British Rule in India

## Section Preview

The British brought stability to India, but destroyed native industries and degraded Indians, while leaders like Mohandas Gandhi worked for Indian independence through nonviolent action.

### Main Idea

- Mistrust and cultural differences between the British and Indians led to violent conflict. (p. 355)
- The British brought order and stability to India, but they also hurt the economy and degraded the Indian people. (p. 356)
- The British presence in India led Indians to organize an independence movement. (p. 358)

- British rule sparked renewed interest among Indians in their own culture and history. (p. 358)

## Content Vocabulary

sepoy, viceroy

## Academic Vocabulary

attitude, transfer

## People and Events to Identify

Queen Victoria, Indian National Congress, Mohandas Gandhi

## Places to Locate

Kanpur, Mumbai

## Reading Objectives

1. Explain the goal of the Indian National Congress.
2. Discuss why India was called the "Jewel in the Crown" of Queen Victoria, the Empress of India.

## Reading Strategy

**Cause and Effect** Using a chart like the one below, identify some causes and effects of British influence on India.

| Cause | Effect |
|---|---|
| 1. British textiles | |
| 2. cotton crops | |
| 3. school system | |
| 4. railroad, telegraph, telephone services | |
| | |

## Preview of Events

| ♦1840 | ♦1850 | ♦1860 | ♦1870 | ♦1880 | ♦1890 | ♦1900 |
|---|---|---|---|---|---|---|

**1853** First passenger train runs from Bombay to Thane

**1857** Sepoy Mutiny fails

**1876** Queen Victoria is named "Empress of India"

**1885** Indian National Congress forms

**1893** Mohandas Gandhi moves to South Africa

## California Standards in This Section

*Reading this section will help you master these California History–Social Science standards.*

**10.4.2:** Discuss the locations of the colonial rule of such nations as England, France, Germany, Italy, Japan, the Netherlands, Russia, Spain, Portugal, and the United States.

**10.4.3:** Explain imperialism from the perspective of the colonizers and the colonized and the varied immediate and long-term responses by the people under colonial rule.

**10.4.4:** Describe the independence struggles of the colonized regions of the world, including the roles of leaders, such as Sun Yat-sen in China, and the roles of ideology and religion.

# The Sepoy Mutiny

**Main Idea** Mistrust and cultural differences between the British and Indians led to violent conflict.

**Reading Connection** Does your family celebrate certain customs or religious traditions? Read to learn how cultural differences helped ignite an Indian rebellion in 1857.

Over the course of the eighteenth century, British power in India had increased while the power of the Mogul rulers had declined. A trading company, the British East India Company, was given power by the British government to become actively involved in India's political and military affairs. Over time, the British in India also had to face social and religious questions, too. How could the British rule a people so very different from themselves?

## *Voices from the Past*

In the minds of most British people, the British culture was superior by far to Indian culture. A famous expression of this **attitude** came from Thomas Macaulay, a government official asked to recommend the kind of education system India should have. Macaulay had no doubt that schools should use the English language, not any language native to India:

> 66What, then, shall the language of education be? [Some] maintain that it should be the English. The other half strongly recommend the Arabic and Sanskrit. The whole question seems to me to be, which language is the best worth knowing? . . . It is, I believe, no exaggeration to say that all the historical information which has been collected from all the books written in the Sanskrit language is less valuable than what may be found in short textbooks used at preparatory schools in England.99

To rule India, the British East India Company had its own soldiers and forts. It also hired Indian soldiers, known as **sepoys,** to protect the company's interests in the region.

In 1857, a growing Indian distrust of the British led to a revolt. The revolt was known to the British as the Great Rebellion or the Sepoy Mutiny. Indians call it the First War of Independence. The immediate cause of the revolt was a rumor that the British were issuing their Indian troops new bullets greased with cow and pig fat. The cow was sacred to Hindus; the pig was taboo to Muslims. A group of sepoys at an army post near Delhi refused to load their rifles with the new bullets. When the British arrested them, the sepoys went on a rampage and killed 50 European men, women, and children.

From this beginning, the revolt quickly spread. Within a year, however, Indian troops loyal to the British, along with fresh British troops, had crushed the rebellion. Although Indian troops fought bravely and outnumbered the British by about 230,000 to 40,000, they were not well organized. Rivalries between Hindus and Muslims kept Indians from working together.

Atrocities were terrible on both sides. At **Kanpur** (Cawnpore), Indians armed with swords and knives massacred two hundred defenseless women and children in a building known as the House of the Ladies. When the British recaptured Kanpur, they took their revenge before executing the Indians.

As a result of the uprising, the British Parliament **transferred** the powers of the East India Company directly to the British government. In 1876, the title of Empress of India was bestowed on **Queen Victoria.** The people of India were now her colonial subjects, and India became her "Jewel in the Crown."

✓**Reading Check** **Describing** What were two effects of the Great Rebellion?

▼ *Schools in India used English—the language "best worth knowing," according to some Britons.*

*Indian sepoy*

## Colonial Rule

**Main Idea** The British brought order and stability to India, but they also hurt the economy and degraded the Indian people.

**Reading Connection** Are there people in your life who have both a positive and a negative influence on you? Read to learn how British rule in India had both positive and negative results for India.

The British government ruled India directly through a British official known as a **viceroy,** a governor who ruled as a representative of a monarch. He was assisted by a British civil service staff. This staff of about 3,500 officials ruled almost 300 million people, the largest colonial population in the world. British rule involved both benefits and costs for Indians.

**Benefits of British Rule** British rule in India had several benefits for subjects. It brought order and stability to a society that had been divided into many states with different political systems. It also led to a fairly honest and efficient government.

Through the efforts of the British administrator and historian Lord Thomas Macaulay, a new school system was set up. Its goal was to train Indian children to serve in the government and army. The new system served only elite, upper-class Indians, however. Ninety percent of the population remained illiterate.

Railroads, the telegraph, and a postal service were introduced to India shortly after they appeared in Great Britain. In 1853 the first trial run of a passenger train traveled the short distance from Bombay to Thane. By 1900, 25,000 miles (40,225 km) of railroads crisscrossed India. *(See page 773 to read an excerpt from Dadabhai Naoroji's speech on the British impact on India in the Primary Sources Library.)*

**Costs of British Rule** The Indian people, however, paid a high price for the peace and stability brought by British rule. Perhaps the greatest cost was economic. British entrepreneurs and a small number of Indians reaped financial benefits from British rule, but it brought hardship to millions of others in both the cities and the countryside. British manufactured goods destroyed local industries. The introduction of British textiles put thousands of women out of work and severely damaged the Indian textile industry.

In rural areas, the British sent zamindars, or local officials, to collect taxes. The British believed that using zamindars would make it easier to collect taxes from the peasants. However, the zamindars in India took advantage of their new authority. They increased taxes and forced the less fortunate peasants to become tenants or lose their land entirely. Peasant unrest grew.

The British also encouraged many farmers to switch from growing food to growing cotton. This policy was one factor that contributed to the famines that devastated India from time to time. Between 1800 and 1900, 30 million Indians died of starvation.

Finally, British rule was degrading, even for the newly educated upper classes who benefited the most from it. The best jobs and the best housing were reserved for Britons. Although many British colonial officials sincerely tried to improve the lot of the people in India, British arrogance cut deeply into the pride of many Indians.

Despite their education, the Indians were never considered equals of the British. Lord Kitchener, one of Britain's military commanders in India, said, "It is this consciousness of the inherent superiority of the European which has won for us India. However well educated and clever a native may be, and however brave he may prove himself, I believe that no rank we can bestow on him would cause him to be considered an equal of the British officer."

Often, the British failed to respect India's cultural heritage. The Taj Mahal, for example, a tomb for the beloved wife of an Indian ruler, became a favorite site for English weddings and parties. Many partygoers even brought hammers to chip off pieces as souvenirs. British racial attitudes led to the rise of an Indian nationalist movement.

**Reading Check** **Examining** In your opinion, was British rule more beneficial or detrimental to India? Explain.

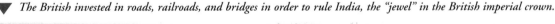

▼ *The British invested in roads, railroads, and bridges in order to rule India, the "jewel" in the British imperial crown.*

## An Indian Nationalist Movement

**Main Idea** The British presence in India led Indians to organize an independence movement.

**Reading Connection** What methods did Martin Luther King, Jr., use in the civil rights movement of the 1960s? Read to learn about Gandhi, the Indian leader who practiced nonviolent protest.

The first Indian nationalists were upper class and English-educated. Many of them were from urban areas, such as **Mumbai** (then called Bombay), Chennai (Madras), and Calcutta. Some were trained in British law and were members of the civil service.

At first, many preferred reform to revolution, but the slow pace of reform convinced many Indian nationalists that relying on British goodwill was futile. In 1885, a small group of Indians met in Bombay to form the **Indian National Congress** (INC). The INC did not demand immediate independence but did call for a share in the governing process.

The INC had difficulties because of religious differences. The goal of the INC was to seek independence for all Indians, regardless of class or religious background. However, many of its leaders were Hindu and reflected Hindu concerns. Eventually, Muslims began to call for the creation of a separate Muslim League to represent the interests of the millions of Muslims in Indian society.

In 1915, the return of a young Hindu from South Africa brought new life to India's struggle for independence. **Mohandas Gandhi** was born in 1869 in Gujarat, in western India. He studied in London and became a lawyer. In 1893, he went to South Africa to work in a law firm serving Indian workers there. He soon became aware of the racial exploitation of Indians living in South Africa.

On his return home to India, Gandhi became active in the independence movement. Using his experience in South Africa, he set up a movement based on nonviolent resistance. Its aim was to force the British to improve the lot of the poor and grant independence to India. In Gandhi's philosophy, resisting unjust laws was the moral path, but if resistance became violent, Gandhi would withdraw support. Gandhi's reputation for morality was so high that he was called Mahatma, or "great soul." Ultimately, his movement would lead to Indian independence.

✔ **Reading Check** **Inferring** Why were Hindus and Muslims able to overcome their differences?

▲ *Mohandas Gandhi at his law office in 1895*

## Colonial Indian Culture

**Main Idea** British rule sparked renewed interest among Indians in their own culture and history.

**Reading Connection** Can a writer or filmmaker inspire people to connect around certain ideas? Read to learn about the Indian author who helped awaken a new interest in Indian culture in the early 1900s.

The love-hate tension in India that arose from British domination led to a cultural, as well as a political, awakening. Indian teachers, writers, and journalists wanted to preserve their own culture and often looked back to their own past to do so. The cultural revival began in the early 1800s when the British established a college in the major city of Calcutta. A publishing house was opened, too, and it published books not only on science and Western literature, but also on India's ancient language of Sanskrit, as well as grammars and dictionaries in some of the many Indian languages.

This new interest soon spread to other regions and led writers to search for modern literary forms to express national identity. Indian novelists and poets began writing historical romances and epics. Although some wrote in English, most were uncomfortable doing so. They preferred to use their own regional tongues.

The most illustrious Indian author was Rabindranath Tagore. A great writer and poet, Tagore was also a social reformer, spiritual leader, educator, philosopher, and international spokesperson for the moral concerns of his age. At his country estate he set up a school that became an international university.

Tagore's life mission was to promote pride in a national Indian consciousness in the face of British domination. He wrote a widely read novel in which he portrayed the love-hate relationship of India toward its colonial mentor. The novel reflected an Indian people who admired and imitated the British but who agonized over how to establish their own identity.

Tagore was more than an Indian nationalist, however. His life's work was one long prayer for human dignity, world peace, and the mutual understanding and union of East and West. As he once said, "It is my conviction that my countrymen will truly gain their India by fighting against the education that teaches them that a country is greater than the ideals of humanity."

▲ *Rabindranath Tagore*

✓**Reading Check** **Comparing** How did the nationalist movement parallel cultural developments in India?

**HISTORY** **Online** **Study Central**

For help with the concepts in this section of *Glencoe World History–Modern Times,* go to wh.mt.glencoe.com and click on **Study Central.**

# SECTION 3 ASSESSMENT

## Checking for Understanding

1. **Vocabulary** Define. attitude, sepoy, transfer, viceroy.

2. **People and Events** Identify: Queen Victoria, Indian National Congress, Mohandas Gandhi.

3. **Places** Locate: Kanpur, Mumbai.

### Reviewing Big Ideas

4. **List** the economic costs to the Indian people that resulted from India being ruled by the British. What benefits to the Indian population, if any, resulted from British rule?

## Critical Thinking

5. **Predicting Consequences** Many British lived in India for decades. Do you think living in India would have changed British attitudes toward Indians? Explain.

6. **Organizing Information** Draw a graph like the example below to show the percentage of India's population that died of starvation in the 1800s.

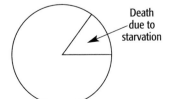

Death due to starvation

## Analyzing Visuals

7. **Interpret** the message conveyed by the image on page 356. Describe your reactions in a paragraph or two. Why might your reactions be different from reactions of English teenagers in the 1850s?

### Writing About History

8. **Descriptive Writing** Imagine you are a member of India's upper class. You have just attended a reception at the home of a British official. Describe in writing your impressions of the home, making a comparison to your own residence.
   **CA** 10WA2.1

# FOCUS ON EVERYDAY LIFE

## A British Official's Home in India

During the time that India was a British colony, many British government officials spent a considerable amount of time there fulfilling their administrative duties. Their families usually came with them during their tours of duty, bringing their Victorian lifestyle and many of the furnishings that went with it.

British officials in India built comfortable bungalows, as they were called. *Bungalow* comes from *bungla,* a word referring to the one-story houses found in Bengal, a region of India. Bungalows were spacious country houses with large porches that were open to breezes but gave protection from the sun. Surrounding the bungalows were cottages where dozens of Indian servants lived with their families.

The official was the sahib—the master. The official's wife was the memsahib, or madam-sahib. The memsahib was expected to oversee the running of the household on a daily basis, especially since the sahib was often away on official business. At the beginning of each day, she assigned duties to all the servants. For example, she fixed the menu for the day with the cook and directed the gardeners about how to plant the gardens with seeds from home. In the evening, she was expected to entertain. Supper parties with other British families were the usual form of entertainment.

Many British officials had a high standard of living and were expected to have a large number of servants. One woman wrote in 1882: "It is one of the social duties of Indian life that you must keep three servants to do the work of one." A well-to-do family had at least 25 servants. Even bachelors had at least a dozen. Indians served as cooks, maids, butlers, gardeners, tailors, and nursemaids for the children. All household servants wore uniforms—usually white with bands on their turbans—and went barefoot in the house.

◀ This painting from 1785 is a miniature in the Mogul style of the Muslims who ruled India officially until 1857. It is easy to date the picture from a Western point of view because the British officer is dressed in typical breeches of the eighteenth century. The house is European, but there are Indian touches, like the louvred shutters to keep out the heat, and, especially, the Indian carpet. In later centuries, the homes of wealthy Indians also reflected features from British styles.

In 1911, Britain's King George V and Queen Mary made a state visit to India. In their honor, the Gateway of India was built at the edge of the harbor in Bombay, the city we know today as Mumbai. The architecture, with its turrets and Roman arches, is a blend of India's Mogul and European styles. For British citizens, the Gateway of India became a familiar symbol for the power and glory of the British Empire.

An Englishman receives a pedicure from an Indian servant. The wide veranda was typical of the bungalows the British lived in. The British ruling class in India was made up of soldiers and a larger group of civil service officials, known as the ICS (Indian Civil Service). Many served in India for their entire career and retired to England with a very good income.

State visits, such as this one in 1922, were great events. Long before the British ruled India, durbars, or formal receptions for visiting royalty, had been held. Here the Prince of Wales, who reigned briefly as Edward VII in 1936 before abdicating to marry a commoner, walks with the princess, or begum, of Bhopal. Female begums ruled this small kingdom beginning in 1819, when the first begum took over for a husband who was assassinated. Begums succeeded to the throne until 1947 when India became independent.

## CONNECTING TO THE PAST

1. **Identifying** What were the responsibilities of the wife of a British officer in India?

2. **Writing about History** What do you learn about British-Indian social relations from this reading?

# Nation Building in Latin America

## Guide to Reading

### Section Preview
Latin American countries served as a source of raw materials for Europe and the United States.

**Main Idea**

- Revolutionary ideas in Latin America were sparked by the successes of revolutions in North America. (p. 363)
- After they became independent, Latin American nations faced a staggering range of problems. (p. 365)
- Many Latin American governments patterned their new constitutions after the United States. (p. 368)

- Changes in the economies of Latin American countries expanded the middle class. (p. 369)

### Content Vocabulary
creole, *peninsulare*, mestizo, Monroe Doctrine, caudillo

### Academic Vocabulary
dominate, emphasis, expand

### People to Identify
José de San Martín, Simón Bolívar, Antonio López de Santa Anna, Benito Juárez

### Places to Locate
Puerto Rico, Panama Canal, Haiti, Nicaragua

### Reading Objectives
1. Explain how the American Revolution inspired political changes in Latin America.
2. Describe the challenges Latin American nations faced in establishing representative governments.

### Reading Strategy
**Compare and Contrast** Create a Venn diagram comparing and contrasting colonial rule in Africa and in Latin America.

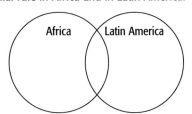

### Preview of Events

| ♦1800 | ♦1805 | ♦1810 | ♦1815 | ♦1820 | ♦1825 | ♦1830 |

**1810**
Mexico experiences its first revolt

**1821**
Mexico declares independence

**1825**
Most of Latin America becomes independent

## California Standards in This Section

*Reading this section will help you master these California History–Social Science standards.*

**10.2.1:** Compare the major ideas of philosophers and their effects on the democratic revolutions in England, the United States, France, and Latin America (e.g., John Locke, Charles-Louis Montesquieu, Jean-Jacques Rousseau, Simón Bolívar, Thomas Jefferson, James Madison.

**10.2.3:** Understand the unique character of the American Revolution, its spread to other parts of the world, and its continuing significance to other nations.

**10.4:** Students analyze patterns of global change in the era of New Imperialism in at least two of the following regions or countries: Africa, Southeast Asia, China, India, Latin America, and the Philippines.

**10.4.1:** Describe the rise of industrial economies and their link to imperialism and colonialism (e.g., the role played by national security and strategic advantage; moral issues raised by the search for national hegemony, Social Darwinism, and the missionary impulse; material issues such as land, resources, and technology.)

**10.4.2:** Discuss the locations of the colonial rule of such nations as England, France, Germany, Italy, Japan, the Netherlands, Russia, Spain, Portugal, and the United States.

# Nationalist Revolts

**Main Idea** Revolutionary ideas in Latin America were sparked by the successes of revolutions in North America.

**Reading Connection** Can you name a famous and successful slave revolt? Learn how a revolt on Hispaniola led to the creation of the first independent state in Latin America.

By the end of the eighteenth century, the new political ideals stemming from the successful revolution in North America were beginning to affect Latin America, and European control would soon be in peril. One of the men who took the lead in liberating South America from Spanish and Portuguese control was Simón Bolívar.

## Voices from the Past

On August 10, 1819, Simón Bolívar issued a proclamation to the people of New Granada (present-day Colombia):

> 66 Granadans! America's day is come; no human power can stay the course of nature guided by the hand of Providence. Join your efforts to those of your brothers: Venezuela marches with me to free you, as in past years you marched with me to free Venezuela. Already our advance guard fills whole provinces of your territory with the luster of its arms; and the same advance guard, powerfully aided, will hurl the destroyed of New Granada into the seas. The sun will not have completed the course of its present round through the heavens without beholding in all your territory the proud altars of liberty. 99

Many revolutionaries in South America were idealistic, just like the revolutionaries in the British colonies. They wanted to amend society. The social class structure that existed in Latin America, however, played a big role in how the revolutions occurred and what they achieved.

Social classes divided Latin America. *Peninsulares,* at the top, held all important positions. Creoles controlled land and business but were seen as second-class citizens by *peninsulares.* Mestizos were the largest group but worked as servants or laborers.

**Prelude to Revolution** The creole elites were especially influenced by revolutionary ideals. **Creoles** were descendants of Europeans born in Latin America and lived there permanently. They found the principles of the equality of all people in the eyes of the law, free trade, and a free press very attractive. In addition, they, along with a growing class of merchants, disliked the domination of their trade by Spain and Portugal.

Creoles deeply resented the *peninsulares,* Spanish and Portuguese officials who resided temporarily in Latin America for political and economic gain and then returned to their mother countries. These Europeans **dominated** Latin America and drained the Americas of their wealth.

The creole elites soon began to denounce the rule of the Spanish and Portuguese. At the beginning of the nineteenth century, Napoleon's wars provided them with an opportunity for change. When Napoleon overthrew the monarchies of Spain and Portugal, the authority of the Spaniards and Portuguese in their colonial empires was severely weakened. Between 1807 and 1825, revolutionary movements were able to succeed against the Spanish and Portuguese. Most of Latin America became independent.

Before the main independence movements began, an unusual revolution took place in the French colony of Saint Domingue, on the island of Hispaniola. Led by François-Dominique Toussaint-Louverture (TOO•SAN LOO•vuhr•TYUR), more than 100,000 slaves rose in revolt and seized control of all of Hispaniola. On January 1, 1804, the western part of Hispaniola, now called Haiti, announced its freedom and became the first independent state in Latin America.

✓ **Reading Check** **Describing** How did Napoleon's wars affect Latin America?

▼ *Portrait of Simón Bolívar*

▲ *Father Hidalgo leads Mexicans in revolt against the Spaniards.*

**Revolt in Mexico** Beginning in 1810, Mexico, too, experienced a revolt. The first real hero of Mexican independence was Miguel Hidalgo, a parish priest in a small village about a hundred miles (160 km) from Mexico City.

Hidalgo, who had studied the French Revolution, roused the local Native Americans and **mestizos** (people of European and Native American descent) to free themselves from the Spanish: "My children, this day comes to us as a new dispensation. Are you ready to receive it? Will you be free? Will you make the effort to recover from the hated Spaniards the lands stolen from your forefathers 300 years ago?"

On September 16, 1810, a crowd of Native Americans and mestizos, armed with clubs, machetes, and a few guns, formed a mob army to attack the Spaniards. Hidalgo was an inexperienced military leader, however, and his forces were soon crushed. A military court sentenced Hidalgo to death, but his memory lived on. In fact, September 16, the first day of the uprising, is Mexico's Independence Day.

The participation of Native Americans and mestizos in Mexico's revolt against Spanish control frightened both creoles and *peninsulares* there. Afraid of the masses, they cooperated in defeating the popular revolutionary forces. Conservative elites—both creoles and *peninsulares*—then decided to overthrow Spanish rule as a way of preserving their own power. They selected a creole military leader, Agustín de Iturbide (ee•tur•BEE•thay), as their leader.

In 1821, Mexico declared its independence from Spain. Iturbide named himself emperor in 1822 but was deposed in 1823. Mexico then became a republic.

**Revolts in South America** **José de San Martín** of Argentina and **Simón Bolívar** of Venezuela, both members of the creole elite, were hailed as the "Liberators of South America." These men led revolutions throughout the continent. San Martín believed that the Spaniards must be removed from all of South America if any South American nation was to be free.

By 1810, the forces of San Martín had liberated Argentina from Spanish authority. Bolívar began the struggle for independence in Venezuela in 1810 and then went on to lead revolts in New Granada (Colombia) and Ecuador.

In January 1817, San Martín led his forces over the Andes to attack the Spanish in Chile. The journey was an amazing feat. Two-thirds of the pack mules and horses died during the trip. Soldiers suffered from lack of oxygen and severe cold while crossing mountain passes that were more than two miles (3.2 km) above sea level.

The arrival of San Martín's forces in Chile completely surprised the Spaniards. Spanish forces were badly defeated at the Battle of Chacabuco on February 12, 1817. In 1821, San Martín moved on to Lima, Peru, the center of Spanish authority.

Convinced that he could not complete the liberation of Peru alone, San Martín welcomed the arrival of Bolívar and his forces. The last significant Spanish force in Peru was crushed at Ayacucho on December 9, 1824.

By the end of 1824, Peru, Uruguay, Paraguay, Colombia, Venezuela, Argentina, Bolivia, and Chile had all become free states. Earlier, in 1822, the prince regent of Brazil had declared Brazil's independence from Portugal. The Central American states had become independent in 1823. In 1838 and 1839, they divided

**HISTORY Online**

**Web Activity** Visit the *Glencoe World History–Modern Times* Web site at **wh.mt.glencoe.com** and click on **Chapter 6–Student Web Activity** to learn more about independence movements in Latin America.

▲ *Painting of early twentieth-century coffee plantation by Candido Portinari*

into five republics: Guatemala, El Salvador, Honduras, Costa Rica, and Nicaragua.

In the early 1820s, only one major threat remained to the newly won independence of the Latin American states. Ever since the Congress of Vienna of 1815, the leading nations of Europe, the Concert of Europe, had agreed to act together on international issues. Most of them now favored the use of troops to restore Spanish control in Latin America. The British, however, disagreed because they were building up a profitable trade with these countries. They proposed joint action with the United States to block European action.

Distrustful of British motives, United States president James Monroe acted alone in 1823. He declared that the American continents were "henceforth not to be considered as subjects for future colonization by any European powers." The president's proclamation, later called the **Monroe Doctrine,** was a bold act, because the United States might not have been able to back up its new policy if challenged.

More important to Latin American independence than American words, however, was Britain's navy. Other European powers feared British naval power, which stood between Latin America and any European invasion force.

✓**Reading Check** **Evaluating** How did the French Revolution help inspire the revolution in Mexico?

## Difficulties of Nation Building

**Main Idea** After they became independent, Latin American nations faced a staggering range of problems.

**Reading Connection** Have you heard it said that most Americans describe themselves as middle class? Read to learn about the social groups in Latin America in the 1800s.

Between 1830 and 1870, Latin American nations faced very serious problems. The wars for independence had resulted in a staggering loss of people, property, and livestock. Unsure of their precise boundaries, the new nations also fought with one another in some cases to settle border disputes. Poor roads, a lack of railroads, thick jungles, and mountains made communication, transportation, and national unity difficult. Finally, over the course of the nineteenth century, these new nations became economically dependent on Western nations as they had been during the colonial period.

**Rule of the Caudillos** Most Latin American nations began with republican governments, but they had little political experience. Soon after independence, strong leaders known as **caudillos** gained control.

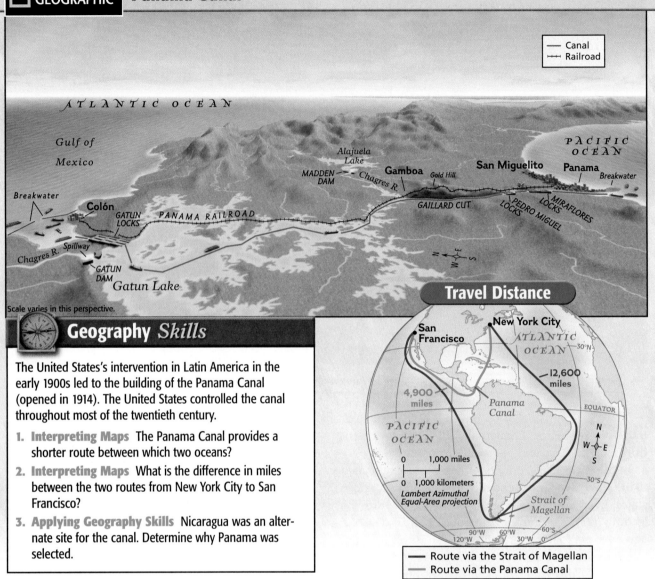

## NATIONAL GEOGRAPHIC  Panama Canal

— Canal
+++ Railroad

*Scale varies in this perspective.*

### Geography *Skills*

The United States's intervention in Latin America in the early 1900s led to the building of the Panama Canal (opened in 1914). The United States controlled the canal throughout most of the twentieth century.

1. **Interpreting Maps** The Panama Canal provides a shorter route between which two oceans?
2. **Interpreting Maps** What is the difference in miles between the two routes from New York City to San Francisco?
3. **Applying Geography Skills** Nicaragua was an alternate site for the canal. Determine why Panama was selected.

**Travel Distance**

— Route via the Strait of Magellan
— Route via the Panama Canal

Caudillos ruled chiefly by military force and were usually supported by the landed elites. Many kept the new national states together. Some were also modernizers who built roads and canals, ports, and schools. Others were destructive.

**Antonio López de Santa Anna,** for example, was often in power in Mexico between 1833 to 1855. He misused state funds, halted reforms, and created chaos. In 1835, American settlers in the Mexican state of Texas revolted.

Texas gained its independence in 1836 and United States statehood in 1845. War between Mexico and the United States soon followed (1846–1848). Mexico was defeated and lost almost one-half of its territory to the United States in the war with Mexico.

Fortunately, Santa Anna's disastrous rule was followed by an era of reform from 1855 to 1876. **Benito Juárez** dominated the era and instituted

many reforms that helped Mexico's poorest citizens. Juárez grew up in a poor family himself. The son of Mexican Indians from the Zapotec nation, he became a national hero for many peasants. His reforms included separation of church and state, education reform, and distributing land to the poor.

Other caudillos, such as Juan Manuel de Rosa in Argentina, gained popular support and brought about radical change. Unfortunately, the caudillo's authority depended on his personal power. When he died or lost power, civil wars often erupted.

**A New Imperialism** Political independence brought economic independence, but old patterns were quickly reestablished. Instead of Spain and Portugal, Great Britain now dominated the Latin American economy. British merchants moved into Latin

## Panama Canal Locks

1. A ship arrives from the Atlantic Ocean or the Pacific Ocean.

2. The ship enters the first lock and steel gates close behind it. Water flows into the lock from an artificial lake. When the water reaches the level of the next higher lock, gates open and the ship moves forward.

3. Electric towing locomotives called mules pull the ship by cables through the locks.

4. In a descending lock, water is drained to the level of the next lower lock and the ship advances.

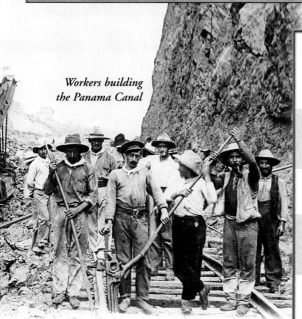

*Workers building the Panama Canal*

## Panama Canal Facts

• In 1534, Holy Roman Emperor Charles V ordered the first survey of a proposed canal route across the Isthmus of Panama. The survey came back "impossible."

• The canal was constructed in two stages: between 1881 and 1888 by a French company and between 1904 and 1914 by the United States.

• The canal is 51 miles (82 km) long. The average time a ship spends in transit is 8 to 10 hours.

• There are 6 pairs of locks, or a total of 12 locks. Each lock is 1,000 feet (305 m) long and 110 feet (34 m) wide. The lock system lifts ships 85 feet (26 m) above sea level.

• About 140 million tons (127 million t) of commercial cargo pass through the canal each year.

America in large numbers, and British investors poured in funds. Old trade patterns soon reemerged.

Latin America continued to serve as a source of raw materials and foodstuffs for the industrial nations of Europe and the United States. Exports included wheat, tobacco, wool, sugar, coffee, and hides. At the same time, finished consumer goods, especially textiles, were imported.

The **emphasis** on exporting raw materials and importing finished products ensured the ongoing domination of the Latin American economy by foreigners. Latin American countries remained economic colonies of Western nations, even though they were no longer political colonies.

**Persistent Inequality** A fundamental, underlying problem for all of the new Latin American nations was the domination of society by the landed elites. Large estates remained a way of life in Latin America. By 1848, for example, the Sánchez Navarro family in Mexico possessed 17 estates made up of 16 million acres (6,480,000 ha). Estates were often so large that they could not even be farmed efficiently.

Land remained the basis of wealth, social prestige, and political power throughout the nineteenth century. Landed elites ran governments, controlled courts, and kept a system of inexpensive labor. These landowners made enormous profits by growing single, specialized crops, such as coffee, for export. The masses, with no land to grow basic food crops, experienced dire poverty.

✓ **Reading Check** **Describing** What were some of the difficulties faced by the new Latin American republics?

# Political Change in Latin America

**Main Idea** Many Latin American governments patterned their new constitutions after the United States.

**Reading Connection** Can you think of a recent example when the United States demonstrated its power in the world? Read to learn how the United States extended its influence over countries in Latin America.

After 1870, Latin American governments, led by large landowners, wrote constitutions similar to those of the United States and European democracies. The ruling elites were careful to keep their power by limiting voting rights, however.

**The United States in Latin America** By 1900, the United States, which had emerged as a world power, had begun to interfere in the affairs of its southern neighbors. As a result of the Spanish-American War (1898), Cuba became a United States protectorate, and **Puerto Rico** was annexed to the United States.

In 1903, the United States supported a rebellion that enabled Panama to separate itself from Colombia and establish a new nation. In return, the United States was granted control of a strip of land 10 miles (16.09 km) wide running from coast to coast in Panama. There, the United States built the **Panama Canal,** which was opened in 1914.

American investments in Latin America soon expanded, as did American resolve to protect those investments. Beginning in 1898, American military forces were sent to Cuba, Mexico, Guatemala, Honduras, Nicaragua, Panama, Colombia, Haiti, and the Dominican Republic to protect American interests.

Some expeditions remained for many years. United States Marines were in **Haiti** from 1915 to 1934, and **Nicaragua** was occupied from 1912 to 1933. Increasing numbers of Latin Americans began to resent this interference from the "big bully" to the north.

**Revolution in Mexico** In some countries, large landowners supported dictators who looked out for the interests of the ruling elite. Porfirio Díaz, who ruled Mexico between 1877 and 1911, created a conservative, centralized government with the support of the army, foreign capitalists, large landowners, and the Catholic Church. All these groups benefited from their alliance. However, forces for change in Mexico led to a revolution.

During Díaz's dictatorial reign, the wages of workers had declined. Much of the Indian population owned no land, whereas about a thousand families owned almost all of Mexico. When a liberal landowner, Francisco Madero, forced Díaz from power in 1911, he opened the door to a wider revolution.

Madero's ineffectiveness increased the demand for agrarian reform. This new call for reform was led by Emiliano Zapata. Zapata aroused the masses of landless peasants and began to seize the estates of wealthy landholders.

Between 1910 and 1920, the Mexican Revolution caused great damage to the Mexican economy. Finally, a new constitution enacted in 1917 set up a government led by a president, created land-reform policies, established limits on foreign investors, and set an agenda to help the workers. The revolution also led to an outpouring of patriotism. Intellectuals and artists sought to capture what was unique about Mexico, with special emphasis on its past.

*Picturing* **History**

United States Marines hoist the American flag following a United States victory in the Spanish-American War. What territories in addition to Cuba came under American control as a result of the Spanish-American War?

**Reading Check** **Interpreting** What were the positive and negative effects of the Mexican Revolution?

# Economic Change

Changes in the economies of Latin American countries expanded the middle class.

**Reading Connection** Can you recall what groups made up the middle classes in Western Europe in the 1800s? As you read, compare those groups with middle-class groups in Latin America.

▲ *The seaside promenade in Montevideo, Uruguay, in the early twentieth century*

After 1870, Latin America began an age of prosperity based to a large extent on the export of a few basic items. These included wheat and beef from Argentina, coffee from Brazil, coffee and bananas from Central America, and sugar and silver from Peru. These foodstuffs and raw materials were largely exchanged for finished goods—textiles, machines, and luxury items—from Europe and the United States. After 1900, Latin Americans also increased their own industrialization, especially by building textile, food-processing, and construction material factories.

One result of the prosperity that came from increased exports was growth in the middle sectors (divisions) of Latin American society—lawyers, merchants, shopkeepers, businesspeople, schoolteachers, professors, bureaucrats, and military officers. These middle sectors accounted for only 5 to 10 percent of the population, hardly enough in numbers to make up a true middle class. Nevertheless, after 1900, the middle sectors of society continued to **expand.**

Regardless of the country in which they lived, middle-class Latin Americans shared some common characteristics. They lived in the cities; sought education and decent incomes; and saw the United States as a model, especially in regard to industrialization.

The middle sectors in Latin America sought liberal reform, not revolution. Once they had the right to vote, they generally sided with the landholding elites.

✓ **Reading Check** **Evaluating** What caused the growth of a middle class in Latin America?

**HISTORY** *Online* **Study Central**

For help with the concepts in this section of *Glencoe World History–Modern Times,* go to wh.mt.glencoe.com and click on **Study Central.**

# SECTION 4 ASSESSMENT

### Checking for Understanding

1. **Vocabulary** Define: creole, *peninsulare,* dominate, mestizo, Monroe Doctrine, caudillo, emphasis, expand.

2. **People** Identify: José de San Martín, Simón Bolívar, Antonio López de Santa Anna, Benito Juárez.

3. **Places** Locate: Puerto Rico, Panama Canal, Haiti, Nicaragua.

### Reviewing Big Ideas

4. **Describe** British motives for protecting Latin American states.

### Critical Thinking

5. **Historical Analysis** **Sequence and Change** Why did eliminating European domination of Latin America not bring significant change? **CA CS 2**

6. **Organizing Information** Fill in a chart like the one below to identify which country exported each product listed.

| Product | Country |
|---|---|
| coffee | |
| bananas and coffee | |
| beef and wheat | |
| sugar and silver | |

### Analyzing Visuals

7. **Describe** the painting on page 364. What action is taking place? How would you describe the emotions of the people in the scene? How has the painter tried to convey the importance of the event?

### Writing About History

8. **Expository Writing** Why did Latin American countries remain economic colonies of Western nations when they were no longer political colonies? Write a brief essay explaining why this happened. **CA 10WA2.3**

*Imperialism has been explained in many different ways. A Social Darwinist, a Presbyterian missionary, and a Marxist account for differing viewpoints of the system in the excerpts below.*

## SOURCE 1: The Standpoint of a Social Darwinist

*In this 1900 lecture, the British mathematician Karl Pearson stated his belief in Social Darwinism, which argued that some nations or races were more fit than others to survive and to rule.*

If you bring the white man into contact with the black, you too often suspend the very process of natural selection on which the evolution of a higher type depends. You get superior and inferior races living on the same soil, and that coexistence is demoralizing for both. They naturally sink into the position of master and servant, if not admittedly or covertly into that of slave-owner and slave. Frequently they inter-cross, and if the bad stock be raised the good is lowered. . . . Thus it comes about that when a struggle for existence between races is suspended, the solution of great problems may be unnaturally postponed; instead of the slow, stern processes of evolution, cataclysmal solutions are prepared for the future. . . .

*Christian missionary in the South Seas*

. . . You may say: Let us cease to struggle; let us leave the lands of the world to the races that cannot profit by them to the full; let us cease to compete in the markets of the world. Well, we could do it, if we were a small nation living off the produce of our own soil, and a soil so worthless that no other race envied it and sought to appropriate it. We should cease to advance; but then we should naturally give up progress as a good which comes through suffering. I say it is impossible for a small rural community to stand apart from the world-contest and to **stagnate**[1], if no more powerful nation wants its possessions.

## SOURCE 2: A Presbyterian Missionary on British Imperialism

*John Patton used religion to argue that the British government should annex the South Sea islands. In an 1883 letter to the government, he listed his reasons, some of which are excerpted below.*

2. The sympathy of the New Hebrides natives are all with Great Britain, hence they long for British protection, while they fear and hate the French, who appear eager to annex the group, because they have seen the way the French have treated the native races in . . . other South Sea islands. . . .

4. All the men and all the money used in civilizing and Christianizing the New Hebrides have been British. Now fourteen missionaries and the Dayspring mission ship, and about 150 native evangelists and teachers are employed in the above work on this group, in which over 6000 yearly of British and British-colonial money is expended. . . .

8. The thirteen islands of this group on which life and property are now comparatively safe, the 8000 professed Christians on the group, and all the

> ———————————
> [1]**stagnate:** stop moving

churches formed from among them are, by God's blessing, the fruits of the labors of British missionaries, who, at great toil, expense, and loss of life have translated, got printed, and taught the natives to read the Bible in part or in whole in nine different languages of this group, while 70,000 at least are longing and ready for the gospel. . . .

For the above reasons . . . we sincerely hope and pray that you will do all possible to get Victoria and the other colonial governments to help and unite in urging Great Britain at once to take possession of the New Hebrides group. Whether looked at in the interests of humanity, or of Christianity, or commercially, or politically, sure it is most desirable that they should at once be British possessions.

## SOURCE 3: Lenin Condemns Imperialism

*Lenin published this attack on imperialism in 1916, a year before he led the Bolshevik Revolution in Russia. Lenin believed that imperialism represented the last stage of monopoly capitalism and that it would be followed by socialism.*

The enormous dimensions of finance capital concentrated in a few hands and creating an extremely extensive and close network of ties and relationships which subordinate not only the small and medium, but also even the very small capitalists and small masters, on the one hand, and the intense struggle waged against other national state groups of financiers for the division of the world and domination over other countries, on the other hand, cause the wholesale transition of the possessing classes to the side of imperialism. . . .

We have seen that the economic **quintessence**[2] of imperialism is monopoly capitalism. . . . We must take special note of the . . . principal form of monopoly, or the . . . principal manifestations of monopoly capitalism, which are characteristic of the epoch under review.

. . . monopolies have accelerated the capture of the most important sources of raw materials . . . The monopoly of the most important sources of raw

➤ ──────────────────────
[2]**quintessence:** the essence of a thing

materials has enormously increased the power of big capital, and has sharpened the **antagonism**[3] between **cartelised**[4] and non-cartelised industry. . . .

. . . monopoly has grown out of colonial policy. To the numerous "old" motives of colonial policy, finance capital has added the struggle for the sources of raw materials, for the export of capital, for "spheres of influence" . . . [and] for economic territory in general. . . . when nine-tenths of Africa had been seized (approximately by 1900), when the whole world had been divided up, there was inevitably ushered in a period of colonial monopoly and, consequently, a period of particularly intense struggle for the division and redivision of the world. . . .

The receipt of high monopoly profits by the capitalists . . . makes it economically possible for them to corrupt certain sections of the working class. . . . The intensification of antagonism between the imperialist nations for the division of the world increases this striving. And so there is created that bond between imperialism and opportunism.

➤ ──────────────────────
[3]**antagonism:** opposition
[4]**cartelised:** businesses that have joined to fix prices and limit competition

## DBQ  Document-Based Questions

### Historical Analysis  CA HR 1, HR 2

**Source 1:** Which statement in this piece best expresses Karl Pearson's belief in Social Darwinism?

**Source 2:** How does John Patton justify Great Britain's right to take possession of the New Hebrides islands?

**Source 3:** According to Lenin, what is the only true motive of imperialists?

### Comparing and Contrasting Sources

1. How do Sources 1 and 2 justify imperialism as being in the best interest of the groups taken over?
   **CA 10RL3.5**

2. Sources 1 and 2 use Social Darwinism and religion to justify imperialism. How would Lenin respond to these justifications?

## Chapter Summary

**The Age Of Imperialism**
The imperialist powers of the nineteenth century conquered weaker countries and carved up the lands they seized. Their actions had a lasting effect on the world, especially the conquered peoples of Asia and Africa. The chart below organizes selected events that occurred during the age of imperialism according to four themes.

### Movement

- Imperialistic nations set up colonies and protectorates.
- Christian missionaries preach in Africa and Asia.
- Cecil Rhodes makes a fortune in South Africa.

### Change

- Ferdinand de Lesseps completes the Suez Canal in 1869.
- King Leopold II of Belgium colonizes the Congo Basin.
- The United States gains new territory after the Spanish-American War.
- The Panama Canal opens in 1914.

### Reaction

- The British East India Company controls India.
- Afrikaners set up independent republics.

### Nationalism

- The United States creates the Monroe Doctrine in 1823.
- In May 1857, the sepoys rebel against British commanders.
- Afrikaners fight the British in the Boer War from 1899 to 1902.

Standards 10.4, 10.4.1, 10.4.2, 10.4.3, 10.4.4

## Reviewing Content Vocabulary

*On a sheet of paper, use each of these terms in a sentence.*

1. New Imperialism
2. protectorate
3. indirect rule
4. direct rule
5. annex
6. indigenous
7. sepoy
8. viceroy
9. creole
10. *peninsulare*
11. mestizo
12. Monroe Doctrine
13. caudillo

## Reviewing Academic Vocabulary

*On a sheet of paper, use each of these terms in a sentence that reflects the term's meaning in the chapter.*

14. exploit
15. impose
16. regime
17. conflicting
18. consequence
19. attitude
20. transfer
21. dominate
22. emphasis
23. expand

## Reviewing the Main Ideas

**Section 1**

24. Why did European states wish to establish colonies?

25. Which country in Southeast Asia remained independent? Why?

**Section 2**

26. By 1914, what European countries had divided up Africa?

27. Describe the zamindar system, which was used by the British in India.

**Section 3**

28. What were the goals of Mohandas Gandhi?

29. What were the effects of British rule in India?

**Section 4**

30. Why was the Haitian revolution unique?

31. List the powers and privileges of the landed elites in Latin America.

## Critical Thinking

32. **Analyzing** Explain the circumstances surrounding the building of the Panama Canal. How did the United States benefit from this undertaking?

33. **Reading Skill** **Comparing and Contrasting** Discuss the various concerns of people under colonial rule. Did social class affect how they viewed colonial power? How were the concerns of different social classes similar? How were they different?

34. **Explaining** Two major European powers settled at different times in southern Africa. What war was fought between them and why?

35. **Evaluating** You are a local ruler in your country. You deeply resent the colonial power that has asked you to rule in its interest. Do you continue to rule or do you resign? What are the consequences of your decision?

36. **Analyzing** Trade, resources, and cheap labor played a large role in the colonization efforts of Europeans. But religion was also a focus. Why would religious missionaries suggest that colonization was a desirable practice?

37. **Drawing Conclusions** Simón Bolívar is considered to be the George Washington of South America. Given what is said about Bolívar in the chapter and what you know about Washington, decide whether or not you think the comparison is fair. Explain your decision.

## Writing About History

38. **Historical Analysis** **Evaluating Evidence** Review what is written in the text about the two different ways colonized people were ruled, direct and indirect rule. Then, consider the evidence and write a short paper evaluating which system stimulated the most resistance. **CA HR3**

39. **Big Idea** Pretend you are a British colonist who has been living abroad for a year. Decide whether you are for or against colonialism and write a letter to your family convincing them of your views. Use examples from the text or your own research. **CA 10WA2.1**

**DBQ** **Document-Based Questions**

**Analyzing Sources** Read the following quote by Miguel Hidalgo:

My children, this day comes to us as a new dispensation. Are you ready to receive it? Will you be free? Will you make the effort to recover from the hated Spanish the lands stolen from your forefathers 300 years ago?""

40. Describe the tone of this quote. What emotions is Hidalgo trying to arouse? Is Hidalgo correct when he claims that the Spanish stole the land? **CA 10RL3.9**

41. Do you think Native Americans in North America are justified in feeling that their lands were stolen? Why or why not?

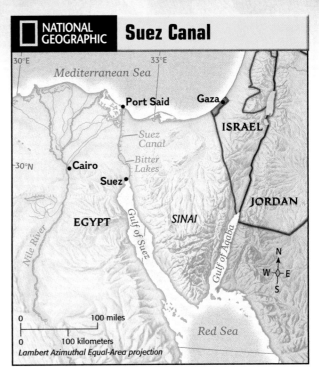

**NATIONAL GEOGRAPHIC** **Suez Canal**

## Analyzing Maps and Charts

Use your text and the map above to answer the following questions.

42. Approximately how long is the Suez Canal?

43. Why is control of the Suez Canal so important?

44. What alternative transportation exists across the land masses surrounding the Suez Canal?

45. What route was used for trade and transportation in this area prior to the building of the Suez Canal?

**Standards Practice**

**Directions: Choose the best answer to the following question.**

46. Which of the following was a consequence of British colonial rule in India?

A the defeat of the Mogul dynasty

B the popularity of the joint-stock company

C the exploitation of resources

D the Berlin Conference of 1884

**CA Standard 10.4.3** Explain imperialism from the perspective of the colonizers and the colonized and the varied immediate and long-term responses by the people under colonial rule.

# East Asia Under Challenge

## ❧ *The Big Ideas* ❧

### SECTION 1: The Decline of the Qing Dynasty

**Nations compete for natural resources and strategic advantages over other nations.** As the Qing dynasty declined, Western nations increased their economic involvement with China.

### SECTION 2: Revolution in China

**Nations compete for natural resources and strategic advantages over other nations.** Reforms by Sun Yat-sen led to a revolution in China, and the arrival of Westerners brought changes to its culture and economy.

### SECTION 3: Rise of Modern Japan

**Nations compete for natural resources and strategic advantages over other nations.** Western intervention opened Japan to trade, and the interaction between Japan and Western nations led to a modern industrial Japanese society.

***World History—Modern Times Video*** *The Chapter 7 video, "The Russo-Japanese War," chronicles the conflict between Russia and Japan.*

*Chinese workers pack tea for export.*

**1854**
Treaty of Kanagawa initiates United States–Japanese relations

**1860**
Europeans seize Chinese capital of Beijing

| 1830 | 1840 | 1850 | 1860 | 1870 |

**1841**
British forces seize island of Hong Kong

**1842**
Treaty of Nanjing establishes trade between China and Great Britain

**1868**
Meiji Restoration begins

A British steamship attacks Chinese naval forces off the coast of China during the Opium War.

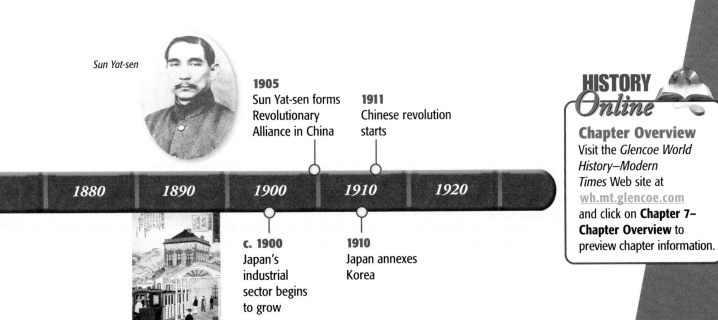

*Sun Yat-sen*

**1905**
Sun Yat-sen forms Revolutionary Alliance in China

**1911**
Chinese revolution starts

1880    1890    1900    1910    1920

**c. 1900**
Japan's industrial sector begins to grow

**1910**
Japan annexes Korea

*Meiji-era train depot*

**HISTORY Online**

**Chapter Overview**
Visit the *Glencoe World History–Modern Times* Web site at **wh.mt.glencoe.com** and click on **Chapter 7– Chapter Overview** to preview chapter information.

## Reading Skill ⟩ Questioning

Authors try to follow logical thinking as they write. They think about the questions a reader would naturally ask and try to handle those questions as they present information. An attentive reader can plug into this method of the author by asking questions of the text.

An easy way to practice asking questions is to turn the headings into questions. For example, the heading "The Boxer Rebellion" in this chapter can be turned into: "What was the Boxer Rebellion?" or "Why would it be called the Boxer Rebellion?" In most cases, you can expect that the question will be answered in the first paragraph. Using this technique will help you remember and understand things more quickly.

*Read the following passage from the chapter and see how the questions about the Boxer Rebellion were answered.*

### QUESTIONING

Take note of the supporting details the author has provided to answer the questions you would naturally ask about the heading.

**Boxer** was the popular name given to members of a secret organization called the Society of Harmonious Fists. Members practiced a system of exercise—a form of shadowboxing, or boxing with an imaginary opponent—that they thought would protect them from bullets.

The Boxers were upset by the foreign takeover of Chinese lands. Their slogan was "destroy the foreigner." They especially disliked Christian missionaries from the West and Chinese converts to Christianity who seemed to threaten Chinese traditions. At the beginning of 1900, Boxer bands roamed the countryside and slaughtered foreign missionaries and Chinese Christians.

### Apply the Skill

Read these headings and turn them into questions. Check to see if the paragraph answers your questions.

- **Decline of the Qing Dynasty**

- **Causes of Decline**

- **The Opium War**

**Historical Interpretation: Standard HI 2** *Students recognize the complexity of historical causes and effects, including the limitations on determining cause and effect.*

Historians recognize that most historical events don't happen in isolation. They occur because of a series of causes and effects, both within a particular geographical area and between various political units. A decision can also have both short-term and long-term results. Effects are not always intended.

*Read the following passage and notice the complex connection between the Meiji policy in Japan and the effect on farmers:*

- The Meiji leaders levied a new land tax, which was set at an annual rate of 3 percent of the estimated value of the land. The new tax was an excellent source of revenue for the government. However, it was quite burdensome for the farmers.

- Under the old system, farmers had paid a fixed percentage of their harvest to the landowners. In bad harvest years, they had owed little or nothing. Under the new system, the farmers had to pay the land tax every year, regardless of the quality of the harvest.

- As a result, in bad years, many peasants were unable to pay their taxes. This forced them to sell their lands to wealthy neighbors and become tenant farmers who paid rent to the new owners. By the end of the nineteenth century, about 40 percent of all farmers were tenants.

## Apply the Skill

Do you think the Meiji leaders originally intended for their taxes to turn farmers into tenants? Write a short paragraph in your own words describing how and why many farmers became tenants. Be sure to include a short bulleted list of the steps that led to this change.

# A Story That Matters

The Summer Palace in Beijing today

Palace interior

## Looting of the Summer Palace

*L*ike the countries of South Asia, Southeast Asia, and Africa, the nations of East Asia faced a growing challenge from the power of the West in the nineteenth century. In China, Westerners used their military superiority to pursue their goals.

In 1860, for example, Great Britain and France decided to retaliate against the Chinese, who had tried to restrict British and French activities. In July, combined British and French forces arrived on the outskirts of Beijing. There, they came upon the Old Summer Palace of the Chinese emperors. The soldiers were astounded by the riches they beheld and could not resist the desire to steal them.

Beginning on October 6, British and French troops moved through the palace. They took anything that looked valuable and smashed what they could not cart away. One British observer wrote, "You would see several officers and men of all ranks with their heads and hands brushing and knocking together in the same box." In another room, he said, "a scramble was going on over a collection of handsome state robes . . . others would be amusing themselves by taking shots at chandeliers."

Lord Elgin, leader of the British forces in China, soon restored order. After the Chinese took hostage and then murdered 20 British and French soldiers, however, Lord Elgin ordered the Old Summer Palace to be burned. Intimidated, the Chinese government agreed to Western demands.

### Why It Matters

The events of 1860 were part of a regular pattern in East Asia in the nineteenth century. Backed by European guns, European merchants and missionaries pressed for the right to carry out their activities in China and Japan. The Chinese and Japanese resisted but were eventually forced to open their doors to the foreigners. Unlike other Asian societies, however, both Japan and China were able to maintain their national independence.

**History and You** International contact continues to shrink differences among nations. Using the information in this chapter and outside research, create a chart comparing the development of the United States and Japan during the twentieth century. Include data on material goods as well as economic, political, or social trends.

# The Decline of the Qing Dynasty

## Guide to Reading

### Section Preview
As the Qing dynasty declined, Western nations increased their economic involvement with China.

**Main Idea**
- Pressure from the West and corruption and unrest from within led to the decline of the Qing dynasty. (p. 380)
- War broke out when the British refused to stop importing opium into China. (p. 380)
- The Tai Ping Rebellion reflected the discontent of the Chinese with the Qing dynasty. (p. 382)
- The Chinese government adopted the self-strengthening policy that reformers called for. (p. 383)
- Western nations and Japan set up spheres of influence in China to gain exclusive trading rights. (p. 384)

- The United States proposed an Open Door policy to guarantee it would have equal trading rights with European countries in China. (p. 385)
- Chinese anger with foreign control in their country led to the Boxer Rebellion. (p. 386)

### Content Vocabulary
extraterritoriality, self-strengthening, spheres of influence, Open Door policy, indemnity

### Academic Vocabulary
decline, ensure

### People to Identify
Hong Xiuquan, Guang Xu, Empress Dowager Ci Xi, John Hay

### Places to Locate
Guangzhou, Chang Jiang, Hong Kong

### Reading Objectives
1. Describe the internal problems that led to the decline of the Qing dynasty.
2. Identify the role that Western nations played in the Qing dynasty's decline.

### Reading Strategy
**Compare and Contrast** Create a chart like the one below comparing the Tai Ping and Boxer Rebellions.

|  | Tai Ping | Boxer |
|---|---|---|
| Reforms Demanded |  |  |
| Methods Used |  |  |

### Preview of Events

| ◆1840 | ◆1850 | ◆1860 | ◆1870 | ◆1880 | ◆1890 | ◆1900 |
|---|---|---|---|---|---|---|

**1839**
Opium War begins

**1850**
Tai Ping Rebellion begins

**1860**
European troops seize Chinese capital of Beijing

**1898**
Ci Xi opposes reforms

**1900**
Boxer Rebellion defeated

## California Standards in This Section

*Reading this section will help you master these California History–Social Science standards.*

**10.4:** Students analyze patterns of global change in the era of New Imperialism in at least two of the following regions or countries: Africa, Southeast Asia, China, India, Latin America, and the Philippines.

**10.4.2:** Discuss the locations of the colonial rule of such nations as England, France, Germany, Italy, Japan, the Netherlands, Russia, Spain, Portugal, and the United States.

**10.4.3:** Explain imperialism from the perspective of the colonizers and the colonized and the varied immediate and long-term responses by the people under colonial rule.

## Causes of Decline

**Main Idea** Pressure from the West and corruption and unrest from within led to the decline of the Qing dynasty.

**Reading Connection** Has your community experienced traffic and congestion because of population growth? Read about population stresses in China during the Qing dynasty.

In 1800, after a long period of peace and prosperity, the Qing dynasty of the Manchus was at the height of its power. A little over a century later, however, humiliated and harassed by the Western powers, the Qing dynasty collapsed.

One important reason for the abrupt **decline** and fall of the Qing dynasty was the intense external pressure applied to Chinese society by the modern West. However, internal changes also played a role.

## Voices from the Past

In the second half of the nineteenth century, calls for political reform were heard in China. A leading court official, Zhang Zhidong, argued against reform:

> ❝The doctrine of people's rights will bring us not a single benefit but a hundred evils. Are we going to establish a parliament? Among the Chinese scholars and people there are still many today who are content to be vulgar and rustic. They are ignorant of the general situation in the world, they do not understand the basic system of the state. They have not the most elementary idea about foreign countries. . . . Even supposing the confused and clamorous people are assembled in one house, for every one of them who is clear-sighted, there will be a hundred others whose vision is clouded; they will converse at random and talk as if in a dream—what use will it be?❞

After an extended period of growth, the Qing dynasty began to suffer from corruption, peasant unrest, and incompetence. Zhang's view prevailed, and no reforms were enacted.

These weaknesses of the Qing dynasty were made worse by rapid growth in the country's population. By 1900, there were 400 million people in China, an increase of 100 million in 100 years. Population growth created a serious food shortage. In the 1850s, one observer wrote, "Not a year passes in which a

▲ *Nobleman of the Qing dynasty*

terrific number of persons do not perish of famine in some part or other of China." The ships, guns, and ideas of foreigners highlighted the growing weakness of the Qing dynasty and probably hastened its end.

**Reading Check** **Examining** What factors led to the decline of the Qing dynasty?

## The Opium War

**Main Idea** War broke out when the British refused to stop importing opium into China.

**Reading Connection** What does the American government do to control illegal drugs? Read to learn how China addressed drug problems in China in the mid-1800s.

By 1800, Europeans had been in contact with China for more than two hundred years. European merchants, however, were restricted to a small trading outlet at **Guangzhou** (GWONG•JO), or Canton. The British did not like this arrangement.

The British also had an unfavorable trade balance in China. That is, they imported more goods from China than they exported to China. For years, Britain had imported tea, silk, and porcelain from the Chinese and sent Indian cotton to China to pay for these imports. The cotton, however, did not cover the entire debt, and the British were forced to pay for their imports with silver. The British sent increasing quantities of silver to China, especially in exchange for tea, which was in great demand by the British.

At first, the British tried to negotiate with the Chinese to improve the trade imbalance. When negotiations failed, the British turned to trading opium.

Opium, a highly addictive drug, was grown in northern India under the sponsorship of the British East India Company and then shipped directly to Chinese markets. Demand for opium in South China jumped dramatically. Soon, silver was flowing out of China and into the pockets of the officials of the British East India Company.

The Chinese reacted strongly. The British were not the first to import opium into China. The Chinese government had already seen opium's dangerous qualities and had made its trade illegal. They appealed to the British government on moral grounds to stop the traffic in opium. A government official wrote to Queen Victoria: "Suppose there were people from another country who carried opium for sale to England and seduced your people into buying and smoking it; certainly your honorable ruler would deeply hate it and be bitterly aroused."

The British refused to halt their activity, however. As a result, the Chinese government blockaded the foreign area in Guangzhou in order to force traders to surrender their chests of opium. The British responded with force, starting the Opium War (1839–1842).

The Chinese were no match for the British. British warships destroyed Chinese coastal and river forts. When a British fleet sailed almost unopposed up the **Chang Jiang** (Yangtze River) to Nanjing, the Qing dynasty made peace.

In the Treaty of Nanjing in 1842, the Chinese agreed to open five coastal ports to British trade, limit taxes on imported British goods, and pay for the costs of the war. China also agreed to give the British the island of **Hong Kong.** Nothing was said in the treaty about the opium trade. Moreover, in the five ports, Europeans lived in their own sections of town. They were subject not to Chinese laws but to their own laws. This practice was known as **extraterritoriality.**

The Opium War marked the beginning of the establishment of Western influence in China. For the time being, the Chinese tried to deal with the problem by pitting foreign countries against one another. Concessions granted to the British were offered to other Western nations, including the United States. Soon, thriving foreign areas were operating in the five treaty ports along the southern Chinese coast.

✓**Reading Check** **Summarizing** What did the British do to adjust their trade imbalance with China?

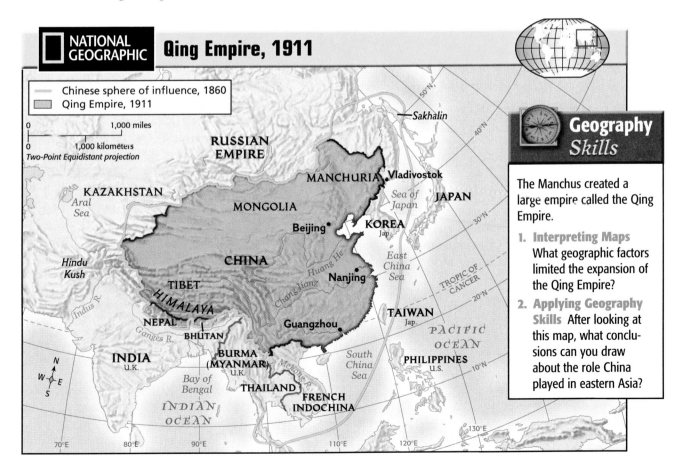

**NATIONAL GEOGRAPHIC**

**Qing Empire, 1911**

Chinese sphere of influence, 1860
Qing Empire, 1911

0        1,000 miles
0        1,000 kilometers
Two-Point Equidistant projection

RUSSIAN EMPIRE

Sakhalin

KAZAKHSTAN
Aral Sea

MANCHURIA · Vladivostok

Sea of Japan    JAPAN

MONGOLIA

Beijing ·

KOREA
Jap.

Hindu Kush

CHINA

Huang He

East China Sea

TIBET

Nanjing ·

Chang Jiang

TROPIC OF CANCER

HIMALAYA

Indus R.

NEPAL

Ganges R.    BHUTAN

Guangzhou ·

TAIWAN
Jap.

PACIFIC OCEAN

INDIA
U.K.

BURMA (MYANMAR)
U.K.

Mekong R.

South China Sea

PHILIPPINES
U.S.

Bay of Bengal    THAILAND

N
W   E
S

INDIAN OCEAN

FRENCH INDOCHINA

**Geography Skills**

The Manchus created a large empire called the Qing Empire.

1. **Interpreting Maps** What geographic factors limited the expansion of the Qing Empire?

2. **Applying Geography Skills** After looking at this map, what conclusions can you draw about the role China played in eastern Asia?

# The Tai Ping Rebellion

**Main Idea** The Tai Ping Rebellion reflected the discontent of the Chinese with the Qing dynasty.

**Reading Connection** Have you read about utopian communities in America in the 1800s? Read to learn about the kinds of social rules that were followed during the Tai Ping Rebellion.

In the meantime, the failure of the Chinese government to deal with pressing internal economic problems led to a peasant revolt, known as the Tai Ping (TIE PING) Rebellion (1850–1864). It was led by **Hong Xiuquan**, a Christian convert who viewed himself as a younger brother of Jesus Christ.

Hong was convinced that God had given him the mission of destroying the Qing dynasty. Joined by great crowds of peasants, Hong captured the town of Yong'an and proclaimed a new dynasty, the Heavenly Kingdom of Great Peace (*Tai Ping Tianguo* in Chinese—hence the name *Tai Ping Rebellion*).

The Tai Ping Rebellion appealed to many people because it called for social reforms. These reforms included giving land to all peasants and treating women as equals of men. Women even served in their own units in the Tai Ping army.

Hong's rebellion also called for people to give up private possessions. Peasants were to hold lands and farms in common, and money, food, and clothing were to be shared equally by all. Hong outlawed alcohol and tobacco and eliminated the practice of binding women's feet. The Chinese Communist Revolution of the twentieth century (see Chapter 16) would have similar social goals.

In March 1853, the rebels seized Nanjing, the second largest city of the empire, and massacred 25,000 men, women, and children. The revolt continued for 10 more years but gradually began to fall apart. Europeans came to the aid of the Qing dynasty when they realized the destructive nature of the Tai Ping forces. As one British observer noted, there was no hope "of any good ever coming of the rebel movement. They do nothing but burn, murder, and destroy."

In 1864, Chinese forces, with European aid, recaptured Nanjing and destroyed the remaining rebel force. The Tai Ping Rebellion was one of the most devastating civil wars in history. As many as 20 million people died in the course of the 14-year struggle.

# CONNECTIONS Past To Present

## The Return of Hong Kong to China

In 1984, Great Britain and China signed a joint declaration in which Britain agreed to return its colony of Hong Kong to China on July 1, 1997. China promised that Hong Kong would keep its free market, its capitalist economy, and its way of life. The formula was "one country, two systems."

In 1841, Hong Kong was a small island with a few fishing villages on the southeastern coast of China. A British naval force seized the island and used it as a port for shipping opium into China. A year later, after a humiliating defeat in the Opium War, China agreed to give the island of Hong Kong to Britain.

Later, the British took advantage of the declining power of China's Qing dynasty to gain additional lands next to Hong Kong. In 1860, the Chinese government granted the Kowloon Peninsula to Britain. In 1898, the Chinese granted the British a 99-year lease on the nearby New Territories, an area that provided much of the food for the colony of Hong Kong.

In the 1950s and 1960s, Hong Kong was filled with refugees from the new Communist regime in mainland China. The population of Hong Kong swelled to six million. The economy of Hong Kong boomed. Today, Hong Kong is the eighth-largest trading nation in the world.

◀ *Troops take down the British flag in Hong Kong in 1997.*

## Comparing Past and Present

Using outside sources, research the current political and cultural situation in Hong Kong. Explain what the formula "one country, two systems" means. Evaluate whether or not the formula has been successful since Hong Kong was returned to China.

▲ *European troops battle Tai Ping soldiers in Guangzhou during the Tai Ping Rebellion.*

Their struggle against Western powers made it hard for the Qing dynasty to deal with internal unrest. From 1856, the British and French were applying force to expand their trading privileges. In the Treaty of Tianjin of 1858, the Chinese agreed to legalize the opium trade and open new ports to foreign trade. They also gave up the Kowloon Peninsula to Britain. When the Chinese resisted parts of the treaty, the British seized Beijing.

**Reading Check** **Summarizing** What social reforms did the Tai Ping Rebellion demand?

## Efforts at Reform

**Main Idea** The Chinese government adopted the self-strengthening policy that reformers called for.

**Reading Connection** Do you know why reforms are adopted in your community? Read to find out why the Chinese government adopted the self-strengthening policy in the 1870s.

During the Tai Ping Rebellion, China's government had relied on regional warlords to recruit the troops necessary to restore order. The warlords had collected taxes to finance these private armies. After crushing the revolt, many warlords refused to dismiss their units. With the support of local leaders, they continued collecting taxes for their own use.

In its weakened state, the Qing court finally began to listen to reformers who supported a policy they called **"self-strengthening."** They wanted China to adopt Western technology, but to keep its Confucian values.

Some reformers wanted to change China's political institutions by introducing democracy. However, such ideas were too radical for most reformers. From the 1870s, the Chinese government tried to modernize its military forces and build up industry without imposing on the basic elements of Chinese culture. Railroads, weapons factories, and shipyards were built, but the Chinese value system remained unchanged.

**HISTORY Online**

**Web Activity** Visit the *Glencoe World History–Modern Times* Web site at wh.mt.glencoe.com and click on **Chapter 7– Student Web Activity** to learn more about Western influence in China.

**Reading Check** **Explaining** What was China's policy of "self-strengthening"?

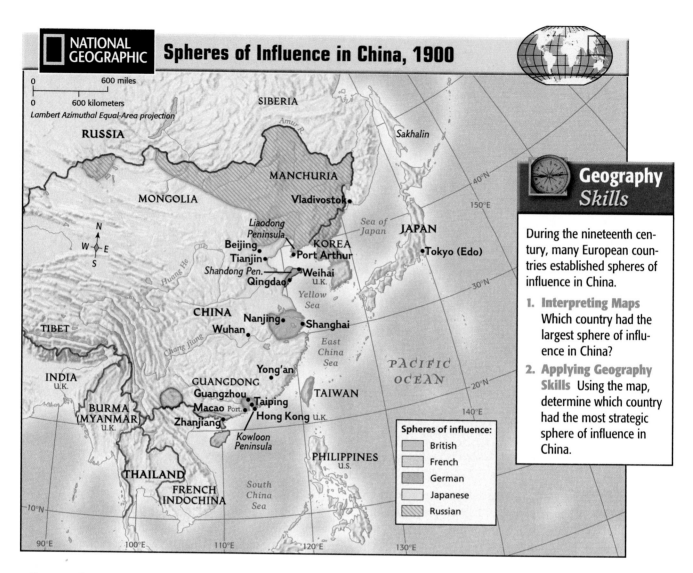

## NATIONAL GEOGRAPHIC
# Spheres of Influence in China, 1900

0 — 600 miles
0 — 600 kilometers
Lambert Azimuthal Equal-Area projection

RUSSIA

SIBERIA

Amur R.

Sakhalin

MANCHURIA

MONGOLIA

Vladivostok

Liaodong
Peninsula

Beijing
Tianjin

Shandong Pen.
Qingdao

KOREA
Port Arthur

Weihai
U.K.

Sea of
Japan

JAPAN

Tokyo (Edo)

Yellow
Sea

TIBET

CHINA
Nanjing
Wuhan

Shanghai

Chang Jiang

East
China
Sea

Huang He

INDIA
U.K.

Yong'an

GUANGDONG
Guangzhou
Macao  Port.
Zhanjiang

Taiping
Hong Kong U.K.

TAIWAN

PACIFIC
OCEAN

BURMA
(MYANMAR)
U.K.

Kowloon
Peninsula

THAILAND
FRENCH
INDOCHINA

South
China
Sea

PHILIPPINES
U.S.

**Spheres of influence:**
- British
- French
- German
- Japanese
- Russian

### Geography Skills

During the nineteenth century, many European countries established spheres of influence in China.

1. **Interpreting Maps** Which country had the largest sphere of influence in China?

2. **Applying Geography Skills** Using the map, determine which country had the most strategic sphere of influence in China.

# The Advance of Imperialism

**Main Idea** Western nations and Japan set up spheres of influence in China to gain exclusive trading rights.

**Reading Connection** Have American military forces ever overpowered another people? Read to learn how European powers gained trading rights in China.

In the end, the reforms did not help the Qing stay in power. The European advance into China continued during the last two decades of the nineteenth century, while internal conditions continued to deteriorate.

**Mounting Pressures** Russia took advantage of China's weakness to force it to give up territories north of the Amur River in Siberia. In Tibet, a struggle between Russia and Great Britain kept both powers from seizing the territory outright. This allowed Tibet to remain free from Chinese influence.

Even more ominous changes were taking place in the Chinese heartland. European states began to create **spheres of influence,** areas where the imperial powers had exclusive trading rights. After the Tai Ping Rebellion, warlords in the provinces began to negotiate directly with foreign nations. In return for money, the warlords granted these nations exclusive trading rights or railroad-building and mining privileges. In this way, Britain, France, Germany, Russia, and Japan all established spheres of influence in China.

In 1894, another blow weakened the Qing dynasty. China went to war with Japan over its inroads into Korea, a land that the Chinese had long controlled. The Chinese were soundly defeated. Japan then demanded and received the island of Taiwan (then called Formosa), and the Liaodong (LYOW•DOONG) Peninsula. Fearing Japan's growing power, however, the European powers forced Japan to give the Liaodong Peninsula back to China.

New pressures for Chinese territory soon arose. In 1897, two German missionaries were murdered by

Chinese rioters. Germany used this pretext to demand territories in the Shandong (SHON•DOONG) Peninsula. When the Chinese government approved the demand, other European nations made new claims on Chinese territory.

**Internal Crisis** This latest scramble for territory took place at a time of internal crisis in China. In the spring of 1898, the young emperor **Guang Xu** (GWANG SHYOO) launched a massive reform program based on changes in Japan (see Section 3). During the following weeks, known as the One Hundred Days of Reform, the emperor issued edicts calling for major political, administrative, and educational reforms. With these reforms, the emperor intended to modernize government bureaucracy by following Western models; to adopt a new educational system that would replace the traditional civil service examinations; to adopt Western-style schools, banks, and a free press; and to train the military to use modern weapons and Western fighting techniques.

Many conservatives at court, however, opposed a policy of copying the West. As one said, "An examination of the causes of success and failure in government reveals that . . . the adoption of foreignism leads to disorder." According to these conservatives, traditional Chinese rules needed to be reformed, not rejected in favor of Western ways.

Most important, the new reform program was opposed by the emperor's aunt, **Empress Dowager Ci Xi** (TSUH•SEE). She became a dominant force at court and opposed the emperor's reforms. With the aid of the imperial army, she eventually imprisoned the emperor and ended his reform efforts.

✓ **Reading Check** **Examining** How did foreign nations obtain trading rights in China at this time?

## Opening the Door to China

**Main Idea** The United States proposed an Open Door policy to guarantee it would have equal trading rights with European countries in China.

**Reading Connection** Have you heard U.S.-Chinese trade policy discussed? Read to learn how America gained access to the Chinese market in 1900.

As foreign pressure on the Qing dynasty grew, Great Britain and the United States feared that other nations would overrun China if its government collapsed. In 1899, U.S. secretary of state **John Hay** presented a proposal to **ensure** equal access to the Chinese market, while preserving China as a nation. When no other imperialist power opposed this idea, Hay proclaimed there was agreement on his Open Door policy.

In part, the **Open Door policy** reflected American concern for the survival of China, but it also reflected the interests of American businesses. These businesses wanted to operate in open markets and disliked the existing division of China into separate spheres of influence dominated by individual states. The Open Door policy did not end the system of spheres of influence, but it did loosen restrictions on trade among the imperialist powers within the spheres. The Open Door policy also helped to reduce imperialist hysteria over access to the China market. The policy lessened fears in Britain, France, Germany, and Russia that other powers would take advantage of China's weakness and attempt to dominate the China market for themselves.

✓ **Reading Check** **Analyzing** Why did the United States want an Open Door policy in China?

## People In History

### Ci Xi
**1835–1908—Chinese empress**

Empress Dowager Ci Xi, through her unwillingness to make significant reforms, helped bring about the overthrow of the Qing dynasty. Ci Xi was at first a low-ranking concubine to Emperor Xian Feng. Her position became influential in 1856, when she gave birth to the emperor's first and only son.

When the emperor died, Ci Xi ruled China on behalf of her son. Later, she ruled on behalf of her nephew Guang Xu. With the aid of conservatives at court and the imperial army, she had Guang Xu jailed in the palace.

Empress Dowager Ci Xi ruled China for almost 50 years, during a crucial period in the nation's history. She was well aware of her own power. "I have often thought that I am the cleverest woman who ever lived . . . I have 400 million people all dependent on my judgement."

# The Boxer Rebellion

**Main Idea** Chinese anger with foreign control in their country led to the Boxer Rebellion.

**Reading Connection** Does your family have particular traditions? Read to find out how Chinese people reacted when they felt their traditions were under threat in the early 1900s.

The Open Door policy came too late to stop the Boxer Rebellion. *Boxer* was the popular name given to members of a secret organization called the Society of Harmonious Fists. Members practiced a system of exercise—a form of shadowboxing, or boxing with an imaginary opponent—that they thought would protect them from bullets.

The Boxers were upset by the foreign takeover of Chinese lands. Their slogan was "destroy the foreigner." They especially disliked Christian missionaries from the West and Chinese converts to Christianity who seemed to threaten Chinese traditions. At the beginning of 1900, Boxer bands roamed the countryside and slaughtered foreign missionaries and Chinese Christians. Their victims also included foreign businessmen and even the German envoy to Beijing.

Response to the killings was immediate and overwhelming. An allied army consisting of 20,000 British, French, German, Russian, American, and Japanese troops attacked Beijing in August 1900. The army restored order and demanded more concessions from the Chinese government. The Chinese

▲ *Boxers are rounded up after the failed rebellion.*

government was forced to pay a heavy **indemnity**—a payment for damages—to the powers that had crushed the uprising. The imperial government was now weaker than ever.

✓**Reading Check** **Explaining** How did the Boxers get their name?

**HISTORY Online** **Study Central**

For help with the concepts in this section of *Glencoe World History–Modern Times,* go to wh.mt.glencoe.com and click on **Study Central.**

# SECTION 1 ASSESSMENT

## Checking for Understanding

1. **Vocabulary** Define: decline, extraterritoriality, self-strengthening, spheres of influence, ensure, Open Door policy, indemnity.

2. **People and Events** Identify: Hong Xiuquan, Guang Xu, Empress Dowager Ci Xi, John Hay.

3. **Places** Locate: Guangzhou, Chang Jiang, Hong Kong.

### Reviewing Big Ideas

4. **Analyze** how the Tai Ping Rebellion helped to weaken the Qing dynasty.

## Critical Thinking

5. **Historical Analysis** **Cause and Effect** Why did European nations agree to follow the Open Door policy proposed by the United States? **CA HI 2**

6. **Organizing Information** Create a diagram listing the factors that led to the decline of the Qing dynasty.

External Factors

Internal Factors

## Analyzing Visuals

7. **Examine** the illustration of the Tai Ping Rebellion on page 383. What visual evidence shows British and Chinese determination?

### Writing About History

8. **Expository Writing** Using outside sources, research, write, and present a report explaining the effects of population on modern China. Remember to include government laws enacted to curtail population growth, and the consequences of disobeying these laws. **CA 10WA2.3**

# Revolution in China

### Section Preview
Reforms by Sun Yat-sen led to a revolution in China, and the arrival of Westerners brought changes to its culture and economy.

**Main Idea**

• Sun Yat-sen led a successful revolution to end the Qing dynasty, but he was unable to establish a stable government. (p. 388)
• General Yuan Shigai's dictatorial ways led to conflict with Sun Yat-sen's Nationalist Party. (p. 390)
• Westerners injected new energy into the Chinese economy, but many economic benefits went to foreigners, not the Chinese. (p. 391)

• Western culture had a dramatic effect on many Chinese people, especially those living in cities. (p. 392)

### Content Vocabulary
provincial, commodity

### Academic Vocabulary
transition, integrate

### People to Identify
Sun Yat-sen, Henry Pu Yi, General Yuan Shigai

### Places to Locate
Shanghai, Wuhan

### Reading Objectives
1. Describe Sun Yat-sen's role in the collapse of the Qing dynasty.
2. Explain how Western influence affected the Chinese economy and culture.

### Reading Strategy
**Compare and Contrast** Create a chart like the one below listing the reforms requested by Sun Yat-sen and those implemented by Empress Dowager Ci Xi.

| Sun Yat-sen's Proposals | Empress Dowager Ci Xi's Reforms |
|---|---|
|  |  |
|  |  |
|  |  |

### Preview of Events

| ♦1902 | ♦1905 | ♦1908 | ♦1911 | ♦1914 | ♦1917 | ♦1920 |
|---|---|---|---|---|---|---|

**1905**
Sun Yat-sen issues reform program

**1908**
Emperor Guang Xu and Empress Dowager Ci Xi die

**1911**
Qing dynasty collapses

**1916**
General Yuan Shigai dies

## California Standards in This Section

*Reading this section will help you master these California History–Social Science standards.*

**10.4:** Students analyze patterns of global change in the era of New Imperialism in at least two of the following regions or countries: Africa, Southeast Asia, China, India, Latin America, and the Philippines.

**10.4.1:** Describe the rise of industrial economies and their link to imperialism and colonialism (e.g., the role played by national security and strategic advantage; moral issues raised by the search for

national hegemony, Social Darwinism, and the missionary impulse; material issues such as land, resources, and technology).

**10.4.4:** Describe the independence struggles of the colonized regions of the world including the roles of leaders, such as Sun Yat-sen in China, and the roles of ideology and religion.

# The Fall of the Qing

**Main Idea** Sun Yat-sen led a successful revolution to end the Qing dynasty, but he was unable to establish a stable government.

**Reading Connection** Why were American revolutionaries able to eventually set up a successful government? Read on to learn about the experiences of the Chinese during the Revolution of 1911.

After the Boxer Rebellion, the Qing dynasty tried desperately to reform in order to save itself. Empress Dowager Ci Xi, who had so long resisted suggestions for change, now embraced a number of reforms. These included reforms in education, in government administration, and in the legal system.

## Voices from the Past

In 1905, a reformer named Sun Yat-sen presented a program that called for the following changes:

66Establish the Republic: Now our revolution is based on equality, in order to establish a republican government. All our people are equal and all enjoy political rights. The president will be publicly chosen by the people of the country. The parliament will be made up of members publicly chosen by the people of the country. Equalize land ownership: The good fortune of civilization is to be shared equally by all the people of the nation. We should assess the value of all the land in the country. Its present price shall be received by the owner, but all increases in value resulting from reform and social improvements after the revolution shall belong to the state, to be shared by all the people.99

The civil service examination system was replaced by a new educational system based on the Western model. In 1909, legislative assemblies were formed at the **provincial,** or local, level. Elections for a national assembly were even held in 1910.

The emerging new elite—composed of merchants, professionals, and reform-minded gentry—soon became impatient with the slow pace of political change. They were angry when they discovered that the new assemblies were not allowed to pass laws but could only give advice to the ruler.

Moreover, the recent reforms had done nothing for the peasants, artisans, and miners, whose living conditions were getting worse as taxes increased. Unrest grew in the countryside as the dynasty continued to ignore deep-seated resentments.

**The Rise of Sun Yat-sen** The first signs of revolution appeared during the last decade of the nineteenth century, when the young radical **Sun Yat-sen** formed the Revive China Society. Sun Yat-sen believed that the Qing dynasty was in a state of decay and could no longer govern the country. Unless the Chinese were united under a strong government, they would remain at the mercy of other countries.

Although Sun believed that China should follow the pattern of Western countries, he also knew that the Chinese people were hardly ready for democracy. He instead developed a three-stage reform process that included: (1) a military takeover, (2) a transitional phase in which Sun's own revolutionary party would prepare the people for democratic rule, and (3) the final stage of a constitutional democracy.

In 1905, at a convention in Tokyo, Sun united radical groups from across China and formed the Revolutionary Alliance, which eventually became the Nationalist Party. The new organization advocated Sun's Three People's Principles, which promoted nationalism, democracy, and the right for people to

▼ *General Yuan Shigai*

Sun Yat-sen's Nationalist soldiers arrive at a village in search of bandits. Sun Yat-sen's revolutionary forces rose against the Qing dynasty in 1911. What stage or stages in his reform process was he trying to carry out with his army?

pursue their own livelihoods. Although the new organization was small, it benefited from the rising discontent generated by the Qing dynasty's failure to improve conditions in China.

## The Revolution of 1911

The Qing dynasty was near its end. In 1908, Empress Dowager Ci Xi died. Her nephew Guang Xu, who was being held prisoner in the imperial palace, died one day before his aunt. The throne was now occupied by China's "last emperor," the infant **Henry Pu Yi.**

In October 1911, followers of Sun Yat-sen launched an uprising in central China. At the time, Sun was traveling in the United States—he read about the uprising in a Denver, Colorado newspaper. In Sun's absence, a brigade commander was asked to lead. Soon, the anti-government rebellion received popular support elsewhere in China. Too weak to resist, the Qing dynasty collapsed, opening the way for new political forces.

Sun's party had neither the military nor the political strength to form a new government. The party was forced to turn to a member of the old order,

**General Yuan Shigai** (YOO•AHN SHUR•GIE), who controlled the army.

Yuan was a prominent figure in military circles, and he had been placed in charge of the imperial army sent to suppress the rebellion. Instead, he abandoned the government and negotiated with members of Sun Yat-sen's party. General Yuan agreed to serve as president of a new Chinese republic and to allow the election of a legislature. Sun himself arrived in China in January 1912, after reading about the revolution while in the United States.

In the eyes of Sun Yat-sen's party, the events of 1911 were a glorious revolution that ended two thousand years of imperial rule. However, the 1911 uprising was hardly a revolution. It produced no new political or social order. Sun Yat-sen and his followers still had much to accomplish.

The Revolutionary Alliance was supported mainly by an emerging urban middle class, and its program was based largely on Western liberal democratic principles. However, the urban middle class in China was too small to support a new political order. Most of the Chinese people still lived on the land, and few peasants supported Sun Yat-sen's party. In effect, then, the events of 1911 were less a revolution than a collapse of the old order.

✓**Reading Check** **Evaluating** What changes did the Revolution of 1911 actually produce in China?

## Sun Yat-sen
### 1866–1925
### Chinese revolutionary

Sun Yat-sen was the leader of the revolutionary movement that overthrew the Qing dynasty. Sun was born to a peasant family in the south and was educated in Hawaii. He returned to China to practice medicine but soon began to use his earnings to finance revolutionary activities.

A failed rebellion forced Sun to flee to Japan and later to the United States and London. He raised money and recruited Chinese exiles to carry out his revolutionary plans. After the Qing government collapsed in 1911, he returned to China. Sun decided to back General Yuan Shigai as president in 1912. He was afraid that more fighting would only lead to chaos and foreign intervention.

Sun never realized his dream of leading a new Chinese republic, but both the Republic of China on Taiwan and the People's Republic of China honor him as the founder of modern China.

## Chiang Kai-shek
### 1887–1975
### General and Politician

A young man who worked closely with Sun Yat-sen was Chiang Kai-shek. Eventually he became president of the Chinese Nationalist government (see Chapter 10). As a young man of 18, Chiang went to Japan for military training. There he learned to believe that an army could shape a nation's future.

Like Sun Yat-sen, Chiang returned home when revolution broke out in 1911. After Sun's death, Chiang became the leader of Sun's Nationalist Party, the Guomindang (GDP).

In the 1920s and 1930s, the GDP and Chinese Communists fought bitterly to become the dominant government—except when they were defending their nation against Japan. The GDP led a republican government from 1928 to 1949, but it was never able to control the entire country.

Chiang's biggest weakness was that his support came from the cities. He offered little to the peasants, who ultimately backed Mao Zedong and the Communists.

# An Era of Civil War

**Main Idea** General Yuan Shigai's dictatorial ways led to conflict with Sun Yat-sen's Nationalist Party.

**Reading Connection** Do you know of a country currently ruled by the head of the army? Read to find out what happened when a general took over the rule of China.

After the collapse of the Qing dynasty, the military took over. Sun Yat-sen and his colleagues had accepted General Yuan Shigai as president of the new Chinese republic in 1911 because they lacked the military force to compete with his control over the army. Many of Sun's supporters feared that if the revolt lapsed into chaos, the Western powers would intervene. If that happened, the last shreds of Chinese independence would be lost. Even the general's new allies distrusted his motives, however, and they had good reason.

Yuan understood little of the new ideas sweeping into China from the West. He ruled in a traditional manner and even tried to set up a new imperial dynasty. Yuan was hated by reformers for using murder and terror to destroy the new democratic institutions. He was hated by traditionalists—those who supported the Qing—for being disloyal to the dynasty he had served.

Yuan's dictatorial efforts rapidly led to clashes with Sun's party, now renamed the *Guomindang,* or Nationalist Party. When Yuan dissolved the new parliament, the Nationalists launched a rebellion. The rebellion failed, and Sun Yat-sen fled to Japan.

Yuan was strong enough to brush off the challenge from the revolutionary forces, but he could not turn back history. He died in 1916 and was succeeded by one of his officers. For the next several years, China slipped into civil war as the power of the central government disintegrated and military warlords seized power in the provinces. Their soldiers caused massive destruction throughout China.

✓ **Reading Check** Explaining Why were there rebellions in China after General Yuan Shigai became president?

## Chinese Society in Transition

**Main Idea** Westerners injected new energy into the Chinese economy, but many economic benefits went to foreigners, not the Chinese.

**Reading Connection** What factors influence your lifestyle? Read to find out how Westerners influenced Chinese ways of life.

When European traders began to move into China in greater numbers in the mid-1800s, Chinese society was already in a state of **transition**. The growth of industry and trade was especially noticeable in the cities, where a national market for such **commodities**, or marketable products, as oil, copper, salt, tea, and porcelain had appeared. Better transportation and a better system of money and banking had begun to create the foundation for a money economy. New crops brought in from abroad increased food production and encouraged population growth. The Chinese economy had never been more productive.

The coming of Westerners to China affected the Chinese economy in three ways. Westerners introduced modern means of transportation and communications; they created an export market; and they **integrated** the Chinese market into the nineteenth-century world economy.

To some, these changes were beneficial. Shaking China out of its old ways quickened a process of change that had already begun in Chinese society. Western influences forced the Chinese to adopt new ways of thinking and acting.

At the same time, however, China paid a heavy price for the new ways. Its local industry was largely destroyed. Also, many of the profits in the new economy went to foreign countries rather than back into the Chinese economy.

During the first quarter of the twentieth century, the pace of change in China quickened even more. One reason was that during World War I, Westerners were unable to continue their domination of Chinese markets. This meant that Chinese businesses had more opportunities. **Shanghai, Wuhan,** Tianjin, and Guangzhou became major industrial and commercial centers with a growing middle class and an industrial working class.

**✓ Reading Check** **Evaluating** How did the arrival of Westerners affect China?

*"As Heaven has unified [the earth] under one sky, it will harmonize the various teachings of the world and bring them back to the same source."*
—*Wang Tao on the need for reform in China, 1800s*

*Picturing* **History**

Sun Yat-sen and his wife, third and second from the left, stand with other members of the Revolutionary Alliance in Hangzhou, China. How does the clothing of the people in the photograph reflect Sun Yat-sen's beliefs about the future of China and Wang Tao's thoughts on the process of reform in the country?

# China's Changing Culture

**Main Idea** Western culture had a dramatic effect on many Chinese people, especially those living in cities.

**Reading Connection** Can you list foreign influences that have shaped American culture? Read to learn how Western ideas and dress influenced the traditional culture of China.

In 1800, daily life for most Chinese was the same as it had been for centuries. Most were farmers, living in one of the millions of villages in rice fields and on hillsides throughout the countryside. A farmer's life was governed by the harvest cycle, village custom, and family ritual. A few men were educated in the Confucian classics. Women remained in the home or in the fields. All children were expected to obey their parents, and wives were expected to submit to their husbands.

A visitor to China 125 years later would have seen a different society, although it would still have been recognizably Chinese. The changes were most striking in the cities. Here the educated and wealthy had been visibly affected by the growing Western cultural presence. Confucian social ideals were declining rapidly in influence and those of Europe and North America were on the rise.

Nowhere in China was the struggle between old and new more visible than in the area of culture. Radical reformers wanted to eliminate traditional culture, condemning it as an instrument of oppression. They were interested in creating a new China that would be respected by the modern world.

The first changes in traditional culture came in the late nineteenth century. Intellectuals began to introduce Western books, paintings, music, and ideas to China. By the first quarter of the twentieth century, China was flooded by Western culture as intellectuals called for a new culture based on that of the modern West.

Western literature and art became popular in China, especially among the urban middle class. Traditional culture remained popular with conservative elements of the population, especially in rural areas. Most creative artists followed foreign trends, while traditionalists held on to Chinese culture.

▼ *Shanghai's harbor was at the mouth of the Chang Jiang. In the 1920s and 1930s, the city's image was something like that of Manhattan in the United States: a center for business, but also for excitement and glamour.*

Literature in particular was influenced by foreign ideas. Western novels and short stories began to attract a larger audience. Although most Chinese novels written after World War I dealt with Chinese subjects, they reflected the Western tendency toward a realistic portrayal of society. Often, they dealt with the new Westernized middle class. Mao Dun's *Midnight,* for example, described the changing customs of Shanghai's urban elites. Most of China's modern authors showed a clear contempt for the past.

Ba Jin, the author of numerous novels and short stories, was one of China's foremost writers in the early twentieth century. Born in 1904, he was well attuned to the rigors and expected obedience of Chinese family life. In his trilogy, *Family, Spring,* and *Autumn,* he describes the disintegration of traditional Confucian ways as the younger members of a large family attempt to break away from their elders.

✓**Reading Check** **Describing** What effects did Western culture have on China?

**HISTORY** *Online* **Study Central**

For help with the concepts in this section of *Glencoe World History–Modern Times,* go to <u>wh.mt.glencoe.com</u> and click on **Study Central.**

# SECTION 2 ASSESSMENT

### Checking for Understanding

1. **Vocabulary** Define: provincial, transition, commodity, integrate.

2. **People** Identify: Sun Yat-sen, Henry Pu Yi, General Yuan Shigai.

3. **Places** Locate: Shanghai, Wuhan.

### Reviewing Big Ideas

4. **Describe** the attitudes toward Western culture held by Chinese in rural and urban areas. Which of these two groups do you think benefited more from Western involvement in the Chinese economy and society?

### Critical Thinking

5. **Historical Analysis** **Sequence and Change** Why did the reforms introduced by Empress Dowager Ci Xi and General Yuan Shigai fail to improve the way China was governed? **CA CS2**

6. **Cause and Effect** Create a diagram like the one below showing the changes resulting from European contact with China in the mid-1800s.

| Contact | | Effects |
|---------|---|---------|
| | → | |
| | → | |
| | → | |

### Analyzing Visuals

7. **Examine** the photograph of Sun Yat-sen's soldiers shown on page 389. What inferences can you draw about his army from looking at the photo? How important was this army in overthrowing the Qing dynasty?

## Writing About History

8. **Expository Writing** Research and compare the reasons why the United States and China experienced civil war. Write an essay offering alternatives to war that might have solved the internal problems of China or the United States. **CA 10WA2.3**

# YOUNG PEOPLE IN . . .

### China

In traditional China, children were thought of not as individuals but as members of a family. Indeed, children were valued because they—especially the sons—would help with the work in the fields, carry on the family name, and care for their parents in old age. By the beginning of the twentieth century, however, these attitudes had changed in some parts of Chinese society.

Some of the changes resulted from the new educational system. After the government abolished the civil service examinations in 1905, a Confucian education was no longer the key to a successful career. New schools based on the Western model were set up. Especially in the cities, both public and private schools educated a new generation of Chinese, who began to have less respect for the past.

By 1915, educated youth had launched an intense attack on the old system and old values. The main focus of the attack was the Confucian concept of the family. Young people rejected the old family ideas of respect for elders, supremacy of men over women, and sacrifice of individual needs to the demands of the family.

The effect of the young people's revolt could be seen mainly in the cities. There, the tyranny of the old family system began to decline. Women sought education and jobs alongside men. Free choice in marriage became commonplace among affluent families in the cities. The teenage children of Westernized elites copied the clothing and even the music of young people in Europe and America.

These changes generally did not reach the villages, where traditional attitudes and customs persisted. Marriages arranged by parents continued to be the rule rather than the exception. According to a survey taken in the 1930s, well over two-thirds of marriages were still arranged, even among urban couples. In one rural area, only 3 villagers out of 170 had even heard of the idea of "modern marriage," or a marriage in which people freely choose their marriage partners.

◄ Young people in rural China in 1900 had much the same experience as previous generations. The family was the most important unit in society, and tradition determined a person's status. Age was greatly respected, and the father was the center of authority. If a child was disobedient, the boy or girl might be severely punished. Hard work was expected.

In this portrait, an urban family look as if they are on the porch or inner courtyard of their handsome home. The wife's elaborate headdress suggests their comfortable upper middle-class status. The father could be a bureaucrat, an influential group in Chinese society.

▲ A person's dress is a badge of social status. Here a young Chinese woman is wearing Western dress of Victorian Britain for her formal portrait (complete with stuffed dog). She may want to say that she is modern—or even that she is Christian if that is a Bible on her lap. Missionary schools were one way that Western customs reached China's young people.

◄ The jaunty stance of this young Chinese man in Western clothing tells another story—that Western dress was partly about being liberated from Chinese traditions and free to choose one's own life.

## CONNECTING TO THE PAST

1. **Contrasting** Contrast the traditional way of life with life after 1915 for young people in China.

2. **Writing about History** How do the teenagers in China during the early twentieth century compare to the young people in the United States today? Write a one-page essay on your ideas, giving specific examples to support your point of view.

# Rise of Modern Japan

## Guide to Reading

### Section Preview
Western intervention opened Japan to trade, and the interaction between Japan and Western nations led to a modern industrial Japanese society.

**Main Idea**
- Under military pressure from the United States, Japan signed the Treaty of Kanagawa, which opened two ports to Western trade. (p. 397)
- Relations with the Western powers brought on the collapse of the shogunate in Japan. (p. 398)
- The Meiji government attempted to modernize Japan's political, economic, and social structures. (p. 398)

- By the early 1900s, Japan strengthened its military and started building an empire. (p. 401)
- Japanese traditional culture was greatly influenced by the culture of Western nations. (p. 402)

### Content Vocabulary
concession, prefecture

### Academic Vocabulary
compensate, equip, succession

### People to Identify
Matthew Perry, Millard Fillmore, Mutsuhito, Ito Hirobumi

### Places to Locate
Edo Bay, Kyoto, Edo, Port Arthur

### Reading Objectives
1. Describe the effect of the Meiji Restoration on Japan.
2. Identify the steps Japan took to become an imperialist nation.

### Reading Strategy
**Categorizing Information** Create a table like the one below listing the promises contained in the Charter Oath of 1868 and the provisions of the Meiji constitution of 1890.

| Charter Oath | Constitution |
|--------------|--------------|
|              |              |
|              |              |
|              |              |

### Preview of Events

♦1850　　♦1860　　♦1870　　♦1880　　♦1890　　♦1900　　♦1910

**1853**
Commodore Perry arrives in Japan

**1871**
Government seizes daimyo's lands to strengthen executive power

**1874**
Japan pursues imperialist policy

**1889**
Adoption of Meiji constitution

**1905**
Japan defeats Russia

## California Standards in This Section

*Reading this section will help you master these California History–Social Science standards.*

**10.4:** Students analyze the patterns of global change in the era of New Imperialism in at least two of the following regions or countries: Africa, Southeast Asia, China, India, Latin America, and the Philippines.

**10.4.1:** Describe the rise of industrial economies and their link to imperialism and colonialism (e.g., the role played by national security and strategic advantage; moral issues raised by the search for national hegemony, Social Darwinism, and the missionary impulse; material issues such as land, resources, and technology).

**10.4.3:** Explain imperialism from the perspective of the colonizers and the colonized and the varied immediate and long-term responses by the people under colonial rule.

**10.4.4:** Describe the independence struggles of the colonized regions of the world, including the roles of leaders, such as Sun Yat-sen in China, and the roles of ideology and religion.

# An End to Isolation

**Main Idea** Under military pressure from the United States, Japan signed the Treaty of Kanagawa, which opened two ports to Western trade. ⌐TURNING POINT¬

**Reading Connection** How would your life be affected if the United States stopped importing goods from other countries? Read to find out why Japan decided to open its ports to trade with other countries.

By the end of the nineteenth century, Japan was emerging as a modern imperialist power. The Japanese accomplished this goal by following the example of Western nations. At the same time, they wanted to be certain that Japanese values were preserved.

## *Voices from the Past*

In 1890, Japanese leaders issued a decree to be read to every schoolchild:

❝You, our subjects, be filial to your parents, affectionate to your brothers and sisters, as husbands and wives be harmonious, as friends true; bear yourselves in modesty and moderation; extend your goodness to all; pursue learning and cultivate arts, and thereby develop intellectual faculties and perfect moral powers; furthermore, advance public good and promote common interests; always respect the Constitution and observe the laws; should emergency arise, offer yourselves to the State; and thus guard and maintain the prosperity of our imperial throne.❞

By 1800, the Tokugawa shogunate had ruled the Japanese islands for two hundred years. It had driven out foreign traders and missionaries and isolated the country from virtually all contact with the outside world. The Tokugawa maintained formal relations only with Korea. Informal trading links with Dutch and Chinese merchants continued at Nagasaki. Foreign ships, which were beginning to prowl along the Japanese coast in increasing numbers, were driven away.

To the Western powers, the continued isolation of Japanese society was a challenge. Western nations were convinced that the expansion of trade on a global basis would benefit all nations. They now began to approach Japan in the hope of opening it up to foreign economic interests.

The first foreign power to succeed with Japan was the United States. In the summer of 1853, an American fleet of four warships under Commodore **Matthew Perry** arrived in **Edo Bay** (now Tokyo Bay). They sought, as Perry said, "to bring a singular and isolated people into the family of civilized nations."

Perry brought with him a letter from President **Millard Fillmore.** The U.S. president asked for better treatment of sailors shipwrecked on the Japanese islands. (Foreign sailors shipwrecked in Japan were treated as criminals and exhibited in public cages.) He also requested the opening of foreign relations between the United States and Japan.

A few months later, Perry, accompanied by an even larger fleet, returned to Japan for an answer. Shogunate officials had been discussing the issue. Some argued that contacts with the West would hurt Japan. Others pointed to the military superiority of the United States and recommended **concessions,** or political compromises. The question was ultimately decided by the guns of Commodore Perry's ships.

Under military pressure, Japan agreed to the Treaty of Kanagawa. It provided for the return of shipwrecked American sailors, the opening of two ports to Western traders, and the establishment of a U.S. consulate in Japan.

In 1858, U.S. consul Townsend Harris signed a more detailed treaty. It called for the opening of several new ports to U.S. trade and residence, as well as an exchange of ministers. Similar treaties were soon signed by Japan and several European nations.

✓**Reading Check** **Identifying** What benefits did the Treaty of Kanagawa grant the United States?

▼ *Commodore Perry meeting Japanese in 1853*

## Resistance to the New Order

**Main Idea** Relations with the Western powers brought on the collapse of the shogunate in Japan.

**Reading Connection** Remember how China's government faced opposition because it failed to deal with foreigners? Read to find out why the Japanese shogunate was replaced.

The decision to open relations with the West was very controversial with some Japanese. Resistance was especially strong among the samurai warriors in two territories in the south, Satsuma and Choshu. Both had strong military traditions, and neither had been exposed to Western military pressure. In 1863, the Sat-Cho alliance (from Satsuma-Choshu) made the shogun promise to end relations with the West.

The rebellious groups soon showed their own weakness, however. When Choshu troops fired on Western ships in the Strait of Shimono-seki, which leads into the Sea of Japan, the Westerners fired back and destroyed the Choshu fortifications.

The incident convinced the rebellious forces that they needed to strengthen their military. They also became more determined not to give in to the West. As a result, Sat-Cho leaders urged the shogun to take a stronger position against the foreigners.

*Mutsuhito*

The Sat-Cho leaders demanded that the shogun resign and the emperor be restored. In January 1868, their armies attacked the shogun's palace in **Kyoto** and proclaimed that the authority of the emperor had been restored. After a few weeks, the shogun's forces collapsed, ending the shogunate system.

**Reading Check** **Identifying** What events led to the collapse of the shogunate system in Japan?

## The Meiji Restoration

**Main Idea** The Meiji government attempted to modernize Japan's political, economic, and social structures.

**Reading Connection** How would you describe the differences in American parties? Read to find out how political parties began in Japan in the late 1800s.

The Sat-Cho leaders had genuinely mistrusted the West, but they soon realized that Japan must change to survive. The new leaders embarked on a policy of reform that transformed Japan into a modern industrialized nation.

The symbol of the new era was the young emperor **Mutsuhito.** He called his reign the Meiji (MAY•jee), or "Enlightened Rule." This period has thus become known as the Meiji Restoration.

The Meiji ruler was controlled by the Sat-Cho leaders, just as earlier emperors had been controlled by the shogunate. In recognition of the real source of political power, the capital was moved from Kyoto to **Edo** (now named Tokyo), the location of the new leaders. The imperial court was moved to the shogun's palace in the center of the city.

**Transformation of Japanese Politics** Once in power, the new leaders moved first to abolish the old order and to strengthen power in their hands. To undercut the power of the daimyo—the local nobles—the new leaders stripped these great lords of the titles to their lands in 1871. As compensation, the lords were given government bonds and were named governors of the territories formerly under their control. The territories were now called **prefectures.**

The Meiji reformers wanted a modern political system based on the Western model. In 1868, the new leaders signed a Charter Oath, in which they promised to create a new legislature within the framework of continued imperial rule. Although senior positions in the new government were given to the daimyo, the key posts were held by modernizing leaders from the Sat-Cho group. The country was divided into 75 prefectures. (The number was reduced to 45 in 1889 and remains at that number today.)

During the next 20 years, the Meiji government undertook a careful study of Western political systems. A commission under **Ito Hirobumi** traveled to Great Britain, France, Germany, and the United States to study their governments.

As the process evolved, two main factions appeared: the Liberals and the Progressives. The Liberals wanted political reform based on the Western liberal democratic model, with supreme authority vested in the parliament as the representative of the people. The Progressives wanted power to be shared between the legislative and executive branches, with the executive branch having more control.

During the 1870s and 1880s, these factions fought for control. In the end, the Progressives won. The Meiji constitution, adopted in 1889, was modeled

## Meiji Restoration: Birth of Modern Japan

**Politics**

**Economics**

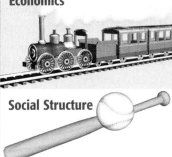

**Social Structure**

### Changes and Events

- Imperial rule reestablished
- Capital moved to Edo
- Most power in executive branch (emperor, prime minister, cabinet)

- Daimyo's lands given to peasants
- Many farmers, unable to pay new land tax, forced into tenancy
- Industrialization encouraged

- New imperial army created
- Universal system of education developed
- Western practices adopted

### Chart *Skills*

The Meiji government began reforms that transformed Japan's political, economic, and social structures.

1. **Cause and Effect** What changes noted on the chart most reflect the influence of Western ideas upon Japan?
2. **Making Generalizations** How are the changes in the three areas of politics, economics, and social structure interrelated?

after that of Imperial Germany. Most authority was given to the executive branch. In theory, the emperor exercised all executive authority. In practice, he was a figurehead. Executive authority rested in the hands of a prime minister and his cabinet of ministers. These ministers were handpicked by the Meiji leaders.

Under the new constitution, the upper house included royal appointments and elected nobles, while the lower house was elected. The two houses were to have equal legislative powers.

The final result was a political system that was democratic in form but authoritarian in practice. Although modern in external appearance, it was still traditional, because power remained in the hands of a ruling oligarchy (the Sat-Cho leaders). Although a new set of institutions and values had emerged, the system allowed the traditional ruling class to keep its influence and economic power.

### Meiji Economics
The Meiji leaders also set up a new system of land ownership. A land reform program made the traditional lands of the daimyo into the private property of the peasants. The daimyo, as mentioned, were **compensated** with government bonds.

The Meiji leaders levied a new land tax, which was set at an annual rate of 3 percent of the estimated value of the land. The new tax was an excellent source of revenue for the government. However, it was quite burdensome for the farmers.

Under the old system, farmers had paid a fixed percentage of their harvest to the landowners. In bad harvest years, they had owed little or nothing. Under the new system, the farmers had to pay the land tax every year, regardless of the quality of the harvest.

As a result, in bad years, many peasants were unable to pay their taxes. This forced them to sell their lands to wealthy neighbors and become tenant farmers who paid rent to the new owners. By the end of the nineteenth century, about 40 percent of all farmers were tenants.

With its budget needs met by the land tax, the government turned to the promotion of industry. The chief goal of the reformers was to create a "rich country and a strong state" to guarantee Japan's survival against the challenge of Western nations.

The Meiji government gave subsidies to needy industries, provided training and foreign advisers, improved transportation and communications, and started a new educational system that stressed applied science. In contrast to China, Japan was able to achieve results with little reliance on foreign money. By 1900, Japan's industrial sector was beginning to grow. Besides tea and silk, other key industries were weapons, shipbuilding, and sake (SAH•kee), or Japanese rice wine.

From the start, a unique feature of the Meiji model of industrial development was the close relationship between government and private business. The government encouraged the development of new industries by providing businesspeople with money and privileges. Once an individual enterprise or industry was on its feet, it was turned over entirely to private ownership. Even then, however, the government continued to play some role in the industry's activities.

**Building a Modern Social Structure** The Meiji reformers also transformed other institutions. A key focus of their attention was the military. The reformers were well aware that Japan would need a modern military force to compete with the Western powers. "Strengthen the Army"—that was their motto.

A new imperial army based on compulsory military service was formed in 1871. All Japanese men now served for three years. The new army was well **equipped** with modern weapons.

Education also changed. The Meiji leaders realized the need for universal education, including instruction in modern technology. A new ministry of education, established in 1871, guided the changes.

After a few years of experimentation, the education ministry adopted the American model of elementary schools, secondary schools, and universities. It brought foreign specialists to Japan to teach in the new schools. In the meantime, it sent bright students to study abroad.

Much of the content of the new educational system was Western in inspiration. However, a great deal of emphasis was still placed on the virtues of loyalty to the family and community. Loyalty to the emperor was especially valued. Both teachers and students were required to bow before a portrait of the emperor each day.

**Daily Life and Women's Rights** Japanese society in the late Tokugawa Era, before the Meiji reforms, could be described by two words: *community* and *hierarchy*. The lives of all Japanese people were determined by their membership in a family, village, and social class. At the same time, Japanese society was highly hierarchical. Belonging to a particular social class determined a person's occupation and social relationships with others. Women were especially limited by the "three obediences": child to father, wife to husband, and widow to son. Whereas husbands could easily obtain a divorce, wives could not. Marriages were arranged, and the average marital age of females was sixteen years. Females did not share inheritance rights with males. Few received any education outside the family.

The Meiji Restoration had a marked effect on the traditional social system in Japan. Special privileges for the aristocracy were abolished. For the first time, women were allowed to seek an education. As the economy shifted from an agricultural to an industrial base, thousands of Japanese began to get new jobs and establish new social relationships.

Western fashions became the rage in elite circles. The ministers of the first Meiji government were known as the "dancing cabinet" because of their love for Western-style ballroom dancing. The game of baseball was imported from the United States.

Young people were increasingly influenced by Western culture and values. A new generation of modern boys and girls began to imitate the clothing styles, eating habits, hairstyles, and social practices of European and American young people.

The social changes of the Meiji Restoration also had an unattractive side. In the effort to industrialize, many commoners were ruthlessly exploited in coal mines and textile mills. Workers labored up to 20 hours a day, often under conditions of incredible hardship. Coal miners employed on a small island in the harbor of Nagasaki worked in temperatures up to 130 degrees Fahrenheit (54 degrees C). When they tried to escape, they were shot.

*Picturing* **History**

For a recital at a music school in 1889, Japanese musicians played Western music and wore Western clothing. In what other ways did Japanese culture change under the Meiji government?

Sometimes people resisted such conditions. A few were beginning to demand attention to human rights. A popular rights movement of the 1870s laid the groundwork for one of Japan's first political parties. It campaigned for a government that would reflect the will of the people.

The transformation of Japan did not detach the country entirely from its old values. Loyalty to family and community was still taught. They also had a firm legal basis in the 1889 constitution, which limited the right to vote to men. The Civil Code of 1898 played down individual rights and placed women within the context of their family role.

✓ Reading Check **Explaining** How was Japan's government structured under the Meiji constitution?

## Joining the Imperialist Nations

**Main Idea** By the early 1900s, Japan strengthened its military and started building an empire.

**Reading Connection** Why did the British set up colonies in America? Read to find out why Japan wanted colonies.

We have seen that the Japanese modeled some of their domestic policies on Western practices. They also copied the imperialist Western approach to foreign affairs. Japan, after all, is small, lacking in resources, and densely populated. There is no natural room for expansion. To some Japanese, the lessons of history were clear. Western nations had amassed wealth and power not only because of their political and economic systems, but also because of their colonies. Colonies provided them with sources of raw materials, inexpensive labor, and markets. To compete, Japan would also have to expand.

**Beginnings of Expansion** The Japanese began their expansion close to home. In 1874, Japan claimed control of the Ryukyu (ree•YOO•KYOO) Islands, which had long been subject to the Chinese Empire. Two years later, Japan's navy forced the Koreans to open their ports to Japanese trade.

The Chinese had long controlled Korea and were concerned by Japan's growing influence there. During the 1880s, Chinese-Japanese rivalry over Korea intensified. In 1894, the two nations went to war. Japanese ships destroyed the Chinese fleet and seized the Manchurian city of **Port Arthur.**

In the treaty that ended the war, the Manchu rulers of China recognized the independence of Korea.

They also ceded Taiwan and the Liaodong Peninsula, with its strategic naval base at Port Arthur, to Japan. Shortly thereafter, the Japanese gave the Liaodong Peninsula back to China. In the early twentieth century, however, the Japanese returned to the offensive.

Rivalry with Russia over influence in Korea had led to increasingly strained relations between Japan and Russia. The Russians thought little of the Japanese and even welcomed the possibility of war. One adviser to Nicholas II said, "We will only have to throw our caps at them and they will run away."

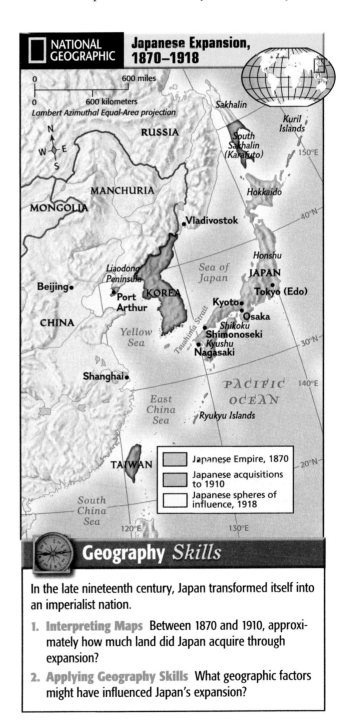

**NATIONAL GEOGRAPHIC**
**Japanese Expansion, 1870–1918**

0 — 600 miles
0 — 600 kilometers
Lambert Azimuthal Equal-Area projection

RUSSIA
Sakhalin
Kuril Islands
South Sakhalin (Karafuto)
150°E
MANCHURIA
MONGOLIA
Hokkaido
Vladivostok
40°N
Honshu
Liaodong Peninsula
Sea of Japan
JAPAN
Beijing•
Port Arthur
KOREA
Kyoto•
Tokyo (Edo)
CHINA
Osaka
Yellow Sea
Shikoku
Shimonoseki
30°N
Kyushu
Nagasaki
Shanghai•
PACIFIC OCEAN
140°E
East China Sea
Ryukyu Islands
Japanese Empire, 1870
Japanese acquisitions to 1910
Japanese spheres of influence, 1918
20°N
TAIWAN
South China Sea
120°E
130°E

**Geography** *Skills*

In the late nineteenth century, Japan transformed itself into an imperialist nation.

1. **Interpreting Maps** Between 1870 and 1910, approximately how much land did Japan acquire through expansion?
2. **Applying Geography Skills** What geographic factors might have influenced Japan's expansion?

**War with Russia** In 1904, Japan launched a surprise attack on the Russian naval base at Port Arthur, which Russia had taken from China in 1898. When Japanese forces moved into Manchuria and the Liaodong Peninsula, Russian troops proved to be no match for them. The Russian commander in chief said, "It is impossible not to admire the bravery and activity of the Japanese. The attack of the Japanese is a continuous **succession** of waves, and they never relax their efforts by day or by night."

In the meantime, Russia had sent its Baltic fleet halfway around the world to East Asia, only to be defeated by the new Japanese navy off the coast of Japan. After their defeat, the Russians agreed to a humiliating peace in 1905. They gave the Liaodong Peninsula back to Japan, as well as the southern part of Sakhalin (SA•kuh•LEEN), an island north of Japan. The Japanese victory stunned the world. Japan had become a leading world power.

**U.S. Relations** During the next few years, Japan consolidated its position in northeastern Asia. It established a sphere of influence in Korea. In 1905, the United States recognized Japan's role in Korea in return for Japanese recognition of American authority in the Philippines. In 1910, Japan annexed Korea outright. Mutual suspicion between the two countries was growing, however. The Japanese resented U.S. efforts to restrict immigration. Moreover, some Americans began to fear Japanese power in East Asia. In 1907, President Theodore Roosevelt made a "gentlemen's agreement" with Japan that essentially stopped Japanese immigration to the United States.

✓ **Reading Check** **Explaining** Why did Japan turn itself into an imperialist power?

## Culture in an Era of Transition

**Main Idea** Japanese traditional culture was greatly influenced by the culture of Western nations.

**Reading Connection** Do you own anything made in Japan? Read to learn about early cultural contact between the United States and Japan.

The wave of Western technology and ideas that entered Japan in the last half of the nineteenth century greatly altered the shape of traditional Japanese culture. Literature was especially affected. Dazzled by European literature, Japanese authors began translating and imitating the imported models.

*Picturing* **History**

The Japanese surprise attack on Port Arthur in 1904 reflected the growing power of Japan and its navy. What impact did the Japanese victory have on Russia? How did it affect relations between Japan and the United States?

▲ *This 1853 print, by famous artists Hiroshige and Toyokuni, shows the Japanese love of their past and traditions. It illustrates a scene from a beloved medieval tale written by a Japanese princess.*

The novel showed the greatest degree of change. People began to write novels that were patterned after the French tradition of realism. Naturalist Japanese authors tried to present existing social conditions and the realities of war as objectively as possible.

Other aspects of Japanese culture were also changed. The Japanese invited technicians, engineers, architects, and artists from Europe and the United States to teach their "modern" skills to eager Japanese students. The Japanese copied Western artistic techniques and styles. Huge buildings of steel and reinforced concrete, adorned with Greek columns, appeared in many Japanese cities.

A national reaction had begun by the end of the nineteenth century, however. Many Japanese artists began to return to older techniques. In 1889, the Tokyo School of Fine Arts was established to promote traditional Japanese art. Japanese artists searched for a new but truly Japanese means of expression. Some artists tried to bring together native and foreign techniques. Others returned to past artistic traditions.

Cultural exchange also went the other way. Japanese arts and crafts, porcelains, textiles, fans, and woodblock prints became fashionable in the West. Japanese art influenced Western painters. Japanese gardens, with their use of rocks and falling water, became popular in the United States.

✓**Reading Check** **Describing** What effect did Japanese culture have on other nations?

**HISTORY** *Online* **Study Central**

For help with the concepts in this section of *Glencoe World History–Modern Times,* go to wh.mt.glencoe.com and click on **Study Central.**

## SECTION 3 ASSESSMENT

### Checking for Understanding

1. **Vocabulary** Define: concession, prefecture, compensate, equip, succession.

2. **People** Identify: Matthew Perry, Millard Fillmore, Mutsuhito, Ito Hirobumi.

3. **Places** Locate: Edo Bay, Kyoto, Edo, Port Arthur.

### Reviewing Big Ideas

4. **List** the professionals that the Japanese invited from abroad to teach "modern" skills.

### Critical Thinking

5. **Historical Analysis** **Examining Trends** How did the Japanese land reform program create internal problems? **CA HI 1**

6. **Cause and Effect** Create a diagram listing the results of Western influence on Japanese culture.

Western Influence on Japanese Culture

### Analyzing Visuals

7. **Study** the image on page 400. Is the woman playing the piano looking at Western musical notation? Is there anything in the image showing the music translated into Japanese? Why?

### Writing About History

8. **Persuasive Writing** Pretend that you wish to study in China or Japan. Write a letter of application stating what you hope to learn, and how you would overcome any cultural barriers. **CA 10WA2.5**

*An American president, a Chinese politician, and a Japanese scholar each had their own ideas about the importance of East-West contacts. Read them to understand this period in Asian history.*

## SOURCE 1: U.S. Trade with Japan

*When U.S. Commodore Matthew C. Perry arrived in Tokyo Bay on his first visit to Japan in July 1853, he carried a letter from Millard Fillmore, the president of the United States. This excerpt is from that letter to the emperor of Japan.*

I have directed Commodore Perry to assure your Imperial Majesty that I entertain the kindest feelings towards your Majesty's person and government; and that I have no other object in sending him to Japan, but to propose to your Imperial Majesty that the United States and Japan should live in friendship, and have [trade] with each other. . . . I have particularly charged Commodore Perry to **abstain**[1] from any act, which could possibly disturb the peace of your Imperial Majesty's lands.

➤ ───────────────
[1]**abstain:** refrain; keep from

*Pu Yi, China's last emperor, standing in a courtyard*

The United States of America reaches from ocean to ocean, and our territory of Oregon and state of California lie directly opposite to the **dominions**[2] of your Imperial Majesty. Our steam-ships can go from California to Japan in eighteen days. Our great state of California produces about sixty millions of dollars in gold, every year, besides silver, quicksilver, precious stones, and many other valuable articles.

Japan is also a rich and fertile country, and produces many very valuable articles. . . . I am desirous that our two countries should trade with each other, for the benefit both of Japan and the United States.

We know that the ancient laws of your Imperial Majesty's government do not allow of foreign trade except with the Dutch. But as the state of the world changes, and new governments are formed, it seems to be wise from time to time to make new laws. . . .

## SOURCE 2: Western Influence in China

*The Chinese politician and scholar Liang Qichao (1873–1929) petitioned the emperor to abolish the old exam system, to resist foreign domination, and to embrace Western technology. He visited Europe in 1918, and promoted progress in all his scholarly writings, including in the excerpt below.*

What is our duty? It is to develop our civilization with that of the West and to supplement Western civilization with ours so as to synthesize and transform them to make a new civilization. . . .

. . . In the past, the ideal and the practical in Western civilization have been sharply divided. Idealism and materialism have both gone to the extreme. Religionists have one-sidedly emphasized the future life. . . . The reaction came from science. Materialism swept over the world and threw overboard all lofty ideals. . . . Now **pragmatism**[3] and evolutionism are being promoted, the aim being to embrace the ideal

➤ ───────────────
[2]**dominions:** royal lands
[3]**pragmatism:** philosophical method of inquiry

in the practical and to harmonize mind and matter. In my opinion, this is precisely the line of development in our ancient systems of thought. . . .

Just think. Weren't the pre-Qin philosophers and the great masters of the Sui and the Tang eras our loving and sagely ancestors who have left us a great heritage? We, being corrupted, do not know how to enjoy them and today we suffer intellectual starvation. . . . Of course, we may laugh at those old folks among us who block their own road of advancement and claim that we Chinese have all that is found in Western learning. But should we not laugh even more at those who are drunk with Western ways and regard everything Chinese as worthless. . . . What we need to learn is the essential spirit of that system and not the conditions under which it was produced. . . . For example, Confucius said a great deal about ethics of an aristocratic nature, which is certainly not suitable today. But we should not take Confucius lightly simply because of this. Shall we cast Plato aside simply because he said that the slavery system should be preserved? . . .

I therefore hope that our dear young people will, first of all, have a sincere purpose of respecting and protecting our civilization; second, that they will apply Western methods to the study of our civilization and discover its true character; third, that they will put our own civilization in order and supplement it with others' so that it will be transformed and become a new civilization. . . .

## SOURCE 3: Comparing the West and the East

*Yukichi Fukuzawa (1835–1901), from a low-ranking samurai family in Japan, traveled to the United States and to Europe. He wrote many influential books on how the Japanese could become strong and independent. His autobiography, from 1899, is excerpted below.*

The final purpose of all my work was to create in Japan a civilized nation as well equipped in the arts of war and peace as those of the Western world. I acted as if I had become the sole functioning agent for the introduction of Western learning. It was natural that I should be disliked by the older type of Japanese as if I were working for the benefit of foreigners. . . .

From my own observations in both **Occidental**[4] and Oriental civilizations, I find that each has certain strong points and weak points. . . . But when I compare the two in a general way as to wealth, **armament**[5], and the greatest happiness for the greatest number, I have to put the Orient below the Occident. Granted that a nation's destiny depends upon the education of its people, there must be some fundamental differences in the education of Western and Eastern peoples.

In the education of the East, so often saturated with Confucian teaching, I find two things lacking; that is to say, a lack of studies in number and reason in material culture, and a lack of the idea of independence in spiritual culture. But in the West I think I see why their statesmen are successful in managing their national affairs, and the businessmen in theirs. . . .

And I reasoned that Chinese philosophy as the root of education was responsible for our obvious shortcomings. . . . And I took every opportunity in public speech, in writing, and in casual conversations, to advocate my doctrine of independence. . . . During my endeavor I came to believe less than ever in the old Chinese teaching.

> ─────────────
> [4]**Occidental:** Western
> [5]**armament:** military equipment

## DBQ  Document-Based Questions

### Historical Analysis  CA HI 1, HR 2, HI 3

**Source 1:** Why can Fillmore's letter be seen as a masterful combination of salesmanship, diplomacy, and firmness?

**Source 2:** What does Liang Qichao mean when he says modern people should look at "the essential spirit" of an ancient work, but not the conditions under which it is produced?

**Source 3:** What does Yukichi Fukuzawa identify as the biggest weakness of Confucius?

### Comparing and Contrasting Sources

1. How is the influence of the West depicted in each of the sources? Do similarities exist between depictions from Japan and China?

2. How do the authors propose to combine Japanese or Chinese traditions with Western ideas?

## Reviewing Content Vocabulary

*On a sheet of paper, use each of these terms in a sentence.*

1. extra-territoriality
2. self-strengthening
3. spheres of influence
4. Open Door policy
5. indemnity
6. provincial
7. commodity
8. concession
9. prefecture

## Reviewing Academic Vocabulary

*On a sheet of paper, use each of these terms in a sentence that reflects the term's meaning in the chapter.*

10. decline
11. ensure
12. transition
13. integrate
14. compensate
15. equip
16. succession

## Reviewing the Main Ideas

### Section 1

17. Explain the One Hundred Days of Reform and their outcome.
18. List the countries that supplied troops for the allied army, which was formed to fight the Boxers in 1900.

### Section 2

19. Summarize the terms of Sun Yat-sen's reform program and tell whether or not they were implemented.
20. What opposing forces formed in China after the civil war?

### Section 3

21. What was the Meiji Restoration?
22. In chronological order, list the territories and countries Japan took control of in its program of expansion.

## Critical Thinking

23. **Summarizing** Summarize the effects of imperialism on nineteenth-century China.
24. **Analyzing** How effective was Japan's territorial expansion program?
25. **Identifying Options** Instead of importing opium to China, what else might the British have done to restore the balance of trade?
26. **Evaluating** To build a "rich country and a strong state," the Japanese government subsidized (provided funds for) its industries. Evaluate the reasons for Japan's decision.
27. **Analyzing** There were "three obediences" in a Japanese woman's life: child to father, wife to husband, and widow to son. How did these values actually affect the rights of women in Japanese society? Did this change after the Meiji Restoration? **CA** 10WA2.5c
28. **Reading Skill** **Questioning** One of the main ideas in Section 1 states that "The Tai Ping Rebellion reflected the discontent of the Chinese with the Qing dynasty." Based on this sentence, what questions would a reader expect to have answered in the following text? What answers does the textbook provide?

## Chapter Summary

Imperialist powers advanced into China and Japan in the nineteenth century. China's government fell, but Japan's modernized and endured.

### Movement
- British secure trade outlets at five coastal ports in China.
- Commodore Perry sails into Edo Bay.
- Japan invades Port Arthur, Manchuria.

### Change
- Japan's Tokugawa shogunate and China's Qing dynasty collapse.
- Meiji reformers institute compulsory military service in Japan.
- United States initiates Open Door policy in China.

### Reaction
- Tai Ping Rebellion breaks out in China.
- Sat-Cho leaders demand the resignation of Japan's shogun.
- Boxer Rebellion occurs in China.

### Nationalism
- Meiji government reforms Japan.
- Japan adopts the Meiji constitution.
- Sun Yat-sen establishes the Republic of China.

## Writing About History

29. **Historical Analysis** Analyzing Cause and Effect The death of Empress Dowager Ci Xi was followed by a series of events that changed the government and culture of China. Write several paragraphs outlining how the empress affected the politics of China. What were the effects on culture and tradition? **CA HI 2**

30. **Describing** The group who formed the Society of Harmonious Fists were opposed to foreign takeover in China. Write a short description about this organization. Describe their motives and beliefs. What was the result of their actions?

31. **Big Idea** Imagine you are a court official living in China during the reign of Emperor Guang Xu. The emperor is planning his reform program and needs advice concerning how to help strengthen China. Write a letter to the emperor telling him how you think China should either change or stay the same. Choose two or three specific issues such as the educational system, the development of the military, or the structure of the government to discuss in your letter. **CA 10WA2.5**

**DBQ** Document-Based Questions

**Analyzing Sources** Zhang Zhidong, a leading Chinese court official, argued:

❝The doctrine of people's rights will bring us not a single benefit but a hundred evils. Are we going to establish a parliament? Among the Chinese scholars and people there are still many today who are content to be vulgar and rustic. They are ignorant of the general situation in the world, they do not understand the basic system of the state.❞

32. Does Zhang Zhidong think that the Chinese people are well informed? Why does he point out scholars specifically?

33. How does Zhang Zhidong's quote apply to China today?

34. Based on what you've learned about the Qing dynasty, why would a court official be against forming a parliament? What did a parliament represent to Chinese traditionalists?

## Analyzing Maps and Charts

Examine the chart of the Meiji Restoration shown on page 399 of your text. Then answer the following questions.

35. What impact did the Meiji Restoration have on the social structure of Japan?

36. How do you think the daimyo felt about the Meiji Restoration?

37. What effect did the Meiji Restoration have on industry?

**Standards Practice**

**Directions: Use the map and your knowledge of world history to answer the following question.**

**Japanese Expansion, 1873–1910**

Sakhalin
MANCHURIA
Liaodong Peninsula
KOREA
Sea of Japan
JAPAN
PACIFIC OCEAN
Yellow Sea
Pescadores Islands
Ryukyu Islands
Formosa (Taiwan)

0 mi. 500
0 km 500

N W E S

- Japanese borders in 1873
- Lands claimed in 1874
- Influence won after Sino-Japanese War
- Territories won after Russo-Japanese War
- Lands annexed in 1910

38. Which of the following resulted from Japanese expansion?

A Japan was humiliated by its losses.

B Japan became an important military force.

C Russia and Japan competed for control of China.

D China's government was strengthened and reformed.

**CA Standard 10.4.2** Discuss the locations of the colonial rule of such nations as England, France, Germany, Italy, Japan, the Netherlands, Russia, Spain, Portugal, and the United States.

# WORLD LITERATURE

## from Shooting an Elephant

### George Orwell

**George Orwell** was the pen name of English author Eric Arthur Blair, who was born in Motihari, India, on June 25, 1903. He lived for 46 years, and during that time, he wrote many influential essays, novels, and newspaper articles. His two most famous works are *1984* and *Animal Farm,* both of which are commentaries against totalitarianism. He served for several years as an assistant superintendent in the Indian Imperial Police but resigned due to his distaste of imperialism. In *Shooting an Elephant,* Orwell describes an incident that happened to him, and he satirizes the problems of colonial rule.

### Read to Discover

Examine the ways in which George Orwell describes the relationship between the British colonial officer and the "natives." Can you think of a modern parallel to this situation?

### Reader's Dictionary

**mahout:** a keeper and driver of an elephant

**dominion:** rule, control

**sahib:** title meaning "sir" or "master"

In Moulmein, in lower Burma, I was hated by large numbers of people—the only time in my life that I have been important enough for this to happen to me. I was subdivisional police officer of the town, and in an aimless, petty kind of way anti-European feeling was very bitter. No one had the guts to raise a riot, but if a European woman went through the bazaars alone somebody would probably spit betel juice over her dress. As a police officer I was an obvious target and was baited whenever it seemed safe to do so. . . .

All this was perplexing and upsetting. For at that time I had already made up my mind that imperialism was an evil thing and the sooner I chucked up my job and got out of it the better. Theoretically—and secretly, of course—I was all for the Burmese and all against their oppressors, the British. . . . But I could get nothing into perspective. . . .

One day something happened which in a roundabout way was enlightening. . . .

Early one morning the subinspector at a police station the other end of the town rang me up on the phone and said that an elephant was ravaging the bazaar. Would I please come and do something about it? . . .

The Burmese subinspector and some Indian constables were waiting for me in the quarter where the elephant had been seen. . . . We began questioning the people as to where the elephant had gone and,

◄ *Colonial hunter*

▲ *Working elephants, 1890s*

as usual, failed to get any definite information. . . . I had almost made up my mind that the whole story was a pack of lies, when we heard yells a little distance away. . . .

The orderly came back in a few minutes with a rifle and five cartridges, and meanwhile some Burmans had arrived and told us that the elephant was in the paddy fields below, only a few hundred yards away. As I started forward practically the whole population of the quarter flocked out of the houses and followed me. They had seen the rifle and were all shouting excitedly that I was going to shoot the elephant. They had not shown much interest in the elephant when he was merely ravaging their homes, but it was different now. . . . I had no intention of shooting the elephant—I had merely sent for the rifle to defend myself if necessary—and it is always unnerving to have a crowd following you. I marched down the hill, looking and feeling a fool, with the rifle over my shoulder and an ever-growing army of people jostling at my heels. . . . The elephant was standing eight yards from the road, his left side towards us. He took not the slightest notice of the crowd's approach. He was tearing up bunches of grass, beating them against his knees to clean them and stuffing them into his mouth.

I had halted on the road. As soon as I saw the elephant I knew with perfect certainty that I ought not to shoot him. It is a serious matter to shoot a working elephant—it is comparable to destroying a huge and costly piece of machinery—and obviously one ought not to do it if it can possibly be avoided. And at that distance, peacefully eating, the elephant looked no more dangerous than a cow. I thought then and I think now that his attack of "must" was already passing off; in which case he would merely wander harmlessly about until the mahout came back and caught him. Moreover, I did not in the least want to shoot him. I decided that I would watch him for a little while to make sure that he did not turn savage again, and then go home.

But at that moment I glanced round at the crowd that had followed me. It was an immense crowd, two thousand at the least and growing every minute. It blocked the road for a long distance on either side. I looked at the sea of yellow faces above the garish clothes—faces all happy and excited over this bit of fun, all certain that the elephant was going to be shot. They were watching me as they would watch a conjurer about to perform a trick. They did not like me, but with the

▲ *Madras governor Lord Goschen completes a shooting expedition in the 1920s.*

magical rifle in my hands I was momentarily worth watching. And suddenly I realized that I should have to shoot the elephant after all. The people expected it of me and I had got to do it; I could feel their two thousand wills pressing me forward irresistibly. And it was at this moment, as I stood there with the rifle in my hands, that I first grasped the hollowness, the futility of the white man's dominion in the East. Here was I, the white man with his gun, standing in front of the unarmed native crowd—seemingly the leading actor of the piece; but in reality I was only an absurd puppet pushed to and fro by the will of those yellow faces behind. I perceived in this moment that when the white man turns tyrant it is his own freedom that he destroys. He becomes a sort of hollow, posing dummy, the conventionalized figure of a sahib. For it is the condition of his rule that he shall spend his life in trying to impress the "natives," and so in every crisis he has got to do what the "natives" expect of him. He wears a mask, and his face grows to fit it. I had got to shoot the elephant. I had committed myself to doing it when I sent for the rifle. A sahib has got to act like a sahib; he has got to appear resolute, to know his own mind and do definite things. To come all that way, rifle in hand, with two thousand people marching at my heels, and then to trail feebly away, having done nothing—no, that was

impossible. The crowd would laugh at me. And my whole life, every white man's life in the East, was one long struggle not to be laughed at.

. . . But I did not want to shoot the elephant. . . . The sole thought in my mind was that if anything went wrong those two thousand Burmese would see me trampled on, and reduced to a grinning corpse. And if that happened it was quite probable that some of them would laugh. That would never do. There was only one alternative. I shoved the cartridges into the magazine and lay down on the road to get a better aim.

The crowd grew very still, and a deep, low, happy sigh, as of people who see the theater curtain go up at last, breathed from innumerable throats. They were going to have their bit of fun after all.

. . . When I pulled the trigger I did not hear the bang or feel the kick—one never does when a shot goes home—but I heard the devilish roar of glee that went up from the crowd. . . . You could see the agony of it jolt [the elephant's] whole body and knock the last remnant of strength from his legs.

. . . In the end I could not stand it any longer and went away. I heard later that it took him half an hour to die. . . .

. . . I often wondered whether any of the others grasped that I had done it solely to avoid looking a fool.

## Interpreting World Literature

1. What is the context of this story? Why is the narrator following an elephant?

2. Why does the narrator ultimately decide that he must shoot the elephant?

3. What does this story reveal about Orwell's attitudes about imperialism? How can you tell?

4. **CRITICAL THINKING** According to Orwell in this piece, who held the power in colonial India?

### Applications Activity

Write a narrative account of an incident when you felt people were pushing you to act in opposition to your original intentions.

# Reading on Your Own

*Here are several books you may want to read on your own.*
*These authors have explored some of the topics covered in this unit.*

## *Things Fall Apart* (Fiction)

Achebe, Chinua (1930–) This Nigerian writer is often thought of as the father of modern African literature. This novel broke new ground for Western audiences because it told about imperialism from the point of view of the colonized people. It vividly recounts the experiences of Okonkwo, a warrior and village hero, and shows how the arrival of white missionaries to his Ibo village in Nigeria in the late nineteenth century changed his life.

## "The Chimney Sweep," "London,"and "Jerusalem," in *The Complete Poems* (Poetry)

Blake, William (1757–1827) A British poet and artist, Blake worked as an engraver all his life. He is often categorized as a Romantic writer, but he was so unusual—a mystic, a revolutionary, and perhaps a little crazy—that he is probably best thought of as being in a category of his own. Usually struggling himself to make ends meet, he was very sensitive to social injustice, and some of his poems reflect the suffering of workers in London where he spent his life.

## *Silence* (Fiction)

Endo, Shusaku (1923–1996) Endo set his best-selling novel, *Silence,* during the period of the early 1600s. Jesuit missionaries were being expelled from Japan, while Japanese converts were put to death. One theme in Endo's work is the conflict between Western and Eastern religion. Endo himself was raised Catholic in Japan, but was bullied by other boys. As a young man, he felt that his religion did not fit Japan. In this novel, he asks whether the Christian message can transcend a national culture and reach the Japanese soul.

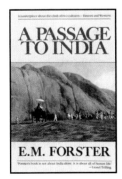

## *A Passage to India* (Fiction)

Forster, Edward (1879–1970) An important British novelist of the 20th century, Forster had his last novel, *A Passage to India,* published in 1924. It was probably also his best novel. The story is set in India when that country was still ruled by the British. It follows the friendship of Dr. Aziz, an Indian, and Cyril Fielding, an English teacher who is sympathetic to the Indian desire for independence. Their friendship is tested when Aziz is falsely accused of trying to rape an English woman.

# The Twentieth-Century Crisis

## *1914–1945*

# **W**hy It Matters

The period between 1914 and 1945 was one of the most destructive in the history of humankind. As many as 60 million people died as a result of World Wars I and II, the global conflicts that began and ended this era. As World War I was followed by revolutions, the Great Depression, totalitarian regimes, and the horrors of World War II, it appeared to many that European civilization had become a nightmare. By 1945, the era of European domination over world affairs had been severely shaken. With the decline of Western power, a new era of world history was about to begin.

## Primary Sources Library

See pages 774–775 for primary source readings to accompany Unit 3.

*Use The World History **Primary Source Document Library CD-ROM** to find additional primary sources about The Twentieth-Century Crisis.*

▲ Gate, Dachau Memorial

▶ Former Russian prisoners of war honor the American troops who freed them.

"*Never in the field of human conflict was so much owed by so many to so few.*"

—Winston Churchill

# *Looking Back...*

# International Peacekeeping

Until the 1900s, with the exception of the Seven Years' War, never in history had there been a conflict that literally spanned the globe. The twentieth century witnessed two world wars and numerous regional conflicts. As the scope of war grew, so did international commitment to collective security, where a group of nations join together to promote peace and protect human life.

**1914–1918**
World War I
is fought

**1919**
League of Nations
created to prevent wars

**1939–1945**
World War II
is fought

## ① *Europe*

## The League of Nations

At the end of World War I, the victorious nations set up a "general association of nations" called the League of Nations, which would settle international disputes and avoid war. By 1920, 42 nations had sent delegates to the League's headquarters in Geneva, Switzerland, and they were eventually joined by another 21.

The United States never joined. Opponents in the U.S. Senate argued that membership in the League went against George Washington's advice to avoid "entangling alliances." When the League failed to halt warlike acts in the 1930s, the same opponents pointed to the failure of collective security.

The League of Nations was seen as a peacekeeper without a sword—it possessed neither a standing army nor members willing to stop nations that used war as diplomacy.

*The League of Nations and Uncle Sam*

# to See Ahead

*UN membership flags*

## ② *The United States*

## The United Nations

After World War II, the United States hosted a meeting to create a new peace-keeping organization. Delegates from 50 nations hammered out the Charter of the United Nations. To eliminate the root causes of war, the UN created agencies that promoted global education and the well-being of children. In 1948, United States delegate Eleanor Roosevelt convinced the UN to adopt the Universal Declaration of Human Rights, which committed the UN to eliminate oppression. The headquarters for the UN are located in New York City.

**1945**
United Nations is founded

**1948**
UN adopts the Universal Declaration of Human Rights

**1950–1953**
UN troops participate in the Korean War

**1988**
Nobel Peace Prize awarded to UN peacekeeping forces

## ③ *South Africa*

## The Power of World Opinion

By 1995, the UN had taken part in 35 peacekeeping missions—some successful, some not. It also had provided protection for over 30 million refugees.

The UN used world opinion to promote justice. In 1977, it urged nations to enforce economic sanctions and an arms embargo against South Africa until apartheid was lifted. In 1994, South Africa held its first all-race elections. Many believed this was a major triumph for collective international action.

*Casting a vote in South Africa*

## Why It Matters

The UN hopes to use collective international actions to promote peace around the world. Often this involves preventing injustice and improving living conditions. What are some recent UN actions that support these principles?

# 8

## *1914–1919*

# War and Revolution

## ✦ *The Big Ideas* ✦

### SECTION 1: The Road to World War I

**The quest for national self-determination is universal.** Militarism, nationalism, and a crisis in the Balkans led to World War I.

### SECTION 2: The War

**War causes immeasurable devastation.** The stalemate at the Western Front led to a widening of World War I, and governments expanded their powers to accommodate the war.

### SECTION 3: The Russian Revolution

**A totalitarian system violates human rights in pursuit of political power.** The fall of the czarist regime and the Russian Revolution put the Communists in power.

### SECTION 4: End of the War

**War causes immeasurable devastation.** After the defeat of the Germans, peace settlements brought political and territorial changes to Europe, creating bitterness and resentment in several nations.

 **World History—Modern Times Video** The Chapter 8 video, "Modern Warfare," chronicles innovations in warfare during the twentieth century.

**1914**
Assassination of Archduke Francis Ferdinand sparks World War I

**1916**
Battle of Verdun leaves more than 700,000 dead, wounded, or missing

*1914*          *1915*          *1916*

**1915**
German submarine sinks the *Lusitania*

*German U-boat*

*Battle of the Somme* by Richard Woodville  The Battle of the Somme was one of the bloodiest battles of World War I.

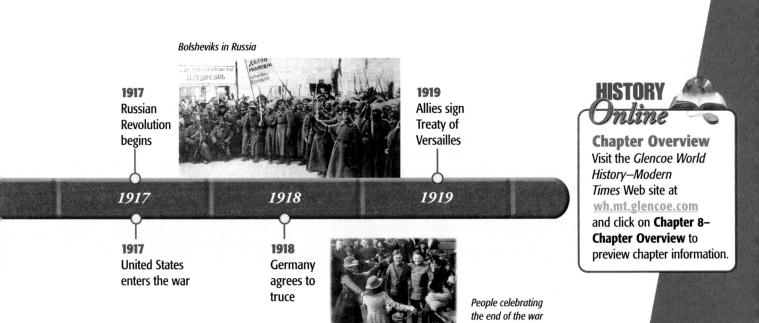

*Bolsheviks in Russia*

**1917**
Russian
Revolution
begins

**1919**
Allies sign
Treaty of
Versailles

*1917*

*1918*

*1919*

**1917**
United States
enters the war

**1918**
Germany
agrees to
truce

*People celebrating
the end of the war*

**HISTORY**
*Online*

**Chapter Overview**
Visit the *Glencoe World
History—Modern
Times* Web site at
wh.mt.glencoe.com
and click on **Chapter 8–
Chapter Overview** to
preview chapter information.

# Preparing to Read Chapter 8

 **Reading Skill** **Time and Sequence**

Time is the basic matter for all history—perhaps like the atom is for physics. Since historians explain change over time, they must first know the <u>order</u> of events. For example, they could not say that one event caused another unless they knew which came first. For this reason, historians often use words or phrases that refer to time or sequence. Time lines also highlight the concern with time or chronology—*chronology* comes from the Greek for time, *chronos*.

You know an author is calling attention to time and sequence when you see certain words and phrases—for example, *first, second, last, finally, next, then, since, after,* and *at last.* The most obvious signal, of course, is a date!

## TIME

That morning . . . Later in the day: Both phrases help fix the time of an event and give the reader a sense of how long it took to come about.

## SEQUENCE

before . . . By 1920: Both phrases explain sequence. The Whites made progress first, then were pushed back, and at the turn of the year were defeated.

*Read the following excerpts from the chapter and notice how the signal words help you anticipate a time-ordered explanation.*

That morning, one of the conspirators threw a bomb at the archduke's car, but it glanced off and exploded against the car behind him. Later in the day, however, Gavrilo Princip, a 19-year-old Bosnian Serb, succeeded in fatally shooting both the archduke and his wife.

. . . In mid-1919, White forces swept through Ukraine and advanced almost to Moscow before being pushed back. By 1920, however, the major White forces had been defeated and Ukraine retaken. The next year, the Communist regime regained control . . . in Georgia, Russian Armenia, and Azerbaijan.

### Apply the Skill

Look for words in each chapter that signal time and sequence. This will make your notes better because you will record information in the right sequence.

 **Historical Interpretation: Standard HI 1** *Students show the connections, causal and otherwise, between particular historical events and larger social, economic, and political trends and developments.*

Historians recognize that dramatic, large-scale events need to be examined closely. Events, such as a huge public demonstration or an assassination of a political leader, are connected to the past, and will affect many people in the future.

In this chapter, you will read about a group of working-class women who marched through the Russian capital in 1917 to protest bread lines. Historians do not look upon this as an isolated incident, but as an event that tells them about the state of Russian society.

*Read this police report to the government, written before the protest:*

> **"Mothers of families, exhausted by endless standing in line at stores, distraught over their half-starving and sick children, are today perhaps closer to revolution than [the liberal opposition leaders] and of course they are a great deal more dangerous because they are the combustible material for which only a single spark is needed to burst into flame."**

Since this happened during World War I, what factors might have led to discontent? Based on what you've learned about the Russian Revolution of 1905, what are the possible consequences of a working-class protest? Might this protest affect Russia's ability to fight the war?

## Apply the Skill

Discuss your answers to the previous questions with a classmate. When the two of you have read the chapter, see whether your conclusions about cause and effect were similar to the actual events in Russia in 1917.

# A Story That Matters

*Advancing troops in the Battle of the Somme*

*British artillery firing on the Germans at the Battle of the Somme*

## The Battle of the Somme

On July 1, 1916, British and French infantry forces attacked German defensive lines along a front about 25 miles (40 km) long near the Somme River in France. Each soldier carried almost 70 (32 kg) pounds of equipment, including a rifle, ammunition, grenades, a shovel, a mess kit, and a full water bottle. This burden made it "impossible to move much quicker than a slow walk."

German machine guns soon opened fire. "We were able to see our comrades move forward in an attempt to cross No-Man's-Land, only to be mown down like meadow grass," recalled one British soldier. Another wrote later, "I felt sick at the sight of this carnage and remember weeping."

Philip Gibbs, an English journalist with the troops, reported on what he found in the German trenches that the British forces overran: "Victory! . . . Groups of dead lay in ditches which had once been trenches, flung into chaos by that bombardment I had seen. . . . Some of the German dead were young boys, too young to be killed for old men's crimes, and others might have been old or young. One could not tell because they had no faces, and were just masses of raw flesh in rags of uniforms. Legs and arms lay separate without any bodies thereabouts."

In the first day of the Battle of the Somme, about 21,000 British soldiers died. After four months of fighting, the British had advanced 5 miles (8 km). About one million Allied and German soldiers lay dead or wounded.

### Why It Matters

World War I (1914–1918) devastated the economic, social, and political order of Europe. People at the time, overwhelmed by the size of the war's battles and the number of casualties, simply called it the Great War. The war was all the more disturbing to Europeans because it came after a period that many believed to have been an age of progress. World War I and the revolutions it spawned can properly be seen as the first stage in the crisis of the twentieth century.

**History and You** Look online or in the library for a speech delivered by Woodrow Wilson or another leader, explaining the reasons for entering the war. Analyze the arguments. How might someone opposed to the war counter those arguments?

# The Road to World War I

## Guide to Reading

### Section Preview
Militarism, nationalism, and a crisis in the Balkans led to World War I.

**Main Idea**

• Feelings of nationalism and a system of alliances contributed to the start of World War I. (p. 422)
• Serbia's determination to become a large, independent state angered Austria-Hungary and started hostilities. (p. 424)

### Content Vocabulary
conscription, mobilization

### Academic Vocabulary
ethnic, alter, anticipate, behalf

### People and Events to Identify
Triple Alliance, Triple Entente, Archduke Francis Ferdinand, Gavrilo Princip, Emperor William II, Czar Nicholas II, General Alfred von Schlieffen

### Places to Locate
Serbia, Bosnia

### Reading Objectives
1. Explain how the assassination of Archduke Francis Ferdinand led to World War I.
2. Describe how the system of alliances helped cause the war.

### Reading Strategy
**Cause and Effect** Use a diagram like the one below to identify the factors that led to World War I.

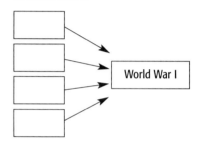

### Preview of Events

| ◆1880 | ◆1890 | ◆1900 | ◆1910 | ◆1920 |
|---|---|---|---|---|

**1882**
Triple Alliance forms

**1907**
Triple Entente forms

**1908**
Austria annexes Ottoman province of Bosnia

**1912–1913**
First and second Balkan wars are fought

**1914**
World War I begins

## California Standards in This Section

*Reading this section will help you master these California History–Social Science standards.*

**10.5.1:** Analyze the arguments for entering into war presented by leaders from all sides of the Great War and the role of political and economic rivalries, ethnic and ideological conflicts, domestic discontent and disorder, and propaganda and nationalism in mobilizing the civilian population in support of "total war."

**10.5.2:** Examine the principal theaters of battle, major turning points, and the importance of geographic factors in military decisions and outcomes (e.g., topography, waterways, distance, climate).

# Nationalism and the System of Alliances

**Main Idea** Feelings of nationalism and a system of alliances contributed to the start of World War I.

**Reading Connection** Have you ever stood up for a friend when he or she was being criticized? Read to find out how a system of alliances led to the start of World War I.

Until about 1850, liberals believed that if European states were organized along national lines, these states could create a peaceful Europe. They were wrong. The system of nation-states that emerged in Europe led later in the century not to cooperation but to competition. Rivalries over colonies and trade grew during an age of frenzied nationalism and imperialist expansion. It took only an assassin's bullet to ignite a world war.

## *Voices from the Past*

On June 28, 1914, the heir to the Austro-Hungarian throne, Archduke Francis Ferdinand, was assassinated in the Bosnian city of Sarajevo. One of the conspirators described the scene:

> 66As the car came abreast, [the assassin] stepped forward from the curb, drew his automatic pistol from his coat and fired two shots. The first struck the wife of the Archduke, the Archduchess Sophia, in the abdomen. She was an expectant mother. She died instantly. The second bullet struck the Archduke close to the heart. He uttered only one word: 'Sophia'—a call to his stricken wife. Then his head fell back and he collapsed. He died almost instantly.99

Why did the archduke's murder lead to war? The answer lies in the European alliance system. For some time, Europe's great powers had been divided into two loose alliances. Germany, Austria-Hungary, and Italy formed the **Triple Alliance** in 1882. France, Great Britain, and Russia created the **Triple Entente** in 1907.

In the early years of the twentieth century, a series of crises tested these alliances. Especially troublesome were the crises in the Balkans between 1908 and 1913. Tensions rose in 1908 when Austria annexed the Ottoman province of Bosnia—the Aus-

trians had already been administering it according to international treaty. Then in 1912 and 1913, different Balkan groups—Serbs, Rumanians, Greeks, and Turks—fought one another for more territory and influence.

These events brought emotions to a boil. European states were angry at each other, especially Austria and Russia. Each state was guided by its own self-interest and success. They were willing to use war as a way to preserve the power of their national states.

The growth of nationalism in the nineteenth century had yet another serious result. Not all **ethnic** groups had become nations. Slavic minorities in the Balkans and the Hapsburg Empire, for example, still dreamed of creating their own national states. The Irish in the British Empire and the Poles in the Russian Empire had similar dreams.

**Internal Dissent** National desires were not the only source of internal strife at the beginning of the twentieth century. Because of industrialization, society had changed. The working class and lower middle class did not want to let wealthy people decide what was best for them. They also wanted a bigger share of the economic wealth they had helped create. Trade unions were demanding better wages. Socialist parties wanted even more radical change—an end to capitalism. Increasingly, both groups used strikes, even violent ones, to achieve their goals.

▼ *Assassination at Sarajevo*

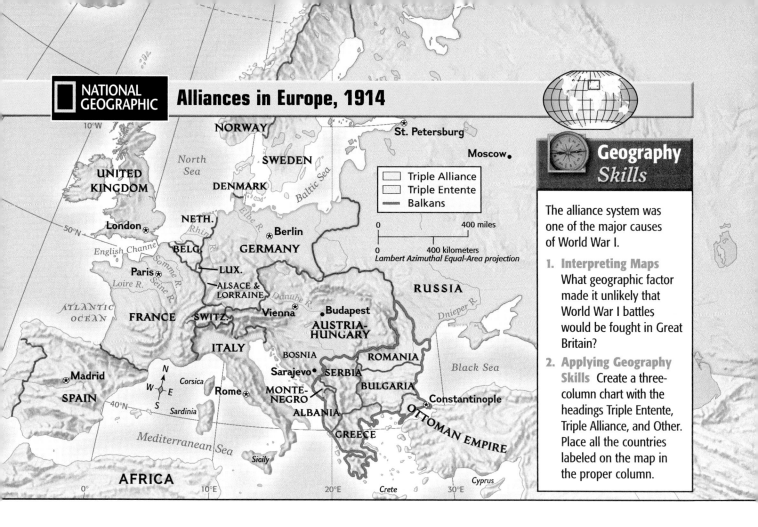

**Legend:**
- Triple Alliance
- Triple Entente
- — Balkans

0 _____ 400 miles
0 _____ 400 kilometers
Lambert Azimuthal Equal-Area projection

### Geography Skills

The alliance system was one of the major causes of World War I.

1. **Interpreting Maps** What geographic factor made it unlikely that World War I battles would be fought in Great Britain?

2. **Applying Geography Skills** Create a three-column chart with the headings Triple Entente, Triple Alliance, and Other. Place all the countries labeled on the map in the proper column.

---

Conservative leaders in a number of European nations were alarmed at this increase in labor conflict and class division. They feared that their nations were on the verge of revolution. A number of historians have argued that this desire to avoid revolution encouraged the plunge into war in 1914. According to this view, the fervent patriotic feeling of wartime was supposed to join all social classes together against a foreign enemy and lessen the appeal of socialism.

**Militarism** The growth of mass armies after 1900 heightened the existing tensions in Europe. The large size of these armies also should have made it obvious that if war did come, it would be highly destructive. There was a second reason that any coming war would be more destructive. The Industrial Revolution had given nations much more destructive guns and weapons than ever before.

Nevertheless, many politicians and generals expected a war that would be like the last one fought in Europe—Bismarck's war against France when he unified Germany. That war was quick and decisive, and the casualties were relatively light. Thus the two sides thought they could take the offensive and win a quick victory.

In the years before 1914, **conscription,** a military draft, had been established as a regular practice in the West. Only the United States and Britain did not have conscription when war broke out. Because of conscription, armies expanded significantly between 1890 and 1914. Many armies doubled in size.

With its 1.3 million men, the Russian army was the largest in Europe. The French and German armies were not far behind, with 900,000 each. The British, Italian, and Austro-Hungarian armies had between 250,000 and 500,000 soldiers each.

Militarism—the aggressive preparation for war—was growing. As armies grew, so too did the influence of military leaders. Generals drew up complex plans for quickly mobilizing millions of men and enormous quantities of supplies in case of war. Generals had spent years planning how to win a war, not how to avoid one.

Military leaders feared that any changes in their plans would cause chaos in the army. Thus they insisted that their plans could not be **altered.** In the 1914 crises, this left European political leaders with little leeway. They were forced to make decisions for military instead of political reasons.

**Reading Check** **Examining** What was the effect of conscription on events leading up to World War I?

# The Outbreak of War: Summer 1914

**Main Idea** Serbia's determination to become a large, independent state angered Austria-Hungary and started hostilities.

**Reading Connection** What circumstances might influence the United States to enter a war on behalf of an ally? Read to learn how an assassination led to a world war.

Militarism, nationalism, and the desire to stifle internal dissent may all have played a role in the starting of World War I. However, it was the decisions made by European leaders in response to another crisis in the Balkans in the summer of 1914 that led directly to the conflict.

**The Serbian Problem** As we have seen, states in southeastern Europe had struggled for many years to free themselves of Ottoman rule. Furthermore, the rivalry between Austria-Hungary and Russia for domination of these new states created serious tensions in the region.

By 1914, **Serbia,** supported by Russia, was determined to create a large, independent Slavic state in the Balkans. Austria-Hungary, which had its own Slavic minorities to contend with, was equally determined to prevent that from happening.

Many Europeans saw the potential danger in this explosive situation. The British ambassador to Vienna **anticipated** war in 1913:

> 66Serbia will some day set Europe by the ears, and bring about a universal war on the Continent. . . . I cannot tell you how exasperated people are getting here at the continual worry which that little country causes to Austria under encouragement from Russia. . . . It will be lucky if Europe succeeds in avoiding war as a result of the present crisis.99

It was against this backdrop of mutual distrust and hatred that the events of the summer of 1914 were played out.

**Assassination in Sarajevo** On June 28, 1914, **Archduke Francis Ferdinand,** the heir to the throne of Austria-Hungary, and his wife Sophia visited Sarajevo (SAR•uh•YAY•voh) in Bosnia. A group of conspirators waited there in the streets. The conspirators were members of the Black Hand, a Serbian terrorist

organization that wanted **Bosnia** to be free of Austria-Hungary and to become part of a large Serbian kingdom.

The conspirators planned to kill the archduke, along with his wife. That morning, one of the conspirators threw a bomb at the archduke's car, but it glanced off and exploded against the car behind him. Later in the day, however, **Gavrilo Princip,** a 19-year-old Bosnian Serb, succeeded in fatally shooting both the archduke and his wife.

**Austria-Hungary Responds** The Austro-Hungarian government did not know whether or not the Serbian government had been directly involved in the archduke's assassination, but it did not care. It saw an opportunity to "render Serbia innocuous [harmless] once and for all by a display of force," as the Austrian foreign minister put it.

Austrian leaders wanted to attack Serbia but feared Russian intervention on Serbia's **behalf,** so they sought the backing of their German allies. **Emperor William II** of Germany and his chancellor responded with a "blank check," saying that Austria-Hungary could rely on Germany's "full support," even if "matters went to the length of a war between Austria-Hungary and Russia."

Strengthened by German support, Austrian leaders sent an ultimatum to Serbia on July 23. In it, they made such extreme demands that Serbia had little choice but to reject some of them in order to preserve its sovereignty. On July 28, Austria-Hungary declared war on Serbia.

**Russia Mobilizes** Russia was determined to support Serbia's cause. On July 28, **Czar Nicholas II** ordered partial mobilization of the Russian army against Austria-Hungary. **Mobilization** is the process of assembling troops and supplies and making them ready for war. In 1914, mobilization was considered an act of war.

Leaders of the Russian army informed the czar that they could not partially mobilize. Their mobilization plans were based on a war against both Germany and Austria-Hungary. Mobilizing against only Austria-Hungary, they claimed, would create chaos in the army. Based on this claim, the czar ordered full mobilization of the Russian army on July 29, knowing that Germany would consider this order an act of war.

**The Conflict Broadens** Indeed, Germany reacted quickly. The German government warned Russia that it must halt its mobilization within 12 hours.

When Russia ignored this warning, Germany declared war on Russia on August 1.

Like the Russians, the Germans had a military plan. It had been drawn up under the guidance of **General Alfred von Schlieffen** (SHLEE•fuhn), and so was known as the Schlieffen Plan. The plan called for a two-front war with France and Russia, who had formed a military alliance in 1894.

According to the Schlieffen Plan, Germany would conduct a small holding action against Russia while most of the German army would carry out a rapid invasion of France. This meant invading France by moving quickly along the level coastal area through Belgium. After France was defeated, the German invaders would move to the east against Russia.

Under the Schlieffen Plan, Germany could not mobilize its troops solely against Russia. Therefore, it declared war on France on August 3. About the same time, it issued an ultimatum to Belgium demanding the right of German troops to pass through Belgian territory. Belgium, however, was a neutral nation.

On August 4, Great Britain declared war on Germany, officially for violating Belgian neutrality. In fact, Britain was concerned about maintaining its own world power. As one British diplomat put it, if Germany and Austria-Hungary won the war, "what would be the position of a friendless England?" By August 4, all the Great Powers of Europe were at war.

▲ *German officer reading the declaration of war in the streets of Berlin*

 **Evaluating** How did the Schlieffen Plan contribute to the outbreak of World War I?

### HISTORY Online — Study Central

For help with the concepts in this section of *Glencoe World History–Modern Times,* go to wh.mt.glencoe.com and click on **Study Central.**

# SECTION 1 ASSESSMENT

### Checking for Understanding

1. **Vocabulary** Define: ethnic, conscription, alter, anticipate, behalf, mobilization.

2. **People and Events** Identify: Triple Alliance, Triple Entente, Archduke Francis Ferdinand, Gavrilo Princip, Emperor William II, Czar Nicholas II, General Alfred von Schlieffen.

3. **Places** Locate: Serbia, Bosnia.

### Reviewing Big Ideas

4. **List** the ethnic groups that were left without nations after the nationalist movements of the nineteenth century.

### Critical Thinking

5. **Historical Analysis Connecting Events** How did the creation of military plans help draw the nations of Europe into World War I? In your opinion, what should today's national and military leaders have learned from the military plans that helped initiate World War I? Explain. **CA HI1**

6. **Sequencing Information** Using a diagram like the one below, identify the series of decisions made by European leaders in 1914 that led directly to the outbreak of war.

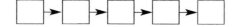

### Analyzing Visuals

7. Examine the photo on this page of the German officer on the streets of Berlin. Compare how German leaders communicated this important event to how it might happen in your own society. Why might the 1914 situation contribute to immediate excitement?

### Writing About History

8. **Expository Writing** Some historians believe that the desire to suppress internal disorder may have encouraged leaders to take the plunge into war. As an adviser, write a memo to your country's leader explaining how a war might benefit the nation. **CA 10WA2.4a**

# THE LUSITANIA

Passengers boarding the British liner *R.M.S. Lusitania* in New York on May 1, 1915, for the voyage to Liverpool, England, knew of Germany's threat to sink ships bound for the British Isles. Britain and Germany had been fighting for nine months. Still, few passengers imagined that a civilized nation would attack an unarmed passenger steamer without warning.

Built eight years earlier, the *Lusitania* was described as a "floating palace." German authorities, however, saw her as a threat. They accused the British government of using the *Lusitania* to carry ammunition and other war supplies across the Atlantic.

With her four towering funnels, the liner looked invincible as she left New York on her last voyage. Six days later, at 2:10 P.M. on May 7, 1915, Walther Schwieger, the 30-year-old commander of the German submarine U 20, fired a single torpedo at the *Lusitania* from a range of about 750 yards (686 m).

Captain William Turner of the *Lusitania* saw the torpedo's wake from the navigation bridge just before impact. It sounded like a "million-ton hammer hitting a steam boiler a hundred feet high," one passenger said. A second, more powerful explosion followed, sending a geyser of water, coal, and debris high above the deck.

Listing to starboard, the liner began to sink rapidly at the bow, sending passengers tumbling down her slanted decks. Lifeboats on the port side were hanging too far inboard to be readily launched, those on the starboard side too far out to be easily boarded. Several overfilled lifeboats spilled occupants into the

sea. The great liner disappeared under the waves in only 18 minutes, leaving behind a jumble of swimmers, corpses, deck chairs, and wreckage. Looking back upon the scene from his submarine, even the German commander Schwieger was shocked. He later called it the most horrible sight he had ever seen.

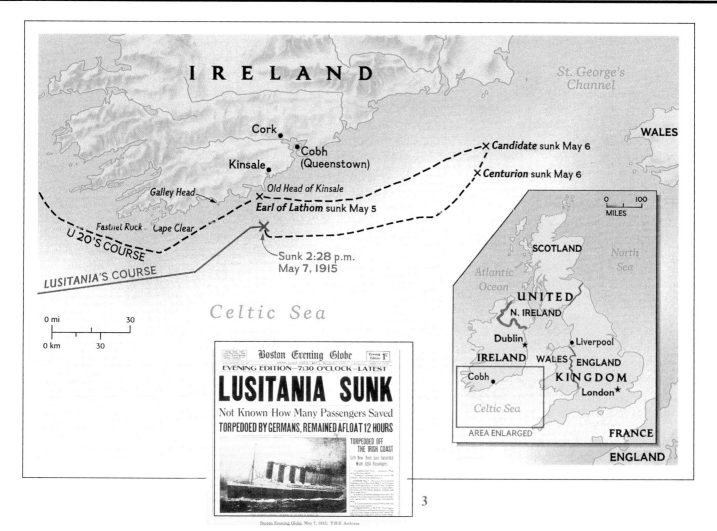

IRELAND

St. George's Channel

WALES

Cork

Cobh (Queenstown)

Kinsale

✕ *Candidate* sunk May 6

✕ *Centurion* sunk May 6

*Galley Head*

*Old Head of Kinsale*

✕ *Earl of Lathom* sunk May 5

*Fastnet Rock*   *Cape Clear*

*U 20'S COURSE*

*LUSITANIA'S COURSE*

✕ Sunk 2:28 p.m. May 7, 1915

0 mi       30

0 km       30

*Celtic Sea*

0       100
MILES

SCOTLAND

*North Sea*

*Atlantic Ocean*

UNITED

N. IRELAND

Dublin ★   • Liverpool

IRELAND   WALES   ENGLAND

Cobh •

KINGDOM

London ★

*Celtic Sea*

AREA ENLARGED

FRANCE

ENGLAND

**Boston Evening Globe**

EVENING EDITION—7:30 O'CLOCK—LATEST

# LUSITANIA SUNK

Not Known How Many Passengers Saved

TORPEDOED BY GERMANS, REMAINED AFLOAT 12 HOURS

TORPEDOED OFF THE IRISH COAST

3

News of the disaster raced across the Atlantic. Of 1,959 people aboard, only 764 were saved. The dead included 94 children and infants.

Questions were immediately raised. Did the British Admiralty give the *Lusitania* adequate warning? How could one torpedo have sunk her? Why did she go down so fast? Was there any truth to the German claim that the *Lusitania* had been armed?

From the moment the *Lusitania* sank, she was surrounded by controversy. Americans were outraged by the attack, which claimed the lives of 123 U.S. citizens. Newspapers called the attack "deliberate murder" and a "foul deed," and former President Theodore Roosevelt demanded

revenge against Germany. The attack on the *Lusitania* is often credited with drawing the United States into World War I. However, President Woodrow Wilson—though he had vowed to hold Germany responsible for its submarine attacks—knew that the American people were not ready to go to war. It was almost two years before the United States joined the conflict in Europe.

A British judge laid full blame on the German submarine commander, while the German government claimed that the British had deliberately made her a military target. Tragically, inquiries following the sinking of the *Lusitania* revealed that Captain Turner had received warnings by wireless from the British Admiralty,

**1** The *Lusitania* arrives in New York on her maiden voyage in 1907 (opposite page).

**2** Captain William Turner of the *Lusitania,* (opposite page, center); Walther Schwieger, commander of the German submarine U 20 (opposite page, right).

**3** Headlines in Boston and New York (above) report the terrible news of the sinking of the *Lusitania* on May 7, 1915. In the two days prior to the attack on the *Lusitania,* the German submarine U 20 had sunk three ships off Ireland's southern coast. Yet the captain of the *Lusitania,* who had received warnings by wireless from the British Admiralty, took only limited precautions as he approached the area.

but took only limited precautions as he approached the area where the U 20 was waiting.

Rumors of diamonds, gold, and valuables locked away in *Lusitania's* safes have prompted salvage attempts over the years. To date, no treasure has ever been reported.

Perhaps the biggest puzzle has been the hardest to solve: Why did the liner sink so fast? Newspapers speculated that the torpedo had struck munitions in a cargo hold, causing the strong secondary explosion. Divers later reported a huge hole in the port side of the bow, opposite where munitions would have been stored.

■

Hoping to settle the issue, a team from the Woods Hole Oceanographic Institution, sponsored by the National Geographic Society, sent their robot vehicle Jason down to photograph the damage. Fitted with cameras and powerful lights, the robot sent video images of the wreck by fiber-optic cable to a control room on the surface ship, *Northern Horizon*. A pilot maneuvered Jason with a joystick, while an engineer relayed instructions to the robot's computers. Other team members watched for recognizable objects on the monitors. In addition to using Jason to make a visual survey of the *Lusitania*, the team of researchers and scientists also used sonar to create a computerized, three-dimensional diagram of how the wreck looks today.

From this data, it was discovered that the *Lusitania's* hull had been flattened—in part by the force of gravity—to half its original width. But when Jason's cameras swept across the hold, looking for the hole reported by divers shortly after the sinking, there was none to be found. Indeed, no evidence was found that would indicate that the torpedo had detonated an explosion in a cargo hold, undermining one theory of why the liner sank.

Questions about her cargo have haunted the *Lusitania* since the day she went down. Was she carrying illegal munitions as the Germans have always claimed? In fact, she was. The manifest for her last voyage included wartime essentials such as motorcycle parts, metals, cotton goods, and food, as well as 4,200 cases of rifle ammunition, 1,250 cases of shrapnel (not explosive), and 18 boxes of percussion fuses. However, the investigation conducted by the Woods Hole team and Jason suggested that these munitions did not cause the secondary blast that sent the *Lusitania* to the bottom. So what did?

One likely possibility was a coal-dust explosion. The German torpedo struck the liner's starboard side about 10 feet (3 m) below the waterline, rupturing one of the long coal

4

4  Homer, a small robot, (opposite page) explores a hole in the stern of the *Lusitania* that was cut by a salvage crew to recover silverware and other items.

5  A provocative poster (left) depicted drowning innocents and urged Americans to enlist in the armed forces.

6  Alice Drury (above left) was a young nanny for an American couple on the *Lusitania*. She and another nanny were caring for the couple's children: Audrey (above right), Stuart, Amy, and Susan. Alice was about to give Audrey a bottle when the torpedo hit. Alice wrapped Audrey in a shawl, grabbed Stuart, and headed for the lifeboats. A crewman loaded Stuart, but when Alice tried to board, the sailor told her it was full. Without a life jacket and with Audrey around her neck, Alice jumped into the water. A woman in the lifeboat grabbed her hair and pulled her aboard. Audrey's parents were rescued too, but Amy, Susan, and the other nanny were lost. Alice and Audrey Lawson Johnston have remained close ever since.

bunkers [storage bins] that stretched along both sides. If that bunker, mostly empty by the end of the voyage, contained explosive coal dust, the torpedo might have ignited it. Such an occurrence would explain all the coal that was found scattered on the seafloor near the wreck.

The *Lusitania's* giant funnels have long since turned to rust, an eerie marine growth covers her hull, and her superstructure is ghostly wreckage. Yet the horror and fascination surrounding the sinking of the great liner live on. With today's high-technology tools, researchers and scientists at Woods Hole and the National Geographic Society have provided another look—and some new answers—to explain the chain of events that ended with the *Lusitania* at the bottom of the sea.

## INTERPRETING THE PAST

1. How did the *Lusitania* contribute to drawing the United States into World War I?

2. Describe the *Lusitania's* route. Where was it when it sank?

3. What mysteries were researchers able to solve by using underwater robot technology?

# SECTION 2  The War

## Guide to Reading

### Section Preview
The stalemate at the Western Front led to a widening of World War I, and governments expanded their powers to accommodate the war.

**Main Idea**

- The war on the Western Front turned into a stalemate as a result of trench warfare, while on the Eastern Front Germany and Austria-Hungary defeated Russia. (p. 431)
- New weapons and trench warfare made World War I far more devastating than any previous wars. (p. 432)
- With the war at a stalemate, both the Allies and the Central Powers looked for new allies to gain an advantage. (p. 433)

- The U.S. attempt at neutrality ended when the Germans refused to stop unrestricted submarine warfare. (p. 434)
- World War I became a total war, with governments taking control of their economies and civilians undergoing rationing of goods. (p. 435)

### Content Vocabulary
propaganda, trench warfare, war of attrition, total war, planned economies

### Academic Vocabulary
suspend, submission, assure

### People to Identify
Lawrence of Arabia, Admiral Holtzendorff, Woodrow Wilson

### Places to Locate
Marne, Tannenberg, Masurian Lakes, Verdun, Gallipoli

### Reading Objectives
1. Describe how trench warfare led to a stalemate.
2. Explain why the United States entered the war.

### Reading Strategy
**Organizing Information** Identify which countries belonged to the Allies and the Central Powers. What country changed allegiance? What country withdrew from the war?

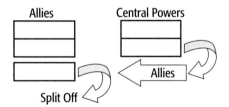

**Preview of Events**

| ◆1914 | ◆1915 | ◆1916 | ◆1917 | ◆1918 | ◆1919 |
|---|---|---|---|---|---|

**1915** *Lusitania* sunk by German forces

**1916** Battle of Verdun

**1917** The United States enters the war

## California Standards in This Section

*Reading this section will help you master these California History–Social Science standards.*

**10.5.1:** Analyze the arguments for entering into war presented by leaders from all sides of the Great War and the role of political and economic rivalries, ethnic and ideological conflicts, domestic discontent and disorder, and propaganda and nationalism in mobilizing the civilian population in support of "total war."

**10.5.2:** Examine the principal theaters of battle, major turning points, and the importance of geographic factors in military decisions and outcomes (e.g., topography, waterways, distance, climate).

# 1914 to 1915: Illusions and Stalemate

**Main Idea** The war on the Western Front turned into a stalemate as a result of trench warfare, while on the Eastern Front Germany and Austria-Hungary defeated Russia.

**Reading Connection** How do political campaigns try to influence voters? Read on to see how governments tried to influence public opinion before World War I.

Before 1914, many political leaders thought that war involved so many political and economic risks that it was something to be avoided. Others thought diplomats would easily be able to control any situation and prevent war. At the beginning of August 1914, both ideas were shattered. When war came, however, another illusion was born—the concept that the war would be a thrilling and positive experience. For the first months of the war, many Europeans shared this belief.

## *Voices from the Past*

The Austrian writer Stefan Zweig described the excitement Austrians felt going to war in 1914:

> ❝What did the people know of war in 1914, after nearly half a century of peace? They did not know war; they had hardly given it a thought. They still saw it in the perspective of their school readers and of paintings in museums; brilliant cavalry attacks in glittering uniforms, the fatal shot always straight through the heart, the entire campaign a resounding march of victory—'We'll be home at Christmas,' the recruits shouted laughingly to their mothers in August of 1914.... The young people were honestly afraid that they might miss this most wonderful and exciting experience of their lives; ... that is why they shouted and sang in the trains that carried them to the slaughter.❞

Why were people so eager for war? First, government **propaganda**—ideas spread to influence public opinion for or against a cause—had stirred up national hatreds. Thus, Europeans responded eagerly to the urgent pleas of their leaders in August 1914 to defend the homeland against aggressors. Most people seemed genuinely convinced that their nation's cause was just.

▲ *Troops going to war*

Second, at the beginning of the war, almost everyone believed it would be over in a few weeks. People were reminded that almost all European wars since 1815 had, in fact, ended in a matter of weeks. Both the soldiers who boarded the trains for the war front in August 1914, and the jubilant citizens who showered them with flowers as they left, believed that the warriors would be home by Christmas.

**The Western Front** German hopes for a quick end to the war rested on a military gamble. The Schlieffen Plan had called for the German army to make a vast encircling movement through Belgium into northern France. According to the plan, the German forces would sweep around Paris. This would enable them to surround most of the French army.

The German advance was halted a short distance from Paris at the First Battle of the **Marne** (September 6–10). To stop the Germans, French military leaders loaded two thousand Parisian taxicabs with fresh troops and sent them to the front line.

The war quickly turned into a stalemate, as neither the Germans nor the French could dislodge each other from the trenches they had dug for shelter. These trenches were ditches protected by barbed wire. Two lines of trenches soon reached from the English Channel to the frontiers of Switzerland. The Western Front had become bogged down in **trench warfare** that kept both sides in virtually the same positions for four years.

**The Eastern Front** In contrast to the Western Front, the war on the Eastern Front was marked by mobility. The cost in lives, however, was equally enormous.

At the beginning of the war, the Russian army moved into eastern Germany but was decisively defeated at the Battle of **Tannenberg** on August 30 and the Battle of **Masurian Lakes** on September 15. As a result of these defeats, the Russians were no longer a threat to German territory.

Austria-Hungary, Germany's ally, fared less well at first. The Austrians had been defeated by the Russians in Galicia and thrown out of Serbia as well. To make matters worse, the Italians betrayed their German and Austrian allies in the Triple Alliance by attacking Austria in May 1915. Italy thus joined France, Great Britain, and Russia, who had formed the Triple Entente. The four nations now were called the Allied Powers, or Allies.

By this time, the Germans had come to the aid of the Austrians. A German-Austrian army defeated the Russian army in Galicia and pushed the Russians far back into their own territory. Russian casualties stood at 2.5 million killed, captured, or wounded. The Russians had almost been knocked out of the war.

Buoyed by their success, Germany and Austria-Hungary, joined by Bulgaria in September 1915, attacked and eliminated Serbia from the war. Their successes in the east would enable the Germans to move back to the offensive in the west.

✓**Reading Check** **Contrasting** How did the war on the Eastern Front differ from the war on the Western Front?

▼ *British women in a munitions factory*

# 1916 to 1917: The Great Slaughter

**Main Idea** New weapons and trench warfare made World War I far more devastating than any previous wars.

**Reading Connection** Have you read about soldiers' experiences in World War II or the Vietnam War? Read on to learn about the trench warfare that characterized World War I.

On the Western Front, the trenches dug in 1914 had by 1916 become elaborate systems of defense. The lines of trenches for both sides were protected by barbed-wire entanglements up to 5 feet (about 1.5 m) high and 30 yards (about 27 m) wide, concrete machine-gun nests, and other gun batteries, supported further back by heavy artillery. Troops lived in holes in the ground, separated from each other by a strip of territory known as no-man's-land.

**Tactics of Trench Warfare** The unexpected development of trench warfare baffled the generals. They had been trained to fight wars of movement and maneuver, and now faced stalemate. They decided that the only solution was to throw masses of men against enemy lines after artillery had bombarded the enemy for hours. Once the decisive breakthrough had been achieved, they thought, they could return to the war of movement that they knew best.

At times, the high command on either side would order an offensive that would begin with an artillery barrage to flatten the enemy's barbed wire and leave the enemy in a state of shock. After "softening up" the enemy in this fashion, a mass of soldiers would climb out of their trenches with fixed bayonets and hope to work their way toward the enemy trenches.

The attacks rarely worked because men advancing unprotected across open fields could be fired at by the enemy's machine guns. In 1916 and 1917, millions of young men died fighting for the elusive breakthrough.

The Battle of **Verdun** was symbolic of the new kind of war that had come about. Verdun was a French fortress city on the German border. The French general in charge encouraged his troops with the phrase, "They shall not pass." Knowing that the French felt honor-bound to defend Verdun, the Germans attacked again and again. The German goal was to bleed the French army white. In the 10 months of fighting at Verdun in 1916, 700,000 French and German young men lost their lives over a few miles of land. World War I had turned into a **war of attrition,** a war based on wearing the other side down by constant attacks and

## Then *and* Now

The introduction of airplanes greatly changed the nature of warfare during the twentieth century.
What kind of aircraft did the Germans use during World War I?

*British fighter plane, c. 1917* ▶

*U.S. jet fighter, 2001* ▼

heavy losses. 📖 *(See page 774 to read an excerpt from Arthur Guy Empey's memoir of World War I in the Primary Sources Library.)*

The Industrial Revolution was largely responsible for bringing about this change in how wars were fought. Railroads were able to supply the troops much more quickly, and to replace worn-out troops with ready reserves. Factories churned out munitions on a scale never seen before, and long bombardments became routine. Shelling and bombing maimed and disfigured many World War I soldiers—yet another sign that the war had been fought by industrialized nations.

**War in the Air** By the end of 1915, airplanes had appeared on the battlefront for the first time in history. At first, planes were used to spot the enemy's position. However, planes soon began to attack ground targets, especially enemy communications.

Fights for control of the air occurred and increased over time. At first, pilots fired at each other with handheld pistols. Later, machine guns were mounted on the noses of planes, which made the skies considerably more dangerous.

The Germans also used their giant airships—the zeppelins—to bomb London and eastern England. This caused little damage but frightened many people. Germany's enemies, however, soon found that zeppelins, which were filled with hydrogen gas, had a fatal weakness. They quickly became raging infernos when hit by antiaircraft guns.

✔**Reading Check** **Explaining** Why were military leaders baffled by trench warfare?

# Widening of the War

**Main Idea** With the war at a stalemate, both the Allies and the Central Powers looked for new allies to gain an advantage.

**Reading Connection** In the American Revolution, what country did the colonists get aid from? Read to learn how nations looked for allies in World War I.

Because of the stalemate on the Western Front, both sides sought to gain new allies who might provide a winning advantage. The Ottoman Empire had already come into the war on Germany's side in August 1914. Russia, Great Britain, and France—the Allies—declared war on the Ottoman Empire in November.

The Allies tried to open a Balkan front by landing forces at **Gallipoli** (guh•LIH•puh•lee), southwest of Constantinople, in April 1915. However, Bulgaria entered the war on the side of the Central Powers, as Germany, Austria-Hungary, and the Ottoman Empire were called. A disastrous campaign at Gallipoli forced the Allies to withdraw.

In return for Italy entering the war on the Allied side, France and Great Britain promised to let Italy have some Austrian territory. Italy on the side of the Allies opened up a front against Austria-Hungary.

By 1917, the war that had started in Europe had truly become a world conflict. In the Middle East, a British officer known as **Lawrence of Arabia** in 1917 urged Arab princes to revolt against their Ottoman overlords. In 1918, British forces from Egypt destroyed the Ottoman Empire in the Middle East.

# World War I in Europe, 1914–1918

**Legend:**
- Allies
- Central Powers
- Neutral nations
- - - - Line of trench warfare, 1915–1917
- —— Farthest advance of Allies with date
- —— Farthest advance of Central Powers with date
- British naval blockade
- - - - Allied mine barrier
- German submarine war zone
- Sinking of the *Lusitania*, May 7, 1915
- - - Armistice line, Nov. 11, 1918
- - - Treaty line of Brest-Litovsk
- Allied victory
- Central Powers victory
- Indecisive
- ← Schlieffen Plan

*Lambert Azimuthal Equal-Area projection*

## Geography Skills

Trench warfare produced a stalemate on the Western Front.

1. **Applying Geography Skills** Create a bar graph with dates as one axis and miles as the other. Using Berlin as the starting point, plot the Central Powers' advances from the earliest to the latest dates shown on the map.
2. **Interpreting Maps** Where did the majority of World War I battles occur?

---

For their Middle East campaigns, the British mobilized forces from India, Australia, and New Zealand.

The Allies also took advantage of the war to seize German colonies in the rest of the world. Japan, a British ally beginning in 1902, seized a number of German-held islands in the Pacific. Australia seized German New Guinea.

**✓ Reading Check** **Describing** What caused the widening of the war?

## Entry of the United States

**Main Idea** The U.S. attempt at neutrality ended when the Germans refused to stop unrestricted submarine warfare.

**Reading Connection** Is it possible today for the United States to ignore problems in other countries? Read to learn what caused the United States to enter World War I.

At first, the United States tried to remain neutral. As World War I dragged on, however, it became more difficult to do so. The immediate cause of United States involvement grew out of the naval war between Germany and Great Britain.

Britain had used its superior naval power to set up a naval blockade of Germany. The blockade kept war materials and other goods from reaching Germany by sea. Germany had retaliated by setting up its own blockade of Britain. Germany enforced its blockade with the use of unrestricted submarine warfare, which included the sinking of passenger liners.

On May 7, 1915, the British ship *Lusitania* was sunk by German forces. There were about 1,100 civilian casualties, including over 100 Americans. After strong United States protests, the German government suspended unrestricted submarine warfare in September 1915 to avoid antagonizing the United States further. Only once did the German and British naval forces actually engage in direct battle—at the Battle of Jutland on May 31, 1916, when neither side won a conclusive victory. By January 1917, however, the Germans were eager to break the deadlock in the war. German naval officers convinced Emperor William II that resuming the use of unrestricted submarine warfare could starve the British into **submission** within six months.

When the emperor expressed concern about the United States, he was told that the British would starve before the Americans could act. Even if the Americans did intervene, **Admiral Holtzendorf assured** the emperor, "I give your Majesty my word as an officer that not one American will land on the continent."

The German naval officers were wrong. The British were not forced to surrender, and the return to unrestricted submarine warfare brought the United States into the war in April 1917. American troops did not arrive in large numbers in Europe until 1918, but they gave the Allied Powers a psychological boost, as well as a major new source of money and war goods.

**Reading Check** **Evaluating** Why did the Germans resort to unrestricted submarine use?

# The Home Front: The Impact of Total War

**Main Idea** World War I became a total war, with governments taking control of their economies and civilians undergoing rationing of goods.

**Reading Connection** Do you think the government should ever be allowed to censor what newspapers publish? Read to learn why many governments resorted to censorship and similar practices during World War I.

As World War I dragged on, it became a **total war,** involving a complete mobilization of resources and people. It affected the lives of all citizens in the warring countries, however remote they might be from the battlefields.

Masses of men had to be organized and supplies had to be manufactured and purchased for years of combat. (Germany alone had 5.5 million men in uniform in 1916.) This led to an increase in government powers and the manipulation of public opinion to keep the war effort going. The home front was rapidly becoming a cause for as much effort as the war front.

**Increased Government Powers** Most people had expected the war to be short, so little thought had

▼ *In December 1915, these Italian troops posed for a camera as they rested in camp.*

been given to long-term wartime needs. Governments had to respond quickly, however, when the war machines failed to achieve their goals. Many more men and supplies were needed to continue the war. To meet these needs, governments expanded their powers. Countries drafted tens of millions of young men for that elusive breakthrough to victory.

Throughout Europe, wartime governments also expanded their power over their economies. Free-market capitalistic systems were temporarily put aside. Governments set up price, wage, and rent controls; rationed food supplies and materials; regulated imports and exports; and took over transportation systems and industries. In effect, in order to mobilize all the resources of their nations for the war effort, European nations set up **planned economies**—systems directed by government agencies.

Under conditions of total war mobilization, the differences between soldiers at war and civilians at home were narrowed. In the view of political leaders, all citizens were part of a national army dedicated to victory. As United States president **Woodrow Wilson** said, the men and women "who remain to till the soil and man the factories are no less a part of the army than the men beneath the battle flags."

### Manipulation of Public Opinion

The war continued, casualties grew worse, and the patriotic enthusiasm that had marked the early stages of World War I waned. By 1916, there were signs that civilian morale was beginning to crack under the pressure of total war. Wartime governments, however, fought back against the growing opposition to the war.

Authoritarian regimes, such as those of Germany, Russia, and Austria-Hungary, relied on force to subdue their populations. Under the pressures of the war, however, even democratic states expanded their police powers to stop internal dissent. The British Parliament, for example, passed the Defence of the Realm Act (DORA). It allowed the government to arrest protesters as traitors. Newspapers were censored, and sometimes their publication was even suspended.

Governments actively used propaganda to arouse enthusiasm for the war. At the beginning, public officials needed to do little to achieve this goal. The British and French, for example, exaggerated German atrocities in Belgium and found that their citizens were only too willing to believe these accounts.

As the war progressed and morale sagged, governments were forced to devise new techniques for motivating the people. In one British recruiting poster, for example, a small daughter asked her father, "Daddy, what did YOU do in the Great War?" while her younger brother played with toy soldiers.

### Total War and Women

World War I created new roles for women. Because so many men left to fight at the front, women were asked to take over jobs that had not been available to them before. Women were employed in jobs that had once been considered beyond their capacity. These included such occupations as chimney sweeps, truck drivers, farm laborers, and factory workers in heavy industry. For example, 38 percent of the workers in the Krupp Armaments works in Germany in 1918 were women.

The place of women in the workforce was far from secure, however. Both men and women seemed to expect that many of the new jobs for women were

## People In History

### Edith Cavell
#### 1865–1915—British nurse

Edith Cavell was born in Norfolk, England. She trained as a nurse and moved to Brussels in 1907 to head the Berkendael Medical Institute. After the outbreak of war, the institute became a Red Cross hospital. Cavell worked to shelter French and British soldiers and help them reach safety in the Netherlands.

Outraged, German military authorities in Brussels put her on trial for aiding the enemy and ordered her to be shot. Before her execution, Cavell said, "I am glad to die for my country." To arouse anti-German sentiment, both the French and British used her as an example of German barbarism. The Germans insisted they had the right to execute a traitor, whether man or woman.

only temporary. This was evident in the British poem "War Girls," written in 1916:

> 66There's the girl who clips your ticket for the train,
> And the girl who speeds the lift from floor to floor,
> There's the girl who does a milk-round in the rain,
> And the girl who calls for orders at your door.
> Strong, sensible, and fit,
> They're out to show their grit,
> And tackle jobs with energy and knack.
> No longer caged and penned up,
> They're going to keep their end up
> Till the khaki soldier boys come marching back.99

At the end of the war, governments would quickly remove women from the jobs they had encouraged them to take earlier. The work benefits for women from World War I were short-lived as men returned to the job market. By 1919, there would be 650,000 unemployed women in Great Britain. Wages for the women who were still employed would be lowered.

Nevertheless, in some countries the role women played in wartime economies had a positive impact on their social and political emancipation. The most obvious gain was the right to vote, which was given to women in Germany, Austria, and the United States immediately after the war. Most British women gained the vote in 1918.

Many upper-class and middle-class women also gained new freedoms. They took jobs, had their own apartments, and showed their new independence.

**Reading Check** **Summarizing** What was the effect of total war on ordinary citizens?

▲ *This famous British recruiting poster put moral pressure on young men to serve in the war.*

**HISTORY** *Online* **Study Central**

For help with the concepts in this section of *Glencoe World History–Modern Times,* go to wh.mt.glencoe.com and click on **Study Central.**

# SECTION 2 ASSESSMENT

## Checking for Understanding

1. **Vocabulary** Define: propaganda, trench warfare, war of attrition, suspend, submission, assure, total war, planned economies.

2. **People** Identify: Lawrence of Arabia, Admiral Holtzendorff, Woodrow Wilson.

3. **Places** Locate: Marne, Tannenberg, Masurian Lakes, Verdun, Gallipoli.

### Reviewing Big Ideas

4. **Explain** why World War I required total warfare.

## Critical Thinking

5. **Historical Analysis** **Connecting Events** What methods did governments use to counter the loss of enthusiasm and opposition to the war at home? **CA HI1**

6. **Organizing Information** Use a diagram like the one below to identify ways in which government powers increased during the war.

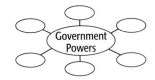

Government Powers

## Analyzing Visuals

7. **Examine** the poster shown on this page. This is a recruiting poster used in World War I. What kind of motivation was it using to encourage young men to enlist?

### Writing About History

8. **Expository Writing** What lasting results occurred in women's rights due to World War I? What were the temporary results? Write an essay discussing the effect of the war on women's rights. **CA 10WA2.3a,b**

# FOCUS ON EVERYDAY LIFE

### Trench Warfare

Warfare in the trenches of the Western Front produced unimaginable horrors. Battlefields were hellish landscapes of barbed wire, shell holes, mud, and injured and dying men. The introduction of poison gas in 1915 produced new forms of injuries. One British writer described them:

"I wish those people who write so glibly about this being a holy war could see a case of mustard gas . . . could see the poor things burnt and blistered all over with great mustard-coloured suppurating [pus-forming] blisters with blind eyes all sticky . . . and stuck together, and always fighting for breath, with voices a mere whisper, saying that their throats are closing and they know they will choke."

At many places along the opposing lines of trenches, a "live and let live" system evolved. It was based on the realization that neither side was going to be successful in driving out the other.

The "live and let live" system resulted in a number of informal arrangements between enemy troops. For example, it was understood that neither side would shell the latrines. It was also considered unfair to attack during breakfast.

On both sides, troops produced their own humor magazines to help pass the time and fulfill the need to laugh in the midst of their daily madness. The British trench magazine, the *B. E. F. Times,* devoted one of its issues to defining military terms, including "DUDS—These are of two kinds. A shell on impact failing to explode is called a dud. They are unhappily not as plentiful as the other kind, which often draws a big salary and explodes for no reason."

◀ These German soldiers were photographed in June 1915. Soldiers in the trenches lived with the presence of death, but since combat went on for months, they had to carry on in the midst of horror. The bodies of those blown apart by artillery barrages lay all around. Many remembered the stench of decomposing bodies and the swarms of rats that grew fat in the trenches.

American nurses with their gas masks file down a trench in France in 1918. For the most part, the only American women active in World War I were nurses. They served in hospitals in France, Belgium, Italy, and England, as well as on trains and transport ships. A number of nurses were decorated for their contribution to the war effort.

▲ *Der Grosse Krieg,* or The Great War, was published during the war by the daily newspaper in Frankfurt, Germany. It chronicled events and included official reports and dispatches. During the war, newspapers and magazines were crammed with war coverage, much of it aimed at keeping up morale.

▲ Daily life in the trenches was predictable. Thirty minutes before sunrise, troops had to "stand to," or be combat-ready to repel attack. If no attack came that day, the day's routine consisted of breakfast followed by inspection, sentry duty, work on the trenches, care of personal items, and attempts to pass the time.

### CONNECTING TO THE PAST

1. **Explain** What was the rationale behind the "live and let live" system?

2. **Writing about History** Write a journal entry as if you were a soldier in the trenches.

# SECTION 3 The Russian Revolution

## Guide to Reading

### Section Preview
The fall of the czarist regime and the Russian Revolution put the Communists in power in Russia.

**Main Idea**

• In March 1917, the czar's failures at the front and worker unrest led to revolution. (p. 441)
• Lenin and the Bolsheviks gained control and quickly overthrew the provisional government. (p. 443)
• A civil war started in Russia between groups opposed to the Bolshevik regime and the Bolsheviks. (p. 444)
• A major reason for Communist victory was that the Bolsheviks were united, while their opponents were not. (p. 445)

### Content Vocabulary
soviets, war communism

### Academic Vocabulary
coincide, irrelevant

### People to Identify
Alexandra, Grigori Rasputin, Alexander Kerensky, Bolsheviks, V. I. Lenin, Leon Trotsky

### Places to Locate
Petrograd, Ukraine, Siberia, Urals

### Reading Objectives
1. Identify the promises the Bolsheviks made to the Russian people after Lenin's arrival in Russia.
2. Explain why the civil war broke out in Russia after the Russian Revolution.

### Reading Strategy
**Categorizing Information** Using a chart like the one below, identify the factors and events that led to Lenin coming to power in 1917.

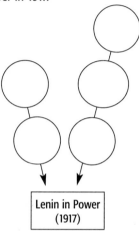

Lenin in Power (1917)

### Preview of Events

| ◆1916 | ◆1917 | ◆1918 | ◆1919 | ◆1920 | ◆1921 |
|-------|-------|-------|-------|-------|-------|
| **1916** Rasputin assassinated | **1917** Czar Nicholas II steps down | **1918** Lenin signs Treaty of Brest-Litovsk | | | **1921** Communists control Russia |

## California Standards in This Section

*Reading this section will help you master these California History–Social Science standards.*

**10.6.2:** Describe the effects of the war and resulting peace treaties on population movement, the international economy, and shifts in geographic and political borders of Europe and the Middle East.

**10.7:** Students analyze the rise of totalitarian governments after World War I.

**10.7.1:** Understand the causes and consequences of the Russian Revolution, including Lenin's use of totalitarian means to seize and maintain control (e.g., the Gulag).

# Background to Revolution

**Main Idea** In March 1917, the czar's failures at the front and worker unrest led to revolution.

**Reading Connection** Do you remember the causes of the 1789 Revolution in France? Read to learn what caused the Russian Revolution.

After its defeat by Japan in 1905 and the Revolution of 1905, Russia was unprepared militarily and technologically for the total war of World War I. Russia had no competent military leaders. Czar Nicholas II insisted on taking charge of the armed forces despite his lack of training. Disastrous leadership in World War I was only one of the causes for the Russian Revolution.

## Voices from the Past

John Reed, an American journalist, described the seizure of the Winter Palace in St. Petersburg, seat of the Russian government, on the night of November 6, 1917. His description captures the moments that heralded the Bolshevik Revolution:

> 66After a few minutes huddling there, some hundreds of men began again to flow forward. By this time, in the light that streamed out of the Winter Palace windows, I could see that the first two or three hundred men were Red Guards [revolutionaries], with only a few scattered soldiers. Over the barricade of firewood we clambered, and leaping down inside gave a triumphant shout as we stumbled on a heap of rifles thrown down by the guards who had stood there. On both sides of the main gateway the doors stood wide open, and from the huge pile came not the slightest sound.99

Besides poor leadership, Russian soldiers suffered other hardships during World War I. They trained using broomsticks because Russian industry was unable to produce the necessary weapons. Other soldiers were sent to the front without rifles and told to pick one up from a dead comrade.

Given these conditions, it is not surprising that the Russian army suffered incredible losses. Between 1914 and 1916, two million soldiers were killed, and another four to six million wounded or captured. By 1917, the Russian will to fight had vanished.

▲ *John Reed, American eyewitness to the Russian Revolution*

**Beginnings of Upheaval** Czar Nicholas II was an autocratic ruler who relied on the army and bureaucracy to hold up his regime. Furthermore, he was increasingly cut off from events by his German-born wife, **Alexandra.** She was a willful and stubborn woman who had fallen under the influence of **Grigori Rasputin** (ra•SPYOO•tuhn), an uneducated Siberian peasant who claimed to be a holy man. Alexandra believed that Rasputin was holy, for he alone seemed able to stop the bleeding of her son Alexis. Alexis, the heir to the throne, had hemophilia (a deficiency in the ability of the blood to clot).

With the czar at the battlefront, Alexandra made all of the important decisions. She insisted on first consulting Rasputin, the man she called "her beloved, never-to-be-forgotten teacher, savior, and mentor." Rasputin's influence made him an important power behind the throne. He did not hesitate to interfere in government affairs.

As the leadership at the top stumbled its way through a series of military and economic disasters, the Russian people grew more and more upset with the czarist regime. Even conservative aristocrats who supported the monarchy felt the need to do something to save the situation.

Rasputin (shown below) had great influence over Czar Nicholas II and his family, seen here in a 1913 photograph. Why was Rasputin able to influence Russian political affairs?

For a start, they assassinated Rasputin in December 1916. It was not easy to kill this man of incredible physical strength. They shot him three times and then tied him up and threw him into the Neva River. He drowned, but not before he had managed to untie the knots underwater. Rasputin's death occurred too late, however, to save the monarchy.

**The March Revolution** At the beginning of March 1917, a series of strikes led by working-class women broke out in the capital city of **Petrograd** (formerly St. Petersburg). A few weeks earlier, the government had started bread rationing in Petrograd after the price of bread had skyrocketed.

Many of the women who stood in the lines waiting for bread were also factory workers who worked 12-hour days. A police report warned the government:

> ❝Mothers of families, exhausted by endless standing in line at stores, distraught over their half-starving and sick children, are today perhaps closer to revolution than [the liberal opposition leaders] and of course they are a great deal more dangerous because they are the combustible material for which only a single spark is needed to burst into flame.❞

On March 8, about 10,000 women marched through the city of Petrograd demanding "Peace and Bread" and "Down with Autocracy." Soon the women and other workers called for a general strike. The strike shut down factories in the city on March 10.

Alexandra wrote her husband Nicholas II at the battlefront, "This is a hooligan movement. If the weather were very cold they would all probably stay at home." Nicholas ordered troops to break up the crowds by shooting them if necessary. Soon, however, large numbers of the soldiers joined the demonstrators and refused to fire on the crowds.

The Duma, or legislative body, which the czar had tried to dissolve, met anyway. On March 12, it established the provisional government, which mainly consisted of middle-class Duma representatives. This government urged the czar to step down. Because he no longer had the support of the army or even the aristocrats, Nicholas II did step down, on March 15, ending the 300-year-old Romanov dynasty.

The provisional government, headed by **Alexander Kerensky** (keh•REHN•skee), now decided to remain in the war to preserve Russia's honor. This decision was a major blunder. It satisfied neither the workers nor the peasants, who wanted an end to the war.

The government was also faced with a challenge to its authority—the **soviets.** The soviets were councils composed of representatives from the workers and soldiers. The soviet of Petrograd had been formed in March 1917. At the same time, soviets sprang up in army units, factory towns, and rural areas. The soviets, largely made up of socialists, represented the more radical interests of the lower classes. One group—the Bolsheviks—came to play a crucial role.

✓ Reading Check  **Identifying** Develop a sequence of events leading to the March Revolution.

## The Rise of Lenin and the Bolsheviks

**Main Idea** Lenin and the Bolsheviks gained control and quickly overthrew the provisional government.

**Reading Connection** How has political change been brought about in the United States? Read to learn how Lenin proposed to make changes in Russia.

The **Bolsheviks** began as a small faction of a Marxist party called the Russian Social Democrats. The Bolsheviks came under the leadership of Vladimir Ilyich Ulianov (ool•YAH•nuhf), known to the world as **V. I. Lenin.**

Under Lenin's direction, the Bolsheviks became a party dedicated to revolution. Lenin believed that only violent revolution could destroy the capitalist system. The vanguard, or forefront of the party leadership, would make the decisions necessary to accomplish the task. Only these disciplined professional revolutionaries could ensure victory.

Between 1900 and 1917, Lenin spent most of his time abroad. When the provisional government was formed in March 1917, he saw an opportunity for the Bolsheviks to seize power. German military leaders, hoping to create disorder in Russia, shipped Lenin to Russia in April 1917. Lenin and his associates were in a sealed train to prevent their ideas from infecting Germany. Lenin's arrival opened a new stage in the

**HISTORY Online**

**Web Activity** Visit the *Glencoe World History– Modern Times* Web site at **wh.mt.glencoe.com** and click on **Chapter 8– Student Web Activity** to learn more about the Russian royal family.

# CONNECTIONS Past To Present

## The Mystery of Anastasia

Czar Nicholas II, his wife Alexandra, and their five children were murdered on the night of July 16, 1918. Soon after, rumors began to circulate that some members of the family had survived.

In 1921, a young woman in Dalldorf, Germany, claimed to be the Grand Duchess Anastasia, youngest daughter of Nicholas II. Some surviving members of the Romanov family became convinced that she was Anastasia. Grand Duke Andrew, Nicholas II's first cousin, said after meeting with her, "For me there is definitely no doubt; it is Anastasia."

Later, the woman claiming to be Anastasia came to the United States. While in New York, she registered at a Long Island hotel as Anna Anderson and soon became known by that name. In 1932, she returned to Germany. During the next 30 years, she pursued a claim in German courts for part of the estate left to Empress Alexandra's German relatives. In the 1960s in the United States, she became even better known as a result of a popular play and film, *Anastasia.*

In 1968, Anna Anderson returned to the United States, where she died in 1984. In 1994, DNA testing of tissues from Anna Anderson revealed that she was not the Grand Duchess Anastasia. In all probability, Anna Anderson was Franziska Schanzkowska, a Polish farmer's daughter who had always dreamed of being an actress.

▲ **Grand Duchess Anastasia**

◄ *Anna Anderson*

## Comparing Past and Present

The woman claiming to be Anastasia convinced many people of the authenticity of her claim. What do you think might have motivated her to act out the part of Anastasia for so many years?

Russian Revolution. Lenin maintained that the soviets of soldiers, workers, and peasants were ready-made instruments of power. He believed that the Bolsheviks should gain control of these groups and use them to overthrow the provisional government.

The Bolsheviks reflected the discontent of the people. They promised an end to the war, the redistribution of all land to the peasants, the transfer of factories and industries from capitalists to committees of workers, and the transfer of government power from the provisional government to the soviets. Three simple slogans summed up the Bolshevik program: "Peace, Land, Bread," "Worker Control of Production," and "All Power to the Soviets."

By the end of October, Bolsheviks made up a slight majority in the Petrograd and Moscow soviets. The number of party members had grown from 50,000 to 240,000. With Leon Trotsky, a dedicated revolutionary, as head of the Petrograd soviet, the Bolsheviks could claim power in the name of the soviets. During the night of November 6, Bolshevik forces seized the Winter Palace, the seat of the provisional government. The government quickly collapsed with little bloodshed.

The overthrow of the provisional government **coincided** with a meeting in Petrograd of the all-Russian Congress of Soviets, which represented soviets from all over the country. Outwardly, Lenin turned over the power of the provisional government to the Congress of Soviets. The real power, however, passed to a Council of People's Commissars, headed by Lenin.

The Bolsheviks, who soon renamed themselves the Communists, still had a long way to go. Lenin had promised peace, and that, he realized, would not be an easy task. It would mean the humiliating loss of much Russian territory. There was no real choice, however.

On March 3, 1918, Lenin signed the Treaty of Brest-Litovsk with Germany and gave up eastern Poland, **Ukraine,** Finland, and the Baltic provinces. To his critics, Lenin argued that it made no difference. The spread of the socialist revolution throughout Europe would make the treaty largely **irrelevant.** In any case, he had promised peace to the Russian people. Real peace did not come, however, because the country soon sank into civil war.

*V. I. Lenin*

☑ **Reading Check** **Examining** What was Lenin's plan when he arrived in Russia?

## Civil War in Russia

**Main Idea** A civil war started in Russia between groups opposed to the Bolshevik regime and the Bolsheviks.

**Reading Connection** What groups were involved in the American Civil War? Read to find out what groups of Russians fought each other between 1918 and 1921.

Many people in Russia were opposed to the new Bolshevik, or Communist, government. They included not only groups loyal to the czar, but also liberals and anti-Leninist socialists. Liberals often supported a constitutional monarchy, while a number of socialists supported gradual reform. These socialists expected to work for a socialist state through much more democratic methods than Lenin. They were joined by the Allies, who were extremely concerned about the Communist takeover. The Allies sent thousands of troops to outlying parts of Russia hoping to bring it back into the war. Although Allied forces rarely fought on Russian soil, they gave material aid to anti-Communist forces.

Between 1918 and 1921, the Communist or Red Army was forced to fight on many fronts. The first serious threat to the Communists came from **Siberia.** Here the anti-Communist or White force attacked westward and advanced almost to the Volga River before being stopped.

Attacks also came from the Ukrainians in the southwest and from the Baltic regions. In mid-1919, White forces swept through Ukraine and advanced almost to Moscow before being pushed back.

By 1920, however, the major White forces had been defeated and Ukraine retaken. The next year, the Communist regime regained control over the independent nationalist governments in Georgia, Russian Armenia, and Azerbaijan (A•zuhr•BY•JAHN).

The royal family was another victim of the civil war. After the czar abdicated, he, his wife, and their five children had been taken into captivity. In April 1918, they were moved to Yekaterinburg, a mining town in the **Urals.** On the night of July 16, members of the local soviet murdered the czar and his family and burned their bodies in a nearby mine shaft.

☑ **Reading Check** **Identifying** Who opposed the new Bolshevik regime?

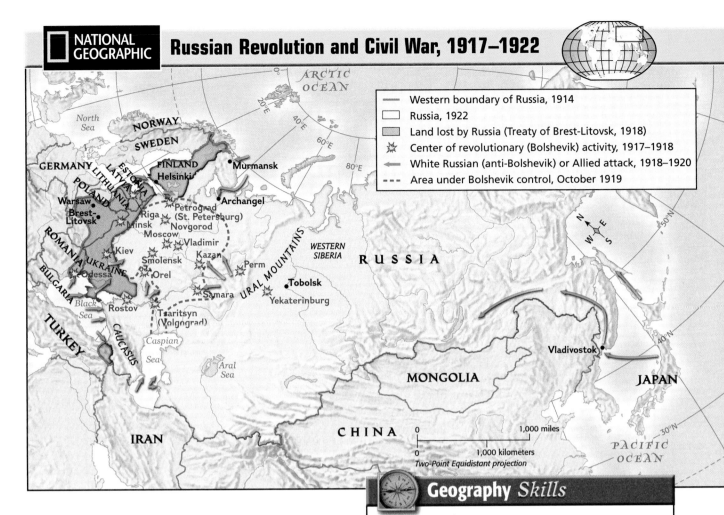

Legend:
— Western boundary of Russia, 1914
□ Russia, 1922
▨ Land lost by Russia (Treaty of Brest-Litovsk, 1918)
✳ Center of revolutionary (Bolshevik) activity, 1917–1918
← White Russian (anti-Bolshevik) or Allied attack, 1918–1920
--- Area under Bolshevik control, October 1919

0    1,000 miles
0    1,000 kilometers
Two-Point Equidistant projection

## Geography *Skills*

The Russian Revolution and civil war resulted in significant changes to Russia's boundaries.

1. **Interpreting Maps** Compare the area of Russia under Bolshevik control in 1919 with the area *not* under Bolshevik control. Which is larger? Which contained Russia's main cities?

2. **Applying Geography Skills** Pose two questions for your classmates to determine whether or not they can describe the changes in Russia's boundaries resulting from the Russian Revolution and World War I.

## Triumph of the Communists

**Main Idea** A major reason for Communist victory was that the Bolsheviks were united, while their opponents were not.

**Reading Connection** Have you seen a group fail because it could not agree on goals? Read to understand the failure of the Whites.

How had Lenin and the Communists triumphed in the civil war over so many opponents? One reason was that the Red Army was a well-disciplined fighting force. This was largely due to the organizational genius of **Leon Trotsky.** As commissar of war, Trotsky reinstated the draft and emphasized rigid discipline. Soldiers who deserted or refused to obey orders were executed on the spot.

A second reason was that the anti-Communist forces were disunited. Political differences created distrust among the Whites and prevented them from cooperating effectively. Some Whites insisted on restoring the czarist regime. Others believed that only a more liberal and democratic program had any chance of success.

The Whites, then, had no common goal. The Communists, in contrast, had a single-minded sense of purpose. Inspired by their vision of a new socialist order, the Communists had the determination that comes from revolutionary zeal and convictions.

The Communists were also able to translate their revolutionary faith into practical instruments of power. A policy of **war communism,** for example, was used to ensure regular supplies for the Red Army. War communism meant government control of banks and most industries, the seizing of grain from peasants, and the centralization of state administration under Communist control.

Another Communist instrument was revolutionary terror. A new Red secret police—known as the Cheka—

*Picturing* **History**

The Red Army is shown marching through Moscow. Between 1918 and 1921, the Red Army faced resistance from both the Allies and the anti-Communist or White forces. Who was the Communist commissar who shaped the Red Army?

began a Red Terror aimed at the destruction of all those who opposed the new regime (much like the Reign of Terror in the French Revolution). The Red Terror added an element of fear to the Communist regime.

Finally, the presence of foreign armies on Russian soil enabled the Communists to appeal to the powerful force of Russian patriotism. At one point, over a hundred thousand foreign troops—mostly Japanese, British, American, and French—were stationed in Russia in support of anti-Communist forces. Their presence made it easy for the Communist govern-

ment to call on patriotic Russians to fight foreign attempts to control the country.

By 1921, the Communists were in total command of Russia. In the course of the civil war, the Communist regime had transformed Russia into a centralized state dominated by a single party. The state was also largely hostile to the Allied powers, because the Allies had tried to help the Communists' enemies in the civil war.

**Reading Check** **Contrasting** Why did the Red Army prevail over the White Army?

**HISTORY Online** **Study Central**

For help with the concepts in this section of *Glencoe World History–Modern Times,* go to <u>wh.mt.glencoe.com</u> and click on **Study Central**.

## SECTION 3 ASSESSMENT

### Checking for Understanding

1. **Vocabulary** Define: soviets, coincide, irrelevant, war communism.

2. **People** Identify: Alexandra, Grigori Rasputin, Alexander Kerensky, Bolsheviks, V. I. Lenin, Leon Trotsky.

3. **Places** Locate: Petrograd, Ukraine, Siberia, Urals.

### Reviewing Big Ideas

4. **Explain** why Lenin accepted the loss of so much Russian territory in the Treaty of Brest-Litovsk.

### Critical Thinking

5. **Historical Analysis** **Connecting Events** How did the presence of Allied troops in Russia ultimately help the Communists? **CA HI1**

6. **Organizing Information** Using a chart like the one below, sequence the steps the Communists took to turn Russia into a centralized state dominated by a single party.

| Steps to Communist Control |
|---|
| 1. |
| 2. |

### Analyzing Visuals

7. **Examine** the photograph of Czar Nicholas II and his family shown on page 442 of your text. Is this photograph an idealized view of royalty? Do you think Russians thought of the royal family like this during World War I?

### Writing About History

8. **Expository Writing** Write an essay comparing the economic, political, and social causes of the American, French, and Russian Revolutions. **CA 10WA2.3a,b**

# SECTION 4 End of the War

## Guide to Reading

### Section Preview

After the defeat of the Germans, peace settlements brought political and territorial changes to Europe and created bitterness and resentment in several nations.

**Main Idea**

- After William II was forced to abdicate, the new German republic and the Allies signed an armistice, ending the war on November 11, 1918. (p. 448)
- The Treaty of Versailles punished Germany, established new nations, and created a League of Nations to solve international problems. (p. 449)

### Content Vocabulary

armistice, reparation, mandate

### Academic Vocabulary

concentrate, consistent, clause

### People to Identify

Erich von Ludendorff, Friedrich Ebert, David Lloyd George, Georges Clemenceau

### Places to Locate

Kiel, Alsace, Lorraine, Poland

### Reading Objectives

1. Identify the key events that brought about the end of World War I.
2. Describe the intended purpose of the League of Nations.

### Reading Strategy

**Organizing Information** At the Paris Peace Conference, the leaders of France, Britain, and the United States were motivated by different concerns. Using a chart like the one below, identify the national interests of each country as it approached the peace deliberations.

| France | Britain | United States |
|--------|---------|---------------|
|        |         |               |
|        |         |               |

### Preview of Events

| ◆1917 | ◆1918 | ◆1919 | ◆1920 |
|-------|-------|-------|-------|

**April 1917**
The United States enters the war

**November 1918**
Germany agrees to an armistice

**January 1919**
Communist revolt crushed in Berlin

**June 1919**
Treaty of Versailles signed at the Paris Peace Conference

## California Standards in This Section

*Reading this section will help you master these California History–Social Science standards.*

**10.5.2:** Examine the principal theaters of battle, major turning points, and the importance of geographic factors in military decisions and outcomes (e.g., topography, waterways, distance, climate).

**10.5.3:** Explain how the Russian Revolution and the entry of the United States affected the course and outcome of the war.

**10.6.1:** Analyze the aims and negotiating roles of world leaders, the terms and influence of the Treaty of Versailles and Woodrow Wilson's Fourteen Points, and the causes and effects of the United States' rejection of the League of Nations on world politics.

**10.6.2:** Describe the effects of the war and resulting peace treaties on population movement, the international economy, and shifts in the geographic and political borders of Europe and the Middle East.

**10.6.3:** Understand the widespread disillusionment with prewar institutions, authorities, and values that resulted in a void that was later filled by totalitarians.

# The Last Year of the War

**Main Idea** After William II was forced to abdicate, the new German republic and the Allies signed an armistice, ending the war on November 11, 1918.

**Reading Connection** Have you heard debates about how large the American military budget should be? Read to understand the role of American army support in the Allied victory of World War I.

The year 1917 had not been a good one for the Allies. Allied offensives on the Western Front were a disaster. The Russian Revolution, which began in November 1917, weakened the Allies when Russia withdrew from the war a few months later. The cause of the Central Powers looked favorable, but the war had taken a tremendous toll on their forces, too. No war had been fought with as much machinery—and as much sheer slaughter.

## *Voices from the Past*

One weapon, the tank, contributed to mortality, but it also played a role in ending the war. The new weapon was introduced in September 1916 on the Western Front. An eyewitness recorded his impressions:

> ❝We heard strange throbbing noises, and lumbering slowly towards us came three huge mechanical monsters such as we had never seen before. My first impression was that they looked ready to topple on their noses, but their tails and the two little wheels at the back held them down and kept them level. . . . Instead of going on to the German lines the three tanks assigned to us straddled our front line, stopped and then opened up a murderous machine-gun fire. . . . They finally realized they were on the wrong trench and moved on, frightening the Germans out of their wits and making them scuttle like frightened rabbits.❞

The main factor that pushed the Allies to victory was the entry of the United States into the war in 1917. The "Yanks" gave the Allies a much-needed psychological boost, as well as fresh troops and materiel. In 1918, the Americans proved crucial.

▲ *An early tank, invented and first used by the British*

**A New German Offensive** For Germany, the withdrawal of the Russians offered new hope for a successful end to the war. Germany was now free to **concentrate** entirely on the Western Front. **Erich von Ludendorff,** who guided German military operations, decided to make one final military gamble—a grand offensive in the west to break the military stalemate.

The German attack was launched in March 1918. By April, German troops were within about 50 miles (80 km) of Paris. However, the German advance was stopped at the Second Battle of the Marne on July 18. French, Moroccan, and American troops (140,000 fresh American troops had just arrived), supported by hundreds of tanks, threw the Germans back over the Marne. Ludendorff's gamble had failed.

With more than a million American troops pouring into France, Allied forces began a steady advance toward Germany. On September 29, 1918, General Ludendorff informed German leaders that the war was lost. He demanded that the government ask for peace at once.

**Collapse and Armistice** German officials soon discovered that the Allies were unwilling to make peace with the autocratic imperial government of Germany. Reforms were begun to create a liberal government, but these efforts came too late for the exhausted and angry German people.

On November 3, sailors in the town of **Kiel,** in northern Germany, mutinied. Within days, councils of workers and soldiers were forming throughout northern Germany and taking over civilian and military offices. William II gave in to public pressure and left the country on November 9.

The Social Democrats under **Friedrich Ebert** then announced the creation of a democratic republic. Two days later, on November 11, 1918, this government signed an **armistice**—a truce or an agreement to stop the fighting.

**Revolutionary Forces** The war was over, but the revolutionary forces it had set in motion were not exhausted yet. A group of radical socialists, unhappy with the moderate policies of the Social Democrats, formed the German Communist Party in December 1918. A month later, they tried to seize power in Berlin.

The new Social Democratic government, backed by regular army troops, crushed the rebels and murdered Rosa Luxemburg and Karl Liebknecht (LEEP•KNEHKT), leaders of the German Communists. A similar attempt at Communist revolution in the city of Munich, in southern Germany, was also crushed.

The new German republic had been saved from radical revolution. The attempt at revolution, however, left the German middle class with a deep fear of communism.

Austria-Hungary, too, experienced disintegration and revolution. As war weariness took hold of the empire, ethnic groups increasingly sought to achieve their independence. By the time the war ended, the Austro-Hungarian Empire was no more.

The empire had been replaced by the independent republics of Austria, Hungary, and Czechoslovakia, along with the large monarchical state called Yugoslavia. Rivalries among the nations that succeeded Austria-Hungary would weaken eastern Europe for the next 80 years.

✓ **Reading Check** **Describing** What happened within Germany after the armistice?

## The Peace Settlements

**Main Idea** The Treaty of Versailles punished Germany, established new nations, and created a League of Nations to solve international problems.

**Reading Connection** What recent world issues has the United Nations focused attention on? Read to learn why the American president wanted a League of Nations after World War I.

In January 1919, representatives of 27 victorious Allied nations met in Paris to make a final settlement of the Great War. Over a period of years, the reasons for fighting World War I had changed dramatically. When European nations had gone to war in 1914 they sought territorial gains. By the beginning of 1918, more idealistic reasons were also being expressed.

**Wilson's Proposals** No one expressed these idealistic reasons better than the U.S. president, Woodrow Wilson. Even before the war ended, Wilson outlined "Fourteen Points" to the United States Congress—his basis for a peace settlement that could justify the enormous military struggle being waged.

Wilson's proposals for a just and lasting peace included reaching the peace agreements openly rather than through secret diplomacy; reducing armaments or military forces to a "point **consistent** with domestic safety"; and ensuring self-determination, the right of each people to have its own nation.

Wilson portrayed World War I as a people's war against "absolutism and militarism." These two enemies of liberty, he argued, could be eliminated only

## People In History

**Georges Clemenceau**
1841–1929—French statesman

**G**eorges Clemenceau was one of France's wartime leaders. He had a long political career before serving as French premier (prime minister) from 1917 to 1920. When Clemenceau became premier in 1917, he suspended basic civil liberties for the rest of the war. He had the editor of an antiwar newspaper executed on a charge of helping the enemy. Clemenceau also punished journalists who wrote negative war reports by having them drafted.

Clemenceau strongly disliked the Germans. "For the catastrophe of 1914 the Germans are responsible," he said. "Only a professional liar would deny this."

by creating democratic governments and a "general association of nations." This association would guarantee "political independence and territorial integrity to great and small states alike."

Wilson became the spokesperson for a new world order based on democracy and international cooperation. When he arrived in Europe for the peace conference, he was enthusiastically cheered by many Europeans. Wilson soon found, however, that more practical motives guided other states.

**The Paris Peace Conference** Delegates met in Paris in early 1919 to determine the peace settlement. Complications soon became obvious. For one thing, secret treaties and agreements that had been made before the war had raised the hopes of European nations for territorial gains. These hopes could not be totally ignored, even if they did conflict with the principle of self-determination put forth by Wilson.

National interests also complicated the deliberations of the Paris Peace Conference. **David Lloyd George,** prime minister of Great Britain, had won a

decisive victory in elections in December 1918. His platform was simple: make the Germans pay.

France's approach to peace was chiefly guided by its desire for national security. To **Georges Clemenceau** (KLEH•muhn•SOH), the premier of France, the French people had suffered the most from German aggression. The French desired revenge and security against future German aggression. Clemenceau wanted Germany stripped of all weapons, vast German payments—**reparations**—to cover the costs of the war, and a separate Rhineland as a buffer state between France and Germany.

The most important decisions at the Paris Peace Conference were made by Wilson, Clemenceau, and Lloyd George. Italy, as one of the Allies, was considered one of the so-called Big Four powers. However, it played a smaller role than the other key powers— the United States, France, and Great Britain, called the Big Three. Germany was not invited to attend, and Russia could not be present because of its civil war.

In view of the many conflicting demands at the peace conference, it was no surprise that the Big

# Opposing Viewpoints

## Who Caused World War I?

Immediately after World War I, historians began to assess which nation was most responsible for beginning the war. As these four selections show, opinions have varied considerably.

"The Allied and Associated Governments affirm and Germany accepts the responsibility of Germany and her allies for causing all the loss and damage to which the Allied and Associated Governments have been subjected as a consequence of the war imposed upon them by the aggression of Germany and her allies."

*Treaty of Versailles, Article 231*, 1919

"None of the powers wanted a European War. . . . But the verdict of the Versailles Treaty that Germany and her allies were responsible for the War, in view of the evidence now available, is historically unsound. It should therefore be revised."

—Sidney Bradshaw Fay
*Origins of the World War*, 1930

Three quarreled. Wilson wanted to create a world organization, the League of Nations, to prevent future wars. Clemenceau and Lloyd George wanted to punish Germany. In the end, only compromise made it possible to achieve a peace settlement.

Wilson's wish that the creation of an international peacekeeping organization be the first order of business was granted. On January 25, 1919, the conference accepted the idea of a League of Nations. In return, Wilson agreed to make compromises on territorial arrangements. He did so because he believed that the League could later fix any unfair settlements.

Clemenceau also compromised to obtain some guarantees for French security. He gave up France's wish for a separate Rhineland and instead accepted a defensive alliance with Great Britain and the United States. The U.S. Senate refused to ratify this agreement, which weakened the Versailles peace settlement.

**The Treaty of Versailles** The final peace settlement of Paris consisted of five separate treaties with the defeated nations—Germany, Austria, Hungary, Bulgaria, and Turkey. The Treaty of Versailles with Ger-

many, signed at Versailles near Paris on June 28, 1919, was by far the most important.

The Germans considered it a harsh peace. They were especially unhappy with Article 231, the so-called War Guilt **Clause,** which declared that Germany (and Austria) were responsible for starting the war. The treaty ordered Germany to pay reparations for all the damage Allied governments and their people had suffered from a war "imposed upon them by the aggression of Germany and her allies."

The military and territorial provisions of the Treaty of Versailles also angered the Germans. Germany had to reduce its army to a hundred thousand men, cut back its navy, and eliminate its air force. **Alsace** and **Lorraine,** taken by the Germans from France in 1871, were now returned. Sections of eastern Germany were awarded to a new Polish state.

German land along both sides of the Rhine was made a demilitarized zone and stripped of all weapons and fortifications. This, it was hoped, would serve as a barrier to any future German military moves westward against France. Outraged by the "dictated peace," the new German government complained but, unwilling to risk a renewal of the war, they accepted the treaty.

**A New Map of Europe** As a result of the war, the Treaty of Versailles, and the separate peace treaties made with the other Central Powers—Austria, Hungary, Bulgaria, and Turkey—the map of eastern Europe was largely redrawn. Both the German and Russian empires lost much territory in eastern Europe. The Austro-Hungarian Empire disappeared.

New nation-states emerged from the lands of these three empires: Finland, Latvia, Estonia, Lithuania, **Poland,** Czechoslovakia, Austria, and Hungary.

New territorial arrangements were also made in the Balkans. Romania acquired additional lands from Russia, Hungary, and Bulgaria. Serbia formed the nucleus of a new state, called Yugoslavia, which combined Serbs, Croats, and Slovenes.

The Paris Peace Conference was supposedly guided by the principle of self-determination. The mixtures of peoples in eastern Europe made it impossible, however, to draw boundaries along neat ethnic lines. Compromises had to be made, sometimes to satisfy the national interests of the victors. France, for example, had lost Russia as its major ally on Germany's eastern border. Thus, France wanted to strengthen and expand Poland, Czechoslovakia, Yugoslavia, and Romania as much as possible. Those states could then serve as barriers against Germany and Communist Russia.

**❝**In estimating the order of guilt of the various countries we may safely say that the only direct and immediate responsibility for the World War falls upon Serbia, France and Russia, with the guilt about equally divided.**❞**

—**Harry Elmer Barnes**
*The Genesis of the World War,* **1927**

**❝**As Germany willed and coveted the Austro-Serbian war and, in her confidence in her military superiority, deliberately faced the risk of a conflict with Russia and France, her leaders must bear a substantial share of the historical responsibility for the outbreak of general war in 1914.**❞**

—**Fritz Fischer**
*Germany's Aims in the First World War,* **1961**

## You Decide

1. Write a quote of your own that reflects your views on which nation caused World War I. Support your quote with passages from the text.

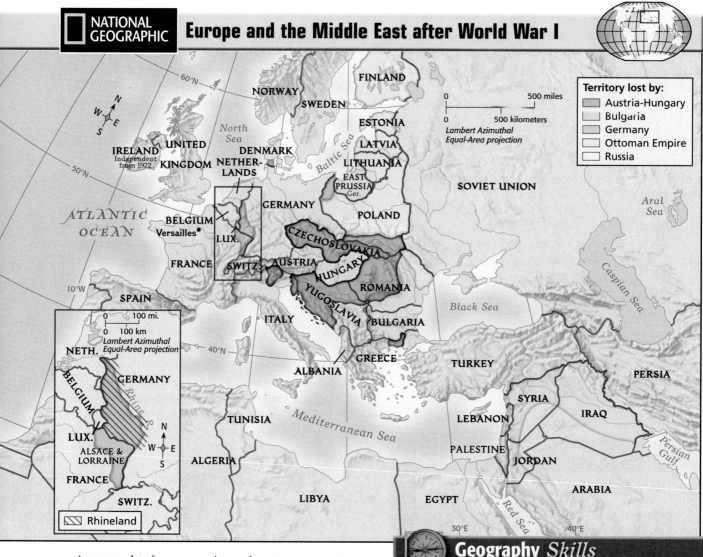

**Territory lost by:**
- Austria-Hungary
- Bulgaria
- Germany
- Ottoman Empire
- Russia

0    500 miles
0    500 kilometers
*Lambert Azimuthal Equal-Area projection*

0    100 mi.
0    100 km
*Lambert Azimuthal Equal-Area projection*

Rhineland

As a result of compromises, almost every eastern European state was left with ethnic minorities. There were Germans in Poland, and Hungarians, Poles, and Germans were living in Czechoslovakia. Romania also had a significant population of Hungarians, while Yugoslavia had a mixture of Serbs, Croats, Slovenes, Macedonians, and Albanians. In some cases, these ethnic groups had a long history of conflict over territory. Not surprisingly, the new boundaries were not always satisfactory.

Yet another centuries-old empire—the Ottoman Empire—was broken up by the peace settlement. To gain Arab support against the Ottoman Turks during the war, the Western Allies had promised to recognize the independence of Arab states in the Ottoman Empire. Once the war was over, however, the Western nations changed their minds. France took control of Lebanon and Syria, and Britain received Iraq and Palestine.

Woodrow Wilson was opposed to the Allies' annexing territory. Therefore these acquisitions were

## Geography *Skills*

World War I dramatically changed political boundaries.

1. **Interpreting Maps** Rank the countries and empires listed in the map legend according to the amount of lost territory, from largest loss to smallest loss.

2. **Applying Geography Skills** Look back at the map on page 423, then examine the map above. Now, knowing the outcome of the war, predict which countries would lose the most territory. Why does the actual loss of territory, as shown above, differ from (or match) your predictions?

officially called **mandates.** As a result, the peace settlement created the mandate system. According to this system, a nation officially governed another nation as a mandate from the League of Nations, but it did not own the territory.

**The War's Legacy** World War I shattered the liberal, rational society that had existed in the late nineteenth and early twentieth century. The death of

▲ *In this painting of the Paris peace talks, American president Woodrow Wilson (second row, center right) shows British leader Lloyd George a report. French premier Georges Clemenceau sits on Wilson's other side.*

almost 10 million people, as well as the incredible destruction caused by the war, undermined the whole idea of progress. Entire populations had participated in a devastating slaughter.

World War I was a total war—one that involved a complete mobilization of resources and people. During its course, the power of governments over the lives of citizens increased. Freedom of the press and speech were limited in the name of national security. World War I thus made the practice of strong central government a way of life.

The turmoil of the war also seemed to open the door to greater insecurity. Revolutions broke up old empires and created new states, which led to new problems. The hope that the world would return to normalcy was, however, soon dashed.

 **Reading Check** **Identifying** What clause in the Treaty of Versailles particularly angered the Germans?

**HISTORY** *Online* **Study Central**

For help with the concepts in this section of *Glencoe World History–Modern Times,* go to **wh.mt.glencoe.com** and click on **Study Central.**

# SECTION 4 ASSESSMENT

## Checking for Understanding

1. **Vocabulary** Define: concentrate, armistice, consistent, reparation, clause, mandate.

2. **People** Identify: Erich von Ludendorff, Friedrich Ebert, David Lloyd George, Georges Clemenceau.

3. **Places** Locate: Kiel, Alsace, Lorraine, Poland.

### Reviewing Big Ideas

4. **List** some of President Wilson's proposals for creating a lasting peace. Why did he feel the need to develop these proposals?

## Critical Thinking

5. **Historical Analysis** **Connecting Events** Although Woodrow Wilson came to the Paris Peace Conference with high ideals, the other leaders had more practical concerns. Why do you think that was so? **CA HI1**

6. **Compare and Contrast** Using a Venn diagram like the one below, compare Wilson's Fourteen Points with the Treaty of Versailles.

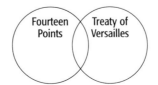

Fourteen Points — Treaty of Versailles

## Analyzing Visuals

7. **Compare** the photograph of troops going to war on page 431 with the painting on page 417. How do you think the soldiers' expectations compared to their actual experiences?

### Writing About History

8. **Informative Writing** You are a reporter for a large newspaper, sent to the Paris Peace Conference to interview one of the leaders of the Big Three. Prepare a written set of questions you would like to ask the leader you have selected. **CA 10WS1.3**

# PRIMARY SOURCES
## EYEWITNESS TO HISTORY

*In these selections, two poems and an excerpt from a novel capture the profound feelings of the war generation.*

## SOURCE 1: An Encounter with Gas Warfare

*Poet Wilfred Owen (1893–1918) served on the Western front and died in the last week of the war. The poem's title, "Dulce et Decorum Est," is taken from Horace, the Roman poet. In Latin, it means "it is sweet and right" to die for one's country.*

Bent double, like old beggars under sacks,
Knocked-kneed, coughing like hags, we cursed
   through sludge.
Till on the haunting flares we turned our backs.
And towards our distant rest began to trudge.
Men marched asleep. Many had lost their boots
But limped on, blood-shod. All went lame; all blind;
Drunk with fatigue; deaf even to the hoots
Of tired, outstripped Five-Nines that dropped behind.
Gas! Gas! Quick Boys!—An ecstasy of fumbling,
Fitting the clumsy helmets just in time;
But someone still was yelling out and stumbling
And flound'ring like a man in fire or **lime**[1] . . .
Dim, through the misty panes and thick green light,
As under a green sea, I saw him drowning,
In all my dreams, before my helpless sight,
He plunges at me, guttering, choking, drowning.
If in some smothering dreams you too could pace
Behind the wagon that we flung him in,
And watch the white eyes writhing in his face,
His hanging face, like a devil's sick of sin;
If you could hear, at every jolt, the blood
Come gargling from the froth-corrupted lungs,
**Obscene**[2] as cancer, bitter as the cud
Of vile, incurable sores on innocent tongues, —
My friend, you would not tell with such high zest
To children ardent for some desperate glory,
The old Lie: Dulce et decorum est Pro patria mori.

➤ ———————————————————————
[1]**lime:** corrosive substance that creates heat
[2]**Obscene:** repulsive

*A fleet of ambulances lined up in front of the veterans hospital in Paris in 1915*

## SOURCE 2: A Soldier's Recollection

*T.S. Eliot (1888–1965), an American-British poet, wrote "The Hollow Men" in 1925 to describe how the war affected the men who fought it.*

We are the hollow men
We are the stuffed men
Leaning together
Headpiece filled with straw.  Alas!
Our dried voices, when
We whisper together
Are quiet and meaningless
As wind in dry grass
Or rats' feet over broken glass
In our dry cellar

Shape without form, shade without colour,
Paralysed force, gesture without motion;

Those who have crossed
With direct eyes, to death's other Kingdom
Remember us—if at all—not as lost
Violent souls, but only
As the hollow men
The stuffed men.

. . . . . . . . . . . . . . . . . . . . . .

*This is the way the world ends*
*This is the way the world ends*
*This is the way the world ends*
*Not with a bang but a whimper.*

## SOURCE 3: A Novelist on the Great War

*Erich Maria Remarque (1897–1970) served in the German army. The following is from his famous novel,* All Quiet on the Western Front, *published in 1929.*

Kantorek had been our schoolmaster, a stern little man in grey tail-coat, with a face like a shrew mouse. . . .

During drill-time Kantorek gave us long lectures until the whole of our class went, under his shepherding, to the District Commandant and volunteered. . . .

There was, indeed, one of us who hesitated and did not want to fall into line. That was Joseph Behm, a plump, homely fellow. But he did allow himself to be persuaded, otherwise he would have been **ostracized**.[3] . . . even one's parents were ready with the word "coward"; no one had the vaguest idea what we were in for. . . .

Strange to say, Behm was one of the first to fall. He got hit in the eye during an attack, and we left him lying for dead. . . .

Naturally we couldn't blame Kantorek for this. . . . There were thousands of Kantoreks, all of whom were convinced that they were acting for the best—in a way that cost them nothing.

And that is why they let us down so badly. . . .

While they continued to write and talk, we saw the wounded and the dying. While they taught that duty to one's country is the greatest thing, we already knew that **death-throes**[4] are stronger. . . . We loved our country as much as they; we went courageously into every action; but we also distinguished the false from the true, we had suddenly learned to see. And we saw that

---

there was nothing of their world left. We were all at once terribly alone; and alone we must see it through.

"I will write to your wife," I say hastily to the dead man, "I will write to her, she must hear it from me, I will tell her everything I have told you, she shall not suffer, I will help her, and your parents too, and your child—"

His **tunic**[5] is half open. The pocket-book is easy to find. But I hesitate to open it. In it is the book with his name. So long as I do not know his name perhaps I may still forget him. . . .

Irresolutely I take the wallet in my hand. It slips out of my hand and falls open. Some pictures and letters drop out. . . .

There are portraits of a woman and a little girl, small amateur photographs taken against an ivy-clad wall.

My brain is taxed beyond endurance. But I realize this much, that I will never dare to write to these people as I intended. Impossible. I look at the portraits once more; they are clearly not rich people. I might send them money anonymously if I earn anything later on. I seize upon that, it is at least something to hold on to.

---

[5]**tunic:** coat of a soldier's uniform

## DBQ Document-Based Questions

### Historical Analysis    CA HR 2

**Source 1:** Why does Owen choose to borrow the words of the Roman poet for his title? How does he want you to take it?

**Source 2:** Eliot wrote his poem after the war. How does his attitude differ from attitudes in 1914?

**Source 3:** In this excerpt, what does the author mean by writing: "And that is why they let us down so badly?" Who are "they"? Who are "us"?

### Comparing and Contrasting Sources

1. What do Source 1 and Source 2 imply about the kind of pressures young men were under to go to war? Why do you say so?

2. What is the main lesson each author wants to convey about the war? **CA 10RL3.5**

---

[3]**ostracized:** shunned; excluded from a group
[4]**death-throes:** struggles when dying

Standards 10.5.1, 10.5.2, 10.5.3, 10.6.1, 10.6.2, 10.6.3, 10.7, 10.7.1

## Reviewing Content Vocabulary

*On a sheet of paper, use each of these terms in a sentence.*

1. conscription
2. mobilization
3. propaganda
4. trench warfare
5. war of attrition
6. total war
7. planned economies
8. soviets
9. war communism
10. armistice
11. reparation
12. mandate

## Reviewing Academic Vocabulary

*On a sheet of paper, use each of these terms in a sentence that reflects the term's meaning in the chapter.*

13. ethnic
14. alter
15. anticipate
16. behalf
17. suspend
18. submission
19. assure
20. coincide
21. irrelevant
22. concentrate
23. consistent
24. clause

## Reviewing the Main Ideas

### Section 1

25. State the significance of the following dates: 1914, 1917, and 1918.

26. Explain why Great Britain became involved in World War I.

### Section 2

27. Describe the role and contribution of women during World War I. What was their status after the war?

28. What innovations in military warfare occurred during World War I?

### Section 3

29. Why were Alexandra and Rasputin able to control the czar's government during much of World War I?

30. Explain the social changes promised by the Bolshevik slogans.

### Section 4

31. What did the creation of a League of Nations have to do with Woodrow Wilson's willingness to sign the Treaty of Versailles?

32. Why was the mandate system created?

## Critical Thinking

33. **Decision Making** Compare Lenin's beliefs and goals with those of Woodrow Wilson. Which leader has had the greater impact on world history? Why?

34. **Analyzing** Why do some people feel that it is unlikely that a lasting peace could have been created at the end of World War I?

## Chapter Summary

The outline below shows four themes of the chapter.

### Cooperation: Alliance System

- Two loose alliances form in Europe: the Triple Alliance (Germany, Austria-Hungary, and Italy) and the Triple Entente (France, Great Britain, and Russia).

- Alliances draw France and Great Britain into a conflict in which they have no direct interest.

### Conflict: World War I

- Combat takes the forms of trench warfare on the Western Front, a war of movement on the Eastern Front, and German submarine warfare in the waters surrounding Great Britain.

- For the first time in history, airplanes are used for reconnaissance, combat, and bombing.

### Revolution: Russian Revolution

- Military and economic crises lead to a spontaneous revolution that ends the reign of the czars.

- The Bolsheviks overthrow the provisional government and establish a Communist regime.

### Internationalism: Peace of Paris

- The peace is a compromise between international and national interests.

- Germany's reparation payments, military reductions, and territorial losses create a lasting bitterness that helps spark World War II.

35. **Reading Skill** **Time and Sequence** Reread the discussion in your textbook on the Bolshevik Revolution that begins on page 443. Track the timing of Lenin's actions between March and November 1917. Does your exercise help you see anything about Lenin as a politician?

36. **Making Conclusions** Some historians argue that the heavy psychological and economic penalties placed on Germany by the Treaty of Versailles created the conditions for World War II. How might the treaty have been written to alleviate worldwide concern over German militarism without exacting such a heavy toll?

## Writing About History

37. **Historical Analysis** **Connecting Events** The assassination of the Archduke Francis Ferdinand and his wife by Gavrilo Princip triggered the outbreak of World War I. What was the underlying dispute between Serbia and Austria-Hungary? Write a paragraph connecting this dispute to the assassination. **CA H1**

38. ***Big Idea*** Both Britain and the United States passed laws during the war to silence opposition and censor the press. Are the ideals of a democratic government consistent with such laws? Provide arguments for and against. **CA 10WA2.4a,c**

**DBQ** **Document-Based Questions**

**Analyzing Sources** Reread the quote below by the British ambassador to Vienna (see page 424), and then answer the questions below.

> I cannot tell you how exasperated people are getting here at the continual worry which that little country [Serbia] causes to Austria under encouragement from Russia. . . . It will be lucky if Europe succeeds in avoiding war as a result of the present crisis.🙶🙷

39. Where is Vienna located? Is the ambassador neutral in his comments or does he favor one country over another?

40. Compare the ways in which the actual events that started World War I mirror this ambassador's concerns.

## Paris Peace Conference: The Big Three

| Country | United States | Great Britain | France |
|---|---|---|---|
| Leader | Wilson | Lloyd George | Clemenceau |
| Goal | Lasting peace | Germany pays | French security |

## Treaty of Versailles

| International Relations | • League of Nations is formed. |
|---|---|
| Responsibility | • Germany accepts responsibility for starting the war and agrees to make reparations to the Allies. |
| Territory | • New nations are formed.<br>• Germany returns Alsace and Lorraine to France.<br>• France and Great Britain acquire mandates in the Middle East. |
| Military Strength | • Germany will reduce its army and navy and eliminate its air force.<br>• German land along the Rhine River is demilitarized. |

## Analyzing Maps and Charts

Using the chart above, answer the following questions:

41. Which of the Big Three nations at the Treaty of Versailles wanted to punish Germany for World War I?

42. What was the effect of the Treaty of Versailles on Germany's military?

43. What territory did France regain after the war?

**Standards Practice**

**Directions: Choose the best answer to the following question.**

44. The role Russia played in World War I can best be described as

A a strong supporter of Germany and Austria.

B a strong supporter of France and Great Britain.

C a weak role due to the Russian Revolution.

D militarily strong because of its vast army.

**CA Standard 10.5.3** Explain how the Russian Revolution and the entry of the United States affected the course and outcome of the war.

CHAPTER

9

*1919–1939*

# The West Between the Wars

## ❧ *The Big Ideas* ❧

### SECTION 1: The Futile Search for Stability

**War causes immeasurable devastation.** Peace and prosperity were short-lived after World War I as a global depression weakened Western democracies.

### SECTION 2: The Rise of Dictatorial Regimes

**A totalitarian system violated human rights in pursuit of political power.** By 1939, many European countries had adopted dictatorial regimes that aimed to control every aspect of their citizens' lives for state goals.

### SECTION 3: Hitler and Nazi Germany

**A totalitarian system violated human rights in pursuit of political power.** Hitler's totalitarian state was widely accepted, but German Jews and minorities were persecuted.

### SECTION 4: Cultural and Intellectual Trends

**New technologies can revolutionize the way people live, work, interact, and govern.** The destruction of the highly mechanized First World War and the turmoil of the Great Depression profoundly affected the work of artists and intellectuals.

 ***World History—Modern Times Video*** *The Chapter 9 video, "The Rise of Dictators," chronicles dictatorial regimes in Europe after 1918.*

*Dorothea Lange's famous photograph, Migrant Mother, 1936, captured the human hardship and suffering resulting from the Great Depression.*

**1929**
The Great Depression begins

| 1920 | 1922 | 1924 | 1926 | 1928 |

**1922**
Communists create the Union of Soviet Socialist Republics

**1924**
Hitler writes first volume of *Mein Kampf*

**1926**
Mussolini creates a Fascist dictatorship in Italy

**1929**
Stalin establishes dictatorship in Soviet Union

Hitler and the Nazi Party used rallies, such as this one at Nuremberg in 1937, to create support for their policies.

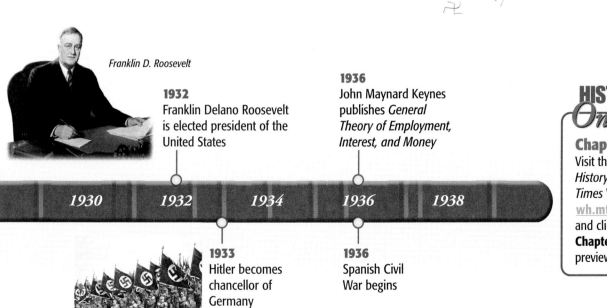

Franklin D. Roosevelt

**1932**
Franklin Delano Roosevelt is elected president of the United States

**1936**
John Maynard Keynes publishes *General Theory of Employment, Interest, and Money*

*1930*  *1932*  *1934*  *1936*  *1938*

**1933**
Hitler becomes chancellor of Germany

**1936**
Spanish Civil War begins

Flags of the Hitler Youth

**HISTORY**
*Online*

**Chapter Overview**
Visit the Glencoe World History–Modern Times Web site at wh.mt.glencoe.com and click on **Chapter 9– Chapter Overview** to preview chapter information.

# Preparing to Read Chapter 9

 **Reading Skill** Cause-and-Effect Chain

All authors structure what they write to get their message across. The structure they choose is like the frame of a house—it holds the information together so it "works." For historians, a favorite structure is cause-and-effect. They use it a lot because they are often explaining why an event or development came about—why a new president was elected, or why rap music came about.

In real life, few events are isolated from the surrounding world: Something you do might affect another person, who then takes an action which has other results. The historian might have to explain a chain reaction like this. When you notice that the historian is listing a series of events or developments, you might suspect that a chain reaction is at work. To help you understand this kind of discussion, use a focus question based on the main idea in the passage.

*Read the following passage from the chapter and use the focus question to find the cause-and-effect chain.*

## FOCUS QUESTION

Your focus question might be: What were the effects of the American stock market crash of 1929?

. . . By 1928, American investors had begun to pull money out of Germany to invest it in the stock market. Then, in October 1929, the American stock market crashed and the prices of stocks plunged.

In a panic, investors throughout the United States withdrew even more funds from Germany and other European markets. This withdrawal weakened the banks of Germany and other European states. The Credit-Anstalt, Vienna's most famous bank, collapsed in May 1931. Other banks soon followed, industrial production declined, and unemployment rose.

## CHAIN OF EFFECTS

The chain of effects is presented in order: the price of stocks plunged, more funds were withdrawn, banks were weakened and collapsed, production declined, and unemployment rose.

### Apply the Skill

As you get practice at seeing how historians use cause-and-effect structures, it will be easier to remember what they are saying about events. You will also gain a better understanding of how multiple effects can flow from a major event like the Great Depression.

# Historical Analysis Skill  Applying Research

**Historical Interpretation: Standard HR 4**  *Students construct and test hypotheses; collect, evaluate, and employ information from multiple primary and secondary sources; and apply it in oral and written presentations.*

When historians write an account of a historical event, or interpret a political decision, they aren't basing their conclusions on information from one book or letter. They could begin their research with one conclusion in mind, but after looking at a variety of sources they could come to an entirely different conclusion. It's their job to look at history from every angle possible, using every source they can find.

Sources used for studying history are broken down into two types: primary and secondary sources. Primary sources include anything that gives you a firsthand account of events, such as a newspaper, diary, song, or book written during the period you're studying. Even objects like a piece of pottery or a guitar tell you something about how things were made, or what people thought was beautiful or useful.

Secondary sources are accounts that are not firsthand, but are based on primary sources. They are written by collecting and synthesizing information. Encyclopedias or this history textbook are examples of secondary sources.

*Read this excerpt from Chapter 9 describing Germany immediately before World War II.*

> **Radio and movies could also be used for political purposes. "Without motor-cars, sound films, and wireless," Hitler once said, "[there would be] no victory of Nazism." Radio offered great opportunities for reaching the masses.**

## Apply the Skill

Write a paragraph listing the sources you would look for if you were going to do further research on the subjects in the excerpt. Be as specific as possible, indicating why you'd use them, and include whether they are primary or secondary sources. Then compare and discuss your list with a partner.

# A Story That Matters

*During the Great
Depression, many
people had to resort
to desperate measures
to find food.*

## The Great Depression

After World War I, Europe was faced with severe economic problems. Most devastating of all was the Great
Depression that began at the end of 1929. The Great Depression brought misery to millions of people. Begging for food
on the streets became widespread, especially when soup
kitchens were unable to keep up with the demand.

More and more people were homeless and moved around
looking for work and shelter. One observer in Germany
reported, "An almost unbroken chain of homeless men
extends the whole length of the great Hamburg-Berlin high-
way . . . [w]hole families had piled all their goods into baby
carriages and wheelbarrows that they were pushing along as
they plodded forward in dumb despair." In the United States,
the homeless set up shantytowns they named "Hoovervilles"
after President Herbert Hoover.

In their misery, some people saw suicide as the only solution. One unemployed person said, "Today, when I am experiencing this for the first time, I think that I should prefer to do
away with myself, to take gas, to jump into the river, or leap
from some high place. . . . Would I really come to such a decision? I do not know."

Social unrest spread rapidly. Some of the unemployed
staged hunger marches to get attention. In democratic countries, people began to listen to, and vote for, radical voices
calling for extreme measures.

### Why It Matters

In the 1920s, many people assumed
that Europe and the world were
about to enter a new era of international peace, economic growth, and
political democracy. These hopes
were not realized, however. Most
people wanted peace but were
unsure how to maintain it. Plans
for economic revival gave way to
inflation and then to the Great
Depression. Making matters worse,
economic hard times gave rise to
dictatorial regimes across much of
Europe. The world was filled with
uncertainty.

**History and You** Make a diagram listing the problems faced by
the United States, Germany, and
France during the Great Depression.
Indicate how the problems were
interrelated. Using what you learn
from your diagram, explain how
recovery would also have a chain
effect.

# SECTION 1 The Futile Search for Stability

## Guide to Reading

### Section Preview
Peace and prosperity were short-lived after World War I as a global depression weakened Western democracies.

**Main Idea**

- Discontent with the peace treaty and a weak League of Nations opened the door to new problems in the interwar years. (p. 464)
- Underlying economic problems and an American stock market crisis triggered the Great Depression. (p. 466)
- Although new democracies were established in Europe after World War I, the depression shook people's confidence in political democracy. (p. 467)

### Content Vocabulary
depression, collective bargaining, deficit spending

### Academic Vocabulary
minimum, circumstance

### People and Events to Identify
Dawes Plan, Treaty of Locarno, Weimar Republic, John Maynard Keynes, Franklin Delano Roosevelt, New Deal

### Places to Locate
Ruhr Valley, Switzerland

### Reading Objectives
1. Evaluate the significance of the Dawes Plan and the Treaty of Locarno.
2. Explain how Germany was affected by the Great Depression.

### Reading Strategy
**Compare and Contrast** Use a table like the one below to compare France's Popular Front with the New Deal in the United States.

| Popular Front | New Deal |
|---|---|
|  |  |
|  |  |
|  |  |
|  |  |

### Preview of Events

| ♦1920 | ♦1925 | ♦1930 | ♦1935 | ♦1940 |
|---|---|---|---|---|

**1921**
German debt determined

**1924**
German debt restructured

**1925**
Treaty of Locarno

**1929**
U.S. stock market crashes

**1936**
Popular Front is formed in France

## California Standards in This Section

*Reading this section will help you master these California History–Social Science standards.*

**10.6.1:** Analyze the aims and negotiating roles of world leaders, the terms and influence of the Treaty of Versailles and Woodrow Wilson's Fourteen Points, and the causes and effects of the United States's rejection of the League of Nations on world politics.

**10.6.2:** Describe the effects of the war and resulting peace treaties on population movement, the international economy, and shifts in the geographic and political borders of Europe and the Middle East.

**10.6.3:** Understand the widespread disillusionment with prewar institutions, authorities, and values that resulted in a void that was later filled by totalitarians.

**10.8.2:** Understand the role of appeasement, nonintervention (isolationism), and the domestic distractions in Europe and the United States prior to the outbreak of World War II.

# Uneasy Peace, Uncertain Security

**Main Idea** Discontent with the peace treaty and a weak League of Nations opened the door to new problems in the interwar years.

**Reading Connection** Why have Israel and the Palestinians been unable to settle their dispute over territory? Read to learn why the League of Nations was too weak to prevent aggression and war.

The peace settlement at the end of World War I had tried to fulfill nineteenth-century dreams of nationalism by creating new boundaries and new states. From the beginning, however, the settlement left nations unhappy. Border disputes poisoned relations in eastern Europe for years. Many Germans vowed to revise the terms of the Treaty of Versailles.

Resentment of the treaty was only one of the problems Europeans faced. The economy in Europe was under tremendous stress.

## Voices from the Past

On October 27, 1932, a group of workers marched in London to protest government policies. One observer reported:

> ❝By mid-day approximately 100,000 London workers were moving towards Hyde Park from all parts of London, to give the greatest welcome to the hunger marchers that had ever been seen in Hyde Park. . . . As the last contingent of marchers entered the park gates, trouble broke out with the police. It started with the special constables [police officers]; not being used to their task, they lost their heads, and, as the crowds swept forward on to the space where the meetings were to be held, the specials drew their truncheons [billy clubs] in an effort to control the sea of surging humanity. This incensed the workers, who turned on the constables and put them to flight.❞

**A Weak League of Nations** American president Woodrow Wilson knew very well that the peace settlement had provisions that might be a source for new conflicts. For this reason, he placed his hopes for peace in the world in the League of Nations. This organization was not able to maintain peace, however.

A major problem was that the United States decided not to join the League. Most Americans did not want to be involved in European affairs. The U.S. Senate reflected this sentiment when it refused to ratify the Treaty of Versailles despite the urging of President Wilson. This meant the United States was not a member of the League of Nations. Since the United States was one of the most powerful countries in the world, the League was seriously weakened.

The League of Nations was weak for another reason, too. As time would prove, when a crisis arose, members of the League would not agree to use force against nations that violated international law.

**French Demands** Between 1919 and 1924, the French government worked to ensure that it would be secure against future attacks. Thus, it demanded that Germany be strictly held to the provisions of the Treaty of Versailles. This tough policy toward Germany began with the levying of reparations, the payments Germany was required to make for war damages.

In April 1921, the Allied Reparations Commission determined that Germany owed 132 billion German marks (33 billion U.S. dollars) for reparations, payable in annual installments of 2.5 billion marks. In 1921, the new German republic made its first payment.

By the following year, however, the German government faced a financial crisis and announced that it could not pay any more reparations. France was outraged and sent troops to occupy the **Ruhr Valley,** Germany's chief industrial and mining center. France planned to collect reparations by operating and using the Ruhr mines and factories.

▼ *Hunger marchers in London, 1932*

**Inflation in Germany** The German government adopted a policy of passive resistance to French occupation. German workers went on strike, and the government mainly paid their salaries by printing more paper money. This only added to the inflation (rise in prices) that had already begun in Germany by the end of the war.

The German mark soon became worthless. In 1914, 4.2 marks equaled 1 U.S. dollar. As Germany's financial situation weakened, the mark began its slide. In 1919, 9 marks were worth 1 dollar. By 1922, it took 500 marks to purchase 1 American dollar. The mark's fall in value then accelerated. By 1923, 1 dollar was worth 18,000 marks in January; 350,000 marks in July; nearly 5,000,000 marks in August; and an incredible 4.2 trillion marks at the end of November.

The German government responded by printing new money as fast as possible. Old notes with additional zeros printed on them were rushed to the banks before they, too, became virtually worthless.

Evidence of runaway inflation was everywhere. Workers used wheelbarrows to carry home their weekly pay. One woman left a basket of money outside while she went into a store. When she came out, the money was there, but the basket had been stolen.

Office workers made sure to buy a newspaper on their way to work, knowing the price would be double or triple if they waited until later in the day.

Economic adversity led to political upheavals, and both France and Germany began to seek a way out of the disaster. In August 1924, an international commission produced a new plan for reparations. The **Dawes Plan,** named after the American banker who chaired the commission, first reduced reparations. It then coordinated Germany's annual payments with its ability to pay.

The Dawes Plan also granted an initial $200 million loan for German recovery. This loan soon opened the door to heavy American investment in Europe. A brief period of European prosperity followed, but it only lasted from 1924 to 1929.

**The Treaty of Locarno** With prosperity came a new European diplomacy. A spirit of cooperation was fostered by the foreign ministers of Germany and France, Gustav Stresemann and Aristide Briand. In 1925, they signed the **Treaty of Locarno,** which guaranteed Germany's new western borders.

The Locarno pact was viewed by many as the beginning of a new era of European peace. On the day after the pact was concluded, enthusiastic headlines

# CONNECTIONS Around The World

## The Great Flu Epidemic

A flu epidemic at the end of World War I proved disastrous to people all over the world. Some observers believe that it began among American soldiers in Kansas. When they were sent abroad to fight, they carried the virus to Europe. By the end of 1918, many soldiers in European armies had been stricken with the flu.

The disease spread quickly throughout Europe. The three chief statesmen at the peace conference—the American president Woodrow Wilson, the British prime minister David Lloyd George, and the French premier Georges Clemenceau—all were sick with the flu during the negotiations that led to the Treaty of Versailles.

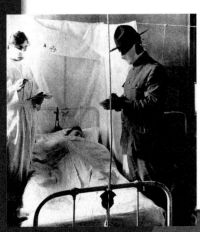

◀ *Flu victim*

The Spanish flu, as this strain of influenza was called, was known for its swift and deadly action. Many people died within a day of being infected. Complications also arose from bacterial infections in the lungs, which caused a deadly form of pneumonia.

In 1918 and 1919, the Spanish flu spread around the world with devastating results. Death tolls were enormous: in Russia, 450,000; in India, at least 6,000,000; in the United States, 550,000. It has been estimated that 22 million people, or more than twice the number of people killed in World War I, died from the great flu epidemic between 1918 and 1919.

## Comparing Cultures

Using outside sources, research the medical advancements made since 1919 in treating and preventing influenza viruses. Could another flu epidemic occur today? Has the flu danger been replaced by other medical concerns?

in *The New York Times* read "France and Germany Ban War Forever," while the London *Times* declared "Peace at Last."

The new spirit of cooperation grew even stronger when Germany joined the League of Nations in March 1926. Two years later, the Kellogg-Briand pact brought even more hope. Sixty-three nations signed this accord written by U.S. secretary of state Frank B. Kellogg and French foreign minister Aristide Briand. These nations pledged "to renounce war as an instrument of national policy." Nothing was said, however, about what would be done if anyone violated the pact.

Unfortunately, the spirit of Locarno was based on little real substance. Promises not to go to war were worthless without a way to enforce these promises. Furthermore, not even the spirit of Locarno could convince nations to cut back on their weapons. The League of Nations Covenant had suggested that nations reduce their military forces to make war less probable. Germany, of course, had been forced to reduce its military forces. At the time, it was thought that other states would later do the same. However, states were simply unwilling to trust their security to anyone but their own military forces.

**Reading Check** **Explaining** Why was the League of Nations unable to maintain peace?

## The Great Depression

**Main Idea** Underlying economic problems and an American stock market crisis triggered the Great Depression.

**Reading Connection** The U.S. stock market plunged in 2001 after terrorist attacks, but what would have happened if it had collapsed? Read to find out the consequences of the 1929 stock market crash.

The brief period of prosperity that began in Europe in 1924 ended in an economic collapse that came to be known as the Great Depression. A **depression** is a period of low economic activity and rising unemployment.

**Causes of the Depression** Two factors played a major role in the start of the Great Depression. One important factor was a series of downturns in the economies of individual nations in the second half of the 1920s. By the mid-1920s, for example, prices for farm products, especially wheat, were falling rapidly because of overproduction.

The second factor in the coming of the Great Depression was an international financial crisis

▼ *Economic downturns led to labor unrest in many countries.*

involving the U.S. stock market. We have seen that much of the European prosperity between 1924 and 1929 was built on U.S. bank loans to Germany. Germany needed the U.S. loans to pay reparations to France and Great Britain.

During the 1920s, the United States stock market was booming. By 1928, American investors had begun to pull money out of Germany to invest it in the stock market. Then, in October 1929, the American stock market crashed, and the prices of stocks plunged.

In a panic, investors throughout the United States withdrew even more funds from Germany and other European markets. This withdrawal weakened the banks of Germany and other European states. The Credit-Anstalt, Vienna's most famous bank, collapsed in May 1931. Other banks soon followed, industrial production declined, and unemployment rose.

**Responses to the Depression** Economic depression was by no means new to Europe. However, the extent of the economic downturn after 1929 truly made this the Great Depression. During 1932, the worst year of the depression, one British worker in every four was unemployed. Six million Germans, or 40 percent of the German labor force, were out of work at the same time. The unemployed and homeless filled the streets.

Governments did not know how to deal with the crisis. They tried a traditional solution of cutting costs by lowering wages and raising protective tariffs to exclude foreign goods from home markets. These measures made the economic crisis worse, however, and had serious political effects.

One effect of the economic crisis was increased government activity in the economy. This occurred even in countries that, like the United States, had a strong laissez-faire tradition—a belief that the government should not interfere in the economy.

Another effect of the crisis was a renewed interest in Marxist doctrines. Marx's prediction that capitalism would destroy itself through overproduction seemed to be coming true. Communism thus became more popular, especially among workers and intellectuals.

Finally, the Great Depression led masses of people to follow political leaders who offered simple solutions in return for dictatorial power. Everywhere, democracy seemed on the defensive in the 1930s.

✔**Reading Check** **Summarizing** What were the results of the Great Depression?

▲ *This German woman is using her worthless money to start a fire in her kitchen stove.*

## Democratic States after the War

**Main Idea** Although new democracies were established in Europe after World War I, the depression shook people's confidence in political democracy.

**Reading Connection** Can you imagine circumstances that would lead you to believe your country would be better off under a military dictator? Read to learn about how hopeless many Europeans felt during the 1930s.

President Woodrow Wilson had claimed that the war had been fought to make the world safe for democracy. In 1919, his claim seemed justified. Most major European states and many minor ones had democratic governments.

In a number of states, women could now vote. Male political leaders had rewarded women for their contributions to the war effort by granting them voting rights. (Exceptions were France, Italy, and **Switzerland.** Women gained the right to vote in 1944 in France, 1945 in Italy, and 1971 in Switzerland.)

In the 1920s, Europe seemed to be returning to the political trends of the prewar era—parliamentary regimes and the growth of individual liberties. This was not, however, an easy process. Four years of total war and four years of post-war turmoil made a "return to normalcy" difficult.

### Germany

The Imperial Germany of William II had come to an end in 1918 with Germany's defeat in the war. A German democratic state known as the **Weimar** (VY•MAHR) **Republic** was then created. The Weimar Republic was plagued by problems.

For one thing, the republic had no truly outstanding political leaders. In 1925, Paul von Hindenburg, a World War I military hero, was elected president at the age of 77. Hindenburg was a traditional military man who did not fully endorse the republic he had been elected to serve.

The Weimar Republic also faced serious economic problems. As we have seen, Germany experienced runaway inflation in 1922 and 1923. With it came serious social problems. Widows, teachers, civil servants, and others who lived on fixed incomes all watched their monthly incomes become worthless, or their life savings disappear. These losses increasingly pushed the middle class toward political parties that were hostile to the republic.

To make matters worse, after a period of relative prosperity from 1924 to 1929, Germany was struck by the Great Depression. In 1930, unemployment had grown to 3 million people by March and to 4.38 million by December. The depression paved the way for fear and the rise of extremist parties.

### France

After the war, France was the strongest European power. Its greatest need was to rebuild the areas that had been devastated in the war. However, France, too, suffered financial problems after the war.

Because it had a more balanced economy than other nations, France did not begin to feel the full

**Europe, 1923**

### Geography Skills

As seen in this 1920s map, the new nationalism did not solve Europe's postwar problems.

1. **Interpreting Maps** Compare the map above to the map on page 423. List all the countries on this map not shown on the earlier map. What can you conclude about the results of World War I?

2. **Applying Geography Skills** Create a table with two columns, Changed Boundaries and Unchanged Boundaries. Use the map above and the one on page 423 to fill out the table, listing countries in the proper columns.

effects of the Great Depression until 1932. The economic instability it then suffered soon had political effects. During a nineteen-month period in 1932 and 1933, six different cabinets were formed as France faced political chaos. Finally, in June 1936, a coalition of leftist parties—Communists, Socialists, and Radicals—formed the Popular Front government.

The Popular Front started a program for workers that some have called the French New Deal. This program was named after the New Deal in the United States (discussed later in this section). The French New Deal gave workers the right to **collective bargaining,** or the right of unions to negotiate with employers over wages and hours. It also gave industrial workers a 40-hour workweek, a paid vacation for two weeks every year, and a **minimum** wage.

The Popular Front's policies, however, failed to solve the problems of the depression. By 1938, the French had little confidence in their political system.

### Great Britain

During the war, Britain had lost many of the markets for its industrial products to the United States and Japan. Such industries as coal, steel, and textiles declined after the war, leading to a rise in unemployment. In 1921, 2 million Britons were out of work. Britain soon rebounded, however, and experienced limited prosperity from 1925 to 1929.

By 1929, Britain faced the growing effects of the Great Depression. The Labour Party, which had become the largest party in Britain, failed to solve the nation's economic problems and fell from power in 1931. A new government, led by the Conservatives, claimed credit for bringing Britain out of the worst stages of the depression. It did so by using the traditional policies of balanced budgets and protective tariffs.

Political leaders in Britain largely ignored the new ideas of a British economist, **John Maynard Keynes,** who published his *General Theory of Employment, Interest, and Money* in 1936. He condemned the old theory that, in a free economy, depressions should be left to resolve themselves without governmental interference.

Keynes argued that unemployment came not from overproduction, but from a decline in demand. Demand, in turn, could be increased by putting people back to work building highways and public buildings. The government should finance such projects even if it had to engage in **deficit spending,** or had to go into debt.

### The United States

Germany suffered tremendously during the Great Depression, but no Western nation was more affected than the United States. By 1932, its industrial production had fallen almost 50 percent from its 1929 level. By 1933, there were more than 12 million unemployed.

Under these **circumstances,** the Democrat **Franklin Delano Roosevelt** was able to win a landslide victory in the 1932 presidential election. A believer in free enterprise, Roosevelt realized that capitalism had to be reformed if it was to be "saved." He pursued a policy of active government intervention in the economy known as the **New Deal.**

The New Deal included an increased program of public works. It also included new social legislation that began the U.S. welfare system. In 1935, the Social Security Act created a system of old-age pensions and unemployment insurance.

The New Deal provided reforms that perhaps prevented a social revolution in the United States. It did not solve the unemployment problem, however. In 1938, U.S. unemployment still stood at more than 10 million. Only World War II and an expanded weapons industry brought back full employment.

☑ **Reading Check** **Explaining** What did John Maynard Keynes think would resolve the Great Depression?

**HISTORY** *Online* **Study Central**

For help with the concepts in this section of *Glencoe World History–Modern Times,* go to wh.mt.glencoe.com and click on **Study Central.**

---

## SECTION 1 ASSESSMENT

### Checking for Understanding

1. **Vocabulary** Define: depression, collective bargaining, minimum, deficit spending, circumstance.

2. **People and Events** Identify: Dawes Plan, Treaty of Locarno, Weimar Republic, John Maynard Keynes, Franklin Delano Roosevelt, New Deal.

3. **Places** Locate: Ruhr Valley, Switzerland.

### Reviewing Big Ideas

4. **Summarize** the intent of the Roosevelt administration's New Deal.

### Critical Thinking

5. **Historical Analysis** **Evaluating** Determine the validity of the following statement: "Promises not to go to war were worthless without a way to enforce these promises." **CA HR 3**

6. **Cause and Effect** Use a diagram like the one below to list the causes of the Great Depression.

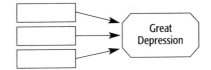

Great Depression

### Analyzing Visuals

7. **Examine** the photograph on page 467. How would you survive if currency became worthless? Who would be at an advantage?

### Writing About History

8. **Informative Writing** Research and write an essay that explains how the Great Depression caused extremist political parties to emerge throughout the world. Identify which parties are still active in the United States. **CA 10WA2.3a**

# The Rise of Dictatorial Regimes

## Guide to Reading

### Section Preview
By 1939, many European countries had adopted dictatorial regimes that aimed to control every aspect of their citizens' lives for state goals.

**Main Idea**
- The totalitarian states did away with individual freedoms. (p. 471)
- In Italy, the Fascist leader Mussolini established a totalitarian state. (p. 471)
- In the Soviet Union, Stalin maintained total power by murdering his political opponents. (p. 473)
- Authoritarian governments in the West worked to preserve the existing social order. (p. 476)

### Content Vocabulary
totalitarian state, fascism, New Economic Policy (NEP), Politburo, Five-Year Plans, collectivization

### Academic Vocabulary
widespread, unrestricted

### People to Identify
Benito Mussolini, Joseph Stalin, Francisco Franco

### Places to Locate
Russia, Madrid

### Reading Objectives
1. Determine the extent of Fascist Italy as a totalitarian state.
2. Explain the methods Stalin used to establish a totalitarian regime in the Soviet Union.

### Reading Strategy
**Categorizing Information** Use a web diagram like the one below to list methods Mussolini used to create a Fascist dictatorship.

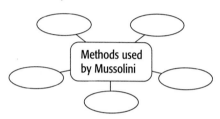

Methods used by Mussolini

### Preview of Events

| ♦1920 | ♦1925 | ♦1930 | ♦1935 | ♦1940 |
|---|---|---|---|---|

**1919**
Mussolini creates the *Fascio di Combattimento*

**1924**
Lenin dies

**1928**
Stalin launches his First Five-Year Plan

**1929**
Mussolini recognizes independence of Vatican City

**1939**
The Spanish Civil War ends

## California Standards in This Section

*Reading this section will help you master these California History–Social Science standards.*

**10.6.3:** Understand the widespread disillusionment with prewar institutions, authorities, and values that resulted in a void that was later filled by totalitarians.

**10.7.1:** Understand the causes and consequences of the Russian Revolution, including Lenin's use of totalitarian means to seize and maintain control (e.g., the Gulag).

**10.7.2:** Trace Stalin's rise to power in the Soviet Union and the connection between economic policies, political policies, the absence of a free press, and systematic violations of human rights (e.g., the Terror Famine in Ukraine).

**10.7.3:** Analyze the rise, aggression, and human costs of totalitarian regimes (Fascist and Communist) in Germany, Italy, and the Soviet Union, noting especially their common and dissimilar traits.

# The Rise of Dictators

**Main Idea** The totalitarian states did away with individual freedoms.

**Reading Connection** What would be your reaction if you could listen only to government-sponsored programs? Read to learn about a form of government that controls all aspects of people's lives.

The apparent triumph of democracy in Europe in 1919 was extremely short-lived. By 1939, only two major European states—France and Great Britain—remained democratic. Italy, the Soviet Union, Germany, and many other European states adopted dictatorial regimes. These regimes took both old and new forms. The new form was first seen in Italy in the Fascist Party led by Benito Mussolini.

## Voices from the Past

In 1932, Mussolini, now the dictator of Italy, published a statement of Fascist principles:

> ❝Anti-individualistic, the Fascist conception of life stresses the importance of the State and accepts the individual only in so far as his interests coincide with those of the State. . . . The Fascist conception of the State is all-embracing; outside of it no human or spiritual values can exist. Thus understood, fascism is totalitarian, and the Fascist State . . . interprets, develops, and potentiates [makes effective] the whole life of a people. . . . fascism does not, generally speaking, believe in the possibility or utility of perpetual peace. . . . War alone keys up all human energies to their maximum tension and sets the seal of nobility on those people who have the courage to face it.❞

Fascism was a new kind of dictatorship, the modern totalitarian state. A **totalitarian state** is a government that aims to control the political, economic, social, intellectual, and cultural lives of its citizens. New totalitarian regimes pushed the power of the central state far beyond what it had been in the past.

These totalitarian states wanted more than passive obedience. They wanted to conquer the minds and hearts of their subjects. They achieved this goal through mass propaganda techniques and high-speed modern communication. Modern technology also provided totalitarian states with an unprecedented ability to impose their wishes on their subjects.

The totalitarian states that emerged were led by a single leader and a single party. They rejected the ideal of limited government power and the guarantee of individual freedoms. Instead, individual freedom was subordinated to the collective will of the masses. This collective will of the masses, however, was organized and determined by the leader. The totalitarian state expected the active involvement of the masses in the achievement of its goals, whether those goals included war, a socialist state, or a thousand-year empire like the one Adolf Hitler wanted to establish.

✓ **Reading Check** **Contrasting** How does a totalitarian state differ from a democracy?

## Fascism in Italy

**Main Idea** In Italy, the Fascist leader Mussolini established a totalitarian state.

**Reading Connection** Do you sometimes read newspaper articles criticizing political leaders or policies? Read to learn how Mussolini reacted to criticism of his government.

In the early 1920s, **Benito Mussolini** (MOO•suh•LEE•nee) established the first European Fascist movement in Italy. Mussolini began his political career as a Socialist. In 1919, he created a new political group, the *Fascio di Combattimento,* or League of Combat. The term *fascist* is derived from that name.

As a political philosophy, **fascism** (FA•SHIH•zuhm) glorifies the state above the individual by emphasizing the need for a strong central government led by a dictatorial ruler. In a fascist state, people are controlled by the government, and any opposition is suppressed.

*"War alone keys up all human energies . . ."*
—*Benito Mussolini*

## NATIONAL GEOGRAPHIC

### Politics of Europe, 1930s

Authoritarian
Democratic
Fascist

NORWAY
FINLAND
SWEDEN
ESTONIA
LATVIA
LITHUANIA
IRELAND
UNITED
KINGDOM
North
Sea
Ger.
NETH.
BELG.
GERMANY
POLAND
LUX.
CZECH.
FRANCE
SWITZ.
AUSTRIA
HUNGARY
ROMANIA
ATLANTIC
OCEAN
SPAIN
YUGOSLAVIA
ITALY
BULGARIA
PORTUGAL
ALBANIA
GREECE
Mediterranean Sea

0          500 miles
0     500 kilometers
Lambert Azimuthal Equal-Area projection

### Geography *Skills*

Many European countries adopted dictatorial regimes to solve their problems in the 1920s and 1930s.

1. **Interpreting Maps** Which countries shown on the map above are Fascist? Which are authoritarian? Which are democratic states?

2. **Applying Geography Skills** Pose and answer a question that creates a comparison between a country's political status as shown on this map and the side that country fought on in World War I.

**Rise of Fascism** Like other European countries, Italy experienced severe economic problems after World War I. Inflation grew, and both industrial and agricultural workers staged strikes. Socialists spoke of revolution. The middle class began to fear a Communist takeover like the one that had recently occurred in **Russia.** Industrial and agricultural strikes created more division. Mussolini emerged from this background of **widespread** unrest.

In 1920 and 1921, Mussolini formed bands of black-shirted, armed Fascists called *squadristi* or Blackshirts. These bands attacked socialist offices and newspapers. They also used violence to break up strikes. Both middle-class industrialists who feared working-class strikes and large landowners who objected to agricultural strikes began to support Mussolini's Fascist movement.

By 1922, Mussolini's movement was growing quickly. The middle-class fear of socialism, commu-

nism, and disorder made the Fascists increasingly attractive to many people. In addition, Mussolini realized that the Italian people were angry over Italy's failure to receive more land in the peace settlement that followed the war. He understood that nationalism was a powerful force. Thus, he demanded more land for Italy and won thousands of converts to fascism with his patriotic and nationalistic appeals.

In 1922, Mussolini and the Fascists threatened to march on Rome if they were not given power. Mussolini exclaimed, "Either we are allowed to govern, or we will seize power." Victor Emmanuel III, the king of Italy, gave in and made Mussolini prime minister.

Mussolini used his position as prime minister to create a Fascist dictatorship. New laws gave the government the right to suspend any publications that criticized the Catholic Church, the monarchy, or the state. The prime minister was made head of the government with the power to make laws by decree. The police were given **unrestricted** authority to arrest and jail anyone for either nonpolitical or political crimes.

In 1926, the Fascists outlawed all other political parties in Italy and established a secret police, known as the OVRA. By the end of the year, Mussolini ruled Italy as *Il Duce* (eel DOO•chay), "The Leader."

**The Fascist State** To establish his totalitarian state, Mussolini used a number of methods. As we have seen, he created a secret police force, the OVRA, whose purpose was to monitor the political activities of individuals and organizations, and also to enforce government policies. The OVRA was never as repressive and brutal as the secret police force in Nazi Germany, however. (See discussion of Nazi Germany in Section 3.)

The Fascists also tried to exercise control over all forms of mass media, including newspapers, radio, and film. The government wanted to use the media to spread the Fascist message. This propaganda was supposed to mold Italians into a single community devoted to Fascist goals. Most of the propaganda, however, was rather clumsy. Often it boiled down to simple slogans, such as, "Mussolini Is Always Right."

To promote their goals, the Fascists also worked through organizations. Prime examples were youth groups. By 1939, for example, Fascist youth groups included about 66 percent of the population between the ages of 8 and 18. Members of such groups wore military-style uniforms and practiced military drills. Mussolini hoped that the youth groups would create a nation of Italians who were fit, disciplined, and war-loving. Meanwhile, school textbooks were also rewritten to reflect Fascist propaganda.

Despite all the Fascist rhetoric, the new state was not so different from the old. In most cases, the Fascists maintained traditional attitudes. This is especially evident in policies toward women. For the Fascists, the family was the pillar of the state and women were at the heart of family life. Women were to be homemakers and mothers. This was "their natural and fundamental mission in life," according to Mussolini.

Despite his attempts, Mussolini never achieved the total control that Hitler did in Germany or that Stalin did in the Soviet Union. Unlike those leaders, Mussolini did not completely destroy the country's old power structure. Some institutions, including the armed forces, were not absorbed into the Fascist state but managed to keep most of their independence. Victor Emmanuel was also retained as king.

Mussolini's compromise with the traditional institutions of Italy was also clear in his relationship to the Catholic Church. In the Lateran Accords of February 1929, Mussolini's regime recognized the sovereignty of the small area within Rome known as Vatican City. The Catholic Church had claimed this area ever since Italy was united in 1870—in fact, the Church had never recognized the legitimacy of the Italian state. When Mussolini formally recognized the Church's claim, the pope recognized the Italian state.

Mussolini's regime also gave the Church a large grant of money and recognized Catholicism as the "sole religion of the state." In return, the Catholic Church urged Italians to support the Fascist regime.

In all areas of life under the Fascists, there was a large gap between ideals and practices. The Italian Fascists promised much but delivered considerably less. They would soon be overshadowed by a much more powerful fascist movement to the north—that of Adolf Hitler, a student and admirer of Mussolini.

✔ **Reading Check** Examining How did Mussolini gain power in Italy?

**Web Activity** Visit the *Glencoe World History–Modern Times* Web site at wh.mt.glencoe.com and click on **Chapter 9– Student Web Activity** to learn more about the rise of fascism.

# A New Era in the Soviet Union

**Main Idea** In the Soviet Union, Stalin maintained total power by murdering his political opponents.

**Reading Connection** If a United States president dies in office, how is he or she replaced? Read to find out the difficulties for succession when Lenin died.

During the Russian civil war, Lenin followed a policy called war communism. The government had extensive control of the economy. It directed most industries and even seized grain from peasants when it wanted in order to ensure supplies for the army.

Once the war was over, peasants began to sabotage the communist program by hoarding food. The situation worsened when drought caused a famine between 1920 and 1922. As many as 5 million lives were lost. With agricultural disaster came industrial collapse. By 1921, industrial output was only 20 percent of its 1913 level.

Russia was exhausted. A peasant banner proclaimed, "Down with Lenin and horseflesh. Bring back the czar and pork." As Leon Trotsky said, "The country, and the government with it, were at the very edge of the abyss."

**Lenin's New Economic Policy** In March 1921, Lenin pulled Russia back from the abyss. He abandoned war communism in favor of his **New Economic Policy (NEP).** The NEP was a modified version of the old capitalist system. Peasants were allowed to sell their produce openly. Retail stores, as well as small industries that employed fewer than 20 workers, could be privately owned and operated. Heavy industry, banking, and mines, however, remained in the hands of the government.

In 1922, Lenin and the Communists formally created a new state called the Union of Soviet Socialist Republics, which is also known as the USSR (by its initials), or as the Soviet Union (by its shortened form). By that time, a revived market and a good harvest had brought an end to famine. Soviet agricultural production climbed to 75 percent of its prewar level.

Lenin's New Economic Policy saved the Soviet Union from complete economic disaster. Lenin and other leading Communists, however, only intended the NEP to be a temporary retreat from the goals of communism.

**The Rise of Stalin** Lenin died in 1924. Immediately, a power struggle began among the seven members of the **Politburo** (PAH•luht•BYOOR•OH)—the committee that made Communist Party policy. The Politburo was split into two on what policy the Soviet Union should follow to create a socialist state.

One group was led by Leon Trotsky. It wanted to end the NEP and launch Russia on a path of rapid industrialization, chiefly at the expense of the peasants. This group also wanted to spread communism abroad and believed that the revolution in Russia would not survive unless other nations adopted communism.

The other group in the Politburo rejected Trotsky's leadership and his ideas for worldwide communist revolution. It wanted to focus on building a socialist state at home and to continue Lenin's NEP. This group believed rapid industrialization was too radical and that such a plan would lower the peasants' standard of living.

This division over policy was underscored by an intense personal rivalry between Leon Trotsky and another Politburo member, **Joseph Stalin.** In 1924, Trotsky held the post of commissar of war, while Stalin was the general secretary for the party. The general secretary appointed the party officials for all regions, districts, cities, and towns. Because of this power of appointment, the general secretary became the most important position in the party.

Stalin used this position to gain complete control of the Communist Party. The thousands of officials Stalin appointed supported him when he made his bid for power. By 1929, Stalin was able to eliminate any Bolsheviks from the revolutionary era from the Politburo and create a dictatorship. Only people loyal to him survived. Trotsky, who was once Lenin's right-hand man, was expelled from the party in 1927. Later he lived in exile in Mexico, but in 1940 he was murdered, probably on Stalin's orders.

**Five-Year Plans** The Stalinist era marked the beginning of an economic, social, and political revolution that was more sweeping in its results than were the revolutions of 1917. Stalin made a significant shift in economic policy in 1928 when he ended the NEP and launched his First Five-Year Plan. The **Five-Year Plans** set economic goals for five-year periods. Their purpose was to transform Russia virtually overnight from an agricultural into an industrial country.

## People In History

### Benito Mussolini
**1883–1945—Italian dictator**

**B**enito Mussolini was the founder of the first Fascist movement. He was an unruly and rebellious child who was expelled from school once for stabbing a fellow pupil. Ultimately, he received a diploma and worked for a short time as an elementary school teacher.

Mussolini became a Socialist and gradually became well known in Italian Socialist circles. In 1912, he obtained the important position of editor of *Avanti (Forward)*, the official Socialist daily newspaper.

After being expelled from the Socialist Party, he formed his own political movement, the Fascist movement. When the Fascists did poorly in the Italian election of November 1919, Mussolini said that fascism had "come to a dead end." He then toyed with the idea of emigrating to the United States to become a journalist.

### Joseph Stalin
**1879–1953—Soviet dictator**

**J**oseph Stalin established a strong personal dictatorship over the Soviet Union. He joined the Bolsheviks in 1903 and came to Lenin's attention after staging a daring bank robbery to get funds for the Bolshevik cause. His real last name was Dzhugashvili, but he adopted the name Stalin, which means "man of steel."

Stalin was neither a dynamic speaker nor a forceful writer. He was a good organizer, however. His fellow Bolsheviks called him "Comrade Index-Card."

Like Hitler, Stalin was one of the greatest mass murderers in human history. It is estimated that his policies and his deliberate executions led to the death of as many as 25 million people. At the time of his death in 1953, he was planning yet another purge of party members.

**Map Legend:**
- Western border of Russia, 1914
- Bolshevik-controlled area, 1919
- Union of Soviet Socialist Republics (USSR), 1938
- Main area of collective farms
- Iron and steel production
- Labor camp

**Geography Skills**

The period from the beginning of World War I to the beginning of World War II was one of dramatic change in Russia.

1. **Interpreting Maps** From Moscow, in which direction would you go to find the Soviet Union's most productive farming area: northeast, southwest, northwest, or southeast?

2. **Applying Geography Skills** Identify a particular area of the Soviet Union as shown on the map and explain why that area would have been of particular interest to Stalin during his First Five-Year Plan.

The First Five-Year Plan emphasized the maximum production of armaments and capital goods—goods, such as heavy machines, that are made to produce other goods. The plan quadrupled the production of heavy machinery and doubled oil production. Between 1928 and 1937, during the first two Five-Year Plans, steel production in Russia increased from 4 million to 18 million tons (3.6 to 16.3 million t) per year.

The social and political costs of industrialization were enormous. Little provision was made to care for the new workers now living in the cities. For example, the number of workers increased by millions between 1932 and 1940, but the total investment in housing actually declined after 1929. The result was that millions of workers and their families lived in pitiful conditions. Real wages in the industrial sector also declined by 43 percent between 1928 and 1940. Strict laws even limited where workers could move. To keep workers content, government propaganda stressed the need for sacrifice to create the new socialist state.

With rapid industrialization came an equally rapid collectivization of agriculture. **Collectivization** was a system in which private farms were eliminated. Instead, the government owned all of the land while the peasants worked it.

Many peasants actively resisted collectivization. Rather than have their crops and animals seized, they hoarded crops or killed livestock. Their resistance only led Stalin to step up his collectivization program. By 1930, 10 million peasant households had been collectivized. Four years later, roughly 26 million family farms had been collectivized into 250,000 units.

CHAPTER 9    The West Between the Wars    **475**

**Costs of Stalin's Programs** Collectivization came at a tremendous cost. The hoarding of food and the slaughter of livestock produced famine. Stalin himself is supposed to have acknowledged that 10 million peasants died in the famines of 1932 and 1933.

Stalin's programs had other costs, too. To achieve his goals, Stalin strengthened his control over the party. Anyone who resisted was sent to forced labor camps in Siberia.

In the 1930s, Stalin's mania for power also led him to purge, or remove, all opponents—or imagined opponents—from Soviet life. His actions are referred to as the Great Purge. First to be removed were the Old Bolsheviks, anyone who had been active in the early years of the movement. Between 1936 and 1938, most of the Old Bolsheviks were put on trial and condemned to death.

During this same time, Stalin purged army officers, diplomats, union officials, party members, intellectuals, and numerous ordinary citizens. An estimated eight million Russians were arrested. Millions were sent to forced labor camps in Siberia, from which they never returned. Others were executed.

The Stalinist era also overturned much of the permissive social legislation enacted in the early 1920s. To promote equal rights for women, the Communists had made the divorce process easier and encouraged women to work outside the home. Once Stalin came to power, divorce became more difficult. The family was praised as a small collective in which parents were supposed to teach their children the value of hard work and duty.

✓ **Reading Check** **Summarizing** What was Lenin's New Economic Policy?

# Authoritarian States in the West

**Main Idea** Authoritarian governments in the West worked to preserve the existing social order.

**Reading Connection** If you were living in a new nation, what kind of government would you want? Read to learn about the types of governments adopted by new states in eastern Europe after World War I.

Some governments in the West were not totalitarian but authoritarian. These states adopted some features of totalitarian states, in particular, their use of police powers. In totalitarian states, the major goal was to create a new kind of mass society. This was not the goal of authoritarian states, however, which focused on preserving the existing social order.

**Eastern Europe** Authoritarian governments developed in some of the new nations in eastern Europe. At first, it seemed that political democracy would be the pattern in these states. Parliamentary systems were adopted in Austria, Poland, Czechoslovakia, Romania, Bulgaria, Hungary, and Yugoslavia (known until 1929 as the kingdom of the Serbs, Croats, and Slovenes). In most of these countries, however, authoritarian regimes soon took power.

Why did parliamentary systems so often fail to succeed in eastern Europe? First, most of these countries had little or no experience with political democracy. Their populations were also largely rural and uneducated. Large landowners still dominated the social and political system, and they did not want to give up power. Finally, eastern European states were usually made up of multiple ethnic groups, which often were at odds or even wanted their own nations.

Powerful landowners, the churches, and even some members of the middle class feared land reform, communist upheaval, and ethnic conflict. For this reason, these groups looked to authoritarian governments to maintain the old system. Only Czechoslovakia, which had a large middle class, a liberal tradition, and a strong industrial base, maintained its political democracy.

---

# What If...

## Trotsky had succeeded Lenin?

Lenin's death in 1924 caused a bitter political struggle to determine his successor. Although he had no influence over the final outcome, Lenin's testament, written in December 1922, predicted a split between Trotsky and Stalin. In his testament, read to delegates at the Thirteenth Congress, Lenin advised removing Stalin from his post as general secretary to prevent a power struggle.

**Consider the Consequences** Consider what would have happened if Stalin had not maintained his position of influence and had lost to Trotsky. Research Trotsky's beliefs, then write a short essay describing the direction the Soviet Union would have taken under his leadership.

---

**Spain** In Spain, too, political democracy failed to survive. Led by General **Francisco Franco,** Spanish military forces revolted against the democratic government in 1936. A bloody civil war began.

Foreign intervention complicated the Spanish Civil War. The Spanish republican government was aided by about 40,000 foreign volunteers and by trucks, planes, tanks, and military advisers from the Soviet Union. The Fascist regimes of Italy and Germany aided Franco's forces with arms, money, and men. Hitler used the Spanish Civil War as an opportunity to test the new weapons of his revived air force. The horrible destruction of Guernica by German bombers in April 1937 was immortalized in a painting by the Spanish artist Pablo Picasso.

The Spanish Civil War came to an end when Franco's forces captured **Madrid** in 1939. Franco established a dictatorship that favored large landowners, businesspeople, and the Catholic clergy. Because it favored traditional groups and did not try to control every aspect of people's lives, Franco's dictatorship is an example of a regime that was authoritarian rather than totalitarian.

✓**Reading Check** **Explaining** How did Czechoslovakia maintain its political democracy?

**HISTORY** *Online* **Study Central**

For help with the concepts in this section of *Glencoe World History–Modern Times,* go to <u>wh.mt.glencoe.com</u> and click on **Study Central.**

# SECTION 2 ASSESSMENT

### Checking for Understanding

1. **Vocabulary** Define: totalitarian state, fascism, widespread, unrestricted, New Economic Policy (NEP), Politburo, Five-Year Plans, collectivization.

2. **People and Events** Identify: Benito Mussolini, Joseph Stalin, Francisco Franco.

3. **Places** Locate: Russia, Madrid.

### Reviewing Big Ideas

4. **Explain** how Stalin gained control of the Communist Party after Lenin died.

### Critical Thinking

5. **Historical Analysis** **Evaluating** What was the major purpose of the Five-Year Plans during the 1920s and 1930s in the Soviet Union? **CA HR 3**

6. **Organizing Information** Use a diagram like the one below to identify ways in which Stalin changed the Soviet Union. Include the economic, social, and political results of his programs.

> How Stalin Changed the Soviet Union

### Analyzing Visuals

7. **Contrast** the above painting with the rally photo on page 459. How do their political messages about war compare? Is one stronger than the other? Why?

### Writing About History

8. **Persuasive Writing** Imagine you are a Communist Party boss who is preparing a short speech. It should convince peasants that they must join a collective farm so that industrialization can succeed. Conduct research to make your speech realistic. **CA 10WA2.4d,c**

# Hitler and Nazi Germany

## Guide to Reading

### Section Preview
Hitler's totalitarian state was widely accepted, but German Jews and minorities were persecuted.

**Main Idea**
- Adolf Hitler's ideas were based on racism and German nationalism. (p. 479)
- Hitler used anti-Semitism, economic policy, and propaganda in an effort to build a Nazi empire. (p. 481)

### Content Vocabulary
Nazi, *Reichstag*, concentration camp

### Academic Vocabulary
academy, ideology

### People and Events to Identify
Adolf Hitler, Enabling Act, Heinrich Himmler, Nuremberg laws, *Kristallnacht*

### Places to Locate
Munich, Nuremberg

### Reading Objectives
1. Explain how Hitler rose to power.
2. Enumerate the chief features of the Nazi totalitarian state.
3. Discuss how the rise of Nazism affected Germany.

### Reading Strategy
**Categorizing Information** Use a chart like the one below to list anti-Semitic policies enforced by the Nazi Party.

| Anti-Semitic Policies |
|---|
|  |
|  |
|  |
|  |

### Preview of Events

| ◆1880 | ◆1890 | ◆1900 | ◆1910 | ◆1920 | ◆1930 | ◆1940 |
|---|---|---|---|---|---|---|

**1889**
Hitler is born

**1921**
Hitler takes control of the National Socialist German Workers' Party

**1933**
*Reichstag* passes Enabling Act

**1935**
Nazis enact Nuremberg laws

**1938**
*Kristallnacht* occurs

## California Standards in This Section

*Reading this section will help you master these California History–Social Science standards.*

**10.7.3:** Analyze the rise, aggression, and human costs of totalitarian regimes (Fascist and Communist) in Germany, Italy, and the Soviet Union, noting especially their common and dissimilar traits.

**10.8.5:** Analyze the Nazi policy of pursuing racial purity, especially against the European Jews; its transformation into the Final Solution; and the Holocaust that resulted in the murder of six million Jewish civilians.

# Hitler and His Views

**Main Idea** Adolf Hitler's ideas were based on racism and German nationalism.

**Reading Connection** What would you say if you were asked to explain your basic ideas about life? Read on to learn about Hitler's ideology.

**Adolf Hitler** was born in Austria on April 20, 1889. A failure in secondary school, he eventually traveled to Vienna to become an artist but was rejected by the Vienna **Academy** of Fine Arts. He stayed in the city, supported at first by an inheritance. It was during these years that Hitler developed the ideas which guided him for the rest of his life. One of the cornerstones of his ideology was an almost mystical belief in the German nation.

## *Voices from the Past*

Hitler also believed that he personally embodied the feelings of a united Germany. In September 1936, Adolf Hitler spoke to a mass rally in the city of Nuremberg:

> ❝Do we not feel once again in this hour the miracle that brought us together? Once you heard the voice of a man, and it struck deep into your hearts; it awakened you, and you followed this voice. . . . When we meet each other here, the wonder of our coming together fills us all. Not everyone of you sees me, and I do not see everyone of you. But I feel you, and you feel me. It is the belief in our people that has made us small men great, that has made brave and courageous men out of us wavering, timid folk; this belief . . . joined us together into one whole!❞

Racism, especially anti-Semitism, was just as basic to Hitler's ideas, and in his view no Jew could be a good German. Finally, at this period of his life, Hitler came to believe in the need for struggle, which he saw as the "granite foundation of the world."

Hitler had a talent for knowing how to use political parties, propaganda, and terror. This talent allowed him to spread his message and his movement very effectively.

At the end of World War I, after four years of service on the Western Front, Hitler remained in Germany and decided to enter politics. In 1919, he joined the little-known German Workers' Party, one of several right-wing extreme nationalist parties in **Munich.**

By the summer of 1921, Hitler had taken total control of the party, which by then had been renamed the National Socialist German Workers' Party (NSDAP), or **Nazi** for short. Within two years, party membership had grown to 55,000 people, with 15,000 in the party militia. The militia was variously known as the SA, the Storm Troops, or the Brownshirts, after the color of their uniforms.

An overconfident Hitler staged an uprising against the government in Munich in November 1923. This so-called Beer Hall Putsch was quickly crushed, and Hitler was sentenced to prison. During his brief stay in jail, Hitler wrote *Mein Kampf,* or *My Struggle,* an account of his movement and its basic ideas.

In *Mein Kampf,* extreme German nationalism, strong anti-Semitism, and anticommunism are linked together by a Social Darwinian theory of struggle. This theory emphasizes the right of superior nations to *lebensraum* (LAY•buhnz•ROWM)—living space—through expansion. It also upholds the right of superior individuals to gain authoritarian leadership.

**Rise of Nazism** While he was in prison, Hitler realized that the Nazis would have to attain power by legal means, and not by a violent overthrow of the Weimar Republic. This meant that the Nazi Party would have to be a mass political party that could compete for votes with the other political parties.

After his release from prison, Hitler expanded the Nazi Party to all parts of Germany. By 1929, it had a national party organization. Three years later, it had 800,000 members and had become the largest party in the *Reichstag*—the German parliament.

▼ *Adolf Hitler*

No doubt, Germany's economic difficulties were a crucial factor in the Nazi rise to power. Unemployment had risen dramatically, growing from 4.35 million in 1931 to 6 million by the winter of 1932. The economic and psychological impact of the Great Depression made extremist parties more attractive.

Hitler promised to create a new Germany. His appeals to national pride, national honor, and traditional militarism struck an emotional chord in his listeners. After attending one of Hitler's rallies, a schoolteacher in Hamburg said, "When the speech was over, there was roaring enthusiasm and applause. . . . —How many look up to him with touching faith as their helper, their saviour, their deliverer from unbearable distress."

After 1930, the German government ruled by decree with the support of President Hindenburg. The *Reichstag* had little power, and thus Hitler clearly saw that controlling the parliament was not very important.

More and more, the right-wing elites of Germany—the industrial leaders, landed aristocrats, military officers, and higher bureaucrats—looked to Hitler for leadership. He had the mass support to create a right-wing, authoritarian regime that would save Germany and people in privileged positions from a Communist takeover. In 1933, Hindenburg, under pressure, agreed to allow Hitler to become chancellor and create a new government.

Within two months, Hitler had laid the foundation for the Nazis' complete control over Germany. The crowning step of Hitler's "legal seizure" of power came on March 23, 1933, when a two-thirds vote of the *Reichstag* passed the **Enabling Act.** This law gave the government the power to ignore the constitution for four years to deal with the country's problems.

The Enabling Act gave Hitler's later actions a legal basis. He no longer needed the *Reichstag* or President Hindenburg. In effect, Hitler became a dictator appointed by the parliamentary body itself.

With their new source of power, the Nazis acted quickly to bring all institutions under Nazi control. The civil service was purged of Jews and democratic elements. Large prison camps called **concentration camps** were set up for people who opposed the new regime. Trade unions were dissolved. All political parties except the Nazis were abolished.

By the end of the summer of 1933, only seven months after being appointed chancellor, Hitler had established the basis for a totalitarian state. When Hindenburg died in 1934, the office of president was abolished. Hitler became sole ruler of Germany. Public officials and soldiers were all required to take a personal oath of loyalty to Hitler as their Führer (FYUR•uhr), or "Leader."

☑ **Reading Check** **Examining** Why was the Enabling Act important to Hitler's control of Germany?

*Picturing* **History**

In *Mein Kampf,* Hitler wrote that mass meetings were important because individuals who feel weak and uncertain become intoxicated with the power of the group. How do you think Hitler viewed the average person?

▲ *The "SS," or* Schutzstaffeln, *were elite Nazi troops who brutally repressed all opposition to Hitler. Their standard reads* Deutschland Erwache—*Germany Forever.*

## The Nazi State, 1933–1939

**Main Idea** Hitler used anti-Semitism, economic policy, and propaganda in an effort to build a Nazi empire.

**Reading Connection** How would you react if the U.S. president declared, "The time of personal happiness is over"? Read to learn how the German people reacted to a similar statement by Hitler.

Hitler wanted to develop a totalitarian state in order to meet his larger goal—the development of his Aryan racial state to dominate Europe and possibly the world for generations.

*Aryan* is a linguistic term used to identify people speaking Indo-European languages. The Nazis misused the term and identified the Aryans with the ancient Greeks and Romans and twentieth-century Germans and Scandinavians. Nazis argued that Germans were the true descendants and leaders of the Aryans and would create another empire like the one ruled by the ancient Romans. The Nazis believed that the world had already seen two German empires, or *Reichs:* the Holy Roman Empire and the German

Empire of 1871 to 1918. It was Hitler's objective to create a Third Reich, the empire of Nazi Germany.

To achieve his goal, Hitler needed the active involvement of the German people. Hitler stated:

❝We must develop organizations in which an individual's entire life can take place. Then every activity and every need of every individual will be regulated by the collectivity represented by the party. There is no longer any arbitrary will, there are no longer any free realms in which the individual belongs to himself. . . . The time of personal happiness is over.❞

The Nazis worked to create a totalitarian state in a variety of ways. Economic policies, mass spectacles, and organizations were employed to further Nazi goals. Terror was freely used. Policies toward women and, in particular, Jews reflected Nazi aims.

**The State and Terror** Nazi Germany was the scene of almost constant personal and institutional conflict. This resulted in administrative chaos. Struggle was a basic feature of relationships within the party, within the state, and between party and state. Hitler, of course, was the ultimate decision maker and absolute ruler.

## Three Dictators: Mussolini, Stalin, and Hitler

| | Benito Mussolini (1883–1945) | Joseph Stalin (1879–1953) | Adolf Hitler (1889–1945) |
|---|---|---|---|
| Country | Italy | USSR | Germany |
| Political Title | Prime Minister | General Secretary | Chancellor |
| Date in Power | 1922 | 1929 | 1933 |
| Political Party | Fascist Party | Communist Party | National Socialist German Workers' Party (NSDAP, or Nazi) |
| Type of Government | Fascist | Communist | Fascist |
| Source(s) of Support | Middle-class industrialists and large landowners | Party officials | Industrial leaders, landed aristocrats, military, and bureaucracy |
| Methods of Controlling Opposition | Secret police (OVRA), imprisonment, outlawing other parties, propaganda, censorship of the press | Purges, prison camps, secret police, state-run press, forced labor camps, executions | *Schutzstaffeln* (SS) police force, propaganda, state-run press, terror, repression, racial laws, concentration and death camps |
| Policies | Support for Catholic Church, nationalism, antisocialism, anticommunism | Five-Year Plans for rapid industrialization, collectivization of farms | Rearmament, public projects to put people to work, anti-Semitism, racism, Social Darwinism, extreme nationalism |

### Chart *Skills*

Mussolini, Stalin, and Hitler all came to power after World War I.

1. **Making Comparisons** Compare the governments of Mussolini, Stalin, and Hitler. How were they similar?
2. **Identifying** What methods do people in a democracy use to express their opposition to government policies? Why would these methods not have worked under these dictators?

For those who needed coercion, the Nazi totalitarian state used terror and repression. The *Schutzstaffeln* ("Guard Squadrons"), known simply as the SS, were an important force for maintaining order. The SS was originally created as Hitler's personal bodyguard. Under the strict direction of **Heinrich Himmler,** the SS came to control not only the secret police forces that Himmler had set up, but also the regular police forces.

The SS was based on two principles: terror and **ideology.** Terror included the instruments of repression and murder—secret police, criminal police, concentration camps, and later, execution squads and death camps (concentration camps where prisoners

are killed). For Himmler, the chief goal of the SS was to further the group they saw as the German master race.

**Economic Policies** In the economic sphere, Hitler used public works projects and grants to private construction firms to put people back to work and end the depression. A massive rearmament program, however, was the key to solving the unemployment problem.

Unemployment, which had reached 6 million in 1932, dropped to 2.6 million in 1934 and fewer than 500,000 in 1937. The regime claimed full credit for this. Its part in bringing an end to the depression was an important reason why many Germans were willing to accept Hitler and the Nazis.

**Spectacles and Organizations** Mass demonstrations and spectacles were also used to make the German people an instrument of Hitler's policies. These meetings, especially the **Nuremberg** party rallies that were held every September, had great appeal. They usually evoked mass enthusiasm and excitement.

Institutions, such as the Catholic and Protestant Churches, primary and secondary schools, and universities, were also brought under the control of the Nazi totalitarian state. Nazi professional organizations and leagues were formed for civil servants, teachers, women, farmers, doctors, and lawyers. In addition, youth organizations taught Nazi ideals.

**Women and Nazism** Women played a crucial role in the Aryan state as bearers of the children who, it was believed, would bring about the triumph of the Aryan race. The Nazis believed men were destined to be warriors and political leaders, while women should be wives and mothers devoted to domestic pursuits. By preserving this clear distinction, each could best serve to "maintain the whole community."

Nazi ideas determined employment opportunities for women. Jobs in heavy industry, it was thought, might hinder women from bearing healthy children. Certain professions, including university teaching, medicine, and law, were also considered unsuitable for women, especially married women. The Nazis instead encouraged women to pursue other occupations, such as social work and nursing. The Nazi regime actively campaigned against working women. It put out posters with slogans like: "Get ahold of pots and pans and broom and you'll sooner find a groom!"

**Anti-Semitic Policies** From its beginning, the Nazi Party reflected the anti-Semitic beliefs of Hitler. For centuries, Jews had suffered discrimination in Europe. Although many laws against Jews had been reformed in the 1800s, anti-Semitism surfaced again during the difficult years after World War I. Once in power, the Nazis translated anti-Semitic ideas into action.

In September 1935, the Nazis announced new racial laws at the annual party rally in Nuremberg. These **Nuremberg laws** excluded Jews from German citizenship. A Jew was defined not by religion but by whether he or she had a Jewish grandparent. Marriage between Jews and German citizens was forbidden. Jews were also required to wear yellow Stars of David and to carry identification cards saying they were Jewish.

A more violent phase of anti-Jewish activity began on the night of November 9, 1938—*Kristallnacht,* or the "night of shattered glass." In a destructive rampage against the Jews, Nazis burned synagogues and destroyed some seven thousand Jewish businesses. At least a hundred Jews were killed. Thirty thousand Jewish males were rounded up and sent to concentration camps.

*Kristallnacht* led to further drastic steps. Jews were barred from all public transportation and all public buildings, including schools and hospitals. They were prohibited from owning, managing, or working in any retail store. The Jews were forced to clean up all the debris and damage due to *Kristallnacht.* Finally, under the direction of the SS, Jews were encouraged to "emigrate from Germany."

☑ **Reading Check** **Summarizing** What steps did Hitler take to establish a Nazi totalitarian state in Germany?

**HISTORY** *Online* **Study Central**

For help with the concepts in this section of *Glencoe World History–Modern Times,* go to wh.mt.glencoe.com and click on **Study Central.**

---

# SECTION 3 ASSESSMENT

### Checking for Understanding

1. **Vocabulary** Define: academy, Nazi, *Reichstag,* concentration camp, ideology.

2. **People and Events** Identify: Adolf Hitler, Enabling Act, Heinrich Himmler, Nuremberg laws, *Kristallnacht.*

3. **Places** Locate: Munich, Nuremberg.

### Reviewing Big Ideas

4. **List** the rights taken from the Jews by the Nazi government.

### Critical Thinking

5. **Historical Analysis** **Cause and Effect** How did mass demonstrations and meetings contribute to the success of the Nazi Party? **CA HI 2**

6. **Organizing Information** Use a table to describe the policies and programs used by the Nazis to create a Third Reich. Identify the goals for each policy or program.

| Policy/Program | Goals |
|---|---|
|  |  |
|  |  |
|  |  |

### Analyzing Visuals

7. **Examine** any two photos from this section. Compare and contrast the two photos. How do you think they relate to Hitler's vision of Nazi Germany?

## Writing About History

8. **Expository Writing** Find a library book by a German who lived under Nazism. Read several chapters that tell about the author's life. In a report, give your opinion about whether that person could have resisted the government and why. **CA 10WA2.3a,b**

# YOUNG PEOPLE IN . . .

## Nazi Germany

In setting up a totalitarian state, the Nazis recognized the importance of winning young people over to their ideas. The Hitler Youth, an organization for young people between the ages of 10 and 18, was formed in 1926 for that purpose.

By 1939, all German young people were expected to join the Hitler Youth. Upon entering, each took an oath: "In the presence of this blood banner [Nazi flag], which represents our Führer, I swear to devote all my energies and my strength to the savior of our country, Adolf Hitler. I am willing and ready to give up my life for him, so help me God."

Members of the Hitler Youth had their own uniforms and took part in a number of activities. For males, these included camping and hiking trips, sports activities, and evenings together in special youth "homes." Almost all activities were competitive and meant to encourage fighting and heroic deeds.

Above all, the Hitler Youth organization worked to foster military values and virtues, such as duty, obedience, strength, and ruthlessness. Uniforms and drilling became a way of life. By 1938, training in the military arts was also part of the routine. Even boys 10 to 14 years old were given small-arms drill and practice with dummy hand grenades. Those who were 14 to 18 years old bore army packs and rifles while on camping trips in the countryside.

The Hitler Youth had a female division, known as the League of German Girls, for girls aged 10 to 18. They, too, had uniforms: white blouses, blue ankle-length skirts, and sturdy hiking shoes. Camping and hiking were also part of the girls' activities. More important, however, girls were taught domestic skills—how to cook, clean houses, and take care of children. In Nazi Germany, women were expected to be faithful wives and dutiful mothers.

◄ Young people were very susceptible to the blind devotion demanded by Nazism. These young girls were probably members of the *Bund Deutscher Madel*, or League of German Girls. Girls and women were among Hitler's most fanatical admirers. Hitler could be sentimental and fatherly, but instantly turn ruthless.

▲ Many Germans who were angry about the outcome of World War I were eager to hear Hitler's message. Public displays of the swastika—a cross with its arms bent 90 degrees to either right or left—were everywhere.

▲ Nazi values were reinforced at mass rallies where thousands of people, including young boys, gathered together for torchlight parades and emotional speeches about German honor and the need to fight and die for the Fatherland.

◄ "A young German must be as swift as a greyhound, as tough as leather, and as hard as Krupp's steel." This saying, like many others attributed to Hitler, was quoted to inspire young Germans with the spirit of militarism.

## CONNECTING TO THE PAST

1. **Explaining** What ideals and values did the Hitler Youth promote?

2. **Analyzing** How did the Hitler Youth help support the Nazi totalitarian state?

3. **Writing about History** Write an essay comparing the youth organizations you know with those of Nazi Germany.

# Cultural and Intellectual Trends

**Section Preview**

The destruction of the highly mechanized First World War and the turmoil of the Great Depression profoundly affected the work of artists and intellectuals.

**Main Idea**

• Hitler used radio and movies as propaganda tools to promote Nazism. (p. 487)

• Hitler extended his control over the German people to how they spent their leisure time. (p. 488)

• Art and literature produced after World War I reflected the horrors of the war and the uncertainty of the future. (p. 488)

• New discoveries in physics after World War I challenged the certainties of the older Newtonian physics. (p. 491)

**Content Vocabulary**

photomontage, surrealism, modernism, uncertainty principle

**Academic Vocabulary**

incapable, abstract, classical

**People and Events to Identify**

*The Triumph of the Will,* Salvador Dalí, James Joyce, Hermann Hesse

**Places to Locate**

Berlin, Dublin

**Reading Objectives**

1. Describe the trends that dominated arts and popular culture after 1918.
2. Explain how the new movements in arts and literature reflect the changes after World War I.

**Reading Strategy**

**Categorizing Information** Use a table like the one below to list literary works by Hesse and Joyce. Describe the techniques used in each work.

| Literary Works | Techniques |
|----------------|------------|
|                |            |
|                |            |
|                |            |

**Preview of Events**

| ♦1915 | ♦1920 | ♦1925 | ♦1930 |
|-------|-------|-------|-------|

**1920**
First Dada show in Berlin

**1922**
James Joyce's *Ulysses* is published

**1927**
Werner Heisenberg explains the uncertainty principle

## California Standards in This Section

*Reading this section will help you master these California History–Social Science standards.*

**10.3.2:** Examine how scientific and technological changes and new forms of energy brought about massive social, economic, and cultural change (e.g., the inventions and discoveries of James Watt, Eli Whitney, Henry Bessemer, Louis Pasteur, Thomas Edison).

**10.6.3:** Understand the widespread disillusionment with prewar institutions, authorities, and values that resulted in a void that was later filled by totalitarians.

**10.6.4:** Discuss the influence of World War I on literature, art, and intellectual life in the West (e.g., Pablo Picasso, the "lost generation" of Gertrude Stein, Ernest Hemingway).

# Mass Culture: Radio and Movies

**Main Idea** Hitler used radio and movies as propaganda tools to promote Nazism.

**Reading Connection** How would you compare advertising in a democracy to propaganda in a totalitarian state? Read to find out how Hitler used movies to promote his beliefs and ideas.

A series of inventions in the late nineteenth century had led the way for a revolution in mass communications. Especially important was Marconi's discovery of wireless radio waves. A musical concert transmitted in June 1920 had a major impact on radio broadcasting. Broadcasting facilities were built in the United States, Europe, and Japan during 1921 and 1922. At the same time, the mass production of radios began. In 1926, there were 2.2 million radios in Great Britain. By the end of the 1930s, there were 9 million.

Radio was only one part of the Western culture that was rapidly changing. The insanity of World War I, new forms of entertainment, and new inventions all gave a sense that the modern world was crazy, and sometimes absurd.

## *Voices from the Past*

One art movement in particular gave expression to the absurdity of modern life. This was dadaism. In 1922, Tristan Tzara, a Romanian-French poet, gave a lecture on this new artistic movement:

> ❝I know that you have come here today to hear explanations. Well, don't expect to hear any explanations about Dada. You explain to me why you exist. You haven't the faintest idea. . . . Dada is a state of mind. Dada applies itself to everything, and yet it is nothing, it is the point where the yes and the no and all the opposites meet, not solemnly in the castles of human philosophies, but very simply at street corners, like dogs and grasshoppers. Like everything in life, Dada is useless. Dada is without pretension, as life should be.❞

One new form of mass culture was destined to dominate the twentieth century: movies, or motion pictures as they were called in the early decades. Although they emerged in the 1890s, full-length features did not appear until right before World War I.

The Italian film *Quo Vadis* and the American film *Birth of a Nation* made it clear movies would be an important form of mass entertainment. By 1939, about 40 percent of adults in the more industrialized countries went to the movies once a week. By the end of World War II, it was 60 percent who did so.

Radio and movies could also be used for political purposes. "Without motor-cars, sound films, and wireless," Hitler once said, "[there would be] no victory of Nazism." Radio offered great opportunities for reaching the masses. This became obvious when people seemed to respond as excitedly to Hitler's radio broadcasts as they did when they heard him in person. The Nazis encouraged radio listening by urging manufacturers to produce inexpensive radios. That way, the average family could buy a radio on an installment plan.

Film, too, had propaganda potential, a fact not lost on Joseph Goebbels (GUH[R]•buhlz), Hitler's propaganda minister. Goebbels believed that film was, as he put it, one of the "most modern and scientific means of influencing the masses." For this reason, he created a film division in the Propaganda Ministry.

The Propaganda Ministry supported the making of both documentaries, or nonfiction films, and popular feature films to convey the Nazi message. *The Triumph of the Will,* for example, was a documentary of the 1934 Nuremberg party rally. This movie was filmed by Leni Riefenstahl, an actress-turned-director. It vividly conveyed the ideas of National Socialism.

✔**Reading Check** **Explaining** Why was the radio an important propaganda tool for the Nazis?

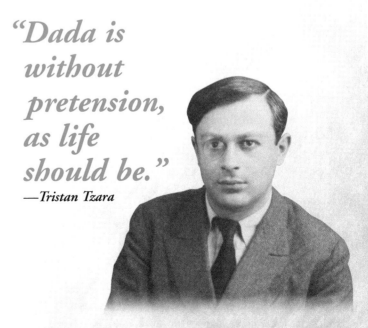

*"Dada is without pretension, as life should be."*
—*Tristan Tzara*

### Picturing History

This 1920s movie camera (far right) and radio were part of a communications revolution. Millions of people could now hear or see the same entertainment, news, and advertisements. A more homogeneous, or uniform, culture resulted. What are the positive and negative results of a uniform culture?

## Mass Leisure

**Main Idea** Hitler extended his control over the German people to how they spent their leisure time.

**Reading Connection** How would you feel if the government had a say in how you spent your free time? Read to see what kind of activities the Nazis set up for the leisure time of ordinary German citizens.

After World War I, new work patterns provided people with more free time to take advantage of the leisure activities that had developed at the turn of the century. By 1920, the eight-hour day had become the norm for many office and factory workers in northern and Western Europe.

Professional sporting events aimed at large audiences were an important aspect of mass leisure. Travel was another favorite activity. Trains, buses, and cars made trips to beaches or holiday resorts increasingly popular and affordable. Beaches, such as the one at Brighton in Great Britain, were mobbed by crowds of people from all social classes.

Mass leisure offered new ways for totalitarian states to control the people. The Nazi regime, for example, adopted a program called *Kraft durch Freude* ("Strength through Joy"). The program offered a variety of leisure activities to fill the free time of the working class. These activities included concerts, operas, films, guided tours, and sporting events. Especially popular were the program's inexpensive vacations, which were similar to modern package tours. A vacation could be a cruise to Scandinavia or the Mediterranean. More likely for workers, it was a shorter trip within Germany.

**Reading Check** **Examining** How did the "Strength through Joy" program help to support the Nazi regime?

## Artistic and Literary Trends

**Main Idea** Art and literature produced after World War I reflected the horrors of the war and the uncertainty of the future.

**Reading Connection** Can you think of a song, book, or movie that reflects the attitudes of your friends? Read to learn about the style and messages in art and literature in the years after World War I.

Four years of devastating war left many Europeans with a profound sense of despair. To many people, the horrors of World War I meant that something was dreadfully wrong with Western values, that human beings were violent animals who were **incapable** of creating a sane and rational world. The Great Depression and the growth of violent fascist movements only added to the despair created by the war.

With political, economic, and social uncertainties came intellectual uncertainties. These were evident in the artistic and intellectual achievements of the years following World War I.

**Art: Nightmares and New Visions** After 1918, artistic trends mainly reflected developments made before the war. **Abstract** art, for example, became ever more popular. In addition, a prewar fascination with the absurd and the unconscious content of the mind seemed even more appropriate in light of the nightmare landscapes of the World War I battlefronts. "The world does not make sense, so why should art?" was a common remark. This sentiment gave rise to both the Dada movement and surrealism.

The dadaists were artists who were obsessed with the idea that life has no purpose. They were revolted by what they saw as the insanity of life and tried to express that feeling in their art. Dada artist Hannah Höch, for example, used **photomontage** (a picture made of a combination of photographs) to comment on women's roles in the new mass culture. Her work was part of the first Dada show in **Berlin** in 1920.

A more important artistic movement than dadaism was **surrealism.** This movement sought a reality beyond the material world and found it in the world of the unconscious. By portraying fantasies, dreams, and even nightmares, the surrealists sought to show the greater reality that exists beyond the world of physical appearances.

The Spaniard **Salvador Dalí** was the high priest of surrealism. Dalí painted everyday objects but separated them from their normal contexts. By placing recognizable objects in unrecognizable relationships, Dalí created a strange world in which the irrational became visible.

Not everybody accepted modern art forms. Many people denounced what they saw as decay in the arts. Nowhere was this more evident than in Nazi Germany. In the 1920s, Weimar Germany was one of the chief European centers for modern arts and sciences. Hitler and the Nazis, however, rejected modern art as "degenerate." In a speech in July 1937, Hitler proclaimed:

> 66The people regarded this art [modern art] as the outcome of an impudent and shameless arrogance or of a simply shocking lack of skill; it felt that . . . these achievements which might have been produced by untalented children of from eight to ten years old—could never be valued as an expression of our own times or of the German future.99

Hitler and the Nazis believed that they could create a new and genuine German art. It would glorify the strong, the healthy, and the heroic—the qualities valued by the Aryan race. The new German art developed by the Nazis, however, was actually derived from nineteenth-century folk art, and emphasized realistic scenes of everyday life.

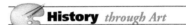

### History *through Art*

***The Persistence of Memory* by Salvador Dalí, 1931**
Surrealism gave everyday objects a dreamlike quality. Dalí, like many surrealist artists, was influenced by Sigmund Freud's theory of the unconscious. Analyze why surrealism developed in the period between the wars.

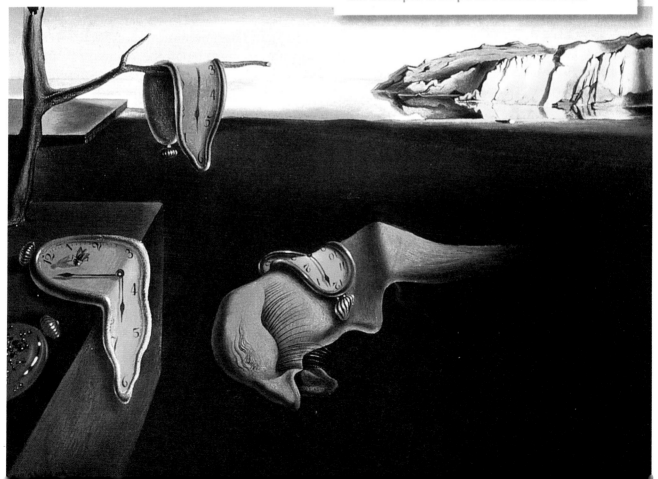

▲ *The* Kornhaus *in Dessau, Germany, served as a gathering place and dance hall for students of the Bauhaus school of architecture. The river beyond is the Elbe.*

## Architecture: The Modernist Spirit

The architects who lived through World War I were driven by the desire to create a new world. They turned their backs on monumental facades and heroic statues on horseback. One man in this generation was Walter Gropius. In 1919, he announced a new school for architects in Weimar, Germany, the Bauhaus, with these words: "Architects, sculptors, painters . . . let us desire, conceive, and create the new structure of the future which will . . . one day rise toward heaven from the hands of a million workers like a crystal symbol of a new faith."

Bauhaus architects wanted to unite function, technology, and craft. Their buildings have clean, horizontal lines and a businesslike look. The artistic spirit that inspired this school and others in the interwar period is called **modernism.** In the United States, a famous modernist structure is the Museum of Modern Art in New York City.

With its faith in technology, America was a natural home for modernism. That connection was aided by Hitler, who shut down the Bauhaus school in 1933. Hitler did not want rational design, but buildings that would glorify the Nazi state. Many Bauhaus leaders emigrated to the United States.

## Literature: The Search for the Unconscious

The interest in the unconscious that was evident in art was also integrated into new literary techniques. For example, "stream of consciousness" was a technique used by writers to report the innermost thoughts of each character. The most famous example of this approach is the novel *Ulysses*, published by the Irish writer **James Joyce** in 1922. *Ulysses* tells the story of one day in the life of ordinary people in **Dublin** by following the flow of their inner thoughts.

The German writer **Hermann Hesse** dealt with the unconscious in a quite different fashion. His novels reflect the influence of both Freud's psychology and Asian religions. The works focus on, among other things, the spiritual loneliness of modern human beings in a mechanized urban society. In both *Siddhartha* and *Steppenwolf*, Hesse uses Buddhist ideas to show the psychological confusion of modern existence. Hesse's novels had a great impact on German youth in the 1920s. He won the Nobel Prize for literature in 1946.

☑ **Reading Check** **Examining** Why were artists and writers after World War I attracted to Freud's theory of the unconscious?

# The Heroic Age of Physics

**Main Idea** New discoveries in physics after World War I challenged the certainties of the older Newtonian physics.

**Reading Connection** Has the possibility of cloning changed your idea of the role of science in society? Read to learn how the observations of a German physicist led to a new picture of the universe.

The prewar revolution in physics begun by Albert Einstein continued in the years between the wars. In fact, Ernest Rutherford, one of the physicists who showed that the atom could be split, called the 1920s the "heroic age of physics."

The new picture of the universe that was unfolding in physics undermined the old certainties of the **classical** physics of Newton. Newtonian physics had made people believe that all phenomena could be completely defined and predicted. In 1927, this belief was shaken when the German physicist Werner Heisenberg explained an observation he called the **uncertainty principle.**

Physicists knew that atoms were made up of smaller parts (subatomic particles). The fact that the behavior of these subatomic particles is unpredictable provides the foundation for the uncertainty principle. Heisenberg's theory essentially suggests that all physical laws are based on uncertainty. The theory's emphasis on randomness challenges Newtonian physics and thus, in a way, represents a new

▲ *German physicist Werner Heisenberg*

worldview. It is unlikely that many nonscientists understood the implications of Heisenberg's work. Nevertheless, the principle of uncertainty fit in well with the other uncertainties of the interwar years.

 **Reading Check** **Explaining** How did Heisenberg's uncertainty principle challenge the Newtonian worldview?

**HISTORY Online** **Study Central**

For help with the concepts in this section of *Glencoe World History—Modern Times,* go to **wh.mt.glencoe.com** and click on **Study Central.**

---

# SECTION 4 ASSESSMENT

### Checking for Understanding

1. **Vocabulary** Define: incapable, abstract, photomontage, surrealism, modernism, classical, uncertainty principle.

2. **People and Events** Identify: *The Triumph of the Will,* Salvador Dalí, James Joyce, Hermann Hesse.

3. **Places** Locate: Berlin, Dublin.

### Reviewing Big Ideas

4. **Explain** how dadaism and surrealism reflected economic and political developments after World War I. Also explain how the painting on page 489, Dalí's *The Persistence of Memory,* supports your explanation.

### Critical Thinking

5. **Historical Analysis** **Evaluating** What impact did technological advances in transportation and communication have on Western culture between the wars? **CA HR 3**

6. **Compare and Contrast** Use a Venn diagram like the one below to compare the Dada movement and surrealism.

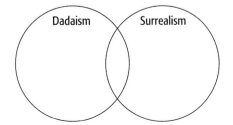

Dadaism   Surrealism

### Analyzing Visuals

7. **Examine** the photographs on page 488. Describe how our culture has been influenced by radio and movies. What communication technology is most influential today?

## Writing About History

8. **Informative Writing** Prepare a poster that shows the development of mass communications from the radio to computers, including photos and illustrations. Write a brief paragraph that summarizes these innovations. **CA 10WA2.3b**

# PRIMARY SOURCES
## EYEWITNESS TO HISTORY

*Three speeches from the 1930s highlight the feeling of crisis in that decade: in Britain and Germany, the Depression crisis; in the Soviet Union, the struggle to establish socialism.*

## SOURCE 1: Ramsay MacDonald on Capitalism

*Ramsay MacDonald was prime minister of Britain's first two Labour governments. In this 1930 speech, he defends the government and argues for reforming capitalism.*

It is not the Labour Government that is on trial; it is Capitalism that is being tried. We told you in those days that the time would come when finance would be more powerful than industry. That day has come. . . . We told you in those days that the time would come when the man who went into the workshop and into the factory, and his employer as well, would no longer be in the simple relationship of mas-

*An out-of-work plumber on the streets of London*

ter and man, but that the master would become impersonal, and that powers that have nothing to do with industry would control industry—the powers of gambling with credit. That day has come. . . .

So, my friends, we are not on trial; it is the system under which we live. It has broken down, not only in this little island, it has broken down in Europe, in Asia, in America; it has broken down everywhere, as it was bound to break down. And the cure, the new path, the new idea is organization—organization which will protect life, not property; organization which may protect property, but protect property in proper relation to life; organization which will see to it that when science discovers and inventors invent, the class that will be crushed down by reason of knowledge shall not be the working class, but the loafing class. This is the policy that we are going to pursue slowly, steadily, persistently, with knowledge and with our minds working upon a plan.

## SOURCE 2: Stalin on Industrialization

*In this 1931 speech, Soviet leader Joseph Stalin says that it is critical for the new socialist state to industrialize.*

It is sometimes asked whether it is not possible to slow down the tempo somewhat, to put a check on the movement. No, **comrades**[1], it is not possible! The tempo must not be reduced! On the contrary, we must increase it as much as is within our powers and possibilities. This is dictated to us by our obligation to the workers and peasants of the USSR. This is dictated to us by our obligations to the working class of the whole world.

To slacken the tempo would mean falling behind. And those who fall behind get beaten. But we do not want to be beaten. No, we refuse to be beaten!

---

➤ [1] **comrades:** a term of address used in Soviet Russia to imply that everyone was equal

. . . In the past we had no fatherland, nor could we have had one. But now that we have overthrown capitalism and power is in our hands, in the hands of the people, we have a fatherland, and we will uphold its independence. Do you want our socialist fatherland to be beaten and to lose its independence? If you do not want this, you must put an end to its backwardness in the shortest possible time and develop a genuine Bolshevik tempo in building up its socialist economy. There is no other way. That is why Lenin said on the eve of the October Revolution: 'Either perish, or overtake and outstrip the advanced capitalist countries.' . . .

We are fifty or a hundred years behind the advanced countries. We must make good this distance in ten years. Either we do it, or they crush us.

That is what our obligations to the workers and peasants of the USSR dictate to us.

## SOURCE 3: Hitler on German Unity

*In 1932, the Nazi Party was concerned about financing its election campaign. Hitler gave this speech to the Industry Club, outlining his plan to develop economic strength and unity.*

Today we stand at the turning-point of Germany's destiny. If the present development continues, Germany will one day of necessity land in Bolshevist chaos, but if this development is broken, then our people must be taken into a school of iron discipline and gradually freed from the prejudices of both camps. A hard schooling, but one we cannot escape!

If one thinks that one can preserve for all time the conceptions of 'bourgeois' and 'proletarian' then one will either preserve the weakness of Germany—which means our downfall—or one ushers in the victory of Bolshevism. If one refuses to surrender to those conceptions, then in my judgment a resurrection of the German nation is no longer possible. The chalk line which **Weltanschauungen**[2] have drawn for peoples in the history of the world already more than once has proved to be the death-line. Either we shall succeed in working out a body-politic hard as iron from this

[2]**Weltanschauungen:** particular worldviews

conglomerate[3] of parties, associations, unions, and conceptions of the world, from this pride of rank and madness of class, or else, lacking this internal consolidation, Germany will fall in final ruin. . . .

And so in contrast to our own official Government I cannot see any hope for the resurrection of Germany if we regard foreign politics of Germany as the primary factor: the primary necessity is the restoration of the sound national German body-politic armed to strike. In order to realize this end I founded thirteen years ago the National Socialist Movement: that Movement I have led during the last twelve years, and I hope that one day it will accomplish this task and that, as the fairest result of its struggle, it will leave behind it a German body-politic completely renewed internally, intolerant of anyone who sins against the nation and its interests, intolerant against anyone who will not acknowledge its vital interests, or who opposes them, intolerant and pitiless against anyone who shall attempt once more to destroy or disintegrate this body-politic, and yet ready for friendship and peace with anyone who has a wish for peace and friendship.

[3]**conglomerate:** gathering; cluster

## DBQ Document-Based Questions

**Historical Analysis** CA HI 3, HR 2, HI 1

**Source 1:** What is MacDonald referring to when he says "the powers of gambling with credit" now control industry?

**Source 2:** Why does Stalin say that the USSR did not previously have a "fatherland"? **CA 10RW1.1**

**Source 3:** What does Hitler view as a primary necessity in the "resurrection of Germany"?

## Comparing and Contrasting Sources

1. In crisis times, political leaders often raise people's fears about what will happen if they do not take action. Look at each speech. Then explain what specific fear each man calls up in his audience.

2. Hitler and Stalin both worry that their countries will be overrun if change is not made. What do they want to do to stop it?

Standards 10.3.2, 10.6.1, 10.6.2, 10.6.3, 10.6.4, 10.7.1, 10.7.2, 10.7.3, 10.8.2, 10.8.5

## Reviewing Content Vocabulary

1. A _____ is a picture made of a combination of photographs.
2. A _____ is a period of low economic activity and rising unemployment.
3. The Soviet government followed a policy of _____ when it took private property after World War I without payments to the former owners.
4. A _____ exists when almost all power in a nation is held by the central government.
5. Lenin abandoned war communism in 1921 in favor of his _____, a modified version of the old capitalist system.
6. The government policy of going into debt to pay for public works projects, such as building highways, is called _____.
7. According to the _____, no one could determine the path of subatomic particles, meaning all physical laws had elements of unpredictability.
8. The German parliament is known as the _____.
9. The _____ was the leading policy maker of the Communist Party.
10. _____ is the right of unions to negotiate with employers.
11. As a political system, _____ glorifies the state above the individual by emphasizing the need for a strong central government.
12. The Nazis set up large prisons called _____ for people who opposed them.
13. _____ sought a reality beyond the material world and found it in the world of the unconscious.

## Reviewing Academic Vocabulary

*On a sheet of paper, use each of these terms in a sentence that reflects the term's meaning in the chapter.*

14. minimum
15. circumstance
16. widespread
17. unrestricted
18. academy
19. ideology
20. incapable
21. abstract
22. classical

## Reviewing the Main Ideas

**Section 1**

23. What did President Roosevelt call the program designed to fight the depression in the United States?
24. List the provisions of the Dawes Plan.

**Section 2**

25. Describe how Stalin defeated Trotsky.
26. The Italian Fascists had a slogan: "Woman into the Home." How did this support their political ideas?

**Section 3**

27. Why did Hitler label modern art as degenerate?
28. Summarize the steps that Hitler took to become the sole ruler of Germany.

**Section 4**

29. List the qualities that the Nazis wanted German art to glorify.
30. What is "stream of consciousness"?

## Chapter Summary

Between 1919 and 1939, the West experienced great economic and political challenges.

### Political and Economic Changes

- In Britain, the Conservative Party implements traditional economic policies.
- In the United States, President Roosevelt develops the New Deal, a policy of active government intervention in the economy.
- In France, the Popular Front establishes the French New Deal, which promotes workers' rights.

### Rise of Totalitarianism

- In Italy, Mussolini leads the Fascists to power.
- Stalin becomes dictator of the Soviet Union and purges the Communist Party of Old Bolsheviks.
- In Germany, Hitler establishes a totalitarian Nazi regime and starts the large-scale persecution of Jews.

### Innovations and Ideas

- The artistic movements of dadaism and surrealism reflect the uncertainty of life created by World War I.
- Radio and film transform communications.
- Literary techniques reflect an interest in the unconscious.
- Heisenberg's uncertainty principle suggests that physical laws are based on uncertainty.

## HISTORY Online

**Self-Check Quiz**
Visit the *Glencoe World History—Modern Times* Web site at <u>wh.mt.glencoe.com</u> and click on **Chapter 9–Self-Check Quiz** to prepare for the Chapter Test.

## Critical Thinking

31. **Reading Skill** Cause-and-Effect Chain Why did the depression help extremist leaders gain power in many nations during the 1930s?

32. **Compare and Contrast** How was Roosevelt's New Deal both similar to and different from Stalin's Five-Year Plan?

33. **Making Generalizations** Describe the influence of the Nazi regime on a young German in the 1930s.

## Writing About History

34. **Historical Analysis** Applying Research Write an essay in which you construct a hypothesis about the leadership of Mussolini, Franco, or Stalin. Find and use at least two primary and two secondary sources. Then prepare a five-minute presentation for your class, describing your research process and sharing your conclusions. **CA HR4**

35. *Big Idea* Write an essay in which you relate one of the following to the interwar mood: mass entertainment, mass leisure, professional sports, dadaism, surrealism, or the "stream of consciousness" in literature. Research your topic and provide a bibliography for your essay. **CA 10WA2.3**

### DBQ Document-Based Questions

**Analyzing Sources** The crisis of confidence in Western civilization ran deep. It was well captured in the words of the French poet Paul Valéry in the early 1920s:

> ❝The storm has died away, and we are still restless, Uneasy, as if the storm were about to break. Almost all the affairs of men remain in a terrible uncertainty. We think of what has disappeared, and we are almost destroyed by what has been destroyed; we do not know what will be born, and we fear the future. . . . Doubt and disorder are in us and with us. There is no thinking man, however shrewd or learned he may be, who can hope to dominate this anxiety, to escape from this impression of darkness.❞

36. If you did not know the poem was written after World War I, how might you guess it?

37. What do the first two lines convey? **CA 10WA2.2**

**NATIONAL GEOGRAPHIC** Spanish Civil War, 1936–1939

- ☐ Nationalist-controlled area, February 1939
- ▨ Republican-controlled area, February 1939
- ✹ Area of intense fighting

## Analyzing Maps and Charts

Study the map above to answer the following questions.

38. What advantage would the Nationalists seem to have had over the Republicans in February 1939?

39. How would the geographic location of the Republicans in 1939 have affected their supply routes?

40. Where was the most intense fighting concentrated?

 **Standards Practice**

**Directions: Choose the best answer to the following question.**

41. The *General Theory of Employment, Interest, and Money* by John Maynard Keynes was published in 1936. The book argued for

A mercantilism.

B disarmament.

C deficit spending.

D isolationism.

**CA Standard 10.6.2** Describe the effects of the war and resulting peace treaties on population movement, the international economy, and shifts in the geographic and political borders of Europe and the Middle East.

# 10

## 1919–1939
# Nationalism Around the World

### ❧ *The Big Ideas* ❧

#### SECTION 1: Nationalism in the Middle East

**The quest for national self-determination is universal.** After World War I, the quest for national self-determination led to the creation of Turkey, Iran, and Saudi Arabia. In the same period, the Balfour Declaration supported the creation of a homeland for Jews in Palestine.

#### SECTION 2: Nationalism in Africa and Asia

**The quest for national self-determination is universal.** Nationalism led the people of Africa and Asia to seek independence.

#### SECTION 3: Revolutionary Chaos in China

**The quest for national self-determination is universal.** During the 1920s, two men struggled to lead a new Chinese state. One leader, Mao Zedong, argued that peasants, not workers, would be the basis for the revolution to establish a Communist China.

#### SECTION 4: Nationalism in Latin America

**The quest for national self-determination is universal.** In Latin America, the Great Depression made politics unstable, and in many cases, military dictatorships were the result.

 *World History—Modern Times Video* The Chapter 10 video, "Gandhi and Passive Resistance," *chronicles India's fight for independence between the two World Wars.*

**1917**
Britain issues
Balfour Declaration

**1923**
Turkish Republic is
formed, ending the
Ottoman Empire

1910        1915        1920        1925

*British enter Jerusalem,
January 1918*

**1928**
Chiang Kai-shek
founds a new
Chinese republic

*Chiang Kai-shek*

*The Destruction of the Old Order* by José Clemente Orozco, c. 1922

**1930**
Gandhi's Salt
March protests
British laws
in India

*Aramco oil refinery in
Ras Tanura, Saudi Arabia*

**1938**
Oil is discovered
in Saudi Arabia

1930    1935    1940    1945

**1931**
Japanese
forces invade
Manchuria

**1933**
Franklin D. Roosevelt
announces the Good
Neighbor policy

*Franklin D. Roosevelt*

**HISTORY**
*Online*

**Chapter Overview**
Visit the *Glencoe World
History–Modern
Times* Web site at
wh.mt.glencoe.com
and click on **Chapter 10–
Chapter Overview** to
preview chapter information.

# Preparing to Read Chapter 10

**Reading Skill** ▸ **Question-Answer Relationships**

Teachers usually ask you questions after you've read a section or chapter in your textbook to help you understand it. You will be able to answer questions more easily if you can quickly see what type of question your teacher is asking.

Some questions use words or phrases that echo the text. These questions point your attention to a single sentence for the answer—the answers are "right there." Other questions require you to "think and search." You have to interpret the words a bit and then search for the answer in more than one sentence or paragraph. Both types of questions, however, are directly from the text.

*Read the paragraph about Mohandas Gandhi's philosophy of non-violent resistance below and then answer the two questions that follow. The highlighted words will help you.*

## QUESTION-ANSWER RELATIONSHIP

Question 1: This is a "right there" question because it echoes key words in the first sentence.

## QUESTION-ANSWER RELATIONSHIP

Question 2: This is a "think-and-search" question since you have to interpret the answer from more than one sentence.

Nonviolence was central to Gandhi's campaign of noncooperation and civil disobedience. To protest unjust British laws, Gandhi told his people: "Don't pay your taxes or send your children to an English-supported school. . . . Make your own cotton cloth by spinning the thread at home, and don't buy English-made goods. Provide yourselves with homemade salt, and do not buy government-made salt."

Question 1: What principle was central to Gandhi's campaign? Answer: Nonviolence.

Question 2: What actions did Gandhi ask fellow Indians to undertake? Answer: Not to pay their taxes, send their children to English-supported schools, or buy English goods, but to make their own cotton cloth and provide their own salt.

### Apply the Skill

Look closely at the Reading Check questions at the end of major headings in each section. Many are either "right-there" or "think-and-search" questions. Practice using the text to find the answers to these kinds of questions.

**Historical Research, Evidence, and Point of View: Standard HR 2**
*Students identify bias and prejudice in historical interpretations.*

Judges and lawyers know that eyewitness accounts of the same event are often different. Versions of an event can differ for several reasons. Maybe the eyewitnesses saw the event from a different angle. Or maybe they brought certain prejudices to what they witnessed. One person might conclude that the frail-looking man getting out of one car in an accident was the cause of it, even though that was not the case. Finally, the passage of time often alters people's memory of an event, especially if they had a role in it. Without realizing it, they may reshape their memory of the event to suit their own self-image.

Historians are trained to recognize how bias and prejudice affect historical accounts. Well-trained historians will also be alert to the fact that their own beliefs and prejudices can influence how they are interpreting the sources they read.

*Read the passage below from this chapter and determine the role of bias in the quote by Atatürk.*

> **President Kemal was now popularly known as Atatürk, or "Father Turk." Over the next several years, he modernized Turkey. . . .**
>
> **Perhaps the most significant reform was Atatürk's attempt to break the power of Islam. He wanted to transform Turkey into a secular state—a state that does not favor particular religions. Atatürk said, "Religion is like a heavy blanket that keeps the people of Turkey asleep."**

## Apply the Skill

What role does bias play in Atatürk's description of religion? Would a devout Muslim of the time describe the changes as a "transformation into a modern state"? As you read this chapter, identify examples of bias or prejudice and their role in how nationalist struggles around the world were shaped.

# A Story That Matters

*Gandhi leading the Salt March to Dandi to protest the British monopoly on salt production*

## Gandhi's March to the Sea

*I*n 1930, Mohandas Gandhi, the 61-year-old leader of the Indian movement for independence from British rule, began a march to the sea with 78 followers. Their destination was Dandi, a little coastal town some 240 miles (386 km) away. The group covered about 12 miles (19 km) a day.

As they went, Gandhi preached his doctrine of nonviolent resistance to British rule in every village through which he passed: "Civil disobedience is the inherent right of a citizen. He dare not give it up without ceasing to be a man." By the time Gandhi reached Dandi, 24 days later, his small group had become a nonviolent army of thousands.

When Gandhi and his followers arrived at Dandi, Gandhi picked up a pinch of crystallized sea salt from the sand. Thousands of people all along the coast did likewise. In so doing, they were openly breaking British laws that prohibited Indians from making their own salt. The British had long profited from their monopoly on the making and selling of salt, an item much in demand in India. They used coastal salt flats to collect crystallized sea salt to sell.

By their simple acts of disobedience, Gandhi and the Indian people had taken yet another step on their long march to independence from the British. The Salt March was one of many nonviolent activities that Gandhi undertook to win India's national independence between World War I and World War II.

### Why It Matters

With Europe in disorder after World War I, people living in colonies controlled by European countries began to think that the independence they desired might now be achieved. In Africa and Asia, movements for national independence began to take shape. In the Middle East, World War I ended the rule of the Ottoman Empire and created new states. For some Latin American countries, the fascist dictatorships of Italy and Germany provided models for change.

**History and You** You have read about many religious conflicts. In this chapter, you will learn about the conflict between the Muslims and the Hindus in India. Make a chart listing the differences between the groups. Explain how religious differences expand into other areas of conflict. How did this rivalry affect the development of India?

# Nationalism in the Middle East

## Section Preview

After World War I, the quest for national self-determination led to the creation of Turkey, Iran, and Saudi Arabia. In the same period, the Balfour Declaration supported the creation of a homeland for Jews in Palestine.

### Main Idea

- The Ottoman Empire, which had been steadily declining since the late 1700s, finally ended after World War I. (p. 502)
- Turkey's President Kemal changed the political system and the Turkish culture to create a modern state. (p. 504)
- Government and economic reforms changed Persia into the modern country of Iran. (p. 505)

- After World War I, Europeans created Middle Eastern states, but a sense of Arab nationalism remained. (p. 505)
- During the 1930s, tensions increased between Jewish immigrants and the existing Muslims in Palestine. (p. 506)

## Content Vocabulary

genocide, ethnic cleansing

## Academic Vocabulary

eliminate, establish

## People to Identify

Abdulhamid II, T. E. Lawrence, Atatürk, Reza Shah Pahlavi, Ibn Saud

## Places to Locate

Tehran, Iran, Saudi Arabia, Palestine

## Reading Objectives

1. Describe the forces that led to the fall of the Ottoman Empire.
2. Explain the relationship between Arab nationalism and the mandate system.

## Reading Strategy

**Compare and Contrast** Make a Venn diagram like the one below comparing and contrasting Atatürk's and Reza Shah Pahlavi's national policies.

Atatürk | Reza Shah Pahlavi

## Preview of Events

♦1910   ♦1915   ♦1920   ♦1925   ♦1930   ♦1935   ♦1940

**1915**
Turkish government massacres Armenians

**1916**
The local governor of Makkah declares Arabia independent

**1924**
Caliphate formally abolished in Turkey

**1932**
Saudi Arabia is established

**1935**
Persia changes name to Iran

## California Standards in This Section

*Reading this section will help you master these California History–Social Science standards.*

**10.5.5:** Discuss human rights violations and genocide, including the Ottoman government's actions against Armenian citizens.

**10.6.2:** Describe the effects of the war and resulting peace treaties on population movement, the international economy, and shifts in the geographic and political borders of Europe and the Middle East.

# Decline and Fall of the Ottoman Empire

**Main Idea** The Ottoman Empire, which had been steadily declining since the late 1700s, finally ended after World War I.

**Reading Connection** Do you think it is possible for an empire to exist in the world today? Read to learn about the fall of the Ottoman Empire.

The empire of the Ottoman Turks had once included parts of eastern Europe, the Middle East, and North Africa. Since about 1800, however, it had been growing steadily weaker. In fact, many Europeans called it "the sick man of Europe." Nationalism was a major reason for the Ottoman "sickness." As ethnic groups gained autonomy or even their own territory, the power of the Ottomans declined.

One group that campaigned for their own nation was the Jews. Although their goal was not realized until 1948, at the end of the next world war, many Jews lived in Palestine within the Ottoman Empire.

## Voices from the Past

In 1925, Hayyim Bialik, a Ukrainian Jew who had settled in Palestine the year before, spoke at the opening of the Hebrew University of Palestine. Bialik supported Zionism, a movement devoted to the establishment of Palestine as a homeland for Jews:

❝Through cruel and bitter trials and tribulations, through blasted hopes and despair of the soul, through innumerable humiliations, we have slowly arrived at the realization that without a tangible homeland, without private national premises that are entirely ours, we can have no sort of a life, either material or spiritual. . . . We have not come here to seek wealth, or dominion, or greatness. How much of these can this poor little country give us? We wish to find here only a domain of our own for our physical and intellectual labor.❞

The size of the Ottoman Empire was no longer as vast as it had once been. Much of its European territory had been lost. Greece, for example, had declared its independence as early as 1821. North African territories were lost, too. In the 1830s, France seized Algeria and Tunisia. In the 1880s, Great Britain gained control of Egypt. These losses led to discontent with the sultan.

In 1876, Ottoman reformers seized control of the empire's government and adopted a constitution aimed at forming a legislative assembly. The sultan they placed on the throne, however, **Abdulhamid II,** suspended the new constitution and ruled by authoritarian means.

Abdulhamid paid a high price for his actions. He lived in constant fear of assassination. He kept a thousand loaded revolvers hidden throughout his guarded estate and insisted that his pets taste his food before he ate it.

The suspended constitution became a symbol of change to a group of reformers named the Young Turks. This group was able to force the restoration of the constitution in 1908 and to depose the sultan the following year. However, the Young Turks lacked strong support for their government. The stability of the empire was also challenged by many ethnic Turks who had begun to envision a Turkish state that would encompass all people of Turkish nationality.

**Impact of World War I** The final blow to the old empire came from World War I. After the Ottoman government allied with Germany, the British sought to undermine Ottoman rule in the Arabian Peninsula by supporting Arab nationalist activities there. The nationalists were aided by the efforts of the dashing British adventurer **T. E. Lawrence,** popularly known as "Lawrence of Arabia."

In 1916, the local governor of Makkah, encouraged by Great Britain, declared Arabia independent from Ottoman rule. British troops, advancing from Egypt, seized Palestine. After suffering more than 300,000 deaths during the war, the Ottoman Empire made peace with the Allies in October 1918.

▼ *Committee planning a Jewish university in Palestine*

Armenian children who have been orphaned wait to board a ship that will take them from Turkey to Greece. During World War I Turks killed over 1 million Armenians and left hundreds of thousands as refugees.

**The Armenian Genocide** During the war, the Ottoman Turks had alienated the Allies with their discriminatory policies toward minority subjects, especially the Armenians. The Christian Armenian minority had been pressing the Ottoman government for reforms for years. In 1915, the Ottoman government accused the Armenians of supporting the Russians and used these allegations as an excuse to begin a brutal campaign to kill or exile all Armenians.

During the deportations carried out from 1915 to the end of the war in 1918, an estimated 1 million to 1.5 million Armenians were killed by massacres and starvation. Several hundred thousand others continued to suffer as refugees in deserts in Syria and other regions.

One eyewitness to the 1915 Armenian deportation recorded this event:

❝[She] saw vultures hovering over children who had fallen dead by the roadside. She saw beings crawling along, maimed, starving and begging for bread. From time to time she passed soldiers driving before them with whips and rifle-butts whole families, men, women and children, shrieking, pleading, wailing. These were the Armenian people setting out for exile into the desert from which there was no return.❞

The Armenians were victims of **genocide,** the deliberate mass murder of a particular racial, political, or cultural group. A similar practice during the 1990s in the Bosnian War was referred to as **ethnic cleansing.**

Russia, France, and Britain denounced the Turkish killing of the Armenians as "crimes against humanity and civilization." In part because of the war, the killings went on without international intervention to stop them. The Armenian refugees eventually formed the worldwide Armenian diaspora, including communities in America. Until today the Turkish government denies that what happened to the Armenians was a genocide.

**Emergence of the Turkish Republic** At the end of World War I, the tottering Ottoman Empire finally collapsed. Great Britain and France made plans to divide up Ottoman territories in the Middle East. Only the area of present-day Turkey remained under Ottoman control. Then, Greece invaded Turkey and seized the western parts of the Anatolian Peninsula.

The invasion alarmed key elements in Turkey, who were organized under the leadership of the war hero Colonel Mustafa Kemal. Kemal resigned from the army and summoned a national congress calling for the creation of an elected government and a new Republic of Turkey. His forces drove the Greeks from the Anatolian Peninsula. In 1923, the last of the Ottoman sultans fled the country, which was now declared to be the Turkish Republic. The Ottoman Empire had finally come to an end.

☑**Reading Check** **Evaluating** How did the Ottoman Empire finally end?

▼ *The bodies of Armenian victims of the genocide lie in a grove of trees in eastern Turkey.*

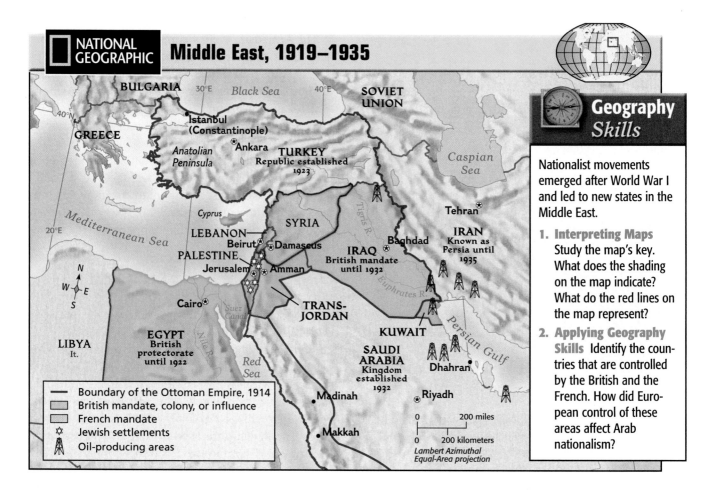

**Geography**
*Skills*

Nationalist movements emerged after World War I and led to new states in the Middle East.

1. **Interpreting Maps** Study the map's key. What does the shading on the map indicate? What do the red lines on the map represent?

2. **Applying Geography Skills** Identify the countries that are controlled by the British and the French. How did European control of these areas affect Arab nationalism?

Map labels:
BULGARIA · 30°E · *Black Sea* · 40°E · SOVIET UNION · 40°N · Istanbul (Constantinople) · GREECE · *Anatolian Peninsula* · Ankara · TURKEY Republic established 1923 · *Caspian Sea* · 20°E · *Mediterranean Sea* · Cyprus · SYRIA · Tehran · *Tigris R.* · LEBANON · Beirut · Damascus · IRAN Known as Persia until 1935 · PALESTINE · Jerusalem · Amman · IRAQ British mandate until 1932 · Baghdad · N W E S · Cairo · *Suez Canal* · TRANS-JORDAN · *Euphrates R.* · KUWAIT · *Persian Gulf* · LIBYA It. · EGYPT British protectorate until 1922 · *Nile R.* · *Red Sea* · SAUDI ARABIA Kingdom established 1932 · Dhahran · Riyadh · Madinah · Makkah · 0 200 miles · 0 200 kilometers · Lambert Azimuthal Equal-Area projection

Key:
— Boundary of the Ottoman Empire, 1914
▢ British mandate, colony, or influence
▢ French mandate
✡ Jewish settlements
⛏ Oil-producing areas

# The Modernization of Turkey

**Main Idea** Turkey's President Kemal changed the political system and the Turkish culture to create a modern state.

**Reading Connection** How would you react if the United States adopted a new alphabet? Read to learn about changes the Turkish people faced after World War I.

President Kemal was now popularly known as **Atatürk** (AT•uh•TUHRK), or "father Turk." Over the next several years, he modernized Turkey. A democratic system was put in place, but the president harshly suppressed his critics.

Atatürk's changes went beyond politics. Many Arabic elements were **eliminated** from the Turkish language, which was now written in the Roman alphabet. Popular education was introduced. All Turkish citizens were forced to adopt family (last) names, in the European style.

Atatürk also took steps to modernize Turkey's economy. Factories were **established,** and a five-year plan provided for state direction over the economy. Atatürk also tried to modernize farming, although he had little effect on the nation's peasants.

Perhaps the most significant reform was Atatürk's attempt to break the power of Islam. He wanted to transform Turkey into a secular state—a state that does not favor particular religions. Atatürk said, "Religion is like a heavy blanket that keeps the people of Turkey asleep."

The caliphate, the system of traditional Muslim rulers, was abolished in 1924. Men were forbidden to wear the fez, the brimless cap worn by Turkish Muslims. When Atatürk began wearing a Western panama hat, one of his critics remarked, "You cannot make a Turk into a Westerner by giving him a hat."

Women were forbidden to wear the veil, a traditional Islamic custom. New laws gave women marriage and inheritance rights equal to men's. In 1934, women received the right to vote. All citizens were also given the right to convert to other religions.

The legacy of Kemal Atatürk was enormous. In practice, not all of his reforms were widely accepted, especially by devout Muslims. However, most of the changes that he introduced were kept after his death in 1938. By and large, the Turkish Republic was the product of Atatürk's determined efforts.

✓ **Reading Check** **Identifying** How did Atatürk modernize Turkey?

# The Beginnings of Modern Iran

**Main Idea** Government and economic reforms changed Persia into the modern country of Iran.

**Reading Connection** If you had the power to make your community more modern, what changes would you make? Read to learn about the changes made in Persia to create the modern state of Iran.

As in Turkey, modernization was the goal of a new leader in the lands known as Persia. For centuries, the Persians had a strong empire, but by 1900, this was no longer true. In the later years of the Qajar dynasty (1794–1925), domestic problems were not addressed. Increasingly the rulers had relied on Russia and Great Britain for help in protecting themselves from their own people. This reliance led to a growing foreign presence in Persia.

Then in 1908, oil was discovered in the southern part of the country, and foreigners became interested in investing in Persia. Oil exports increased rapidly, and most of the profits went to British investors. Persian nationalists resented the growing foreign presence and began to organize.

In 1921, Reza Khan, an army officer, led a mutiny that seized control of the capital, **Tehran.** In 1925, Reza Khan established himself as shah, or king, and was called **Reza Shah Pahlavi.** The name of the new dynasty he created, Pahlavi, was the name of the ancient Persian language.

During the next few years, Reza Shah Pahlavi tried to copy the reforms of Kemal Atatürk in Turkey. He introduced reforms to strengthen and modernize the government, the military, and the economy. Persia became the modern state of **Iran** in 1935.

Unlike Kemal Atatürk, Reza Shah Pahlavi did not try to destroy the power of Islamic beliefs. He did encourage the creation of a Western-style educational system and forbade women to wear the veil in public.

Foreign powers continued to harass Iran. To free himself from Great Britain and the Soviet Union, Reza Shah Pahlavi drew closer to Nazi Germany. During World War II, the shah rejected the demands of Great Britain and the Soviet Union to expel a large number of Germans from Iran. In response, the Soviet Union and Great Britain sent troops into the country. Reza Shah Pahlavi resigned in protest and was replaced by his son, Mohammad Reza Pahlavi.

✔ **Reading Check** **Comparing** How did Persia's modernization process differ from Turkey's?

*Sultan Ibn Saud, who established the kingdom of Saudi Arabia*

# Arab Nationalism

**Main Idea** After World War I, Europeans created Middle Eastern states, but a sense of Arab nationalism remained.

**Reading Connection** Do you or your family feel connected to any peoples outside the United States? Read to find out what Arab unity meant at this time.

World War I offered the Arabs an opportunity to escape from Ottoman rule. However, there was a question as to what would replace that rule. The Arabs were not a nation, though they were united by their language and their Islamic cultural and religious heritage.

Because Britain had supported the efforts of Arab nationalists in 1916, the nationalists hoped this support would continue after the war ended. Instead, Britain made an agreement with France to create a number of mandates in the area. These mandates were former Ottoman territories that were now supervised by the new League of Nations. The League, in turn, granted League members the right to govern particular mandates. Iraq, Palestine, and Jordan were assigned to Great Britain; Syria and Lebanon, to France.

For the most part, Europeans created these Middle Eastern states. The Europeans determined the nations' borders and divided the peoples. In general, the people in these states had no strong identification with their designated country. However, a sense of Arab nationalism remained.

In the early 1920s, a reform leader, **Ibn Saud,** united Arabs in the northern part of the Arabian Peninsula. Devout and gifted, Ibn Saud (from whom came the name *Saudi Arabia*) won broad support. He established the kingdom of Saudi Arabia in 1932.

At first, the new kingdom, which consisted mostly of the vast desert of central Arabia, was desperately poor. Its main source of income came from the Muslim pilgrims who visited Makkah and Madinah.

During the 1930s, however, U.S. prospectors began to explore for oil. Standard Oil made a successful strike at Dhahran, on the Persian Gulf, in 1938. Soon, an Arabian-American oil company, popularly called Aramco, was created. The isolated kingdom was suddenly flooded with Western oil industries that brought the promise of wealth.

**Reading Check** **Analyzing** Why were many Middle Eastern states created after World War I?

## The Problem of Palestine

**Main Idea** During the 1930s, tensions increased between Jewish immigrants and the existing Muslims in Palestine.

**Reading Connection** Have you seen reports on conflicts between Jews and Arabs? Read to learn about the historical background to today's conflicts.

The situation in **Palestine** made matters even more complicated in the Middle East. While Palestine had been the home of the Jews in antiquity, they were forced into exile in the first century A.D. A Jewish presence always remained, but Muslim Arabs made up about 80 percent of the population. In Palestine, the nationalism of Jews and Arabs was in conflict since both groups saw the region as a potential homeland.

Since the 1890s, the Zionist movement had wanted to establish Palestine as a Jewish state, as it was in ancient times. Arabs pointed out that their ancestors had also lived in Palestine for centuries.

As a result of the Zionist movement and growing anti-Semitism in Europe, more Jews began to migrate to Palestine. Then during World War I, the British government, hoping to win Jewish support for the Allies, issued the Balfour Declaration. It expressed support for a national home for the Jews in Palestine, but it also added that this goal should not undermine the rights of the non-Jewish peoples living there.

The Balfour Declaration drew even more Jews to Palestine. In 1933, the Nazi regime in Germany began policies that later led to the Holocaust and the murder of 6 million Jews. During the 1930s, many Jews fled to Palestine. Tensions grew, and violence between Jewish and Muslim inhabitants flared.

Trying to end the violence, the British declared in 1939 that only 75,000 Jewish people would be allowed to immigrate to Palestine over the next five years; after that, no more Jews could do so. This decision, however, only intensified tension and violence.

**Reading Check** **Explaining** How did the Balfour Declaration eventually lead to problems in Palestine?

**HISTORY Online** **Study Central**

For help with the concepts in this section of *Glencoe World History–Modern Times,* go to wh.mt.glencoe.com and click on **Study Central.**

## SECTION 1 ASSESSMENT

### Checking for Understanding

1. **Vocabulary** Define: genocide, ethnic cleansing, eliminate, establish.

2. **People** Identify: Abdulhamid II, T. E. Lawrence, Atatürk, Reza Shah Pahlavi, Ibn Saud.

3. **Places** Locate: Tehran, Iran, Saudi Arabia, Palestine.

### Reviewing Big Ideas

4. **Explain** why the British supported Arab nationalist activities in 1916.

### Critical Thinking

5. **Historical Analysis** **Evaluating** Why was it difficult for the Arab peoples to form one nation? **CA HR3**

6. **Summarizing Information** Make a diagram like the one below showing eight aspects of the modernization of Turkey.

Modernization of Turkey

### Analyzing Visuals

7. **Examine** the photo on page 503 showing Armenian children who lost their parents. Why were hundreds of thousands of Armenians killed or driven from their homes by the Turks?

### Writing About History

8. **Expository Writing** Research the current political policies of Iran. Write two paragraphs comparing these with the policies of Reza Shah Pahlavi. Document your sources. **CA 10WS1.3**

# SECTION 2 Nationalism in Africa and Asia

## Guide to Reading

### Section Preview
Nationalism led the people of Africa and Asia to seek independence.

**Main Idea**
- After World War I, many Africans organized to end colonial rule in their countries. (p. 508)
- Mohandas Gandhi and Jawaharlal Nehru led the independence movement in India. (p. 510)
- By the late 1920s, militant forces in Japan were campaigning for an end to peaceful policies. (p. 511)

- In the 1920s, the Comintern worked to spread communism throughout Asia. (p. 513)

### Content Vocabulary
Pan-Africanism, Mahatma, civil disobedience, *zaibatsu*

### Academic Vocabulary
aware, integrity

### People to Identify
W. E. B. DuBois, Marcus Garvey, Mohandas Gandhi, Jawaharlal Nehru, Ho Chi Minh

### Places to Locate
Kenya, Manchuria

### Reading Objectives
1. Describe the different forms that protest against Western rule took.
2. Explain how communism was received in Asia.

### Reading Strategy
**Contrasting Information** Using a table like the one below, contrast the backgrounds and values of Gandhi and the younger Nehru.

| Mohandas Gandhi | Jawaharlal Nehru |
|---|---|
|  |  |
|  |  |

### Preview of Events

| ◆1915 | ◆1920 | ◆1925 | ◆1930 | ◆1935 | ◆1940 | ◆1945 |
|---|---|---|---|---|---|---|

**1920**
Marcus Garvey issues *Declaration of the Rights of the Negro Peoples of the World*

**1935**
Government of India Act is passed

**1938**
Japan passes military draft law

## California Standards in This Section

*Reading this section will help you master these California History–Social Science standards.*

**10.3.5:** Understand the connections among natural resources, entrepreneurship, labor, and capital in an industrial economy.

**10.4.1:** Describe the rise of industrial economies and their link to imperialism and colonialism (e.g., the role played by national security and strategic advantage; moral issues raised by the search for national hegemony, Social Darwinism, and the missionary impulse; material issues such as land, resources, and technology).

**10.4.2:** Discuss the locations of the colonial rule of such nations as England, France, Germany, Italy, Japan, the Netherlands, Russia, Spain, Portugal, and the United States.

**10.4.4:** Describe the independence struggles of the colonized regions of the world, including the roles of leaders, such as Sun Yat-sen in China, and the roles of ideology and religion.

**10.5.4:** Understand the nature of the war and its human costs (military and civilian) on all sides of the conflict, including how colonial peoples contributed to the war effort.

**10.7:** Students analyze the rise of totalitarian governments after World War I.

**10.8.1:** Compare the German, Italian, and Japanese drives for empire in the 1930s, including the 1937 Rape of Nanking, other atrocities in China, and the Stalin-Hitler Pact of 1939.

# Movements Toward Independence in Africa

**Main Idea** After World War I, many Africans organized to end colonial rule in their countries.

**Reading Connection** What issue would make you want to get involved in politics? Read to learn what Africans did after World War I to achieve their goals.

Black Africans had fought in World War I in British and French armies. Many hoped they would be rewarded with independence. As one newspaper in the Gold Coast argued, if African volunteers who fought on European battlefields were "good enough to fight and die in the Empire's cause, they were good enough to have a share in the government of their countries." Most European leaders, however, were not ready to give up their colonies.

## *Voices from the Past*

One African leader, Jomo Kenyatta, understood that it would take a determined effort to shake off European control. In his autobiography, Kenyatta described the Africans' struggle:

❝By driving the African off his ancestral lands, the Europeans have reduced him to a state of serfdom incompatible with human happiness. The African is conditioned, by the cultural and social institutions of centuries, to a freedom of which Europe has little conception, and it is not in his nature to accept serfdom forever. He realizes that he must fight unceasingly for his own complete emancipation [freedom]; for without this he is doomed to remain the prey of rival imperialisms, which in every successive year will drive their fangs more deeply into his vitality and strength.❞

The peace treaty did nothing to advance independence in Africa. Since Germany lost the war, it was stripped of its colonies, but these were now awarded to Great Britain and France to be administered as mandates for the League of Nations. Britain and France now governed a vast area of Africa.

**African Protests** In the 1920s, Africans became much more active politically. Africans who had fought in World War I were exposed to many new ideas about freedom and nationalism in the West. In Africa itself, missionary schools taught their pupils about liberty and equality. As more Africans became **aware** of the enormous gulf between Western ideals and practices, they decided to seek reform.

Reform movements took different forms. In **Kenya** in 1921, the Young Kikuyu Association, organized by Harry Thuku, a telephone operator, protested the high taxes levied by the British rulers. His message was simple: "Hearken, every day you pay . . . tax to the Europeans of Government. Where is it sent? It is their task to steal the property of the Kikuyu people." Thuku was arrested. When an angry crowd stormed the jail and demanded his release, government authorities fired into the crowd and killed at least 20 people. Thuku was sent into exile.

A struggle against Italian rule in Libya also occurred in the 1920s. Forces led by Omar Mukhtar used guerrilla warfare against the Italians and defeated them a number of times. The Italians reacted ferociously. They established concentration camps and used all available modern weapons to crush the revolt. Mukhtar's death ended the movement.

Although colonial powers typically responded to such movements with force, they also began to make reforms. They hoped this would satisfy African peoples. Reforms, however, were too few and too late. By the 1930s, an increasing number of African leaders were calling for independence, not reform.

▼ *Jomo Kenyatta*

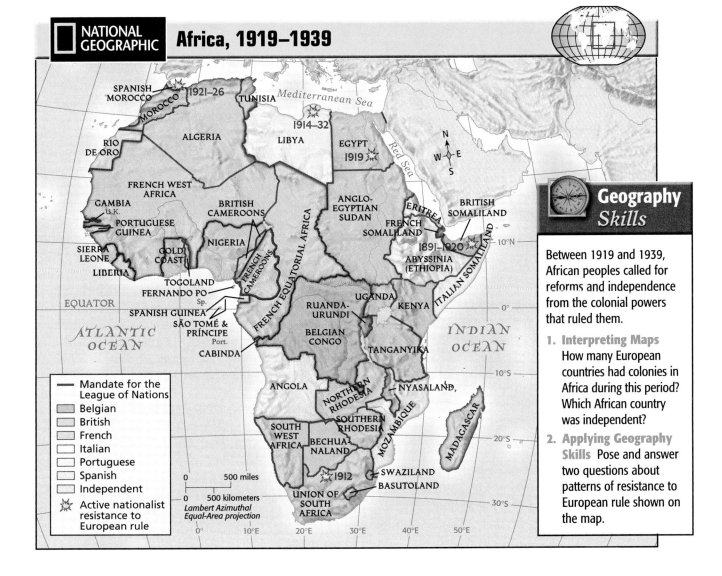

**Geography Skills**

Between 1919 and 1939, African peoples called for reforms and independence from the colonial powers that ruled them.

1. **Interpreting Maps** How many European countries had colonies in Africa during this period? Which African country was independent?

2. **Applying Geography Skills** Pose and answer two questions about patterns of resistance to European rule shown on the map.

**New Leaders** Calls for independence came from a new generation of young African leaders. Many had been educated abroad, in Europe and the United States. Those who had studied in the United States were especially influenced by the ideas of **W. E. B. DuBois** and **Marcus Garvey.**

In the early 1900s, W. E. B. DuBois, an African American educated at Harvard University, led the movement in the United States for full civil and political equality. Marcus Garvey, a Jamaican who lived in Harlem in New York City, urged black Americans to return to Africa. He too stressed the need for the unity of all Africans, a movement known as **Pan-Africanism.** His *Declaration of the Rights of the Negro Peoples of the World,* issued in 1920, had a strong impact on later African leaders. DuBois, too, believed fervently in Pan-Africanism and organized the first Pan-African Congress in Paris, held in 1919. In later life, DuBois left the United States to live in Ghana.

Leaders and movements in individual African nations also appeared. Educated in Great Britain, Jomo Kenyatta of Kenya argued in his book *Facing Mount Kenya* that British rule was destroying the traditional culture of the peoples of Africa. Léopold Senghor, who had studied in France and written poetry about African culture, organized an independence movement in Senegal. Nnamdi Azikiwe, of Nigeria, began a newspaper, *The West African Pilot,* in 1937 and urged nonviolence as a method to gain independence. These are but three of the leaders who worked to end colonial rule in Africa. Success, however, would not come until after World War II.

✓**Reading Check** **Analyzing** Why did many Africans become more politically active after World War I?

**HISTORY** *Online* **Web Activity**

Visit the *Glencoe World History—Modern Times* Web site at **wh.mt.glencoe.com** and click on **Chapter 10– Student Web Activity** to learn more about nationalist movements.

# The Movement for Indian Independence

**Main Idea** Mohandas Gandhi and Jawaharlal Nehru led the independence movement in India.

**Reading Connection** Do you think great leaders always have the same set of character traits? Read to learn about the character traits of Mohandas Gandhi.

**Mohandas Gandhi** had become active in the movement for Indian self-rule before World War I. By the time of World War I, the Indian people had already begun to refer to him as India's "Great Soul," or **Mahatma.** After the war, Gandhi remained an important figure, and new leaders also arose.

**Protest and Reform** Gandhi left South Africa in 1914. When he returned to India, he began to organize mass protests to achieve his aims. A believer in nonviolence, Gandhi protested British laws by using the methods of **civil disobedience**—refusal to obey laws considered to be unjust.

In 1919, the protests led to violence and a strong British reaction. British troops killed hundreds of unarmed protesters in the city of Amritsar, in northwestern India. Horrified at the violence, Gandhi briefly retreated from active politics. He was later arrested for his role in protests against British rule and spent several years in prison.

In 1935, Great Britain passed the Government of India Act. This act expanded the role of Indians in the governing process. Before, the Legislative Council had only given advice to the British governor. Now, it became a two-house parliament. Two-thirds of its Indian members were to be elected. Similar bodies were created at the provincial level. Five million Indians—still only a small percentage of the total population—were given the right to vote.

**A Push for Independence** The Indian National Congress (INC) was founded in 1885 to seek reforms in Britain's government of India (see Chapter 6). Reforms, however, were no longer enough for many members of the INC. Under its new leader, Motilal Nehru, the INC wanted to push for full independence.

Gandhi, now released from prison, returned to his earlier policy of civil disobedience. He worked hard to inform ordinary Indians of his beliefs and methods. It was wrong, he said, to harm any living being. Hate could only be overcome by love, and love, rather than force, could win people over to one's position.

Nonviolence was central to Gandhi's campaign of noncooperation and civil disobedience. To protest unjust British laws, Gandhi told his people: "Don't pay your taxes or send your children to an English-supported school. . . . Make your own cotton cloth by spinning the thread at home, and don't buy English-made goods. Provide yourselves with homemade salt, and do not buy government-made salt."

Britain had introduced measures increasing the salt tax and prohibiting the Indian people from manufacturing or harvesting their own salt. In 1930, Gandhi protested these measures. Accompanied by supporters, he walked to the sea on what became known as the Salt March. On reaching the coast, Gandhi picked up a pinch of salt. Thousands of Indians followed his act of civil disobedience. Gandhi and many other members of the INC were arrested. 📖 *(See page 775 to read excerpts from Gandhi's 1930 statement on civil disobedience in the Primary Sources Library.)*

**New Leaders and New Problems** In the 1930s, a new figure entered the movement. **Jawaharlal Nehru,** who had studied law in Great Britain, was an example of a new kind of Indian politician. He was upper-class and intellectual.

The independence movement split into two paths. The one identified with Gandhi was religious, Indian, and traditional. The other, identified with Nehru, was secular, Western, and modern. The existence of varying approaches created uncertainty about India's future path.

In the meantime, another problem had arisen in the independence movement. Hostility between

▼ *Gandhi with Jawaharlal Nehru in the mid-1940s*

Hindus and Muslims had existed for centuries. Muslims were dissatisfied with the Hindu dominance of the INC and raised the cry "Islam is in danger."

By the 1930s, the Muslim League, under the leadership of Muhammad Ali Jinnah, was beginning to believe in the creation of a separate Muslim state of Pakistan (meaning "the land of the pure") in the northwest.

✓ **Reading Check** **Identifying** What two paths to independence did Nehru and Gandhi represent?

## The Rise of a Militarist Japan

**Main Idea** **By the late 1920s, militant forces in Japan were campaigning for an end to peaceful policies.**

**Reading Connection** Do you own any goods made by Japanese companies like Sony, Mitsubishi, or Toshiba? Read to learn how Japan developed its modern industrial economy.

During the first two decades of the twentieth century, Japanese society developed along a Western model. The economic and social reforms launched during the Meiji Era led to increasing prosperity and the development of a modern industrial and commercial sector.

After World War I, the political system also became more Western. In 1925, the Diet passed a law giving the vote to all adult males.

**A *Zaibatsu* Economy** In the Japanese economy, various manufacturing processes were concentrated within a single enterprise called the *zaibatsu*, a large financial and industrial corporation. These firms gradually developed, often with government help, into vast companies that controlled major segments of the Japanese industrial sector. By 1937, the four largest *zaibatsu* (Mitsui, Mitsubishi, Sumitomo, and Yasuda) controlled 21 percent of the banking industry, 26 percent of mining, 35 percent of shipbuilding, and over 60 percent of paper manufacturing and insurance.

The concentration of wealth led to growing economic inequalities. City workers were poorly paid and housed. Economic crises added to this problem shortly after World War I when inflation in food prices led to food riots. A rapid increase in population led to food shortages. (The population of the Japanese islands increased from 43 million in 1900 to

# CONNECTIONS Around The World

## Paths to Modernization

After World War I, new states in the Middle East and Asia sought to modernize their countries. To many people, modernization meant Westernization, the adoption of political and economic reforms based on Western models. These models included government based on democratic principles and a free-market, or capitalist, economic system based on industrialization.

After the success of the Communist revolution in Russia, however, a second model for modernization appeared. To some people, a Marxist system seemed to offer a better and quicker way to transform an agricultural state into a modern industrial state. The new system would be a socialist model in which an authoritarian state, not private industry, would own and control the economy.

◀ *Dubai, United Arab Emirates, a thriving, modern port city*

Between World War I and World War II, some new republics combined features of both systems. In Turkey, Kemal Atatürk, creator of the new Turkish Republic, set up a national assembly but ruled with an iron fist. His economic modernization combined private industries with state direction of the economy.

In China, the Nanjing Republic under Chiang Kai-shek supported the idea of democracy but maintained the need for dictatorial government as a first stage to prepare the Chinese people for democracy. Economic modernization in the new Chinese republic combined a modern industrial state with the traditional Chinese values of hard work and obedience.

## Comparing Cultures

Using outside sources, research the current government of Turkey. How has the government developed since the rule of Kemal Atatürk? Does the current government reflect the influence of Western principles, or has it evolved according to a Marxist model?

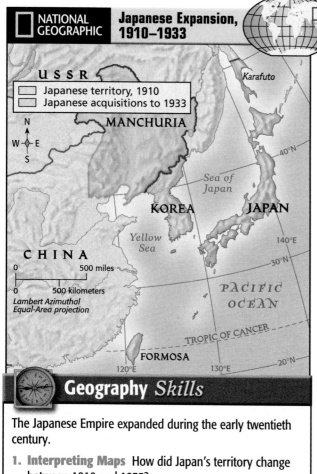

## NATIONAL GEOGRAPHIC
### Japanese Expansion, 1910–1933

Japanese territory, 1910
Japanese acquisitions to 1933

USSR

Karafuto

MANCHURIA

Sea of Japan

KOREA

JAPAN

Yellow Sea

CHINA

0    500 miles

0    500 kilometers

Lambert Azimuthal Equal-Area projection

PACIFIC OCEAN

TROPIC OF CANCER

FORMOSA

120°E    130°E    20°N

40°N

140°E

30°N

## Geography Skills

The Japanese Empire expanded during the early twentieth century.

1. **Interpreting Maps** How did Japan's territory change between 1910 and 1933?

2. **Applying Geography Skills** Describe Japan's geographical features. How was geography a factor in Japanese expansion?

73 million in 1940.) Later, when the Great Depression struck, workers and farmers suffered the most.

With hardships came calls for a return to traditional Japanese values. Traditionalists especially objected to the growing influence of Western ideas and values on Japanese educational and political systems. At the same time, many citizens denounced Japan's attempt to find security through cooperation with the Western powers. Instead, they demanded that Japan use its own strength to dominate Asia and meet its needs.

**Japan and the West** In the early twentieth century, Japanese leaders began to have trouble finding the raw materials and the foreign markets for manufactured goods. Until World War I, Japan had dealt with the problem by seizing territories—Formosa, Korea, and southern Manchuria on mainland China, for example—and making them part of a Japanese empire. This policy solved their problem, but it also aroused the concern of the Western nations.

The United States was especially worried about Japanese expansion because it wanted to keep Asia open for American trade. In 1922, the United States held a major conference of nations with interests in the Pacific. This Washington Conference resulted in a nine-power treaty that recognized the territorial **integrity** of China and that the Open Door policy of 1899 should be maintained. Japan accepted the treaty in return for recognition that it controlled southern Manchuria.

During the rest of the decade, the Japanese government tried to follow the rules of the Washington Conference. This meant using diplomatic and economic means to reach their goals in Asia. This approach was not popular, however, with influential groups in Japan.

In the 1920s and 1930s, Japanese industrialists were expanding into new areas, such as heavy industry, mining, chemicals, and the manufacturing of appliances and automobiles. These industries desperately needed resources that were scarce in Japan. More and more, industry leaders pressured the Japanese government to help them find raw materials in other countries.

**The Rise of Militarism** During the first two decades of the twentieth century, Japan was moving toward a more democratic government. The parliament and political parties grew stronger. The influence of the old ruling oligarchy, however, remained strong. At the end of the 1920s, new problems led to the emergence of militant nationalists who wanted a militaristic state.

These militant nationalists became influential when they gained control of the political system. Who were these people and what did they believe? Some of them were civilians who felt that Japan's parliamentary system had been corrupted by Western ideas. Others were members of the army and navy who were angered by the cuts in military spending and the government's pacifist policies in the early 1920s.

There were other signs of aggressive nationalism. During the early 1930s, army and navy officers and some civilians formed extremist patriotic organizations, such as the Black Dragon Society.

In the fall of 1931, one group of middle-level army officers even invaded **Manchuria,** a northern province of China, without government approval. Within a short time, all of Manchuria had been conquered.

The Japanese government opposed this unlawful conquest of Manchuria, but the Japanese people supported it. Soon military leaders who supported the Manchurian conquest, like Hideki Tojo, dominated the government. They were behind Japanese expansionism completely. Emperor Hirohito, fearing that the monarchy would be abolished, refused to oppose the action of the military leaders.

Japanese society was put on wartime status. A military draft law was passed in 1938. All political parties were merged into the Imperial Rule Assistance Association, which called for Japanese expansion abroad. Culture was purged of most Western ideas. Militant leaders insisted on the need for stressing traditional Japanese values instead.

**Reading Check** **Examining** How did the Japanese government change in the 1920s and 1930s?

# Nationalism and Revolution in Asia

**Main Idea** In the 1920s, the Comintern worked to spread communism throughout Asia.

**Reading Connection** Do you remember the Marxist theory that industrial workers would defeat capitalism? Read to learn how Lenin's revised idea of Marxism was spread in Asia.

Before World War I, the Marxist doctrine of social revolution had no appeal for Asian intellectuals. After all, most Asian societies were still agricultural and were hardly ready for a workers' revolution.

That situation changed after the revolution in Russia in 1917. The rise to power of Lenin and the Bolsheviks showed that a Marxist party could overturn an outdated system—even one that was not fully industrialized—and begin a new one.

**The Spread of Communism** In 1920, Lenin adopted a new revolutionary strategy aimed at non-Western societies which did not have a fully industrialized

economy. In the Russian Revolution, Lenin adapted Marx's theory and argued that peasants as well as workers would make the revolution. Because the Bolsheviks were successful in Russia, Marxism became very attractive to many poor people around the world.

The chief means of spreading the ideas of Karl Marx was through the Communist International, or Comintern. Founded in 1919, it was a worldwide organization of Communist parties dedicated to spreading revolution. At its headquarters in Moscow, revolutionaries from many countries were trained. They then returned home to promote revolution. By the late 1920s, practically every colonial society in Asia had a Communist party.

**Communist Parties in Asia** How successful were these new parties? In some countries, the local Communists were briefly able to cooperate with nationalist parties in the struggle against Western imperialism. This was true in French Indochina, where Vietnamese Communists were organized by the Moscow-trained revolutionary **Ho Chi Minh** in the 1920s. The strongest Communist-nationalist alliance was formed in China (see Section 3). In most colonial societies, though, Communist parties in the 1930s failed to build a base of support among the mass of the population.

**Reading Check** **Evaluating** What was the relationship between communism and imperialism?

**HISTORY** *Online* **Study Central**

For help with the concepts in this section of *Glencoe World History—Modern Times,* go to wh.mt.glencoe.com and click on **Study Central.**

---

# SECTION 2 ASSESSMENT

### Checking for Understanding

1. **Vocabulary** Define: aware, Pan-Africanism, Mahatma, civil disobedience, *zaibatsu,* integrity.

2. **People** Identify: W. E. B. DuBois, Marcus Garvey, Mohandas Gandhi, Jawaharlal Nehru, Ho Chi Minh.

3. **Places** Locate: Kenya, Manchuria.

### Reviewing Big Ideas

4. **List** at least three leaders who worked to end colonial rule in Africa.

### Critical Thinking

5. **Historical Analysis** **Identifying Bias** In what ways did black Africans who had fought in World War I face prejudice when they returned home? **CA HR2**

6. **Sequencing Information** On a sequence chain like the one below, show five events that contributed to Japan's becoming a military state in the 1930s.

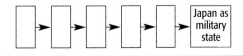

Japan as military state

### Analyzing Visuals

7. **Examine** the photo of Dubai in the feature on page 511. What do you see that tells you this is a modern port city?

### Writing About History

8. **Expository Writing** Japanese conglomerates today are called *keiretsu.* Research one of them, such as Mitsui or Mitsubishi, and write two paragraphs comparing their operations to American industry. **CA 10WS1.3**

# SECTION 3 Revolutionary Chaos in China

## Guide to Reading

### Section Preview
During the 1920s, two men struggled to lead a new Chinese state. One leader, Mao Zedong, argued that peasants, not workers, would be the basis for the revolution to establish a Communist China.

### Main Idea
• The Nationalists and Communists cooperated to drive the imperialists from China, but fought one another fiercely for the right to rule China. (p. 515)
• Mao Zedong relied on peasant support and guerrilla tactics to defeat the Nationalists. (p. 516)
• Many members of Mao's People's Liberation Army died on their Long March to the hills of northern China. (p. 517)

• Chiang Kai-shek was committed to building a new China with a republican government. (p. 518)

### Content Vocabulary
guerrilla tactics, redistribution of wealth

### Academic Vocabulary
pursue, constitutional

### People and Events to Identify
Sun Yat-sen, Chiang Kai-shek, Shanghai Massacre, Mao Zedong, PLA

### Places to Locate
Shanghai, Chang Jiang, Nanjing

### Reading Objectives
1. Explain the alliance between the Nationalist and the Chinese Communist parties.
2. Describe the obstacles facing Chiang Kai-shek in building a new China.

### Reading Strategy
**Summarizing Information** Make a cluster diagram like the one below showing the Confucian values that Chiang Kai-shek used to bring modern Western ideas into a culturally conservative population.

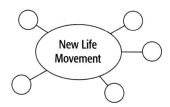

New Life Movement

### Preview of Events

♦1921   ♦1923   ♦1925   ♦1927   ♦1929   ♦1931   ♦1933

**1921**
Chinese Communist Party is formed in Shanghai

**1923**
Nationalists and Communists form an alliance

**1928**
Chiang Kai-shek founds new Chinese republic at Nanjing

**1934**
Mao's troops begin Long March

## California Standards in This Section

*Reading this section will help you master these California History–Social Science standards.*

**10.4.4:** Describe the independence struggles of the colonized regions of the world, including the roles of leaders, such as Sun Yat-sen in China, and the roles of ideology and religion.

**10.9.4:** Analyze the Chinese Civil War, the rise of Mao Zedong, and the subsequent political and economic upheavals in China (e.g., the Great Leap Forward, the Cultural Revolution, and the Tiananmen Square uprising).

# Nationalists and Communists

**Main Idea** The Nationalists and Communists cooperated to drive the imperialists from China, but fought one another fiercely for the right to rule China.

**Reading Connection** Are you able to work with people you do not trust? Read to learn how the alliance between the Chinese Nationalists and the Chinese Communists worked out.

Revolutionary Marxism had its greatest impact in China. By 1920, China was in such chaos that central authority had almost ceased to exist. Two political forces emerged as competitors for the right to rule China: Sun Yat-sen's Nationalist Party, which had been driven from the political arena several years earlier, and the Chinese Communist Party. Ultimately, the Chinese Communists were successful. The reason was that their leader saw that success depended upon winning the support of the vast majority of the Chinese—the peasants.

## Voices from the Past

In the fall of 1926, the young Communist Mao Zedong submitted a report to the Chinese Communist Party Central Committee calling for a massive peasant revolt against the ruling order:

> ❝In a very short time, in China's Central, Southern, and Northern provinces, several hundred million peasants will rise like a mighty storm, like a hurricane, a force so swift and violent that no power, however great, will be able to hold it back. They will smash all the restraints that bind them and rush forward along the road to liberation. They will sweep all the imperialists, warlords, corrupt officials, local tyrants, and evil gentry into their graves. . . . In force and momentum the attack is tempestuous; those who bow before it survive and those who resist perish.❞

It was a group of young radicals from Beijing University who founded the Chinese Communist Party (CCP) in 1921 in **Shanghai,** a commercial and industrial city. Comintern agents soon advised the new party to join with the more experienced Nationalist Party.

**Sun Yat-sen,** leader of the Nationalists (see Chapter 7), welcomed the cooperation of the CCP. After all, both groups wanted to oppose the warlords and drive the imperialist powers out of China. Sun Yat-sen also needed the expertise that the Soviet Union could provide, and he had little support from any Westerners. His anti-imperialist words had alienated many Western powers. One English-language newspaper in Shanghai wrote, "All his life, all his influence, are devoted to ideas that keep China in turmoil, and it is utterly undesirable that he should be allowed to prosecute those aims here."

In 1923, the two parties—Nationalists and Communists—formed an alliance. For three years, they overlooked their mutual suspicions. They mobilized and trained a revolutionary army to march north and seize control of China. This Northern Expedition began in the summer of 1926. By the following spring, these forces had taken control of all China south of the **Chang Jiang** (Yangtze), including the major river ports of Wuhan and Shanghai.

Tensions between the two parties eventually rose to the surface. Sun Yat-sen died in 1925 and was succeeded as head of the Nationalist Party by the general **Chiang Kai-shek** (JEE•AHNG KY•SHEHK). Chiang pretended to support the alliance with the Communists. In April 1927, however, he struck against the Communists and their supporters in Shanghai, killing thousands in what is called the **Shanghai Massacre.** The alliance ceased to exist.

In 1928, Chiang Kai-shek founded a new Chinese republic at **Nanjing.** During the next three years, he worked to reunify China. Although Chiang saw Japan as a serious threat to the Chinese nation, he believed that Japan was less dangerous than his other enemy, the Communists. He once remarked that "the Communists are a disease of the heart."

**✓ Reading Check** **Drawing Conclusions** Why did Chiang Kai-shek end the alliance with the CCP?

▼ *Mao Zedong (at left)*

# The Communists in Hiding

**Main Idea** Mao Zedong relied on peasant support and guerrilla tactics to defeat the Nationalists.

**Reading Connection** Think about how the revolutions you've read about so far were organized. Read to learn about how Mao Zedong attempted to organize a Chinese revolution.

After the Shanghai Massacre, most of the Communist leaders went into hiding in Shanghai. They tried to revive the Communist movement among the working class. Shanghai was a rich recruiting ground for the party. People were discontented and looking for leadership.

Some party members left the city, however, and went to the mountainous Jiangxi (jee•AHNG•SHEE) Province south of the Chang Jiang. They were led by the young Communist organizer **Mao Zedong** (MOW DZUH•DOONG).

Unlike most other leading members of the CCP, Mao was convinced that a Chinese revolution would have to depend on the peasants, not the working class. Lenin had appealed to the peasants in Russia for a similar reason as Mao did—peasants were a large part of the population. In Russia, however, workers were still the engine of the Russian Revolution. Mao made peasants the heart and soul of Chinese communism.

Meanwhile, Chiang Kai-shek was trying to root the Communists out of their urban base in Shanghai and their rural base in Jiangxi Province. He succeeded in the first task in 1931. Most party leaders in Shanghai were forced to flee to Mao's base in southern China.

Chiang Kai-shek then turned his forces against Mao's stronghold in Jiangxi Province. Chiang's forces far outnumbered Mao's, but Mao made effective use of **guerrilla tactics,** using unexpected maneuvers like sabotage and subterfuge. Four slogans describe his methods: "When the enemy advances, we retreat! When the enemy halts and camps, we trouble them! When the enemy tries to avoid battle, we attack! When the enemy retreats, we **pursue**!"

✓**Reading Check** **Identifying** Why did Mao believe a Chinese revolution would depend on peasants in the countryside rather than the working class?

*Picturing* **History**

Members of the Communist forces prepare to evacuate Shanghai during the Nationalists' takeover in 1927. Why did Chiang Kai-shek initiate this military action against the Communists?

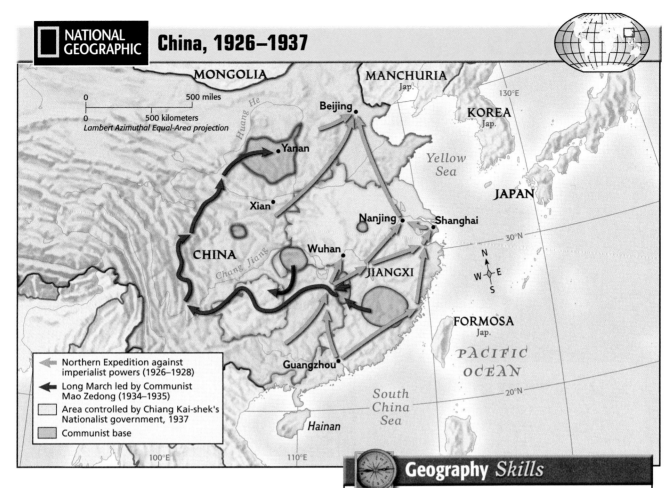

MONGOLIA

0 ——— 500 miles
0 ——— 500 kilometers
Lambert Azimuthal Equal-Area projection

Huang He

Yanan

Xian

CHINA

Chang Jiang

Wuhan

JIANGXI

Nanjing

Shanghai

Beijing

MANCHURIA
Jap.

KOREA
Jap.

130°E

Yellow
Sea

JAPAN

30°N

N
W — E
S

Guangzhou

South
China
Sea

Hainan

FORMOSA
Jap.

PACIFIC
OCEAN

20°N

100°E        110°E

→ Northern Expedition against
imperialist powers (1926–1928)

→ Long March led by Communist
Mao Zedong (1934–1935)

☐ Area controlled by Chiang Kai-shek's
Nationalist government, 1937

▨ Communist base

## The Long March

**Main Idea** Many members of Mao's People's Liberation Army died on their Long March to the hills of northern China.

**Reading Connection** Do you remember Napoleon's "Great Retreat" across Russia? Read on to compare that "Great Retreat" with Mao's Long March.

Using their superior military strength, Chiang's troops surrounded the Communist base in Jiangxi in 1934. Mao's army, the People's Liberation Army (**PLA**), was able, however, to break through the Nationalist lines. It then began its famous Long March.

Moving on foot through mountains, marshes, and deserts, Mao's army traveled almost 6,000 miles (9,600 km) to reach the last surviving Communist base in northern China. His troops had to fight all the way. Many froze or starved. One survivor remembered, "As the days went by, there was less and less to eat. After our grain was finished, we ate the horses, and then we lived on wild vegetables. When even the wild vegetables were finished, we ate our leather belts. After that we had to march on empty stomachs."

### Geography Skills

Communists and Nationalists fought imperialist powers and each other for control of China in the 1920s and 1930s.

1. **Interpreting Maps** What major cities were the destination of the Northern Expedition? Why do you think the Northern Expedition headed toward these cities?

2. **Applying Geography Skills** Use this map and others of China in this text to identify the mountains, rivers, and deserts Mao's army crossed during the Long March.

One year later, Mao's troops reached safety in the dusty hills of northern China. Of about 90,000 troops who began the journey, only some 9,000 remained. During the course of this ordeal, Mao Zedong had established himself as the heroic and unquestioned leader of the Chinese Communist Party. He would hold this role for the rest of his life.

To people who lived at the time, it must have seemed that the Communist threat to the Nanjing regime was over. The Communists, however, anticipated that a better time would come. They had not given up their fight.

✓**Reading Check** **Explaining** Why did communism no longer seem a threat to China after the Long March?

**Picturing History**

Chinese Communists gather in northern China following the year-long, 6,000-mile (9,600-km) Long March. Describe the difficulties Mao Zedong's forces had to overcome to reach safety in northern China.

# The New China of Chiang Kai-shek

**Main Idea** Chiang Kai-shek was committed to building a new China with a republican government.

**Reading Connection** What is your definition of a republican government? Read to learn what Chiang Kai-shek believed must happen before China could become a republic.

In the meantime, Chiang Kai-shek had been trying to build a new nation. Chiang had publicly declared his commitment to the plans of Sun Yat-sen, which called for a republican government. First, however, there would be a transitional period. In Sun's words:

❝China . . . needs a republican government just as a boy needs school. As a schoolboy must have good teachers and helpful friends, so the Chinese people, being for the first time under republican rule, must have a farsighted revolutionary government for their training. This calls for the period of political tutelage, which is a necessary transitional stage from monarchy to republicanism. Without this, disorder will be unavoidable.❞

In keeping with Sun's program, Chiang announced a period of training to prepare people for a democratic **constitutional** government. In the meantime, the Nationalists would use their dictatorial power to carry out land reform and to modernize industry.

It would take more than plans on paper to create a new China, however. Years of neglect and civil war had severely weakened the political, economic, and social fabric of the nation. Most rural people, who made up 80 percent of the population, were drained by civil strife. They were still very poor and overwhelmingly illiterate.

In the cities, though, a Westernized middle class had begun to develop. It was there that the new Nanjing government of Chiang Kai-shek found most of its support. The Westernized elite had very little in common with the peasants in the countryside. They pursued the typical middle-class value of individual achievement. They wanted to accumulate wealth and high social status.

Chiang Kai-shek was aware that introducing Western ideas into a conservative rural society would be difficult. While attempting to build a modern industrial state through Western innovation, he also stressed the traditional Confucian values of hard

### Mao Zedong
**1893–1976—Chinese leader**

Mao Zedong was the creator of the People's Republic of China. The son of a prosperous peasant, he insisted that the Communist Party support peasant demands for land reform. In 1949, Communist forces under Mao drove out Chiang Kai-shek's Nationalists and assumed complete control of China. Mao's sayings were collected in *Quotations from Chairman Mao Zedong,* which came to be known simply as *The Little Red Book.*

work, obedience, and integrity. With his American-educated wife Mei-ling Soong, Chiang set up a "New Life Movement." It promoted Confucian values and rejected what was seen as the excessive individualism and materialism of Western capitalism.

Chiang Kai-shek faced a host of other serious problems. First, the Nanjing government did not control the entire country, but only a few provinces in the Chang Jiang Valley. As will be discussed in the next chapter, the Japanese were threatening to take control of northern China. Second, the Great Depression was hurting the Chinese economy.

In spite of these problems, Chiang had some success. He undertook a massive road-building project and repaired and extended much of the country's railroad system. He also established a national bank and improved the education system.

In other areas, Chiang's government was less successful. For example, a land-reform program was enacted in 1930, but it was ineffective. This was not surprising since Chiang's support came from the landed gentry in the countryside and the urban middle class. Neither group wanted land reform. Chiang did not, therefore, press for programs that would lead to a **redistribution of wealth,** the shifting of wealth from a rich minority to a poor majority. Chiang's government was also repressive because it feared Communist influence. It suppressed all opposition, but by doing so, it alienated many intellectuals and political moderates.

☑ **Reading Check** **Evaluating** How successful was Chiang Kai-shek in establishing a republican government in China?

**Study Central**

For help with the concepts in this section of *Glencoe World History–Modern Times,* go to wh.mt.glencoe.com and click on **Study Central.**

## SECTION 3 ASSESSMENT

### Checking for Understanding

1. **Vocabulary** Define: guerrilla tactics, pursue, constitutional, redistribution of wealth.

2. **People and Events** Identify: Sun Yat-sen, Chiang Kai-shek, Shanghai Massacre, Mao Zedong, PLA.

3. **Places** Locate: Shanghai, Chang Jiang, Nanjing.

### Reviewing Big Ideas

4. **Explain** why the Communist Party aligned with the Nationalist Party.

### Critical Thinking

5. **Historical Analysis** **Contextualizing** What did Mao's Long March accomplish? Why was it successful? **CA HI3**

6. **Summarizing Information** Use a diagram like the one below to show Chiang Kai-shek's successes during the 1930s.

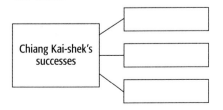

Chiang Kai-shek's successes

### Analyzing Visuals

7. **Describe** the action taking place in the photo on page 516. What clues in the photo indicate the different kinds of warfare undertaken by soldiers during this time?

### Writing About History

8. **Persuasive Writing** Conduct research to learn how the United States supported Chiang Kai-shek and why. Write an editorial for or against United States intervention in China. **CA 10WA2.4a,c**

# Nationalism in Latin America

## California Standards in This Section

Reading this section will help you master these California History–Social Science standards.

**10.3.5:** Understand the connections among natural resources, entrepreneurship, labor, and capital in an industrial economy.

**10.4.1:** Describe the rise of industrial economies and their links to imperialism and colonialism (e.g., the role played by national security and strategic advantage; moral issues raised by the search for national hegemony, Social Darwinism, and the missionary impulse; material issues such as land, resources, and technology).

**10.6.4:** Discuss the influence of World War I on literature, art, and intellectual life in the West (e.g., Pablo Picasso, the "lost generation" of Gertrude Stein, Ernest Hemingway).

**10.9:** Students analyze the international developments in the post–World War II world.

# The Latin American Economy

**Main Idea** During the 1920s and 1930s, dictators took over in many Latin American nations, and some emphasized domestic industry to balance the economy.

**Reading Connection** Do you ever purchase goods made in Latin America? Read to learn how the Great Depression affected economic relations between Latin America and the United States.

At the beginning of the twentieth century, the Latin American economy was based mostly on exporting foodstuffs and raw materials. Some countries relied on only one or two products for sale abroad. For example, **Argentina** sent beef and wheat; **Chile,** nitrates and copper; **Brazil** and Caribbean nations, sugar; and Central America, bananas. A few became rich from this export trade, but for most of the people, the returns were small. Political instability and economic crises in many Latin American countries during the 1920s and 1930s eventually led to military dictatorships.

## *Voices from the Past*

In July 1938, Getúlio Vargas spoke to the Brazilian nation to explain his dictatorial regime, which he called the New State:

> ❝If you would ask me what is the program of the New State, I would tell you that its program is to crisscross the nation with railroads, highways, and airlines; to increase production; to provide for the workers and to encourage agriculture; to expand exports; to prepare the armed forces; to organize public opinion so that there is, body and soul, one Brazilian thought . . . finally [that] the preparation of internal and external defense by the rearmament of our brave armed forces and the simultaneous education of the new generations [is] inculcating [implanting] in them the spirit and love of the fatherland.❞

**Role of the United States** In the 1920s, the United States began to replace Great Britain as the top investor in Latin America. British investors had put money into stocks and other forms of investment. American investors put their funds directly into companies and ran them themselves.

In this way, American firms became the owners of a large part of the Latin American export companies. Even though a number of smaller Central American countries were independent republics, their economies were often dependent on large, wealthy nations. The U.S.-owned United Fruit Company, for example, owned land, packing plants, and railroads in Central America. American firms also gained control of the copper-mining industry in Chile and **Peru,** as well as of the oil industry in **Mexico,** Peru, and Bolivia.

The fact that investors in the United States controlled many Latin American industries angered the people of Latin America. A growing nationalist consciousness led many of them to see the United States as an imperialist power. It was not difficult for Latin American nationalists to show that profits from U.S. businesses were sometimes used to keep ruthless dictators in power. In Venezuela, for example, U.S. oil companies had a close relationship with the dictator **Juan Vicente Gómez.**

The United States had always cast a large shadow over Latin America. It had intervened militarily in Latin American affairs for years. This was especially true in Central America and the Caribbean. Many Americans felt their involvement was justified since they saw these regions as vital to American security.

The United States made some attempts to change its relationship with Latin America in the 1930s. In 1933, President Franklin D. Roosevelt announced the **Good Neighbor policy,** rejecting the use of military force in Latin America on principle. Adhering to his word, Roosevelt withdrew the last U.S. Marines from Haiti in 1934. For the first time in 30 years, there were no U.S. troops in Latin American countries.

*Getúlio Vargas*

**Impact of the Great Depression** The Great Depression was a disaster for Latin America. Weak American and European economies meant that there was decreased demand for Latin American foodstuffs and raw materials, especially coffee beans, sugar, metals, and meat. The total value of Latin American exports in 1930 was almost 50 percent below the figures for the years 1925 to 1929. Worst hit were countries that depended on the export of one product.

The Great Depression had one positive effect on the Latin American economy. With the decline in exports, Latin American countries no longer had the money to buy manufactured goods. Thus, their governments encouraged the development of new industries to produce manufactured goods at home. The hope was that industrial development would bring greater economic independence.

Often, however, the new industries were not started by individuals. Because of a shortage of capital in the private sector, governments frequently invested in the new industries. This led to government-run steel industries in Chile and Brazil, along with government-run oil industries in Argentina and Mexico.

✔ **Reading Check** **Comparing** How did the American method of investing in Latin America differ from that of Britain?

## The Move to Authoritarianism

**Main Idea** In most Latin American countries, a small group of church leaders, military leaders, and large landowners controlled politics.

**Reading Connection** Do you think fear of social chaos could ever lead the American Congress to suspend the U.S. Constitution? Read to learn about Latin American governments in the 1930s.

Most Latin American countries had republican forms of government. In reality, a relatively small group of church leaders, military officers, and large landowners dominated each country. This elite group controlled the masses of people, who were mostly poverty-stricken peasants. Military forces were crucial in keeping these special-interest groups in power. Indeed, military leaders often took control of the government.

This trend toward authoritarianism increased during the 1930s, largely because of the Great Depression. Domestic instability caused by economic crises led to the creation of military dictatorships. This trend was especially evident in Argentina

**Geography Skills**

The economic and political stability of Latin America was strongly affected by World War I and the Great Depression.

1. **Interpreting Maps** How many countries made up Latin America in 1939?
2. **Applying Geography Skills** What evidence of the European occupation of Latin America can you find on this map? What inferences can you draw about this occupation by looking at northern South America?

and Brazil. Along with Mexico, these nations possessed over half of the land and wealth of Latin America.

**Argentina** Argentina was controlled by an **oligarchy,** a government where a select group of people exercises control. This oligarchy of large landowners who had grown wealthy from the export of beef and wheat failed to realize the growing importance of industry and cities in their country. It also ignored the growing middle class, which reacted by forming the Radical Party in 1890.

In 1916, **Hipólito Irigoyen** (ee•PAW•lee•TOH IHR•ih•GOH•YEHN), leader of the Radical Party, was elected president of Argentina. The Radical Party, however, feared the industrial workers, who were using strikes to improve working conditions. The party thus drew closer to the large landowners and became more corrupt.

The military was also concerned with the rising power of the industrial workers. In 1930, the Argentine army overthrew President Irigoyen and reestablished the power of the large landowners. Through this action, the military hoped to **stimulate** the old export economy and thus stop the growth of working-class power that would come with more industrialization.

During World War II, restless military officers formed a new organization, known as the Group of United Officers (GOU). Discontented with the government, they overthrew it in June 1943. Three years later, one GOU member, Juan Perón, was elected president of Argentina (see Chapter 14).

**Brazil** In 1889, the army had overthrown the Brazilian monarchy and established a republic. The republic was controlled chiefly by the landed elites, who had become wealthy by growing coffee on large plantations.

By 1900, three-fourths of the world's coffee was grown in Brazil. As long as coffee prices remained high, the ruling oligarchy was able to **maintain** its power. The oligarchy largely ignored the growth of urban industry and the working class that came with it.

The Great Depression devastated the coffee industry. By the end of 1929, coffee prices had hit a record low. In 1930, a military coup made **Getúlio Vargas,** a wealthy rancher, president of Brazil. Vargas ruled Brazil from 1930 to 1945. Early in his rule, he appealed to workers by instituting an eight-hour day and a minimum wage.

Faced with strong opposition in 1937, Vargas made himself dictator. Beginning in 1938, he established his New State, an authoritarian state with fascist-like features. Political parties were outlawed and civil rights restricted. A secret police used torture to force Vargas's opponents into submission.

Vargas also pursued a policy of stimulating new industries. The government established the Brazilian steel industry and set up a company to explore for oil. By the end of World War II, Brazil had become Latin America's chief industrial power. In 1945, the army, fearing that Vargas might prolong his power illegally after calling for new elections, forced him to resign.

**Mexico** Mexico was not an authoritarian state, but neither was it truly democratic. The Mexican Revolution of the early twentieth century had been the first significant effort in Latin America to overturn the system of large landed estates. It also raised the living standards for most people (see Chapter 6). The revolution led to a relatively stable political order.

The government was democratic in form, but one party dominated. The official party of the Mexican Revolution, known as the Institutional Revolutionary Party or **PRI,** controlled the major groups in society. Every six years, party bosses of the PRI chose the party's presidential candidate. That candidate was then dutifully elected by the people.

A new wave of change began with **Lázaro Cárdenas** (KAHR•duhn•AHS), president of Mexico from 1934 to 1940. He moved to fulfill some of the original goals of the revolution. His major step was to distribute 44 million acres (17.8 million ha) of land to landless Mexican peasants, an action that made him enormously popular with the peasants.

Cárdenas also took a strong stand with the United States, especially over oil. By 1900, Mexico was known to have enormous oil reserves. Over the next 30 years, foreign oil companies from Britain and, in particular, the United States, made large investments in Mexico. After a dispute with the foreign-owned oil companies over workers' wages, the Cárdenas government seized control of the oil fields and the property of the oil companies.

The U.S. oil companies were furious and asked President Franklin D. Roosevelt to intervene. He refused, reminding them of his promise in the Good Neighbor policy not to send U.S. troops into Latin America. Mexicans cheered Cárdenas as the president who had stood up to the United States.

▼ *The price of coffee affects every aspect of life in Brazil.*

| | Latin America | | | Africa and Asia | | | Middle East | | |
|---|---|---|---|---|---|---|---|---|---|
| **Country** | Argentina | Brazil | Mexico | Kenya | Libya | India | Turkey | Persia | Northern Arabian Peninsula |
| **Leader** | Argentine army; Group of United Officers | Getúlio Vargas | Lázaro Cárdenas | Harry Thuku (Young Kikuyu Association); Jomo Kenyatta | Omar Mukhtar | Mohandas Gandhi | Mustafa Kemal (Atatürk) | Reza Khan (Reza Shah Pahlavi) | Ibn Saud |
| **Driving Force** | Fear of workers; dissatisfaction with government | Bad economy | Foreign control of oil industry | High taxes; British rule | Italian rule | British rule | Greek seizure of Anatolian Peninsula | British and Soviet presence | European creation of states |
| **Outcome** | New governments (1930, 1943) | Vargas's New State (1938) | Seizure of oil and property (1938); PEMEX | Exile of Thuku (1922) | Revolt crushed (1920s) | Government of India Act (1935) | Turkish Republic (1923) | Iran (1935) | Saudi Arabia (1932) |

## Chart Skills

Between World War I and World War II, many countries around the world struggled to achieve independence and national identity.

1. **Analyzing** What was the most frequent motivation for revolt in the countries identified above?

2. **Summarizing** How successful were those who sought to create a new nation or a new form of government? Using the information above and in this chapter, write a paragraph that summarizes the attempts at independence and nationalism made by the countries on the chart.

Eventually, the Mexican government did pay the oil companies for their property. It then set up PEMEX, a national oil company, to run the oil industry.

✓ **Reading Check** **Examining** How was the Mexican government democratic in form but not in practice?

# Culture in Latin America

**Main Idea** In this period, Latin American artists created a national art by combining European techniques and their own native traditions.

**Reading Connection** If you could paint a mural for your community, what scene would you create? Read how Diego Rivera painted murals with political and social messages in public spaces.

During the early twentieth century, Latin American artists were following European artistic and literary trends. In major cities, such as Buenos Aires in Argentina and São Paulo in Brazil, wealthy elites expressed great interest in the work of modern artists.

Latin American artists went abroad and brought back modern techniques. Often they adapted European styles to their own traditions. Many artists and writers used their work to promote the emergence of a new national spirit. An example was the Mexican artist Diego Rivera.

Rivera had studied in Europe, where he was especially influenced by Italian frescoes—the murals or wall paintings done on fresh plaster. When he returned home, he filled wall after wall with monumental shapes and bold colors. His murals can be found in such diverse places as the Ministry of Education, the Chapel of the Agriculture School at Chapingo, and the Social Security Hospital. His works were aimed at average and even poor Mexicans, many of whom could not read.

▲ *This image is part of a huge mural by Diego Rivera in the Palacio National in Mexico City.*

Although Rivera trained in Europe, his goal was to celebrate his own country and culture. He used European styles like cubism, but he looked for inspiration to the Mexican past. He especially liked to portray his own interpretations of Aztec legends, Mexican festivals, and folk customs.

Rivera's work also carried a political and social message. For example, the large mural in the Palacio National in Mexico City, completed between 1929 and 1935, is titled *The Arrival of Cortez at Veracruz* (see above). In it, he expressed his attitude toward the Spanish conquest of Mexico. A favorite theme was the Mexican Revolution. Rivera did not want people to forget the event that had overthrown the large landowners and the foreign interests that supported them.

✓**Reading Check** **Examining** How did Diego Rivera use his artistic talent as a political tool?

**HISTORY** *Online* **Study Central**

For help with the concepts in this section of *Glencoe World History–Modern Times,* go to wh.mt.glencoe.com and click on **Study Central.**

# SECTION 4 ASSESSMENT

### Checking for Understanding

1. **Vocabulary** Define: oligarchy, stimulate, maintain.

2. **People and Events** Identify: Juan Vicente Gómez, Good Neighbor policy, Hipólito Irigoyen, Getúlio Vargas, PRI, Lázaro Cárdenas.

3. **Places** Locate: Argentina, Chile, Brazil, Peru, Mexico.

### Reviewing Big Ideas

4. **Explain** how Vargas's dictatorship ended.

### Critical Thinking

5. **Historical Analysis** **Cause and Effect** Why did the Great Depression cause many Latin American countries to improve their economic systems and gain more independence from foreign economic dominance? **CA HI2**

6. **Compare and Contrast** Make a chart comparing and contrasting political struggles in Argentina and Brazil.

| Argentina | Brazil |
|---|---|
| | |
| | |

### Analyzing Visuals

7. **Analyze** the photo on page 523. What does this photo reveal about what working conditions were like on Brazilian coffee plantations?

### Writing About History

8. **Descriptive Writing** Using outside sources, find two of Diego Rivera's murals. In an essay, compare these to the frescoes of medieval Italian painters like Giotto. How do Rivera's murals reflect the influence of Italian frescoes? How do they differ? **CA 10WA2.3a,b**

As the twentieth century progressed, so did various nationalist movements. The excerpts below express nationalist feelings of some Arab, African, and Chinese groups.

## SOURCE 1: An Arab Students' Declaration

*This manifesto was written by Arab students in Brussels in 1938, at the first Arab Students' Congress in Europe.*

### I. Our National Pact

I am an Arab, and I believe that the Arabs constitute one nation. The sacred right of this nation is to be **sovereign**[1] in the Arab homeland, to unite all its parts, and to found political, economic, and social institutions more sound and more compatible than the existing ones. . . .

I pledge myself to God, that I will strive in this path to my utmost, putting the national interest above any other consideration.

### II. First Principles

*The Arabs:* All who are Arab in their language, culture, and loyalty . . . those are the Arabs. . . .

*The Arab Homeland:* It is the land which has been, or is, inhabited by an Arab majority, in the above sense, in Asia and Africa. As such it is a whole which

---

> [1] **sovereign:** free from external control

*A Harlem march supporting Marcus Garvey*

cannot be divided or **partitioned**[2]. It is a sacred heritage no inch of which may be trifled with. Any compromise in this respect is invalid and is national treason.

*Arab Nationalism:* It is the feeling for the necessity of independence and unity which the inhabitants of the Arab lands share. . . . It is based on the unity of the homeland, of language, culture, history, and a sense of the common good.

*The Arab Movement:* . . . Its motive force is her glorious past, her remarkable vitality and the awareness of her present and future interests. This movement strives . . . to liberate and unite the Arab homeland, to found political, economic, and social organizations more sound than the existing ones, and to attempt afterward to work for the good of the human **collectivity**[3] and its progress. These aims . . . will be realized without subscribing to any particular creed of the modern Western ones such as Fascism, Communism, or Democracy.

## SOURCE 2: A Call for African Freedom

*Marcus Garvey, living in New York City in the 1920s, wrote the following passage to promote pride in people of African descent.*

George Washington was not God Almighty. He was a man like any Negro in this building, and if he and his associates were able to make a free America, we too can make a free Africa. Hampden, Gladstone, Pitt and Disraeli were not the representatives of God in the person of Jesus Christ. They were but men, but in their time they worked for the expansion of the British Empire, and today they boast of a British Empire upon which "the sun never sets." As Pitt and Gladstone were able to work for the expansion of the British Empire, so you and I can work for the expansion of a great

---

> [2] **partitioned:** broken into different political units
> [3] **collectivity:** people as a whole

African Empire. Voltaire and Mirabeau were not Jesus Christs, they were but men like ourselves. They worked and overturned the French Monarchy. They worked for the Democracy which France now enjoys, and if they were able to do that, we are able to work for a democracy in Africa. . . .

It falls to our lot to tear off the shackles that bind Mother Africa. Can you do it? You did it in the Revolutionary War; you did it in the Civil War. . . . You can do it marching up the battle heights of Africa. Let the world know that 400,000,000 Negroes are prepared to die or live as free men. . . . We are coming 400,000,000 strong. We are coming with our woes behind us, with the memory of suffering behind us— woes and suffering of three hundred years—they shall be our inspiration. My **bulwark**[4] of strength in the conflict for freedom in Africa, will be the three hundred years of persecution and hardship left behind in this Western Hemisphere. The more I remember the sufferings of my fore-fathers, the more I remember lynchings and burnings in the Southern States of America, the more I will fight. . . . [C]ease not in well doing until you have planted the banner of the Red, the Black and the Green on the hilltops of Africa.

## SOURCE 3: A Revolutionary's Vision

*This passage is part of a lecture given on February 17, 1924, by the Chinese revolutionary Sun Yat-sen.*

Now we want to revive China's lost nationalism and use the strength of our four hundred millions to fight for mankind against injustice; this is our divine mission. The Powers are afraid that we will have such thoughts and are setting forth a specious doctrine. They are now advocating **cosmopolitanism**[5] to inflame us, declaring that, as the civilization of the world advances and as mankind's vision enlarges, nationalism becomes too narrow, unsuited to the present age, and hence that we should espouse cosmopolitanism. . . . But it is not a doctrine which wronged races should talk about. We, the wronged race, must first recover our position of national free-

> ─────────────────────────────
[4]**bulwark:** safeguard; support

[5]**cosmopolitanism:** an international scope

dom and equality before we are fit to discuss cosmopolitanism . . . if we discard the nationalism and go and talk cosmopolitanism we . . . put the cart before the horse.

European superiority to China is not in political philosophy but altogether in the field of material civilization. . . . It was after the seventeenth and eighteenth centuries, when Bacon, Newton and other great scholars advocated the use of observation, experiment, and investigation of all things, that science came into being. So when we speak of Europe's scientific progress and of the advance of European material civilization, we are talking about something which has only two hundred years' history. A few hundred years ago, Europe could not compare with China, so now if we want to learn from Europe we should learn what we ourselves lack—science—but not political philosophy. Europeans are still looking to China for the fundamentals of political philosophy. . . . Cosmopolitanism has just flowered out in Europe during this generation, but it was talked of two thousand years ago in China. . . . our four hundred millions have devoted [themselves] to the principle of world peace . . .

## DBQ Document-Based Questions

**Historical Analysis** CA HR 1, HI 3

**Source 1:** According to the Arab students in 1938, what were the goals of the Arab nationalist movement?

**Source 2:** When Marcus Garvey mentions a number of famous Americans and Europeans and writes that they "were not the representatives of God," what is he trying to tell Africans?

**Source 3:** According to Sun Yat-sen, in which ways is China behind Europe and, at the same time, ahead of Europe?

### Comparing and Contrasting Sources

1. All three excerpts are trying to deal with the problems of a particular nationality. Identify these problems. **CA 10RL3.5**

2. After reading these three passages, can you come up with one general definition of nationalism? **CA 10RW1.1**

## Reviewing Content Vocabulary

*On a sheet of paper, use each of these terms in a sentence.*

1. genocide
2. ethnic cleansing
3. Pan-Africanism
4. Mahatma
5. civil disobedience
6. *zaibatsu*
7. guerrilla tactics
8. redistribution of wealth
9. oligarchy

## Reviewing Academic Vocabulary

*On a sheet of paper, use each of these terms in a sentence that reflects the term's meaning in the chapter.*

10. eliminate
11. establish
12. aware
13. integrity
14. pursue
15. constitutional
16. stimulate
17. maintain

## Reviewing the Main Ideas

### Section 1

18. What reforms did Atatürk implement to transform the Turkish Republic into a modern and secular state?

19. Why did foreign investment in Persia increase in the early 1900s?

20. What role did Ibn Saud play in promoting Arab nationalism?

21. Why were many Arabs opposed to the Balfour Declaration?

### Section 2

22. What message did Jomo Kenyatta use as the basic theme of his book *Facing Mount Kenya?*

23. What did the British do to make the people of India less opposed to their colonial government in 1935?

24. Why did industrialists want Japan to expand?

### Section 3

25. Identify the Comintern and explain why it was formed.

26. Why did the Nationalists and Communists in China form an alliance in 1928?

27. What happened to cause Chinese Communists to undertake the Long March in 1933?

### Section 4

28. What did the United States hope to accomplish through its Good Neighbor policy toward Latin America?

29. What single positive effect did the Great Depression have on Latin America?

30. Why did people in some apparently democratic Latin American nations have little voice in their country's government?

31. How did Diego Rivera seek to create a national style of art?

## Critical Thinking

32. **Cause and Effect** How did harsh treatment of Jewish people in Europe create problems for Arab people in the Middle East?

33. **Evaluating** How did Chiang Kai-shek's fear of communism cause him to alienate many Chinese intellectuals and political moderates?

34. **Making Generalizations** What was the cultural impact of World War I on Africans? How did the political status of Africa change after the war?

35. **Making Decisions** Imagine that you are a female American foreign exchange student. Which Middle Eastern country would you choose to live in for a year? Discuss the reasons for your choice and also the concessions that would be required of you.

## Chapter Summary

Between the two World Wars, a growing sense of nationalism inspired many countries to seek their independence from foreign rulers, as shown in the chart below.

| Middle East | Africa and Asia | China | Latin America |
|---|---|---|---|
| The decline of the Ottoman Empire results in the emergence of many new Arab states. | Black Africans who fought in World War I become more politically active. They organize reform movements and then call for independence. | In 1923, the Nationalists and the Communists form an alliance to oppose the warlords and drive the imperialist powers out of China. | After the Great Depression, Latin American countries work to become economically independent by creating new industries to produce goods that were formerly imported. |

**36. Compare and Contrast** What were the attitudes of Mao Zedong and Chiang Kai-shek toward the roles of the middle class and the peasants in the new Chinese nation?

**37.** **Reading Skill** Question-Answer Relationships Reread question 4 on page 506. Is this a "right there" or a "think-and-search" question?

## Writing About History

**38.** **Historical Analysis** Identifying Bias and Prejudice Find an English account and an Indian account of Mohandas Gandhi's work toward Indian independence. Write a one-page essay identifying any possible bias or prejudice each author has. Be sure to identify specific passages to support your conclusions. **CA HR2**

**39.** *Big Idea* Nationalism first became a significant political force in the movement against Napoleon. Write an essay comparing the early nationalist movements to the later nationalist battles against colonial powers discussed in this chapter. **CA 10WA2.3a,b**

**DBQ** **Document-Based Questions**

**Analyzing Sources** Chiang Kai-shek declared his commitment to Sun Yat-sen's plans for building a new nation. Chiang announced a period of political training, as described by Sun in the following quote.

> ❝China . . . needs a republican government just as a boy needs school. As a schoolboy must have good teachers and helpful friends, so the Chinese people, being for the first time under republican rule, must have a farsighted revolutionary government for their training. This calls for the period of political tutelage, which is a necessary transitional stage from monarchy to republicanism. Without this, disorder will be unavoidable.❞

**40.** What did Chiang Kai-shek mean when he compared China to a boy in school? **CA 10RW1.1**

**41.** What does the quote seem to say, compared to what you think it really means? Is there a self-serving bias in Sun Yat-sen's statement? If so, explain.

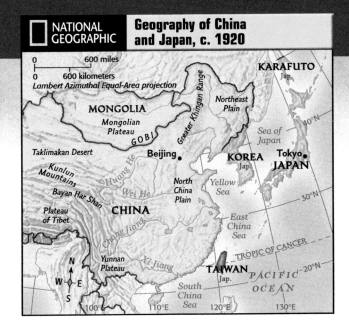

**NATIONAL GEOGRAPHIC** **Geography of China and Japan, c. 1920**

## Analyzing Maps and Charts

Use the map above to answer the following questions.

**42.** Near what latitudes are the cities of Beijing and Tokyo located?

**43.** Name the bodies of water that separate Japan from Korea, and Japan from China.

**44.** List three geographical features of China.

**45.** Compare this map to the map shown on page 512. What major territory did Japan acquire between the date indicated on the above map and 1933?

 **Standards Practice**

**Directions: Choose the best answer to the question below.**

**46.** Which of the following is a true statement about the relationship between World War I and nationalism?

**A** World War I brought nationalist movements to a standstill.

**B** Most nationalist movements had reached their goals by the conclusion of World War I.

**C** The weakening of European countries fostered national independence movements.

**D** World War I helped the European economy, which fueled nationalist movements.

**CA Standard 10.6.2** Describe the effects of the war and resulting peace treaties on population movement, the international economy, and shifts in the geographic and political borders of Europe and the Middle East.

# CHAPTER 11

## 1939–1945

# World War II

## ∿ The Big Ideas ∿

### SECTION 1: Paths to War

**Nations compete for natural resources and strategic advantages over other nations.** Nationalistic competition and ambitions on the part of Japan and Germany paved the way for the outbreak of World War II.

### SECTION 2: The Course of World War II

**War causes immeasurable devastation.** The devastation of the war was brought to an end by Allied perseverance, effective military operations, and Axis miscalculations.

### SECTION 3: The New Order and the Holocaust

**War causes immeasurable devastation.** Devastation and suffering resulted during World War II when Germany set up a New Order in Europe and Japan set up a Greater East Asia Co-Prosperity Sphere in Asia.

### SECTION 4: The Home Front and the Aftermath of the War

**International rivalry between superpowers and growing nationalism in the Third World led to major conflicts in the Cold War.** In the wake of World War II, a new set of Cold War problems faced the international community.

***World History—Modern Times Video*** *The Chapter 11 video,* "The Holocaust," *illustrates the horrors of Hitler's Final Solution.*

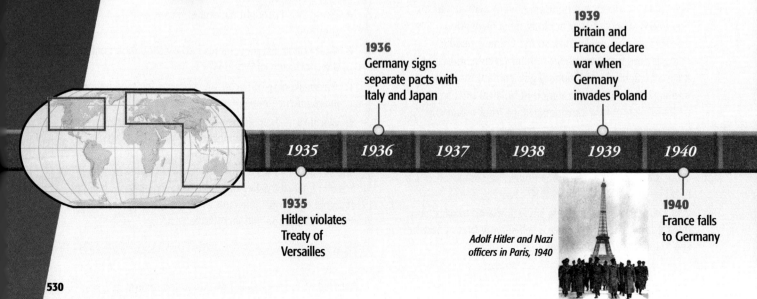

**1936**
Germany signs separate pacts with Italy and Japan

**1939**
Britain and France declare war when Germany invades Poland

| 1935 | 1936 | 1937 | 1938 | 1939 | 1940 |

**1935**
Hitler violates Treaty of Versailles

*Adolf Hitler and Nazi officers in Paris, 1940*

**1940**
France falls to Germany

The Marine Corps War Memorial in Arlington County, Virginia, depicts Marines raising the American flag on Iwo Jima in February 1945.

*Self-Portrait with a Jewish Identity Card by Felix Nussbaum, 1943*

**1942**
Nazi death camps in full operation

*Atomic bomb dropped on Hiroshima*

**1945**
Japanese surrender after United States drops atomic bombs on Japan

1941     1942     1943     1944     1945     1946

**1941**
United States enters war after Japan attacks Pearl Harbor

*Soldiers and civilians celebrate VE-Day, Paris*

**1945**
Germany surrenders

**1946**
Churchill proclaims existence of "iron curtain" in Europe

**HISTORY Online**

**Chapter Overview**
Visit the *Glencoe World History–Modern Times* Web site at wh.mt.glencoe.com and click on **Chapter 11– Chapter Overview** to preview chapter information.

# Preparing to Read Chapter 11

 **Reading Skill** **Inferring**

Often, you answer a teacher's questions directly from the text. Other questions, however, require you to turn to your own knowledge and experience. Readers have to supply additional ideas and information because authors could never write down every single thing that supports their message.

When you supply this additional information, you are *inferring*, based on what the author has suggested in the text. After the excerpt below, you will find two questions. Both of them ask you to make an inference—come to a logical conclusion by combining your general knowledge of the world with what the text says. See if the example below helps make clear what an inference is.

*Read the following paragraph from this chapter about German and Soviet teenagers during World War II and discuss the answers with a partner.*

## INFERRING

Question #1: Combine your understanding of how difficult war is with the text to answer this.

Question #2: Think about what would motivate you to undertake such work to answer this.

At times, young people were expected to carry the burden of fighting the war. In the last year of the war, Hitler Youth members, often only 14 or 15 years old, could be found in the front lines. In the Soviet Union, children as young as 13 or 14 spied on German positions and worked with the resistance movement. Some were even given decorations for killing the enemy.

Question #1: How did the governments of Germany and the Soviet Union view teenagers during World War II?

Question #2: Why would German and Russian youth do work that would place them in so much physical danger?

### Apply the Skill

Look closely at the questions in each of the Section Assessments in this chapter. These questions are often examples of "author-plus-you" or "on-your-own" questions. Make a chart indicating which questions fall into the first category and which ones fall into the second category.

## Historical Analysis Skill — Alternative History

**Historical Interpretation: Standard HI 4** *Students understand the meaning, implication, and impact of historical events and recognize that events could have taken other directions.*

Consider the following hypothetical events: The colonists lose the American Revolutionary War in 1776; Thomas Jefferson decides not to make the Louisiana Purchase in 1803; and, women are denied the vote in 1919. Historians analyze events to understand their consequences, but they must also consider what would have happened if events had turned out differently. In this chapter, consider the situation of Asians during World War II. Many were torn between their hatred of European colonial rulers and of Japanese invaders.

*Read the following excerpt from pages 556–557 of your text:*

> The Japanese had conquered Southeast Asia under the slogan 'Asia for the Asiatics.' Japanese officials in occupied territories quickly made contact with anticolonialists. They promised the people that local governments would be established under Japanese control. Such governments were eventually set up in Burma, the Dutch East Indies, Vietnam, and the Philippines.
>
> In fact, real power rested with Japanese military authorities in each territory.... The economic resources of the colonies were used for the benefit of the Japanese war machine. The native peoples in occupied lands were recruited to serve in local military units or were forced to work on public works projects.
>
> In some cases, these policies brought severe hardships to peoples living in the occupied areas. In Vietnam, for example, local Japanese authorities forcibly took rice and shipped it abroad. This led directly to a food shortage that caused over a million Vietnamese to starve to death in 1944 and 1945.

### Apply the Skill

How would Asians under European control have reacted if the Japanese had acted differently? What if the Japanese had actually worked to create a new order that benefited all Asians equally? Would you want the Allies to win World War II?

# A Story That Matters

*Poster, c. 1938, which proclaims "One People, one State, one Leader!"*

*After becoming dictator in 1933, Hitler often held large rallies to inspire the loyalty of Germans.*

## Hitler's Vision

On February 3, 1933, Adolf Hitler met secretly with Germany's leading generals. He had been appointed chancellor of Germany only four days before and was by no means assured that he would remain in office for long. Nevertheless, he spoke with confidence.

Hitler told the generals about his desire to remove the "cancer of democracy," create "the highest authoritarian state leadership," and forge a new domestic unity. All Germans would need to realize that "only a struggle can save us and that everything else must be subordinated to this idea." The youth especially would have to be trained and their wills strengthened "to fight with all means."

Hitler went on to say that Germany must rearm by instituting a military draft. Leaders must ensure that the men who were going to be drafted were not "poisoned by pacifism, Marxism, or Bolshevism." Once Germany had regained its military strength, how should this strength be used? Hitler had an answer. Because Germany's living space was too small for its people, it must prepare for "the conquest of new living space in the east and its ruthless Germanization."

Even before he had consolidated his power, Hitler had a clear vision of his goals. Reaching those goals meant another European war. Although World War I has been described as a total war, World War II was even more so. It was fought on a scale unprecedented in history and led to the most widespread human-made destruction that the world had ever seen.

### Why It Matters

World War II in Europe was clearly Hitler's war. Other countries may have helped make the war possible by not resisting Germany earlier, before it grew strong, but it was Nazi Germany's actions that made the war inevitable. Globally, World War II was more than just Hitler's war. It consisted of two conflicts. One arose, as mentioned above, from the ambitions of Germany in Europe. The other arose from the ambitions of Japan in Asia. By 1941, with the involvement of the United States in both conflicts, these two conflicts merged into one global world war.

**History and You** The decision by the United States to use atomic bombs against Japan led to the end of World War II. Find two contrasting views on the potential of nuclear warfare today and analyze the perspectives.

# SECTION 1 Paths to War

## Section Preview
Nationalistic competition and ambitions on the part of Japan and Germany paved the way for the outbreak of World War II.

**Main Idea**
- Adolf Hitler's theory of Aryan racial domination laid the foundation for aggressive expansion outside of Germany. (p. 536)
- The need for natural resources fueled the Japanese plan to seize other countries. (p. 539)

## Content Vocabulary
demilitarized, appeasement, New Order, sanction

## Academic Vocabulary
labor, achieve, conference, assume

## People to Identify
Adolf Hitler, Benito Mussolini, Joseph Stalin, Chiang Kai-shek

## Places to Locate
Rhineland, Sudetenland, Manchukuo

## Reading Objectives
1. Describe the agreement reached at the Munich Conference.
2. Explain why Germany believed it needed more land.

## Reading Strategy
**Categorizing Information** Create a chart like the one below listing examples of Japanese aggression and German aggression prior to the outbreak of World War II.

| Japanese Aggression | German Aggression |
|---|---|
|  |  |
|  |  |
|  |  |

## Preview of Events

| ♦1931 | ♦1932 | ♦1933 | ♦1934 | ♦1935 | ♦1936 | ♦1937 | ♦1938 | ♦1939 |
|---|---|---|---|---|---|---|---|---|

**1931**
Japanese forces invade Manchuria

**1936**
Hitler and Mussolini create Rome-Berlin Axis

**1937**
Japanese seize Chinese capital

**1938**
Hitler annexes Austria

**1939**
World War II begins

---

## California Standards in This Section

*Reading this section will help you master these California History–Social Science standards.*

**10.7.3:** Analyze the rise, aggression, and human costs of totalitarian regimes (Fascist and Communist) in Germany, Italy, and the Soviet Union, noting especially their common and dissimilar traits.

**10.8:** Students analyze the causes and consequences of World War II.

**10.8.1:** Compare the German, Italian, and Japanese drives for empire in the 1930s, including the 1937 Rape of Nanking, other atrocities in China, and the Stalin-Hitler Pact of 1939.

**10.8.2:** Understand the role of appeasement, nonintervention (isolationism), and the domestic distractions in Europe and the United States prior to the outbreak of World War II.

## The German Path to War

**Main Idea** Adolf Hitler's theory of Aryan racial domination laid the foundation for aggressive expansion outside of Germany.

**Reading Connection** Have you ever been forsaken by a friend? Read to find out how Czechoslovakia was abandoned by its Western allies.

World War II in Europe had its beginnings in the ideas of **Adolf Hitler,** the head of the Nazi Party and leader of Germany. He believed that Germans belonged to a so-called Aryan race that was superior to all other races and nationalities. Thus, Hitler felt that Germany was capable of building a great civilization. To do so, however, Germany needed more land to support a larger population. During the 1930s, Hitler became more aggressive, but no nation opposed him, even when he demanded a part of neighboring Czechoslovakia. One British politician, however, Winston Churchill, believed that Hitler's actions could only lead to war.

### *Voices from the Past*

In 1938, after France and Great Britain gave in to Hitler's demands for territory in Czechoslovakia, Churchill gave a stern warning to the British House of Commons:

> ❝I will begin by saying what everybody would like to ignore or forget but which must nevertheless be stated, namely, that we have sustained a total and unmitigated defeat. . . . And I will say this, that I believe the Czechs, left to themselves and told they were going to get no help from the Western Powers, would have been able to make better terms than they have got. . . . We are in the presence of a disaster of the first magnitude which has befallen Great Britain and France. . . . And do not suppose that this is the end. This is only the beginning of the reckoning.❞

As early as the 1920s, Hitler had indicated that a Nazi regime would find this land to the east—in the Soviet Union. Germany therefore must prepare for war with the Soviet Union. Once the Soviet Union had been conquered, Hitler planned to resettle it with German peasants. The Slavic peoples could be used

as slave **labor** to build the Third Reich, an "Aryan" racial state that Hitler thought would dominate Europe for a thousand years.

**The First Steps** After World War I, the Treaty of Versailles had limited Germany's military power. As chancellor, Hitler, posing as a man of peace, stressed that Germany wished to revise the unfair provisions of the treaty by peaceful means. Germany, he said, only wanted its rightful place among the European states.

On March 9, 1935, however, Hitler announced the creation of a new air force. One week later, he began a military draft that would expand Germany's army from 100,000 to 550,000 troops. These steps were in direct violation of the Treaty of Versailles.

France, Great Britain, and Italy condemned Germany's actions and warned against future aggressive steps. In the midst of the Great Depression, however, these nations were distracted by their own internal problems and did nothing further.

Hitler believed the Western states would not use force to maintain the Treaty of Versailles. Hence, on March 7, 1936, he sent troops into the **Rhineland.** The Rhineland was part of Germany, but, according to the Treaty of Versailles, it was a **demilitarized** area. That is, Germany was not permitted to have weapons or fortifications there. France had the right to use force against any violation of the demilitarized Rhineland but would not act without British support.

Great Britain did not support the use of force against Germany, however. The British government viewed the occupation of German territory by German troops as a reasonable action by a dissatisfied power. The London *Times* noted that the Germans were only "going into their own back garden." Great Britain thus

*Winston Churchill*

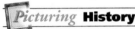 **History**

This 1937 Italian illustration depicts Hitler and Mussolini. What ideology brought Hitler and Mussolini together?

**Union With Austria** By 1937, Germany was once more a "world power," as Hitler proclaimed. He was convinced that neither France nor Great Britain would provide much opposition to his plans. In 1938, he decided to pursue one of his goals: *Anschluss* (ANSH•luhs), or union, with Austria, his native land.

By threatening Austria with invasion, Hitler forced the Austrian chancellor to put Austrian Nazis in charge of the government. The new government promptly invited German troops to enter Austria and "help" in reinforcing law and order. One day later, on March 13, 1938, after his triumphal return to his native land, Hitler annexed Austria to Germany.

**Demands and Appeasement** Hitler's next objective was the destruction of Czechoslovakia. On September 15, 1938, he demanded that Germany be given the **Sudetenland,** an area in northwestern Czechoslovakia that was inhabited largely by Germans. He expressed his willingness to risk "world war" to achieve his objective.

At a hastily arranged **conference** in Munich, British, French, German, and Italian representatives did not object to Hitler's plans but instead reached an agreement that met virtually all of Hitler's demands. German troops were allowed to occupy the Sudetenland. Abandoned by their Western allies, the Czechs stood by helplessly.

The Munich Conference was the high point of Western appeasement of Hitler. When Neville Chamberlain, the British prime minister, returned to Britain from Munich, he boasted that the agreement meant "peace for our time." Hitler had promised Chamberlain that he would make no more demands. Like many others, Chamberlain believed Hitler's promises.

**Great Britain and France React** In fact, Hitler was more convinced than ever that the Western democracies were weak and would not fight. Increasingly, Hitler was sure that he could not make a mistake, and he had by no means been satisfied at Munich.

In March 1939, Hitler invaded and took control of Bohemia and Moravia in western Czechoslovakia. In the eastern part of the country, Slovakia became a puppet state controlled by Nazi Germany. On the evening of March 15, 1939, Hitler triumphantly declared in Prague that he would be known as the greatest German of them all.

At last, the Western states reacted to the Nazi threat. Hitler's aggression had made clear that his promises were worthless. When Hitler began to demand the Polish port of Danzig, Great Britain saw

began to practice a policy of **appeasement.** This policy was based on the belief that if European states satisfied the reasonable demands of unsatisfied powers, the unsatisfied powers would be content, and stability and peace would be **achieved** in Europe.

**New Alliances** Meanwhile, Hitler gained new allies. **Benito Mussolini** had long dreamed of creating a new Roman Empire in the Mediterranean, and, in October 1935, Fascist Italy invaded Ethiopia. Angered by French and British opposition to his invasion, Mussolini welcomed Hitler's support. He began to draw closer to the German dictator.

In 1936, both Germany and Italy sent troops to Spain to help General Francisco Franco in the Spanish Civil War. In October 1936, Mussolini and Hitler made an agreement recognizing their common political and economic interests. One month later, Mussolini spoke of the new alliance between Italy and Germany, called the Rome-Berlin Axis. Also in November, Germany and Japan signed the Anti-Comintern Pact, promising a common front against communism.

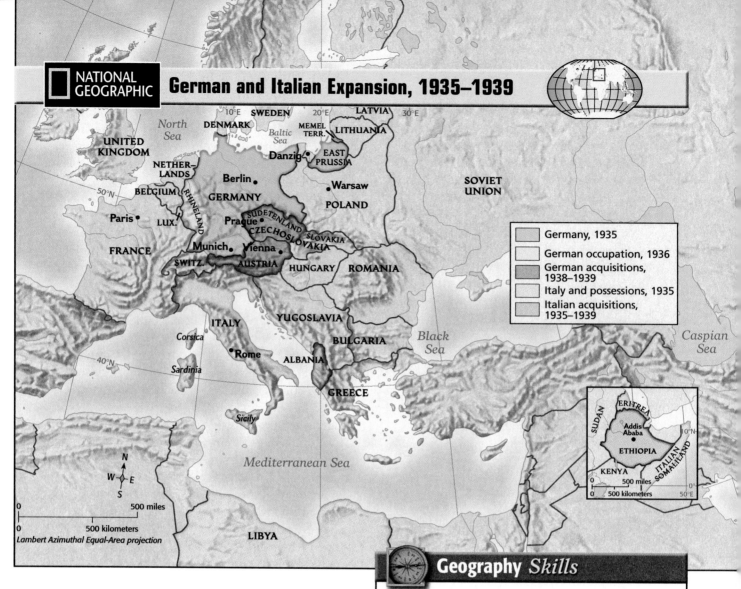

## German and Italian Expansion, 1935–1939

Germany, 1935
German occupation, 1936
German acquisitions, 1938–1939
Italy and possessions, 1935
Italian acquisitions, 1935–1939

Lambert Azimuthal Equal-Area projection

### Geography Skills

Germany and Italy expanded their territories in the years leading up to World War II.

1. **Interpreting Maps** Approximately how much territory did Germany annex between 1936 and 1939? How did Italy's size in 1939 compare to its size in 1935?

2. **Applying Geography Skills** Use the information on the map to create a chart comparing German and Italian expansion. What geographic factors made it easier for Germany to expand more readily?

the danger and offered to protect Poland in the event of war. At the same time, both France and Britain realized that only the Soviet Union was powerful enough to help contain Nazi aggression. They began political and military negotiations with **Joseph Stalin,** the Soviet dictator.

**Hitler and the Soviets** Meanwhile, Hitler pressed on in the belief that the West would not fight over Poland. He now feared, however, that the West and the Soviet Union might make an alliance. Such an alliance could mean a two-front war for Germany. To prevent this possibility, Hitler made his own agreement with Joseph Stalin.

On August 23, 1939, Germany and the Soviet Union signed the Nazi-Soviet Nonaggression Pact. In it, the two nations promised not to attack each other. As compensation for signing the pact, Hitler offered Stalin control of eastern Poland and the Baltic states. Because he expected to fight the Soviet Union anyway, it did not matter to Hitler what he promised— he was accustomed to breaking promises.

Hitler shocked the world when he announced the nonaggression pact. The treaty gave Hitler the freedom to attack Poland. He told his generals, "Now Poland is in the position in which I wanted her. . . . I am only afraid that at the last moment some swine will submit to me a plan for mediation."

Hitler need not have worried. On September 1, German forces invaded Poland. Two days later, Britain and France declared war on Germany.

**Reading Check** **Explaining** Why were the Western allies willing to appease Hitler?

# The Japanese Path to War

**Main Idea** The need for natural resources fueled the Japanese plan to seize other countries.

**Reading Connection** Have you heard about possible oil shortages in the United States in the next 30 years? Read to learn about how the Japanese reacted when they needed certain natural resources in the 1930s.

In September 1931, Japanese soldiers had seized Manchuria, which had natural resources that Japan needed. To justify their seizure, Japan cited a Chinese attack on a Japanese railway near the city of Mukden. In fact, the "Mukden incident" had been carried out by Japanese soldiers disguised as Chinese.

World protests against the Japanese led the League of Nations to send investigators to Manchuria. When the investigators issued a report condemning the seizure, Japan withdrew from the League. Over the next several years, Japan strengthened its hold on Manchuria, which was renamed **Manchukuo.** Japan now began to expand into northern China.

By the mid-1930s, militants connected to the government and the armed forces had gained control of Japanese politics. The United States refused to recognize the Japanese takeover of Manchuria but was unwilling to threaten force.

**War with China** Chiang Kai-shek tried to avoid a conflict with Japan so that he could deal with what he considered the greater threat from the Communists. When clashes between Chinese and Japanese troops broke out, he appeased Japan by allowing it to govern areas in northern China. As Japan moved steadily southward, protests grew stronger in Chinese cities. In December 1936, Chiang ended his military efforts against the Communists and formed a united front against the Japanese. In July 1937, Chinese and Japanese forces clashed south of Beijing.

This 1937 incident eventually turned into a major conflict. The Japanese seized the Chinese capital of Nanjing in December. Chiang Kai-shek refused to surrender and moved his government upriver, first to Hankou, then to Chongqing.

**The New Asian Order** Japanese military leaders had hoped to force Chiang to agree to join a **New Order** in East Asia, comprising Japan, Manchuria, and China. Japan would attempt to establish a new system of control in Asia with Japan guiding its Asian neighbors to prosperity. After all, who could

better teach Asian societies how to modernize than the one Asian country that had already done it?

Part of Japan's plan was to seize Soviet Siberia, with its rich resources. During the late 1930s, Japan began to cooperate with Nazi Germany. Japan **assumed** that the two countries would ultimately launch a joint attack on the Soviet Union and divide Soviet resources between them.

When Germany signed a nonaggression pact with the Soviets in August 1939, Japanese leaders had to rethink their goals. Japan did not have the resources to defeat the Soviet Union without help. Instead Japan turned its attention to raw materials that could be found in Southeast Asia to fuel its military machine. A move southward, however, would risk war with Europe and the United States. Japan's

**NATIONAL GEOGRAPHIC**

**Japanese Expansion, 1933–1941**

Japanese territory, 1933
Japanese acquisitions to November 1941

0 — 1,000 miles
0 — 1,000 kilometers
Two-Point Equidistant projection

**Geography** *Skills*

Like Germany, Japan attempted to expand its territories prior to the beginning of the war.

1. **Applying Geography Skills** Pose and answer your own question about the territories Japan did *not* acquire but wanted to acquire.

attack on China in the summer of 1937 had already aroused strong criticism. Nevertheless, in the summer of 1940, Japan demanded the right to exploit economic resources in French Indochina.

The United States objected. It warned Japan that it would apply economic **sanctions**—restrictions intended to enforce international law—unless Japan withdrew to the borders of 1931. Japan badly needed the oil and scrap iron it was getting from the United States. If these resources were cut off, Japan would have to find them elsewhere.

Japan was now caught in a dilemma. To guarantee access to the raw materials it wanted in Southeast

Asia, Japan had to risk losing raw materials from the United States. Japan's military leaders, guided by Hideki Tojo, decided to launch a surprise attack on U.S. and European colonies in Southeast Asia.

☑ **Reading Check** **Explaining** Why did Japan want to establish a New Order in East Asia?

**HISTORY Online** **Study Central**

For help with the concepts in this section of *Glencoe World History–Modern Times*, go to wh.mt.glencoe.com and click on **Study Central.**

# SECTION 1 ASSESSMENT

## Checking for Understanding

1. **Vocabulary** Define: labor, demilitarized, appeasement, achieve, conference, New Order, assume, sanction.

2. **People** Identify: Adolf Hitler, Benito Mussolini, Joseph Stalin, Chiang Kai-shek.

3. **Places** Locate: Rhineland, Sudetenland, Manchukuo.

### Reviewing Big Ideas

4. **List** the reasons why Hitler's pact with Stalin was a key factor in forcing Britain and France to declare war on Germany.

## Critical Thinking

5. **Historical Analysis** **Cause and Effect** In what sense was World War II a product of World War I? **CA HI 2**

6. **Sequencing Information** Create a chart like the one below listing in chronological order the agreements that emboldened Hitler in his aggressive expansion policies.

| Agreements Encouraging Hitler's Aggression Leading to World War II |
|---|
| |
| |
| |

## Analyzing Visuals

7. **Analyze** the illustration on page 537 to determine what opinion the artist had about Italy's alliance with Germany. What aspects of the illustration indicate that its creator and its publisher either did or did not support Hitler's relationship with Mussolini and Italy?

### Writing About History

8. **Persuasive Writing** Imagine you are the editor of a British newspaper in 1938. Write an editorial that captures the essence of your viewpoint on how war can be avoided. **CA** 10WA2.4a,c

# The Course of World War II

## Guide to Reading

### Section Preview
The devastation of the war was brought to an end by Allied perseverance, effective military operations, and Axis miscalculations.

**Main Idea**
- Germany used a "lightning war" to gain control of much of western and central Europe, but Britain was undefeated and German troops were stopped in Russia. (p. 542)
- The Japanese attack on Pearl Harbor outraged Americans and led to the entry of the United States into the war. (p. 544)
- The Allied forces stopped the advance of the Germans and the Japanese. (p. 546)

- Allied victories forced Germany and Japan to surrender unconditionally. (p. 548)

### Content Vocabulary
blitzkrieg, partisan

### Academic Vocabulary
isolationism, neutrality, indefinite

### People to Identify
Franklin D. Roosevelt, Douglas MacArthur, Winston Churchill, Harry S. Truman

### Places to Locate
Stalingrad, Midway Island, Normandy, Hiroshima

### Reading Objectives
1. Explain why the United States did not enter the war until 1941.
2. Identify the major events that helped end the war in Europe and Asia.

### Reading Strategy
**Cause and Effect** Create a chart like the one below listing key events during World War II and their effect on the outcome of the war.

| Event | Effect |
|-------|--------|
|       |        |
|       |        |
|       |        |
|       |        |

### Preview of Events

| ♦1939 | ♦1940 | ♦1941 | ♦1942 | ♦1943 | ♦1944 | ♦1945 |
|-------|-------|-------|-------|-------|-------|-------|

**1940**
Germans bomb British cities

**1942**
Japanese defeated at the Battle of Midway Island

**1943**
Germans defeated at Stalingrad

**1944**
Allied forces invade France on D-Day

## California Standards in This Section

*Reading this section will help you master these California History–Social Science standards.*

**10.8.3:** Identify and locate the Allied and Axis powers on a map and discuss the major turning points of the war, the principal theaters of conflict, key strategic decisions, and the resulting war conferences and political resolutions, with emphasis on the importance of geographic factors.

**10.8.4:** Describe the political, diplomatic, and military leaders during the war (e.g., Winston Churchill, Franklin Delano Roosevelt, Emperor Hirohito, Adolf Hitler, Benito Mussolini, Joseph Stalin, Douglas MacArthur, Dwight Eisenhower).

**10.8.6:** Discuss the human costs of war, with particular attention to the civilian and military losses in Russia, Germany, Britain, the United States, China, and Japan.

# Europe at War

**Main Idea** Germany used a "lightning war" to gain control of much of western and central Europe, but Britain was undefeated and German troops were stopped in Russia.

**Reading Connection** Have you ever been in the middle of two people fighting, but you refused to take a side? Read how the United States remained neutral even though the British asked for its help.

Hitler stunned Europe with the speed and efficiency of the German attack on Poland. His innovative **blitzkrieg,** or "lightning war," used armored columns, called panzer divisions, supported by airplanes. Each panzer division was a strike force of about 300 tanks with support forces. Hitler had committed Germans to a life-or-death struggle.

## *Voices from the Past*

No one described the sacrifices this struggle would demand better than Hitler himself. On September 1, 1939, after the attack on Poland began, Hitler addressed the German *Reichstag* with these words:

> ❝I do not want to be anything other than the first soldier of the German Reich. I have once more put on the uniform which was once most holy and precious to me. I shall only take it off after victory or I shall not live to see the end. . . . As a National Socialist and as a German soldier, I am going into this struggle strong in heart. My whole life has been nothing but a struggle for my people, for their revival, for Germany. . . . Just as I myself am ready to risk my life any time for my people and for Germany, so I demand the same of everyone else. But anyone who thinks that he can oppose this national commandment, whether directly or indirectly, will die! Traitors can expect death.❞

The forces of the blitzkrieg broke quickly through Polish lines and encircled the bewildered Polish troops. Regular infantry units then moved in to hold the newly conquered territory. Within four weeks, Poland had surrendered. On September 28, 1939, Germany and the Soviet Union divided Poland.

**Hitler's Early Victories** After a winter of waiting (called the "phony war"), Hitler resumed the attack on April 9, 1940, with another blitzkrieg against Denmark and Norway. One month later, on May 10, Germany launched an attack on the Netherlands, Belgium, and France. The main assault was through Luxembourg and the Ardennes (ahr•DEHN) Forest. German panzer divisions broke through weak French defensive positions there and raced across northern France.

French and British forces were taken by surprise when the Germans went around, instead of across, the Maginot Line—a series of concrete and steel fortifications armed with heavy artillery along France's border with Germany. The Germans' action split the Allied armies, trapping French troops and the entire British army on the beaches of Dunkirk. Only by the heroic efforts of the Royal Navy and civilians in private boats did the British manage to evacuate 338,000 Allied troops. Most of them were British.

The French signed an armistice on June 22. German armies now occupied about three-fifths of France. An authoritarian regime under German control was set up over the remainder of the country to the south of the parts of France the Nazis occupied. It was known as Vichy France and was led by an aged French hero of World War I, Marshal Henri Pétain. Germany was now in control of western and central Europe, but Britain had still not been defeated. After Dunkirk, the British appealed to the United States for help.

▼ *Hitler addresses the* Reichstag *on September 1, 1939.*

President **Franklin D. Roosevelt** denounced the aggressors, but the United States followed a strict policy of **isolationism.** A series of **neutrality** acts, passed in the 1930s, prevented the United States from taking sides or becoming involved in any European wars. Many Americans felt that the United States had been drawn into World War I due to economic involvement in Europe, and they wanted to prevent a recurrence. Roosevelt was convinced that the neutrality acts actually encouraged Axis aggression and wanted the acts repealed. They were gradually relaxed as the United States supplied food, ships, planes, and weapons to Britain.

## The Battle of Britain

Hitler realized that an amphibious (land-sea) invasion of Great Britain could succeed only if Germany gained control of the air over the island nation. At the beginning of August 1940, the Luftwaffe (LOOFT•vah•fuh)—the German air force—launched a major offensive. German planes bombed British air and naval bases, harbors, communication centers, and war industries.

The British fought back with determination. They were supported by an effective radar system that gave them early warning of attacks. Nevertheless, by the end of August, the British air force had suffered critical losses. In September, in retaliation for a British attack on Berlin, Hitler had the Luftwaffe begin massive bombing of British cities. Hitler hoped to break British morale. Instead, because military targets were not being hit, the British were able to rebuild their air strength quickly. Soon, the British air force was inflicting major losses on Luftwaffe bombers. At the end of September, Hitler postponed the invasion of Britain **indefinitely.**

▲ *London buildings collapse as a result of nightly German bombing.*

**Attack on the Soviet Union** Although he had no desire for a two-front war, Hitler was convinced that Britain stayed in the war only because it expected Soviet support. If the Soviet Union was smashed, Britain's last hope would be eliminated. Hitler was also convinced that the Soviet Union had a pitiful army and could be defeated quickly.

Hitler's invasion of the Soviet Union was scheduled for the spring of 1941, but the attack was delayed because of problems in the Balkans. Hitler had already gained the political cooperation of Hungary, Bulgaria, and Romania, but the failure of Mussolini's invasion of Greece in 1940 had exposed Hitler's southern flank to British air bases in Greece. To secure his Balkan flank, Hitler seized both Greece and Yugoslavia in April.

Reassured, Hitler invaded the Soviet Union on June 22, 1941, believing it could be decisively defeated before the brutal winter weather set in. The

**NORWAY**
**SWEDEN**
**FINLAND**

*ATLANTIC OCEAN*
*North Sea*

Leningrad (Sept. 1941–Jan. 1944)
• Moscow

**ESTONIA**
*Baltic Sea*
**LATVIA**
**LITHUANIA**

**SOVIET UNION**

**IRELAND**
**UNITED KINGDOM**
Liverpool • Manchester
Birmingham • Hull
Bristol • Coventry
Plymouth • London

**DENMARK**

Minsk (July 1944)
Kursk (July 1943)
Stalingrad (Aug. 1942– Feb. 1943)
*Volga R.*

Battle of Britain (July–Oct. 1940)
*English Channel*

Bremen • Hamburg
NETH. Berlin (Apr.– May 1945)
Rotterdam
Hanover
BELG. Düsseldorf
Cologne
Dresden
Frankfurt

**POLAND**
Warsaw (Aug. 1944–Jan. 1945)
• Kiev

Normandy (June 1944)
Battle of the Bulge (Dec. 1944–Jan. 1945)
Paris (Aug. 1944)
Mannheim
**GERMANY**
Stuttgart
Munich

**SLOVAKIA**
**AUSTRIA**
Budapest
**HUNGARY**

Vichy

SWITZ.

*Caspian Sea*

**FRANCE**

**ITALY**
Belgrade
**ROMANIA**
• Ploiesti

**PORTUGAL**

**SPAIN**

Corsica
Anzio (Jan.–Mar. 1944)
• Rome
Monte Cassino (Jan.–May 1944)
Sardinia

**YUGOSLAVIA**
**BULGARIA**
*Black Sea*

**ALBANIA** It.

**GREECE**

**TURKEY**

**IRAN**

**SP. MOROCCO**

*Mediterranean Sea*

Tunis (May 1943)
Malta • Valletta

Sicily (July 1943)

Crete

Cyprus

**SYRIA**

**IRAQ**

**MOROCCO**
North Africa Landings (Nov. 1942)

**TUNISIA**

El Alamein (Oct.– Nov. 1942)
Tobruk (April 1941)
Alexandria
• Cairo

**LEBANON**
**PALESTINE**
**TRANS-JORDAN**

**ALGERIA**

**LIBYA**

**EGYPT**

**SAUDI ARABIA**

| | Axis Powers | | Neutral nations |
| | Axis-controlled area, November 1942 | | Major battle with date |
| | Farthest Axis advance, December 1941 | | Major city severely damaged by bombing |
| | Vichy France and territories | | Air battle |
| | Allied Powers | | Maginot Line |
| | Allied-controlled area, November 1942 | | |

0  400 miles
0  400 kilometers
*Lambert Azimuthal Equal-Area projection*

---

massive attack stretched out along a front some 1,800 miles (about 2,900 km). German troops advanced rapidly, capturing two million Russian soldiers. By November, one German army group had swept through Ukraine. A second army was besieging the city of Leningrad, while a third threatened Moscow, the Soviet capital.

An early winter and fierce Soviet resistance, however, halted the German advance. Because of the planned spring date for the invasion, the Germans had no winter uniforms. For the first time in the war, German armies had been stopped. A counterattack in December 1941 by a Soviet army came as an ominous ending to the year for the Germans.

✓ **Reading Check** **Evaluating** In the spring of 1941, what caused Hitler to delay his invasion of the Soviet Union?

## Japan at War

**Main Idea** The Japanese attack on Pearl Harbor outraged Americans and led to the entry of the United States into the war. ⌐TURNING POINT⌐

**Reading Connection** Do you think the terrorist attacks of 2001 unified or divided Americans? Read to find out how the Japanese attack on Pearl Harbor affected American opinion about World War II.

On December 7, 1941, Japanese aircraft attacked the U.S. naval base at Pearl Harbor in the Hawaiian Islands. The same day, other Japanese units launched additional assaults on the Philippines and began advancing toward the British colony of Malaya.

## Geography *Skills*

Heavy fighting took place in Europe and North Africa.

1. **Interpreting Maps** Name at least six major land battles of the war in Europe. Which side, the Allies or the Axis Powers, was more aggressive at the beginning of the war? Summarize the changes in direction of this side's offensives during the first three years of the war.

2. **Applying Geography Skills** Using information from all of the maps on pages 544 and 545, create an imaginary model of the war's outcome had Hitler chosen not to invade the Soviet Union. Your model could take the form of a map, a chart, or a database and include such items as battles, offensives, and casualties.

Soon after, Japanese forces invaded the Dutch East Indies and occupied a number of islands in the Pacific Ocean. In some cases, as on the Bataan Peninsula and the island of Corregidor in the Philippines, resistance was fierce. By the spring of 1942, however, almost all of Southeast Asia and much of the western Pacific had fallen into Japanese hands.

A triumphant Japan now declared the creation of a community of nations. The name given to this new "community" was the Greater East Asia Co-Prosperity Sphere. The entire region would now be under Japanese direction.

Japan also announced its intention to liberate the colonial areas of Southeast Asia from Western colonial rule. For the moment, however, Japan needed the resources of the region for its war machine, and it

treated the countries under its rule as conquered lands.

Japanese leaders had hoped that their lightning strike at American bases would destroy the American fleet in the Pacific. The Roosevelt administration, they thought, would now accept Japanese domination of the Pacific. Why did the Japanese predict such a reaction from the United States government? The answer is that in the eyes of many Japanese leaders, the American people were soft. Their prosperous and easy life had made them unable to fight.

The Japanese miscalculated. The attack on Pearl Harbor unified American opinion. Up to this time, many Americans wanted to remain neutral. Now they were ready to become involved in the war. The United States now joined with European nations and Nationalist China in a combined effort to defeat Japan.

This decision quickly brought a declaration of war against the United States from the Nazis. The German navy had been fighting an undeclared sea war with American ships helping the British. Now that Hitler's ally Japan had attacked the United States, the long-expected war with America had come. Four days after the Pearl Harbor attack, Germany and the United States were at war. Another European conflict had turned into a global war.

**Reading Check** **Determining** Why did the Japanese attack Pearl Harbor?

CHAPTER 11    World War II    **545**

# World War II: Attack and Counterattack

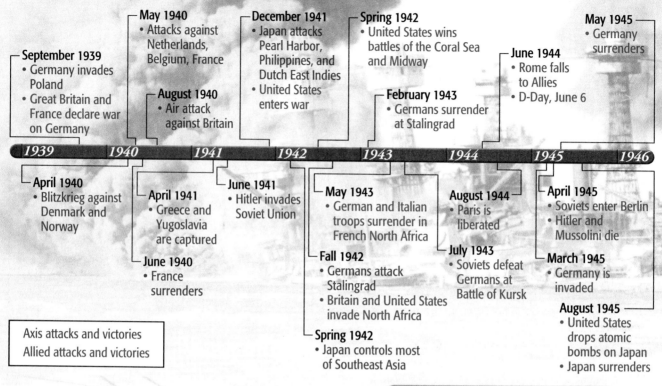

**September 1939**
• Germany invades Poland
• Great Britain and France declare war on Germany

**May 1940**
• Attacks against Netherlands, Belgium, France

**August 1940**
• Air attack against Britain

**December 1941**
• Japan attacks Pearl Harbor, Philippines, and Dutch East Indies
• United States enters war

**Spring 1942**
• United States wins battles of the Coral Sea and Midway

**February 1943**
• Germans surrender at Stalingrad

**June 1944**
• Rome falls to Allies
• D-Day, June 6

**May 1945**
• Germany surrenders

**April 1940**
• Blitzkrieg against Denmark and Norway

**April 1941**
• Greece and Yugoslavia are captured

**June 1941**
• Hitler invades Soviet Union

**May 1943**
• German and Italian troops surrender in French North Africa

**August 1944**
• Paris is liberated

**April 1945**
• Soviets enter Berlin
• Hitler and Mussolini die

**June 1940**
• France surrenders

**Fall 1942**
• Germans attack Stalingrad
• Britain and United States invade North Africa

**July 1943**
• Soviets defeat Germans at Battle of Kursk

**March 1945**
• Germany is invaded

**Spring 1942**
• Japan controls most of Southeast Asia

**August 1945**
• United States drops atomic bombs on Japan
• Japan surrenders

Axis attacks and victories
Allied attacks and victories

1939  1940  1941  1942  1943  1944  1945  1946

## The Allies Advance

**Main Idea** The Allied forces stopped the advance of the Germans and the Japanese.

**Reading Connection** Have you ever had to fight obstacles to achieve a goal? Read to find out how the Allied forces fought the Germans and the Japanese to work for the unconditional surrender of Germany and Japan.

The entry of the Americans into the war created a new coalition, the Grand Alliance: the United States, Great Britain, and the Soviet Union. Ever since the Russian Revolution of 1917, the Soviet Union had been relatively isolated from the West. Now they had to come together to fight a common enemy, Nazi Germany. To overcome mutual suspicions, the Allies agreed to stress military operations and ignore political differences.

At the beginning of 1943, the Allies agreed to fight until the Axis Powers—Germany, Italy, and Japan—surrendered unconditionally. The unconditional surrender principle, which required the Axis nations to surrender without any favorable condition, cemented the Grand Alliance by making it nearly impossible for Hitler to divide his foes.

**Graphic Organizer → Skills**

The time line above traces the major events of World War II.

1. **Identifying** How much time elapsed from France's defeat until Paris was liberated?

2. **Cause and Effect** What were the effects of three dramatic events in 1939, 1941, and 1945?

**The European Theater** Defeat was far from Hitler's mind at the beginning of 1942. As Japanese forces advanced into Southeast Asia and the Pacific, Hitler continued fighting the war in Europe against the armies of Britain and the Soviet Union.

Until late 1942, it appeared that the Germans might still prevail on the battlefield. In North Africa, Erwin Rommel, whose daring exploits and willingness to use trickery to outwit his foes had earned him the nickname "Desert Fox," commanded the Reich's Afrika Korps. Rommel's clever tactics helped the Germans break through the British defenses in Egypt and advance toward Alexandria. Meanwhile, a renewed German offensive in the Soviet Union led to the capture of the entire Crimea in the spring of 1942. In August, Hitler confidently boasted:

> 66As the next step, we are going to advance south of the Caucasus and then help the rebels in Iran and Iraq against the English. Another thrust will be directed along the Caspian Sea toward Afghanistan and India. Then the English will run out of oil. In two years we'll be on the borders of India. Twenty to thirty elite German divisions will do. Then the British Empire will collapse.99

This would be Hitler's last optimistic outburst. By the fall of 1942, the war had turned against the Germans.

In North Africa, British forces had stopped Rommel's troops at El Alamein (EL A•luh•MAYN) in the summer of 1942. The Germans then retreated back across the desert. In November 1942, British and American forces invaded French North Africa. They forced the German and Italian troops there to surrender in May 1943.

On the Eastern Front, after the capture of the Crimea, Hitler's generals wanted him to concentrate on the Caucasus and its oil fields. Hitler, however, decided that **Stalingrad,** a major industrial center on the Volga, should be taken first.

In perhaps the most terrible battle of the war, between November 1942 and February 2, 1943, the Soviets launched a counterattack. German troops were stopped, then encircled, and supply lines were cut off, all in frigid winter conditions. The Germans were forced to surrender at Stalingrad. The entire German Sixth Army, considered the best of the German troops, was lost.

By February 1943, German forces in Russia were back to their positions of June 1942. By the spring of 1943, even Hitler knew that the Germans would not defeat the Soviet Union.

**The Asian Theater** In 1942, the tide of battle in the East changed dramatically. In the Battle of the Coral Sea on May 7 and 8, 1942, American naval forces stopped the Japanese advance and saved Australia from the threat of invasion.

# CONNECTIONS Around The World

## Women as Spies in World War II

For thousands of years, governments have relied on spies to gather information about their enemies. Until the twentieth century, most spies were men. During World War II, however, many women became active in the world of espionage.

Yoshiko Kawashima was born in China but raised in Japan. In 1932, she was sent to China by Japanese authorities to gather information for the invasion of China. Disguised as a young man, Kawashima was an active and effective spy until her arrest by the Chinese in 1945. The Chinese news agency announced that "a long-sought-for beauty in male costume was arrested today in Beijing." She was executed soon after her arrest.

Hekmath Fathmy was an Egyptian dancer. Her hatred of the British, who had occupied Egypt, caused her to become a spy for the Germans. Fathmy sang and danced for British troops in the Kit Kat Club, a nightclub in Cairo. After shows, she took British officers to her houseboat on the banks of the Nile. Any information she was able to obtain from her guests was passed on to John Eppler, a German spy in Cairo. Eventually, she was caught, but she served only a year in prison for her spying activities.

Violette Szabo of French/English background became a spy after her husband died fighting the Germans in North Africa. She joined Special Operations Executive, an arm of British Intelligence, and was sent to France several times. In August 1944, she parachuted into France to spy on the Germans. Caught by Gestapo forces at Salon La Tour, she was tortured and then shipped to Ravensbruck, a women's concentration camp near Berlin. She was executed there in April 1945.

▲ *Violette Szabo spied for the Allies to avenge her husband's death.*

## Comparing Cultures

People have different motives for becoming spies. List several motives that might draw someone to espionage. Do you think the motives are different in peacetime? Investigate current espionage activities using the Internet or library. What various methods do governments use today to gather intelligence?

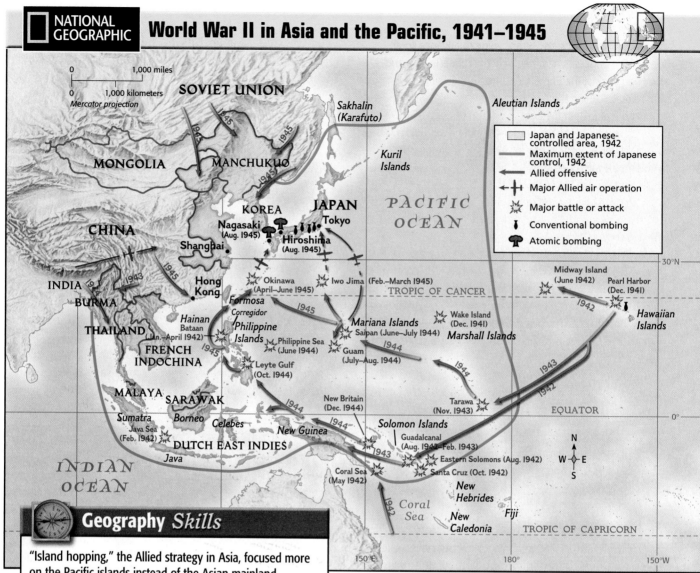

## World War II in Asia and the Pacific, 1941–1945

NATIONAL GEOGRAPHIC

**Legend:**
- Japan and Japanese-controlled area, 1942
- Maximum extent of Japanese control, 1942
- Allied offensive
- Major Allied air operation
- Major battle or attack
- Conventional bombing
- Atomic bombing

0    1,000 miles
0    1,000 kilometers
*Mercator projection*

SOVIET UNION

Sakhalin (Karafuto)

Aleutian Islands

MONGOLIA    MANCHUKUO

Kuril Islands

KOREA    JAPAN

PACIFIC OCEAN

CHINA    Nagasaki (Aug. 1945)    Tokyo
Shanghai    Hiroshima (Aug. 1945)

Hong Kong    Okinawa (April–June 1945)    Iwo Jima (Feb.–March 1945)    TROPIC OF CANCER    Midway Island (June 1942)    Pearl Harbor (Dec. 1941)    30°N

INDIA    Formosa    Hawaiian Islands
BURMA    Corregidor    Mariana Islands    Wake Island (Dec. 1941)
Hainan    Philippine    Saipan (June–July 1944)    Marshall Islands
THAILAND    Bataan (Jan.–April 1942)    Islands    Philippine Sea (June 1944)
FRENCH INDOCHINA    Guam (July–Aug. 1944)
Leyte Gulf (Oct. 1944)

MALAYA    SARAWAK    Tarawa (Nov. 1943)    EQUATOR    0°
Sumatra    Borneo    Celebes    New Britain (Dec. 1944)
Java Sea (Feb. 1942)    New Guinea    Solomon Islands
DUTCH EAST INDIES    Guadalcanal (Aug. 1942–Feb. 1943)
Java    Eastern Solomons (Aug. 1942)
INDIAN OCEAN    Coral Sea (May 1942)    Santa Cruz (Oct. 1942)    N W-E S
New Hebrides
Coral Sea    Fiji
New Caledonia    TROPIC OF CAPRICORN

150°E    180°    150°W

### Geography Skills

"Island hopping," the Allied strategy in Asia, focused more on the Pacific islands instead of the Asian mainland.

1. **Interpreting Maps** What was the approximate distance from Japan to its farthest point of control?

2. **Applying Geography Skills** Compare this map to the maps in the chapter on the war in Europe. Then analyze the effects of geographic factors on the major events in the two different theaters of war.

The turning point of the war in Asia came on June 4, at the Battle of **Midway Island.** U.S. planes destroyed four attacking Japanese aircraft carriers. The United States defeated the Japanese navy and established naval superiority in the Pacific.

By the fall of 1942, Allied forces in Asia were gathering for two operations. One, commanded by U.S. general **Douglas MacArthur,** would move into the Philippines through New Guinea and the South Pacific Islands. The other would move across the Pacific with a combination of U.S. Army, Marine, and Navy attacks on Japanese-held islands. The policy was to capture some Japanese-held islands and

bypass others, "island hopping" up to Japan. After a series of bitter engagements in the waters off the Solomon Islands from August to November 1942, Japanese fortunes were fading.

**Reading Check** **Summarizing** Why was the German assault on Stalingrad a crushing defeat for the Germans?

## Last Years of the War

**Main Idea** Allied victories forced Germany and Japan to surrender unconditionally.

**Reading Connection** In wartime, does the end justify the means? Read to learn about President Truman's decision to use the atomic bomb.

By the beginning of 1943, the tide of battle had turned against Germany, Italy, and Japan. Axis forces in Tunisia surrendered on May 13, 1943. The Allies then crossed the Mediterranean and carried the war to Italy, an area that **Winston Churchill** had called the "soft underbelly" of Europe. After taking Sicily, Allied troops began an invasion of mainland Italy in September.

## The European Theater

After the fall of Sicily, Mussolini was removed from office and placed under arrest by Victor Emmanuel III, king of Italy. A new Italian government offered to surrender to the Allied forces. However, Mussolini was liberated by the Germans in a daring raid and then set up as the head of a puppet German state in northern Italy. At the same time, German troops moved in and occupied much of Italy.

The Germans set up effective new defensive lines in the hills south of Rome. The Allied advance up the Italian Peninsula turned into a painstaking affair with very heavy casualties. Rome did not fall to the Allies until June 4, 1944. By that time, the Italian war had assumed a secondary role as the Allied forces opened their long-awaited "second front" in western Europe.

Since the autumn of 1943, the Allies had been planning an invasion of France from Great Britain, across the English Channel. Finally, on June 6, 1944 (D-Day), Allied forces under U.S. general Dwight D. Eisenhower landed on the beaches of **Normandy** in history's greatest naval invasion. The Allies fought their way past underwater mines, barbed wire, and horrible machine-gun fire. There was heavy German resistance even though the Germans thought the battle was a diversion and the real invasion would occur elsewhere. Their slow response enabled the Allied forces to set up a beachhead. Within three months, the Allies had landed two million men and a half million vehicles. Allied forces then pushed inland and broke through German defensive lines.

After the breakout, Allied troops moved south and east. In Paris, resistance fighters rose up against the occupying Germans. The Allies liberated Paris by the end of August. In March 1945, they crossed the Rhine River and advanced into Germany. At the end of April 1945, Allied armies in northern Germany moved toward the Elbe River, where they linked up with the Soviets.

The Soviets had come a long way since the Battle of Stalingrad in 1943. In the summer of 1943, Hitler gambled on taking the offensive using newly developed heavy tanks. German forces were soundly defeated by the Soviets at the Battle of Kursk (July 5 to 12), the greatest tank battle of World War II.

Soviet forces now began a steady advance westward. They had reoccupied Ukraine by the end of 1943 and moved into the Baltic states by the beginning of 1944. Advancing along a northern front, Soviet troops occupied Warsaw in January 1945 and entered Berlin in April. Meanwhile, Soviet troops, along a southern front, swept through Hungary, Romania, and Bulgaria.

By January 1945, Adolf Hitler had moved into a bunker 55 feet (almost 17 m) under the city of Berlin to direct the final stages of the war. In his final political testament, Hitler, consistent to the end in his anti-Semitism, blamed the world's Jews for the war. He wrote, "Above all I charge the leaders of the nation and those under them to scrupulous observance of

## People In History

### Winston Churchill
**1874–1965**
**British prime minister**

Winston Churchill was Great Britain's wartime leader. At the beginning of the war, Churchill had already had a long political career. He had advocated a hardline policy toward Nazi Germany in the 1930s. On May 10, 1940, he became British prime minister.

Churchill was confident that he could guide Britain to ultimate victory. "I thought I knew a great deal about it all," he later wrote, "and I was sure I should not fail." Churchill proved to be an inspiring leader who rallied the British people with stirring speeches: "We shall fight on the beaches, we shall fight on the landing grounds, in the fields, in the streets, and in the hills. We shall never surrender." *Time* magazine designated Churchill the Man of the Year in 1940 and named him the Man of the Half Century in 1950.

| Battle Deaths in World War II | |
|---|---|
| **Country** | **Battle Deaths** |
| USSR | 7,500,000 |
| Germany | 3,500,000 |
| Yugoslavia | 410,000 |
| Poland | 320,000 |
| Romania | 300,000 |
| United States | 292,000 |
| United Kingdom | 245,000 |
| France | 210,000 |
| Hungary | 140,000 |
| Finland | 82,000 |
| Italy | 77,000 |
| Greece | 74,000 |
| Canada | 37,000 |

the laws of race and to merciless opposition to the universal poisoner of all peoples, international Jewry."

Hitler committed suicide on April 30, two days after Mussolini had been shot by Italian **partisans,** or resistance fighters. On May 7, 1945, German commanders surrendered. The war in Europe was finally over.

**The Asian Theater** The war in Asia continued. Beginning in 1943, U.S. forces had gone on the offensive and advanced, slowly at times, across the Pacific. As Allied military power drew closer to the main Japanese islands in the first months of 1945, **Harry S. Truman,** who had become president on the death of Roosevelt in April, had a difficult decision to make.

Should he use newly developed atomic weapons to bring the war to an end or find another way to defeat the Japanese forces?

Using atomic weapons would, Truman hoped, enable the United States to avoid an invasion of Japan. The Japanese had made extensive preparations to defend their homeland. Truman and his advisers had become convinced that American troops would suffer heavy casualties if they invaded Japan. At the time, however, only two bombs were available, and no one knew how effective they would be.

Truman decided to use the bombs. The first bomb was dropped on the Japanese city of **Hiroshima** on August 6. Three days later, a second bomb was dropped on Nagasaki. Both cities were leveled. Thousands of people died immediately, and thousands more died later from radiation. Emperor Hirohito now stepped in and forced the Japanese military leaders to surrender unconditionally, which they did on August 14.

World War II was finally over. Seventeen million had died in battle. Perhaps 20 million civilians had perished as well. Some estimates place total losses at 50 million.

**✓Reading Check** **Evaluating** Why is the invasion of Normandy considered one of history's greatest naval invasions?

**HISTORY Online** **Study Central**

For help with the concepts in this section of *Glencoe World History–Modern Times,* go to wh.mt.glencoe.com and click on **Study Central.**

# SECTION 2 ASSESSMENT

### Checking for Understanding
1. **Vocabulary** Define: blitzkrieg, isolationism, neutrality, indefinite, partisan.

2. **People** Identify: Franklin D. Roosevelt, Douglas MacArthur, Winston Churchill, Harry S. Truman.

3. **Places** Locate: Stalingrad, Midway Island, Normandy, Hiroshima.

### Reviewing Big Ideas
4. **Explain** Hitler's strategy of attacking the Soviet Union. Why did his delay in launching the attack ultimately contribute to the Soviet victory over the Germans?

### Critical Thinking
5. **Historical Analysis** **Evaluating** How might the Allied demand for unconditional surrender have helped Hitler maintain control over Germany? **CA HR 3**

6. **Sequencing Information** Using a chart like the one below, place the events of World War II in chronological order.

| Year | Country | Event |
|---|---|---|
| 1939 | | |
| | | |
| | | |

### Analyzing Visuals
7. **Examine** the photo on page 543 showing the destruction caused by the Luftwaffe's bombing raids on London. Explain how this strategy of Hitler's hurt, rather than helped, Germany's efforts.

### Writing About History
8. **Descriptive Writing** Imagine you lived in California during World War II. Write an essay about your expectations of a Japanese invasion of California. You can choose to believe that an invasion was possible or impossible. **CA 10WA2.1**

# The New Order and the Holocaust

## Section Preview
Devastation and suffering resulted during World War II when Germany set up a New Order in Europe and Japan set up a Greater East Asia Co-Prosperity Sphere in Asia.

**Main Idea**
- The German conquest of continental Europe forced millions of native peoples to labor for the Nazi war machine. (p. 552)
- Adolf Hitler's philosophy of Aryan superiority led to the Holocaust. (p. 553)

- The Japanese conquest of Southeast Asia forced millions of native peoples to work for the Japanese war machine. (p. 556)

## Content Vocabulary
genocide, collaborator

## Academic Vocabulary
implement, adjust

## People to Identify
Heinrich Himmler, Reinhard Heydrich

## Places to Locate
Poland, Auschwitz

## Reading Objectives
1. Describe how the Nazis carried out their Final Solution.
2. Explain how the Japanese created a dilemma for nationalists in the lands they occupied.

## Reading Strategy
**Compare and Contrast** Using a Venn diagram like the one below, compare and contrast the New Order of Germany with the New Order of Japan.

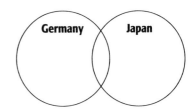

Germany    Japan

## Preview of Events

| ◆1940 | ◆1941 | ◆1942 | ◆1943 | ◆1944 | ◆1945 |
|---|---|---|---|---|---|

**1941**
*Einsatzgruppen* active in Poland

**1942**
Two million ethnic Germans resettled in Poland

**1943**
Japan uses forced labor to build Burma-Thailand railroad

**1944**
Nazis continue Final Solution even as they start losing the war

## California Standards in This Section

*Reading this section will help you master these California History–Social Science standards.*

**10.8.5:** Analyze the Nazi policy of pursuing racial purity, especially against the European Jews; its transformation into the Final Solution; and the Holocaust that resulted in the murder of six million Jewish civilians.

**10.8.6:** Discuss the human costs of the war, with particular attention to the civilian and military losses in Russia, Germany, Britain, the United States, China, and Japan.

# The New Order in Europe

**Main Idea** The German conquest of continental Europe forced millions of native peoples to labor for the Nazi war machine.

**Reading Connection** Did you know that four million enslaved African Americans were freed after the Civil War in the United States? Read to learn about the Nazi plan to use slave labor.

In 1942, the Nazi regime stretched across continental Europe from the English Channel in the west to the outskirts of Moscow in the east. Nazi Europe was usually organized in one of two ways. Some areas, such as western Poland, were directly annexed and made into German provinces. Most of occupied Europe, however, was run by German military or civilian officials with help from local people willing to collaborate with the Nazis. Because the Nazis controlled all Europe, they were able to carry out one of the most horrible atrocities in human history—the murder of some six million Jews, as well as other people they judged unfit for the new German Reich.

## *Voices from the Past*

Many of Europe's Jews perished in the death camps. The most notorious was at Auschwitz where Rudolf Höss was the commanding officer. Höss described what happened to Jews when they arrived at the camp:

> ❝We had two SS doctors on duty at Auschwitz to examine the incoming transports of prisoners. The prisoners would be marched by one of the doctors who would make spot decisions as they walked by. Those who were fit for work were sent into the camp. Others were sent immediately to the extermination plants. Children of tender years were invariably exterminated since by reason of their youth they were unable to work. . . . At Auschwitz we fooled the victims into thinking that they were to go through a delousing process. Frequently they realized our true intentions and we sometimes had riots and difficulties due to that fact.❞

The camps were the final stage of genocide, but the Nazi plan for exterminating the Jews began with the movement of Jews and other "undesirables."

**Resettlement in the East** Nazi administration in the conquered lands to the east was especially ruthless. These lands were seen as the living space for German expansion. They were populated, Nazis thought, by racially inferior Slavic peoples. Hitler's plans for an Aryan racial empire were so important to him that he and the Nazis began to **implement** their racial program soon after the conquest of **Poland.**

**Heinrich Himmler,** the leader of the SS, was put in charge of German resettlement plans in the east. Himmler's task was to move the Slavic peoples out and replace them with Germans. Slavic peoples included Czech, Polish, Serbo-Croatian, Slovene, and Ukrainian. This policy was first applied to the new German provinces created from the lands of western Poland.

One million Poles were uprooted and transferred to southern Poland. Hundreds of thousands of ethnic Germans (descendants of Germans who had migrated years ago from Germany to different parts of southern and eastern Europe) were brought in to colonize the German provinces in Poland. By 1942, two million ethnic Germans had been settled in Poland.

The invasion of the Soviet Union made the Nazis even more excited about German colonization in the east. Hitler spoke to his intimate circle of a colossal project of social engineering after the war. Poles, Ukrainians, and Russians would be removed from their lands and become slave labor. German peasants would settle on the abandoned lands and "Germanize" them.

Himmler told a gathering of SS officers that 30 million Slavs might die in order to achieve German

*Rudolf Höss*

## Anne Frank
**1929–1945**
**Dutch Holocaust victim**

Anne Frank was one of the millions of victims of the Holocaust. When the Nazis began to round up Jews in the Netherlands, the Frank family, along with another family, moved into a secret annex above a warehouse owned by the family business. Employees of the Frank family provided food and a lifeline to the outside world.

Anne remained hopeful. She kept a diary to while away the time spent in hiding. On July 15, 1944, she wrote, "In spite of everything I still believe that people are really good at heart."

On August 4, 1944, the Nazis found the secret annex of the Frank family. Anne and her sister were sent to Bergen-Belsen, a concentration camp in Germany. There they died of typhus. Anne's father, Otto Frank, who survived, later found Anne's diary. Published in 1947, *The Diary of Anne Frank* became an international best-seller.

plans in the east. He continued, "Whether nations live in prosperity or starve to death interests me only insofar as we need them as slaves for our culture. Otherwise it is of no interest."

**Slave Labor in Germany** German labor shortages led to a policy of rounding up foreign workers. In 1942, a special office was set up to recruit labor for German enterprises. By mid-1944, seven million Europeans were working in Germany. Another seven million workers were forced to labor for the Nazis in their own countries, sometimes in military camps.

The use of forced labor often caused problems, however. Sending so many workers to Germany disrupted industrial production in the occupied countries that could have helped Germany. Then, too, the brutal way in which Germany recruited foreign workers led more and more people to resist the Nazi occupation forces.

**Reading Check** **Describing** What was Hitler's vision for the residents of eastern Europe?

## The Holocaust

**Main Idea** Adolf Hitler's philosophy of Aryan superiority led to the Holocaust.

**Reading Connection** Have you seen films about the Holocaust? Read to find out how the Nazis planned to exterminate the Jews.

No aspect of the Nazi New Order was more terrifying than the deliberate attempt to exterminate the Jews. Racial struggle was a key element in Hitler's world of ideas. To him, racial struggle was a clearly defined conflict of opposites. On one side were Hitler's "master German race," creators of human progress. On the other side were the Jews, parasites, in Hitler's view, who were trying to destroy Germans and control the world.

Himmler and the SS closely shared Hitler's racial ideas. The SS was given responsibility for what the Nazis called their Final Solution to the Jewish problem. The Final Solution was **genocide,** the physical extermination of the Jewish people.

**The *Einsatzgruppen*** **Reinhard Heydrich,** head of the SS's Security Service, was given the task of administering the Final Solution. Heydrich created special strike forces, called *Einsatzgruppen*, to carry out the Nazi plans for the extermination of the Jews. After the defeat of Poland, he ordered these forces to round up all Polish Jews and put them in ghettos set up in a number of Polish cities.

Conditions in the ghettos were horrible. Families were crowded together in unsanitary housing. The Nazis attempted to starve residents by allowing only minimal amounts of food. Despite suffering, residents tried to **adjust,** and some ghettos organized resistance against the Nazis.

In June 1941, the *Einsatzgruppen* were given the new job of acting as mobile killing units. These SS death squads followed the regular army's advance into the Soviet Union. Their job was to round up Jews in their villages, execute them, and bury them in mass graves. The graves were often giant pits dug by the victims themselves before they were shot.

The leader of one death squad described their methods:

> 66 The unit selected for this task would enter a village or city and order the prominent Jewish citizens to call together all Jews for the purpose of resettlement. They were requested to hand over their valuables to the leaders of the unit, and shortly before the execution to surrender their outer clothing. The men, women, and children were led to a place of execution which in most cases was located next to a more deeply excavated anti-tank ditch. Then they were shot, kneeling or standing, and the corpses thrown into the ditch. 99

**The Death Camps** Probably one million Jews were killed by the *Einsatzgruppen*. As appalling as that sounds, it was too slow by Nazi standards. They decided to kill the European Jewish population in specially built death camps.

Beginning in 1942, Jews from countries occupied by Germany (or sympathetic to Germany) were rounded up, packed like cattle into freight trains, and shipped to Poland. Six extermination centers were built in Poland for this purpose. The largest was **Auschwitz** (OWSH•VIHTS).

About 30 percent of the arrivals at Auschwitz were sent to a labor camp, where many were starved or worked to death. The remainder went to the gas chambers. Some inmates were subjected to cruel and painful "medical" experiments.

By the spring of 1942, the death camps were in full operation. First priority was given to the elimination of the ghettos in Poland. By the summer of 1942, however, Jews were also being shipped from France, Belgium, and Holland. Even as the Allies were winning the war in 1944, Jews were being shipped from Greece and Hungary. Despite desperate military needs, even late in the war when Germany faced

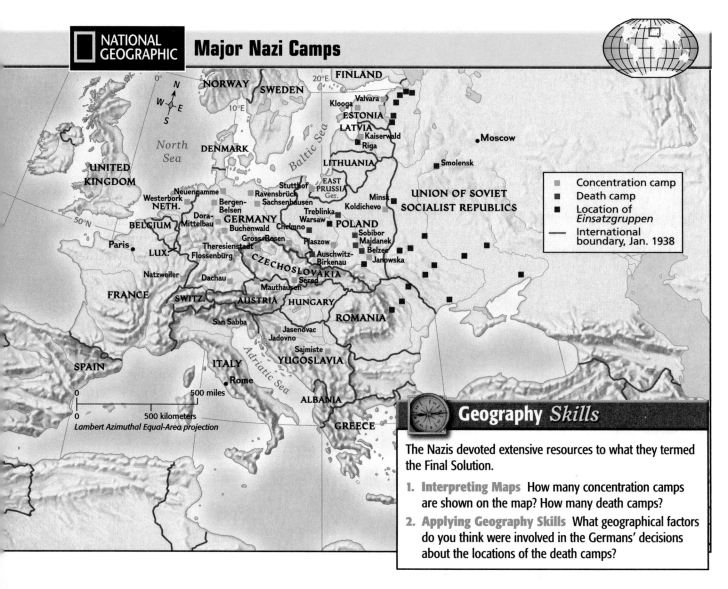

**NATIONAL GEOGRAPHIC Major Nazi Camps**

**Geography** *Skills*

The Nazis devoted extensive resources to what they termed the Final Solution.

1. **Interpreting Maps** How many concentration camps are shown on the map? How many death camps?
2. **Applying Geography Skills** What geographical factors do you think were involved in the Germans' decisions about the locations of the death camps?

▲ *Jews from the Warsaw ghetto surrendering after their rebellion in 1943*

utter defeat, the Final Solution had priority in using railroad cars to ship Jews to death camps.

**The Death Toll** The Germans killed between five and six million Jews, over three million of them in the death camps. Virtually 90 percent of the Jewish populations of Poland, the Baltic countries, and Germany were killed. Overall, the Holocaust was responsible for the death of nearly two out of every three European Jews.

The Nazis were also responsible for the deliberate death by shooting, starvation, or overwork of at least another nine to ten million non-Jewish people. The Nazis considered the Roma, sometimes known as Gypsies, to be an alien race. The Roma were rounded up for mass killing. About 40 percent of Europe's one million Roma were killed in the death camps.

The leading citizens of the Slavic peoples—the clergy, intellectuals, civil leaders, judges, and lawyers—were arrested and killed. Probably an additional four million Poles, Ukrainians, and Belorussians lost their lives as slave laborers for Nazi Germany. Finally, at least three million to four million Soviet prisoners of war were killed in captivity.

This mass slaughter of European civilians, particularly European Jews, is known as the Holocaust. Jews in and out of the camps attempted to resist the Nazis. Some were aided by friends and even strangers, hidden in villages or smuggled into safe areas. Foreign diplomats would try to save Jews by issuing exit visas. The nation of Denmark saved almost its entire Jewish population.

Some people did not believe the accounts of death camps because, during World War I, the Allies had greatly exaggerated German atrocities to arouse enthusiasm for the war. Most often, people pretended not to notice what was happening. Even worse, **collaborators** (people who assisted the enemy) helped the Nazis hunt down Jews. The Allies were aware of the concentration camps and death camps but chose to concentrate on ending the war. Not until after the war did they learn the full extent of the horror and inhumanity of the Holocaust. 📖 *(See page 775 to read an excerpt from a French doctor's description of the Holocaust in the Primary Sources Library.)*

**Children in the War** Young people of all ages were also victims of World War II. Because they were unable to work, Jewish children, along with their mothers, were the first ones selected for the gas

**HISTORY Online Web Activity**

Visit the *Glencoe World History—Modern Times* Web site at wh.mt.glencoe.com and click on **Chapter 11– Student Web Activity** to learn more about concentration camps.

chambers upon their arrival in the death camps of Poland. Young Jewish males soon learned to look as adult as possible in order to survive. Altogether, 1.2 million Jewish children died in the Holocaust.

Many children were evacuated from cities during the war in order to avoid the bombing. The Germans created about 9,000 camps for children in the countryside. In Japan, 15,000 children were evacuated from Hiroshima before its destruction. The British moved about 6 million children and their mothers in 1939. Some British parents even sent their children to Canada and the United States. This, too, could be dangerous. When the ocean liner *Arandora Star* was hit by a German torpedo, it had 77 British children on board. They never made it to Canada.

Children evacuated to the countryside did not always see their parents again. Some of them, along with many other children, became orphaned when their parents were killed. In 1945, there were perhaps 13 million orphaned children in Europe.

In eastern Europe, children especially suffered under the harsh occupation policies of the Germans. All secondary schools in German-occupied eastern Europe were closed. Their facilities and equipment were destroyed.

Heinrich Himmler, head of the SS, said of these Slavic children that their education should consist only "in teaching simple arithmetic up to 500, the writing of one's name, and that God has ordered obedience to the Germans, honesty, diligence, and politeness. I do not consider an ability to read as necessary."

At times, young people were expected to carry the burden of fighting the war. In the last year of the war, Hitler Youth members, often only 14 or 15 years old, could be found in the front lines. In the Soviet Union, children as young as 13 or 14 spied on German positions and worked with the resistance movement. Some were even given decorations for killing the enemy.

✓ **Reading Check** **Summarizing** What was the Nazis' Final Solution?

## The New Order in Asia

**Main Idea** The Japanese conquest of Southeast Asia forced millions of native peoples to work for the Japanese war machine.

**Reading Connection** How would you feel if you were separated from your family and forced to work for a foreign country? Read to learn about the Japanese policies in the occupied areas of Southeast Asia.

Japanese war policy in the areas in Asia occupied by Japan was basically defensive. Japan hoped to use its new possessions to meet its need for raw materials, and also as an outlet for manufactured goods. To organize these possessions, Japanese leaders included them in the Greater East Asia Co-Prosperity Sphere, the economic community supposedly designed to provide benefits to the occupied areas and the home country.

**Japanese Policies** The Japanese had conquered Southeast Asia under the slogan "Asia for the Asiatics." Japanese officials in occupied territories quickly made contact with anticolonialists. They promised the people that local governments would be established under Japanese control. Such governments were eventually set up in Burma, the Dutch East Indies, Vietnam, and the Philippines.

*Picturing* **History**

American and Filipino prisoners of war were held in the Philippines. What role did prisoners of war play in the Japanese war effort?

In fact, real power rested with Japanese military authorities in each territory. In turn, the local Japanese military command was directly subordinated to the Army General Staff in Tokyo. The economic resources of the colonies were used for the benefit of the Japanese war machine. The native peoples in occupied lands were recruited to serve in local military units or were forced to work on public works projects.

In some cases, these policies brought severe hardships to peoples living in the occupied areas. In Vietnam, for example, local Japanese authorities forcibly took rice and shipped it abroad. This led directly to a food shortage that caused over a million Vietnamese to starve to death in 1944 and 1945.

**Japanese Behavior** At first, many Southeast Asian nationalists took Japanese promises at face value and agreed to cooperate with the Japanese authorities. In Burma, for example, an independent government was set up in 1943 and declared war on the Allies. Eventually, the nature of Japanese occupation policies became clear, and sentiment turned against Japan.

Japanese officials provoked such attitudes by their arrogance and contempt for local customs. In the Dutch East Indies, for example, Indonesians were required to bow in the direction of Tokyo and to recognize the divinity of the Japanese emperor. In Burma, Buddhist pagodas were used as military latrines.

Like German soldiers in occupied Europe, Japanese military forces often had little respect for the lives of their subject peoples. After their conquest of Nanjing, China, in 1937, Japanese soldiers spent several days killing, raping, and looting. After the conquest

of Korea, almost 800,000 Korean people were sent to Japan, most as forced laborers.

In construction projects to help their war effort, the Japanese made extensive use of labor forces composed of both prisoners of war and local peoples. In building the Burma-Thailand railway in 1943, for example, the Japanese used 61,000 Australian, British, and Dutch prisoners of war and almost 300,000 workers from Burma, Malaya, Thailand, and the Dutch East Indies. An inadequate diet and appalling work conditions in an unhealthy climate led to the death of 12,000 Allied prisoners of war and 90,000 workers by the time the railway was completed.

Such Japanese behavior created a dilemma for nationalists in occupied countries. They had no desire to see the return of the colonial powers, but they did not like what the Japanese were doing. Some turned against the Japanese. Others simply did nothing.

Indonesian patriots tried to have it both ways. They pretended to support Japan while actually sabotaging the Japanese administration. In French Indochina, Ho Chi Minh's Communist Party made contact with U.S. military units in southern China. The Communists agreed to provide information on Japanese troop movements and to rescue downed American fliers in the area. By the end of the war, little support remained in the region for the Japanese "liberators."

✓**Reading Check** **Examining** What was Japan's war policy in the occupied areas of Southeast Asia?

**HISTORY** **Study Central**
*Online*

For help with the concepts in this section of *Glencoe World History–Modern Times,* go to **wh.mt.glencoe.com** and click on **Study Central.**

# SECTION 3 ASSESSMENT

### Checking for Understanding

1. **Vocabulary** Define: implement, genocide, adjust, collaborator.

2. **People** Identify: Heinrich Himmler, Reinhard Heydrich.

3. **Places** Locate: Poland, Auschwitz.

### Reviewing Big Ideas

4. **Explain** what the Nazis meant by the Final Solution. How did Hitler's commitment to the Final Solution hinder Germany's war effort?

### Critical Thinking

5. **Historical Analysis** **Evaluating** What was the impact of the Holocaust on history? What lessons does the Holocaust have for us today? **CA HR 3**

6. **Cause and Effect** Create a chart giving examples of Hitler's actions to create a New World Order in Europe and the outcome of his efforts.

| Hitler's Actions | Outcome |
|---|---|
| | |
| | |

### Analyzing Visuals

7. **Examine** the scene pictured on page 555. Based on your reading, describe the series of events that will most likely follow.

## Writing About History

8. **Persuasive Writing** Imagine you are a member of Hitler's inner circle who is alarmed about the Final Solution. Compose a letter to Hitler, outlining why he should abandon plans to send Jews to the death camps. **CA 10WA2.4a,c**

# The Home Front and the Aftermath of the War

## Guide to Reading

### Section Preview

In the wake of World War II, a new set of Cold War problems faced the international community.

**Main Idea**

- The Soviet Union, the United States, Germany, and Japan all mobilized for the war with an emphasis on personal sacrifice. (p. 559)
- The bombing of cities in Britain, Germany, and Japan destroyed buildings and killed thousands of civilians. (p. 562)
- Political tensions, suspicions, and a conflict of ideas led the United States and the Soviet Union into the Cold War. (p. 563)

### Content Vocabulary

mobilization, kamikaze, Cold War

### Academic Vocabulary

impact, alternative

### People to Identify

Albert Speer, General Hideki Tojo

### Places to Locate

London, Dresden

### Reading Objectives

1. Explain why the Japanese were encouraged to serve as kamikaze pilots.
2. Describe the outcome of the Yalta Conference in 1945.

### Reading Strategy

**Compare and Contrast** Create a chart like the one below comparing and contrasting the impact of World War II on the lives of civilians.

| Country | Impact on Lives of Civilians |
|---|---|
| Soviet Union | |
| United States | |
| Japan | |
| Germany | |

### Preview of Events

| ◆1942 | ◆1943 | ◆1944 | ◆1945 | ◆1946 | ◆1947 |
|---|---|---|---|---|---|

**1942**
Major bombing raids on German cities begin

**1943**
Stalin, Roosevelt, and Churchill meet in Tehran to determine future course of war

**1945**
Allies bomb Dresden

**1946**
Churchill proclaims existence of "iron curtain" in Europe

## California Standards in This Section

*Reading this section will help you master these California History–Social Science standards.*

**10.8.3:** Identify and locate the Allied and Axis powers on a map and discuss the major turning points of the war, the principal theaters of conflict, key strategic decisions, and the resulting war conferences and political resolutions, with emphasis on the importance of geographic factors.

**10.8.4:** Describe the political, diplomatic, and military leaders during the war (e.g., Winston Churchill, Franklin Delano Roosevelt, Emperor Hirohito, Adolf Hitler, Benito Mussolini, Joseph Stalin, Douglas MacArthur, Dwight Eisenhower).

**10.9.1:** Compare the economic and military power shifts caused by the war, including the Yalta Pact, the development of nuclear weapons, Soviet control over Eastern European nations, and the economic recoveries of Germany and Japan.

# The Mobilization of Peoples: Four Examples

**Main Idea** The Soviet Union, the United States, Germany, and Japan all mobilized for the war with an emphasis on personal sacrifice.

**Reading Connection** Can you think of a time when you felt all citizens should cooperate in a national crisis? Read on to understand the feelings of sacrifice during the crisis of the Second World War.

Even more than World War I, World War II was a total war. Fighting was much more widespread and covered most of the world. Outside of the damage done to Japanese cities in the last month of the war in Asia, German cities were the hardest hit.

## *Voices from the Past*

A German civilian described an Allied bombing raid on Hamburg in 1943:

❝As the many fires broke through the roofs of the burning buildings, a column of heated air rose more than two and a half miles high and one and a half miles in diameter. . . . This column was fed from its base by in-rushing cooler ground-surface air. One and one half miles from the fires this draft increased the wind velocity from eleven to thirty-three miles per hour. At the edge of the area the velocities must have been much greater, as trees three feet in diameter were uprooted. In a short time the temperature reached ignition point for all combustibles, and the entire area was ablaze. In such fires, complete burnout occurred, that is, no trace of combustible material remained.❞

The bombing of civilians made the home front far more dangerous than in previous wars. The home front was also more affected by economic **mobilization,** the act of assembling and preparing for war. Mobilization affected women far more than in other wars. Finally, the number of civilians killed—almost 20 million—was far higher. Many of these victims were children.

World War II had an enormous **impact** on civilian life in the Soviet Union, the United States, Germany, and Japan. We consider the home fronts of those four nations next.

**The Soviet Union** The initial defeats of the Soviet Union led to drastic emergency measures that affected the lives of the civilian population. Leningrad, for example, experienced nine hundred days of siege. Its inhabitants became so desperate for food that they ate dogs, cats, and mice. Probably 1.5 million people died in the city.

As the German army made its rapid advance into Soviet territory, Soviet workers dismantled and shipped the factories in the western part of the Soviet Union to the interior—to the Urals, western Siberia, and the Volga regions. Machines were placed on the bare ground. As laborers began their work, walls went up around them.

Stalin called the widespread military and industrial mobilization of the nation a "battle of machines." The Soviets won, producing 78,000 tanks and 98,000 artillery pieces. In 1943, 55 percent of the Soviet national income went for war materials, compared with 15 percent in 1940. As a result of the emphasis on military goods, Soviet citizens experienced severe shortages of both food and housing.

Soviet women played a major role in the war effort. Women and girls worked in industries, mines, and railroads. Overall, the number of women working in industry increased almost 60 percent. Soviet women were also expected to dig antitank ditches and work as air-raid wardens. In addition, the Soviet Union was the only country in World War II to use women in battle. Soviet women served as snipers and also in aircrews of bomber squadrons.

▼ *A B-26 drops bombs on Germany.*

**The United States** The home front in the United States was quite different from that of the other major powers. The United States was not fighting the war in its own territory. Eventually, the United States became the arsenal of the Allied Powers; it produced much of the military equipment the Allies needed. At the height of war production in November 1943, the country was building six ships a day and about 96,000 planes a year.

The mobilization of the American economy led to some social turmoil. The construction of new factories created boomtowns that attracted thousands, but often the workers faced a shortage of houses and schools.

During the war, there was widespread migration. About 16 million men and women in military service moved to join up, and moved often thereafter. Another 16 million were moving often, too. These were mostly wives and girlfriends of servicemen or of workers looking for jobs.

Over a million African Americans moved from the rural South to the cities of the North and West to find jobs in industry. Since African Americans were now living in places where they had not before, racial tensions increased. Sometimes there were race riots. In Detroit in June 1943, for example, white mobs roamed the streets attacking African Americans.

One million African Americans joined the military. There they were segregated in their own battle units. Angered by discrimination, some became militant and were determined to fight for their civil rights after the war.

Japanese Americans faced even more serious discrimination. On the West Coast, 110,000 Japanese Americans, 65 percent of whom had been born in the United States, were removed to camps surrounded by barbed wire and required to take loyalty oaths. Public officials claimed this policy was necessary for security reasons.

The racism in the treatment of Japanese Americans was evident when the California governor, Culbert Olson, said, "You know, when I look out at a group of Americans of German or Italian descent, I can tell

**_Picturing_ History**

Many Japanese American families in southern California were transported to internment camps. Would you have supported the internment policy for Japanese Americans during the war? Explain.

whether they're loyal or not. I can tell how they think and even perhaps what they are thinking. But it is impossible for me to do this with inscrutable Orientals, and particularly the Japanese."

**Germany** In August 1914, Germans had enthusiastically cheered their soldiers marching off to war. In September 1939, the streets were quiet. Many Germans did not care. Even worse for the Nazi regime, many feared disaster.

▲ *Kamikaze attacker being shot down in the Pacific, 1945*

Hitler was well aware of the importance of the home front. Despite the facts, Hitler believed that the Germans had lost World War I because of a "stab in the back"—a collapse of the will to win by those on the home front. Determined to avoid this same result, Hitler adopted certain economic policies that may have cost Germany the war.

To maintain the morale at home during the first two years of the war, Hitler refused to cut the production of consumer goods or increase the production of armaments. After German defeats on the Russian front and the American entry into the war, however, the economic situation in Germany changed.

Early in 1942, Hitler finally ordered a massive increase in armaments production and in the size of the army. Hitler's architect, **Albert Speer,** was made minister for armaments and munitions in 1942. In one year, Speer was able to triple armaments production despite Allied air raids.

In July 1944, the economy was totally mobilized. Schools, theaters, and cafes were closed. Total mobilization came too late to save Germany, however.

Nazi attitudes toward women changed over the course of the war. Before the war, the Nazis had worked to keep women out of the job market. As the war progressed and more and more men were called up for military service, this position no longer made sense. Nazi magazines now proclaimed, "We see the woman as the eternal mother of our people, but also as the working and fighting comrade of the man."

In spite of this change, the number of women working in industry, agriculture, commerce, and domestic service increased only slightly. The total number of employed women in September 1944 was 14.9 million, compared with 14.6 million in May 1939. Many women, especially those of the middle class, did not want jobs, particularly in factories.

**Japan** Wartime Japan was a highly mobilized society. To guarantee its control over all national resources, the government created a planning board to control prices, wages, labor, and resources. Traditional habits of obedience and hierarchy were used to encourage citizens to sacrifice their resources, and sometimes their lives, for the national cause.

The calls for sacrifice reached a high point in the final years of the war. Young Japanese men were encouraged to volunteer to serve as pilots in suicide missions against U.S. fighting ships at sea. These pilots were known as **kamikaze,** or "divine wind."

Japan was extremely reluctant to mobilize women on behalf of Japan's war effort. **General Hideki Tojo,** prime minister from 1941 to 1944, opposed female employment. He argued that "the weakening of the family system would be the weakening of the nation . . . we are able to do our duties only because we have wives and mothers at home."

The number of women working outside the home increased during the war, but only in areas like the textile industry and farming, where women had traditionally worked. Instead of using women to meet labor shortages, the Japanese government brought in Korean and Chinese laborers as an **alternative.**

✓ **Reading Check** **Evaluating** How did World War II contribute to racial tensions in the United States?

# Frontline Civilians: The Bombing of Cities

**Main Idea** The bombing of cities in Britain, Germany, and Japan destroyed buildings and killed thousands of civilians.

**Reading Connection** Has a relative told you about living someplace where military attacks were a threat? Read to learn about the bombing of cities during World War II.

Bombing was used in World War II against a variety of targets, including military targets, enemy troops, and civilian populations. The bombing of civilians in World War II made the home front a dangerous place.

A few bombing raids had been conducted in the last year of World War I. The bombing of civilian populations had led to a public outcry. The bombings and the reaction to them had given rise to the argument that bombing civilian populations would be an effective way to force governments to make peace. As a result, European air forces began to develop long-range bombers in the 1930s.

**Britain** The first sustained use of civilian bombing began in early September 1940. Londoners took the first heavy blows. For months, the German air force bombed **London** nightly. Thousands of civilians were killed or injured, and enormous damage was done. Nevertheless, Londoners' morale remained high.

The blitz, as the British called the German air raids, soon became a national experience. The blitz was carried to many other British cities and towns. The ability of Londoners to maintain their morale set the standard for the rest of the British population. The theory that the bombing of civilian targets would force peace was proved wrong.

**Germany** The British failed to learn from their own experience, however. Churchill and his advisers believed that destroying German communities would break civilian morale and bring victory. Major bombing raids on German cities began in 1942. On May 31, 1942, Cologne became the first German city to be attacked by a thousand bombers.

Bombing raids added an element of terror to circumstances already made difficult by growing shortages of food, clothing, and fuel. Germans especially feared the incendiary bombs, which created firestorms that swept through cities. The ferocious bombing of **Dresden** from February 13 to 15, 1945, created a firestorm that may have killed as many as 100,000 inhabitants and refugees.

Germany suffered enormously from the Allied bombing raids. Millions of buildings were destroyed, and possibly 500,000 civilians died. Nevertheless, it is highly unlikely that Allied bombing sapped the morale of the German people. Instead, Germans, whether pro-Nazi or anti-Nazi, fought on stubbornly, often driven simply by a desire to live.

*Dresden after the bombing in 1945*

*Dresden in 2000*

# The Atomic Bomb

Early in the twentieth century, scientists began to think about the possibilities of splitting the atom to release energy and create a devastating weapon, an atomic bomb. During World War II, the fear that the Germans might make such a weapon convinced the U.S. government to try to develop one first. In 1942, the United States set in motion the Manhattan Project.

The Manhattan Project was a code name for creating the first atomic bomb. It was an enormous industrial and technical enterprise that cost 2 billion dollars and employed 600,000 people. Physicist J. Robert Oppenheimer directed the center in Los Alamos, New Mexico, where the bomb was built. The bomb was successfully tested on July 16, 1945, near Alamogordo, New Mexico. Although the war in Europe was over, the war in Japan was not.

On August 6, 1945, a B-29 bomber nicknamed *Enola Gay* dropped the bomb on Hiroshima. An area of about 5 square miles (13 sq km) was turned to ashes. Of the 76,000 buildings in the city, 70,000 were flattened. Of its 350,000 inhabitants, 140,000 had died by the end of 1945. By the end of 1950, another 50,000 had died from the effects of radiation. A second bomb was dropped on Nagasaki on August 9. The world had entered the Nuclear Age.

**Evaluating** *Was the decision to use the atomic bomb different from Allied decisions to bomb civilian population centers in Europe? Why or why not?*

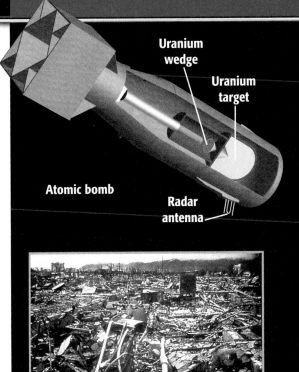

Uranium wedge

Uranium target

Atomic bomb

Radar antenna

**Hiroshima after atomic bomb dropped, August 1945**

---

Nor did the bombing destroy Germany's industrial capacity. Production of war materials actually increased between 1942 and 1944, despite the bombing. Nevertheless, the widespread destruction of transportation systems and fuel supplies made it extremely difficult for the new materials to reach the German military.

**Japan** In Japan, the bombing of civilians reached a new level with the use of the first atomic bomb. Japan was open to air raids toward the end of the war because its air force had almost been destroyed. Moreover, its crowded cities were built of flimsy materials that were especially vulnerable to fire.

Attacks on Japanese cities by the new U.S. B-29 Superfortresses, the biggest bombers of the war, had begun on November 24, 1944. By the summer of 1945, many of Japan's industries had been destroyed, along with one-fourth of its dwellings.

The Japanese government decreed the mobilization of all people between the ages of 13 and 60 into a People's Volunteer Corps. Fearing high U.S. casualties in a land invasion of Japan, President Truman and his advisers decided to drop the atomic bomb on Hiroshima and Nagasaki in August 1945.

**Reading Check** **Explaining** Why were civilian populations targeted in bombing raids?

## Peace and a New War

**Main Idea** Political tensions, suspicions, and a conflict of ideas led the United States and the Soviet Union into the Cold War.

**Reading Connection** How do you react to people you do not trust? Read to learn how the United States and the Soviet Union reacted to one another in this era.

The total victory of the Allies in World War II was followed not by a real peace but by a period of political tensions, known as the **Cold War.** Primarily an

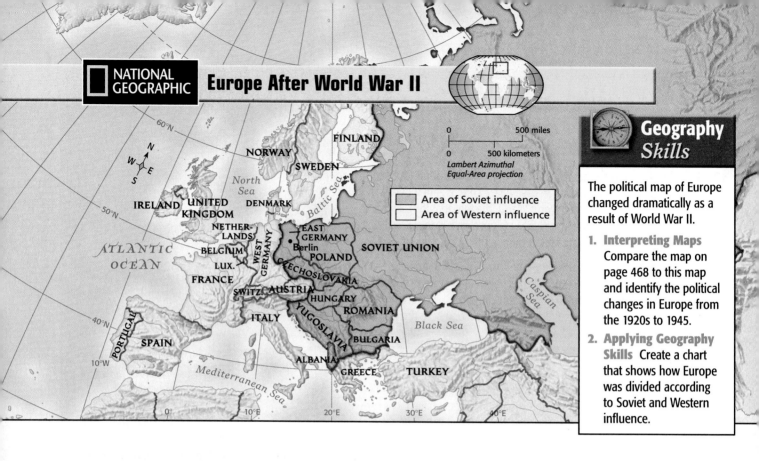

FINLAND
NORWAY
SWEDEN
North Sea
IRELAND UNITED KINGDOM DENMARK
NETHER-LANDS
EAST GERMANY
Berlin
BELGIUM
WEST GERMANY
LUX.
POLAND
SOVIET UNION
FRANCE
CZECHOSLOVAKIA
SWITZ. AUSTRIA
HUNGARY
ROMANIA
ITALY
YUGOSLAVIA
BULGARIA
Black Sea
Caspian Sea
SPAIN
PORTUGAL
ALBANIA
Mediterranean Sea
GREECE
TURKEY
ATLANTIC OCEAN
Baltic Sea

0  500 miles
0  500 kilometers
Lambert Azimuthal Equal-Area projection

☐ Area of Soviet influence
☐ Area of Western influence

## Geography Skills

The political map of Europe changed dramatically as a result of World War II.

1. **Interpreting Maps** Compare the map on page 468 to this map and identify the political changes in Europe from the 1920s to 1945.

2. **Applying Geography Skills** Create a chart that shows how Europe was divided according to Soviet and Western influence.

ideological conflict between the United States and the Soviet Union, the Cold War was to dominate world affairs until the end of the 1980s.

## The Tehran Conference

Stalin, Roosevelt, and Churchill were the leaders of what was called the Big Three (the Soviet Union, the United States, and Great Britain) of the Grand Alliance. They met at Tehran in November 1943 to decide the future course of the war. Their major tactical decision concerned the final assault on Germany. Stalin and Roosevelt had argued successfully for an American-British invasion through France. This was scheduled for the spring of 1944.

This plan had important consequences. It meant that Soviet and British-American forces would meet in defeated Germany along a north-south dividing line. Most likely, Eastern Europe would be liberated by Soviet forces. The Allies also agreed to a partition of postwar Germany.

## The Yalta Conference

The Big Three powers met again at Yalta in southern Russia in February 1945. By then, the defeat of Germany was obvious. The Western powers, which had once believed that the Soviets were in a weak position, were now faced with the reality of 11 million Soviet soldiers taking possession of Eastern and much of Central Europe.

Stalin was deeply suspicious of the Western powers. He wanted a buffer to protect the Soviet Union

from possible future Western aggression. This would mean establishing pro-Soviet governments along the border of the Soviet Union.

Roosevelt, however, favored the idea of self-determination for Europe. This involved a pledge to help liberated Europe in the creation of "democratic institutions of their own choice." Liberated countries would hold free elections to determine their political systems.

At Yalta, Roosevelt wanted Soviet military help against Japan. At this point, the atomic bomb was not yet a certainty. Roosevelt therefore agreed to Stalin's price for military aid against Japan: possession of Sakhalin and the Kuril Islands, which were ruled by Japan, as well as two warm-water ports and railroad rights in Manchuria.

The creation of the United Nations was a major American concern at Yalta. Roosevelt wanted the Big Three powers to pledge to be part of such an international organization before difficult issues divided them into hostile camps. Both Churchill and Stalin accepted Roosevelt's plans for the establishment of a United Nations organization and set the first meeting for San Francisco in April 1945.

Differences over Germany and Eastern Europe were treated less decisively. The Big Three reaffirmed that Germany must surrender unconditionally. It would be divided into four zones, which would be occupied and governed by the military forces of the United States, Great Britain, France, and the Soviet Union.

A compromise was also worked out on Poland. Stalin agreed to free elections in the future to determine a new government in that country. The issue of free elections in Eastern Europe, however, caused a split between the Soviets and Americans, as soon became evident at the next conference of the Big Three powers at Potsdam, Germany.

**The Potsdam Conference** The Potsdam Conference of July 1945 began under a cloud of mistrust. Roosevelt had died on April 12 and was succeeded by Harry S. Truman. At Potsdam, Truman demanded free elections in Eastern Europe. Stalin responded, "A freely elected government in any of these East European countries would be anti-Soviet, and that we cannot allow."

After a war in which the Soviets had lost more people than any other country, Stalin sought absolute military security. Only the presence of Communist states in Eastern Europe could guarantee this.

**War Crimes Trials** By the summer of 1945, the Allies had agreed to hold a trial of war leaders for committing aggressive war and crimes against humanity. Nazi leaders were tried and condemned as war criminals at the Nuremberg war crimes trials in Germany in 1945 and 1946. War crimes trials were also held in Japan and Italy.

**A New Struggle** Even while memories of the war were fading, the Cold War struggle began. Many in the West thought Soviet policy was part of a global Communist conspiracy. The Soviets viewed Western, and especially American, policy as nothing less than global capitalist expansionism.

Churchill, Roosevelt, and Stalin at Yalta

In March 1946, in a speech, the former British prime minister Winston Churchill declared that "an iron curtain" had "descended across the continent," dividing Europe into two hostile camps. Stalin branded Churchill's speech a "call to war with the Soviet Union." Only months after the world's most devastating conflict had ended, the world was bitterly divided again.

**Reading Check** **Identifying** Why did Stalin want to control Eastern Europe after World War II?

**HISTORY Online** **Study Central**

For help with the concepts in this section of *Glencoe World History–Modern Times,* go to wh.mt.glencoe.com and click on **Study Central.**

# SECTION 4 ASSESSMENT

## Checking for Understanding

1. **Vocabulary** Define: mobilization, impact, kamikaze, alternative, Cold War.

2. **People and Events** Identify: Albert Speer, General Hideki Tojo.

3. **Places** Locate: London, Dresden.

### Reviewing Big Ideas

4. **List** examples of Japan's vulnerability to Allied air attack in late 1944. What type of U.S. aircraft was used for the heaviest bombing of Japanese targets?

## Critical Thinking

5. **Historical Analysis** **Contextualizing** Why did General Hideki Tojo oppose having Japanese women join the labor force? **CA HI 3**

6. **Organizing Information** Create a chart listing countries where bombing of heavily populated cities took place.

| Country | City |
|---------|------|
|         |      |
|         |      |
|         |      |
|         |      |

## Analyzing Visuals

7. **Analyze** the photo of the leaders of the Big Three at the top of this page. How might the seating arrangement for the three leaders be significant?

### Writing About History

8. **Persuasive Writing** President Truman concluded that dropping the atomic bomb on Japan was justifiable. Write an essay that takes a position on Truman's decision. **CA 10WA2.4a,c**

# PRIMARY SOURCES
## Eyewitness to History

*During the Holocaust, over six millions Jews were murdered. Read these accounts to understand more about the atrocities of this period.*

## SOURCE 1: Escape from Poland

*After the Nazi invasion and occupation of Poland, the border into the Soviet Union remained open throughout 1939, and over 300,000 Jews crossed it. The following survivor describes the dangers involved in making the trip across the border in November 1939.*

. . . There is no present and no future for young Jews. They escape for their lives. They get away by different methods: on foot, by auto, train, carts and every other kind of transport. The border is open. The Soviets do nothing to prevent it. The occupying forces have no fixed system. You can never know what is forbidden and what is allowed. In a word—one day they are lenient and one day severe. . . . At the beginning of the Occupation the border was open . . . the roads were beset with dangers. According to the "Regulations" persons crossing the border could take only 20 **zloty**[1] with them. . . . Devices were therefore thought up in order to smuggle larger sums across, and here many failed. People were robbed and beaten on the way and left naked, with everything gone. The Border Guards know that the blood and the money of Jews were outside the law. . . . From this time the border crossers preferred to cross without permission. They had no confidence in the legalisms of the Occupying Power. When they crossed quietly they were more secure. There simply was no refugee who did not take with him a sum of money larger than that which the "Regulations" permitted. . . .

It is reliably estimated that more than a million refugees escaped to Russia. However many came they were still well received. But—where was the great mass of people to go? A small part, particularly those with a trade, have already been moved to the interior of Russia. As to the majority—either they had money with them and could eat, or they had nothing and hungered and thirsted. . . .

*The entrance to Auschwitz death camp*

## SOURCE 2: A Survivor of Auschwitz

*Auschwitz was the largest Nazi death camp where the greatest number of Jews were murdered during the Holocaust. This interview of Hadassah M. begins in 1943.*

In Auschwitz my block was right across from the **crematorium**[2]. Perhaps thirty meters separated the crematorium from me. I had occasion to witness everything. It was entirely open. They didn't even try to cover it up. . . . The transports arrived there, huge transports. In ten minutes by the clock we already saw the fire coming from the chimneys. . . . There were seasons when the ovens weren't able to burn as many transports as there were, [so] they dug ditches, pits . . . almost as if they were burning people who were still quite alive. . . .

---

[1] **zloty:** Polish currency

[2] **crematorium:** building where the deceased are incinerated

*Without having the people gassed?*

. . . The people were only like they had lost consciousness. They even begrudged [them] a little gas. We had occasion to hear all the cries of **Shema Yisroeil**[3] and sometimes the singing of the **Hatikveh**[4]. I myself saw how the oven [gas chamber] was being opened and the people were being pushed in. . . .

*You happened to pass by, yourself?*

No. Our work crew passed along the road that time. So we observed quite well. There were also cases that out of giant transports nobody, nobody was let into the camp alive. Children were altogether out of the question. If they want to claim that they only burned weak people, the living witnesses can tell that they took away the most beautiful, the youngest, the healthiest people, still sufficiently capable and strong [enough] for work. There was a time when they installed a children's block. The children were given the finest and best, but it was only when they had to present proof for an inspection or such. During one nice, bright morning the children were taken away and all burned.

## SOURCE 3: A Jewish Girl in Hiding

*The Holocaust produced many who risked their lives in order to ensure the survival of some Jews. This survivor describes how her governess, Marisia, helped her to escape from the Polish ghetto and hid her.*

. . . When the Germans invaded Poland in September 1939, my father, a captain in the Cavalry, pitted his horses against steel tanks. The horses lost. . . . [T]he Germans ordered all Jews to move immediately into a specified area. It came to be known as the Warsaw **Ghetto**[5]. . . .

At the end of 1942, the Germans announced that all workers of certain factory complexes in the ghetto would be transported to "more suitable and comfort-

able quarters." My parents knew what that meant. How right they were—both soon perished at Poniatowa Concentration Camp. . . .

. . . [O]ne day, I left the ghetto in the column of cleaning women, marched to the hospital, changed clothes with the woman who wanted to return, and was taken away by a waiting Marisia. She took me to the suburbs, then found a priest who was willing to sell her a birth certificate of a girl my age who had died. With this document, she was able to pass me off as her niece. She worked whenever possible to feed and house us. . . .

She took me to a cousin with whom she had not been in contact for many years. She introduced me as her child out of wedlock. As unpleasant as this admission was to her religious cousin, she allowed us to rent a room in an apartment she was renting to a prostitute who made home-made whiskey on the side to supplement her income. She and Marisia made an arrangement whereby Marisia would hide the whiskey in a basket under some slaughtered chickens, take them to Warsaw, sell them, and split the profits. That's how we stayed alive.

---

**DBQ** **Document-Based Questions**

**Historical Analysis** CA HI 2, HI 3

**Source 1:** According to this survivor, why was it so risky for Jews to cross the *open* border between Poland and the Soviet Union?

**Source 2:** According to Hadassah M.'s account, how did the overseers of Auschwitz go to great lengths to disguise their activities because of possible inspections by the Red Cross?

**Source 3:** According to this account, how was it possible for Jews to escape and hide throughout the Holocaust?

**Comparing and Contrasting Sources**

1. Comparing each of these accounts, is it surprising that many Jews risked their lives to avoid being sent to the camps? Explain. **CA 10RL3.5**

2. Why do you believe some groups took advantage of escaping Jews (Source 1), while others risked their lives in order to save them (Source 3)?

---

[3]**Shema Yisroeil (usually spelled "Yisroel"):** declaration of one God. It's Jewish custom to make these the final words before death.

[4]**Hatikveh:** Israel's national anthem, meaning "the Hope"

[5]**Ghetto:** city quarter to which Jews were restricted

# CHAPTER 11 ASSESSMENT and ACTIVITIES

 Standards 10.7.3, 10.8, 10.8.1, 10.8.2, 10.8.3, 10.8.4, 10.8.5, 10.8.6, 10.9.1

## Reviewing Content Vocabulary

*On a sheet of paper, use each of these terms in a sentence.*

1. demilitarized
2. appeasement
3. sanction
4. blitzkrieg
5. partisan
6. genocide
7. mobilization
8. kamikaze
9. Cold War

## Reviewing Academic Vocabulary

*On a sheet of paper, use each of these terms in a sentence that reflects the term's meaning in the chapter.*

10. labor
11. achieve
12. conference
13. assume
14. isolationism
15. neutrality
16. indefinite
17. implement
18. adjust
19. impact
20. alternative

## Reviewing the Main Ideas

**Section 1**

21. Where was the Sudetenland? Why was it important?

22. Explain why Japan felt the need to control other nations.

**Section 2**

23. What significant military action occurred at Midway Island in 1942?

24. What event triggered the entry of the United States into the war?

**Section 3**

25. What percentage of the Jewish populations of Poland, the Baltic countries, and Germany were killed during the Holocaust?

26. List examples of questionable Japanese occupation policies in Asia.

**Section 4**

27. In what way were Japanese Americans treated differently than German Americans and Italian Americans?

28. Explain the significance of the Yalta Conference.

## Chapter Summary

World War II was the most devastating total war in human history. Events engaged four continents, involved countless people and resources, and changed subsequent history. The chart below summarizes some of the themes and developments.

| Country | Movement | Cooperation | Conflict |
|---|---|---|---|
| United States | • Retakes Japanese positions in Southeast Asia | • Relaxes neutrality acts<br>• Meets with Allies at Tehran, Yalta, and Potsdam | • Leads war effort<br>• Conducts island-hopping counterattacks<br>• Drops atomic bombs on Japan |
| Great Britain | • Makes huge troop movements at Dunkirk and Normandy | • Meets with Allies at Tehran, Yalta, and Potsdam | • Stops Rommel at El Alamein<br>• Withstands heavy German bombing |
| Soviet Union | • Occupies Kuril and Sakhalin Islands<br>• Takes control of much of eastern Europe | • Meets with Allies at Tehran, Yalta, and Potsdam | • Defeats Germany at Stalingrad<br>• Forces Germany to fight war on two fronts |
| Germany | • Takes over Austria, Poland, and Sudetenland | • Forms Rome-Berlin Axis<br>• Signs Anti-Comintern Pact | • Uses blitzkrieg tactics<br>• Conducts genocide of Jews and others<br>• Besieges Leningrad |
| Italy | • Invades Ethiopia | • Forms Rome-Berlin Axis | • Becomes German puppet state (northern Italy) |
| Japan | • Seizes Manchuria and renames it Manchukuo<br>• Invades China | • Signs Anti-Comintern Pact | • Attacks Pearl Harbor<br>• Conquers Southeast Asia from Indochina to Philippines |

## Self-Check Quiz
Visit the *Glencoe World History–Modern Times* Web site at **wh.mt.glencoe.com** and click on **Chapter 11– Self-Check Quiz** to prepare for the Chapter Test.

## Critical Thinking

**29. Cause and Effect** What factors caused President Truman to order the dropping of atomic bombs in Japan?

**30. Drawing Conclusions** How did World War II affect the world balance of power? What nations emerged from the conflict as world powers?

**31.** **Reading Skill** **Inferring** Hitler, a Nazi, and Mussolini, a Fascist, had similar beliefs. What did these two men have in common as World War II approached?

## Writing About History

**32.** **Historical Analysis** **Alternative History** In an essay, examine whether events leading to World War II, or even the war itself, would have occurred if England, France, and Italy had enforced the conditions of the Treaty of Versailles when Germany initially broke them. **CA HI 4**

**33.** *Big Idea* Write an essay that examines the different approaches to colonial governing in Asia taken by the Japanese during World War II and by Europeans before the war. Be sure to include information about key people, places, and events from each of the two periods in history.

**34. Persuasive Writing** Some historians believe that President Truman dropped atomic weapons on Japan not to end the war in the Pacific, but to impress the Soviet Union with U.S. military power. Write a position paper evaluating this hypothesis in light of what you have learned about Stalin and the United States. **CA 10WA2.4a,c**

**DBQ** **Document-Based Questions**

**Analyzing Sources** Heinrich Himmler, head of the German SS, argued:

“Whether nations live in prosperity or starve to death interests me only insofar as we need them as slaves for our culture. Otherwise it is of no interest.”

**35.** Describe Heinrich Himmler's opinion of the people that Germany conquered.

**36.** Compare the Nazi philosophy of creating a New Order with the Japanese philosophy of Asia for the Asiatics.

## Analyzing Maps and Charts

Refer to the map on page 548 to answer the following questions.

**37.** Why did the Allies not retake every Japanese-held island?

**38.** How far is it from Pearl Harbor to Japan?

## Standards Practice

**Directions: Use the map and your knowledge of world history to answer the following question.**

German-Controlled Territory, 1943

**39.** What geographic factors influenced German military advances?

**A** German troops had to cover long distances.

**B** Colder climates created problems that the German military could not overcome.

**C** The blitzkrieg relied on tanks that were most effective on flatter terrain.

**D** All of the above.

**CA Standard 10.8.3** Identify and locate the Allied and Axis powers on a map and discuss the major turning points of the war, the principal theaters of conflict, key strategic decision, and the resulting war conferences and political resolutions, with emphasis on the importance of geographic factors.

# WORLD LITERATURE

## from A Room of One's Own

### by Virginia Woolf

**Virginia Woolf** was born in 1882 in London. Her work changed the ways many modern novels were written. She used an experimental narrative technique known as stream of consciousness, in which characters are portrayed through their inner lives and thoughts without explanation from the writer. She is also known for her feminist writings. One of the most famous of these is *A Room of One's Own.* Its title reflects her belief that a woman "must have money and a room of her own" in order to write.

### Read to Discover

How does Virginia Woolf express her belief that gender influences the development of talent? Do you think Woolf is being fair in her assessment? Does her analysis of the differences between treatment of men and women apply today?

### Reader's Dictionary

**agog:** full of intense interest or excitement

**moon:** to dream

. . . Let me imagine, since facts are so hard to come by, what would have happened had Shakespeare had a wonderfully gifted sister, called Judith, let us say. Shakespeare himself went, very probably—his mother was an heiress—to the grammar school, where he may have learnt Latin—Ovid, Virgil and Horace—and the elements of grammar and logic. He was, it is well known, a wild boy who poached rabbits, perhaps shot a deer, and had, rather sooner than he should have done, to marry a woman in the neighbourhood, who bore him a child rather quicker than was right. That escapade sent him to seek his fortune in London. He had, it seemed, a taste for the theatre; he began by holding horses at the stage door. Very soon he got work in the theatre, became a successful actor, and lived at the hub of the universe, meeting everybody, knowing everybody, practising his art on the boards, exercising his wits in the street, and even getting access to the palace of the queen. Meanwhile

◀ *A surviving manuscript shows London's Globe theater where Shakespeare's plays were performed. Woolf asks what would have happened to a sister of Shakespeare if she had wanted to write.*

his extraordinarily gifted sister, let us suppose, remained at home. She was as adventurous, as imaginative, as agog to see the world as he was. But she was not sent to school. She had no chance of learning grammar and logic, let alone of reading Horace and Virgil. She picked up a book now and then, one of her brother's perhaps, and read a few pages. But then her parents came in and told her to mend the stockings or mind the stew and not moon about with books and papers. They would have spoken sharply but kindly, for they were substantial people who knew the conditions of life for a woman and loved their daughter—indeed, more likely than not she was the apple of her father's eye. Perhaps she scribbled some pages up in an apple loft on the sly, but was careful to hide them or set fire to them. Soon, however, before she was out of her teens, she was to be betrothed to the son of a neighbouring wool-stapler. She cried out that marriage was hateful to her, and for that she was severely beaten by her father. Then he ceased to scold her. He begged her instead not to hurt him, not to shame him in this matter of her marriage. He would give her a chain of beads or a fine petticoat, he said; and there were tears in his eyes. How could she disobey him? How could she break his heart? The force of her own gift alone drove her to it. She made up a small parcel of her belongings, let herself down by a rope one summer's night and took the road to London. She was not seventeen. The birds that sang in the hedge were not more musical than she was. She had the quickest fancy, a gift like her brother's, for the tune of words. Like him, she had a taste for the theatre. She stood at the stage door; she wanted to act, she said. Men laughed in her face. The manager—a fat, loose-lipped man—guffawed. He bellowed something about poodles dancing and women acting—no woman, he said could possibly be an actress. He hinted—you can imagine what. She could get no training in her craft. Could she even seek her dinner in a tavern or roam the streets at midnight? Yet her genius was for fiction. . . . At

last—for she was very young, oddly like Shakespeare the poet in her face, with the same grey eyes and rounded brows—at last Nick Greene the actor-manager took pity on her; [but] she . . . killed herself one winter's night and lies buried at some cross-roads where the omnibuses now stop outside the Elephant and Castle.

But for my part, it is unthinkable that any woman in Shakespeare's day should have had Shakespeare's genius. For genius like Shakespeare's is not born among labouring, uneducated, servile people. How, then, could it have been born among women whose work began, almost before they were out of the nursery, who were forced to it by their parents and held to it by all the power of law and custom? Yet genius of a sort must have existed among women as it must have existed among the working classes. Now and again an Emily Brontë or a Robert Burns blazes out and proves its presence. But certainly it never got itself on to paper. When, however, one reads of a witch being ducked, of a woman possessed by devils, of a wise woman selling herbs, or even of a very remarkable man who had a mother, then I think we are on the track of a lost novelist, a suppressed poet, of some mute and inglorious Jane Austen, some Emily Brontë who dashed her brains out on the moor or mopped and mowed about the highways crazed with the torture that her gift had put her to. . . .

This may be true or it may be false—who can say?—but what is true in it, so it seemed to me, reviewing the story of Shakespeare's sister as I had made it, is that any woman born with a great gift in the sixteenth century would certainly have gone crazed, shot herself, or ended her days in some lonely cottage outside the village, half witch, half wizard, feared and mocked at. For it needs little skill in psychology to be sure that a highly gifted girl who had tried to use her gift for poetry would have been so thwarted and hindered by other people, so tortured and pulled asunder by her own contrary instincts, that she must have lost her health and sanity to a certainty. No girl could have

walked to London and stood at a stage door and forced her way into the presence of actor-managers without doing herself a violence and suffering an anguish which may have been irrational. . . . To have lived a free life in London in the sixteenth century would have meant for a woman who was poet and playwright a nervous stress and dilemma which might well have killed her. Had she survived, whatever she had written would have been twisted and deformed, issuing from a strained and morbid imagination. And undoubtedly, I thought, looking at the shelf where there are no plays by women, her work would have gone unsigned. . . . Currier Bell, George Eliot, George Sand, all the victims of inner strife as their writings prove, sought ineffectively to veil themselves by using the name of a man. Thus they did homage to the convention, which if not implanted by the other sex was liberally encouraged by them (the chief glory of a woman is not to be talked of, said Pericles, himself a much-talked-of man) that publicity in women is detestable. Anonymity runs in their blood. . . .

That woman, then, who was born with a gift of poetry in the sixteenth century, was an unhappy woman, a woman at strife against herself. All the conditions of her life, all her own instincts, were hostile to the state of mind which is needed to set free whatever is in the brain. But what is the state of mind that is most propitious to the act of creation? I asked.

But for women, I thought, looking at the empty shelves, these difficulties were infinitely more formidable. In the first place, to have a room of her own, let alone a quiet room or a sound-proof room, was out of the question. . . .

## Interpreting World Literature

1. What were "the conditions of life for a woman" that made Judith's parents scold her for attempting to read and write? **CA 10RL 3.12**

2. Why does Judith's father beat her?

3. What is Woolf's conclusion about the possibility of a woman becoming Shakespeare?

4. **CRITICAL THINKING** Why does Virginia Woolf have Shakespeare marry, but Shakespeare's sister run away from marriage?

## Applications Activity

What does a person today need to succeed as a writer or artist? Write a descriptive account to illustrate your argument.

# Reading on Your Own

*Here are several books you may want to read on your own.*
*These authors have explored some of the topics covered in this unit.*

## *All Quiet on the Western Front* (Fiction)

Erich Maria Remarque (1897–1970) wrote this classic novel of World War I. It captures the despair and anger of the young Germans who faced the senseless conditions of trench warfare. Remarque himself served in the war, and the authentic note is on every page. Hitler saw it as dangerous because it seemed to question whether war could ever be justified, and the Nazis ordered all copies to be burned.

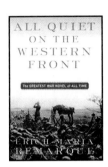

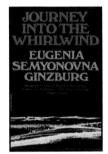

## *Journey into the Whirlwind* (Autobiography)

Eugenia Ginzburg (1906?–1977) experienced the purges of Stalinist Russia and lived to write about it. A devoted Communist Party member and intellectual, she was arrested because she worked with an editor targeted by Stalin's police. She spent about 18 years in prisons and labor camps. This gripping tale of survival in desperate circumstances also shows how strong the commitment was to socialist goals in 20th century Russia.

## *God's Bits of Wood* (Fiction)

Sembene Ousmane (1923–) a prominent Senegal writer and filmmaker, set his novel in Senegal before it gained its independence from France in 1960. Ousmane tells the story of Senegal railroad workers who go on strike against their French bosses for better pay. The French use ruthless tactics to pressure the workers. As the story unfolds, the workers' wives are drawn into the struggle, and gain a new sense of what women can contribute to community life.

## *The Death of Artemio Cruz* (Fiction)

Carlos Fuentes (1928–) has achieved international recognition for his novels. The son of a Mexican diplomat, Fuentes himself had a diplomatic career before focusing entirely on literature. Like other of Fuentes's novels, *The Death of Artemio Cruz* explores themes in Mexican history. The tragic hero is an idealist as a young man, fighting bravely during the Mexican Revolution, but he later marries for money and becomes selfish and greedy.

# Civilization

## 1945–Present

# **W**hy It Matters

World War II can be seen as the end of an era of European domination of the world. After the war, Europe quickly divided into hostile camps as the Cold War rivalry between the United States and the Soviet Union forced nations to take sides. In the late 1980s, however, the Soviet Empire began to come apart, and the Cold War quickly ended.

World War II severely undermined the stability of the colonial order in Asia and Africa. By the end of the 1940s, most colonies in Asia had gained their independence. Later, African colonies, too, would become independent nations.

## Primary Sources Library

See pages 776–777 for primary source readings to accompany Unit 4.

Use The World History **Primary Source Document Library CD-ROM** to find additional primary sources about Global Civilization.

▲ Contemporary African art featuring Nelson Mandela

▶ African National Congress campaign rally

*". . . there is no easy walk to freedom anywhere . . ."*

—Nelson Mandela

# Communication

The invention of writing and printing reshaped history. Today, electronic technology is moving communications forward at a startling rate. People can now be instantaneously linked around the world by satellites and the Internet.

**1901**
Guglielmo Marconi sends first radio waves across Atlantic

**1930s**
Television developed

**1948**
First electronic computer with stored memory is developed

**1957**
Soviet Union launches *Sputnik I*

## ❶ *The United States*

## Satellite Communication

The first telephone developed by Alexander Graham Bell in 1876 was nothing more than a wooden stand with a funnel, some wires, and a cup of acid, but the telephone was soon to revolutionize communication worldwide.

Similarly, when the Soviet Union launched a tiny communications satellite named *Sputnik I* in 1957, the device could do little more than transmit radio signal beeps. However, this satellite also represented a major step in communication technology.

Three years later, the United States launched its first satellites, which could relay telephone calls between Europe and the United States. In 1962, the United States satellite *Telstar* was the first to relay live television programs to distant locations.

By the 1980s, people around the world with satellite-dish antennas could tune in to hundreds of television programs. The effect was revolutionary. Repressive governments in Eastern Europe and elsewhere could not legislate against free speech beamed down from the skies.

*Telstar*

*Cybercafe*

## ❷ *Africa*

## The Internet

In Africa, UNESCO is helping the Pan-African News Agency and others to link to the Internet. Project leaders see the Internet as one of the keys to unlocking Africa's economic potential. Currently, there is one Internet access site for every 200 Africans, compared to a world average of one site for every 30 people. Internet access will improve, and as it does, African communications, education, business, and government endeavors will be profoundly impacted.

**1960**
United States launches its first satellites

**1971**
Microprocessor is invented

**1977**
Apple II computer introduced

**1990**
African agencies link to the Internet

**2001**
China orders removal of illegal satellite dishes

## ❸ *China*

## Satellite Dishes

Satellite dishes made it possible for people across the People's Republic of China to listen to Mandarin-speaking rappers out of Hong Kong, English broadcasts of CNN News, and movies from Japan. The uncensored broadcasts enraged government officials, who tried to ban satellite dishes in 1993. However, even as officials dismantled thousands of large dishes, kits for smaller dishes were being smuggled into the country.

Other countries with repressive policies, such as Iran and Myanmar, tried and failed to ban satellite reception. Even free governments, like India's, were concerned about the "cultural invasion," but satellite television was here to stay.

*Satellite dish, Tibet*

## Why It Matters

While it used to take months to send a letter from the United States to Africa, today it can take only seconds. How has instantaneous communication made the world smaller? What are the good and bad results of this phenomenon?

# 12

## *1945–1970*

# Cold War and Postwar Changes

### ⁓❈ *The Big Ideas* ❈⁓

### SECTION 1: Development of the Cold War

**International rivalry between superpowers and growing nationalism in the Third World led to major conflicts in the Cold War.** A period of conflict called the Cold War developed between the United States and the Soviet Union after 1945, forcing European nations to support one of the two major powers.

### SECTION 2: The Soviet Union and Eastern Europe

**A totalitarian system violates human rights in pursuit of political power.** The Soviet Union faced revolts and protests in its attempt to gain and maintain control over Eastern Europe.

### SECTION 3: Western Europe and North America

**Throughout history people have struggled for rights.** Post–World War II societies rebuilt their economies and communities, but not without upheaval and change.

 ***World History—Modern Times Video*** *The Chapter 12 video,* "The Berlin Airlift," *shows how American and British planes circumvented the Soviet blockade.*

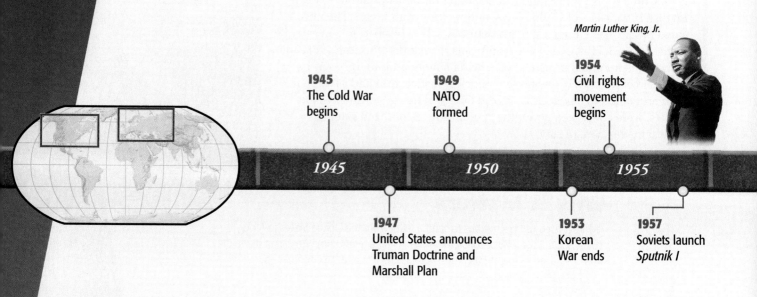

*Martin Luther King, Jr.*

**1945**
The Cold War
begins

**1949**
NATO
formed

**1954**
Civil rights
movement
begins

*1945*　　　　*1950*　　　　*1955*

**1947**
United States announces
Truman Doctrine and
Marshall Plan

**1953**
Korean
War ends

**1957**
Soviets launch
*Sputnik I*

The Soviet government displays its military strength in Moscow's annual May Day parade.

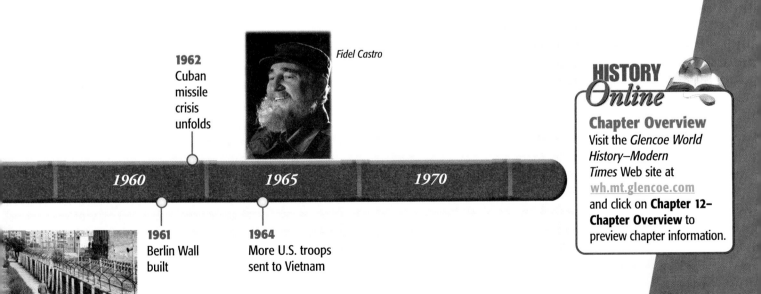

**1962**
Cuban missile crisis unfolds

*Fidel Castro*

1960

1965

1970

**1961**
Berlin Wall built

**1964**
More U.S. troops sent to Vietnam

*Berlin Wall*

**HISTORY**
*Online*

**Chapter Overview**
Visit the *Glencoe World History–Modern Times* Web site at wh.mt.glencoe.com and click on **Chapter 12– Chapter Overview** to preview chapter information.

## Reading Skill — Evaluating

When you read, you don't take each piece of information in isolation. You need to think critically about what you've read, constantly evaluating and drawing conclusions. For example, your first reaction in reading about Napoleon might be that he was foolish to invade Russia and get thousands of French soldiers killed. This is an immediate reaction, but to have a well-formed evaluation of the past, you want to look at decisions and policies in context. What led up to that decision or policy?

While reading about the past, you should consider all the circumstances of a situation. Think of yourself as a judge, objectively taking in information from a variety of perspectives and thinking about motivation. Once you've done that, you are ready to evaluate decisions, policies, and behaviors, and come to a conclusion.

*Read the following excerpt about Joseph Stalin from this chapter and write down your first impression of his leadership skills.*

### EVALUATING

Discuss why you think Stalin was motivated to compare his colleagues to blind kittens. Why was this comparison appropriate for Stalin's way of thinking?

Stalin remained the undisputed master of the Soviet Union. He distrusted competitors, exercised sole power, and had little respect for other Communist Party leaders. He is reported to have said to members of his inner circle in 1952, "You are as blind as kittens. What would you do without me?"

Stalin's suspicions added to the increasing repression of the regime. In 1946, the government decreed that all literary and scientific work must conform to the political needs of the state.

### Apply the Skill

As you read this chapter, write a short paragraph explaining the state of the Soviet Union after World War II. Then look at your initial impression of Stalin. With a classmate, evaluate what Stalin's words tell us about how he led the Soviet government.

**Historical Interpretation: Standard HI 6** *Students conduct cost-benefit analyses and apply basic economic indicators to analyze the aggregate economic behavior of the U.S. economy.*

Historians know that national and global economies play a vital role in influencing history. When a nation's economy is weak, people might vote for new leaders, or even an entirely new political system. Economic trends affect the kinds of jobs people have, the way different social classes relate to one another, and how much money consumers spend.

As the Great Depression demonstrated, economic crises are a springboard for a variety of economic, political, and social problems. Historians also look at economic upturns, which often predict the economic behavior of social groups.

*Read the following statements from Chapter 12 about American economic activity after World War II.*

- **An economic boom followed World War II. A shortage of consumer goods during the war had left Americans with both extra income and the desire to buy goods after the war.**

- **In addition, the growth of labor unions brought higher wages and gave more workers the ability to buy consumer goods. Between 1945 and 1973, real wages (the actual purchasing power of income) grew an average of 3 percent a year, the most prolonged advance in American history.**

## Apply the Skill

Based on what you've read in the previous chapter, write a brief summary on the home front in the United States during World War II. Then discuss whether the fact that there was an economic boom after the war was surprising. After reading this chapter, draw comparisons with the postwar economies of other former Allied and Axis powers.

581

# A Story That Matters

*Cleaning up after the London Blitz*

## A Sober Victory

*T*he end of World War II in Europe had been met with great joy. One visitor in Moscow reported, "I looked out of the window [at 2 A.M.], almost everywhere there were lights in the windows—people were staying awake. Everyone embraced everyone else, someone sobbed aloud."

After the victory parades and celebrations, however, Europeans awoke to a devastating realization: their civilization was in ruins. As many as fifty million people (both soldiers and civilians) had been killed over the last six years. Massive air raids had reduced many of the great cities of Europe to heaps of rubble.

An American general described Berlin: "Wherever we looked we saw desolation. It was like a city of the dead. Suffering and shock were visible in every face. Dead bodies still remained in canals and lakes and were being dug out from under bomb debris."

Millions of Europeans faced starvation. Grain harvests were only half of what they had been in 1939. Millions were also homeless. In the parts of the Soviet Union that had been occupied by the Germans, almost twenty-five million people were without homes. Fifteen million Germans and East Europeans were driven out of countries where they were no longer wanted. Millions of people had been uprooted by the war and became "displaced persons" who tried to find food and a way home.

### Why It Matters

Despite the chaos, Europe was soon on the road to a remarkable recovery. However, World War II had destroyed European supremacy in world affairs, and from this, Europe did not recover. As the Cold War between the world's two superpowers–the United States and the Soviet Union–grew stronger, European nations were divided into two armed camps dependent on one of these two major powers. The United States and the Soviet Union, whose rivalry brought the world to the brink of nuclear war, seemed to hold the survival of Europe and the world in their hands.

**History and You** Create a world map. As you read the chapter, color the map as a United States policy maker might have during the Cold War. Indicate the Soviet and United States spheres of influence as well as areas under contention.

# Development of the Cold War

## Section Preview

A period of conflict called the Cold War developed between the United States and the Soviet Union after 1945, forcing European nations to support one of the two major powers.

### Main Idea

- After World War II, the differences between the United States and Soviet Union became very apparent, and the two powers became fierce rivals. (p. 584)
- As Cold War tensions increased, nations were forced to choose to support the Soviet Union or the United States. (p. 586)

- With the goal of stopping the spread of communism, the United States entered the war in Vietnam. (p. 589)

## Content Vocabulary

satellite state, policy of containment, arms race, deterrence, domino theory

## Academic Vocabulary

aid, occupy, creation, administration, communications

## People and Events to Identify

Truman Doctrine, Dean Acheson, Marshall Plan, NATO, Warsaw Pact, SEATO, CENTO, Nikita Khrushchev

## Places to Locate

Berlin, Federal Republic of Germany, German Democratic Republic

## Reading Objectives

1. Explain the major turning points in the development of the Cold War.
2. Describe the Cuban missile crisis.

## Reading Strategy

**Summarizing Information** Use a table like the one below to list the American presidents who held office during the Cold War and major events related to the Cold War that took place during their administrations.

| President | Major Event |
|-----------|-------------|
|           |             |
|           |             |
|           |             |

## Preview of Events

◆1945    ◆1950    ◆1955    ◆1960    ◆1965

**1948**
Berlin Air Lift begins

**1949**
Chinese Communists take control of China

**1950**
Korean War begins

**1961**
Soviets and East Germans build the Berlin Wall

**1964**
Lyndon B. Johnson increases number of troops sent to Vietnam

## California Standards in This Section

*Reading this section will help you master these California History–Social Science standards.*

**10.9.2:** Analyze the causes of the Cold War, with the free world on one side and Soviet client states on the other, including competition for influence in such places as Egypt, the Congo, Vietnam, and Chile.

**10.9.3:** Understand the importance of the Truman Doctrine and the Marshall Plan, which established the pattern for America's postwar policy of supplying economic and military aid to prevent the spread of Communism and the resulting economic and political competition in arenas such as Southeast Asia (i.e., the Korean War, Vietnam War), Cuba, and Africa.

**10.9.8:** Discuss the establishment and work of the United Nations and the purposes and functions of the Warsaw Pact, SEATO, NATO, and the Organization of American States.

# Confrontation of the Superpowers

**Main Idea** After World War II, the differences between the United States and Soviet Union became very apparent, and the two powers became fierce rivals.

**Reading Connection** Can you remember a time when you wanted to perform better than one of your rivals? Read to learn how the not-so-friendly rivalry between the United States and Soviet Union began.

Once the Axis Powers were defeated, the differences between the United States and the Soviet Union became clear. Stalin still feared the capitalist West, while the United States and other Western leaders feared communism. No one identified the coming conflict so clearly as British prime minister Winston Churchill.

## Voices from the Past

On March 5, 1946, Winston Churchill gave a speech in Fulton, Missouri, expressing his growing concern about the rift between the Soviets and the West:

> 66From Stettin in the Baltic to Trieste in the Adriatic, an iron curtain has descended across the continent. Behind that line lie all the capitals of the ancient states of central and eastern Europe, Warsaw, Berlin, Prague, Vienna, Budapest, Belgrade, Bucharest, and Sofia; all these famous cities and the populations around them lie in the Soviet sphere and all are subject, in one form or another, not only to Soviet influence but to a very high and increasing measure of control from Moscow.99

It did not take long for Soviet leader Joseph Stalin to reply: "In substance, Mr. Churchill now stands in the position of a firebrand of war." Who, then, was responsible for beginning the Cold War between the United States and the Soviet Union? Both nations took steps that were unwise and might have been avoided, but it was not surprising that two nations, so different in policy and nature, would conflict.

Because of a need to feel secure on its western border, the Soviet government was not prepared to give up its control of Eastern Europe after Germany's defeat. American leaders were not willing to give up the power and prestige the United States had gained throughout the world. Suspicious of each other's motives, the United States and the Soviet Union soon became rivals. Between 1945 and 1949, a number of events led the two superpowers (countries whose military power is combined with political influence) to oppose each other.

**Rivalry in Europe** Eastern Europe was the first area of disagreement. The United States and Great Britain believed that the liberated nations of Eastern Europe should freely determine their own governments. Stalin, fearful that the Eastern European nations would be anti-Soviet if they were permitted free elections, opposed the West's plans. Having freed Eastern Europe from the Nazis, the Soviet army stayed in the conquered areas.

A civil war in Greece created another area of conflict between the superpowers. The Communist People's Liberation Army and anticommunist forces (supported by Great Britain) were fighting each other for control of Greece in 1946. But due to internal economic problems, Britain withdrew its **aid** from Greece.

**The Truman Doctrine** President Harry S. Truman of the United States, alarmed by the British withdrawal and the possibility of Soviet expansion into the eastern Mediterranean, responded in early 1947 with the Truman Doctrine. The **Truman Doctrine** stated that the United States would provide money to countries (in this case, Greece) threatened by Communist expansion. If the Soviets were not stopped in Greece, the Truman argument ran, then the United States would have to face the spread of communism throughout the free world.

*Winston Churchill*

▲ *President Truman asked Congress for money to aid European recovery.*

As **Dean Acheson,** the U.S. secretary of state, explained, "Like apples in a barrel infected by disease, the corruption of Greece would infect Iran and all the East . . . likewise Africa, Italy, France. . . . Not since Rome and Carthage had there been such a polarization of power on this earth."

**The Marshall Plan** The Truman Doctrine was followed in June 1947 by the European Recovery Program. Proposed by General George C. Marshall, U.S. secretary of state, it is better known as the **Marshall Plan.** Marshall, who had been the chief of staff for the U.S. Army during World War II, won the Nobel Peace Prize for his work on the European Recovery Program.

The Marshall Plan was designed to rebuild the prosperity and stability of war-torn Europe. It included $13 billion in aid for Europe's economic recovery. Underlying the Marshall Plan was the belief that Communist aggression was successful in countries where there were economic problems.

The Marshall Plan was not meant to shut out the Soviet Union or its economically and politically dependent Eastern European **satellite states.** These nations refused to participate, however. The Soviets saw the Marshall Plan as an attempt to buy the support of countries.

In 1949, the Soviet Union responded to the Marshall Plan by founding the Council for Mutual Economic Assistance (COMECON) for the economic cooperation of the Eastern European states. COMECON largely failed, however, because the Soviet Union was unable to provide the necessary financial aid.

By 1947, the split in Europe between the United States and the Soviet Union had become a fact of life. In July 1947, George Kennan, a well-known U.S. diplomat with crucial knowledge of Soviet affairs, argued for a **policy of containment** to keep communism within its existing boundaries and prevent further Soviet aggressive moves. Containment became U.S. policy.

**The Division of Germany** The fate of Germany also became a source of heated contention between the Soviets and the West. At the end of the war, the Allied Powers had divided Germany into four zones, each **occupied** by one of the Allies—the United States, the Soviet Union, Great Britain, and France. **Berlin,** located deep inside the Soviet zone, was also divided into four zones.

The foreign ministers of the four occupying powers met repeatedly in an attempt to arrive at a final peace treaty with Germany but had little success. By February 1948, Great Britain, France, and the United States were making plans to unify the three Western sections of Germany (and Berlin) and create a West German government.

The Soviets opposed the **creation** of a separate West German state. They attempted to prevent it by mounting a blockade of West Berlin. Soviet forces did not allow trucks, trains, or barges to enter the city's three Western zones. Food and supplies could no longer get through to the 2.5 million people in these zones.

The Western powers faced a dilemma. No one wanted World War III, but how could the people in the Western zones of Berlin be kept alive, when the whole city was inside the Soviet zone? The solution was the Berlin Airlift—supplies would be flown in by American and British airplanes. For over 10 months, more than 200,000 flights carried 2.3 million tons (2.1 million t) of supplies into the zone. The Soviets, who also wanted to avoid war, finally gave in and lifted the blockade in May 1949.

In September 1949, the **Federal Republic of Germany,** or West Germany, was formally created. Its capital was Bonn. Less than a month later, a separate East German state, the **German Democratic Republic,** was set up by the Soviets. East Berlin became that nation's capital. Berlin, which only a few years earlier had been the center of the 1,000-year Reich, was now divided into two parts, a reminder of the division of West and East.

✓**Reading Check** **Describing** What was the intention of the Marshall Plan?

**NATIONAL GEOGRAPHIC**

**Divided Germany and the Berlin Airlift**

EAST GERMANY

FRENCH SECTOR

EAST BERLIN

BRITISH SECTOR

SOVIET SECTOR

WEST BERLIN

AMERICAN SECTOR

0   10 miles
0   10 kilometers
Lambert Azimuthal Equal-Area projection

EAST GERMANY

DENMARK

Hamburg

NETHER-LANDS

British Zone

POLAND

Hannover

Braunschweig

Berlin

WEST GERMANY (FEDERAL REPUBLIC OF GERMANY)

EAST GERMANY (GERMAN DEMOCRATIC REPUBLIC)

BELG.

LUX.

French Zone

Frankfurt

CZECHOSLOVAKIA

American Zone

FRANCE

AUSTRIA

SWITZ.

☐ Allied occupation zone
☐ Soviet occupation zone
◄╌╂ Routes of the Berlin Airlift, 1948–1949
— Iron Curtain
╌╌ Division of Allied zone

ITALY   YUGOSLAVIA

0   100 miles
0   100 kilometers
Chamberlin Trimetric projection

**Geography** *Skills*

During the Berlin Airlift, Western planes delivered food and supplies to the people of West Berlin.

1. **Interpreting Maps** Approximately how much German land was occupied by the Allies? How much was occupied by the Soviets?

2. **Applying Geography Skills** Why could the Allies not deliver food to West Berlin by land?

# Spread of the Cold War

**Main Idea** As Cold War tensions increased, nations were forced to choose to support the Soviet Union or the United States.

**Reading Connection** In the war on terrorism in the early 2000s, did some nations attempt to stay neutral? Read to learn how communist and noncommunist alliances came about.

In 1949, Chinese Communists took control of the government in China, strengthening U.S. fears about the spread of communism. The Soviet Union exploded its first atomic bomb in 1949. All too soon, the United States and the Soviet Union were involved in a growing **arms race,** in which both countries built up their armies and weapons. Nuclear weapons became increasingly destructive.

Both sides believed that an arsenal of nuclear weapons would prevent war. They believed that if one nation attacked with nuclear weapons, the other nation would still be able to respond and devastate the attacker. According to this policy, neither side could risk using their massive supplies of weapons.

**New Military Alliances** The search for security during the Cold War led to the formation of new military alliances. The North Atlantic Treaty Organization **(NATO)** was formed in April 1949 when Belgium, Luxembourg, France, the Netherlands, Great Britain, Italy, Denmark, Norway, Portugal, and Iceland signed a treaty with the United States and Canada. All the powers who signed agreed to provide mutual help if any one of them was attacked. A few years later, West Germany, Turkey, and Greece also joined.

In 1955, the Soviet Union joined with Albania, Bulgaria, Czechoslovakia, East Germany, Hungary, Poland, and Romania in a formal military alliance known as the **Warsaw Pact.** Now, Europe was once again divided into hostile alliance systems, just as it had been before World War I.

New military alliances spread to the rest of the world after the United States became involved in the Korean War (discussed in Chapter 16). The war began in 1950 as an attempt by the Communist government of North Korea, which was allied with the Soviet Union, to take over South Korea. The Korean War confirmed American fears of Communist expansion. More determined than ever to contain Soviet power, the United States extended its military alliances around the world.

A Soviet scientist is shown working on *Sputnik I.* The launch of *Sputnik I,* which orbited the earth for 57 days, stunned the United States and enhanced the prestige of the Soviet Union. Today, many space endeavors are international efforts. Why?

To stem Soviet aggression in the East, the United States, Great Britain, France, Pakistan, Thailand, the Philippines, Australia, and New Zealand formed the Southeast Asia Treaty Organization (**SEATO**). The Central Treaty Organization (**CENTO**), which included Turkey, Iraq, Iran, Pakistan, Great Britain, and the United States, was meant to prevent the Soviet Union from expanding to the south. By the mid-1950s, the United States found itself allied militarily with 42 states around the world.

### The Arms Race
The Soviet Union had set off its first atomic bomb in 1949. In the early 1950s, the Soviet Union and the United States developed the even more deadly hydrogen bomb. By the mid-1950s, both had intercontinental ballistic missiles (ICBMs) capable of sending bombs anywhere.

The search for security soon took the form of **deterrence.** This policy held that huge arsenals of nuclear weapons on both sides prevented war. The belief was that neither side would launch a nuclear attack because the other side would be able to strike back with devastating power.

In 1957, the Soviets sent *Sputnik I,* the first human-made space satellite, to orbit the earth. New fears seized the American public. Did the Soviet Union have a massive lead in building missiles? Was there a "missile gap" between the United States and the Soviet Union?

### A Wall in Berlin
Nikita Khrushchev (kroosh•CHAWF), who emerged as the new leader of the Soviet Union in 1955, tried to take advantage of the American concern over missiles to solve the problem of West Berlin. West Berlin remained a "Western island" of prosperity in the midst of the relatively poverty-stricken East Germany. Many East Germans, tired of Communist repression, managed to escape East Germany by fleeing through West Berlin.

Khrushchev realized the need to stop the flow of refugees from East Germany through West Berlin. In August 1961, the East German government began to build a wall separating West Berlin from East Berlin. Eventually it became a massive barrier guarded by barbed wire, floodlights, machine-gun towers, minefields, and vicious dog patrols. The Berlin Wall became a striking symbol of the division between the two superpowers.

✔ Reading Check  **Identifying** Name the military alliances formed during the Cold War.

### The Cuban Missile Crisis
During the **administration** of John F. Kennedy, the Cold War confrontation between the United States and the Soviet Union reached frightening levels. In 1959, a left-wing revolutionary named Fidel Castro overthrew the Cuban dictator Fulgencio Batista and set up a Soviet-supported totalitarian regime in Cuba (see Chapter

NATO and the Warsaw Pact map showing:
- North Atlantic Treaty Organization (NATO) member nations, 1949
- Nations joining NATO as of 1955
- Warsaw Pact members as of 1955
- Nonmember nations as of 1955

Inset map legend: Dates indicate when countries came under Communist control.

DENMARK — Copenhagen
Berlin · POLAND 1947 · Warsaw
EAST GERMANY 1949
Prague
WEST GERMANY · CZECH. 1948 · SOVIET UNION
Vienna
SWITZ. AUSTRIA · Budapest
HUNGARY 1947 · ROMANIA 1947
Belgrade · Bucharest
ITALY · YUGOSLAVIA 1945 · BULGARIA 1946
Rome · Tirana · Sofia
Yugoslavia left the Communist Bloc in 1948.
ALBANIA 1946 · GREECE · TURKEY

0   200 mi.
0   200 km
Lambert Azimuthal Equal-Area projection

0   1,000 miles
0   1,000 kilometers
Orthographic projection

## Geography *Skills*

After World War II, the spread of the Cold War created new military alliances.

1. **Interpreting Maps** Are there any geographic factors that could have determined whether a country became a member of NATO or of the Warsaw Pact?

2. **Applying Geography Skills** Use the map to create a chart listing all of the countries in NATO and all the members of the Warsaw Pact.

14). President Kennedy approved a secret plan for Cuban exiles to invade Cuba in the hope of causing a revolt against Castro. The invasion was a disaster. Many of the exiles were killed or captured when they attempted a landing at the Bay of Pigs.

After the Bay of Pigs, the Soviet Union sent arms and military advisers to Cuba. Then, in 1962, Khrushchev began to place nuclear missiles in Cuba.

The United States was not willing to allow nuclear weapons within such close striking distance of its mainland. In October 1962, Kennedy found out that Soviet ships carrying missiles were heading to Cuba. He decided to blockade Cuba and prevent the fleet from reaching its destination. This approach gave each side time to find a peaceful solution. Khrushchev agreed to turn back the fleet and remove Soviet missiles from Cuba if Kennedy pledged not to invade Cuba. Kennedy quickly agreed.

The Cuban missile crisis brought the world frighteningly close to nuclear war. Indeed, in 1992 a high-ranking Soviet officer revealed that short-range nuclear devices would have been used against U.S. troops if the United States had invaded Cuba, an option that Kennedy fortunately had rejected. The realization that the world might have been destroyed in a few days had a profound influence on both sides. A hotline **communications** system between Moscow and Washington, D.C., was installed in 1963. The two superpowers could now communicate quickly in times of crisis.

✓ **Reading Check**   **Making Inferences** What proved to be most important to both the United States and Soviet Union during the Cuban missile crisis?

# Vietnam and the Domino Theory

**Main Idea** With the goal of stopping the spread of communism, the United States entered the war in Vietnam.

**Reading Connection** Remember how Germany forced its own government and ideas on the European countries it invaded during World War II? Read to learn how the United States feared the spread of communism.

The United States soon became drawn into a new struggle that had an important impact on the Cold War—the Vietnam War (see Chapter 16). In 1964, under President Lyndon B. Johnson, increasing numbers of U.S. troops were sent to Vietnam. Their purpose was to keep the Communist regime of North Vietnam from gaining control of South Vietnam.

U.S. policy makers saw the conflict in terms of a **domino theory.** If the Communists succeeded in South Vietnam, other countries in Asia would also fall (like dominoes) to communism.

Despite the massive superiority in equipment and firepower of the American forces, the United States failed to defeat the determined North Vietnamese. The growing number of American troops sent to Vietnam soon produced an antiwar movement in the United States, especially among college students of draft age. The images of war brought into American homes on television also turned American public opinion against the war.

President Johnson, condemned for his handling of the costly and indecisive war, decided not to run for reelection. Former vice president Richard M. Nixon won the election with his pledge to stop the war and bring the American people together. Ending the war was difficult, and Nixon's administration was besieged by antiwar forces.

Finally, in 1973, President Nixon reached an agreement with North Vietnam's leaders that allowed the United States to withdraw its armed forces. Within two years after the American withdrawal, Vietnam had been forcibly reunited by Communist armies from the North.

Despite the success of the North Vietnamese Communists, the domino theory proved unfounded. A split between Communist China and the Soviet Union, including border clashes and different implementations of communism, put an end to the Western idea that there was a single form of communism directed by Moscow. Under President Nixon, American relations with China were resumed. New nations in Southeast Asia, such as the Philippines, managed to avoid Communist governments.

Above all, Vietnam helped show the limitations of American power. By the end of the Vietnam War, a new era in American-Soviet relations had begun to emerge.

✓ **Reading Check** **Examining** What did the Vietnam War prove about the state of global communism?

**HISTORY Online** **Study Central**

For help with the concepts in this section of *Glencoe World History–Modern Times,* go to <u>wh.mt.glencoe.com</u> and click on **Study Central.**

---

# SECTION 1 ASSESSMENT

### Checking for Understanding

1. **Vocabulary** Define: aid, satellite state, policy of containment, occupy, creation, arms race, deterrence, administration, communications, domino theory.

2. **People and Events** Identify: Truman Doctrine, Dean Acheson, Marshall Plan, NATO, Warsaw Pact, SEATO, CENTO, Nikita Khrushchev.

3. **Places** Locate: Berlin, Federal Republic of Germany, German Democratic Republic.

### Reviewing Big Ideas

4. **Explain** why the Berlin Wall was built.

### Critical Thinking

5. **Historical Analysis** **Evaluating** In your opinion, why did the United States assume global responsibility for containing communism? **CA HR 3**

6. **Organizing Information** Use a table like the one below to list the military alliances formed during the Cold War. In the next column list the countries belonging to the alliance.

| Alliance | Countries |
|---|---|
|  |  |
|  |  |

### Analyzing Visuals

7. **Examine** the map on page 588. Why do you think the Soviets were able to install Communist governments in so many countries after World War II?

## Writing About History

8. **Informative Writing** Imagine that you are a resident of Berlin in 1948. Write a letter to a friend living in another part of Germany explaining what is happening in Berlin and your reaction to the actions of the foreign governments involved. **CA 10WA2.1a**

# FOCUS ON EVERYDAY LIFE

### Youth Protest in the 1960s

The decade of the 1960s witnessed a dramatic change in traditional manners and morals. The new standards were evident in dramatically higher divorce rates. Movies, plays, and books broke new ground in dealing with taboo subjects.

The youth movement was the most obvious sign of the times. New attitudes toward sex and the use of drugs were two of its features. Young people also questioned authority and rebelled against the older generation. Spurred on by the Vietnam War, the youth rebellion in the United States had become a youth protest movement by the second half of the 1960s. People active in the movement were often called "hippies." Although it started in the United States, the youth movement was found in other countries, too, as the Paris student protest of 1968 showed.

In the 1960s, the lyrics of rock music reflected the rebellious mood of many young people. Bob Dylan, a well-known recording artist, expressed their feelings. His 1964 song "The Times They Are A-Changin'" has been called an "anthem for the protest movement." Some of its words show why:

Come gather round people
Wherever you roam
And admit that the waters
Around you have grown
And accept it that soon
You'll be drenched to the bone
If your time to you
Is worth savin'
Then you better start swimmin'
Or you'll sink like a stone
For the times they are a-changin' . . .
Come mothers and fathers
Throughout the land
And don't criticize
What you can't understand
Your sons and your daughters
Are beyond your command
Your old road
Is rapidly agin'
Please get out of the new one
If you can't lend your hand
For the times they are a-changin'

◀ Young people expressed their rebellion through clothing, music, and protests. In clothing, a new informality defied old rules about what was proper—today's informal wear is a direct result. Styles in the 1960s ranged from the colorful, to folk-inspired, to mock-military. The styles spread and helped create a sense that a new generation would shape a better future.

American student opposition to the Vietnam War was one of the strongest causes for student unity. The anti-war movement had support in other countries and among all age groups. In this 1966 photo, Australians protested the war. The sign reading "Children Burnt for LBJ" is a reference to Vietnamese children, while "LBJ" stands for American president Lyndon Baines Johnson.

In May 1968, French students joined with workers in a general strike that paralyzed the nation. Inspired partly by American and Czech students, the French students were protesting what they saw as an outdated university system, while workers were protesting low salaries. In late May, the French riot police restored order, and many students were arrested and taken to jail.

The 1960s generation lent energy to political protests. Here, Czech youths demonstrate against the Soviet tanks which rolled into Prague on August 21, 1968, to damp down a reform movement. The student sign reads, "The USSR—Never Again." The protesters did not oppose socialism, but a Soviet system that repressed free speech. In March 1969, the Soviets brutally suppressed all remaining opposition.

## CONNECTING TO THE PAST

1. **Identifying** What does Bob Dylan say is the consequence of not changing?

2. **Comparing** Are there artists today who have the same outlook as Bob Dylan?

3. **Writing about History** What social or political issues concern young people around the world today? Are they being expressed in music, literature, TV, or movies? Write a brief essay focusing on one or two examples.

# The Soviet Union and Eastern Europe

## Guide to Reading

### Section Preview
The Soviet Union faced revolts and protests in its attempt to gain and maintain control over Eastern Europe.

**Main Idea**

- The Soviet Union recovered rapidly after World War II, but it could not maintain high levels of industrial production. (p. 593)
- After World War II, Soviet control of Eastern Europe became firmly entrenched. (p. 594)

### Content Vocabulary
heavy industry, de-Stalinization

### Academic Vocabulary
conform, symbol

### People to Identify
Alexander Solzhenitsyn, Tito, Imre Nagy, Alexander Dubček

### Places to Locate
Soviet Union, Poland, Hungary, Czechoslovakia, Albania, Yugoslavia

### Reading Objectives
1. List Khrushchev's policies of de-Stalinization.
2. Explain how the Soviet Union exerted power over Eastern Europe.

### Reading Strategy
**Categorizing Information** Use a diagram like the one below to identify how the Soviet Union carried out Communist policies.

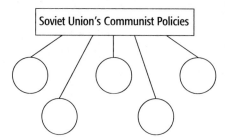
Soviet Union's Communist Policies

### Preview of Events

| ♦1950 | ♦1955 | ♦1960 | ♦1965 | ♦1970 |
|---|---|---|---|---|

**1953**
Khrushchev named general secretary

**1962**
Solzhenitsyn's *One Day in the Life of Ivan Denisovich* is published

**1964**
Khrushchev is voted out of office

**1968**
The Soviet Army invades Czechoslovakia

## California Standards in This Section

*Reading this section will help you master these California History–Social Science standards.*

**10.9:** Students analyze the international developments in the post-World War II world.

**10.9.5:** Describe the uprisings in Poland (1952), Hungary (1956), and Czechoslovakia (1968) and those countries' resurgence in the 1970s and 1980s as people in Soviet satellites sought freedom from Soviet control.

**10.9.7:** Analyze the reasons for the collapse of the Soviet Union, including the weakness of the command economy, burdens of military commitments, and growing resistance to Soviet rule by dissidents in satellite states and the non-Russian Soviet republics.

## Recovery Soviet-Style

**Main Idea** The Soviet Union recovered rapidly after World War II, but it could not maintain high levels of industrial production.

**Reading Connection** In a democracy, does a change in the administration drastically alter American life? Read to learn how the Soviet Union changed after the death of Joseph Stalin.

World War II devastated the **Soviet Union.** To create a new industrial base, Soviet workers were expected to produce goods for export. The incoming capital was used to buy machinery or Western technology, not consumer goods, so Soviet workers got little in return for their hard labor. This same strict life was found in Eastern Europe where the Soviet Union controlled the communist governments of this region. Periodically, the peoples of Eastern Europe rebelled.

### *Voices from the Past*

In 1956, Hungary revolted against the harsh control of the Soviets. As it sent in troops, the Soviet Union claimed that anti-democratic forces were responsible for the discontent:

> ❝Forces of reaction and counterrevolution . . . are trying to take advantage of the discontent of part of the working people to undermine the foundations of the people's democratic order in Hungary and to restore the old landlord and capitalist order. The Soviet government and all the people deeply regret that the development of events in Hungary has led to bloodshed. On the request of the Hungarian People's Government the Soviet government consented to the entry into Budapest of the Soviet Army units to assist the Hungarian authorities to establish order in the town.❞

**The Reign of Stalin** Economic recovery under Stalin was spectacular in some respects. By 1950, Russian industrial production had surpassed prewar levels by 40 percent. New power plants, canals, and giant factories were built. **Heavy industry,** the manufacture of machines and equipment for factories and mines, also increased. This increased production was targeted for military use. Meanwhile, the Soviet Union's reputation as a world power grew when it tested hydrogen bombs in 1953 and sent the first satellite, *Sputnik I,* into space in 1957.

Ordinary people were shortchanged, however. For example, the growth rate for heavy industry was three times that for consumer goods, and the housing shortage was severe. An average Russian family lived in a one-room apartment. A British official in Moscow reported that "every room is both a living room by day and a bedroom by night."

Stalin remained the undisputed master of the Soviet Union. He distrusted competitors, exercised sole power, and had little respect for other Communist Party leaders. He is reported to have said to members of his inner circle in 1952, "You are as blind as kittens. What would you do without me?"

Stalin's suspicions added to the increasing repression of the regime. In 1946, the government decreed that all literary and scientific work must **conform** to the political needs of the state. Along with this anti-intellectual campaign came political terror. A new series of purges seemed likely in 1953, but Stalin's death on March 5 prevented more bloodletting.

**✓ Reading Check** **Summarizing** What costs did Stalin's economic policy impose on the Russian people?

**The Khrushchev Era** A group of leaders succeeded Stalin, but the new general secretary of the Communist Party, Nikita Khrushchev, soon emerged as the chief Soviet politician. Once in power, Khrushchev took steps to undo some of the worst features of Stalin's regime.

At the Twentieth Congress of the Communist Party in 1956, Khrushchev condemned Stalin for his "administrative violence, mass repression, and terror." The process of eliminating the more ruthless policies of Stalin became known as **de-Stalinization.**

Khrushchev loosened government controls on literary works. In 1962, for example, he allowed the

▼ *Soviet tanks in Hungary*

publication of *One Day in the Life of Ivan Deniso-vich*, a grim portrayal of life in a Siberian forced-labor camp written by **Alexander Solzhenitsyn** (SOHL•zhuh•NEET•suhn). Each day, as Solzhenitsyn related, prisoners were marched from the prison camp in a remote location to a work project through subzero temperatures: "There were escort guards all over the place, ... their machine guns sticking out and pointed right at your face. And there were guards with gray dogs." Many Soviets identified with Ivan as a **symbol** of the suffering they had endured under Stalin.

Khrushchev tried to place more emphasis on satisfying consumers by producing more consumer goods. He also attempted to increase agricultural output by growing corn and cultivating vast lands east of the Ural Mountains. His agricultural policies were not successful, however, and damaged his reputation in the party.

The agricultural weaknesses, combined with increased military spending, hurt the Soviet economy. The industrial growth rate, which had soared in the early 1950s, now declined dramatically from 13 percent in 1953 to 7.5 percent in 1964.

Foreign policy failures also damaged Khrushchev's reputation. His rash plan to place missiles in Cuba was the final straw. While he was away on vacation in 1964, a special meeting of the Soviet leaders voted him out of office—the public statement was that his health had deteriorated—and forced him into retirement.

✓**Reading Check** **Explaining** Why did the Soviet leaders vote Khrushchev out of power?

# Eastern Europe: Behind the Iron Curtain

**Main Idea** After World War II, Soviet control of Eastern Europe became firmly entrenched.

**Reading Connection** During the age of imperialism, European powers controlled their colonial peoples in a number of ways. Read to learn how the Soviet Union maintained tight control over Eastern Europe.

At the end of World War II, Soviet military forces occupied all of Eastern Europe and most of the Balkans except for Greece, Albania, and Yugoslavia. All of the occupied states came under Soviet control.

**Communist Patterns of Control** The timetable of the Soviet takeover varied from country to country. Between 1945 and 1947, Soviet-controlled Communist governments became firmly entrenched in East Germany, Bulgaria, Romania, **Poland,** and **Hungary.** In **Czechoslovakia,** where there was a strong tradition of democracy and a multiparty system, the Soviets did not seize control of the government until 1948. At that time they dissolved all parties but the Communist Party.

**Albania** and **Yugoslavia** were exceptions to this pattern of Soviet dominance. During the war, both countries had had strong Communist movements that resisted the Nazis. After the war, local Communist parties took control. Communists in Albania set up a Stalinist-type regime that grew more and more independent of the Soviet Union.

## People In History

### Nikita Khrushchev
**1894–1971—Soviet leader**

First secretary of the Communist Party after Stalin's death, Khrushchev eventually came to be the sole Soviet ruler. In 1956, he denounced the rule of Stalin, arguing that "Stalin showed in a whole series of cases his intolerance, his brutality and his abuse of power. . . . He was a very distrustful man, sickly suspicious. Everywhere and in everything he saw enemies, two-facers, and spies."

Khrushchev alienated other Soviet leaders by his policy in Cuba. He had other problems with the higher Soviet officials as well. They frowned on his tendency to crack jokes and play the clown. They also were displeased when he tried to curb their privileges.

▲ *Polish teenagers armed with clubs and bottles protest communism.*

In Yugoslavia, Josip Broz, known as **Tito,** had been the leader of the Communist resistance movement. After the war, he moved toward the creation of an independent communist state in Yugoslavia. Stalin hoped to take control of Yugoslavia, just as he had done in other Eastern European countries. Tito, however, refused to give in to Stalin's demands. He gained the support of the people by portraying the struggle as one of Yugoslav national freedom. Tito ruled Yugoslavia until his death in 1980. Although Yugoslavia had a Communist government, it was not a Soviet satellite state.

Between 1948 and Stalin's death in 1953, the Eastern European satellite states, directed by the Soviet Union, followed Stalin's example. They instituted Soviet-type five-year plans with emphasis on heavy industry rather than consumer goods. They began to collectivize agriculture. They eliminated all non-communist parties and set up the institutions of repression—secret police and military forces.

**Revolts Against Communism** Communism did not develop deep roots among the peoples of Eastern Europe. In some cases, there was a long history of hostility between Russia and certain countries, such as Poland. Since the Soviets exploited them economically and made living conditions harsh, Eastern Europeans disliked the Soviet system.

After Stalin's death, many Eastern European states felt freer to pursue a new course. In the late 1950s and 1960s, the Soviet Union decided that this was unacceptable. The Soviet Union made it clear that it would not allow its satellite states—especially Poland, Hungary, and Czechoslovakia—to be independent.

In 1956, protests erupted in Poland. In response, the Polish Communist Party adopted a series of reforms in October 1956 and elected Wladyslaw Gomulka as first secretary. Gomulka declared that Poland had the right to follow its own socialist path. Fearful of Soviet armed response, however, the Poles compromised. Poland pledged to remain loyal to the Warsaw Pact.

Developments in Poland in 1956 led Hungarian Communists to seek the same kinds of reforms. Unrest in Hungary, combined with economic difficulties,

**HISTORY Online** **Web Activity**

Visit the *Glencoe World History—Modern Times* Web site at wh.mt.glencoe.com and click on **Chapter 12– Student Web Activity** to learn more about the Cold War.

# TIME

## THE WEEKLY NEWSMAGAZINE

Self-Determination for Czechoslovakia

PARTY BOSS
DUBČEK

### Picturing History

Relatively unknown outside his native Czechoslovakia before 1968, Alexander Dubček captured international attention with his bold moves toward reforming a communist society. **Why do you think the Soviets crushed the reform movement?**

led to calls for revolt. To quell the rising rebellion, **Imre Nagy,** the Hungarian leader, declared Hungary a free nation on November 1, 1956, and promised free elections. It soon became clear that this might spell the end of Communist rule there.

Khrushchev was in no position at home to allow this to happen. Three days after Nagy's declaration,

the Soviet army attacked the Hungarian capital of Budapest and the Soviets reestablished control in the country. The Soviets seized Nagy, who was executed two years later.

The situation in Czechoslovakia in the 1950s was different. There, Stalin had placed "Little Stalin," Antonin Novotny, in power himself in 1953. By the late 1960s, however, Novotny had alienated many members of his own party. He was especially disliked by Czechoslovakia's writers. A writers' rebellion, which encouraged the people to take control of their own lives, led to Novotny's resignation in 1968.

In January 1968, **Alexander Dubček** (DOOB•chehk) was elected first secretary of the Communist Party. He introduced a number of reforms, including freedom of speech and press and the freedom to travel abroad. He relaxed censorship, began to pursue an independent foreign policy, and promised a gradual democratization of the political system. Dubček hoped to create "socialism with a human face." A period of euphoria broke out that came to be known as the "Prague Spring."

The euphoria proved to be short-lived. To forestall the spreading of this "spring fever," the Soviet army invaded Czechoslovakia in August 1968 and crushed the reform movement. Gustav Husák replaced Dubček and did away with his reforms, reestablishing the old order.

✔ **Reading Check** **Evaluating** What caused the battles between the Eastern European states and the Soviet Union?

## HISTORY Online · Study Central

For help with the concepts in this section of *Glencoe World History—Modern Times,* go to wh.mt.glencoe.com and click on **Study Central.**

---

# SECTION 2 ASSESSMENT

### Checking for Understanding

1. **Vocabulary** Define: heavy industry, conform, de-Stalinization, symbol.

2. **People** Identify: Alexander Solzhenitsyn, Tito, Imre Nagy, Alexander Dubček.

3. **Places** Locate: Soviet Union, Poland, Hungary, Czechoslovakia, Albania, Yugoslavia.

### Reviewing Big Ideas

4. **List** two countries in Eastern Europe that resisted Soviet dominance.

### Critical Thinking

5. **Historical Analysis** **Connecting Ideas** Why did Yugoslavia and Albania not come under the direct control of the Soviet Union? **CA HI 1**

6. **Organizing Information** Use a table like the one below to identify the policies of Stalin and those of Khrushchev.

| Stalin | Khrushchev |
|--------|------------|
|        |            |
|        |            |
|        |            |

### Analyzing Visuals

7. **Compare** the photographs on pages 593 and 595. How does each photograph symbolize different reactions to Communist rule?

### Writing About History

8. **Informative Writing** Imagine you are a Western journalist in Hungary in 1956. Write an article for an American newspaper that describes the events leading to the Soviet attack on Budapest and what effect the attack will have on the Cold War. **CA 10WA2.1a**

# Western Europe and North America

## Guide to Reading

### Section Preview
Post–World War II societies rebuilt their economies and communities, but not without upheaval and change.

**Main Idea**
- After the end of World War II, most of Western Europe recovered economically and the region became more unified. (p. 598)
- In the years following World War II, the United States faced a range of difficult social and political issues. (p. 600)
- After World War II, advances in technology and the struggle for rights led to rapid change in Western society. (p. 603)

### Content Vocabulary
welfare state, bloc, real wages, civil rights movement, consumer society, women's liberation movement

### Academic Vocabulary
role, publish

### People and Events to Identify
Charles de Gaulle, European Economic Community, John F. Kennedy, Martin Luther King, Jr., Simone de Beauvoir

### Places to Locate
France, West Germany

### Reading Objectives
1. Describe how the EEC benefited its members.
2. List the major social changes in Western society after 1945.

### Reading Strategy
**Categorizing Information** Use a table like the one below to list programs instituted by Great Britain, the United States, and Canada to promote social welfare.

| Great Britain | United States | Canada |
|---------------|---------------|--------|
|               |               |        |
|               |               |        |
|               |               |        |

### Preview of Events

| ♦1945 | ♦1950 | ♦1955 | ♦1960 | ♦1965 | ♦1970 | ♦1975 |
|-------|-------|-------|-------|-------|-------|-------|

**1949**
Simone de Beauvoir publishes *The Second Sex*

**1957**
The Rome Treaty establishes the EEC

**1964**
The Civil Rights Act is passed

**1968**
Student revolts peak

## California Standards in This Section

*Reading this section will help you master these California History–Social Science standards.*

**10.9:** Students analyze the international developments in the post–World War II world.

**10.9.1:** Compare the economic and military power shifts caused by the war, including the Yalta Pact, the development of nuclear weapons, Soviet control over Eastern European nations, and the economic recoveries of Germany and Japan.

# Western Europe: Recovery and New Unity

**Main Idea** After the end of World War II, most of Western Europe recovered economically and the region became more unified.

**Reading Connection** Do you remember reading about the economic recovery of Germany after World War I? Read to learn how West Germany and East Germany recovered after World War II.

With the economic aid of the Marshall Plan, Western Europe recovered relatively rapidly from World War II. Between 1947 and 1950, European countries received $9.4 billion for new equipment and raw materials. By 1950, industrial output in Europe was 30 percent above prewar levels. This economic recovery continued well into the 1950s and 1960s, decades of dramatic growth and unequaled prosperity. This economic wealth brought cultural changes in society, too, and youth were often at the forefront.

## *Voices from the Past*

Student revolts were a part of larger problems that faced Western society after 1945. The 1960s were a major period of cultural shifts. In 1968, student protesters scribbled these words on the walls of a building at the University of Paris:

> ❝May 1968. World revolution is the order of the day.
> To be free in 1968 is to take part.
> Make love, not war.
> The mind travels faster than the heart but it doesn't go as far.
> Exam = servility, social promotion, hierarchic society.
> Love each other.
> Are you consumers or participants?
> Revolution, I love you.❞

**France and de Gaulle** The history of **France** for nearly a quarter of a century after the war was dominated by one man—the war hero **Charles de Gaulle.** In 1946, de Gaulle helped establish a new government called the Fourth Republic. It featured a strong parliament and a weak presidency. No party was strong enough to dominate, and the government was largely ineffective.

Unhappy with the Fourth Republic, de Gaulle withdrew from politics. Then, in 1958, he returned. Leaders of the Fourth Republic, frightened by bitter divisions caused by a crisis in the French colony of Algeria (discussed in Chapter 15), asked de Gaulle to form a new government and revise the constitution.

In 1958, de Gaulle drafted a new constitution for the Fifth Republic that greatly enhanced the power of the president. The president would now have the right to choose the prime minister, dissolve parliament, and supervise both defense and foreign policy. The constitution was overwhelmingly approved by French voters, and de Gaulle became the first president of the Fifth Republic.

As the new president, de Gaulle sought to return France to a position of great power. To achieve the status of a world power, de Gaulle invested heavily in nuclear arms. In 1960, France exploded its first nuclear bomb.

During de Gaulle's presidency, the French economy grew at an annual rate of 5.5 percent, faster than that of the United States. France became a major industrial producer and exporter, especially of automobiles and weapons.

Nevertheless, problems remained. Large government deficits and a rise in the cost of living led to unrest. In May 1968, a series of student protests was followed by a general labor strike. Tired and discouraged, de Gaulle resigned from office in April 1969 and died within a year.

▼ *Student protester facing policeman in Paris*

## People In History

### Charles de Gaulle
#### 1890–1970—French president

Charles de Gaulle had an unshakable faith in his mission to restore the greatness of the French nation. De Gaulle followed a military career and, before World War II, he argued for a new type of mobile tank warfare. After France fell to the Nazis, he fled to Britain and became leader of the French Resistance.

As president of France, de Gaulle realized that France was wasting its economic strength by maintaining its colonial empire. By 1962, he had granted independence to France's black African colonies and to Algeria. At the same time, he believed that playing an important role in the Cold War would enhance France's stature. For that reason, he pulled France out of NATO, saying that France did not want to be an American "vassal state."

**The Economic Miracle of West Germany** The three Western zones of Germany were unified as the Federal Republic of Germany in 1949. From 1949 to 1963, Konrad Adenauer (A•duhn•OWR), the leader of the Christian Democratic Union (CDU), served as chancellor (head of state). Adenauer sought respect for **West Germany.** He cooperated with the United States and other Western European nations and especially wanted to work with France—Germany's long-time enemy.

Under Adenauer, West Germany experienced an "economic miracle." The finance minister, Ludwig Erhard, played a major role in the West German economic revival. Unemployment fell from 8 percent in 1950 to 0.4 percent in 1965. To maintain its economic expansion, West Germany even brought in hundreds of thousands of "guest workers" on visas from Italy, Spain, Greece, Turkey, and Yugoslavia.

Adenauer resigned in 1963, after 14 years of guiding West Germany through its postwar recovery. Ludwig Erhard succeeded Adenauer as chancellor and largely continued his policies.

An economic downturn in the mid-1960s opened the door to the Social Democratic Party, which became the leading party in 1969. The leader of the Social Democrats, a moderate socialist party, was Willy Brandt, the mayor of West Berlin.

**The Decline of Great Britain** The end of World War II left Great Britain with massive economic problems. In elections immediately after the war, the Labour Party overwhelmingly defeated the Conservative Party headed by Churchill—a shock for the man who had led the fight against Hitler.

The Labour Party had promised far-reaching reforms, especially in the area of social welfare. Under Clement Attlee, the new prime minister, the Labour government set out to create a modern **welfare state**—a state in which the government takes responsibility for providing citizens with services and a minimal standard of living.

In 1946, the new government passed the National Insurance Act and the National Health Service Act. The insurance act provided funds for the unemployed, the sick, and the aged. The health act created a system of socialized medicine that ensured medical care for all. The British welfare state soon became the norm for most European states.

The cost of building a welfare state at home forced Britain to reduce expenses abroad. This meant the dismantling of the British Empire. Economic necessity forced Britain to give in to the demands of its many colonies for national independence. Britain was no longer able to play the **role** of a world power.

Continuing economic problems brought the Conservatives back into power from 1951 to 1964. Although they favored private enterprise, the Conservatives accepted the welfare state and even extended it by financing an ambitious building program to improve British housing.

√ **Reading Check** **Explaining** Why did de Gaulle invest heavily in nuclear arms?

## Geography *Skills*

The signing of the Rome Treaty in 1957 established the European Economic Community (EEC).

1. **Interpreting Maps** What countries were members of the EEC in 1957?

2. **Applying Geography Skills** What geographical factors could help to explain why some European countries joined the EEC in 1957 but others did not?

**The Move Toward Unity** As we have seen, the divisions created by the Cold War led the nations of Western Europe to form the North Atlantic Treaty Organization in 1949. The destructiveness of two world wars caused many thoughtful Europeans to consider the need for some additional form of European unity. National feeling was still too powerful, however, for European nations to give up their political sovereignty. As a result, the desire for unity focused chiefly on the economic arena, not the political one.

In 1957, France, West Germany, the Benelux countries (Belgium, the Netherlands, and Luxembourg), and Italy signed the Rome Treaty. This treaty created the **European Economic Community** (EEC), also known as the Common Market.

The EEC was a free-trade area made up of the six member nations. These six nations would impose no tariffs, or import charges, on each other's goods. However, as a group, they would be protected by a tariff imposed on goods from non-EEC nations. In this way, the EEC encouraged cooperation among the member nations' economies. All the member nations benefited economically.

By the 1960s, the EEC had become an important trading **bloc**—a group of nations with a common purpose. With a total population of 165 million, the EEC was the world's largest exporter and purchaser of raw materials.

**Reading Check** **Making Comparisons** Compare the economic recoveries of France and Great Britain.

## American Dominance

**Main Idea** In the years following World War II, the United States faced a range of difficult social and political issues.

**Reading Connection** Are the issues politicians debate today most often political or economic? Read to learn about the controversies in American history from 1945 to 1970.

Between 1945 and 1970, the ideals of President Franklin Delano Roosevelt's New Deal largely determined the agenda in American domestic politics. The New Deal had brought basic changes to American society. They included a dramatic increase in the role of the federal government, the rise of unions as a force in the economy and politics, the beginning of a welfare state, and a greater emphasis on the need to deal fairly with minorities in society, especially African Americans.

Since Roosevelt was a Democrat, the New Deal tradition was reinforced when other Democrats were elected president—Harry S. Truman in 1948, John F. Kennedy in 1960, and Lyndon B. Johnson in 1964. Even the election of a Republican, Dwight D. Eisenhower, in 1952 and 1956 did not change the basic direction of the New Deal. "Should any political party attempt to abolish Social Security and eliminate labor laws," President Eisenhower once said, "you would not hear of that party again in our political history."

An economic boom followed World War II. A shortage of consumer goods during the war had left Americans with both extra income and the desire to buy goods after the war. In addition, the growth of labor unions brought higher wages and gave more workers the ability to buy consumer goods. Between 1945 and 1973, **real wages** (the actual purchasing power of income) grew an average of 3 percent a year, the most prolonged advance in American history.

Prosperity was not the only characteristic of the early 1950s, however. Cold War struggles abroad led to the widespread fear that Communists had infiltrated the United States. President Truman's attorney general warned that Communists were "everywhere—in factories, offices, butcher stores, on street corners, in private businesses." For many Americans, proof of this threat became more evident when thousands of American soldiers were sent to Korea to fight and die in a war against Communist aggression.

This climate of fear produced a dangerous political agitator, Senator Joseph R. McCarthy of Wisconsin. His charges that hundreds of supposed Communists were in high government positions helped create a massive "Red Scare"—fear of Communist subversion. Under McCarthy, several individuals, including intellectuals and movie stars, were questioned about Communist activities. When McCarthy attacked alleged "Communist conspirators" in the U.S. Army, he was condemned by the Senate in 1954. Very quickly, his anti-Communist crusade came to an end.

✓ **Reading Check** **Describing** What effect did the Cold War have on many Americans?

**The 1960s and President Johnson** The 1960s began on a youthful and optimistic note. At age 43, **John F. Kennedy** became the youngest elected president in the history of the United States. His administration was cut short when the president was killed by an assassin on November 22, 1963. Vice President Lyndon B. Johnson then became president. Johnson won a new term as president in a landslide victory in 1964.

President Johnson used his stunning victory to pursue the growth of the welfare state, begun in the New Deal. Johnson's programs included health care for the elderly, various measures to combat poverty, and federal assistance for education.

Johnson's other domestic passion was the **civil rights movement,** or equal rights for African Americans. The civil rights movement had its beginnings in 1954, when the United States Supreme Court ruled that the practice of racial segregation (separation) in public schools was illegal. According to Chief Justice Earl Warren, "separate educational facilities are inherently unequal." African Americans also boycotted segregated buses, restaurants, and other public places.

# CONNECTIONS Around The World

## Economic Miracles: Germany and Japan

Both Germany and Japan were devastated by World War II. Their economies were in shambles. Their cities lay in ruins. At the end of the twentieth century, though, Germany and Japan were two of the world's greatest economic powers. What explains their economic miracles?

Because of the destruction of the war, both countries were forced to build new industrial plants. For many years, neither country spent much on defense. Their governments focused instead on rebuilding the infrastructure (roads, bridges, canals, and buildings) that had been destroyed during the war. Both German and Japanese workers had a long tradition of hard work and basic skills. In both countries, U.S. occupation policy was committed to economic recovery, a goal that was made easier by American foreign aid.

◀ *German bridge*

Today, Germany and Japan share many similarities in economic structure. Both rely on imports of raw materials for their industries. Both depend for their prosperity on exports of manufactured goods, including machinery, automobiles, steel, textiles, electrical and electronic equipment, and ships. Both nations must import food to feed their populations.

▲ *Japanese railroad station*

## Comparing Cultures

The United States has never experienced the kind of destruction experienced by Germany and Japan during World War II. How might your life be different if the United States was in the process of rebuilding after a war? What cultural, political, and economic factors might influence the process of rebuilding in the United States?

Gunfire breaks up an antiwar protest at Kent State University, Ohio, in 1970. Today, a memorial inscribed "Inquire, Learn, Reflect" marks the site where four students were killed by the National Guard. What message or lesson is conveyed to you by the events at Kent State?

In August 1963, the Reverend **Martin Luther King, Jr.,** leader of a growing movement for racial equality, led a march on Washington, D.C., to dramatize the African American desire for equality. King advocated the principle of passive disobedience practiced by Mohandas Gandhi. King's march and his impassioned plea for racial equality had an electrifying effect on the American people. By the end of 1963, a majority of the American people called civil rights the most significant national issue.

President Johnson took up the cause of civil rights. The Civil Rights Act in 1964 created the machinery to end segregation and discrimination in the workplace and all public places. The Voting Rights Act the following year made it easier for African Americans to vote in Southern states.

Laws alone, however, could not guarantee the Great Society that Johnson talked about creating. He soon faced bitter social unrest.

**Social Upheaval** In the North and West, African Americans had had voting rights for many years. Local patterns of segregation, however, meant that African Americans had higher unemployment rates than whites. In the summer of 1965, race riots broke out in the Watts district of Los Angeles. Thirty-four people died, and over a thousand buildings were destroyed. In 1968, Martin Luther King, Jr., was assassinated. Riots hit at least a hundred cities, including Washington, D.C. The riots led to a "white

backlash," meaning that whites now became less sympathetic to the cause of racial equality. Racial tensions continued to divide the nation.

Antiwar protests also divided the American people after President Johnson sent American troops to war in Vietnam (see Chapter 16). As the war progressed through the second half of the 1960s, the protests grew. Then, in 1970, four students at Kent State University were killed and nine others were wounded by the Ohio National Guard during a student demonstration. The tragedy startled the nation. By this time many Americans were less willing to continue the war.

The combination of antiwar demonstrations and riots in the cities caused many people to call for "law and order." This was the appeal used by Richard Nixon, the Republican presidential candidate in 1968. With Nixon's election in 1968, a shift to the political right in American politics began.

**Reading Check** **Interpreting** In your opinion, what was President Johnson's most important policy?

**American-Canadian Relations** In some ways, Canada had a parallel experience to the United States. For 25 years after World War II, a prosperous Canada set out on a new path of industrial development. Canada had always had a strong export economy based on abundant natural resources. Now it developed electronic, aircraft, nuclear, and chemical engineering industries on a large scale. Much of the Canadian growth, however, was financed by American capital, which led to U.S. ownership of Canadian businesses.

Some Canadians feared American economic domination of Canada. Canadians also worried about playing a secondary role politically and militarily to the United States. They sought to establish their own identity in world politics, and were a founding member of the United Nations in 1945 and the North Atlantic Treaty Organization in 1949.

The Liberal Party dominated Canadian politics throughout most of this period. Under Lester Pearson, the Liberal government created Canada's welfare state by enacting a national social security system (the Canada Pension Plan) and a national health insurance program.

✓**Reading Check** **Explaining** Why did some Canadians fear U.S. domination of their economy?

# Changing Values in Western Society

**Main Idea** After World War II, advances in technology and the struggle for rights led to rapid change in Western society.

**Reading Connection** Have you or your family members ever used credit cards? Read to learn how easy credit was only one change of the 1950s.

After World War II, Western society witnessed rapid change. Such new inventions as computers, televisions, and jet planes altered the pace and nature of human life. The rapid changes in postwar society led many to view it as a new society.

**A New Social Structure** Postwar Western society was marked by a changing social structure. The most noticeable changes were in the middle class. In the United States, the middle class expanded significantly, as the average income of families roughly tripled between 1940 and 1955.

By now the middle class included many types of occupations. Traditionally, businesspeople, merchants, lawyers, doctors, and teachers made up the middle class. Since early in the twentieth century, however, new groups such as the managers and technicians for corporations and government agencies had joined the ranks of the middle class. After World War II, these occupations multiplied, especially with the growth of government agencies.

Changes also occurred among the lower classes. The shift of people from rural to urban areas continued. The number of people in farming had been declining for a long time, but now it declined drastically. By the 1950s, the number of farmers in most parts of Europe had dropped by 50 percent. The number of industrial workers also began to decline while the number of white-collar workers increased.

At the same time, a noticeable increase in the real wages of workers made it possible for them to imitate the buying patterns of the middle class. Already in the 1920s, some historians have suggested that a new kind of society was developing, a **consumer society**— one that was preoccupied with buying goods, not producing them. By the 1950s, consumption patterns had definitely changed in many Western countries.

Buying on credit became widespread in the 1950s. Workers could now buy such products as televisions, washing machines, refrigerators, vacuum cleaners, and stereos. The automobile was the most visible symbol of the new consumerism. In 1948, there were 5 million cars in all of Europe. By the 1960s, there were almost 45 million.

**Women in the Postwar World** Women's participation in both World Wars led to important gains for them. They achieved one of the major aims of the

▼ *Early 1950s television*

nineteenth-century women's movement, the right to vote. After World War I, many governments had expressed thanks to women by granting them voting rights. Sweden, Great Britain, Germany, Poland, Hungary, Austria, and Czechoslovakia did so in 1918, followed by the United States in 1920. French women finally gained the vote in 1944, while Italian women did so in 1945.

During World War II, women had entered the workforce in huge numbers. At the war's end, however, they were removed to provide jobs for soldiers returning home. For a time, women fell back into traditional roles. Birthrates rose, creating a "baby boom" in the late 1940s and the 1950s.

By the end of the 1950s, however, the birthrate had begun to fall, and with it, the size of families. The structure of the workplace changed once again as the number of married women in the workforce increased in both Europe and the United States.

These women, especially working-class women, faced an old problem. They still earned less than men for equal work. For example, in the 1960s, women earned 60 percent of men's wages in Britain, 50 percent in France, and 63 percent in West Germany.

In addition, women still tended to enter traditionally female jobs. Many faced the double burden of earning income and raising a family. Such inequalities led increasing numbers of women to rebel.

By the late 1960s, women had begun to assert their rights again. In the late 1960s came renewed interest in feminism, or the **women's liberation movement,** as it was now called.

The work of **Simone de Beauvoir** (duh•boh•VWAHR) was very important to the emergence of the postwar women's liberation movement. In 1949,

she **published** her highly influential work, *The Second Sex.* In it, she argued that as a result of male-dominated societies, women had been defined mostly by how they were different from men and consequently they were treated as second-class citizens. De Beauvoir's book influenced both the American and European women's movements.

**Student Revolt** As we have seen, students in American universities in the mid- to late 1960s launched an antiwar protest movement. At the same time, European students were engaging in protests of their own.

Before World War II, it was mostly members of Europe's wealthier classes who went to universities. After the war, European states began to encourage more people to gain higher education by eliminating fees. As a result, universities saw an influx of students from the middle and lower classes. Enrollments grew dramatically. In France, 4.5 percent of young people went to universities in 1950. By 1965, the figure had increased to 14.5 percent.

There were problems, however. Many European university classrooms were overcrowded, and many professors paid little attention to their students. Growing discontent led to an outburst of student revolts in the late 1960s.

This student radicalism had several causes. Many of these protests were an extension of the revolts in U.S. universities, which were often sparked by student opposition to the Vietnam War. Some students, particularly in Europe, wished to reform the university system. They did not believe that universities responded to their needs or to the realities of the modern world. Others felt that they were becoming

## People In History

### Simone de Beauvoir
#### 1908–1986—French author

A prominent French intellectual, Simone de Beauvoir became a major voice in the European feminist movement. Born into a Catholic middle-class family and educated at the Sorbonne in Paris, she supported herself as a teacher and later as a novelist and writer.

De Beauvoir believed that she lived a "liberated" life for a twentieth-century European woman. Despite all her freedom, she still came to perceive that, as a woman, she faced limits that men did not: "What particularly signalizes the situation of woman is that she—a free autonomous being like all human creatures—nevertheless finds herself in a world where men compel her to assume the status of the Other."

Students threw cobblestones and the police retaliated with tear gas during the 1968 Paris demonstrations. Later, the streets were repaved with asphalt and concrete. After this incident, why do you think the authorities wanted paved streets rather than cobblestone?

small cogs in the large and impersonal bureaucratic wheels of the modern world. Student protest movements in both Europe and the United States reached a high point in 1968. By the early 1970s, the movements had largely disappeared.

The student protests of the late 1960s caused many people to rethink some of their basic assumptions. Looking back, however, we can see that the student upheavals were not a turning point in the history of postwar Europe, as some people thought at the time.

In the 1970s and 1980s, student rebels would become middle-class professionals. The vision of revolutionary politics would remain mostly a memory.

**Reading Check** **Identifying** What was the women's liberation movement trying to accomplish?

**HISTORY** *Online* **Study Central**

For help with the concepts in this section of *Glencoe World History–Modern Times,* go to wh.mt.glencoe.com and click on **Study Central.**

# SECTION 3 ASSESSMENT

### Checking for Understanding

1. **Vocabulary** Define: welfare state, role, bloc, real wages, civil rights movement, consumer society, women's liberation movement, publish.

2. **People and Events** Identify: Charles de Gaulle, European Economic Community, John F. Kennedy, Martin Luther King, Jr., Simone de Beauvoir.

3. **Places** Locate: France, West Germany.

### Reviewing Big Ideas

4. **Explain** why many British colonies gained their independence after World War II.

### Critical Thinking

5. **Historical Analysis** **Connecting Events** Do you think the student revolts of this period contributed positively or negatively to society? Why?
   **CA HI 1**

6. **Cause and Effect** Use a diagram like the one below to identify factors leading to the emergence of the postwar women's liberation movement.

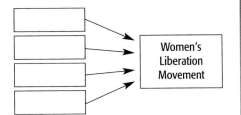

### Analyzing Visuals

7. **Compare** the Kent State photo on page 602 with the photo above. What do these two scenes have in common? In your opinion, were the costs of these protests justified? What causes today could motivate this type of passion and sacrifice?

## Writing About History

8. **Persuasive Writing** Demonstrations, marches, and riots were used in the 1960s and 1970s to communicate popular opinion. Write an essay that argues for or against the effectiveness of these methods for changing public opinion and policy.
   **CA 10WA2.4a,c**

# PRIMARY SOURCES
## EYEWITNESS TO HISTORY

*The following excerpts represent Soviet and American viewpoints during the early Cold War period. Read them to learn how each viewed Soviet power.*

## SOURCE 1: A Communist's Speech

*After the Soviet Union's defeat of Germany on the Eastern Front in the Second World War, the Soviet dictator Joseph Stalin delivered the following speech in February 1946.*

It would be wrong to believe that the Second World War broke out accidentally or as a result of the mistakes of some or other statesmen. . . . In reality, the war broke out as an inevitable result of the development of world economic and political forces on the basis of modern monopoly capitalism. . . .

As to our country, for her the war was the severest and hardest of all the wars our Motherland has ever experienced in her history. But the war . . . laid bare all the facts and events in the rear and at the front, it mercilessly tore off all the veils and covers which had concealed the tired faces of States, governments, and parties, and placed them on the stage without masks, without embellishments, and with all their shortcomings and virtues. . . .

And so, what are the results of the war . . .

Our victory means, in the first place, that our Soviet social system has won, that the Soviet social system successfully withstood the trial in the flames of war and proved its perfect **viability**[1].

It is well known that the foreign press more than once asserted that the Soviet social system . . . was doomed to failure, that the Soviet system is a "house of cards" . . . imposed upon the people by the organs of the "Cheka," [secret police] that a slight push from outside would be enough to blow this "house of cards" to smithereens.

Now we can say that the war swept away all these assertions of the foreign press as groundless. The war has shown that the Soviet social system is a truly popular system, which has grown from the people and enjoys its powerful support. . . .

*The Kremlin in Moscow*

More than that, the point is now not whether the Soviet social system is viable . . . since after the objective lessons of the war no single skeptic now . . . [has] doubts concerning the viability of the Soviet social system. The point now is that the Soviet social system has proved more viable and stable than a non-Soviet social system, that the Soviet social system is a better form of organization than any non-Soviet social system.

## SOURCE 2: The American Reaction to Communism

*This passage is an excerpt from a once-classified report of the National Security Council. Completed in 1950, it discusses American foreign policy during the Cold War.*

Our overall policy at the present time may be described as one designed to foster a world environment in which the American system can survive and

---

[1]**viability:** ability to continue

flourish. It therefore rejects the concept of isolation and affirms the necessity of our positive participation in the world community.

This broad intention embraces two **subsidiary**[2] policies. One is a policy which we would probably pursue even if there were no Soviet threat. It is a policy of attempting to develop a healthy international community. The other is the policy of "containing" the Soviet system. . . .

As for the policy of "containment," it is one which seeks by all means short of war to (1) block further expansion of Soviet power, (2) expose the falsities of the Soviet pretensions, (3) induce a retraction of the **Kremlin's**[3] control and influence and (4) in general, so foster the seeds of destruction within the Soviet system that the Kremlin is brought at least to the point of modifying its behavior to conform to generally accepted international standards. . . .

It is quite clear from Soviet theory and practice that the Kremlin seeks to bring the free world under its dominion by the methods of the cold war. The preferred technique is to subvert by infiltration and intimidation. Every institution of our society is an instrument which it is sought to stultify and turn against our purposes. Those that touch most closely our material and moral strength are obviously the prime targets, labor unions, civil enterprises, schools, churches, and all media for influencing opinion. The effort is not so much to make them serve obvious Soviet ends as to prevent them from serving our ends, and thus to make them sources of confusion in our economy, our culture, and our body politic . . .

## SOURCE 3: An American Diplomat on the Soviets

*In February 1946, George Kennan, an American diplomat in Russia, wired his government—in telegraph style—his opinion about the goals of Soviet leaders.*

1. To undermine general political and strategic potential of major Western powers. Efforts will be made in such countries to disrupt national self-confidence, to hamstring measures of national defense, to increase social and industrial unrest, to stimulate all forms of disunity. . . .

2. On unofficial plane particularly violent efforts will be made to weaken power and influence of Western powers over colonial, backward, or dependent peoples. . . . Resentment among dependent peoples will be stimulated. And while latter are being encouraged to seek independence of Western powers, Soviet-dominated puppet political machines will be undergoing preparation to take over domestic power in respective colonial areas when independence is achieved.

5. Everything possible will be done to set major Western powers against each other. . . . Where suspicions exist, they will be fanned; where not, ignited. No effort will be spared to discredit and combat all efforts which threaten to lead to any sort of unity or cohesion among others from which Russia might be excluded. . . .

6. In general, all Soviet efforts on unofficial international plane will be negative and destructive in character, designed to tear down sources of strength beyond reach of Soviet control. This is only in line with basic Soviet instinct that there can be no compromise with rival power and that constructive work can start only when Communist power is dominant. . . .

### DBQ Document-Based Questions

**Historical Analysis** CA HR 2, HI 3

**Source 1:** According to Stalin, what has the Soviet victory in World War II proven?

**Source 2:** What two major foreign policies did the American National Security Council propose?

**Source 3:** According to Kennan, what is the Soviet plan of attack?

#### Comparing and Contrasting Sources

1. According to the above passages, how would Soviet goals conflict with those of the Americans?
2. Why do both American accounts view the Soviets as a global, not just an American, concern? CA 10RL3.5

---

[2]**subsidiary:** supplementary; supporting
[3]**Kremlin:** seat of government for the USSR

## Reviewing Content Vocabulary

Standards 10.9, 10.9.1, 10.9.2, 10.9.3, 10.9.5, 10.9.7, 10.9.8

1. The actual purchasing power of income is called ___ .

2. The idea that allowing communist aggressors to take over one country will encourage them to take over other nations has been called the ___ .

3. The process of removing Stalin's influence from the Soviet government, economy, and social system was called ___ .

4. A nation that is preoccupied with the desire to provide its people with material goods may be said to be a ___ .

5. Governments that intervene in the economy to assure a minimal standard of living for all are said to be ___ .

6. The attempt of noncommunist world powers to prevent a further spread of communism to other states was called a ___ .

7. The ___ is a force that is working for greater equality and rights for women.

8. A country that was economically and politically dependent on the Soviet Union was called a ___ .

9. The United States and the Soviet Union were involved in a growing ___ in which both countries built up their armies and weapons.

10. After World War II, the Soviets concentrated on developing ___ , the manufacture of machines and equipment for factories.

11. The policy of ___ held that huge arsenals of nuclear weapons on both sides prevented nuclear war.

12. Nations grouped together for a common purpose are called a ___ .

13. The ___ is the pursuit of equal rights for African Americans.

## Reviewing Academic Vocabulary

*On a sheet of paper, use each of these terms in a sentence that reflects the term's meaning in the chapter.*

14. aid
15. occupy
16. creation
17. administration
18. communications
19. conform
20. symbol
21. role
22. publish

## Reviewing the Main Ideas

### Section 1

23. What was COMECON and why was it formed?

24. What happened during the Cuban missile crisis in 1962?

### Section 2

25. Describe what happened when satellite states tried to become independent of the Soviet Union.

26. Explain Khrushchev's relationship to Stalinism.

## Chapter Summary

Following World War II, two new superpowers, the United States and the Soviet Union, engaged in a Cold War that was fought around the globe.

| | Conflict/Crisis | Significant Event(s) | Result(s) |
|---|---|---|---|
| Greece (1944–1949) | Civil war erupts. | Great Britain aids government forces against communism. | United States creates Truman Doctrine. |
| Berlin (1949) | Soviets and Western powers divide Germany. | Western powers airlift supplies to Soviet-blockaded West Berlin. | Blockade is lifted. |
| Korea (1950–1953) | Civil war begins when North Korea invades South Korea. | United Nations forces fight to save South Korea from communism. | United States extends military alliances around the world. |
| Berlin (1961) | Refugees escape from East to West Berlin. | Soviets build Berlin Wall. | Berlin Wall becomes symbol of divided Germany. |
| Cuba (1962) | Soviets support Castro's totalitarian regime in Cuba. | United States invades Bay of Pigs; Soviets place nuclear missiles in Cuba; United States blockades Cuba. | Soviets withdraw missiles; hotline is established between Moscow and Washington, D.C. |
| Vietnam (1964–1973) | Civil war erupts between North and South Vietnam. | United States intervenes to prevent North Vietnam from taking over South Vietnam. | United States withdraws from Vietnam; Vietnam is reunited by Communists. |

## HISTORY Online

**Self-Check Quiz**

Visit the *Glencoe World History–Modern Times* Web site at wh.mt.glencoe.com and click on **Chapter 12– Self-Check Quiz** to prepare for the Chapter Test.

**Section 3**

27. Name the social movements that altered American society after World War II.

28. What book influenced the women's movement in America and Europe? What was its significance to the movement?

## Critical Thinking

29. **Analyzing** How did de-Stalinization help Khrushchev gain control of the Soviet government?

30. **Explaining** Is containment an important or pressing issue in American foreign policy today? Explain your reasoning.

31. **Reading Skill** **Evaluating** The Cuban missile crisis developed out of a tense power struggle between two nuclear powers. What decisions created the crisis? What else might have been done?

## Writing About History

32. **Historical Analysis** **Interpreting Economics** Look up how much money the United States government spent on the arms race during a year in the 1950s. Write a one-page essay exploring why this expenditure was a priority in the post–World War II economy. **CA HI 6**

33. **Big Idea** In an essay, identify and explain possible reasons for the comparatively slow growth of social benefits provided to Americans, compared to the rapid growth of these programs in Europe, after World War II. **CA 10WA2.3**

**DBQ** **Document-Based Questions**

**Analyzing Sources** Read the following excerpt from Solzhenitsyn's *One Day in the Life of Ivan Denisovich* in which prisoners march from the prison camp to a work project through temperatures of seventeen degrees below zero:

66 There were escort guards all over the place, . . . their machine guns sticking out and pointed right at your face. And there were guards with gray dogs. 99

34. Why might Soviets identify with this story?

35. Why did Khrushchev allow this book to be published?

## Analyzing Maps and Charts

Using the map on this page, answer the following questions.

36. How many miles did the blockade zone of Cuba extend from west to east?

**NATIONAL GEOGRAPHIC** **Cuban Missile Crisis, 1962**

| Soviet missile site
— U.S. blockade zone
U.S. naval base

37. Why was the United States so concerned that the Soviets were placing missiles in Cuba? What other islands fall within the blockade zone?

## Standards Practice

**Directions: Use the quote and your knowledge of world history to answer the following question.**

66 And even today woman is heavily handicapped, though her situation is beginning to change. Almost nowhere is her legal status the same as man's, and frequently it is much to her disadvantage. Even when her rights are legally recognized in the abstract, long-standing custom prevents their full expression. . . . 99

—*The Second Sex*, **Simone de Beauvoir**

38. Simone de Beauvoir's book *The Second Sex* was published in 1949. Her book was influential because it

A helped women gain the right to vote.

B contributed to a women's movement in the 1950s and 1960s.

C greatly increased the number of married women in the labor force.

D influenced and shaped the student protest movement.

**CA Standard 10.10.3** Discuss the important trends in the regions today and whether they appear to serve the cause of individual freedom and democracy.

*1970–Present*

# The Contemporary Western World

## ❧ *The Big Ideas* ❧

### SECTION 1: Decline of the Soviet Union

**The quest for national self-determination is universal.** A change in Soviet leadership led to a freer political system in the Soviet Union and Eastern Europe, but change has also presented serious economic challenges.

### SECTION 2: Eastern Europe

**The quest for national self-determination is universal.** Popular revolutions helped end Communist regimes in Eastern Europe.

### SECTION 3: Europe and the United States

**Nations compete for natural resources and strategic advantages over other nations.** Postwar Western societies rebuilt their communities, but shifting social structures led to upheaval and change.

### SECTION 4: Western Society and Culture

**New technologies can revolutionize the way people live, work, interact and govern.** Western society has been shaped by science and technology, changes in family structures and population trends, a renewed interest in religion, and popular culture.

 ***World History—Modern Times Video*** *The Chapter 13 video,* "*Solidarity," chronicles the history of the movement for democracy in Poland.*

**1980**
Lech Walesa
organizes trade
union Solidarity
in Poland

**1987**
Soviet Union
and United
States sign
INF Treaty

*1970*      *1974*      *1978*      *1982*      *1986*

**1972**
Equal Pay Act
passed in United
States

*Women's
liberation march*

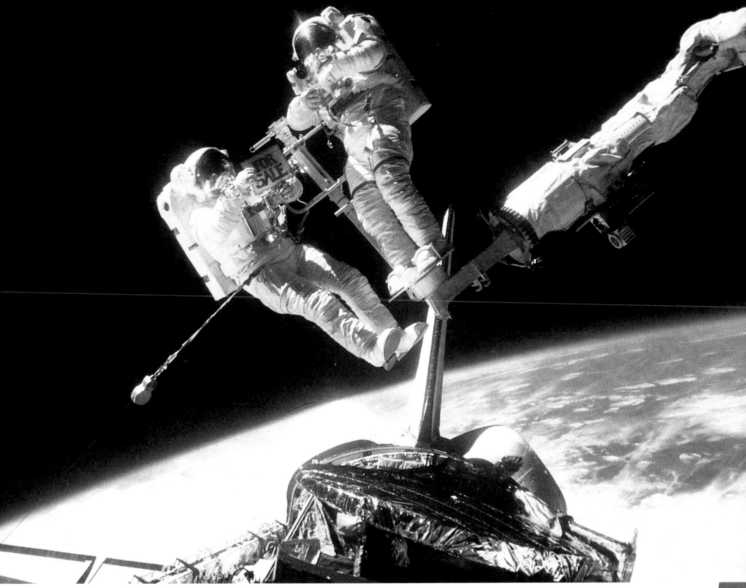

Advances in space exploration have been made possible by new technology.

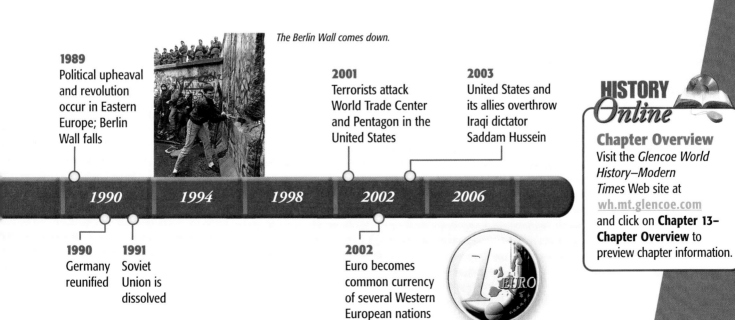

The Berlin Wall comes down.

**1989**
Political upheaval and revolution occur in Eastern Europe; Berlin Wall falls

**2001**
Terrorists attack World Trade Center and Pentagon in the United States

**2003**
United States and its allies overthrow Iraqi dictator Saddam Hussein

1990

1994

1998

2002

2006

**1990**
Germany reunified

**1991**
Soviet Union is dissolved

**2002**
Euro becomes common currency of several Western European nations

*Euro coin*

**HISTORY** *Online*

**Chapter Overview**
Visit the *Glencoe World History–Modern Times* Web site at **wh.mt.glencoe.com** and click on **Chapter 13– Chapter Overview** to preview chapter information.

## Reading Skill    Connecting

Alert readers make a connection to any text they read. There are usually three ways this happens. Someone reads a feature about a local woman who turns 105 and thinks, "My grandmother is old, but she's not that old!" (You are connecting the text to yourself.). Or maybe you think to yourself, "I remember reading in school about the Middle Ages and the book said the average age was only 50!" (You are connecting the text to another text.) Finally, you might think, "I've heard that new drugs are curing diseases—I wonder if soon a lot of people will live to be 105." (You are connecting the text to your world.)

Stop after a paragraph or passage and ask yourself a connecting question. Does it remind you of something that has happened in your life? Does it remind you of something you have read? Does it make you think of a person or event in the world around you?

### TEXT-TO-TEXT

The phrase *young neo-Nazis who believed in Hitler's idea of a pure Aryan race* might easily trigger a text-to-text connection, reminding you of what you read in Chapter 9 about Germany in the 1930s.

*Read the following paragraph from this chapter about unrest in Germany in the 1990s and ask yourself a connecting question about it.*

Economic problems also led to attacks on foreigners, who were seen as taking jobs from Germans. For years, illegal immigrants and foreigners seeking political refuge were able to move to Germany because of its liberal immigration laws.... As economic conditions throughout Europe worsened, so, too, did tensions between some Germans and immigrant groups. Attacks against foreigners by right-wing extremists—especially young neo-Nazis who believed in Hitler's idea of a pure Aryan race—became part of German life.

### TEXT-TO-SELF and TEXT-TO-WORLD

After you read the paragraph, you think about how you feel about an immigrant you know— that's text-to-self. Or, you wonder whether terrorism makes immigrants more likely to be attacked—that's text-to-world.

### Apply the Skill

As you read this chapter, pause periodically to make one of the three types of connections: text-to-self, text-to-text, or text-to-world. If you do, the idea or topic will have greater meaning to you—and be easier to remember.

 **Historical Analysis Skill** Analyzing Sequence and Change

 **Historical Interpretation: Standard CS 2** *Students analyze how change happens at different rates at different times; understand that some aspects can change while others remain the same; and understand that change is complicated and affects not only technology and politics but also values and beliefs.*

Studying history means to study how things change over time. That's why one of the first things a historian does is to figure out when events occurred and the order in which they occurred. This is an important step to understanding how events are related. Through this kind of analysis, a historian learns that change can be slow or fast, and it can occur in some areas but not in others. Analyzing sequence and change helps a historian pinpoint the most important factors in major developments.

In the late 1980s, the Communist system unraveled in the nations of Eastern Europe. These nations reacted against the Soviet system in different ways. In some, well-organized workers' movements took the lead. In others, mass demonstrations against dictatorial policies or general suppression of peoples' rights pressured Communist leaders to accept the need for change. If you keep timing and sequence in mind, however, you will be better able to understand the important overall outcome.

*Read this general description from Chapter 13 of what happened when Eastern European governments lost Soviet support:*

**Many Eastern Europeans were discontented with their Soviet-controlled governments. Freedom of speech was limited, and housing and consumer goods were often in short supply. When Gorbachev decided the Soviets would no longer send troops to support these governments, popular demonstrations and revolutions occurred across Eastern Europe.**

## Apply the Skill

Create a time line that reflects the decline of Soviet control in Poland and Czechoslovakia. Use information from the previous chapter and add to it as you read this chapter. What does this time line tell you about how change occurs? Did both countries react to events in the Soviet Union in the same way?

# A Story That Matters

*Near Berlin's Brandenburg Gate in 1990, crowds of people celebrate the reunification of Germany.*

## *"Tear Down This Wall"*

*I*n 1988, the American president, Ronald Reagan, traveled to West Berlin. Facing the Berlin Wall, he challenged Mikhail Gorbachev, leader of the Soviet bloc, to "tear down this wall." During his own visit to West Germany a year later, Gorbachev responded, "The wall could disappear once the conditions that generated the need for it disappear. I do not see much of a problem here."

East Germany's Communist leaders, however, did see a problem, and they refused to remove the wall. In the summer of 1989, tens of thousands of East Germans fled their country while hundreds of thousands took to the streets to demand the resignation of the hard-line Communist leader, Erich Honecker.

Honecker finally relented. On November 9, 1989, a new East German government opened the wall and allowed its citizens to travel freely between West and East Berlin. The next day, government workers began to knock down the wall. They were soon joined by thousands of West and East Berliners who used sledgehammers and crowbars to rip apart the Cold War symbol.

Germans were overcome with joy. Many danced on the wall while orchestras played in the streets. Churches, theaters, and shops remained open day and night in West Germany as East Germans took advantage of their new freedom to travel. In 1990, West and East Germany became a single nation, and Berlin was once again the capital of Germany.

### Why It Matters

In 1970, after more than two decades of the Cold War, the division of Europe between West and East seemed well established to most Europeans. A prosperous Western Europe that was allied to the United States stood opposed to a still-struggling Eastern Europe that remained largely subject to the Soviet Union. However, within 20 years, a revolutionary upheaval in the Soviet Union and Eastern Europe brought an end to the Cold War and the long-standing division of postwar Europe.

**History and You** Research contemporary Berlin. Use sources ranging from academic histories to travel guides. Make a list of the ways the East/West split still affects Berlin today. Which of these reminders of the past did you expect, and which surprised you? Why?

# Decline of the Soviet Union

## Guide to Reading

### Section Preview
A change in Soviet leadership led to a freer political system in the Soviet Union and Eastern Europe, but change has also presented serious economic challenges.

**Main Idea**
- The Soviet Union was unable to survive a combination of domestic and foreign problems. (p. 616)
- Mikhail Gorbachev's reforms contributed to the end of the Cold War and of the Soviet system. (p. 617)

### Content Vocabulary
détente, dissident, perestroika

### Academic Vocabulary
apparent, expansion

### People and Events to Identify
Mikhail Gorbachev, Leonid Brezhnev, Brezhnev Doctrine, Ronald Reagan, Boris Yeltsin, Vladimir Putin

### Places to Locate
Afghanistan, Ukraine, Belarus

### Reading Objectives
1. List reasons for the end of the Cold War.
2. Describe the problems that arose when the Soviet Union disintegrated.

### Reading Strategy
**Compare and Contrast** Create a chart like the one below comparing the policies of Brezhnev and Gorbachev.

|  | Leonid Brezhnev | Mikhail Gorbachev |
|---|---|---|
| Foreign Policy |  |  |
| Economic Policy |  |  |
| Military Policy |  |  |
| Personal Policy |  |  |

### Preview of Events

♦1985　　♦1990　　♦1995　　♦2000　　♦2005

**1985**
Mikhail Gorbachev assumes leadership of Soviet Union

**1988**
Communist Party conference initiates political reforms

**1991**
Boris Yeltsin becomes president of Russia

**2000**
Ex-KGB agent Vladimir Putin becomes president of Russia

**2004**
300 hostages die when Russian soldiers end the rebel siege of a Chechnyan school

## California Standards in This Section

*Reading this section will help you master these California History–Social Science standards.*

**10.9.7:** Analyze the reasons for the collapse of the Soviet Union, including the weakness of the command economy, burdens of military commitments, and growing resistance to Soviet rule by dissidents in satellite states and the non-Russian Soviet republics.

# The Soviet System Under Stress

**Main Idea** The Soviet Union was unable to survive a combination of domestic and foreign problems.

**Reading Connection** Do you listen to regular reporting on the domestic and foreign challenges of the American president? Read to learn why Soviet leaders could not solve domestic and foreign problems that intensified in the 1980s.

Between 1964 and 1982, drastic change in the Soviet Union had seemed highly unlikely. What happened to create such a dramatic turnaround by the late 1980s? The major reason lies with a man named **Mikhail Gorbachev** (GAWR•buh•CHAWF).

## *Voices from the Past*

Gorbachev, who became the Soviet leader in 1985, wrote a 1978 book that explained his goals for change in the Soviet Union:

> ❝There is a great thirst for mutual understanding and mutual communication in the world. It is felt among politicians, it is gaining momentum among the intelligentsia, representatives of culture, and the public at large. And if the Russian word 'perestroika' has easily entered the international lexicon [vocabulary], this is due to more than just interest in what is going on in the Soviet Union. Now the whole world needs restructuring, i.e., progressive development, a fundamental change. . . . I believe that more and more people will come to realize that through RESTRUCTURING in the broad sense of the word, the integrity of the world will be enhanced.❞

It is hard to understand how dramatic Gorbachev's words were unless we look at Soviet events of that era. When Nikita Khrushchev was removed from office in 1964, two men, Alexei Kosygin and **Leonid Brezhnev** (BREHZH•NEHF), replaced him. Brezhnev emerged as the dominant leader in the 1970s. He was determined to keep Eastern Europe in Communist hands and was uninterested in reform. Brezhnev insisted on the right of the Soviet Union to intervene if communism was threatened in another Communist state (known as the **Brezhnev Doctrine**).

At the same time, Brezhnev benefited from the more relaxed atmosphere associated with **détente,** a relaxation of tensions and improved relations between the two superpowers. The Soviet Union was roughly equal to the United States in nuclear arms. Its leaders thus felt secure and were willing to relax their rigid rule. There was more access to Western literature and pop culture, although **dissidents**—those who spoke out against the regime—were still punished.

In economic policy, Brezhnev continued to emphasize heavy industry. He also stuck with two policies that weakened the economy. Central government planning had created a huge bureaucracy that discouraged efficiency in industry. In agriculture, too, there was inefficiency. Farmers had no incentive to work hard on huge state-owned collectives—they worked much harder on their own tiny plots. Brezhnev also made no effort to reform the Communist ruling class, which by now was corrupt. Party officials and army and secret-police personnel enjoyed a high standard of living, while average Russians struggled to make ends meet.

By the 1970s, improved American-Soviet relations allowed grain and consumer goods to be sold to the Soviet Union. Beginning in 1979, however, the **apparent** collapse of détente began a new period of East-West confrontation. Détente suffered a major setback in 1979 when the Soviet Union invaded **Afghanistan.** The Soviet Union wanted to restore a pro-Soviet regime there, which the United States viewed as an act of **expansion.** To show his disapproval, President Jimmy Carter canceled American participation in the 1980 Olympic Games to be held in Moscow. He also put an embargo on the shipment of American grain to the Soviets.

*Mikhail Gorbachev*

When **Ronald Reagan** was elected president of the United States in 1980, relations with the Soviets became even chillier. Calling the Soviet Union an "evil empire," Reagan began a military buildup, which stimulated a new arms race. He also gave military aid to rebels fighting a pro-Soviet regime in Afghanistan. By doing so, Reagan believed he would force the Soviet Union to waste resources on a foreign war.

✓ **Reading Check** **Making Inferences** Why did détente between Soviets and Americans come to an end?

## Gorbachev and Soviet Reform

**Main Idea** Mikhail Gorbachev's reforms contributed to the end of the Cold War and of the Soviet system.

**Reading Connection** Can you think of an American president who dramatically changed the course of the nation? Read to learn how a Communist Party leader changed the course of Russian history.

By 1980, the Soviet Union was seriously ailing, with a declining economy, a rise in infant mortality rates, a surge in alcoholism, and poor working conditions. It was clear that the system was in trouble. Within the Communist Party, a small group of reformers emerged who wanted to address these problems. One of these was Mikhail Gorbachev. When the party chose him as leader in March 1985, a new era began. From the start, he preached the need for radical reforms. The basis of these reforms was **perestroika** (PEHR•uh•STROY•kuh), or restructuring.

At first, this meant restructuring economic policy. Gorbachev wanted to start a market economy more responsive to consumers. It was to have limited free enterprise so that some businesses would be privately owned and operated.

Soon Gorbachev realized that an attempt to reform the economy would not work without political reform. Therefore at the 1988 Communist Party conference, he established a new Soviet parliament with elected members, the Congress of People's Deputies. It met in 1989—the first such meeting in Russia since 1918. Early in 1990, Gorbachev decreed that non-communist political parties could organize. He also abolished a constitutional provision saying that the Communist Party had a "leading role" in the state.

Gorbachev then created a new state presidency as the leading executive office—under the old system, the first secretary of the Communist Party had been

▲ *Gorbachev and Reagan meeting in the 1980s*

the most important. In March 1990, Gorbachev became the Soviet Union's first president. Ironically, he was also its last.

**End of the Cold War** When Mikhail Gorbachev came to power in the Soviet Union, the Cold War came suddenly to an end. Gorbachev's "New Thinking"—his willingness to rethink Soviet foreign policy—had resulted in stunning changes.

First, Gorbachev made an agreement with the United States in 1987, often called the INF Treaty, to eliminate intermediate-range nuclear weapons. Both superpowers wanted to slow down the arms race. Instead of spending so much on weapons, Gorbachev hoped to focus resources on social and economic change. In the United States, too, cutting military expenditures would be helpful. It would help balance the national debt, which had tripled during the Reagan presidency. The country had moved from being a creditor nation—a country that exports more than it imports—to being the world's biggest debtor nation. By 1990, both countries wanted to reduce their military budgets in order to solve domestic problems.

For the Soviets, another important change resulted from the reduced military budget: Gorbachev stopped giving military support to Communist governments in Eastern Europe. This change opened the door to the overthrow of these Communist regimes. In 1989, a mostly peaceful revolutionary movement swept through Eastern Europe.

When this peaceful popular revolution occurred in East Germany, it was not long before the two

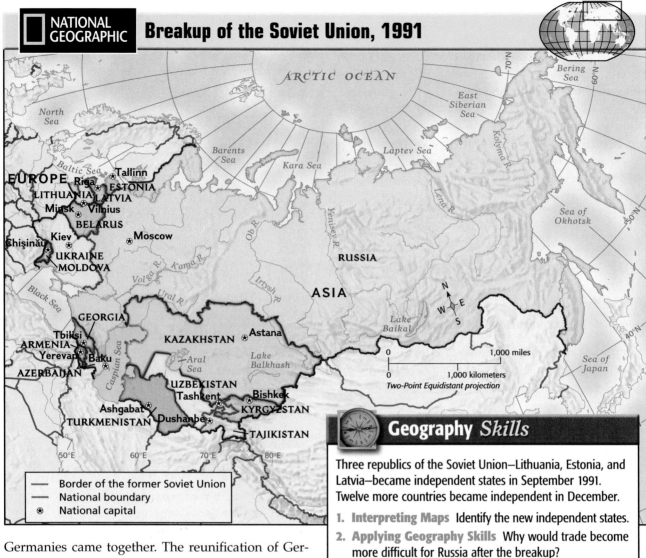

**Map legend:**
- Border of the former Soviet Union
- National boundary
- ⊛ National capital

### Geography *Skills*

Three republics of the Soviet Union—Lithuania, Estonia, and Latvia—became independent states in September 1991. Twelve more countries became independent in December.

1. **Interpreting Maps** Identify the new independent states.
2. **Applying Geography Skills** Why would trade become more difficult for Russia after the breakup?

Germanies came together. The reunification of Germany on October 3, 1990, was a powerful symbol of the end of the Cold War. In 1991, the Soviet Union was dissolved. The long rivalry between the two superpowers was over.

**The End of the Soviet Union** One of Gorbachev's most serious problems was the multi-ethnic nature of the Soviet Union. It included 92 nationalities and 112 different languages. The iron hand of the Communist Party, centered in Moscow, had kept centuries-old ethnic tensions contained.

As Gorbachev released this iron grip, these tensions again came to the fore. Nationalist movements emerged in the republics that made up the Soviet Union. In 1989 and 1990, there were calls for independence, first in Soviet Georgia and then in Latvia, Estonia, Moldavia, Uzbekistan, Azerbaijan, and Lithuania.

During 1990 and 1991, Gorbachev struggled to deal with the problems unleashed by his reforms. By 1991, the conservative leaders of the traditional Soviet institutions like the army and the secret police were worried. The possible breakup of the Soviet

Union would mean an end to their privileges. On August 19, 1991, a group of these conservatives arrested Gorbachev and tried to seize power. The attempt failed, however, when **Boris Yeltsin,** president of the Russian Republic, and thousands of Russians bravely resisted the rebel forces in Moscow.

The Soviet republics now moved for complete independence. **Ukraine** voted for independence on December 1, 1991. A week later, the leaders of Russia, Ukraine, and **Belarus** announced that the Soviet Union had "ceased to exist." Gorbachev resigned on December 25, 1991, and turned over his responsibilities as commander in chief to Boris Yeltsin, the new Russian president. By the end of 1991, one of the largest empires in world history had ended. A new era began.

**The New Russia** Boris Yeltsin was committed to introducing a free market economy as quickly as possible, but the transition was not easy. Economic hardships and social disorder were made worse by a rise in organized crime. Another problem Yeltsin faced was in Chechnya, a province in the south that wanted to be independent. Yeltsin used force to keep Chechnya in Russia. Yeltsin also dealt with former Soviet states like Poland, Hungary, and the Czech Republic who wanted to join NATO. Yeltsin opposed their wishes, but in the 1990s, these countries succeeded.

At the end of 1999, Yeltsin resigned and was replaced by **Vladimir Putin,** who was elected president in 2000. Putin, a former officer in the KGB, or secret police, was widely seen as someone who wanted to keep a tight rein on government power. In July 2001, Putin launched reforms aimed at boosting growth and budget revenues and keeping Russia on a strong economic track. The reforms included the free sale and purchase of land and tax cuts. Since then, Russia has experienced a budget surplus and a growing economy. The business climate remains somewhat uncertain, however, and this has stifled foreign investment.

In foreign policy Putin worked to have Russia take on a bigger role in international affairs. He applied for Russia's admission to the World Trade Organization and worked out a special partnership with the European Union.

Putin followed a hard-line policy in Chechnya, vowing to return the breakaway state to Russian authority. Fighting in this largely Muslim state intensified and the capital of Grozny was nearly reduced to ruins. As more Russian troops were sent, the rebels became even more radical and religious motives became more important. Some claimed that al-Qaeda,

*Vladimir Putin*

the terrorist organization, was funding the rebels, though others doubted that this was true.

Bombings and assassinations continued. In early September 2004, Chechnyan rebels seized a school in the town of Beslan. When Russian troops moved in to end the siege, more than 300 died. Many were young schoolchildren. Putin continued to refuse to negotiate with the Chechnyan rebels, but critics began to question his hard-line position, as well as how fully this event was reported in state-owned media. In response Putin cracked down on media outlets, and in the fall of 2004, he proposed that regional leaders be appointed rather than popularly elected.

**Reading Check** **Cause and Effect** How did Gorbachev contribute to the fall of the Soviet Union?

## HISTORY Online — Study Central

For help with the concepts in this section of *Glencoe World History—Modern Times,* go to wh.mt.glencoe.com and click on **Study Central.**

# SECTION 1 ASSESSMENT

### Checking for Understanding

1. **Vocabulary** Define: détente, dissident, apparent, expansion, perestroika.

2. **People and Events** Identify: Mikhail Gorbachev, Leonid Brezhnev, Brezhnev Doctrine, Ronald Reagan, Boris Yeltsin, Vladimir Putin.

3. **Places** Locate: Afghanistan, Ukraine, Belarus.

### Reviewing Big Ideas

4. **Explain** why the conservative leaders of the traditional Soviet institutions opposed the breakup of the Soviet Union. Name the institutions these leaders represented.

### Critical Thinking

5. **Drawing Inferences** Why did the former Soviet Union have problems adapting to a free-market society?

6. **Organizing Information** Create a diagram like the one below showing the problems the Soviet Union faced under communism and the problems the former Soviet republics face today.

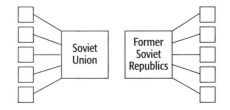

### Analyzing Visuals

7. **Examine** the photograph on page 611 of a man tearing down the Berlin Wall. How would you describe the reaction of the Soviet soldiers standing on top of the wall?

## Writing About History

8. **Expository Writing** Locate biographical information on Leonid Brezhnev, Mikhail Gorbachev, Boris Yeltsin, and Vladimir Putin. In an essay, analyze each leader's strengths and weaknesses.
   **CA 10WA2.3**

## Guide to Reading

### Section Preview
Popular revolutions helped end Communist regimes in Eastern Europe.

**Main Idea**
- Without the backing of the Soviet Union, Communist governments in Eastern Europe fell to popular revolutions. (p. 621)
- Nationalism and ethnic tensions led to armed conflict in the former Yugoslavia. (p. 623)

### Content Vocabulary
ethnic cleansing, autonomous

### Academic Vocabulary
found, settlement, cooperation

### People to Identify
Lech Walesa, Václav Havel, Slobodan Milošević

### Places to Locate
Bosnia-Herzegovina, Kosovo

### Reading Objectives
1. List reasons for East Germany opening its border in 1989.
2. Describe the effect of the collapse of communism in Yugoslavia in 1990.

### Reading Strategy
**Categorizing Information** In a chart like the one below, list reasons for, and the results of, revolution.

| Country | Reasons for Revolution | Results of Revolution |
|---|---|---|
| Poland | | |
| Czechoslovakia | | |
| Romania | | |
| East Germany | | |
| Yugoslavia | | |

### Preview of Events

♦1988    ♦1992    ♦1996    ♦2000    ♦2004

**1988**
Poles hold free elections

**1989**
Berlin Wall falls; communism falls in Czechoslovakia, Romania

**1991**
Slovenia and Croatia declare independence

**1992**
Serbs carry out ethnic cleansing in Bosnia-Herzegovina

**2003**
Serbia and Montenegro unite under new charter

## California Standards in This Section

*Reading this section will help you master these California History–Social Science standards.*

**10.9.5:** Describe the uprisings in Poland (1952), Hungary (1956), and Czechoslovakia (1968) and those countries' resurgence in the 1970s and 1980s as people in Soviet satellites sought freedom from Soviet control.

**10.9.7:** Analyze the reasons for the collapse of the Soviet Union, including the weakness of the command economy, burdens of military commitments, and growing resistance to Soviet rule by dissidents in satellite states and the non-Russian Soviet republics.

**10.10.1:** Understand the challenges in the regions, including their geopolitical, cultural, military, and economic significance and the international relationships in which they are involved.

**10.10.2:** Describe the recent history of the regions, including political divisions and systems, key leaders, religious issues, natural features, resources, and population patterns.

**10.10.3:** Discuss the important trends in the regions today and whether they appear to serve the cause of individual freedom and democracy.

# Revolutions in Eastern Europe

**Main Idea** Without the backing of the Soviet Union, Communist governments in Eastern Europe fell to popular revolutions.

**Reading Connection** Remember Churchill's "Iron Curtain" speech on the split between Eastern and Western Europe? Read to learn how the "iron curtain" was finally brought down.

Many Eastern Europeans were discontented with their Soviet-style governments. Freedom of speech was limited, and housing and consumer goods were often in short supply. When Gorbachev decided the Soviets would no longer send troops to support these governments, popular demonstrations and revolutions occurred across Eastern Europe.

Other consequences of Gorbachev's reforms were not so positive. Ethnic conflicts that had been long suppressed in Eastern Europe soon came to the surface. Some of the worst conflicts were in Bosnia, a part of Yugoslavia.

## Voices from the Past

In July 1992, a *Newsday* journalist, Roy Gutman, reported on ethnic conflict between Serbs and Muslims in Bosnia, an area that had proclaimed its independence from Yugoslavia:

“Visegrad, with a population of about 30,000, is one of a number of towns where Serb forces carried out 'ethnic cleansing' of Muslims in the past two weeks, according to the Bosnian government. 'There was chaos in Visegrad. Everything was burned, looted and destroyed,' said [one man], 43, who spoke of the terrible events but would give neither his name nor his profession. He escaped only because he was an invalid with a gangrenous [diseased] leg. The survivors of the massacre are the old, the infirm, the women and the children. They are traumatized by what they witnessed, barely able to speak or to control their emotions.”

The upheaval in Eastern Europe that began in 1989 dramatically changed the world at the end of the twentieth century. By looking at four Eastern European states, we can see how the process worked.

**Poland** Workers' protests led to demands for change in Poland. In 1980, a worker named **Lech Walesa** (lehk vah•LEHN•suh) organized a national trade union known as Solidarity. Solidarity gained the support of the workers and of the Roman Catholic Church. During a period of military rule in the 1980s, Walesa was arrested, but the movement continued. Finally, after a new wave of demonstrations in 1988, the Polish regime agreed to free parliamentary elections—the first in Eastern Europe in 40 years. A new government was elected, ending 45 years of Communist rule.

In December 1990, Walesa was chosen as president. Poland's new path, however, was not easy. Rapid free-market reforms led to severe unemployment and popular discontent. At the end of 1995, former Communist Aleksander Kwasniewski defeated Walesa, but he continued Poland's move toward an increasingly prosperous free-market economy.

**Czechoslovakia** After Soviet troops crushed the reform movement in 1968, the Communist government in Czechoslovakia used massive repression to maintain its power. Writers and other intellectuals continued to oppose the government, but at first they had little success. Then these reformers could see that the Soviet leader, Mikhail Gorbachev, was loosening the tight grip on Eastern Europe. In 1988 and 1989, mass demonstrations took place in Czech cities. By November 1989, crowds as large as 500,000 were forming in the capital of Prague.

▼ *Bosnian man mourning in graveyard*

▲ *Lech Walesa, the Polish leader who inspired many Eastern Europeans*

In December 1989, the Communist government collapsed. At the end of that month, **Václav Havel** (VAHT•SLAHF HAH•vehl), a writer who had played an important role in bringing down the Communist government, became the new president. Havel became an eloquent spokesperson for Czech democracy and a new order in Europe.

In Czechoslovakia itself, the new government soon faced old ethnic conflicts. On January 1, 1993, the two ethnic groups of the nation, Czechs and Slovaks, agreed to a peaceful division of the country: Czechoslovakia split into the Czech Republic and Slovakia. Havel was elected the first president of the new Czech Republic, while Michal Kovác was elected president of Slovakia.

**Romania** In 1965, the Communist leader Nicolae Ceauşescu, (NEE•koh•lay chow•SHEHS•koo) and his wife, Elena, set up a rigid and dictatorial regime in Romania. Ceauşescu ruled Romania with an iron grip, using secret police to crush all dissent. Nonetheless, opposition to his regime grew.

Ceauşescu's economic policies led to a sharp drop in living standards, including food shortages and the rationing of bread, flour, and sugar. His plan for rapid urbanization, especially a program that called for the bulldozing of entire villages, further angered the Romanian people.

One incident ignited the flames of revolution. In December 1989, the secret police murdered thousands of men, women, and children who were peacefully demonstrating. In protest, the army then refused to support any more repression. Ceauşescu and his wife were captured on December 22 and executed on Christmas Day. A new government was quickly formed.

**German Reunification** In 1971, Erich Honecker became head of the Communist Party in East Germany. He used the Stasi, the secret police, to rule for the next 18 years. In 1989, however, popular unrest, fueled by Honecker's harsh regime, led many East Germans to flee their country. In the fall of 1989, mass demonstrations against the regime broke out.

On November 9, the Communist government surrendered to popular pressure by opening its entire border with the West. Hundreds of thousands of East Germans swarmed across the border. Families and friends who had not seen each other in decades were reunited. People on both sides of the wall began tearing it down. The government, helpless before this popular uprising, ordered the rest of the wall torn down. The Berlin Wall, long a symbol of the Cold War, was no more.

During East Germany's first free elections in March 1990, the Christian Democrats won almost 50 percent of the vote. The Christian Democrats supported political union with West Germany, and they carried out this policy almost immediately. The historic reunification of East and West took place on October 3, 1990, ending just over 40 years of separation. What had seemed almost impossible at the beginning of 1989 had become a reality in 1990—the countries of West and East Germany had reunited to form one Germany.

✔ **Reading Check** **Explaining** Why did the Eastern Europeans begin popular revolutions against their governments in the late 1980s?

**Web Activity** Visit the *Glencoe World History–Modern Times* Web site at wh.mt.glencoe.com and click on **Chapter 13–Student Web Activity** to learn more about the fall of the Berlin Wall.

# The Disintegration of Yugoslavia

**Main Idea** Nationalism and ethnic tensions led to armed conflict in the former Yugoslavia.

**Reading Connection** Can you remember earlier examples in your textbook of ethnic conflict? Read to learn about the ethnic cleansing in the Bosnian war.

Although Yugoslavia had a Communist government, it had never been a Soviet satellite state. After World War II, its dictatorial leader, Josip Broz Tito, worked to keep the six republics and two provinces of Yugoslavia together. After Tito died in 1980, a collective federal government composed of representatives from the separate republics and provinces kept Yugoslavia under Communist rule. At the end of the 1980s, Yugoslavia was caught up in the reform movements sweeping Eastern Europe. By 1990, new parties had emerged, and the authority of the Communist Party had collapsed.

## Calls for Independence
The Yugoslav political scene was complex. In 1990, the Yugoslav republics of Slovenia, Croatia, **Bosnia-Herzegovina,** and Macedonia began to lobby for independence. **Slobodan Milošević** (SLOH•buh•DAHN muh•LOH•suh•VIHCH), who became leader of the Yugoslav republic of Serbia in 1987, rejected these efforts. The populations of these republics included Serb minorities. In Milošević's view, the republics could only be independent if their borders were redrawn to include the Serb minorities in a new Greater Serbian state.

After negotiations failed, Slovenia and Croatia declared their independence in June 1991. In September 1991, the Yugoslavian army began a full assault against Croatia. Increasingly, the Serbs of Yugoslavia dominated the Yugoslavian army. It was aided by Serbian minorities in Croatia. Before a cease-fire was arranged, the Serbian forces had captured one-third of Croatia's territory in brutal fighting.

## The War in Bosnia
Early in 1992, the Serbs turned their guns on Bosnia-Herzegovina. By mid-1993, Serbian forces had acquired 70 percent of Bosnian territory.

Many Bosnians were Muslims. Toward them, the Serbs followed a policy they called **ethnic cleansing**—killing them or forcibly removing them from their lands. Ethnic cleansing revived memories of Nazi atrocities in World War II. By 1995, 250,000 Bosnians, most of them civilians, had been killed. Two million more were left homeless.

In 1995, new offensives by Bosnian government army forces and by the Croatian army regained considerable territory that had been lost to Serbian forces. Under pressure from U.S. president Bill Clinton, NATO bombers carried out air strikes in retaliation for the Serb attacks on civilians.

The air attacks forced the Serbs to sign a formal peace treaty on December 14. The agreement split Bosnia into a loose union of a Serb republic and a Muslim-Croat federation. NATO sent a force of about 60,000 troops to monitor the frontier between the new political entities. In 2004, Bosnia-Herzegovina was still under international supervision.

## The War in Kosovo
Peace in Bosnia did not bring peace to the region. A new war erupted in 1998 over **Kosovo.** In 1974, Tito had made Kosovo an **autonomous** (self-governing) province within Yugoslavia. Kosovo's inhabitants were mainly ethnic Albanians who had kept their own language and customs.

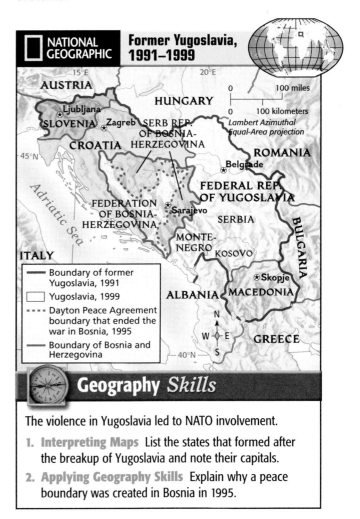

**NATIONAL GEOGRAPHIC** **Former Yugoslavia, 1991–1999**

Boundary of former Yugoslavia, 1991
Yugoslavia, 1999
Dayton Peace Agreement boundary that ended the war in Bosnia, 1995
Boundary of Bosnia and Herzegovina

### Geography *Skills*

The violence in Yugoslavia led to NATO involvement.

1. **Interpreting Maps** List the states that formed after the breakup of Yugoslavia and note their capitals.
2. **Applying Geography Skills** Explain why a peace boundary was created in Bosnia in 1995.

Picturing **History**

In 1999, Serbs forced hundreds of thousands of ethnic Albanians from their homes in Kosovo, creating a massive refugee crisis. What issues led to conflict in Kosovo?

In 1989, Slobodan Milošević stripped Kosovo of its autonomous status. Some groups of ethnic Albanians **founded** the Kosovo Liberation Army (KLA) in the mid-1990s and began a campaign against Serbian rule in Kosovo. In an effort to crush the KLA, Serb forces began to massacre ethnic Albanians. The United States and its NATO allies then sought to arrange a **settlement.**

In 1999, the Albanians in Kosovo gained autonomy within Serbia. When Milošević objected, a NATO bombing campaign forced Yugoslav **cooperation.** Elections held in 2000 ended Milošević's rule, and he was brought to trial for his role in the Balkans'

bloodshed. In 2002, Serbia and Montenegro formed a looser union of two republics, dropping the name "Yugoslavia." In 2003, lawmakers agreed that voters would vote on full independence in 2006.

✓**Reading Check** **Identifying** What events resulted from the disintegration of Yugoslavia?

**HISTORY**
*Online* **Study Central**

For help with the concepts in this section of *Glencoe World History—Modern Times,* go to wh.mt.glencoe.com and click on **Study Central.**

---

# SECTION 2 ASSESSMENT

### Checking for Understanding

1. **Vocabulary** Define: ethnic cleansing, autonomous, found, settlement, cooperation.

2. **People** Identify: Lech Walesa, Václav Havel, Slobodan Milošević.

3. **Places** Locate: Bosnia-Herzegovina, Kosovo.

### Reviewing Big Ideas

4. **Explain** why the Communist government ordered the Berlin Wall to be torn down.

### Critical Thinking

5. **Historical Analysis** **Cause and Effect** Why did Eastern Europeans feel it was safe to rebel in 1989? **CA HI 2**

6. **Summarizing Information** Create a chart like the one below listing the Yugoslav republics seeking independence after 1990, their ethnic groups, and the reasons for conflict.

| Republics | Ethnic Groups | Causes of Fighting |
|-----------|---------------|--------------------|
|           |               |                    |
|           |               |                    |

### Analyzing Visuals

7. **Study** the photo on this page. What do these ethnic Albanians have in common with other victims of oppression?

## Writing About History

8. **Informative Writing** Research and write an essay about the Polish Solidarity movement begun by Lech Walesa in 1980. Why was it successful? Be sure to discuss Walesa's supporters, his adversaries, and the status of the movement today. **CA 10WA2.3**

# Europe and the United States

## Section Preview
Postwar Western societies rebuilt their communities, but shifting social structures led to upheaval and change.

### Main Idea
• Dramatic changes in Western Europe after World War II led to the formation of the European Economic Community. (p. 626)

• Since 1970, mainstream views in America have moved toward the right on social and fiscal issues. (p. 628)

## Content Vocabulary
Thatcherism, budget deficit, weapons of mass destruction (WMDs)

## Academic Vocabulary
currency, method

## People to Identify
Willy Brandt, Margaret Thatcher, Richard Nixon, George W. Bush

## Places to Locate
France, West Germany

## Reading Objectives
1. Describe the problems that Western Europe faced after 1980.
2. Explain the focus of U.S. domestic politics in the 1970s.

## Reading Strategy
**Compare and Contrast** Draw a Venn diagram comparing and contrasting economic policies of Thatcherism with those of the Reagan Revolution.

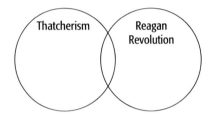

## Preview of Events

| ♦1970 | ♦1975 | ♦1980 | ♦1985 | ♦1990 | ♦1995 | ♦2000 |
|---|---|---|---|---|---|---|

**1971**
West German chancellor Willy Brandt wins Nobel Peace Prize

**1974**
Richard Nixon resigns the presidency of the United States

**1995**
Canadian voters reject independence for Quebec

## California Standards in This Section

*Reading this section will help you master these California History–Social Science standards.*

**10.10:** Students analyze instances of nation-building in the contemporary world in at least two of the following regions or countries: the Middle East, Africa, Mexico and other parts of Latin America, and China.

**10.11:** Students analyze the integration of countries into the world economy and the information, technological, and communications revolutions (e.g., television, satellites, computers).

# Winds of Change in Western Europe

**Main Idea** Dramatic changes in Western Europe after World War II led to the formation of the European Economic Community.

**Reading Connection** Can you imagine what it would be like if there were 50 separate currencies for every state in the Union? Read to learn how Europe adopted a single currency.

Between the early 1950s and late 1970s, Western Europe experienced virtually full employment. An economic downturn, however, occurred in the mid-1970s and early 1980s. Inflation and unemployment rose dramatically, partly because of increases in oil prices after the Arab-Israeli conflict in 1973 (see Chapter 15). During the 1980s, Western European economies recovered, but significant problems remained. In Germany, some economic strains came from the reunification of East and West Germany. When the economy is under stress, people sometimes take out their resentment on others.

## *Voices from the Past*

In the Germany of 1991, foreigners were sometimes blamed for economic troubles. A German reporter described attacks he witnessed against immigrant workers:

> ❝The municipality in northern Saxony has a population of just under 70,000, including 70 people from Mozambique and Vietnam who live in a hostel [inn] at the other end of town. The 'political situation' was triggered by an attack by a neo-Nazi gang on Vietnamese traders selling their goods on the market square on 17 September. After being dispersed by the police the Faschos [neo-Nazis] carried out their first attack on the hostel for foreigners. The attacks then turned into a regular evening hunt by a growing group of right-wing radicals, some of them minors, who presented their idea of a clean Germany by roaming the streets armed with truncheons, stones, steel balls, bottles and Molotov cocktails.❞

Long before this, of course, a bigger economic transition had begun in Western Europe: the move toward economic union had its origin in 1957

(see Chapter 12). In 1973, the European Economic Community (EEC) expanded to include Great Britain, Ireland, and Denmark. By 1986, Spain, Portugal, and Greece had become members. Austria, Finland, and Sweden joined in 1995.

The EEC or European Community (EC) was chiefly an economic union. By 1992, it comprised 344 million people and made up the world's largest single trading bloc. The Treaty on European Union, which went into effect on January 1, 1994, turned the EC into the principal organization within the even more solidified European Union (EU). One of the EU's first goals was to establish a common European **currency,** the euro. Twelve of the fifteen EU nations abandoned their currency in favor of the euro on January 1, 2002. In 2004, the EU added ten new members, mostly states from Eastern Europe.

**Uncertainties in France** In **France,** a deteriorating economic situation in the 1970s caused a political shift to the left. By 1981, the Socialists had become the chief party in the National Assembly. The Socialist leader, François Mitterrand, was elected president.

Mitterrand initiated a number of measures to aid workers: an increased minimum wage, a 39-hour workweek, and higher taxes for the rich. The Socialist government also nationalized, or took over, major banks, the steel industry, the space and electronics industries, and insurance firms.

▼ *Neo-Nazis at a 1990 demonstration in East Germany*

Original members, 1957
**Additional members:**
by 1973
by 1986
by 1995
by 2004
Candidate countries

FINLAND

North Sea

SWEDEN    ESTONIA

Baltic Sea

UNITED KINGDOM    DENMARK    LATVIA

IRELAND    LITHUANIA

NETH.

BELG.    GERMANY    POLAND

LUX.    CZECH REPUBLIC

FRANCE    SLOVAKIA

AUSTRIA HUNGARY

ATLANTIC OCEAN

SLOVENIA    ROMANIA

CROATIA

PORTUGAL    SPAIN    ITALY    BULGARIA

Black Sea

40°N    GREECE    TURKEY

500 miles

500 kilometers

Mediterranean Sea    CYPRUS

Lambert Azimuthal Equal-Area projection

*Flag of the European Union*

*Euro coin*

## Geography *Skills*

The European Union (EU) allows members to work together to increase trade and develop favorable economic policies.

1. **Interpreting Maps** How long have the original members been part of the EU?

2. **Applying Geography Skills** What does the EU's growth suggest about its value to European states?

Socialist Party policies largely failed to work, and France's economic decline continued. In 1993, French unemployment stood at 10.6 percent. In the elections in March of that year, the Socialists won only 28 percent of the vote. A coalition of conservative parties won 80 percent of the seats in the National Assembly. The move to the right was strengthened when conservative Jacques Chirac was elected president in May 1995.

**From West Germany to Germany** In 1969, the Social Democrats, a moderate Socialist party, replaced the Christian Democrats as the leading party in the Federal Republic of Germany, usually referred to as **West Germany.** The first Social Democratic chancellor of West Germany was **Willy Brandt.** In December 1972, Brandt signed a treaty with East Germany that led to greater cultural, personal, and economic contacts between West and East Germany.

For this, he received the Nobel Peace Prize for 1971. In 1982, the Christian Democratic Union of Helmut Kohl formed a new, more conservative government. Kohl was a smart politician who benefited greatly from an economic boom in the mid-1980s. When Germany was reunified in 1990, Kohl was the leader of Europe's most powerful nation.

The joy over reunification soon faded. First, it became clear that rebuilding eastern Germany would take far more money than had originally been thought. Kohl's government was forced to raise taxes. In addition, the virtual collapse of the economy in eastern Germany resulted in very high unemployment. One result was that the Social Democrats were returned to power in the 1998 elections.

Economic problems also led to attacks on foreigners, who were seen as taking jobs from Germans. For years, illegal immigrants and foreigners seeking political refuge were able to move to Germany because of its liberal immigration laws. In 1992, over 440,000 immigrants came to Germany—123,000 of these were from the former Yugoslavia. As economic conditions throughout Europe worsened, so too, did tensions between some Germans and immigrant groups. Attacks against foreigners by right-wing extremists—especially young neo-Nazis who believed in Hitler's idea of a pure Aryan race—became part of German life.

**Great Britain and Thatcherism** Between 1964 and 1979, two parties in Great Britain alternated in power: the Conservative Party and the Labour Party. One problem both parties faced was the intense fighting between Catholics and Protestants in Northern Ireland. An ailing economy and frequent labor strikes were two other issues that the government struggled to solve.

In 1979, the Conservatives came to power under **Margaret Thatcher.** Thatcher pledged to limit social welfare, restrict union power, and end inflation. Although she did not eliminate the basic parts of the social welfare system, she broke the power of the labor unions and brought down inflation.

**Thatcherism,** as her economic policy was termed, improved the British economic situation, but at a price. The south of England prospered, but in old industrial areas in the north, unemployment and poverty were common.

Thatcher dominated British politics through the 1980s, but in 1990, the Labour Party began to revive. In that year, Thatcher's government tried to replace local property taxes with a flat-rate tax that every adult had to pay. Anti-tax riots broke out, and when Thatcher's popularity fell to an all-time low, she resigned as prime minister.

Now led by John Major, the Conservative Party held a narrow majority for several years, but in 1997, the Labour Party won a landslide victory. Tony Blair, a moderate, became prime minister.

✓**Reading Check** **Explaining** What were the policies of Thatcherism?

## The U.S. Domestic Scene

**Main Idea** Since 1970, mainstream views in America have moved toward the right on social and fiscal issues.

**Reading Connection** What have been the main issues the current American president has faced? Read to learn about the challenges of American presidents from Richard Nixon to George W. Bush.

With the election of **Richard Nixon** as president in 1968, politics in the United States shifted to the right. By the mid-1970s, economic issues had become the focus of most domestic politics.

**Nixon and Watergate** In his campaign for the presidency, Nixon believed that "law and order" issues and a slowdown in racial desegregation would appeal to Southern whites. The South, which had once been a stronghold for the Democrats, began to form a new allegiance to the Republican Party.

As president, Nixon began to use illegal **methods** to gain political information about his opponents. Nixon's zeal led to the Watergate scandal. A group of men working for Nixon's reelection committee broke into the Democratic national headquarters in the Watergate Hotel in Washington, D.C. They were caught there trying to install electronic listening devices.

Nixon repeatedly lied to the American public about his involvement in the Watergate incident. Secret tapes of his conversations in the White House

**Picturing History**
Richard Nixon bids his staff good-bye after resigning his job as president of the United States. What events led Nixon to decide to leave office?

*Ayatollah Khomeini*

Total federal spending rose from $631 billion in 1981 to over a trillion dollars by 1987. These expenditures produced record government **budget deficits.** A budget deficit exists when the government spends more than it collects in revenues. In the 1970s, the total deficit was $420 billion. Between 1981 and 1987, budget deficits were three times that amount.

**The Clinton Years** George Bush, Reagan's vice president, succeeded him as president. Bush's inability to deal with the deficit problem, as well as an economic downturn, allowed Democrat Bill Clinton to be elected president in 1992.

The new president was a Southern Democrat who called himself a new Democrat—one who favored certain Republican policies of the 1980s. This was a clear indication that the shift to the right in American politics by no means ended when Clinton was elected.

President Clinton's political fortunes were aided considerably by a lengthy economic revival. Much

were discovered, however, that revealed the truth. On August 9, 1974, Nixon resigned the presidency rather than face almost certain impeachment.

**The Carter Administration** Vice President Gerald Ford became president when Nixon resigned, only to lose in the 1976 election to the former governor of Georgia, Jimmy Carter. By 1980, the Carter administration was faced with two devastating problems.

First, high inflation and a decline in average earnings caused living standards to drop. Second, a crisis abroad erupted when 52 Americans were held hostage by the Iranian government of the Ayatollah Ruhollah Khomeini (koh•MAY•nee) (see Chapter 15). Carter was unable to gain the hostages' release, and this contributed to his overwhelming loss to Ronald Reagan in the election of 1980.

**The Reagan Revolution** The Reagan Revolution, as it has been called, pointed the United States in a new direction. Reversing decades of policy, Reagan cut back on the welfare state by decreasing spending on food stamps, school lunch programs, and job programs. In foreign affairs, many credited Reagan with speeding the collapse of the Soviet Union by his staunch opposition to Communist ideology. Others suggested that the Soviet collapse was a result of the country's inability to keep up with American military spending and its own economic weaknesses.

The largest peacetime military buildup in U.S. history took place during Reagan's administration.

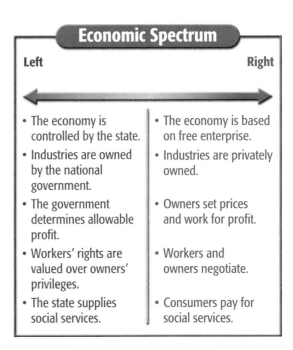

**Economic Spectrum**

Left                                    Right

| The economy is controlled by the state. | The economy is based on free enterprise. |
| Industries are owned by the national government. | Industries are privately owned. |
| The government determines allowable profit. | Owners set prices and work for profit. |
| Workers' rights are valued over owners' privileges. | Workers and owners negotiate. |
| The state supplies social services. | Consumers pay for social services. |

**Chart** *Skills*

The chart above represents a simplified view of two opposite economic models.

1. **Identifying** Select five countries from this chapter. On which side of the economic spectrum would their economies belong?

2. **Describing** Find definitions for the following: *laissez-faire, command economy, capitalism, invisible hand, communism, socialism.* Do the terms belong on the left or the right?

of Clinton's second term, however, was overshadowed by charges of presidential misconduct. Clinton was threatened with removal from office when the House of Representatives voted two articles of impeachment—formal charges of misconduct—against him. He was tried in the Senate, but acquitted after a bitter partisan struggle.

**George W. Bush** In the election of 2000, **George W. Bush** of Texas narrowly defeated Vice President Al Gore in one of the most hotly contested elections in American history. However, Bush faced major challenges in winning over public and congressional support after the controversial election. Some of Bush's major policies included a $1.6 trillion tax cut and the No Child Left Behind Act, an overhaul of federal education legislation.

The terrorist attacks of September 11, 2001, led to the president's call for a war on terrorism. The United States entered armed conflict in Afghanistan, the training ground for terrorists, and also in Iraq. Unlike the war in Afghanistan, the war in Iraq was very controversial.

The U.S.-led invasion of Iraq was based on statements that the dictator Saddam Hussein possessed **weapons of mass destruction (WMDs).** WMDs are nuclear, chemical, and biological weapons that can kill tens of thousands of people at once. The intelligence information about WMDs was hard to verify, and the UN did not back the timing of the U.S. action. Though American forces ousted dictator Saddam Hussein, no WMDs were discovered (see Chapter 15). During the 2004 presidential campaign race between President Bush and Democratic challenger Senator John Kerry of Massachusetts, the war and the sluggish economy were major issues.

*Saddam Hussein*

The campaign, one of the most expensive in American history, was bitterly fought. Intense feelings on both sides resulted in a record turnout. President Bush was elected for a second term, winning the popular vote by a margin of 51 to 48 percent. Besides the war in Iraq, voters were divided over how to handle the threat of terrorism. Some analysts concluded that in a more threatening world, many Americans chose to reelect the leader who had proclaimed the war on terrorism.

✓ **Reading Check** **Summarizing** Describe the political shift in American politics from the 1960s to the present.

**HISTORY Online** **Study Central**

For help with the concepts in this section of *Glencoe World History–Modern Times,* go to **wh.mt.glencoe.com** and click on **Study Central**.

---

# SECTION 3 ASSESSMENT

### Checking for Understanding

1. **Vocabulary** Define: currency, Thatcherism, method, budget deficit, weapons of mass destruction (WMDs).

2. **People** Identify: Willy Brandt, Margaret Thatcher, Richard Nixon, George W. Bush.

3. **Places** Locate: France, West Germany.

### Reviewing Big Ideas

4. **List** some of the changes initiated by François Mitterrand's government in France. How successful were Mitterrand's socialist policies?

### Critical Thinking

5. **Historical Analysis** **Cause and Effect** What factors led to the economic downturn of the 1970s? How did European nations respond? **CA HI 2**

6. **Organizing Information** Create a chart like the one below listing the problems faced by Germany when it was unified in 1990.

| Problems Created by German Unification |
| --- |
|  |
|  |
|  |
|  |

### Analyzing Visuals

7. **Compare** the photo on page 626 with the Nazi photos on pages 459 and 485. What similarities and differences do you see among the photos?

## Writing About History

8. **Expository Writing** When a country faces economic problems, its inhabitants often blame a person or a group. Look up the word *scapegoating*. Write an essay about the use of scapegoating, including two examples from history, and one from the contemporary world. **CA 10WA2.3**

# Western Society and Culture

## Section Preview

Western society has been shaped by science and technology, changes in family structures and population trends, a renewed interest in religion, and popular culture.

**Main Idea**

- Since 1970, societies have faced new population and health issues, changing roles for women, and technological change. (p. 632)
- As popular culture and technology bring all parts of the world closer together, individual nations struggle to maintain their identities. (p. 635)

## Content Vocabulary

globalization, gender parity, cultural imperialism

## Academic Vocabulary

percentage, liberation

## People and Events to Identify

Equal Pay Act, *Roe* v. *Wade,* Ervin (Magic) Johnson, Elvis Presley, Fest Noz, "Bloody Sunday"

## Places to Locate

Munich, Brittany, Basque region, Northern Ireland

## Reading Objectives

1. Explain the major social changes since 1970.
2. Describe the important scientific, technological, and cultural trends since World War II.

## Reading Strategy

**Categorizing Information** Complete a chart like the one below on the issues and outcomes for the women's movement since 1970.

| Issues | Outcomes |
|--------|----------|
|        |          |
|        |          |
|        |          |

### Preview of Events

| ♦1970 | ♦1975 | ♦1980 | ♦1985 | ♦1990 | ♦1995 | ♦2000 |
|-------|-------|-------|-------|-------|-------|-------|

**1972**
Fighting escalates in Northern Ireland

**1981**
Women protest presence of American nuclear missiles in Britain

**1999**
World population reaches 6 billion

## California Standards in This Section

*Reading this section will help you master these California History–Social Science standards.*

**10.10.2:** Describe the recent history of the regions, including political divisions and systems, key leaders, religious issues, natural features, resources, and population patterns.

**10.11:** Students analyze the integration of countries into the world economy and the information, technological, and communications revolutions (e.g., television, satellites, computers).

# The Quickening Pace of Change

**Main Idea** Since 1970, societies have faced new population and health issues, changing roles for women, and technological change.

**Reading Connection** Do you depend on a technology that did not exist for a grandparent? Read about how new technologies are transforming Western society.

Ever since the first Industrial Revolution, Western societies have tended to pride themselves on expanding democracy and material progress. Since 1970, the pace of material change has quickened and promoted a global economy. An important question today is how this global economy will affect each country. Will all nations adopt market-style capitalism? Will democracy expand? Will the United States dominate the global economy and popular culture in this trend toward **globalization**?

## Voices from the Past

Different people give very different answers to these questions. One scholar, Jan Aart Scholte, has captured the extremes of the debate:

> ❝Globalization has . . . become a heavily loaded word. People have linked the notion to well-nigh every . . . contemporary social change, including an emergent information age, a retreat of the state, the demise of traditional cultures, and the advent of a postmodern [era]. . . . [S]ome people have associated 'globalization' with progress, prosperity and peace. For others, however, the word has conjured up deprivation, disaster and doom. No one is indifferent. Most of us are confused.❞

**Science and Technology** Science and technology are important forces for change in today's world. Since World War II, they have revolutionized people's lives. During the war, governments recruited scientists to develop new weapons. Perhaps the most famous product of this research was the atomic bomb, created by scientists working at Los Alamos, New Mexico. By funding projects, governments created a new model for scientific research. Complex projects required teams of scientists, huge laboratories, and sophisticated equipment that only governments or large corporations could fund.

A stunning example of such projects is the space race. In 1961, four years after the Soviet Union launched *Sputnik I*, President Kennedy predicted that Americans would land men on the moon within a decade. The United States did so in 1969. 📖 (*See page 776 to read an excerpt from a speech by astronaut John Glenn in the Primary Sources Library.*)

The postwar alliance of science and technology led to a fast rate of change. More than ever, people believed that scientific knowledge gave society the ability and the right to manipulate the environment for everyone's benefit. Critics in the 1960s and 1970s, however, argued that some technology had far-reaching effects that damaged the environment. The use of chemical fertilizers, for example, produced higher-yield crops, but also destroyed the ecological balance of streams, rivers, and woodlands. In the early 2000s, debates over organic farming and genetically enhanced foods intensified. People continue to disagree over the proper role of science.

**Population Issues** In October 1999, the United Nations announced that the world's population had reached 6 billion people only 12 years after passing 5 billion. The world population is expected to reach 9.3 billion by 2050. In wealthy regions such as Western Europe, though, population is declining and

▼ *Opponents of a global economy demonstrating at a meeting of the World Trade Organization (WTO)*

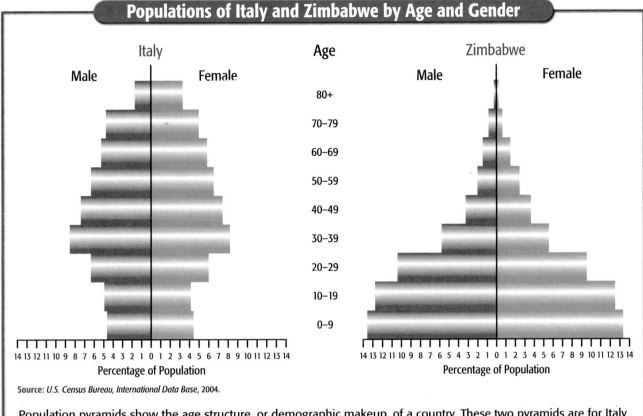

## Populations of Italy and Zimbabwe by Age and Gender

**Italy**

Male / Female

**Age**

80+
70–79
60–69
50–59
40–49
30–39
20–29
10–19
0–9

**Zimbabwe**

Male / Female

14 13 12 11 10 9 8 7 6 5 4 3 2 1 0 1 2 3 4 5 6 7 8 9 10 11 12 13 14
Percentage of Population

14 13 12 11 10 9 8 7 6 5 4 3 2 1 0 1 2 3 4 5 6 7 8 9 10 11 12 13 14
Percentage of Population

Source: *U.S. Census Bureau, International Data Base,* 2004.

Population pyramids show the age structure, or demographic makeup, of a country. These two pyramids are for Italy and Zimbabwe. They are good examples of the contrast between highly industrialized countries in Europe and developing countries in Africa or other parts of the world. When you look at the pyramids, notice where the largest percentage of the population is located. Think about the consequences of the demographic makeup of these two countries.

"graying"—a larger **percentage** of the population is reaching retirement. Soon, the most populous nations in the world will be developing countries. In fact, by 2050, the United States is expected to be the only wealthy nation with a growing population.

In 2000, European nations had the oldest population of any region in the world: 15 percent of the population was 65 or older. By 2050, 28 percent are expected to be in this age group. An older population places a demand on the economy because the taxes of workers must be stretched further to cover the expenses of the elderly.

### Changes in the Family and in Women's Lives

One reason for an older population in Europe is changing trends in marriage and divorce. Over the past 40 years, the number of people in Europe getting married has decreased and people tend to get married at a slightly older age. Between 1980 and 1995, for example, the average age of French women marrying for the first time went up from 23 to 27 years. The divorce rate has also gone up. Between 1970 and 1995, Belgium, France, the Netherlands, and the

United Kingdom all saw enormous increases in divorce rates. The highest divorce rate was in the United Kingdom, where 42 of 100 marriages ended in divorce. These social trends have meant a lower birthrate and thus an older population overall.

To some extent, women's changing roles in the workforce have also affected family size, and thus population growth. More and more women were working because they chose to, but also because two incomes were seen as necessary to support a family.

Since 1970, the number of women in the workforce has continued to rise. In Britain, for example, the number of women in the labor force went from 32 percent to 44 percent between 1970 and 1990. More women went to college, and more of them pursued careers in law, medicine, and government.

In the 1960s and 1970s, the women's movement emerged in the United States. It quickly spread to Western Europe and in recent decades to other parts of the world. Supporters wanted to change the basic conditions of women's lives. They formed small "consciousness-raising" groups that worked to make people aware of women's demands. Politicians now had to address the issue of "gender stereotyping," restricting what a person could do just because of the person's gender. Could a woman be a bricklayer? Could a man be a nurse? Other issues, such as contraception and equality, took center stage. A milestone was reached in the United States in 1963 when the **Equal Pay Act** was passed. It required women to be paid the same as men for performing the same work.

One of the most controversial issues was abortion, which some women campaigned to have legalized. In the United States, the Supreme Court legalized abortion in the *Roe v. Wade* decision in 1973. While abortion is covered by national health insurance in most of Europe, the procedure is still hotly debated in the United States because many religious groups do not believe it is ethical.

In the 1990s, there was a backlash, or reaction against, the women's movement. Some women urged that they were better off returning to traditional gender roles. Others adopted a different tactic by stressing that women needed to find a way to balance career and family goals. The women's movement also led many men to reexamine their family role.

Despite the gains made by the women's movement, women in Western societies still earn significantly less on average than men. Many women also face the double burden of working outside the home, while continuing to do most of the child rearing and domestic work.

Finally, women remain underrepresented in most national legislatures. Some European countries have adopted **gender parity,** policies that encourage more women to become part of government. This policy requires that women make up either a certain number of the candidates in an election, or a certain number of those elected. Such measures went into effect in Norway and Denmark in the 1970s. Many other European nations followed suit in the 1980s and 1990s. France passed a constitutional amendment instituting gender parity in politics in 1999–2000. It is not yet clear if French measures will be as successful as those elsewhere in Europe.

### Health Issues (The AIDS Crisis)

AIDS, or *a*cquired *i*mmuno*d*eficiency *s*yndrome, a terrifying and incurable disease that attacks the immune system, was discovered in 1981. The disease was especially frightening during the first few years after its discovery because no one knew exactly how it was transmitted. This fear led police in some areas to equip crews with protective masks and gloves when dealing with suspected AIDS patients.

▲ *In Ho Chi Minh City, a Vietnamese woman sells newspapers in front of a poster warning about the link between drug addiction and AIDS.*

Fear also led to discrimination against people with AIDS, especially against homosexual men, the group from which most early reported cases in the United States came. Discrimination continued even after scientists proved that AIDS was not transmitted through casual contact.

During the late 1980s and 1990s public education campaigns helped to promote awareness and tolerance. People's attitudes changed, too, when it was understood that HIV, the virus that causes AIDS, could strike anyone—even NBA standout **Ervin (Magic) Johnson** or tennis star Arthur Ashe.

Today AIDS remains a global issue of great seriousness. More than 3 million people died of AIDS in 2003, and an estimated 40 million people live with HIV. National governments and multinational organizations like the World Health Organization and the UN continue to sponsor initiatives to educate the public about the disease, provide treatment to those already infected, and search for a cure.

✓ **Reading Check** **Evaluating** Why did publicity about sports figures with AIDS help to improve awareness?

# Popular Culture and National Identity

**Main Idea** As popular culture and technology bring all parts of the world closer together, individual nations struggle to maintain their identities.

**Reading Connection** How often do you hear songs or see movies produced outside the United States or Europe? Read to learn how Western movies and music dominate popular culture abroad.

The effects of globalization are not limited to politics and economics. With new technology, such as Internet chat rooms, online music services, and relatively inexpensive DVDs, culture can be mass-produced and marketed globally. More people enjoy the same music and films, but the dominance of Western culture also raises questions.

**Movies and Music** In December 2003, moviegoers around the world eagerly waited for the opening of the third and final installment of the *Lord of the Rings* trilogy, *The Return of the King.* The film itself was an international project. It was produced by an American studio, directed by a New Zealander, interpreted by actors from many countries, and based on the story by British author J.R.R. Tolkien.

Breaking with tradition, the film was released simultaneously in 28 different countries, instead of opening first in the United States and taking months or years to open elsewhere. From Mexico City to Stockholm, from Paris to Singapore, people of many countries, religions, and political views shared the harrowing adventures of hobbits, elves, and men. The worldwide success of the *Lord of the Rings* is an example of the globalization of modern popular culture.

Popular culture is entertainment created for a mass audience to make a profit. Ever since the 1920s, popular culture has become more important. Today people often talk about movies, television, or sports before they talk about anything else.

By the 1990s, popular culture was also becoming similar the world over. Although many countries have their own movies and music celebrities, it is mainly American performers and filmmakers who are known throughout the world. In the 1950s and 1960s, **Elvis Presley,** Little Richard, and Chuck Berry combined jazz, gospel, traditional African, and country music to create rock 'n' roll. Rock music was a major way that American popular culture spread to other parts of the world.

When MTV, the American cable-TV music channel, was established, a rock group's image became as important as their music in selling records. Stars like Madonna and Michael Jackson, who were known as much for their flamboyant image as their voices, became the icons of the 1980s and early 1990s. In the late 1990s, teen and preteen consumers made performers such as 'N Sync and Britney Spears into multimillion-dollar musical acts.

Films also played a big role in spreading American culture. During the 1980s and 1990s, Hollywood

### *Picturing* History

Young people in Chile display their enthusiasm for the world movie hit, *Lord of the Rings.* In what ways was the film trilogy an example of the globalization of modern popular culture?

studios spent enormous sums of money producing "blockbusters" for world audiences. By the 1990s, studios could spend hundreds of millions of dollars on a single film, showcasing the latest in special effects.

Some people worried that American entertainment was weakening their own language and culture. Critics referred to **cultural imperialism,** meaning that a Western nation controlled other world cultures, much as they had controlled colonial governments in the 1800s. To protect their own musical heritage, the French even passed a law saying that at least 40 percent of radio time had to be reserved for French-language music.

Although Western music and movies dominate, there are trends in the opposite direction, too. One trend is that non-Western music is being played in Western rock and pop. Paul Simon's *Graceland,* a smash-hit album in the 1980s, was an early example. Simon spiced many of his songs with *mbaqanga*—the dance music of the black townships of South Africa.

The reggae music native to Jamaica has an enormous following, especially with resistance movements. Yet another trend is the popularity of world music programming on public radio stations. Finally, Latin pop has become so popular that there have been Latin Grammy awards since 1999.

**Television and Sports** More and more since the 1960s, television has created a sense that Americans and Europeans share a culture. When American networks sold shows abroad, the appropriate language was "dubbed" in. Europeans watched American shows like *The Simpsons, Baywatch,* and *ER,* even if they spoke no English and had never been to the United States. As they watched, viewers became familiar with American brand names—and American attitudes about family, work, and money.

After World War II, sports became another cultural export. The Olympic Games, for example, could be broadcast across the globe from any location. With televised sports, fans could enjoy an event without buying a ticket. For this reason, some sports organizations at first resisted televising events. They soon found, however, that they were receiving most of their revenues from advertisers who paid millions to sponsor TV football, soccer, or baseball.

Sports have become big politics, as well as big business. The most telling example of how politics and sports mix came with the 1972 Olympic Games in **Munich.** There a Palestinian terrorist group seized 11 Israeli athletes as hostages. All of them subsequently were killed. Mirroring Cold War political tensions, the USSR refused to participate in the 1984 Los Angeles Games after the United States boycotted the 1980 Moscow Olympics.

Sporting events can also be a positive political force. In 1998 when France hosted the soccer World Cup, its team, affectionately called "Les Bleus" for their blue uniforms, was expected to finish near the bottom of the tournament.

Surprising everyone, "Les Bleus" advanced to the final match, where they defeated world soccer powerhouse Brazil. The spontaneous celebrations across France were larger than any since France's **liberation** in World War II, and were made even sweeter because the hero of the final match, Zinedine Zidane, was the son of Algerian immigrants. Zidane gave many French people a positive image of North African immigrants.

**National Religious Trends** From the Middle Ages through the early part of the twentieth century, Christianity dominated the spiritual life of Western society. After World War II, however, many immigrants from former colonies moved to Europe to find jobs. The result has been much greater religious diversity in Europe. Millions of immigrants from Africa, for example, have established large Muslim communities in France, Germany, and Great Britain.

Religion is one of the ways that any people define themselves, and it influences national customs and social attitudes. This is why some Europeans feel that non-Christian immigrants are threatening their culture.

In the United States, where religious toleration was a founding principle of the nation, there is a different trend. Since the 1980s, an evangelical Protestant revival has gathered strength. Some observers suggest that one cause lies with the aging baby-boom generation. Some people who were in the 1960s protest movement may have become more religious when they got older. It is also possible that religion serves as a way to strengthen a sense of community in an increasingly complex society. Whatever the reasons, religious fervor has also translated into a powerful political force in America. Ever since the 1980 election of Republican Ronald Reagan, conservative Christian groups have played a larger role in American politics.

# CONNECTIONS Around The World

## Global Migrations

Since 1945, tens of millions of people have migrated from one part of the world to another. There are many reasons for these migrations. Persecution for political reasons caused many people from Pakistan, Bangladesh, Sri Lanka, Eastern Europe, and East Germany to seek refuge in Western European countries. Brutal civil wars in Asia, Africa, the Middle East, and Europe led millions of refugees to seek safety in neighboring countries. A devastating famine in Africa in 1984–1985 drove hundreds of thousands of Africans to relief camps throughout the continent to find food.

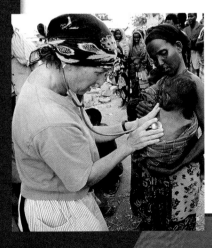

◀ *Mobile clinic in Somalia, Africa*

Most people who have migrated, however, have done so to find jobs. Latin Americans seeking a better life have migrated to the United States. Guest workers from Turkey, southern and Eastern Europe, North Africa, and South Asia have entered more prosperous Western European lands. In the 1980s, about fifteen million guest workers worked and lived in Europe.

Many host countries allowed guest workers to stay for several years. In the 1980s and 1990s, however, foreign workers often became scapegoats when countries faced economic problems. Political parties in France and Norway, for example, called for the removal of blacks and Arabs.

## Comparing Cultures

Are there immigrant populations where you live? Describe some of the attitudes your friends and families have toward foreign workers. Think of several reasons why foreign populations have migrated to the United States.

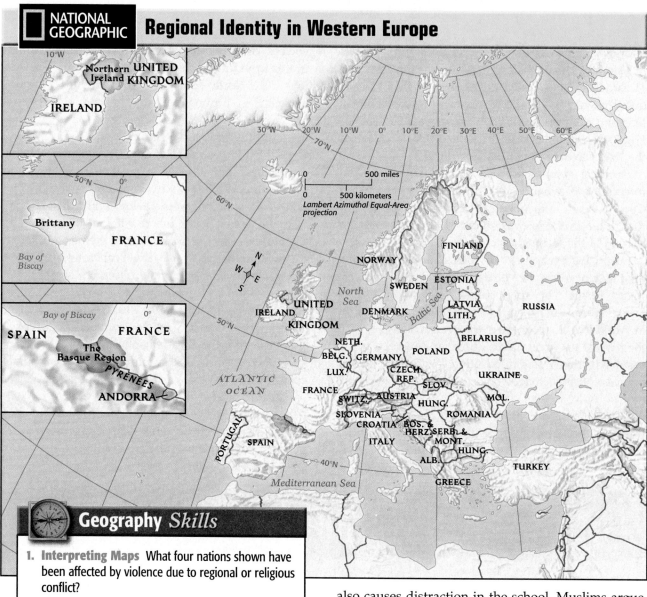

1. **Interpreting Maps** What four nations shown have been affected by violence due to regional or religious conflict?

2. **Applying Geography Skills** Is there a geographic factor that could contribute to the Basque people feeling separate?

Religious trends in the United States and Europe have raised an important issue: what role should religion play in a democracy? In the United States, controversies have erupted over the precise extent to which religion and government should be separated. Conflicts have arisen, for example, about the place of prayer in public schools, and the use of federal money to fund programs that certain Christians oppose.

In Europe, non-Christians struggle to find a balance between their identities as citizens of the West and as devout believers in a non-Christian religion. In France, for example, there is an ongoing struggle over whether Muslim girls should be allowed to wear headscarves to public schools. The government argues that by forcing a girl to wear a headscarf, her family sets her apart for ridicule from her peers and

also causes distraction in the school. Muslims argue that a girl needs to obey the dictates of her religion.

**Nationalism and Regional Identity** A global American-style culture is not the only challenge to national identity. There are also minorities in Europe and North America who want to preserve their culture, or even have their own nation. Sometimes these are ethnic groups, and sometimes they are religious groups. These minorities use many different tactics, from peaceful demonstrations to terrorism, to reach their goals.

Most minority movements are peaceful. In **Brittany,** a western region of France that is Celtic in its language and culture, local communities organize festivals called **Fest Noz** to celebrate their culture. These festivals feature traditional Breton costumes, dancing, music, and the Breton language, which closely resembles the Gaelic spoken in Ireland. In Canada, in the province of Quebec, which, unlike the rest of Canada, is French in language and culture, many have campaigned for independence for decades. They have

▲ *A building crumbling in a Belfast, Ireland fire during the often violent Catholic-Protestant clashes of the early 1970s*

used legal means to try to achieve their goal, and in 1995 Canadian voters decided the issue. The separatists were defeated but only by about 50,000 votes. Although many in Quebec are still fighting to secede, the 1995 vote reflects how close they are to winning and to becoming an entirely independent country.

Some minorities use violence as a tool to win concessions or gain independence. The **Basque region** is in the western Pyrenees, and part of the territory belongs to Spain and part to France. Although most Basques accept the status quo and work peacefully to protect their language and culture, Basque extremists do not. The group Basque Fatherland and Liberty (ETA) employ violence and terrorism.

**Northern Ireland** has also faced ongoing problems with violent extremists. In 1921, Ireland was partitioned between the independent Irish Republic, which has a mostly Catholic population, and Northern Ireland, which remained under British control. The five counties that make up Northern Ireland have a powerful Protestant majority, but they also contain many Catholics.

Clashes between Catholics and Protestants in Northern Ireland escalated on January 30, 1972. On this date, which is known as **"Bloody Sunday,"** British troops fired on a crowd of civil rights protesters and killed 13 people.

For the next three decades, the Catholic Irish Republican Army (IRA) employed violence and terror in an effort to unite Northern Ireland with the Republic of Ireland. Often aimed against British officials or local Protestant leaders, this violence continued despite many peace talks. By 2000, about 3,600 people had been killed and 36,000 injured in what are termed the "Troubles." Exhausted by years of violence, the two sides began talks in the 1990s, and signed the Good Friday Agreement in April 1996. The reluctance of the IRA and other militants to disarm, however, threatens the peace process.

✓ **Reading Check** **Explaining** Why did conflict between Catholics and Protestants in Northern Ireland begin?

**HISTORY** *Online* **Study Central**

For help with the concepts in this section of *Glencoe World History—Modern Times*, go to wh.mt.glencoe.com and click on **Study Central.**

# SECTION 4 ASSESSMENT

## Checking for Understanding

1. **Vocabulary** Define: globalization, percentage, gender parity, cultural imperialism, liberation.

2. **People and Events** Identify: Equal Pay Act, *Roe* v. *Wade,* Ervin (Magic) Johnson, Elvis Presley, Fest Noz, "Bloody Sunday."

3. **Places** Locate: Munich, Brittany, Basque region, Northern Ireland.

### Reviewing Big Ideas

4. **Explain** why some critics questioned technological progress in postwar society. Name a technological achievement and tell why it was criticized.

## Critical Thinking

5. **Summarize** What are the components of the new scientific establishment? Explain their benefits and shortcomings.

6. **Organizing Information** Create a chart showing the social effects and political effects of the following on society.

| | Social Effects | Political Effects |
|---|---|---|
| TV Sports | | |
| Movies | | |
| Music | | |

## Analyzing Visuals

7. **Examine** the photograph of the sports figures on page 636. Do you think the emotions conveyed in this kind of photograph can change how people feel about a specific minority group? Why or why not?

### Writing About History

8. **Expository Writing** List recent societal trends in Western Europe. In an essay, discuss the possible influences of these trends on future generations. **CA** 10WA2.3

*In the following passages, Russian political thinkers Mikhail Gorbachev and Aleksandr Solzhenitsyn discuss the future of the Soviet Union after the Cold War.*

## SOURCE 1: Gorbachev on Nuclear War

*In his book* Perestroika, *published in 1987, before the collapse of the Soviet Union, Soviet leader Mikhail Gorbachev argues that nuclear warfare is senseless.*

The fundamental principle of the new political outlook is very simple: *nuclear war cannot be a means of achieving political, economic, ideological or any other goals.* . . . Nuclear war is senseless; it is irrational. There would be neither winners nor losers in a global nuclear conflict: world civilization would inevitably perish. It is a suicide, rather than a war in the conventional sense of the word.

A way of thinking and a way of acting, based on the use of force in world politics, have formed over centuries, even millennia. It seems they have taken root as something unshakable. Today, they have lost all reasonable grounds. . . . For the first time in history, basing international politics on moral and ethical norms that are common to all humankind . . . has become a vital requirement.

. . . There is a great thirst for mutual understanding and mutual communication in the world. It is felt among politicians, it is gaining momentum among the

intelligentsia, representatives of culture, and the public at large. And if the Russian word **"perestroika**[1]**"** has easily entered the international **lexicon**[2], this is due to more than just interest in what is going on in the Soviet Union. Now the whole world needs restructuring, i.e., progressive development, a fundamental change. . . .

We are all students, and our teacher is life and time. I believe that more and more people will come to realize that through RESTRUCTURING in the broad sense of the word, the integrity of the world will be enhanced. Having earned good marks from our main teacher—life—we shall enter the twenty-first century well prepared and sure that there will be further progress.

## SOURCE 2: Gorbachev's Communist Party

*Gorbachev spoke to the Central Committee of the Soviet Communist Party on February 6, 1990, about the future of the party in the Soviet Union.*

. . . The main thing that now worries Communists and all citizens of the country is the fate of perestroika, the fate of the country and the role of the Soviet Communist Party at the current, probably most crucial, stage of revolutionary transformation. . . .

Of no less importance is the understanding of the fact . . . that the party will only be able to fulfill the mission of political **vanguard**[3] if it drastically restructures itself, masters the art of political work in the present conditions and succeeds in cooperating with forces committed to perestroika. . . .

The **platform**[4] says, Our ideal is a humane, democratic socialism, expressing the interests of the working class and all working people and relying on the great

▼ *Russian children gathered around a fallen statue of Lenin, the Communist Party founder*

[1]**perestroika:** restructuring; Gorbachev's policy of reform
[2]**lexicon:** vocabulary
[3]**vanguard:** at the head of an action or movement
[4]**platform:** plan of political action

legacy of Marx, Engels and Lenin. The Soviet Communist Party is creatively developing socialist ideals to match present-day realities and with due account for the entire experience of the 20th century.

The platform states clearly what we should abandon. We should abandon the ideological dogmatism that became ingrained during past decades, outdated stereotypes in domestic policy and outmoded view on the world revolutionary process and world development as a whole.

We should abandon everything that led to the isolation of socialist countries from the mainstream of world civilization. . . .

The party in a renewing society can exist and play its role as vanguard only as a democratically recognized force. This means that its status should not be imposed through constitutional endorsement.

The Soviet Communist Party . . . intends to struggle for the status of the ruling party.

But it will do so strictly within the framework of the democratic process by giving up any legal and political advantages . . . cooperating with other social and political forces, always working amidst the masses, living by their interests and their needs.

## SOURCE 3: Solzhenitsyn on Russian Democracy

*In a* **New York Times** *editorial of January 1997, author Aleksandr Solzhenitsyn questioned whether Russia had finally achieved a democracy.*

What is known today as "Russian democracy" masks a Government of a completely different sort. **Glasnost**[5]—freedom of the press—is only an instrument of democracy, not democracy itself. And to a great extent freedom of the press is **illusory,**[6] since the owners of newspapers erect strict taboos against discussion of issues of vital importance. . . .

Democracy in the unarguable sense of the word means the rule of the people—that is, a system in which the people are truly in charge of their daily lives and can influence the course of their own historical fate. There is nothing of the sort in Russia today.

> [5] **Glasnost:** Soviet policy of openness
> [6] **illusory:** deceptive

In August 1991, the "councils of people's deputies," though only window dressing under the rule of the Communist Party, were abolished throughout the country. Since then, the united resistance of the President's machine, the Government, State Duma, leaders of the political parties and majority of governors has prevented the creation of any agencies of local self-government. . . .

There exists no legal framework or financial means for the creation of local self-government; people will have no choice but to achieve it through social struggle. All that really exists is the government hierarchy, from the President and national Government on down. . . .

. . . Russia has been exhausted by crime, by the transfer into private hands of billions of dollars' worth of the nation's wealth. Not a single serious crime has been exposed, nor has there been a single public trial. . . .

The destructive course of events over the last decade has come about because the Government, while ineptly imitating foreign models, has completely disregarded the country's creativity and particular character, as well as Russia's centuries-old spiritual and social traditions. Only if those paths are freed up can Russia be delivered from its near-fatal condition.

## DBQ Document-Based Questions

**Historical Analysis** CA HI 1, HR 3, CS 2

**Source 1:** Why does Gorbachev say that nuclear warfare is irrational?

**Source 2:** In the second excerpt, Gorbachev proposes that the Soviet Communist Party's mission is to be a political vanguard. What does he mean?

**Source 3:** Why does Solzhenitsyn argue that there is still no democracy in Russia?

### Comparing and Contrasting Sources

1. Compare Gorbachev's attitude and mood on what communism has to offer in Source 1 and Source 2.
2. Compare Gorbachev's hopes for democracy in the second passage with Solzhenitsyn's analysis of Russia's progress toward democracy seven years later.

Standards 10.9.5, 10.9.7, 10.10, 10.10.1, 10.10.2, 10.10.3, 10.11

## Chapter Summary

The end of the Cold War brought dramatic economic, political, and social changes to Europe and North America. Many of these changes can be understood through the themes of conflict, change, regionalism, and cooperation. Below, some of the major events in postwar society are categorized according to these themes.

### Conflict

- Serb forces carry out "ethnic cleansing" of Muslims.
- Terrorism becomes a regular aspect of modern society.
- Soviet troops crush a reform movement in Czechoslovakia.
- Nicolae Ceauşescu is arrested and executed.

### Change

- The Soviet Union adopts a policy of perestroika under Gorbachev.
- Lech Walesa becomes the first elected president of an Eastern European nation in 40 years.
- The national debt triples in the United States during Ronald Reagan's presidency.
- Television, movies, and music spread American culture throughout the world.

### Regionalism

- Ethnic Albanians declare Kosovo an independent province.
- Bosnian Serbs fight Bosnian Muslims and Croats.
- Bands of German youths attack immigrants.
- Intense fighting breaks out between Protestants and Catholics in Northern Ireland.

### Cooperation

- British women hold an antinuclear protest.
- American culture spreads through popular media.
- East Germany and West Germany are reunited into one nation.
- The Soviet Union and the United States sign the INF Treaty.

## Reviewing Content Vocabulary

*On a sheet of paper, use each of these terms in a sentence.*

1. détente
2. dissident
3. perestroika
4. ethnic cleansing
5. autonomous
6. Thatcherism
7. budget deficit
8. weapons of mass destruction
9. globalization
10. gender parity
11. cultural imperialism

## Reviewing Academic Vocabulary

*On a sheet of paper, use each of these terms in a sentence that reflects the term's meaning in the chapter.*

12. apparent
13. expansion
14. found
15. settlement
16. cooperation
17. currency
18. method
19. percentage
20. liberation

## Reviewing the Main Ideas

### Section 1

21. What doctrine gave the Soviet Union the right to intervene if communism in another Communist state was threatened?

22. What problems arose in Russia after the Soviet Union dissolved?

### Section 2

23. How did religion contribute to changes in Bosnia and Poland?

24. List the three Eastern European countries that made peaceful transitions from Communist to free-market societies.

### Section 3

25. What caused the economic downturn in Western Europe from the mid-1970s to the early 1980s?

26. What problems surfaced in Germany as a result of reunification?

### Section 4

27. What goal did women in the United States and Europe work toward when the women's movement began?

28. List the recent societal changes in Europe due to population trends.

## Critical Thinking

29. **Evaluating** What were the results of the Reagan administration's military buildup?

30. **Analyzing** Explain why the United States, Great Britain, and France alternated between liberal and conservative government leaders from 1970 through 2000.

31. **Analyzing** The United States has been accused of "cultural imperialism." What positive and negative effects does the spread of American popular culture have? How has American popular culture been influenced in return?

32. **Reading Skill** **Connecting** Who do you consider as influential musicians, artists, and entertainers in the popular culture of the 2000s? What values do these individuals model? Who are the heroes and who are the superstars? Is there a difference?

## Writing About History

33. **Historical Analysis** **Analyzing Sequence and Change** Write an essay discussing Ireland's struggle to maintain a national identity. Look at the issues and events chronologically while exploring what changes have or have not occurred. **CA CS 2**

34. *Big Idea* In the latter part of the twentieth century, communist governments ceased to exist in the Soviet Union and Eastern Europe. Countries experienced problems converting their economic systems from socialist to free-market societies. Write a paper listing the problems created by the fall of communism and describe solutions that would have made the transition easier. **CA 10WA2.3**

**DBQ** **Document-Based Questions**

**Analyzing Sources** In his book *Perestroika,* Mikhail Gorbachev wrote:

> ❝There is a great thirst for mutual understanding and mutual communication in the world. It is felt among politicians, it is gaining momentum among the intelligentsia, representatives of culture, and the public at large. . . . Now the whole world needs restructuring, i.e., progressive development, a fundamental change. . . . I believe that more and more people will come to realize that through RESTRUCTURING in the broad sense of the word, the integrity of the world will be enhanced.❞

35. What does Gorbachev think is gaining momentum among the public at large?

36. How does Gorbachev's quote apply to today's world?

**Caucasus Region, 1991**

## Analyzing Maps and Charts

Study the map above to answer the following questions.

37. Which of these states is completely landlocked?

38. Which state's territory is separated by Armenia? What problems might that present?

 **Standards Practice**

**Directions: Choose the best answer to the following question.**

39. What happened in Czechoslovakia after the Communist Party collapsed?

**A** Rival ethnic states could not agree on national borders.

**B** East Germany remained loyal to the Soviets.

**C** Conservative movements came to power in America and Great Britain.

**D** Mikhail Gorbachev invaded Czechoslovakia to regain control.

**CA Standard 10.9.5** Describe the uprisings in Poland (1952), Hungary (1956), Czechoslovakia (1968), and those countries' resurgence in the 1970s and 1980s as people in Soviet satellites sought freedom from Soviet control.

## CHAPTER 14

*1945–Present*

# Latin America

## ✧ The Big Ideas ✧

### SECTION 1: General Trends in Latin America

**The quest for national self-determination is universal.** Many Latin American nations began to build democratic systems in the late 1980s.

### SECTION 2: Mexico, Cuba, and Central America

**The quest for national self-determination is universal.** Mexico and Central America faced political and economic crises after World War II that hampered national progress.

### SECTION 3: The Nations of South America

**Throughout history people have struggled for rights.** South American nations have experienced economic, social, and political problems, but democracy has advanced since the late 1980s.

 **World History—Modern Times Video** *The Chapter 14 video, "The Cuban Revolution," chronicles the causes and effects of Castro's revolution in Cuba.*

*Juan Perón*

**1951**
Juan Perón elected to second term as president of Argentina

**1961**
Bay of Pigs invasion fails

**1962**
Cuban missile crisis resolved

*1940*　　　*1950*　　　*1960*

**1946**
Juan Perón establishes authoritarian regime in Argentina

**1948**
Organization of American States formed

**1959**
Fidel Castro seizes power in Cuba

Sugarloaf Mountain overlooks Rio de Janeiro, one of Brazil's most populous cities.

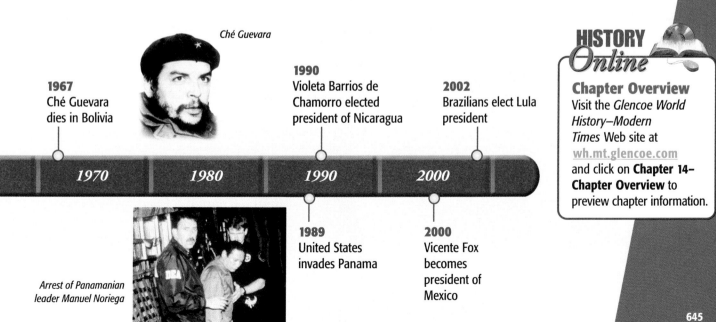

*Ché Guevara*

**1967**
Ché Guevara
dies in Bolivia

**1990**
Violeta Barrios de
Chamorro elected
president of Nicaragua

**2002**
Brazilians elect Lula
president

*1970*     *1980*     *1990*     *2000*

*Arrest of Panamanian
leader Manuel Noriega*

**1989**
United States
invades Panama

**2000**
Vicente Fox
becomes
president of
Mexico

**HISTORY**
*Online*

**Chapter Overview**
Visit the *Glencoe World
History–Modern
Times* Web site at
wh.mt.glencoe.com
and click on **Chapter 14–
Chapter Overview** to
preview chapter information.

# Preparing to Read Chapter 14

## Reading Skill | Comparing and Contrasting

Good readers make comparisons across sections and chapters. Getting used to making comparisons is a big help when you are reading about many different people, places, and events. If you see headings in your textbook that are similar, that is a logical time to stop and think about making comparisons.

In this chapter, Section 2 is about Mexico, Cuba, and Central America, while Section 3 is about the nations of South America. When you look quickly over the sections, you will notice that many headings are by country. You might expect that similar information will be presented for each country. If you find this to be the case when you read, it is a good idea to think about what is similar or different.

*Read the following excerpts from this chapter that describe the economic challenges faced by each country.*

### COMPARING

Each excerpt refers to a group that has or is gaining power in a country. Look to see if you find a similarity in the power structure of Argentina and Chile before the workers' actions.

Economic weakness forced the Castro regime to depend on the Soviets and on selling sugar to Soviet bloc countries. (Cuba)

For years, it had been ruled by a powerful oligarchy whose wealth was based on growing wheat and raising cattle. (Argentina)

Wealthy landowners were angry because the government did nothing when radical workers began to take control of their estates. (Chile)

### CONTRASTING

How do the dominant groups differ in the three countries—Cuba, Argentina, and Chile—that are described here?

### Apply the Skill

As you read this chapter, make comparisons between countries to understand how they are alike and different. You can also remember to look for the signal words mentioned in the Chapter 6 Reading Skill to make comparisons.

# Historical Analysis Skill ⟩ Characterizing Current Events

**Chronological and Spatial Thinking: Standard CS4** *Students relate current events to the physical and human characteristics of places and regions.*

Historians understand that current events are tied to trends and characteristics of a given nation or region. Therefore, knowing about trends and traditions in a region makes it easier to understand how a contemporary event will affect it.

If you read about a political event, try to remember whatever you already know about that topic. This will give you additional background or context for understanding the new information.

Over time, you will be building up your ability to recognize and trace the direction of trends. For example, let's say that you often hear a reference to huge inflation problems in a South American country. If you later heard that a new government had lowered inflation, you would quickly know that this was an unusual event—one that might open the door to a new and more hopeful trend.

*Read the following passage from pages 666–667 depicting one of Peruvian president Alejandro Toledo's political decisions.*

> **Toledo presided over the completion of the Camisea Gas Project, a pipeline to carry natural gas from deep in the Amazon jungle to Lima. The project has been financed by a consortium that is dominated by a Texas oil company. Peruvian politicians welcome the project, but it has been criticized for ignoring the damage to the Camisea rain forest and the indigenous peoples living there.**

## Apply the Skill

After reading the chapter, discuss with a partner the factors that connect this current event to Latin American trends and traditions. For instance, is the involvement of an American company unusual? What role does conservation play? Why would Peruvian politicians "welcome the project"?

# A Story That Matters

*A victorious Fidel Castro rides through the streets of Havana in 1959.*

## The Castro Brothers

On July 26, 1953, two brothers, Fidel and Raul Castro, led a band of 165 young people in an attack on the Moncada army camp at Santiago de Cuba. While a law student at the University of Havana, Fidel Castro had become a revolutionary. He was determined to overthrow the government of Fulgencio Batista, the dictator of Cuba.

The attack on Moncada, however, was a disaster. Many of the troops led by the Castro brothers were killed, wounded, or arrested. Fidel and Raul Castro escaped but were later captured and sentenced to prison for 15 years.

The Castro brothers could easily have died in prison, where political prisoners were routinely tortured. Instead, they were released after 11 months. By freeing political prisoners, Batista hoped to win the favor of the Cuban people.

He certainly did not gain the favor of the Castros. After his release, Fidel Castro fled to Mexico and built a new revolutionary army. Six years later, on January 1, 1959, Fidel Castro and his forces finally seized control of Cuba. Hundreds of thousands of Cubans swept into the streets, overcome with joy. One person remarked, "We were walking on a cloud." To the many Latin Americans who wanted major social and economic changes, Castro soon became a source of hope.

### Why It Matters

Since 1945, the nations of Latin America have followed different paths of change. In some countries military dictators have maintained political stability and initiated economic changes. A few nations, like Cuba, have used Marxist revolutions to create a new political, economic, and social order. Many Latin American nations have struggled to build democratic systems, especially since the late 1980s. The Cold War has also had an impact on Latin America.

**History and You** As you read this chapter, document the struggle between democracy and dictatorship in the Latin American states. Make a chart or diagram comparing the different states, their leadership, and reasons why the regimes were able to gain power.

# General Trends in Latin America

## Section Preview

Many Latin American nations began to build democratic systems in the late 1980s.

### Main Idea

- Because many Latin American economies depend too much on exporting raw materials, they have had serious economic and political problems. (p. 650)

- Economic and population problems have been critical to shaping modern Latin America. (p. 653)

- Latin American artists and writers are seen as important national figures. (p. 654)

## Content Vocabulary

multinational corporation, megacity, favela, magic realism

## Academic Vocabulary

finance, trend

## People and Events to Identify

Organization of American States (OAS), Gabriel García Márquez, Oscar Niemeyer

## Places to Locate

São Paulo, Mexico City, Rio de Janeiro, Brasília

## Reading Objectives

1. List the factors that undermined the stability of Latin American countries.
2. Describe how the role of women changed in the decades after 1945.

## Reading Strategy

**Categorizing Information** Use a chart like the one below to identify social and political challenges in Latin America since 1945.

## Preview of Events

| ◆1940 | ◆1950 | ◆1960 | ◆1970 | ◆1980 | ◆1990 |
|---|---|---|---|---|---|

**1948**
Organization of American States is formed

**1980**
Movement toward democracy takes place in Latin America

**1982**
Gabriel García Márquez wins Nobel Prize for literature

**1990**
Twenty-nine Latin American cities have over a million people

## California Standards in This Section

*Reading this section will help you master these California History–Social Science standards.*

**10.10:** Students analyze instances of nation-building in the contemporary world in at least two of the following regions or countries: the Middle East, Africa, Mexico and other parts of Latin America, and China.

**10.10.2:** Describe the recent history of the regions, including political divisions and systems, key leaders, religious issues, natural features, resources, and population patterns.

**10.10.3:** Discuss the important trends in the regions today and whether they appear to serve the cause of individual freedom and democracy.

# Economic and Political Developments

**Main Idea** Because many Latin American economies depend too much on exporting raw materials, they have had serious economic and political problems.

**Reading Connection** Have you heard reports about the "outsourcing" of American jobs? Read to learn how multinational firms affect Latin American economies.

Ever since colonial times, Latin American countries have had economies that relied heavily on exporting raw materials to buy manufactured goods they needed. As we saw in Chapter 10, industry made some progress during the Depression. The world economy slowed down, and Latin American nations had to become more self-sufficient and create new industry. Overall their economies remained fragile, however. Whenever world prices for raw goods fell, their economies threatened to go into a slump.

These countries were especially dependent on "the giant to the north." American business investment was one of the reasons the United States often intervened in Latin American affairs. American investors would pressure the U.S. government to prevent political and social change in Latin America—even if that meant backing dictators.

## Voices from the Past

One of the most influential American businesses in Latin America was the United Fruit Company, based in Boston. One analysis estimated the extent of its holdings in Guatemala in the 1950s:

> ❝United Fruit controlled directly or indirectly nearly 40,000 jobs in Guatemala. Its investments in the country were valued at $60 million. It functioned as a state within a state, owning Guatemala's telephone and telegraph facilities, administering its only important Atlantic harbor and monopolizing its banana export. The company's subsidiary, the International Railways of Central America (IRCA), owned 887 miles of railroad track in Guatemala, nearly every mile in the country.❞

In 1952, Jacobo Arbenz, who was elected president of Guatemala in 1950, began a land reform program and seized some of the United Fruit property. The company lobbied the U.S. government to take action

▲ *Jacobo Arbenz (left) in Mexico after his overthrow*

against Arbenz, citing a link to communism. With help from the U.S. Central Intelligence Agency, military forces overthrew Arbenz in 1954.

The United States has long played a major role in Latin America. In the early 1900s, it often sent troops into Latin American countries to protect U.S. interests and bolster dictators friendly to them. Then in the 1930s, President Franklin D. Roosevelt began a "Good Neighbor" policy, an effort to end such intervention. In 1948, the states of the Western Hemisphere formed the **Organization of American States (OAS)**. The OAS also emphasized the need for Latin American independence. It passed a resolution calling for an end to military action by one state in the affairs of another. The founding of the OAS did not end American involvement in Latin America, however.

Why did American involvement continue? A major reason was the onset of the Cold War. American leaders became more anxious about instability in Latin America. They feared that the poverty in these countries made them ripe for communist takeover. The Soviet Union, they concluded, would then have more power to threaten American interests around the globe. When a communist government took over in Cuba in 1959, these anxieties reached a fever pitch (see Section 2).

During much of the Cold War era, the United States kept a close watch on radical movements in Latin America. In some cases, it used its influence if it felt that Communist-backed parties were gaining power in South and Central America. As part of the mission to fight communism around the world, the United States also provided massive amounts of military aid to anti-Communist regimes.

Radical social and political movements did have an appeal for many people in Latin America. The reason was that weak economies and the gap between rich and poor had continued. During the 1960s, many nations were still unable to move away from relying too heavily on exporting food and natural resources to get finished products. Now, instead of manufactured goods, it was often the advanced technology required for modern industry that they needed to import. Despite their best efforts, Latin American industry was unable to compete effectively in the world. Their economies remained vulnerable to the ups and downs of the world market for products like coffee, cotton, tin, and copper.

With their economies so rocky, their governments tended to be unstable. When unemployment rose and workers demonstrated, dictators were able to take power because they had the support of the military and conservative elites. In the 1960s, repressive military regimes in Chile, Brazil, and Argentina abolished political parties and returned to export-import economies **financed** by foreigners.

These regimes also encouraged **multinational corporations**—companies with divisions in more than two countries—to come to Latin America. This practice was a new twist on the existing model of dependence. Latin American nations were now even more dependent on industrialized nations.

In the 1970s, the cycle of dependence took a turn for the worse. In an effort to maintain their weak economies, Latin American nations borrowed money from other nations. Between 1970 and 1982, debt to foreigners grew from $27 billion to $315.3 billion. By 1982, a number of Latin American economies had begun to crumble. Wages fell, and unemployment and inflation skyrocketed.

With such a staggering debt load, many nations could not even afford to make the interest payments on their loans. They needed new loans and turned to foreign banks and international organizations like the World Bank, a UN agency that promotes development in poorer countries. These institutions would only agree to make more loans if financial and other reforms were made. For example, they insisted that governments give up running some state-run industries so that free enterprise would be strengthened. The debt crisis of the 1980s was seen again in Mexico in the mid-1990s.

Recurring economic crisis has had one positive effect on Latin American politics—it led to a demand for greater democracy. This occurred for two reasons. First, some military leaders did not want to deal with

# CONNECTIONS Around The World

## International Women's Conferences

As women around the world organized movements to change the conditions of their lives, an international women's movement emerged. Between 1975 and 1985, the United Nations celebrated the Decade for Women by holding conferences in such cities as Mexico City, Copenhagen, and Nairobi. These conferences made it clear that there were significant differences between the problems facing women in Western and non-Western countries.

Women from Western countries spoke about political, economic, cultural, and sexual rights. In contrast, women from developing countries in Latin America, Africa, and Asia focused on bringing an end to the violence, hunger, and disease that haunt their lives.

At the International Women's Year Tribunal in Mexico in 1974, sponsored by the United Nations, Domitila Barrios de Chungara, a miner's wife from Bolivia, expressed her lack of patience with professional women at the conference: "So, I went up and spoke. I made them see that they don't live in our world. I made them see that in Bolivia human rights aren't respected. . . . Women like us, housewives, who get organized to better our people, well, they [the Bolivian police] beat us up and persecute us."

◀ *Latin American mother with children*

## Comparing Cultures

Women from industrialized and developing nations focus on different issues.
1. Does the Bolivian woman believe she will see progress?
2. What purposes might conferences serve other than identifying issues?

# U.S. Involvement in Latin America since 1945

**⑤ CHILE**
1940s–1970: Support for left-leaning parties grows
1970: President Allende nationalizes some industry and institutes land reform
1973: Army overthrows Allende; General Pinochet becomes dictator
1989: Pinochet forced out; Aylwin elected president by popular vote

**⑥ CUBA**
1959: Marxist Castro overthrows dictator Batista
1960: U.S. declares trade embargo
1961: U.S. supports Bay of Pigs invasion
1962: Cuban Missile Crisis
1989: Soviet military subsidies to Cuba end, hurting Cuban economy
1996: U.S. continues trade embargo
2000: U.S. approves sale of food and medicines to Cuba

**① MEXICO**
1946: One-party rule by PRI continues
1950s–1960s: Industrialization under way, often with U.S. capital
1986: continuing wave of immigrants prompts new U.S. law
1994: U.S., Mexico, and Canada form NAFTA
2000: Vicente Fox elected, ending 70 years of PRI rule

**② NICARAGUA**
1937–1979: Somoza family, with strong U.S. support, controls country
1979: Marxist Sandinistas overthrow Somoza regime
1981–1990: U.S. aids right-wing "contras" against Sandinistas
1990: Chamorro elected; U.S. lifts trade embargo
2004: World Bank writes off 80% of Nicaragua's debt

**③ PANAMA**
1968–1981: military junta controls country
1977: By treaty, canal reverts to Panama in 1999
1983: Dictator Noriega profits from illegal drug trade
1989: U.S. invades Panama and captures Noriega
1999: Canal reverts to Panama

**④ COLOMBIA**
1960s–present: guerrillas, illegal drug gangs and paramilitary groups create violence and chaos
2003: U.S. forces protecting oil pipeline from terrorist attacks

**⑦ BRAZIL**
1946–1980s: Industrial development begins, surging in the 1970s and 1980s
1964–85: military dictatorship rules
1989: first direct election held
1994–95: new president introduces reforms
1995: annual rate of deforestation of Amazon rain forests estimated at 29,000 sq. kilometers
2002: new president heads first left-wing government in more than 40 years
2003: annual rate of Amazon deforestation reaches its highest rate since 1995

**⑧ ARGENTINA**
1946: Peron begins to nationalize industry and expand unions; economic growth is slow
1976–83: period of military rule and "Dirty War"; thousands disappear
1982 Argentina invades British Falkland Islands; defeat leads to political reform
2003: International Monetary Fund approves $6.78 million loan for financial crisis

0 ____ 1,000 miles
0 ____ 1,000 kilometers
*Lambert Azimuthal Equal-Area projection*

---

the monstrous debt problem and were willing to step aside. Second, more and more people recognized that military power without popular consent could not maintain a strong modern state. By the mid-1990s, several democratic regimes had been established.

While the economies of Latin America improved in the late 1990s and early 2000s, their forward progress is not assured. The debt load remains high and a large percentage of the population lives in poverty. Because so many people are impoverished, they cannot buy many consumer goods—which is necessary to stimulate a vibrant domestic economy based on consumption.

One serious by-product of continuing rural poverty is the drug trade. Starving peasants in Bolivia, Peru, and Colombia have been drawn to growing coca and opium to make a living. The products they grow supply drug lords who make millions feeding the world demand for cocaine and heroin. The majority of the illegal drugs consumed in the United States are produced in Latin America.

Wars between competing drug gangs have brought violence to the cities as well as the countryside. With American backing, governments have fought to suppress the drug industry, but it has been a difficult battle. In some cases, the judges who dared to sentence a drug criminal have been assassinated.

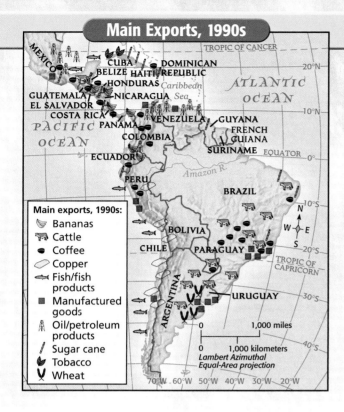

**Main Exports, 1990s**

Main exports, 1990s:
- 🍌 Bananas
- 🐂 Cattle
- ● Coffee
- Copper
- 🐟 Fish/fish products
- ■ Manufactured goods
- ⛽ Oil/petroleum products
- Sugar cane
- 🍃 Tobacco
- V Wheat

0   1,000 miles

0   1,000 kilometers
Lambert Azimuthal
Equal-Area projection

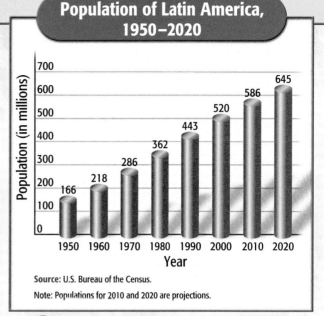

**Population of Latin America, 1950–2020**

Source: U.S. Bureau of the Census.

Note: Populations for 2010 and 2020 are projections.

The revival of democracy remains very fragile. Without a strong economy and a more even distribution of wealth to all citizens, any government faces a challenge. In 1992, Peru's President Alberto Fujimori, who had campaigned on reforming the nation's economy, returned to an authoritarian system.

**✓ Reading Check** **Explaining** Why did the debt crisis of the 1980s create a movement toward democracy?

# Latin American Society

**Main Idea** Economic and population problems have been critical to shaping modern Latin America.

**Reading Connection** Do you know a city where fast growth has created traffic jams and "urban sprawl"? Read to learn about megacities in Latin America.

Latin America's economic problems were made worse by dramatic growth in population. By the mid-1980s, the population in Latin America had grown from about 165 million people in 1950 to 400 million.

The birthrate in many Latin American nations was relatively high for much of the twentieth century. As late as 1970, it was still higher than the birthrate in Western Europe or North America. A high birthrate is one reason for the phenomenal population growth. For example, between 1940 and 1994, the Mexican population grew from 47 million to more than 90 million. In recent decades, population growth has

**Geography** *Skills*

Over the past 50 to 60 years, the United States has been actively involved in Latin American affairs.

1. **Interpreting Maps** What information can you find in the map on page 652 that shows that Latin Americans oppose American intervention in Latin America?

2. **Applying Geography Skills** Examine the bar graph above on Latin American population. What is the population increase from 1950 to the year 2000?

slowed. The population remains high, however, especially compared to the low economic productivity.

Since the colonial era, cities have been a feature of South American life, but in recent decades, the size of cities has increased. By 2000, 50 cities in Latin America and the Caribbean had more than a million people. Poverty drives poor villagers to the cities to find work, but they end up living in slums. The most striking part of this migration is how gargantuan some cities have become. In 2004, an estimated 17 million people lived in São Paulo (compared to about 8 million in New York City). Mexico City, the world's largest city, has an estimated 18 million people.

Analysts refer to such cities as megacities. A **megacity** not only has a huge population, but also has mushroomed so fast that regular urban services cannot be provided. Housing, plumbing, water supply, schools—this normal infrastructure can be nearly nonexistent in the suburbs of a megacity.

As vast streams of poor people move from the countryside to São Paulo or **Rio de Janeiro,** their hopes for a better life die quickly. They build shacks in front of glittering high-rise condos and roam the streets looking for work and food. Many live in **favelas,** Brazilian squatter settlements where clean water and electricity are in short supply. This migration has been dramatic in Brazil, Chile, and Venezuela. In other Latin American countries, most of the poor still live in villages. Everywhere, however, the enormous gap between the poor and the rich remains.

For women in Latin America, there has been great change for some, and less so for others. In Hispanic cultures, the traditional roles of wife and mother are highly respected. Like women in other parts of the world, though, some Latin American women have moved into jobs in industry, law, and medicine.

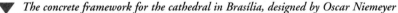

✓ **Reading Check** **Describing** What effects has population expansion had on Latin American cities?

## Latin American Culture

**Main Idea** Latin American artists and writers are seen as important national figures.

**Reading Connection** Can you name major American artists and writers who influence your view of society? Read to learn about the impact of writers and artists in Latin America.

Writers and artists have played important roles in Latin America. They have been given a status granted to writers and artists in few other regions of the world. Latin Americans often look to them to express their hopes and their criticisms of government and society.

One of the distinctive styles in Latin American literature is called **magic realism.** Magic realism brings together realistic events with dreamlike or fantastic backgrounds.

Perhaps the best example of magic realism is *One Hundred Years of Solitude,* a novel by the Colombian **Gabriel García Márquez.** Márquez is one of the world's best-known modern writers. Born in Colombia, he began to write after he read the "The Metamorphosis" by Franz Kafka: "That's how my grandmother used to tell stories, the wildest things with a completely natural tone of voice." Márquez's book made a huge impact around the world and focused attention on Latin American culture. In 1982, Márquez was awarded the Nobel Prize for literature.

Márquez was raised by his grandmother and had great respect and love for her. He set his story in the fictional town of Macondo, a town inspired by her stories of village life in Colombia. In Macondo, the point-of-view slips easily between fact and fantasy. Tall tales abound, and villagers are not surprised when a local priest rises into the air and floats.

Yet when the villagers are introduced to magnets, telescopes, and magnifying glasses, they are dumbfounded. Such things seem more magical to them than the myths and folklore of their village. Márquez's work suggests that whether something is fantasy or fact depends on a person's perspective. In many of

▼ *The concrete framework for the cathedral in Brasília, designed by Oscar Niemeyer*

▲ *Nobel Prize–winning author Gabriel García Márquez*

Marquez's works, readers will also find reflections of the rebellions and civil wars that have occurred in Colombia's past.

The art and architecture of Latin America in the postwar period was strongly influenced by international **trends**. In painting, abstract styles predomi-nated, while Bauhaus and Modernist styles were seen in architecture (see Chapter 9). Outstanding examples of Latin American architecture can be seen in Brasília. **Brasília** was built as Brazil's new capital in the 1950s and 1960s—the then-capital of Rio de Janeiro was on the coast. Government leaders wanted a new capital to attract development to the middle of Brazil and to lessen the population pressures on Rio de Janeiro.

Brazilian architect **Oscar Niemeyer** was appointed chief architect for the new capital. Niemeyer already had an international reputation as one of the two architects who designed the United Nations building. Niemeyer's outlook is evident in his description of his work in Brasília:

❝. . . I did my very best in the structures, trying to make them different with their columns narrow, so narrow that the palaces would seem to barely touch the ground. And I set them apart from the facades, creating an empty space through which, as I bent over my work table, I could see myself walking, imagining their forms and the different resulting points of view they would provoke.❞

 **Evaluating** What has had the most impact on Latin American countries in the past 50 years?

**HISTORY** *Online* **Study Central**

For help with the concepts in this section of *Glencoe World History–Modern Times*, go to wh.mt.glencoe.com and click on **Study Central.**

# SECTION 1 ASSESSMENT

### Checking for Understanding

1. **Vocabulary** Define: finance, multinational corporation, megacity, favela, magic realism, trend.

2. **People and Events** Identify: Organization of American States (OAS), Gabriel García Márquez, Oscar Niemeyer.

3. **Places** Locate: São Paulo, Mexico City, Rio de Janeiro, Brasília.

### Reviewing Big Ideas

4. **Explain** how the Great Depression hurt Latin American economies. Have these economies recovered from the problems caused by the Great Depression?

### Critical Thinking

5. **Historical Analysis** **Cause and Effect** Why did the rapid rate of population growth in many Latin American countries cause problems for their government and economy? **CA HI 2**

6. **Organizing Information** Draw a chart like the one below to list economic challenges in Latin America since 1945.

Economic Challenges

### Analyzing Visuals

7. **Examine** the photograph of a Latin American mother with her children shown on page 651 of the text. From the evidence, how does this Latin American mother do her housekeeping and prepare food?

### Writing About History

8. **Descriptive Writing** A uniquely Latin American literary form is magic realism. Do some research on your own about magic realism. Then write a short account of a real event that blends fact and fantasy in the style of magic realism. **CA WA2.1a**

# YOUNG PEOPLE IN . . .

## Argentina

For hundreds of years, the Catholic Church, European traditions, and a blending of cultures have shaped life in Argentina. For many Argentines, life begins and ends with Catholic rituals: baptism at birth and a Catholic funeral mass when they die. The government reflects this Catholic culture, too. For example, by law, all children must be registered at birth with names from a specific registry. Usually these are the Spanish names of Catholic saints.

Though Catholic traditions are honored, Argentines take a relaxed view toward religion. Less than 20 percent attend church regularly. Some Argentines who are Native American combine their worship in church on Sunday with prayer to nature spirits during the week.

Teenagers in Argentina are more likely to hear their parents talk passionately about politics, the arts, sports—especially soccer—and what it means *to be* an Argentine. About 40 percent of Argentines are of Italian descent, and 30 percent have Spanish roots. Another 15 percent are descendants of British, German, French, and Polish immigrants.

The Buenos Aires *porteños,* or "people of the port," are Argentina's elite. They view themselves as sophisticated trendsetters, and young people there grow up wearing Calvin Klein and other designer clothing. *Porteños* usually see those who live outside Buenos Aires as campesinos—mere country folk.

Social trends are changing, but Argentinian boys still learn machismo characteristics—to be strong, respected, and protective. They expect they will grow up to be the breadwinners in their family, while girls are encouraged to learn the feminine arts. As in many South American countries, Argentinian girls celebrate their 15th birthday with a "coming out" party. Hundreds are invited to this lavish party to announce that a daughter is now a woman.

Most young people in Argentina grow up under the watchful eyes of parents, aunts, uncles, and other relatives. They have a sense of duty toward their parents and usually live at home until they finish college.

◄ A young farmworker harvests grapes in the mountainous wine-growing country of Mendoza province. About 15 percent of Argentina's population includes mestizos. In this region, young workers might also herd llamas or farm mountainside plots.

Gauchos, or cowhands, are the national symbol of Argentina, admired for their fierce independence, strength, and horse-riding skills. In the past, gauchos roamed the pampas, or Argentina's grasslands, taming wild horses and herding cattle. Few in number today, gauchos still tend livestock, a vital part of the country's economy.

The tango, Argentina's folk dance, is known for its long, gliding steps and dramatic poses. Here tango dancers perform for tourists in the capital and port city of Buenos Aires.

These young people respond to the opening of the film *Evita* starring Madonna and based on the life of Eva Peron, a national heroine for many. These are *porteños*—residents of the port city of Buenos Aires, which is distinctly European.

## CONNECTING TO THE PAST

1. **Analyzing** How might the self-image of the *porteños* have caused conflict in Argentina?

2. **Writing about History** Research the time of the traditional gauchos. Write an essay describing their lifestyle and skills, as well as their continuing effect on the nationalistic image of Argentines today.

# SECTION 2 Mexico, Cuba, and Central America

## Guide to Reading

### Section Preview
Mexico and Central America faced political and economic crises after World War II that hampered national progress.

**Main Idea**

- Political and economic problems have plagued Mexico since the Mexican Revolution. (p. 659)
- The Cuban Revolution established the communist dictatorship of Fidel Castro. (p. 660)
- Fearing the spread of communism, the United States involved itself in affairs of Central America on a number of occasions. (p. 661)

### Content Vocabulary
PRI, privatization, trade embargo, contra

### Academic Vocabulary
challenge, element

### People to Identify
César Chávez, Vicente Fox, Fidel Castro, Manuel Noriega

### Places to Locate
Havana, El Salvador, Nicaragua, Panama

### Reading Objectives
1. List the problems Mexico and Central America faced after World War II.
2. Explain the main features and impact of the Cuban Revolution.

### Reading Strategy
**Categorizing Information** Use a table like the one below to identify the political and economic challenges faced by El Salvador, Nicaragua, and Panama after 1945.

| El Salvador | Nicaragua | Panama |
|---|---|---|
|  |  |  |
|  |  |  |
|  |  |  |

### Preview of Events

| ♦1950 | ♦1960 | ♦1970 | ♦1980 | ♦1990 | ♦2000 |
|---|---|---|---|---|---|

**1959**
Castro's revolutionaries seize Havana

**1961**
United States breaks diplomatic relations with Cuba

**1979**
Sandinistas overthrow Somoza rule in Nicaragua

**1983**
Noriega takes control of Panama

**2000**
Vicente Fox defeats PRI candidate to become Mexico's president

## California Standards in This Section

*Reading this section will help you master these California History–Social Science standards.*

**10.9.1:** Compare the economic and military power shifts caused by the war, including the Yalta Pact, the development of nuclear weapons, Soviet control over Eastern European nations, and the economic recoveries of Germany and Japan.

**10.10:** Students analyze instances of nation-building in the contemporary world in at least two of the following regions or countries: the Middle East, Africa, Mexico and other parts of Latin America, and China.

**10.10.2:** Describe the recent history of the regions, including political divisions and systems, key leaders, religious issues, natural features, resources, and population patterns.

**10.10.3:** Discuss the important trends in the regions today and whether they appear to serve the cause of individual freedom and democracy.

# The Mexican Way

**Main Idea** Political and economic problems have plagued Mexico since the Mexican Revolution.

**Reading Connection** Do economic issues influence American politics? Read how economic troubles ended the reign of the Institutional Revolutionary Party in Mexico.

Mexico stands out from many other countries in Latin America. The Mexican Revolution of 1911 aimed at a fair and democratic society. That goal was not completely achieved, but the revolution created a stable, if often corrupt, political order.

During the 1950s and 1960s, steady economic growth led to real gains in wages for more and more people in Mexico. At the end of the 1960s, however, students began to protest Mexico's one-party government system. On October 2, 1968, university students gathered in Mexico City to **challenge** government policies. Police forces opened fire and killed hundreds.

## *Voices from the Past*

The official government report of the conflict said that Mexican authorities were fired upon, and they returned the gunfire. This excerpt from an account of the events by the student National Strike Council gave a different account:

> ❝After an hour and a half of a peaceful meeting attended by 10,000 people and witnessed by scores of domestic and foreign reporters, a helicopter gave the army the signal to attack by dropping flares into the crowd. Simultaneously, the plaza was surrounded and attacked by members of the army and police forces. . . . The results of this brutal military operation include hundreds of dead (including women and children), thousands of wounded, an unwarranted search of all the apartments in the area, and thousands of violent arrests. . . .❞

For most of the twentieth century, Mexico did not have a strong two-party system. The official party of the Mexican Revolution was the Institutional Revolutionary Party, or **PRI.** It dominated Mexico for many decades. Every six years, PRI leaders chose the party's presidential candidate, who was then dutifully elected by Mexicans.

▲ In the 1960s, César Chávez organized many of the Mexican farm workers who migrated north.

With the strike, PRI leaders saw a need for reform. They allowed more freedom of debate in the press and on college campuses. Economic problems made democratic reform difficult, however. There were also accusations of corruption against presidents Luís Echeverría and José López Portillo, who were in office between 1970 and 1982.

In the late 1970s, vast new reserves of oil were discovered in Mexico. The sale of oil abroad increased dramatically, and the government became more dependent on oil revenues. When world oil prices dropped in the mid-1980s, Mexico was not able to make its payments on foreign debt. The government was forced to adopt new economic policies. One **element** of the policies was **privatization,** the sale of government-owned companies to private firms.

The debt crisis and unemployment increased dissatisfaction with the PRI government to the breaking point. In 2000, **Vicente Fox** defeated the PRI candidate and was elected president—the first person elected from an opposition party since 1910.

Fox grew up in a wealthy family and was educated at Harvard. He rose to become an executive for the Coca-Cola Company in Mexico and later the National Action Party (PAN) in the 1980s. His election as president brought high hopes, but so far he has been unable to deliver on many of his promises. Police corruption and making the bureaucracy more efficient have proved very difficult problems to solve.

The number of poor people also troubles today's Mexico. This poverty has pushed many Mexicans north to the United States. In 2002, 30 percent of all immigrants to the United States were Mexican. Many crossed the border illegally. This stream of immigrants highlights two issues in the global economy: What policy should nations adopt toward illegal immigrants? How will that policy also honor the demands of its citizens?

One man who devoted his life to these issues is **César Chávez.** Chávez was born in Arizona in 1927. When his family lost their farm during the Depression, they became migrant workers. In 1965, he founded the United Farm Workers union. At first, Chávez opposed "illegals." Chávez felt his union could only bargain with employers if they could not turn to illegal workers during a strike. Chávez gradually changed his thinking about illegal immigrants.

One of Fox's top priorities was finding a solution to the immigration problem. He met with U.S. president George W. Bush several times on the subject. In early 2004, at a special Summit of the Americas in Monterrey, Mexico, Bush backed a program to give temporary visas to illegal workers. President Fox went further and argued for a grant of amnesty to illegal Mexican workers in the United States.

Neither approach is favored by many Americans, who believe immigration reform would take jobs away from Americans. Still, the mere fact that a Mexican president took the initiative with an American president signals that relations with the "giant to the north" are changing.

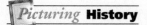 **Reading Check** **Evaluating** How has Mexico's oil industry affected its economy?

## The Cuban Revolution

**Main Idea** The Cuban Revolution established the communist dictatorship of Fidel Castro.

**Reading Connection** Do you remember reading about how Lenin led the Russian Revolution? Read to learn about Castro's role in the Cuban Revolution.

In the 1950s, a strong opposition movement arose in Cuba. Led by **Fidel Castro,** the movement aimed to overthrow the government of the dictator Fulgencio Batista, who had controlled Cuba since 1934. Castro's army used guerrilla warfare against Batista's regime. As the rebels gained more support, the regime collapsed. Castro's revolutionaries seized **Havana** on January 3, 1959. Many Cubans who disagreed with Castro fled to the United States.

Relations between Cuba and the United States quickly deteriorated when the Castro regime began to receive aid from the Soviet Union. Arms from Eastern Europe also began to arrive in Cuba. In October 1960, the United States declared a **trade embargo** prohibiting trade with Cuba and just three months later, on January 3, 1961, broke all diplomatic relations with Cuba.

Soon after that, in April 1961, American president John F. Kennedy supported an attempt to overthrow Castro's government. When the invasion at the Bay of Pigs failed, the Soviets were encouraged to make an even greater commitment to Cuba. In December 1961, Castro declared himself a Marxist. The Soviets began placing nuclear missiles in Cuba in 1962, an act that led to a showdown with the United States.

The Cuban missile crisis caused Castro to realize that the Soviet Union had been unreliable. If the revolutionary movement in Cuba was to survive, the Cubans would have to start a social revolution in the rest of Latin America. They would do this by starting guerrilla wars and encouraging peasants to overthrow the old regimes. Ernesto Ché Guevara, an Argentinian and an ally of Castro, led such a war in Bolivia but was killed by the Bolivian army in the fall of 1967. The Cuban strategy failed.

*Picturing* **History**

A Cuban refugee is carried ashore by a U.S. Marine in 1975. Over the past few decades, thousands of Cuban refugees have entered the United States. In what year did the United States break diplomatic relations with Cuba?

## Rigoberta Menchú
**1959– Guatemalan activist**

Rigoberta Menchú is a reformer who worked to save her fellow Quiché Indians from the murder squads of the Guatemalan government. She grew up in a poor family. Her father helped organize a peasant movement, but he and other family members were killed by government troops.

Rigoberta Menchú then began to play an active role in her father's movement. Condemned by the Guatemalan government, she fled to Mexico. Her autobiography, *I . . . Rigoberta Menchú,* brought world attention to the fact that 150,000 Native Americans had been killed by the Guatemalan authorities. In 1992, she received the Nobel Peace Prize and used the money from the award to set up a foundation to help Native Americans.

Nevertheless, in Cuba, Castro's Marxist regime continued, but with mixed results. The Cuban people did secure some social gains. The regime provided free medical services for all citizens, and illiteracy was nearly eliminated.

The Cuban economy continued to rely on sugar production. Economic weakness forced the Castro regime to depend on the Soviets and on selling sugar to Soviet bloc countries. Once Communist regimes in Eastern Europe collapsed in 1989, Cuba lost their support. Since then, economic conditions in Cuba have declined, but Castro has managed to stay in power.

✔ **Reading Check** **Describing** How was Castro's Cuba affected by the collapse of Communist governments in Eastern Europe?

## Upheaval in Central America

**Main Idea** Fearing the spread of communism, the United States involved itself in affairs of Central America on a number of occasions.

**Reading Connection** Remember the United States's actions in Korea and Vietnam during the Cold War. Read to learn about how the Cold War affected American policy in Central America.

Central America includes seven countries: Costa Rica, Nicaragua, Honduras, El Salvador, Panama, Belize, and Guatemala. Economically, Central America has depended on the export of bananas, coffee, and cotton. Prices for these products have fluctuated a great deal, often creating severe economic problems. As in other parts of Latin America, the enormous gulf between a wealthy elite and poor peasants has made society unstable.

Fear of the spread of communism often led to American support for repressive regimes in the area. American involvement was especially noticeable in El Salvador, Nicaragua, and Panama.

**El Salvador** After World War II, the wealthy elite and the military controlled the government in **El Salvador.** The rise of an urban middle class led to some hopes for a more democratic government. The army, however, refused to accept the results of free elections that were held in 1972.

In the late 1970s and the 1980s, El Salvador was rocked by a bitter civil war. Marxist-led leftist guerrillas and right-wing groups battled one another. During the presidency of Ronald Reagan, the United States provided weapons and training to the Salvadoran army to defeat the guerrillas.

In 1984, a moderate, José Duarte, was elected president, but his election failed to stop the savage killing. By the early 1990s, the civil war had led to the deaths of at least 75,000 people. Finally, in 1992, a peace settlement brought the war to an end.

**Web Activity** Visit the *Glencoe World History–Modern Times* Web site at wh.mt.glencoe.com and click on **Chapter 14–Student Web Activity** to learn more about Fidel Castro.

▲ *Contra soldiers*

**Nicaragua** In **Nicaragua,** the Somoza family seized control of the government in 1937 and kept control for the next 42 years. For most of this time, the United States government supported the Somoza regime. The Somozas used their position to enrich themselves, rather than promoting social programs to benefit all citizens. When opposition arose, the Somoza regime used murder and torture to silence it.

By 1979, American president Jimmy Carter was unwilling to continue American support for the Somozas. In the same year, Marxist guerrilla forces, the Sandinista National Liberation Front, won a number of military victories against the government and gained virtual control of the country. Soon, a group opposed to the Sandinistas' policies, called the **contras,** began to try to overthrow the new government.

The American government, worried by the Sandinistas' alignment with the Soviet Union, supported the contras. In 1990, the Sandinistas held free elections, and they lost to a coalition headed by Violeta Barrios de Chamorro. The Sandinista party again lost an election in 2001, but it remained one of the strongest parties.

**Panama** **Panama** became a nation in 1903, when it broke away from Colombia with help from the United States. In return for this aid, the United States was able to build the Panama Canal and gained influence in Panama. A wealthy oligarchy ruled, with American support.

After 1968, power in Panama came into the hands of the military leaders of Panama's National Guard. One such leader was **Manuel Noriega,** who took control of Panama in 1983.

At first, Noriega was supported by the United States. His brutality and involvement with the drug trade, however, turned American leaders against him. In 1989, President George Bush sent U.S. troops to Panama. Noriega was arrested and sent to prison in the United States on charges of drug trafficking.

✓**Reading Check** **Summarizing** What factors led to conflicts in Central America from the 1970s to the 1990s?

**HISTORY** *Online* **Study Central**

For help with the concepts in this section of *Glencoe World History–Modern Times,* go to wh.mt.glencoe.com and click on **Study Central.**

# SECTION 2 ASSESSMENT

### Checking for Understanding

1. **Vocabulary** Define: PRI, challenge, element, privatization, trade embargo, contra.

2. **People** Identify: Vicente Fox, César Chávez, Fidel Castro, Manuel Noriega.

3. **Places** Locate: Havana, El Salvador, Nicaragua, Panama.

### Reviewing Big Ideas

4. **List** the political reforms enacted by Mexican presidents Luís Echeverría and José López Portillo.

### Critical Thinking

5. **Historical Analysis** **Evaluating Evidence** Why did relations between the Soviet Union and Cuba become more difficult after 1962? **CA HR 3**

6. **Cause and Effect** Use a chart like the one below to show how Mexico has reacted to political and economic crises since World War II.

| Crisis | Reaction |
|--------|----------|
|   →    |          |
|   →    |          |

### Analyzing Visuals

7. **Examine** the photo of Castro on page 648 and the photo of a Cuban refugee on page 660. What inferences can you draw about Castro's reign in Cuba from looking at these photos?

### Writing About History

8. **Persuasive Writing** The United States has increasingly tried to negotiate conflicts using economic tools. Research the trade embargo on Cuba. Write a persuasive argument for or against this embargo. **CA WA2.4a,c**

# The Nations of South America

## Guide to Reading

### Section Preview
South American nations have experienced economic, social, and political problems, but democracy has advanced since the late 1980s.

**Main Idea**
- Brazil's super-sized economy has the potential to influence the global economy, but still struggles to meet the needs of its people. (p. 664)
- Ideological battles drove politics in Argentina and Chile in the 1970s and 1980s, but current governments focus on the economy. (p. 664)

- Violence and poverty have challenged Colombia and Peru, but both nations have made economic progress in recent years. (p. 666)

### Content Vocabulary
*Desaparecidos,* cooperative, Shining Path, Camisea Gas Project

### Academic Vocabulary
accurate, parallel

### People to Identify
Lula, Juan Perón, Salvador Allende, Augusto Pinochet, Juan Velasco Alvarado, Alberto Fujimori, Alejandro Toledo, Alvaro Uribe

### Places to Locate
Falkland Islands, Lima, Colombia

### Reading Objectives
1. List the obstacles faced by the new democratic government of Brazil.
2. Describe the causes of instability in South America.

### Reading Strategy
**Categorizing Information** Use a table like the one below to describe the factors leading to the change from military rule to civilian rule in Argentina, Brazil, and Chile.

| Argentina | Brazil | Chile |
|-----------|--------|-------|
|           |        |       |
|           |        |       |

### Preview of Events

| ♦1945 | ♦1955 | ♦1965 | ♦1975 | ♦1985 | ♦1995 | ♦2005 |
|-------|-------|-------|-------|-------|-------|-------|

**1946**
Juan Perón is elected president of Argentina

**1973**
Military forces overthrow Allende presidency in Chile

**1982**
Argentina sends troops to the Falkland Islands

**2001**
Alejandro Toledo is elected president of Peru

## California Standards in This Section

*Reading this section will help you master these California History–Social Science standards.*

**10.9.1:** Compare the economic and military power shifts caused by the war, including the Yalta Pact, the development of nuclear weapons, Soviet control over Eastern European nations, and the economic recoveries of Germany and Japan.

**10.10:** Students analyze instances of nation-building in the contemporary world in at least two of the following regions or countries: the Middle East, Africa, Mexico and other parts of Latin America, and China.

**10.10.2:** Describe the recent history of the regions, including political divisions and systems, key leaders, religious issues, natural features, resources, and population patterns.

**10.10.3:** Discuss the important trends in the regions today and whether they appear to serve the cause of individual freedom and democracy.

## Brazil, the Colossus of Latin America

**Main Idea** Brazil's super-sized economy has the potential to influence the global economy, but still struggles to meet the needs of its people.

**Reading Connection** Do you remember reading about the 1960s War on Poverty in American history? Read to learn how poverty has been a continuing problem in Brazil.

After World War II, Brazil faced many economic problems. Even when these began to be solved, the benefits did not reach most Brazilians.

### Voices from the Past

In 1974, a group of Brazilian Catholic priests discussed an economic miracle that had taken place:

❝Beginning in 1968, Brazil's gross domestic product grew at an annual rate of about 10 percent. . . . The consequences of this 'miracle' were the impoverishment of the Brazilian people. Between 1960 and 1970 the 20 percent of the population with the highest income increased its share of the national income from 54.5 percent to 64.1 percent, while the remaining 80 percent saw its share reduced from 45.5 percent to 36.8 percent. . . . In the same period the 1 percent of the population that represents the richest group increased its share of the national income from 11.7 percent to 17 percent.❞

Despite efforts by the government, priests, and missionaries, Brazil has been unable to fix this underlying problem. Its failure to distribute wealth more equally led to political instability. In the 1940s and 1950s, its democratic governments faced a series of economic crises. Then in 1964, the military seized control. Military regimes continued their control for the next 20 years, focusing economic policies on attracting foreign investment to expand industry.

These policies seemed to be working **accurately**. In the 1960s and 1970s, Brazil experienced an "economic miracle," but inflation was extremely high. Overwhelmed by the debt crisis, the generals retreated, thus opening the door to democratic reform in 1985.

The new government faced enormous obstacles—a massive foreign debt and inflation that stood at about 800 percent in 1987. The people were also bit-terly divided. Still, by the 1990s, some stability was restored, though the gap between rich and poor remained wide. Dissatisfaction with this gap helped elect Luiz Inacio **Lula** da Silva in 2002. Lula was Brazil's first left-wing president in four decades. He has pursued a mission of making Brazil more independent in global trade, but social problems remain severe. Millions of children have never seen the inside of a school, and about 15 percent of the people in major cities were unemployed in 2003.

✔ **Reading Check** **Explaining** What factors led to the return to democracy in Brazil in 1985?

## Argentina and Chile

**Main Idea** Ideological battles drove politics in Argentina and Chile in the 1970s and 1980s, but current governments focus on the economy.

**Reading Connection** Do American voters choose candidates based on party identification or on how well the economy is doing? Read to learn about transitions in politics in southern Latin America.

Argentina is South America's second largest country. For years, it had been ruled by a powerful oligarchy whose wealth was based on growing wheat and raising cattle. Support from the army was crucial to the continuing power of the oligarchy.

▼ *Brazilian city, 1971*

## Eva Perón
### 1919–1952—Argentine first lady

Eva Perón, known as Evita to her followers, was the first lady of Argentina from 1946 to 1952. Raised in poverty, Eva dreamed of being an actress. At 15, she moved to Buenos Aires, Argentina's largest city, where she eventually gained fame as a radio performer.

Eva met Juan Perón in 1944 and became his wife a year later. She was an important force in her husband's rise to power. Together, they courted the working-class poor with promises of higher wages and better working conditions. As first lady, Eva Perón formed a charitable organization that built hospitals, schools, and orphanages. She campaigned for women's rights. The masses adored her. To this day, monuments and street names in Argentina keep her memory alive. The American musical and movie *Evita* are based on her life.

In 1943, in the midst of World War II, a group of army officers overthrew the oligarchy. The new military regime was unsure of how to deal with the working classes until one of its members, **Juan Perón,** devised a new strategy.

Using his position as labor secretary in the military government, Perón sought to win over the workers, known as the *descamisados,* or the "shirtless ones." He encouraged them to join labor unions. He also increased job benefits, as well as the number of paid holidays and vacations.

In 1944, Perón became vice president of the military government and made sure that people knew he was responsible for the better conditions for workers. As Perón grew more popular, however, other army officers began to fear his power, and they arrested him. An uprising by workers forced the officers to back down.

Perón was elected president of Argentina in 1946. His chief support came from labor and the urban middle class, and to please them, he followed a policy of increased industrialization. At the same time, he tried to free Argentina from foreign investors. The government bought the railways and took over the banking, insurance, shipping, and communications industries.

Perón's regime was authoritarian. He created Fascist gangs **parallel** to Hitler's Brownshirts. The gangs used violence to terrify Perón's opponents. Fearing his power, the military overthrew him in September 1955. Perón went into exile in Spain. Overwhelmed by problems, however, military leaders later allowed Perón to return. He was reelected as president in 1973 but died a year later.

In 1976, the military once again took over power. The new regime tolerated no opposition. As many as 36,000 people were killed during their rule.

Economic problems continued to plague the nation. In April 1982, to divert people's attention, the military regime appealed to nationalistic feeling by invading the **Falkland Islands,** off the coast of Argentina. Great Britain, which had controlled the islands since the nineteenth century, sent ships and troops and took the islands back. This humiliating defeat discredited the military and opened the door to civilian rule.

In 1983, Raúl Alfonsín was elected president and worked to restore democracy. The Perónist Carlos Saúl Menem won the presidential election of 1989. This peaceful transfer of power made Argentinians hopeful that the nation was on a democratic path. Inflation and foreign debt have handicapped growth, but since 2003, the administration of President Nestor Kirchner has seen expanded growth.

The history of Chile has mirrored the experience of other Latin American nations, but it took a dramatic step in the elections of 1970. **Salvador Allende** (ah•YEHN•day), a Marxist, became president of Chile. Allende tried to create a socialist society through constitutional means. His first steps were to increase wages and to nationalize the largest corporations.

Allende's policies were unpopular with powerful groups. Nationalization of the copper industry angered the copper companies' American owners, as well as the American government. Wealthy landowners were angry because the government did nothing when radical workers began to take control of their estates.

In March 1973, new elections increased the number of Allende's supporters in the Chamber of Deputies. Afraid of Allende's growing strength, the army, led by General **Augusto Pinochet** (PEE•noh•CHEHT), moved against the government. In September 1973, while the military forces were seizing the presidential palace, Allende was killed. The military then set up a dictatorship.

The Pinochet regime was one of the most brutal in Latin American history. Thousands of opponents were imprisoned. Thousands more were tortured and murdered. The regime outlawed all political parties and did away with the Chamber of Deputies. While some estates and industries were returned to their owners, the copper industries remained in government hands.

The regime's horrible abuses of human rights led to growing unrest in the mid-1980s. Thousands of Pinochet opponents and other civilians were arrested and were never seen again—they came to be known as *Desaparecidos,* or "The Disappeared."

In 1989, a plebiscite led to Pinochet's defeat. Chile has since moved toward democracy. Economic policies have improved life in Chile for many, but unemployment remains high. The current president, Ricardo Lagos, signed a free trade agreement with the United States in January 2004. It is hoped that this will accelerate economic growth.

✓ **Reading Check** **Explaining** Why did the armed forces of Chile overthrow the government of Salvador Allende in 1973?

## Colombia and Peru

**Main Idea** Violence and poverty have challenged Colombia and Peru, but both nations have made economic progress in recent years.

**Reading Connection** Have you heard news stories about American efforts to suppress drug imports? Read to learn more about what fuels drug production.

Both Colombia and Peru, situated in the northwest part of South America, have had volatile economies. Historically, Colombia has been dependent on the price of coffee, while Peru has been dependent on the export of minerals and metals.

In Peru, economic ups and downs have led to many changes in government. A large peasant population, most poor and landless, has often been a source of unrest. Many peasants are Amerindian—about 45 percent of all Peruvians are of Amerindian descent.

In 1968, a military takeover led to some change. General **Juan Velasco Alvarado** sought to help the peasants. His government seized almost 75 percent of landed estates and put ownership into the hands of peasant **cooperatives,** farm organizations owned by and operated for the peasants' benefit. The government also nationalized many foreign-owned companies and held food prices down to help workers in the cities.

When economic problems continued, Peruvian military leaders removed General Alvarado in 1975. Five years later, unable to cope with Peru's economic problems, the military returned Peru to civilian rule.

Terrorism made the task of the civilian government even more difficult. **Shining Path,** a group of communist guerrillas in the countryside, killed mayors, priests, missionaries, and peasants. Shining Path wanted to smash all authority and create a classless society.

In 1990, Peruvians chose **Alberto Fujimori** as president. Fujimori, the son of a Japanese immigrant, promised reforms. Hopes were high that the new president would create a sort of Japanese miracle of a vigorous economy. These hopes were disappointed, and two years after his election, Fujimori suspended the constitution and the congress.

One of the missions Fujimoro pursued with his dictatorial powers was to fight the Shining Path guerrillas. Terrorism has subsided, although there have been signs in recent years that the Shining Path is still active. In March 2002, days before the American president George W. Bush visited, a car bomb exploded near the U.S. embassy in the capital of **Lima.**

In 2000, Fujimori's reputation for corruption led the Peruvian people to oust him from power. In June 2001, they elected **Alejandro Toledo.** Toledo became the first freely elected president of Native American descent to fill that position.

Toledo presided over the completion of the **Camisea Gas Project,** a pipeline to carry natural gas from deep in the Amazon jungle to Lima. The project

## What If...

### Salvador Allende had lost the Chilean election?

In 1970, Salvador Allende beat Jorge Alessandri, former president of Chile, by 40,000 votes out of almost 3 million cast. Since Allende won by a plurality rather than a majority, the election was referred to the Chilean National Congress for a final decision. The Congress chose Allende, bringing the Western world its first democratically elected Marxist president.

**Consider the Consequences** What if Alessandri had been reelected to continue his regime? Why might the United States have supported Alessandri?

has been financed by a consortium that is dominated by a Texas oil company. Peruvian politicians welcome the project, but it has been criticized for ignoring the damage to the Camisea rain forest and the indigenous peoples living there.

Despite strong economic growth, President Toledo's popularity had plummeted by the spring of 2004. Like Fujimori before him, President Toledo was suspected of corruption.

**Colombia** has long had a democratic political system. A conservative elite, led by the owners of coffee plantations, however, has dominated the government.

After World War II, Marxist guerrilla groups began to organize Colombian peasants against this elite. The government responded violently. More than 200,000 peasants had been killed by the mid-1960s. Violence remained a constant feature of Colombian life in the 1980s and 1990s.

Peasants who lived in poverty turned to a new cash crop—coca leaves, used to make cocaine. The drug trade increased, and so, too, did the number of drug lords. Drug lords formed cartels—groups of drug businesses—that used bribes and violence to force government cooperation in the drug traffic and to eliminate competitors. Attempts to stop the traffic in drugs had little success, and drug traffickers thrived. Currently, Colombia supplies the majority of cocaine to the international drug market. The government has begun an aerial eradication program.

High unemployment, around 17 percent in 2004, continues to hamper Colombia's economic growth.

▲ *Drug lords often use terrorism to threaten those people who try to stop the flow of illegal drugs.*

Colombia's leading exports, coffee and oil, are subject to price fluctuations. Under President Andres Pastrana, the economy was kept on track, but his failure to control Marxist guerrilla groups contributed to his defeat in 2002. Instead, voters gave **Alvaro Uribe** a landslide victory. Uribe has taken a hard line against guerrilla rebels. They have responded by trying to assassinate him.

 **Identifying** Name some similarities and differences between Colombia and Peru.

**HISTORY Online** **Study Central**

For help with the concepts in this section of *Glencoe World History–Modern Times*, go to wh.mt.glencoe.com and click on **Study Central.**

# SECTION 3 ASSESSMENT

### Checking for Understanding

1. **Vocabulary** Define: accurate, parallel, *Desaparecidos,* cooperative, Shining Path, Camisea Gas Project.

2. **People** Identify: Lula, Juan Perón, Salvador Allende, Augusto Pinochet, Juan Velasco Alvarado, Alberto Fujimori, Alejandro Toledo, Alvaro Uribe.

3. **Places** Locate: Falkland Islands, Lima, Colombia.

### Reviewing Big Ideas

4. **List** the obstacles Brazil's new democratic government faced in 1985. How did economic conditions help this democratic government come to power?

### Critical Thinking

5. **Historical Analysis** **Connecting Ideas** Why is it often easier for the military to seize power in a nation than for it to rule? Which countries discussed in this chapter seem to support this theory? **CA HI 1**

6. **Organizing Information** Use a chart like the one below to show how democracy has advanced in South America since the late 1980s.

How Democracy Advanced

### Analyzing Visuals

7. **Examine** the photograph of a Brazilian city shown on page 664 of your text. How does this photograph reflect the problems created by the Brazilian "economic miracle"?

### Writing About History

8. **Informative Writing** Pretend you are an American journalist sent to Argentina to cover Perón's presidency. Write an article based on your interviews with the workers and government officials. Include the pros and cons of living under the Perón regime. **CA 10WS1.3**

# PRIMARY SOURCES
## EYEWITNESS TO HISTORY

*Poetry, a soup-kitchen menu, and letters to a politician all reveal the problems of Latin American life in the last half of the twentieth century.*

## SOURCE 1: A Poem on Poverty

*Nicaraguan poet Leonel Rugama (1950–1970) criticized the world's neglect of poverty in "The Earth is a Satellite of the Moon." He died fighting against Nicaraguan dictator Anastasio Somoza.*

**Apollo**[1] 2 cost more than Apollo 1
Apollo 1 cost plenty.

Apollo 3 cost more than Apollo 2
Apollo 2 cost more than Apollo 1
Apollo 1 cost plenty.

Apollo 4 cost more than Apollo 3
Apollo 3 cost more than Apollo 2
Apollo 2 cost more than Apollo 1
Apollo 1 cost plenty.

Apollo 8 cost a fortune but no one minded because the astronauts were Protestants they read the Bible from the moon astounding and delighting every Christian and on their return Pope Paul VI gave them his blessing.

Apollo 9 cost more than all these put together including Apollo 1 which cost plenty.

The great-grandparents of the people of **Acahualinca**[2]
    were less hungry than the grandparents.
The great-grandparents died of hunger.
The grandparents of the people of Acahualinca were
    less hungry than the parents.
The grandparents died of hunger.
The parents of the people of Acahualinca were less
    hungry than the children of the people there.
The parents died of hunger.
The people of Acahualinca are less hungry than the
    children of the people there.
The children of the people of Acahualinca, because of
    hunger, are not born
they hunger to be born, only to die of hunger.
Blessed are the poor, for they shall inherit the moon.

---

[1]**Apollo:** NASA programs to land humans on the moon
[2]**Acahualinca:** neighborhood in Managua, Nicaragua's capital

## SOURCE 2: Peruvian Diet

*This menu comes from a soup kitchen in Lima, the capital of Peru, when the country was facing an economic crisis during the early 1990s.*

*Monday*
Beef Head Noodle Soup
Fried Fish with Rice, Lentils, and Mixed Salad
Sweetened Yerbaluisa Herb Tea

*Tuesday*
Cream of Green Pea and Egg Soup
Beef Intestine Stew with Rice and Mixed Salad
Sweetened Manzanilla Herb Tea

*Wednesday*
Polenta and Chicken Giblet Soup
Chicken and Fried Rice with Chopped Beets
Sweetened Yerbaluisa Herb Tea

*Thursday*
Beef Head Cream of Wheat Soup
Noodles in Red Sauce with Tomato, Carrot, and Tuna
Sweetened Manzanilla Herb Tea

*Friday*
Fishhead and Mussel Noodle Soup
Fish with Beans and Rice
Sweetened Yerbaluisa Herb Tea

## SOURCE 3: Mexicans' Pleas for Help

*Three Mexican citizens wrote letters in 1988 to Cuauhtémoc Cárdenas. Cárdenas was running for president against the candidate of the official political party, the Institutional Revolutionary Party (PRI).*

Sir:
    You are the Hope of all The Poor You must sit in the presidential chair so as to put a stop to all these **diabolical**[3] functionaries who only think about how to

---

[3]**diabolical:** having characteristics of the devil

*In 1991, children looking for food—or anything of value—at the municipal garbage dump in Managua, the capital of Nicaragua*

the word that they can't work anywhere . . . they've sent people to kill us look here my oldest son was kidnapped and I was beaten by this man's thugs through some miracle of God they didn't kill me how do you think I live here with such fear and so much repression thinking that whenever my kids go out in the street to ask for help just so as to get a tortilla in their mouths they go out with their children and I stay here thinking that only God knows if they will return alive and if I'll ever see them again . . .

*August 15, 1988*

I put my situation in your hands we the women are very mistreated by our husbands they persecute us and want to kill the children and much more persecuting them and wanting to kill them I ask for a solution to this problem and also in our ***colonia***[4] there is no drainage or pavement or public service. I ask for a solution.

Thank you for listening to me Mr. Cardenas.

*June 1988*

---

[4]***colonia:*** low-income neighborhoods/subdivisions

raise the price of everything with you as president in 6 years you will be able to put everything in order you will visit all of the poor neighborhoods and get to know the poor people you will hear all of the commentaries of the people who have been dragged along by the PRI in its cycle the people are very wrought up they no longer believe in it. You are the hope you must give all you have to the poor people you being president we are going to invite the people to sell all they can and give you all the money we collect so as to pay the debt sir. forgive the poor writing and lack of penmanship but go with all the heart of a Mexican citizen who desires with all his family and friends your triumph for the well being of the Mexican people thank you.

*Tampico, undated*

I am that humble woman who with tears in my eyes asks you for help for all of the fishermen who for three years have been fighting for the liberation of this cooperative, but the man . . . because he has money to buy the corresponding authorities for that reason we cannot do anything because here he is king . . . it's been three seasons that all the members of this cooperative have not gone out to work because this man spreads

## DBQ Document-Based Questions

**Historical Analysis**  CA CS 2, HI 2

**Source 1:** In Rugama's poem, what connection is made between America's space program and the people of Acahualinca?

**Source 2:** From reading the menu of the whole week, what can you conclude about how food is used?

**Source 3:** What do the letters tell you about the education and background of the writers? Do you think Cárdenas will meet their expectations if elected? Why or why not?

### Comparing and Contrasting Sources

1. What do these three passages tell you about the economic and political situation in Latin America?

2. Describe the tone and attitude of Source 1 and Source 3. How are they similar? How are they different?  **CA 10RL3.5**

10.9.1, 10.10, 10.10.2, 10.10.3

## Reviewing Content Vocabulary

*On a sheet of paper, use each of these terms in a sentence.*

1. multinational corporation
2. megacity
3. favela
4. magic realism
5. PRI
6. privatization
7. trade embargo
8. contra
9. *Desaparecidos*
10. cooperative
11. Shining Path
12. Camisea Gas Project

## Reviewing Academic Vocabulary

*On a sheet of paper, use each of these terms in a sentence that reflects the term's meaning in the chapter.*

13. finance
14. trend
15. challenge
16. element
17. accurate
18. parallel

## Reviewing the Main Ideas

### Section 1

19. What literary style is often associated with Latin American writers?

20. What effect does the wide gap between the rich and the poor have in Latin American countries?

### Section 2

21. How was the United States involved in El Salvador?

22. What happened that ended Manuel Noriega's control of Panama in 1989?

### Section 3

23. What was the goal of the guerrilla group known as Shining Path?

24. Explain why the Argentine military invaded the Falkland Islands. What was the impact of this invasion on the government of Argentina?

## Critical Thinking

25. **Reading Skill** Compare and Contrast In an essay, compare the policies of the United States toward Latin American countries to those of the Soviet Union toward countries in Eastern Europe. **CA** WA2.3a,b

26. **Drawing Inferences** Analyze why the United States used its military power to arrest Manuel Noriega after ignoring many other dishonest and corrupt leaders in Latin America.

27. **Analyzing** What factors contributed to the American policy of intervention in Latin American affairs in the early 1900s? Why did the political situation of many Latin American nations cause their leaders to welcome such intervention?

## Chapter Summary

Several Latin American countries have moved from conflict to cooperation.

| Country | Conflict | Revolution | Change | Cooperation |
|---|---|---|---|---|
| Cuba | Corruption and canceled elections create unrest. | Castro ousts Batista. | Castro improves social welfare system but suspends elections. | Castro allows limited foreign investment, improving relations with Canada and other countries. |
| Nicaragua | Repressive Somoza regime owns a quarter of the country's land. | Social movement led by Sandinistas overthrows Somoza in 1979. | Sandinistas initiate social reforms but are hampered by contras. | Sandinista regime agrees to hold free elections in 1990; Chamorro is elected president. |
| Mexico | PRI dominates. | University students protest government policies. | PRI allows new political parties and more freedoms. | Mexico elects non-PRI candidate as president. |
| Argentina | Economy is poor. | Argentine military overthrows Perón. | Economy recovers; many citizens lose lives to death squads. | Democracy is gradually restored after Falkland Islands disaster. |
| El Salvador | Elites control most wealth and land. | Leftist guerrillas and right-wing groups battle. | U.N.-sponsored peace agreement ends civil war in 1992. | Economy grows; ties with neighbors are renewed. |

## Writing About History

28. **Historical Analysis** **Characterizing Current Events** Review the role of writers in Latin American society. Based on what you've learned about modern Colombia, write a one-page essay on how Gabriel García Márquez's style of writing reflects something about the Colombian people. **CA CS4**

29. *Big Idea* Analyze how Cuba's revolution affected the United States and the Soviet Union. Explain the background and context of the revolution. How were these events particular to the time period?

30. **Expository Writing** Identify one of the challenges faced by the countries of Latin America today. In an essay, discuss the background of the challenge, and key individuals or countries involved with the issue. Identify options, predict consequences, and offer possible solutions. **CA 10WA2.3**

**DBQ** **Document-Based Questions**

**Analyzing Sources** Read this report from an Arizona newspaper on whether the former president of Chile should be forced to return there to stand trial:

> ❝One of the tragedies of 20th-century Latin America was the dirty war of the 1970s waged against anyone who might be considered remotely attracted to left-wing ideology. It was a war waged primarily in Argentina under a military junta and in Chile by the dictator Gen. Augusto Pinochet. At age 88, Pinochet has managed to avoid prosecution for crimes against the Chilean people. But a Chilean judge is determined to drag this murderer into a court of law. And rightly so. Pinochet is a criminal.❞

31. What is the writer implying about those who hold left-wing views and about how governments should see them?

## Analyzing Maps and Charts

Using the map on this page, answer the following questions:

32. Which South American country has the largest geographic area? Which countries have the largest populations?

**NATIONAL GEOGRAPHIC** **Population of Latin America, 2004**

Population:
- Under 15 million
- 15–30 million
- 30–100 million
- Over 100 million

33. How do the populations of Central American countries compare to the populations of other Latin American countries?

34. Which South American countries are landlocked? Between what degrees of latitude and longitude are they located?

## Standards Practice

**Directions: Choose the best answer to the following question.**

35. Why are Latin American countries economically important to the United States?

A American banks need countries such as Brazil and Mexico to default on their loans.

B Latin American countries are popular destinations for American tourists.

C Latin American countries are colonies of European nations.

D America imports raw goods such as oil, coffee, and copper from Mexico, El Salvador, Colombia, and Chile.

**CA Standard 10.10.1** Understand the challenges in the regions, including their geopolitical, cultural, military, and economic significance and the international relationships in which they are involved.

# 15

*1945–Present*

# Africa and the Middle East

## ⊰ The Big Ideas ⊱

### SECTION 1: Independence in Africa

**The quest for national self-determination is universal.** Although most African nations won independence from colonial rulers after World War II, many fell victim to military regimes and one-party states.

### SECTION 2: Conflict in the Middle East

**Throughout history people have struggled for rights.** Nationalism, fired by religious passion, has led to frequent armed conflict and continuing efforts at international mediation.

### SECTION 3: The Challenge of Terrorism

**War causes immeasurable devastation.** Death and destruction have resulted from the terrorist acts of Islamic militants who want to defeat pro-Western governments in the Middle East and establish their idea of a pure Islamic society.

 ***World History—Modern Times Video*** *The Chapter 15 video, "Apartheid," chronicles segregation and its demise in South Africa.*

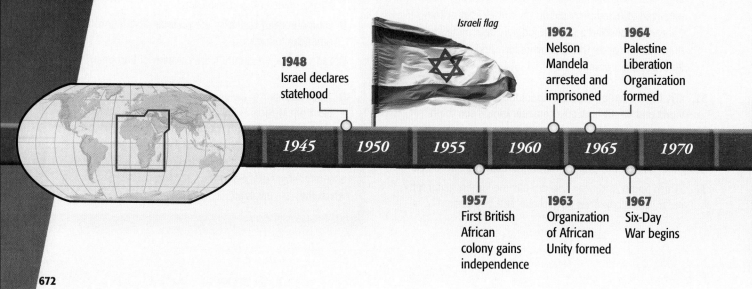

*Israeli flag*

**1948** Israel declares statehood

**1962** Nelson Mandela arrested and imprisoned

**1964** Palestine Liberation Organization formed

1945    1950    1955    1960    1965    1970

**1957** First British African colony gains independence

**1963** Organization of African Unity formed

**1967** Six-Day War begins

Kwame Nkrumah celebrates independence. Ghana gained its independence from Great Britain in 1957.

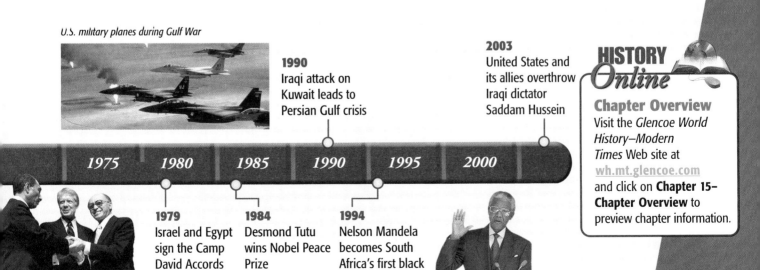

*U.S. military planes during Gulf War*

**1990**
Iraqi attack on Kuwait leads to Persian Gulf crisis

**2003**
United States and its allies overthrow Iraqi dictator Saddam Hussein

1975    1980    1985    1990    1995    2000

**1979**
Israel and Egypt sign the Camp David Accords

**1984**
Desmond Tutu wins Nobel Peace Prize

**1994**
Nelson Mandela becomes South Africa's first black president

*Inauguration of Nelson Mandela*

*Leaders of Camp David Accords*

**HISTORY Online**

**Chapter Overview**
Visit the *Glencoe World History–Modern Times* Web site at
wh.mt.glencoe.com
and click on **Chapter 15– Chapter Overview** to preview chapter information.

673

## Reading Skill — Identifying Problems and Solutions

When they analyze the past, historians often organize their discussions around identifying problems and how a society solved them. This approach is natural to historians since change tends to occur when leaders or communities are responding to a crisis. After considering how a problem looked to the people at the time, historians try to evaluate the solution that was chosen.

Historians usually present the problems and solutions they have identified over the course of several paragraphs. When you notice that problems and solutions are being described, ask yourself focused questions like the following: Who has the problem and what are its causes? What leader or group came up with a solution? What are the effects of the solution in the short and long run? Did the solution create new problems for the group or society?

### IDENTIFYING PROBLEMS

Notice the many negative words that suggest the problem—such as fearing, seized, and demand.

### IDENTIFYING SOLUTIONS

The words suggesting the problem words are very often followed by words that suggest the solution: agreement and treaty.

*Read the following excerpt from pages 690–691 to identify a problem and solution in the Middle East:*

In 1967, Egyptian president Nasser set up a blockade against Israeli ships.... Fearing attack ... Israel launched air strikes against Egypt and several of its Arab neighbors.... Israel seized territory.... Over the next few years, Arab states continued to demand the return of the occupied territories.... In September 1978, Carter met with President Sadat of Egypt and Israeli prime minister Menachem Begin.... The result was the Camp David Accords, an agreement to sign an Israeli-Egyptian peace treaty. The treaty, signed by Sadat and Begin in March 1979, ended the war between Egypt and Israel. Many Arab countries, however, continued to refuse to recognize Israel.

### Apply the Skill

A good way to understand problems and solutions is to make a table when you are taking notes. For this passage, create a simple table for the problems with column headings such as: What's the Problem? What Are the Causes? and Who Do They Affect? A second table will help you track the solution.

## Historical Analysis Skill   Analyzing Landscapes

**Historical Interpretation: Standard HI 5**  *Students analyze human modifications of landscapes and examine the resulting environmental policy issues.*

Many of us are familiar with stories of how landscapes change because of a flood, hurricane, or tornado. Historians recognize that human actions can also change the natural landscape and environment.

Industrialization, population growth, and migration are leading examples of human developments that can radically change an environment. Historians examine these changes and reactions to them, both locally and internationally, to draw conclusions about major concerns for specific historical periods.

In Africa, drought, famine, and genocide have often caused the landscape, both environmental and human, to change dramatically in many countries.

*Read this excerpt from Chapter 15 about the effects of drought and political instability in Africa.*

> **Drought conditions led to widespread hunger and starvation, first in West African countries such as Niger and Mali and then in the East African nations of Ethiopia, Somalia, and Sudan. Millions have starved to death, and major outbreaks of disease have swept through the region. Millions more fled to neighboring countries in search of food. . . . Many nations in Africa do not produce enough food to feed their populations. . . . Political unrest and civil war have made food problems even worse . . . [and] have made it impossible for normal farming to occur.**

### Apply the Skill

How would starvation and illness change a landscape? Make a list of the local effects these conditions would have on a particular area. Then, as you read this chapter, make another list covering what kinds of policy changes would have to be made nationally and internationally to deal with the problems of hunger and refugees.

# A Story That Matters

*Mohammad Reza Pahlavi*

*Anti-American protesters in Iran*

## Revolution in Iran

*I*n the 1970s, many Iranians began to grow dissatisfied with their ruler, Mohammad Reza Pahlavi, the shah of Iran. An opposition movement, led by the Muslim clergy under the guidance of the Ayatollah Ruhollah Khomeini, grew in strength. (An ayatollah is a major religious leader. The word means "the sign of God.")

One observer described a political rally in the capital city of Tehran in 1978: "On Sunday, December 11, hundreds of thousands of people held a procession in the center of Tehran. . . . Slogans against the shah rippled in the wind—'Death to the Shah!' 'Death to the Americans!' 'Khomeini is our leader,' and so on. People from all walks of life could be found in the crowd."

In January 1979, the shah left Iran, officially for a "period of rest and holiday." Three weeks later, the Ayatollah Khomeini returned to Iran from exile in Paris. On April 1, his forces seized control and proclaimed Iran to be an Islamic republic. Included in the new government's program was an attack on the United States, viewed by Khomeini as the "Great Satan."

On November 4, after the shah had gone to the United States for medical treatment, Iranian revolutionaries seized the United States Embassy in Tehran, taking 52 Americans hostage. Not until the inauguration of a new American president, Ronald Reagan, in January 1981 did the Iranians free their American captives.

### Why It Matters

These revolutionary events in Iran are examples of the upheavals that changed both Africa and the Middle East after 1945. In both these areas of the world, Europeans were forced to give up their control and allow independent states to emerge. The change from colony to free nation was not easy. In Africa, the legacy of colonialism left arbitrary boundaries, political inexperience, and continued European economic domination. In the Middle East, ethnic and religious disputes persist.

### History and You
The Arab-Israeli war is not one war but a continual series of struggles. Using your textbook and outside resources, make a time line of the conflict. Choose three points on your time line to highlight, then describe the events that led to those specific episodes. **CA** 10WS1.3

# SECTION 1 Independence in Africa

## Guide to Reading

### Section Preview
Although most African nations won independence from colonial rulers after World War II, many fell victim to military regimes and one-party states.

**Main Idea**

- After World War II, most nations in Africa gained independence from colonial rule. (p. 678)
- The newly independent African states faced significant political, economic, and health challenges. (p. 679)
- In recent decades, dictators fell in several African nations, and in 1994, apartheid ended in South Africa. (p. 683)

- Tension between old and new, and between African and Western, affects the societies of many African nations. (p. 684)

### Content Vocabulary
apartheid, Pan-Africanism

### Academic Vocabulary
significant, arbitrary

### People to Identify
Kwame Nkrumah, Nelson Mandela, Jomo Kenyatta, Desmond Tutu, Chinua Achebe

### Places to Locate
South Africa, Ghana, Kenya, Nigeria, Rwanda, Democratic Republic of the Congo, Sudan

### Reading Objectives
1. Identify economic problems that faced the newly independent African nations.
2. Assess the impact of social tensions in modern African culture.

### Reading Strategy
**Categorizing Information** As you read this section, complete a chart like the one below identifying the problems in Africa during its first stages of independence.

| Africa | |
|---|---|
| Economic | |
| Social | |
| Political | |

### Preview of Events

| ♦1960 | ♦1970 | ♦1980 | ♦1990 | ♦2000 |
|---|---|---|---|---|

**1960**
Blacks massacred in Sharpeville

**1989**
Chinua Achebe awarded Nobel Prize for literature

**1994**
Mass murder of Tutsis in Rwanda

Apartheid ends and Mandela elected president of South Africa

**2003**
Ethnic conflict in Darfur region of Sudan

---

## California Standards in This Section

*Reading this section will help you master these California History–Social Science standards.*

**10.9.2:** Analyze the causes of the Cold War, with the free world on one side and Soviet client states on the other, including competition for influence in such places as Egypt, the Congo, Vietnam, and Chile.

**10.10:** Students analyze instances of nation-building in the contemporary world in at least two of the following regions or countries: the Middle East, Africa, Mexico and other parts of Latin America, and China.

**10.10.1:** Understand the challenges in the regions, including their geopolitical, cultural, military, and economic significance and the international relationships in which they are involved.

**10.10.2:** Describe the recent history of the regions, including political divisions and systems, key leaders, religious issues, natural features, resources, and population patterns.

**10.10.3:** Discuss the important trends in the regions today and whether they appear to serve the cause of individual freedom and democracy.

# The Transition to Independence

**Main Idea** After World War II, most nations in Africa gained independence from colonial rule.

**Reading Connection** When and from whom did American colonists declare their independence? Read to learn how and when Africans won independence from European nations.

By 1900, European rule had been imposed on nearly all of Africa. After World War II, however, many Europeans realized that colonial rule would have to end. This belief was supported by the United Nations Charter, which stated that all colonial peoples should have the right to self-determination. In some African nations, the whites who had held political power refused to give it up easily.

## Voices from the Past

A dramatic example of white resistance in South Africa was reported on March 21, 1960, by Humphrey Taylor. Taylor, a reporter, saw what happened when black South Africans—a majority of the population—marched against white rule at Sharpeville:

66We went into Sharpeville the back way, around lunch time last Monday, driving along behind a big grey police car and three armoured cars. As we went through the fringes of the township many people were shouting the Pan-Africanist slogan 'Our Land.' They were grinning and cheerful. . . . Then the shooting started. We heard the chatter of a machine gun, then another, then another. . . . One woman was hit about ten yards from our car. . . . Hundreds of kids were running, too. Some of the children, hardly as tall as the grass, were leaping like rabbits. Some of them were shot, too.99

**South Africa** was one of the few African countries with a **significant** minority of whites who had settled centuries earlier. In most African nations, the process was not so complicated. Independence led quickly to governments headed by indigenous African leaders.

In 1957, the Gold Coast, renamed **Ghana** and under the guidance of **Kwame Nkrumah,** became the first former British colony to gain independence. Nigeria, the Belgian Congo (now the Democratic Republic of the Congo), Kenya, and others soon followed. Seventeen new African nations emerged in 1960. Another 11 nations followed between 1961 and 1965. After a series of brutal guerrilla wars, the Portuguese finally surrendered their colonies of Mozambique and Angola in the 1970s.

In North Africa, the French granted full independence to Morocco and Tunisia in 1956. Because Algeria was home to one million French settlers, France chose to keep control there. Meanwhile, however, Algerian nationalists had organized the National Liberation Front (FLN) and in 1954 initiated a guerrilla war to liberate their homeland. The French leader, Charles de Gaulle, granted Algeria its independence in 1962.

In South Africa, the black population began organizing against white rule as early as 1912 when they formed the African National Congress (ANC). Its campaign for reform met with little success, however. In fact, the ruling white class was more repressive than ever. These Afrikaners—descendants of Dutch settlers from the 1600s and 1700s—were determined to keep control of South Africa. In the 1950s, they strengthened the laws separating whites and blacks. The result was a system of racial segregation known as **apartheid** ("apartness").

Blacks demonstrated against the apartheid laws, but the white government brutally repressed the demonstrators. In 1960, police opened fire on people who were leading a peaceful march in Sharpeville, killing 69, two-thirds of whom were shot in the back. After the arrest of ANC leader **Nelson Mandela** in 1962, members of the ANC called for armed resistance to the white government.

✓**Reading Check** **Describing** How did Algeria gain independence from France?

▼ *Demonstration against white rule*

▲ *Jomo Kenyatta, third from left, meets with African leaders in 1964 in Nairobi.*

## The New Nations

**Main Idea** The newly independent African states faced significant political, economic, and health challenges.

**Reading Connection** Were you ever surprised to find there were still problems to face after you had achieved a goal? Read to learn about what confronted nations in Africa after independence.

Once they achieved independence, many African nations found that they faced daunting problems. Independence did not automatically give the people of these new nations a stable government or a prosperous economy. For many, the dream of a good society is still unrealized.

**New African Leaders** Most of the leaders of the newly independent African states came from the urban middle class and had studied in either Europe or the United States. They spoke and read European languages and believed that the Western democratic model was the one to copy.

One of these leaders was **Jomo Kenyatta.** Educated in Great Britain, Kenyatta returned to **Kenya** in 1946 and founded the Kenya African National Union, which sought independence for Kenya. British authorities imprisoned him on a charge of support-

ing the Mau Mau movement, which used terrorism to gain freedom from the British. He led his country to independence in 1963 and served as its president from 1964 until his death in 1978.

African leaders held diverse views on economics. Some leaders, such as Jomo Kenyatta, believed in Western-style capitalism. Others, such as Kwame Nkrumah of Ghana, preferred an "African form of socialism." Such a system would put ownership of the country's wealth into the hands of the people.

Some leaders believed in the dream of **Pan-Africanism,** the unity of all black Africans, regardless of national boundaries. Pan-Africanism was supported by several of the new African leaders, including Léopold Senghor of Senegal, Julius Nyerere of Tanzania, Kwame Nkrumah, and Jomo Kenyatta.

Nkrumah in particular hoped that a Pan-African union would bring African nations together. Although this dream never became a reality, the Organization of African Unity (OAU), founded with 32 African states in 1963, was a concrete result of the belief in

**HISTORY**
*Online*

**Web Activity** Visit the *Glencoe World History– Modern Times* Web site at <u>wh.mt.glencoe.com</u> and click on **Chapter 15– Student Web Activity** to learn more about African independence.

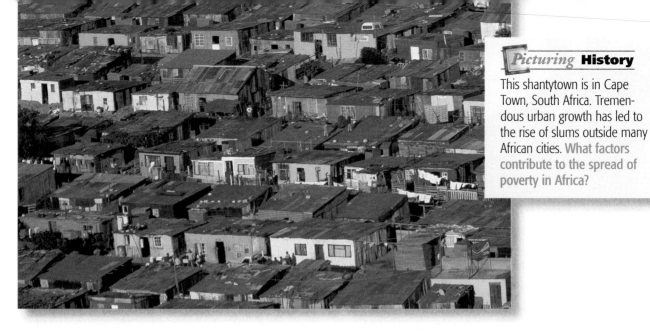

Pan-Africanism. In 2002 the African Union (AU) replaced the OAU. This 53-nation group promotes democracy and economic growth.

**Economic Problems** For the most part, independence did not change the kind of economy these countries had. Most still relied on the export of a single crop or natural resource, just as they had during the colonial era. Liberia, for example, depended on the export of rubber; **Nigeria,** Africa's most populous nation, on oil. When the price of major exports dropped, their economies suffered. To make matters worse, most African states imported technology and manufactured goods from the West, causing many of them to have a poor balance of trade. If they borrowed funds to sustain their economy and economic growth remained low, they could owe huge debts to foreign banks.

The new states also sometimes created their own problems. Scarce resources were spent on military equipment or luxury goods for an elite minority rather than on what was needed to industrialize. In addition, corruption and bribery became common.

Population growth also crippled efforts to create modern economies. By the 1980s, population growth averaged nearly 3 percent throughout Africa, the highest rate of any continent.

Drought conditions led to widespread hunger and starvation, first in West African countries such as Niger and Mali and then in the East African nations of Ethiopia, Somalia, and Sudan. Millions have starved to death, and major outbreaks of disease have swept through the region. Millions more fled to neighboring countries in search of food.

Drought, however, is not the only reason for famine in Africa. Many nations in Africa do not produce enough food to feed their populations and must therefore import food. Many countries cannot afford to feed all of their residents. According to UN statistics, between 40 and 50 percent of the people living in nations south of the Sahara lack sufficient food and are malnourished. In fact, Africa's population is the most undernourished in the world.

Political unrest and civil war have made food problems even worse. In countries like Ethiopia, Angola, and Eritrea, war and political instability have made it impossible for normal farming to occur. These conditions also disrupt the normal networks for distributing food from one region to another, or even from one village to another.

Poverty is worst in rural Africa, where roughly 75 percent of the people live. To survive, many flee to the cities, which have grown tremendously. When they first arrive, the rural immigrants usually live in massive slums or shantytowns that ring the city. This growth has overwhelmed sanitation and transportation systems. Pollution and huge traffic jams are the result.

Millions live in homes with no water or electricity. In the meantime, the fortunate few enjoy lavish lifestyles. In a number of East African countries, the rich are known as the *wabenzi*—the Mercedes-Benz people.

**Health Problems** AIDS, or acquired immunodeficiency syndrome, is a worldwide problem, but in Africa it is an epidemic. AIDS is caused by the virus known as HIV, which is spread through bodily fluids. HIV weakens the immune system so that people with the disease cannot fight other illnesses.

According to a UN estimate, about 8 percent of the adult population of Africa south of the Sahara is infected. Of nearly 38 million people worldwide infected with HIV, about two-thirds—25 million—live in Africa south of the Sahara. In Swaziland and Botswana, more than 35 percent of the population has HIV.

One of the most striking effects of AIDS in Africa is the impact on children and families. As many as 12 million children have lost both parents to AIDS. Very often, other relatives are too poor to take these children into their homes. Many orphans thus become heads of households filled with younger brothers and sisters. For centuries, extended families have been the source of support in difficult times, especially in rural parts of Africa. The AIDS epidemic, however, has overwhelmed this traditional support system.

African nations have taken steps to fight the epidemic. It has proved a tremendous burden, however, because many of these countries do not have the money or health facilities to educate their citizens about the disease—or to purchase the drugs that would extend the lives of those with HIV.

Uganda is one nation that has been able to mount an impressive effort to fight AIDS. Early on, President Yoweri Museveni involved a wide range of natural leaders in Ugandan society—religious and tribal leaders, for example, as well as international health and social service agencies. As a result of a major campaign promoting health and sex education, Uganda has made significant progress and the rate of new AIDS infections has been lowered.

**Political Challenges** Many people had hoped that independence would lead to a stable political order based on "one person, one vote." They were soon disappointed as democratic governments gave way to military regimes and one-party states.

The Cold War also created problems for Africa as the superpowers competed for influence. For example, when the Soviet Union supported a Marxist government in Ethiopia, the United States established military bases in neighboring Somalia. Similarly, in Nigeria and

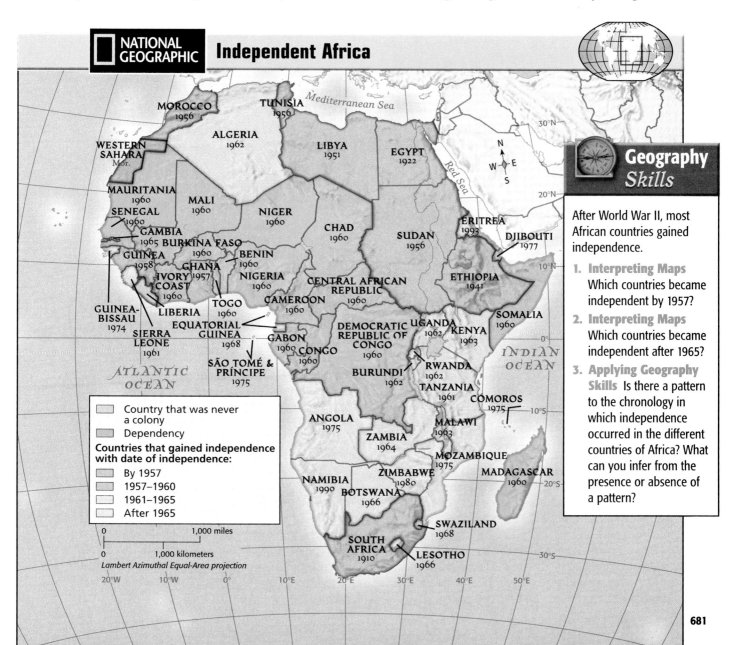

**NATIONAL GEOGRAPHIC**

## Independent Africa

**Geography Skills**

After World War II, most African countries gained independence.

1. **Interpreting Maps** Which countries became independent by 1957?

2. **Interpreting Maps** Which countries became independent after 1965?

3. **Applying Geography Skills** Is there a pattern to the chronology in which independence occurred in the different countries of Africa? What can you infer from the presence or absence of a pattern?

Country that was never a colony

Dependency

Countries that gained independence with date of independence:

By 1957

1957–1960

1961–1965

After 1965

0   1,000 miles
0   1,000 kilometers
*Lambert Azimuthal Equal-Area projection*

the Republic of the Congo (now the Democratic Republic of the Congo), the United States and the Soviet Union backed leaders and political groups that they believed would support their interests.

Within many African nations, the concept of nationhood was also undermined by warring ethnic groups. Conflict among ethnic groups has survived in part as a result of Western imperialism. Most national borders were **arbitrarily** drawn by Britain, France, and other colonial powers, rather than evolving from natural alliances among those working to found a new nation. Thus most African nations include widely different ethnic, linguistic, and territorial groups.

One of the first examples of ethnic conflict occurred in the late 1960s when civil war tore Nigeria apart. When northerners began to kill the Ibo people, thousands of Ibo fled to their home region in the eastern part of Nigeria. There, Lieutenant Colonel Odumegu Ojukwu organized the Ibo and declared that the eastern region of Nigeria was an independent state, Biafra. After two and a half years of bloody civil war, Biafra finally surrendered and accepted the authority of the Nigerian government. Conflicts also broke out among ethnic groups in Zimbabwe.

In recent years, political and ethnic conflict has ravaged neighboring countries in central Africa. The heart of the conflict is the competition between the Hutu and Tutsi peoples to control the area.

During the colonial period, Hutu and Tutsi peoples lived together under European control, but when independence came in 1962, two new countries were created: **Rwanda** and Burundi. The Hutus dominated Rwanda, and the Tutsis controlled Burundi, but the population in both countries was mixed. In Rwanda the Hutus were in a majority and killed thousands of Tutsis, who fled to neighboring countries. Fighting flared across the borders in the next decades.

Then in 1994, violent civil war broke out in Rwanda. It has been estimated that about 500,000 people, mostly Tutsis, were killed in a campaign of genocide. Then the tables turned as Tutsi soldiers won control. Fearing revenge, as many as a million Hutus fled to nearby countries, especially to the **Democratic Republic of the Congo.** To put down the Hutu militias in that country, Tutsi forces invaded. As a result, a large-scale civil war broke out in the Democratic Republic of the Congo in 1998. As many as 3.5 million people died from hunger and disease created by the war.

The same kind of ethnically inspired conflict has occurred in **Sudan,** the largest nation in Africa. In the Darfur region of western Sudan, government-backed Arab militias stand accused of waging a "reign of terror" of ethnic cleansing and genocide against African tribal groups. According to the UN, tens of thousands have died in this conflict, which escalated in 2003. The UN further reported that 2 million people need "acute assistance," more than a million people have been forced to abandon their homes, and at least 150,000 have fled to Chad.

**Reading Check** **Explaining** Why was the Organization of African Unity formed?

## People In History

### Nelson Mandela
**1918–**
**South African leader**

Nelson Mandela was the first black president of South Africa. Mandela was trained to be a leader of the Thembu people, and, later, he received a Western education.

In 1952, Mandela became one of the leaders of the African National Congress (ANC). The ANC at first advocated a policy of passive resistance to white rule in South Africa. Later, it supported more violent methods. The result was a sentence of life imprisonment for Mandela.

During his stay in prison, Mandela's reputation grew throughout Africa and the world. Finally, the South African government released Mandela and agreed to hold free elections. In 1994, he became president.

### Desmond Tutu
**1931–**
**South African activist**

Head of the Anglican Church in South Africa, Archbishop Desmond Tutu became a leader of the nonviolent movement against apartheid. Raised in Johannesburg, he studied theology and was ordained an Anglican priest in 1961. He rose quickly through the ranks and became an archbishop and head of the Anglican Church in South Africa in 1986. As a passionate believer in nonviolence, he supported a policy of economic sanctions against his own country in order to break the system of apartheid peacefully. He wrote: "If we cannot consider all peaceful means then people are in effect saying that there are no peaceful means." For his efforts, he was awarded the Nobel Peace Prize in 1984.

*Picturing* **History**
President F. W. de Klerk agreed to hold South Africa's first democratic national elections in 1994. Here you see people waiting to vote for the first time. Who was the first freely elected president of South Africa?

## New Hopes

**Main Idea** In recent decades, dictators fell in several African nations, and in 1994, apartheid ended in South Africa.

**Reading Connection** Are you familiar with the term *political prisoner,* and can you think of one in American history? Read to learn about how a former political prisoner became South Africa's first black president. ⊢TURNING POINT⊣

Not all the news in Africa has been bad. In recent years, popular demonstrations have led to the collapse of one-party regimes and the emergence of democracies in several countries. One case was that of Idi Amin of Uganda. After ruling by terror and brutal repression throughout the 1970s, Amin was deposed in 1979. Dictatorships also came to an end in Ethiopia, Liberia, and Somalia. In these nations, however, the fall of the regime was later followed by bloody civil war.

In South Africa, the move toward democracy was especially dramatic. In 1994, Nelson Mandela, a man who spent nearly three decades of his life in prison, was elected president of the Republic of South Africa.

Mandela had been sentenced to life imprisonment in 1962 for his activities with the African National Congress. He spent 27 years in maximum-security prisons on an island off the South African coast.

In January 1985, the South African president offered Mandela his freedom if he would accept certain conditions. By then Mandela was 66 years old and had been in prison for more than 20 years. Yet he refused to accept a conditional freedom: "Only free men can negotiate; prisoners cannot enter into contracts. Your freedom and mine cannot be separated."

For much of this period, Nobel Peace Prize winner (1984) Bishop **Desmond Tutu** and others worked to free Mandela and to end apartheid in South Africa. World pressure in the form of economic boycotts led to reforms and the gradual dismantling of apartheid laws. In 1990, Mandela was at last released.

In 1993, President F. W. de Klerk agreed to hold democratic national elections, the first in South Africa's history, and Mandela became South Africa's first black president in 1994. In his inaugural address, Mandela expressed his hopes for unity: "We shall build a society in which all South Africans, both black and white, will be able to walk tall, without any fear in their hearts, assured of their inalienable right to human dignity—a rainbow nation at peace with itself and the world." 📖 (*See page 777 to read an excerpt from a speech Nelson Mandela made during his 1964 trial in the Primary Sources Library.*)

✓**Reading Check** **Identifying** Which African countries overthrew dictatorships?

# Society and Culture in Modern Africa

**Main Idea** Tension between old and new, and between African and Western, affects the societies of many African nations.

**Reading Connection** Have you heard an older person say that something was lost when people began to e-mail instead of writing letters? Read to learn about the tensions between tradition and modernity in many African nations.

Industrialization and industrial cities bring a dramatic transformation to any society. They have in African nations, too. In Western nations, these changes came about from within their society. In African nations, however, industrialization and industrial cities were introduced by colonial powers of the West. This has made Africa a study in contrasts. Old and new, native and foreign live side by side. One result is a constant tension between traditional ways and Western culture.

**City and Countryside** In general, the impact of the West has been greater in the cities than in the countryside. After all, the colonial presence was first and most firmly established in the cities. Many cities are the direct product of colonial rule—for example: Lagos, the former capital of Nigeria; Cape Town in South Africa; and Nairobi, the capital of Kenya. Most African cities today have the typical urban features—high-rises, neon lights, movie theaters, and, of course, traffic jams.

Outside the major cities, where about 75 percent of the people live, the traditional cultures have survived. Millions live much as their ancestors did, in thatched dwellings without modern plumbing and electricity. They farm, hunt, or raise livestock by traditional methods, wear traditional clothing, and practice traditional beliefs.

Agricultural disasters like drought or flooding have had a traumatic effect on rural societies. When their crops dry up and their herds die off, many Africans migrate to the cities. If the most productive workers move to the cities, the people left behind often suffer. Family and village life is disrupted.

Even though this migration has been transforming African society, traditional attitudes have continued. City dwellers tend to think that rural people are backward, while village people tend to feel that the cities are corrupt and destroy the most important African values and customs.

**Women's Roles** Independence has changed the lives of many women in African nations. Almost without exception, women were allowed to vote and run for political office. Few women, however, hold political office.

Women dominate some professions, such as teaching, child care, and clerical work, but they still do not have access to the range of careers that men do. Most women work in low-paid jobs on farms, in factories, and in people's homes as servants. In rural areas, the attitudes toward women have not changed much. Most women, for example, would expect their families to choose the man whom they will marry.

▼ *Tea pickers on a plantation in Kenya*

▲ *Modern office buildings and contemporary art in Pretoria, South Africa, show the Westernization of Africa's cities.*

## *Picturing* **History**

The contrast between modern and traditional lifestyles often creates tension in African society. About what percentage of African people live in cities?

**African Culture** In contemporary Africa, a tension exists between traditional and modern, as well as between indigenous and Western culture. Many Africans have kept their traditional artistic traditions, but they have adapted them to foreign influences. For many African artists, the challenge is to find a balance between Western techniques and training on the one hand, and the rich heritage of African art forms on the other.

In some countries, governments make the artists' decisions for them. Artists are told to depict scenes of traditional African life. These works are designed to serve the tourist industry.

These cultural tensions are reflected in African literature. Especially in the 1960s and 1970s, novelists, poets, and journalists wrote about people who were caught in a struggle between their rural roots and a new urban environment. These themes certainly characterize the work of **Chinua Achebe,** a Nigerian novelist and winner of the Nobel Prize for literature in 1989. Achebe's novels show the problems of Africans caught up in the conflict between traditional and Western values.

Most famous of Achebe's novels is *Things Fall Apart,* in which the author portrays the simple dignity of traditional African village life. Set in the 1890s, this novel tells the story of what happens to a powerful village leader when Europeans arrive.

✓ **Reading Check** **Summarizing** What themes characterize the work of Chinua Achebe?

*Picturing* **History**

A Nigerian craftsman is in the process of carving a wooden drum. How do you think tourism has affected traditional African art forms?

**HISTORY** *Online* **Study Central**

For help with the concepts in this section of *Glencoe World History–Modern Times,* go to wh.mt.glencoe.com and click on **Study Central.**

## SECTION 1 ASSESSMENT

**Checking for Understanding**

1. **Vocabulary** Define: significant, apartheid, Pan-Africanism, arbitrary.

2. **People** Identify: Kwame Nkrumah, Nelson Mandela, Jomo Kenyatta, Desmond Tutu, Chinua Achebe.

3. **Places** Locate: South Africa, Ghana, Kenya, Nigeria, Rwanda, Democratic Republic of the Congo, Sudan.

**Reviewing Big Ideas**

4. **Explain** how the history of imperialism contributed to the ethnic conflict in Rwanda, Burundi, and the Democratic Republic of the Congo.

**Critical Thinking**

5. **Historical Analysis** **Assessing Alternative History** Why was the idea of Pan-Africanism never realized? **CA HI 4**

6. **Organizing Information** Create a chart comparing city and rural areas in Africa.

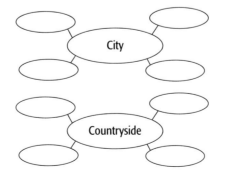

**Analyzing Visuals**

7. **Examine** the photographs on page 684 of your text. How do these photographs capture what is traditional and what is modern in Africa today? Use specific visual evidence from the photographs to support your answer.

**Writing About History**

8. **Persuasive Writing** Assume the role of an African leader of a newly independent nation. Write a speech to your citizens in which you explain Pan-Africanism and convince them that Pan-Africanism will benefit them. **CA 10WA2.4a,c**

# YOUNG PEOPLE IN . . .

## Nigeria

Nigerian young people grow up in as many diverse environments as there are ethnic groups. Africa's most populous country has more than 250 ethnic groups, each with its own culture and language. The four largest ethnic groups are the Hausa, the Fulani, the Yoruba, and the Ibo—together they account for about 65 percent of Nigerians.

In Nigeria's cities, life for young people is much like modern urban life everywhere. Children go to school, watch TV, help with chores, and play soccer. They are surrounded by tall office buildings, large department stores, banks, restaurants, and, of course, traffic jams.

About 64 percent of Nigeria's young people grow up in rural areas, helping on family farms. Teenage boys and men also work in the cities or in petroleum fields to earn money. In the city, it is easy to tell it is Friday: Bus stations are packed with workers on their way home for the weekend.

Girls typically remain in the villages with their mothers. They tend gardens, collect firewood and water, watch younger children, tend the animals, and sell crops at the local market. All Nigerians aged 6 to 15 are required to go to school, but many girls are pulled out of school after a few years. Since they marry at a younger age than boys, education is considered wasted on them.

Almost half of Nigeria's population is younger than 15. Large families are the norm because parents see their children as a sign of wealth and prestige. Family networks are large, too, in the countryside. Aunts, uncles, older cousins, and grandparents all take a hand in raising the children. Elders are treated with respect, and the good of the community is seen as more important than that of the individual. Every ethnic group has its own traditional festivals to honor the ancestors and spirits who protect the community.

◄ Here, Nigerian women are shown enjoying themselves while having their hair done at an outdoor salon in the Oshodi market of Lagos. Lagos, a port city, is estimated to have anywhere from 8 to 13 million people. In an effort to redistribute population, the government moved the capital inland in 1991 to Abuja.

▲ This young Fulani herder waits at the bank of a river for a festival to begin. The Fulani, one of northern Nigeria's ethnic groups, were originally nomadic. Today many Fulani have settled in towns, often intermarrying with the Hausa, another major ethnic group.

▲ In the southwestern city of Ibadan, two Egba women chat under an umbrella. The Egba are one of many different ethnic groups who identify themselves as belonging to the Yoruba people. The Yoruba played a big role in Nigeria's independence movement.

◀ A Hausa girl waits for the next train in the northern city of Gusau. Following Islamic tradition, most Hausa men have one or more wives who practice *purdah,* or a life of seclusion. The women are busy, however. They run businesses from the family compound, using their children to run errands and trade goods.

## CONNECTING TO THE PAST

1. **Identifying** What percentage of Nigeria's population is younger than 15?

2. **Writing About History** Write a short essay analyzing why Nigerian and American governments required high school education when they did.

# SECTION 2 Conflict in the Middle East

## Guide to Reading

### Section Preview
Nationalism, fired by religious passion, has led to recurring violence and continuing efforts at international mediation.

**Main Idea**

- The creation of Israel as a Jewish state in Palestine led to decades of conflict between Israelis and Palestinian Arabs. (p. 689)
- In 1979, an Iranian revolution set up an Islamic republic headed by the Ayatollah Ruhollah Khomeini, while in Iraq, the dictator Saddam Hussein tried to strengthen his role in the Middle East. (p. 691)

### Content Vocabulary
Pan-Arabism, OPEC, *intifada*

### Academic Vocabulary
motive, prime

### People to Identify
Gamal Abdel Nasser, Anwar el-Sadat, Menachem Begin, Yasir Arafat, Shah Mohammad Reza Pahlavi, Ayatollah Khomeini, Saddam Hussein

### Places to Locate
Israel, Egypt, Sinai Peninsula, West Bank, Iran, Iraq

### Reading Objectives
1. Explain how the state of Israel was created.
2. Identify causes of the Iranian revolution of 1979.

### Reading Strategy
**Categorizing Information** As you read this section, create a table and fill in the important events in the history of the Arab-Israeli conflicts.

| YEAR | EVENT |
| --- | --- |
|  |  |
|  |  |
|  |  |

### Preview of Events

| ♦1950 | ♦1960 | ♦1970 | ♦1980 | ♦1990 | ♦2000 |
| --- | --- | --- | --- | --- | --- |
| **1948** State of Israel founded | **1956** Nasser takes over Suez Canal | **1967** Six-Day War begins | **1979** Revolution in Iran establishes Islamic republic | **1993** PLO recognizes the state of Israel | **2003** Israel accepts principle of a Palestinian state |

## California Standards in This Section

*Reading this section will help you master these California History–Social Science standards.*

**10.9:** Students analyze the international developments in the post-World War II world.

**10.9.6:** Understand how the forces of nationalism developed in the Middle East, how the Holocaust affected world opinion regarding the need for a Jewish state, and the significance and effects of the location and establishment of Israel on world affairs.

**10.10:** Students analyze instances of nation-building in the contemporary world in at least two of the following regions or countries: the Middle East, Africa, Mexico and other parts of Latin America, and China.

**10.10.1:** Understand the challenges in the regions, including their geopolitical, cultural, military, and economic significance and the international relationships in which they are involved.

**10.10.2:** Describe the recent history of the regions, including political divisions and systems, key leaders, religious issues, natural features, resources, and population patterns.

**10.10.3:** Discuss the important trends in the regions today and whether they appear to serve the cause of individual freedom and democracy.

# The Middle East and Palestine

**Main Idea** The creation of Israel as a Jewish state in Palestine led to decades of conflict between Israelis and Palestinian Arabs. ⌐TURNING POINT⌐

**Reading Connection** Have your relatives or neighbors ever had a long-standing grudge or dispute with another group? Read to learn about the origins of Israeli-Arab conflict in the Middle East.

In the Middle East, as in Asia and Africa, a number of new nations emerged after World War II. Syria and Lebanon gained their independence just before the end of the war, and Jordan achieved complete self-rule soon afterward. These new states were predominantly Muslim, but one was not.

## Voices from the Past

A very dramatic proclamation of independence came from the new state of Israel, however, a homeland for Jews. On May 14, 1948, in Museum Hall in Tel Aviv, David Ben-Gurion announced the state of **Israel:**

66The land of Israel was the birthplace of the Jewish people. Here their spiritual, religious and national identity was formed. In their exile from the land of Israel the Jews remained faithful to it in all the countries of their dispersal, never ceasing to hope and pray for the restoration of their national freedom. Therefore by virtue of the natural and historic right of the Jewish people to be a nation as other nations, and of the Resolution of the General Assembly of the United Nations, we hereby proclaim the establishment of the Jewish nation in Palestine, to be called the State of Israel.99

The creation of Israel made Arab-Israeli conflict a certainty. Both Jews and Muslim Arabs claimed the area known in ancient times as Palestine. The movement known as Zionism had been working for a Jewish state in Palestine for many decades (see Chapter 10). During the 1920s and 1930s, significant numbers of Jews moved to Palestine, fleeing from persecution in Hitler's Nazi Germany.

After World War II, when world opinion faced the full horror of the Holocaust, sympathy for the Jewish desire for a homeland grew. In 1948, by UN resolution, Palestine was divided into a Jewish state and an Arab state.

Arab nations in the Middle East saw the creation of Israel as a betrayal of the majority population in Palestine, most of whom were Muslim. Outraged, several Arab countries invaded the new Jewish state. The invasion failed, but Arab states still refused to recognize Israel's right to exist.

As a result of the division of Palestine, hundreds of thousands of Palestinians fled to neighboring Arab countries, where they lived in refugee camps. Other Palestinians came under Israeli rule. The issue of a homeland and self-governance for the Palestinians remains a problem today. The failure to solve this long-standing dispute has also contributed to terrorist attacks and violent retaliation in the region.

**Nasser and Pan-Arabism** In **Egypt,** a new leader arose who would play an important role in the Arab world. Colonel **Gamal Abdel Nasser** took control of the Egyptian government in the early 1950s. Then on July 26, 1956, Nasser took a dramatic step. He seized the Suez Canal Company, which had been under British and French administration since the nineteenth century.

Great Britain and France were upset by this threat to their world position. The Suez Canal was an important waterway linking the Mediterranean Sea and Asia. Great Britain and France decided to strike back. They were quickly joined by Israel. The three nations launched a joint attack on Egypt, starting the Suez War of 1956.

The United States and the Soviet Union joined in supporting Nasser. Normally, these Cold War enemies

▼ *David Ben-Gurion, the first prime minister of Israel*

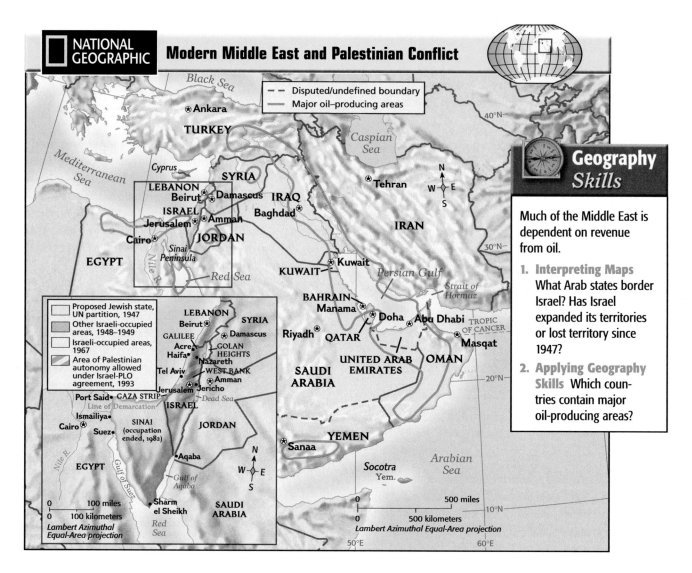

## NATIONAL GEOGRAPHIC
## Modern Middle East and Palestinian Conflict

Disputed/undefined boundary
Major oil–producing areas

**Geography Skills**

Much of the Middle East is dependent on revenue from oil.

1. **Interpreting Maps** What Arab states border Israel? Has Israel expanded its territories or lost territory since 1947?

2. **Applying Geography Skills** Which countries contain major oil-producing areas?

Proposed Jewish state, UN partition, 1947
Other Israeli-occupied areas, 1948–1949
Israeli-occupied areas, 1967
Area of Palestinian autonomy allowed under Israel-PLO agreement, 1993

were on opposite sides of international disputes, but both opposed French and British influence in the Middle East. They forced Britain, France, and Israel to withdraw their troops from Egypt.

Nasser emerged from the Suez conflict as a powerful leader and hero to his nation. He began to promote **Pan-Arabism,** or Arab unity. In February 1958, Egypt formally united with Syria in the United Arab Republic (UAR). Nasser was named the first president. Egypt and Syria hoped that the union would eventually include all the Arab states.

Other Arab leaders were suspicious of Pan-Arabism, however. Oil-rich Arab states did not want to have to share oil revenues with poorer states. In fact, it was Nasser's **motive** to share resources. He wanted the wealth of Arab oil of a few states and the foreign interests there to be used to improve the standard of living throughout the Middle East. In 1961, however, military leaders took over Syria. They then withdrew Syria from its union with Egypt. Nasser continued to work on behalf of Arab interests.

**The Arab-Israeli Dispute** During the late 1950s and 1960s, the dispute between Israel and other states became more heated. In 1967, Egyptian president Nasser set up a blockade against Israeli ships so they could not move through the Gulf of Aqaba. "Now we are ready to confront Israel," Nasser declared. "We are ready to deal with the entire Palestine question."

Fearing attack, on June 5, 1967, Israel launched air strikes against Egypt and several of its Arab neighbors. Israeli warplanes were thus able to wipe out most of the Egyptian air force. Israeli armies then broke the blockade and occupied the **Sinai Peninsula.**

Israel seized territory on the **West Bank** of the Jordan River, occupied Jerusalem, and took control of the Golan Heights. During this Six-Day War, Israel tripled the size of its territory. As a result, another million Palestinians now lived inside Israel's new borders. Most of them lived on the West Bank.

Over the next few years, Arab states continued to demand the return of the occupied territories. Nasser died in 1970 and was succeeded by **Anwar el-Sadat.**

In 1973, Arab forces led by Sadat launched a new attack against Israel. This conflict was ended in 1974 by a cease-fire agreement negotiated by the UN.

Meanwhile, the war had a significant impact on Western nations. In 1960, several Arab oil-producing nations had formed **OPEC,** the Organization of Petroleum Exporting Countries, to control the price of oil. During the 1973 war, some OPEC nations announced large increases in the price of oil. The price hikes, coupled with cuts in production, led to oil shortages and serious economic problems in the West.

In 1977, U.S. president Jimmy Carter began to press for a compromise peace between Arabs and Israelis. In September 1978, Carter met with President Sadat of Egypt and Israeli **prime** minister **Menachem Begin** (BAY•giluı) at Camp David in the United States. The result was the Camp David Accords, an agreement to sign an Israeli-Egyptian peace treaty. The treaty, signed by Sadat and Begin in March 1979, ended the war between Egypt and Israel. Many Arab countries, however, continued to refuse to recognize Israel.

**The PLO and the *Intifada*** In 1964, the Egyptians formed the Palestine Liberation Organization (PLO) to represent the interests of the Palestinians. The PLO believed that only the Palestinian Arabs should have a nation in the Palestine region. At the same time, a guerrilla movement called al-Fatah, headed by the PLO political leader **Yasir Arafat,** began to launch terrorist attacks on Israeli territory.

During the early 1980s, Palestinian Arabs, frustrated by their failure to achieve self-rule, became even more militant. This militancy led to a movement called the

▼ *Palestinians clash with Israeli soldiers.*

*intifada* ("uprising") among PLO supporters living in Israel. The *intifada* was marked by protests throughout the nation. A second *intifada* began in September 2000 and continued for over a year.

As the 1990s began, Israel and Arab nations took part in U.S.-sponsored peace talks to address the Palestinian issue. Finally, in 1993, Israel and the PLO agreed that there would be Palestinian autonomy in certain areas of Israel. In return, the PLO recognized Israel. Yasir Arafat became the head of the semi-independent area known as the Palestinian Authority.

Even with this change, little progress was made toward Palestinian statehood. Some Israelis did not want to give up the occupied territories for a Palestinian state, and some Palestinians would not accept the state of Israel at all. These Palestinians continued to carry out deadly terrorist attacks in Israel.

✓**Reading Check** **Summarizing** How did the 1993 agreement between Israel and the PLO expand on the Camp David Accords?

## Turmoil in Iran and Iraq

**Main Idea** In 1979, an Iranian revolution set up an Islamic republic headed by the Ayatollah Ruhollah Khomeini, while in Iraq, the dictator Saddam Hussein tried to strengthen his role in the Middle East.

**Reading Connection** How is a new president chosen in the United States? Read to learn how a government came to power in Iran in 1979.

The leadership of **Shah Mohammad Reza Pahlavi** and revenue from oil helped **Iran** become a rich country. Iran was also the chief ally of the United States in the Middle East in the 1950s and 1960s.

Many Iranians opposed the shah, however. Devout Muslims found the new Iranian culture distasteful. In their eyes, it was based on greed and materialism, which they identified with American influence.

Leading the opposition was the **Ayatollah Ruhollah Khomeini** (ko•MAY•nee). *Ayatollah* is a title Shiite Muslims give to religious leaders known for their holiness and wisdom. Khomeini regularly denounced the Westernizing policies of the shah. Although Khomeini lived in exile in Iraq, many Iranians were responding to his message. Mass protests were organized against the shah, and he fled the country in 1979.

The Iranian revolution led to an Islamic republic, led by Khomeini. The shah's supporters were executed or fled Iran. Anti-American sentiment erupted in November 1979 when militants seized 52 Americans in the American embassy in Tehran and held them hostage for over a year.

To the west of Iran was a militant and hostile **Iraq,** led by **Saddam Hussein** since 1979. Iran and Iraq have long had an uneasy relationship. Their disputes have been fueled by religious differences. Although both are Muslim nations, the Iranians are mostly Shiite Muslims, and the leaders of Iraq are predominantly Sunni Muslims. Iran and Iraq have fought over territory, too, especially over the Strait of Hormuz. The strait is strategically very important because it connects the Persian Gulf and the Gulf of Oman.

In 1980, Iraqi president Saddam Hussein launched an attack on Iran. The war was a brutal one. Children were used to clear dangerous minefields. Poison gas was used against civilians, especially the Kurds, an ethnic minority in the north who wanted their own state. The war dragged on, but its basic issues were never resolved. Finally, a cease-fire was signed in 1988.

After Khomeini died in 1989, a new government under President Hashemi Rafsanjani began to loosen control over social activities. Some Iranians were dissatisfied with the government's economic performance, while many young people pressed for more freedoms and an end to the power of conservative Muslim clerics. Rising criticism of official corruption and a high rate of inflation sparked a new wave of government repression in the mid-1990s.

✓**Reading Check** **Summarizing** List the reasons that the shah's government collapsed in Iran.

▲ *The 1979 hostage crisis symbolized the aggressive attitude of the new Islamic republic in Iran.*

**HISTORY Online** **Study Central**

For help with the concepts in this section of *Glencoe World History–Modern Times,* go to wh.mt.glencoe.com and click on **Study Central.**

## SECTION 2 ASSESSMENT

### Checking for Understanding

1. **Vocabulary** Define: Pan-Arabism, motive, OPEC, prime, *intifada.*

2. **People** Identify: Gamal Abdel Nasser, Anwar el-Sadat, Menachem Begin, Yasir Arafat, Shah Mohammad Reza Pahlavi, Ayatollah Ruhollah Khomeini, Saddam Hussein.

3. **Places** Locate: Israel, Egypt, Sinai Peninsula, West Bank, Iran, Iraq.

### Reviewing Big Ideas

4. **Summarize** the events that led to the Six-Day War. What gains and losses resulted from the war?

### Critical Thinking

5. **Historical Analysis** **Understanding Chronology** Evaluate the changes that occurred in Iran after the revolution in 1979. **CA CS 1**

6. **Taking Notes** Organize the information presented in this section in outline form, following the model below.

   I. Palestine
     A. Great Britain limits Jewish immigration.
     B. Zionists want Jewish homeland.
   II. Nasser takes control of Egypt.

### Analyzing Visuals

7. **Examine** the photograph of Palestinians clashing with Israeli soldiers on page 691. How old do the Palestinians appear to be? What effect do you think the age factor has on the future of relations between Israel and Palestine?

### Writing About History

8. **Persuasive Writing** Choose the role of an Arab Palestinian or a Jewish settler. Write a letter to the UN General Assembly arguing your position on the Palestine issue. Use rational arguments in making your case. **CA 10WA2.4a,c**

# SECTION 3 The Challenge of Terrorism

## Guide to Reading

### Section Preview
Death and destruction have resulted from the terrorist acts of Islamic militants who want to defeat pro-Western governments in the Middle East and establish their idea of a pure Islamic society.

**Main Idea**

- Terrorists kill civilians, take hostages, and hijack planes to advance their goals. (p. 694)
- Following the attacks of September 11, 2001, the United States and its allies attacked terrorists in Afghanistan. (p. 697)
- In March 2003, a U.S.-led coalition attacked Iraq, believing that it possessed weapons of mass destruction; when none were found, many questioned the decision to begin the war. (p. 698)

### Content Vocabulary
Irish Republican Army (IRA), state-sponsored terrorism, al-Qaeda, Taliban, Patriot Act

### Academic Vocabulary
federal, design

### People to Identify
Osama bin Laden, Hamid Karzai, Iyad Allawi

### Places to Locate
Kabul, Kuwait

### Reading Objectives
1. Describe the development of Middle East terrorism.
2. Explain the response of the United States and its allies to the terrorist attacks of September 11, 2001.

### Reading Strategy
As you read about modern terrorism, complete a graphic organizer similar to the one below to show the different reasons that terrorists launch attacks.

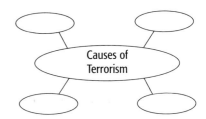

Causes of Terrorism

### Preview of Events

| ♦1980 | ♦1985 | ♦1990 | ♦1995 | ♦2000 | ♦2005 |
|---|---|---|---|---|---|

**1979**
Soviet Union invades Afghanistan

**1988**
Al-Qaeda is organized

**1998**
Bombs explode at U.S. embassies in Kenya and Tanzania

**2001**
Attacks on the World Trade Center and Pentagon

**2003**
U.S.-led coalition invades Iraq

**2004**
Interim Iraqi government is established

## California Standards in This Section

*Reading this section will help you master these California History–Social Science standards.*

**10.10:** Students analyze instances of nation-building in the contemporary world in at least two of the following regions or countries: the Middle East, Africa, Mexico and other parts of Latin America, and China.

**10.10.1:** Understand the challenges in the regions, including their geopolitical, cultural, military, and economic significance and the international relationships in which they are involved.

**10.10.2:** Describe the recent history of the regions, including political divisions and systems, key leaders, religious issues, natural features, resources, and population patterns.

**10.10.3:** Discuss the important trends in the regions today and whether they appear to serve the cause of individual freedom and democracy.

# Modern Terrorism

**Main Idea** Terrorists kill civilians, take hostages, and hijack planes to advance their goals.

**Reading Connection** What do you remember about the use of terror in other times? Read to learn about the background to terrorism in recent decades.

Acts of terror have become a regular aspect of modern society around the globe. Terrorists try to intimidate states and institutions as a way of advancing their political goals. They do not believe that their goals will be won by organizing or negotiating. This belief is so strong that many terrorists are willing to die themselves as they carry out their attacks. They bomb buses and schools, take hostages, and hijack planes. In some Muslim countries, terrorists often target places where Westerners are often found.

## Voices from the Past

On the Indonesian island of Bali, young Australians knew that the Sari Club was the place to go. Two Australians, Glen DuBois and Peter Cooper, showed up around 10:30 P.M. on Saturday, October 12, 2002. A little later, DuBois heard a loud explosion.

❝I said to Peter, 'What do you think that is?' I remember looking outside and saw people scurrying . . . it was all happening to the left of the entrance. I saw the flash and then I woke up, flat on my back, with about five or six bodies on top of me, from the lower ribcage down. We'd been standing shoulder to shoulder and it knocked us down like a field of wheat. When I got up on my elbows, there was no one in the room standing. It's led me to believe that I may have been the last person to get out of the club alive. I must have had an immense rush of adrenaline, because everything seemed so crystal clear. I saw arms and legs everywhere. It was dark. The ceiling had spot fires on it and looked like it was alight on top. It was the most macabre, surreal experience. There was a deathly silence.❞

In the deadly Bali bombings, about 200 people died. Similar events have filled news reports in recent years. What is it that terrorists of recent decades want? Some are militant nationalists who want to create their own state or expand national territory. The goal of the **Irish Republican Army (IRA),** for example, is to unite Northern Ireland, which is now governed by Great Britain, with the Irish Republic. Since the 1970s, thousands of people have died at the hands of IRA terrorists.

Other terrorists work for one nation to undermine the government of another. This kind of terrorism is called **state-sponsored terrorism.** Militant governments in Iraq, Iran, Syria, Libya, and North Korea have sponsored terrorist acts. There are also states that secretly finance, train, or hide terrorists.

**Islamic Militants: A Clash of Cultures** Terrorism has been practiced since ancient times. In the modern period, one example occurred in Russia in the late 1800s, when radical reformers bombed trains or assassinated officials to fight the czar's repression.

The causes of recent world terrorism are complex. Some analysts say this terrorism is rooted in the clash of modern and Islamic cultures. They argue that because many states in the former Ottoman Empire did not modernize along Western lines, Muslims have not accommodated their religious beliefs to the modern world. Other analysts note that the Christians and Muslims have viewed each other with hostility since at least the time of the Crusades. Others suggest that poverty and ignorance lie at the root of the problem—extremists find it easy to stir up resentment against wealthy Western societies. Finally, some say terrorism would be rare if the Israeli-Palestinian conflict could be solved. For years, peace talks were

▼ *Indonesian police inspecting Bali bombing site*

held between Israel and the PLO, led by Yasir Arafat, but no permanent solutions were found. In November 2004, Arafat died. Arafat had led the PLO since 1969 and symbolized the Palestinian cause. Because he had dominated the PLO for so long, there were hopes that a new leader might be more successful in negotiations with Israel. The path toward peace remained unclear, however.

Many terrorist attacks since World War II have been carried out by Middle Eastern groups against Western countries. One reason Middle Eastern terrorists have targeted Americans can be traced to developments in the 1900s. As oil became important to the American economy in the 1920s, the United States invested heavily in the Middle East oil industry. This industry brought great wealth to the ruling families in some Middle Eastern kingdoms, but most ordinary citizens remained poor. Some became angry at the United States for supporting the wealthy kingdoms and families.

The oil business soon increased Middle Eastern contact with the West. Some Muslims began to fear that this contact would weaken their religion and their way of life. Some Muslims began organizing movements to overthrow their pro-Western governments. Muslims who support these movements are called fundamentalist militants. They promote their own vision of what a pure Islamic society should be. Most Muslims around the world do not share this vision, nor do they agree with the use of terrorism.

American support of Israel also angered many in the Middle East. After Israel was created in 1948, Palestinians who wanted their own nation began staging guerrilla raids and terrorist attacks. Since the United States gave aid to Israel, it, too, became a target. In the 1970s, several Middle Eastern nations realized they could fight Israel and the United States by giving terrorists money, weapons, and training.

The movement for a conservative Islamic society was first seen in Iran under the Ayatollah Khomeini. After the revolution of 1979, clothing styles, social practices, and the legal system were regulated by a strict interpretation of Islam. These practices spread to other Muslim countries.

Because militants have received so much media attention, some believed that most Muslims were extremists. They are in a minority, however, especially in their view toward women. In the early 1900s, many Middle Eastern women had few rights. This situation had existed for centuries, but it was not seen in the earliest Islamic societies. In Muhammad's time, Muslim women had extensive political and social rights. Restrictions on women came later.

In the nineteenth and twentieth centuries, Muslim scholars began debating women's roles. Many argued that Muslims needed to rethink outdated interpretations that narrowed the lives of women. In nations like Turkey and Iran, these debates led to an expansion of women's rights and freedoms.

This trend continued, especially in urban areas of many Islamic societies, until the 1970s. Since that time,

# CONNECTIONS Around The World

## Global Terrorism

Terrorist acts became more frequent in the later twentieth century. By May 2003, the U.S. State Department had designated 36 groups as Foreign Terrorist Organizations. These groups include urban guerrilla groups in Latin America; militants dedicated to the liberation of Palestine; Islamic militants fighting Western influence in the Middle East; and separatists seeking independent states.

Terrorists have not limited their targets to their own countries. In 1972, three members of a Japanese terrorist group, who were hired by the Popular Front for the Liberation of Palestine, killed 24 people at the Tel Aviv airport in Israel. The terrorists' goal was to discourage people from visiting Israel.

TV has encouraged global terrorism to some extent because terrorists know that newscasts create instant publicity. TV images of American jetliners flying into the World Trade Center in New York City in 2001, for example, created immediate awareness of the goals of the Islamic fundamentalist militants.

## Comparing Cultures

Using outside sources, locate recent acts of terrorism that occurred in two separate countries. Compare how these acts were similar and how they were different. Do you think the terrorists will achieve their goals by performing these acts?

## NATIONAL GEOGRAPHIC Terrorist Activity in the Middle East and Central Asia

Hezbollah terrorists are dedicated to setting up an Islamic republic in Lebanon.

Terrorists fight new Iraqi government after the fall of Saddam Hussein.

Al-Qaeda–trained terrorists prepared in camps for the September 11, 2001, attacks on the United States.

Some al-Qaeda leaders were suspected of hiding in northern Pakistan.

Members of Hamas have conducted numerous suicide bombings against Israel.

0  200 miles
0  200 kilometers
Lambert Azimuthal Equal-Area projection

### Geography *Skills*

Terrorism has been found in many regions, especially the Middle East and Central Asia.

1. **Interpreting Maps** Why was it relatively easy for terrorists to hide in Afghanistan?

however, there has been a shift toward more traditional roles for women. This trend was especially noticeable in Iran.

### The War in Afghanistan and Its Aftermath

After World War II, the king of Afghanistan needed economic assistance for his country. He turned to the Soviet Union and developed close ties with that country. In 1973, the king was overthrown by his cousin, who was in turn overthrown in a pro-Soviet coup in 1978.

The new communist leaders were opposed by Afghans who wanted an Islamic state. Soon, conflict developed, and in 1979, the Soviets launched a full-scale invasion and set up their own man, Babrak Karmal, as prime minister.

Because of the Cold War, the United States feared any expansion of Soviet influence. Thus the American government supported the Afghans against the Soviets. Muslims from across the Middle East headed to Afghanistan to join the effort against the Soviets. Among them was a 22-year-old Muslim named **Osama bin Laden,** who came from one of Saudi Arabia's wealthiest families. He used his wealth to support the Afghan resistance. In 1988 bin Laden founded **al-Qaeda** (al KY-duh), or "the Base." Al-Qaeda recruited Muslims and sent money and arms to Afghanistan.

When the Afghan fighters succeeded in defeating the Soviet Union, bin Laden became convinced that superpowers could be beaten. He believed that Western ideas had contaminated Muslim societies. He was outraged when Saudi Arabia allowed American troops on Saudi soil after Iraq invaded Kuwait.

Bin Laden dedicated himself to driving Westerners out of countries with a largely Muslim population. When a Muslim fundamentalist group, the **Taliban,** took control of Afghanistan in 1996, bin Laden began using Afghanistan to train al-Qaeda recruits.

By the fall of 1998, the Taliban controlled more than two-thirds of the country, while other Afghan factions controlled the north. Condemned for its human rights abuses and imposition of harsh social policies, the Taliban was also suspected of sheltering bin Laden and his al-Qaeda organization. In 1998, bin Laden called on Muslims to kill Americans. Later that year, bin Laden's followers set off bombs at the American embassies in Kenya and Tanzania, killing 224 people.

Shortly after these bombings, President Bill Clinton ordered Cruise missiles launched at terrorist facilities in Afghanistan and Sudan. The attacks did not deter bin Laden. In October 2000, al-Qaeda terrorists crashed a boat loaded with explosives into the American warship USS *Cole,* which was docked near the Middle Eastern country of Yemen. In 1999 and again in 2000, the United Nations Security Council demanded the Taliban hand over bin Laden for trial, but it refused.

✓**Reading Check** **Explaining** What are the primary goals of militant Islamic fundamentalists?

## The Attacks of 9/11

**Main Idea** Following the attacks of September 11, 2001, the United States and its allies attacked terrorists in Afghanistan.

**Reading Connection** In American history, has the government limited civil liberties during war? Read to learn about the controversy over the Patriot Act after the attacks of 2001.

One of the most destructive acts of terrorism in history occurred on September 11, 2001. Terrorists directed by al-Qaeda's leader, Osama bin Laden, hijacked four commercial jets in Boston, Newark, and Washington, D.C. The hijackers flew two of the airplanes directly into the World Trade Center towers in New York City, demolishing the buildings and damaging a number of buildings in the area. A third hijacked plane slammed into the Pentagon in Arlington, Virginia. The fourth plane crashed into an isolated field in Pennsylvania, diverted from its apparent target in Washington, D.C., by heroic passengers. In all, thousands of people were killed.

On September 14, President George W. Bush declared a national emergency. Congress voted to authorize the use of force to fight the terrorists. Intelligence sources and the FBI quickly identified the attacks as the work of bin Laden and the al-Qaeda network.

In October 2001, Bush led a coalition of nations in launching a war against the Taliban in Afghanistan. American and NATO air strikes targeted their command centers, airfields, and al-Qaeda hiding places. The Northern Alliance, an Afghan coalition that had fought the Taliban for several years, led the ground attack and helped force the Taliban out of the capital, **Kabul.** By December, the Taliban government collapsed.

The United States and its allies then worked with Afghan leaders to create a new government. Nations around the world pledged more than $4 billion for this effort. Allied troops arrived to act as peacekeepers and to hunt for terrorists who had fled to the rugged highlands of Afghanistan. Many Afghans rejoiced at the Taliban defeat. Men no longer had to

wear beards, and urban women celebrated by removing their burkas—the head-to-toe garment the Taliban had required them to wear. Afghan leaders selected **Hamid Karzai** as the new president, but Karzai faced many challenges. Poverty still stalked the land, and after decades of civil war, reaching political agreement was very difficult.

In the United States, President Bush asked Congress to pass legislation to help track down terrorist suspects. An antiterrorist bill known as the **Patriot Act** was passed in October 2001. The Patriot Act allowed secret searches to avoid tipping off terrorism suspects. The law made it easier to wiretap suspects and to track e-mail, seize voice mail, and monitor library records. These sweeping and controversial measures led some Americans to debate how far constitutional rights should be restricted to protect against attacks.

In November 2002, Congress passed a bill establishing a new cabinet department—the Department of Homeland Security—to coordinate the dozens of **federal** agencies, such as the Coast Guard, Customs, and Immigration and Naturalization, that work against terrorism.

▼ *An Afghan man rides through a ruined Kabul in November 2001.*

Worldwide, one of the most noticeable changes in public policies since September 11, 2001, has been increased security at airports. Many European and Asian governments have also begun working more closely together in their intelligence and police activities to track down terrorists.

✓ **Reading Check** **Examining** What was the response of the U.S. government to the attacks of 9/11?

## The Iraq Factor

**Main Idea** In March 2003, a U.S.-led coalition attacked Iraq, believing that it possessed weapons of mass destruction; when none were found, many questioned the decision to begin the war.

**Reading Connection** When do you believe one country is justified in invading another country? Read to learn how and why the United States decided to invade Iraq in 2003.

The attacks of September 11, 2001, created fear that groups such as al-Qaeda might acquire nuclear, chemical, or biological weapons. These weapons of mass destruction could kill thousands at one time.

In his State of the Union speech in January 2002, President Bush told the American people that an "axis of evil," made up of Iraq, Iran, and North Korea, posed a grave threat to the world. Each of these countries sponsored terrorism and was suspected of trying to develop weapons of mass destruction.

**Iraq's Aggression** President Bush considered Iraq a more immediate threat than North Korea or Iran. Saddam Hussein had already used chemical weapons in Iraq's war against Iran in the 1980s and in 1988 against the Kurds, an ethnic minority in northern Iraq.

Fears about Iraqi aggression were underscored by the 1990 Gulf War. Iraqi troops moved across the border and occupied **Kuwait,** a country at the head of the Persian Gulf. The invasion sparked an international outcry. The United States led an international force that freed Kuwait and destroyed a large part of Iraq's armed forces. The allies hoped an internal revolt would overthrow Hussein, but he remained in power.

In 1991, following the Gulf War, UN inspectors found evidence that Iraq had developed biological weapons and was working on a nuclear bomb. In the early 1990s, UN Security Council resolutions called for Iraq to disarm its weapons programs. Iraq repeatedly violated these resolutions.

▲ *Iyad Allawi (center), Iraq's interim prime minister, on a state visit to Jordan in July 2004*

**War on Iraq** In the summer of 2002, American president George W. Bush increased pressure on Iraq, calling for a regime change in the country. At the urging of Secretary of State Colin Powell, Bush tried to gain UN support for a war against Iraq. On September 12, 2002, he asked for a new resolution demanding that Iraq give up weapons of mass destruction. Bush made it clear, however, that if the UN did not pass such a resolution, the United States would act without UN support.

While the UN Security Council debated, Bush asked Congress to authorize the use of force against Iraq. Congress voted in October 2002 to approve the president's request. The next month, the United Nations approved a new resolution. It stated that Iraq must allow UN inspectors to return to Iraq by a certain date. Iraq was supposed to declare all its weapons of mass destruction, stop supporting terrorism, and stop persecuting opponents of Hussein within Iraq. The resolution threatened "serious consequences" if Iraq did not comply.

Weapons inspectors returned to Iraq, but some Americans doubted their effectiveness. The Bush administration argued that the Iraqis were still hiding weapons of mass destruction. Others wanted to give the inspectors more time to work.

The Bush administration then asked the UN Security Council for a resolution for war, but France and Russia, two permanent Council members with veto power, refused and said they wanted to wait.

At that point, the United States and Great Britain, with the support of about 30 other countries, prepared for war. Antiwar protesters in the United States and other countries argued that war was not justified. They argued that Iraq had not been involved in the September 11 attacks and that the weapons evidence was inconclusive. Thus Iraq did not pose an immediate threat.

On March 20, 2003, the U.S.-led coalition attacked Iraq. Over the next six weeks, much of the Iraqi army seemed to dissolve as many soldiers refused to risk their lives for Hussein. The coalition forces were able to gain control of Iraq quickly, and on May 1, President Bush declared that the major combat was over. About 140 Americans, and several thousand Iraqis, had died.

The controversy over Iraq continued, however, as did the fighting. By December 2003, Americans had found no evidence of weapons of mass destruction. In January 2004, David Kay, who had served as the Bush administration's top weapons inspector, stated that "we're very unlikely to find large stockpiles of weapons. I don't think they exist." Kay added that the American intelligence agencies had provided flawed information to the American president.

In Iraq, a majority of Iraqis rejoiced because the invasion ended the dictatorial and brutal regime of Saddam Hussein. Many Iraqis were unhappy, however, that American and British forces stayed on in Iraq to set up an interim government. Establishing a new government was difficult because there were differences among the three major groups in Iraqi society: Shiite Muslims, Sunni Muslims, and ethnic Kurds.

In December 2003, Saddam Hussein was captured. The Bush administration hoped that this would bring stability, but insurgents continued increasingly deadly attacks on coalition forces and a newly organized Iraqi police. Who were these insurgents? Some may have been former members of Saddam Hussein's ruling party who feared they would have no power in an American-**designed** government. Some were young radicals who wanted a strict Islamic republic, not a democracy based on the Western model.

Bombings and sporadic battles plagued American soldiers as well as Iraqis who cooperated with the interim government. The war was officially declared over in May 2004, but violence continued. By mid-January 2005, the Pentagon reported that 1,365 American soldiers had died in the war. Rebuilding Iraq was also costly. American president George W. Bush continued to seek the support of other countries to help stabilize the war-torn nation.

On June 28, 2004, the U.S. had officially transferred sovereignty to Iraq. **Iyad Allawi,** who was officially sworn in as Iraq's interim prime minister, called it "a historic day" and vowed to bring an end to the violence that continued to plague Iraq. Coalition troops stayed on in Iraq, however, to fight insurgents who did not support the new Iraqi government.

Some Iraqi citizens seemed willing to support their new government, but a difficult road lay ahead. First the new government must succeed in keeping order and rebuilding the country's infrastructure. An even greater challenge was to create a national consensus among groups that disagreed about the role of religion in society and the kind of government they would accept.

✓**Reading Check** **Analyzing** What were the arguments for and against the American-led invasion of Iraq?

**HISTORY Online** **Study Central**

For help with the concepts in this section of *Glencoe World History—Modern Times,* go to wh.mt.glencoe.com and click on **Study Central.**

---

# SECTION 3 ASSESSMENT

### Checking for Understanding

1. **Vocabulary** Define: Irish Republican Army (IRA), state-sponsored terrorism, al-Qaeda, Taliban, Patriot Act, federal, design.

2. **People** Identify: Osama bin Laden, Hamid Karzai, Iyad Allawi.

3. **Places** Locate: Kabul, Kuwait.

### Reviewing Big Ideas

4. **Identify** possible reasons that a person would turn to terrorism.

### Critical Thinking

5. **Historical Analysis** **Contextualizing** Why was it possible to believe that Saddam Hussein was developing weapons of mass destruction? **CA HI 3**

6. **Organizing** Complete a graphic organizer similar to the one below to list the factors that contribute to the rise of terrorist groups.

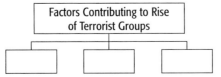

### Analyzing Visuals

7. **Examine** the map of terrorist activity on page 696. What major terrorist group has been active in Lebanon? What is its goal?

---

### Writing About History

8. **Assess** The American decision to go to war against Iraq was later criticized because weapons of mass destruction were never found. How would you assess the original decision to go to war? **CA 10WA2.3a,b**

---

# PRIMARY SOURCES
## Eyewitness to History

*Both Jews and Arabs have historic ties to the region known as Palestine, and both peoples have claimed their rights to it. These three sources describe the views of the two groups on the long-simmering conflict in the Middle East.*

## SOURCE 1: The Jewish Claim to Palestine

*The "Proclamation of the State of Israel" in May 1948 defined both the Jewish claim to the land and the State itself.*

The Land of Israel was the birthplace of the Jewish people. Here their spiritual, religious and political identity was formed. Here they first achieved independence and created a culture of national and universal significance. Here they wrote and gave the Bible to the world.

Exiled from Palestine, the Jewish people remained faithful to it in all the countries of their dispersion, never ceasing to pray and hope for their return and the restoration of their national freedom. Impelled by this historic association, Jews strove throughout the centuries to go back to the land of their fathers and regain their statehood. In recent decades they returned in masses. They reclaimed the wilderness, revived their language, built cities . . . with [their] own economic and cultural life. . . .

The Nazi holocaust, which engulfed millions of Jews in Europe, proved anew the urgency of the re-establishment of the Jewish State, which would solve the problem of Jewish homelessness by opening the gates to all Jews and lifting the Jewish people to equality in the family of nations. . . .

On November 29, 1947, the General Assembly of the United Nations adopted a Resolution for the establishment of an independent Jewish State in Palestine. . . .

This recognition by the United Nations of the right of the Jewish people to establish their independent State may not be revoked. . . .

THE STATE OF ISRAEL . . . will uphold the full social and political equality of all its citizens, without distinction of race, creed or sex . . . [and] will guarantee full freedom of conscience, worship, education and culture. . . .

In the midst of **wanton**[1] aggression, we yet call upon the Arab inhabitants of the State of Israel to return to the ways of peace and play their part in the development of the state, with full and equal citizenship. . . .

## SOURCE 2: The Arab Claim to Palestine

*The "Palestinian National Charter" (1968) established the Palestine Liberation Organization (PLO) and stated its view of the rights of Palestinians.*

Article 1: Palestine is the homeland of the Arab Palestinian people; it is an indivisible part of the Arab homeland, and the Palestinian people are an integral part of the Arab nation. . . .

Article 3: The Palestinian Arab people possess the legal right to their homeland. . . .

Article 5: The Palestinians are those Arab nationals who, until 1947, normally resided in Palestine regardless of whether they were evicted from it or have stayed there. Anyone born, after that date, of a Palestinian father—whether inside Palestine or outside it—is also a Palestinian.

Article 6: The Jews who had normally resided in Palestine until the beginning of the Zionist invasion will be considered Palestinian. . . .

*Girls in a PLO training camp*

---

[1]**wanton** having no just foundation

Article 8: The phase in their history, through which the Palestinian people are now living, is that of national (watani) struggle for the liberation of Palestine. . . .

Article 9: Armed struggle is the only way to liberate Palestine. . . . The Palestinian Arab people assert their absolute determination and firm resolution to continue their armed struggle and to work for an armed popular revolution for the liberation of their country and their return to it. . . .

Article 19: The partition of Palestine in 1947 and the establishment of the state of Israel are entirely illegal, regardless of the passage of time, because they were contrary to the will of the Palestinian people and to their natural right in their homeland. . . .

Article 25: For the realization of the goals of this Charter and its principles, the Palestine Liberation Organization will perform its role in the liberation of Palestine in accordance with the Constitution of this Organization. . . .

## SOURCE 3: The View of an Israeli Prime Minister

*In a June 9, 2002 article in the* New York Times, *Israel's prime minister, Ariel Sharon, gave his view on the Middle East conflict.*

Thirty-five years ago, on June 5, 1967, the start of the Six Day War, Israel faced a threat to its very existence as a coalition of Arab armies massed their troops along the fragile armistice lines that had separated Arab and Israeli forces since 1949. . . . The declared goal of the attack was Israel's elimination.

Israel entered the West Bank only after its cities and airports had come under heavy fire. Israeli actions were legal—resulting from a clear-cut war of self-defense. . . . The United Nations Security Council determined in . . . Resolution 242, that Israel . . . was not expected to withdraw from all the territories that its forces had entered . . . in the Six Day War. . . .

Under Resolution 242, which became the cornerstone of peacemaking, Israel withdrew from the Sinai Peninsula in accordance with the 1979 peace treaty with Egypt. . . . And again in line with Resolution 242, Israel, operating under the 1993 Oslo agreement, withdrew its military government over the Palestinian population so that by 1999, 98 percent of the Pales-

tinians in the West Bank and Gaza were under Palestinian rule.

Nonetheless, the Palestinian leadership decided to initiate the current war against Israel after the failure of the Camp David summit in July 2000.

Despite this situation, there is a way forward. First, Israel must defeat terrorism; it cannot negotiate under fire. Israel has made painful concessions for peace before and will demonstrate diplomatic flexibility to make peace again, but it requires first and foremost a reliable partner for peace. . . .

In the nearly two years of the Palestinian **intifada**[2], the people of Israel have seen Israel's vulnerabilities exploited, its holy sites desecrated and massive weaponry smuggled and used against Israel's cities. For this reason, Israel will not return to the vulnerable 1967 armistice lines, redivide Jerusalem or concede its right to defensible borders. . . .

---

➤ [2] **intifada**  a Palestinian uprising against Israel's occupation of the West Bank and the Gaza Strip

## DBQ  Document-Based Questions

### Historical Analysis  CA HR 1

**Source 1:** According to this source, why do Jews have a right to the land?

**Source 2:** According to the Palestinian National Charter, to whom does the same land belong?

**Source 3:** What does the Israeli prime minister propose to achieve peace? What does he offer the Palestinians? Based on the excerpts, how do you assess his plan?

### Comparing and Contrasting Sources

1. Comparing Source 1 and Source 2, are Palestinians welcome in Israel, and are Jews welcome in Palestine?

Standards 10.9, 10.9.2, 10.9.6, 10.10, 10.10.1, 10.10.2, 10.10.3

## Reviewing Content Vocabulary

*On a sheet of paper, use each of these terms in a sentence.*

1. apartheid
2. Pan-Africanism
3. Pan-Arabism
4. OPEC
5. *intifada*
6. Irish Republican Army
7. state-sponsored terrorism
8. al-Qaeda
9. Taliban
10. Patriot Act

## Reviewing Academic Vocabulary

*On a sheet of paper, use each of these terms in a sentence that reflects the term's meaning in the chapter.*

11. significant
12. arbitrary
13. motive
14. prime
15. federal
16. design

## Reviewing the Main Ideas

### Section 1

17. Why did France grant independence to Morocco and Tunisia in 1956, but not to Algeria?

18. What was the philosophy behind African socialism?

19. Why was Nelson Mandela imprisoned by the white South African government?

### Section 2

20. What did Nelson Mandela achieve in 1994?

21. Why is Desmond Tutu an important international leader?

22. How was Israel created? What factors led to its founding?

23. Name some accomplishments of Gamal Abdel Nasser that elevated his status as a leader in the Arab world.

24. How did price increases and production cuts by OPEC nations in 1973 affect the United States and Europe?

25. Why did Shah Mohammad Reza Pahlavi lose popular support despite growth in Iran's economy and standard of living?

26. Give two reasons for the war that broke out in 1980 between Iran and Iraq.

### Section 3

27. What does the Irish Republican Army hope to accomplish?

28. How did the United States respond to the attacks of 9/11?

29. What did President George W. Bush mean by "axis of evil"?

30. What action did the United Nations take against the regime of Saddam Hussein in October 2002?

31. Why did the United States and a coalition of 30 other countries send troops into Iraq in 2003?

## Critical Thinking

32. **Evaluating** Why have English and French been used as official languages of government in many African nations?

33. **Predicting** Could a lasting peace have been established between Iraq and its neighbors if the United States had not defeated Saddam Hussein? Explain your answer.

34. **Evaluating** Compare the legacy of European colonialism in Africa and the Middle East. Discuss its consequences.

## Chapter Summary

In the postwar period, Africa and the Middle East faced many challenges that threatened their stability. Terrorism challenged the peace and security of all nations in the modern world.

| | **Politics** | **Economy** | **Society** |
|---|---|---|---|
| **Africa** | • Civil war undermines many nations.<br>• Democracy is threatened by military regimes.<br>• Democratic national elections are held in South Africa. | • Most new nations rely on the export of a single crop or resource.<br>• Population growth cripples economies.<br>• Poverty is widespread. | • Tensions grow between traditional and Western cultures. |
| **Middle East** | • Palestine is divided into two states.<br>• Arab-Israeli disputes lead to conflicts.<br>• Israel and PLO reach agreement about autonomy. | • Much of the Middle East is dependent on oil revenue.<br>• OPEC is formed to gain control over oil prices. | • Revival asserts Islamic values over foreign ones. |
| **Modern Terrorism** | • Some states sponsor terrorist groups.<br>• National coalitions form to oppose terrorism.<br>• Fear of terrorism affects national policies. | • Resentment of Western wealth fuels many terrorists.<br>• Security costs affect national budgets. | • Security affects privacy.<br>• Terrorism leads to increased awareness about religious identity. |

**Self-Check Quiz**

Visit the *Glencoe World History–Modern Times* Web site at wh.mt.glencoe.com and click on **Chapter 15– Self-Check Quiz** to prepare for the Chapter Test.

**35. Analyzing** Why do you think Israel was able to seize so much territory during the Six-Day War?

**36.** **Reading Skill** **Identifying Problems and Solutions** Why do the Israelis and the Palestinians need a peace accord? What country would both parties agree to accept as an intermediary to help them settle their problems?

**37. Evaluating** What developments in the Middle East explain the rise of terrorist groups that want to attack Americans?

## Writing About History

**38.** **Historical Analysis** **Analyzing Landscapes** Write a one-page paper exploring how genocide or ethnic cleansing changed a specific country's landscape in Africa or the Middle East after 1945. Be sure to include how the international community responded. **CA HI 5**

**39.** *Big Idea* Compare and contrast the role of women and their social position in the Middle East and Africa.

**DBQ** **Document-Based Questions**

**Analyzing Sources** Read the following quote describing a political rally in Tehran in 1978.

> ❝On Sunday, December 11, hundreds of thousands of people held a procession in the center of Tehran . . . . Slogans against the shah rippled in the wind–'Death to the Shah!' 'Death to the Americans!' 'Khomeini is our leader,' and so on. People from all walks of life could be found in the crowd.❞

**40.** When the phrase "people from all walks of life" is used, what is the writer trying to convey? **CA 10RW1.1**

**41.** Why were the people protesting the shah? Why were anti-American slogans included in the protest? What resulted when the shah left Iran and the Ayatollah Khomeini became the leader? Who are the leaders of Iran today? Does the quote above reflect current sentiments?

## Analyzing Maps and Charts

Refer to the map on page 690 of your textbook to answer the following questions.

**42.** What do you think Iraq hoped to gain by invading the country of Kuwait?

**43.** How far is Tehran from Baghdad?

**44.** What is the significance of the Strait of Hormuz for oil-producing countries?

 **Standards Practice**

**Directions: Use the time line and your knowledge of world history to answer the following question.**

## Selected Events in Middle Eastern Politics

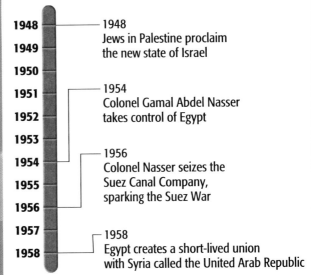

| | |
|---|---|
| 1948 | **1948** Jews in Palestine proclaim the new state of Israel |
| 1949 | |
| 1950 | |
| 1951 | **1954** Colonel Gamal Abdel Nasser takes control of Egypt |
| 1952 | |
| 1953 | |
| 1954 | **1956** Colonel Nasser seizes the Suez Canal Company, sparking the Suez War |
| 1955 | |
| 1956 | |
| 1957 | **1958** Egypt creates a short-lived union with Syria called the United Arab Republic |
| 1958 | |

**45.** Which of the following events resulted from the events on this time line?

**A** Shock over the Holocaust helped Jews realize their goals for a homeland.

**B** Nasser imposed a blockade against Israeli shipping.

**C** Iraq launched an attack on its enemy, Iran.

**D** The Balfour Declaration gave support to Zionist Jews.

**CA Standard 10.9.6** Understand how the forces of nationalism developed in the Middle East, how the Holocaust affected world opinion regarding the need for a Jewish state, and the significance and effects of the location and establishment of Israel on world affairs.

# CHAPTER

# 16

## 1945–Present

# Asia and the Pacific

## ❧ The Big Ideas ❧

### SECTION 1: Communist China

**A totalitarian system violates human rights in pursuit of political power.** The policies of the Chinese Communist government set up in 1949 failed to bring prosperity; since the 1980s, its economy has moved toward free enterprise, but political freedom is still very limited.

### SECTION 2: Independent States in South and Southeast Asia

**The quest for national self-determination is universal.** British India and colonies throughout Southeast Asia gained independence following World War II, but independence was often followed by continued conflict.

### SECTION 3: Japan and the Pacific

**New technologies can revolutionize the way people live, work, interact, and govern.** Since 1945, Japan and the four "Asian tigers" have become economic powerhouses, while Australia and New Zealand remain linked culturally to Europe.

 **World History—Modern Times Video** The Chapter 16 video, "Vietnam," *chronicles the history and impact of the Vietnam War.*

*Mao Zedong*

**1949**
Communist Party takes over China

**1953**
Korean War ends

**1965**
Lyndon Johnson sends U.S. troops to South Vietnam

| 1935 | 1945 | 1955 | 1965 |

**1947**
India and Pakistan become independent nations

**1966**
Indira Gandhi elected prime minister of India

*Indira Gandhi*

704

Singapore's architecture is a mixture of modern and colonial buildings.

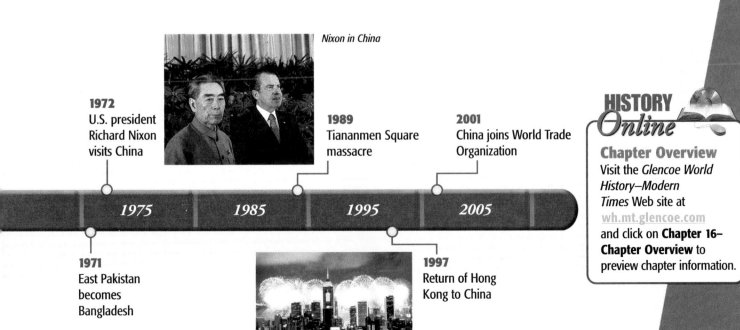

*Nixon in China*

**1972**
U.S. president Richard Nixon visits China

**1989**
Tiananmen Square massacre

**2001**
China joins World Trade Organization

1975　　　1985　　　1995　　　2005

**1971**
East Pakistan becomes Bangladesh

**1997**
Return of Hong Kong to China

*Fireworks celebrate the handover of Hong Kong to China.*

**HISTORY**
*Online*
**Chapter Overview**
Visit the *Glencoe World History–Modern Times* Web site at
wh.mt.glencoe.com
and click on **Chapter 16–Chapter Overview** to preview chapter information.

# Preparing to Read Chapter 16

**Reading Skill**    **Determining Importance**

The volume of information in any textbook can seem overwhelming. How do you know what are the most important points to remember? The answer lies in knowing when an author is giving you some guideposts.

Often, the guideposts are found in three places: at the beginning of a chapter; in headings; and in the first, or topic, sentence of a paragraph. For example, Chapter 16 contains a Guide to Reading with a Section Preview describing the theme of the chapter. Next, notice the Main Idea heading in the Guide. It describes the main idea for each important heading in the text. Finally, focus on the first sentence of each paragraph. It describes the general topic of a paragraph, while supporting details follow.

*Read the following paragraph from Chapter 16 to practice how to determine importance.*

## DETERMINING IMPORTANCE

*Topic sentence:* The first or topic sentence of this paragraph explains the reason why the Red Guards were formed.

## DETERMINING IMPORTANCE

*Supporting details:* After the topic sentence, there is further description to illustrate what the Red Guards did to achieve the goal stated in the topic sentence.

To further the Cultural Revolution, the Red Guards were formed. These were bands of revolutionaries, mostly students and teenagers, who set out across the nation to eliminate the "Four Olds"— old ideas, old culture, old customs, and old habits. They destroyed temples, books written by foreigners, and foreign music. They replaced street signs so that they now had revolutionary names. The Red Guards made vicious attacks on people who had supposedly deviated from Mao's plan. Intellectuals and artists seen as pro-Western were especially open to attack.

### Apply the Skill

As you read through Chapter 16, notice any special features like People in History or Connections Around the World. Make a list of them and show how they offer support for a main idea in the section.

# Historical Analysis Skill — Validating Arguments

**Historical Research, Evidence, and Point of View: Standard HR 1**
*Students distinguish valid arguments from fallacious arguments in historical interpretations.*

A good researcher investigates whether an argument is valid before accepting it. One way to check validity is to consider what the author's bias might be (see the Historical Analysis Skill for Chapter 3). Even if an author does not seem biased strongly in one direction, there is a second validity check—considering *how* an author reaches a particular conclusion.

How do you recognize a valid argument? First, if it seems that an author is considering an argument from different points of view, the argument is probably valid. Second, if an author seems to be using information from various sources and most of the information is readily available, the argument is probably valid. Finally, you can suspect that an argument is fallacious, or false, if the conclusion does not match the information presented.

*Examine the following excerpt from Chapter 16 to determine whether it is a valid or a fallacious argument.*

> **The Japanese are group-oriented and believe strongly in cooperation with other members of the community. Hardworking and frugal, they are more inclined to save than to buy. This boosts the savings rate and labor productivity. The labor force is highly skilled. Japanese people also share common values and respond in similar ways to the challenges of the modern world.**

## Apply the Skill

What do you think is the context of this argument? After reading this chapter, look at this excerpt again and make a list of the evidence offered for this argument about Japanese postwar culture. Do you think this interpretation is valid? Does it use its sources correctly?

# A Story That Matters

*The events in Tiananmen Square ended tragically for pro-democracy protesters.*

# A Movement for Democracy

*I*n the spring of 1989, China began to experience a remarkable series of events. Crowds of students, joined by workers and journalists, filled Tiananmen Square in Beijing day after day to demonstrate in favor of a democratic government for China. Some students waged a hunger strike, and others carried posters calling for democracy.

To China's elderly rulers, calls for democracy were a threat to the dominant role that the Communist Party had played in China since 1949. Some leaders interested in reform advised restraint in handling the protesters. Most of the Communist leaders, however, wanted to repress the movement. When students erected a 30-foot (9-m)-high statue called "The Goddess of Democracy" that looked similar to the American Statue of Liberty, party leaders became especially incensed.

On June 3, 1989, the Chinese army moved into the square. Soldiers carrying automatic rifles fired into the unarmed crowds. Tanks and troops moved in and surrounded the remaining students. At 5:30 in the morning on June 4, the mayor of Beijing announced that Tiananmen Square had been "handed back to the people." Even then, the killing of unarmed citizens continued. At least 500 civilians were killed—perhaps as many as 2,000. The movement for democracy in China had ended.

## Why It Matters

The movement for democracy in China in the 1980s was only one of many tumultuous events in Asia after World War II. In China, a civil war gave way to a new China under Communist control. Japan recovered from the devastation of World War II and went on to build an economic powerhouse. In South Asia and Southeast Asia, nations that had been dominated by Western colonial powers struggled to gain their freedom. Throughout Asia, nations worked to develop modern industrialized states.

**History and You** Find online or in the library a commentary on the Tiananmen Square incident written from the perspective of the Chinese government. Analyze the work to determine whether or not it displays bias. Support your opinion.

# SECTION 1 Communist China

## Section Preview
The policies of the Chinese Communist government set up in 1949 failed to bring prosperity; since the 1980s, its economy has moved toward free enterprise, but political freedom is still very limited.

### Main Idea
- Mao Zedong led the Communists to victory in the civil war, but the human and economic costs of establishing communism were severe. (p. 710)
- After Mao's death, Deng Xiaoping led an effort to modernize the nation, but he faced increased pressures for democratic reform. (p. 712)

- Under Mao, the Communist Party undermined the traditional family system; after Mao's death, the state reversed this policy, but it still works to limit family size. (p. 713)
- In 1950, Cold War tensions between the United States and China led to the Korean War, but by the 1970s, tensions had eased. (p. 714)

### Content Vocabulary
commune, permanent revolution, one-child policy

### Academic Vocabulary
release, injure

### People and Events to Identify
Great Proletarian Cultural Revolution, *Little Red Book,* Deng Xiaoping, Tiananmen Square

### Places to Locate
Taiwan, South Korea, North Korea

### Reading Objectives
1. Explain how the Great Leap Forward and the Great Proletarian Cultural Revolution affected China.
2. Discuss the major economic, social, and political developments in China after the death of Mao Zedong.

### Reading Strategy
**Cause and Effect** Use a chart like the one below to list communism's effects on China's international affairs.

```
                                    Effects
              ┌──────────┐       →  ┌──────────┐
              │Communism │       →  └──────────┘
              └──────────┘          ┌──────────┐
                                 →  └──────────┘
                                    ┌──────────┐
                                    └──────────┘
```

### Preview of Events

| ◆1950 | ◆1960 | ◆1970 | ◆1980 |
|---|---|---|---|

**1950**
A marriage law guarantees women equal rights with men in China

**1958**
Mao Zedong institutes the Great Leap Forward

**1972**
President Nixon visits China

**1979**
China establishes diplomatic ties with the United States

## California Standards in This Section

*Reading this section will help you master these California History–Social Science standards.*

**10.9.4:** Analyze the Chinese Civil War, the rise of Mao Zedong, and the subsequent political and economic upheavals in China (e.g., the Great Leap Forward, the Cultural Revolution, and the Tiananmen Square uprising).

**10.10:** Students analyze instances of nation-building in the contemporary world in at least two of the following regions or countries: the Middle East, Africa, Mexico and other parts of Latin America, and China.

**10.10.1:** Understand the challenges in the regions, including their geopolitical, cultural, military, and economic significance and the international relationships in which they are involved.

**10.10.2:** Describe the recent history of the regions, including political divisions and systems, key leaders, religious issues, natural features, resources, and population patterns.

**10.10.3:** Discuss the important trends in the regions today and whether they appear to serve the cause of individual freedom and democracy.

# The Leadership of Chairman Mao

**Main Idea** Mao Zedong led the Communists to victory in the civil war, but the human and economic costs of establishing communism were severe.

**Reading Connection** Remember what you read earlier about Lenin's transformation of Russia in 1917? Read to learn about the changes Mao Zedong brought to China when he took power in 1949.

As World War II ended, two opposing groups were vying for power: the Nationalists led by Chiang Kai-shek, who were based in southern and central China, and the Communists led by Mao Zedong, who were based in northern China. In 1945, civil war broke out between them. In the countryside, the Communists won the favor of millions of peasants with promises of land. Many joined Mao's People's Liberation Army, and in the spring of 1949, the Nationalists were defeated. The Communist Party, under its chairman, Mao Zedong, now ruled the People's Republic of China. Chiang Kai-shek and two million Nationalists fled to the island of **Taiwan,** which they declared the Republic of China.

In the coming years, Mao's communist zeal became clear. To transform Chinese society, Mao undertook a number of radical programs, at times even setting young people against their parents.

## *Voices from the Past*

One of Mao's instruments for creating his ideal society were the Red Guards, usually squads of young people. One widow of a Nationalist Party official wrote about the actions of the Red Guards when they came to her home:

> ❝Mounting the stairs, I was astonished to see several Red Guards taking pieces of my porcelain collection out of their padded boxes. One young man . . . was stepping on them. . . . Impulsively I leapt forward and caught his leg just as he raised his foot to crush the next cup. He toppled. We fell in a heap together. . . . The young man whose revolutionary work of destruction I had interrupted said angrily, 'You shut up! These things belong to the old culture. . . . Our Great Leader Chairman Mao taught us, "If we do not destroy, we cannot establish." The old culture must be destroyed to make the way for the new socialist culture.'❞

The Red Guard campaign was not Mao's first large-scale initiative. In 1955, he launched a program to build a socialist society. About two-thirds of peasant households received land the government had taken from wealthy landlords. Most of the peasant land was collectivized, while most industry and commerce was nationalized, or owned and operated by the state. The goal was for the collectives to increase food production so that more people could work in industry. Food production, however, did not increase. Meanwhile, China's vast population continued to expand—in 1957, China had approximately 657 million people.

**The Great Leap Forward** To speed up economic growth, Mao began a radical program in 1958 known as the Great Leap Forward. Existing collective farms, most the size of a village, were combined into vast **communes,** each containing more than 30,000 people who lived and worked cooperatively. Mao hoped this program would allow China to reach the final stage of communism—a classless society—before the end of the twentieth century. The government's official slogan promised the following: "Hard work for a few years, happiness for a thousand."

Despite such slogans, the Great Leap Forward was a disaster. Bad planning and bad weather drove food production down. At least 16 million starved to death, and in 1960, the government began breaking up the communes into collectives and some private plots.

**The Cultural Revolution** Despite this failure and even opposition within the party, Mao still dreamed of a classless society. In his eyes, only **permanent revolution,** an atmosphere of constant revolutionary fervor, would bring the Chinese people to the final stage of communism. Thus in 1966, Mao launched

*Students in support of Mao Zedong*

# China, 1949–1989

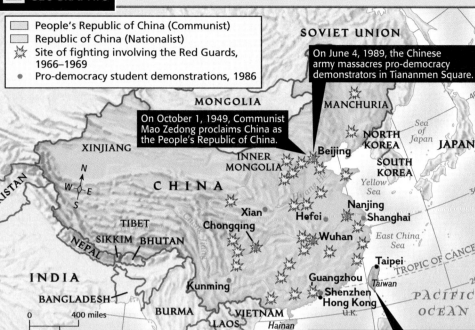

- ▢ People's Republic of China (Communist)
- ▢ Republic of China (Nationalist)
- ✷ Site of fighting involving the Red Guards, 1966–1969
- ● Pro-democracy student demonstrations, 1986

On June 4, 1989, the Chinese army massacres pro-democracy demonstrators in Tiananmen Square.

On October 1, 1949, Communist Mao Zedong proclaims China as the People's Republic of China.

In late 1949, Nationalist Chiang Kai-shek and his followers flee to Taiwan and re-establish the Republic of China.

SOVIET UNION

MONGOLIA
MANCHURIA
NORTH KOREA
SOUTH KOREA
JAPAN
Sea of Japan
Yellow Sea
XINJIANG
Beijing
INNER MONGOLIA
CHINA
TIBET
Xian
Hefei
Nanjing
Shanghai
Chongqing
Wuhan
East China Sea
SIKKIM
BHUTAN
NEPAL
PAKISTAN
INDIA
Kunming
Guangzhou
Taipei
Taiwan
TROPIC OF CANCER
BANGLADESH
Shenzhen
Hong Kong
U.K.
PACIFIC OCEAN
BURMA
VIETNAM
Hainan
LAOS
THAILAND

0    400 miles
0    400 kilometers
Two-Point Equidistant projection
80°E    90°E    100°E    110°E
40°N    30°N    20°N

## Geography *Skills*

The People's Republic of China originated in 1949.

1. **Interpreting Maps** Identify the places where pro-democracy student demonstrations took place in 1986. Which of these cities had also been sites of fighting involving the Red Guards 20 years earlier?

2. **Applying Geography Skills** Use the map's scale to determine the approximate distance from Taiwan to mainland China. Use an atlas to help you name two U.S. cities that are about this same distance apart.

▲ *Chinese workers in a state-owned factory*

the **Great Proletarian Cultural Revolution.** The Chinese name literally meant "great revolution to create a proletarian (working class) culture." A collection of Mao's thoughts, called the ***Little Red Book,*** became a sort of bible for Chinese Communists—the ultimate source of all knowledge.

To further the Cultural Revolution, the Red Guards were formed. These were bands of revolutionaries, mostly students and teenagers, who set out across the nation to eliminate the "Four Olds"—old ideas, old culture, old customs, and old habits. They destroyed temples, books written by foreigners, and foreign music. They replaced street signs so that they now had revolutionary names. The Red Guards made vicious attacks on people who had supposedly deviated from Mao's plan. Intellectuals and artists seen as pro-Western were especially open to attack.

Many party members, military officers, and professionals were disgusted at the Red Guards and turned against this early phase of the Cultural Revolution. Mao himself grew tired of the chaos and reined in the Red Guards. More moderate policies were followed, but Mao's doctrines still prevailed.

✓ **Reading Check** **Explaining** What motivated the Cultural Revolution and why did it fail?

**HISTORY** *Online*

**Web Activity** Visit the *Glencoe World History–Modern Times* Web site at <u>wh.mt.glencoe.com</u> and click on **Chapter 16–Student Web Activity** to learn more about the Cultural Revolution.

# China After Mao

**Main Idea** After Mao's death, Deng Xiaoping led an effort to modernize the nation, but he faced increased pressures for democratic reform.

**Reading Connection** If you wanted to protest a government policy, would you worry that you were risking your life? Read to learn about the risks of public protest in China.

In September 1976, Mao Zedong died at the age of 82. A group of practical-minded reformers, led by **Deng Xiaoping** (DUNG SHOW•PIHNG), seized power and brought the Cultural Revolution to an end.

**Policies of Deng Xiaoping** Deng Xiaoping called for Four Modernizations—new policies in industry, agriculture, technology, and national defense. He also wanted to **release** China from its isolation. He invited foreign investment and sent thousands of students abroad to study.

In agriculture, peasants were allowed to lease land from the collectives and to sell crops or goods they made on the private market. Industrial output also skyrocketed. During the 1980s, per capita, or per person, income doubled. In the early 1980s, the average citizen earned barely enough to buy a bicycle or radio, but by the 1990s, many could buy refrigerators and color TVs.

After Deng's death in 1997, his successors continued his policies. China attracted record-setting levels of foreign investment. China is now one of the world's leading exporters and has the world's fastest-growing economy. In 2001, China joined the World Trade Organization.

There are still major challenges, however. Although farmers' income is rising, it is harder for them to make a profit because of high taxes and other fees. The nation's 750 million rural citizens often feel that economic policy favors the cities and ignores their interests. As in many poor African nations, there is a huge gap between the incomes of the urban rich and the rural poor.

**Movement for Democracy** Many Chinese complained that Deng Xiaoping's program ignored one key part of modernization—democracy. Communist Party officials did not allow direct criticism of the party. Those who called for party reform or for democracy were often sentenced to long prison terms.

Dissatisfaction with the government began to build as more Chinese were studying abroad and

# Opposing Viewpoints

## What U.S. Trade Status Should China Have?

**The debate over granting Permanent Normal Trade Relations to China turned on two points: China's human rights policy and the effect a new trade treaty would have on American business.**

❝Trade should not be used as a weapon of war against China. . . . Such a short-sighted policy fails to recognize the significant advances China has made. . . . [I]t has given the Chinese people greater autonomy and has already weakened the power of the Communist Party. . . . [I]solating China from the West would be disastrous.❞

—**James Dorn**
*"Advancing Human Rights in China"*

❝. . . human rights abuses have changed for the worse . . . there has yet to be any serious, credible linkage of trade and human rights, yet we are being asked today to forgo any possibility of linkage in the future . . . Deny China's PNTR today—require them to move in the direction of reform and the protection of human rights.❞

—**Congressman Chris Smith**
*May 24, 2000 debate*

learning about the West. As the economy prospered, students and other groups felt they could ask for better living conditions and greater freedom. In the late 1980s, rising inflation and government corruption led to more criticism of China's Communist Party. In May 1989, student protesters called for the aging party leaders to resign. This protest had widespread support, especially in the cities. The most dramatic outpouring came in massive demonstrations in **Tiananmen Square** in the capital of Beijing (see page 719).

China's leaders were split over how to respond, but Deng believed the protesters were calling for an end to Communist rule. He ordered tanks and troops into Tiananmen Square to remove the protesters. Between 500 and 2,000 were killed and many more **injured.** Yet by the late 1990s, Chinese citizens were again demonstrating against official corruption, high rural taxes, and economic and social inequality.

These human rights violations, increasing military strength, and determination to unify with Taiwan have all placed a strain on China's relations with the West. Diplomatic relations, however, have been maintained.

**✓ Reading Check** **Analyzing** How has China's economic modernization contributed to demands for democracy?

**❝**Since the last presidential election the U.S. textile and apparel sector has lost 323,000 jobs, representing 31% of its workforce. . . . The textile crisis in the United States has been precipitated by a record-breaking flood of illegally subsidized Chinese imports. . . . Studies have shown that the removal of all remaining Chinese quotas will destroy the textile sector in the United States. . . . **❞**

—**Statement from the American Textile Manufacturing Institute, 2004**

## You Decide

1. Should concerns about human rights play a significant role in making trade policy?

2. How would you vote to decide the first question? Should economic interests be separated from consequences to workers? Can you think of another example of economic progress which came at the cost of human rights?

# Chinese Society Under Communism

**Main Idea** Under Mao, the Communist Party undermined the traditional family system; after Mao's death, the state reversed this policy, but it still works to limit family size.

**Reading Connection** Can you think of a modern society where a person might be torn between duty to family and duty to the state? Read to learn about family policies in China.

From the start, the Communist Party wanted to create a new kind of citizen, one who would give the utmost for the good of all China. In Mao's words, the people "should be resolute, fear no sacrifice, and surmount every difficulty to win victory."

During the 1950s, the Chinese government made some basic changes affecting families and women. Women, for example, were now allowed to participate in politics. Another change in 1950 was a new law guaranteeing women equal rights with men in marriage—a dramatic shift from Chinese custom.

Mao wanted to get rid of the traditional family values rooted in Confucianism. He feared that loyalty to the family would interfere with loyalty to the state. During the Cultural Revolution, for example, children were encouraged to report negative comments their parents made about the government. Red Guards expected students to report on their teachers. At the time, many foreign observers feared that China would be transformed into a nation of robots spouting communist slogans. This did not happen, however.

After Mao's death, there was a noticeable shift away from revolutionary fervor and a return to family traditions, a change welcomed by most citizens. People now had more freedom in everyday matters. Parents who themselves had been given patriotic names such as "Protect Mao Zedong" and "Build the Country" chose more traditional names for their own children. Clothing choices were no longer restricted to a baggy "Mao suit" in olive drab or dark blue. Today, young Chinese people wear jeans, sneakers, and sweatsuits. *(See page 777 to read an excerpt from an article on changes in China in the 1990s in the Primary Sources Library.)*

Mao's successors have followed one of his goals to the present day—the effort to control population growth. In 1949, the population stood at 550 million, and in 2000, at more than 1.29 billion. In 1979, the state began advocating a **one-child policy.** Incentives such as education benefits, child care, and housing were offered to couples who limited their families to

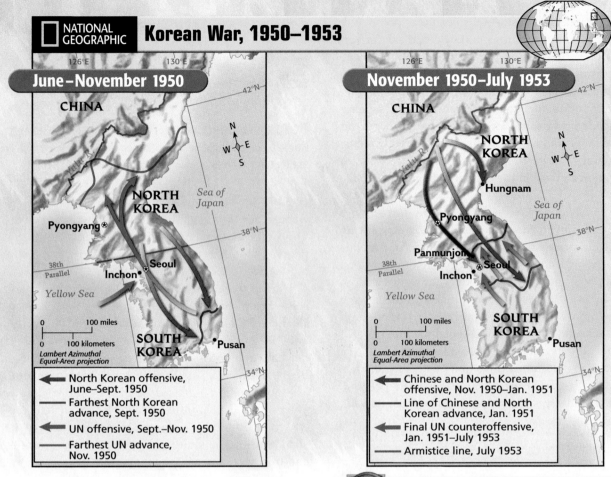

## NATIONAL GEOGRAPHIC — Korean War, 1950–1953

### June–November 1950

CHINA

NORTH KOREA

Sea of Japan

Pyongyang

38th Parallel

Inchon • Seoul

Yellow Sea

0    100 miles
0    100 kilometers
Lambert Azimuthal
Equal-Area projection

SOUTH KOREA • Pusan

◄── North Korean offensive, June–Sept. 1950
─── Farthest North Korean advance, Sept. 1950
◄── UN offensive, Sept.–Nov. 1950
─── Farthest UN advance, Nov. 1950

### November 1950–July 1953

CHINA

NORTH KOREA

Hungnam

Sea of Japan

Pyongyang

Panmunjom

38th Parallel

Inchon • Seoul

Yellow Sea

0    100 miles
0    100 kilometers
Lambert Azimuthal
Equal-Area projection

SOUTH KOREA • Pusan

◄── Chinese and North Korean offensive, Nov. 1950–Jan. 1951
─── Line of Chinese and North Korean advance, Jan. 1951
◄── Final UN counteroffensive, Jan. 1951–July 1953
─── Armistice line, July 1953

---

one child. The UN and other international groups criticized the policy for using coercion and intense psychological pressure. Overall, the policy has been much more successful in cities than in rural areas.

✓ **Reading Check** **Evaluating** How did Chinese communism affect women and family institutions?

## China and the World: The Cold War in Asia

**Main Idea** In 1950, Cold War tensions between the United States and China led to the Korean War, but by the 1970s, tensions had eased.

**Reading Connection** Remember reading that U.S.-Soviet relations improved during the 1970s? Read about how the United States also worked to improve Chinese relations at this time.

When Chinese Communists came to power, American fears intensified that communism was spreading. In 1950, China signed a pact of friendship and cooperation with the Soviet Union. This treaty

### Geography Skills

Three years of fighting resulted in no significant change to the boundary between North and South Korea.

1. **Interpreting Maps** Identify the offensive shown in the map on the left that caused the Chinese to enter the war.

2. **Applying Geography Skills** What differences explain the UN offensives in the two maps?

between two large Communist powers set the stage for an increase in the tensions of the Cold War. Many Americans worried that the Communists wanted to dominate the world. Their fears were reinforced when the Korean War broke out. The Cold War had arrived in Asia.

**The Korean War** From 1905 until 1945, Korea was a part of the Japanese Empire. As World War II was ending, the Soviet army was positioned in the north of Korea, and the U.S. army was in the south. When the Japanese surrendered in August 1945, the Soviets and the Americans agreed to divide Korea into two zones along the 38th parallel and to hold elections later to reunify Korea.

American-Soviet relations grew worse, however, and in Korea two separate governments emerged: a Communist one in the north, and an anti-Communist one in the south.

Tension quickly escalated between the two governments. With the approval of Joseph Stalin, North Korean troops invaded **South Korea** on June 25, 1950. The United Nations then approved President Harry Truman's decision to send American troops to repel the Communist forces. In October 1950, UN forces, made up of mostly American soldiers, marched northward across the 38th parallel with the aim of unifying Korea. Alarmed, the Chinese sent hundreds of thousands of Chinese troops into **North Korea** and pushed UN forces back across the 38th parallel.

Three more years of fighting produced no final victory. An armistice was finally signed in 1953. The 38th parallel remained, and remains today, the boundary line between North and South Korea. In June 2000, the leaders of North and South Korea took part in the first North-South summit, but tensions between the two countries remain high. North Korea's government continues to pour money into the military while the country's economic situation grows worse. As many as two million North Koreans may have died as a result of food shortages since the mid-1990s. In 2002, fears arose that North Korea's leaders were pursuing nuclear weapons despite their worsening economy.

**The Shifting Power Balance in Asia** In the early decades of Mao's rule, China had become isolated. It had to rely almost entirely on the Soviet Union for technological and economic aid. In the late 1950s, however, relations between China and the Soviet Union deteriorated. China did not want to follow the Soviet model in everything, and it expected more in Soviet aid than it got. In the 1960s there were also frequent clashes along their frontier over boundary disputes.

Faced with a security threat from the Soviets and internal problems, Chinese leaders decided to improve relations with the United States. In 1972, President Richard Nixon made a state visit to China, the first U.S. president to visit the People's Republic of China since it became a nation. The two nations agreed then to improve relations and in 1979 established diplomatic ties. In the 1980s, Chinese relations with the Soviet Union also improved. By the 1990s, China was playing an increasingly active role in Asian and world affairs. In 2001, it joined the World Trade Organization.

✓**Reading Check** **Examining** Why did China decide to improve relations with the United States?

**HISTORY** _Online_ **Study Central**

For help with the concepts in this section of *Glencoe World History–Modern Times,* go to wh.mt.glencoe.com and click on **Study Central.**

# SECTION 1 ASSESSMENT

### Checking for Understanding

1. **Vocabulary** Define: commune, permanent revolution, release, injure, one-child policy.

2. **People and Events** Identify: Great Proletarian Cultural Revolution, *Little Red Book,* Deng Xiaoping, Tiananmen Square.

3. **Places** Locate: Taiwan, South Korea, North Korea.

### Reviewing Big Ideas

4. **List** the actions the Chinese government took to promote modernization and economic development.

### Critical Thinking

5. **Compare and Contrast** Identify the changes the Communist takeover brought to China during the 1950s. Then, compare and contrast how policies have changed in China since the 1970s.

6. **Contrasting Information** Use a table like the one below to contrast the policies of the two Chinese leaders Mao Zedong and Deng Xiaoping.

| Mao Zedong | Deng Xiaoping |
|---|---|
|  |  |
|  |  |

### Analyzing Visuals

7. **Compare** the photographs on pages 708 and 710. Imagine that you are taking part in the demonstrations in Tiananmen Square and that you are participating in a rally in support of Mao Zedong. What are you expressing at each event? Are other points of view being expressed? What might happen to you after each event? How will you be remembered by historians?

## Writing About History

8. **Descriptive Writing** Pretend that you are a visitor to China during the Cultural Revolution. Write a letter to a friend at home describing your reaction to the Red Guards.

# TRANSFORMING BEIJING

In 1979, after decades of watching China's economy stagnate, Communist Party leader Deng Xiaoping took a gamble. He began relaxing the state's tight economic controls while trying to keep a firm grip on political power. In the Chinese capital of Beijing, the result of Deng's "second revolution" has been a big construction boom, new foreign investment—and the kind of Western cultural influence that China has resisted for centuries.

Geographically, Beijing's location in Asia is roughly similar to New York's in North America. Both lie near the 40th parallel, and in both places the most comfortable seasons are autumn and spring. But the similarities end there. The city now known as Beijing began as a frontier outpost nearly 3,000 years ago. It was built to guard the North China Plain against marauding groups who attacked through mountain passes in the north.

Without access to the sea or a significant river to link it to the outside world, Beijing might have remained a dusty outpost. But in the seventh century A.D., a 1,000-mile (1,609-km) canal was dug to link the city with the fertile Chang Jiang Valley in the south. Three centuries later the city became the capital of the Liao dynasty. Then came the Mongols under Genghis Khan, who sacked and burned the capital in 1215.

About 50 years later, however, Genghis's grandson, Kublai Khan, rebuilt the city so gloriously that the Venetian traveler Marco Polo marveled at its streets "so straight and wide that you can see right along from end to end and from one gate to another." Kublai Khan's Dadu (meaning "Great Capital"), Marco Polo wrote, "is arranged like a chessboard."

Indeed, Beijing is laid out on a precise north-south axis, in harmony with the ancient practice of *feng shui* ("wind and water"). According to this tradition, buildings (and the furnishings inside them) must be properly aligned to take advantage of the natural energy (*qi*) that flows through all things. The proper placement of a house or temple will thus attract positive *qi* and good luck; the wrong placement invites disaster.

The north-south axis passes directly through Qian Men (Front Gate), proceeds through the red walls of Tian An Men (Gate of Heavenly Peace), and then on to Wu Men (Meridian Gate), beyond which lies the Forbidden City.

An area once barred to everyone except the emperor, his family, and his most favored concubines, guards, and

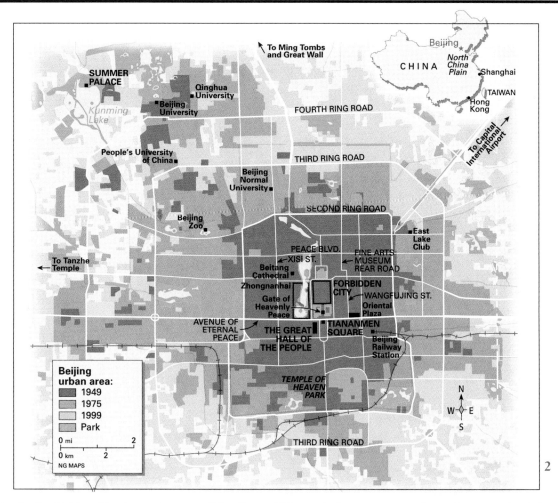

2

officials, the Forbidden City lay at the very center of a series of cities-within-cities, concentric rectangles defined by their high walls. Today the walls are largely gone and the Forbidden City is a museum overflowing with tourists.

The Gate of Heavenly Peace, on the north side of nearby Tiananmen Square, is the spiritual heart of all China. Centuries ago, orders from the emperor were sent down from the top of the gate to officials waiting below.

**1  A migrant worker balances on his cart as he stacks bricks at the construction site of a large apartment complex.**

**2  The Forbidden City (above map) was once considered the stable core of the empire. In spite of its growth, urban Beijing accounts for only a fraction of the territory the city includes. By an administrative decision of 1959, Beijing's boundaries now cover a 6,600 square-mile (17,094 square-km) municipality that includes satellite towns and agricultural communes as well as such tourist attractions as the Ming Tombs and the Great Wall.**

**3  Mao Zedong's mausoleum and the Monument to the People's Heroes dominate Tiananmen Square.**

3

4

5

From that same high place, on the afternoon of October 1, 1949, Mao Zedong formally proclaimed the establishment of the People's Republic of China. His portrait now hangs on the wall of the gate, staring out at the square and providing a backdrop for tourist photographs.

In the late 1950s, during the Great Leap Forward, homes around Tiananmen Square were torn down to expand the square from 27 acres (10.9 ha) to 98 acres (39.7 ha)—large enough to hold a million people. In the center stands the 124-foot (37.8-m) high Monument to the People's Heroes. On the west side is the many-columned Great Hall of the People, where the government meets and visiting dignitaries are entertained. Across the square on the east side is the Historical Museum. To the south, opposite his portrait on Tian An Men, is the huge mausoleum where Mao Zedong's body is on display.

■

In the 20-some years since Deng Xiaoping's experiment in free enterprise began, the blocky Soviet-style monuments built by Mao have been overtaken by the bright lights of McDonald's, Kentucky Fried Chicken, and thousands of private restaurants and nightclubs catering to foreign visitors and investors.

The building boom has swept away much of what was once a major characteristic of the old city: the low, walled alleyways called *hutong*. Some of the family compounds were hundreds of years old and housed three generations. The government is moving more than 2 million of the city's 11 million residents out to the suburbs to make room for new tourism centers, department stores, and expensive apartment compounds.

As one longtime Beijing resident put it, "The old city is gone. Old things like the Forbidden City or a temple are scattered between skyscrapers like toys thrown here and there. Old Beijing is dismembered."

Along with all the tearing down

德先生,你好
HELLO, Mr. DEMOCRACY

6

and building up that has occurred in the last two decades, China's production has climbed steadily. Per capita annual income for city dwellers has almost doubled since 1990 to more than $600. Foreign businesses hoping for a share of the vast Chinese market have rushed in.

Not all of these entrepreneurs have been welcomed by Beijing's residents, however. A mammoth complex called the Oriental Plaza, for example, has been the focus of controversy. Built by a Hong Kong business partnership, the complex contains eight office towers, two apartment towers, and a five-star international hotel. It also includes more than a million square feet (93,000 square m) of retail mall and a parking structure for 2,000 cars and 10,000 bicycles.

Even for a city of large monuments, the Oriental Plaza is beyond big. Residents complain that the project destroys the character of the old city, dwarfing as it does the Gate of Heavenly Peace.

As the site of countless demonstrations over the years, Tiananmen Square has become familiar to television viewers around the world. The most vivid scenes in recent memory are from early June 1989, when the Chinese army attacked unarmed demonstrators who had been protesting government corruption. Perhaps as many as 2,000 people were killed. Although the government would prefer the event be forgotten, the anniversary of the June 4th attack has been marked repeatedly with some form of protest.

Yet even as the government clamps down on highly visible political demonstrations, activists have found a more subtle way to make their points—the Internet. More and more young Chinese are making their way online. Their access to an open market of ideas and uncensored information brings with it a new sense of individualism. Undoubtedly this will have a lasting impact on the future of their city and their nation.

**4** Demolition of the old makes way for the new as downtown Beijing undergoes a massive face-lift.

**5** Residents of old family compounds haul out their belongings as they load a truck to move to housing projects in the suburbs.

**6** Students protest in Tiananmen Square in 1989. The peaceful protests turned violent when the army attacked.

## INTERPRETING THE PAST

**1. Why was Beijing established?**

**2. How is the capital city laid out ?**

**3. How has Beijing changed during the last twenty years?**

**4. Do you think the lives of the residents of Beijing have improved or deteriorated during the last two decades?**

# Independent States in South and Southeast Asia

## Guide to Reading

### Section Preview

British India and colonies throughout Southeast Asia gained independence following World War II, but independence was often followed by continued conflict.

**Main Idea**

- At independence, British India became two nations, India and Pakistan; both have faced problems of poverty, over-population, and ethnic and religious strife. (p. 721)
- Colonies in Southeast Asia gained independence, but politics were often unstable; in Vietnam, conflict led to war with the United States. (p. 723)

- In recent years, some nations in Southeast Asia have moved toward democracy. (p. 725)

### Content Vocabulary

outsourcing, stalemate, discrimination

### Academic Vocabulary

involvement, gender

### People to Identify

Sikhs, Vietminh, Khmer Rouge, Pol Pot, Ferdinand Marcos

### Places to Locate

Punjab, Kashmir, Bangladesh

### Reading Objectives

1. Discuss the policies that Jawaharlal Nehru put into effect in India.
2. Analyze the internal and external problems the Southeast Asian nations faced after 1945.

### Reading Strategy

**Categorizing Information** Use a web diagram like the one below to identify challenges India faced after independence.

Challenges in India

### Preview of Events

| ♦1945 | ♦1965 | ♦1985 | ♦2005 |
|---|---|---|---|

**1948**
A Hindu militant assassinates Mohandas Gandhi

**1949**
Republic of Indonesia is established

**1966**
Indira Gandhi becomes India's prime minister

**1971**
East Pakistan becomes Bangladesh

**1992**
Hindu militants destroy Muslim shrine at Ayodhya

**2002**
India-Pakistan fighting over Kashmir eases

## California Standards in This Section

*Reading this section will help you master these California History–Social Science standards.*

**10.9:** Students analyze the international developments in the post-World War II world.

**10.9.3:** Understand the importance of the Truman Doctrine and the Marshall Plan, which established the pattern for America's postwar policy of supplying economic and military aid to prevent the spread of Communism and the resulting economic and political competition in arenas such as Southeast Asia (i.e., the Korean War, Vietnam War), Cuba, and Africa.

**10.11:** Students analyze the integration of countries into the world economy and the information, technological, and communications revolutions (e.g., television, satellites, computers).

# British India Divided: India and Pakistan

**Main Idea** At independence, British India became two nations, India and Pakistan; both have faced problems of poverty, overpopulation, and ethnic and religious strife.

**Reading Connection** The population of the United States in 2004 was 294 million, but India's is more than three times that large—about 1 billion. Read to learn about population and economic challenges in South Asia.

When British rule in India ended, its population was bitterly divided. Most Indians were Hindu, but many were Muslim. The decision was made to create two countries: India would be predominantly Hindu, and Pakistan predominantly Muslim. The new Pakistan would have two regions: West Pakistan to the northwest of India, and East Pakistan to the northeast.

When independence day arrived on August 15, 1947, millions fled across the new borders—Hindus toward India and Muslims toward Pakistan. Extreme violence broke out, fed in the previous months by rumor, fear, and thugs willing to take advantage of chaos. If Muslims or Hindus were a minority in an area, they might kill first for fear of being killed. Likewise, the killing might begin with majority Hindus.

## *Voices from the Past*

Some of the worst violence was in Punjab, a rich land that was to be divided on independence day. Prakash Tandon wrote about his uncle's experience then. A Hindu lawyer, his uncle at first believed his Muslim friends could keep him safe. He soon changed his mind.

    ❝One day, a train crammed with two thousand [Hindu] refugees came from the more predominantly Muslim areas of Jhelum and beyond. At Gujarat station the train was stopped, and Muslims from the neighbourhood, excited by the news of violence in East Punjab, began to attack and loot. There was indescribable carnage. Several hours later the train moved on, filled with a bloody mess of corpses, without a soul alive. At Amritsar, when the train with its load of dead arrived, [Hindus] took revenge on a trainload of Muslim refugees. . . .❞

That night the uncle and his family prepared to join the vast convoy of trucks, carts, and people on foot leaving their homeland. Over a million people were killed in this mass migration. On January 30, 1948, violence claimed one more victim: A Hindu militant murdered Gandhi, the man who had preached nonviolence during the struggle for freedom.

**The New India** With independence, the Indian National Congress, now called the Congress Party, began to rule India. Jawaharlal Nehru (jah•WAH•huhr•LAHL NAY•roo), the new prime minister, was a popular figure who had worked with Gandhi. Nehru admired Britain's political institutions and especially the socialist ideals of its Labour Party. His vision of the new India combined a parliamentary form of government with moderate socialism in the economy. The state, therefore, took over ownership of major industries, utilities, and transportation. Private enterprise was permitted at the local level, and farmland remained in private hands. Industrial production almost tripled between 1950 and 1965.

Nehru died in 1964. In 1966, the leaders of the Congress Party selected Nehru's daughter, Indira Gandhi (who was not related to Mohandas Gandhi), as the new prime minister. Except for 22 months in the late 1970s, she retained that office until 1984.

During this time, India faced serious problems. Population growth was probably the most serious. Even in 1948, India had been unable to support its population. In the 1950s and 1960s, its population grew at a rate of more than 2 percent per year. One result was worsening poverty for many people. Millions lived in vast city slums.

▼ *Muslims and Hindus piling on trains to escape violence in 1947*

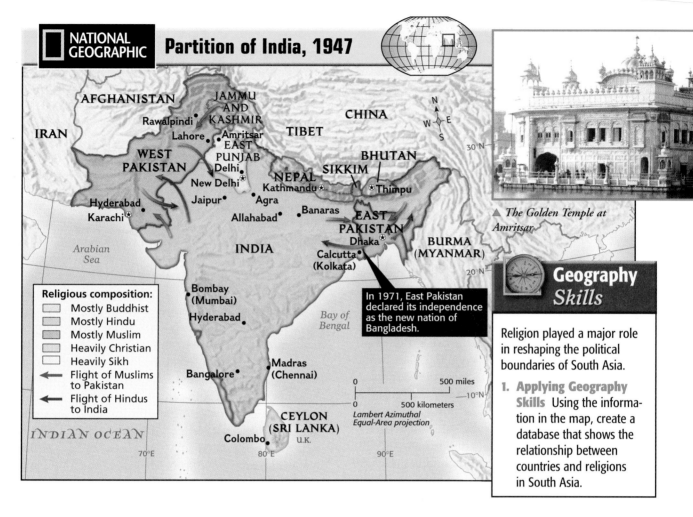

AFGHANISTAN

JAMMU AND KASHMIR

CHINA

Rawalpindi

Lahore

TIBET

IRAN

WEST PAKISTAN

Amritsar

EAST PUNJAB

Delhi

BHUTAN

NEPAL

SIKKIM

New Delhi

Kathmandu

Thimpu

Hyderabad

Jaipur

Agra

Karachi

Allahabad

Banaras

EAST PAKISTAN

BURMA (MYANMAR)

Arabian Sea

INDIA

Dhaka

Calcutta (Kolkata)

In 1971, East Pakistan declared its independence as the new nation of Bangladesh.

Bombay (Mumbai)

Hyderabad

Bay of Bengal

**Religious composition:**
- Mostly Buddhist
- Mostly Hindu
- Mostly Muslim
- Heavily Christian
- Heavily Sikh
- ← Flight of Muslims to Pakistan
- ← Flight of Hindus to India

Bangalore

Madras (Chennai)

0    500 miles

0    500 kilometers

Lambert Azimuthal Equal-Area projection

INDIAN OCEAN

CEYLON (SRI LANKA) U.K.

Colombo

70°E    80°E    90°E

▲ *The Golden Temple at Amritsar*

## Geography Skills

Religion played a major role in reshaping the political boundaries of South Asia.

1. **Applying Geography Skills** Using the information in the map, create a database that shows the relationship between countries and religions in South Asia.

---

Another problem was conflict involving the **Sikhs,** followers of a religion based on both Hindu and Muslim ideas. Many Sikhs lived in a northern province called the **Punjab.** Militant Sikhs wanted this province to be independent. Gandhi refused and, in 1984, she used military force against Sikh rebels who had taken refuge in the Golden Temple, one of the Sikhs' most important shrines. More than 450 Sikhs were killed. Seeking revenge for these killings, two Sikh members of Gandhi's personal bodyguard assassinated her later that year.

Indira Gandhi's son Rajiv replaced his mother as prime minister and began new economic policies. He started to encourage private enterprise and to transfer state-run industries into private hands. These policies led to a growth in the middle class.

Rajiv Gandhi served as prime minister until 1989. While campaigning for reelection in 1991, he was assassinated. Since then, the Congress Party has lost its leadership position and must compete with new parties.

One part of the Indian economy that is thriving is technology. India is a leading exporter of software services and workers, and U.S. firms in the 1990s began outsourcing jobs to India. **Outsourcing** occurs when companies send certain types of jobs—such as data entry or customer service—to countries where wages are lower. Outsourcing is controversial because it reduces the number of jobs in the United States or in the other advanced societies which practice it. For India, outsourcing is seen as an opportunity. While Western attitudes have spread, in rural villages where one-quarter of the people live in poverty, traditional attitudes remain.

Conflict between Hindus and Muslims remains a problem in India. In 1992, Muslims and Hindus fought to control a historic holy place in the town of Ayodhya. Hindu militants destroyed an ancient shrine there that had great symbolic value for Muslims. Hindu-Muslim riots then followed all over India.

India is also involved in an ongoing dispute with Pakistan over **Kashmir,** a territory between the two nations. Today, Pakistan controls one-third of Kashmir and the rest is held by India. Troops from both countries patrol the border between the two areas. This conflict became an international concern in 1998, when both nations tested nuclear weapons. Tensions had eased by the end of 2002.

**Pakistan** Unlike its neighbor India, Pakistan was a completely new nation in 1947. Its early years were marked by intense internal conflict. Most dangerous was the growing division between East and West Pakistan. These two regions are very different. West Pakistan is dry and mountainous, while East Pakistan has marshy land densely populated with rice farmers.

Many people in East Pakistan felt that the government, based in West Pakistan, ignored them. In 1971, East Pakistan declared its independence. After a brief civil war, it became the new nation of **Bangladesh.**

Both Bangladesh and Pakistan, as West Pakistan is now known, have struggled to establish stable governments. Often military officials have seized control. Both nations also remain very poor. Bangladesh, in particular, is vulnerable to frequent and damaging floods.

☑ **Reading Check** **Explaining** How did the two independent nations of India and Pakistan come about?

# Southeast Asia

**Main Idea** Colonies in Southeast Asia gained independence, but politics were often unstable; in Vietnam, conflict led to war with the United States.

**Reading Connection** Do you remember reading about the formal treaty ending World War I? Read how the Korean and Vietnam wars ended without a settlement.

In Southeast Asia, as in other parts of the world, the colonies of Western powers gained their independence after World War II. Independence came about in different ways across the region.

**Independence** In 1946, the Philippines became independent of the United States. Britain was also willing to end its colonial rule in Southeast Asia. Burma became independent in 1948, Malaya in 1957.

The Netherlands and France were less willing to abandon their colonial empires in Southeast Asia. The Dutch tried to suppress a new Indonesian republic led by Achmed Sukarno. When the Indonesian Communist Party attempted to seize power, however, the United States decided to pressure the Netherlands to grant independence to Sukarno and his non-Communist Nationalist Party. In 1949, the Netherlands recognized the new Republic of Indonesia.

The situation was very different in Vietnam. The local Communist Party, led by Ho Chi Minh, was the most active group fighting colonial French rule. In

August 1945, the **Vietminh,** an alliance of forces under Communist leadership, was organized. It seized power in much of Vietnam. Ho Chi Minh was elected president of a provisional republic, but France refused to accept this government and seized the southern part of the country.

**The Vietnam War** Over the following years, France fought Ho Chi Minh's forces for control of Vietnam, but it could not defeat them. In 1954, France agreed to a peace settlement. Vietnam was divided into two parts. In the north, the Communists were based in Hanoi, and in the south, the non-Communists were based in Saigon. Both sides agreed to hold elections in two years to create a single government.

Because the United States was opposed to the spread of communism, it began to provide aid to the South Vietnamese government of Ngo Dinh Diem. In spite of this aid, South Vietnamese Communist guerrillas known as Viet Cong, supported by military units from North Vietnam, were on the verge of seizing control of the entire country by early 1965.

In March 1965, President Lyndon Johnson decided to send U.S. troops to South Vietnam to prevent a Communist victory. The Communist government of North Vietnam responded by sending more forces to the south. By the end of the 1960s, the war had reached a **stalemate**—neither side was able to make significant gains. With support for the war weakened and no military victory in sight, President Richard Nixon reached an agreement with North Vietnam in 1973. American troops were withdrawn. In 1975, North Vietnamese troops forcibly reunited Vietnam.

The reunification of Vietnam under a Communist government had an immediate impact on the region. By the end of 1975, both Laos and Cambodia had Communist governments. Cambodia was ruled by a brutal revolutionary regime called the **Khmer Rouge** (kuh•MEHR ROOZH), led by the dictator **Pol Pot.** The Khmer Rouge is estimated to have massacred 1.5 million Cambodians between 1975 and 1979, or one-fifth to one-third of the population. Many victims were members of Cambodia's middle and upper classes or were suspected "enemies of the state."

The Communist triumph in Indochina did not, however, lead to the "falling dominoes" that many U.S. policy makers had feared. (See Chapter 12.)

**Vietnam, Cambodia, and Laos Today** Since 1986, Vietnam has increasingly relied on the free market and private enterprise. Its leaders have vowed to make Vietnam an industrialized nation by 2020.

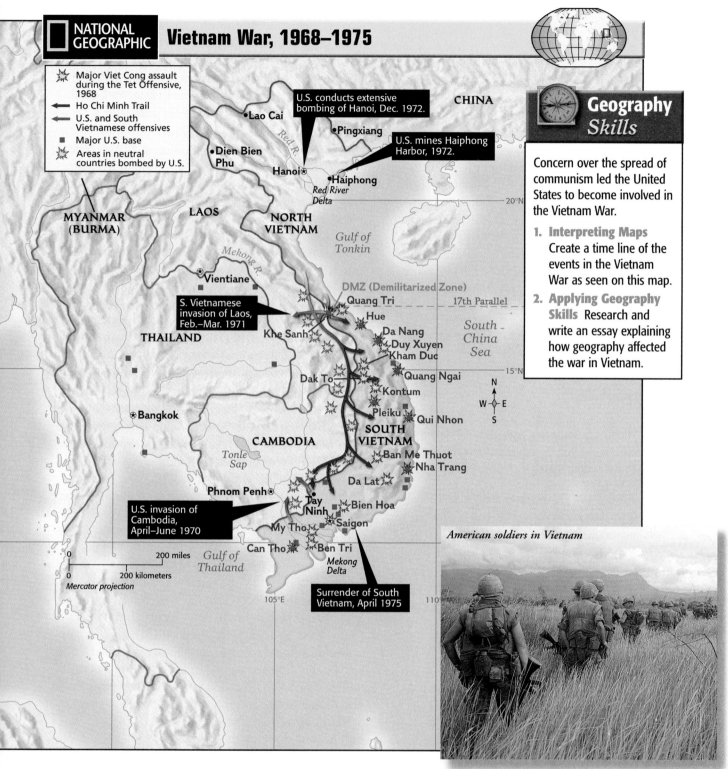

## Vietnam War, 1968–1975

Major Viet Cong assault during the Tet Offensive, 1968

Ho Chi Minh Trail

U.S. and South Vietnamese offensives

Major U.S. base

Areas in neutral countries bombed by U.S.

U.S. conducts extensive bombing of Hanoi, Dec. 1972.

CHINA

•Lao Cai

•Pingxiang

•Dien Bien Phu

Red R.

Hanoi⊛

•Haiphong

U.S. mines Haiphong Harbor, 1972.

Red River Delta

20°N

MYANMAR (BURMA)

LAOS

NORTH VIETNAM

Gulf of Tonkin

Mekong R.

⊛Vientiane

S. Vietnamese invasion of Laos, Feb.–Mar. 1971

DMZ (Demilitarized Zone)

Quang Tri

17th Parallel

Hue

THAILAND

Khe Sanh

Da Nang

Duy Xuyen

Kham Duc

South China Sea

Dak To

Quang Ngai

15°N

Kontum

N

Pleiku

W  E

⊛Bangkok

Qui Nhon

S

CAMBODIA

SOUTH VIETNAM

Tonle Sap

Ban Me Thuot

Nha Trang

Phnom Penh⊛

Da Lat

U.S. invasion of Cambodia, April–June 1970

Tay Ninh

Bien Hoa

My Tho

Saigon

0        200 miles

Gulf of Thailand

Can Tho

Ben Tri

0      200 kilometers

Mekong Delta

Mercator projection

105°E

110

Surrender of South Vietnam, April 1975

### Geography Skills

Concern over the spread of communism led the United States to become involved in the Vietnam War.

1. **Interpreting Maps** Create a time line of the events in the Vietnam War as seen on this map.

2. **Applying Geography Skills** Research and write an essay explaining how geography affected the war in Vietnam.

*American soldiers in Vietnam*

Relations with the United States have significantly improved, and President Bill Clinton visited Vietnam in November 2000. The U.S.-Vietnam Bilateral Trade Agreement took effect at the end of 2001.

In Cambodia, the Khmer Rouge were driven from power in the late 1970s by a Vietnamese invasion. During the 1980s, various groups competed for power. In 1987, a peace treaty was signed and in 1993, democratic elections were held for the first time.

Today, Laos, along with Vietnam and North Korea, is one of the few remaining Communist nations. Cambodia and Laos are among the world's poorest countries. In both countries, economic progress has been held back because of the poor quality of roads, bridges, and railroads.

✔ **Reading Check** **Explaining** Why did the United States enter the Vietnam War, and why did it withdraw from it?

# Democratic Reform in Southeast Asia

**Main Idea** In recent years, some nations in Southeast Asia have moved toward democracy.

**Reading Connection** Do you remember how protests ended Communist regimes in Eastern Europe? Read to learn how citizens in Southeast Asia forced dictators to step down.

At first, the leaders of new nations in Southeast Asia wanted to establish capitalist democracies. By the end of the 1950s, the economies were failing, however, and the support for democracy weakened. The door was opened to military governments or one-party regimes. In recent years, some Southeast Asian societies have once again moved toward democracy, but serious obstacles remain for these peoples.

**The Philippines and Indonesia** In the Philippines, two presidents have been forced out of office in recent years. In 1986, a public uprising forced **Ferdinand Marcos** to flee the country after 20 years in office. His regime was very corrupt, and in the early 1980s, he was also accused of **involvement** in the killing of a popular opposition leader, Benigno Aquino. In 1986, Aquino's widow, Corazon Aquino, became president and worked for democratic reforms.

Another public uprising in 2001 forced President Joseph Estrada from office over charges of corruption. He was succeeded by Gloria Macapagal-Arroyo. She promised to create jobs and improve living standards. Although the Philippines once had one of the strongest economies in the region, it now has a huge national debt and poverty is widespread. The nation also faces terrorist threats. Muslim rebels on the island of Mindanao, for example, have used terror to promote their demands for independence.

In Indonesia, General Suharto came to power in 1965 and imposed authoritarian rule for more than 30 years. In 1998, widespread rioting forced him to step down. Since then the government has struggled to improve the economy, which has suffered from slow growth and high unemployment. The nation has also been torn by ethnic and religious conflict and scandals about corruption in government.

**Women in South and Southeast Asia** Across the region, the rights and roles of woman have changed. In India, women's rights expanded after independence. Its constitution of 1950 forbade **discrimination,** or prejudicial treatment, based on **gender** and called for equal pay for equal work. Child marriage was also outlawed. Women were encouraged to attend school and to enter the labor market. In Southeast Asia, virtually all of the newly independent states gave women full legal and political rights, but in rural areas, old customs and attitudes survive.

**Reading Check** **Identifying** List the challenges to democracy faced by nations in Southeast Asia.

**HISTORY** *Online* **Study Central**

For help with the concepts in this section of *Glencoe World History–Modern Times,* go to wh.mt.glencoe.com and click on **Study Central.**

---

# SECTION 2 ASSESSMENT

### Checking for Understanding

1. **Vocabulary** Define: outsourcing, stalemate, involvement, discrimination, gender.

2. **People** Identify: Sikhs, Vietminh, Khmer Rouge, Pol Pot, Ferdinand Marcos.

3. **Places** Locate: Punjab, Kashmir, Bangladesh.

### Reviewing Big Ideas

4. **Explain** how the reunification of Vietnam under Communist rule affected the region.

### Critical Thinking

5. **Historical Analysis** **Understanding Chronology** Has the division of British India into two countries been beneficial? Explain. **CA CS 1**

6. **Organizing Information** Use a table like the one below to list the type of government of each Southeast Asian country discussed in this section.

| Country | | | |
|---|---|---|---|
| Government | | | |

### Analyzing Visuals

7. **Examine** the photograph on page 722 and then locate Amritsar on the map. How does Amritsar's location support the statement that Sikhism has been influenced by both Hinduism and Islam?

### Writing About History

8. **Expository Writing** Write an essay comparing political, economic, and cultural developments in India and Pakistan from World War II to the present. **CA 10WA2.3**

# Japan and the Pacific

## Guide to Reading

### Section Preview
Since 1945, Japan and the four "Asian tigers" have become economic power-houses, while Australia and New Zealand remain linked culturally to Europe.

**Main Idea**
- After World War II, Allied forces occupied Japan and helped to lay the groundwork for postwar Japanese society. (p. 727)
- By the end of the twentieth century, Japan was the world's second greatest industrial power. (p. 727)
- Four other Asian nations, known as the "Asian tigers," have become successful industrial societies. (p. 730)

- Australia and New Zealand identify with Europe culturally and politically but have drawn closer to their Asian neighbors in recent years. (p. 733)

### Content Vocabulary
occupied, state capitalism

### Academic Vocabulary
subsidize, derive

### People to Identify
Douglas MacArthur, Kim Il Sung, Syngman Rhee

### Places to Locate
Taipei, Singapore, Hong Kong

### Reading Objectives
1. Discuss the important political, economic, and social changes that have occurred in Japan since 1945.
2. List the accomplishments of the "Asian tigers."

### Reading Strategy
**Categorizing Information** Use a table like the one below to list the key areas of industrial development in South Korea, Taiwan, and Singapore.

| South Korea | Taiwan | Singapore |
|---|---|---|
|  |  |  |
|  |  |  |
|  |  |  |

### Preview of Events

| ♦1940 | ♦1950 | ♦1960 | ♦1970 | ♦1980 | ♦1990 | ♦2000 |
|---|---|---|---|---|---|---|

**1947**
Japan adopts new constitution

**1951**
A peace treaty restores Japanese independence

**1963**
General Chung Hee Park is elected president of South Korea

**1997**
Great Britain returns control of Hong Kong to mainland China

## California Standards in This Section

*Reading this section will help you master these California History–Social Science standards.*

**10.9:** Students analyze the international developments in the post-World War II world.

**10.9.1:** Compare the economic and military power shifts caused by the war, including the Yalta Pact, the development of nuclear weapons, Soviet control over Eastern European nations, and the economic recoveries of Germany and Japan.

**10.11:** Students analyze the integration of countries into the world economy and the information, technological, and communications revolutions (e.g., television, satellites, computers).

# The Allied Occupation

**Main Idea** After World War II, Allied forces occupied Japan and helped to lay the groundwork for postwar Japanese society.

**Reading Connection** Do you follow the news about efforts to create a new government in Iraq since Saddam Hussein was defeated? Read to learn what happened in Japan at the end of World War II.

From 1945 to 1952, Japan was an **occupied** country—it was held and controlled by Allied military forces. An Allied administration led by U.S. general **Douglas MacArthur** governed. It had three main tasks: to destroy Japan's war machine, to try Japanese officials charged with war crimes, and to lay the foundations for a new Japanese society.

## Voices from the Past

After World War II, many Japanese women began to abandon old roles. In a 1995 book, Kumiko Fujimura-Fanselow reported on this trend:

❝A quick glance at educational statistics reveals a higher percentage of female as compared to male high school graduates entering colleges and universities. The overwhelming majority of female college and university graduates, over 80 percent, are taking up employment and doing so in a wider range of fields than in the past. Better education and the availability of more job opportunities have increasingly made it possible for women to look upon marriage as an option rather than a prescribed lifestyle. . . . A dramatic development has been the advancement by married women, including those with children, into the labor force.❞

Social customs, such as the attitudes toward women's roles, take a long time to change. The basis for change, however, began with the Allied government of Japan. Under MacArthur, Japanese society was remodeled along Western lines. A new constitution adopted in 1947 renounced war as a national policy. Japan agreed to maintain armed forces at levels sufficient only for self-defense. The constitution also established a more democratic system. The constitution reduced the power of the emperor, who was forced to announce that he was not divine. It also guaranteed basic civil and political rights and gave women the right to vote.

Finally, a peace treaty restoring Japanese independence was signed on September 8, 1951, by the United States and other former World War II allies. The Soviet Union was not included—although it had been a World War II ally, it was now at odds with the West in the Cold War. On the same day, Japan and the United States signed a defensive alliance that allowed the United States to maintain military bases in Japan. This arrangement gave the United States a military presence in Asia. At the same time, since the size of the Japanese military was limited by the peace treaty, the presence of American troops provided Japan with additional national security.

✓**Reading Check** **Identifying** What were the main tasks MacArthur had in Japan after the war?

# The Japanese Miracle

**Main Idea** By the end of the twentieth century, Japan was the world's second greatest industrial power.

**Reading Connection** Remember reading about German economic progress after World War II? Read to understand how Japan made dramatic economic progress in this same period.

In August 1945, Japan was in ruins and its land was occupied by a foreign army. A mere 50 years later, it was the second greatest industrial power in the world. This transformation has been described as the "Japanese miracle." How did the miracle occur? The causes were not only economic, but also political and social.

**Politics and Government** Japan's new constitution was modeled on the U.S. Constitution. It embodied the principles of universal suffrage and a balance of

▼ *Japanese woman at work in a Toyota factory*

## Foundations of Postwar Japan

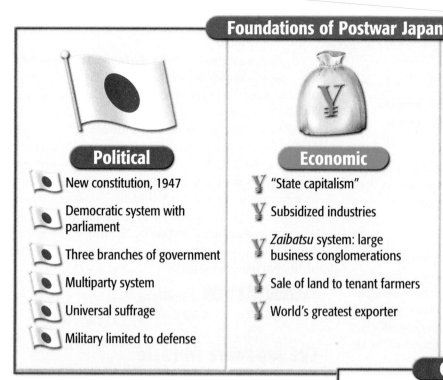

### Political

- New constitution, 1947
- Democratic system with parliament
- Three branches of government
- Multiparty system
- Universal suffrage
- Military limited to defense

### Economic

- "State capitalism"
- Subsidized industries
- *Zaibatsu* system: large business conglomerations
- Sale of land to tenant farmers
- World's greatest exporter

### Social

- Reduction in emperor's power
- Removal of references to patriotism from educational system
- Guaranteed human rights
- Increased women's rights
- Maintenance of traditional values and a strong work ethic

### Chart *Skills*

After 1945, Japan's society, government, and economy were modernized.

1. **Compare and Contrast** Pick another country discussed in this chapter and compare its economy to that of postwar Japan.

power among the executive, legislative, and judicial branches of government. These principles have held firm. Japan today is a stable democratic society.

At the same time, the current Japanese political system retains some of Japan's nineteenth-century features of the Meiji period. One example can be seen in how political power is distributed. Japan has a multiparty system with two major parties—the Liberal Democrats and the Socialists. In practice, however, the Liberal Democrats have dominated the government. At one point, they remained in office for 30 years. During this period decisions on key issues, such as who should become prime minister, were decided by a small group within the party.

A dramatic change did occur in 1993 when the Liberal Democrats were defeated on charges of government corruption. Mirohiro Hosokawa was elected prime minister and promised to clean up politics.

*Junichiro Koizumi*

Today, the central government plays an active role in the economy. It establishes price and wage policies and **subsidizes** vital industries. This government role in the economy is widely accepted in Japan. In fact, many Western observers often point to the government's role to explain why Japanese industry is so efficient and why Japan has become an industrial giant. The term often used to describe Japan's economic system is **state capitalism.**

Japan faces some problems in its political leadership. Two recent prime ministers have been forced to resign over improper financial dealings with business associates. Unemployment and economic slumps also plagued Japan throughout the 1990s.

The current prime minister, Junichiro Koizumi, is a member of Japan's most conservative party, the Liberal Democrats (LP). Koizumi was elected in 2001 because he was from the LP's reform wing. His maverick image, outspoken style, and promises of reform made him wildly popular. Since 2003, people have been less enthusiastic, however, because Koizumi has not taken dramatic action and even fired a reform minister in the cabinet. Koizumi has worked to address the huge government debt and Japan's ailing banking system. So far results have been modest. Some observers feel the economic recovery will be a long process.

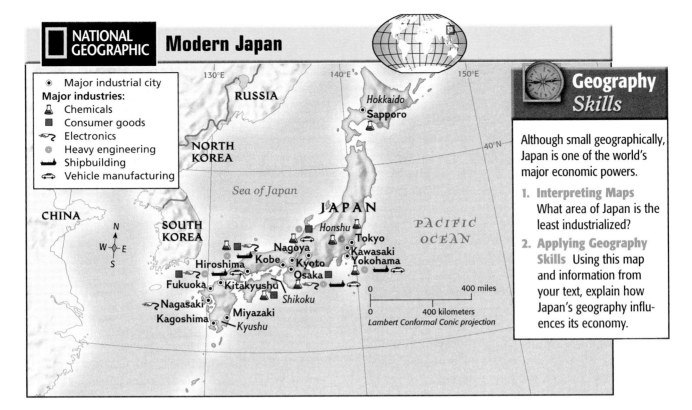

Major industrial city
**Major industries:**
🧪 Chemicals
⬛ Consumer goods
〜? Electronics
⦿ Heavy engineering
🚢 Shipbuilding
🚗 Vehicle manufacturing

130°E    140°E    150°E

RUSSIA

Hokkaido
● Sapporo

NORTH
KOREA

40°N

Sea of Japan

JAPAN

CHINA

SOUTH
KOREA

N
W   E
S

Honshu

Nagoya

Hiroshima   Kobe   Kyoto

Fukuoka   Kitakyushu   Osaka

Nagasaki

Kagoshima   Miyazaki

Kyushu

Shikoku

● Tokyo
● Kawasaki
Yokohama

PACIFIC
OCEAN

0        400 miles

0    400 kilometers
Lambert Conformal Conic projection

### Geography Skills

Although small geographically, Japan is one of the world's major economic powers.

1. **Interpreting Maps** What area of Japan is the least industrialized?

2. **Applying Geography Skills** Using this map and information from your text, explain how Japan's geography influences its economy.

**The Economy** During their occupation of Japan, Allied officials had planned to dismantle the large business conglomerations known as the *zaibatsu*. With the rise of the Cold War, however, the policy was scaled back. Only the 19 largest companies were affected. In addition, the new policy did not keep Japanese companies from forming loose ties with each other, which basically gave rise to another *zaibatsu* system, similar to a monopoly.

The occupation administration had more success with its land-reform program. Half of the population lived on farms, and half of all farmers were tenants of large landowners. Under the program, lands were sold on easy credit terms to tenants. This reform program created a strong class of independent farmers.

At the end of the Allied occupation in 1952, the Japanese gross national product was one-third that of Great Britain or France. Today, it is larger than both put together and well over half that of the United States. Japan is one of the largest exporting nations in the world and a leading producer of cars and consumer electronics. Its per capita income equals or surpasses that of most Western nations.

What explains the Japanese success? Some analysts point to cultural factors. The Japanese are group-oriented and believe strongly in cooperation with other members of the community. Hardworking and frugal, they are more inclined to save than to buy. This boosts the savings rate and labor productivity. The labor force is highly skilled. Japanese people also share common values and respond in similar ways to the challenges of the modern world.

Other analysts have cited more practical reasons for the Japanese success. For example, because its industries were destroyed in World War II, Japan was forced to build entirely new, modern factories. Japanese workers also spend a substantially longer period of time at their jobs than do workers in most other advanced societies. Corporations reward innovation and maintain good management-labor relations. Finally, some experts contend Japan has an advantage because it uses unfair trade practices—that it dumps goods at prices below cost to break into a foreign market and restricts imports from other countries.

**Social Changes** During the occupation, Allied planners wanted to eliminate the aggressiveness that characterized Japanese behavior before and during the war. They designed a new educational system, removing all references to patriotism and loyalty to the emperor. It also stressed individualism.

Efforts to remake Japanese behavior through laws were only partly successful. Many of the distinctive characteristics of traditional Japanese society have persisted into the present day, although in altered form. Emphasis on the work ethic, for example, remains strong. The tradition of hard work is stressed in the educational system.

Women's roles are another example of the difficulty of social change. After the war, women gained the vote and were encouraged to enter politics, yet the subordinate role of women in society has not been entirely eliminated. Women are now legally protected against discrimination in employment, yet very few have reached senior levels in business, education, or politics. Japan has had no female prime ministers, although in recent years about 10 percent of the Diet, or parliament, have been women. Women now make up more than 40 percent of the workforce, but most are in retail or service jobs. Their average salary is only about 60 percent that of men. (In the United States, women make on average about 77 percent of the average salary of men.)

**Culture** After the Japanese defeat in World War II, many of the writers who had been active before the war resurfaced. Their works now were much more sober and sad. This "lost generation" described its anguish and piercing despair. Several writers committed suicide. For them, defeat was made worse by fear that their Japanese culture would be Americanized.

Since the 1970s, increasing wealth and a high literacy rate have led to a massive outpouring of books. Already in 1975, Japanese authors were producing twice as many fiction titles as American authors. This trend continued into the 1990s.

Much of this new literature deals with the common concerns of all wealthy industrialized nations. Contemporary Japanese authors, raised in the crowded cities of postwar Japan, soaked up movies, television, and rock music. These writers speak the universal language of today's world.

Haruki Murakami is one of Japan's most popular authors. He discarded the somber style of the earlier postwar period to speak the contemporary language. *A Wild Sheep Chase*, published in 1982, is an excellent example of his gripping, yet humorous, writing.

✓ **Reading Check** **Contrasting** How does the Japanese system of state capitalism differ from the capitalist system in the United States?

## The "Asian Tigers"

**Main Idea** Four other Asian nations, known as the "Asian tigers," have become successful industrial societies.

**Reading Connection** Do you own clothing or products from "Asian tiger" countries? Read to learn how their economic success depends largely on their exports to the United States.

A number of Asian nations have imitated Japan in creating successful industrial societies. Sometimes called the "Asian tigers," they are South Korea, Taiwan, Singapore, and Hong Kong. Along with Japan, they have become economic powerhouses.

# CONNECTIONS Around The World

## Cities and Cars

Since the beginning of the Industrial Revolution in the nineteenth century, the growth of industrialization has been accompanied by the growth of cities. In both industrialized and developing countries, congested and polluted cities have become a way of life. In recent years, as more people have been able to buy cars, traffic jams have also become a regular feature.

In São Paulo, Brazil, for example, traffic jams in which nobody moves last for hours. There are 4.5 million cars in São Paulo, twice the number in New York City, although both cities have about the same population (16 million people). Workers in auto factories in Brazil work around the clock to meet the demand for cars.

*Traffic in Thailand*

The same situation is evident in other cities around the world. In Cairo, a city of 10.6 million people, pollution from stalled traffic erodes the surface of the Sphinx outside the city. In Bangkok, the capital city of Thailand, it can take six hours to reach the airport.

A major cause of traffic congestion is lack of roads. As more and more poor people have fled the countryside for the city, many cities have tripled in population in just 20 years. At the same time, few new roads have been built.

## Comparing Cultures

Using outside sources, research traffic problems in three cities in different parts of the world (for example, Los Angeles, Hong Kong, and Paris). How are the traffic problems in these cities similar, and how are they different? What solutions are people developing to solve traffic problems in these particular cities?

▲ *North Korea's Kim Jong Il (left) and South Korea's Kim Dae-jung met in June 2000—the first time leaders of these countries did so in more than 50 years.*

**South Korea** In 1953, the Korean Peninsula was exhausted from three years of bitter war. Two heavily armed countries now faced each other across the 38th parallel. North of this line was the People's Republic of Korea (North Korea), under the dictatorial rule of the Communist leader **Kim Il Sung.** To the south was the Republic of Korea (South Korea), under the dictatorial president **Syngman Rhee.**

After several years of harsh rule and government corruption in South Korea, demonstrations broke out in the spring of 1960 in Seoul, the capital. President Rhee was forced to retire. The next year, a coup d'etat put General Chung Hee Park in power. Two years later, Park was elected president and began to strengthen the South Korean economy with land reform and the promotion of free-market policies.

South Korea gradually emerged as a major industrial power in the region. The key areas for industrial development were chemicals, textiles, and shipbuilding. By the 1980s, South Korea was moving into automobile production. The largest Korean corporations are Samsung, Daewoo, and Hyundai. Today South Korea enjoys a per capita income that is roughly 18 times that of North Korea.

Like many other countries in the region, South Korea was slow to develop democratic principles. Park ruled by autocratic means and suppressed protest. Opposition to his military rule began to develop, however, with the growth of the middle class.

Often it was students and city dwellers who demonstrated against Park's harsh policies. Democracy finally came in the 1990s. Elections held during an economic crisis in 1997 brought the reformer Kim Dae-jung to the presidency.

**Taiwan: The Other China** After they were defeated by the Communists and forced to retreat to Taiwan, Chiang Kai-shek and his followers established a capital at **Taipei.** The government continued to call itself the Republic of China, although it was dwarfed by Communist China. Chiang Kai-shek's government maintained that it was the legitimate government of all the Chinese people and would eventually return in triumph to the mainland. Similarly, Communist leaders in Beijing claimed that their government represented all of China, including Taiwan.

Protection by American military forces allowed the Taiwanese government to concentrate on economic growth without worrying about a Communist invasion. Making good use of foreign aid and the efforts of its own energetic people, the Republic of China built a modern industrialized society.

▲ *Hong Kong has one of the most vibrant economies in the world. Since Hong Kong was returned to China in 1997, its economy has been more integrated with that nation's.*

A land-reform program, which put farmland in the hands of peasants, doubled food production in Taiwan. With government help, local manufacturing and commerce expanded. During the 1960s and 1970s, industrial growth averaged well over 10 percent a year. Taiwan is now one of the world's largest producers of computer technology. By 2000, over three-fourths of the population lived in urban areas.

Prosperity did not at first lead to democracy. Under Chiang Kai-shek, the government ruled by emergency decree and refused to allow new political parties to form. After Chiang died in 1975, the Republic of China began to evolve toward representative government. By 2000, free elections gave opposition parties control of the presidency and the legislature.

What will happen to Taiwan in the future? Will it become an independent state, or will it be united with mainland China? The United States has taken the position that the people of Taiwan should be able to determine their future and that any final decision must be made through peaceful means. Meanwhile, the People's Republic of China on the mainland remains committed to eventual unification.

### Singapore and Hong Kong

**Singapore,** once a British colony and briefly a part of the state of Malaysia, is now an independent state.

Under the leadership of Prime Minister Lee Kuan Yew (kwahn yoo), Singapore developed an industrial economy based on shipbuilding, oil refineries, and electronics. Its port is one of the busiest in the world. Singapore's leaders are committed to making it the financial and high-tech center of Southeast Asia. Its citizens enjoy one of the highest standards of living in the world.

Singapore's authoritarian system has created a stable environment for economic growth. The prime minister once stated that Western democracy was not suitable for Singapore, but its citizens are beginning to demand more political freedoms.

Like Singapore, **Hong Kong** became an industrial powerhouse with standards of living well above those of other urban areas in the region. For over 150 years, Hong Kong was under British rule. In 1997, Great Britain finally returned control of Hong Kong to mainland China. China, in turn, promised that, for the next 50 years, the people of Hong Kong would live under a capitalist system and be self-governing. The Chinese government refers to this as "one country, two systems." The shape of Hong Kong's future remains uncertain.

✔ **Reading Check** **Analyzing** What is the relationship between Taiwan and China?

# Australia and New Zealand

**Main Idea** Australia and New Zealand identify with Europe culturally and politically but have drawn closer to their Asian neighbors in recent years.

**Reading Connection** What history helps explain the economic ties between the United States and Europe? Read about the economic ties of this region.

In the past, both Australia and New Zealand, located to the south and east of Asia, have identified with Europe, not with Asia. Their political institutions, economies, and values are **derived** from European models. Both are members of the British Commonwealth. Both are also part of the United States–led ANZUS defensive alliance (Australia, New Zealand, the United States).

In recent years, new trends have drawn the two nations closer to Asia. First, Asian immigration has increased rapidly—more than half of all immigrants to Australia come from East Asia, and it is estimated that 13 percent of New Zealand's population will be Asian by 2021. Second, trade relations with Asia are increasing rapidly and this, too, contributes to closer ties. About 60 percent of Australia's export markets today are in East Asia. New Zealand is also expanding its trade with Asia.

Whether these two nations will become an integral part of the Asia-Pacific region is not certain. Most citizens still have European origins, and cultural differences often hinder understanding.

**Reading Check** **Examining** How have Australia and New Zealand been drawn closer to their Asian neighbors?

▲ *A Japanese garden in New South Wales, Australia*

**HISTORY** **Online** **Study Central**

For help with the concepts in this section of *Glencoe World History–Modern Times,* go to wh.mt.glencoe.com and click on **Study Central.**

# SECTION 3 ASSESSMENT

## Checking for Understanding

1. **Vocabulary** Define: occupied, subsidize, state capitalism, derive.

2. **People** Identify: Douglas MacArthur, Kim Il Sung, Syngman Rhee.

3. **Places** Locate: Taipei, Singapore, Hong Kong.

### Reviewing Big Ideas

4. **Explain** the impact of Japan's land-reform program.

## Critical Thinking

5. **Predicting Consequences** What further impact do you think the return of Hong Kong to China will have?

6. **Organizing Information** Use a diagram like this to show factors contributing to Japan's economic success.

Japan's Economic Success

## Analyzing Visuals

7. **Examine** the photo on page 731. How would you describe its purpose? Do you think the leaders' warmth signals the end of their diplomatic differences?

### Writing About History

8. **Informative Writing** Research Japan and the "Asian tigers" further and analyze their sources of growth. Explain in an essay why these states have been so successful. **CA** 10WA2.3

# PRIMARY SOURCES
## Eyewitness to History

*These three selections reflect aspects of modern Japanese society in government, education, and gender relations.*

## SOURCE 1: Preamble to the Japanese Constitution

*The Preamble to the Japanese Constitution of 1946 was written after Japan's defeat in World War II.*

We, the Japanese people, acting through our duly elected representatives in the National **Diet,**[1] determined that we shall secure for ourselves and our **posterity**[2] the fruits of peaceful cooperation with all nations and the blessings of liberty throughout this land, and resolved that never again shall we be visited with the horrors of war through the action of government, do proclaim the sovereignty of the people's will and do ordain and establish this Constitution, founded upon the universal principle that government is a sacred trust the authority for which is derived from the people, the powers of which are exercised by the representatives of the people, and the benefits of which are enjoyed by the people; and we reject and revoke all constitutions, laws, ordinances, and rescripts in conflict herewith.

Desiring peace for all time and fully conscious of the high ideals controlling human relationship now stirring in mankind, we have determined to rely for our security and survival upon the justice and good faith of the peace-loving peoples of the world. We desire to occupy an honored place in an international society designed and dedicated to the preservation of peace, and the banishment of tyranny and slavery, oppression and intolerance, for all time from the earth. We recognize and acknowledge that all people have the right to live in peace, free from fear and want.

We hold that no people is responsible to itself alone, but that laws of political morality are universal; and that obedience to such law is incumbent upon all peoples who would sustain their own sovereignty and justify their sovereign relationship with other peoples.

To these high principles and purposes we, the Japanese people, pledge our national honor, determined will and full resources.

---

[1] **Diet:** the Japanese parliament
[2] **posterity:** future generations

*Japanese schoolchildren in their uniforms*

## SOURCE 2: School Regulations in Japan

*Japanese children are exposed to a regimented environment. The following are examples of rules for middle school systems in various parts of Japan.*

1. Boys' hair should not touch the eyebrows, the ears, or the top of the collar.
2. No one should have a permanent wave, or dye his or her hair. Girls should not wear ribbons or accessories in their hair. Hair dryers should not be used. . . .
3. Keep your uniform clean and pressed at all times. Girls' middy blouses should have two buttons on the back collar. Boys' pant cuffs should be of the prescribed width. No more than 12 eyelets should be on shoes.

4. Wear your school badge at all times. It should be positioned exactly.
5. Going to school in the morning, wear your book bag strap on the right shoulder; in the afternoon on the way home, wear it on the left shoulder.
6. When you raise your hand to be called on, your arm should extend forward and up at the angle prescribed in your handbook.
7. Your own route to and from school is marked in your student rule handbook; carefully observe which side of each street you are to use on the way to and from school.
8. After school you are to go directly home, unless your parent has written a note permitting you to go to another location. Permission will not be granted by the school unless this other location is a suitable one. You must not go to coffee shops.
9. Before and after school, no matter where you are, you represent our school, so you should behave in ways we all can be proud of.

## SOURCE 3: Women's Rights in Japan

*In 1982, Higuchi Keiko captured new trends for Japanese women in "Japanese Women in Transition."*

"The Age of Women"—so ran the catch-phrase adorning a Japanese newspaper advertisement on New Year's Day 1979, the eve of the 80s. The ad went on in part to say: "Dazzling—simply dazzling, the women of today . . . Expressing themselves freely, without fear or hesitation, these are women who know the art of enjoying life to the full. . . . Today's women are off the sidelines to stay."

The slogan notwithstanding, this message is probably best understood as a gift of flattery from male salesmen to female buyers. . . . In any case, the emergence of language such as this in newspaper advertising is surely a sign of change in the situation of Japanese women.

The **consciousness**[3] of Japanese women is now in a state of transition. Their attitude toward the idea that

> ---
> [3]**consciousness:** awareness, especially of a social or political cause

"men should work outside the home, women inside" has changed greatly in the last 10 years . . . [but] acceptance of sex-differentiated work roles is still deep-rooted in Japan. . . .

Women in Japan are stepping out of the house in ever-swelling numbers. Yet men persist in clinging to the notion that "women's work is in the home. . . ." It appears inevitable, therefore, that discord will arise between the sexes. . . .

The husband expects his wife to look after the home, and in the home he seeks a place of recreation and relaxation in which to **garner**[4] strength for the coming day's work. This is the view of the wife's role, and of the function of the home, given often in Japanese textbooks of the lower, compulsory levels of school. . . . The wife, however, has begun to entertain misgivings about an existence spent for the most part waiting passively at home for her husband's return. . . .

The new women's liberation movement which spread to Japan in the early 70s brought pressure for change in the lives of both men and women. . . . At the same time, the extremely rapid aging of Japanese society . . . is forcing upon us, willy-nilly, a reevaluation of relationships between the sexes, married and unmarried alike.

> ---
> [4]**garner:** gather

## DBQ Document-Based Questions

### Historical Analysis  CA HR 2, HI 3

**Source 1:** What phrases in the first excerpt refer to the Japanese experience in World War II?

**Source 2:** What kinds of words in the second excerpt show how careful students must be in dress?

**Source 3:** How does the author of the third excerpt view the new trends in women's lives?

### Comparing and Contrasting Sources

1. Comparing Source 1 and Source 2, which one is sensitive to the world community, and which one to the Japanese community?
2. Analyzing Source 2 and Source 3, how would you compare the position of women and of children in traditional Japanese society?

Standards 10.9, 10.9.1, 10.9.3, 10.9.4, 10.10, 10.10.1, 10.10.2, 10.10.3, 10.11

## Chapter Summary

Since 1945, Asia and the Pacific region have seen many changes, as shown below.

### Change

*Out of defeat comes a new political and economic system.*
- After gaining independence, Japan becomes an economic powerhouse.
- Imitating Japan, other Asian nations also develop strong economies.

### Revolution

*Communists assume power and introduce socialist methods.*
- In China, Mao Zedong initiates programs like the Great Leap Forward and the Great Proletarian Cultural Revolution. After Mao, Deng Xiaoping institutes the Four Modernizations.

### Regionalism

*Decades of rivalry and suspicion cause divisions.*
- Tensions between Communist North Korea and non-Communist South Korea lead to war.
- China resists Taiwanese independence.

### Conflict

*Nationalism and Cold War competition lead to war.*
- The United States enters the war in Vietnam.
- The Khmer Rouge devastates Cambodia.

### Diversity

*Religious and ethnic rivalries hinder unity and lead to violence.*
- Religious and ethnic differences produce conflict between Hindus and Muslims in India and Pakistan.

### Cultural Diffusion

*Political and economic changes link Asian countries to the world.*
- Democracy develops in the Philippines.
- Chinese students demand democratic reforms.
- Increased immigration and trade draw Australia and New Zealand closer to their Asian neighbors.

## Reviewing Content Vocabulary

*On a sheet of paper, use each of these terms in a sentence.*

1. commune
2. permanent revolution
3. one-child policy
4. outsourcing
5. stalemate
6. discrimination
7. occupied
8. state capitalism

## Reviewing Academic Vocabulary

*On a sheet of paper, use each of these terms in a sentence that reflects the term's meaning in the chapter.*

9. release
10. injure
11. involvement
12. gender
13. subsidize
14. derive

## Reviewing the Main Ideas

### Section 1

15. What help did China require to improve its economy after the Cultural Revolution?

16. What events took place in Tiananmen Square in 1989?

### Section 2

17. What policy did the Khmer Rouge follow toward the people they regarded as enemies after they gained control of Cambodia?

18. Who was Indira Gandhi?

### Section 3

19. How did promises of military protection from the United States help Taiwan develop its economy?

20. What nations are called the "Asian tigers" and why?

## Critical Thinking

21. **Making Predictions** Analyze the conditions in India that contributed to the assassinations of political leaders. Do you believe it is possible for India to maintain a stable democratic government?

22. **Drawing Conclusions** Evaluate the impact Japan's recovery has had on global affairs since World War II.

23. **Analyzing** What is the conflict regarding Taiwan's independence? How could this conflict best be resolved?

24. **Reading Skill** **Determining Importance** Write out the headings and first sentences of each paragraph from page 730 to page 732. Then use them in order to write a short summary paragraph of what is most important in this section.

## Writing About History

25. **Historical Analysis** **Validating Arguments** Select a historical interpretation from this chapter. Write a one-page analysis on how the argument is validated in the text. Could anything have been added to make this argument stronger? **CA HR 1**

26. *Big Idea* Compare North Korea and South Korea. In what ways are they similar? In what ways are they different? Do supplementary research online or at the library to learn about their cultures and histories. **CA 10WS1.3**

**DBQ** **Document-Based Questions**

**Analyzing Sources** Read the following excerpt from a 1992 article, "Women in Japanese Society: Their Changing Roles":

> ❝Much of the work which women are involved in is part time. Many women work in the "kagyo"— household business. A kagyo can range from sewing or typing to running a farm or a fishing enterprise. By engaging in a kagyo a wife can attempt to balance the responsibilities of being a Japanese wife with the desire or need to work. . . . A kagyo also offers more opportunity for a woman. In corporate Japan a woman must compete with overt sex discrimination, and a clique network that is almost impossible to break. A Japanese wife who started her own kagyo said: 'The odds are so high against a woman succeeding in a a Japanese company that women like me are much better off working on their own. . . .'❞

27. What does this passage suggest about why women work in the kagyo?

28. What does the article suggest about women's progress since World War II?

29. Read the last quotation in the excerpt. Based on your knowledge of the civil rights and women's rights movements in the United States, how do you assess her strategy for addressing discrimination in the workplace?

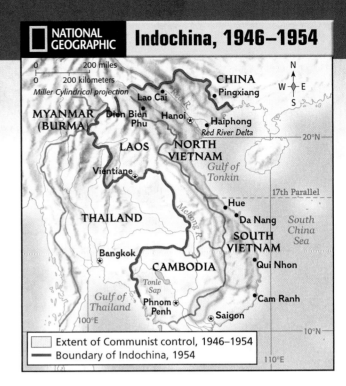

**NATIONAL GEOGRAPHIC** **Indochina, 1946–1954**

- Extent of Communist control, 1946–1954
- Boundary of Indochina, 1954

## Analyzing Maps and Charts

Study the map above to answer the following questions.

30. Approximately how much of Vietnam was controlled by the Communists between 1946 and 1954?

31. Which countries separate North and South Vietnam from Thailand?

32. What river runs from China to the Gulf of Tonkin?

 **Standards Practice**

**Directions: Choose the best answer to the following question.**

33. Between 1966 and 1976, the destruction of many temples, the seizure of many books, and the imprisonment of some artists and intellectuals were closely related to which movement?

   **A** China's Cultural Revolution

   **B** conservatism

   **C** women's rights movement

   **D** humanism

**CA Standard 10.10.3** Discuss the important trends in the regions today and whether they appear to serve the cause of individual freedom and democracy.

# CHAPTER 17

# Challenges and Hopes for the Future

### ❧ *The Big Ideas* ❧

### SECTION 1: The Challenges of Our World

**New technologies can revolutionize the way people live, work, interact, and govern.**
Today's societies face many political and social challenges, especially the challenge of how to
balance the costs and benefits of the technological revolution.

### SECTION 2: Global Visions

**Moral and ethical principles influence the development of political thought.** The
global economy and new global threats have stimulated individuals and international organizations to work on global problems.

 ***World History—Modern Times Video*** *The Chapter 17 video,*
*"In the 21st Century," explores various issues that the world is facing today.*

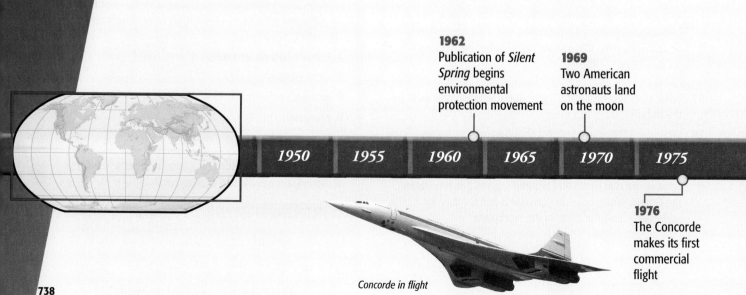

**1962**
Publication of *Silent
Spring* begins
environmental
protection movement

**1969**
Two American
astronauts land
on the moon

| 1950 | 1955 | 1960 | 1965 | 1970 | 1975 |

**1976**
The Concorde
makes its first
commercial
flight

*Concorde in flight*

The International Space Station, shown here in 2000, combines the scientific and technological resources of 16 nations.

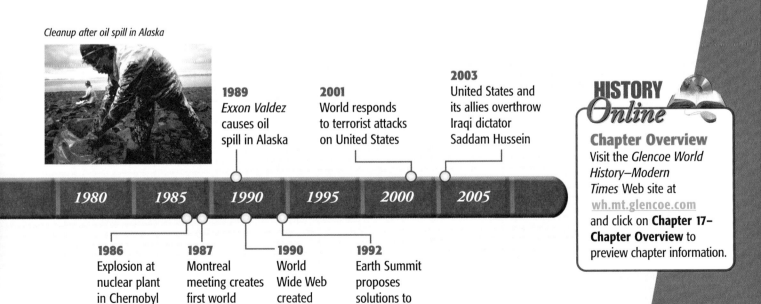

Cleanup after oil spill in Alaska

**1989**
*Exxon Valdez*
causes oil
spill in Alaska

**2001**
World responds
to terrorist attacks
on United States

**2003**
United States and
its allies overthrow
Iraqi dictator
Saddam Hussein

1980   1985   1990   1995   2000   2005

**1986**
Explosion at
nuclear plant
in Chernobyl
releases deadly
radiation

**1987**
Montreal
meeting creates
first world
environmental
pact

**1990**
World
Wide Web
created

**1992**
Earth Summit
proposes
solutions to
environmental
challenges

**HISTORY**
*Online*

**Chapter Overview**
Visit the *Glencoe World
History–Modern
Times* Web site at
wh.mt.glencoe.com
and click on **Chapter 17–
Chapter Overview** to
preview chapter information.

# Preparing to Read Chapter 17

## Reading Skill    Inferring

When readers come to conclusions that aren't written by the author, but are based on facts presented by the author, they are making inferences. It is the job of readers of history to analyze facts and quotations presented to them before reaching conclusions. In a textbook, an author usually doesn't have the space or time to explain the significance of every phrase. It is the reader's job to analyze facts and quotations based on general information and experience.

Now that you've come to the last chapter in the textbook, you can infer a great deal based on the knowledge you've gained. You can also apply information you've learned from other classes, such as government, science, or language courses, to make inferences about the state of the world and its future.

*Read the following paragraph from this chapter to practice inferring:*

### INFERRING

Based on the highlighted words in the excerpt, what can you infer about the populations of "rich nations"?

One of the features of the global economy is the wide gap between rich and poor nations. Rich nations are mainly in the Northern Hemisphere and include the United States, Canada, countries in western Europe, and Japan. They have well-organized industrial and education systems and use advanced technologies. Poor nations, often called developing countries, are mainly in the Southern Hemisphere and include many nations in Africa, Asia, and Latin America. Developing countries are mainly farming nations with little technology.

### Apply the Skill

Drawing on what you already know about various regions in the world, what can you infer about the meaning of "the wide gap between rich and poor nations"? How did they get to that point and what might their future hold?

# Historical Analysis Skill    Contextualizing Events

**Historical Interpretation: Standard HI 3** *Students interpret past events and issues within the context in which an event unfolded rather than solely in terms of present-day norms and values.*

Have you ever had to explain your actions without being able to explain your circumstances, knowing that your audience's opinion would change if they knew the full story? Historians have to keep this in mind and not come to conclusions based on an isolated incident. For example, you could take the assassination of Archduke Franz Ferdinand as an isolated terrorist incident. Placed into context with Austro-Hungarian and Serbian relations, European alliances, or leaders in charge, however, historians see the bigger picture of what led to World War I.

When you contextualize events, you utilize the other history skills covered in this textbook. While analyzing a particular event you need to explore cause and effect, examine trends, and recognize bias, among other skills.

*Read the following passage from page 750 about the founding of the United Nations.*

> **The UN was founded in 1945 at the end of World War II. American president Franklin Delano Roosevelt was especially eager to create an organization to work for peace. Already at the Yalta Conference of February 1945, with the war still being fought, the "Big Three"—Roosevelt, British prime minister Winston Churchill, and Joseph Stalin of the Soviet Union—had agreed to found an international organization.**
>
> **Roosevelt died two months later, but his successor, President Harry Truman, arranged for the founding meeting to be held in San Francisco in April 1945. There the representatives of the Allied forces worked out the mission and structure of the United Nations.**

## Apply the Skill

Write a paragraph identifying the factors leading to the formation of the United Nations. Be sure to include the post–World War II context. Then share your paragraph with a partner to see if you placed the event in the same context. Because you each have a different bias, what you identify might vary.

# A Story That Matters

*Rescue workers search for survivors in the ruins of the World Trade Center.*

## A Time for Heroes

On September 11, 2001, international terrorists hijacked four commercial airplanes, two of which were used to destroy the twin towers of the World Trade Center in New York City. Thousands of people died in the attack when first one tower, and then the other, collapsed. Many of those who died were firefighters, police officers, and other rescue workers who rushed into the buildings to help people to safety.

In the days following the attack, countless tales of unimaginable bravery emerged. Two office workers carried a disabled woman down 68 floors to safety. Peter Ganci, a 33-year veteran of the New York City Fire Department, survived the collapse of the first tower but died trying to evacuate people from the second tower. Father Mychal Judge, the Fire Department chaplain, removed his helmet to give last rites to a dying firefighter but died himself when he was hit by debris. One firefighter, as he climbed toward the flames, stopped to give a fleeing woman a bottle of water. She escaped, but he did not.

George Howard, a Port Authority officer, raced to help people, even though it was his day off, and died in the effort. In an address to the American nation, President George W. Bush said that he would carry Howard's badge as a reminder of the horrors of terrorism, for "Freedom and fear are at war. The advance of human freedom, the great achievement of our time and the great hope of every time, now depends on us. . . . We will not falter and we will not fail."

### Why It Matters

The destruction of the World Trade Center was not an attack on the United States alone. People from over 80 countries were killed in what the United Nations condemned as a "crime against humanity." More and more, people are coming to understand that destructive forces unleashed in one part of the world soon affect the entire world. As British prime minister Tony Blair said, "We are realizing how fragile are our frontiers in the face of the world's new challenges. Today, conflicts rarely stay within national boundaries." Terrorism, worldwide hunger, nuclear proliferation, global warming—these issues make us aware of the global nature of contemporary problems. Increasingly, the world's nations must unite to create lasting solutions.

**History and You** What contemporary global problem concerns you the most? Write an essay explaining what the world's nations should do, together, to solve this problem.

# The Challenges of Our World

## Section Preview

Today's societies face many political and social challenges, especially the challenge of how to balance the costs and benefits of the technological revolution.

**Main Idea**

- Economic development and population growth pose a challenge to the world's environment. (p. 744)
- The benefits of the technological revolution must be balanced against its costs. (p. 746)
- Developing nations face continuing problems of poverty, population growth, and ethnic conflict. (p. 747)

## Content Vocabulary

ecology, deforestation, ozone layer, greenhouse effect, acid rain, sustainable development, biowarfare, bioterrorism

## Academic Vocabulary

nuclear, mental

## People and Events to Identify

Rachel Carson, Kyoto Protocol, Neil Armstrong, World Trade Organization

## Places to Locate

Bhopal, Chernobyl

## Reading Objective

1. Explain the challenges facing the contemporary world.
2. Describe the benefits and costs of the technological revolution.

## Reading Strategy

**Cause and Effect** Complete a table like the one below as you read the chapter.

| Concern | Cause | Effect |
|---|---|---|
| Deforestation | | |
| Loss of ozone layer | | |
| Greenhouse effect | | |
| Acid rain | | |
| Weapons | | |
| Hunger | | |

### Preview of Events

◆1980     ◆1985     ◆1990     ◆1995     ◆2000

**1984**
Toxic fumes kill 3,800 people in Bhopal, India

**1989**
Oil spill from tanker in Alaska devastates environment

**1997**
Indonesian wildfires destroy rain forests and endanger species

**2003**
Seven astronauts die when *Columbia* space shuttle explodes

## California Standards in This Section

*Reading this section will help you master these California History–Social Science Standards.*

**10.10.1:** Understand the challenges in the regions, including their geopolitical, cultural, military, and economic significance and the international relationships in which they are involved.

**10.10.2:** Describe the recent history of the regions, including political divisions and systems, key leaders, religious issues, natural features, resources, and population patterns.

**10.10.3:** Discuss the important trends in the regions today and whether they appear to serve the cause of individual freedom and democracy.

**10.11:** Students analyze the integration of countries into the world economy and the information, technological, and communications revolutions (e.g., television, satellites, computers).

# The Environmental Crisis

**Main Idea** Economic development and population growth pose a challenge to the world's environment.

### Reading Connection
Have you seen newly designed cars that run on alternative forms of energy? Read to learn about environmental challenges in today's world.

Most people today are aware that protecting the environment is a public policy issue—politicians campaign on it, and voters make choices on it. On a regular basis, we in advanced societies hear about the quality of the air we breathe, the water we drink, and the chemicals in the food we eat.

Such concerns are addressed by the field of science known as **ecology,** the study of the relationship between living things and their environment. The field of ecology is relatively new and emerged only after people began to be aware of the serious threats to the environment that modern economies can pose.

## Voices from the Past

The person most responsible for the modern movement to protect the environment was an American scientist, **Rachel Carson.** In 1962, her book *Silent Spring* was published. In one part of this work, Carson wrote:

> 66It is not my contention that chemical pesticides must never be used. I do contend that we have put poisons and biologically potent chemicals into the hands of persons largely or wholly ignorant of their potentials for harm. We have subjected enormous numbers of people to contact with these poisons, without their consent and often without their knowledge. . . . I contend, furthermore, that we have allowed these chemicals to be used with little or no advance investigation of their effect on soil, water, wildlife, and man himself. Future generations are unlikely to condone our lack of prudent concern for the integrity of the natural world that supports all life.99

Rachel Carson argued that the use of pesticides—chemicals sprayed on crops to kill insects—was having deadly, unforeseen results. Besides insects, birds, fish, and other wild animals were being killed by the buildup of pesticides in the environment. Also, the pesticide residue on food was harming humans.

Carson's warnings alarmed many scientists. As they conducted research and published studies, they showed that dangers to the environment have many sources.

One source is the rapid increase in world population. Many fear that Earth's resources cannot support the ever-expanding population. A specific environmental by-product of population growth is **deforestation**—the clearing of forests. Forests and jungles have been cut down to provide more farmland and firewood, removing the natural dwelling places for plants and animals. In 1997, fires in Indonesia raged out of control, destroying thousands of acres of rain forest that were home to many species. The fires, which have recurred in recent years, also caused intense smog.

Especially worrisome is the rapid destruction of tropical rain forests near Earth's equator. Although the tropical rain forests cover only 6 percent of Earth's surface, they support 50 percent of the world's species of plants and animals. The tropical rain forests are also crucial to human survival. They remove carbon dioxide from the air and return oxygen to it.

**Chemical Wastes and Disasters** Another danger to the environment is chemical waste. One concern involves chlorofluorocarbons, which are gases used in aerosol cans, refrigerators, and automobile air conditioners. Many scientists warn that the release of

▼ *Biologist and author Rachel Carson*

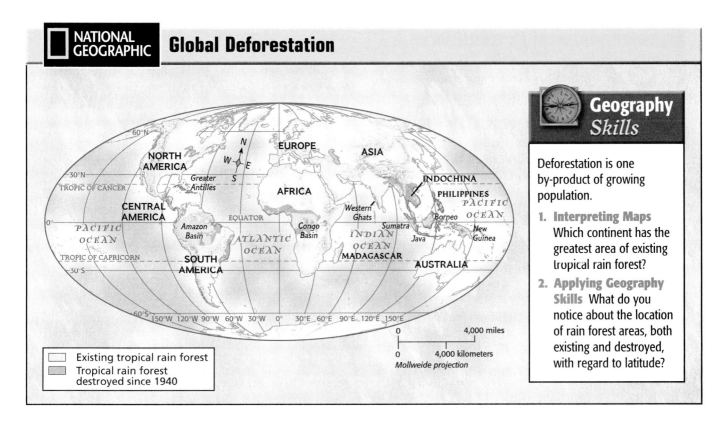

Geography Skills

Deforestation is one by-product of growing population.

1. **Interpreting Maps** Which continent has the greatest area of existing tropical rain forest?

2. **Applying Geography Skills** What do you notice about the location of rain forest areas, both existing and destroyed, with regard to latitude?

Legend:
☐ Existing tropical rain forest
▨ Tropical rain forest destroyed since 1940

0 — 4,000 miles
0 — 4,000 kilometers
*Mollweide projection*

---

chlorofluorocarbons is destroying the **ozone layer,** a thin layer of gas in the upper atmosphere that shields Earth from the Sun's ultraviolet rays.

Other scientists have proposed the existence of a **greenhouse effect,** global warming caused by the buildup of carbon dioxide in the atmosphere. Global warming could create various problems. Sea levels could rise because of melting polar ice, for example, and cause flooding of coastal areas. Yet another problem is **acid rain,** the rainfall that results when sulfur produced by factories mixes with moisture in the air. Acid rain has been held responsible for killing forests in both North America and Europe.

Major ecological disasters have also occurred during the last 20 years. In 1984, a chemical plant at **Bhopal,** India, released toxic fumes into the air, killing 3,800 people and injuring another 100,000. A **nuclear** explosion at **Chernobyl** in 1986 released radiation that killed hundreds and had long-lasting health and environmental consequences. In 1989, the oil tanker *Exxon Valdez* ran aground in Alaska. Thousands of birds were killed, fishing grounds were polluted, and the local environment was devastated.

These ecological disasters made people more aware of the need to deal with environmental problems. In 1987, representatives of 43 nations meeting in Montreal agreed to protect Earth's ozone layer by reducing the use of chlorofluorocarbons. In 1997, a conference on global warming was held in Kyoto,

Japan. To reduce emissions, more than 150 nations signed the **Kyoto Protocol.** The European Union and Japan ratified the treaty in 2002, but in 2001, President George W. Bush withdrew the United States from the agreement, arguing that the treaty was flawed.

**Sustainable Development** Economic development that does not limit the ability of future generations to meet their basic needs is known as **sustainable development.** The UN has promoted sustainable development by urging nations to work to conserve all natural resources.

One of the most basic necessities of life is water. In a 2003 report, the UN noted that one-sixth of the world's population is without water for drinking or agriculture. Women in Africa and Asia must walk nearly 4 miles (6 km) to collect water. Those who cannot get clean water often get sick with cholera, typhoid, and diarrhea. More than 5 million people die every year from the lack of water or drinking untreated water.

Many nations have reacted to environmental threats by enacting recycling and water conservation programs and by curbing the dumping of toxic materials. It is not yet clear if these measures will be enough to achieve sustainable development.

 **Reading Check** **Summarizing** What global concerns have arisen since the 1960s?

# The Technological Revolution

**Main Idea** The benefits of the technological revolution must be balanced against its costs.

**Reading Connection** Have you heard news reports about laws to limit research methods in science? Read on to learn about the medical and technological advances that raise new questions of public policy.

Since World War II, but especially since the 1970s, a stunning array of changes has created a technological revolution. Like the first and second Industrial Revolutions, this revolution, too, is having a profound effect on people's daily lives and on entire societies.

**Transportation, Communications, and Space** Modern transportation and communication systems are transforming the world community. Since the 1970s, jumbo jet airliners have moved millions of people around the world each year. The Internet—the world's largest computer network—provides quick access to enormous quantities of information. The development of the World Wide Web in the 1990s made the Internet even more accessible to people everywhere. Satellites, cable television, facsimile (fax) machines, and cellular telephones allow people to communicate with each other practically everywhere on Earth.

▼ *Astronaut Buzz Aldrin on the moon with the* **Apollo 11** *lunar module*

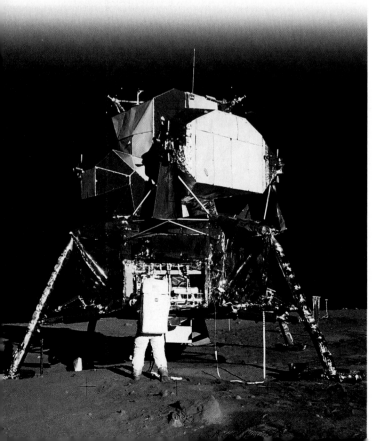

Space exploration is yet another world-changing development. In 1969, the American astronauts **Neil Armstrong** and Buzz Aldrin landed on the moon. Space probes and shuttle flights have increased scientific knowledge and contributed indirectly to practical gains in medicine, engineering, and other fields. A visible sign of continuing scientific research through the space program is the Hubble Space Telescope. Launched in 1990 by NASA (the National Aeronautics and Space Administration), the telescope orbits Earth, takes pictures of objects billions of miles away, and gathers data on the chemical makeup of matter.

The benefits have not come without great human costs. In 1986, the space shuttle *Challenger* exploded a minute or so after liftoff, killing all onboard. In 2003, seven astronauts died when the shuttle *Columbia* abruptly disintegrated over Texas in the last minutes of a 16-day mission. In both cases, Americans responded with a profound sense of grief.

**Health Care and Agriculture** In the field of health, new medicines allow doctors to treat both physical and **mental** illnesses, while new technologies, such as computer-aided imaging, let them perform "miracle" operations. Organ transplants and mechanical valves and pumps for the heart have allowed people to live longer, more productive lives.

Technological changes in the field of health have raised new concerns, however, and have led to a new field of study called bioethics, which deals with moral choices in medical research. For example, genetic engineering is a new scientific field that alters the genetic information of cells to produce new variations. Some scientists have questioned whether genetic engineering might accidentally create new strains of deadly bacteria that could not be controlled. The issues of stem-cell research and human cloning have also generated intense debate.

In agriculture, the Green Revolution was heralded as a technological solution to feeding the world's population. The Green Revolution refers to the development of new strains of rice, corn, and other grains that have greater yields. The drawbacks are that immense quantities of chemical fertilizers are needed to grow the new strains, and many farmers cannot afford them. In addition, the new crops are often vulnerable to insects that must be controlled by pesticides that damage the environment.

**Weapons** The technological revolution has also led to frightening weapons, such as nuclear, biological, and chemical weapons. The end of the Cold War reduced the risk of major nuclear conflict, but regional nuclear conflicts seem possible. There are also fears that terrorists will obtain and use nuclear materials.

The potential threat from biological and chemical weapons was raised when anthrax-filled letters were used to kill several Americans in 2001. **Biowarfare,** the use of disease and poison against civilians and soldiers in wartime, is not new. The first known incident occurred in Europe in the 1300s when, during a siege, plague-infested corpses were launched over city walls to infect the populace. Chemical weapons were used extensively in World War I and during the Iran-Iraq war in the 1980s.

Governments have made agreements to limit the research, production, and use of biological and chemical weapons. The 1925 Geneva Protocol, for example, prohibited the use of such weapons, though not research or production of them. In 1972, the United States and the Soviet Union agreed only to permit work on defensive biological weapons.

These measures have not prevented terrorists from practicing **bioterrorism,** the use of biological and chemical weapons. In 1995, members of a Japanese religious sect named Aum Shinrikyo released a chemical agent, sarin gas, in a Tokyo subway, killing 12 people and injuring thousands.

☑ **Reading Check** **Identifying** List industries affected by the technological revolution since World War II.

# Political and Economic Challenges

**Main Idea** Developing nations face continuing problems of poverty, population growth, and ethnic conflict.

**Reading Connection** Have you heard news reports on the "outsourcing" of American jobs? Read further to learn about the challenges of a global economy.

The global economy began to develop after World War II and gathered momentum in the 1980s and 1990s. In 1995, the **World Trade Organization** (WTO) was established. Trade agreements are made and upheld by its more than 140 members. The WTO has been criticized for placing commercial interests over environmental and health concerns and leaving out small and developing countries. Still, the WTO is the only global international organization dealing with rules of trade among nations.

Another symbol of the global economy is the multinational corporation. There are a growing number of multinationals—banks, computer companies,

▲ *People in the Sahara waiting for relief supplies*

airlines, and fast-food chains that do business around the world. In this way, multinationals are creating a more interdependent world.

**The Gap Between Rich and Poor Nations** One of the features of the global economy is the wide gap between rich and poor nations. Rich nations are mainly in the Northern Hemisphere and include the United States, Canada, countries in western Europe, and Japan. They have well-organized industrial and education systems and use advanced technologies. Poor nations, often called developing countries, are mainly in the Southern Hemisphere and include many nations in Africa, Asia, and Latin America. Developing countries are mainly farming nations with little technology.

A serious problem in developing countries is explosive population growth. The world's population today is 6.2 billion. By 2050, the UN projects that it will reach 9 billion. Much of the growth is occurring in poor countries that can least afford it. Hunger has also become a staggering problem. Every year, over 8 million people die of hunger, many young children. Poor and eroded soil, natural catastrophes, and economic and political factors contribute to hunger.

**Food Shortages and Civil Wars** In recent years, civil wars have been devastating in creating food shortages. Not only does war disrupt normal farming, but enemies deliberately limit access to food to civilian populations in order to defeat their opponents. This tactic was practiced on a grand scale in the Soviet Union in the early 1930s. When Russian peasants in the Ukraine resisted the order to join a collective farm, the Soviet leader Joseph Stalin responded brutally,

▲ *Sudanese woman holding her baby at a refugee camp*

purging the population and confiscating food. Between 1932 and 1933, Stalin's famine resulted in as many as seven million deaths.

During a civil conflict in the African nation of Sudan, combatants prevented food from reaching people living in enemy territory. By the early 1990s, 1.3 million had died from starvation. In the early 2000s, as unrest in Sudan continued, families in Darfur, a region in the west, were forced to leave their farms and prevented from returning. As a result, some estimate that at least 70,000 men, women, and children starved to death by mid-2004.

**The Outlook for Democracy** After World War II, African and Asian leaders identified democracy as the defining theme of their new political cultures. Within a decade, however, democratic systems in many developing countries had been replaced by military dictatorships or one-party governments. Many leaders underestimated the difficulties of building democratic political institutions.

In recent years, there have been signs of renewed interest in democracy, especially in Asia, Africa, and Latin America. Examples are the free elections held in South Korea, Taiwan, and the Philippines. Similar developments have taken place in a number of African countries and throughout Latin America.

Regional, ethnic, and religious differences continue to create conflict. In Europe, Yugoslavia has been torn apart by ethnic divisions. In the Middle East, the conflict between Israelis and Palestinians continues to produce acts of terror. Conflicts among hostile ethnic groups in Africa have led to genocide. It remains to be seen how such conflicts can be resolved.

✓**Reading Check** **Explaining** Describe the connection between hunger and civil war.

**HISTORY** *Online* **Study Central**

For help with the concepts in this section of *Glencoe World History–Modern Times*, go to **wh.mt.glencoe.com** and click on **Study Central.**

# SECTION 1 ASSESSMENT

### Checking for Understanding

1. **Vocabulary** Define: ecology, deforestation, ozone layer, greenhouse effect, acid rain, nuclear, sustainable development, mental, biowarfare, bioterrorism.

2. **People and Events** Identify: Rachel Carson, Kyoto Protocol, Neil Armstrong, World Trade Organization.

3. **Places** Locate: Bhopal, Chernobyl.

### Reviewing Big Ideas

4. **Explain** why technological advance and environmental problems are sometimes connected.

### Critical Thinking

5. **Historical Analysis** **Examining Trends** What are the individual and global consequences of overpopulation? **CA HI 1**

6. **Summarizing Information** Create a chart like the one below listing technological advances and their costs.

| Advances | Drawback or Cost |
|---|---|
| Transportation | |
| Communications | |
| Space Exploration | |
| Health Care | |
| Agriculture | |
| Weaponry | |

### Analyzing Visuals

7. **Evaluate** Study the photographs on this page and on page 747. How would such photos spark increased aid efforts from developed nations?

### Writing About History

8. **Expository Writing** By now, many nations recognize that environmental damage can be significant and their leaders hold formal meetings on them. In an essay, describe why some leaders disagree over the best solutions to global environmental problems. **CA 10WA2.3a,b**

# SECTION 2 Global Visions

## Section Preview
The global economy and new global threats have stimulated individuals and international organizations to work on global problems.

### Main Idea
- International organizations have evolved that focus on a variety of international problems. (p. 750)

- Voluntary organizations and average citizens have become more active in working on global problems. (p. 752)

### Content Vocabulary
peacekeeping force, disarmament group

### Academic Vocabulary
approach, professional, constant

### People to Identify
Franklin Delano Roosevelt

### Places to Locate
China

### Reading Objectives
1. Name the international organization that arose at the end of World War II to help maintain peace.
2. Describe how ordinary citizens have worked to address the world's problems.

### Reading Strategy
**Organizing Information** Create a pyramid like the one below to depict how the United Nations is organized.

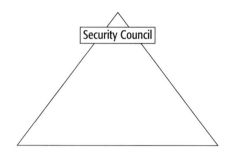

Security Council

### Preview of Events

| ♦1945 | ♦1946 | ♦1947 | ♦1948 | ♦1949 |
|---|---|---|---|---|

**1945**
United Nations founded

**1946**
United Nations International Children's Emergency Fund (UNICEF) founded

**1948**
United Nations General Assembly adopts Universal Declaration of Human Rights

## California Standards in This Section

*Reading this section will help you master these California History–Social Science Standards.*

**10.9.8:** Discuss the establishment and work of the United Nations and the purposes and functions of the Warsaw Pact, SEATO, NATO, and the Organization of American States.

**10.10.2:** Describe the recent history of the regions, including political divisions and systems, key leaders, religious issues, natural features, resources, and population patterns.

**10.10.3:** Discuss the important trends in the regions today and whether they appear to serve the cause of individual freedom and democracy.

# The United Nations

**Main Idea** International organizations have evolved that focus on a variety of international problems.

**Reading Connection** Did you hear debates on whether the United States needed UN cooperation for the Iraqi invasion? Read further to learn about the origins of the UN.

By 1945, two world wars had killed millions of people and devastated the material resources of many nations around the globe. The experience of the Holocaust during World War II made many people painfully aware of the need for an international organization to monitor world conflicts that could lead to genocide and war. This awareness was obvious at an early session of the newly founded United Nations.

## *Voices from the Past*

On December 10, 1948, the UN General Assembly adopted the Universal Declaration of Human Rights. It took the lead in affirming the basic human rights of all peoples in the following statement:

❝All human beings are born free and equal in dignity and rights. . . . Everyone is entitled to all the rights and freedoms set forth in this Declaration, without distinction of any kind, such as race, color, sex, language, religion, political or other opinion, national or social origin, property, birth or other status. . . . Everyone has the right to life, liberty, and security of person. . . . Everyone has the right to freedom of movement. . . . Everyone has the right to freedom of opinion and expression.❞

In recent decades, many nations have become more convinced that there are many significant problems—not just war and peace, but economic and environmental problems—that can only be solved by working with other nations. Today, the UN is one of the most visible symbols of the new globalism.

The UN was founded in 1945 at the end of World War II. American president **Franklin Delano Roosevelt** was especially eager to create an organization to work for peace. Already at the Yalta Conference of February 1945, with the war still being fought, the "Big Three"—Roosevelt, British prime minister Winston Churchill, and Joseph Stalin of the Soviet Union—had agreed to found an international organization.

Roosevelt died two months later, but his successor, President Harry Truman, arranged for the founding meeting to be held in San Francisco in April 1945. There the representatives of the Allied forces worked out the mission and structure of the United Nations.

The United Nations has two chief goals: peace, and human dignity and welfare. These goals were clearly stated in its charter. Members pledged:

❝to save succeeding generations from the scourge of war, which twice in our lifetime . . . brought untold sorrow to mankind, and to reaffirm faith in fundamental human rights, in the dignity and worth of the human person, in the equal rights of men and women and of nations large and small, and to promote social progress and better standards of life in larger freedom.❞

The UN has two main bodies. The first is the General Assembly, made up of representatives from all member nations. It has the power to discuss any important question and to recommend action. The second main body is the Security Council, the most important advisory group to the General Assembly. Five nations have permanent seats on the Security Council: the United States, Russia, Great Britain, France, and **China.** Ten other members serve for limited terms.

The Security Council decides what actions the United Nations should take to settle international disputes. Because each permanent member can veto a decision, deliberations can often end in a stalemate. Overall administration of the UN is under the secretary-general.

▼ *Eleanor Roosevelt holds the Universal Declaration of Human Rights.*

Many specialized agencies carry out the UN's mission to promote human dignity and welfare. Among these agencies are: the United Nations Educational, Scientific, and Cultural Organization (UNESCO), the World Health Organization (WHO), and the United Nations International Children's Emergency Fund (UNICEF). The International Monetary Fund (IMF), another specialized agency, focuses on economic needs and provides funds for economic development to developing nations.

These agencies have been relatively successful in addressing economic and social problems. Around the world, UN agencies have worked to prevent the spread of AIDS, to eradicate polio, and to supplement basic nutrition. They have also worked to develop new fisheries, new farming practices, or to counter practices that harm the environment.

With the second broad mission of the UN—promoting peace—it is more difficult to measure success. Until recently, the basic weakness of the United Nations was that for much of its existence, it was subject to the whims of the two superpowers. The rivalry between the United States and the Soviet Union during the Cold War was often played out at the expense of the United Nations. The United Nations had little success, for example, in reducing the arms race between the two superpowers.

Since the end of the Cold War, the United Nations has played a more active role in keeping alive a vision of international order. Even in the past decade, however, the basic dilemma that faced the UN remains. If an international conflict is serious, the UN is hampered by at least two factors. First, few sovereign nations are willing to allow an outside body to make peace or establish order within its borders. Second, member nations do not often agree on the best solution for an international problem.

▲ *United Nations troops giving food to starving Bosnian Muslims*

A dramatic example of the weakness of the UN in an international dispute came in the Iraq war of 2003–2004. In the early months of 2003, the United States tried to win the support of the United Nations for its decision to invade Iraq to look for weapons of mass destruction. When the UN did not pass a resolution of support, the American government proceeded alone.

On a number of occasions, the UN has been able to provide **peacekeeping forces**—military forces drawn from neutral member states to settle conflicts and supervise truces in "hot spots" around the globe. Such missions can be successful, but if warring forces are not ready to consider peace, the UN effort may fail.

 **Analyzing** Why is the UN Security Council so important?

**Web Activity** Visit the *Glencoe World History—Modern Times* Web site at <u>wh.mt.glencoe.com</u> and click on **Chapter 17–Student Web Activity** to learn more about the United Nations.

# New Global Visions

**Main Idea** Voluntary organizations and average citizens have become more active in working on global problems.

**Reading Connection** Have you ever heard of Doctors Without Borders or the International Red Cross? Read to learn about the role of NGOs in world affairs.

In recent decades, an awareness of global problems has led to new social movements. The **approach** in these social movements is to get ordinary citizens involved.

These movements try to address problems that are shared by many nations. They have focused their efforts on many different areas, including threats to the environment, women's and men's liberation, child labor issues, the development of human potential, the appropriate use of technology, and promoting peaceful solutions to conflict.

Sometimes individual citizens are motivated to join voluntary organizations that draw their membership from people in many different countries. The Red Cross and church-related charitable organizations fall into this category.

At other times, individuals decide that acting at the grassroots level, that is, in their own community, is the best way to work on solving a global problem. One of the favorite slogans of grassroots groups is: "Think globally, act locally."

Hazel Henderson, a British-born economist, has been especially active in founding public interest groups that focus on problems like these. Henderson believes that citizen groups can be an important force for greater global unity and justice.

In *Creating Alternative Futures*, Henderson presented her argument for the role of ordinary people:

> ❝These aroused citizens are by no means all mindless young radicals. Well-dressed, clean-shaven, middle-class businessmen and their suburban wives comprise the major forces in California fighting against nuclear power. Hundreds of thousands of middle-class mothers are bringing massive pressure to ban commercials and violent programs from children's television.❞

Another movement that has emerged to address world problems is the growth of NGOs, or nongovernmental organizations. NGOs include **professional,** business, and cooperative organizations; foundations; religious, peace, and **disarmament groups** that work to limit the size of military forces and weapon stocks; organizations to protect the welfare of women and children; environmental groups; and human rights groups.

American educator Elise Boulding has been active in promoting NGOs. Boulding believes that NGOs can educate people to think about problems from a global perspective. "Since NGOs by definition are identified

▼ *Marches and demonstrations are one way that citizens express their concerns about global issues.*

with interests that transcend national boundaries," she says, "we expect all NGOs to define problems in global terms, to take account of human interests and needs as they are found in all parts of the planet." The number of international NGOs increased from 176 in 1910 to nearly 37,000 in 2000.

Global approaches to global problems, however, have been hindered by political, ethnic, and religious disputes. The Palestinian-Israeli conflict keeps much of the Middle East in **constant** turmoil. Religious differences between Hindus and Muslims help inflame relations between India and Pakistan. The United States and Canada have argued about the effects of acid rain on Canadian forests.

National and ethnic disputes increased at the end of the twentieth century when the Soviet Union collapsed. Many new nations emerged from the old Soviet empire. Both in Eastern Europe and central and southwestern Asia, some of these nations have become involved in ethnic or boundary conflicts.

One of the worst examples of such conflict occurred in the lands of the former Yugoslavia. The Bosnian war that broke out there clearly indicates the dangers in unchecked nationalist sentiment and religious passion. Even though people around the world share in a global culture and are more interdependent in a global economy, old ethnic and nationalistic conflicts continue to disrupt peace and progress.

Many lessons can be learned from the study of world history. One of them is especially clear: a lack of involvement in the affairs of society can easily lead to a sense of powerlessness. For each generation, an

▲ *A Doctors Without Borders worker examines a patient in Afghanistan.*

understanding of our world heritage and its lessons can offer the opportunity to make wise choices in a complex and sometimes chaotic world. We are all creators of history. The choices we make in our everyday lives will affect the future of world civilization.

✓ **Reading Check** **Examining** List two ways people have attempted to resolve global problems and describe the obstacles to solving these problems.

**HISTORY Online** **Study Central**

For help with the concepts in this section of *Glencoe World History–Modern Times*, go to wh.mt.glencoe.com and click on **Study Central.**

# SECTION 2 ASSESSMENT

### Checking for Understanding

1. **Vocabulary** Define: peacekeeping force, approach, professional, disarmament group, constant.

2. **People** Identify: Franklin Delano Roosevelt.

3. **Places** Locate: China.

### Reviewing Big Ideas

4. **Explain** why global approaches to global problems are sometimes difficult to coordinate.

### Critical Thinking

5.  **Historical Analysis** **Contextualizing** What motivated world leaders to create an international peacekeeping organization after World War II? **CA HI 3**

6. **Categorizing Information** Create a chart like the one below listing areas that have political, ethnic, and religious disputes. Place each country in the most appropriate category.

| Nature of Dispute | Country |
|---|---|
| Political | |
| Ethnic | |
| Religious | |

### Analyzing Visuals

7. **Describe** the photo on page 751 in your own words. Then explain why peacekeepers wear military clothing.

### Writing About History

8. **Descriptive Writing** Thousands of NGOs represent citizens' interests throughout the world. Choose one NGO to research. Write an essay about the organization's mission, its goals, accomplishments, and failures. How has it affected world problems? **CA 10WA2.4a,c**

# PRIMARY SOURCES
## *Eyewitness to History*

*The authors of the following passages try to predict the state of the world in the near future in terms of conflicts, ecology, and national and cultural interests.*

## SOURCE 1: The World in Conflict

*Harvard University professor Samuel P. Huntington wrote the following article entitled "The Clash of Civilizations" in the journal* Foreign Affairs *in 1993.*

It is my **hypothesis**[1] that the fundamental source of conflict in this new world will not be primarily ideological or primarily economic. The great divisions among humankind and the dominating source of conflict will be cultural. Nation states will remain the most powerful actors in world affairs, but the principal conflicts of global politics will occur between nations and groups of different civilizations. . . .

. . . differences between civilizations are real and important; civilization-consciousness is increasing; conflict between civilizations will supplant ideological and other forms of conflict as the dominant global form of conflict [and] conflicts between groups in different civilizations will be more frequent, more sustained and more violent than conflicts between groups in the same civilization. . . .

In the longer term other measures would be called for. Western civilization is both Western and modern.

---

> [1]**hypothesis:** a stated proposal or principle

---

*Women in Kuala Lumpur, Malaysia, near a vending machine for Western soft drinks*

Non-Western civilizations have attempted to become modern without becoming Western. To date only Japan has fully succeeded in this quest. . . . This will require the West to maintain the economic and military power necessary to protect its interests in relation to these civilizations. It will also, however, require the West to develop a more profound understanding of the basic religious and philosophical assumptions underlying other civilizations and the ways in which people in those civilizations see their interests. It will require an effort to identify elements of commonality between Western and other civilizations. For the relevant future, there will be no universal civilization, but instead a world of different civilizations, each of which will have to learn to coexist with the others.

## SOURCE 2: Ecological Concern for the Future

*Author Jeremy Brecher and union activist Tim Costello co-authored the following passage from the book* Global Village or Global Pillage *in 1994, which details their concerns about globalization.*

Globalization has affected every economic structure from the World Bank to local governments and workplaces. Correcting its devastating impact will take changes in each of these interlocking structures. . . .

As long as democracy remains exclusively national it will remain largely powerless to address the economic problems of ordinary people. It will take **democratization**[2] at each level from the local to the global to implement an effective alternative economic program. And it will take continuing grassroots mobilization to see that such a program actually works. . . .

The current industrial system is already destroying the earth's air, water, land, and biosphere. Global warming, desertification, pollution, and resource exhaustion will make the earth uninhabitable long before every Chinese has a private car and every American a private boat or plane.

---

> [2]**democratization:** the act of becoming democratic

The solution to this dilemma lies in converting the system of production and consumption to an ecologically sound basis. The technology to do this exists or can be developed, from solar energy to public transportation and from reusable products to resource-minimizing production processes. However, a system in which the search for ever-expanding profits has no regulation or limits will continue to use environmentally destructive processes to produce luxuries, pollutants, and waste. . . .

The energies now directed to the race to the bottom need to be redirected to rebuilding the global economy on a humanely and environmentally sound basis. . . .

## SOURCE 3: The End of Globalism

*Canadian author John Ralston Saul's essay "The Collapse of Globalism" first appeared in* Harper's Magazine *in 2004. He argues that a form of nationalism is replacing globalism as a world ideology.*

Despite that initial certainty, a growing vagueness now surrounds the original promise of Globalization; we seem to have lost track of what was repeatedly declared thirty years ago, even ten years ago, to be inevitable:

That the power of the nation-state was on its way out, to be replaced by that of **global markets**[3]. That in the future, economics, not politics or arms, would determine the course of human events. That freed markets would quickly establish natural international balances, impervious to the old boom-and-bust cycles . . . That prosperous markets would turn dictatorships into democracies. That all of this would discourage irresponsible nationalism, racism, and political violence. That global economics would produce stability through the creation of ever larger corporations impervious to bankruptcy. That these transnational corporations would provide a new kind of international leadership, free of local political prejudices. That the rise of global marketplace leadership and the decline of national politics, with its tendency to deform healthy economic processes, would force the emergence of debt-free governments. By then wedding our governments to a permanent state of deficit-free public accounting, our societies would thus be stabilized.

[In the mid 1990s] [t]here were three particularly obvious signs that Globalization would not deliver on its promises. First, the leadership of a movement devoted to "real competition" was made up largely of . . . private-sector bureaucrats—managing large **joint-stock companies**[4]. Most of the changes they sought were aimed at reducing competition.

Second, the idea of transnationals as new virtual nation-states missed the obvious. Natural resources are fixed in place, inside nation-states. And consumers live on real land in real places. These are called countries. . . . It would be only a matter of time before elected leaders noticed that their governments were far stronger than the large corporations.

Finally, the new approach to debt—public versus private, First World versus Third World—revealed a fatal confusion. Those who preached Globalization couldn't tell the difference between ethics and morality. Ethics is the measurement of the public good. . . . Globalization had shoved ethics to the side from the very beginning and insisted upon a curious sort of moral righteousness that included maximum trade, unrestrained self-interest, and governments alone respecting their debts. . . .

---

[4]**joint-stock companies:** capital provided by a number of people

## DBQ — Document-Based Questions

### Historical Analysis — CA HR 2, HI 1

**Source 1:** According to Huntington, what will be the source of future conflict in the world? What were the sources of conflict previously?

**Source 2:** What solutions do Brecher and Costello propose to fix the global economy?

**Source 3:** In Saul's essay, what does he claim globalizaton promised to do and failed?

### Comparing and Contrasting Sources

1. How do Huntington, Brecher and Costello, and Saul view nationalism and the role of nation-states in a global economy?
2. How do you see globalism in your own life?

---

[3]**global markets:** international area for commodities or services

Standards 10.9.8, 10.10.1, 10.10.2, 10.10.3, 10.11

## Reviewing Content Vocabulary

*On a sheet of paper, use each of these terms in a sentence.*

1. ecology
2. deforestation
3. ozone layer
4. greenhouse effect
5. acid rain
6. sustainable development
7. biowarfare
8. bioterrorism
9. peacekeeping force
10. disarmament group

## Reviewing Academic Vocabulary

*On a sheet of paper, use each of these terms in a sentence that reflects the term's meaning in the chapter.*

11. nuclear
12. mental
13. approach
14. professional
15. constant

## Reviewing the Main Ideas

### Section 1

16. What environmental message was the theme of *Silent Spring?*

17. Explain the greenhouse effect and the problems it could create.

18. When and where did the world's nations meet to discuss environmental issues?

19. What problems do developing nations face?

20. What contributes to the hunger problem in developing nations?

### Section 2

21. What is the United Nations Security Council? Why is it difficult for this council to make decisions?

22. Why does the goal of any nongovernmental organization support a global perspective?

23. Why are nongovernmental organizations taking greater responsibility for protecting the world's environment?

24. What is one of the major slogans of grassroots public interest groups? What kinds of issues do these groups address, and what kinds of members do these groups usually attract?

## Critical Thinking

25. **Evaluating** Analyze the interdependency of developing and industrialized nations. **CA** 10WA2.3a,b

26. **Cause and Effect** Explain the increased potential for regional nuclear wars since the Soviet Union disintegrated.

## Chapter Summary

At the beginning of the twenty-first century, the world has become a global society. Nations are politically and economically dependent on each other, and the world's problems are of a global nature, as shown in the chart below.

### Cultural Diffusion

- Jumbo jetliners transport passengers around the world.
- Corporations have offices in more than one country.
- Advances in communication, such as the Internet, connect people around the globe.

### Technological Innovation

- The science of ecology is born.
- American astronauts land on the moon.
- Super strains of corn, rice, and other grains produce greater crop yields.
- Health care advances prolong lives.
- Developments in transportation and communication transform the world community.

### Cooperation

- The Earth Summit meets in Rio de Janeiro.
- Nations enact recycling programs and curb the dumping of toxic materials.
- The United Nations forms to promote world peace.
- Nongovernmental organizations advocate social and environmental change.

### Conflict

- Massive growth in world population causes overcrowding and hunger in many countries.
- Regional, ethnic, and religious differences continue to produce violence around the world.
- International terrorists remain a threat to peace and security.

27. **Reading Skill** **Inferring** Grassroots organizations
have created more opportunities for an individual citizen to
influence policy. After you read this chapter, consider what
global issues affect you in some way. Make an inference
about what you could do to affect policy on these issues.

## Writing About History

28. **Historical Analysis** **Contextualizing Events** Select a
current event covered in this chapter and write a one-page
essay identifying all the factors needed to understand this
event in context. Be sure to consider national and global
causes and effects. **CA HI 3**

29. ***Big Idea*** Write an essay comparing the nuclear disaster
at Chernobyl with the chemical plant accident in Bhopal and
the grounding of the *Exxon Valdez* in Alaska. Which disaster
was the most devastating to the environment, in your opinion? Why do you have this opinion, and how would you prevent a future disaster?

**DBQ** **Document-Based Questions**

**Analyzing Sources** In the following excerpt from her book *Silent
Spring*, Rachel Carson cautioned about the dangers of harmful
chemicals:

> ❝It is not my contention that chemical pesticides
> must never be used. I do contend that we have put poi-
> sons and biologically potent chemicals into the hands
> of persons largely or wholly ignorant of their potentials
> for harm. . . . Future generations are unlikely to con-
> done our lack of prudent concern for the integrity of
> the natural world that supports all life.❞

30. Summarize the argument that Carson is presenting in this
quotation.

31. Who will question the lack of concern shown for the natural
world, in Carson's opinion?

32. Why was *Silent Spring* a groundbreaking book? How has it
influenced the ways in which people view the relationship
between humans and the natural world? **CA 10RL3.12**

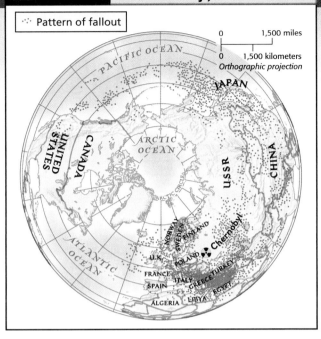

**NATIONAL GEOGRAPHIC** **Radioactive Fallout from Chernobyl, 1986**

## Analyzing Maps and Charts

Use the map above and the text to answer the following
questions.

33. Where is the radioactive fallout most concentrated?

34. Where are the furthest traces of radioactive fallout found
(using Chernobyl as the point of origin)?

35. What global effects did the explosion at Chernobyl have?

**Standards Practice**

**Directions: Choose the best answer to the
following question.**

36. Which of the following statements is true about the
UN?

A There are seven permanent members of the Security
Council.

B Its chief goals are peace and the protection of human
rights.

C It is easy to get UN members to agree on a course of
action.

D The UN was founded after World War I.

**CA Standard 10.9.8** Discuss the establishment and work of
the United Nations and the purposes and functions of the
Warsaw Pact, SEATO, NATO, and the Organization of
American States.

# WORLD LITERATURE

## Civil Peace *from* Girls at War and Other Stories

### by Chinua Achebe

**Chinua Achebe** was born in Nigeria and was christened Albert Chinualamogu. He rejected his British name while studying at the University College of Ibadan. Many of his works deal with the impact of Western values and culture on African society. He has done more than almost any other author to spread the understanding and influence of African literature worldwide. "Civil Peace" is one of the stories from *Girls at War and Other Stories* in which Achebe responds to the Nigerian civil war.

### Read to Discover
How does Chinua Achebe describe the conditions of the civil war? Do you think this story accurately reflects conditions for African families following civil war?

### Reader's Dictionary
**commandeer:** to seize for military purposes

**Biro:** a British term for a ballpoint pen

**raffia:** fiber of a type of palm tree

Jonathan Iwegbu counted himself extraordinarily lucky. "Happy survival!" meant so much more to him than just a current fashion of greeting old friends in the first hazy days of peace. It went deep to his heart. He had come out of the war with five inestimable blessings—his head, his wife Maria's head and the heads of three out of their four children. As a bonus he also had his old bicycle—a miracle too but naturally not to be compared to the safety of five human heads.

The bicycle had a little history of its own. One day at the height of the war it was commandeered "for urgent military action." Hard as its loss would have been to him he would still have let it go without a thought had he not had some doubts about the genuineness of the officer. It wasn't his disreputable rags, nor the toes peeping out of one blue and one brown canvas shoes, nor yet the two stars of his rank done obviously in a hurry in Biro, that troubled Jonathan; many good and heroic soldiers looked the same or worse. It was rather a certain lack of grip and firmness in his manner. So Jonathan, suspecting he might be

▲ *Soldier in the Biafran War in Nigeria in 1968*

charge per trip was six pounds and those who had the money were only glad to be rid of some of it in this way. At the end of a fortnight he had made a small fortune of one hundred and fifteen pounds.

Then he made the journey to Enugu and found another miracle waiting for him. It was unbelievable. He rubbed his eyes and looked again and it was still standing there before him. But, needless to say, even that monumental blessing must be accounted also totally inferior to the five heads in the family. This newest miracle was his little house in Ogui Overside. Indeed nothing puzzles God! Only two houses away a huge concrete edifice some wealthy contractor had put up just before the war was a mountain of rubble. And here was Jonathan's little zinc house of no regrets built with mud blocks quite intact! Of course the doors and windows were missing and five sheets off the roof. But what was that? And anyhow he had returned to Enugu early enough to pick up bits of old zinc and wood and soggy sheets of cardboard lying around the neighborhood before thousands more came out of their forest holes looking for the same things. He got a destitute carpenter with one old hammer, a blunt plane and a few bent and rusty nails in his tool bag to turn this assortment of wood, paper and metal into door and window shutters for five Nigerian shillings or fifty Biafran pounds. He paid the pounds, and moved in with his overjoyed family carrying five heads on their shoulders.

His children picked mangoes near the military cemetery and sold them to soldiers' wives for a few pennies—real pennies this time—and his wife started making breakfast akara balls for neighbours in a hurry to start life again. With his family earnings he took his bicycle to the villages around and bought fresh palm-wine which he mixed generously in his rooms with the water which had recently started running again in the public tap down the road, and opened up a bar for soldiers and other lucky people with good money.

At first he went daily, then every other day and finally once a week, to the offices of the Coal

amenable to influence, rummaged in his raffia bag and produced the two pounds with which he had been going to buy firewood which his wife, Maria, retailed to camp officials for extra stock-fish and corn meal, and got his bicycle back. That night he buried it in the little clearing in the bush where the dead of the camp, including his own youngest son, were buried. When he dug it up again a year later after the surrender all it needed was a little palm-oil greasing. "Nothing puzzles God," he said in wonder.

He put it to immediate use as a taxi and accumulated a small pile of Biafran money ferrying camp officials and their families across the four-mile stretch to the nearest tarred road. His standard

Corporation where he used to be a miner, to find out what was what. The only thing he did find out in the end was that that little house of his was even a greater blessing than he had thought. Some of his fellow ex-miners who had nowhere to return at the end of the day's waiting just slept outside the doors of the offices and cooked what meal they could scrounge together in Bourn-vita tins. As the weeks lengthened and still nobody could say what was what Jonathan discontinued his weekly visits altogether and faced his palm-wine bar.

But nothing puzzles God. Came the day of the windfall when after five days of endless scuffles in queues and counter-queues in the sun outside the Treasury he had twenty pounds counted into his palms as ex-gratia award for the rebel money he had turned in. It was like Christmas for him and for many others like him when the payments began. They called it (since few could manage its proper official name) *egg-rasher.*

As soon the palm notes were placed in his palm Jonathan simply closed it tight over them and buried fist and money inside his trouser pocket. He had to be extra careful because he had seen a man a couple of days earlier collapse into near-madness in an instant before that oceanic crowd because no sooner had he got his twenty pounds than some heartless ruffian picked it off him. Though it was not right that a man in such an extremity of agony should be blamed yet many in the queues that day were able to remark quietly on the victim's careless-ness, especially after he pulled out the innards of his pocket and revealed a hole in it big enough to pass a thief's head. But of course he had insisted that the money had been in the other pocket, pulling it out too to show its comparative wholeness. So one had to be careful.

▲ **Children Dancing, c. 1948, by Robert Gwathmey**

Jonathan soon transferred the money to his left hand and pocket so as to leave his right free for shaking hands should the need arise, though by fix-ing his gaze at such an elevation as to miss all approaching human faces he made sure that the need did not arise, until he got home.

## Interpreting World Literature

1. What does Jonathan's encounter with the false offi-cer reveal about the conditions of the war?

2. Biafra lost the civil war. What clues in the text indi-cate this outcome?

3. Why was having a bicycle a "miracle"?

4. **CRITICAL THINKING** Do you think it is effective for Achebe to discuss the war through an individual account rather than as a direct discussion of the devastation created? Why or why not?

### Applications Activity

Choose a contemporary problem and describe it through the effect it has on an individual or family.

# Reading on Your Own

*Here are several books you may want to read on your own.*
*These authors have explored some of the topics covered in this unit.*

### Against All Hope: The Prison Memoirs of Armando Valladares (Nonfiction)

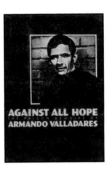

**Valladares, Armando** (1937?–) served 22 years in a Cuban prison because he resisted a decree of Fidel Castro. He was released in 1982 after an international campaign of protest. Valladares's memoir focuses on the suffering Castro's regime has imposed on Cubans, and especially on the prison conditions he knows from personal experience.

### The Frozen Waterfall (Fiction)

**Hicyilmaz, Gaye** (1947–) was born in England and raised in Turkey, but moved to Switzerland when she was young. In this novel, she tells the story of a 12-year-old girl who makes a similar journey. In Switzerland, she struggles to adapt to a new language and culture. Her friendships with an illegal Turkish immigrant and a wealthy Swiss classmate help her to cope with the taunts of her classmates. The title refers to her first holiday in the Swiss mountains where she sees a frozen waterfall.

### When Heaven and Earth Changed Places: A Vietnamese Woman's Journey from War to Peace (Autobiography)

As a young girl, author Le Ly Hayslip survived during the Vietnam War by working at many things—as a courier and lookout for the Vietcong, as part of the guerrilla army of the North Vietnamese Communists, as a bar girl, and hospital aide. This book tells the story of her experiences, including her capture by the South Vietnamese army. Years later she returned to Vietnam to search for the family she left behind. The title comes from a saying that, in war, heaven and earth change places not once but many times.

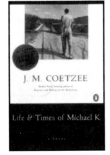

### Life and Times of Michael K (Fiction)

This novel of J. M. Coetzee (1940–) was published in 1983. It tells the story of a simple-minded man who struggles against great odds to live with dignity in a war-torn world. Set in South Africa when apartheid is still a reality, Michael manages to survive poverty, violence, and cruelty by retreating into his own thoughts and the natural world.

# Appendix

## Contents

An almanac is a book or table that contains a variety of statistical, tabular, or general information. The most common almanacs in history have been those that kept astronomical data or that gave weather predictions and related advice to farmers. In agricultural societies it was important to keep accounts of natural phenomena so that farmers would have an idea of when to plant and harvest their crops. Ancient Egyptians carved their almanacs on sticks of wood and called them "fingers of the sun." The first printed almanac was prepared in Europe in 1457. The *Old Farmer's Almanac* has been published continuously since 1792. Because almanacs are compact and concise, they are a popular way of presenting a wide variety of information.

## World Population, A.D. 1–2004

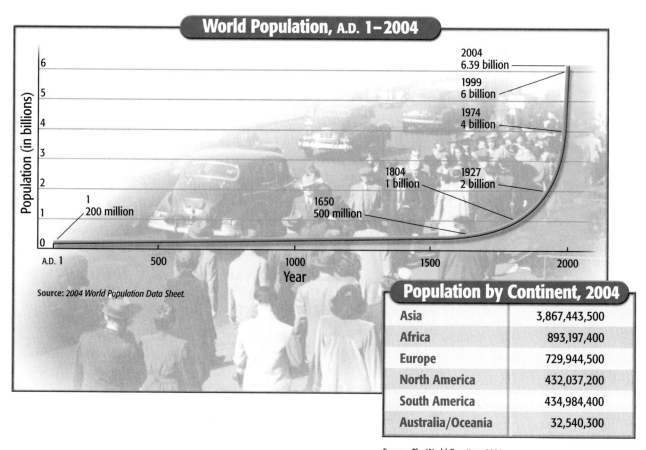

Source: *2004 World Population Data Sheet.*

### Population by Continent, 2004

| | |
|---|---|
| Asia | 3,867,443,500 |
| Africa | 893,197,400 |
| Europe | 729,944,500 |
| North America | 432,037,200 |
| South America | 434,984,400 |
| Australia/Oceania | 32,540,300 |

Source: *The World Gazetteer*, 2004
Note: Populations are estimates.

### Life Expectancy

| Country | Years |
|---|---|
| Andorra | 83.50 |
| Japan | 81.04 |
| France | 79.44 |
| Israel | 79.17 |
| New Zealand | 78.49 |
| United Kingdom | 78.27 |
| United States | 77.43 |
| Chile | 76.38 |
| China | 71.96 |
| Russia | 66.39 |
| Egypt | 70.71 |
| Brazil | 71.41 |
| India | 63.99 |
| South Africa | 44.19 |
| Mozambique | 37.10 |

Source: *The CIA World Factbook*, 2004.

### Infant Mortality

| Country | Infant Deaths per 1,000 Live Births |
|---|---|
| South Africa | 62.18 |
| India | 57.92 |
| Egypt | 33.90 |
| Brazil | 30.66 |
| China | 25.28 |
| Russia | 16.96 |
| Chile | 9.05 |
| South Korea | 7.18 |
| United States | 6.63 |
| United Kingdom | 5.22 |
| Canada | 4.82 |
| Germany | 4.20 |
| France | 4.31 |
| Japan | 3.28 |

Source: *The CIA World Factbook*, 2004.

### Most Populous Countries

| Country | Population |
|---|---|
| China | 1,295,480,400 |
| India | 1,088,056,200 |
| United States | 293,271,500 |
| Indonesia | 221,777,700 |
| Brazil | 179,383,500 |
| Pakistan | 157,056,000 |
| Nigeria | 154,491,100 |
| Russia | 146,697,800 |
| Bangladesh | 133,581,700 |
| Japan | 127,853,600 |

Source: *The World Gazetteer*, 2004.
Note: Populations are estimates.

## World's Richest Countries

| Country | Gross Domestic Product, per Capita (in U.S. dollars) |
| --- | --- |
| Luxembourg | 55,100 |
| United States | 37,800 |
| Norway | 37,700 |
| Bermuda | 36,000 |
| Cayman Islands | 35,000 |

Source: *The CIA World Factbook,* 2004.

## World's Poorest Countries

| Country | Gross Domestic Product, per Capita (in U.S. dollars) |
| --- | --- |
| East Timor | 500 |
| Somalia | 500 |
| Sierra Leone | 500 |
| Gaza Strip | 600 |
| Malawi | 600 |

Source: *The CIA World Factbook,* 2004.

## Highest Inflation Rates

| Country | Rate of Inflation (percent) |
| --- | --- |
| Zimbabwe | 383.40 |
| Angola | 106.00 |
| Burma | 52.80 |
| Haiti | 37.30 |
| Venezuela | 31.10 |
| Belarus | 30.00 |
| Iraq | 27.50 |
| Malawi | 27.40 |
| Ghana | 26.40 |
| Uzbekistan | 21.90 |

Source: *The CIA World Factbook,* 2004.
Note: Estimates are for 2003.

## Lowest Inflation Rates

| Country | Rate of Inflation (percent) |
| --- | --- |
| Nauru | −3.60* |
| Hong Kong | −2.60 |
| Macau | −2.60 |
| Brunei | −2.00 |
| Lithuania | −1.00 |
| New Caledonia | −0.60 |
| Barbados | −0.50 |
| St Vincent and the Grenadines | −0.40 |
| Japan | −0.30 |
| Taiwan | −0.20 |

Source: *The CIA World Factbook,* 2004.
Note: Estimates are for 2003.
*1993 information

## World's Ten Leading Companies, 2004

| Rank | Company | Profits (in billions of U.S. dollars) |
| --- | --- | --- |
| 1. | Exxon Mobil (United States) | 20.96 |
| 2. | Citigroup (United States) | 17.85 |
| 3. | General Electric (United States) | 15.59 |
| 4. | Bank of America (United States) | 10.81 |
| 5. | BP (United Kingdom) | 10.27 |
| 6. | Freddie Mac (United States) | 10.09 |
| 7. | Altria Group (United States) | 9.20 |
| 8. | Wal-Mart Stores (United States) | 9.05 |
| 9. | Microsoft (United States) | 8.88 |
| 10. | Total (France) | 8.84 |

Source: *Forbes,* 2004.

## Most Livable Countries

| Rank | Country | Rank | Country | Rank | Country |
|------|---------|------|---------|------|---------|
| 1. | Norway | 10. | Ireland | 19. | Germany |
| 2. | Sweden | 11. | Switzerland | 20. | Spain |
| 3. | Australia | 12. | United Kingdom | 21. | Italy |
| 4. | Canada | 13. | Finland | 22. | Israel |
| 5. | Netherlands | 14. | Austria | 23. | Hong Kong, China (SAR)* |
| 6. | Belgium | 15. | Luxembourg | 24. | Greece |
| 7. | Iceland | 16. | France | 25. | Singapore |
| 8. | United States | 17. | Denmark | | |
| 9. | Japan | 18. | New Zealand | | |

Source: United Nations Human Development Index, 2004.
Note: The criteria include life expectancy, adult literacy, school enrollment, educational attainment, and per capita gross domestic product (GDP).
* Special Administrative Region of China

## Highest Adult Literacy Rates

| Country | Rate of Literacy (percent) |
|---------|---------------------------|
| Andorra | 100 |
| Australia | 100 |
| Denmark | 100 |
| Finland | 100 |
| Liechtenstein | 100 |
| Luxembourg | 100 |
| Norway | 100 |
| Czech Republic | 99.9 |
| Iceland | 99.9 |
| Estonia | 99.8 |

Source: *The CIA World Factbook,* 2004.
Note: Literacy is defined by each country.

## Lowest Adult Literacy Rates

| Country | Rate of Literacy (percent) |
|---------|---------------------------|
| Niger | 17.6 |
| Burkina Faso | 26.6 |
| Sierra Leone | 31.4 |
| Guinea | 35.9 |
| Afghanistan | 36.0 |
| Somalia | 37.8 |
| The Gambia | 40.1 |
| Senegal | 40.2 |
| Iraq | 40.4 |
| Benin | 40.9 |

Source: *The CIA World Factbook,* 2004.
Note: Literacy is defined by each country.

## World Adult Illiteracy by Gender

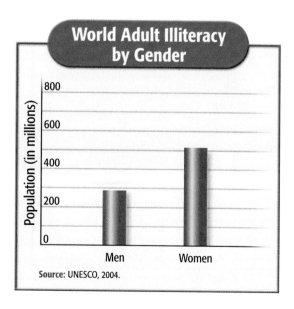

Source: UNESCO, 2004.

## Years, by Country, in Which Women Gained the Right to Vote

| Year | Country | Year | Country |
|------|---------|------|---------|
| 1893 | New Zealand | 1945 | Italy |
| 1902 | Australia | 1945 | Japan |
| 1913 | Norway | 1947 | Argentina |
| 1918 | United Kingdom | 1947 | Mexico |
| 1918 | Canada | 1950 | India |
| 1919 | Germany | 1952 | Greece |
| 1920 | United States | 1956 | Egypt |
| 1930 | South Africa | 1963 | Kenya |
| 1934 | Brazil | 1971 | Switzerland |
| 1944 | France | 1980 | Iraq |

## Highest Military Expenditures

| | Billions of U.S. Dollars per Year | Percentage of Gross Domestic Product (GDP) |
|---|---|---|
| United States | 399.0 | 3.9 |
| China | 60.0 | 3.5–5.0 |
| France | 45.2 | 2.6 |
| United Kingdom | 42.8 | 2.4 |
| Japan | 42.4 | 1.0 |
| Germany | 35.0 | 1.5 |
| Italy | 28.1 | 1.9 |
| Saudi Arabia | 18.0 | 10.0 |
| South Korea | 14.5 | 2.7 |
| Australia | 14.1 | 2.8 |

**Source:** *The CIA World Factbook,* 2004.

## Nuclear Weapons Capability

| Country | Date of First Test |
|---|---|
| United States | 1945 |
| Russia (Soviet Union) | 1949 |
| United Kingdom | 1952 |
| France | 1960 |
| China | 1964 |
| India | 1974 |
| Pakistan | 1998 |

Sources: U.S. Department of State and *Time* magazine.

## Communication Around the World

| | Daily newspaper circulation per 1,000 persons | Radios per 1,000 persons | Televisions per 1,000 persons | Telephone main lines per 1,000 persons | Cellular phone subscribers per 1,000 persons | Estimated personal computers per 1,000 persons |
|---|---|---|---|---|---|---|
| Canada | 159 | 1,047 | 691 | 676 | 362 | 487 |
| China | n/a | 339 | 350 | 137 | 110 | 28 |
| Cuba | 118 | 185 | 251 | 51 | 1 | 32 |
| France | 201 | 950 | 632 | 574 | 605 | 347 |
| Germany | 305 | 570 | 661 | 634 | 682 | 431 |
| Italy | 104 | 878 | 494 | 472 | 883 | 231 |
| Japan | 578 | 956 | 785 | 586 | 588 | 382 |
| Mexico | 94 | 330 | 282 | 137 | 217 | 82 |
| Russia | 105 | 418 | 538 | 243 | 38 | 89 |
| South Africa | 32 | 336 | 177 | 111 | 242 | 73 |
| United Kingdom | 329 | 1,445 | 950 | 588 | 770 | 406 |
| United States | 213 | 2,117 | 938 | 667 | 451 | 659 |

Sources: World Bank, *World Development Indicators,* 2004; *Time Almanac* 2004.

# Primary Sources Library

## CONTENTS

## What Is It and How Do I Use It?

The primary sources as defined here are written testimony or documents from a particular era in history or about an important development. The source may be the writings of a noted historian or political leader, or it may be from the diary of someone who lived at the time and recorded the events of the day.

Reading primary sources is an excellent way to understand how and why people believed and acted as they did in the past. While many people might have written down their stories or beliefs, the sources chosen here are from witnesses who were close to events or especially sensitive to them.

## Checking Your Sources

When you read primary or secondary sources, you should analyze them to determine if they are dependable or reliable. Historians usually prefer primary sources to secondary sources, but both can be reliable or unreliable, depending on the following factors.

## Time Span

With primary sources, it is important to consider how much time passed from the date the event occurred to the date that the primary source was written. Generally, the longer the time span between the event and the account, the less reliable the account is. As time passes, people often forget details and fill in gaps with events that never took place. Although we like to think we remember things exactly as they happened, the fact is, we often remember them very differently than they occurred.

## Reliability

Another factor to consider when evaluating a primary source is the writer's background and reliability. When reading a historical document, try to determine if the statements and information can be proved. If the information can be verified as true by independent sources, then it probably is fact.

## Opinions

When evaluating a primary source, you should also decide whether or not the account has been influenced by emotion, opinion, or exaggeration. Writers sometimes distort the truth to suit their personal purposes. Ask yourself: Why did the person write the account? Do any words or expressions reveal the author's emotions or opinions? Again, you may wish to compare the account with another primary source document about the same event. If the two accounts differ, ask yourself why they differ and then conduct your own outside research to determine which account can be verified by other authoritative sources.

## Interpreting Primary Sources

To help you analyze a primary source, use the following steps:

• **Examine the origins of the document.**
  You need to determine if it is indeed a primary source.

• **Find the main ideas.**
  Read the document and summarize the main ideas in your own words.

• **Reread the document.**
  Difficult ideas and historical documents are not always easily understood on the first reading.

• **Use a variety of resources.**
  Use a dictionary, an encyclopedia, and maps to further your understanding of the topic. These resources are tools to help you discover new ideas and knowledge and check the validity of sources.

## Classifying Primary Sources

Primary sources fall into different categories. While the documents presented here are primarily printed publications, there are other types of primary sources.

Printed publications include books such as autobiographies. Printed publications also include newspapers and magazines.

Visual materials include a wide range of forms: original paintings, drawings, sculpture, photographs, film, videos, and maps.

Oral history collects spoken memories and personal observations through recorded interviews. In contrast, oral tradition involves stories that people have passed along by word of mouth from generation to generation.

Personal records are accounts of events kept by an individual who is a participant in or witness to these events. Personal records include diaries, journals, and letters.

Artifacts are objects such as tools or ornaments. Artifacts provide archaeologists and historians with information about a particular culture or a stage of technological development.

# Early Modern Europe

*The Reformation paved the way for people in European nations to begin challenging established ideas about religion and politics. This tradition continued through the Enlightenment when new philosophies were debated. The most dramatic evidence for new political and social ideas was the French Revolution, which began in 1789.*

## Reader's Dictionary

**Scripture:** passage from the Bible

**revered:** honored or respected

**contention:** point made in an argument

**judicature:** court of justice or judicial authority

**imprescriptible:** cannot be taken away by law

▲ *Martin Luther*

*Ulrich Zwingli* ▶

# A Reformation Debate

**Printed Publications**

*In 1529, Martin Luther and Ulrich Zwingli debated over the sacrament of the Lord's Supper, or Communion.*

LUTHER: Although I have no intention of changing my mind, which is firmly made up, I will nevertheless present the grounds of my belief and show where the others are in error. . . . Your basic contentions are these: In the last analysis you wish to prove that a body cannot be in two places at once, and you produce arguments about the unlimited body which are based on natural reason. I do not question how Christ can be God and man and how the two natures can be joined. For God is more powerful than all our ideas, and we must submit to his word.

Prove that Christ's body is not there where the Scripture says, "This is my body!" God is beyond all mathematics and the words of God are to be revered and carried out in awe. It is God who commands, "Take, eat, this is my body." I request, therefore, valid scriptural proof to the contrary.

ZWINGLI: I insist that the words of the Lord's Supper must be figurative. This is ever apparent, and even required by the article of faith; "taken up into heaven, seated at the right hand of the Father." Otherwise, it would be absurd to look for him in the Lord's Supper at the same time that Christ is telling us that he is in heaven. One and the same body cannot possibly be in different places. . . .

LUTHER: I call upon you as before: your basic contentions are shaky. Give way, and give glory to God!

ZWINGLI: And we call upon you to give glory to God and to quit begging the question! The issue at stake is this: Where is the proof of your position?

LUTHER: It is your point that must be proved, not mine. But let us stop this sort of thing. It serves no purpose.

ZWINGLI: It certainly does! It is for you to prove that the passage in John 6 speaks of a physical meal.

LUTHER: You express yourself poorly. . . . You're going nowhere.

# Second Treatise of Government

*John Locke wrote* Two Treatises of Government *in the early 1680s when the English Parliament was in conflict with the monarchy. The work was published in 1690. By then, the Stuart king James II had been replaced by a constitutional monarch, William of Orange.*

Man . . . hath by nature a power, not only to preserve his property, that is, his life, liberty and estate, against the injuries and attempts of other men; but to judge of, and punish the breaches of that law in others, as he is persuaded the offence deserves, even with death itself, in crimes where the heinousness of the fact, in his opinion, requires it . . . [In political society] every one of the members hath quitted this natural power, resigned it up into the hands of the community in all cases that exclude him not from appealing for protection to the law established by it. And thus all private judgment of every particular member being excluded, the community comes to be umpire . . . Those who are united into one body, and have a common

established law and judicature to appeal to, with authority to decide controversies between them, and punish offenders, are in civil society one with another . . .

. . . absolute monarchy, which by some men is counted the only government in the word, is indeed inconsistent with civil society, and so can be no form of civil-government at all . . .

*Illustration of the defeat of James II*

# Declaration of the Rights of Woman and the Female Citizen

*Olympe de Gouges composed her own Declaration of the Rights of Woman and the Female Citizen in 1791. Following are excerpts.*

1. Woman is born free and lives equal to man in her rights. Social distinctions can be based only on the common utility.
2. The purpose of any political association is the conservation of the natural and imprescriptible rights of woman and man; these rights are liberty, property, security, and especially resistance to oppression. . . .
4. Liberty and justice consist of restoring all that belongs to others; thus, the only limits on the exercise of the natural rights of woman are perpetual male tyranny; these limits are to be reformed by the laws of nature and reason. . . .
6. The law must be . . . the same for all: male and female citizens. . . .
7. No woman is an exception; she is accused, arrested, and detained in cases determined by law. Women, like men, obey this rigorous law. . . .
11. The free communication of thoughts and opinions is one of the most precious rights of woman, since that liberty assured the recognition of children by their fathers. . . .

## Analyzing Primary Sources

1. Was a conclusion reached in the debate presented between Luther and Zwingli?
2. According to Locke, why can't a civil society have an absolute monarchy?
3. What are the rights of women as listed in the excerpts from *Declaration of the Rights of Woman and the Female Citizen*?
4. Olympe de Gouges states that free communication of thoughts is one of the most precious rights of women. Do you agree or disagree?

# An Era of European Imperialism

*During the late 1700s and throughout the 1800s, the nations of Europe and North America began an Industrial Revolution that had far-reaching effects, including the demand for social and political reforms. At the same time, Western nations extended their hold on new lands and on foreign markets.*

## Reader's Dictionary

**autocrat:** a monarch who rules with unlimited authority

**close:** an enclosed area of land

**enumerated:** counted

**abject:** existing in a low state or condition

**infanticide:** killing an infant

**resuscitation:** restoration or renewal

*Czar Alexander II*

# Imperial Decree to Free the Serfs

**Printed Publications**

*I*n 1861, the Russian czar Alexander II issued the Emancipation Manifesto, *an imperial decree to free his country's serfs.*

By the grace of God, we, Alexander II, Emperor and Autocrat of all the Russias, King of Poland, Grand Duke of Finland, etc., to all our faithful subjects, make known:

Examining the condition of classes and professions comprising the state, we became convinced that the present state legislation favors the upper and middle classes, . . . but does not equally favor the serfs. . . . These facts had already attracted the attention of our predecessors, and they had adopted measures aimed at improving the conditions of the peasants. But decrees on free farmers and serfs have been carried out on a limited scale only.

We thus came to the conviction that the work of a serious improvement of the condition of the peasants was a sacred inheritance bequeathed to us by our ancestors, a mission which, in the course of events Divine Providence called upon us to fulfill. . . .

In virtue of the new dispositions above mentioned, the peasants attached to the soil will be invested within a term fixed by the law with all the rights of free cultivators. . . .

At the same time, they are granted the right of purchasing their close, and, with the consent of the proprietors, they may acquire in full property the arable lands and other appurtenances [rights of way] which are allotted to them as a permanent holding. By the acquisition in full property of the quantity of land fixed, the peasants are free from their obligations towards the proprietors for land thus purchased, and they enter definitely into the condition of free peasants-landholders.

# The Unfortunate Situation of Working Women

T*his article was published in* L'Atelier, *a Parisian workingman's newspaper, in 1842.*

Although women's work is less productive for society than that of men, it does, nevertheless, have a certain value, and, moreover, there are professions that only women can practice. For these, women are indispensable. . . . It is these very workers in all these necessary trades who earn the least and who are subject to the longest layoffs. Since for so much work they earn only barely enough to live from day to day, it happens that during times of unemployment they sink into abject poverty.

Who has not heard of the women silkworkers' dirty, unhealthy, and badly paid work; of the women in the spinning and weaving factories working fourteen to sixteen hours (except for one hour for both meals); always standing, without a single minute for repose, putting forth an enormous amount of effort. And many of them have to walk a league or more, morning and evening, to get home. Nor should we neglect to mention the danger that exists merely from working in these large factories, surrounded by wheels, gears, enormous leather belts that always threaten to seize you and pound you to pieces.

The existence of women who work as day laborers, and are obliged to abandon . . . the care of their children to indifferent neighbors is no better. . . . We believe that the condition of women will never really improve until workingmen can earn enough to support their families, which is only fair. Woman is so closely linked to man that the position of the one cannot be improved without reference to the position of the other.

# The Impact of British Rule in India

I*n 1871, Dadabhai Naoroji commented on the benefits and the problems of British rule in India.*

**Benefits of British Rule:**
*In the Cause of Humanity:* Abolition of suttee and infanticide. *Civilization:* Education, both male and female. . . . Resuscitation of India's own noble literature. *Politically:* Peace and order. Freedom of speech and liberty of the press. . . . Improvement of government in the native states. Security of life and property. Freedom from oppression. . . . *Materially:* Loans for railways and irrigation. Development of a few valuable products, such as indigo, tea, coffee, silk, etc. Increase of exports. Telegraphs.

**The Detriments of British Rule:**
*In the Cause of Humanity:* Nothing. *Civilization:* [T]here has been a failure to do as much as might have been done. *Politically:* Repeated breach of pledges to give the natives a fair and reasonable share in the higher administration of their own country, . . . an utter disregard of the feelings and views of the natives. *Financially:* [N]ew modes of taxation, without any adequate effort to increase the means of the people to pay.

*Summary:* British rule has been: morally, a great blessing; politically, peace and order on one hand, blunders on the other; materially, impoverishment. . . . Our great misfortune is that you do not know our wants. When you will know our real wishes, I have not the least doubt that you would do justice. The genius and spirit of the British people is fair play and justice.

## Analyzing Primary Sources

1. What reason does Czar Alexander II give for freeing the serfs?
2. What physical and economic problems of women workers are described in the Parisian newspaper article? What solution(s) does the author offer?
3. What is the attitude of the *L'Atelier* writer toward women and women's work? Is the author of the article more likely to be a woman or a man? What makes you think so?
4. Summarize the benefits and problems of British rule in India.

# The Twentieth-Century Crisis

*During the first half of the 1900s, two destructive wars raged throughout the world and brought tremendous political and social change. World War I destroyed the power of European monarchies, while Nazi aggression in Germany eventually led to World War II and the Holocaust.*

## Reader's Dictionary

**parapet:** wall of earth piled on top of a trench

**snipers:** people who shoot at exposed individuals from a concealed location

**civil disobedience:** refusal to obey governmental demands

**exploitation:** unfair use for one's own advantage

**disarmament:** reducing or eliminating weapons

*Battle of the Somme*

# An American Soldier Remembers World War I

**Personal Records**

*A*rthur Guy Empey reflects upon his experiences during World War I in the trenches in France.

Suddenly, the earth seemed to shake and a thunderclap burst in my ears. I opened my eyes,—I was splashed all over with sticky mud, and men were picking themselves up from the bottom of the trench. The parapet on my left had toppled into the trench, completely blocking it with a wall of tossed-up earth. The man on my left lay still. . . . A German "Minnie" (trench mortar) had exploded in the [trench]. . . . Stretcher-bearers came up the trench on the double. After a few minutes of digging, three still, muddy forms on stretchers were carried down the communication trench to the rear. Soon they would be resting "somewhere in France," with a little wooden cross over their heads. They had done their bit for King and Country, had died without firing a shot. . . . I was dazed and motionless. Suddenly a shovel was pushed into my hands, and a rough but kindly voice said: "Here, my lad, lend a hand clearing the trench, but keep your head down, and look out for snipers. . . ."

Lying on my belly on the bottom of the trench, I filled sandbags with the sticky mud. . . . The harder I worked, the better I felt.

Occasionally a bullet would crack overhead, and a machine gun would kick up the mud on the bashed-in parapet. At each crack I would duck and shield my face with my arm. One of the older men noticed this action of mine, and whispered: "Don't duck at the crack of a bullet, Yank; the danger has passed,—you never hear the one that wings you. Always remember that if you are going to get it, you'll get it, so never worry." . . . [Days later] we received the cheerful news that at four in the morning we were to go over the top and take the German frontline trench. My heart turned to lead.

# Gandhi Takes the Path of Civil Disobedience

**Printed Publications**

Mohandas Gandhi explains why British rule in India must end.

Before embarking on civil disobedience and taking the risk I have dreaded to take all these years, I would fain approach you and find a way out.

My personal faith is absolutely clear. I cannot intentionally hurt anything that lives, much less fellow human beings, even though they may do the greatest wrong to me and mine. Whilst, therefore, I hold the British rule to be a curse, I do not intend harm to a single Englishman or to any legitimate interest he may have in India.

I must not be misunderstood. Though I hold the British rule in India to be a curse, I do not, therefore, consider Englishmen in general to be worse than any other people on earth. I have the privilege of claiming many Englishmen as dearest friends. Indeed much that I have learned of the evil of British rule is due to the writings of frank and courageous Englishmen who have not hesitated to tell the truth about that rule.

And why do I regard British rule as a curse? It has impoverished the ignorant millions by a system of progressive exploitation and by a ruinously expensive military and civil administration which the country can never afford.

It has reduced us politically to serfdom. It has sapped the foundations of our culture. And, by the policy of cruel disarmament, it has degraded us spiritually. Lacking the inward strength, we have been reduced . . . to a state bordering on cowardly helplessness. . . .

# The Holocaust— The Camp Victims

**Printed Publications**

A French doctor describes the victims of one of the crematoriums at Auschwitz-Birkenau during the Holocaust.

It is mid-day, when a long line of women, children, and old people enter the yard. The senior official in charge . . . climbs on a bench to tell them that they are going to have a bath and that afterwards they will get a drink of hot coffee. They all undress in the yard. . . . The doors are opened and an indescribable jostling begins. The first people to enter the gas chamber begin to draw back. They sense the death which awaits them. The SS men put an end to the pushing and shoving with blows from their rifle butts beating the heads of the horrified women who are desperately

hugging their children. The massive oak double doors are shut. For two endless minutes one can hear banging on the walls and screams which are no longer human. And then—not a sound. Five minutes later the doors are opened. The corpses, squashed together and distorted, fall out like a waterfall. The bodies which are still warm pass through the hands of the hairdresser who cuts their hair and the dentist who pulls out their gold teeth . . . One more transport has just been processed through No. IV crematorium.

## Analyzing Primary Sources

1. How did Arthur Empey feel and act during his time in the trenches of World War I?
2. According to Gandhi, what had British rule done to India?
3. Why do you think Gandhi believed that nonviolent civil disobedience would encourage the British to free India?
4. What is the French doctor's point of view about the events he describes at the Auschwitz-Birkenau death camp?

# Toward a Global Civilization

*Following World War II, the balance of power in the world shifted dramatically. Many nations and peoples came under the political and ideological influence of the United States, which promoted capitalism and individual rights and liberties.*

## Reader's Dictionary

**reserve:** a reservation; land set aside for use by a particular group

**squatters:** those who settle on public land without rights or permission

**perturbation:** major change or disturbance

*John Glenn*

# Progress Never Stops

### Printed Publications

*In 1962, John J. Glenn, Jr. was commander of the first U.S. crewed spacecraft to orbit the earth. Glenn spoke to a joint meeting of Congress six days after he returned from orbit.*

What did we learn from the flight? . . . The Mercury spacecraft and systems design concepts are sound and have now been verified during manned flight. We also proved that man can operate intelligently in space and can adapt rapidly to this new environment.

Zero G or weightlessness appears to be no problem. As a matter of fact, lack of gravity is a rather fascinating thing. Objects within the cockpit can be parked in midair. For example, at one time during the flight, I was using a hand-held camera. Another system needed attention; so it seemed quite natural to let go of the camera, take care of the other chore, then reach out, grasp the camera, and go back about my business.

There seemed to be little sensation of speed although the craft was traveling at about five miles per second—a speed that I too find difficult to comprehend.

The view from that altitude defies description. The horizon colors are brilliant and sunsets are spectacular. It is hard to beat a day in which you are permitted the luxury of seeing four sunsets. . . .

Our efforts today and what we have done so far are but small building blocks in a huge pyramid to come.

But questions are sometimes raised regarding the immediate payoffs from our efforts. Explorations and the pursuit of knowledge have always paid dividends in the long run—usually far greater than anything expected at the outset. Experimenters with common, green mold, little dreamed what effect their discovery of penicillin would have.

We are just probing the surface of the greatest advancements in man's knowledge of his surroundings that has ever been made. . . . Knowledge begets knowledge. Progress never stops.

# An Ideal for Which I Am Prepared to Die

Nelson Mandela gave this speech during his trial in South Africa in 1964. Following the trial, he was sentenced to life in prison.

The whites enjoy what may well be the highest standard of living in the world, whilst Africans live in poverty and misery. Forty percent of the Africans live in hopelessly overcrowded and, in some cases, drought-stricken reserves, where soil erosion and the overworking of the soil make it impossible for them to live properly off the land. Thirty percent are labourers, labour tenants, and squatters on white farms. The other thirty percent live in towns where they have developed economic and social habits which bring them closer, in many respects, to white standards. Yet forty-six percent of all African families in Johannesburg do not earn enough to keep them going.

The complaint of Africans, however, is not only that they are poor and whites are rich, but that the laws which are made by the whites are designed to preserve this situation. . . .

During my lifetime I have dedicated my life to this struggle of the African people. I have fought against white domination, and I have fought against black domination. I have cherished the ideal of a democratic and free society in which all persons live together in harmony with equal opportunities. It is an ideal which I hope to live for, and to see realized. But my lord, if needs be, it is an ideal for which I am prepared to die.

# China's Gilded Age

Xiao-huang Yin recounts his trip through China in 1994.

Recently I took a six week journey across China. It was my first trip back since . . . 1985. In the course of my visit I saw—I felt—the perturbations of profound and chaotic social change. China's stunning hurtle from a centrally planned economy to a free market has set off an economic explosion and generated tremendous prosperity. Its economic growth was 13 percent in 1993, and average personal income in urban areas had doubled since 1985. With the state-owned sector accounting for less than 30 percent of total economic output, the socialist system is becoming an empty shell. Across China the lines between the state and private economies are blurring. At the largest national department store in Shanghai, a symbol of Chinese socialist business, customers now bargain for better prices. The counters within the store have been contracted out to shop clerks, who decide the prices. Dual ownership has in essence turned this state enterprise into a private business. . . .

Not everyone gets rich quick, but the economic boom has brought most urban Chinese a huge improvement in their standard of living. Color TV sets, refrigerators, and VCRs, considered luxuries when I lived in China, can be found in almost every working-class urban household— at least in the prosperous coastal cities.

## Analyzing Primary Sources

1. What are the immediate and long-term "payoffs" of John Glenn's 1962 space mission, according to his report to Congress?
2. Summarize the demographics of the African population discussed by Nelson Mandela.
3. What ideal does Nelson Mandela discuss?
4. Why does Xiao-huang Yin believe that socialism is becoming an "empty shell" in China?

# Honoring America

## Flag Etiquette

Over the years, Americans have developed rules and customs concerning the use and display of the flag. One of the most important things every American should remember is to treat the flag with respect.

- The flag should be raised and lowered by hand and displayed only from sunrise to sunset. On special occasions, the flag may be displayed at night, but it should be illuminated.

- The flag may be displayed on all days, weather permitting, particularly on national and state holidays and on historic and special occasions.

- No flag may be flown above the American flag or to the right of it at the same height.

- The flag should never touch the ground or floor beneath it.

- The flag may be flown at half-staff by order of the president, usually to mourn the death of a public official.

- The flag may be flown upside down only to signal distress.

- The flag should never be carried flat or horizontally, but always carried aloft and free

- When the flag becomes old and tattered, it should be destroyed by burning. According to an approved custom, the Union (stars on blue field) is first cut from the flag; then the two pieces, which no longer form a flag, are burned.

## The Star-Spangled Banner

O! say can you see, by the dawn's early light,
What so proudly we hail'd at the twilight's last gleaming?
Whose broad stripes and bright stars through the perilous fight,
O'er the ramparts we watched, were so gallantly streaming?
And the rockets' red glare, the bombs bursting in air,
Gave proof through the night that our flag was still there;
O! say, does that star-spangled banner yet wave
O'er the land of the free and the home of the brave?

## The Pledge of Allegiance

I pledge allegiance to the Flag of the United States of America and to the Republic for which it stands, one Nation under God, indivisible, with liberty and justice for all.

# SKILLBUILDER Handbook

## Table of Contents

The exercises in the Glencoe Skillbuilder Handbook give you hands-on practice with the skills you need to master the California content standards for world history. The range of skills in the Handbook reflect all three categories in the California Historical and Social Sciences Analysis Skills: Chronological and Spatial Thinking; Historical Research, Evidence, and Point of View; and, Historical Interpretation.

Using these Skillbuilders will help you learn key history skills, such as interpreting points of view and distinguishing fact from opinion in historical interpretations. The 17 Skillbuilders listed are designed to go with each chapter. You will get the most from them if you use them as you are study. Each Skillbuilder has three parts:

- an explanation of why the skill is valuable

- step-by-step pointers for learning the skill

- an exercise to practice the skill that *uses the content of the chapter*

# CRITICAL THINKING
# SKILLBUILDER

## Making Comparisons

*For use with Chapter 1*

### Why Learn This Skill?

*When making comparisons, you identify the similarities and differences among two or more ideas, objects, or events.*

### Learning the Skill

Follow these steps to make comparisons:
- Find two subjects that can be compared. They should be similar enough to have characteristics that are common to both. For example, it would be more appropriate to compare a Greek statue to an Egyptian statue than to an abstract modern painting.
- Determine which features the subjects have in common that are suitable for comparison.
- Look for similarities and differences within these areas.
- If possible, find information that explains the similarities and differences.

### Practicing the Skill

The following excerpts from the text discuss Spartan and Athenian models for raising children. Read both excerpts, then answer the questions.

### Passage A

In Sparta, boys were trained to be soldiers. State officials examined all children at birth and decided whether they were fit to live. The "unfit" were left in the open on a mountainside to die. Boys judged fit were put under control of the state at age seven. They lived in military-style barracks and were subjected to harsh discipline. Their education stressed military training and obedience to authority.

### Passage B

Athenian children were nurtured by their mothers until the age of seven, when boys of the upper class were turned over to a male servant, known as a pedagogue. The pedagogue accompanied the child to school and was responsible for teaching his charge good manners. He could punish the child with a birch rod to impose discipline.

The purpose of an education for upper-class Athenian boys was to create a well-rounded person. A boy had three teachers. One taught reading, writing, and arithmetic; a second taught physical education; and a third taught music. Education ended at eighteen when a male formally became a citizen.

1. Make a chart with one column labeled Sparta and one labeled Athens. List the similarities in how the two states raised children, then list the differences.
2. How did the similarities and differences in raising children suit the needs of each city-state?

*Athena*

### Applying the Skill

Survey your classmates about an issue in the news. Summarize their opinions and compare the different results in a paragraph.

Glencoe's **Skillbuilder Interactive Workbook, Level 2,** provides instruction and practice in key social studies skills.

# CRITICAL THINKING
# SKILLBUILDER

## Understanding Cause and Effect

*For use with Chapter 2*

### Why Learn This Skill?

*It is important to understand how or why an event occurred. What action or situation caused an event? What were the effects or consequences of that action or situation?*

### Learning the Skill

To understand causes and effects, you need to know how or why an event occurred. A cause is the action or situation that produces an event. An effect is the result or consequence of an action or situation. To identify cause-and-effect relationships, follow these steps:

- Identify two or more events or developments.

- Decide whether one event caused the other. Look for "clue words," such as *because, led to, brought about, produced, as a result of, so that, since,* and *therefore.*

- Identify the outcomes of events.

Making a graphic organizer can help your understanding of cause and effect.

Read the passage below to see how it relates to the graphic organizer:

> George Grenville's financial program included the Stamp Act, requiring colonists to buy stamps for legal documents. This Act drew the boldest protests. The Massachusetts legislature issued a series of "Resolves" that insisted the people have "the Right of Representation." The Sons of Liberty, a protest group in Boston, held protest parades, destroyed stamps, and forced the stamp distributors to resign. Edmund Burke, a noted political thinker in Britain, defended the position of the colonists. In 1766, Parliament repealed the Act.

### Cause and Effect

**Cause**

- Stamp Act requires colonists to buy stamps.

**Effects**

- Massachusetts issues Resolves.
- Sons of Liberty lead protests.
- Edmund Burke speaks out.
- Parliament repeals the Stamp Act.

### Practicing the Skill

On a separate piece of paper, make a cause-and-effect diagram for each of these statements. Some statements may have more than one cause and effect.

1. When George Grenville became prime minister of England, he decided to help King George III solve some of the nation's financial problems. Parliament adopted Grenville's proposal of a Stamp Act.

2. The Stamp Act included a provision that anyone evading the stamp tax would be tried without a jury.

3. Colonial merchants decided not to import any British goods until the hated Stamp Act was repealed. When British merchants began to lose money, they pressured Parliament to repeal the law.

### Applying the Skill

Read about a current event in your local newspaper. Determine at least one cause and one effect of that event. Show the cause-and-effect relationship in a chart.

**GO TO** Glencoe's **Skillbuilder Interactive Workbook, Level 2,** provides instruction and practice in key social studies skills.

# SOCIAL STUDIES SKILLBUILDER

## Interpreting Graphs

*For use with Chapter 3*

### Why Learn This Skill?

*Graphs are one method of illustrating dates, facts, and figures. With a graph, you can compare change or differences easily. For example, your parents say you are spending too much money on clothes. They have a bar graph of your weekly expenses, and the clothing bar is higher each week. With a quick glance, you see that they are right and decide to make a graph illustrating that your allowance is not keeping up with inflation.*

### Learning the Skill

There are basically three types of graphs:

- **Circle graphs** They look like a pizza that has been divided into different size slices. They are useful for showing comparisons and percentages.

- **Bar graphs** Individual bars are drawn for each item being graphed. The length of the bars easily illustrates differences or changes over time.

- **Line graph** Each item is indicated by a point on the graph. The points are then connected by a line. You can tell how values have changed by whether the line is going up or down.

Most graphs also use words to label information. The steps below will help you interpret graphs.

- **Read the captions and title** If the graph is called "Randy's Weekly Clothing Expenses," then it will be plotting Randy's expenses every week. Each bar would be captioned with a weekly date, and the amounts that each bar represents would be clearly marked.

- **Determine the relationships among all sections of the graph** By looking at each bar, you can see the amount spent for that week. By comparing the bars with each other, you can see how Randy's expenses have changed from week to week.

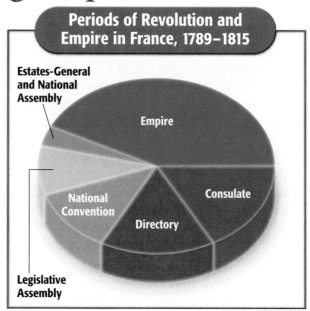

**Periods of Revolution and Empire in France, 1789–1815**

### Practicing the Skill

The circle graph above compares the length of time for different periods. Answer the following:

1. What was the longest of the six periods of the French Revolution?

2. What was the shortest of the six periods?

3. About what percentage of the total time did Napoleon rule France (he ruled during the Consulate and Empire)?

4. About what percentage of the time did the Directory rule?

### Applying the Skill

Pick a recent day and make a list of all of your activities in a 24-hour period. Now create a circle graph that shows the division of the day.

 Glencoe's **Skillbuilder Interactive Workbook, Level 2,** provides instruction and practice in key social studies skills.

# CRITICAL THINKING
# SKILLBUILDER

## Identifying an Argument

*For use with Chapter 4*

### Why Learn This Skill?

*In everyday conversation, the word **argument** refers to a conflict involving two or more opinions. In writing and in formal debate, an argument is the full presentation of a single opinion. An argument uses facts to support a particular opinion. After hearing these facts, it is up to you to determine whether the argument is valid.*

### Learning the Skill

There are three basic elements to consider:

- **What is the thesis?** The main idea of an argument is its thesis, or the basic position on the subject. In some arguments the thesis is stated explicitly. In others, you must read carefully to determine it.

- **What are the supporting reasons, examples, and facts?** The writer supports the thesis with reasons and supports the reasons with examples or facts.

- **What are its strengths and weaknesses?** First, evaluate the strengths and weaknesses of an argument. How well is it supported by facts and examples?

### Practicing the Skill

Read the following quotation published in 1842 in *L'Atelier (The Workshop)*, a Parisian newspaper. Then answer the following questions.

66Who has not heard of the women silkworkers . . . working fourteen to sixteen hours (except for one hour for both meals); always standing, without a single minute for repose [rest], putting forth an enormous amount of effort. And many of them have to walk a league or more, morning and evening, to get home, which is often a cause for moral disorder. Nor should we neglect to mention the danger that exists merely from working in these large factories, surrounded by wheels, gears, enormous leather belts that always threaten to seize you and pound you to pieces. There is not a factory in which some kind of accident has not happened—some woman worker

*Men, women, and children working in a factory*

caught by the hair or her clothing, and thereby pulverized; some mutilation of the fingers or the hands.99

❶ What is the writer's thesis?

❷ What reasons does the writer give to support this thesis?

❸ What facts support the statement that danger exists for the workers in the workplace?

❹ What is your reaction to the author's argument?

### Applying the Skill

Find a recent article that states an argument about a political or historical issue. Identify the thesis of the argument and the major reasons and evidence supporting it. Decide whether you accept or reject this argument and explain why.

Glencoe's **Skillbuilder Interactive Workbook, Level 2,** provides instruction and practice in key social studies skills.

# CRITICAL THINKING
# SKILLBUILDER

## Detecting Bias

*For use with Chapter 5*

### Why Learn This Skill?

*Suppose you see an ad showing two happy customers shaking hands with a used-car salesman. The ad says, "Visit Honest Harry for the best deal on wheels." That evening you see a television program that investigates used-car sales businesses. The report says that many of these businesses cheat their customers.*

*Each message expresses a bias—an inclination or prejudice that inhibits impartiality. Harry wants to sell cars; the television program wants to attract viewers. Most people have preconceived opinions that affect their judgment. Ideas stated as facts may be opinions. Detecting bias enables us to evaluate the accuracy of information.*

### Learning the Skill

In detecting bias:

- Identify the writer's or speaker's purpose.

- Watch for emotionally charged language such as *exploit, terrorize,* and *cheat.*

- Look for visual images that provoke a strong emotional response.

- Look for overgeneralizations such as *unique, honest,* and *everybody.*

- Notice italics, underlining, and punctuation that highlight particular ideas.

- Examine the material to determine whether it presents equal coverage of differing views.

### Practicing the Skill

Industrialization produced widespread changes in society and disagreement on its effects. Karl Marx and Friedrich Engels presented their viewpoint on industrialization in *The Communist Manifesto* in 1848. Read the following excerpt and then answer these questions.

> 66The bourgeoisie . . . has put an end to all feudal, patriarchal, idyllic relations. It has pitilessly torn asunder the motley feudal ties that bound man to his 'natural superiors,' and has left remaining no other nexus [link] between man and man than naked self-interest, than callous 'cash payment.' It has drowned the most heavenly of ecstasies of religious fervor, of chivalrous enthusiasm . . . in the icy water of egotistical calculation. . . . In one word, for exploitation, veiled by religious and political illusions, it has substituted naked, shameless, direct, brutal exploitation.99

1. What are three examples of emotionally charged language?

2. According to Marx and Engels, which is more inhumane—the exploitation by feudal lords or by the bourgeoisie? Why?

3. What bias about the bourgeoisie is expressed in this excerpt?

### Applying the Skill

Find written material about a topic of interest in your community. Possible sources include editorials, letters to the editor, and pamphlets from political candidates and interest groups. Write a short report analyzing the material for evidence of bias.

Glencoe's **Skillbuilder Interactive Workbook, Level 2,** provides instruction and practice in key social studies skills.

# TECHNOLOGY SKILLBUILDER

## Evaluating a Web Site

*For use with Chapter 6*

### Why Learn This Skill?

*Your little sister has developed a strange rash on her back, so you decide to check the Internet to see if it might be chicken pox and how the rash should be treated. When you look for a Web site, however, you find dozens, and they are all giving different advice. How do you determine which site is giving the most accurate and up-to-date information?*

*The Internet has become a valuable research tool. It is convenient to use and contains plentiful information. Unfortunately, some Web site information is not necessarily reliable. The user must distinguish between quality information and inaccurate information.*

### Learning the Skill

To evaluate a Web site, ask yourself the following questions:

- Where does the site originate? If it is a university, a well-known organization or agency, or a respected publication, then the information is likely to be trustworthy.

- Are the facts on the site documented? Where did this information originally come from? Is the author clearly identified?

- Are the links to other parts of the site appropriate? Do they take you to information that helps you learn more about the subject?

- Is more than one source used for background information within the site? If so, does the site contain a bibliography?

- When was the last time the site was updated?

- Does the site explore the topic in-depth?

- Does the site contain links to other useful and up-to-date resources? Some sites are more interested in sales than in providing accurate information.

- Is the information easy to access? Is it properly labeled?

### Practicing the Skill

Visit the Web site about Emilio Aguinaldo at *http://www.loc.gov/rr/hispanic/1898/aguinaldo.html* Then, answer the following questions.

1. Who is the author or sponsor of the Web site?

2. What information does the home page link you to? Are the links appropriate to the topic?

3. What sources were used for the information contained on the site? When was it last updated?

4. Does the site explore the topic in-depth? Why or why not?

5. Are there links to other useful sources and are they up-to-date?

6. When was Aguinaldo born? How easy or difficult was it to locate this information?

### Applying the Skill

**Comparing Web Sites** Locate two other Web sites that provide information about Emilio Aguinaldo. Evaluate each one for accuracy and usefulness, and then compare them to the site featured above (http://www.loc.gov/rr/hispanic/1898/aguinaldo.html).

# SOCIAL STUDIES SKILLBUILDER

## Finding Exact Location on a Map

*For use with Chapter 7*

### Why Learn This Skill?

*A friend tells you that she lives at the northwest corner of Vine Street and Oak Avenue. By giving you the names of two streets that cross, she has pinpointed her exact location. We use a similar system to identify the exact location of any place on Earth.*

### Learning the Skill

Over many centuries, cartographers developed a grid system of imaginary lines—lines of latitude and longitude. Lines of latitude run east and west around the earth. They are also called parallels. The parallel lines of latitude measure distance north and south of the Equator, which is located at 0 degrees latitude. Each line of latitude is one degree, or 69 miles (110 km), from the next. There are 90 latitude lines between the Equator and each pole. For example, New York City lies 41 degrees north of the Equator, or 41°N.

Lines of longitude, or meridians, run north and south from pole to pole. Lines of longitude are not always the same distance from each other. Lines of longitude are farthest apart at the Equator, and they intersect at the North and South Poles. The prime meridian marks 0 degrees longitude and runs through Greenwich, England, and western Africa. Longitude lines are measured by their distance east and west of the prime meridian up to 180 degrees. New York City, for example, lies 74 degrees west of the prime meridian, or 74°W.

With this system we can pinpoint the "grid address" of any place on Earth. For example, if we wanted to find a grid address for New York City, we would first find the line of latitude closest to it. Then, by following this line, we would locate the nearest line of longitude to cross it. The point where the lines intersect is the grid address. New York City's grid address would be 41°N, 74°W.

NATIONAL GEOGRAPHIC **Early Japan**

### Practicing the Skill

Use the map to answer these questions.

1. What is Ise's approximate grid address?
2. What city sits at approximately 35°N, 140°E?
3. What is Osaka's approximate grid address?
4. What is Mt. Fuji's approximate grid address?

### Applying the Skill

Create a travel itinerary for a tour of ancient Egypt, Greece, or Southwest Asia. Choose 10 sites to visit. Draw a map of each region, including grid lines. Then, identify each site's grid location.

 Glencoe's **Skillbuilder Interactive Workbook, Level 2,** provides instruction and practice in key social studies skills.

# CRITICAL THINKING
# SKILLBUILDER

# Interpreting Military Movements on Maps

*For use with Chapter 8*

## Why Learn This Skill?

*Wars begin over many different issues. Because wars are often fought over land, maps are particularly useful tools for seeing the "big picture" of a war.*

## Learning the Skill

The map key is essential in interpreting military maps. The key explains what the map's colors and symbols represent. Use the following steps to study the key:

- Determine the meanings of the colors on the map. Usually, colors represent different sides in the conflict.

- Identify all symbols. These may include symbols for battle sites, victories, and types of military units and equipment.

- Study the arrows, which show the direction of military movements. Because these movements occur over time, some maps give dates showing when and where troops advanced and retreated.

Once you have studied the key and the map, follow the progress of the campaign that is shown. Notice where each side began, in which direction it moved, where the two sides fought, and which side claimed victory.

## Practicing the Skill

The map on this page shows the Middle East front during World War I. Study the map and then answer the following questions.

➊ On which side did Arabia and Egypt fight?

➋ Who won the battle at the Dardanelles?

➌ Describe the movement of the Central Powers.

➍ When did the Allies win the most battles in the Middle East?

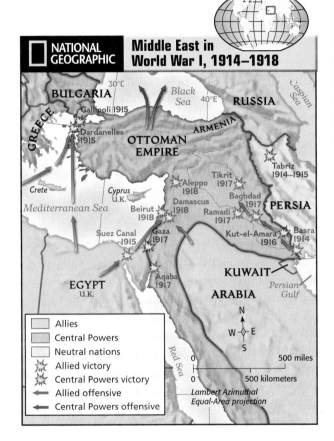

NATIONAL GEOGRAPHIC

**Middle East in World War I, 1914–1918**

Key:
- Allies
- Central Powers
- Neutral nations
- Allied victory
- Central Powers victory
- Allied offensive
- Central Powers offensive

*Lambert Azimuthal Equal-Area projection*

## Applying the Skill

Choose a military map from this text. Study the map carefully. Write a paragraph about the war or conflict as it is depicted. You should respond to issues such as where most of the fighting occurred; the year in which the most significant advance was made and whether there was a decisive victory. Attach a copy of the map to your report.

 Glencoe's **Skillbuilder Interactive Workbook, Level 2,** provides instruction and practice in key social studies skills.

# CRITICAL THINKING
# SKILLBUILDER

# Analyzing Political Cartoons

*For use with Chapter 9*

## Why Learn This Skill?

*What is your favorite comic strip? Why do you read it? Many people enjoy comics because they use interesting or amusing visuals to convey a story or idea.*

*Cartoons do not only appear in the newspaper's funny pages. They are also in the editorial section, where they give opinions on political issues. Political cartoons have been around for centuries and are good historical sources because they reflect the popular views on current affairs.*

## Learning the Skill

Using caricature and symbols, political cartoonists help readers see relationships and draw conclusions about events. A caricature exaggerates a detail such as a subject's features. Cartoonists use caricature to create a positive or negative impression. For example, if a cartoon shows one figure three times larger than another, it implies that one figure is more powerful than the other.

A symbol is an image or object that represents something else. Symbols often represent nations or political parties. Uncle Sam is a common symbol for the United States.

To analyze a political cartoon:

- Examine the cartoon thoroughly.
- Identify the topic and principal characters.
- Read labels and messages.
- Note relationships between the figures and symbols.
- Determine what point the cartoon is making.

## Practicing the Skill

In the next section of this chapter, you will be reading about several dictators who rose to power in Europe in the years following World War I.

This 1938 political cartoon makes a statement about dictators and the reaction of the Western democracies toward them. Study the cartoon and then answer these questions.

1. What do the figures represent?
2. Why is the standing figure so large?
3. What is the standing figure holding and what is it attached to?
4. What is the sitting figure doing?
5. What is the message of the cartoon?

*WOULD YOU OBLIGE ME WITH A MATCH PLEASE?*

**David Low,** *London Evening Standard*

## Applying the Skill

Choose a current issue on which you hold a strong opinion. Draw a political cartoon expressing your opinion on this issue. Show it to a friend to find out if the message is clear. If not, revise the cartoon to clarify its point.

 **GO TO** Glencoe's **Skillbuilder Interactive Workbook, Level 2,** provides instruction and practice in key social studies skills.

# CRITICAL THINKING SKILLBUILDER

## Making Inferences and Drawing Conclusions

*For use with Chapter 10*

### Why Learn This Skill?

*While driving, you hear a news story about a fire downtown. As you approach downtown, traffic is very heavy. You cannot see any smoke, but infer that the traffic is caused by the fire.*

*To infer means to evaluate information and arrive at a conclusion. When you make inferences, you draw conclusions that are not stated directly.*

### Learning the Skill

Follow the steps below to make inferences and draw conclusions:

- Read to determine the main facts and ideas and then write them down.

- Consider any information you know that relates to the topic. Then determine how your knowledge affects what you have read.

- What inferences can you make that are not specifically stated in the facts?

- Use your knowledge and reason to develop conclusions about the facts.

- If possible, find specific information that proves or disproves your inference.

### Practicing the Skill

Read the passage below. Then answer the questions that follow.

In 1930 the Indian National Congress, India's leading body of nationalists, declared that it wanted complete independence. The resistance movement against British rule began. In March, Mohandas Gandhi sent Viceroy Lord Irwin a letter, informing him that unless Indian demands were met, he would be compelled to break the salt laws. The letter simply amused the viceroy, so Gandhi set off with a few followers towards Dandi on the sea. There Gandhi

picked up a lump of natural salt, signaling thousands of people to defy the law. . . . Gandhi and thousands of others were hauled into jail. To break the deadlock, Irwin agreed to hold talks with Gandhi. Later the British agreed to hold a conference in London to negotiate possible terms for independence. Gandhi went to London in 1931, but the negotiations were inconclusive. On his return to India, he was once again arrested.

❶ What events does the writer describe?

❷ What facts are presented?

❸ What can you infer about the British government during this time?

❹ What conclusions can you make about Gandhi and the Indian people, other than those the author specifically states?

### Applying the Skill

Scan a newspaper or magazine for a political cartoon. Paste it on a piece of paper or poster board. Underneath, list three inferences based on the cartoon.

Glencoe's **Skillbuilder Interactive Workbook, Level 2,** provides instruction and practice in key social studies skills.

# CRITICAL THINKING
# SKILLBUILDER

## Synthesizing Information

*For use with Chapter 11*

### Why Learn This Skill?

*Consider what it would be like to get funding for a new after-school club. In order to present your case, you would need to talk to other students, school administrators, and read reports and articles. Once you had gathered all the information you needed, you would synthesize the most important points.*

*Synthesizing information involves combining information from two or more sources. The ability to synthesize information is important because information gained from one source often sheds new light upon other information. It is like putting the pieces of a puzzle together to form a complete picture. Being able to synthesize information will help you read and write more effectively.*

### Learning the Skill

To write a research report, you study several sources. Once you have gathered information, you synthesize it into a report. Before doing this, analyze each source separately. Determine its value and reliability. Then, look for connections and relationships among the different sources.

### Practicing the Skill

Study the passage and the photo on this page.

> Bombing was used in World War II against a variety of targets, including military targets, enemy troops, and civilian populations. The bombing of civilians in World War II made the home front a dangerous place. A few bombing raids had been conducted in the last year of World War I. The bombings and the reaction to them had given rise to the argument that bombing civilian populations would be an effective way to force governments to make peace.
>
> Beginning in early September 1940, the German air force bombed London and many other British cities

*Scottish city bombed in 1941*

and towns nightly. The blitz, as the British called the German air raids, became a national experience. Londoners took the first heavy blows. Their ability to maintain their morale set the standard for the rest of the British population.

❶ What is the main idea of the passage?

❷ What does the photo tell you about this topic?

❸ By synthesizing the two sources, what information do you have about the bombing of Britain?

### Applying the Skill

Find two sources of information about a current event and write a short report. For your report, try to use a primary and a secondary source, if possible. Answer these questions: What are the main ideas from these sources? How does each source add to your understanding of the topic? Do the sources support or contradict each other? If there are contradictions, how would you include the conflicting information in your report?

Glencoe's **Skillbuilder Interactive Workbook, Level 2,** provides instruction and practice in key social studies skills.

# CRITICAL THINKING
# SKILLBUILDER

## Analyzing Primary and Secondary Sources

*For use with Chapter 12*

### Why Learn This Skill?

*Suppose for a moment that a devastating tornado has struck a nearby town. On television that night, you watch an interview with an eyewitness. The eyewitness begins to cry as he describes the destruction of his own home and neighborhood. The next day, you read a newspaper account that describes the tornado's path. Is one of these accounts of the same event more accurate than the other?*

### Learning the Skill

To determine the accuracy of an account, you must analyze its source. There are two main types of sources—primary and secondary.

Primary sources are produced by eyewitnesses to events. Diaries, letters, autobiographies, interviews, artifacts, and paintings are primary sources. Because primary sources convey direct experiences, they often include emotions and opinions.

Secondary sources use information gathered from others. Newspapers, textbooks, and biographies are secondary sources. Secondary sources are written later to put events in a larger context or time frame.

To determine reliability of a source, consider first what kind of source you are using. If it is a primary source, determine when it was written and who wrote it. An account written during or immediately after an event may have information available nowhere else, but it might also come from someone who was a participant. Thus a primary source is more likely to reflect only one point of view. If you are using a secondary source, look for good documentation. Researchers should cite their sources in footnotes and bibliographies.

For both types of sources, evaluate the author. Is he or she biased? What background and authority does he or she have?

### Practicing the Skill

Read the following excerpts and answer the questions:

> ❝Stalin wrote to Churchill that elections were the only way to solve the problem of what political course Poland would follow. A date for the election was set. It was to be basically a referendum to decide whom the Polish people trusted and whom they wanted to have in their leadership. . . . The elections were a success for us and a failure for Churchill. . . . The Polish Workers' Party and the parties allied with it received an absolute majority of the votes.❞
>
> ***Khrushchev Remembers*, 1974, pp. 171–173**

> ❝From Stettin in the Baltic to Trieste in the Adriatic, an iron curtain has descended across the Continent. Behind that line lie all the capitals of the ancient states of Central and Eastern Europe. . . . All these famous cities and the populations around them lie in what I must call the Soviet sphere. . . . The Communist parties, which were very small in all these Eastern States of Europe, have been raised to pre-eminence and power far beyond their numbers and are seeking everywhere to obtain totalitarian control.❞
>
> **Winston Churchill, Westminster College, 1946**

❶ What is the general topic of the two sources?

❷ Identify the primary sources.

❸ Is one account more reliable than the other? If so, why? How do you know?

### Applying the Skill

Find two accounts of a recent event or a historical event. Analyze the reliability of each. Be sure to document how you reached your conclusions.

Glencoe's **Skillbuilder Interactive Workbook, Level 2,** provides instruction and practice in key social studies skills.

# Summarizing Information

*For use with Chapter 13*

## Why Learn This Skill?

*Imagine you have begun to read a chapter on the end of the Cold War in preparation for a quiz. After taking a short break, you realize that you cannot recall important information. What can you do to avoid this problem?*

*When you read a long selection, it is helpful to take notes. Summarizing information—reducing large amounts of information to a few key phrases—can help you remember the main ideas and important facts.*

## Learning the Skill

To summarize information, follow these guidelines when you read:

- Distinguish the main ideas from the supporting details. Use the main ideas in the summary.

- Use your own words to describe the main ideas. Do not copy the selection word for word.

- Summarize the author's opinion if you think it is important.

- If the summary is almost as long as the reading selection, you are including too much information. The summary should be very short.

## Practicing the Skill

Read the selection below, and then answer the questions that follow.

As the Soviet Union tried to compete with America's rapidly expanding technology in the 1980s, several obstacles faced the Communist Party. An inefficient system provided little incentive for workers. The Soviets could not build and maintain a vast weapons arsenal and provide basic food, shelter, and clothing for their people. Pressure for change was already building when President Reagan visited Berlin and said: "Mr. Gorbachev, tear down this wall." By 1989 the Communists had lost control of Eastern Europe. Soon after the United States and the Soviet Union signed the START treaty, the Soviet Union ceased to exist as a nation.

➊ What are the main ideas of this paragraph?
➋ What are the details that support the main ideas?
➌ Write a brief summary of two or three sentences that will help you remember what the paragraph is about.

## Applying the Skill

Read and summarize two articles from the front page of a newspaper. Have a classmate ask you questions about them. How much were you able to remember after summarizing the information?

 Glencoe's **Skillbuilder Interactive Workbook, Level 2,** provides instruction and practice in key social studies skills.

# STUDY & WRITING
# SKILLBUILDER

# Writing a Report

*For use with Chapter 14*

## Why Learn This Skill?

*You have learned about taking notes, making outlines, and finding sources for researching a paper. Now how do you put all those skills together to actually write a report?*

## Learning the Skill

Use the following guidelines to help you in writing a report:

- **Select an interesting topic.** As you identify possible topics, focus on resources that are available. Do preliminary research to determine whether your topic is too broad or too narrow. For example, Brazil in the twentieth century is a very broad topic. Narrow it down to one event in the twentieth century, such as the construction of the capital city, Brasília, or to a certain time period. If you find it difficult to find information, your topic is probably too narrow.

- **Write a thesis statement.** The thesis defines what you want to prove, discover, or illustrate in your report.

- **Prepare and do research on your topic.** Make a list of main idea questions, and then do research to answer those questions. Prepare note cards on each main idea question, listing the source information.

- **Organize your information.** Use an outline or another kind of organizer. Then follow your outline or organizer in writing a rough draft of your report.

- **Include an introduction, main body, and conclusion.** The introduction briefly presents the topic and gives your thesis statement. The main body should follow your outline to develop the important ideas in your argument. The conclusion summarizes and restates your findings.

- **Revise the first draft.** Before writing the final draft of your report, wait one day and then reread and revise your first draft.

## Practicing the Skill

Suppose you are writing a report on the Changing Ecology of the Amazon Rain Forest. Answer the following questions about the writing process.

1. What is a possible thesis statement?
2. What are three main idea questions?
3. What are three possible sources of information?
4. What are the next two steps in the process of writing a report?

## Applying the Skill

Review the thesis, questions, and resources you found for the report on the Changing Ecology of the Amazon Rain Forest. Using this information, continue your research, organize your information, and write a short report.

Glencoe's **Skillbuilder Interactive Workbook, Level 2,** provides instruction and practice in key social studies skills.

# CRITICAL THINKING
# SKILLBUILDER

# Distinguishing Between Fact and Opinion

*For use with Chapter 15*

## Why Learn This Skill?

*Imagine that you are watching two candidates for president debate the merits of the college loan program. One says, "In my view, the college loan program must be reformed. Sixty percent of students do not repay their loans on time."*

*The other replies, "College costs are skyrocketing, but only 30 percent of students default on their loans for more than one year. I believe we should spend more on this worthy program."*

*How can you tell who or what to believe?*

## Learning the Skill

A fact is a statement that can be proved to be true. In the example above, the statement "Sixty percent of students do not repay their loans on time" is a

fact. By reviewing statistics on who repay their loans, we can determine whether it is true or false. To identify facts, look for words and phrases indicating specific people, places, events, dates, and times.

An opinion expresses a personal belief, viewpoint, or emotion. Because opinions are subjective, we cannot prove or disprove them. Opinions often include qualifying words and phrases such as *I think, I believe, probably,* or *in my view.* Also, look for expressions of approval or disproval such as *good, bad, poor,* and *satisfactory.*

## Practicing the Skill

Read each set of statements below about terrorism by Tony Blair, Britain's Prime Minister. Determine which one is fact and which is an interpretative statement. Give a reason for your answer.

### Set 1

- No decision I have ever made in politics has been as divisive as the decision to go to war in Iraq.
- We have had three inquiries, including the one by Lord Hutton conducted over six months.

### Set 2

- We spent October and November in the U.N. negotiating U.N. Resolution 1441.
- Here is where I feel so passionately that we are in mortal danger of mistaking the nature of the new world in which we live.

## Applying the Skill

Find a news article and an editorial pertaining to the same subject in your local newspaper. Identify three facts and three opinions from these sources.

**GO TO** Glencoe's **Skillbuilder Interactive Workbook, Level 2,** provides instruction and practice in key social studies skills.

# SKILLBUILDER

# Reading a Cartogram

*For use with Chapter 16*

## Why Learn This Skill?

*Maps show countries in proportion to their amount of land area. For example, Japan is much smaller than China and is depicted that way on a map. Japan, however, has a greater gross national product than China. If we wanted to depict GNP size on a map, how would it look?*

*Cartograms are maps that show countries according to a value other than land area. They might portray features such as populations or economies. Cartograms distort countries' sizes and shapes. This makes it possible to see at a glance how each country or region compares with another. Therefore, on a cartogram showing gross national products, Japan looks larger than China.*

## Learning the Skill

To use a cartogram:

- Read the title and key to identify what value the cartogram illustrates.

- Examine the cartogram to see which countries or regions appear.

- Find the largest and smallest countries.

- Compare the cartogram with a conventional land-area map to determine the degree of distortion of particular countries.

## Practicing the Skill

Study the cartogram and answer the questions.

❶ What is the subject of the cartogram?

❷ What countries are represented?

❸ Which country appears largest on the cartogram? Which appears smallest?

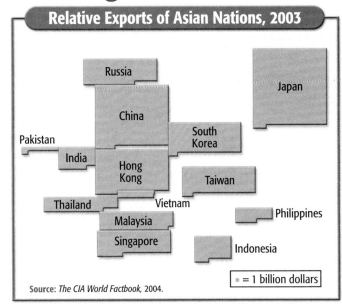

**Relative Exports of Asian Nations, 2003**

Russia • China • Japan • Pakistan • India • South Korea • Hong Kong • Taiwan • Thailand • Vietnam • Philippines • Malaysia • Singapore • Indonesia

■ = 1 billion dollars

Source: *The CIA World Factbook,* 2004.

❹ Compare the cartogram to the map of Asia found in the Atlas. Which countries are most distorted in size compared to a land-area map?

❺ What accounts for these distortions?

## Applying the Skill

At the library, find statistics that compare different countries. For example, you might compare the amount of oil in North America.

Convert these statistics into a cartogram. Determine the relative size of each country according to the chosen value. If the United States consumes five times more oil than Mexico, then the United States should appear five times larger than Mexico.

Glencoe's **Skillbuilder Interactive Workbook, Level 2,** provides instruction and practice in key social studies skills.

# CRITICAL THINKING
# SKILLBUILDER

# Making Generalizations

*For use with Chapter 17*

## Why Learn This Skill?

*Generalizations are broad statements or principles derived from specific facts. Here are some facts about world population growth.*

| World Population | 1750 | 1800 | 1950 | 2000 |
|---|---|---|---|---|
| | 760 million | 1 billion | 1.2 billion | 6.1 billion |

One generalization that can be made from these facts is that world population is growing at an increasingly rapid rate. Generalizations are useful when you want to summarize large amounts of information and when detailed information is not required.

## Learning the Skill

To make a valid generalization, follow these steps:

- **Identify the subject matter.** The example above compares world population at four different dates.

- **Gather related facts and examples.** The two sets of dates are 50 years apart (1750 and 1800; 1950 and 2000).

- **Identify similarities and differences among these facts.** In the examples, there is an increase in population, but the increase is greater between 1950 and 2000.

- **Use these observations to form a general statement about the subject.** How much faster did world population grow in the period 1950 to 2000?

## Practicing the Skill

Read the following excerpt from an on–line report of the Population Reference Bureau, a standard source for population trends. Then answer the questions that follow.

In 1800, the vast majority of the world's population (86 percent) resided in Asia and Europe, with 65 percent in Asia alone. By 1900, Europe's share of world population had risen to 25 percent, fueled by the population increase that accompanied the Industrial Revolution. Some of this growth spilled over to the Americas, increasing their share of the world total.

World population growth accelerated after World War II, when the population of less developed countries began to increase dramatically. . . . The human population indeed grew explosively, doubling again and again; a billion people were added between 1960 and 1975; another billion were added between 1975 and 1987. Throughout the 20th century each additional billion has been achieved in a shorter period of time. Human population entered the 20th century with 1.6 billion people and left the century with 6.1 billion. The growth of the last 200 years appears explosive on the historical timeline. The overall effects of this growth on living standards, resource use, and the environment will continue to change the world landscape long after.

**–from the Population Reference Bureau, 2004**

Based on this excerpt, identify whether each statement is valid.

1. The population growth of less developed countries contributed to the population explosion.

2. New technologies of the twentieth century were largely responsible for the population growth.

3. Soon the world will not have enough food to sustain its population.

## Applying the Skill

Over the next three weeks, read the editorials in your local newspaper. Write a list of generalizations about the newspaper's position on issues that have been discussed, either national or local.

Glencoe's **Skillbuilder Interactive Workbook, Level 2,** provides instruction and practice in key social studies skills.

# Glossary

This glossary includes all the content vocabulary words and academic vocabulary words from your text. Content vocabulary relates to history content. These words are boldfaced and highlighted in yellow in your text. Academic vocabulary will help you understand all of your school subjects. These words are boldfaced in your text and are shown with an asterisk in the glossary.

## A

*abandon to give up control or influence to another person or idea (p. 282)

abolitionism a movement to end slavery (p. 279)

*abstract having only intrinsic form with little or no attempt at pictorial representation or narrative content (p. 488)

*academy a high school or college where special subjects or skills are taught (p. 480)

*accurate free from error as the result of attention to detail (p. 664)

*achieve to reach a goal; accomplish (p. 537)

acid rain the rainfall that results when sulfur produced by factories mixes with moisture in the air (p. 745)

*adapt to make fit for a specific or new use or situation by modifying or changing (p. 284)

*adjust to conform to fit into a new place or situation (p. 553)

*administration the group of political executives who help the President run the country (p. 587)

*adult a man or woman who has reached a certain age declared by law (p. 135)

*affect to produce an effect upon someone or something (p. 185)

*aid to give assistance (p. 584)

al-Qaeda terrorist group led by Osama bin Laden which recruited Muslims and sent money and arms to Afghanistan to support the Afghan resistance (p. 696)

*alter to give a different position, course, or direction to something or someone (p. 423)

*alternative something that can be chosen instead of something else (p. 561)

*amendment an alteration proposed or effected by the process of parliamentary or constitutional procedure (p. 197)

annex incorporate territory into an existing political unit, such as a city or country (p. 343)

*annual occurring or happening every year or once a year; yearly (p. 323)

*anticipate to give advance thought to an action expected to occur (p. 424)

apartheid "apartness," the system of racial segregation in South Africa from the 1950s until 1991 (p. 678)

*apparent open to view; obvious (p. 616)

appeasement satisfying demands of dissatisfied powers in an effort to maintain peace and stability (p. 537)

*approach to take preliminary steps toward a particular purpose (p. 752)

*arbitrary not restrained or fixed by law (p. 682)

armistice a truce or agreement to end fighting (p. 449)

arms race building up armies and stores of weapons to keep up with an enemy (p. 586)

Articles of Confederation the American nation's first constitution approved in 1781 (p. 196)

*assembly a company of persons gathered for deliberation and legislation, worship, or entertainment (p. 197)

assembly line a production system with machines and workers arranged so that each person performs an assigned task again and again as the item passes before him or her (p. 297)

*assume to believe that something is true even if it has not been stated directly; suppose (p. 539)

*assure to inform or promise a positive result (p. 435)

*attitude a belief about something or someone (p. 355)

*attribute to give credit to someone for their words or actions (p. 176)

autonomous self-governing (p. 623)

*aware having or showing realization, perception, or knowledge (p. 508)

## B

*behalf in the interest of something or someone else (p. 424)

*beneficial conducive to personal or social well-being (p. 265)

Bill of Rights the first ten amendments to the Constitution ratified in 1789 (p. 197)

bioterrorism the use of biological and chemical weapons in terrorist attacks (p. 747)

biowarfare the use of disease or poison against civilians and soldiers in wartime (p. 747)

blitzkrieg German for "lightning war," a swift and sudden military attack; used by the Germans during World War II (p. 542)

bloc a group of nations with a common purpose (p. 600)

bourgeoisie the middle class, including merchants, industrialists, and professional people (p. 213)

Buddhism a religious doctrine introduced in northern India in the sixth century B.C. by Siddhartha Gautama, known as the Buddha, or "Enlightened One" (p. 128)

budget deficit the state that exists when a government spends more than it collects in revenues (p. 629)

**Camisea Gas Project** a pipeline carrying natural gas from the Amazon jungle through Peru (p. 666)

*__capable__ a person having attributes (such as intelligence) required for performance or accomplishment (p. 231)

**capital** money available for investment (p. 254)

**caste system** a set of rigid categories in ancient India that determined a person's occupation and economic potential as well as his or her position in society (p. 127)

**Catholic Church** the first major organized Christian institution in Europe (p. 151)

**caudillo** in post-revolutionary Latin America, a strong leader who ruled chiefly by military force, usually with the support of the landed elite (p. 365)

*__challenge__ to dispute as being unjust, invalid, or outdated (p. 659)

**Christianity** monotheistic religion that emerged during the first-century (p. 147)

*__circumstance__ a condition, fact, or event accompanying, conditioning, or determining another (p. 469)

**civil disobedience** refusal to obey laws that are considered to be unjust (p. 510)

**civilization** a complex culture in which large numbers of people share basic elements such as a social structure, religion, and art (p. 122)

**civil rights movement** equal rights movement for African Americans beginning in 1954 (p. 601)

*__classical__ not involving relativity, wave mechanics, or quantum theory (p. 491)

*__clause__ a distinct article in a formal document (p. 451)

*__code__ a system of principles or rules (p. 122)

*__coincide__ to happen at the same time or place (p. 444)

**Cold War** the period of political tension following World War II and ending with the fall of communism in the Soviet Union at the end of the 1980s (p. 563)

**collaborator** a person who assists the enemy (p. 555)

**collective bargaining** the right of unions to negotiate with employers over wages and hours (p. 468)

**collectivization** a system in which private farms are eliminated and peasants work land owned by the government (p. 475)

**colony** a settlement of people living in a new territory, linked with the parent country by trade and direct government control (p. 191)

**commodity** a marketable product (p. 391)

**common law** a uniform system of law developed in England based on court decisions and on customs and usage rather than on written law codes; replaces law codes that varied from place to place (p. 156)

**commonwealth** a republic (p. 180)

**commune** in China during the 1950s, a group of collective farms each of which contained more than 30,000 people who lived and worked together (p. 710)

*__communications__ systems for communicating, like telephones or the Internet (p. 588)

*__compensate__ to make an appropriate and usually counterbalancing payment to (p. 399)

*__compensation__ payment to unemployed or injured workers or their dependants (p. 314)

*__concentrate__ to focus all attention on something or someone (p. 448)

**concentration camp** a camp where prisoners of war, political prisoners, or members of minority groups are confined, typically under harsh conditions (p. 480)

*__concept__ an abstract or generic idea generalized from particular instances (p. 185)

**concession** political compromise (p. 397)

*__confer__ to bestow, or give, from a position of superiority to someone of lesser power (p. 156)

*__conference__ a meeting of two or more people to discuss common problems and concerns (p. 537)

*__conflict__ struggle resulting from opposing needs, drives, wishes, or external or internal demands (p. 346)

*__conform__ to be obedient or compliant (p. 593)

**Confucianism** the system of political and ethical ideas formulated by the Chinese philosopher Confucius toward the end of the Zhou dynasty; it was intended to help restore order to a society that was in a state of confusion. (p. 129)

**conscription** military draft (p. 423)

*__consensus__ a general agreement (p. 181)

*__consequence__ something produced by a cause or unavoidably following from a set of conditions (p. 348)

**conservatism** a political philosophy based on tradition and social stability, favoring obedience to political authority and organized religion (p. 265)

*__consistent__ marked by harmony, regularity, or steady continuity; free from variation or contradiction (p. 449)

*__constant__ continually occurring or recurring (p. 753)

*__constitutional__ loyal to or supporting an established constitution or form of government (p. 518)

**consulate** government established in France after the overthrow of the Directory in 1799, with Napoleon as first consul in control of the entire government (p. 230)

*__consumer__ a person who buys economic goods (p. 213)

**consumer society** a society that is preoccupied with buying goods, not producing one (p. 603)

**contras** rebels financed by the United States who began a guerrilla war against the Sandinista government in Nicaragua (p. 662)

*__controversy__ a discussion marked by the opposing views of individuals or groups (p. 284)

**Glossary**

**\*cooperation** the act of working with others; acting together (p. 624)

**cooperative** a farm organization owned by and operated for the benefit of the farmers (p. 666)

**\*core** a central and often foundational part of something larger (p. 128)

**\*correspondence** communication by letters (p. 193)

**cottage industry** a method of production in which tasks are done by individuals in their rural homes (p. 255)

**coup d'état** a sudden overthrow of the government (p. 225)

**covenant** contract (p. 126)

**\*creation** the act of making, inventing, or producing (p. 585)

**creole** a person of European descent born in the Americas and living there permanently (p. 363)

**\*crucial** important or essential (p. 313)

**cultural imperialism** the idea that a Western nation controls other world cultures, much as they had actual governments of colonies in the age of imperialism (p. 636)

**\*currency** paper money in circulation (p. 626)

**Declaration of Independence** a document written by Thomas Jefferson in 1789 outlining why American colonies were free from Britain (p. 194)

**\*decline** to move toward an inferior state or weaker condition (p. 380)

**deficit spending** when a government pays out more money than it takes in through taxation and other revenues, thus going into debt (p. 469)

**deforestation** the clearing of forests (p. 744)

**deism** an eighteenth-century religious philosophy based on reason and natural law (p. 185)

**demilitarize** eliminate or prohibit weapons, fortifications, and other military installations (p. 536)

**democracy** "the rule of the many," government by the people, either directly or through their elected representatives (p. 136)

**depression** a period of low economic activity and rising unemployment (p. 466)

**\*derive** to take, receive, or obtain from a specified source (p. 733)

**Desaparecidos** "the Disappeared," opponents of the Pinochet regime in Chile who were arrested and never seen again (p. 666)

**\*design** to create, fashion, execute, or construct according to plan (p. 699)

**de-Stalinization** the process of eliminating Stalin's more ruthless policies (p. 593)

**détente** a phase of relaxed tensions and improved relations between two adversaries (p. 616)

**deterrence** security policy which holds that if two sides in a political conflict have huge arsenals of nuclear weapons, war can be prevented (p. 587)

**dictatorship** a form of government in which a person or small group has absolute power (p. 300)

**direct democracy** a system of government in which the people participate directly in government decision making through mass meetings (p. 138)

**direct rule** colonial government in which local elites are removed from power and replaced by a new set of officials brought from the mother country (p. 339)

**Directory** a committee of five created by France's Constitution of 1795, lasting until 1799 (p. 225)

**disarmament groups** organizations working toward limiting or reducing armed forces and weapons (p. 752)

**discrimination** prejudice, usually based on race, religion, class, sex, or age (pp. 322, 725)

**dissident** a person who speaks out against the regime in power (p. 616)

**divine right of kings** the belief that kings receive their power from God and are responsible only to God (p. 176)

**\*domestic** relating to or originating in a country, especially one's own country (p. 220)

**\*dominate** to rule or control (p. 363)

**domino theory** idea that, if one country falls to communism, neighboring countries will also fall (p. 589)

**Duma** the Russian legislative assembly (p. 315)

**\*dynamic** marked by a continuous and productive activity or change (p. 254)

**ecology** the study of the relationships between living things and their environment (p. 744)

**elector** an individual qualified to vote in an election (p. 225)

**\*element** one of the a number of distinct groups composing a larger group (p. 660)

**\*eliminate** to cast out or get rid of (p. 504)

**emancipation** the act of setting free (p. 278)

**\*emerge** to rise from an obscure or inferior position (p. 299)

**\*emphasis** to place importance on something (p. 367)

**enclosure movement** landowners fence off common land previously used by peasants (p. 254)

**\*ensure** to make certain or safe (p. 385)

**entrepreneur** a person interested in finding new business opportunities and new ways to make profits (p. 254)

**\*equip** to make ready for service or action by gathering the needed supplies (p. 400)

**\*establish** to introduce (p. 504)

Glossary

**\*estate** one of the three classes into which French society was divided before the revolution: the clergy (first estate), the nobles (second estate), and the townspeople (third estate); a person's property, usually with a large house located within (pp. 212, 146)

**\*ethnic** of or relating to large groups of people belonging to the same racial, national, tribal, religious, linguistic, or cultural origin or background (p. 422)

**ethnic cleansing** a policy of killing or forcibly removing an ethnic group from its lands; used by the Serbs against the Muslim minority in Bosnia (pp. 503, 623)

**\*evidence** legitimate proof of an idea, occurrence, or action that has been questioned by an individual or society (p. 184)

**\*exclusion** the act of preventing or restricting a person from belonging to a group (p. 215)

**\*expand** to increase the number or volume of something (p. 369)

**\*expansion** the act or process of expanding or gaining land (p. 616)

**\*exploit** to make productive use of, sometimes selfishly or unjustly (p. 339)

**\*external** of or relating to dealings or relationships with foreign countries (p. 221)

**extraterritoriality** living in a section of a country set aside for foreigners but not subject to the host country's laws (p. 381)

---
**F**
---

**faction** a dissenting group (p. 220)

**fascism** a political philosophy that glorifies the state above the individual by emphasizing the need for a strong central government led by a dictatorial ruler (p. 471)

**favelas** in Brazil, squatter settlements lacking basic urban services (p. 654)

**\*federal** operating on behalf of the national government (p. 697)

**federal system** a form of government in which power is shared between the national government and state governments (p. 196)

**feminism** the movement for women's rights (p. 307)

**feudalism** political and social system that developed during the Middle Ages, when royal governments were no longer able to defend their subjects; nobles offered protection and land in return for service (p. 155)

**finance** to provide with necessary funds (p. 651)

**Five-Year Plan** economic goals set by Stalin for five-year periods to transform Russia virtually overnight from an agricultural into an industrial country (p. 474)

**\*focus** to concentrate attention or effort (p. 123)

**\*found** to establish an institution often with terms of future maintenance (p. 624)

**\*foundation** basis on which something stands or is supported (p. 140)

---

**G**
---

**\*gender** a person's sexual identity (p. 725)

**gender parity** policies that encourage more women to become part of government (p. 634)

**\*generator** a machine that changes mechanical energy into electrical energy (p. 296)

**genocide** the deliberate mass murder of a particular racial, political, or cultural group (pp. 503, 553)

**globalization** a term with both positive and negative connotations referring to the trend toward development of a global economy and culture (p. 632)

**\*goal** something that one works for; aim (p. 135)

**\*grant** to consent to carry out for a person or entity (p. 154)

**greenhouse effect** global warming caused by the buildup of carbon dioxide in the atmosphere (p. 745)

**guerrilla tactics** the use of unexpected maneuvers like sabotage and subterfuge to fight an enemy (p. 516)

---
**H**
---

**heavy industry** the manufacture of machines and equipment for factories and mines (p. 593)

**Hinduism** a major Indian religious system, which had its origins in the religious beliefs of the Aryans who settled India after 1500 B.C. (p. 128)

**\*hypothetical** a statement that is a part of an assumption or concession made for the sake of argument (p. 181)

---

**I**
---

**\*ideology** a systematic body of ideas, especially about human life or culture (p. 482)

**\*impact** a significant or major effect (p. 559)

**\*implement** to begin or carry out a plan or course of action (p. 552)

**\*impose** to establish or bring about as if by force (p. 339)

**\*incapable** lacking capacity or ability to accomplish a goal (p. 488)

**\*indefinite** not precise; undetermined (p. 543)

**indemnity** payment for damages (p. 386)

**indigenous** native to a region (p. 347)

**indirect rule** colonial government in which local rulers are allowed to maintain their positions of authority and status (p. 339)

**industrial capitalism** an economic system based on industrial production or manufacturing (p. 260)

*injure to physically hurt someone (p. 713)

*innovation the introduction of a new idea, method, or device (p. 303)

*integrate to incorporate into a larger unit (p. 391)

*integrity the quality or state of being complete and undivided (p. 512)

*intifada* "uprising," militant movement that arose during the 1980s among supporters of the Palestine Liberation Organization living in Israel (p. 691)

*involvement participation (p. 725)

Irish Republican Army (IRA) militant nationalists who want to unite Northern Ireland (p. 694)

*irrelevant insignificant or unimportant (p. 444)

Islam monotheistic religion that emerged in the Arabian Peninsula during the seventh century (p. 153)

*isolationism a policy of national isolation by not forming alliances or other international political and economic relations (p. 543)

Judaism monotheistic religion developed among the Israelites (p. 125)

kaiser German for "caesar," the title of the emperors of the Second German Empire (p. 275)

kamikaze Japanese for "divine wind," a suicide mission in which young Japanese pilots intentionally flew their airplanes into U.S. fighting ships at sea (p. 561)

*labor human activity that provides the goods or services in the economy (p. 536)

laissez-faire literally, "let [people] do [what they want]," the concept that the state should not impose government regulations but should leave the economy alone (p. 187)

*levy to impose or collect by legal authority (p. 274)

*liberal an individual, group, or idea that does not strictly observe orthodox, traditional, or established forms or ways (p. 232)

liberalism a political philosophy originally based largely on Enlightenment principles, holding that people should be as free as possible from government restraint and that civil liberties—the basic rights of all people—should be protected (p. 266)

*liberation the act of freeing a country from domination by a foreign power (p. 637)

literacy the ability to read and write (p. 308)

magic realism a form of expression unique to Latin American literature; it combines realistic events with dreamlike or fantastic backgrounds (p. 654)

Magna Carta the "Great Charter" of rights, which King John was forced to sign by the English nobles at Runnymede in 1215 (p. 156)

Mahatma "Great Soul," title given to Mohandas Gandhi by the Indian people (p. 510)

*maintain to sustain against opposition or danger; uphold and defend (p. 523)

mandate a nation governed by another nation on behalf of the League of Nations (p. 452)

mass production the production of large quantities of goods using machinery and often an assembly line (p. 297)

megacities cities with rapidly increasing populations, having trouble keeping up with urban services (p. 653)

*mental of or relating to the total emotional and intellectual response of an individual to external reality (p. 746)

mestizo a person of mixed European and native American Indian descent (p. 364)

*method a way, technique, or process of or for doing something (p. 628)

*migrate to move from one country, place, or locality to another (p. 257)

militarism reliance on military strength (p. 274)

*minimum the lowest amount possible (p. 469)

ministerial responsibility the idea that the prime minister is responsible to the popularly elected executive body and not to the executive officer (p. 313)

*minority a smaller group within society, usually differing from the majority (pp. 149, 559)

mobilization the process of assembling troops and supplies and making them ready for war (p. 424)

modernism a movement in which writers and artists between 1870 and 1914 rebelled against the traditional literary and artistic styles that had dominated European cultural life since the Renaissance (pp. 323, 490)

monotheistic having one god (p. 126)

Monroe Doctrine the United States policy guaranteeing the independence of Latin American nations and warning against European intervention in the Americas, made by President James Monroe in 1823 (p. 365)

*motive something, like a need or desire, that causes a person to act (p. 690)

multinational corporation a company with divisions in more than two countries (p. 651)

multinational state a political area made up of people with different ethnicities (p. 269)

Glossary

**\*mutual** obligations, expenses, or various other responsibilities shared with another individual or group (p. 181)

**nationalism** the unique cultural identity of a people based on common language, religion, and national symbols (p. 234)

**natural rights** rights with which all humans are supposedly born, including the rights to life, liberty, and property (p. 181)

**natural selection** the principle set forth by Darwin that some organisms are more adaptable to the environment than others; in popular terms, "survival of the fittest" (p. 284)

**Nazi** the National Socialist German Workers' Party (NSDAP) led by Adolf Hitler (p. 480)

**\*network** a group of interconnected people who exchange services (p. 127)

**\*neutrality** remaining impartial by refusing to participate in a war between other powers (p. 543)

**New Economic Policy (NEP)** a modified version of the old capitalist system adopted by Lenin in 1921 to replace war communism in Russia; peasants were allowed to sell their produce, and retail stores and small industries could be privately owned, but heavy industry, banking, and mines remained in the hands of the government (p. 473)

**New Imperialism** the extension of direct control by European power over other regions of the world, especially Africa, in the late 1800s (p. 336)

**New Order** a new Asian order including Japan, China, and Manchuria, that would result in Asian prosperity (p. 539)

**\*nuclear** of or relating to the atomic nucleus (p. 745)

**\*objective** something toward which effort is directed; an aim, goal, or end of action (p. 305)

**occupied** held by a foreign power (p. 727)

**\*occupy** to take or hold possession or control of (p. 585)

**oligarchy** "the rule of the few," a form of government in which a small group of people exercises control (pp. 136, 522)

**one-child policy** a policy in China that awards families with only one child education benefits, child care, and housing (p. 714)

**Open Door policy** a proposal that ensured equal access to the Chinese market for all nations and preserved the unity of the Chinese Empire (p. 385)

**OPEC** the Organization of Petroleum Exporting Countries formed in 1960 by several Arab oil-producing nations to control the price of oil (p. 691)

**organic evolution** the principle set forth by Darwin that every plant or animal has evolved, or changed, over a long period of time from earlier, simpler forms of life to more complex forms (p. 283)

**outsourcing** a practice in which companies send certain jobs, such as data entry or customer service, to countries with lower wages (p. 722)

**ozone layer** a thin layer of gas in the upper atmosphere that shields Earth from the Sun's ultraviolet rays (p. 745)

**Pan-Africanism** the unity of all black Africans, regardless of national boundaries (pp. 509, 679)

**Pan-Arabism** Arab unity, regardless of national boundaries (p. 690)

**\*parallel** similar or analogous in tendency or development (p. 665)

**parliament** a representative body of advisers to a king or other chief executive (p. 156)

**partisan** a resistance fighter in World War II (p. 550)

**patriarchal** dominated by men (p. 123)

**patrician** great landowners, they formed the ruling class in the Roman Republic (p. 145)

**Patriot Act** an antiterrorist bill passed after 9/11 that allows secret searches to avoid tipping off terrorism suspects. The law made it easier to wiretap suspects and to track e-mail, seize voice mail, and monitor library records. (p. 697)

**peacekeeping force** a military force drawn from neutral members of the United Nations to settle conflicts and supervise truces (p. 751)

*peninsulare* a person born on the Iberian Peninsula; typically, a Spanish or Portuguese official who resided temporarily in Latin America for political and economic gain and then returned to Europe (p. 363)

**\*percentage** a part of a whole expressed in hundredths obtained by multiplying a number by a percent (p. 633)

**perestroika** Mikhail Gorbachev's plan to reform the Soviet Union by restructuring its economy (p. 617)

**permanent revolution** an atmosphere of constant revolutionary fervor favored by Mao Zedong to enable China to overcome the past and achieve the final stage of communism (p. 710)

**pharaoh** an Egyptian monarch originally meaning "great house" or "palace" (p. 124)

**philosophe** French for "philosopher"; applied to intellectuals, writers, journalists, economists, and social reformers during the Enlightenment (p. 184)

**philosophy** an organized system of thought. The term comes from the Greek word meaning "love of wisdom." (p. 139)

**Glossary**

**photomontage** a picture made of a combination of photographs (p. 489)

**planned economy** an economic system directed by government agencies (p. 436)

**plebeian** in the Roman Republic, a social class made up of minor landholders, craftspeople, merchants, and small farmers (p. 145)

**plebiscite** a popular vote (p. 276)

**pogrom** organized persecution or massacre of a minority group, especially Jews (p. 322)

**policy of containment** a plan to keep something, such as communism, within its existing geographical boundaries and prevent further aggressive moves (p. 585)

**polis** the early Greek city-state, consisting of a city or town and its surrounding territory (p. 135)

**Politburo** a seven-member committee that became the leading policy-making body of the Communist Party in Russia (p. 474)

**\*potential** something that can develop or become actual; possible (p. 148)

**prefecture** in the Japanese Meiji Restoration, a territory governed by its former daimyo lord (p. 398)

**PRI** abbreviation for the Institutional Revolutionary Party, the official party of the Mexican Revolution; Mexican presidents were from this party until 2000 (pp. 523, 659)

**\*prime** first in rank, authority, or significant (p. 691)

**principle of intervention** idea that great powers have the right to send armies into countries where there are revolutions to restore legitimate governments (p. 265)

**privatization** the sale of government-owned companies to private firms (p. 659)

**\*professional** of, relating to, or characteristic of a profession (p. 752)

**proletariat** the working class (p. 299)

**propaganda** ideas spread to influence public opinion for or against a cause (p. 431)

**prophets** religious teachers (p. 126)

**protectorate** a political unit that depends on another government for its protection (p. 338)

**provincial** local; of or relating to a province (p. 388)

**psychoanalysis** a method by which a therapist and patient probe deeply into the patient's memory; by making the patient's conscious mind aware of repressed thoughts, healing can take place (p. 321)

**\*publish** to make the work of an author public in the form of a book or novel (p. 604)

**puddling** process in which coke derived from coal is used to burn away impurities in crude iron to produce high-quality iron (p. 256)

**\*pursue** to follow in order to overtake, capture, kill, or defeat (p. 516)

**real wages** the actual purchasing power of income (p. 600)

**realism** mid-nineteenth century movement that rejected romanticism and sought to portray lower- and middle-class life as it actually was (p. 284)

**redistribution of wealth** the shifting of wealth from a rich minority to a poor majority (p. 519)

**\*regime** a government in power (p. 341)

**Reichstag** the German parliament (p. 480)

**\*reinforce** to strengthen by additional assistance, material, or support; make stronger (p. 325)

**\*release** to set free from restraint, confinement, or servitude (p. 712)

**\*reliance** the state of being dependent on someone or something (p. 274)

**reparation** payment made to the victors by the vanquished to cover the costs of a war (p. 450)

**republic** a form of government in which the leader is not a king and certain citizens have the right to vote (p. 145)

**\*restraint** not succumbing to one's every whim by maintaining a control over one's actions (p. 178)

**revisionist** a Marxist who rejected the revolutionary approach, believing instead in evolution by democratic means to achieve the goal of socialism (p. 300)

**\*role** a function or part performed in a particular development or process (p. 599)

**romanticism** an intellectual movement that emerged at the end of the eighteenth century in reaction to the ideas of the Enlightenment; it stressed feelings, emotion, and imagination as sources of knowing (p. 281)

**salon** the elegant drawing rooms of great urban houses where, in the eighteenth century, writers, artists, aristocrats, government officials, and wealthy middle-class people gathered to discuss the ideas of the philosophes, helping to spread the ideas of the Enlightenment (p. 188)

**sanction** a restriction intended to enforce international law (p. 540)

**sans-culottes** "without breeches," French revolutionaries who considered themselves ordinary patriots (in other words, they wore long trousers instead of fine knee-length breeches) (p. 218)

**satellite state** a country that is economically and politically dependent on another country (p. 585)

**secede** to withdraw (p. 279)

**secularization** indifference to or rejection of religion or religious consideration (p. 283)

**Glossary**

**self-strengthening** a policy promoted by reformers toward the end of the Qing dynasty under which China would adopt Western technology while keeping its Confucian values and institutions (p. 383)

**Senate** a select group of about 300 landowners in the Roman Republic who served for life (p. 145)

**separation of powers** a form of government in which the executive, legislative, and judicial branches limit and control each other through a system of checks and balances (p. 185)

**sepoy** an Indian soldier hired by the British East India Company to protect the company's interests in the region (p. 355)

*__settlement__ an agreement resolving differences (p. 624)

**Shining Path** a radical Communist guerrilla group based in rural areas of Peru whose goal was to smash all authority and create a classless society (p. 666)

*__significant__ having or likely to have an influence or effect on (p. 678)

**social contract** the concept proposed by Rousseau that an entire society agrees to be governed by its general will, and all individuals should be forced to abide by the general will since it represents what is best for the entire community (p. 186)

**Social Darwinism** a theory used to justify the dominance of Western nations in the late nineteenth century; falsely based on Dawin's theory of the survival of the fittest (p. 321)

**socialism** a system in which society, usually in the form of the government, owns and controls the means of production (p. 261)

**Socratic method** teaching method that uses a question-and-answer format to lead pupils to see things for themselves (p. 139)

**soviet** a Russian council composed of representatives from the workers and soldiers (p. 442)

**sphere of influence** an area in which a foreign power has been granted exclusive rights and privileges, such as trading rights and mining privileges (p. 384)

*__stability__ the quality, state, or degree of being stable; the strength to stand or endure (p. 265)

**stalemate** the condition that exists when neither of two opposing sides is able to make significant gains (p. 723)

**Stamp Act** an act that required certain printed materials, such as legal documents and newspapers, to carry a stamp showing that a tax had been paid to Britain (p. 192)

**state capitalism** an economic system in which the central government plays an active role in the economy, establishing price and wage policies and subsidizing vital industries (p. 728)

**state-sponsored terrorism** terrorism in which terrorists who work for one nation undermine the government of another (p. 694)

*__stimulate__ to motivate activity or growth (p. 523)

*__submission__ an act of yielding to the authority or control of another (p. 435)

*__subsidize__ to aid or promote a private enterprise with public money (p. 728)

*__succession__ a number of persons or things that follow each other in sequence (p. 402)

*__successor__ one that follows, especially to a throne, title, estate, or office (p. 278)

**surrealism** artistic movement that seeks to depict the world of the unconscious (p. 489)

*__suspend__ to stop temporarily (p. 435)

**sustainable development** economic development that does not limit the ability of future generations to meet their basic needs (p. 745)

*__symbol__ something that stands for something else by reason of relationship, association, or convention; a visible sign of something invisible (p. 594)

*taille* French for the "chief tax" (p. 212)

**Taliban** a Muslim fundamentalist group (p. 696)

*__tension__ a state of latent hostility or opposition between opposing individuals or groups (p. 192)

**Thatcherism** the economic policy of British prime minister Margaret Thatcher, which limited social welfare and restricted union power (p. 628)

**totalitarian state** a government that aims to control the political, economic, social, intellectual, and cultural lives of its citizens (p. 471)

**total war** a war that involves the complete mobilization of resources and people, affecting the lives of all citizens in the warring countries, even those remote from the battlefields (p. 435)

**trade embargo** a policy prohibiting trade with a particular country (p. 660)

*__transfer__ to move control from one person or group to another (p. 355)

*__transform__ to change in composition or structure (p. 296)

*__transition__ a subtle change from one state or place to another (p. 391)

**trench warfare** fighting from ditches protected by barbed wire, as in World War I (p. 431)

*__trend__ current style or preference (p. 655)

**tyrant** ruler who seizes power by force and not subject to the law (p. 135)

**uncertainty principle** the idea put forth by Heisenberg in 1927 that the behavior of subatomic particles is uncertain, suggesting that all of the physical laws governing the universe are based in uncertainty (p. 491)

Glossary

**universal male suffrage** the right of all males to vote in elections (p. 268)

**\*unrestricted** to have power without limits or restrictions (p. 472)

**\*variation** difference in the characteristics of an organism from the species or population average (p. 284)

**viceroy** a governor who ruled as a representative of a monarch (p. 356)

**war communism** in World War I Russia, government control of banks and most industries, the seizing of grain from peasants, and the centralization of state administration under Communist control (p. 445)

**war of attrition** a war based on wearing the other side down by constant attacks and heavy losses, such as World War I (p. 432)

**weapons of mass destruction** nuclear, chemical, and biological weapons that can kill tens of thousands of people at once (p. 630)

**welfare state** a state in which the government takes responsibility for providing citizens with services such as health care (p. 599)

**\*widespread** generalized; common almost everywhere (p. 472)

**women's liberation movement** late 1960s equal rights movement for women (p. 604)

*zaibatsu* in the Japanese economy, a large financial and industrial corporation (p. 511)

Glossary

Este glosario incluye todas las palabras del contendio y vocabulario académico en tu texto. El vocabulario de contenido se relaciona con el contenido de historia. Estas palabras se encuentran en negrillas y están resaltadas en amarillo en tu texto. El vocabulario académico te facilitará la comprensión de todas la materias escolares. Estas palabras están en negrillas en tu texto y se muestran con un asterisco en el glosario.

## A

*abandon/*abandono* ceder el control o la influencia a otra persona o idea (pág. 282)

abolitionism/*abolicionismo* un movimiento para poner fin a la esclavitud (pág. 279)

*abstract/*abstracto* que sólo tiene forma intrínseca, sin tratar de incluir representación pictórica o contenido narrativo o muy poco contenido de estos últimos dos (pág. 488)

*academy/*academia* bachillerato o universidad donde se enseñan materias o destrezas especiales (pág. 480)

*accurate/*preciso* sin error como resultado de la atención a los detalles (pág. 664)

*achieve/*alcanzar* lograr una meta (pág. 537)

acid rain/*lluvia ácida* la lluvia que resulta cuando azufre producido por industrias se mezcla con la humedad en el aire (pág. 745)

*adapt/*adaptar* acomodar algo a un uso o situación específica o nueva mediante la modificación o el cambio (pág. 284)

*adjust/*ajustarse* lograr una meta (pág. 553)

*administration/*administración* grupo de ejecutivos políticos que le ayudan al presidente a manejar el país (pág. 587)

*adult/*adulto* persona que ha alcanzado cierta edad según la ley (pág. 135)

*affect/*afectar* producir un efecto en alguien o en algo (pág. 185)

*aid/*ayuda* prestar asistencia (pág. 584)

al-Qaeda/*Al-Qaeda* grupo terrorista encabezado por Osama bin Laden que reclutaba musulmanes y enviaba fondos monetarios y armas a Afganistán para apoyar la resistencia afgana (pág. 696)

*alter/*alterar* dar una posición, curso o dirección diferente a algo (pág. 423)

*alternative/*alternativa* algo que se puede escoger en lugar de algo más (pág. 561)

*amendment/*enmienda* alteración propuesta o afectada por el proceso parlamentario o constitucional (pág. 197)

annex/*anexar* unir un territorio a una unidad política, tal como una ciudad o un país (pág. 343)

*annual/*anual* que ocurre cada año o una vez al año; anualmente (pág. 323)

*anticipate/*anticipar* considerar con antelación una acción esperada (pág. 424)

apartheid/*segregación racial* "separación," el sistema de segregación racial aplicado en Sudáfrica desde la década de 1950 hasta 1991 (pág. 678)

*apparent/*aparente* a la vista; obvio (pág. 616)

appeasement/*apaciguamiento* satisfacción de las demandas razonables de poderes insatisfechos en un esfuerzo por mantener la paz y la estabilidad (pág. 537)

*approach/*abordar* tomar pasos preliminares hacia una meta particular (pág. 752)

*arbitrary/*arbitrario* que no está restringido por la ley (pág. 682)

armistice/*armisticio* una tregua o acuerdo para dar fin a una guerra (pág. 449)

arms race/*carrera armamentista* constitución de ejércitos y acopio de armas mantenerse a la par con un enemigo (pág. 586)

Articles of Confederation/*Artículos de la Confederación* la primera constitución de Estados Unidos aprobada en 1781 (pág. 196)

*assembly/*asamblea* grupo de personas reunidas para deliberar y legislar, para orar o para entretenerse (pág. 197)

assembly line/*cadena de montaje* sistema de producción con máquinas y trabajadores acomodados de modo que cada persona realiza repetidamente una tarea asignada a medida que el producto pasa frente a ella (pág. 297)

*assume/*presumir* creer que algo es cierto aunque no haya sido enunciado directamente; suponer (pág. 539)

*assure/*asegurar* informar o prometer un resultado positivo (pág. 435)

*attitude/*actitud* creer en algo o en alguien (pág. 355)

*attribute/*atributo* dar crédito a alguien por sus palabras o acciones (pág. 176)

autonomous/*autónomo* de gobierno propio (pág. 623)

*aware/*consciente* que tiene o que muestra comprensión, percepción o conocimiento (pág. 508)

## B

*behalf/*a favor de* en beneficio de algo o alguien (pág. 424)

*beneficial/*benéfico* que conduce al bienestar personal o social (pág. 265)

Bill of Rights/*Carta de Derechos* las primeras diez enmiendas a la Constitución, ratificadas en 1789 (pág. 197)

bioterrorism/*terrorismo biológico* el uso de armas biológicas y químicas en ataques terroristas (pág. 747)

biowarfare/*guerra biológica* el uso de enfermedades comunicables y agentes tóxicos contra el público y el ejército en tiempo de guerra (pág. 747)

blitzkrieg/*guerra relámpago* término alemán para "guerra relámpago," una táctica utilizada por los alemanes durante la Segunda Guerra Mundial (pág. 542)

**bloc/*bloque*** un grupo de naciones con un objetivo común (pág. 600)

**bourgeoisie/*burguesía*** la clase media (pág. 213)

**Buddhism/*budismo*** una doctrina religiosa introducida en el norte de la India en el siglo sexto A.C. por Siddhartha Gautama, conocido como el Buda (o "el Iluminado") (pág. 128)

**budget deficit/*déficit presupuestario*** el estado que existe cuando un gobierno gasta más de lo que cobra en la forma de ingresos (pág. 629)

**Camisea Gas Project/*proyecto Camisea*** oleoducto que transporta gas natural de la selva amazónica a través de Perú (pág. 666)

**\*capable/*capaz*** persona que posee atributos (como la inteligencia) requeridos para desenvolverse y lograr metas (pág. 231)

**capital/*capital*** dinero disponible para inversiones (pág. 254)

**caste system/*sistema de castas*** un conjunto de categorías rígidas en la antigua India que determinaba la ocupación de una persona y su potencial económico, así como también su posición en la sociedad (pág. 127)

**Catholic Church/*Iglesia católica*** la primera institución cristiana organizada en Europa (pág. 151)

**caudillo/*caudillo*** en Latinoamérica post revolucionaria, un líder poderoso que gobernaba principalmente mediante la fuerza militar, a menudo con el respaldo de la elite hacendada (pág. 365)

**\*challenge/*desafiar*** disputar algo injusto, inválido u obsoleto (pág. 659)

**Christianity/*cristianismo*** religión monoteísta que surgió en el siglo primero (pág. 147)

**\*circumstance/*circunstancia*** condición, hecho o evento que acompaña, condiciona o determina otro evento (pág. 469)

**civil disobedience/*desobediencia civil*** rechazo a obedecer leyes que son consideradas injustas (pág. 510)

**civilization/*civilización*** una compleja cultura en la que grandes números de personas comparten un gran número de elementos tales como la estructura social, la religión y el arte (pág. 122)

**civil rights movement/*movimiento de derechos civiles*** movimiento de igualdad de derechos para los afroamericanos que comenzó en 1954 (pág. 601)

**\*classical/*clásico*** que no involucra relatividad, mecánica de ondas o teoría cuántica (pág. 419)

**\*clause/*cláusula*** artículo distintivo en un documento formal (pág. 451)

**\*code/*código*** sistema de principios o reglas (pág. 122)

**\*coincide/*coincidir*** que ocurre al mismo tiempo o en el mismo lugar (pág. 444)

**Cold War/*Guerra fría*** el período de tensión política que siguió a la Segunda Guerra Mundial y que culminó con la caída del comunismo en la Unión Soviética a fines de la década de 1980 (pág. 563)

**collaborator/*colaborador*** una persona que ayuda al enemigo (pág. 555)

**collective bargaining/*convenio colectivo*** el derecho de los sindicatos a negociar con los empleadores acerca de remuneraciones y horarios (pág. 468)

**collectivization/*colectivización*** un sistema en el cual se eliminan las fincas privadas y los campesinos trabajan la tierra de propiedad del gobierno (pág. 475)

**colony/*colonia*** un asentamiento de personas que están viviendo en un nuevo territorio, enlazado a la madre patria por el comercio y el control directo del gobierno (pág. 191)

**commodity/*mercancía*** un producto vendible (pág. 391)

**common law/*derecho consuetudinario*** sistema de leyes desarrollado en Inglaterra y que era uniforme en todo el país; reemplazó los códigos legales que variaban de lugar en lugar (pág. 156)

**commonwealth/*mancomunidad*** nación o estado gober-nando por el pueblo o representantes del mismo (pág. 180)

**commune/*comuna*** en China durante la década de los 1950s, un grupo de granjas colectivas cada una de las cuales contenía más de 30,000 personas que vivían y trabajaban juntas (pág. 710)

**\*communications/*comunicaciones*** sistema para comunicarse, por ejemplo, los teléfonos o el Internet (pág. 588)

**\*compensate/*compensar*** pagar apropiadamente y por lo general de manera equilibrada (pág. 399)

**\*compensation/*compensación*** pago a trabajadores lesionados o desempleados o a sus cargas familiares (pág. 314)

**\*concentrate/*concentrar*** enfocar toda la atención en algo o alguien (pág. 448)

**concentration camp/*campo de concentración*** un campo donde se confina a prisioneros de guerra, prisioneros políticos, o miembros de grupos minoritarios, típicamente bajo condiciones duras (pág. 480)

**\*concept/*concepto*** idea genérica abstracta o que se generaliza a partir de una ocasión en particular (pág. 185)

**concession/*concesión*** acción y efecto de ceder en una posición ideológica para llegar a un acuerdo (político) (pág. 397)

**\*confer/*conferir*** otorgar, o donar desde una posición de superioridad a alguien más necesitado (pág. 156)

**\*conference/*conferencia*** reunión de dos o más personas para hablar sobre problemas y asuntos comunes (pág. 537)

**\*conflict/*conflicto*** lucha que resulta de necesidades, empujes, deseos o demandas internas o externas y en contraposición (pág. 346)

**\*conform/*conformar*** el acto de obedecer o ser complaciente (pág. 593)

**Confucianism/*confucianismo*** el sistema de ideas políticas y éticas formuladas por el filósofo chino Confucio hacia fines de la dinastía Zhou; fue concebido para restaurar el orden en una sociedad que estaba en estado de confusión (pág. 129)

**conscription/*conscripción*** llamado obligatorio al servicio militar (pág. 423)

**\*consensus/*consenso*** acuerdo general (pág. 181)

Spanish Glossary

*consequence/*consecuencia* algo que produce una causa o que inevitablemente ocurre a partir de un conjunto de condiciones (pág. 348)

conservatism/*conservatismo* una filosofía política basada en la tradición y estabilidad social sobre la base de la obediencia a la autoridad política y la religión organizada (pág. 265)

*consistent/*consistente* arcado por armonía, regularidad o continuidad permanente; libre de variación o contradicción (pág. 449)

*constant/*constante* que ocurre continuamente (pág. 753)

*constitutional/*constitucional* que es leal o apoya una constitución o forma de gobierno establecida (pág. 518)

consulate/*consulado* el nuevo gobierno establecido en Francia después del derrocamiento del Directorio en 1799, siendo Napoleón el primer cónsul en control de todo el gobierno (pág. 230)

*consumer/*consumidor* persona que compra bienes económicos (pág. 213)

consumer society/*sociedad consumidora* sociedad preocupada por la compra de bienes y que no produce ningún bien (pág. 603)

contras/*contras* rebeldes financiados por los Estados Unidos que empezaron una guerra guerrillera contra el gobierno sandinista en Nicaragua (pág. 662)

*controversy/*controversia* discusión marcada por los puntos de vista opuestos de individuos o grupos (pág. 284)

*cooperation/*cooperación* el acto de trabajar bien con los demás; actuar en conjunto (pág. 624)

cooperative/*cooperativa* una sociedad agrícola perteneciente a y a menudo administrada para beneficio de los agricultores (pág. 666)

*core/*corazón, núcleo* parte central y a menudo fundamental de algo más grande (pág. 128)

*correspondence/*correspondencia* comunicarse mediante cartas (pág. 193)

cottage industry/*industria de casa de campo* un método de producción en el que las tareas las realizan las personas en sus hogares (pág. 255)

coup d'état/*golpe de estado* un súbito derrocamiento del gobierno (pág. 225)

covenant/*convenio* contrato (pág. 126)

*creation/*creación* el acto de hacer, inventar o producir (pág. 585)

creole/*criollo* descendiente de europeos nacido en las Américas (pág. 363)

*crucial/*crucial* importante o esencial (pág. 313)

cultural imperialism/*imperialismo cultural* la idea que una nación occidental controla a otras culturas mundiales, como si fueran gobiernos coloniales en la era del imperialismo (pág. 636)

*currency/*moneda* papel moneda en circulación (pág. 626)

**D**

Declaration of Independence/*Declaración de la Independencia* documento escrito por Thomas Jefferson en 1789 en el cual señalaba por qué las colonias estadounidenses eran independientes de la Gran Bretaña (pág. 194)

*decline/*declinar* reducirse a un estado inferior o condición más baja (pág. 380)

deficit spending/*gastos deficitarios* los gastos gubernamentales que exceden a lo que se recibe a través de los impuestos y otros ingresos, por ende entrando en deuda (pág. 469)

deforestation/*deforestación* la tala de bosques (pág. 744)

deism/*deísmo* una filosofía religiosa del siglo XVIII basada en la razón y en la ley natural (pág. 185)

demilitarize/*desmilitarizar* eliminar o prohibir las armas, fortificaciones y otras instalaciones militares (pág. 536)

democracy/*democracia* gobierno por mandato del pueblo directamente o por medio de sus representantes elegidos (pág. 136)

depression/*depresión* un período de baja actividad económica y aumento del desempleo (pág. 466)

*derive/*derivar* tomar, recibir u obtener de una fuente específica (pág. 733)

*Desaparecidos/*desaparecidos* opositores al régimen de Pinochet en Chile, quienes fueron encarcelados y a quienes nunca se les volvió a ver (pág. 666)

*design/*designar* crear, modelar, ejecutar o construir según un plan (pág. 699)

de-Stalinization/*de-Stalinización* el proceso de eliminar las políticas más crueles de Stalin (pág. 593)

détente/*disminución* una fase de relajamiento de relaciones o tensiones entre dos adversarios (pág. 616)

deterrence/*disuasión* una política de seguridad que mantiene que si dos lados de un conflicto político tengan arsenales masivas de armas nucleares, se puede impedir la guerra (pág. 587)

dictatorship/*dictadura* una forma de gobierno en la cual una persona o pequeño grupo tiene el poder absoluto (pág. 300)

direct democracy/*democracia directa* un sistema de gobierno en que las personas participan directamente en la toma de decisiones del gobierno a través de asambleas (pág. 138)

direct rule/*dominio directo* gobierno colonial en el que las elites locales son removidos del poder y reemplazadas por un nuevo grupo de oficiales traídos desde la madre patria (pág. 339)

Directory/*Directorio* comité de cinco que creó la constitución francesa de 1795 y que duró hasta 1799 (pág. 225)

disarmament groups/*grupos de desarme* organizaciones que se esfuerzan en limitar o reducir las fuerzas armadas y las armas (pág. 752)

discrimination/*discriminación* prejuicio, habitualmente sobre la base de la raza, la religión, clase, sexo, o edad (págs. 322, 725)

dissident/*disidente* una persona que critica abiertamente al régimen que tiene el poder (pág. 616)

divine right of kings/*derecho divino de reyes* la creencia de que los reyes reciben su poder de parte de Dios y de que son responsables sólo ante Dios (pág. 176)

*domestic/*doméstico* relacionado con o que tiene su origen en un país, especialmente el país propio (pág. 220)

*dominate/*dominar* gobernar o controlar (pág. 363)

**domino theory/*teoría dominó*** la idea de que, si un país cae ante el comunismo, los países colindantes también lo harán (pág. 589)

**Duma/*Duma*** la asamblea legislativa rusa (pág. 315)

*****dynamic/*dinámico*** marcado por una actividad o cambio continuo y productivo (pág. 254)

## E

**ecology/*ecología*** el estudio de las relaciones entre cosas vivas y su ambiente (pág. 744)

**elector/*elector*** una persona calificada para votar en una elección (pág. 225)

*****element/*elemento*** uno de entre un número de distintos grupos que componen un grupo más grande (pág. 660)

*****eliminate/*eliminar*** desechar o descartar (pág. 504)

**emancipation/*emancipación*** liberación (pág. 278)

*****emerge/*emerger*** surgir de una posición oscura o inferior (pág. 299)

*****emphasis/*énfasis*** dar importancia a algo (pág. 367)

**enclosure movement/*movimiento de cercado*** los terratenientes ponen cercas alrededor de las tierras comunes que antes usaban los campesinos (pág. 254)

*****ensure/*asegurar*** dar por sentado o seguro (pág. 385)

**entrepreneur/*empresario*** una persona interesada en hallar nuevas oportunidades de negocios y nuevas formas de obtener ganancias (pág. 254)

*****equip/*equipar*** alistar para un servicio o acción al reunir el equipo necesario (pág. 400)

*****establish/*establecer*** introducir (pág. 504)

*****estate/*estado*** una de las tres clases en las que se dividía la sociedad francesa medieval: el clero (primer estado), los nobles (segundo estado) y la plebe (tercer estado) (págs. 212, 146)

*****ethnic/*etnia*** relacionado con o que pertenece a un grupo de personas de la misma raza, nacionalidad, tribu, religión, lengua, origen o antecedente cultural (pág. 422)

**ethnic cleansing/*purificación étnica*** una política de matar o sacar por la fuerza a un grupo étnico desde sus territorios (págs. 503, 623)

*****evidence/*evidencia*** prueba legítima de una idea, ocurrencia o acción, la cual un individuo o la sociedad ha puesto en duda (pág. 184)

*****exclusion/*exclusión*** el acto de prevenir o impedir que una persona pertenezca a un grupo (pág. 215)

*****expand/*ensanchar*** aumentar el número o volumen de algo (pág. 369)

*****expansion/*expansión*** el acto o proceso de expandir o ganar tierras (pág. 616)

*****exploit/*explotar*** usar productivamente, a veces, egoísta o injustamente (pág. 339)

*****external/*externo*** se relaciona con el trato o las relaciones con países extranjeros (pág. 221)

**extraterritoriality/*extraterritorialidad*** vivir en una sección de un país apartada para extranjeros pero no sujeta a las leyes del país anfitrión (pág. 381)

## F

**faction/*facción*** un grupo de personas disidentes (pág. 220)

**fascism/*fascismo*** filosofia política basada en el nacionalismo y en un estado todopoderoso (pág. 471)

**favelas/*favelas*** en el Brazil, barracas que carecen de los servicios urbanos básicos (pág. 654)

*****federal/*federal*** agencia u organización que opera en nombre del gobierno nacional (pág. 697)

**federal system/*sistema federal*** una forma de gobierno en la cual el poder es compartido entre el gobierno nacional y los gobiernos estatales (pág. 196)

**feminism/*feminismo*** el movimiento para promover los derechos e intereses de las mujeres (pág. 307)

**feudalism/*feudalismo*** sistema político y social que se desarrolló durante la Edad Media cuando gobiernos reales ya no podían defender a su pueblo; los nobles ofrecían protección y tierras a cambio de servicio (pág. 155)

**finance/*financiar*** proveer los fondos necesarios (pág. 651)

**Five-Year Plan/*Plan de Cinco Años*** metas económicas delineadas por Stalin para períodos de cinco años con el fin de transformar a Rusia de la noche a la mañana, prácticamente, de un país basado en la agricultura a uno industrial (pág. 474)

*****focus/*enfocar*** concentrar la atención o el esfuerzo (pág. 123)

*****found/*fundar*** establecer una institución, por lo general, con arreglos para el futuro mantenimiento de la misma (pág. 624)

*****foundation/*cimientos*** base sobre la cual se funda o se apoya algo (pág. 140)

## G

*****gender/*género*** la identidad sexual de una persona (pág. 725)

**gender parity/*paridad de género*** políticas que se esfuerzan por aumentar el número de mujeres en el gobierno (pág. 634)

*****generator/*generador*** máquina que cambia la energía mecánica en energía eléctrica (pág. 296)

**genocide/*genocidio*** la matanza masiva de un grupo racial, político o cultural en particular (págs. 503, 553)

**globalization/*globalización*** término con connotaciones tanto positivas como negativas que referir a tendencia hacia un desarrollo de un economia y cultura globales (pág. 632)

*****goal/*meta*** algo hacia lo cual uno trabaja; propósito (pág. 135)

*****grant/*concesión*** consentir a la ejecución de una obra en nombre de una persona o entidad (pág. 154)

**greenhouse effect/*efecto invernadero*** calentamiento global causado por la acumulación de dióxido de carbono en la atmósfera (pág. 745)

**guerrilla tactics/*táctica de guerrillas*** el uso de maniobras inesperadas tales como el sabotaje y subterfugio para luchar contra un enemigo (pág. 516)

**Spanish Glossary**

## H

**heavy industry/*industria pesada*** la manufactura de máquinas y equipo para fábricas y minas (pág. 593)

**Hinduism/*hinduismo*** el mayor sistema religioso de la India, que tuvo sus orígenes en las creencias religiosas de los arios que se establecieron en la India después del año 1500 A.C. (pág. 128)

***hypothetical/*hipotético*** enunciado que forma parte de una suposición o concesión hecha sólo por el bien de un argumento (pág. 181)

## I

***ideology/*ideología*** conjunto de ideas sistemáticas, especialmente en lo que se refiere a la vida humana o la cultura (pág. 482)

***impact/*impacto*** efecto grande o significativo (pág. 559)

***implement/*implementar*** comenzar a llevar a cabo un plan o curso de acción (pág. 552)

***impose/*imponer*** establecer o llevar a cabo como si por la fuerza (pág. 339)

***incapable/*incapaz*** que carece de capacidad o habilidad para lograr una meta (pág. 488)

***indefinite/*indefinido*** impreciso; indeterminado (pág. 543)

**indemnity/*indemnización*** un pago por daños (pág. 386)

**indigenous/*indígena*** nativo a una región (pág. 347)

**indirect rule/*dominio indirecto*** gobierno colonial en el que los gobernantes locales pueden mantener sus posiciones de autoridad y estatus (pág. 339)

**industrial capitalism/*capitalismo industrial*** un sistema económico basado en la producción industrial o la fabricación (pág. 260)

***injure/*lastimar*** causar daño físico a alguien (pág. 713)

***innovation/*innovación*** la introducción de una idea, método o dispositivo (pág. 303)

***integrate/*integrar*** incorporar en una unidad más grande (pág. 391)

***integrity/*integridad*** la cualidad o estado de una cosa que tiene todas sus partes y que no ha sido alterado (pág. 512)

***intifada/*intifada*** "levantamiento," un movimiento que surgió durante la década de 1980 entre quienes respaldaban a la Organización Para la Liberación de Palestina radicada dentro de Israel (pág. 691)

***involvement/*implicación*** participación (pág. 725)

**Irish Republican Army (IRA)/*Ejército republicano irlandés (I.R.A.)*** nacionalistas militantes que desean unificar el norte de Irlanda (pág. 694)

***irrelevant/*ajeno*** insignificativo o sin importancia (pág. 444)

**Islam/*Islam*** religión monoteísta que surgió en la Península Arábiga en el siglo séptimo (pág. 153)

***isolationism/*aislacionismo*** política de aislamiento nacional al no formar alianzas u otras relaciones políticas y económicas internacionales (pág. 543)

## J

**Judaism/*judaísmo*** religión monoteísta desarrollada por los israelitas (pág. 125)

## K

**kaiser/*káiser*** término alemán para "césar," el título de los emperadores del Segundo Imperio Alemán (pág. 275)

**kamikaze/*kamikaze*** término japonés para "viento divino," una misión suicida en la que jóvenes pilotos japoneses intencionalmente estrellaban sus aviones contra buques de guerra de los EE.UU. (pág. 561)

## L

***labor/*mano de obra*** actividad humana que provee los bienes y servicios en la economía (pág. 536)

**laissez-faire/*laissez-faire*** literalmente, "dejar [a las personas] hacer [lo que quieran]," el concepto de que el estado no debe imponer regulaciones gubernamentales si no que debe dejar la economía sola (pág. 187)

***levy/*gravar*** imponer o recaudar con autoridad legal (pág. 274)

***liberal/*liberal*** individuo, grupo o idea que no observa estrictamente normas ortodoxas, tradicionales o establecidas (pág. 232)

**liberalism/*liberalismo*** una filosofía política originalmente basada principalmente en principios de Ilustración, que sostenía que las personas deberían ser lo más libres dentro de lo posible de las restricciones gubernamentales y que las libertades civiles—los derechos básicos de las personas—deberían ser protegidos (pág. 266)

***liberation/*liberación*** el acto de liberar a un país de la dominación de una potencia extranjera (pág. 637)

**literacy/*alfabetización*** la capacidad de leer y escribir (pág. 308)

## M

**magic realism/*realismo mágico*** una singular forma de expresión de la literatura latinoamericana; combina eventos realistas con fondos como sueños o fantásticos (pág. 654)

**Magna Carta/*Carta Magna*** la Gran Cédula de derechos, que el Rey Juan Sin Tierra fue obligado a firmar por los nobles ingleses en Runnymede en 1215 (pág. 156)

**Mahatma/*Mahatma*** "Gran Alma," un título que los indios utilizaron para referirse a Mohandas Gandhi (pág. 510)

***maintain/*mantener*** sostener contra oposición o peligro; apoyar y defender (pág. 523)

**mandate/*mandato*** una nación gobernada por otra nación en nombre de la Liga de Naciones (pág. 452)

Spanish Glossary

**mass production/*producción en masa*** producción de grandes cantidades de bienes mediante el uso de máquinas y con frecuencia cadenas de montaje (pág. 297)

**megacities/*megaciudades*** ciudades cuyas poblaciones aumentan rápidamente; tienen problemas con el abastecimiento de servicios urbanos (pág. 653)

*****mental/*mental*** relacionado con la respuesta emocional total e intelectual de un individuo a la realidad externa (pág. 746)

**mestizo/*mestizo*** la progenie de europeos e indígenas americanos (pág. 364)

*****method/*método*** manera, técnica o proceso de hacer algo o para hacer algo (pág. 628)

*****migrate/*migrar*** mudarse de un país, lugar o ubicación a otro (pág. 257)

**militarism/*militarismo*** política nacional basada en la fuerza militar y la glorificación de la guerra (pág. 274)

*****minimum/*mínimo*** a cantidad mínima posible (pág. 469)

**ministerial responsibility/*responsabilidad ministerial*** la idea de que el primer ministro es responsable ante el ejecutivo popularmente electo y no ante el oficial ejecutivo (pág. 313)

*****minority/*minoría*** grupo más pequeño dentro de una sociedad, generalmente diferente a la mayoría (pág. 149)

**mobilization/*movilización*** el proceso de agrupar tropas y suministros y prepararlos para la guerra (pág. 424, 559)

**modernism/*modernismo*** un movimiento resultante de la rebelión por parte de escritores y artistas entre 1870 y 1914 en contra de los estilos literarios y artísticos tradicionales que habían dominado la vida cultural europea desde el Renacimiento (págs. 323, 490)

**monotheistic/*monoteísta*** con un solo dios (pág. 126)

**Monroe Doctrine/*Doctrina Monroe*** la política de los Estados Unidos que garantiza la independencia de las naciones latinoamericanas y advierte contra la intervención europea en las Américas, promulgada por el presidente James Monroe en 1823 (pág. 365)

*****motive/*motivo*** algo, como una necesidad o un deseo, que hace que exista o se haga algo (pág. 690)

**multinational corporation/*compañía multinacional*** una compañía con divisiones en más de dos países (pág. 651)

**multinational state/*estado multinacional*** área política compuesta por personas de diferentes etnias (pág. 269)

*****mutual/*mutuo*** obligaciones, gastos u otras responsabilidades que se comparten con otro individuo o grupo (pág. 181)

**nationalism/*nacionalismo*** la singular identidad cultural de un pueblo basada en un idioma, religión y símbolos nacionales en común (pág. 234)

**natural rights/*derechos naturales*** derechos con los que todos los humanos supuestamente nacen, incluyendo el derecho a la vida, la libertad y la propiedad (pág. 181)

**natural selection/*selección natural*** el principio establecido por Darwin en el sentido de que algunos organismos son más adaptables al medio que otros; en términos populares, "supervivencia de los aptos" (pág. 284)

**Nazi/*nazismo*** partido nacionalsocialista alemán que acaudilló Adolfo Hitler (pág. 480)

*****network/*red*** grupo de personas interconectadas que intercambian servicios (pág. 127)

*****neutrality/*neutralidad*** que permanece imparcial al rehusarse a participar en una guerra entre otras potencias (pág. 543)

**New Economic Policy (NEP)/*Nueva Política Económica*** una versión modificada del antiguo sistema capitalista adoptado por Lenin en 1921 para reemplazar el comunismo de guerra en Rusia; se permitió a los campesinos vender su producto, las tiendas y pequeñas industrias podían ser privadas, pero la gran industria, la banca y las minas permanecieron en manos del gobierno (pág. 473)

**New Imperialism/*Nuevo Imperialismo*** imperialismo de fines del siglo XIX, durante el cual los europeos buscaban nada menos que el control directo de vastos territorios, especialmente en África (pág. 336)

**New Order/*Nuevo orden*** nuevo orden en Asia que incluye el Japón, la China y Manchuria y el cual resultaría en prosperidad para Asia (pág. 539)

*****nuclear/*nuclear*** relacionado con el núcleo atómico (pág. 745)

*****objective/*objetivo*** algo hacia lo cual uno se esfuerza; un propósito, o fin de una acción (pág. 305)

**occupied/*ocupado*** país cuyas tierras son poseídas por un poder extranjero (pág. 727)

*****occupy/*ocupar*** tomar posesión o controlar (pág. 585)

**oligarchy/*oligarquía*** literalmente, el gobierno de unos pocos, en el cual un pequeño grupo de personas controla el gobierno (págs. 136, 522)

**one-child policy/*política de un sólo hijo*** política china que recompensa a las familias que tienen un sólo hijo con beneficios de educacion, guardería infantil y vivienda (pág. 714)

**Open Door Policy/*Política de Puertas Abiertas*** propuesta que aseguraba que todas las naciones tengan equidad de acceso al mercado chino y que conservaba la unidad del imperio chino (pág. 385)

**OPEC/*O.P.E.P.*** la Organización de Países Exportadores de Petróleo formada en 1960 por varias naciones árabes productoras de petróleo con el fin de controlar el precio del petróleo (pág. 691)

**organic evolution/*evolución orgánica*** el principio establecido por Darwin de que cada planta o animal ha evolucionado, o cambiado, durante un largo periodo desde formas más primitivas y simples de vida hasta formas más complejas (pág. 283)

**outsourcing/*enviar fuera*** práctica en que las compañías envían ciertos empleos, como la entrada de datos o los servicios al cliente, a países con salarios más bajos (pág. 722)

**ozone layer/*capa de ozono*** delgada capa de gas en la atmósfera superior que protege a la Tierra de los rayos ultravioleta provenientes del Sol (pág. 745)

**Pan-Africanism/*Panafricanismo*** movimiento que promociona la unidad de todos los africanos por todo el mundo (págs. 509, 679)

**Pan-Arabism/*Panarabismo*** política que promueve la unidad árabe internacional (pág. 690)

**\*parallel/*paralelo*** semejante o análogo en tendencia o desarrollo (pág. 665)

**parliament/*parlamento*** asamblea representativa de consejeros a un rey u otro alto ejecutivo (pág. 156)

**partisan/*partisano*** guerreo de resistencia en la Segunda Guerra Mundial (pág. 550)

**patriarchal/*patriarcal*** dominado por los hombres (pág. 123)

**patrician/*patricio*** grandes terratenientes, formaban la clase dominante en la República Romana (pág. 145)

**Patriot Act/*Ley Patriota*** proyecto de ley antiterrorista pasado después del once de Septiembre que permite indagaciones secretas para impedir poner sobre aviso a sospechos de terrorismo. La ley facilitó la interceptación de líneas telefónicas de sospechosos y también permite el seguimiento de correos electrónicos, apoderarse de mensajes telefónicos y monitorear los récords bibliotecarios. (pág. 697)

**peacekeeping force/*fuerza para mantener la paz*** fuerza militar traída de miembros neutrales de las Naciones Unidas para resolver conflictos y supervisar treguas (pág. 751)

**peninsulare/*peninsulare*** persona nacida en la Península Ibérica; comúnmente, un oficial español o portugués que residía temporalmente en Latinoamérica para obtener ganancia política y económica y luego regresaba a Europa (pág. 363)

**\*percentage/*porcentaje*** parte de un todo expresada en centésimas mediante un por ciento (pág. 633)

**perestroika/*perestroika*** plan de Mikhail Gorbachev para reformar la URSS, reestructurando su economía (pág. 617)

**permanent revolution/*revolución permanente*** una atmósfera constante de fervor revolucionario apoyado por Mao Zedong para permitir que China venza a su pasado y logre la etapa final del comunismo (pág. 710)

**pharaoh/*faraón*** monarca egipcio; la palabra significó originalmente "gran casa" o "palacio" (pág. 124)

**philosophe/*filósofo*** término francés para "filósofo", se aplica los intelectuales, escritores, periodistas, economistas y reformadores sociales durante la Ilustración (pág. 184)

**philosophy/*filosofía*** sistema organizado de creencias. El término proviene de la palabra griega que significa "amor por la sabiduría." (pág. 139)

**photomontage/*fotomontaje*** una imagen compuesta de una combinación de fotografías (pág. 489)

**planned economy/*economía planificada*** sistema económico dirigido por agencias gubernamentales (pág. 436)

**plebeian/*plebe*** en la República romana, era la clase social compuesta por terratenientes pequeños, artesanos, mercaderes y agricultores (pág. 145)

**plebiscite/*plebiscito*** voto popular (pág. 276)

**pogrom/*pogrom*** persecución organizada de un grupo minoritario, usualmente judíos, en la Rusia de los zares (pág. 322)

**policy of containment/*política de contención*** plan para mantener algo, como por ejemplo el comunismo, dentro de sus fronteras geográficas existentes e impedir posteriores movimientos agresivos (pág. 585)

**polis/*polis*** la ciudad-estado de la antigua Grecia, que constaba de una ciudad o pueblo y el territorio de sus alrededores que existe como entidad política (pág. 135)

**Politburo/*Politburó*** comité de siete miembros que se convirtió en el organismo dominante de determinación de normas del partido comunista en Rusia (pág. 474)

**\*potential/*potencial*** algo que puede desarrollarse o convertirse en realidad; posible (pág. 148)

**prefecture/*prefectura*** en la Restauración Meiji japonesa, un territorio gobernado por su anterior señor daimyo (pág. 398)

**PRI/*PRI*** abreviatura para Partido Revolucionario Institucional, el partido oficial de la Revolución mejicana; los presidentes mejicanos pertenecieron a este partido hasta el año 2000 (págs. 523, 659)

**\*prime/*primero*** principal en rango, autoridad o significativo (pág. 691)

**principle of intervention/*principio de intervención*** la idea de que las grandes potencias tienen el derecho de enviar ejércitos a países donde existen revoluciones a fin de restaurar los gobiernos legítimos (pág. 265)

**privatization/*privatización*** la venta de compañías del Estado a firmas privadas (pág. 659)

**\*professional/*profesional*** que se relaciona o que es característico de una profesión (pág. 752)

**proletariat/*proletariado*** la clase trabajadora (pág. 299)

**propaganda/*propaganda*** ideas que se difunden para influir en la opinión pública a favor de una causa o en contra de ella (pág. 431)

**prophets/*profetas*** maestros religiosos (pág. 126)

**protectorate/*protectorado*** unidad política que depende de otro gobierno para su protección (pág. 338)

**provincial/*provincial*** local; relativo a una provincia (pág. 388)

**psychoanalysis/*psicoanálisis*** método mediante el cual un terapeuta y un paciente indagan profundamente en la memoria del paciente; haciendo que la mente consciente del paciente tenga consciencia pensamientos reprimidos, podrá ocurrir una cura (pág. 321)

**\*publish/*publicar*** difundir la obra de un autor para hacerla conocer de todos en la forma de un libro o una novela (pág. 604)

**puddling/*pudelación*** procesos en el cual se utiliza coque derivado del carbón para extraer impurezas por medio del fuego en hierro bruto y producir un hierro de alta calidad (pág. 256)

**\*pursue/*perseguir*** seguir en orden o alcanzar, capturar, aniquilar o derrotar (pág. 516)

## R

**real wages/*salario efectivo*** el poder adquisitivo de los ingresos (pág. 600)

**realism/*realismo*** estilo y literatura de mediados del Siglo XIX, que reflejaba las realidades de la vida cotidiana (pág. 284)

**redistribution of wealth/*redistribución de la riqueza*** el cambio de la riqueza de una minoría rica a una mayoría pobre (pág. 519)

**\*regime/*régimen*** gobierno que está en el poder (pág. 341)

**Reichstag/*Reichstag*** el parlamento alemán (pág. 480)

**\*reinforce/*reforzar*** fortalecer mediante asistencia, material o apoyo adicional; fortificar (pág. 325)

**\*release/*liberar*** poner en libertad de restricciones, reclusión o servidumbre (pág. 712)

**\*reliance/*seguridad*** facultad de depender de alguien o algo (pág. 274)

**reparation/*reparación*** pago hecho a los victoriosos por los derrotados para cubrir los costos de una guerra (pág. 450)

**republic/*república*** forma de gobierno en la cual el líder no es un rey y ciertos ciudadanos tienen derecho a votar (pág. 145)

**\*restraint/*restricción*** no ceder a todos los caprichos propios al controlar uno sus acciones (pág. 178)

**revisionist/*revisionista*** un marxista que rechazó el enfoque revolucionario, creyendo en cambio en una evolución por medio de una democracia para lograr el objetivo del socialismo (pág. 300)

**\*role/*papel*** parte o función que se realiza en un desarrollo o proceso particular (pág. 599)

**romanticism/*romanticismo*** un movimiento intelectual que surgió e finales del siglo XVIII en reacción a las ideas de la Ilustración, daba énfasis a los sentimientos, la emoción y la imaginación como fuentes del conocimiento (pág. 281)

## S

**salon/*salón*** las elegantes salas de las grandes casas urbanas donde, en el siglo VIII, escritores, artistas, aristócratas, funcionarios de gobierno y gente de la clase media se reunían y hablaban de las ideas de los filósofos y ayudaban a difundir las ideas de la Ilustración (pág. 188)

**sanction/*sanción*** restricción para hacer cumplir la ley internacional (pág. 540)

**sans-culottes/*revolucionarios*** "sin pantalones," los revolucionarios francés, que se consideraban patriotas ordinarios (en otras palabras, usaban pantalones largos en vez de pantalones hasta la rodilla) (pág. 218)

**satellite state/*estado satélite*** país que depende económica y políticamente de otro país (pág. 585)

**secede/*separar*** separarse (pág. 279)

**secularization/*secularización*** viendo el mundo en términos materiales, no espirituales (pág. 283)

**self-strengthening/*autofortalecimiento*** política promovida por reformadores hacia fines de la dinastía Qing en China bajo la cual China adoptaría la tecnología occidental aunque manteniendo sus valores e instituciones confucianos (pág. 383)

**Senate/*senado*** grupo selecto de unos 300 terratenientes en la República romana quienes servían de por vida (pág. 145)

**separation of powers/*separación de los poderes*** forma de gobierno en la cual las divisiones ejecutiva, legislativa y judicial se limitan y controlan entre sí a través de un sistema de revisiones y balances (pág. 185)

**sepoy/*cipayo*** soldado indio contratado por la British East India Company para proteger los intereses de la compañía en la región (pág. 355)

**\*settlement/*convenio*** acuerdo que se hace con el fin de resolver las diferencias (pág. 624)

**Shining Path/*Sendero Luminoso*** grupo de guerrilla radical en Perú con lazos con la China comunista (pág. 666)

**\*significant/*significativo*** que tiene o que es posible que tenga influencia o efecto sobre algo (pág. 678)

**social contract/*contrato social*** el concepto propuesto por Rousseau de que una sociedad completa accede a ser gobernada por su voluntad general y que todos los individuos deben ser forzados a soportar por el deseo general, lo que representa qué es lo mejor para la comunidad completa (pág. 186)

**Social Darwinism/*darwinismo social*** teoría que se usó para justificar la dominancia de las naciones occidentales a fines del siglo XIX; se basó falsamente en la teoría de Darwin sobre la sobrevivencia del más fuerte (pág. 321)

**socialism/*socialismo*** sistema en el cual la sociedad, por lo general en la forma del gobierno, posee y controla el medio de producción (pág. 261)

**Socratic method/*método socrático*** método didáctico que usa un formato de pregunta y respuesta para guiar a los alumnos a ver las cosas por sí mismos (pág. 139)

**soviet/*soviet*** consejo ruso compuesto de representantes de los trabajadores y los soldados (pág. 442)

**sphere of influence/*esfera de influencia*** área en la que a un poder extranjero se le ha garantizado derechos y privilegios exclusivos, tales como derechos de comercio y privilegios de minería (pág. 384)

**\*stability/*estabilidad*** cualidad, estado o grado de estable; la fortaleza para mantenerse firme o aguantar (pág. 265)

**stalemate/*estancamiento*** la condición que existe cuando ninguno de los dos lados puede obtener ganancias significativas (pág. 723)

**Stamp Act/*Ley del Timbre*** ley que requería que ciertos materiales impresos, como los documentos legales y los periódicos, llevaran una estampilla mostrando que se le había pagado un impuesto a la Gran Bretaña (pág. 192)

**state capitalism/*capitalismo del estado*** sistema económico en el cual el gobierno central tiene una función activa en la economía, estableciendo políticas de precios y sueldos y subsidiando industrias vitales (pág. 728)

**Spanish Glossary**

**state-sponsored terrorism/*terrorismo patrocinado por el estado*** terrorismo en que terroristas que trabajan para una nación con el fin de debilitar el gobierno de otra nación (pág. 694)

**\*stimulate/*estimular*** motivar actividad o crecimiento (pág. 523)

**\*submission/*sumisión*** el acto de ceder a la autoridad o control de otro (pág. 435)

**\*subsidize/*subsidiar*** prestar ayuda o promover una empresa privada con fondos públicos (pág. 728)

**\*succession/*sucesión*** un número de personas o cosas que se siguen una tras otra en orden (pág. 402)

**\*successor/*sucesor*** aquél que sucede a otro, especialmente a un trono, titulo, herencia u cargo (pág. 278)

**surrealism/*surrealismo*** movimiento artístico que trata de representar la vida del inconsciente (pág. 489)

**\*suspend/*suspender*** detener temporalmente (pág. 435)

**sustainable development/*desarrollo sostenible*** desarrollo económico que no limita la capacidad de generaciones futuras de abastecer sus necesidades básicas (pág. 745)

**\*symbol/*símbolo*** algo que representa otra cosa abstracta mediante relación, asociación o convención; una señal visible de algo invisible (pág. 594)

**taille/*taille*** palabra francesa que significa "impuesto directo" (pág. 212)

**Taliban/*talibán*** grupo musulmán fundamentalista (pág. 696)

**\*tension/*tensión*** estado de latente hostilidad u oposición entre individuos o grupos opuestos (pág. 192)

**Thatcherism/*thatcherismo*** la política económica de la Primera Ministra británica Margaret Thatcher, que limitaba el bienestar social y restringía el poder de sindicatos (pág. 628)

**totalitarian state/*estado totalitario*** gobierno que se centra en controlar no sólo el lado político de la vida, sino también la vida económica, social, intelectual y cultural de sus ciudadanos (pág. 471)

**total war/*guerra total*** guerra que implica la movilización completa recursos y personas, afecta las vidas de todos los ciudadanos en los países en guerra, incluso aquellos alejados de los campos de batalla (pág. 435)

**trade embargo/*embargo comercial*** política que prohibe el comercio con un país en particular (pág. 660)

**\*transfer/*transferir*** trasladar a una persona o grupo el control que se tiene (pág. 355)

**\*transform/*transformar*** cambio en composición o estructura (pág. 296)

**\*transition/*transición*** cambio sutil de un estado o lugar a otro (pág. 391)

**trench warfare/*guerra de trincheras*** pelea desde trincheras protegidas por alambres de púa, como en la Primera Guerra Mundial (pág. 431)

**\*trend/*tendencia*** estilo o preferencia contemporáneos (pág. 655)

**tyrant/*tirano*** gobernante que toman el poder por la fuerza y no están sujeto a las leyes (pág. 135)

**uncertainty principle/*principio de incertidumbre*** la idea establecida por Heiseneberg en 1927 de que el comportamiento de las partículas subatómicas no es certero, lo que sugiere que en el fondo de todas las leyes físicas que rigen el universo está la incertidumbre (pág. 491)

**universal male suffrage/*sufragio masculino universal*** el derecho de todos los hombres a votar en elecciones (pág. 268)

**\*unrestricted/*ilimitado*** tener poder sin límites ni restricciones (pág. 472)

**\*variation/*variación*** diferencia en los rasgos de un organismo en relación con la especie o los promedios de la población (pág. 284)

**viceroy/*virrey*** gobernanate que representa a un monarca (pag. 356)

**war communism/*comunismo de guerra*** en la Rusia de la Primera Guerra Mundial, el control del gobierno de bancos y la mayoría de las industrias, la confiscación de granos de los campesinos y la centralización de la administración estatal bajo el control comunista (pág. 445)

**war of attrition/*guerra de desgaste*** guerra que se basa en desgastar al otro bando con constantes ataques y grandes pérdidas, tal como en la Primera Guerra Mundial (pág. 432)

**weapons of mass destruction/*armas de destrucción masiva*** armas biológicas, químicas y nucleares que pueden aniquilar a decenas de millares de personas al mismo tiempo (pág. 630)

**welfare state/*estado benefactor*** estado en el cual el gobierno tiene responsabilidad de entregarle a los ciudadanos servicios tales como la atención de salud (pág. 599)

**\*widespread/*difundido*** generalizado; común casi en todas partes (pág. 472)

**women's liberation movement/*movimiento de liberación femenina*** movimiento femenino de fines de la década de 1960 en la lucha por igualdad de derechos (pág. 604)

**zaibatsu/*zaibatsu*** en la economía japonesa, una gran sociedad financiera e industrial (pág. 511)

Spanish Glossary

*Italicized page numbers refer to illustrations. The following abbreviations are used in the index:
m = map, c = chart, p = photograph or picture, g = graph, crt = cartoon, ptg = painting, q = quote*

**Balfour Declaration**, *c496*, 506

**Bali**, 694, *p694*; bombings in, 694, *q694*

**Balkans**: Crimean War and, 272; crises in, 317–18, 424–25; Paris Peace Conference and, 451; Second Industrial Revolution and, 297; Slavic minorities in, 422; Soviet control over, 594

**Baltic states**: Jews shipped to death camps from, 554; Treaty of Brest-Litovsk and Baltic provinces, 444; World War II and, 549

**Bangkok, Thailand**, 730, *p730*

**Bangladesh, People's Republic of**, *c705, c720, m722*, 723. *See also* East Pakistan

**Barton, Clara**, 307

**Basque Fatherland and Liberty (ETA)**, 639

**Basque region**, 639

**Bastille Day parade**, *p217*

**Bastille, fall of**, 210, *p210, p212*, 214

**Bataan Peninsula**, 545

**Batista, Fulgencio**, 587, 648, 660

*Battle of the Somme* (Woodville), *ptg417*

**Bauhaus school of architecture**, 490, *p490*, 655

**Bay of Pigs**, 588, *c644*, 660

*Baywatch*, 636

**Beauvoir, Simone de**. *See* de Beauvoir, Simone

**Beccaria, Cesare**, 187

**Beer Hall Putsch**, 479

**Beethoven, Ludwig van**, 282

*B.E.F. Times*, 438

**Begin, Menachem**, *p673, 691*; Camp David Peace Accords, 691

**begums**, 361, *p361*

**Beijing, China**, 383, 386, 539, 716–19, *m717*; British and French seize, *c374*, 378; economy of, 716, 719; feng shui and, 716; Gate of Heavenly Peace (*Tian An Men*), 716, 717–18, *m717*; geography of, 716; Imperial (Forbidden) City in, 716–17, *m717*; Mongols conquer, 716; Monument to the People's Heroes, *p717*, 718; Oriental Plaza in, 719; Summer Palace in, 378, *p378*; Tiananmen Square in, 717, *p717*, 718; tourism in, 717–18; urbaniza-

tion of, *p716*, 717–19, *p718, p719*

**Belarus**, 618

**Belfast, Ireland**, *p639*

**Belgian Congo (Democratic Republic of the Congo)**, 345, 678, 682

**Belgium**: colonial interests of, 345, 346; divorce in, 633; EEC and, 600; growth of cities and town, 260; Industrial Revolution in, 257, 258, *m258*; NATO and, 586; Nazi invasion, 542; rebellion in, 268; Second Industrial Revolution and, 296, 297; World War I, 425; World War II, 542, 554

**Belize**, 661

**Bell, Alexander Graham**, *c290*, 296, 576

**Belorussians**, 555

**Bengali language**, *c202*

**Ben-Gurion, David**, 689, *p689, q689*

**Bennett, James Gordon**, 350, 352

**Benz, Karl**, 298

**Bergen-Belsen**, 553

**Berkendael Medical Institute**, 436

**Berlin Airlift**, *c583*, 585, *m586*

**Berlin Conference**, *c342*, 346

**Berlin, Germany**, 299, *c447*, 449, 585; Brandenburg Gate and, *p614*; British attack on, 582; Dada show in, 489; postwar division of, 585–86; reunification of, 622; Soviet troops enter, 549. *See also* Berlin Wall; East Berlin; West Berlin

**Berlin Wall**: building of, *c579, p579*, 587; comes down, *c611, p611*, 614, *p614, c620*, 622

**Bernhardi, Friedrich von**, 321

**Berry, Chuck**, 635

**Beslan**, 619

**Bessemer, Henry**, *c247*

**Beveridge, Albert**, *q338*

**Bhopal, India**, 361, *p361*; chemical plant disaster, *c743*, 745

**Biafra**, 682

**Bialik, Hayyim**, *q502*

**"Big Three,"** 741. *See also* Grand Alliance

**Bill of Rights, English**, *c170*, 174, 181

**Bill of Rights, U.S.**, 181, 197, 266

**bin Laden, Osama**, 696–97

**bioethics**, 746

**bioterrorism**, 747

**biowarfare**, 747

*Birth of a Nation*, 487

**Bismarck, Otto von**, 274, *p274*, 284, 300, 315, 317, *crt317*, 346

**Black Death**, 157

**Black Dragon Society**, 512

**Black Hand**, 424

**Blackpool, England**, 294

**Black Sea**, 131, 132, 272

**Blackshirts** (*squadristi*), 472

**Blair, Tony**, 628, *q742*

**Blake, William**, 282

**blitzkrieg**, 542

**bloc**, 600

**"bloodless revolution,"** 182

**"Bloody Sunday,"** 315, 639

*Body of Civil Law* (Justinian Code), 114, *c114, p114*

**Boers (Afrikaners)**, 347, 678

**Boer War**, 347

**Bohemia**, 537

**Bolívar, Simón**, *p363, q363*, 363

**Bolivia**, 660; drug trade and, 652; human rights in, 651; oil industry in, 521

**Bolsheviks**, 313, *p417*, 441, 474, 513; Old, 476; power seized by, 443–44; renamed as Communists, 444

**Bombay (Mumbai), India**, 358, *p361*

**Bonaparte, Josephine**, *p230*

**Bonaparte, Napoleon**. *See* Napoleon I, emperor of France

**Bonn, Germany**, 585

**Borodino, Russia**, 234

**Bosnia**, 424; Austria-Hungary annexes, 318; war in, 621, *p621*, 623, *p751*, 753

**Bosnia-Herzegovina**, 318, *c620*, 623

**Bossuet, Jacques**, *q176*

**Boston Tea Party**, 193, *p193*

**Bouchot, François**, 225

**Boulding, Elise**, 752–53, *q752–53*

**bourgeoisie (burghers)**, 213, 222, 260, 299

**Boxer Rebellion**, *c379*, 386

**Boxers**, 386, *p386*

**Brahman, the**, 127

**Brahmins**, 128

**Brandenburg Gate**, *p614*

**Brandt, Willy**, 599, 627; Nobel Peace Prize awarded to, *c625*, 627

**Brasília**, *p654*, 655

**Brazil**, 521, 730; authoritarianism in, 523; economic challenges, 664; Getúlio Vargas 's New State in, *c520*, 523; Great Depression and, 523; independence, 364; inflation, 664; military regime in, 522, 523, 651, 664; nationalist movement in, *c524*; plantations in, 523, *p523*; rural to urban migration, 654; social problems, 664; trade and, 298, 369, 521; U.S. involvement in, *m652*; wealth gap in, 664, *p664*

**Brecher, Jeremy**, 754–55

**Brest-Litovsk, Treaty of**, *c440*, 444

**Brezhnev Doctrine**, 616

**Brezhnev, Leonid**, 616

**Briand, Aristide**, 465, 466

**Britain, Battle of**, 543

**British civil service**, *p331*, 356, 360, *p360, p361*

**Brittany**, 638

**Brownshirts**, 479

**Broz, Josip (Tito)**, 595, 623

**Budapest, Hungary**, 269, 277

**Buddha, the**, *p128*, 166

**Buddhism**: beginnings of, *c121*, 128; beliefs in, 128, 166; Eightfold Path in, 166; followers of, *c164, m164*, 166; nirvana, 168; Wheel of Law, 166, *p166*; worship and celebrations, 168

**Buddhist monks**, 168, *p168*

**budget deficits**, 629

**Buenos Aires, Argentina**, 524, 657

**Bulgaria**, 317–18; authoritarian regime in, 476; Paris Peace Conference and, 451; Soviet control over, 594; Warsaw Pact and, 586; World War I and, 432, 433; World War II and, 549

**bungalow**, 360, *p361*

**Bunker Hill, Battle of**, 194

**bureaucracy**, 231, 659

**burghers (bourgeoisie)**, 260

**Burke, Edmund**, *q222*

**Burma (Myanmar)**: colonial rule resisted in, 340–41; economy of, 340; Great Britain's control over, 337, 339, 723;

Index

**Index**

Index

Index

**Index**

Index

**Index**

Index

Index

Index

Index

Index

**Index**

**Index**

Index

# Acknowledgements and Photo Credits

## Acknowledgements
### World History: Modern Times, California Edition

160 Excerpt from *The Republic of Plato,* translated by Frances MacDonald Cornford, 1941. By permission of Oxford University Press.

160 Excerpt from *The Politics by Aristotle,* translated by T.A. Sinclair, revised and re-presented by Trevor J. Saunders (Penguin Classics, 1962, Revised Edition 1981). The 1962 translation copyright © the Estate of T.A. Sinclair, 1962. Reprinted by permission of Penguin Books Ltd.

161 Excerpt from *The Politics of Aristotle,* translated by Ernest Barker, 1946. By permission of Oxford University Press.

198 from "Encyclopedie," by Denis Diderot, from *The Portable Enlightenment Reader,* edited by Isaac Kramnick. Copyright © 1995 Penguin Books USA, Inc. Reprinted by permission.

199 from *The Social Contract,* by Jean-Jacques Rousseau, translation copyright © 1968 by Maurice Cranston. Reprinted by permission of The Penguin Group UK.

236-237 From *The French Revolution and Human Rights,* edited and translated by Lynn Hunt. Copyright © 1996 by Bedford/St. Martin's. Reprinted by permission of Bedford/St. Martin's.

371 Excerpts from *Lenin: Imperialism, the Highest Stage of Capitalism.* International Publishers, 1939. Reprinted by permission of International Publishers, Inc.

454 "Dulce et Decorum Est" by Wilfred Owens, from *The Collected Poems of Wilfred Owens,* copyright © 1963 by Chatto & Windus Ltd. Reprinted by permission of New Directions Publishing Corp.

454 Excerpts from Part I and Part V of "The Hollow Men" in *Collected Poems 1909-1962* by T.S. Eliot, copyright 1936 by Harcourt Inc., copyright © 1964, 1963 by T.S. Eliot, reprinted by permission of the publisher.

526 From *Arab Nationalism,* selected and edited by Sylvia G. Haim. Copyright © 1962 by The Regents of the University of California. Reprinted by permission of Sylvia G. Haim.

566 Reprinted with the permission of Scribner, an imprint of Simon & Schuster Adult Publishing Group, from *Scroll of Agony,* by Abraham I. Katsh. Copyright © 1965, 1973 by Abraham I. Katsh.

566 From *Fresh Wounds: Early Narratives of Holocaust Survival* by Donald L. Niewyk. Copyright © 1998 the University of North Carolina Press. Used by permission of the publisher.

567 from *Heroes of the Holocaust,* by Arnold Geier. Reprinted by permission of Londonbooks/USA.

640 Excerpt from *Perestroika* by Mikhail Gorbachev. Copyright © 1987 by Mikhail Gorbachev. Reprinted by permission of HarperCollins Publishers Inc.

640 "Excerpts From Remarks by Gorbachev Before Central Committee of Party," *New York Times,* February 6, 1990. Copyright © 1990 by The New York Times Co. Reprinted with permission.

641 from "What Kind of 'Democracy' Is This?" by Aleksandr Solzhenitsyn. Copyright © 1997 The New York Times Company. Reprinted by permission.

668 "The Earth is a Satellite of the Moon," from *The Earth is a Satellite of the Moon,* by Leonel Rugama (Curbstone Press, 1984). Reprinted with permission of Curbstone Press. Distributed by Consortium.

668 Excerpts from *The Peru Reader,* edited by Orin Starn, Carlos Ivan Degregori and Robin Kirk, copyright © 1995 by Duke University Press. Reprinted by permission of the publisher.

668 Excerpts from *The Mexico Reader,* edited by Gilbert M. Joseph and Timothy J. Henderson, copyright © 2002 by Duke University Press. Reprinted by permission of the publisher.

701 from "The Way Forward in the Middle East," by Ariel Sharon. *New York Times,* June 9, 2002. Copyright © 2002 by The New York Times Co. Reprinted with permission.

735 from "Japanese Women in Transition" by Miguchi Keiko, *Japan Quarterly,* 1982. Reprinted by permission.

754 From "The Clash of Civilizations," by Samuel P. Huntington. Reprinted by permission of *Foreign Affairs,* Summer 1993. Copyright © 1993 by the Council on Foreign Relations, Inc.

754 From *Global Village or Global Pillage,* by Jeremy Brecher and Tim Costello (1994). Reprinted by permission of the publisher, South End Press.

755 From "The Collapse of Globalism" by John Ralston Saul. Copyright © 2004 by Harper's Magazine. All rights reserved. Reproduced from the March issue by special permission.

Glencoe would like to acknowledge the artists and agencies who participated in illustrating this program: Morgan-Cain & Associates; Ortelius Design, Inc.; QA Digital.

## Photo Credits

vi Erich Lessing/Art Resource, NY; vii The Metropolitan Museum of Art, Gift of Lincoln Kirstein, 1959 (JP 3276), photograph by Otto E. Nelson; viii Christopher Morris/Black Star; xii The Bodleian Library, Oxford, Ms. Bodl. 264, fol.219R; xiv Snark/Art Resource, NY; 2–3 Panoramic Images; 3 Getty Images; 5 Panoramic Images; 6–7 Panoramic Images; 8–9 Panoramic Images; 10 Robert Landau/CORBIS; 12 Masterfile; 48 (l)AKG London, (tc r)AP/Wide World Photos, (bc)CORBIS; 49 (t)Bettmann/CORBIS, (b)Matt Meadows; 50 (t)AP/Wide World Photos, (others)PhotoDisc/Getty Images; 51 Digital Stock; 64 Ric Ergenbright; 65 PhotoDisc/Getty images; 101 (t)Dallas and John Heaton/CORBIS, (c)Jamie Harron/CORBIS, (b)Owen Franken/CORBIS; 102 103 Getty Images 109 AFP/CORBIS; 112 Reunion des Musees Nationaux/Art Resource, NY; 112–113 SuperStock; 113 Hulton/Archive by Getty Images; 114 Bodleian Library, University of Oxford; 115 (l)Joseph Sohm/Visions of America/CORBIS, (r)Giraudon/Art Resource; 116 Art Resource, NY; 116–117 SuperStock; 117 Mary Evans Picture Library; 120 Stock Montage; 122 Musee de Louvre, Paris/E.T. Archives/SuperStock; 123 Ancient Art & Architecture Collection Ltd.; 124 SuperStock; 125 Bettmann/CORBIS; 126 (l)The Israel Museum, Jerusalem, (r)SuperStock; 127 Victoria & Albert Museum, London/Art Resource, NY; 128 Christies, London/Bridgeman Art Library/SuperStock; 129 Giraudon/Art Resource, NY; 130 Kunsthistorisches Museum, Vienna; 132 Robert Frerck/Woodfin Camp/PictureQuest; 133 (t)James L. Stanfield, (b)Mykonos Archaelogical Museum, Mykonos, courtesy of the Hellenic Republic Ministry of Culture; 135 Bill Bachmann/Photo Researchers; 137 Christie's Images/CORBIS; 138 (t)Ronald Sheridan/Ancient Art & Architecture Collection, (b)Museo Delle Terme, Rome/E.T. Archives/SuperStock; 139 SuperStock International; 140 Reunion des Musees Nationaux/Art Resource, NY; 141 Bettmann/CORBIS; 142 Nimatallah/Art Resource, NY; 143 (t)Massimo Listri/CORBIS, ©Michael Holford, (b)Réunion des Musées Nationaux/Art Resource, NY; 145 Cathedral St. Bavo, Ghent./Art Resource; 146 Art Resource, NY; 148 Bridgeman Art Library; 150 Art Resource, NY; 151 Scala/Art Resource, NY; 153 Giraudon/Art Resource, NY; 155 Scala/Art Resource, NY; 156 SuperStock; 158 Vatican Museums & Galleries, Rome/Fratelli Alinari/SuperStock; 159 Photo Researchers; 160 Bettmann/CORBIS; 165 (tl)Paul Chesley/Getty Images, (tr)Edward Parker/Hutchison Library, (bl)Michael Freeman/CORBIS, (br)L. Clarke/CORBIS; 166 (t)The Newark Museum/Art Resource, ©Victoria & Albert Museum, London/Art Resource, (b)Bibliotheque Nationale, Paris, France/Bridgeman Art Library Int'l. Ltd.; 167 (t c)CORBIS, (b)The Jewish Museum, NY/Art Resource; 168 (t)Bettmann/CORBIS, ©Phil Schermeister/CORBIS, (b)Ma Wenlin/Sovfoto/Eastfoto/PictureQuest; 169 (t)FPG International, ©Peter Sanders/HAGA/The Image Works, (b)Bill Aron/Stone, Inc.; 170 (l)Scala/Art Resource, NY, (r)Bettmann/CORBIS; 170–171 Giraudon/Art Resource, NY; 171 Tate Gallery, London/Art Resource, NY; 174 Bettmann/CORBIS; 176 Reunion des Musees Nationaux/Art Resource, NY; 177 National Museum and Gallery of Wales/Bridgeman Art Library; 178 AKG London/AKG London; 179 Giraudon/Art Resource, NY; 180 Ronald Sheridan/Art & Architecture Collection, Ltd.; 181 Peter Hoadley, William III and Mary Stuart, Rijksmuseum, Amersterdam; 182 Bettmann/CORBIS; 184 North Wind Picture Archives; 185 (t)Art Resource, NY, (b)Giraudon/Art Resource, NY; 187 Tate Gallery, London/Art Resource, NY; 188 Pablo Corral V/CORBIS; 191 Giraudon/Art Resource, NY; 192 Library of Congress; 193 CORBIS; 194 Courtesy of the Historical Society of Pennsylvania Collection, Atwater Kent Museum of Philadelphia; 195 The Valley Forge Historical Society; 196 Fraunces Tavern Museum, New York, (inset)Picture Research Consultants; 198 Giraudon/Art Resource, NY; 203 (t)PhotoDisc/Getty Images, ©The Huntington Library, Art Collections and Botanical Gardens, San Marino, CA/SuperStock, (b)Bettmann/CORBIS; 205 (t)Getty Images, (b)Robert Holmes/CORBIS; 206 (t) Reunion des Musees Nationaux /Art Resource, NY, (b)Bridgeman Art Library Int'l. Ltd. (U.S.); 206–207 Erich Lessing/Art Resource, NY; 207 (t)Giraudon/Bridgeman Art Library Int'l. Ltd. (U.S.), (b)Mary Evans Picture Library/Bridgeman Art Library Int'l. Ltd. (U.S.); 210 AKG London; 212 Giraudon/Art Resource, NY; 214 Giraudon/Bridgeman Art Library Int'l. Ltd. (U.S.); 215 AKG London; 216 (t)Stock Montage, (b)Giraudon/Art Resource, NY; 217 Rueters NewMedia Inc./CORBIS; 218 Giraudon/Art Resource, NY; 220 AKG London/Jerome da Cunha/AKG London; 221 (l)Giraudon/Art Resource, NY, (r)Mary Evans Picture Library; 224 (l)Hulton-Deutsch Collection/CORBIS, ©Stock Montage, (r)Giraudon/Art Resource, NY; 225 Reunion des Musees Nationaux/Art Resource, NY; 226 Roger-Viollet, Paris/Bridgeman Art Library Int'l. Ltd. (U.S.); 227 (tl)Archivo Iconografico, S.A./CORBIS, (tr)Gianni Dagli

Orti/CORBIS, (b)Dupelessis-Bertaux, engraved by Malapeau/Mary Evans Picture Library; 229 Museum of Art History, Vienna/AKG, Berlin/SuperStock International; 230 Giraudon/Art Resource, NY; 231 Gianni Dagli Orti/CORBIS; 232 Giraudon/Art Resource, NY; 234 AKG London; 236 Bettmann/CORBIS; 237 Stefano Bianchetti/CORBIS; 240 (l)Giraudon/Art Resource, (r)CORBIS; 241 Reunion des Musees Nationaux/Art Archive; 242 Robbie Jack/CORBIS; 243 Doug Martin; 244 SuperStock International; 244–245 Hulton Deutsch Collection/CORBIS; 245 Bridgeman Art Library Int'l. Ltd. (U.S.); 246 Stock Montage; 247 (t)Library of Congress, (b)Laurie Platt Winfrey; 248 Bettmann/CORBIS; 248–249 Science Museum/Science & Society Picture Library; 249 (t)Archivo Iconografico, S.A./CORBIS, (bl br)Mary Evans Picture Library; 252 (l)Stock Montage/SuperStock, (r)Bettmann/CORBIS; 254 Culver Pictures, Inc.; 255 (tl)National Trust/Art Resource, NY, (tr)Ronald Sheridan/Ancient Art and Architecture, (b)Ronald Sheridan/Ancient Art and Architecture; 256 Superstock; 259 Lambert/Archive Photos/Hulton Archive; 260 Mary Evans Picture Library; 262 CORBIS; 263 (tl)Library of Congress, (tr)Time Life Pictures/Getty Images, (b)CORBIS; 265 Woldemar Friedrich in Die Deutschen Befreigskriege/Mary Evans Picture Library; 267 (t)Giraudon/Art Resource, NY; (t)Austrian Information Service; 268 Stock Montage; 269 Hulton-Deutsch Collection/CORBIS; 272 Museo Civico Modigliana, Italy/Dagli Orti/Art Archive; 274 "Proclamation of the German Empire at Versailles", 1871, Anton von Werner, Photo Bildarchiv Preussicher Kulturbesitz, Berlin; 275 Gianni Dagli Orti/CORBIS; 276 Hulton-Deutsch Collection/CORBIS; 277 David David Gallery, Philadelphia/SuperStock, (inset)Musee du Chateau de Versailles/Dagli Orti/Art Archive; 278 Ullstein Bilderdeinst, Berlin; 279 Bettmann/CORBIS; 281 Larry Fisher/Masterfile; 282 (tl)Archivo Iconografico, S.A./CORBIS; 283 Burstein Collection/CORBIS; 284 Michael Nicholson/CORBIS; 285 Staatliche Kunstsammlungen, Dresden, Germany/Bridgeman Art Library, London/SuperStock; 286 Stapleton Collection/CORBIS; 290 (t)CORBIS, (b)Culver Pictures; 290–291 CORBIS; 291 (t)Bridgeman Art Library, (b)AKG London; 294 Underwood & Underwood/CORBIS; 296 Bettmann/CORBIS; 298 (l)Reuters/CORBIS, (r)Tom Burnside/Photo Researchers; 299 AP/Wide World Photos; 304 Bettmann/CORBIS; 305 Hulton-Deutsch Collection/CORBIS; 306 Musee de la Poste, Paris, photo J.L.Charmet; 307 Snark/Art Resource, NY; 308 Christies, London/SuperStock; 309 Library of Congress; 310 Hulton-Deutsch Collection/CORBIS; 311 (tl)Bettmann/CORBIS, (tr)Topical Press Agency/Getty Images, (b)North Wind Picture Archives; 313 AKG London; 316 Hawaii State Archives; 317 318 Bettmann/CORBIS; 320 Hulton/Archive by Getty Images; 322 Getty Images; 323 SuperStock; 324 The Museum of Modern Art, NY/Licensed by Scala/Art Resource, NY; 325 Photo ©E. Louis Lankford; 327 Bettmann/CORBIS; 330 (t)Hulton/Archive by Getty Images, (b)Frans Lemmens/The ImageBank; 330–331 Hulton/Archive by Getty Images; 331 (t)Hulton-Deutsch Collection/CORBIS, (b)Brown Brothers; 334 (l)Image Select/Art Resource, NY, (r)Hulton/Archive by Getty Images; 339 340 North Wind Picture Archives; 341 Sipahioglu/Sipa Press; 343 Hulton/Archive by Getty Images; 345 Bridgeman Art Library; 348 Hulton-Deutsch Collection/CORBIS; 350 North Wind Picture Archives; 351 (tl)Royal Geographical Society, London, UK/Bridgeman Art Library, (tr)Royal Geographical Society, London, ©From The Last Journels of David Livingstone, in Central Africa, Harper & Brothers, Publishers, 1875; photograph by Mark Thiessen, (b)Royal Geographical Society, London; 353 (l)The Picture Desk, (r)Hulton-Deutsch Collection/CORBIS; 355 The Image Works; 356 North Wind Picture Archives, (inset)The Stapleton Collection/Bridgeman Art Library; 357 akg-images; 358 359 Hulton-Deutsch Collection/CORBIS; 361 (t)Getty Images, (b)Hulton-Deutsch Collection/CORBIS; 363 Giraudon/Art Resource, NY; 364 Schalkwijk/Art Resource; 365 Museo Nacional de Belas Artes Rio de Janeiro Brazil/Dagli Orti/Art Archive; 368 Bettmann/CORBIS; 369 Hulton-Deutsch Collection/CORBIS; 370 akg-images; 374 Peabody Essex Museum, Salem, Mass. Photo by Mark Sexton; 374–375 National Maritime Museum, London; 375 (t)Camera Press/Globe Photos, (b)Asian Art & Archaeology/CORBIS; 378 (l)SuperStock, (r)CORBIS; 380 Royal Ontario Museum; 382 TimePix; 383 Harper's Weekly/CORBIS; 385 Courtesy of the Freer Gallery of Art, Smithsonian Institution, Washington, DC; 386 Bettmann/CORBIS; 388 Getty Images; 389 Hulton-Deutsch Collection/CORBIS; 390 (l)Keystone, Paris/Sygma, (r)Hulton-Deutsch Collection/CORBIS; 391 UPI/Bettmann; 392 Mary Evans Picture Library; 393 ChinaStock; 394 POPPERFOTO/Alamy; 395 (tl)POPPERFOTO/Alamy, (tr)Getty Images, (b)Bettmann/CORBIS; 397 Courtesy of the United States Naval Academy Museum; 398 CORBIS; 400 The Metropolitan Museum of Art, Gift of Lincoln Kirstein, 1959 (JP 3276), photograph by Otto F. Nelson; 402 Culver Pictures, Inc.; 403 Private Collection/Bridgeman Art Library/SuperStock; 404 Bettmann/CORBIS; 408 Hulton/Archive by Getty Images; 409 Mary Evans Picture Library; 410 Underwood & Underwood/CORBIS; 411 Doug Martin; 412 Ira Nowinski/CORBIS; 412–413 Hulton Archive; 413 Hulton/Archive by Getty Images; 414 Bettmann/CORBIS; 415 (t)United Nations Photo Library, (b)David Turnley/CORBIS; 416 Hulton Getty Picture Collection; 416–417 Bridgeman Art Library Int'l. Ltd.; 417 Bettmann/CORBIS; 420 (l)Hulton/Archive by Getty Images, (r)Hulton-Deutsch Collection/CORBIS; 422 Bettmann Archive; 425 Getty Images; 426 (t bl)Brown Brothers, (br)Bettmann/CORBIS; 427 Titanic Historical Society Inc., Indian Orchard, Massachusetts; 428 Jonathan Blair; 429 (l)Bowman Gray Collection, Rare Book Collection, The University of North Carolina at Chapel Hill, (r)Jonathan Blair; 431 ©Roger-Viollet, Paris; 432 Getty Images; 433 (l)John H. Clark/CORBIS, (r)Hulton/Archive by Getty Images; 435 Bettmann/CORBIS; 436 CORBIS; 437 Victoria and Albert Museum, London/Art Resource, NY; 438 CORBIS; 439 (l)Stapleton Collection/CORBIS, (tr)Hulton-Deutsch Collection/CORBIS, (br)Hulton Getty Picture Collection; 441 CORBIS; 442 (l)Hulton/Archive by Getty Images, (r)Bettmann/CORBIS; 443 (l)Rykoff Collection/CORBIS, (r)Hulton Getty Picture Collection; 444 446 Bettmann/CORBIS; 448 Hulton/Archive by Getty Images; 449 Reunion des Musees Nationaux/Art Resource, NY; 453 National Portrait Gallery, Smithsonian Institution/Art Resource, NY; 454 Hulton-Deutsch Collection/CORBIS; 457 Doug Martin; 458 Hulton/Archive by Getty Images; 458–459 Hugo Jaeger/TimePix; 459 (t)National Portrait Gallery, Smithsonian Institution/Art Resource, NY, (b)AKG London; 462 Archive Photos/Getty Images New Service; 464 CORBIS; 465 Culver Pictures; 466 467 Bettmann Archive; 471 Hulton/Archive by Getty Images; 474 (l)L'Illustration/Sygma, (r)SuperStock; 477 Centro de Arte Reina Sofia, Madrid, Spain/Giraudon, Paris/Superstock; 479 CORBIS; 480 Hulton-Deutsch Collection/CORBIS; 481 CORBIS; 482 (l)Bettmann/CORBIS, ©Seidman Collection/Culver Pictures, (r)Mary Evans Picture Library; 484 Mary Evans Picture Library; 485 (tl)Snark/Art Resource, NY, (tr)AP/Wide World, (b)Time Life Pictures/Getty Images; 487 CORBIS; 488 (l)CORBIS, (r)AKG London; 489 Bridgeman Art Library Int'l.Ltd. (U.S.); 490 ForestierYves/CORBIS SYGMA; 491 Bettmann/CORBIS; 492 Hulton-Deutsch Collection/CORBIS; 496 Hulton/Archive by Getty Images; 496–497 Schalkwijk/Art Resource, NY; 497 (t)Barry Iverson/TimePix, (b)Stock Montage; 500 Hulton/Archive by Getty Images; 502 Hulton-Deutsch Collection/CORBIS; 503 (t)CORBIS, (b)Bettmann/CORBIS; 505 Bettmann/CORBIS; 508 Black Star; 510 Bettmann/CORBIS; 511 H. Rogers/Art Directors & TRIP Photo Library; 515 AFP Worldwide; 516 Getty Images; 518 Hulton-Deutsch Collection/CORBIS; 519 521 Getty Images; 523 Underwood & Underwood/CORBIS; 525 Peter Menzel/Stock Boston; 526 Underwood & Underwood/CORBIS; 530 Hulton Getty/Tony Stone Images; 530–531 Dallas and John Heakon/CORBIS; 531 (tl)AKG Berlin/AKG London, (tr)Culver Pictures, (b)AKG London; 534 (l)AKG London, (r)Hugo Jaeger/LIFE Magazine, Time, Inc.; 536 Bettmann/CORBIS; 537 Mary Evans Picture Library; 540 CORBIS; 542 National Archives (#306-NT-1222E); 543 Bettmann Archive; 547 Hulton/Archive by Getty Images; 549 552 CORBIS; 553 AKG London; 556 555 Bettmann/CORBIS; 559 CORBIS; 560 AKG London; 561 Bettmann/CORBIS 562 CORBIS; 563 J.R. Eyerman, Life Magazine, ©Time Warner Inc.; 565 E.T. Archive; 566 Getty Images; 570 (l)CORBIS, (r)Bridgeman Art Library/Art Resource, NY; 572 Alinari Archives/CORBIS; 574–575 David & Peter Turnley/CORBIS, Contemporary African Art Collection Limited/CORBIS; 576 UPI/Bettmann/CORBIS; 577 (t)Eye Ubiquitous/CORBIS, (b)Scott Peterson/Liaison/Getty/Liaison Agency; 578 Charles Moore/Black Star; 578–579 Sovfoto/Eastfoto; 579 (l)Bettmann/CORBIS, (r)John Lopinot/Black Star; 582 Hulton-Deutsch Collection/CORBIS; 584 Woodfin Camp & Associates; 585 AP/Wide World Photos; 587 Sovfoto/Eastfoto; 590 Henry Diltz/CORBIS; 591 (tl b)Bettmann/CORBIS, (tr)Alain Nogues/CORBIS SYGMA; 593 Bettmann/CORBIS; 594 Semyon Raskin/Magnum Photos; 595 Bettmann/CORBIS; 596 Time Life Pictures/Getty Images; 598 Marc Riboud/Magnum Photos; 599 UPI/Bettmann; 601 (l)Hulton-Deutsch Collection/CORBIS, (r)Bettmann/CORBIS; 602 Black Star; 603 Lido/SIPA Press; 604 Elliott Erwitt/Magnum Photos; 605 ©C. Raimond-Dityvon/Viva, Woodfin Camp and Associates; 606 Yevgeny Khaldei/CORBIS; 610 Black Star; 610–611 NASA; 611 (l)Reuters/Bettmann, (r)AP/Wide World Photos; 614 Reuters Bettmann; 616 Novosti/Sipa Press; 617 Joseph C. Marquette; 619 Reuters Newmedia, Inc./CORBIS; 621 David Turnley/CORBIS; 622 AP/Wide World Photos; 624 AFP/Bettmann; 626 Reuters/CORBIS; 627 (t)Getty Images, (b)AP/Wide World Photos; 628 Wally McNamee/CORBIS; 629 CORBIS; 630 Woodfin Camp & Associates; 632 Paul A. Souders/CORBIS; 634 AFP/Getty Images; 635 Reuters/CORBIS; 636 Thierry Orban/CORBIS; 637 Woodfin Camp & Associates; 639 Abbas/Magnum Photos; 640 AP/Wide World Photos; 644 UPI/Bettmann; 644–645 Stone; 645 (t)Hulton/Archive by Getty Images, (b)AFP Worldwide; 648 AFP/CORBIS; 650 Bettmann/CORBIS; 651 Vera Lentz/Black Star; 654 Getty Images; 655 Colita/CORBIS; 656 Alamy Images; 657 (tl)Yann Arthus-Bertrand/CORBIS, (tr)Diego Giudice/CORBIS, (b)Carlos Carrion/CORBIS SYGMA; 659 660 Bettmann/CORBIS; 661 Chip Hires/Gamma Presse; 662 Woodfin Camp & Associates; 664 Bettmann/CORBIS; 665 AFP Worldwide; 667 Richard Emblin/Black Star; 669 Magnum Photos; 672 CORBIS; 672–673 UPI/Bettmann; 673 (t)Hulton/Archive by Getty Images, (b)CORBIS; 674 (l)Bettmann/CORBIS, (r)Woodfin Camp & Associates; 678 Gamma Presse; 679 Bettmann/CORBIS; 680 CORBIS;